The American Journey
A History of the United States

FIFTH EDITION

VOLUME TWO

DAVID GOLDFIELD
University of North Carolina, Charlotte

CARL ABBOTT
Portland State University

PETER H. ARGERSINGER
Southern Illinois University

VIRGINIA DEJOHN ANDERSON
University of Colorado, Boulder

WILLIAM L. BARNEY
University of North Carolina, Chapel Hill

JO ANN E. ARGERSINGER
Southern Illinois University

ROBERT M. WEIR
University of South Carolina

PEARSON

Upper Saddle River, New Jersey 07458

Library of Congress Cataloging-in-Publication Data

The American journey : a history of the United States / David Goldfield—[et al.]. —5th ed.
   p. cm.
   "Combined volume."
   Includes bibliographical references and index.
      ISBN 0-13-603281-8 (combined) — ISBN 0-13-603255-9 (v. 1) —
   ISBN 0-13-603256-7 (v. 2)
      1. United States–History. 2. United States—History–Software.
   I. Goldfield, David R.
   E178.1.A4925 2009
   973—dc22   2008040113

For our students, who helped us write this book.

Publisher: Charlyce Jones Owen
Executive Marketing Manager: Sue Westmoreland
Editorial Assistant: Maureen Diana
Operations Supervisor: Mary Ann Gloriande
Operations Specialist: Maura Zaldivar
Director of Media and Assessment: Brian Hyland
Media Editor: Sarah Kinney
Senior Art Director/Cover Design: Maria Lange
Interior Design: iDesign
AV Project Manager: Mirella Signoretto

Senior Managing Editor: Ann Marie McCarthy
Project Manager: Denise Brown
Full-Service Production and Composition: Patty Donovan/Pine Tree Composition, Inc.
Manager, Rights and Permissions: Zina Arabia
Manager, Visual Research: Beth Brenzel
Manager, Cover Visual Research and Permissions: Karen Sanatar
Image Permission Coordinator: Craig Jones
Printer/Binder: Courier/Kendallville
Cover Printer: Phoenix Color/Hagerstown

Cover art: The unemployed in New York City during the Great Depression are depicted in an illustration "Corteo di Disoccupati a New York" by Achille Beltrame (Italian, 1871–1945). The illustration was first published in the Italian Sunday newsletter *Domenica del Corrier,* number 45, November 9, 1930.

Credits and acknowledgments from other sources and reproduced, with permission, in this textbook appear on appropiate page within text (or on page C-1).

10 9 8 7 6 5 4 3 2 1

PEARSON

Volume II
ISBN 13: 978-0-13-603256-4
ISBN 10:   0-13-603256-7

BRIEF CONTENTS

CONTENTS

16

RECONSTRUCTION 1865–1877   433

17

A NEW SOUTH: ECONOMIC PROGESS AND SOCIAL TRADITION 1877–1900   465

21

THE PROGRESSIVE ERA 1900–1917
579

VOICES FROM THE AMERICAN JOURNEY:
"GENERAL" ROSALIE JONES   579

22

CREATING AN EMPIRE 1865–1917   611

VOICES FROM THE AMERICAN JOURNEY:
MAJOR-GENERAL LEONARD WOOD   611

23

AMERICA AND THE GREAT WAR 1914–1920   637

24

TOWARD A MODERN AMERICA: THE 1920s   665

25

THE GREAT DEPRESSION AND THE NEW DEAL 1929–1939   693

26

WORLD WAR II 1939–1945   725

27

THE COLD WAR AT HOME AND ABROAD 1946–1952   759

VOICES FROM THE AMERICAN JOURNEY:
BERNADETTE WHEELER   759

28

THE CONFIDENT YEARS 1953–1964   787

VOICES FROM THE AMERICAN JOURNEY:
MELBA PATILLO   787

29

SHAKEN TO THE ROOTS 1965–1980   819

VOICES FROM THE AMERICAN JOURNEY:
BUZZ ALDRIN AND NEIL ARMSTRONG   819

30

THE REAGAN REVOLUTION AND A CHANGING WORLD 1981–1992   851

VOICES FROM THE AMERICAN JOURNEY:
CELIA NOUP   851

31
COMPLACENCY, CRISIS, AND GLOBAL REENGAGEMENT 1993–2007   885

SPECIAL FEATURES

American Views

Global Perspectives

From Then To Now

Maps

*Denotes a map exploration is available on *myhistorylab* and online.

Figures and Tables

Overview Tables

PREFACE

The path that led us to *The American Journey* began in the classroom with our students. Our goal is to make American history accessible to students. The key to that goal—the core of the book—is a strong clear narrative. American history is a compelling story, and we seek to tell it in an engaging, forthright way. But we also provide students with an abundance of tools to help them absorb that story and put it in context. We introduce them to the concerns of the participants in America's history with primary source documents. The voices of contemporaries open each chapter, describing their own personal journeys toward fulfilling their dreams, hopes, and ambitions as part of the broader American journey. These voices provide a personal window on our nation's history, and the themes they express resonate throughout the narrative.

But if we wrote this book to appeal to our students, we also wrote it to engage their minds. We wanted to avoid academic trendiness, particularly the restricting categories that have divided the discipline of history over the last twenty years or so. We believe that the distinctions involved in the debates about multiculturalism and identity, between social and political history, between the history of the common people and the history of the elite, are unnecessarily confusing.

What we seek is integration—to combine political and social history, to fit the experience of particular groups into the broader perspective of the American past, to give voice to minor and major players alike because of their role in the story we have to tell.

Approach

In telling our story, we had some definite ideas about what we might include and emphasize that other texts do not—information we felt that the current and next generations of students will need to know about our past to function best in a new society.

CHRONOLOGICAL ORGANIZATION A strong chronological backbone supports the book. We have found that the jumping back and forth in time characteristic of some American history textbooks confuses students. They abhor dates but need to know the sequence of events in history. A chronological presentation is the best way to be sure they do.

GEOGRAPHICAL LITERACY We also want students to be geographically literate. We expect them not only to know what happened in American history, but where it happened as well. Physical locations and spatial relationships were often important in shaping historical events. The abundant maps in *The American Journey*—all numbered and called out in the text—are an integral part of our story.

REGIONAL BALANCE *The American Journey* presents balanced coverage of all regions of the country. In keeping with this balance, the South and the West receive more coverage in this text than in comparable books.

POINT OF VIEW *The American Journey* presents a balanced overview of the American past. But "balanced" does not mean bland. We do not shy away from definite positions on controversial issues, such as the nature of early contacts between Native Americans and Europeans, why the political crisis of the 1850s ended in a bloody Civil War, and how Populism and its followers fit into the American political spectrum. If students and instructors disagree, that's great; discussion and dissent are important catalysts for understanding and learning.

RELIGION This text stresses the importance of religion in American society both as a source of strength and a reflection of some its more troubling aspects.

Historians mostly write for each other. That's too bad. We need to reach out and expand our audience. An American history text is a good place to start. Our students are not only our future historians, but more important, our future. Let their American journey begin.

Features of the Text

The American Journey includes an array of features designed to make American history accessible to students. It provides more learning tools than any other U.S. history text.

- The **Student Tool Kit** that follows this preface helps students get the most out of the text and its features. It introduces students to key conventions of historical writing and it explains how to work with maps, documents, and visuals.

- **Personal Journeys,** brief primary source excerpts, open each chapter. Consisting of letters, diary entries, and other first-hand accounts, these voices highlight the personal dimension of the American journey and show students the wealth and variety of experiences that make up this country's history. From Olaudah Equiano's narrative of his forced journey to Virginia as a slave, to the ultimate journey Sullivan Ballou made during the Civil War defending the Union, to Cambodian refugee Celia Noup's harrowing journey to California where she took her place as one of the thousands of new immigrants who are reshaping the face of our nation, **Personal Journeys** set the stage for the key themes that are explored in each chapter.

- The **American Views** box in each chapter contains a relevant primary source document. Taken from letters, diaries, newspapers, government papers, and other sources, these bring the people of the past and their concerns vividly alive. An introduction and prereading questions relate the documents to the text and direct students' attention to important issues.

- **From Then to Now,** relates important issues and events in each chapter to the issues and events of today, letting students see the relevance of history to their lives. In the fifth edition, this feature has been expanded to a two-page spread with thought-provoking visuals to support and enhance the narrative.

- **Global Perspectives,** included in each chapter, make an appropriate and substantive global connection that links the United States to other nations in the world, thereby enhancing students' understanding of America's development. *Global Perspectives* informs students that globalization is not something new. America was part of global trends long before we were a nation. This feature acknowledges that fact and places the American journey within a broader worldwide context. That journey not only influenced other countries and peoples, but, we in turn have been shaped by global economic, migratory, technological, and political trends.

- **Overview Tables** summarize complex issues.

- **Chapter Chronologies** help students build a framework of key events.

- **Key Terms** are highlighted within each chapter and defined in an alphabetical end of text glossary.

- **Review Questions** at the end of each chapter are organized by key subtopics in each chapter to help students review material and relate it to broader themes.

- A **Recommended Readings** section introduces students to relevant outside reading suggestions that expand on topics within the chapters.

- **Where to Learn More** sections, found at relevant places in the margin, and listed at the end of each chapter, describe important historical sites (both real and virtual) that students can visit to gain a deeper understanding of the events discussed in the chapter.

- Abundant **maps** help students understand the spatial dimension of history. The topographical detail in many of the maps helps students understand the influence of geography on history.

- **Illustrations and photographs** — tied to the text with detailed captions — provide a visual dimension to history.

Changes to the Fifth Edition

Every chapter has been thoroughly revised and improved with new special features as well as updated scholarship.

New to the Fifth Edition

Personal Journeys: References to additional documents from individuals that relate to the content of chapter. These additional voices are included in the *myhistorylab* website.

From Then to Now: This feature is now included in every chapter and includes references to additional documents related to the topic that are available on *myhistorylab*. These online *From Then to Now* activities provide research and writing opportunities for students.

Chapter 16 Reconstruction
- New discussion on black gender relations.
- Renamed section "Northern Indifference" now makes clear that racism was a national, not merely a southern phenomenon from the beginning of the Reconstruction era and was central to both the growing indifference toward violence against blacks and the willingness to believe southern white propaganda concerning Republican governments in the South.
- New subhead called "Economic Transformation." The vast economic transformation of the 1870s affected the lives of millions of Americans, especially in the North where the transformation was most notable. This transformation pushed Reconstruction policy and the South generally to the back burner of public consciousness.

Chapter 17 A New South
- Expanded coverage of the growth of evangelical Protestant churches in the South.
- New discussion of black women's clubs in the section on Women's Clubs.

Chapter 18 Industry, Immigrants, and Cities
- Added discussion on cultural institutions of immigrants.
- New section, "The Ideal City," discusses one of the signal events of the late nineteenth century, the World's Columbian Exposition in Chicago and its meaning.

Chapter 19 Transforming the West
- New material on the difficulty of settling in the West and on corporate and California aspects of the cattle industry.
- Revised treatments of American Indians to direct more attention to Navajos and resistance to Americanization.

Chapter 20 Politics and Government
- Added new material dealing with non-electoral politics, including a discussion on lobbying and legal activities of business and labor groups and a discussion of Christian reformers seeking to promote morality through government action.
- Expanded discussion on Southern Populism (including a reference to Texas Populists).

Chapter 21 The Progressive Era
- New **Global Perspective:** *The New Zealand Way* discusses that country's reform initiatives and their influence in the United States.
- Revised discussion of woman suffrage to emphasize its centrality to progressivism.
- Revised discussions of muckrakers and of progressive attitudes toward immigration to include new material.
- Revised discussion of Wilson's presidency to clarify his attitudes toward government.

Chapter 22 Creating an Empire
- Revised discussions of Secretaries of State Seward and Blaine.
- Revised discussion of U.S.- Latin American relations.

Chapter 23 America and the Great War, 1914-1920
- New opening journey: excerpts from speeches by Woodrow Wilson calling for a declaration of war and from Senator Robert LaFollette opposing U.S. intervention. They suggest different journeys for America's future, point up the opposition to an unpopular war, and correspond to several critical themes in the chapter, including the government's efforts to build support for the war.
- The new opening discussion highlights Wilson's ultimate failure at peacemaking in Versailles.

Chapter 24 Toward a Modern America, The 1920s
- More information on religion in the cultural conflicts of the 1920s.
- New **American Views:** Features Aimee Semple McPherson, the remarkably popular female evangelist who defied traditional roles and embraced modern marketing techniques in broadcasting her religious message.

Chapter 26 World War II
- Expanded coverage of World War II homefront.
- Deepened coverage of women, Native Americans, and Latinos in the war effort.

Chapter 27 The Cold War at Home and Abroad
- Incorporates new discoveries about the character and extent of Cold War espionage.

Chapter 29 Shaken to the Roots
- Rewritten sections on urban violence and minority self-determination in the later 1960s.

Chapter 30 The Reagan Revolution and a Changing World
- New tables on U.S. cities compared to world cities and on economic status by ethnicity and race.
- Deepened discussion of relations between religious belief and political action.

Chapter 31 Complacency and Crisis
- Reduced coverage of domestic politics during Clinton administration
- Expanded and updated coverage of Bush administration domestic and foreign policy.

Supplementary Instructional Materials

The American Journey comes with an extensive package of supplementary print and multimedia materials for both instructors and students.

Print Supplements

Instructor's Resource Manual   A time-saver in developing and preparing lecture presentations, the *Instructor's Resource Manual* contains chapter outlines, detailed chapter overviews, lecture outlines, topics for discussion, and information about audiovisual resources.

Test Item File   The test item file contains more than 1,500 multiple-choice, identification, matching, true-false, and essay test questions and 10–15 questions per chapter on the maps found in each chapter.

Prentice Hall Test Generator   Suitable for both Windows and Macintosh environments, this commerical-quality, computerized test-management program allows instructors to select items from the test-item file and design their own exams. Available at www.ivc.com for download.

Transparency Package   Over 100 full-color transparency acetates of all the maps, charts, and graphs in the text are available as transparency acetates for use in the classroom.

American Stories: Biographies in United States History (Volume I and II)   This two-volume collection of sixty-two biographies provides insight into the lives and contributions of key figures as well as ordinary citizens to American history. Introductions, pre-reading questions, and suggested resources helps students connect the relevance of these individuals to historical events.

Retrieving the American Past: A Customized U.S. History Reader   This collection of documents is an on-demand history database written and developed by leading historians and educators. It offers eighty-six compelling modules on topics in American history, such as "Women on the Frontier," "The Salem Witchcraft Scare," "The Age of Industrial Violence," and "Native American Societies, 1870–1995." Approximately thirty-five pages in length, each module includes an introduction, several primary documents and secondary sources, follow-up questions, and recommendations for further reading. Instructor-originated material, including other readings and exercises, can be incorporated. Contact your local Prentice Hall representative for more information about this custom-publishing option.

Prentice Hall and Penguin Bundle Program   Prentice Hall is pleased to provide adopters of *The American Journey* with an opportunity to receive significant discounts when copies of the text are bundled with Penguin titles in American history. Contact your local Prentice Hall representative for details.

Multimedia Supplement

myhistorylab

Myhistorylab   www.myhistorylab.com
MyHistoryLab means access to a wealth of study resources. Organized by major sections within chapters, these resources focus students using an easy-to-use learning system—*Read, Review and Assess, Interact,* and *Research*—that will help them to reinforce and apply what they are learning in class and from the text.

For Students

- Over 300 primary source documents with questions for analysis, classic works from the *History Bookshelf* like Thomas Paine's *Common Sense,* and the e-textbook version of *The American Journey* give students the opportunity to explore historical events in more depth. The e-book online makes the textbook accessible for study and review while students are working with *MyHistoryLab.*
- Chapter review materials include a study guide, learning objectives, PPT review presentations, overview activities, and key term flashcards to help students master the contents of the textbook and prepare for exams. In addition, students have access to *The Tutor Center,* where they can obtain one-on-one assistance with *MyHistorylab* and a *History Toolkit* for guidance on how to read and analyze documents. Each chapter includes pre- and post-tests self-study quizzes with targeted feedback for review and testing of content mastery.
- Hands-on activities and exercises let students explore content in the text in more depth and experience history beyond the textbook. *Exploring America* and other interactive learning activities, map explorations, anima-

tions, audio, and videos take students into the key events that have shaped our nation and strengthen geographic literacy and document analysis skills.
- From finding the right articles and journals, to citing sources, drafting and writing effective papers, and completing research assignments, students will turn to Pearson's **Research Navigator**™ for help with the research process.

For Instructors

For instructors using course management, *MyHistoryLab* means access to the student's resources, *and* all of the instructional material available to use in teaching with the text, including the instructor's manual, the test item file, images, maps, charts, and graphs from the text, video and audio clips, and Powerpoint™ lecture presentations and questions for use with CRS technology in the classroom. These are resources are also available to download from the Pearson Instructor Resource Center online at www.irc.com.

Acknowledgments

We would like to thank the reviewers whose thoughtful and often detailed comments helped shape this fourth edition and the previous editions of *The American Journey:*

Alfred Hunt, SUNY Purchase
Andrew Cayton, Miami University
Andrew Wallace, Northern Arizona University
Armand LaPotin, SUNY Oneonta
Benjamin Newcomb, Texas Technological University
Betsy Powers, Montgomery College
Bill Cecil-Fronsman, Washburn University
Brian Wills, Clinch Valley Community College
Bryan LeBeau, Creighton University
Bufford Satcher, University of Arkansas at Pine Bluff
Caroline Cox, University of the Pacific
Charles Bolton, University of Arkansas at Little Rock
Chris Padgett, Weber State University
Christopher Moss, University of Texas at Arlington
Christopher Phillips, Emporia State University
Colleen O'Connor, San Diego Mesa College
Craig Ferguson, Oklahoma Community College
Dale Carnagey, Blinn College
Dale Schmitt, East Tennessee State University
David Aldstadt, Houston Community College
David Castle, Ohio University, Eastern Campus
David Conrad, Southern Illinois University
David G. Hogan, Heidelberg College
David Hamilton, University of Kentucky
David McFadden, Fairfield University
David Parker, Kennesaw State College
David Sloan, University of Arkansas

Dean Dunlap, Rose State College
Donald Dewey, California State University
Donald Jacobs, Northeastern University
Donald McCoy, University of Kansas
E. Wayne Carp, Pacific Lutheran University
Ed Lukes, Hillsborough Community College
Edward Weller, San Jacinto College, South
Elizabeth Nybakken, Mississippi State University
Emily Teipe, Fullerton College
Eric J. Bolsteri, University of Texas at Arlington
Eugene Berwanger, Colorado State University
Eugene Demody, Cerritos College
Frank Marmolejo, Irvine Valley College
Frank Siltman, U.S. Military Academy
Frank Towers, Clarion University
Fred Blue, Youngstown State University
Frederick Jaher, University of Illinois
Gary Reichard, Florida Atlantic University
Gary Topping, Salt Lake Community College
Gene Kirkpatrick, Tyler Junior College
George Gerdow, Northeastern Illinois University
Gerald Ghelfi, Rancho Santiago College
Gerald MacFarland, University of Massachusetts
Gilbert Cruz, Glendale Community College
Gregory Goodwin, Bakersfield College
Gwendolyn Hall, Rutgers University
Hal Rothman, University of Nevada, Las Vegas
Harland Hagler, University of North Texas
Harmon Mothershead, Northwest Missouri State University
Harry Bralley, Surry Community College
Harry Ward, University of Richmond
Henry Sage, Northern Virginia Community College, Alexandria
Henry William Brands, Texas A&M University
Howard Rock, Florida International University
Ira Gruber, U.S. Military Academy
Iris Engstrand, University of San Diego
J. Edward Lee, Winthrop University
J.B. Smallwood, University of North Texas
James Bradford, Texas A&M University
James Goode, Grand Valley State University
James Matray, New Mexico State University
James Seymour, CY-Fair
James Whittenberg, College of William and Mary
James Woods, Georgia Southern University
Janet Allured, McNeese State University
Jay Fell, University of Colorado
JoAnn Carpenter, Florida Community College
Joe Hapak, Moraine Valley Community College
John Chalberg, Normandale Community College
John Ingham, University of Toronto
John Johnson, University of Northern Iowa
John LaSaine, University of Georgia

John Rector, Western Oregon State University
John Wiseman, Frostburg State University
Jonathan Earle, University of Kansas
Joseph Adams, Saint Louis Community College
Joseph Devine, Stephen F. Austin State University
Joseph E. King, Texas Tech University
Joseph Reidy, Howard University
Juli Jones, St. Charles Community College
Karen Miller, Oakland University
Kay Pulley, Trinity Valley Community College
Ken Weatherbie, Del Mar College
Kenneth Stevens, Texas Christian University
LaShonda Mims, Central Piedmont Community College
Laura Graves, South Plains College
Lawrence Kohl, University of Alabama at Tuscaloosa
Leflett Easley, Campbell University
Leo Lyman, Victor Valley College
Leonard Dinnerstein, University of Arizona
Light T. Cummins, Austin College
Louis Gimelli, Eastern Michigan University
Marilyn Geiger, Washburn University
Mark Grimsley, Ohio State University
Mark Leff, University of Illinois, Urbana-Champaign
Mark Summers, University of Kentucky
Mark Wyman, Illinois State University
Marvin Dulaney, University of Texas at Arlington
Michael Batinski, Southern Illinois University
Michael Bradley, Motlow State Community College
Michael Krenn, University of Miami
Michael Krutz, Southeastern Louisiana University
Michael Schaller, University of Arizona
Michael Weiss, Linn-Benton Community College
Michael Welsh, University of Northern Colorado
Myles Clowers, San Diego City College
Nancy Gabin, Purdue University
Nancy Shoemaker, University of Connecticut
Nancy Smith Midgette, Elon College
Nancy Zen, Central Oregon Community College
Neal Brooks, Essex Community College
Neil York, Brigham Young University
Norman Markowitz, Rutgers University
Norman Raiford, Greenville Technical College
Otis Miller, Belleville Area College
Paul K. Davis, University of Texas at San Antonio
Paula Trekel, Allegheny College
Peggy Pascoe, University of Utah
Peter C. Mancell, University of Kansas
Priscilla Jackson-Evans, Longview Community College
Quintard Taylor, University of Oregon
Ralph Goodwin, East Texas State University
Randolph Campbell, University of North Texas
Rebecca Shoemaker, Indiana State University
Richard Brown, University of Connecticut

Richard Crepeau, University of Central Florida
Richard Lowe, University of North Texas
Richard Sadler, Weber State University
Rick Elder Bay Mills Community College
Robert Cray, Montclair State College
Robert Greene, Morgan State University
Robert Hinkle, Lexington Community College
Robert LaPorte, North Texas University
Robin Fabel, Auburn University
Ronald Hatzenbuchler, Idaho State University
Ronald McArthur, Atlantic Community College
Ronald Reitvald, California State University, Fullerton
Ronald Schultz, University of Wyoming
Samuel Crompton, Holyoke Community College
Sandra Schackel, Boise State University
Scott Garrett, Paducah Community College
Scott Martin, Bowling Green State University
Sheri David, Northern Virginia Community College
Sherry Smith, University of Texas at El Paso
Stanley Underal, San Jose University
Stephen Stein, University of Memphis
Stephen Webre, Louisiana Tech University
Steve Haley, Shelby State Community College
Terry Bilhartz, Sam Houston State University
Thomas C. Reeves, University of Wisconsin, Parkside
Thomas L. Powers, University of South Carolina, Sumter
Thomas McLuen, Spokane Falls Community College
Timothy D. Hall, Central Michigan University
Timothy Morgan, Christopher Newport University
Tom Bryan, Alvin Community College
Tyler Anbinder, George Washington University
Wade Shaffer, West Texas A&M
Wendy St. Jean, Dickinson College
Wilbur Johnson, Rock Valley College
William Allison, Weber State University
William Corbett, Northeastern State University
William Paquette, Tidewater Community College
William Stockton, Johnson County Community College

William Tanner, Humbolt State University
William Young, Johnson County Community College
Worth Robert Miller, Southwest Missouri State University
Yasuhide Kawashima, University of Texas at El Paso
Yvonne Johnson, Central Missouri State University

All of us are grateful to our families, friends, and col-
leagues for their support and encouragement. Jo Ann and
Peter Argersinger would like in particular to thank Anna
Champe, Linda Hatmaker, and John Willits; William Barney
thanks Pamela Fesmire and Rosalie Radcliffe; Virginia Ander-
son thanks Fred Anderson, Kim Gruenwald, Ruth Helm,
Eric Hinderaker, and Chidiebere Nwaubani; and David
Goldfield thanks Frances Glenn and Jason Moscato, Jim
Miller, Sylvia Mallory, and Sally Constable played key roles in
the book's inception and initial development.

Finally, we would like to acknowledge the members of
our Prentice Hall family. They are not only highly competent professionals but also pleasant people. We regard them
with affection and appreciation. None of us would hesitate
to work with this fine group again. We would especially like
to thank our editorial team: Charlyce Jones Owen, Publisher;
Priscilla McGeehon, VP/Publisher; our marketing team: Sue
Westmoreland, Executive Marketing Manager, and Brandy
Dawson, Director of Marketing; our production team: Anne
Marie McCarthy, Patty Donovan, Pine Tree Composition,
Denise Brown, Production Liaison, Maura Zaldovar, Manufacturing Manager, and Mary Ann Gloriande, Manufacturing;
and Yolanda deRooy, President of Prentice Hall's Humanities
and Social Sciences division.

DG
CA
VDJA
JEA
PHA
WLB
RMW

About the Authors

David Goldfield received his Ph.D. in history from the University of Maryland. Since 1982 he has been Robert Lee Bailey Professor of History at the University of North Carolina in Charlotte. He is the author or editor of thirteen books on various aspects of southern and urban history. Two of his works—*Cotton Fields and Skyscrapers: Southern City and Region, 1607–1980* (1982) and *Black, White, and Southern: Race Relations and Southern Culture, 1940 to the Present* (1990)—received the Mayflower Award for nonfiction and were nominated for the Pulitzer Prize in history. His most recent book is *Still Fighting the Civil War: The American South and Southern History* (2002). When he is not writing history, Dr. Goldfield applies his historical craft to history museum exhibits, voting rights cases, and local planning and policy issues.

Carl Abbott is a professor of Urban Studies and planning at Portland State University. He taught previously in the history departments at the University of Denver and Old Dominion University and held visiting appointments at Mesa College in Colorado and George Washington University. He holds degrees in history from Swarthmore College and the University of Chicago. He specializes in the history of cities and the American West and serves as co-editor of the Pacific Historical Review. His books include *The New Urban America: Growth and Politics in Sunbelt Cities* (1981, 1987), *The Metropolitan Frontier: Cities in the Modern American West* (1993), *Planning a New West: The Columbia River Gorge National Scenic Area* (1997), and *Political Terrain: Washington, D.C. from Tidewater Town to Global Metropolis* (1999). He is currently working on a comprehensive history of the role of urbanization and urban culture in the history of western North America.

Virginia DeJohn Anderson is Professor of History at the University of Colorado at Boulder. She received her B.A. from the University of Connecticut. As the recipient of a Marshall Scholarship, she earned an M.A. degree at the University of East Anglia in Norwich, England. Returning to the United States, she received her A.M. and Ph.D. degrees from Harvard University. She is the author of *New England's Generation: The Great Migration and the Formation of Society and Culture in the Seventeenth Century* (1991) and several articles on colonial history, which have appeared in such journals as the *William and Mary Quarterly* and the *New England Quarterly*. Her most recent book is *Creatures of Empire: How Domestic Animals Transformed Early America* (2004).

Jo Ann E. Argersinger received her Ph.D. from George Washington University and is Professor of History at Southern Illinois University. A recipient of fellowships from the Rockefeller Foundation and the National Endowment for the Humanities, she is a historian of social, labor, and business policy. Her publications include *Toward a New Deal in Baltimore: People and Government in the Great Depression* (1988) and *Making the Amalgamated: Gender, Ethnicity, and Class in the Baltimore Clothing Industry* (1999).

Peter H. Argersinger received his Ph.D. from the University of Wisconsin and is Professor of History at Southern Illinois University. He has won several fellowships as well as the Binkley-Stephenson Award from the Organization of American Historians, and he is currently president of the Society for Historians of the Gilded Age and Progressive Era. Among his books on political and rural history are *Populism and Politics* (1974), *Structure, Process, and Party* (1992), and *The Limits of Agrarian Radicalism* (1995). His current research focuses on the political crisis of the 1890s.

William L. Barney is Professor of History at the University of North Carolina at Chapel Hill. A native of Pennsylvania, he received his B.A. from Cornell University and his M.A. and Ph.D. from Columbia University. He has published extensively on nineteenth century U.S. history and has a particular interest in the Old South and the coming of the Civil War. Among his publications are *The Road to Secession* (1972), *The Secessionist Impulse* (1974), *Flawed Victory* (1975), *The Passage of the Republic* (1987), and *Battleground for the Union* (1989). He is currently finishing an edited collection of essays on nineteenth-century America and a book on the Civil War. Most recently, he has edited *A Companion to 19th-Century America* (2001) and finished *The Civil War and Reconstruction: A Student Companion* (2001).

Robert M. Weir is Distinguished Professor of History Emeritus at the University of South Carolina. He received his B.A. from Pennsylvania State University and his Ph.D. from Case Western Reserve University. He has taught at the University of Houston and, as a visiting professor, at the University of Southampton in the United Kingdom. His articles have won prizes from the Southeastern Society for the Study of the Eighteenth Century and the *William and Mary Quarterly*. Among his publications are *Colonial South Carolina: A History, "The Last of American Freemen": Studies in the Political Culture of the Colonial and Revolutionary South,* and, more recently, a chapter on the Carolinas in the new *Oxford History of the British Empire* (1998).

STUDENT TOOL KIT

When writing history, historians use maps, tables, graphs, and visuals to help their readers understand the past. What follows is an explanation of how to use the historian's tools that are contained in this book.

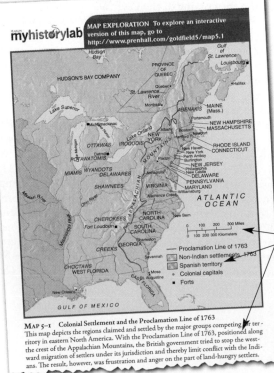

TEXT

Whether it is a biography of George Washington, an article on the Civil War, or a survey of American history such as this one, the text is the historian's basic tool for discussing the past. Historians write about the past using narration and analysis. Narration is the story line of history. It describes what happened in the past, who did it, and where and when it occurred. Narration is also used to describe how people in the past lived, how they passed their daily lives and even, when the historical evidence makes it possible for us to know, what they thought, felt, feared, or desired. Using analysis, historians explain why they think events in the past happened the way they did and offer an explanation for the story of history. In this book, narration and analysis are interwoven in each chapter.

MAPS

Maps are important historical tools. They show how geography has affected history and concisely summarize complex relationships and events. Knowing how to read and interpret a map is important to understanding history. Map 5-1 from Chapter 5 shows the British colonies on the eastern seaboard of North America in 1763, about twelve years before the American Revolution. It has three features to help you read it: a caption, a legend, and a scale. The caption explains the historical significance of the map. Here the caption tells us that in 1763 the British government sought to restrict colonial settlement west of the Appalachian Mountains to prevent conflict between colonists and Indians. Colonial frustration with this policy contributed to the outbreak of the American Revolution.

The legend and the scale appear in the lower right corner of the map. The legend provides a key to what the symbols on the map mean. The solid line stretching along the Appalachian Mountains from Maine to Georgia represents the Proclamation Line of 1763. Cities are marked with a dot, capitals with a star, and forts by a black square. Spanish territory west of the Mississippi River is represented in blue; territory settled by Europeans is represented in green. The scale tells us that 7/8ths of an inch on the map represents 300 miles (about 480 kilometers) on the ground. With this information, estimates of the distance between points on the map are easily made. Some maps also shows the topography of the region-its mountains, rivers, and lakes. This helps us understand how geography influenced history in this case.

MAP 5-1   Colonial Settlement and the Proclamation Line of 1763
This map depicts the regions claimed and settled by the major groups competing for territory in eastern North America. With the Proclamation Line of 1763, positioned along the crest of the Appalachian Mountains, the British government tried to stop the westward migration of settlers under its jurisdiction and thereby limit conflict with the Indians. The result, however, was frustration and anger on the part of land-hungry settlers.

For example, the Appalachian Mountains divide the eastern seaboard from the rest of the continent. The mountains obstructed colonial migration to the west for a long time. By running the Proclamation Line along the Appalachians, the British hoped to use this natural barrier to separate Indians and colonists. A critical-thinking question asks for careful considersation of the spatial connections between geography and history.

MAP EXPLORATIONS

Many of the maps in each chapter are provided in a useful interactive version on the text's *Myhistorylab* website. These maps are easily identified by a bar along the top that reads "Map Explorations." An interactive version of Colonial Settlements and the Proclamation Line of 1763 can also be accessed at www.prenhall.com/goldfield5/map5.1. The interactive version of this particular map provides an opportunity to pan over an enlarged version of the territory in question. Cities, forts, settlements, and terrain are shown in detail. By moving the cursor north, south, east, or west one can gain a bird's-eye view of the entire region.

VISUALS

Visual images embedded thoughout the text can provide as much insight into our nation's history as the written word. Within photographs and pieces of fine art lies emotional and historical meaning. Captions provide valuable information, such as in the example below. When studying the image, consider questions such as: "Who are these people?"; "How were they feeling?"; "What event motivated this photograph or painting?"; and "What can be learned from the backdrop surrounding the focal point?" Such analysis allows for a fuller understanding of the people who lived theAmerican journey.

122   *Chapter 5   Imperial Breakdown 1763–1774*

Cunne Shote, one of three Cherokee chiefs who visited London in 1762, had this portrait painted there by Francis Parsons.

by giving them blankets that smallpox victims had used. Settlers in Paxton township (near modern Harrisburg, Pennsylvania) also committed atrocities. Angered by the Pennsylvania Assembly's lack of aggressive action against the Indians, the settlers lashed out at their peaceful neighbors, the Conestogas. Facing arrest and trial for this outrage, the so-called Paxton Boys marched on Philadelphia, threatening the Pennsylvania Assembly. Benjamin Franklin persuaded them to disperse. Despite the government's efforts, the Paxton Boys were never effectively prosecuted for their acts.

Pontiac's Rebellion and the Cherokee War were costly for both sides. Hoping to prevent such outbreaks, British officials began experimenting with centralized control of Indian affairs during the 1750s. Following the recommendations of the Albany Congress in 1754 (see Chapter 4), they had already created two districts, northern and southern, for the administration of Indian affairs, each with its own superintendent. The Proclamation of 1763, and the line it established restricting further white settlement, gave these officials increased responsibility for protecting the Indians against encroachments by settlers. But land-hungry Americans objected to efforts to keep them off Indian lands, and white traders resented restrictions on their activities. Centralized control of the fur and deerskin trades also proved to be expensive for the British government. British authorities therefore permitted several adjustments in the Indian boundary line and in 1768 returned supervision of the Indian

trauers to the individual colonies. But such tacit recognition of local autonomy conflicted with imperial plans to restrict the powers of the colonial assemblies.

Curbing the Assemblies

As early as the 1750s, a dispute over the salaries of Anglican ministers known as the **Parson's Cause** prompted British officials to instruct the governor of Virginia not to sign any legislation that modified existing laws unless it contained a clause making the change inoperative until the king approved it. This restriction, which severely hampered the assembly's ability to respond to emergencies, alarmed Virginians who maintained that their legislators had the "Right to enact ANY Law they shall think necessary for their INTERNAL Government."

British authorities of course disagreed, and in 1764 Parliament bowed to the wishes of British merchants, who suffered from depreciating colonial paper money, by extending an earlier measure to forbid all American legislatures from making such issues legal tender. Because the Currency Act of 1764 came when most colonies were in an economic recession, Americans considered this step especially burdensome or, as one said, "downright Robbery." Worse, however, was yet to come.

The Sugar and Stamp Acts

In 1764, the British Parliament, under Prime Minister George Grenville, passed the American Revenue Act, commonly known as the **Sugar Act**. In order to generate increased revenue, the Sugar Act and accompanying legislation combined new and revised duties on colonial imports with strict enforcement provisions. In particular, Parliament sought to minimize motivation for smuggling by reducing the duty on French West Indian molasses by 50 percent.

The Sugar Act legislation also lengthened the list of enumerated products—goods that could be sent only to England or destinations within the empire—and required that ships carry elaborate new documentation of their cargoes; these requirements were a reasonable attempt to prevent illegal trade with other countries, but unintentional mistakes by a shipper could result in the unreasonable seizure of entire cargoes.

To enforce these cumbersome regulations, the British government continued to use the Royal Navy to seize smugglers' ships, a practice authorized by the Revenue Act of 1762 during the French and Indian War. It also ordered colonial customs collectors to discharge their duties personally. Previously, the collectors had often lived in England, leaving the work of collection in the colonies to poorly paid deputies, who were susceptible to bribes. Finally, Parliament gave responsibility for trying violations of the laws to a new vice-admiralty court in Halifax, Nova Scotia. Vice-admiralty courts had jurisdiction over maritime affairs. Unlike other courts, they normally operated without a jury and were therefore more likely to enforce trade restrictions. For this reason, and because of the remote location of the Halifax court—getting to it would be a hardship—Americans immediately opposed this provision of the Sugar Act. In response, Parliament created three other vice-admiralty courts in the more conven-

STUDENT TOOL KIT

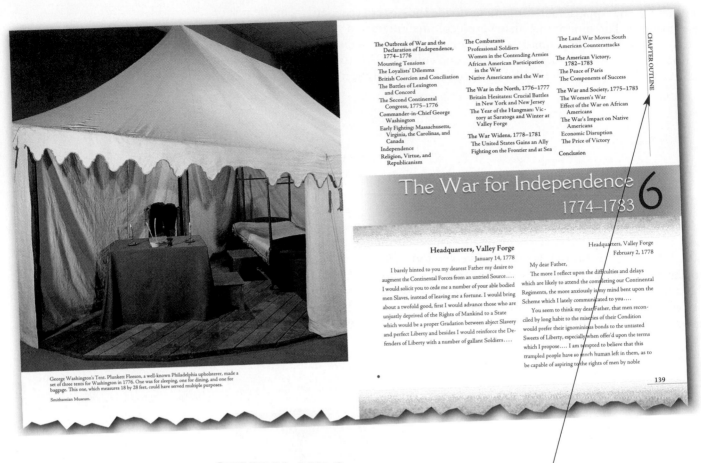

George Washington's Tent. Plunkett Fleeson, a well-known Philadelphia upholsterer, made a set of three tents for Washington in 1776. One was for sleeping, one for dining, and one for baggage. This one, which measures 18 by 28 feet, could have served multiple purposes.

Smithsonian Museum.

STUDY AIDS

Each chapter begins with a stunning visual and a Chapter Outline that provides a road map for study and review.

KEY TERMS/ GLOSSARY

Significant historical terms are called out in heavy type throughout the text and listed at the end of each chapter with appropriate page numbers. All key terms in the text are listed alphabetically and defined in a glossary at the end of the book.

STUDENT TOOL KIT

OVERVIEW

Predominant Colonial Labor Systems, 1750

	Colony	Labor System
New England	Massachusetts	Family farms
	Connecticut	Family farms
	New Hampshire	Family farms
	Rhode Island	Family farms
Middle Colonies	New York	Family farms, tenancy
	Pennsylvania and Delaware	Indentured servitude, tenancy, family farms
	New Jersey	Family farms, tenancy
South	Maryland	Slavery
	Virginia	Slavery
	North Carolina	Family farms, slavery

OVERVIEWS

The Overview tables in this text are a special feature designed to highlight and summarize important topics within a chapter. The Overview table shown here, for example, shows the predominant colonial labor systems in 1750 by geographic area.

CHRONOLOGY

1861	Tsar Alexander II frees the serfs of Russia.
1863	Lincoln proposes his Ten Percent Plan.
1864	Congress proposes the Wade-Davis Bill.
1865	Sherman issues Field Order No. 15.
	Freedmen's Bureau is established.
	Andrew Johnson succeeds to the presidency, unveils his Reconstruction plan.
	Massachusetts desegregates all public facilities.
	Black citizens in several southern cities organize Union Leagues.
	Former Confederate states begin to pass black codes.
1866	Congress passes Southern Homestead Act, Civil Rights Act of 1866.
	Ku Klux Klan is founded.

CHRONOLOGIES

Each chapter includes a Chronology, a list of the key events discussed in the chapter arranged in chronological order. The chronology for Chapter 16 lists the dates of key events during the Reconstruction era from 1865 to 1877. Chronologies provide a review of important events and their relationship to one another.

STUDENT TOOL KIT

Page 136 sample:

136   Chapter 5   *Imperial Breakdown 1763–1774*

to call themselves **Whigs** and condemned their opponents as **Tories**. These traditional English party labels dated from the late seventeenth century, when the Tories had supported the accession of the Catholic King James II, whereas the Whigs had opposed it. By calling themselves Whigs and their opponents Tories (loyalist was a more accurate label), the advocates of colonial rights cast themselves as champions of liberty and their enemies as defenders of religious intolerance and royal absolutism.

Conclusion

All Americans, Whigs and loyalists alike, considered themselves good British subjects. But Americans were a more diverse and more democratic people than the English. A considerably larger percentage of them could participate in government, and for all practical purposes, they had been governing themselves for a long time. British officials recognized the different character of American society and feared it might lead Americans to reject British control. But the steps they took to prevent this outcome had the opposite effect.

Attempts to protect their accustomed autonomy first brought the colonial assemblies into conflict with Parliament. Asserting their rights led to greater cooperation among individual colonies. This development, in turn, led to increasingly widespread resistance, then to rebellion, and finally to revolution. Moving imperceptibly from one stage to the next, Americans grew conscious of their common interests and their differences from the English. They became aware, as Benjamin Franklin would later write, of the need to break "through the bounds, in which a dependent people had been accustomed to think, and act" so that they might "properly comprehend the character they had assumed."

That workingmen and members of the elite dressed as Indians had joined in the dangerous act of defiance known as the Boston Tea Party also foreshadowed coming developments. No one now knows for certain why they adopted that particular disguise, but Indians were a traditional symbol of the New World. And those who were making a new political world were risking much—even, it would shortly turn out, life itself.

Review Questions

1. What do Eliza Farmar's letters tell us about the crisis over dutied tea in 1773 and 1774? What does she think has caused the crisis and who was at fault? What makes her think the colonists have any chance of success in resisting British impositions?

2. How did the British victory and French withdrawal from North America after the French and Indian War affect the relations between Native Americans and white settlers? Between British authorities and Americans?

3. What was the relationship between the French and Indian War and changes in British policy toward America? How did the expectations of Americans and Britons differ in 1763? Why were the new policies offensive to Americans?

4. How was stationing British troops in America related to British taxation of the colonists? Why did the colonists consider taxation by Parliament an especially serious threat to their freedom as well as to their pocketbooks?

5. How did Americans oppose the new measures? Who participated in the various forms of resistance? How effective were the different kinds of resistance? What effect did resistance to British measures have on Americans' internal politics and sense of identity as Americans?

6. What led to the meeting of the First Continental Congress? What steps did the Congress take? What did it expect to achieve? What were the differences between Whigs and Tories?

Key Terms

Boston Massacre (p. 129)
Boston Tea Party (p. 131)
British Constitution (p. 123)
Cherokee War (p. 121)
Coercive Acts (p. 131)
Committees of correspondence (p. 129)

First Continental Congress (p. 133)
Intolerable Acts (p. 131)
Nonimportation movement (p. 125)
Parson's Cause (p. 122)
Pontiac's Rebellion (p. 121)
Proclamation of 1763 (p. 120)

Stamp Act (p. 123)
Stamp Act Congress (p. 125)
Sugar Act (p. 122)
Suffolk Resolves (p. 133)
Tea Act of 1773 (p. 129)
Tories (p. 136)

Page 137 sample:

Imperial Breakdown 1763–1774   Chapter 5   137

Recommended Reading

Bailyn, Bernard. *The Ideological Origins of the American Revolution*, 2nd ed. (1992). A clear and illuminating account of how the colonists' ideas about politics prepared them to resist British measures.

Countryman, Edward. *The American Revolution*, 2nd ed. (2003). A brief, readable general history of the Revolutionary period that focuses on the involvement of the common people.

Morison, Samuel Eliot, ed. *Sources and Documents Illustrating the American Revolution, 1764–1788, and the Formation of*

the Federal Constitution, 2nd ed. (1965). The most readily available and conveniently used collection of documents (mostly official) from the era of the American Revolution.

Raphael, Ray. *A People's History of the American Revolution: How Common People Shaped the Fight for Independence* (2001). A readable, popular synthesis of much recent scholarship.

Where to Learn More

■ **Charleston, South Carolina.** Many buildings date from the eighteenth century. Officials stored tea in one of them, the Exchange, to prevent a local version of the Boston Tea Party. The website for Historic Charleston, www.cr.nps.gov/nr/travel/charleston, provides a map, a list of buildings, and information about them.

■ **Philadelphia, Pennsylvania.** Numerous buildings and sites date from the eighteenth century. Independence National Historical Park, between Second and Sixth streets on Walnut and Chestnut streets, contains Carpenter's Hall, where the First Continental Congress met, and the Pennsylvania State House (now known as Independence Hall), where the Declaration of Independence was adopted. Philadelphia's Historic Mile, www.ushistory.org/tour/index.html, provides a virtual tour of the great landmarks of the city, including Independence Hall.

■ **Boston, Massachusetts.** Many important buildings and sites in this area date from the seventeenth and eigh-

teenth centuries. They include Faneuil Hall (Dock Square), where many public meetings took place prior to the Revolution, and the Old State House (Washington and State streets), which overlooks the site of the Boston Massacre. The Freedom Trail, www.thefreedomtrail.org/virtual_tour.html, provides a well-illustrated virtual tour of the historic sites.

■ **Fort Michilimackinac National Historic Landmark, Mackinaw City, Michigan.** Near the south end of the Mackinac Bridge, the present structure is a modern restoration of the fort as it was when Pontiac's Rebellion took a heavy toll of its garrison. The Mackinac State Historic Park's website, www.mackinacparks.com/michilimackinac/html, provides a brief description and photographs of the reconstructed colonial village and fort.

Study Resources

PEARSON
myhistorylab

For study resources for this chapter, go to www.myhistorylab.com and choose *The American Journey*. You will find a wealth of study and review material for this chapter, including pre- and post-tests, customized study plan, key term review flash cards, interactive map and document activities, and documents for analysis.

CONCLUSION

The conclusion at the end of each chapter puts the subject of the chapter in the broader perspective of U.S. history.

REVIEW QUESTIONS, RECOMMENDED READING, WHERE TO LEARN MORE

At the end of each chapter there are a number of review and enrichment resources. Review questions reconsider the main topics of each chapter. Annotated Recommended Reading introduce students to interesting books and articles that can expand their knowledge on the topics outlined the chapter. The section called Where to Learn More lists important historical sites and museums around the country and related Websites that provide first-hand exposure to historical artifacts and settings. A new section, Study Resources, notes the availability of materials related to the chapter on the *Myhistorylab* website; this is an excellent resource for additional study aids.

SPECIAL FEATURES

Historians find most of their information in written records and original documents that have survived from the past. These include government publications, letters, diaries, newspapers–whatever people wrote or printed, including many private documents never intended for publication. Several features in the text highlight the written record so important to understanding historical events.

VOICES FROM THE AMERICAN JOURNEY

Each chapter begins with a brief firsthand account from an individual that powerfully recounts the personal journey he or she took in their lives. Each of these "voices" relates to the themes that follow in the chapter. For example, in Chapter 18 is an excerpt from a letter written by Mary Antin, a Russian-Jewish immigrant who came to America at the turn of the last century.

New! Personal Journeys Online
At the end of each document is a list of additional firsthand accounts that are included on the *Myhistorylab* website.

STUDENT TOOL KIT

AMERICAN VIEWS

Each chapter contains a selection from a primary source document. The example shown here is the published account of Mary Rowlandson from Lancaster, Massachusetts, who in 1676 was taken captive with two of her children by Indian warriors. Each American Views feature begins with a brief introduction followed by several questions–for discussion or written response–on what the document reveals about key issues and events.

American Views

Mary Rowlandson Among the Indians

In February 1676, in the midst of King Philip's War, Indian warriors attacked the town of Lancaster, Massachusetts. They killed many inhabitants and took 23 colonists captive, including Mary Rowlandson and three of her children. Rowlandson spent the next three months traveling with various groups of Nipmucs, Narragansetts, and Wampanoags. She suffered physically and emotionally, watching her youngest daughter die in her arms and worrying about her other two children, from whom she was frequently separated. During her captivity, Rowlandson survived by accepting her fate and adapting to the Indians' way of life. Finally, with an English victory imminent, Rowlandson was ransomed and rejoined her husband (who had been away at the time of the attack) and family. In 1682, she published an account of her captivity in which she explored the meaning of her experience. Rowlandson's narrative proved so popular that three editions were printed in the first year.

- How did Rowlandson describe the Indians? How did she characterize her encounter with King Philip?
- In what ways did Rowlandson accommodate herself to the Indians' way of life? How did she employ her skills to fit in? Did her gender make a difference in her experience of captivity?
- How did Rowlandson's Puritan faith shape her narrative?

We travelled on till night; and in the morning, we must go over the River to Philip's crew. When I was in the Cannoo, I could not but be amazed at the numerous crew of Pagans that were on the Bank on the other side. When I came ashore, they gathered all about me, I sitting alone in the midst: I observed they asked one another questions, and laughed, and rejoiced over their Gains and Victories. Then my heart began to fail: and I fell a weeping which was the first time to my remembrance that I wept before them. Although I had met with so much Affliction, and my heart was many times ready to break, yet could I not shed one tear in their sight: but rather had been all this while in a maze, and like one astonished: but now I may say as, Psal. 137.1 *By the rivers of Babylon, there we sat down: yea, we wept when we remembered Zion.* There one of them asked me, why I wept, I could hardly tell what to say: yet I answered, they would kill me: No, said he, none will hurt you. Then came one of them and gave me two spoon-fulls of Meal to comfort me…. Then I went to see King Philip, he bade me come in and sit down, and asked me whether I would smoke (a usual Complement now adayes amongst Saints and Sinners) but this no way suited me. For though I had formerly used Tobacco, yet I had left it ever since I was first taken,

It seems to be a bait, the devil lays to make men loose their precious time….

During my abode in this place, Philip spake to me to make a shirt for his boy, which I did, for which he gave me a shilling: I offered the money to my master, but he bade me keep it: and with it I bought a piece of Horse flesh. Afterwards he asked me to make a Cap for his boy, for which he invited me to Dinner. I went, and he gave me a Pancake, about as big as two fingers; it was made of parched wheat, beaten, and fryed in Bears grease, but I thought I never tasted pleasanter meat in my life. There was a Squaw who spake to me to make a shirt for her *Sannup* [husband], for which she gave me a piece of Bear. Another asked me to knit a pair of Stockins, for which she gave me a quart of Pease…. Hearing that my son was come to this place, I went to see him, and found him lying flat upon the ground: I asked him how he could sleep so? He answered me, *That he was not asleep, but at Prayer*; and lay so, that they might not observe what he was doing. I pray God he may remember these things now he is returned in safety.

Source: Neal Salisbury, ed., *The Sovereignty and Goodness of God, Together with the Faithfulness of His Promises Displayed…* (Boston, 1997), pp. 82–83.

66

GLOBAL PERSPECTIVES

This feature places the American journey within a broader worldwide context. That journey not only influenced other countries and peoples, but we in turn have been shaped by global economic, migratory, technological, and political trends. The example shown here is about a mass exodus of German-speaking people from the Rhineland to various parts of the world, including the United States.

New! Critical thinking questions encourage analysis of the global connections.

Global Perspectives

Early Modern Europe's Biggest Mass Migration

The stream of German immigrants moving to America in the late seventeenth and eighteenth centuries formed only a small part of a much larger flow of emigrants from the Rhineland to many parts of the globe. The Rhineland was not a single political unit, but a region of small states and principalities located along one of Europe's major rivers. Political fragmentation brought religious diversity, with German Reformed or Lutheran churches dominant in some areas and Catholics in others.

Large-scale emigration of Rhineland inhabitants stemmed from many causes, especially warfare. During the Thirty Years' War (1618–1648), much of the Rhineland area was devastated by intense religious conflict and famine. In the 1680s and 1690s, Louis XIV of France invaded the region, sparking more turmoil. Almost continual warfare from the 1730s to the 1760s made the lives of Rhineland inhabitants even worse.

Economic hardship and political repression also spurred emigration. Harsh winters in 1708–1709 and 1709–1710, for instance, destroyed orchards and vineyards, threatening many farmers with impoverishment and even starvation. Harvests failed in many parts of the Rhineland in the 1740s. In addition, religious minorities suffered from persecution, and everyone bore the burden of increasing taxes and arbitrary rule by local princes. For all of these reasons, over the course of the eighteenth century, hundreds of thousands of Rhinelanders decided to flee their homeland.

Many promoters, land speculators, and even governments sought to direct the flow of emigrants to a favored region. Officials from Russia and Prussia offered cheap land and tax exemptions to lure migrants to their countries. As a result of this promotional campaign, by far the largest number of Rhineland refugees relocated to various parts of Eastern Europe, including Prussia, Russia, Hungary, and Poland. A smaller flow of emigrants, mostly Protestants, made their way to North America, settling principally in Pennsylvania, New York, and the Carolinas. Still others moved to Cayenne (French Guiana) in South America. The exodus of these German-speaking emigrants to destinations in the Old and New Worlds constituted the most significant mass migration in early modern Europe.

- Why might more Rhineland migrants have moved within Europe instead of going to the North American colonies?

equipment, including boats, provisions, and salt (used for preserving fish). Merchants recruited fishermen by advancing credit to coastal villagers so that they could outfit their own boats. To pay off the debt, the fishermen were legally bound to bring their catch to the merchant, who then sold it to Europe and the West Indies. Many fishermen ran up such large debts that they were obliged to continue supplying fish to their creditors, whether they wanted to or not. Toward the end of the seventeenth century, as the rising population of coastal villages lowered the cost of labor, merchants abandoned the credit system and paid wages to fishermen instead.

In the northern colonies, the same conditions that made men reluctant to become fishermen deterred them from becoming farm laborers, except perhaps for high wages. Paying high wages, however, was difficult for New Englanders with farms or slaves was difficult for New Englanders with farms that produced no export crops and could not be worked during cold winter months. So northern farmers turned to the cheapest and most dependable workers they could find—their children.

Children as young as 5 or 6 years old began with simple tasks and moved on to more complex work as they grew older. By the time they were in their late teens, girls knew how to run households, and boys knew how to farm. Instead of contracts or outright coercion, fathers used their ownership of property to prolong the time their sons worked for them. Young men could not marry until they could set up their own households and relied on their fathers to provide them with land to do so. Fathers often waited until their sons were in their mid-twenties, compelling them until then to invest their labor in the paternal estate.

Thus New England's labor shortage produced strong ties of dependency between generations. Fathers kept their sons working for them as long as possible; sons accepted this arrangement because they had no other way to become

79

FROM THEN TO NOW

This feature connects events and trends in the past to issues that confront Americans today, illustrating the value a historical perspective can contribute to our understanding of the world we live in. The example here, from Chapter 3, discusses the continuing legacy of slavery in American life.

New! From Then to Now Online
This new section lists additional text and visual primary source documents on the topic that are included on the *Myhistorylab* website.

"A Hunger to Learn." This 1863 watercolor by Henry L. Stephens depicts an elderly African American, probably a former slave, learning to read. The newspaper's headline states, "Presidential Proclamation, Slavery." Learning transcended age among freed blacks in the South.

Reconstruction 16
1865–1877

Marianna, Florida 1866

The white academy opened about the same time the church opened the school for the Negro children. As the colored children had to pass the academy to reach the church it was easy for the white children to annoy them with taunts and jeers. The war passed from words to stones which the white children began to hurl at the colored. Several colored children were hurt and, as they had not resented the rock-throwing in kind because they were timid about going that far, the white children became more aggressive and abusive.

One morning the colored children armed themselves with stones and determined to fight their way past the academy to their school. [They] approached the academy in formation whereas in the past they had been going in pairs or small groups. When they reached hailing distance, a half dozen white boys rushed out and hurled their missiles. Instead of scampering away, the colored children not only stood their ground and hurled their missiles but maintained a solemn silence. The white children, seeing there was no backing down as they expected, came rushing out of the academy and charged the colored children.

During some fifteen minutes it was a real tug of war. In the close fighting the colored children got the advantage gradually and began to shove the white children back. As they pressed the advantage the white children

433

broke away and ran for the academy. The colored fighters did not follow them but made it hot for the laggards until they also took to their heels. There were many bruises on both sides, but it taught the white youngsters to leave the colored ones alone thereafter.

T. Thomas Fortune, *Norfolk Journal and Guide*

T. Thomas Fortune, "Norfolk Journal and Guide," August 20, 1927, reprinted in Dorothy Sterling, ed., *The Trouble They Seen: Black People Tell the Story of Reconstruction* (Garden City, NY: Doubleday, 1976): 22–24.

myhistorylab

Personal Journeys Online

- N. J. Bell, *Southern Railroad Man,* 1865. A railroad conductor recalls the aftermath of the Civil War and its impact on a white family in Wilmington, NC.

- Adelbert Ames, *Letter from the Republican Governor of Mississippi,* 1875. Letter to his wife expressing frustration at the violence against black voters in his state and his hope for federal intervention.

T. Thomas Fortune, a New York newspaper editor, recalled this battle between black and white schoolchildren sixty years after it occurred at the beginning of the Reconstruction era. In the scheme of things, it did not amount to much. However, for 10-year-old Thomas, born a slave in Marianna, the incident encapsulated the dilemma of Reconstruction. In the journey from slavery to freedom, education emerged as an important element of full citizenship for African Americans. The eagerness with which black children (and adults) flooded schools, often spaces converted in churches and staffed initially by white missionaries from the North, was matched by the hostility of the white community, which resented any social advance or pretense of equality in the former bondsmen.

Reconstruction was not merely a series of white aggressions against African American aspirations, followed by black retreats. The former slaves did not shy away from asserting their rights. The violence and disorder that punctuated southern society after the Civil War was due in part to the refusal of blacks to relinquish their dreams of equal citizenship, including the right to a decent education.

Young Thomas did not back down, although by 1878 he understood that the promise of his schoolboy days could not be realized in the South. The journey from slavery to freedom, he felt, would always be incomplete in the South. Together with his young bride, Carrie Smiley of Jacksonville, Florida, Thomas left for New York City, where he obtained a job as a printer for the *New York Sun.* Shaped by his early years in Florida, and the difficulties involved in obtaining a decent education, Fortune used the pages of the *Sun* to promote equality of education for all races and integrated public schools in New York State. He died there in 1928. New York's gain was the South's loss, a process repeated many times over in the decades after the Civil War as talented young black men and women migrated north. It was a double tragedy for the South: losing people who could have rebuilt a shattered region and missing the opportunity to create a society based on racial equality.

The position of African Americans in American society was one of the two great issues of the Reconstruction era. Americans of both sections disagreed about how much freedom to grant the former slaves, almost all of whom lived in the South. The other great issue was how and under what terms to readmit the former Confederate states. The Constitution was silent on the subject. As with the issue of black equality, opinions in both sections varied widely.

◆ African American aspirations and southern white expectations

◆ Federal government plans to bring the South back into the Union and secure freedom for former slaves

◆ Southern Republican efforts to keep the allegiance of black voters and win white support

◆ Why and how Reconstruction ended

KEY TOPICS

The formation of a national consensus on freedom and reunification began with the demands and hopes of three broad groups. One was the Republican Party, which controlled the federal government. Most Republicans were unwilling to accept the seceding states back in the Union without an expression of loyalty and a commitment to protect the rights of freedmen. A second group, the more than 4 million former slaves, demanded voting rights, access to education, and the opportunity to seek economic self-sufficiency. Few black northerners yet enjoyed all these benefits, and few white southerners could conceive of former slaves possessing them. The third group, white southerners, hoped to restore their shattered lives, fortunes, and dignity. In their vision of a renewed South, black people remained subservient, and the federal government stopped interfering in southern affairs.

Between 1865 and 1867, under President Andrew Johnson's Reconstruction plan, white southerners pretty much had their way with the former slaves and with their own state governments. Congressional action between 1867 and 1870 attempted to balance black rights and home rule, with mixed results. After 1870, white southerners gradually regained control of their states and localities, often through violence and intimidation, denying black southerners their political gains while Republicans in Washington and white northerners lost interest in policing their former enemies.

By the time the last federal troops left the South in 1877, the white southerners had prevailed. The Confederate states had returned to the Union with all of their rights and many of their leaders restored. And the freed slaves remained in mostly subservient positions with few of the rights and privileges enjoyed by other Americans.

CHRONOLOGY

1861	Tsar Alexander II frees the serfs of Russia.
1863	Lincoln proposes his Ten Percent Plan.
1864	Congress proposes the Wade-Davis Bill.
1865	Sherman issues Field Order No. 15.
	Freedmen's Bureau is established.
	Andrew Johnson succeeds to the presidency, unveils his Reconstruction plan.
	Massachusetts desegregates all public facilities.
	Black citizens in several southern cities organize Union Leagues.
	Former Confederate states begin to pass black codes.
1866	Congress passes Southern Homestead Act, Civil Rights Act of 1866.
	Ku Klux Klan is founded.
	Fourteenth Amendment to the Constitution is passed (ratified in 1868).
1867	Congress passes Military Reconstruction Acts, Tenure of Office Act.
1868	President Johnson is impeached and tried in the Senate for defying the Tenure of Office Act.
	Republican Ulysses S. Grant is elected president.
1869	Fifteenth Amendment passed (ratified 1870).
1870	Congress passes Enforcement Act.
	Republican regimes topple in North Carolina and Georgia.
1871	Congress passes Ku Klux Klan Act.
1872	Freedmen's Bureau closes down.
	Liberal Republicans emerge as a separate party.
	Ulysses S. Grant is reelected.
1873	Severe depression begins.
	Colfax Massacre occurs.
	U.S. Supreme Court's decision in the *Slaughterhouse* cases weakens the intent of the Fourteenth Amendment.
	Texas falls to the Democrats in the fall elections.
1874	White Leaguers attempt a coup against the Republican government of New Orleans.
	Democrats win off-year elections across the South amid widespread fraud and violence.
1875	Congress passes Civil Rights Act of 1875.
1876	Supreme Court's decision in *United States v. Cruikshank* nullifies Enforcement Act of 1870.
	Outcome of the presidential election between Republican Rutherford B. Hayes and Democrat Samuel J. Tilden is contested.
1877	Compromise of 1877 makes Hayes president and ends Reconstruction.

White Southerners and the Ghosts of the Confederacy, 1865

Confederate soldiers, generals and troops alike, returned to devastated homes. General Braxton Bragg returned to his "once prosperous" Alabama home to find "all, all was lost, except my debts." Bragg and his wife found temporary shelter in a slave cabin. Yeomen farmers, the backbone of the Confederacy, found uprooted fences, farm animals dead or gone, and buildings destroyed. They and their families wandered about in a living nightmare, seeking shelter where they could. They lived in morbid fear of vengeful former slaves or the hated Yankee soldiers wreaking more damage.

Nathaniel Bell, a former Confederate soldier, was lucky enough to get a job on the North Carolina Railroad in 1865. Every two weeks, Bell enjoyed a two-day layover in the coastal city of Wilmington. "On one of these occasions," he wrote, "a small boy and little girl, both pretty children, came to me and asked me for something to eat. I gave them all the meat, bread, potatoes, and syrup that they could carry away. They were very proud of this. They said their father was killed in the war, and that their mother and grandmother were both sick. Some months afterwards I was passing by the same place where I saw the children, and a man got on my train.... I asked him about the two children.... He said the little boy and girl starved to death."

The casualties of war in the South continued long after the hostilities ceased. These were hardly the only cases of starvation that stalked the defeated region in the months after the surrender. Although soldiers of both sides would experience difficulty in reentering civilian life, the southerner's case was the more difficult because of the economic devastation, the psychological burdens of defeat, and the break-up of families through death, migration, or poverty. Cities such as Richmond, Atlanta, Savannah, Charleston, and Columbia lay in ruins; farmsteads were stripped of everything but the soil; infrastructure, especially railroads, was damaged or destroyed; factories and machinery were demolished; and at least 5 million bales of cotton, the major cash crop, had gone up in smoke. Add a worthless currency, and the loss was staggering, climbing into hundreds of billions of dollars in today's currency.

Law and order, when not closely supervised by federal troops, often broke down. Deserters, guerilla fighters, and just plain hungry people stole and fought to survive. As a Georgia woman explained, "We have no currency, no law, save the primitive code that might makes right."

Their cause lost and their society destroyed, white southerners lived through the summer and fall of 1865 surrounded by ghosts, the ghosts of lost loved ones, joyful times, bountiful harvests, self-assurance, and slavery. Defeat shook the basic tenets of their religious beliefs. A North Carolinian cried, "Oh, our God! What sins we must have been guilty of that we should be so humiliated by Thee now!" Some praised God for delivering the South from the sin of slavery. A Virginia woman expressed thanks that "we white people are no longer permitted to go on in such wickedness, heaping up more and more wrath of God upon our devoted heads." But many other white southerners refused to accept their defeat as a divine judgment. How could they, as a devout people, believe that God had abandoned them? Instead, they insisted, God had spared the South for a greater purpose. They came to view the war as the **Lost Cause** and interpreted it, not as a lesson in humility, but as an episode in the South's journey to salvation. Robert E. Lee became the patron saint of this cause, his poignant nobility a contrast to the crassness of the Yankee warlords. White southerners transformed the bloody struggle into a symbol of courage against great odds and piety against sin. Eventually, they believed, redemption would come.

The southern white view of the Civil War (and of Reconstruction) was not a deliberate attempt to falsify history, but rather a need to justify and rationalize the devastation that accompanied defeat. This view, in which the war became the Lost Cause, and Reconstruction became the Redemption, also served to forge a community among white southerners at a time of great unrest. A common religion solidified the bond and sanctified it. The Lost Cause also enabled white southerners to move on with their lives and concentrate on rebuilding their shattered region. The Lost Cause was a historical rationalization that enabled believers to hope for a better future. The regrettable feature of elevating the Civil War to a noble, holy enterprise was that it implied a stainless Old South, a civilization worth fighting and dying for. This new history required the return of the freedmen, if not to the status of slaves, then at least to a lowly place in society. This new history also ignored the savagery of the war by romanticizing the conflict.

The Lost Cause would not merely exist as a memory, but also as a three-dimensional depiction of southern history, in rituals and celebrations, and as the educational foundation for future generations. The statues of the Confederate common soldier erected typically on the most important site in a town, the courthouse square; the commemorations of Confederate Memorial Day, the birthdays of prominent Confederate leaders, and the reunions of veterans, all marked with flourishing oratory, brass bands, parades, and related spectacles; and the textbooks implanting the white history of the South in young minds and carrying the legacy down through the generations—all of these ensured that the Lost Cause would not only be an interpretation of the past, but also the basic reality of the present and the foundation for the future.

Fifteen years after the war, Mark Twain traveled the length of the East Coast. After visiting a gentlemen's club in Boston, he recalled that the conversation had covered a va-

This engraving shows Southerners decorating the graves of rebel soldiers at Hollywood Memorial Cemetery in Virginia in 1867. Northerners and southerners alike honored their war dead. But in the South, the practice of commemorating fallen soldiers became an important element in maintaining the myth of the Lost Cause that colored white southerners' view of the war.

riety of topics, none of which included the Civil War. Northerners had relegated the conflict to history books and moved on. Such was not the case in the South. There, Twain reported, gentlemen's talk inevitably wandered to the war and to heroism and sacrifice. "In the South," Twain wrote, "the war is what A.D. is elsewhere: they date from it." White southerners would not accept the changes implied by defeat. They would fight to preserve as much of their past as the victors allowed. For the past was both their present and their future.

Most white southerners approached the great issues of freedom and reunification with unyielding views. They saw African Americans as adversaries whose attempts at self-improvement were a direct challenge to white people's belief in their own racial superiority. White southerners saw outside assistance to black southerners as another invasion. The Yankees might have destroyed their families, their farms, and their fortunes, but they would not destroy the racial order. The war may have ended slavery, but white southerners were determined to preserve strict racial boundaries.

More Than Freedom: African American Aspirations in 1865

Black southerners had a quite different perspective on the Civil War and Reconstruction, seeing the former as a great victory for freedom and the latter as a time of great possibility. But their view did not matter; it was invisible or,

worse, distorted, in books, monuments, and official accounts. If, as the British writer George Orwell later argued, "who controls the present controls the past, and who controls the past controls the future," then the vanishing black perspective is not surprising. The ferocity with which white southerners attempted to take back their governments and their social structure was not only about nostalgia; it was about power and the legitimacy that power conferred.

And, of course, the black perspective was decidedly different from that of whites. To black southerners the Civil War was a war of liberation, not a Lost Cause. At an emancipation parade in Norfolk in 1863, black women took joy in stomping on Confederate flags and burning an effigy of Jefferson Davis. Less raucous displays followed the war, especially on July 4, which in the South, until well into the 1880s, was primarily a black holiday. The response of southern whites to black aspirations still stunned African Americans, who believed, naively perhaps, that what they sought—education, land, access to employment, and equality in law and politics—were basic rights and modest objectives. The former slaves did not initially even dream of social equality; far less did they plot murder and mayhem, as white people feared. They did harbor two potentially contradictory aspirations. The first was to be left alone, free of white supervision. But the former slaves also wanted land, voting and civil rights, and education. To secure these, they needed the intervention and support of the white power structure.

In 1865, African Americans had reason to hope that their dreams of full citizenship might be realized. They enjoyed a reservoir of support for their aspirations among some Republican leaders. The views of James A. Garfield, Union veteran, U.S. congressman, and future president, were typical of these Republicans. Commenting on the ratification of the Thirteenth Amendment, Garfield asked, "What is freedom? Is it the bare privilege of not being chained? . . . If this is all, then freedom is a bitter mockery, a cruel delusion."

The first step Congress took beyond emancipation was to establish the Bureau of Refugees, Freedmen, and Abandoned Lands in March 1865. Congress envisioned the **Freedmen's Bureau,** as it came to be called, as a multipurpose agency to provide social, educational, and economic services, advice, and protection to former slaves and destitute white southerners. The Bureau marked the federal government's first foray into social welfare legislation. Congress also authorized the bureau to rent confiscated and abandoned farmland to freedmen in 40-acre plots, with an option to buy. This auspicious beginning belied the great disappointments that lay ahead.

Education

The greatest success of the Freedmen's Bureau was in education. The bureau coordinated more than fifty northern philanthropic and religious groups, which, in turn, established 3,000 freedmen's schools in the South, serving 150,000 men, women, and children.

Initially, single young women from the Northeast comprised much of the teaching force. One of them, 26-year-old Martha Schofield, came to Aiken, South Carolina, from rural Pennsylvania in 1865. Like many of her colleagues, she had joined the abolitionist movement as a teenager and decided to make teaching her life's work. Her strong Quaker beliefs reflected the importance of Protestant Christianity in motivating the young missionaries. When her sponsoring agency, the Pennsylvania Freedmen's Relief Association, folded in 1871, her school closed. Undaunted, she opened another school on her own, and, despite chronic financial problems and the hostility of Aiken's white citizens, she and the school endured. (Since 1953, her school has been part of the Aiken public school system.)

By the time Schofield opened her school in 1871, black teachers outnumbered white teachers in the "colored" schools. The financial troubles of northern missionary societies and white northerners' declining interest in the freedmen's condition opened opportunities for black teachers. Support for them came from black churches, especially the African Methodist Episcopal (AME) Church.

The former slaves crowded into basements, shacks, and churches to attend school. "The children...hurry to school as soon as their work is over," wrote a teacher in Norfolk, Virginia, in 1867. "The plowmen hurry from the field at night to get their hour of study. Old men and women strain their dim sight with the book two and a half feet distant from the eye, to catch the shape of the letter. I call this heaven-inspired interest."

At the end of the Civil War, only about 10 percent of black southerners were literate, compared with more than 70 percent of white southerners. Within a decade, black literacy had risen above 30 percent. Joseph Wilson, a former slave, attributed the rise to "this longing of ours for freedom of the mind as well as the body."

The Freedmen's Bureau, northern churches, and missionary societies established more than 3,000 schools, attended by some 150,000 men, women, and children in the years after the Civil War. At first, mostly young white women from the Northeast staffed these schools.

Some black southerners went on to one of the thirteen colleges established by the American Missionary Association and black and white churches. Between 1860 and 1880 more than 1,000 black southerners earned college degrees at institutions still serving students today, such as Howard University in Washington, DC, Fisk University in Nashville, Hampton Institute (now University), Tuskegee Institute, and Biddle Institute (now Johnson C. Smith University) in Charlotte.

Pursuing freedom of the mind involved challenges beyond those of learning to read and write. Many white southerners condemned efforts at "Negro improvement." They viewed the time spent on education as wasted, forcing the former slaves to catch their lessons in bits and pieces between work, often by candlelight or on Sundays. White southerners also harassed white female teachers, questioning their morals and threatening people who rented rooms to them. After the Freedmen's Bureau folded in 1872 and many of the northern societies that supported freedmen's education collapsed or cut back their involvement, education for black southerners became more haphazard.

"Forty Acres and a Mule"

Although education was important to the freed slaves in their quest for civic equality, land ownership offered them the promise of economic independence. For generations, black people had worked southern farms and had received nothing for their labor.

An overwhelmingly agricultural people, freedmen looked to farm ownership as a key element in their transition from slavery to freedom. "Gib us our own land and we take care of ourselves," a Charleston freedman asserted to a northern visitor in 1865. "But without land, de ole massas can hire or starve us, as dey please." Even before the war's end, rumors circulated through black communities in the South that the government would provide each black family with 40 acres and a mule. These rumors were fueled by General William T. Sherman's **Field Order No. 15** in January 1865, which set aside a vast swath of abandoned land along the South Atlantic coast from the Charleston area to northern Florida for grants of up to 40 acres. The Freedmen's Bureau likewise raised expectations when it was initially authorized to rent 40-acre plots of confiscated or abandoned land to freedmen.

By June 1865, about 40,000 former slaves had settled on Sherman land along the southeastern coast. In 1866, Congress passed the **Southern Homestead Act,** giving black people preferential access to public lands in five southern states. Two years later, the Republican government of South Carolina initiated a land-redistribution program financed by the sale of state bonds. The state used proceeds from the bond sales to purchase farmland, which it then resold to freedmen, who paid for it with state-funded long-term low-interest loans. By the late 1870s, more than 14,000 African American families had taken advantage of this program.

The highest concentration of black land ownership was in the Upper South and in areas of the Lower South with better economic conditions and less white hostility toward black people. By 1890, one out of three black farmers in the Upper South owned his land, compared to one out of five for the South as a whole. In Virginia, 43 percent of black farmers owned the land they farmed.

Land ownership did not ensure financial success. Most black-owned farms were small and on marginal land. The value of these farms in 1880 was roughly half that of white-owned farms. Black farmers also had trouble obtaining credit to purchase or expand their holdings. A lifetime of fieldwork left some freedmen without the managerial skills to operate a farm. The hostility of white neighbors also played a role in thwarting black aspirations. Black farmers often had the most success when groups of families settled together, as in the farm community of Promise Land in upcountry South Carolina.

The vast majority of former slaves, however, especially those in the Lower South, never fulfilled their dreams of land ownership. Rumors to the contrary, the federal government never intended to implement a land-redistribution program in the South. General Sherman viewed his field order as a temporary measure to support freedmen for the remainder of the war. President Andrew Johnson nullified the order in September 1865, returning confiscated land to its former owners. Even Republican supporters of black land ownership questioned the constitutionality of seizing privately owned real estate. Most of the land-redistribution programs that emerged after the war, including government-sponsored programs, required black farmers to have capital. But in the impoverished postwar economy of the South, it was difficult for them to acquire it.

Republican Party rhetoric of the 1850s extolled the virtues and dignity of free labor over the degradation of slave labor. Free labor usually meant working for a wage or under some other contractual arrangement. But unlike slaves, according to the then prevailing view, free laborers could enjoy the fruits of their work and might someday become owners or entrepreneurs themselves. It was self-help, not government assistance, that guaranteed individual success. After the war, many white northerners envisioned former slaves assuming the status of free laborers, not necessarily of independent landowners.

Most of the officials of the Freedmen's Bureau shared these views and therefore saw reviving the southern economy as a higher priority than helping former slaves acquire farms. They wanted both to get the crop in the field and start the South on the road to a free labor system. Thus, they encouraged freedmen to work for their former masters under contract and to postpone their quest for land. Bureau and military officials lectured former slaves on the virtues of staying home and working "faithfully" in the fields.

Freed women washing laundry along a creek near Circleville, Texas, circa 1866. Other than farming, domestic service was the only work open to freed women after the Civil War.

At first, agents of the Freedmen's Bureau supervised labor contracts between former slaves and masters. But after 1867, bureau surveillance declined. Agents assumed that both black laborers and white landowners had become accustomed to the mutual obligations of contracts. The bureau, however, underestimated the power of white landowners to coerce favorable terms or to ignore those they did not like. Contracts implied a mutuality that most planters could not accept in their relations with former slaves. As the northern journalist Whitelaw Reid noted in 1865, planters "have no sort of conception of free labor. They do not comprehend any law for controlling laborers, save the law of force."

By the late 1870s, most former slaves in the rural South had been drawn into a subservient position in a new labor system called **sharecropping**. The premise of this system was relatively simple: The landlord furnished the sharecroppers with a house, a plot of land to work, seed, some farm animals, and farm implements and advanced them credit at a store the landlord typically owned. In exchange, the sharecroppers promised the landlord a share of their crop, usually one-half. The croppers kept the proceeds from the sale of the other half to pay off their debts at the store and save or spend as they and their families saw fit. In theory, a sharecropper could save enough to secure economic independence.

But white landlords perceived black independence as both contradictory and subversive. With landlords keeping the accounts at the store, black sharecroppers found that the proceeds from their share of the crop never left them very far ahead. In exchange for extending credit to sharecroppers, storeowners felt justified in requiring collateral, but sharecroppers had no assets other than the cotton they grew. So southern states passed crop-lien laws, which gave the storeowner the right to the following year's crop in exchange for the current year's credit. If the following year's harvest could not pay off the debt, the sharecropper sank deeper into dependence. Some found themselves in perpetual debt and worked as virtual slaves. They could not simply abandon their debts and go to another farm, because the new landlord would check their references. Those found to have jumped their debts could end up on a prison chain gang. Not all white landlords cheated their tenants, but given the sharecroppers' innocence regarding accounting methods and crop pricing, the temptation to do so was great. Thus weak cotton prices conspired with white chicanery to keep black people economically dependent.

Migration to Cities

Even before the hope of land ownership faded, African Americans looked for alternatives to secure their personal and economic independence. Before the war, the city had offered slaves and free black people a measure of freedom unknown in the rural South. After the war, African Americans moved to cities to find families, seek work, escape the tedium and supervision of farm life, or simply to test their right to move about.

For the same reasons, white people disapproved of black migration to the city. It reduced the labor pool for farms. It also gave black people more opportunities to associate with white people of similar social status, to compete for jobs, and to establish schools, churches, and social organizations, fueling their hopes for racial equality. Between 1860 and 1870, the African American population in every major southern city rose significantly. In Atlanta, for example, black people accounted for one in five residents in 1860 and nearly one in two by 1870. Some freedmen came to cities initially to reunite with their families. Every city newspaper after the war carried advertisements from former slaves seeking their mates and children. In 1865, the Nashville *Colored Tennessean* carried this poignant plea: "During the year 1849, Thomas Sample carried away from this city, as his slaves, our daughter, Polly, and son. . . . We will give $100 each for them to any person who will assist them . . . to get to Nashville, or get word to us of their whereabouts."

Once in the city, freedmen had to find a home and a job. They usually settled on the outskirts of town, where building codes did not apply. Rather than developing one large ghetto, as happened in many northern cities, black southerners lived in small concentrations in and around cities. Sometimes armed with a letter of reference from their former masters, black people went door to door to seek employment. Many found work serving white families, as guards, laundresses, or maids, for very low wages. Both skilled and unskilled laborers found work rebuilding war-torn cities like Atlanta. Frederick Ayer, a Freedmen's Bureau agent in Atlanta, reported to a colleague in 1866 that "many of the whites are making most vigorous efforts to retrieve their broken fortunes and . . . rebuild their dwellings and shops. . . . This furnished employment to a large number of colored people as Masons, Carpenters, Teamsters, and Common Workmen."

Most rural black southerners, however, worked as unskilled laborers. The paltry wages men earned, when they could find work, pushed black women into the work force. They often had an easier time securing a job in cities as domestics and laundresses. Black men had hoped to assert their patriarchal prerogatives, like white men, by keeping wives and daughters out of the labor market, but necessity dictated otherwise. In both Atlanta and Nashville, black people comprised more than 75 percent of the unskilled workforce in 1870. Their wages were at or below subsistence level. A black laborer in Richmond admitted to a journalist in 1870 that he had difficulty making ends meet on $1.50 a day. "It's right hard," he reported. "I have to pay $15 a month rent, and only two little rooms." His family survived because his wife took in laundry, while her mother watched the children. Considering the laborer's struggle, the journalist wondered, "Were not your people better off in slavery?" The man replied, "Oh, no sir! We're a heap better off now. . . . We're men now, but when our masters had us we was only change in their pockets."

The black church was the center of African-American life in the postwar urban South. Most black churches were founded after the Civil War, but some, such as the first African Baptist Church in Richmond, shown here in an 1874 engraving, traced their origins to before 1861.

Global Perspectives

Emancipation and Freedom in the United States and Russia

Tsar Alexander II (1855–1881) freed Russia's serfs in 1861, two years before Abraham Lincoln's Emancipation Proclamation. Although Russian serfs had more rights than American slaves, both were tied to the land and to their landlords/masters. The liberation of the serfs was part of a broader reform plan designed to help modernize Russia.

On becoming tsar in 1855, Alexander II had relaxed the speech, travel, and press restrictions imposed by his predecessors, resulting in an influx of Western ideas into Russia. These ideas helped create widespread public support for the liberation of the serfs. The tsar couched his emancipation proclamation in the ideals of God and country, but its origin lay primarily in Russia's economic aspirations and the tsar's political strategy. While most Americans perceived their liberated slaves as forming an agricultural working class, Alexander made land ownership one of the major attractions of emancipation. The government divided farms equally between the landlords and the former serfs, compensating the owners for the divided property.

In theory at least, Russian serfs seemed in a better position than the southern freedmen to secure economic independence, given the land they received. One Russian official exulted, "The people are erect and transformed; the look, the walk, the speech, everything is changed." But the Russian serfs found their economic situation little improved. The land chosen for redistribution was marginal, and redistribution came with a major catch: The former serfs were required to repay the state on the installment plan. Given the quality of the land, the relatively high interest rates attached to the loans, and the vast numbers of serfs and their families, repayment was unrealistic even in the long term. To ensure that the former serfs would pay up, the tsar allowed local governments to keep the peasants on their land until they fulfilled their financial obligations. In other words, they were as much tied to the land after emancipation as before. And, as a method to improve the quality of agricultural cultivation, the multiplicity of small plots and impoverished peasants was also a failure.

As in the United States, violence marred the transition from bondage to freedom. Rebellions flared in several parts of Russia, but the tsar's armies put these uprisings down quickly. Some of the former serfs managed to escape to towns and cities and become part of the growing laboring class, much as freedmen went to southern cities. In the cities, both former serfs and slaves came closer to the free-labor ideal posited but not supported by their respective governments. In rural areas, reform broke down through a lack of planning and a failure of will.

■ After emancipation, did the Russian serf or the American slave have a better opportunity to establish economic independence?

Faith and Freedom

Religious faith framed and inspired the efforts of African Americans to test their freedom on the farm and in the city. White southerners used religion to transform the Lost Cause from a shattering defeat to a premonition of a greater destiny. Black southerners, in contrast, saw emancipation in biblical terms as the beginning of an exodus from bondage to the Promised Land.

Some black churches in the postwar South had originated during the slavery era, but most split from white-dominated congregations after the war. White churchgoers deplored the expressive style of black worship, and black churchgoers were uncomfortable in congregations that treated them as inferiors. A separate church also reduced white surveillance.

The church became a primary focus of African American life. It gave black people the opportunity to hone skills in self-government and administration that white-dominated society denied them. Within the supportive confines of the congregation, they could assume leadership positions, render important decisions, deal with financial matters, and engage in politics. The church also operated as an educational institution. Local governments, especially in rural areas, rarely constructed public schools for black people; churches often served that function.

The desire to read the Bible inspired thousands of former slaves to attend the church school. The church also spawned other organizations that served the black community, such as burial societies, Masonic lodges, temperance groups, trade unions, and drama clubs. African Americans took great pride in their churches, which became visible measures of their progress. In Charleston, the first building erected after the war was a black church. The First Colored Baptist Church in Nashville became a landmark for its imposing brick and stone façade. Black people donated a greater proportion of their earnings to their churches than white people. The church and the congregation were a cohesive force in black communities. They supported families under stress from discrimination and poverty. Husbands and wives joined church-affiliated societies together. Their children joined organizations such as the Young Rising Sons and Daughters of the New Testament. The church enforced family and religious values, punishing violators guilty of such infractions as adultery. Black churchwomen, both working-class and middle-class, were especially prominent in the family-oriented organizations.

Most black churches looked inward to strengthen their members against the harsh realities of postwar southern society. Few ministers dared to engage in or even support protest activities. Some, especially those in the Colored Methodist Episcopal Church, counseled congregants to abide by the rules of second-class citizenship and to trust in God's will to right the wrongs of racism. Northern-based denominations, however, notably the AME Church, were more aggressive advocates of black rights. AME ministers stressed the responsibility of individual black people to realize God's will of racial equality.

The efforts of former slaves in the classroom, on the farm, in cities, and in the churches reflect the enthusiasm and expectations with which black southerners greeted freedom. But the majority of white southerners were unwilling to see those expectations fulfilled. For this reason, African Americans could not secure the fruits of their emancipation without the support and protection of the federal government. The issue of freedom was therefore inextricably linked to the other great issue of the era, the rejoining of the Confederacy to the Union, as expressed in federal Reconstruction policy.

Federal Reconstruction, 1865–1870

When the Civil War ended in 1865, no acceptable blueprint existed for reconstituting the Union. President Lincoln believed that a majority of white southerners were Unionists at heart, and that they could and should undertake the task of reconstruction. He favored a conciliatory policy toward the South in order, as he put it in one of his last letters, "to restore the Union, so as to make it . . . a Union of hearts and hands as well as of States." He counted on the loyalists to be fair with respect to the rights of the former slaves.

As early as 1863, Lincoln had proposed to readmit a seceding state if 10 percent of its prewar voters took an oath of loyalty to the Union, and it prohibited slavery in a new state constitution. But this Ten Percent Plan did not require states

to grant equal civil and political rights to former slaves, and many Republicans in Congress thought it was not stringent enough. In 1864, a group of them responded with the Wade-Davis Bill, which required a majority of a state's prewar voters to pledge their loyalty to the Union and demanded guarantees of black equality before the law. The bill was passed at the end of a congressional session, but Lincoln kept it from becoming law by refusing to sign it (an action known as a "pocket veto").

Lincoln, of course, died before he could implement a Reconstruction plan. His views on reconstructing the Union during the war did not necessarily prefigure how his views would have unfolded after the war. Given his commitment in the Gettysburg Address to promote "a new birth of freedom," it is likely that had white southerners resisted black civil rights, Lincoln would have responded with harsher terms. Above all, Lincoln was a savvy politician: He would not have allowed a stalemate to develop between himself and the Congress, and, if necessary, he would have moved closer to the radical camp. On April 11, 1865, in one of his last pronouncements on Reconstruction, Lincoln stated that he favored a limited suffrage for the freedmen, though he admitted that each state had enough peculiarities that a blanket policy might not work. In a cabinet meeting on April 14, he dismissed an idea for military occupation, though he acknowledged that allowing the states to reconstruct themselves might not work either. In any case, his successor, Andrew Johnson, lacked his flexibility and political acumen.

The controversy over the plans introduced during the war reflected two obstacles to Reconstruction that would continue to plague the ruling Republicans after the war. First, neither the Constitution nor legal precedent offered any guidance on whether the president or Congress should take the lead on Reconstruction policy. Second, there was no agreement on what that policy should be. Proposals requiring various preconditions for readmitting a state, loyalty oaths, new constitutions with certain specific provisions, guarantees of freedmen's rights, all provoked vigorous debate.

President Andrew Johnson, some conservative Republicans, and most Democrats believed that because the Constitution made no mention of secession, the southern states had been in rebellion but had never left the Union, and therefore that there was no need for a formal process to readmit them. Moderate and radical Republicans disagreed, arguing that the defeated states had forfeited their rights. Moderates and radicals parted company, however, on the conditions necessary for readmission to the Union. The radicals wanted to treat the former Confederate states as territories, or "conquered provinces," subject to congressional legislation. Moderates wanted to grant the seceding states more autonomy and limit federal intervention in their affairs while they satisfied the conditions of readmission. Neither group held a majority in Congress, and legislators sometimes changed their positions (see the Overview table, Contrasting Views of Reconstruction).

Presidential Reconstruction, 1865–1867

When the Civil War ended in April 1865, Congress was not in session and would not reconvene until December. Thus, the responsibility for developing a Reconstruction policy initially fell on Andrew Johnson, who succeeded to the presidency upon Lincoln's assassination. Johnson seemed well suited to the difficult task. He was born in humble circumstances in North Carolina in 1808. He learned the tailoring trade and struck out for Tennessee as a teenager to open a tailor shop in the eastern Tennessee town of Greenville. Obtaining his education informally, he prospered modestly, purchased a few slaves, and began to pursue politics. He was elected alderman, mayor, state legislator, congressman, governor, and then, in 1856, U.S. senator. Johnson was the only southern senator to remain in the U.S. Senate after secession. This defiant Unionism won him acclaim in the North and credibility among Republican leaders, who welcomed him into their party. During the war, as military governor of Tennessee, he solidified his Republican credentials by advocating the abolition of slavery in Tennessee and severe punishment of Confederate leaders. His views landed him on the Republican ticket as the candidate for vice president in 1864. Indiana Republican congressman George W. Julian, who advocated harsh terms for the South and broad rights for black people, viewed Johnson's accession to the presidency in 1865 as "a godsend."

Most northerners and many Republicans approved Johnson's Reconstruction plan when he unveiled it in May 1865. Johnson extended pardons and restored property rights, except in slaves, to southerners who swore an oath of allegiance to the Union and the Constitution. Southerners who had held prominent posts in the Confederacy, however, and those with more than $20,000 in taxable property, had to petition the president directly for a pardon, a reflection of Johnson's disdain for wealthy whites. The plan said nothing about the voting rights or civil rights of former slaves.

Northern Democrats applauded the plan's silence on these issues and its promise of a quick restoration of the southern states to the Union. They expected the southern states to favor their party and expand its political power. Republicans approved the plan because it restored property rights to white southerners, although some wanted it to provide for black suffrage. Republicans also hoped that Johnson's conciliatory terms might attract some white southerners to the Republican Party.

On the two great issues of freedom and reunion, white southerners quickly demonstrated their eagerness to reverse the results of the Civil War. Although most states accepted President Johnson's modest requirements, several objected to one or more of them. Mississippi and Texas refused to ratify the Thirteenth Amendment, which abolished slavery. Alabama accepted only parts of the amendment. South Carolina declined to nullify its secession ordinance. No southern state authorized black voting. When Johnson ordered special congressional elections in the South in the fall of 1865, the all-white electorate returned many prominent Confederate leaders to office.

In late 1865, the newly elected southern state legislatures revised their antebellum slave codes. The updated **black codes** allowed local officials to arrest black people who could not document employment and residence or who were "disorderly" and sentence them to forced labor on farms or road crews. The codes also restricted black people to certain occupations, barred them from jury duty, and forbade them to possess firearms. Apprenticeship laws permitted judges to take black children from parents who could not, in the judges' view, adequately support them. Given the widespread poverty in the South in 1865, the law could apply to almost any freed black family. Northerners looking for contrition in the South found no sign of it. Worse, President Johnson did not seem perturbed about this turn of events.

The Republican-dominated Congress reconvened in December 1865 in a belligerent mood. A few radical Republicans pushed for swift retribution. George W. Julian thundered that he would "indict, convict and hang Jefferson Davis in the name of God; as for Robert E. Lee, unmolested in Virginia, hang him too." His colleague, Benjamin F. Wade, suggested that "if the negroes by insurrection would contrive to slay one-half of the White Southerners, the remaining half would then hold them in respect and treat them with justice." Few in Congress took such statements seriously. Nonetheless, a consensus formed among radical Republicans, who comprised nearly half of the party's strength in Congress, that to gain readmission, a state would have to extend suffrage to black citizens, protect freedmen's civil rights, and have its white citizens officially acknowledge these rights. Some radicals also supported the redistribution of land to former slaves, but few pressed for social equality. They envisioned a new South of modest farms, some owned by former slaves, and a Republican Party built on an alliance between black people and white loyalists.

But the radicals could not unite behind a program, and it fell to their moderate colleagues to take the first step toward a congressional Reconstruction plan. The moderates shared the radicals' desire to protect the former slaves' civil rights. But they would not support land-redistribution schemes or punitive measures against prominent Confederates, and disagreed on extending voting rights to the freedmen. The moderates' first measure, passed in early 1866, extended the life of the Freedmen's Bureau and authorized it to punish state officials who failed to extend equal civil rights to black citizens. But President Johnson vetoed the legislation.

Undeterred, Congress passed the Civil Rights Act of 1866 in direct response to the black codes. The act specified the civil rights to which all U.S. citizens were entitled. In creating a category of national citizenship with rights that su-

Selling a Freeman to Pay his Fine at Monticello, Florida. This 1867 engraving shows how the black codes of the early Reconstruction era reduced former slaves to virtually their pre–Civil War status. Scenes like this convinced northerners that the white South was unrepentant and prompted congressional Republicans to devise their own Reconstruction plans.

perseded state laws, the act changed federal-state relations (and in the process overturned the *Dred Scott* decision). President Johnson vetoed the act, but it became law when Congress mustered a two-thirds majority to override his veto, the first time in American history that Congress passed major legislation over a president's veto.

Andrew Johnson's position reflected both his view of government and his racial attitudes. The Republican president remained a Democrat in spirit. Republicans had expanded federal power during the Civil War. Johnson, however, like most Democrats, favored more of a balance between federal and state power. He also shared with many whites a belief in black inferiority. In supporting abolition, Johnson had assumed that black people, once free, would emigrate to Africa.

Given the president's views and his inflexible temperament, a clash between him and Congress became inevitable.

To keep freedmen's rights safe from presidential vetoes, state legislatures, and federal courts, the Republican-dominated Congress moved to incorporate some of the provisions of the 1866 Civil Rights Act into the Constitution. The **Fourteenth Amendment,** which Congress passed in June 1866, addressed the issues of civil and voting rights. It guaranteed every citizen equality before the law. The two key sections of the amendment prohibited states from violating the civil rights of their citizens, thus outlawing the black codes, and gave states the choice of enfranchising black people or losing representation in Congress. Some radical Republicans expressed disappointment that the amendment, in a reflec-

American Views

Mississippi's 1865 Black Codes

White southerners, especially landowners and business owners, feared that emancipation would produce a labor crisis; freedmen, they expected, would either refuse to work or strike hard bargains with their former masters. White southerners also recoiled from the prospect of having to treat their former slaves as full social equals. Thus, beginning in late 1865, several southern states, including Mississippi, enacted laws designed to control black labor, mobility, and social status. Northerners responded to the codes as a provocation, a bold move to deny the result of the war and its consequences.

- How did the black codes fit into President Andrew Johnson's Reconstruction program?
- Some northerners charged that the black codes were a backdoor attempt at reestablishing slavery. Do you agree?
- If southern states enacted black codes to stabilize labor relations, how did the provisions below effect that objective?

From An Act to Confer Civil Rights on Freedmen, and for other Purposes

Section 1. All freedmen, free negroes and mulattoes may sue and be sued, implead and be impleaded, in all the courts of law and equity of this State, and may acquire personal property, and choose in action, by descent or purchase, and may dispose of the same in the same manner and to the same extent that white persons may: Provided, That the provisions of this section shall not be so construed as to allow any freedman, free negro or mulatto to rent or lease any lands or tenements except in incorporated cities or towns, in which places the corporate authorities shall control the same.

Section 7. Every civil officer shall, and every person may, arrest and carry back to his or her legal employer any freedman, free negro, or mulatto who shall have quit the service of his or her employer before the expiration of his or her term of service without good cause; and said officer and person shall be entitled to receive for arresting and carrying back every deserting employee aforesaid the sum of five dollars, and ten cents per mile from the place of arrest to the place of delivery; and the same shall be paid by the employer, and held as a set off for so much against the wages of said deserting employee: Provided, that said arrested party, after being so returned, may appeal to the justice of the peace or member of the board of police of the county, who, on notice to the alleged employer, shall try summarily whether said appellant is legally employed by the alleged employer, and has good cause to quit said employer. Either party shall have the right of appeal to the county court, pending which the alleged deserter shall be remanded to the alleged employer or otherwise disposed of, as shall be right and just; and the decision of the county court shall be final.

From An Act to Amend the Vagrant Laws of the State

Section 2. All freedmen, free negroes and mulattoes in this State, over the age of eighteen years, found on the second Monday in January, 1866, or thereafter, with no lawful employment or business, or found unlawfully assembling themselves together, either in the day or night time, and all white persons assembling themselves with freedmen, Free negroes or mulattoes, or usually associating with freedmen, free negroes or mulattoes, on terms of equality, or living in adultery or fornication with a freed woman, freed negro or mulatto, shall be deemed vagrants, and on conviction thereof shall be fined in a sum not exceeding, in the case of a freedman, free negro or mulatto, fifty dollars, and a white man two hundred dollars, and imprisonment at the discretion of the court, the free negro not exceeding ten days, and the white man not exceeding six months.

Source: "Laws in Relation to Freedmen," 39 Congress, 2 Session, Senate Executive Document 6, Freedmen's Affairs, 182–86.

tion of northern ambivalence, failed to give the vote to black people outright.

The amendment also disappointed advocates of woman suffrage, for the first time using the word *male* in the Constitution to define who could vote. Wendell Phillips, a prominent abolitionist, counseled women, "One question at a time. This hour belongs to the Negro." Susan B. Anthony, who had campaigned for the abolition of slavery before the war and helped mount a petition drive that collected 400,000 signatures for the Thirteenth Amendment, founded the American Equal Rights Association in 1866 with her colleagues to push for woman suffrage at the state level.

The Fourteenth Amendment had little immediate impact on the South. Although enforcement of black codes diminished, white violence against black people increased. In the 1870s, several decisions by the U.S. Supreme Court weakened the amendment's provisions. Eventually, however, it would play a major role in securing the civil rights of African Americans.

President Johnson encouraged southern white intransigence by openly denouncing the Fourteenth Amendment. In August 1866, at the start of the congressional election campaign, he undertook an unprecedented tour of key northern states to sell his message of sectional reconciliation to the public. Although listeners appreciated Johnson's desire for peace, they questioned his claims of southern white loyalty to the Union. The president's diatribes against the Republican Congress won him followers in those northern states with a reservoir of opposition to black suffrage. But the tone and manner of his campaign offended many as undignified. In the November elections, the Democrats suffered embarrassing defeats in the North as Republicans managed better than two-thirds majorities in both the House and Senate, sufficient to override presidential vetoes. Radical Republicans, joined by moderate colleagues buoyed by the election results and revolted by the president's and the South's intransigence, seized the initiative when Congress reconvened.

Congressional Reconstruction, 1867–1870

The radicals' first salvo in their attempt to take control of Reconstruction occurred with the passing over President Johnson's veto of the Military Reconstruction Acts. The measures, passed in March 1867, inaugurated a period known as **Congressional Reconstruction** or Radical Reconstruction. With the exception of Tennessee, the only southern state that had ratified the Fourteenth Amendment and been readmitted to the Union, Congress divided the former Confederate states into five military districts, each headed by a general (see Map 16–1). The commanders' first order of business was to conduct voter-registration campaigns to enroll black people and bar white people who had held office before the Civil War and supported

the Confederacy. The eligible voters would then elect delegates to a state convention to write a new constitution that guaranteed universal manhood suffrage. Once a majority of eligible voters ratified the new constitution and the Fourteenth Amendment, their state would be eligible for readmission to the Union.

The Reconstruction Acts fulfilled the radicals' three major objectives. First, they secured the freedmen's right to vote. Second, they made it likely that southern states would be run by Republican regimes that would enforce the new constitutions, protect former slaves' rights, and maintain the Republican majority in Congress. Finally, they set standards for readmission that required the South to accept the preeminence of the federal government and the end of slavery.

To limit presidential interference with their policies, Republicans passed the **Tenure of Office Act,** prohibiting the president from removing certain officeholders without the Senate's consent. Johnson, angered at what he believed was an unconstitutional attack on presidential authority, deliberately violated the act by firing Secretary of War Edwin M. Stanton, a leading radical, in February 1868. The House responded by approving articles of impeachment against a president for the first time in American history. That set the stage for the next step prescribed by the Constitution: a Senate trial to determine whether the president should be removed from office.

MAP 16–1 Congressional Reconstruction, 1865–1877
When Congress wrested control of Reconstruction policy from President Andrew Johnson, it divided the South into the five military districts depicted here. The commanding generals for each district held the authority both to hold elections and to decide who could vote.

Johnson had indeed violated the Tenure of Office Act, a measure of dubious constitutionality even to some Republicans, but enough Republicans felt that his actions fell short of the "high crimes and misdemeanors" standard set by the Constitution for dismissal from office. Seven Republicans deserted their party, and Johnson was acquitted. Defiant to the end, he continued to issue pardons to leading Confederates, even to Robert E. Lee and Jefferson Davis, and he refused to follow the traditional courtesy of accompanying and welcoming his successor, Ulysses S. Grant, into office. The seven Republicans who voted against their party did so not out of respect for Johnson but because they feared that a conviction would damage the office of the presidency and violate the constitutional separation of powers. The outcome weakened the radicals and eased the way for Grant, a moderate Republican, to gain the party's nomination for president in 1868.

The Republicans viewed the 1868 presidential election as a referendum on Congressional Reconstruction. They supported black suffrage in the South but equivocated on allowing African Americans to vote in the North. Black northerners could vote in only eight of the twenty-two northern states, and between 1865 and 1869, white northerners rejected equal suffrage referendums in eight of eleven states. Republicans "waved the bloody shirt," reminding voters of Democratic disloyalty, the sacrifices of war, and the peace only Republicans could redeem. Democrats denounced Congressional Reconstruction as federal tyranny and, in openly racist appeals, warned white voters that a Republican victory would mean black rule. Grant won the election, but his margin of victory was uncomfortably narrow. Reflecting growing ambivalence in the North over issues of race and federal authority, New York's Horatio Seymour, the Democratic presidential nominee, probably carried a majority of the nation's white vote. Black voters' overwhelming support for Grant probably provided his margin of victory.

The Republicans retained a strong majority in both houses of Congress and managed to pass another major piece of Reconstruction legislation, the **Fifteenth Amendment,** in February 1869. In response to growing concerns about voter fraud and violence against freedmen, the amendment guaranteed the right of American men to vote, regardless of race. Although the amendment provided a loophole allowing states to restrict the right to vote based on literacy or property qualifications, it was nonetheless a milestone. It made the right to vote perhaps the most distinguishing characteristic of U.S. citizenship.

The Fifteenth Amendment allowed states to keep the franchise a male prerogative, angering many in the woman-suffrage movement more than had the Fourteenth Amendment. The resulting controversy severed the ties between the movement and Republican politics. Susan B. Anthony broke with her abolitionist colleagues and opposed the amendment. A fellow abolitionist and woman suffragist, Elizabeth Cady Stanton, charged that the amendment created an "aristocracy of sex." In an appeal brimming with ethnic and racial animosity, Stanton warned that "if you do not wish the lower orders of Chinese, African, Germans and Irish, with their low ideas of womanhood to make laws for you and your daughters…awake to the danger…and demand that woman, too, shall be represented in the government!" Such language created a major rift in the nascent women's movement.

The Democratic Party ran an openly racist presidential campaign in 1868. This pro-Republican drawing by noted cartoonist Thomas Nast includes three Democratic constituencies: former Confederate soldiers (note the "CSA: on the belt buckle); the Irish or immigrant vote (note the almost Simian depiction of the Irishman), and the well-dressed man sporting a "5th Avenue" button and waving a wallet full of bills, a reference to the corrupt Democratic politics in New York City. The three have their feet on an African American soldier. In the background note the "colored orphan asylum" and southern school" ablaze, and the lynching of black children. *Courtesy of the Library of Congress.*

African American Voting Rights in the South

Right from the end of the Civil War, white southerners resisted African American voting rights. Black people, with equal determination, used the franchise to assert their equal right to participate in the political process. Black voting rights proved so contentious that Congress sought to secure them with the Fourteenth and Fifteenth Amendments to the U.S. Constitution. But U.S. Supreme Court decisions in *United States v. Cruikshank* (1876) and in the Civil Rights Cases (1883) undermined federal authority to protect the rights of freedmen, including voting rights. A combination of violence, intimidation, and legislation effectively disfranchised black southerners by the early twentieth century.

During the 1960s, Congress passed legislation designed to override state prohibitions and earlier court decisions limiting African American voting rights. The key measure, the 1965 Voting Rights Act, not only guaranteed black southerners (and later, other minorities) the right to register and vote but also protected them from procedural subterfuges. These protections proved necessary because of the extreme racial polarization of southern elections.

Official photograph Congressional Black Caucus, 106th Congress.

To ensure African American candidates an opportunity to win elections, the federal government after 1965 insisted that states and localities establish procedures to increase the likelihood of such a result. By the early 1990s, states were being directed to draw districts with majority-black voting populations to ensure African American representation in the U.S. Congress and in state legislatures. The federal government cited the South's history of racial discrimination and racially polarized voting to justify these districts. But white southerners challenged such claims, as they had more than a century earlier, and their challenges proved partially successful in federal court.

As with the First Reconstruction, the U.S. Supreme Court has narrowed the scope of black voting rights in several decisions since the early 1990s. Despite the history of racial discrimination with respect to voting rights, the Court has often championed the standard of "colorblindness," which justices insist was codified in the Fourteenth Amendment. The principle of colorblindness, however wonderful in the abstract, ignores the history of black voting rights from the Reconstruction era to the present. The framers of the Reconstruction Amendments had the protection of the rights of the freedmen in mind (including and especially voting rights) when they wrote those measures. The issue of African American voting rights in the South and the degree to which the federal goverment may or may not intercede to protect those rights remains as much at issue as it was more than a century ago.

■ There is considerable debate as to whether the U.S. Constitution is colorblind with respect to voting rights. Should it be?

Southern black men during Reconstruction went to great lengths to vote and to protect themselves on election day as these voters fording a stream with rifles aloft attest.

PEARSON myhistorylab
From Then to Now Online

Additional Documents and Brief Descriptions

16–1 "An Eloquent Appeal," *Harper's Weekly*, September 26, 1868.

16–2 U.S. Supreme Court Justice Sandra Day O'Connor strikes down a North Carolina Congressional district, in *Shaw v. Reno*, 509 U.S. 360 (1993).

Contrasting Views of Reconstruction: President and Congress

Politician or Group	Policy on Former Slaves	Policy on Readmission of Former Confederate States
President Johnson	Opposed to black suffrage	Maintained that rebellious states were already readmitted
	Silent on protection of black civil rights	Granted pardons and restoration of property to all who swore allegiance to the United States
	Opposed to land redistribution	
Radical Republicans	Favored black suffrage	Favored treating rebellious states as territories and establishing military districts*
	Favored protection of black civil rights	Favored limiting franchise to black people and loyal white people
	Favored land redistribution	
Moderate Republicans	Favored black suffrage*	Favored some restrictions on white suffrage**
	Favored protection of civil rights	Favored requiring states to meet various requirements before being readmitted*
	Opposed land redistribution	Split on military rule

*After 1866.

**True of most but not all members of the group.

Southern Republican Governments, 1867–1870

Away from Washington, the first order of business for the former Confederacy was to draft state constitutions. The documents embodied progressive principles new to the South. They mandated the election of numerous local and state offices. Self-perpetuating local elites could no longer appoint themselves or cronies to powerful positions. The constitutions committed southern states, many for the first time, to public education. Lawmakers enacted a variety of reforms, including social welfare, penal reform, legislative reapportionment, and universal manhood suffrage.

The Republican regimes that gained control in southern states promoted vigorous state government and the protection of civil and voting rights. Three Republican constituencies supported these governments: native whites, native blacks, and northern transplants. The native white group was mostly made up of yeomen farmers. Residing mainly in the upland regions of the South and long ignored by lowland planters and merchants in state government, they were left devastated by the war. They struggled to keep their land and hoped for an easing of credit and for debt-stay laws to help them escape foreclosure. They wanted public schools for their children and good roads to get their crops to market. Some urban merchants and large planters also called themselves Republicans. They were attracted to the party's emphasis on economic development, especially railroad

construction, and would become prominent in Republican leadership after 1867, forming a majority of the party's elected officials.

Collectively, opponents called these native white southerners **scalawags.** Although their opponents perceived them as a unified group, scalawags held a variety of views. Planters and merchants opposed easy debt and credit arrangements and the use of their taxes to support programs other than railroads or port improvements. Yeomen farmers desperately needed the debt and credit legislation to retain their land. And even though they supported public schools and road building, which would require increased state revenues, they opposed higher taxes.

Northern transplants, or **carpetbaggers,** as many southern whites called them, constituted a second group of southern Republicans. Cartoonists depicted carpetbaggers as shoddily dressed and poorly groomed, their worldly possessions in a ratty cloth satchel, slinking into a town and swindling the locals before departing with their ill-gotten gains. The reality was far different from the caricature. Thousands of northerners came south during and after the war. Many were Union soldiers who simply enjoyed the climate and perhaps married a local woman. Most were drawn by economic opportunity. Land was cheap and the price of cotton high. Although most carpetbaggers had supported the Republican Party before they moved south, few became politically active until the cotton economy nosedived in 1866. Financial

"Time Works Wonders." This Thomas Nast cartoon has Jefferson Davis, former President of the Confederacy, dressed as Iago in William Shakespeare's play *Othello*, declaring with considerable anguish, "For that I suspect the lusty moor [Othello] hath leap'd into my seat: the thought where of doth like a poisonous mineral gnaw my inwards," Indeed, Hiram Revels occupies Davis's old seat in the U.S. Senate representing the state of Mississippi in 1870.

concerns were not all that motivated carpetbaggers to enter politics; some hoped to aid the freedmen.

Carpetbaggers never comprised more than 2 percent of any state's population. Most white southerners viewed them as an alien presence, instruments of a hated occupying force. They estranged themselves from their neighbors by supporting and participating in the Republican state governments that most white people despised. In Alabama, local editors organized a boycott of northern-owned shops. Because many of them tended to support extending political and civil rights to black southerners, carpetbaggers were

also often at odds with their fellow white Republicans, the scalawags.

African Americans constituted the Republican Party's largest southern constituency. In three states, South Carolina, Mississippi, and Louisiana, they also constituted the majority of eligible voters. They viewed the franchise as the key to civic equality and economic opportunity and demanded an active role in party and government affairs.

Black people began to take part in southern politics even before the end of the Civil War, especially in cities occupied by Union forces. In February 1865, black people in Norfolk,

Virginia, gathered to demand a say in the new government that Union supporters were forming in that portion of the state. In April, they created the Colored Monitor Union club, modeled after regular Republican Party organizations in northern cities, called **Union Leagues.** They demanded "the right of universal suffrage" for "all loyal men, without distinction of color." Black people in other southern cities held similar meetings, seeking inclusion in the democratic process to protect their freedom. White southerners viewed these developments with alarm but could not at first counter them. Despite white threats, black southerners thronged to Union League meetings in 1867, even forging interracial alliances in states such as North Carolina and Alabama. Focusing on political education and recruitment, the leagues successfully mobilized black voters. In 1867, more than 90 percent of eligible black voters across the South turned out for elections. Black women, even though they could not vote, also played a role. During the 1868 presidential campaign, for example, black maids and cooks in the South wore buttons touting the candidacy of the Republican presidential nominee, Ulysses S. Grant.

Black southerners were not content just to vote; they also demanded political office. White Republican leaders in the South often took the black vote for granted. But on several occasions after 1867, black people threatened to run independent candidates, support rival Democrats, or simply stay home unless they were represented among Republican nominees. These demands brought them some success. The number of southern black congressmen in the U.S. House of Representatives increased from two in 1869 to seven in 1873, and more than 600 African Americans, most of them former slaves from plantation counties, were elected to southern state legislatures between 1867 and 1877.

White fears that black officeholders would enact vengeful legislation proved unfounded. African Americans generally did not promote race-specific legislation. Rather, they supported measures such as debt relief and state funding for education that benefited all poor and working-class people. Like all politicians, however, black officials in southern cities sought to enact measures beneficial to their constituents, such as roads and sidewalks. And they succeeded in having a black police commissioner appointed in Jacksonville, Florida. Gains like these underscored the advantages of suffrage for the African American community.

During the first few years of Congressional Reconstruction, Republican governments walked a tightrope, attempting to lure moderate Democrats and unaffiliated white voters into the party without slighting the black vote. They used the lure of patronage power and the attractive salaries that accompanied public office. In 1868, for example, Louisiana's Republican governor, Henry C. Warmoth, appointed white conservatives to state and local offices, which he divided equally between Confederate veterans and black people, and repealed a constitutional provision disfranchising former Confederate officials.

Republicans also gained support by expanding the role of state government to a degree unprecedented in the South. Southern Republican administrations appealed to hard-pressed upland white constituents by prohibiting foreclosure and passing stay laws that allowed farm owners additional time to repay debts. They undertook building programs that benefited black and white citizens, erecting hospitals, schools, and orphanages. Stepping further into social policy than most northern states at the time, Republican governments in the South expanded women's property rights, enacted legislation against child abuse, and required child support from fathers of mulatto children. In South Carolina, the Republican government provided medical care for the poor; in Alabama, it provided free legal aid for needy defendants.

Despite these impressive policies, southern Republicans were unable to hold their diverse constituency together. Although the party had some success among white yeoman farmers, the liberal use of patronage failed to attract white conservatives. At the same time, it alienated the party's core supporters, who resented seeing their former enemies rewarded with lucrative offices.

The high costs of their activist policies further undermined the Republicans by forcing them to raise state taxes. In Mississippi, where the Republican governor built a public school system for both black and white students, founded a black university, reorganized the state judiciary, built new courthouses and two state hospitals, and pushed through legislation giving black people equal access to public facilities, the state debt soared to $1.5 million between 1869 and 1873. This was in an era in which state budgets rarely exceeded $1 million.

Unprecedented expenditures and the liberal use of patronage sometimes resulted in waste and corruption. Officials charged with selecting railroad routes, appointing lesser officials, and erecting public buildings were well positioned to benefit from their power. Their high salaries offended many in an otherwise impoverished region. Problems like these were not limited to the South, but the perception of dishonesty was nonetheless damaging to governments struggling to build legitimacy among a skeptical white electorate.

The excesses of some state governments, high taxes, contests over patronage, and conflicts over the relative roles of white and black party members opened rifts in Republican ranks. Patronage triggered intraparty warfare. Every office secured by a Democrat created a disappointed Republican. Class tensions erupted in the party as economic development policies sometimes superseded relief and social service legislation supported by small farmers. The failure of Alabama Republicans to deliver on promises of debt relief and land redistribution eroded the party's support among upcountry white voters. There were differences among black voters too. In the Lower South, divisions that had developed in the prewar era between urban, lighter-skinned free black people and darker, rural slaves persisted into the Reconstruction era. In many southern states, black clergy, because of their independence from white support and their important spiritual and educational role, became leaders. But most preached salvation in the next world rather than equality in this one, conceding more to white people than their rank-and-file constituents.

Counter-Reconstruction, 1870–1874

Republicans might have survived battles over patronage, policy, expenditures, and taxes. But they could not overcome racism and the violence it generated. Racism killed Republican rule in the South because it deepened divisions within the party, encouraged white violence, and eroded support in the North. Southern Democrats discovered that they could use race baiting and racial violence to create solidarity among white people that overrode their economic and class differences. Unity translated into election victories.

Northerners responded to the persistent violence in the South, not with outrage, but with a growing sense of tedium. They came to accept the arguments of white southerners that it was folly to allow black people to vote and hold office. Racism became respectable. Noted intellectuals and journalists espoused "scientific" theories that claimed to demonstrate the natural superiority of white people over black people. These theories influenced the Liberal Republicans, followers of a new political movement that splintered the Republican Party, further weakening its will to pursue Reconstruction policy.

By 1874, Americans were concerned with an array of domestic problems that overshadowed Reconstruction. An economic depression left them more preoccupied with survival than racial justice. Corruption convinced many that politics was part of the nation's problems, not a solution to them. With the rest of the nation thus distracted and weary, white southerners reclaimed control of the South.

The Klan directed violence at African Americans primarily for engaging in political activity. Here, a black man, John Campbell, vainly begs for mercy in Moore County, North Carolina, in August 1871.

The Uses of Violence

Racial violence preceded Republican rule. As African Americans moved about, attempted to vote, haggled over labor contracts, and carried arms as part of the occupying Union forces, they tested the patience of white southerners, to whom any black assertion of equality seemed threatening.

White paramilitary groups were responsible for much of the violence directed against African Americans. Probably the best-known of these groups was the **Ku Klux Klan.** Founded in Tennessee by six Confederate veterans in 1866, the Klan was initially a social club. Prominent ex-Confederates such as General John B. Gordon and General Nathan Bedford Forrest saw the political potential of the new organization. Within a year, the Klan had spread throughout the South. In 1867, when black people entered politics in large numbers, the Klan unleashed a wave of terror against them. Klan nightriders in ghostlike disguises intimidated black communities. The Klan directed much of its violence toward subverting the electoral process. One historian has estimated that roughly 10 percent of all black delegates to the 1867 state constitutional conventions in the South became victims of political violence during the next decade.

Not all Klan attacks had political objectives. Klansmen struck against anyone, black or white, who they believed had violated racial boundaries. A Georgia Klansman murdered a freedman because he could read and write. Klansmen in Florence, South Carolina, killed a black man who rented a plantation "because such a thing ought not to be." And in 1868, Klansmen murdered three southern white Republican Georgia state legislators. Membership in the Klan crossed class lines. Race became an issue on which white people, regardless of differing economic interests, could agree.

By 1868, white paramilitary organizations permeated the South. Violence was particularly severe in election years in Louisiana, which had a large and active black electorate. Before the presidential election of 1868, for example, white Louisianans killed at least 700 Republicans, including the black leader William R. Meadows, who was dragged from his home and shot and beheaded in front of his family. As the election neared, white mobs roamed New Orleans, attacking black people and breaking up Republican rallies. The violence cut the Republican vote in the state by 50 percent from the previous spring.

The most serious example of political violence in Louisiana, if not in the entire South, occurred in Colfax in 1873, when a white Democratic mob attempted to wrest control of local government from Republicans. For three weeks, black defenders held the town against the white onslaught. When the white mob finally broke through, they massacred the remaining black defenders, including those who had surrendered and laid down their weapons.

Racial violence and the combative reaction it provoked both among black people and Republican administrations energized white voters. Democrats regained power in North Carolina, for example, after the state's Republican governor enraged white voters by calling out the militia to counter white violence during the election of 1870. That same year, the Republican regime in Georgia fell as well. Some Republican governments countered the violence successfully for a time. Governor Edmund J. Davis of Texas, for example, organized a special force of 200 state policemen to round up Klan nightriders. Between 1870 and 1872, Davis's force arrested 6,000 and broke the Klan in Texas. Arkansas Governor Powell Clayton launched an equally successful campaign against the Klan in 1869. But other governors hesitated to enforce laws directed at the Klan, fearing that to do so would further alienate white people.

The federal government responded with a variety of legislation. One example was the Fifteenth Amendment, ratified in 1869, which guaranteed the right to vote. Another was the Enforcement Act of 1870, which authorized the federal government to appoint supervisors in states that failed to protect voting rights. When violence and intimidation persisted, Congress followed with a second, more sweeping measure, the Ku Klux Klan Act of 1871. This law permitted federal authorities, with military assistance, if necessary, to arrest and prosecute members of groups that denied a citizen's civil rights if state authorities failed to do so. The Klan Act was not successful in curbing racial violence, as the Colfax Massacre in 1873 made vividly clear. But with it, Congress, by claiming the right to override state authority to bring individuals to justice, established a new precedent in federal-state relations.

Northern Indifference

The success of political violence after 1871 reflected both a declining commitment on the part of northern Republicans to support southern Republican administrations and a growing indifference of northerners to the major issues of Reconstruction. The erosion of northern support for Congressional Reconstruction began as early as the presidential campaign of 1868. Republican candidate Ulysses S. Grant did not articulate a Reconstruction policy beyond his campaign slogan, "Let Us Have Peace." In fairness to President Grant, Reconstruction policy required a delicate balance between supporting southern Republican governments without alienating the party's northern base that brought it to power in the first place.

That northern base grew increasingly skeptical about Reconstruction policy in general and assistance to the freedmen in particular. Northern Republicans looked around their cities and many saw the local political scene infested with unqualified immigrant voters and corruption. New York City's Democratic boss William M. Tweed and his associates bilked the city of an astounding $100 million dollars. When white southerners charged that unqualified blacks and grasping carpetbaggers corrupted the political process in the South, northerners recognized the argument. Republican

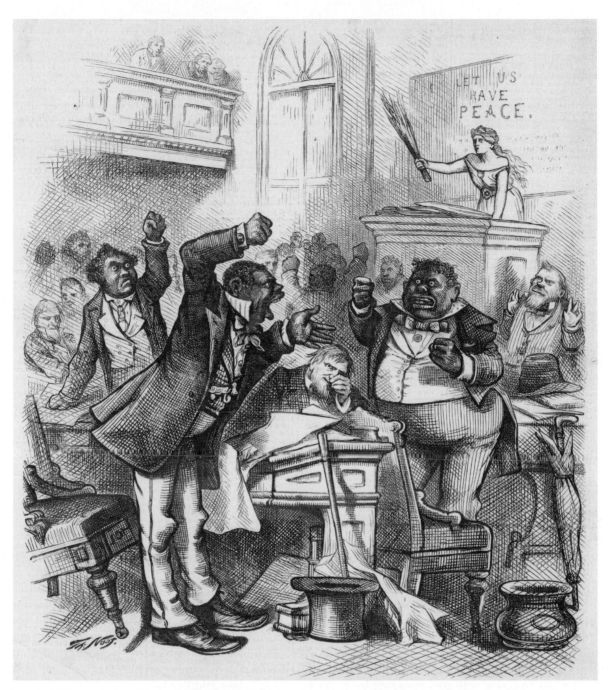

By the early 1870s, northern public opinion had shifted greatly with respect to black suffrage, in part because of the growing concern about the immigrant vote in northern cities; whereas in the late 1860s cartoons and the press depicted newly enfranchised African Americans nobly, later representations were hostile as this caricature of the South Carolina legislature by Thomas Nast demonstrates.

leader Carl Schurz, an early champion of African American civil rights, reflected the change in northern opinion, allowing that black voters and officeholders "were ignorant and inexperienced; that the public business was an unknown world to them, and that in spite of the best intentions they were easily misled."

Changing perceptions in the North also indicated a convergence of racial views with white southerners. As radical Republican Congressman from Indiana, George W. Julian admitted in 1865, white northerners "*hate the negro.*" They expressed this hatred in their rejection of black suffrage, racially segregated their African American population, and in periodic violence against black residents, such as during the New York draft riots of 1863. Northerners' views were bolstered by prevailing scientific theories of race that "proved" blacks' limited capacities and, therefore, unfitness for either the ballot or skilled occupations.

Northerners also grew increasingly wary of federal power. The emerging scandals of the Grant administration, fueled, it seemed, by government subsidies to railroads and other private businesses, demanded a scaling back of federal power and discretion. The Civil War had grown government bureaucracy without corresponding checks on power. Intervening in southern elections, taking sides with a particular faction, ordering troops to put down local disturbances now seemed less an exercise in establishing law and order and protecting civil rights than bullying citizens to comply with the whims of Republicans in Washington, DC. When white southerners complained about federal meddling, again, they found resonance in the North.

The excesses and alleged abuses of federal power inspired a reform movement among a group of northern Republicans and some Democrats. In addition, business leaders decried the ability of wealthy lobbyists to influence economic decisions. An influential group of intellectuals and opinion makers lamented the inability of politicians to understand "natural" laws, particularly those related to race. And some Republicans joined the reform movement out of fear that Democrats would capitalize on the turmoil in the South and the political scandals in the North to reap huge electoral victories in 1872.

Liberal Republicans and the Election of 1872

Liberal Republicans, as the reformers called themselves, put forward an array of suggestions to improve government and save the Republican Party. They advocated civil service reform to reduce reliance on patronage and the abuses that accompanied office seeking. To limit government and reduce artificial economic stimuli, the reformers called for tariff reduction and an end to federal land grants to railroads. For the South, they recommended a general amnesty for white people and a return to "local self-government" by men of "property and enterprise."

When the Liberals failed to convince other Republicans to adopt their program, they broke with the party. Taking advantage of this split, the Democrats forged an alliance with the Liberals. Together, they nominated journalist Horace Greeley to challenge Ulysses S. Grant for the presidency in the election of 1872. Grant won resoundingly, helped by high turnout among black voters in the South. He carried every southern state except Georgia, Tennessee, and Texas. Elsewhere, Republicans again used the tactic of waving the bloody shirt to good effect. It was the Republicans, they declared, who had saved the Union, the Democrats who had

almost destroyed it. Greeley had been a staunch Republican during the Civil War and had spent most of his career attacking Democrats. Republicans used his own words against him. Many Democratic voters stayed home.

The election suggested that the Grant administration had not yet exhausted public tolerance and that the Republican experiment in the South retained some public support. But Greeley had helped the Republicans by running an inept campaign. Within a year, an economic depression, continued violence in the South, and the persistent corruption of the Grant administration would erode the last remnants of support for Reconstruction and black rights in the South.

Economic Transformation

After 1873, the Republican Party in the South became a liability for the national party, especially as Americans fastened on economic issues. The major story of the decade would not be equal rights for African Americans—a long-shot even in the heady days following freedom—but the changing nature of the American economy. An overextended banking and credit system generated the Panic of 1873 and caused extended suffering, particularly among working-class Americans. But the depression masked a remarkable economic transformation as the nation moved toward a national industrial economy.

During the 1870s, the economy grew annually between 4.5 and 6 percent, among the fastest decadal growth rates on record. Consumption grew even faster; Americans purchased more food, more fuel, and more manufactured products than at any other previous time in the nation's history. While unemployment was severe, overall, employment grew by 40 percent between 1870 and 1880 and productivity increased at least as fast. This seeming contradiction is explained by the rapid expansion of new industries such as oil refining and meatpacking, and the application of technology in iron and steel production. Technology also eliminated jobs, and those that remained were primarily low-skilled, low-paying positions—painful, to be sure, for those caught in the change, but liberating for those with education and ability who populated a burgeoning middle-management sector of the growing urban middle class.

The depression and the economic transformation occupied center stage in the American mentality of the mid-1870s, at least in the North. Most Americans had mentally forsaken Reconstruction long before the Compromise of 1877 made its abandonment a political fact. The sporadic violence against black and white Republicans in the South, and the cries of help from freedmen as their rights and persons were abused by white Democrats, became distant echoes from another era, the era of the Civil War, now commemorated and memorialized, but no longer an active part of the nation's present and future. Of course, for white southerners, the past was not yet past. There was still work to do.

Redemption, 1874–1877

For southern Democrats, the Republican victory in 1872 underscored the importance of turning out larger numbers of white voters and restricting the black vote. They accomplished these goals over the next four years with a surge in political violence, secure in the knowledge that federal authorities would rarely intervene against them. Preoccupied with corruption and economic crisis and increasingly indifferent, if not hostile, to African American aspirations, most Americans looked the other way. The elections of 1876 confirmed the triumph of white southerners.

In a religious metaphor that matched their view of the Civil War as a lost crusade, southern Democrats called their victory "Redemption" and depicted themselves as **Redeemers,** holy warriors who had saved the South from the hell of black Republican rule. Generations of American boys and girls would learn this interpretation of the Reconstruction era, and it would affect race relations for nearly a century.

The Democrats' Violent Resurgence

The violence between 1874 and 1876 differed in several respects from earlier attempts to restore white government by force. Attackers operated more openly and more closely identified themselves with the Democratic Party. Mounted, gray-clad ex-Confederate soldiers flanked Democratic candidates at campaign rallies and "visited" black neighborhoods afterward to discourage black men from voting. With black people intimidated and white people already prepared to vote, election days were typically quiet.

Democrats swept to victory across the South in the 1874 elections. "A perfect reign of terror" redeemed Alabama for the Democrats. The successful appeal to white supremacy inspired a massive white turnout to unseat Republicans in Virginia, Florida (legislature only), and Arkansas. Texas had fallen to the Democrats in 1873. Only South Carolina, Mississippi, and Louisiana, states with large black populations, survived the debacle. But the relentless tide of terror would soon overwhelm them as well.

As this Thomas Nast cartoon makes clear, the paramilitary violence against black southerners in the early 1870s threatened not only the voting rights of freedmen, but their dreams of education, prosperity, and family life. In this context, the slogan "The Union As It Was" is highly ironic.

In Louisiana, a group of elite Democrats in New Orleans organized a military organization, known as the White League, in 1874 to challenge the state's Republican government. In September 1874, more than 8,000 White Leaguers staged a coup to overthrow the Republican government of New Orleans. The city's police, commanded by the former Confederate general, James Longstreet, and the intervention of nearby federal troops saved the government and prevented a wholesale slaughter. But the incident only inspired White Leaguers to redouble their efforts.

The Weak Federal Response

Unrest like the events in Louisiana also plagued Mississippi and South Carolina. When Governor Daniel H. Chamberlain could no longer contain the violence in South Carolina in 1876, he asked the president for help. Grant acknowledged the gravity of Chamberlain's situation but would offer him only the lame hope that South Carolinians would exercise "better judgment and cooperation" and assist the governor in bringing offenders to justice "without aid from the federal Government."

Congress responded to blacks' deteriorating status in the South with the Civil Rights Act of 1875. The act prohibited discrimination against black people in public accommodations, such as theaters, parks, and trains, and guaranteed freedmen's rights to serve on juries. It had no provision for voting rights, which Congress presumed the Fifteenth Amendment protected. A Texas judge fined a Galveston theater $500 for refusing to allow black people to sit wherever they wanted, but most judges either interpreted the law narrowly or declared it unconstitutional. In 1883, the U.S. Supreme Court agreed and overturned the act, declaring that only the states, not Congress, could redress "a private wrong, or a crime of the individual."

The Election of 1876 and the Compromise of 1877

Reconstruction officially ended with the presidential election of 1876, in which the Democrat Samuel J. Tilden ran against the Republican Rutherford B. Hayes. Republicans again waved the bloody shirt, touting their role in preserving the Union during the Civil War, but they ignored Reconstruction. The Democrats hoped that their resurgent strength in the South and a respectable showing in the North would bring them the White House. The scandals of the Grant administration, northern weariness with southern Republican governments, and the persisting economic depression worked in the Democrats' favor.

When the ballots were counted, it appeared that Tilden, a conservative New Yorker respectable enough for northern voters and Democratic enough for white southerners, had won. But despite a majority in the popular vote, disputed returns in three southern states left him with only 184 of the 185 electoral votes needed to win (see Map 16–2). The three

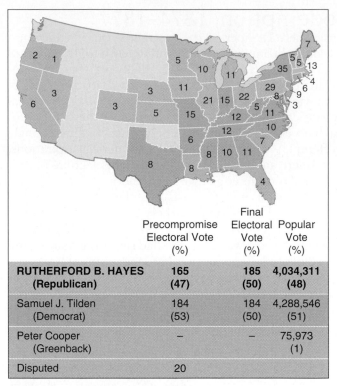

	Precompromise Electoral Vote (%)	Final Electoral Vote (%)	Popular Vote (%)
RUTHERFORD B. HAYES (Republican)	**165** (47)	**185** (50)	**4,034,311** (48)
Samuel J. Tilden (Democrat)	184 (53)	184 (50)	4,288,546 (51)
Peter Cooper (Greenback)	–	–	75,973 (1)
Disputed	20		

MAP 16–2   The Election of 1876
The Democrat Samuel F. Tilden won a majority of the popular vote but eventually fell short of an electoral vote majority when the contested electoral votes of Florida, Louisiana, and South Carolina went to his Republican opponent, Rutherford B. Hayes. The map also indicates the Republicans' failure to build a base in the South after more than a decade of Reconstruction.

states—Florida, South Carolina, and Louisiana—were the last in the South still to have Republican administrations.

Both camps maneuvered intensively in the following months to claim the disputed votes. Congress appointed a 15-member commission to settle the issue. Because the Republicans controlled Congress, they held a one-vote majority on the commission.

Southern Democrats wanted Tilden to win, but they wanted control of their states more. They were willing to deal. As one South Carolina newspaper editorialized in February 1877, "It matters little to us who rules in Washington, if South Carolina is allowed to have [Democratic governor Wade] Hampton and Home Rule." Hayes intended to remove federal support from the remaining southern Republican governments anyway. It thus cost him nothing to promise to do so in exchange for the contested electoral votes. Republicans also made vague promises to invest in the southern economy and support a southern transcontinental railroad, but these were secondary. What the South wanted most was to be left alone, and that is what it got. The so-called **Compromise of 1877** installed Hayes in the

White House and gave Democrats control of every state government in the South. Congress never carried through on the economic promises, and southern Democrats never pressed it to. Southern Democrats emerged the major winners from the Compromise of 1877. President Hayes and his successors into the next century left the South alone. In practical terms, the Compromise signaled the revocation of civil rights and voting rights for black southerners. The Fourteenth and Fifteenth Amendments would be dead letters in the South until well into the twentieth century. On the two great issues confronting the nation at the end of the Civil War, reunion and freedom, the white South had won. It reentered the Union largely on its own terms with the freedom to pursue a racial agenda consistent with its political, economic, and social interests.

The Memory of Reconstruction

Southern Democrats used the memory of Reconstruction to help maintain themselves in power. Reconstruction joined the Lost Cause as part of the glorious fight to preserve the civilization of the Old South. As white southerners elevated Civil War heroes into saints and battles into holy struggles, they equated Reconstruction with Redemption. For white southerners, white Democrats in particular, had rescued the South from a purgatory of black rule and federal oppression. Whenever southern Democrats felt threatened over the next century, they reminded their white constituents of the sacrifices and heroism of the war, the "horrors of Reconstruction," the menace of black rule, and the cruelty of the Yankee occupiers. The southern view of Reconstruction permeated textbooks, films, and standard accounts of the period. By the early 1900s, professional historians at the nation's finest institutions concurred in this view, ignoring contrary evidence and rendering the story of African Americans invisible. By that time, therefore, most Americans believed that the policies of Reconstruction had been misguided and had brought great suffering to the white South. The widespread acceptance of this view allowed the South to maintain its system of racial segregation and exclusion without interference from the federal government.

Not all memories of Reconstruction conformed to this thesis. In 1913, John R. Lynch, a former black Republican congressman from Mississippi, published *The Facts of Reconstruction* to "present the other side." He hoped that his book would "bring to public notice those things that were commendable and meritorious, to prevent the publication of which seems to have been the primary purpose of nearly all who have thus far written upon that important subject." But most Americans ignored his book. Two decades later, a more forceful defense, W. E. B. Du Bois's *Black Reconstruction* (1935), met a similar fate. An angry Du Bois attacked the prevailing view of Reconstruction as "one of the most stupendous efforts the world ever saw to discredit human beings, an effort involving universities, history, science, social life and religion."

The national historical consensus grew out of a growing national reconciliation concerning the war, a mutual agreement that both sides had fought courageously and that it was time to move on. Immediately after the Civil War, a number of prominent white southerners urged their neighbors to work on rebuilding the South rather than hating the Yankees. But general reconciliation remained on hold until the end of Reconstruction, when white southerners reclaimed both their governments and their dominance over African Americans. Once that recovery occurred, joint battlefield commemorations stressed mutual bravery and shared sacrifice. Hidden in all the goodwill was the tacit agreement between southern and northern whites that the South was now free to work out its own resolution to race relations. Reconstruction rested on a national consensus of African American inferiority.

There is much to be said in favor of sectional reconciliation as opposed to persistent animosity. There are enough examples in the world today of antagonists in the same country never forgetting or never forgiving their bloody histories. Ideally, Americans could have had *both* healing and justice, but instead they settled for the former. Frederick Douglass, prescient as ever, worried about the peace that followed the Civil War and what it would mean for race relations: "If war among the whites brought peace and liberty to the blacks, what will peace among the whites bring?"

The Failed Promise of Reconstruction

If the demise of Reconstruction elicited a resounding indifference from most white Americans, black southerners greeted it with frustration. Their dreams of land ownership faded as a new labor system relegated them to a lowly position in southern agriculture. Redemption reversed their economic and political gains and deprived them of most of the civil rights they had enjoyed under Congressional Reconstruction. Although they continued to vote into the 1890s, they had by 1877 lost most of the voting strength and political offices they held. Rather than becoming part of southern society, they were increasingly set apart from it, valued only for their labor.

Still, the former slaves were better off in 1877 than in 1865. They were free, however limited their freedom. Some owned land; some held jobs in cities. They raised their families in relative peace and experienced the spiritual joys of a full religious life. They socialized freely with relatives and friends, and they moved about. The Reconstruction amendments to the Constitution guaranteed an array of civil and political rights, and eventually these guarantees would form the basis of the civil rights revolution after World War II. But that outcome was long, too long, in the future. By 1877, the "golden moment," an unprecedented opportunity for the na-

OVERVIEW

Constitutional Amendments and Federal Legislation of the Reconstruction Era

Amendment or Legislation	Purpose	Significance
Thirteenth Amendment (passed and ratified in 1865)	Prevented southern states from reestablishing slavery after the war	Final step toward full emancipation of slaves
Freedmen's Bureau Act (1865)	Oversight of resettlement, labor for former slaves	Involved the federal government directly in relief, education, and assisting the transition from slavery to freedom; worked fitfully to achieve this objective during its seven-year career
Southern Homestead Act (1866)	Provided black people preferential access to public lands in five southern states	Lack of capital and poor quality of federal land thwarted the purpose of the act
Civil Rights Act of 1866	Defined rights of national citizenship	Marked an important change in federal-state relations, tilting balance of power to national government
Fourteenth Amendment (passed 1866; ratified 1868)	Prohibited states from violating the rights of their citizens	Strengthened the Civil Rights Act of 1866 and guaranteed all citizens equality before the law
Military Reconstruction Acts (1867)	Set new rules for the readmission of former Confederate states into the Union and secured black voting rights	Initiated Congressional Reconstruction
Tenure of Office Act (1867)	Required congressional approval for the removal of any official whose appointment had required Senate confirmation	A congressional challenge to the president's right to dismiss cabinet members; led to President Andrew Johnson's impeachment trial
Fifteenth Amendment (passed 1869; ratified 1870)	Guaranteed the right of all American male citizens to vote regardless of race	The basis for black voting rights
Civil Rights Act of 1875	Prohibited racial discrimination in jury selection, public transportation, and public accommodations	Rarely enforced; Supreme Court declared it Unconstitutional in 1883

tion to live up to its ideals by extending equal rights to all its citizens, black and white alike, had passed.

Modest Gains and Future Victories

Black southerners experienced some advances in the decade after the Civil War, but these owed little to Reconstruction. Black families functioned as economic and psychological buffers against unemployment and prejudice. Black churches played crucial roles in their communities. Self-help and labor organizations offered mutual friendship and financial assistance. All of these institutions had existed in the slavery era, although on a smaller scale. And some of them, such as black labor groups, schools, and social welfare associations, endured because comparable white institutions excluded black people.

Black people also scored some modest economic successes during the Reconstruction era, mainly from their own pluck. In the Lower South, black per capita income increased

46 percent between 1857 and 1879, compared with a 35 percent decline in white per capita income. Sharecropping, oppressive as it was, represented an advance over forced and gang labor. Collectively, black people owned more than $68 million worth of property in 1870, a 240 percent increase over 1860, but the average worth of each was only $408. Those who had been free before the war sometimes fared worse after it, especially property-owning free black people in the Lower South. Black city dwellers, especially in the Upper South, fared somewhat better. The overwhelming majority of black people, however, were landless agricultural laborers eking out a meager income that merchants and landlords often snatched to cover debts.

The Fourteenth and Fifteenth Amendments to the Constitution are among the few bright spots in Reconstruction's otherwise dismal legacy. The Fourteenth Amendment guaranteed former slaves equality before the law; the Fifteenth Amendment protected their right to vote. Both amendments elevated the federal government over the states by protecting freedmen from state attempts to deny them their rights. But the benefits of these two landmark amendments did not accrue to African Americans until well into the twentieth century. White southerners effectively nullified the Reconstruction amendments, and the U.S. Supreme Court virtually interpreted them, and other Reconstruction legislation, out of existence.

In the ***Slaughterhouse* cases** (1873), the Supreme Court contradicted the intent of the Fourteenth Amendment by decreeing that most citizenship rights remained under state, not federal, control. In ***United States v. Cruikshank*** (1876), the Court overturned the convictions of some of those responsible for the Colfax Massacre, ruling that the Enforcement Act applied only to violations of black rights by states, not individuals. Within the next two decades, the Supreme Court would uphold the legality of racial segregation and black disfranchisement, in effect declaring that the Fourteenth and Fifteenth Amendments did not apply to African Americans. The Civil War had killed secession forever, but states' rights enjoyed a remarkable revival.

As the historian John Hope Franklin accurately concluded, Reconstruction "had no significant or permanent effect on the status of the black in American life.... [Black people] made no meaningful steps toward economic independence or even stability."

Conclusion

Formerly enslaved black southerners had entered freedom with many hopes, among the most prominent of which was to be left alone. White southerners, after four bloody years of unwanted attention from the federal government, also longed to be left alone. But they did not include their ex-slaves as equals in their vision of solitude. Northerners, too, began to seek escape from the issues and consequences of the war abandoning their weak commitment to secure civil and voting rights for black southerners.

White southerners robbed black southerners of their gains and sought to reduce them again to servitude and dependence, if not to slavery. But in the process, the majority of white southerners lost as well. Yeoman farmers missed an opportunity to break cleanly from the Old South and establish a more equitable society. Instead, they allowed the old elites to regain power and gradually ignore their needs. They preserved the social benefit of a white skin at the cost of almost everything else. Many lost their farms and sank into tenancy. Few had a voice in state legislatures or the U.S. Congress. A new South, rid of slavery and sectional antagonism, had indeed emerged—redeemed, regenerated, and disenthralled. But the old South lingered on.

As federal troops left the South, an era of possibility for American society ended, and a new era began. "The southern question is dead," a Charleston newspaper proclaimed in 1877. "The question of labor and capital, work and wages" had moved to the forefront. The chance to redeem the sacrifice of a bloody civil war with a society that fulfilled the promise of the Declaration of Independence and the Constitution for all citizens slipped away. It would take a new generation of African Americans a long century later to revive it.

Review Questions

1. Both Russia and America hoped to develop a free-labor agricultural class after their respective emancipations. Why didn't these governments follow through on their own objectives?

2. Given the different perspectives on the Civil War's outcome and what the social structure of a postwar South should be, was there any common ground between southern white and southern black on which to forge a Reconstruction policy?

3. Black people did achieve some notable gains during Reconstruction, despite its overall failure. What were those gains?

4. In T. Thomas Fortune's recollection of a boyhood incident, why was it important for him and his friends to fight back?

Key Terms

Black codes (p. 444)

Carpetbaggers (p. 450)

Compromise of 1877 (p. 458)

Congressional Reconstruction (p. 447)

Field Order No. 15 (p. 439)

Fifteenth Amendment (p. 448)

Fourteenth Amendment (p. 445)

Freedmen's Bureau (p. 437)

Ku Klux Klan (p. 454)

Lost Cause (p. 436)

Redeemers (p. 457)

Scalawags (p. 450)

Sharecropping (p. 440)

Slaughterhouse cases (p. 461)

Southern Homestead Act (p. 439)

Tenure of Office Act (p. 447)

Union Leagues (p. 452)

United States v. Cruikshank (p. 461)

Recommended Reading

Du Bois, W. E. B. *Black Reconstruction in America, 1860–1880* (1935). An early and long-ignored study by the foremost black scholar of his time that refuted the contemporary historical wisdom that Reconstruction was a horror visited on the South by an overbearing federal government and ignorant, willful black people.

Foner, Eric. *Reconstruction: America's Unfinished Revolution, 1863–1877* (1988). The standard work on Reconstruction, notable for its emphasis on the experience and aspirations of black southerners.

Foster, Gaines M. *Ghosts of the Confederacy: Defeat, the Lost Cause, and the Emergence of the New South, 1865 to 1913* (1987). A fine picture of how the memory of the Civil War affected white southerners and their views on Reconstruction policy.

Litwack, Leon. *Been in the Storm So Long: The Aftermath of Slavery* (1979). An eloquent account of the early days of freedom from the freedmen's perspective, up to 1867.

Tourgée, Albion W. *A Fool's Errand* (1879). A novel written by an Ohioan who migrated to North Carolina in 1865 to take advantage of economic opportunities in the state and eventually became involved in politics; his frustrations with Reconstruction and his keen analysis of racism are important themes.

Where to Learn More

- **Penn Center Historic District, St. Helena Island, South Carolina.** The Penn School was a sea-island experiment in the education of free black people established by northern missionaries Laura Towne and Ellen Murray in 1862. They operated it until their deaths in the early 1900s. The Penn School became Penn Community Services in 1948, serving as an educational institution, health clinic, and a social service agency. See its website at www.penncenter.com

- **Hampton University Museum, Hampton, Virginia.** Hampton University was founded by the Freedmen's Bureau in 1868 to provide "practical" training in the agricultural and mechanical fields for former slaves. In addition to a history of the institution, the museum includes one of the oldest collections of African art in the United States. Its website is at www.hamptonu.edu/museum

- **Beauvoir, Biloxi, Mississippi.** The exhibits at Beauvoir, the home of Jefferson Davis, evoke the importance of the Lost Cause for the white survivors of the Confederacy. Especially interesting is the Jefferson Davis Soldiers Home on the premises and the Confederate Veterans Cemetery. Davis spent his retirement in Beauvoir. Go to www.beauvoir.org

- **Levi Jordan Plantation, Brazoria County, Texas.** This site provides an excellent depiction and interpretation of the lives of sharecroppers and tenants during and immediately after the Reconstruction era. The site is especially valuable for demonstrating the transition from slavery to sharecropping. Go to www.webarchaeology.com

Study Resources

For study resources for this chapter, go to www.myhistorylab.com and choose *The American Journey*. You will find a wealth of study and review material for this chapter, including pre- and post-tests, customized study plan, key term review flash cards, interactive map and document activities, and documents for analysis.

The economic advance of African Americans in the South during the decades after the Civil War against great odds provided one of the more inspiring success stories of the era. But it was precisely this success, as depicted here at Dr. McDougald's Drug Store in Georgia, in 1900, that infuriated whites who believed that the African American's place in the South resided in menial and subservient occupations.

A New South: Economic Progress and Social Tradition 17

1877–1900

The colored woman of to-day occupies…a unique position in this country.…She is confronted by both a woman question and a race problem.…While the women of the white race can with calm assurance enter upon the work they feel by nature appointed to do [including reform efforts both inside and outside the home], while their men give loyal support and appreciative countenance to [these] efforts, recognizing in most avenues of usefulness the propriety and the need of woman's distinctive co-operation, the colored woman too often finds herself hampered and shamed by a less liberal sentiment…on the part of those for whose opinion she cares most.…

You do not find the colored woman selling her birthright for a mess of pottage.…It is largely our women in the South to-day who keep the black men solid in the Republican Party. The black woman can never forget, however lukewarm the party may to-day appear, that it was a Republican president who struck the manacles from her own wrists and gave the possibilities of manhood to her helpless little ones; and to her mind a Democratic Negro is a traitor and a time-server.

465

To be a woman in a…[new] age carries with it a privilege and an opportunity never implied before. But to be a woman of the Negro race in America, and to be able to grasp the deep significance of the possibilities of the crisis, is to have a heritage, it seems to me, unique in the ages. In the first place, the race is young and full of the elasticity and hopefulness of youth. All its achievements are before it.…Everything to this race is new and strange and inspiring. There is a quickening of its pulses and a glowing of its self-consciousness. Aha, I can rival that! I can aspire to that! I can honor my name and vindicate my race! Something like this, it strikes me, is the enthusiasm which stirs the genius of young Africa in America; and the memory of past oppression and the fact of present attempted repression only serve to gather momentum for its irrepressible power.…What a responsibility then to have the sole management of the primal lights and shadows! Such is the colored woman's office. She must stamp weal or woe on the coming history of this people. May she see her opportunity and vindicate her high prerogative.

Anna J. Cooper,
A Voice from the South, 1892

Anna Julia Cooper, *A Voice from the South* (Xenia, OH: Aldine Printing House, 1892): pp. 134–135, 138–140, 142–145. The book may be accessed from the Internet: http://docsouth.unc.edu/church/cooper/cooper.html

myhistorylab
PEARSON

Personal Journeys Online

- Booker T. Washington, *Atlanta Compromise Address*, 1895. Speech in which Washington accepts segregation and disfranchisement of southern blacks in return for white southerners' economic assistance.

- W. E. B. Du Bois, *Of Mr. Booker T. Washington and Others*, 1903. Du Bois declares that Washington's compromise places African Americans in the South on a journey to failure.

Anna J. Cooper undertook an incredible journey that took her from slavery at her birth in Raleigh, North Carolina, in 1858 to a doctoral degree at the Sorbonne in Paris, France, and to a prominent career as an educator. Throughout her life she remained a firm believer in the role women, especially black women, should play in striking down both white supremacy and male domination. In 1892, Dr. Cooper published *A Voice from the South*, excerpted here. The book appeared at a time when the first African American generation raised in freedom generated a relatively prosperous, educated middle class intent on challenging the limits of race in the New South. The assertiveness of this generation alarmed their white counterparts, who launched a campaign of violence and repression, mainly directed at black men.

Despite these tensions and threats, Cooper's tone reflects the optimism of the New South and an enthusiasm for the expanding public role of women. At the same time, her critical assessment of black men is scarcely concealed. She implies that black men have held black women back,

KEY TOPICS

◆ Continuity and change between the Old South and the New South

◆ Problems in southern agriculture

◆ Women's roles in the New South

◆ How and why segregation and disfranchisement changed race relations in the South

CHRONOLOGY

1872	Texas and Pacific Railway connects Dallas to eastern markets.
1880	First southern local of the Women's Christian Temperance Union is formed in Atlanta.
1881	Booker T. Washington establishes Tuskegee Institute.
1882	Agricultural Wheel is formed in Arkansas.
1883	Laura Haygood founds the home mission movement in Atlanta.
1884	James B. Duke automates his cigarette factory.
1886	Dr. John Pemberton creates Coca-Cola.
	Southern railroads conform to national track gauge standards.
1887	Charles W. Macune expands the Southern Farmer's Alliance from its Texas base to the rest of the South.
1888	The Southern Farmers' Alliance initiates a successful boycott of jute manufacturers.
1890	Mississippi becomes the first state to restrict black suffrage with literacy tests.
1892	The Populist Party forms.
1894	United Daughters of the Confederacy is founded.
1895	Booker T. Washington delivers his "Atlanta Compromise" address.
1895	Publication of Theodor Herzl's *The Jewish State* outlining his ideas for a Jewish homeland in Palestine in response to rising anti-Semitism in Europe.
	In *Plessy v. Ferguson,* the Supreme Court permits segregation by law.
1897	First Zionist Congress meets in Switzerland.
1898	North Carolina Mutual Life Insurance is founded.
1899	Publication of *Die Grundlagen des neunzehnten Jahrhunderts* ["The Foundations of the Nineteenth Century"] by British scientist Houston Stewart Chamberlain, promoting the superiority of the German "race."
1903	W. E. B. Du Bois publishes *The Souls of Black Folk.*
1905	James B. Duke forms the Southern Power Company.
	Thomas Dixon publishes *The Clansman.*
1906	Bloody race riots break out in Atlanta.
1907	Pittsburgh-based U.S. Steel takes over Birmingham's largest steel producer.

unlike their white counterparts, though Cooper overestimated white women's freedom of choice outside the home. Cooper also suggests that black men share at least some of the blame for the white assault on their political rights. Her solution for racial advancement and, presumably, for white hostility to black aspirations is to increase the public profile of black women. But however "new" the New South may have been, traditional views of southern whites on race and gender rendered that solution untenable.

By the early 1900s, Cooper was living in Washington, DC and had immersed herself in the woman-suffrage movement and the promotion of female education. She would live to see the dawn of a new racial and gender era in the South and in America, but the journey would take many years and many lives. Cooper died at the age of 106 in 1964.

The Newness of the New South

Southerners of both races and genders shared Anna J. Cooper's optimism in the decades after Reconstruction. Despite the destruction of war and the turmoil of Reconstruction, southerners worked to rebuild their stricken region as both a testimony to their ability to rise from the ashes and as a way to secure a measure of economic independence from their former Civil War enemies. Southerners did what other Americans were doing between 1877 and 1900; they built railroads, erected factories, and moved to towns and cities, only on a smaller scale and with more modest results. The factories did not dramatically alter the South's rural economy, and the towns and cities did not make it an urban region. The changes, nonetheless, brought political and social turmoil, emboldening black people like Cooper to assert their rights, encouraging women to work outside the home and pursue public careers, and frightening some white men.

By 1900, southern white leaders, urban and rural, had used the banner of white supremacy to stifle dissent. They removed African Americans from political life and constricted their social and economic role. The New South, however, is not solely a southern story. The racial solutions that emerged from the South by 1900 established a legacy only partially dissolved by the civil rights movement of the 1960s. If, as the black leader W. E. B. Du Bois predicted in 1903, the major American problem of the twentieth century would be "the problem of the color line," that line was drawn most emphatically down South.

The New South's "newness" was to be found primarily in its economy, not in its social relations, although the two were complementary. After Reconstruction, new industries absorbed tens of thousands of first-time industrial workers from impoverished rural areas. Southern cities grew faster than those in any other region of the country. A burst of railroad construction linked these cities to one another and to the rest of the country, giving them increased commercial prominence. Growing in size and taking on new functions, cities extended their influence into the countryside with newspapers, consumer products, and new values. But this urban influence had important limits. It did not bring electricity, telephones, public health services, or public schools to the rural South. It did not greatly broaden the rural economy with new jobs. And it left the countryside without the daily contact with the outside world that fostered a broader perspective.

The Democratic Party dominated southern politics after 1877, significantly changing the South's political system. Through various deceits, Democrats purged most black people and some white people from the electoral process and suppressed challenges to their leadership. The result was the emergence by 1900 of the **Solid South,** a period of white Democratic Party rule that lasted into the 1950s.

Although most southern women remained at home or on the farm, piecing together families shattered by war, some enjoyed new options after 1877. Middle-class women in the cities, both white and black, became increasingly active in civic work and reform. They organized clubs, preserved and promoted memories of the war, lobbied for various causes, and assumed regional leadership on a number of important issues. Tens of thousands of young white women from impoverished rural areas found work in textile mills, in city factories, or as servants. These new options posed a challenge to prevailing views about the role of women but ultimately did not change them.

The status of black southerners changed significantly between 1877 and 1900. The members of the first generation born after Emancipation sought more than just freedom as they came of age. They also expected dignity and self-respect and the right to work, to vote, to go to school, and to travel freely. White southerners responded with the equivalent of a second Civil War, and they won. By 1900, black southerners found themselves more isolated from white southerners and with less political power than at any time since 1865. Despite these setbacks, they succeeded, especially in the cities, in building a rich community life and spawning a vibrant middle class.

An Industrial and Urban South

Since the 1850s, public speakers calling for economic reform in the South had been rousing audiences with the tale of the burial of a southern compatriot. The man's headstone, his clothes, the coffin, and the gravediggers' tools all came from the North. Only the corpse and the earth of his grave were southern. The speakers urged their listeners to found industries, build railroads, and grow great cities, so that the South could make its own goods and no one in the future would have to suffer the indignity of journeying to the next world accompanied by Yankee artifacts.

It is unclear whether such admonitions worked. Certainly, southerners manufactured very little in 1877, less than 10 percent of the national total. By 1900, however, they boasted a growing iron and steel industry, textile mills that rivaled those of New England, a world-dominant tobacco industry, and a timber-processing industry that helped make the South a leading furniture-manufacturing center. A variety of regional enterprises also rose to prominence, among them the maker of what would become the world's favorite soft drink, Coca-Cola.

Steel mills and textiles.   Birmingham, barely a scratch in the forest in 1870, exemplified one aspect of what was new about the New South. Within a decade, its iron and steel mills were belching the smoke of progress across the northern Alabama hills. By 1889, Birmingham had surpassed the older southern iron center of Chattanooga, Tennessee, and was preparing to challenge Pittsburgh, the nation's preeminent steelmaking city.

The southern textile industry also experienced significant growth during the 1880s. Although the South had manufactured cotton products since the early decades of the nineteenth century, chronic shortages of labor and capital kept the industry small. In the 1870s, however, several factors drew local investors into textile enterprises. The population of the rural South was rising, but farm income was low, ensuring a steady supply of cheap labor. Cotton was plentiful and cheap. Mixing profit and southern patriotism, entrepreneurs promoted a strong textile industry as a way to make the South less dependent on northern manufactured products and capital. The entrepreneurs located their mills mostly in rural areas. The center of the industry was in the Carolina Piedmont, a region with good railroads, plentiful labor, and cheap energy. By 1900, the South had surpassed New England to become the nation's foremost textile-manufacturing center.

Tobacco and Coca-Cola.   The South's tobacco industry, like its textile industry, predated the Civil War. Virginia was the dominant producer, and its main product was chewing tobacco. The discovery of bright-leaf tobacco, a strain suitable for smoking in the form of cigarettes, changed Americans' tobacco habits. In 1884, James B. Duke installed the first cigarette-making machine in his Durham, North Carolina, plant. By 1900, Duke's American Tobacco Company controlled 80 percent of all tobacco manufacturing in the United States.

Although not as important as textiles or tobacco in 1900, a soft drink developed by an Atlanta pharmacist Dr. John Pemberton eventually became the most renowned southern product worldwide. Pemberton developed the drink, a mixture of oils, caffeine, coca leaves, and cola nuts, in his backyard in an effort to find a good-tasting cure for headaches. He called his concoction Coca-Cola. It was not an overnight success, and Pemberton, short of cash, sold the rights to it to another Atlantan, Asa Candler, in 1889. Candler tinkered with the formula to improve the taste and marketed the product heavily. By the mid-1890s, Coca-Cola enjoyed a national market. Southerners were such heavy consumers that the Georgia Baptist Association felt compelled to warn its members "The more you drink, the more you want to drink. We fear great harm will grow out of this sooner or later, to our young people in particular." The Baptists may have been onto something, as Coca-Cola's original formula did, in fact, include chemically active coca leaves.

Railroads and growth.   Southern railroad construction boomed in the 1880s, outpacing the rest of the nation. Overall, southern track mileage doubled between 1880 and 1890, with the greatest increases in Texas and Georgia (see Map 17–1). In 1886, the southern railroads agreed to conform to a national standard for track width, firmly linking the region into a national transportation network and ensuring quick and direct access for southern products to the booming markets of the Northeast.

The railroads connected many formerly isolated small southern farmers to national and international agricultural markets. At the same time, it gave them access to a whole new range of products, from fertilizers to fashions. Drawn into commercial agriculture, the farmers were now subject to market fluctuations, their fortunes rising and falling with the market prices for their crops. To an extent unknown before the Civil War, the market now determined what farmers planted, how much credit they could expect, and on what terms.

The railroad also opened new areas of the South to settlement and economic development. In 1892, according to one guidebook, Florida was "in the main inaccessible to the ordinary tourist, and unopened to the average settler." But railroad construction boomed in the state in the 1890s, and by 1912 there were tourist hotels as far south as Key West. Railroads also penetrated the Appalachian Mountains, expanding markets for farmers but also opening the area to outside timber and coal-mining interests.

The railroad increased the prominence of interior cities at the expense of older coastal cities. Antebellum ports such as New Orleans, Charleston, and Savannah declined as commerce took to the rails. Cities such as Dallas, Atlanta, Nashville, and Charlotte, astride great railroad trunk lines, emerged to lead southern urban growth. When the Texas and Pacific Railway linked Dallas to eastern markets in 1872, it was a small town of 3,000 people. Eight years later, its population had grown to more than 10,000, and within thirty years it had become the South's twelfth-largest city. By 1920, New Orleans and Norfolk were the only coastal ports still among the ten most populous southern cities.

The Limits of Industrial and Urban Growth

Rapid as it was, urban and industrial growth in the South barely kept pace with that in the booming North (see Chapter 18). Between 1860 and 1900, the South's share of the nation's manufacturing increased only marginally from 10.3 percent to 10.5 percent, and its share of the nation's capital declined slightly from 11.5 percent to 11 percent. About the same percentage of people worked in manufacturing in the southern states east of the Mississippi in 1900 as in 1850. Between 1860 and 1880, the per capita income of the South declined from 72 percent of the national average to 51 percent, and by 1920 it had recovered to only 62 percent (see Figure 17–1).

A weak agricultural economy and a high rural birthrate depressed wages in the South. Southern industrial workers earned roughly half the national average manufacturing wage during the late nineteenth century. Business leaders promoted the advantages of this cheap labor to northern investors. In 1904, a Memphis businessman boasted that his city "can save the northern manufacturer…who employs 400 hands, $50,000 a year on his labor bill."

Effects of low wages.   Despite their attractiveness to industrialists, low wages undermined the southern economy in several ways. Poorly paid workers did not buy much, keeping consumer demand low and limiting the market for southern manufactured goods. They also could not provide much tax revenue, restricting the southern states' ability to fund services like public education. Low wages meant that mostly low-skilled, labor-intensive industries flourished in the South. Well-educated workers would either go north, where factories needed skilled labor to produce high-quality goods and run complicated machinery, or agitate for higher wages and better working conditions in the South. Birmingham, Alabama, for example, probably spent more on public education than any other southern city, but the skilled workers in its steel mills tended to leave for higher-wage opportunities in northern cities like Pittsburgh and Cleveland. As a result, investment in education lagged in the South. Per-pupil expenditure in the region was at least 50 percent below that of the rest of the nation in 1900. North Dakota, not a wealthy state, spent ten times more per pupil than North Carolina, not the poorest state in the South.

Finally, low wages kept immigrants, and the skills and energy they brought with them, out of the South. With steady work available at higher wages in the North, only a scattering of Italian farm laborers, Chinese railroad workers, and Jewish peddlers ventured south. Between 1860 and 1900, during one of the greatest waves of immigration the United States has yet experienced, the foreign-born

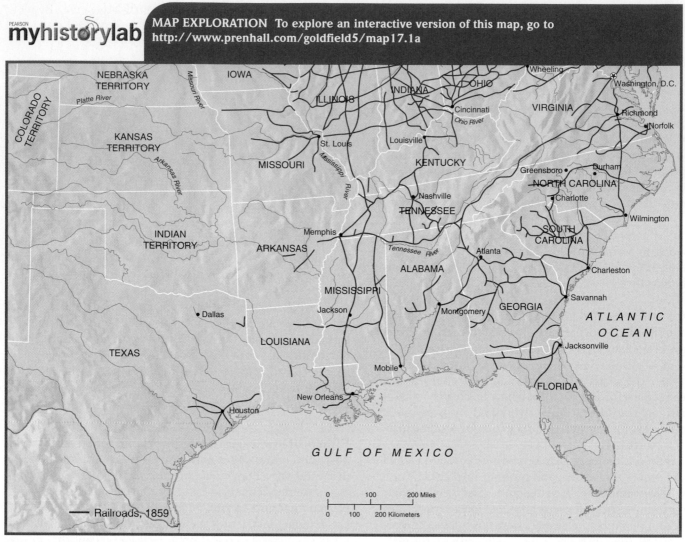

MAP EXPLORATION To explore an interactive version of this map, go to
http://www.prenhall.com/goldfield5/map17.1a

MAP 17–1A   Railroads in the South, 1859 and 1899
A postwar railroad construction boom promoted commercial agriculture and industry in the South. Unlike the railroads of the prewar South, uniform gauges and connections to major trunk lines in the North linked southerners to the rest of the nation. Northern interests, however, owned the major southern railroads in 1899, and most of the products flowing northward were raw materials to be processed by northern industry or shipped elsewhere by northern merchants.

population of the South actually declined from about 10 percent to less than 2 percent.

Limited capital.   Why did the South not do better? Why did it not benefit more from the rapid expansion of the national economy in the last three decades of the nineteenth century? The simple answer is that, despite its growing links to the national economy, the South remained a region apart.

The Civil War had wiped out the South's capital resources, leaving it, in effect, an economic colony of the North. Northern goods flowed into the South, but northern capital, technology, and people did not. Northern-based national banks emerged in the wake of the Civil War to fund northern economic expansion. The South, in contrast, had few banks, and they lacked sufficient capital reserves to fuel

an equivalent expansion. In 1880, Massachusetts alone had five times as much bank capital as the entire South.

Investment in the South seemed riskier and less promising than investment in the vibrant northern economy. As a result, northern banks imposed higher interest rates and shorter terms on loans to southerners than on loans to their northern customers. Some northern capital came south nonetheless. When southern rail lines failed during a depression in the 1870s, northern financiers purchased the companies at bargain prices. By the 1890s, northern firms owned the five major rail lines serving the South.

With limited access to other sources of capital, the South's textile industry depended on thousands of small investors in towns and cities. These investors avoided risk and shunned innovation. Most textile operations remained small-

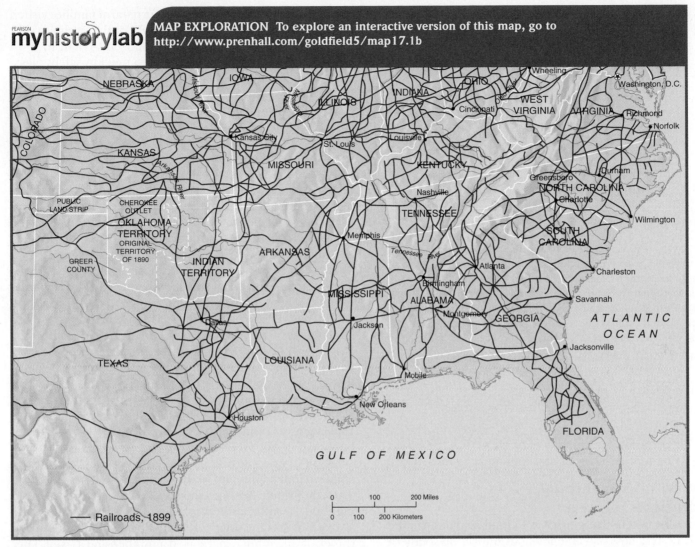

MAP EXPLORATION To explore an interactive version of this map, go to http://www.prenhall.com/goldfield5/map17.1b

MAP 17–1B   (Continued)

scale. The average southern firm in 1900 was capitalized at $11,000, compared with an average of $21,000 elsewhere.

The lumber industry, the South's largest, typified the shortcomings of southern economic development in the late nineteenth century. It required little capital, relied on unskilled labor, and processed its raw materials on site. After clear-cutting (i.e., felling all the trees) in one region, sawmills moved quickly to the next stand of timber, leaving behind a bare landscape, rusting machinery, and a workforce no better off than before. This process, later repeated by the coal-mining industry, inflicted environmental damage on once remote areas such as Appalachia, and displaced their residents.

The tobacco industry, however, avoided the problems that plagued other southern enterprises. James B. Duke's American Tobacco Company was so immensely profitable that he became, in effect, his own bank. With more than enough capital to install the latest technology in his plants, Duke bought out his competitors. He then diversified into electric power generation, investing in an enterprise that be-

came the Southern Power Company in 1905 (and later the Duke Power Company). He also endowed what became Duke University.

Southern industry fit into a narrow niche of late-nine-teenth-century American industrialization. With an unskilled and uneducated work force, poor access to capital and technology, and a weak consumer base, the South processed raw agricultural products and produced cheap textiles, cheap lumber products, and cheap cigarettes. "Made in the South" became synonymous with bottom-of-the-line goods. In the North, industrialization usually occurred in an urban context and promoted rapid urban growth. In the South, textile mills were typically located in the countryside, often in mill villages where employers could easily recruit families and keep them isolated from the distractions and employment alternatives of the cities. The timber industry similarly remained a rural-based enterprise. Tobacco manufacturing helped Durham and Winston, North Carolina, grow, but they remained small compared to northern industrial cities. Duke

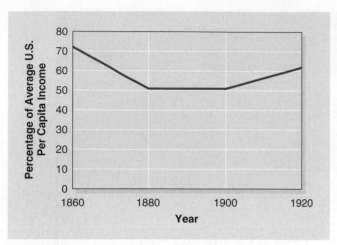

FIGURE 17–1　Per Capita Income in the South as a Percentage of the U.S. Average, 1860–1920
This graph illustrates the devastating effect of the Civil War on the southern economy. Southerners began a slow recovery during the 1880s that accelerated after 1900. But even as late as 1920, per capita income in the South was still lower relative to the country as a whole than it had been before the Civil War.

Data Source: Richard A. Easterlin, "Regional Economic Trends, 1840–1950," in *American Economic History*, ed. Seymour E. Harris (1961).

moved his corporate headquarters to New York to be near that city's financial, advertising, and communications services.

Farms to Cities: Impact on Southern Society

If industrialization in the South was limited compared to the North, it nonetheless had an enormous impact on southern society. In the southern Piedmont, for example, textile mills transformed a portion of the farm population into an industrial workforce. Failed farmers moved to textile villages to earn a living. Entire families secured employment and often a house in exchange for their labor. Widows and single young men also moved to the mills, usually the only option outside farm work in the South. Nearly one-third of the textile-mill labor force by 1900 consisted of children under the age of 14 and women. They worked 12 hours a day, six days a week, although some firms allowed a half-day off on Saturday. They had worked long hours on the farm, too, but now they became the target of concern of middle-class urban reformers, who viewed factory work as destructive of individual and family life.

In 1880, southern towns often did not differ much from the countryside in appearance, economy, religion, and outlook. Over the next twenty years, the gap between town and country widened. By 1900, a town in the New South would boast a business district and more elegant residences than before. It would have a relatively prosperous economy and more frequent contact with other parts of the country. Its influence would extend into the countryside. Mail, the telegraph, the railroad, and the newspaper brought city life to

the attention of farm families. In turn, farm families visited nearby towns and cities more often. A South Carolina writer related in 1900 that "country people who … went to town annually or semiannually, can now go quickly, safely, pleasantly, and cheaply several times a day." Many never returned to the farm. "Cheap coal, cheap lights, convenient water supply offer inducements; society and amusements draw the young; the chance to speculate, to make a sudden rise in fortunes, to get in the swim attracts others."

The urban South drew the region's talented and ambitious young people. White men moved to cities to open shops or take jobs as bank clerks, bookkeepers, merchants, and salesmen. White women worked as retail clerks, telephone operators, and office personnel. Black women filled the growing demand for laundresses and domestic servants. And black men also found prospects better in towns than on the farm, despite a narrow and uncertain range of occupations available to them. The excitement that drew some southerners to their new cities repelled others. To them, urbanization and the emphasis on wealth, new technology, and display represented a second Yankee conquest. The cities, they feared, threatened to infect the South with northern values, undermining southern grace, charm, faith, and family. Ministers warned against trafficking with the urban devil, whose temptations could overcome even the most devout individual. Evangelist Sam Jones, a reformed alcoholic, chose Atlanta for his largest revivals in the 1890s, challenging its residents to keep the Sabbath holy, reject alcohol, and obey the Golden Rule.

Country people held ambivalent views of the city. Farm children looked forward to the Saturday excursion to town, when they would gaze into shop windows, watch people rushing about, wonder at the workings of electricity, and drink a "Coka Cola" at the drugstore. Their parents shared some of this excitement but experienced apprehension as well. They were disturbed by the easy blurring of class and racial distinctions in town and offended by the scorn with which town folk sometimes treated them.

White southerners in town and country, who not long before had lived similar lives, grew distant. Small landholding white farmers and their families had fallen on hard times. The market that lured them into commercial agriculture threatened to take away their independence. They faced the loss of their land and livelihood. Their way of life no longer served as the standard for the South. New South spokesmen promoted cities and industries and ordered farmers to get on board the train of progress before it left the station without them.

The Southern Agrarian Revolt

Even more than before the Civil War, cotton dominated southern agriculture between 1877 and 1900. And the economics of cotton brought despair to cotton farmers. Those who grew two other traditional southern cash crops, rice and tobacco, fared better. Rice and tobacco production increased,

By the 1890s, textile mills were a common sight in towns throughout the South. The mills provided employment for impoverished rural families, especially women and children.

and Louisiana and Arkansas overtook South Carolina in rice production. Steady demand allowed rice and tobacco growers to maintain a decent standard of living. Cotton was another matter. The size of the cotton crop continued to set annual records after 1877. Fertilizers revived supposedly exhausted soils in North and South Carolina, turning them white with cotton. The railroad opened new areas for cultivation in Mississippi and eastern Texas. But the price of cotton fell while the price of fertilizers, agricultural tools, food, and most other necessities went up (see Figure 17–2). As a result, the more cotton the farmers grew, the less money they made.

Before the Civil War, the South fed itself. After the war, with railroads providing direct access to major cotton-marketing centers, farmers produced more cotton and less food. The South became an importer of food. As a common lament went in 1893, "Five-cent cotton, forty-cent meat, how in the world can a poor man eat?"

Cotton and Credit

The solution to this agrarian dilemma seemed simple: Grow less cotton. But that course was not possible for several reasons. In a cash-poor economy, credit ruled. Cotton was the only commodity instantly convertible into cash and thus the only commodity accepted for credit. Food crops generated less income per acre than cotton. Local merchants, themselves bound in a web of credit to merchants in larger cities, accepted cotton as collateral. As cotton prices plummeted, the merchants required their customers to grow more cotton to make up the difference. "No cotton, no credit" became a standard refrain throughout the South after 1877.

For small landowning farmers, credit proved addictive. Trapped in debt by low cotton prices and high interest rates, they lost their land in record numbers. Both black farmers and white farmers were affected. But white farmers were more likely than black farmers to own their farms, so the effect on them was more dramatic. Just after the Civil War, less than one-third of white farmers in the South were tenants or sharecroppers. By the 1890s, nearly half were.

Some areas were able to diversify. Good rail connections in Georgia, for example, made peach farming profitable for some farmers. Railroads likewise helped cattle ranching spread in Texas. But few crops or animals had the geographical range of cotton. Soil type, rainfall, animal parasites, and frost made alternatives unfeasible. Cotton required no machinery or irrigation system. James Barrett, a farmer outside Augusta, Georgia, said of his experiment with diversification in 1900: "I have diversified, and I have not made any money by diversification. . . . I grow green peas and everything I know of. I have raised horses, cows, and hogs, and I have diversified it for the last three years and have not been able to make a dollar."

Southern Farmers Organize, 1877–1892

As their circumstances deteriorated, southern farmers fought back. They engaged in barter when they could. They supplemented their income with occasional jobs off the farm and by selling eggs or vegetables. They lobbied for debt-stay laws and formed farmer organizations. They had lived a communal life of church, family, and kin. Now they would widen the circle of their community to include other farmers sharing the same plight. These were not naive country folk; most

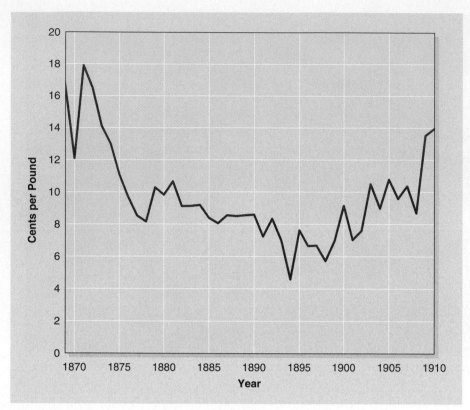

FIGURE 17–2   The Price of Cotton, 1869–1910
The steadily declining price of cotton after the Civil War, from 18 cents a pound to 5 cents a pound by the early 1890s, reflected extreme overproduction. Behind the numbers lay an impoverished rural South.

Data Source: U.S. Department of Commerce, *Historical Statistics of the United States: Colonial Times to 1957.*

owned their own land and participated in the market economy. They just wanted to make the market fairer, to lower interest rates and ease credit, to regulate railroad freight rates, and to keep the prices of necessities in check.

But these goals required legislation that neither the federal government nor southern state governments were inclined to support. Therefore, southern farmers joined their colleagues nationwide to address common grievances related to pricing, credit, and tax policies. Although some of the southern farmers' problems resulted from conditions peculiar to the South, agricultural distress became widespread after 1870. By 1875, nearly 250,000 southern landowners had joined the National Grange of the Patrons of Husbandry or, more popularly, simply the **Grange** (see Chapter 20). The leaders of the Grange, however, were large landowners. They did not have the same interests as the small farmers who made up the organization's rank and file.

Salvation and cooperation.   The most powerful agricultural reform organization, the **Southern Farmers' Alliance,** originated in Texas in the late 1870s. Alliance-sponsored farmers' cooperatives provided their members with discounts on supplies and credit. Members also benefited from marketing their cotton crops collectively. The Alliance was not the only organization to form cooperatives, but it was unique in the messianic zeal with which it promoted them. Although it sometimes endorsed candidates for office, the Alliance was not a political party and did not challenge Democratic domination of the South.

The Alliance was still very much a Texas organization in 1887 when Charles W. Macune, a Wisconsin native, became its driving force. Macune sent a corps of speakers to create a network of southern cooperatives. Within two years, the Alliance had spread throughout the South and into the North and West. By 1890, it claimed more than a million members. With the exception of a few large landowners and some tenant farmers, almost all were small farmers who owned their own land. The success of the Alliance reflected both the desperate struggle of these small farmers to keep their land and the failure of other organizations to help them.

The Alliance operated like a religious denomination. Its leaders preached a message of salvation through cooperation to audiences of as many as 20,000 people at huge revival-like rallies. Qualifications for membership included a belief in the divinity of Jesus and the literal truth of the Bible. Alliance speakers, many of them rural ministers, often held meetings in churches. In their talks, they combined biblical nostrums with economic policy and stressed the importance of doing good as much as good farming. They urged members to visit "the homes where lacerated hearts are bleeding, to assuage the suffering of a brother or a sister, bury the dead, care for the widows and educate the orphans." The Alliance lobbied state legislatures to fund rural public schools. To increase the sense of community, the Alliance sponsored picnics, baseball games, and concerts.

The Alliance became for many small farmers a surrogate government and church in a region where public officials and many mainline Protestant ministers ignored their needs. It imposed strict morality on its members, prohibiting drinking, gambling, and sexual misconduct. Alliance leaders criticized the many Baptist, Methodist, and Presbyterian ministers who had strayed from the traditional emphasis on individual salvation and were defending a status quo that benefited large planters and towns. Cyrus Thompson, the president of the North Carolina Alliance and a prominent Methodist, declared in 1889 that "the church today stands where it has always stood, on the side of human slavery."

Black sharecroppers in Georgia cotton fields, 1898; the scene is reminiscent of the slavery era. Southern agriculture contradicted New South rhetoric both in social and economic terms.

much as 14 cents a yard. The Alliance initiated a jute boycott throughout the South, telling farmers to use cotton bagging as an alternative. The protest worked, forcing the chastened jute manufacturers to offer farmers their product at a mere 5 cents per yard.

Storing cotton. This success encouraged Macune to pursue a more ambitious project. Low cotton prices and a lack of cash kept farmers poor. To address these problems, Macune proposed his **subtreasury plan.** Alliance members were to store their crops in a subtreasury (i.e., warehouse), keeping their cotton off the market until the price rose. In the meantime, the government would loan the farmers up to 80 percent of the value of the stored crops at a low interest rate of 2 percent per year. This arrangement would free farmers from merchants' high interest rates and crop liens. Macune urged Alliance members to endorse political candidates who supported the subtreasury scheme. Many Democratic candidates for state legislatures throughout the South did endorse it and were elected, with Alliance backing, in 1890. Once in office, however, they failed to deliver.

The failure of the subtreasury plan, combined with a steep drop in cotton prices after 1890, undermined the Alliance. Its cooperatives collapsed as crop liens cut down small landowners as though with scythes. A Georgia Alliance man wrote in 1891 that "Hundreds of farmers will be turned adrift, and thousands of acres of our best land allowed to grow up in weeds through lack of necessary capital to work them." Alliance membership declined by two-thirds in Georgia that year. Desperate Alliance leaders merged their organization with a new national political party in 1892, the People's Party, better known as the **Populist party.** The Populists appropriated the Alliance program and challenged Democrats in the South and Republicans in the West. The merger reflected desperation more than calculation. As we will see in Chapter 20, the Populists stirred up national politics between 1892 and 1896. In the South, they challenged the Democratic Party, sometimes courting Republicans, including black voters.

Some Alliance members left their churches for new religious groups. The Holiness movement, which began in the North before the Civil War, revived among Texas farmers in the mid-1880s. Holiness disciples advocated simple dress, avoided coffee and pork, and swore off all worldly amusements. The members of the Church of God, which was founded in the mountains of Tennessee and North Carolina in 1886, similarly sought to cleanse themselves of secular evils. The new churches promoted a vision of an egalitarian South. They accepted women on an equal basis, and occasionally black people as well. As many as a third of Holiness preachers were women.

Women also found an active role as officers and speakers in the Alliance. As a Texas woman declared, "The Alliance has come to redeem woman from her enslaved condition. She is admitted into the organization as the equal of her brother, and the ostracism which has impeded her intellectual progress in the past is not met with."

Unlike some of the new religious movements, however, the Alliance did not accept black members. Black farmers formed the first **Colored Farmers' Alliance** in Texas in 1886. The Colored Alliance had fewer landowners and more tenants and sharecroppers in its ranks than the white organization. It concerned itself with issues relevant to this constituency, such as higher wages for cotton pickers. In 1891, the Colored Alliance attempted a region-wide strike over farm wages but was unable to enforce it in the worsening southern economy.

The white Alliance had better results with a protest over price fixing. To protect cotton shipped to market, farmers wrapped it in a burlap-like material called jute. In 1888, jute manufacturers combined to raise the price from 7 cents to as

Women in the New South

Just as farmwomen found their voices in the Alliance movement of the 1880s, a growing group of middle-class white and black urban women entered the public realm and engaged in policy issues. In the late-nineteenth-century North, women became increasingly active in reform movements, including woman suffrage, labor legislation, social welfare, and city planning. Building on their antebellum activist traditions, northern women, sometimes joining with men, sought to improve the status of women.

Because the antebellum reform movements included abolitionism, they had made little headway in the South. As a result, southern women had a meager reform tradition to build on. The war also left them ambivalent about independence. With husbands, fathers, and brothers dead or incapacitated, many women had to care for themselves and their families in the face of defeat and deprivation. Some determined never again to depend on men. Others, responding to the stress of running a farm or business, would have preferred less independence.

The response of southern white men to the war also complicated women's efforts to improve their status. Southern men had been shaken by defeat. They had lost the war and placed their families in peril. Many responded with alcoholism and violence. To regain their self-esteem, they recast the war as a noble crusade rather than a defeat. And they imagined southern white women as paragons of virtue and purity who required men to defend them. Demands for even small changes in traditional gender roles would threaten this image. Southern women understood this and never mounted an extensive reform campaign like their sisters in the North. Some middle-class women were openly hostile to reform, and others adopted conservative causes more inclined to reinforce the role of men in southern society than to challenge it.

Despite such limitations, middle-class southern women found opportunities to broaden their social role and enter the public sphere in the two decades after 1880. They found these opportunities primarily in the cities, where servants, stores, and schools freed them of many of the productive functions, such as making clothing, cooking, and childcare, that burdened their sisters in the country and kept them tied to the home.

Church Work and Preserving Memories

Southern women waded warily into the public arena, using channels men granted them as natural extensions of the home, such as church work. By the 1880s, evangelical Protestant churches had become prominent in many aspects of southern life. The need to rationalize the loss and devastation of the war, the dislocation and the broken families, and the weakness of post-Reconstruction state and local governments thrust the church into many aspects of southern life. The South became the most church-going region of the country. Women took advantage of the church's prominence to build careers using the moral gravity of church affiliation to political advantage. Most of the major reform efforts in the South during this era emanated from the church, and from the women for whom church work was an approved role for their gender.

The movement to found home mission societies, for example, was led by single white women in the Methodist Church. Home missions promoted industrial education among the poor and helped working-class women become self-sufficient. The home mission movement reflected an increased interest in missionary work in white southern evangelical churches. Laura Haygood, an Atlantan who had served as a missionary in China, founded a home mission in Atlanta when she returned in 1883. Lily Hammond, another Atlantan, extended the mission concept when she opened settlement houses in black and white neighborhoods in Atlanta in the 1890s. **Settlement houses,** pioneered in New York in the 1880s, promoted middle-class values in poor neighborhoods and provided them with a permanent source of services. In the North, they were privately sponsored. In the South, they were supported by the Methodist Church and known as Wesley Houses, after John Wesley, the founder of Methodism.

Religion also prompted southern white women to join the **Women's Christian Temperance Union (WCTU).** The first southern local was organized in Lucy Haygood's church in Atlanta in 1880. Temperance reform, unlike other church-inspired activities, involved women directly in public policy. Women framed temperance and the prohibition of alcohol as a family issue—alcohol ruined families, victimizing innocent women and children. WCTU members visited schools to educate children about the evils of alcohol, addressed prisoners, and blanketed men's meetings with literature. As a result, they became familiar with the South's abysmal school system and its archaic criminal justice system. They soon began advocating education and prison reform as well as legislation against alcohol.

By the 1890s, many WCTU members realized that they could not achieve their goals unless women had the vote. Rebecca Latimer Felton, an Atlanta suffragist and WCTU member, reflected the frustration of her generation of southern women in an address to working women in 1892: "But some will say, you women might be quiet, you can't vote, you can't do anything! Exactly so, we have kept quiet for nearly a hundred years hoping to see relief come to the women of this country, and it hasn't come. How long must our children be slain? If a mad dog should come into my yard, and attempt to bite my child or myself, would you think me out of my place, if I killed him with a dull meat axe?...[You] would call that woman a brave woman...and yet are we to sit by while drink ruins our homes?"

Rebecca Felton's own career highlighted the essentially conservative nature of the reform movement among middle-class white women in the New South. Born in 1835 to a wealthy planter family, she attended college and married Dr. William H. Felton, a physician and minister twelve years her senior. During the Civil War and its aftermath, the Feltons eked out a modest living teaching school and working a small farm. Four of their five children died. Seeing southern families worse off than her own, Felton threw herself into a variety of reform activities, ranging from woman suffrage to campaigns against drinking, smoking, and Coca-Cola. She fought for childcare facilities and sex education, as well as compulsory school attendance, and she pushed for the admission of women to the University of Georgia. But she strongly supported textile operators over textile workers and defended white supremacy. She had no qualms about the lynching of black men, executing them without trial "a thousand times a week if necessary" to preserve the purity of white women. In 1922, she became the first woman member of the U.S. Senate. By any definition, Felton was a reformer, but like most middle-class southern women, she had no interest in challenging the class and racial inequities of the New South.

The dedication of southern women to commemorating the memory of the Confederate cause also indicates the conservative nature of middle-class women's reform in the New South. Ladies' Memorial Associations formed after the war to ensure the proper burial of Confederate soldiers and suitable markings for their graves. The associations joined with men to erect monuments to Confederate leaders and, by the 1880s, to the common soldier. These activities reinforced white solidarity and constructed a common heritage for all white southerners regardless of class or location. By the 1890s, women were planning monuments in prominent civic spaces in the urban South. Their efforts sparked interest in city planning and city beautification. A new organization, the United Daughters of the Confederacy (UDC), appeared in 1894 to preserve southern history and honor its heroes. Although men formed similar associations, women remained the most active protectors of regional memory. Work for the Lost Cause reflected traditional roles, but it also offered a way for women to hone leadership and organizational skills, preparing them for less traditional public activities in the 1890s. Gertrude Thomas, for example, one of the South's leading suffragists, played an important role in the Georgia UDC.

Women's Clubs

A broader spectrum of southern middle-class women joined women's clubs than joined church-sponsored organizations or memorial associations. Most women's clubs began in the 1880s as literary or self-improvement societies that had little interest in reform. By 1890, most towns and cities boasted at least several women's clubs and perhaps a federated club organization. But by that time, some clubs and their members had also begun to discuss political issues, such as child labor reform, educational improvement, and prison reform. The Arkansas Federation of Women's Clubs launched a boycott of goods produced by "exploited" labor in 1903. The Lone Star (Texas) Federation scrutinized public hospitals, almshouses, and orphanages at the turn of the century. Its president asserted, "The Lone Star Federation stands for the highest and truest type of womanhood, that which lends her voice as well as her hand." Southern women's club members sought out their sisters in the North. As Georgia's federated club president, Mrs. A.O. Granger, wrote in 1906, "Women of intellectual keenness in the South could not be left out of the awakening of the women of the whole country to a realization of the responsibility which they properly had in the condition of their fellow-women and of the children."

The activities of black women's clubs paralleled those of white women's clubs. Most African American women in southern cities worked as domestics or laundresses. Black

Southern white women played a major role in memorializing the Civil War and Confederate veterans. Here, a float prepared for a Confederate Veterans parade includes the major symbols of the Lost Cause, including the prominent pictures of Robert E. Lee, Thomas "Stonewall" Jackson, and Jefferson Davis, as well as the Confederate Battle Flag. The sponsorship of a casket company affords some irony to the photograph.

women's clubs supported daycare facilities for working mothers and settlement houses in poor black neighborhoods modeled after those in northern cities. Atlanta's Neighborhood Union, founded by Lugenia Burns Hope in 1908, provided playgrounds and a health center and obtained a grant from a New York foundation to improve black education in the city. Black women's clubs also established homes for single black working women to protect them from sexual exploitation, and they worked for woman suffrage "to reckon with men who place no value on her [black woman's] virtue," as Nannie H. Burroughs of the National Association of Colored Women argued at the turn of the century.

Only rarely, however, as at some meetings of the Young Women's Christian Association (YWCA) or occasional meetings in support of prohibition, did black and white club members interact. Some white clubwomen expressed sympathy for black women privately, but publicly they maintained white solidarity. Most were unwilling to sacrifice their own reform agenda to the cause of racial reconciliation. Women suffragists in the South, for example, did not make common cause with black people. On the contrary, some used racial solidarity as a weapon to promote white women's right to

Global Perspectives

The Race "Problem" in Europe

Like the United States, Europe became more race conscious toward the end of the nineteenth century. A combination of factors, including the misapplication of Charles Darwin's *Origin of Species* (1859) to imply a hierarchy of races, increasing mobility and urbanization, rising nationalism, and imperialist ventures in Asia and Africa, generated a greater awareness of racial differences. Scientists and academics singled out the Nordics, Teutons (Germans), and Anglo-Saxons as the "fittest" of the globe's races; they considered such groups as Jews, Slavs, and southern Europeans to be inferior. Although today we would classify all of these as ethnic groups, Europeans at the time called them races. Some Europeans believed that the "superior" races had an obligation to protect and help the "inferior" ones. For others, the racial hierarchy represented nature's ordering of peoples, and human intervention would therefore serve no purpose. These attitudes justified imperialism abroad and discrimination at home.

These racial attitudes emerged at a time when many European nations had already granted Jewish citizens full legal equality. Freed from occupational, educational, and residential restrictions, the Jewish population flourished as never before, rising and assimilating into European society. Their ascension troubled some Europeans, much as contemporary southern whites felt threatened by African American mobility. During the 1880s and 1890s, Germany and Austria founded right-wing parties that utilized anti-Semitism to win votes among groups that were wary of modern trends such as urbanization and industrialization. For such people, newly enfranchised Jews were a natural target of hatred and fear. By the 1890s, Europe had a "Jewish problem" that resembled the American South's "Negro problem."

In 1895, Theodor Herzl, an Austrian Jewish journalist, posed an answer to the problem: the voluntary removal of Europe's Jews to Palestine. Surveying the rising tide of European anti-Semitism, Herzl proposed a Jewish nation-state. "Palestine is our ever memorable historic home…the great symbol of the solution of the Jewish Question after eighteen centuries of Jewish suffering."

The first Zionist Congress met in Switzerland in 1897, declaring its aim to create a "home in Palestine secured by public law" for world Jewry. Between 1904 and 1914, about 3,000 Jews per year migrated to the Holy Land. Throughout the first half of the twentieth century, Jewish migration to Palestine was restricted, first by the Ottoman Turks and then by the British. Large numbers of Jews settled instead in the northern cities of the United States.

Blacks in the American South also contemplated separate homelands, either in Africa or in the United States. Back-to-Africa movements appeared periodically in the decades after the Civil War. But as with European Jews, the greatest number of migrants went to the cities of the North, especially after the turn of the twentieth century.

■ Why did most blacks in the American South and Jews in Europe during the late nineteenth century decide against migrating to a separate homeland?

---

vote, arguing that the combined vote of white men and women could be used to further white interests.

The primary interest of most southern white women's clubs was the plight of young white working-class and farm women. This interest reflected the growing number of such women in the workforce. Single and adrift in the city, many worked for low wages, and some slipped into prostitution. The clubs sought to help them make the transition from rural to urban life or to improve their lives on the farm. To this end, they focused on child labor reform and on upgrading public education.

Settling the Race Issue

The assertiveness of a new generation of African Americans in the 1880s and 1890s, especially in urban areas, provided the impetus and opportunity for white leaders to secure white solidarity. To counter black aspirations, white leaders enlisted the support of young white southerners, convincing them that the struggle for white supremacy would place them beside the larger-than-life heroes of the Civil War generation. African Americans resisted the resulting efforts to deprive them of their remaining freedoms. Although some left the South, many more built new lives and communities within the restricted framework white southerners allowed them.

The Fluidity of Southern Race Relations, 1877–1890

Race relations remained remarkably fluid in the South between the end of Reconstruction and the early 1890s. Despite the departure of federal troops and the end of Republican rule, many black people continued to vote and hold office. Some Democrats even courted the black electorate. Although segregation ruled in churches, schools, and in some organizations and public places after the Civil War, black people and white people continued to mingle, do business with each other, and often maintain cordial relations.

In 1885, T. McCants Stewart, a black journalist from New York, traveled to his native South Carolina, expecting a rough reception once his train headed south from Washington, DC. To his surprise, the conductor allowed him to remain in his seat while white riders sat on baggage or stood. He provoked little reaction among white passengers when he entered the dining car. Some of them struck up a conversation with him. Stewart, who admitted he had begun his journey with "a chip on my shoulder…[daring] any man to knock it off," now observed that "the whites of the South are really less afraid to [have] contact with colored people than the whites of the North." In Columbia, South Carolina, Stewart found that he could move about with no restrictions. "I can ride in first class cars…. I can go into saloons and get refreshments even as in New York. I can stop in and drink a glass of soda and be more politely waited upon than in some parts of New England."

Other black people corroborated Stewart's experiences in different parts of the South. During the 1880s, black people joined interracial labor unions and continued to be active in the Republican Party. They engaged in business with white people. In the countryside, African Americans and white people hunted and fished together, worked side by side at sawmills, and traded with each other. Cities were segregated more by class than by race, and people of both races sometimes lived in the same neighborhoods. To be sure, black people faced discrimination in employment and voting and random retaliation for perceived violations of racial barriers. But the barriers were by no means fixed.

The White Backlash

The black generation that came of age in this environment demanded full participation in American society. As the young black editor of Nashville's *Fisk Herald* proclaimed in 1889, "We are not the Negro from whom the chains of slavery fell a quarter of a century ago…. We are now qualified, and being the equal of whites, should be treated as such." Charles Price, an educator from North Carolina, admonished colleagues in 1890, "If we do not possess the manhood and patriotism to stand up in the defense of…constitutional rights and protest long, loud and unitedly against their continual infringements, we are unworthy of heritage as American citizens and deserve to have fastened on us the wrongs of which many are disposed to complain."

For many in the generation of white southerners who came of age in the same period, this assertiveness rankled. These young white people, raised on the myth of the Lost Cause, were continually reminded of the heroism and sacrifice of their fathers during the Civil War. For them, black people replaced the Yankees as the enemy; they saw it as their mission to preserve white purity and dominance. Echoing these sentiments, David Schenck, a Greensboro, North Carolina, businessman, wrote in 1890 that "the breach between the races widens as the young free negroes grow up and intrude themselves on white society and nothing prevents the white people of the South from annihilating the negro race but the military power of the United States Government."

The South's deteriorating rural economy and the volatile politics of the late 1880s and early 1890s exacerbated the growing tensions between assertive black people and threatened white people. So too did the growth of industry and cities in the South. In the cities, black and white people came into close contact, competing for jobs and jostling each other for seats on streetcars and trains. Racist rhetoric and violence against black people accelerated in the 1890s.

Lynch Law

In 1892, three prominent black men, Tom Moss, Calvin McDowell, and William Stewart, opened a grocery on the south side of Memphis, an area with a large African American population. The People's Grocery prospered, while a white-owned store across the street struggled. The proprietor of the white-owned store, W. H. Barrett, was incensed. He obtained an indictment against Moss, McDowell, and Stewart for maintaining a public nuisance. Outraged black community leaders called a protest meeting at the grocery, during which two people made threats against Barrett. Barrett learned of the threats, notified the police, and warned the gathering at the People's Grocery that white people planned to attack and destroy the store. Nine sheriff's deputies, all white, approached the store to arrest the men who had threatened Barrett. Fearing Barrett's threatened white assault, the people in the grocery fired on the deputies, unaware who they were, and wounded three. When the deputies identified themselves, thirty black people surrendered, including Moss, McDowell, and Stewart, and were imprisoned. Four days later, deputies removed the three owners from jail, took them to a deserted area, and shot them dead.

The men at the People's Grocery had violated two of the unspoken rules that white southerners imposed on black southerners to maintain racial barriers: They had prospered, and they had forcefully challenged white authority. During 1892, a year of political agitation and economic depression, 235 **lynchings** occurred in the South. White mobs lynched nearly 2,000 black southerners between 1882 and 1903. During the 1890s, lynchings occurred at the rate of 150 a year.

Lynching became a public spectacle, a ritual designed to reinforce white supremacy. Note the matter-of-fact satisfaction of the spectators at this gruesome murder of a black man.

Most lynchers were working-class whites with rural roots, who were struggling in the depressed economy of the 1890s and enraged at the fluidity of urban race relations. The men who murdered Moss, McDowell, and Stewart, for example, had recently moved to Memphis from the countryside, where they had been unable to make a living farming.

The silence or tepid disapproval of white leaders condoned this orgy of violence. The substitution of lynch law for a court of law seemed a cheap price to pay for white solidarity at a time when political and economic pressures threatened entrenched white leaders. In 1893, Atlanta's Methodist bishop, Atticus G. Haygood, usually a spokesman for racial moderation, objected to the torture some white lynchers inflicted on their victims but added, "Unless assaults by Negroes on white women and little girls come to an end, there will most probably be still further displays of vengeance that will shock the world."

Haygood's comments reflect the most common justification for lynching, the presumed threat posed by black men to the sexual virtue of white women. Sexual "crimes" could include remarks, glances, and gestures. Yet only 25 percent of the lynchings that took place in the thirty years after 1890 had an alleged sexual connection. Certainly, the men of the People's Grocery had committed no sex crime. Lynchers did not carry out their grisly crimes to end a rape epidemic; they killed to keep black men in their place and to restore their own sense of manhood and honor.

Ida B. Wells, who owned a black newspaper in Memphis, used her columns to publicize the People's Grocery lynchings. The great casualty of the lynchings, she noted, was her faith that education, wealth, and upright living guaranteed

black people the equality and justice they had long sought. The reverse was true. The more black people succeeded, the greater was their threat to white people. She investigated other lynchings, countering the claim that they were the result of assaults on white women. When she suggested that, on the contrary, perhaps some white women were attracted to black men, the white citizens of Memphis destroyed her press and office. Exiled to Chicago, Wells devoted herself to the struggle for racial justice.

Segregation by Law

Southern white lawmakers sought to cement white solidarity and ensure black subservience in the 1890s by instituting **segregation** by law and the **disfranchisement** of black voters. Racial segregation restricting black Americans to separate and rarely equal public facilities had prevailed nationwide before the Civil War. After 1870, the custom spread rapidly in southern cities. In Richmond by the early 1870s, segregation laws required black people registering to vote to enter through separate doors and registrars to count their ballots separately. The city's prison and hospitals were segregated. So too were its horsedrawn street railways, its schools, and most of its restaurants, hotels, and theaters.

During the same period, many northern cities and states, often in response to protests by African Americans, were ending segregation. Massachusetts, for example, had passed the nation's first public accommodations law in May 1865, desegregating all public facilities. Cities such as New York, Cleveland, and Cincinnati desegregated their streetcars. Chicago, Cleveland, Milwaukee, and the entire state of Michigan desegregated their public school systems. Roughly 95 percent of the nation's black population, however, lived in the South. Integration in the North, consequently, required white people to give up very little to black people. And as African American aspirations increased in the South during the 1890s while their political power waned, they became more vulnerable to segregation by law at the state level. At the same time, migration to cities, industrial development, and technologies such as railroads and elevators increased the opportunities for racial contact and muddled the rules of racial interaction.

Much of the new legislation focused on railroads, a symbol of modernity and mobility in the New South. Local laws and customs could not control racial interaction on interstate railroads. White passengers objected to black passengers' implied assertion of economic and social equality when they sat with them in dining cars and first-class compartments. Black southerners, by contrast, viewed equal access

Ida B. Wells, an outspoken critic of lynching, fled to Chicago following the People's Grocery lynchings in Memphis in 1892 and became a national civil-rights leader.

to railroad facilities as a sign of respectability and acceptance. When southern state legislatures required railroads to provide segregated facilities, black people protested.

Segregation laws required the railroads to provide "separate but equal" accommodations for black passengers. Railroads balked at the expense involved in doing so and provided black passengers with distinctly inferior facilities. Many lines refused to sell first-class tickets to black people and treated them roughly if they sat in first-class seats or tried to eat in the dining car. In 1890, Homer Plessy, a black Louisianan, refused to leave the first-class car of a railroad traveling through the state. Arrested, he filed suit, arguing that his payment of the first-class fare entitled him to sit in the same first-class accommodations as white passengers. He claimed that under his right of citizenship guaranteed by the Fourteenth Amendment, neither the state of Louisiana nor the railroad could discriminate against him on the basis of color. The Constitution, he claimed, was colorblind.

The U.S. Supreme Court ruled on the case, *Plessy v. Ferguson,* in 1896. In a seven-to-one decision, the Court held that Louisiana's railroad segregation law did not violate the Constitution as long as the railroads or the state provided equal accommodations for black passengers. The decision left unclear what "equal" meant. In the Court's view, "Legislation is powerless to eradicate racial instincts," meaning that segregation of the races was natural and transcended constitutional considerations. The only justice to vote against the decision was John Marshall Harlan, a Kentuckian and former slave owner. In a stinging dissent, he predicted that the decision would result in an all-out assault on black rights. "The destinies of the two races...are indissolubly linked together," Harlan declared, "and the interests of both require that the common government of all shall not permit the seeds of race hate to be planted under the sanction of law."

Harlan's was a prophetic dissent. Both northern and southern states enacted new segregation laws in the wake of *Plessy v. Ferguson.* In practice, the separate facilities for black people these laws required, if provided at all, were rarely equal. A sense of futility, time, expense, and physical danger dissuaded black people from challenging the statutes. Protests in the press, appeals to white leaders, and occasional boycotts failed to stem the rising tide. By 1900, segregation by law extended to public conveyances, theaters, hotels, restaurants, parks, and schools.

The segregation statutes came to be known collectively as **Jim Crow laws,** after the blackface stage persona of Thomas Rice, a white northern minstrel-show performer in the 1820s. Reflecting white stereotypes of African Americans, Rice had caricatured Crow as a foolish, elderly, lame slave who spoke in an exaggerated dialect.

Economic segregation followed social segregation. Before the Civil War, black men had dominated such crafts as carpentry and masonry. By the 1890s, white men were replacing them in these trades and excluding them from new ones, such as plumbing and electrical work. Trade unions, composed primarily of craft workers, began systematically to exclude African Americans. Although the steel and tobacco industries hired black workers, most other manufacturers turned them away. Confined increasingly to low or unskilled positions in railroad construction, the timber industry, and agriculture, black people underwent deskilling, a decline in workforce expertise, after 1890. With lower incomes from unskilled labor, they faced reduced opportunities for better housing and education.

Disfranchisement

With economic and social segregation came political isolation. The authority of post-Reconstruction Redeemer governments had rested on their ability to limit and control the black vote. Following the political instability of the late 1880s and the 1890s, however, white leaders determined to disfranchise black people altogether, thereby reinforcing white solidarity and eliminating the need to consider black interests. Obstacles loomed—the Fifteenth Amendment, which guaranteed freedmen the right to vote, and a Republican-dominated Congress—but with a national consensus emerging in support of white supremacy, they proved easy to circumvent.

"JIM CROW" CARS

For Virginia Afro-Americans, as Well as Those of Kentucky, Tennessee and Several Other Southern States.

An Attempt to Extend the Provisions of the Outrageous Law to Street Cars.

The Constitutionality of the Law to be Attacked in the Courts by an Electric Street Car Company and Prominent Virginia Afro-Americans.

Richmond, Va.—Since Sunday week, July 1, the "Jim Crow" car law passed by the Virginia legislature last January, and signed by Gov. Tyler in spite of the remonstrance of nearly every influential colored man in Virginia, has been in force. It requires every railroad and, some attorneys say, every street car company in the state to provide separate cars for the exclusive use of colored people. Negroes are not allowed to ride on the cars intended for the use of the whites, and vice versa; but any Negro forcing himself upon a car for whites, and refusing to leave when requested to do so, may be forcibly ejected

Segregation by law accelerated after the 1896 *Plessy v. Ferguson* decision, but public conveyances often failed to abide by the "equal" portion of the separate-but-equal ruling. African Americans in the South fought racial separation and exclusion vigorously, as this excerpt from a black newspaper in Cleveland attests. July 14, 1900.

Support for disfranchisement was especially strong among large landowners in the South's plantation districts, where heavy concentrations of black people threatened their political domination. Urban leaders, especially after the turmoil of the 1890s, looked on disfranchisement as a way to stabilize politics and make elections more predictable.

The movement to reduce or eliminate the black vote in the South began in the 1880s and continued through the early 1900s (see Overview table, The March of Disfranchisement across the South, 1889–1908). Democrats enacted a variety of measures to attain their objectives without violating the letter of the Fifteenth Amendment. They complicated the registration and voting processes. States enacted **poll taxes**, requiring citizens to pay to vote. They adopted the secret ballot, which confused and intimidated illiterate black voters accustomed to using ballots with colors to identify parties. States set literacy and educational qualifications for voting or required prospective registrants to "interpret" a section of the state constitution. To avoid disfranchising poor, illiterate white voters with these measures, states enacted **grandfather clauses,** granting the vote automatically to anyone whose grandfather could have voted prior to 1867 (the year Congressional Reconstruction began). The grandfathers of most black men in the 1890s had been slaves, ineligible to vote.

Tennessee was the first state to pass disfranchising legislation. In 1889, it required the secret ballot and a poll tax in four cities, Nashville, Memphis, Chattanooga, and Knoxville, where African Americans often held the balance of power. A year later, Mississippi amended its constitution to require voters to pass a literacy test and to prove that they "understood" the state constitution. The laws granted the registrar wide latitude in interpreting the accuracy of the registrant's understanding. When a journalist asked an Alabama lawmaker if Jesus Christ could pass his state's "understanding" test, the legislator replied, "That would depend entirely on which way he was going to vote."

Lawmakers sold white citizens on franchise restrictions with the promise that they would apply only to black voters and would scarcely affect white voters. This promise proved untrue. Alarmed by the Populist uprising, Democratic leaders used disfranchisement to gut dissenting parties. During the 1880s, minority parties in the South consistently polled an average of 40 percent of the statewide vote; by the mid-1890s, the figure had diminished to 30 percent despite the Populist insurgency. Turnout dropped even more dramatically. In Mississippi, for example, voter turnout in gubernatorial races during the 1880s averaged 51 percent; during the 1890s, it was 21 percent. Black turnout in Mississippi, which averaged 39 percent in the 1880s, plummeted to near zero in the 1890s. Overall turnout, which averaged 64 percent during the 1880s, fell to only 30 percent by 1910.

Black people protested disfranchisement vigorously. When 160 South Carolina delegates gathered to amend the state constitution in 1895, the six black delegates among them

OVERVIEW

The March of Disfranchisement Across the South, 1889–1908

Year	State	Strategies
1889	Florida	Poll tax
1889	Tennessee	Poll tax
1890	Mississippi	Poll tax, literacy test, understanding clause
1891	Arkansas	Poll tax
1893, 1901	Alabama	Poll tax, literacy test, grandfather clause
1894, 1895	South Carolina	Poll tax, literacy test, understanding clause
1894, 1902	Virginia	Poll tax, literacy test, understanding clause
1897, 1898	Louisiana	Poll tax, literacy test, grandfather clause
1899, 1900	North Carolina	Poll tax, literacy test, grandfather clause
1902	Texas	Poll tax
1908	Georgia	Poll tax, literacy test, understanding clause, grandfather clause

mounted a passionate but futile defense of their right to vote. Black delegate W. J. Whipper noted the irony of white people clamoring for supremacy when they already held the vast majority of the state's elected offices. Robert Smalls, the state's leading black politician, urged delegates not to turn their backs on the state's black population (see American Views, Robert Smalls Argues Against Disfranchisement). Such pleas fell on deaf ears.

A National Consensus on Race

How could the South get away with it? How could southerners openly segregate, disfranchise, and lynch African Americans without a national outcry? Apparently, the majority of Americans in the 1890s subscribed to the notion that black people were inferior to white people and deserved to be treated as second-class citizens. Contemporary depictions of black people show scarcely human stereotypes: black men with bulbous lips and bulging eyes, fat black women wearing turbans and smiling vacuously, and black children contentedly eating watermelon or romping with jungle animals. These images appeared on cereal boxes, in advertisements, in children's books, in newspaper cartoons, and as lawn ornaments. Popular theater of the day featured white men in blackface cavorting in ridiculous fashion and singing songs such as "All Coons Look Alike to Me" and "I Wish My Color Would Fade." Among the widely read books of the era was *The Clansman*, a glorification of the rise of the Ku Klux Klan. D. W. Griffith transformed *The Clansman* into an immensely popular motion picture epic under the title *Birth of a Nation*.

Intellectual and political opinion in the North bolstered southern policy. So-called scientific racism purported to establish white superiority and black inferiority on biological grounds. Northern-born professional historians reinterpreted the Civil War and Reconstruction in the white South's favor. Historian William A. Dunning, the generation's leading authority on Reconstruction, wrote in 1901 that the North's "views as to the political capacity of the blacks had been irrational." Respected journals openly supported disfranchisement and segregation. The progressive journal *Outlook* hailed disfranchisement because it made it "impossible in the future for ignorant, shiftless, and corrupt negroes to misrepresent their race in political action." Harvard's Charles Francis Adams, Jr., chided colleagues who disregarded the "fundamental, scientific facts" that, he claimed, demonstrated black inferiority. The *New York Times,* summarizing this national consensus in 1903, noted that "practically the whole country" supported the "southern solution" to the race issue, because "there was no other possible settlement."

These views permeated Congress, which made no effort to block the institutionalization of white supremacy in the South after 1890, and the courts, which upheld discriminatory legislation. As a delegate at the Alabama disfranchisement convention of 1901 noted, "The race problem is no longer confined to the States of the South, [and] we have the sympathy instead of the hostility of the North."

By the mid-1890s, Republicans were so entrenched in the North and West that they did not need southern votes to win presidential elections or to control Congress. Besides, business-oriented Republicans found common ground with conservative southern Democrats on fiscal policy and foreign affairs. Their attention, diverted by economic problems and labor unrest, no longer rested on the South. The emerging consensus on the meaning of the Civil War and Reconstruction, part of the national reconciliation discussed in the

American Views

Robert Smalls Argues against Disfranchisement

Born in Beaufort, South Carolina, in 1839, Robert Smalls worked as a slave pilot in Charleston harbor. In 1862, he emancipated himself, with his family and friends, when he delivered a Confederate steamer, *The Planter*, to the Union fleet blockading the harbor. He entered politics in 1864 as a delegate from his state to the Republican National Convention. He helped write South Carolina's Reconstruction constitution, which, among its provisions, guaranteed the right of former slaves to vote and hold office. Smalls won election to the state house of representatives in 1869, the state senate in 1871, and the U.S. House of Representatives in 1875. With opportunities for African Americans to hold public office declining following Reconstruction, Smalls secured appointment as collector of the port of Beaufort, a federal post he occupied until his death in 1915. In the speech excerpted here, delivered to the South Carolina Constitutional Convention of 1895, he bitterly assails the state's plan to disfranchise black voters.

- From the white perspective, what is Smalls's most telling argument against the disfranchisement and the planned strategies to implement it?

- How does Smalls depict the black citizens of South Carolina?

- Why were white political leaders unmoved by Smalls's plea?

Mr. President, this convention has been called for no other purpose than the disfranchisement of the negro.... The negroes are paying taxes in the south on $263,000,000 worth of property. In South Carolina, according to the census, the negroes pay tax on $12,500,000 worth of property. That was in 1890. You voted down without discussion...a proposition for a simple property and education qualification [for voting]. What do you want?...In behalf of the 600,000 negroes in the State and the 132,000 negro voters all that I demand is that a fair and honest election law be passed. We care not what the qualifications imposed are, all that we ask is that they be fair and honest, and honorable, and with these provisos we will stand or fall by it. You have 102,000 white men over 21 years of age, 13,000 of these cannot read nor write. You dare not disfranchise them, and you know that the man who proposes it will never be elected to another office in the State of South Carolina....Fifty-eight thousand negroes cannot read nor write. This leaves a majority of 14,000 white men who can read and write over the same class of negroes in this State. We are willing to accept a scheme that provides that no man who cannot read nor write can vote, if you dare pass it. How can you expect an ordinary man to "understand and explain" any section of the Constitution, to correspond to the interpretation put upon it by the manager of election, when by a very recent decision of the supreme court, composed of the most learned men in the State, two of them put one construction upon a section, and the other justice put an entirely different construction upon it. To embody such a provision in the election law would be to mean that every white man would interpret it aright and every negro would interpret it wrong....Some morning you may wake up to find that the bone and sinew of your country is gone. The negro is needed in the cotton fields and in the low country rice fields, and if you impose too hard conditions upon the negro in this State there will be nothing else for him to do but to leave. What then will you do about your phosphate works? No one but a negro can work them; the mines that pay the interest on your State debt. I tell you the negro is the bone and sinew of your country and you cannot do without him. I do not believe you want to get rid of the negro, else why did you impose a high tax on immigration agents who might come here to get him to leave?

Now, Mr. President we should not talk one thing and mean another. We should not deceive ourselves. Let us make a Constitution that is fair, honest and just. Let us make a Constitution for all the people, one we will be proud of and our children will receive with delight.

Source: *The Columbia State*, October 27, 1895.

The offices of the North Carolina Mutual Life Insurance Company, around 1900. Founded by John Merrick, C. C. Spaulding, and Dr. A. M. Moore (all of whom appear in the picture), this Durham-based insurance company became one of the most successful black enterprises in the country.

A few black people chose to leave the South. In 1879, Benjamin "Pap" Singleton, a Nashville real estate agent, led several thousand black migrants to Kansas. Henry McNeal Turner of Georgia, an African Methodist Episcopal (AME) bishop, promoted migration to Liberia, but only a few hundred made the trip in the late 1870s, Turner not included, and most of them returned disappointed. Most black people who moved in the 1890s stayed within the South, settling in places like Mississippi, Louisiana, and Texas, where they could find work with timber companies or farming new lands that had opened to cotton and rice cultivation.

An urban middle class.   More commonly, black people withdrew to develop their own rich community life within the restricted confines white society permitted them. Particularly in the cities of the South, they could live relatively free of white surveillance and even white contact. In 1890, fully 70 percent of black city dwellers lived in the South; and between 1860 and 1900, the proportion of black people in the cities of the South rose from one in six to more than one in three. The institutions, businesses, and families that black people had begun painstakingly building during Reconstruction continued to grow, and in some cases flourish, after 1877.

By the 1880s, a new black middle class had emerged in the South. Urban-based, professional, business-oriented, and serving a primarily black clientele, its members fashioned an interconnected web of churches, fraternal and self-help organizations, families, and businesses. Black Baptists, AME, and AME Zion churches led reform efforts that sought to eliminate drinking, prostitution, and other vices in black neighborhoods.

African American fraternal and self-help groups, led by middle-class black people, functioned as surrogate welfare organizations for the poor. Some groups, such as the Colored Masons and the Colored Odd Fellows, paralleled white organizations. Black membership rates usually exceeded those in the white community. More than 50 percent of Nashville's black men, for example, belonged to fraternal associations in the city. Fraternal orders also served as the seedbed for such business ventures as the North Carolina Mutual Life Insurance Company, founded in Durham in 1898. Within two decades, North Carolina Mutual became the largest black-owned business in the nation and helped transform Durham into the "capital of the black middle class." Durham's thriving black business district included several black-owned insurance firms, banks, and a textile mill. Most southern cities boasted active black business districts by the 1890s.

preceding chapter, also worked against a federal response to the elimination of black rights in the South.

As the white consensus on race emerged, the status of African Americans slipped in the North as well as the South. Although no northern states threatened to deny black citizens the right to vote, they did increase segregation. The booming industries of the North generally did not hire black workers. Antidiscrimination laws on the books since the Civil War went unenforced. In 1904, 1906, and 1908, race riots erupted in Springfield, Ohio; Greensburg, Indiana; and Springfield, Illinois, matching similar disturbances in Wilmington, North Carolina; and Atlanta, Georgia.

Response of the Black Community

American democracy had, it seemed, hung out a "whites only" sign. How could African Americans respond to the growing political, social, and economic restrictions on their lives? Given white America's hostility, protest proved ineffective, even dangerous. African Americans organized more than a dozen boycotts of streetcar systems in the urban South between 1896 and 1908 in an effort to desegregate them, but not one succeeded. The Afro-American Council, formed in 1890 to protest the deteriorating conditions of black life, accomplished little and disbanded in 1908. W. E. B. Du Bois organized an annual Conference on Negro Problems at Atlanta University beginning in 1896, but it produced no effective plan of action.

The Confederate Battle Flag

Memories of the Civil War and Reconstruction formed a crucial part of southern civic and religious culture from the late nineteenth century onward. White Southerners perceived themselves and the rest of the nation through the lens of the heroic Lost Cause and the alleged abuses of Reconstruction, and the symbols associated with those events took on the status of icons. During the 1890s, the memory industry that white political and religious leaders had promoted since the end of the war became institutionalized. Organizations such as the United Daughters of the Confederacy and the Sons of Confederate Veterans strove to educate a new generation of white southerners on the sacrifices of the war generation, bolstering white supremacy through racial segregation and disfranchisement. The Confederate battle flag emerged from this process as an icon of the Lost Cause and a symbol of white supremacy.

The Confederate battle flag was displayed mostly at veterans' reunions and only rarely on other public occasions until the late 1940s, that is, when civil rights for African Americans reemerged as a national issue. Proponents argued that the battle flag represented heritage, not hate. Opponents denounced it as a symbol of white supremacy. Controversies and referenda over the display and location of battle flags and the design of state flags flared in South Carolina, Georgia, and Mississippi from 1999 through 2004, and an NAACP boycott of South Carolina over the battle flag persists to this day. When people in other parts of the country sometimes remark that white southerners are still fighting the Civil War, it is controversies like the one over the battle flag that they have in mind. But the controversy is less about the past than it is about the way we use history to shape our understanding of the society we live in and our vision of its future. At issue is not just history, but whose history. In this sense the flag controversy can at least generate positive dialogue. Even so, in the interests of reconciliation, it may be time for southerners to follow Robert E. Lee's final order to his men and "Furl the flag, boys."

A "Keep the Flag Change the Governor" political sign is shown in a yard in Louisville, Miss., Oct. 9, 2003. Two years after Mississippi voters decided to keep a Confederate battle emblem on their state banner, the flag has again become an issue in the governor's race. In a television ad, Republican gubernatorial nominee Haley Barbour said Democratic Gov. Ronnie Musgrove "attacked" the state flag when he insisted on giving voters a change to decide the banner's design in 2001. Barbour's campaign office in Yazoo City, Miss., was also distributing "Keep the Flag. Change the Governor" campaign materials.

■ Is the current conflict over the Confederate battle flag a reflection of differing views of history or does it derive from present-day issues?

The South Surrenders by Richard N. Brooke.

PEARSON myhistorylab

From Then to Now Online

17-1 *Savannah Morning News*, April 23, 1863; April 28, 1863; May 4, 1863. As early as 1863, white southerners identified the various versions of the Confederate battle flag as a standard for white supremacy.

17-2 http://usgovinform.about.com/library/news/aa070200a.htm. Excerpts from chat rooms and blogs concerning the removal of the Confederate battle flag from atop the South Carolina state capitol in Columbia in July 2000.

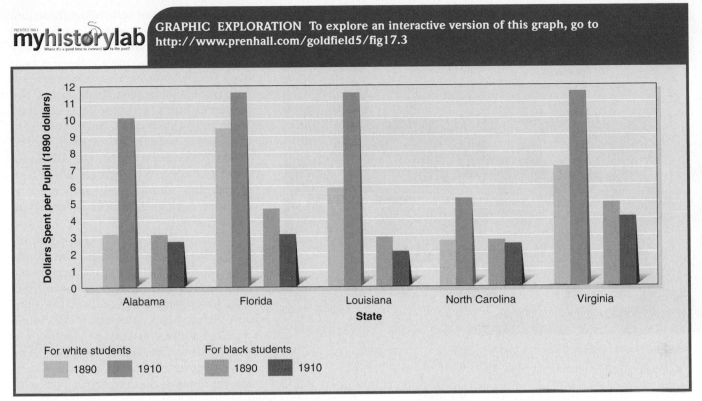

FIGURE 17–3   Disfranchisement and Educational Spending in the South, 1890–1910
By barring black people from the political process, franchise restrictions limited their access to government services. Educational expenditures, which increased for white people but decreased for black people following disfranchisement, provide one measure of the result.

Data Source: Robert A. Margo, "Disfranchisement, School Finance, and the Economics of Segregated Schools in the United States South, 1890–1910," Ph.D. diss., Harvard University, 1982.

The African American middle class worked especially hard to improve black education (see Figure 17–3). Declining black political power encouraged white leaders to reduce funding for black public education. Black students in cities had only makeshift facilities; those in the countryside had almost no facilities. By the early 1900s, the student-teacher ratio in Nashville's segregated school system was 33 to one for white schools but 71 to one for black schools. To improve these conditions, black middle-class leaders solicited educational funds from northern philanthropic organizations.

Black women's roles.   After disfranchisement, middle-class black women assumed an even more pivotal role in the black community. They often used their relations with prominent white women and organizations such as the WCTU and the Young Women's Christian Association (YWCA) to press for public commitments to improve the health and education of African Americans. Absent political pressure from black men, and given the danger of African American males asserting themselves in the tense racial climate after 1890, black women became critical spokespersons for their race.

The extension of black club work into rural areas of the South, where the majority of the African American population lived, to educate families about hygiene, nutrition, and childcare, anticipated similar efforts among white women after 1900. But unlike their white counterparts, these middle-class black women worked with limited resources in a context of simmering racial hostility and political and economic impotence. In response, they nurtured a self-help strategy to improve the conditions of the people they sought to help. One of the most prominent African American leaders of the late nineteenth and early twentieth centuries, Booker T. Washington, adopted a similar approach to racial uplift.

Booker T. Washington's accommodation.   Born a slave in Virginia in 1856, Washington and his family worked in the salt and coal mines of West Virginia after the Civil War. Ambitious and flushed with the postwar enthusiasm for advancement that gripped freedmen, he enrolled in Hampton Normal and Agricultural Institute, the premier black educational institution in the South. Washington worked his way through Hampton, graduated, taught for a time, and

Booker T. Washington at his desk, Tuskegee Institute, 1902.

then, in 1881, founded the Tuskegee Institute for black students in rural Alabama. Washington thought that his students would be best served if they learned a trade and workplace discipline. By learning industrial skills, he maintained, black people could acquire self-respect and economic independence. As a result, Tuskegee emphasized vocational training over the liberal arts.

Washington argued that African Americans should accommodate themselves to segregation and disfranchisement until they could prove their economic worth to American society. In exchange for this accommodation, however, white people should help provide black people with the education and job training they would need to gain their independence. Washington articulated this position, known as the **Atlanta Compromise,** in a speech at the Atlanta Cotton States and International Exposition in 1895. Despite his conciliatory public stance, Washington secretly helped to finance legal challenges to segregation and disfranchisement. The social and economic realities of the South, meanwhile, frustrated his educational mission. Increasingly, black people were shut out of the kinds of jobs for which Washington hoped to train them. Facing a depressed rural economy and growing racial violence, they had little prospect of advancement.

W. E. B. Du Bois attacks the Atlanta Compromise. Another prominent African American leader, W. E. B. Du Bois, challenged Washington's acceptance of black social inequality. Born in Massachusetts in 1868, Du Bois was the first African American to earn a doctorate at Harvard.

Du Bois promoted self-help, education, and black pride. A gifted teacher and writer, he taught at Atlanta University and wrote 18 books on various aspects of black life in America. In *The Souls of Black Folk,* published in 1903, he described the strengths of black culture and attacked Washington's Atlanta Compromise. Du Bois was a cofounder, in 1910, of the **National Association for the Advancement of Colored People (NAACP),** an interracial organization dedicated to restoring African American political and social rights.

Despite their differences, which reflected their divergent backgrounds, Washington and Du Bois agreed on many issues. Both had reservations about allowing illiterate black people to vote, and both believed that black success in the South required some white assistance. As Du Bois wrote in *The Souls of Black Folk,* "Any movement for the elevation of the Southern Negro needs the cooperation, the sympathy, and the support of the best white people in order to succeed." But it became apparent to Du Bois that "the best white people" did not care to elevate black southerners. In 1906, after a bloody race riot in Atlanta, Du Bois left the South, a decision millions of black southerners would make over the next two decades.

A curtain had descended between black and white, in both the North and the South, on the issue of race. Northerners did not care to look behind that curtain to acknowledge the injustice of southern treatment of black people. As long as it provided the raw materials for the North's new urban industrial economy and maintained the peace, the South could count on the rest of the country not to interfere in its solution to race relations. Indeed, to the extent that most white Americans concerned themselves with race, they agreed with the southern solution.

Conclusion

In many respects, the South was more like the rest of the nation in 1900 than at any other time since 1860. Southern cities hummed with activity, and industries from textiles to steel dotted the southern interior. Young men and women migrated to southern cities to pursue opportunities unavailable to their parents. Advances in the production and marketing of cigarettes and soft drinks would soon make southern entrepreneurs and their products household names. Southerners ordered fashions from Sears, Roebuck catalogs and enjoyed electric lights, electric trolleys, and indoor plumbing as much as other urban Americans.

Americans idealized the South—not the urban industrial South, but a mythical South of rural grace and hospitality. National magazines and publishers rushed to print stories about this land of moonlight and magnolias, offering it as a counterpoint to the crowded, immigrant-infested, factory-fouled, money-grubbing North. It was this fantasy South that white people in both the North and the South imagined as they came to a common view on race and reconciled their differences. Northern journalists offered admiring portraits of such southern heroes as Robert E. Lee, of whom one declared in 1906, "the nation has a hero to place beside her greatest." The Republican-dominated Congress agreed to care for the graves of the Confederate dead and ordered the return to the South of captured Confederate flags. White southerners cultivated national reconciliation but remained fiercely dedicated to preserving the peculiarities of their region: a one-party political system, disfranchisement of African Americans, and segregation by law. The region's urban and industrial growth, impressive from the vantage of 1865, paled before that of the North. The South remained a colonial economy characterized more by deep rural poverty than urban prosperity.

How one viewed the New South depended on one's vantage point. White northerners accepted at face value the picture southerners painted for them of a chastened and prosperous, yet still attractive, region. Middle-class white people in the urban South enjoyed the benefits of a national economy and a secure social position. Middle-class white women enjoyed increased influence in the public realm, but not to the extent of their northern sisters. And the institutionalization of white supremacy gave even poor white farmers and factory workers a place in the social hierarchy a rung or two above the bottom.

For black people, the New South proved a crueler ruse than Reconstruction. No one now stepped forward to support their cause and stem the erosion of their economic independence, political freedom, and civil rights. Yet they did not give up the American dream, nor did they give up the South for the most part. They built communities and worked as best they could to challenge restrictions on their freedom.

The New South was thus both American and southern. It shared with the rest of the country a period of rapid urban and industrial growth. But the legacy of war and slavery still lay heavily on the South, manifesting itself in rural poverty, segregation, and black disfranchisement. The burdens of this legacy would limit the attainments of both black and white southerners for another half-century, until Americans finally rejected racial inequality as an affront to their national ideals.

Review Questions

1. In what ways did the growing activism of white middle-class women, the increasing assertiveness of young urban black people, and the persistence of the agricultural depression affect the politics of the South in the late 1880s and early 1890s?

2. We associate segregation and disfranchisement with reactionary political and social views. Yet many white people who promoted both seriously believed them to be reforms. How could white people hold such a view?

3. What strategies did black southerners employ in response to the narrowing of economic and political opportunities in the New South?

4. What accounted for Anna J. Cooper's optimism for African American women in the South at a time when southern whites were beginning an extensive legal and physical assault on black civil rights?

5. Why did racial "problems" emerge as a major issue in Europe and the United States in the late nineteenth century?

Key Terms

Atlanta Compromise (p. 488)

Colored Farmer's Alliance (p. 475)

Disfranchisement (p. 480)

Grandfather clause (p. 482)

Grange (p. 474)

Jim Crow laws (p. 481)

Lynching (p. 479)

National Association for the Advancement of Colored People (NAACP) (p. 488)

Plessy v. Ferguson (p. 481)

Poll taxes (p. 482)

Populist party (p. 475)

Segregation (p. 480)

Settlement house (p. 476)

Solid South (p. 468)

Southern Farmers' Alliance (p. 474)

Subtreasury plan (p. 475)

Women's Christian Temperance Union (WCTU) (p. 476)

Recommended Reading

Gaston, Paul M. *The New South Creed: A Study in Southern Mythmaking* (1970). An important assessment of how New South booster rhetoric matched up against the economic reality; especially good at examining how New South spokesmen turned images of the Old South and other southern traditions to the ends of urban and industrial development.

Rabinowitz, Howard N. *Race Relations in the Urban South, 1865–1890* (1978). A fine survey of how African Americans built communities in the urban South despite the worsening racial situation after Reconstruction.

Williamson, Joel. *The Crucible of Race: Black-White Relations in the American South since Emancipation* (1984). An innovative work that details the racial attitudes of white southerners and reveals how elites in particular used race to further political and social objectives.

Woodward, C. Vann. *Origins of the New South, 1877–1913* (1951). A classic interpretation of the New South era that stresses the discontinuities between Old South and New.

Where to Learn More

- **Levine Museum of the New South, Charlotte, North Carolina.** The museum has exhibits on various New South themes and a permanent exhibit on the history of Charlotte and the Carolina Piedmont. www.museumofthenewsouth.org

- **Atlanta History Center, Atlanta, Georgia.** The major exhibit, "Metropolitan Frontiers, 1835–2000," includes a strong segment on the New South era, including the development of separate black and white economies in At-

lanta. The Herndon home, on the grounds of the center, has an exhibit on black upper-class life in Atlanta from 1880 to 1930. www.atlhist.org/exhibitions/html/metropolitan_frontiers.htm

- **Sloss Furnaces National Historical Landmark, Birmingham, Alabama.** The site recalls the time when Birmingham challenged Pittsburgh as the nation's primary steel-producing center. www.slossfurnaces.com

Study Resources

For study resources for this chapter, go to www.myhistorylab.com and choose *The American Journey*. You will find a wealth of study and review material for this chapter, including pre- and post-tests, customized study plan, key term review flash cards, interactive map and document activities, and documents for analysis.

Photographer Lewis Hine's portrait of a young Jewish woman arriving from Russia at Ellis Island in 1905. Like hundreds of thousands of other immigrants who passed through the portals of New York harbor, this young woman's expression carries the hope, fear, and remembrance that touched her fellow wanderers as they embarked on their new life in America.

Industry, Immigrants and Cities 1870–1900 18

We were homeless, houseless, and friendless in a strange place. We had hardly money enough to last us through the voyage for which we had hoped and waited for three long years. We had suffered much that the re-union we longed for might come about; we had prepared ourselves to suffer more in order to bring it about, and had parted with those we loved, with places that were dear to us in spite of what we passed through in them, never again to see them, as we were convinced, all for the same dear end. With strong hopes and high spirits that hid the sad parting, we had started on our long journey. And now we were checked so unexpectedly but surely.... When my mother had recovered enough to speak, she began to argue with the *gendarme*, telling him our story and begging him to be kind. The children were

frightened and all but I cried. I was only wondering what would happen....Here we had been taken to a lonely place;...our things were taken away, our friends separated from us; a man came to inspect us, as if to ascertain our full value; strange-looking people driving us about like dumb animals, helpless and unresisting; children we could not see crying in a way that suggested terrible things; ourselves driven into a little room where a great kettle was boiling on a little stove; our clothes taken off, our bodies rubbed with a slippery substance that might be any bad thing; a shower of warm water let down on us without warning....We are forced to pick out our clothes from among all the others, with the steam blinding us; we choke, cough, entreat the women to give us time; they persist, "Quick! Quick!, or you'll miss the train!", Oh, so

493

we really won't be murdered! They are only making us ready for the continuing of our journey, cleaning us of all suspicions of dangerous sickness. Thank God! ...

Oh, what solemn thoughts I had! How deeply I felt the greatness, the power of the scene! The immeasurable distance from horizon to horizon;...the absence of any object besides the one ship;...I was conscious only of sea and sky and something I did not understand. And as I listened to its solemn voice, I felt as if I had found a friend, and knew that I loved the ocean.

Mary Antin

Mary Antin, *The Promised Land* (Boston: Houghton Mifflin Co., 1912), chap. VIII.

myhistorylab

Personal Journeys Online

- *Young Chinese immigrant memoir, 1882.* A Chinese immigrant recalls his migration to America and his early days in San Francisco.

- *Letters of Negro Migrants, 1917.* Letters from southern black migrants to the North back home.

Mary Antin, a 13-year-old Jewish girl from Russia, describes her family's perilous journey from persecution in tsarist Russia to the ship that would take her from Hamburg, Germany, to faraway America. In 1894, Mary and her mother and sisters set out from their village to join her father in Boston.

Millions of European immigrants made similar journeys across the Atlantic (as did Chinese and Japanese immigrants, across the Pacific), a trip fraught with danger, unpredictable detours, occasional heartbreak, the sundering of family ties, and the fear of the unknown. So powerful was the promise of American life for the migrants that they willingly risked these obstacles to come to the United States. Mary wrote this extended letter to her uncle, who remained behind, during the first few months after her arrival in Boston. The letter was a way both of conveying the details of her family's exodus and of maintaining contact with a world and a family she had left behind.

Mary recalls the fear and frustration of being removed from the train at the Russian-German border by Russian police because of improper documents. Once her mother had settled the issue with the help of a local Jewish family, they reboarded the train to Berlin. Outside that city, they were once again removed from the train and, although they did not immediately understand what was happening, German authorities had arranged for a thorough cleansing and health inspection, since a cholera epidemic was raging in Russia. As the excerpt ends, you can sense Mary's exultation of joy and freedom as the ship leaves Hamburg for the open ocean and the place that lay beyond the horizon.

For Mary, America did indeed prove to be *The Promised Land,* as she titled her emigration memoir, pub-

KEY TOPICS

- ◆ The technological and organizational innovations behind the emergence of large industrial corporations

- ◆ Changes in the American workforce in the urban-industrial economy and the reaction of organized labor

- ◆ The impact of the new immigration and the start of African American migration to the cities of the North

- ◆ The changing physical and social structure of the industrial city

- ◆ New patterns of residence and recreation in the consumer society

lished in 1912. At the age of 15, she published her first poem in the *Boston Herald* and, after attending Barnard College in New York City, she wrote on immigrant issues, lectured widely, and worked for Theodore Roosevelt's Progressive Party. She fought against immigration-restriction legislation and promoted public education as the main channel of upward mobility for immigrants. Although some have viewed her work as a bit too optimistic and perhaps naive, her own life is a strong testament of how a teenage girl moved from a medieval life in tsarist Russia to a career as a respected writer in the United States.

Mary and her family were part of a major demographic and economic transformation in the United States between 1870 and 1900. Rapid industrial development changed the nature of the workforce and the workplace.

CHRONOLOGY

1869	The Knights of Labor is founded in Philadelphia.
1870	John D. Rockefeller organizes the Standard Oil Company.
	Congress passes the Naturalization Act barring Asians from citizenship.
1871	Unification of Germany in the wake of rising nationalism following the Franco-Prussian War.
1876	The Centennial Exposition opens in Philadelphia.
	Beginning of the rule of dictator Porfirio Diaz in Mexico, whose regime is ended by the Mexican Revolution.
1877	Execution of ten Molly Maguires in Pennsylvania.
	The Great Uprising railroad strike, the first nationwide work stoppage in the United States, provokes violent clashes between workers and federal troops.
1879	Thomas Edison unveils the electric light bulb.
1880	Founding of the League of American Wheelmen helps establish bicycling as one of urban America's favorite recreational activities.
1881	Assassination of Tsar Alexander II begins a series of pogroms that triggers a wave of Russian Jewish immigration to the United States.
1882	Congress passes the Chinese Exclusion Act.
	First country club in the United States founded in Brookline, Massachusetts.
1883	National League merges with the American Association and opens baseball to working-class fans.
1884	Berlin Conference on Africa to set rules for competing European powers annexing African territory.

1886	The Neighborhood Guild, the nation's first settlement house, opens in New York City.
	Riot in Chicago's Haymarket Square breaks the Knights of Labor.
	American Federation of Labor is formed.
1887	Anti-Catholic American Protective Association is formed.
1888	Wanamaker's department store introduces a "bargain room," and competitors follow suit.
1889	Jane Addams opens Hull House, the nation's most celebrated settlement house, in Chicago.
1890	Jacob A. Riis publishes *How the Other Half Lives.*
1891	African American Chicago physician Daniel Hale Williams establishes Provident Hospital, the nation's first interracially staffed hospital.
1892	General Electric opens the first corporate research and development division in the United States.
	Strike at Andrew Carnegie's Homestead steelworks fails.
1894	Pullman Sleeping Car Company strike fails.
	Immigration Restriction League is formed.
1895	American-born Chinese in California form the Native Sons of the Golden State to counter nativism.
1897	George C. Tilyou opens Steeplechase Park on Coney Island in Brooklyn, New York.
	First Zionist Congress meets in Switzerland proclaiming its aim to create a home in Palestine for the Jewish people.
1898	Congress passes the Erdman Act to provide for voluntary mediation of railroad labor disputes.

Large factories staffed by semiskilled laborers displaced the skilled artisans and small shops that had dominated American industry before 1870. Industrial development also accelerated urbanization. Between the Civil War and 1900, the proportion of the nation's population living in cities, swelled by migrants from the countryside and immigrants from Europe and Asia, increased from 20 to 40 percent, a rate of growth twice that of the population as a whole. During the 1880s alone, more than 5 million immigrants came to the United States, twice as many as in any previous decade.

The changes in American life were exhilarating for some, tragic for others. New opportunities opened as old opportunities disappeared. Vast new wealth was created, but poverty increased. New technologies eased life for some but left others untouched. It would be the great dilemma of early-twentieth-century America to reconcile these contradictions and satisfy the American quest for a decent life for all within the new urban industrial order.

Few locations encapsulated this dilemma better than Philadelphia during the Centennial Exposition of 1876, marking the nation's hundredth birthday. More than 8 million people would visit the site over the following six months. There they witnessed the ingenuity of the world's newest industrial power. Thomas Edison explained his new automatic telegraph, and Alexander Graham Bell demonstrated his telephone to the wonder of onlookers. A giant Corliss steam engine loomed over the entrance to Machinery Hall, dwarfing the other exhibits and providing them with power. "Yes," a visitor concluded, "it is in these things of iron and steel that the national genius most freely speaks."

For many Americans, however, the fanfare of the exposition rang hollow. The country was in the midst of a depression that had begun in 1873 and would not bottom out until 1877. Tens of thousands were out of work, and countless others had lost their savings in bank failures and sour investments. With the typical daily wage a dollar, most Philadelphians could not afford the exposition's 50-cent admission price. They celebrated instead at "Centennial City," a ragtag collection of cheap bars, seedy hotels, small restaurants, and circus sideshows hurriedly constructed of wood and tin along a muddy mile-long strip across the street from the exposition's sturdy halls and manicured lawns.

This small area of Philadelphia reflected the promise and failure of late-nineteenth-century America, a period often called the **Gilded Age**. The term is taken from the title of a novel by Mark Twain that satirizes the materialistic excesses of the day. It serves as a shorthand description of the shallow worship of wealth, and the veneer of respectability and prosperity covering deep economic and social divisions, that characterized the period.

New Industry

Between 1870 and 1900, the United States transformed itself from an agricultural nation, a nation of farmers, merchants, and artisans, into the world's foremost industrial power, producing more than one-third of the world's manufactured goods. By the early twentieth century, factory workers made up one-fourth of the workforce, and agricultural workers had dropped from a half to less than a third (see Figure 18–1). A factory with a few dozen employees would have been judged fair-sized in 1870. By the early twentieth century, many industries employed thousands of workers in a single plant. Some industries—petroleum, steel, and meatpacking, for example—had been unknown before the Civil War.

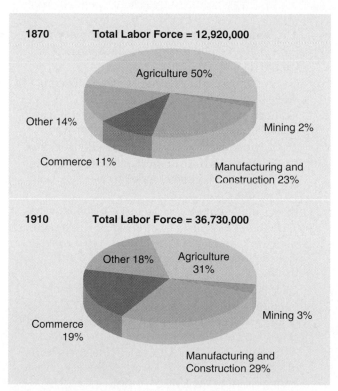

FIGURE 18–1   Changes in the American Labor Force, 1870–1910
The transformation of the American economy in the late nineteenth century changed the nature and type of work. By 1910, the United States was an urban, industrial nation with a matching workforce that toiled in factories and commercial establishments (including railroads) and, less frequently, on farms.

Although the size of the industrial workforce increased dramatically, the number of firms in any given industry shrank. Mergers, changes in corporate management and the organization of the workforce, and a compliant government left a few companies in control of vast segments of the American economy. Workers, reformers, and eventually government challenged this concentration of economic power.

Inventing Technology: The Electric Age

Technology played a major role in transforming factory work and increasing the scale of production. Steam engines, like the giant Corliss engine at the Centennial Exposition and, later, electricity, freed manufacturers from dependence on water power. Factories no longer had to be located by rivers. They could be built anywhere accessible to the transportation system and a concentration of labor. Technology also enabled managers to substitute machines for workers, skewing the balance of power in the workplace toward employers. And it transformed city life, making available a host of new conveniences. By the early twentieth century, electric lights, appliances, ready-made clothing, and store-bought food eased middle-class life. Electric trolleys whisked clerks, salespeople, bureaucrats, and bankers to new urban and suburban subdivisions. Electric streetlights lit up city streets at night. Amusement parks drew crowds with mechanical attractions scarcely imaginable a generation earlier. Movies entertained the masses. As the historian and novelist Henry Adams put it at the turn of the century, "In the essentials of life…the boy of 1854 stood nearer [to] the year one than to the year 1900."

For much of the nineteenth century, the United States was dependent on the industrial nations of Europe for technological innovation. American engineers often went to England and Germany for education and training, and the textile industry, railroads, and the early steel industry benefited from German and English inventions. In the late nineteenth century, the United States changed from a technology borrower to a technology innovator. By 1910, a million patents had been issued in the United States, 900,000 of them after 1870.

Nothing represented this shift better than Thomas A. Edison's development of a practical electric light bulb and electric generating system. Edison's invention transformed electricity into a new and versatile form of industrial energy. It also reflected a change in the relationship between science and technology. Until the late nineteenth century, advances in scientific theory usually followed technological innovation, rather than the other way around. Techniques for making steel, for example, developed before scientific theories emerged to explain how they worked. Textile machinery and railroad technology developed similarly. In contrast, a theoretical understanding of electricity preceded its practical use as a source of energy. Scientists had been experimenting with electricity for half a century before Edison unveiled his light bulb in 1879. Edison's research laboratory at Menlo Park,

New Jersey, also established a model for corporate-sponsored research and development that would rapidly increase the pace of technological innovation.

Scientists had already discovered that passing an electric current through a filament in a vacuum produced light. They had not yet found a filament, however, that could last for more than a few minutes. Edison tried a variety of materials, from grass to hair from a colleague's beard, before succeeding with charred thread. In 1879, he produced a bulb that burned for an astounding 45 hours. Then he devised a circuit that provided an even flow of current through the filament. After thrilling a crowd with the spectacle of 500 lights ablaze on New Year's Eve in 1879, Edison went on to build a power station in New York City to serve businesses and homes by 1882. The electric age had begun.

Edison's initial success touched off a wave of research and development in Germany, Austria, Great Britain, France, and the United States. Whoever could light the world cheaply and efficiently held the key to an enormous fortune. Ultimately, the prize fell not to Edison but to Elihu Thomson, a high school chemistry teacher in Philadelphia. Leaving teaching to devote himself to research full-time, Thomson founded his own company and in 1883 moved to Connecticut, where he experimented with transformers and electric trolley equipment. Thomson purchased Edison's General Electric Company in 1892 and established the country's first corporate research and development division. His scientists produced what was then the most efficient light bulb design, and by 1914, General Electric was producing 85 percent of the world's light bulbs.

Following this precedent, other American companies established research and development laboratories. Standard Oil, U.S. Rubber, the chemical giant Du Pont, and the photographic company Kodak all became world leaders in their respective industries because of innovations their laboratories developed.

The process of invention that emerged in the United States gave the country a commanding technological lead. But the modernization of industry that made the United States the world's foremost industrial nation after 1900 reflected organizational as well as technological innovation. As industries sought efficient ways to apply technology and expand their markets within and beyond national borders, their workforces expanded, and their need for capital mounted. Coping with these changes required significant changes in corporate management.

The Corporation and Its Impact

The modern corporation provided the structural framework for the transformation of the American economy. A corporation is an association of individuals that is legally authorized to act as a fictional "person" and thus relieves its individual members of certain legal liabilities. This form of business organization had existed since colonial times but became a

Electricity conquered space and the night. The yellow glow of incandescent bulbs, the whiz of trolleys, and the rumble of elevated railways energize the Bowery, an emerging entertainment district in lower Manhattan at the end of the nineteenth century.

W. Louis Sonntag, Jr., *The Bowery at Night*, watercolor, 1895. Copyright Museum of the City of New York. 32.275.2

significant factor in the American economy with the growth of railroad companies in the 1850s. A key feature of a corporation is the separation of ownership from management. A corporation can raise capital by selling ownership shares, or stock, to people who have no direct role in running it. The shareholders benefit from dividends drawn on profits and, if the corporation thrives, from the rising value of its stock.

The corporation had two major advantages over other forms of business organization that made it attractive to investors. First, unlike a partnership, which dissolves when a partner dies, a corporation can outlive its founders. This durability permits long-term planning. Second, a corporation's officials and shareholders are not personally liable for its debts. If it goes bankrupt, they stand to lose only what they have invested in it.

As large corporations emerged in major American industries, they had a ripple effect on the economy. To build plants, merge with or acquire other companies, develop new technology, and hire workers, large corporations needed huge supplies of capital. They turned to the banks to help meet these needs, and the banks grew in response. The corporations stimulated technological change as they looked for ways to speed production, improve products, and lower costs. As they grew, they generated jobs.

Large industrial corporations also changed the nature of work. Into the late nineteenth century, well-paid skilled artisans, typically native-born, dominated the industrial workplace. Operating alone or in groups, they controlled the pace of their work, their output, and even the hiring and firing of coworkers. By the early twentieth century, control of the workplace was shifting to managers, and semiskilled and unskilled workers were replacing skilled artisans. These new workers, often foreign-born, performed repetitive tasks for low wages.

Because corporations usually located factories in cities, they stimulated urban growth. Large industrial districts sprawled along urban rivers and rail lines. There were exceptions. Southern textile manufacturers tended to locate plants in villages and small towns and on the outskirts of larger cities. A few northern entrepreneurs also constructed industrial communities outside major cities to save on land costs and ensure control over labor. George Pullman, for example, built his railway car manufacturing plant outside Chicago in 1880. Nonetheless, by 1900, fully 90 percent of all manufacturing occurred in cities.

Two organizational strategies, vertical integration and horizontal integration, helped successful corporations reduce competition and dominate their industries. **Vertical integration** involved the consolidation of all functions related to a particular industry, from the extraction and transport of raw materials to manufacturing and finished-product distribution and sales. Vertical integration reduced a company's dependence on outside suppliers, cutting costs and delays. Geographical dispersal went hand in hand with vertical integration. Different functions, a factory and its source of raw materials, for example, were likely to be in different places, a development made possible by such advances in communication as the telephone. The multiplication of functions also prompted the growth of corporate bureaucracy.

The meatpacking industry provides a good example of vertical integration. Meat is perishable and cannot be transported long distances without refrigeration. To reach eastern markets, cattlemen had to ship live animals in cattle cars from western ranges to major rail centers like Chicago. Since only 40 percent of a steer is edible, shippers were paying freight charges for a lot of commercially useless weight. In addition, some animals died in transit, and many lost weight.

Gustavus Swift, a Boston native who moved to Chicago in 1875, realized that refrigerated railway cars would make it possible to ship butchered meat, eliminating the need to transport live cattle. He invented a refrigerated car but could not sell it to the major railroads because they feared losing their substantial investment in cattle cars and pens. Swift had the cars built himself and convinced a Canadian railroad with only a small stake in cattle shipping to haul them to eastern markets. He established packinghouses in Omaha and Kansas City near the largest cattle markets, built refrigerated warehouses at key distribution points, and hired a sales force to convince eastern butchers of the quality of his product. He now controlled the production, transportation, and distribution of his product, the essence of vertical integration. By 1881, he was shipping $200,000 worth of beef a week. Competitors soon followed his example.

Horizontal integration involved the merger of competitors in the same industry. John D. Rockefeller's Standard Oil Company pioneered horizontal integration in the 1880s. He began investing in Cleveland oil refineries by his mid-twenties and formed Standard Oil in 1870. Using a variety of tactics, including threats, deceit, and price wars, Rockefeller rapidly acquired most of his competitors. Supported by investment bankers like J. P. Morgan, Standard Oil controlled

A family takes a spin in their Model T Ford with the boys up front. The Ford Motor Company built affordable machines for the expanding middle-class, changing patterns of recreation and expanding work commutes and tourism.

90 percent of the nation's oil refining by 1890. Acquiring oil fields and pipelines as well as refineries, it achieved both vertical and horizontal integration. Rockefeller's dominant position allowed him to impose order and predictability on the industry, ensuring a continuous flow of profits. He closed inefficient refineries, opened new ones, and kept his operations up to date with the latest technologies.

The invention of the internal combustion engine and the growth of automobile and truck manufacturing after 1900 suddenly made an inconsequential by-product of the refining process, gasoline, an indispensable fuel. By that time, the refining and production of oil had spread to Texas and Oklahoma, with the discovery of oil at Spindletop Hill, near Beaumont, Texas. The Texas oil fields dwarfed the Pennsylvania basin and soon surpassed their eastern rivals in output, spawning towns from the Gulf Coast to the Permian Basin in West Texas, and new companies such as the Texas Oil Company (Texaco) and Gulf Oil, breaking Rockefeller's near-monopoly. The petroleum industry represented one of the earliest shifts of industrial wealth from the Northeast and Midwest to the South and Southwest.

Other entrepreneurs achieved similar dominance in other industries and amassed similarly enormous fortunes. James B. Duke, who automated cigarette manufacturing, gained control of most of the tobacco industry. Andrew Carnegie consolidated much of America's steel industry within his Carnegie Steel Company (later U.S. Steel). By 1900, Carnegie's company was producing one-quarter of the country's steel.

The concentration of industry in the hands of a few powerful corporate monopolies or **trusts**, as they came to be known, alarmed many Americans. Giant corporations set prices, influenced politicians, and threatened to restrict opportunities for small entrepreneurs like the shopkeepers, farmers, and artisans who abounded at mid-century. In the words of one historian, the corporations "seemed to signal the end of an open, promising America and the beginning of a closed, unhappier society." Impersonal and governed by profit, the modern corporation challenged the ideal of the self-made man and the belief that success and advancement would reward hard work. These concerns eventually prompted the federal and state governments to respond with antitrust and other regulatory laws (see Chapters 20 and 21).

Tabloid newspapers reinforced distrust of the corporations with exposés of the sharp business practices of corporate barons such as Rockefeller and Carnegie and accounts of the sumptuous lifestyles of the corporate elite. Public concern notwithstanding, however, the giant corporations helped increase the efficiency of the American economy, raise the national standard of living, and transform the United States into a major world power. Corporate expansion generated jobs that attracted rural migrants and immigrants by the millions from Europe and Asia to American cities.

The Changing Nature of Work

From the perspective of the workers, immigrant and native-born alike, the growth of giant corporations was a mixed blessing. The corporations provided abundant jobs, but they firmly controlled working conditions. A Pennsylvania coal miner spoke for many of his fellows in the 1890s when he remarked, "The working people of this country...find monopolies as strong as government itself. They find capital as rigid as absolute monarchy. They find their so-called independence a myth."

As late as the 1880s, shops of skilled artisans were responsible for most manufacturing in the United States. Since the mid-century, however, industrialists had been introducing ways to simplify manufacturing processes so that they could hire low-skilled workers. This deskilling process accelerated in the 1890s in response to new technologies, new workers, and workplace reorganization. By 1906, according to a U.S. Department of Labor report, industrial labor had been reduced to minute, low-skilled operations, making skilled artisans obsolete.

Mechanization and technological innovation did not reduce employment, although they did eliminate some jobs, most of them skilled. On the contrary, the birth of whole new industries—steel, automobiles, electrical equipment, cigarettes, food canning, and machine tools—created a huge demand for workers. Innovations in existing industries, like railroads, similarly spurred job growth. The number of people working for U.S. railroads increased from 80,000 to more than 1 million between 1860 and 1910.

Ironically, it was a shortage of skilled workers as much as other factors that encouraged industrialists to mechanize. Unskilled workers cost less than the scarce artisans. And with massive waves of immigrants arriving from Europe and Asia between 1880 and 1920 (joined after 1910 by migrants from the American South), the supply of unskilled workers seemed limitless.

Low salaries and long hours.   The new workers shared little of the wealth generated by industrial expansion and enjoyed few of the gadgets and products generated by the new manufacturing. The East European immigrants who comprised three-quarters of U.S. Steel's workforce during the first decade of the twentieth century received less than $12.50 a week, significantly less than the $15.00 a week a federal government survey in 1910 calculated that an urban family needed to subsist.

Nor did large corporations put profits into improved working conditions. In 1881, on-the-job accidents maimed or killed 30,000 railroad workers. Safety equipment existed that could have prevented many of these injuries, but the railroads refused to purchase it. At a U.S. Steel plant in Pittsburgh, injuries or death claimed one out of every four workers between 1907 and 1910. In Chicago's meat plants, injuries were commonplace. Workers grew careless from fatigue and long-term exposure to the extreme temperatures of the workplace. Meat cutters working rapidly with sharp knives often sliced fingers off their numb hands. Upton Sinclair wrote in his novel *The Jungle* (1906), a chronicle of the killing floors of meatpacking plants in Chicago, "It was to be counted as a wonder that there were not more men slaughtered than cattle."

Factory workers typically worked 10 hours a day, six days a week in the 1880s. Steel workers put in 12 hours a day. The mills operated around the clock, so once every two weeks, when the workers changed shifts, one group had to take a "long turn" and stay on the job for 24 hours.

Long hours affected family life. By Sunday, most factory workers were too tired to do more than sit around home. During the week, they had time only to eat and sleep. As one machinist testified before a U.S. Senate investigative committee in 1883: "They were pretty well played out when they come home, and the first thing they think of is having something to eat and sitting down, and resting, and then of striking a bed. Of course when a man is dragged out in that way he is naturally cranky, and he makes all around him cranky...and staring starvation in the face makes him feel sad, and the head of the house being sad, of course the whole family are the same, so the house looks like a dull prison."

Workers lived as close to the factory as possible, to reduce the time and expense of getting to work. The environment around many factories, however, was almost as unwholesome as the conditions inside. A visitor to Pittsburgh in 1884 noticed "a drab twilight" hanging over the areas around the steel mills, where "gas-lights, which are left burning at mid-day, shine out of the murkiness with a dull, reddish glare." Industrial wastes fouled streams and rivers around many plants. The factories along the Cuyahoga River in Cleveland turned that waterway into an open sewer by the turn of the century.

Big factories were not characteristic of all industries after 1900. In some, like the "needle," or garment, trade, operations remained small scale. But salaries and working conditions in these industries were, if anything, worse than in the big factories. The garment industry was dominated by small manufacturers who assembled clothing for retailers from cloth provided by textile manufacturers. The manufacturers squeezed workers into small, cramped, poorly ventilated **sweatshops.** These might be in attics or lofts or even in the workers' own dwellings. Workers pieced together garments on the manufacturer's sewing machines. A government investigator in Chicago in the 1890s described one sweatshop in a three-room tenement where the workers, a family of eight, both lived and worked: "The father, mother, two daughters, and a cousin work together making trousers at seventy-five cents a dozen pairs.... They work seven days a week.... Their destitution is very great."

Child Labor

Child labor was common in the garment trade and other industries. Shocked reformers in the 1890s told of the devastating effect of factory labor on children's lives, citing cases like that of a 7-year-old girl whose legs were paralyzed and deformed because she toiled "day after day with little legs crossed, pulling out bastings from garments."

Industries that employed many children were often dangerous, even for adults. In the gritty coal mines of Pennsylvania, breaker boys, youths who stood on ladders to pluck waste matter from coal tumbling down long chutes, breathed harmful coal dust all day. Girls under 16 made up half the workforce in the silk mills of Scranton and Wilkes-Barre, Pennsylvania. Girls with missing fingers from mill accidents were a common sight in those towns.

By 1900, Pennsylvania and a few other states had passed legislation regulating child labor, but enforcement of these laws was lax. Parents desperate for income often lied about their children's age, and government officials were often sympathetic toward mill or mine owners, who paid taxes and provided other civic benefits.

Working Women

Women accompanied children into the workforce outside the home in increasing numbers after 1870. The comparatively low wages of unskilled male workers often required women family members to work as well. The head of the Massachusetts Bureau of Labor Statistics observed in 1882, "A family of workers can always live well, but the man with a family of small children to support, unless his wife works also, has a small chance of living properly." Between 1870 and 1920, the number of women and children in the workforce more than doubled.

Like child labor, the growing numbers of women in the workforce alarmed middle-class reformers. They worried about the impact on family life and on the women themselves. Streets in working-class districts teemed with unsupervised children. Working-class men were also concerned. The trend toward deskilling favored women. Employers, claiming that women worked only for supplemental money, paid them less than men. A U.S. Department of Labor commissioner asserted that women worked only for "dress or pleasure." In one St. Louis factory in 1896, women received $4 a week for work for which men were paid $16 a week. Women chafed under this wage system but had no recourse other than to quit. An Iowa shoe saleswoman complained in 1886, "I don't get the salary the men clerks do, although this day I am 600 sales ahead! Call this justice? But I have to grin and bear it, because I am so unfortunate as to be a woman."

Most women worked out of economic necessity. In 1900, fully 85 percent of wage-earning women were unmarried and under the age of 25. They supported siblings and contributed to their parents' income. A typical female factory worker earned $6 a week in 1900. On this wage, a married woman might help pull her family up to subsistence level. For a single woman on her own, however, it allowed little more, in the writer O. Henry's words, "than marshmallows and tea." Her lodging rarely consisted of more than one room.

Noted urban and labor photographer Lewis Hine's crusade against child labor included this photo of breaker boys at a Pennsylvania coal mine, 1910. The boys worked in a constant cloud of coal dust picking out refuse from coal coming down chutes. Note the overseer with a stick at right.

Yet, even with their limited wages, working women found ways to enjoy their leisure time. They went to dances, visited amusement parks such as Brooklyn's Coney Island (formerly a mostly male preserve), and crowded into theaters. They met young men at these venues under relatively safe conditions because proprietors ensured order to attract and keep female customers, who would, in turn, draw the young men. Although these cheap amusements sometimes scandalized middle-class reformers, working women viewed them as both an escape from the restrictions of work and a declaration of independence from their families.

Over time, more work options opened to women, but low wages and poor working conditions persisted. Women entered the needle trades after widespread introduction of the sewing machine in the 1870s. Factories gradually replaced sweatshops in the garment industry after 1900, but working conditions improved little.

On the factory floor, young women had less room for negotiation because the customer was far removed from the manufacturing process, but they banded together, sometimes in labor unions after 1900, to demand and receive concessions from management. Working women, no less than working men, refused to be inanimate recipients of bosses' decrees and working conditions. The factory, though less so than the department store, was a space for negotiation between worker and management. And if a young woman could obtain some basic skills, other opportunities loomed as well.

The introduction of the typewriter transformed office work, dominated by men until the 1870s, into a female preserve. Women were alleged to have the dexterity and tolerance for repetition that the new technology required. But they earned only half the salary of the men they replaced. Middle-class parents saw office work as clean and honorable compared with factory or sales work. Consequently, clerical positions drew growing numbers of native-born women into the urban workforce after 1890. A top-paid office worker in the 1890s earned as much as $900 a year. Teaching, another acceptable occupation for middle-class women, typically paid only $500 a year.

By the turn of the century, women were gaining increased access to higher education. Coeducational colleges were rare, but by 1900 there were many women-only institutions. By 1910, women comprised 40 percent of all American college students, compared to 20 percent in 1870. Despite these gains, many professions, including those of physician and attorney, remained closed to women. Men still accounted for more than 95 percent of all doctors in 1900. Women also were rarely permitted to pursue doctoral degrees.

Most women college graduates found employment in such "nurturing" professions as nursing, teaching, and library work. Between 1900 and 1910, the number of trained women nurses increased sevenfold. In response to the growing problems of urban society, a relatively new occupation, social work, opened to women. There were 1,000 women social workers in 1890 and nearly 30,000 by 1920. Reflecting new theories on the nurturing role of women, school boards after 1900 turned exclusively to female teachers for the elementary grades. Despite these gains, women's work remained segregated. More than 90 percent of all wage-earning women in 1900 worked at occupations in which women comprised the great majority of workers. Some reforms meant to improve working conditions for women reinforced this state of affairs. Protective legislation restricted women to "clean" occupations and limited their ability to compete with men in other jobs. As an economist explained in 1901, "The wage bargaining power of men is weakened by the competition of women and children, hence a law restricting the hours of women and children may also be looked upon as a law to protect men in their bargaining power."

Women also confronted negative stereotypes. Most Americans in 1900 believed a woman's proper role was to care for home and family. The single working woman faced doubts about her virtue. The system of "treating" on dates reinforced stories about loose salesgirls, flirtatious secretaries, and easy factory workers. Newspapers and magazines published exposés of working girls descending into prostitution. These images encouraged sexual harassment at work, which was rarely punished.

Working women faced a difficult dilemma. To justify their desire for education and training, they had to argue that these would enhance their roles as wives and mothers. To gain improved wages and working conditions, they increasingly supported protective legislation that restricted their opportunities in the workplace.

Responses to Poverty and Wealth

Concerns about working women merged with larger anxieties about the growing numbers of impoverished workers in the nation's cities during the 1890s and the widening gap between rich and poor. While industrial magnates flaunted their fabulous wealth, working men and women led hard lives on meager salaries and in crowded dwellings. In his exposé of poverty in New York, *How the Other Half Lives* (1890), the Danish-born urban reformer Jacob Riis wrote that "the half that is on top cares little for the struggles, and less for the fate of those who are underneath so long as it is able to hold them there and keep its own seat."

The urban poor included workers as well as the unemployed, aged, widowed, and disabled. The industrial economy strained working-class family life. Workplace accidents and deaths left many families with only one parent. Infant mortality among the working poor was nearly twice the citywide norm in 1900. Epidemic diseases, especially typhoid, an illness spread by impure water, devastated crowded working-class districts. Poverty compounded itself in various ways. For example, the poor paid twice as much for coal to heat their homes as better-off people, because they could afford to buy it only in small quantities.

Inadequate housing was the most visible badge of poverty. Crammed into four- to six-story buildings on tiny

The new industrial age created great wealth and abject poverty, and the city became the stage upon which these hard economic lessons played out. Here a "modest" Fifth Avenue mansion in turn-of-the-century New York City; farther downtown, Jacob Riis found this tenement courtyard.

Getty Images Inc., Hulton Archive Photos. Photograph by Jacob A. Riis, 22 Baxter Street Court. The Jacob A. Riis Collection, Museum of the City of New York

lots, **tenement** apartments in urban slums were notorious for their lack of ventilation and light. According to Jacob Riis, a typical apartment in New York's Mulberry Bend neighborhood consisted of a parlor, a combined living room and kitchen, and "two pitch-dark coops called bedrooms." The furniture included three beds, "if the old boxes and heaps of foul straw can be called by that name," which gave off an appalling smell. In 90-degree July heat, temperatures inside soared to 115 degrees.

Authorities did nothing to enforce laws prohibiting overcrowding for fear of leaving people homeless. The population density of New York's tenement district in 1894 was 986.4 people per acre, the highest in the world at the time. (Today, the densest areas of American cities rarely exceed 400 people per acre, and only Calcutta, India, and Lagos, Nigeria, approach the crowding of turn-of-the-century New York; today Manhattan has 84 residents per acre.)

One early attempt to deal with these conditions was the settlement house. The settlement house movement, which originated in England, sought to moderate the effects of poverty through neighborhood reconstruction. New York's

Neighborhood Guild, established in 1886, was the first settlement house in the country; Chicago's **Hull House,** founded in 1889 by Jane Addams, a young Rockford (Illinois) College graduate, became the most famous. Addams had visited settlement houses in England and thought the idea would work well in American cities.

The Gospel of Wealth. Late-nineteenth-century political ideology discouraged more comprehensive efforts to remedy urban poverty until the Progressive Era (discussed in Chapter 21). According to the **Gospel of Wealth,** a theory popular among industrialists, intellectuals, and some politicians, any intervention on behalf of the poor was of doubtful benefit. Hard work and perseverance, in this view, led to wealth. Poverty, by implication, resulted from the flawed character of the poor. Steel tycoon Andrew Carnegie sought to soften this doctrine by stressing the responsibility of the affluent to set an example for the working class and to return some of their wealth to the communities in which they lived. Carnegie, accordingly, endowed libraries, cultural institutions, and schools throughout the country. Beneficial as

Workers Organize

Organization	History	Strategies
Knights of Labor	Founded in 1869; open to all workers; declined after 1886	Disapproved of strikes; supported an array of labor reforms, including cooperatives; favored broad political involvement
American Federation of Labor	Founded in 1886; open only to craft workers and organized by craft; hostile to blacks and women; became the major U.S. labor organization after 1880s	Opposed political involvement; supported a limited number of labor reforms; approved of strikes

they might be, however, these philanthropic efforts scarcely addressed the causes of poverty, and few industrialists followed Carnegie's example.

A flawed attempt to apply Charles Darwin's theory of biological evolution to human society emerged as a more common justification than the Gospel of Wealth for the growing gap between rich and poor. According to the theory of **Social Darwinism,** the human race evolves only through competition. The fit survive, the weak perish, and humanity moves forward. Wealth reflects fitness; poverty, weakness. For governments or private agencies to interfere with this natural process is futile. Thus, Columbia University president Nicholas Murray Butler, claiming that "nature's cure for most social and political diseases is better than man's," warned against charity for the poor in 1900. Standard Oil's John D. Rockefeller concurred, asserting that the survival of the fittest—Darwin never used that phrase—is "the working out of a law of nature and a law of God."

The era's popular literature contributed to the notion that the individual, armed with his wits and a determination to work hard, was responsible for his own fate. The press circulated stories of self-made men. Luxuries, such as suburban residences, carriages, and household appliances, came within the grasp of the growing urban middle class. Moving up the economic ladder, even dramatic improvement in one's status, seemed not only possible but probable. Few cultural icons contributed to these sentiments more than the **Horatio Alger stories.**

Alger captured the country's imagination beginning in the late 1860s with a series of best-selling stories about rags-to-riches heroes. He was an unlikely hero himself. Born in Massachusetts in 1832 in a comfortable family, he overcame a stuttering defect to climb the academic ladder and enter Harvard's Divinity School, where he graduated as a Unitarian minister in 1860. In 1866, allegations that he had molested two children forced him to resign from the ministry and move to New York City, where he began his writing career.

In New York, Alger saw an opportunity to atone for his sins and save the children of the city. The result was his first rags-to-riches novel, *Ragged Dick,* published in 1867. Dick shines shoes for his meager living and sleeps on the streets. One day he overhears a conversation between a wealthy businessman and his newly arrived nephew. Dick volunteers to show the young lad about the city. His contact with the nephew opens Dick to another life and to a desire to succeed, which he does after improving his personal habits and having another chance encounter with a wealthy businessman.

Ragged Dick and Alger's subsequent novels stressed the importance of order: neat clothes, cleanliness, thrift, and hard work. But the books also highlighted the importance of chance and the responsibility of those better off to serve as positive role models. The city may be a place of fantastic wealth and abysmal poverty, but the two worlds can and should be mutually supportive and smooth out the rough spots of capitalism. But many workers could not afford to wait for a chance encounter to lift themselves out of poverty.

Workers Organize

The growing power of industrial corporations and the declining power of workers generated social tensions reminiscent of the sectional crisis that triggered the Civil War. Wild swings in the business cycle, the fluctuation between periods of growth and contraction in the economy, aggravated these tensions. Two prolonged depressions, one beginning in 1873 and the other in 1893, threw as many as 2 million laborers out of work. Skilled workers, their security undermined by deskilling, were hit particularly hard. Their hopes of becoming managers or starting their own businesses disappearing, they saw the nation "drifting," as a carpenter put it in 1870, "to that condition of society where a few were rich, and the many very poor."

Beginning after the Civil War and continuing through World War I, workers fought their loss of independence to industrial capital by organizing and striking (see the Overview table, Workers Organize). Violence often accompanied these actions. Some of the earliest confrontations occurred in the Pennsylvania anthracite coal region, where the mostly Irish miners gathered in a secret labor organization, the **Molly Maguires,** named after a woman who led a massive protest against landlords in Ireland in the 1840s. The Molly Maguires carried out selective murders of coal company officials until 1877, when an infiltrator exposed the group and its activities. Twenty members were found guilty of murder and executed. The trials themselves generated controversy because Irish Catholics were excluded from the juries.

More widespread and violent was the railroad strike of 1877, sometimes referred to as the **Great Uprising.** The four largest railroads, in the midst of a depression and in the wake of a series of pay cuts over the preceding four years, agreed to slash wages yet again. When Baltimore & Ohio Railroad workers struck in July to protest the cut, President Rutherford B. Hayes dispatched federal troops to protect the line's property. The use of federal troops infuriated railroad workers throughout the East and Midwest, and they stopped work. Violence erupted in Pittsburgh when the state militia opened fire on strikers and their families, killing 25, including a woman and three children. As news of the violence spread, so did the strike, as far as Galveston, Texas, and San Francisco. Over the next two weeks, police and federal troops continued to clash with strikers. By the time this first nationwide work stoppage in American history ended, more than 100 had been killed. The wage cuts remained.

Despite its ultimate failure, the Great Uprising was notable for the way workers cooperated with one another across ethnic and, in some cases, racial lines. The experience proved important in the next major upheaval, nine years later.

The **Knights of Labor,** a union of craft workers founded in Philadelphia in 1869, grew dramatically after the Great Uprising under the leadership of Terence V. Powderly. Reflecting the views of many skilled workers, the Knights saw "an inevitable…conflict between the wage system of labor and [the] republican system of government." Remarkably inclusive for its time, the Knights welcomed black workers and women to its ranks. Victories in several small railroad strikes in 1884 and 1885 boosted its membership to nearly 1 million workers by 1886.

In that year, the Knights led a movement for an eight-hour workday. Ignoring the advice of the national leadership to avoid strikes, local chapters staged more than 1,500 strikes involving more than 340,000 workers. Employers fought back. They persuaded the courts to order strikers back to work and used local authorities to arrest strikers for trespassing or obstructing traffic. In early May 1886, police killed four unarmed workers during a skirmish with strikers in Chicago. Rioting broke out when a bomb exploded at a meeting in Haymarket Square to protest the slayings. The bomb killed seven policemen and four strikers and left 100 people

wounded. Eight strike leaders were tried for the deaths, and despite the lack of evidence linking them to the bomb, four were executed.

The Haymarket Square incident, and a series of disastrous walkouts that followed it, weakened the Knights of Labor. By 1890, it had fewer than 100,000 members. Thereafter, the **American Federation of Labor** (AFL), found in 1886, became the major organizing body for skilled workers.

The AFL was much less ambitious, and less inclusive, than the Knights of Labor. Led by a British immigrant, Samuel Gompers, it emphasized **collective bargaining,** negotiations between management and union representatives, to secure workplace concessions. The AFL also discouraged political activism. With this business unionism, the AFL proved more effective than the Knights of Labor at meeting the needs of skilled workers, but it left out the growing numbers of unskilled workers, black workers, and women workers, to whom the Knights had given a glimmer of hope.

Rather than including all workers in one large union, the AFL organized skilled workers by craft. It then focused on a few basic workplace issues important to each craft. The result was greater cohesion and discipline. In 1889 and 1890, more than 60 percent of AFL-sponsored strikes were successful, a remarkable record in an era when most strikes failed. Responding to this success, employers determined to break the power of craft unions just as they had destroyed the Knights. In 1892, Andrew Carnegie dealt the steelworkers' union a major setback in the Homestead strike. Carnegie's manager, Henry Clay Frick, announced to workers at

During the Great Uprising of 1877, federal troops clashed with striking workers. Here the Maryland militia fires at strikers in Baltimore, killing 12. As Reconstruction ended, government attention shifted from the South to quelling labor unrest.

Carnegie's Homestead plant in Pennsylvania that he would negotiate only with workers individually and not renew the union's collective bargaining contract. Expecting a strike, Frick locked the union workers out of the plant and hired 300 armed guards to protect the nonunion ("scab") workers he planned to hire in their place. Union workers, with the help of their families and unskilled workers, seized control of Homestead's roads and utilities. In a bloody confrontation, they drove back Frick's forces. Nine strikers and seven guards died. But Pennsylvania's governor called out the state militia to open the plant and protect the nonunion workers. After four months, the union capitulated. With this defeat, skilled steelworkers lost their power on the shop floor. Eventually, mechanization cost them their jobs.

In 1894, workers suffered another setback in the Pullman strike, against George Pullman's Palace Sleeping Car Company. The strike began when the company cut wages for workers at its plant in the "model" suburb it had built outside Chicago, without a corresponding cut in the rent it charged workers for their company-owned housing. When Pullman rejected their demands, the workers appealed for support to the American Railway Union (ARU), led by Eugene V. Debs. The membership of the ARU, an independent union not affiliated with the AFL, had swelled to more than 150,000 workers after it won a strike earlier in 1894 against the Great Northern Railroad. On behalf of the Pullman strikers, Debs ordered a boycott of any trains with Pullman cars, disrupting train travel in several parts of the country. The railroads claimed to be innocent victims of a local dispute, and with growing public support, they fired workers who refused to handle trains with Pullman cars. Debs called for all ARU members to walk off the job, crippling rail travel nationwide. When Debs refused to honor a federal court injunction against the strike, President Cleveland, at the railroads' request, ordered federal troops to enforce it. Debs was arrested, and the strike and the union were broken.

These setbacks, and the depression that began in 1893, left workers and their unions facing an uncertain future. But growing public opposition to the use of troops, the high-handed tactics of industrialists, and the rising concerns of Americans about the power of big business sustained the unions. Workers would call more than 22,000 strikes over the next decade, the majority of them union-sponsored. Still, no more than 7 percent of the American workforce was organized by 1900. By that time, a dramatic change in the industrial workforce was afoot. As the large factories installed labor- and time-saving machinery, unskilled foreign-born labor flooded onto the shop floor. For many reasons, not least of which were the adjustments required for life in a new country, labor radicalism was not a high priority for many of the newcomers. Immigrants transformed not only the workplace, but also the cities where they settled and the nation many eventually adopted. In the process, they changed themselves.

New Immigrants

The late nineteenth century was a period of unprecedented worldwide population movements. The United States was not the only New World destination for the migrants of this period. Many also found their way to Brazil, Argentina, and Canada. The scale of overseas migration to the United States after 1870, however, dwarfed all that preceded it. Between 1870 and 1910, the country received more than 20 million immigrants. Before the Civil War, most immigrants came from northern Europe. Most of the new immigrants, by contrast, came from southern and eastern Europe. Swelling their ranks were migrants from Mexico and Asia, as well as internal migrants moving from the countryside to American cities (see Map 18–1 and Figure 18–2).

Old World Backgrounds

The people of southern and eastern Europe had long been accustomed to migrating within Europe on a seasonal basis to find work to support their families. In the final quarter of the nineteenth century, however, several factors drove migrants beyond the borders of Europe and into the Western Hemisphere.

A growing rural population combined with unequal land distribution to create economic distress in late-nineteenth-century Europe. With land ownership concentrated in increasingly fewer hands, more and more people found themselves working ever smaller plots as laborers rather than owners.

For Russian Jews, religious persecution compounded economic hardship. After the assassination of Tsar Alexander II in 1881, which was falsely blamed on Jews, the government sanctioned a series of violent attacks on Jewish settlements; these attacks were known as **pogroms.** At the same time, the government forced Jews into fewer towns, deepening their poverty and making them easier targets for violence.

Sometime during the 1880s, an agent from the Hamburg-American Line, a German steamship company, visited a village in the Russian Ukraine where the great-grandparents of one of this book's authors lived. Shortly after his visit, they boarded a train to Austrian-occupied Poland and Hamburg. There they boarded a Hamburg-American steamer emblazoned with a large banner proclaiming *Willkommen* ("Welcome"). Like Mary Antin, whose recollection begins this chapter, just boarding that ship, they felt that they were entering the United States. Millions of others like them sailed on ocean liners from Germany, Italy, and Great Britain over the next 30 years.

Chinese and Japanese immigrants also came to the United States in appreciable numbers for the first time during the late nineteenth century. Most Chinese immigrants came from Canton in South China, a region of great rural poverty. They worked on railroads and in mines throughout the West and as farm laborers in California. Many eventu-

FROM THEN TO NOW

The Nature of Work

The growth of American corporate capitalism and the emergence of the United States as a major industrial power transformed the nature of work in the late nineteenth century. As machines took over sophisticated tasks, laborers were left to drudge at repetitive, dead-end jobs. Wages fell as certain jobs became obsolete, and a wave of mergers reduced competition and forced layoffs. In the late twentieth century, as the country began a transition to an economy based on service and information technology, many workers felt similar pressures. Job losses and social dislocation accompanied both the industrialization of the late nineteenth century and the transition to an information economy in the late twentieth. Both also generated new wealth and created new types of work.

There are important contrasts, however, between then and now. The great moguls of industry at the turn of the twentieth century made their fortunes from natural resources such as oil and iron ore. The entrepreneurial wizards of the twenty-first century derive wealth from knowledge. Although a global economy existed in 1900, today's version relies more on electronic mobility to shift labor and capital rapidly. Firms cast about for the best and, in some cases, the cheapest places to do business to gain a competitive edge. These factors have made work less secure. Today, workers are likely to have several employers over time. Employers today expect more flexibility and initiative from their employees, and workers have more opportunities for responsibility and advancement. But workers pay a price in diminished job security and employers in diminished worker loyalty.

Although technology of the post-industrial global economy is considerably more sophisticated than its industrial predecessor, gender segregation still exists in clerical work.

- Textile workers in both excerpts confronted job loss, in one instance due to technology, and in another due to foreign competition. Yet, the benefit to American consumers is cheaper clothing in both cases. Can this "creative destruction" of the changing nature of work in the textile industry be avoided, or is this the price of progress?

Before the typewriter was invented, most office workers were men. However, employers believed that women exhibited greater dexterity with the new machines, and besides, they could pay them less. Note the male supervisor.

PEARSON myhistorylab

From Then to Now Online

18-1 *Report of Senate Committee upon the Relations between Capital and Labor.* In 1883, in response to worker unrest and sporadic violence, this Senate committee held hearings to determine the depth and nature of the problem. The excerpt is from the testimony of a textile worker in Fall River, Massachusetts.

18-2 Mark Levinson, *Witness Testimony,* House Committee on Energy and Commerce. In testimony given in 2004 before a U.S. House of Representatives committee, a textile union economist charged that China exploits its workers resulting in the loss of tens of thousands of American jobs and that the U.S. government should impose trade sanctions on China until working conditions improve.

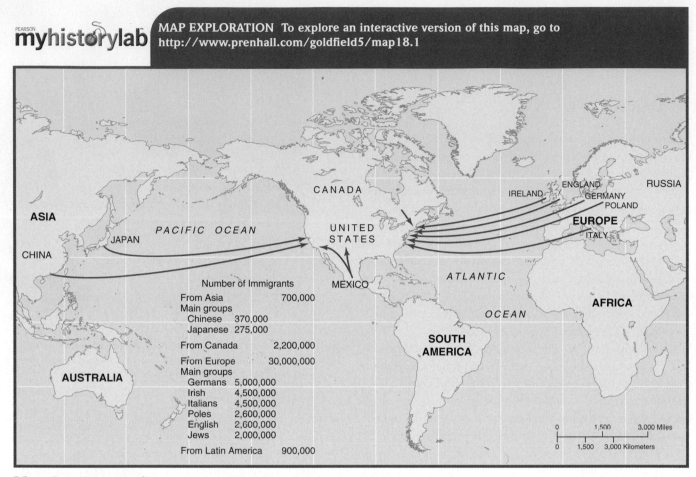

MAP EXPLORATION To explore an interactive version of this map, go to
http://www.prenhall.com/goldfield5/map18.1

Number of Immigrants

From Asia		700,000
Main groups		
Chinese	370,000	
Japanese	275,000	
From Canada		2,200,000
From Europe		30,000,000
Main groups		
Germans	5,000,000	
Irish	4,500,000	
Italians	4,500,000	
Poles	2,600,000	
English	2,600,000	
Jews	2,000,000	
From Latin America		900,000

MAP 18–1   Patterns of Immigration, 1820–1914
The migration to the United States was part of a worldwide transfer of population that accelerated with the industrial revolution and the accompanying improvement in transportation.

ally settled in cities such as San Francisco, where they established residential enclaves referred to as Chinatowns. The Chinese population in the United States peaked at about 125,000 in 1882.

Japanese began immigrating to the United States in the late 1880s, driven by a land shortage even more acute than the one in Europe. The first wave came by way of Hawaii to work on farms in California, taking the place of Chinese workers who had moved to the cities. By 1900, there were some 50,000 Japanese immigrants in the United States, nearly all on the West Coast.

Some immigrants came from right on our borders. In the late nineteenth century, Mexicans came across the border to work on the ranches and cotton farms of South and West Texas. Unlike their counterparts from Asia and Europe, these migrants settled primarily in rural areas. In 1900, 76 percent of Mexican immigrants resided in rural parts of Texas. But the urban population swelled after 1910 in the wake of the Mexican Revolution. Whether on farms, in squalid quarters in the *barrios* of El Paso or San Antonio, or in the smaller urban centers in South Texas, such as Laredo,

living and working conditions were harsh. By the turn of the century, Mexican laborers in urban areas began to organize into unions.

Wherever they came from, most migrants saw their route as a two-way highway. They intended to stay only a year or two, long enough to earn money to buy land or, more likely, to start a business back home and improve life for themselves and their families. Roughly half of all immigrants to the United States between 1880 and World War I returned to their country of origin. Some made several round trips. Jews, unwelcome in the lands they left, were the exception. No more than 10 percent of Jewish immigrants returned to Europe, and very few Jews from Russia, who accounted for almost 80 percent of Jewish immigrants after 1880, went back home.

Most of the newcomers were young men. (Jews, again, were the exception: Reflecting their intention to stay in their new home, they tended to migrate in families.) Immigrants easily found work in the nation's booming cities. The quickest way to make money was in the large urban factories, with their voracious demands for unskilled labor. Except for the Japanese, few immigrants came to work on farms after 1880.

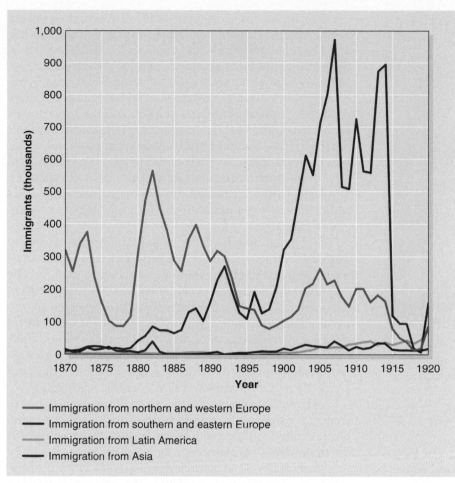

FIGURE 18–2   Immigration to the United States, 1870–1915
The graph illustrates the dramatic change in immigration to the United States during the late nineteenth and early twentieth centuries. As immigration from northern and western Europe slackened, the numbers of newcomers from southern and eastern Europe swelled. Latin American and Asian immigration also increased during this period.

— Immigration from northern and western Europe
— Immigration from southern and eastern Europe
— Immigration from Latin America
— Immigration from Asia

The desire of the new immigrants to retain their cultural traditions led contemporary observers to doubt their ability to assimilate into American society. Even sympathetic observers, such as social workers, marveled at the utterly foreign character of immigrant districts. In 1900, a Philadelphia social worker, Emily Dinwiddie, visited an Italian neighborhood and described "black-eyed children, rolling and tumbling together, the gaily colored dresses of the women and the crowds of street vendors, that give the neighborhood a wholly foreign appearance."

Cultural Connections in a New World

Immigrants maintained their cultural traditions through the establishment of religious and communal institutions. Charitable organizations were frequently connected to religious institutions. The church or synagogue became the focal point for immigrant neighborhood life. Much more than a place of worship, it was a school for transmitting Old World values and language to American-born children. The church or synagogue also functioned as a recreational facility and a gathering place for community leaders. In Jewish communities, associations called *landsmanshaften* arranged for burials, jobs, housing, and support for the sick, poor, and elderly. Because religious institutions were so central to their lives, immigrant communities insisted on maintaining control over them. Polish parishioners wanted Polish priests, and Russian Jewish communities wanted Russian rabbis. The nationality of parish priests became such a heated topic for some Catholic national groups that they threatened to secede from the church, a movement the hierarchy squelched.

Religious institutions played a less formal role among Chinese and Japanese neighborhoods. For them, the family functioned as the source of religious activity and communal organization. Chinatowns were organized in clans of people with the same surname. An umbrella organization called the Chinese Consolidated Benevolent Association emerged; it functioned like the Jewish *landsmanshaften*. Perhaps most important, the association shipped the bones of deceased members back to China for burial in ancestral cemeteries. A similar association, the Japanese Association of America, governed the Japanese community in the United States. This organization was sponsored by the Japanese government, which was sensitive to mistreatment of its citizens abroad

By 1900, women began to equal men among all immigrant groups as young men who had decided to stay sent for their families. In a few cases, entire villages migrated, drawn by the good fortune of one or two compatriots, a process called **chain migration.** The success of Francesco Barone, a Buffalo tavern owner, induced 8,000 residents of his former village in Sicily to migrate to that city, many arriving on tickets Barone purchased.

Immigrants tended to live in neighborhoods among people from the same homeland. Their native culture helped shape their response to their new home. For Italians from the Mezzogiorno (southern Italy), for example, the family was the basic institution for obtaining work and rendering assistance in times of stress, death, or sickness. Family ties were so strong that voluntary associations in the towns of the Mezzogiorno were rare. In the United States, immigrants from the Mezzogiorno, almost alone among European and Asian migrants, rarely formed neighborhood or ethnic associations.

Hope for a new generation. Victoria de Ortiz came to Nebraska with her family around 1915 to escape the turmoil in Mexico and, like millions of other immigrants of that era, to make a better life for herself and her family. The black lines are part of the photograph.

and anxious that immigrants set a good example. The Japanese Association, unlike other ethnic organizations, actively encouraged assimilation and stressed the importance of Western dress and learning English.

Ethnic newspapers, theaters, and schools supplemented associational life for immigrants. These institutions reinforced Old World culture while informing immigrants about American ways. Thus, the *Jewish Daily Forward,* first published in New York in 1897, reminded readers of the importance of keeping the Sabbath while admonishing them to adopt American customs.

The Job

If immigrant culture provided newcomers with a supportive environment, work offered the ultimate reward for coming to America. All immigrants perceived the job as the way to independence and as a way out, either back to the Old World or into the larger American society.

Immigrants typically got their first job with the help of a countryman. Italian, Chinese, Japanese, and Mexican newcomers worked with contractors who placed them in jobs. These middlemen often provided housing, loans, and other services for recent arrivals. They exacted a fee, sometimes extortionate, for their services. In an era before employment agencies, however, they efficiently matched immigrants with jobs. Other immigrant groups, such as Poles and Russian Jews, often found work through their ethnic associations or village or family connections. Poles in the meatpacking industries in

Chicago, for example, recommended relatives to their bosses. Family members sometimes exchanged jobs with one another.

The type of work available to immigrants depended on their skills, the local economy, and local discrimination. Mexican migrants to southern California, for example, concentrated in railroad construction. Mostly unskilled, they replaced Chinese laborers when the federal government prohibited Chinese immigration after 1882. Mexicans built the interurban rail lines of Los Angeles in 1900 and established communities at their construction camps. Los Angeles businessmen barred Mexicans from other occupations. Similarly, Chinese immigrants were confined to work in laundries and restaurants within the boundaries of Los Angeles's Chinatown.

The Japanese who came to Los Angeles around 1900 were forced into sectors of the economy that native-born white people had either shunned or failed to exploit. The Japanese turned this discrimination to their benefit when they transformed the cultivation of market-garden crops into a major agricultural enterprise. By 1904, Japanese farmers owned more than 50,000 acres in California. George Shima, who came to California from Japan in 1889 with a little capital, made himself the "Potato King" of the Sacramento Delta. By 1913, Shima owned 28,000 acres of farmland.

Other ethnic groups in other parts of the country had to conform to similar constraints. Greeks in Chicago, for example, restricted to food services, established restaurants, fruit distributorships, and ice-cream factories throughout the city.

Stereotypes also channeled immigrants' work options, sometimes benefiting one group at the expense of another. Jewish textile entrepreneurs, for example, sometimes hired only Italians because they thought them less prone to unionization than Jewish workers. Other Jewish bosses hired only Jewish workers, hoping that ethnic loyalty would overcome the lure of the unions. Pittsburgh steelmakers preferred Polish workers to the black workers who began arriving in northern cities in appreciable numbers after 1900. This decision began the decades-long tradition of handing down steel mill jobs through the generations in Polish families.

Jews, alone among European ethnic groups, found work almost exclusively with one another. Among the factors contributing to this pattern may have been the discrimination Jews faced in eastern Europe, the existence of an established Jewish community when they arrived, and their domination of the needle trades. Jews comprised three-quarters of the more than half-million workers in New York City's garment industry in 1910. Jews were also heavily concentrated in the retail trade.

Like their native-born counterparts, few married immigrant women worked outside the home, but unlike the native-born, many Italian and Jewish women did piecework for the garment industry in their apartments. Unmarried Polish women often worked in factories or as domestic servants. Japanese women, married and single, worked with their families on farms. Until revolution in China in 1911 began to

Mulberry Street, New York, 1905. The vibrant, predominantly Russian-Jewish Lower East Side of New York at first reflected more the culture of the homeland than of the United States. Language, dress, ways of doing business, keeping house, and worshiping, all followed Old World patterns. Gradually, thanks especially to the influence of school-age children, a blend of Russian Jewish and American traditions emerged.

Nativism

Despite the openness of America's borders in the nineteenth century, and contrary to the nation's reputation as a refuge from foreign persecution and poverty, immigrants did not always receive a warm reception. Ben Franklin groused about the "foreignness" of German immigrants during the colonial era. From the 1830s to 1860, nativist sentiment, directed mainly at Irish Catholic immigrants, expressed itself in occasional violence and job discrimination. Anti-immigrant sentiment gave rise to an important political party, the Know-Nothings, in the 1850s.

When immigration revived after the Civil War, so did antiforeign sentiment. But late-nineteenth-century **nativism** differed in two ways from its antebellum predecessor. First, the target was no longer Irish Catholics, but the even more numerous Catholics and Jews of southern and eastern Europe, people whose languages and usually darker complexions set them apart from the native-born majority. Second, late-nineteenth-century nativism had a pseudoscientific underpinning. As we saw in Chapter 17, the "scientific" racism of the period maintained that some people are inherently inferior to others. There was, in this view, a natural hierarchy of race. At the top, with the exception of the Irish, were northern Europeans, especially those of Anglo-Saxon ancestry. Below them in descending order were French, Slavs, Poles, Italians, Jews, Asians, and Africans. Social Darwinism, which justified the class hierarchy, reinforced scientific racism.

When the "inferior" races began to arrive in the United States in significant numbers after 1880, nativists sounded the alarm. A prominent Columbia University professor wrote in 1887 that Hungarians and Italians were "of such a character as to endanger our civilization." Nine years later, the director of the U.S. census warned that eastern and southern Europeans were "beaten men from beaten races. They have none of the ideas and aptitudes which fit men to take up readily and easily the problem of self-care and self-government." The result of unfettered migration would be "race suicide."

The popular press translated these scientific pronouncements into blunter language. In the mid-1870s, a Chicago newspaper described recently arrived immigrants from Bohemia (the present-day Czech Republic) as "depraved beasts, harpies, decayed physically and spiritually, mentally and morally, thievish and licentious." A decade later, with eastern Europeans still pouring into Chicago, another newspaper suggested: "Let us whip these slavic wolves back to the European dens from which they issue, or in some way

erode traditional gender roles, married Chinese immigrant women typically remained at home.

The paramount goal for many immigrants was to work for themselves rather than for someone else. Some immigrants, like George Shima, parlayed their skills and a small stake into successful businesses. Most new arrivals, however, had few skills, and no resources beyond their wits, with which to realize their dreams. Major banks at the time were unlikely to extend even a small business loan to a budding ethnic entrepreneur. Family members and small ethnic-based community banks provided the initial stake for most immigrant businesses. Many of these banks failed, but a few prospered. For example, the Bank of Italy, established by Amadeo Pietro Giannini in San Francisco in 1904, eventually grew into the Bank of America, today one of the nation's largest financial institutions.

Immigrants could not fully control their own destinies in the United States, any more than native-born Americans could. The vagaries of daily life, including death, disease, and bad luck, thwarted many immigrants' dreams. Hard work did not always ensure success. Add to these the difficulty of cultural adjustment to an unfamiliar environment, and the newcomer's confident hopes could fade quickly. Almost all immigrants, however, faced an obstacle that by its nature white native-born Americans did not. They faced it on the job, in the city at large, and even in their neighborhoods: the antiforeign prejudice of American nativism.

American Views

Tenement Life

In 1890, the Danish immigrant Jacob A. Riis published *How the Other Half Lives*, an exposé of living conditions among immigrants in New York City's Lower East Side neighborhood. The book, complete with vivid photographs, caused a sensation. At a time when newspapers and magazines competed for readers with lurid tales of urban life, Riis's detailed and gruesome depictions shocked readers and provided an impetus for housing reform in New York and, eventually, across the urban nation. Riis's scientific tone, devoid of sensationalism, rendered the scenes that much more dramatic. For a nation that valued family life and the sanctity of childhood, Riis's accounts of how the environment, inside and outside the tenement, destroyed young lives provided moving testimony that for some and perhaps many immigrants, the "promise" had been taken out of the Promised Land.

- What is Jacob Riis's attitude toward the tenement dwellers?
- Considering the destitute character of the family Riis describes, what sort of assistance do you think they receive?
- Why do you suppose the authorities were reluctant to enforce sanitary, capacity, and building regulations in these neighborhoods?

Look into any of these houses, everywhere the same piles of rags, of malodorous bones and musty paper all of which the sanitary police flatter themselves they have banished....Here is a "parlor" and two pitch-dark coops called bedrooms. Truly, the bed is all there is room for. The family teakettle is on the stove, doing duty for the time being as a wash-boiler. By night it will have returned to its proper use again, a practical illustration of how poverty...makes both ends meet. One, two, three beds are there, if the old boxes and heaps of foul straw can be called by that name; a broken stove with crazy pipe from which the smoke leaks at every joint, a table of rough boards propped up on boxes, piles of rubbish in the corner. The closeness and smell are appalling....

Well do I recollect the visit of a health inspector to one of these tenements on a July day when the thermometer outside was climbing high in the nineties; but inside, in that awful room, with half a dozen persons washing, cooking, and sorting rags, lay the dying baby alongside the stove, where the doctor's thermometer ran up to 115 degrees! Perishing for the want of a breath of fresh air in this city of untold charities! ...

A message came one day last spring summoning me to a Mott Street tenement in which lay a child dying from some unknown disease. With the "charity doctor" I found the patient on the top floor, stretched upon two chairs in a dreadfully stifling room. She was gasping in the agony of peritonitis [abdominal infection] that had already written its death-sentence on her wan and pinched face. The whole family, father, mother, and four ragged children, sat around looking on with the stony resignation of helpless despair that had long since given up the fight against fate as useless. A glance around the wretched room left no doubt as to the cause of the children's condition. "Improper nourishment," said the doctor, which translated to suit the place, meant starvation. The father's hands were crippled from lead poisoning. He had not been able to work for a year. A contagious disease of the eyes, too long neglected, had made the mother and one of the boys nearly blind. The children cried with hunger....For months the family had subsisted on two dollars a week from the priest, and a few loaves and a piece of corned beef which the sisters sent them on Saturday. The doctor gave direction for the treatment of the child, knowing that it was possible only to alleviate its sufferings until death should end them, and left some money for food for the rest. An hour later, when I returned, I found them feeding the dying child with ginger ale, bought for two cents a bottle at the pedlar's cart down the street. A pitying neighbor had proposed it as the one thing she could think of as likely to make the child forget its misery.

Source: Jacob A. Riis, *How the Other Half Lives: Studies Among the Tenements of New York* (New York: Charles Scribner's Sons, 1890).

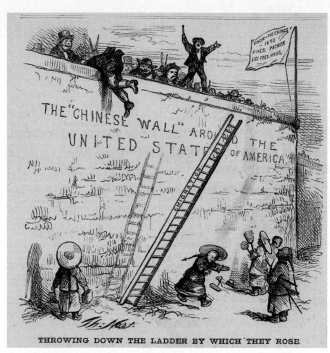

THROWING DOWN THE LADDER BY WHICH THEY ROSE.

"Throwing Down the Ladder by Which They Rose," Thomas Nast's 1870 attack on nativism. White workers, many of them immigrants themselves, objected to labor competition from Chinese immigrants and eventually helped to persuade Congress to pass the Chinese Exclusion Act in 1882.

exterminate them." The *New York Times,* demurring from such an extreme, suggested instead some form of restriction. Referring to Russian Jewish and Italian immigrants, the *Times* concluded that Americans "pretty well agreed" that these foreigners were "of a kind which we are better without." The rhetoric of the scientific press was scarcely less extreme. *Scientific American* magazine warned immigrants to "assimilate" quickly or "share the fate of the native Indians" and face "a quiet but sure extermination."

Such sentiments generated proposals to restrict foreign immigration. The treatment of the Chinese provided a precedent. Chinese immigrants had long worked for low wages, under harsh conditions, in mining and railroad construction in the West. Their different culture and their willingness to accept low wages provoked resentment among native- and European-born workers. Violence against Chinese laborers increased during the 1860s and 1870s. In 1870, the Republican-dominated Congress passed the Naturalization Act, which limited citizenship to "white persons and persons of African descent." The act was specifically intended to prevent Chinese from becoming citizens, a ban not lifted until 1943, but it affected other Asian groups also. The Chinese Exclusion Act of 1882, passed following another decade of anti-Chinese pressure, made the Chinese the only ethnic group in the world that could not immigrate freely into the United States. Even this drastic measure did not satisfy one Knights of Labor official, who in 1885 viewed the conflict between Chinese and native-born labor in the perspective of the 1850s sectional crisis (with a modern Darwinian twist): "This is the old irrepressible conflict between slave and white labor. God grant there may be survival of the fittest." Anti-Asian violence raced through mining communities in the West for the next two years.

Labor competition also contributed to the rise of another anti-immigrant organization. A group of skilled workers and small businessmen formed the American Protective Association (APA) in 1887 and claimed half a million members a year later. The APA sought to limit Catholic civil rights in the United States to protect the jobs of Protestant workingmen.

The Immigration Restriction League (IRL), formed in 1894 in the midst of a depression, took a more modest and indirect approach. The IRL proposed to require prospective immigrants to pass a literacy test that most southern and eastern Europeans would presumably fail. Cynically reaching out to native-born workers, the IRL vowed that its legislation would protect "the wages of our workingmen against the fatal competition of low-price labor."

The IRL ultimately failed to have its literacy requirement enacted. The return of prosperity and the growing preference of industrialists for immigrant labor put an end to calls for formal restrictions on immigration for the time being. Less than 30 years later, however, Congress would enact major restrictive legislation aimed at southern and eastern European immigrants. In the meantime, IRL propaganda encouraged northern universities to establish quotas limiting the admission of new immigrants, especially Jews.

Immigrants and their communal associations fought attempts to restrict immigration. The Japanese government even hinted at violent retaliation if Congress ever enacted restrictive legislation on Japanese similar to that imposed on the Chinese. But most immigrants believed that the more "American" they became, the less prejudice they would encounter. Accordingly, leaders of immigrant groups stressed the importance of assimilation.

In 1895, a group of American-born Chinese in California formed a communal association called the Native Sons of the Golden State (a deliberate response to a nativist organization that called itself the Native Sons of the Golden West). Stressing the need to assimilate, the association's constitution declared, "It is imperative that no members shall have sectional, clannish, Tong [a secret fraternal organization] or party prejudices against each other.... Whoever violates this provision shall be expelled." A handbook written at the same time for immigrant Jews recommended that they "hold fast," calling that attitude "most necessary in America. Forget your past, your customs, and your ideals.... A bit of advice to you: do not take a moment's rest. Run, do, work, and keep your own good in mind." Although it is doubtful whether most Jewish immigrants followed this advice whole, it nonetheless reflects the way the pressure to conform modified the cultures of all immigrant groups.

Global Perspectives

The Era of Global Migrations

The massive wave of immigration from Europe and Asia to the United States was part of a worldwide migration in the late nineteenth century. Italian peasants, for example, migrated to major cities in their newly unified country, to Berlin and London, to South America, and to Canada and Australia as well as to the United States. A major objective of the migrants was to improve their lot so that they and their families would have a better life. Countries undergoing industrialization, particularly those in the Western Hemisphere, provided opportunities that did not exist in China, Japan, Italy, and Eastern Europe.

In Italy, too little land, too many people, and the lack of educational and social opportunities aided the migration stream. Italy experienced a sudden surge in fertility in the 1880s. That, combined with a declining mortality rate, resulted in sharply reduced resources and land, especially in the mostly rural regions of southern Italy

and Sicily. It was a region where tax policies favored the wealthy landlords. High tariffs protected northern Italian industry but not southern enterprises, resulting in high unemployment. Adding to the misery, a blight eradicated vineyards in southern Italy, and, in 1905, a series of earthquakes rattled the region. In 1908, a tsunami in the Straits of Messina between Sicily and the Italian mainland leveled the city of Messina. None of these economic, political, and natural misfortunes by themselves caused people to pull up roots in a very rooted society. But in combination, their effect was powerful.

The same combination spurred immigration from other countries. Economic policies that ruined farm workers in southern China touched off migrations to the West Coast of the United States. In Japan, soaring inflation and unemployment during the 1870s and 1880s, worsened by a destructive typhoon in 1884, prompted nearly 30,000 Japanese to leave for Hawaii. Russian Jewish migrants

feared not only for their livelihoods but their lives. Emigration was more of a necessity than a choice in these cases.

While opportunities provided the attraction, and economic, political, and religious oppression at home provided the push, technology enhanced the means to get to far-flung places. The migration of labor was something that had gone on since ancient times. But by the late nineteenth century, the advent of railroads and steamships shrunk the world, making jobs accessible anywhere. These new modes of transportation, combined with inexpensive newspapers, letters from countrymen, and the telegraph, also spread information quickly and more widely than ever before. As Mary Antin wrote about her Russian town in the early 1890s, "America was in everybody's mouth."

■ **Why did such massive immigration occur in the late nineteenth century?**

Assimilation connotes the loss of one culture in favor of another. The immigrant experience of the late nineteenth and early twentieth centuries might better be described as a process of adjustment between old ways and new. It was a dynamic process that resulted in entirely new cultural forms. The Japanese, for example, had not gone to Los Angeles to become truck farmers, but circumstances led them to that occupation, and they used their cultural heritage of hard work, strong family ties, and sober living to make a restricted livelihood successful. Sometimes economics and the availability of alternatives resulted in modifications of traditions that nonetheless maintained their spirit. In the old country, Portuguese held *festas* every Sunday honoring a patron saint. In New England towns, they confined the tradition to their churches instead of parading through the streets. And instead

of baking bread themselves, Portuguese immigrant women were happy to buy all the bread they needed from local bakers.

Despite the antagonism of native-born white people toward recent immigrants, the greatest racial divide in America remained that between black and white. Newcomers quickly caught on to this distinction and sought to assert their "whiteness" as a common bond with other European immigrant groups and a badge of acceptance into the larger society. Nativists, however, often lumped immigrants into the "black" category. The word *guinea,* for example, which originally referred to African slaves, emerged as a derogatory epithet for Italians and, occasionally, Greeks, Jews, and Puerto Ricans. When the Louisiana legislature debated disfranchisement in 1898, a lawmaker explained that "according to the spirit of our meaning when we speak of 'white man's government,' Italians are as black as the blackest negro in existence." For immigrants, therefore, becoming "white," distancing themselves from African American culture and people, was often part of the process of adjusting to American life, especially as increasing numbers of black southerners began moving to northern cities.

Roots of the Great Migration

Nearly 90 percent of African Americans still lived in the South in 1900, most in rural areas. Between 1880 and 1900, however, black families began to move into the great industrial cities of the Northeast and Midwest. They were drawn by the same economic promise that attracted overseas migrants and were pushed by growing persecution in the South. Job opportunities probably outweighed all other factors in motivating what became known as the **Great Migration.**

In most northern cities in 1900, black people typically worked as common laborers or domestic servants. They competed with immigrants for jobs, and in most cases they lost. Immigrants even claimed jobs that black workers had once dominated, such as barbering and service work in hotels, restaurants, and transportation. Fannie Barrier Williams, a turn-of-the-century black activist in Chicago, complained that between 1895 and 1905, "the colored people of Chicago have lost...nearly every occupation of which they once had almost a monopoly."

Black women had very few options in the northern urban labor force outside of domestic service, although they earned higher wages than they had for similar work in southern cities. The retail and clerical jobs that attracted young working-class white women remained closed to black women. Employers rejected them for any job involving direct contact with the public. As one historian concluded, advertisers and corporate executives demanded "a pleasing physical appearance (or voice), one that conformed to a native-born white American standard of female beauty [and served] as an important consideration in hiring office receptionists, secretaries, department store clerks, and telephone operators." Addie W. Hunter, who qualified for a civil-service clerical position in Boston, could not find work to match her training. She concluded in 1916, "For the way things stand at present, it is useless to have the requirements. Color...will always be in the way."

The lack of options black migrants confronted in the search for employment matched similar frustrations in their quest for a place to live. Even more than foreign immigrants, they were restricted to segregated urban ghettos. Small black ghettos existed in antebellum northern cities. In 1860, four out of every five black residents of Detroit lived in a clearly defined district, for example. After the Civil War, black ghettos emerged in southern and border cities. In Washington, DC, black residents comprised nearly 80 percent of the population in a 20-block area in the southwestern quadrant of the city. In the 1890s, black people dominated an area east of downtown Atlanta known as Sweet Auburn after the avenue that cut through the neighborhood. As black migration to northern cities accelerated after 1900, the pattern of residential isolation became more pronounced. The black districts in northern cities were more diverse than those in southern cities. Migration brought rural southerners, urban southerners, and West Indians together with the black northerners already living there. People of all social classes lived in these districts.

The difficulties that black families faced to make ends meet paralleled in some ways those of immigrant working-

An African-American religious meeting, New York City, early 1900s. Black migrants from the South found vibrant communities in northern cities typically centered around black churches and their activities. Like immigrants from Asia and Europe, who sought to transplant the culture of their homelands within the urban United States, black migrants reestablished southern religious and communal traditions in their new homes.

class families. Restricted job options, however, limited the income of black families, even with black married women five times more likely to work than married white women. In black families, moreover, working teenage children were less likely to stay home and contribute their paychecks to the family income.

Popular culture reinforced the marginalization of African Americans. Vaudeville and minstrel shows, popular urban entertainments around 1900, featured songs belittling black people and black characters with names like Useless Peabody and Moses Abraham Highbrow. Immigrants frequented these shows and absorbed the culture of racism from them. The new medium of film perpetuated the negative stereotypes.

In the North as in the South, African Americans sought to counter the hostility of the larger society by building their own communal institutions. An emerging middle-class leadership sought to develop black businesses. Despite these efforts, chronic lack of capital kept black businesses mostly small and confined to the ghetto. Immigrant groups often pooled extended-family capital resources or tapped ethnic banks. With few such resources at their disposal, black businesses failed at a high rate. Most black people worked outside the ghetto for white employers. Economic marginalization often attracted unsavory businesses—dance halls, brothels, and bars—to black neighborhoods. One recently arrived migrant from the South complained that in his Cleveland neighborhood, his family was surrounded by loafers, "gamblers [and] pocket pickers; I can not raise my children here like they should be."

Other black institutions proved more lasting than black businesses. In Chicago in 1891, black physician Daniel Hale Williams established Provident Hospital, the nation's first interracially staffed hospital, with the financial help of wealthy white Chicagoans. Although it failed as an interracial experiment, the hospital thrived, providing an important training ground for black physicians and nurses.

Black branches of the Young Men's and Young Women's Christian Association provided living accommodations, social facilities, and employment information for black young people. Many black migrants to northern cities, perhaps a majority, were single, and the Y provided them with guidance and a "home." White people funded many black Y projects but did not accept black members in their chapters. By 1910, black settlement houses modeled on the white versions appeared in several cities.

New Cities

Despite the hardships associated with urban life, the American city continued to act, in the words of the contemporary novelist Theodore Dreiser, as a "giant magnet." Immigration from abroad and migration from American farms to the cities resulted in an urban explosion during the late nineteenth century (see Map 18–2). In 1850, six cities had a population

exceeding 100,000; by 1900, thirty-eight did. In 1850, only 5 percent of the nation's population lived in cities of more than 100,000 inhabitants; by 1900, the figure was 19 percent. The nation's population tripled between 1860 and 1920, but the urban population increased ninefold. Of the 1,700 cities listed in the 1900 census, fewer than 2 percent even existed in 1800.

In Europe, a few principal cities, such as Paris and Berlin, absorbed most of the urban growth during this period. In the United States, by contrast, growth was more evenly distributed among many cities. In 1820, about 18 percent of the urban population of the United States lived in New York, the nation's largest city; by 1890, its share had fallen to 7 percent. Put another way, many U.S. cities experienced the pains of rapid growth and industrialization in the late nineteenth century.

Despite the relative evenness of growth, a distinctive urban system had emerged by 1900, with New York and Chicago anchoring an urban-industrial core extending in a crescent from New England to the cities bordering the Great Lakes. This region included nine of the nation's ten largest cities in 1920. Western cities like Denver, San Francisco, and Los Angeles emerged as dominant urban places in their respective regions but did not challenge the urban core for supremacy. Southern cities, limited in growth by low consumer demand, low wages, and weak capital formation, were drawn into the orbit of the urban core. Atlanta, an offspring of the railroad, prospered as the region's major way station for funneling wealth into the urban North. Dallas emerged as Atlanta's counterpart in the western South (see Chapter 17).

Urban growth highlighted the growing divisions in American society. The crush of people and the emergence of new technologies expanded the city outward and upward as urban dwellers sorted themselves by social class and ethnic group. While the new infrastructure of water and sewer systems, bridges, and trolley tracks kept steel mills busy, it also fragmented the urban population by allowing settlements well beyond existing urban boundaries. The way people satisfied their needs for food, clothing, and shelter stimulated the industrial economy while distinguishing one class from another. Although urban institutions emerged to counter these divisive trends, they could not overcome them completely.

Centers and Suburbs

The centers of the country's great cities changed in scale and function in this era, achieving a prominence they would eventually lose in the twentieth century. Downtowns expanded up and out as tall buildings arose, monuments to business and finance, creating towering urban skylines. Residential neighborhoods were pushed out, leaving the center dominated by corporate headquarters and retail and entertainment districts.

Corporate heads administered their empires from downtown, even if their factories were located on the urban pe-

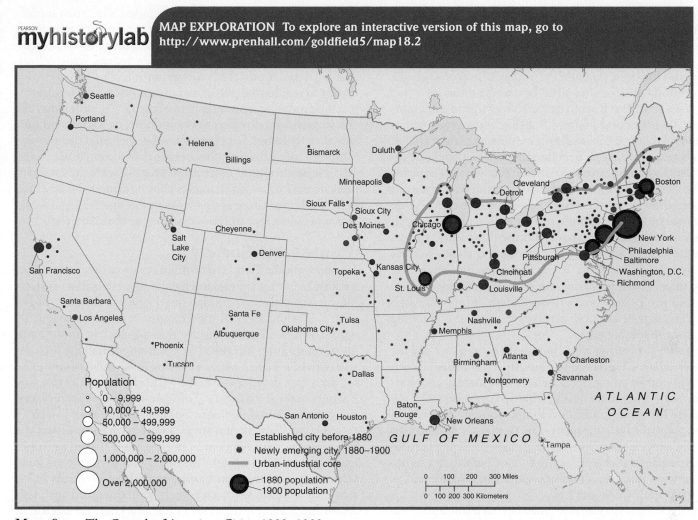

Population

- ° 0 – 9,999
- ○ 10,000 – 49,999
- ◯ 50,000 – 499,999
- ◯ 500,000 – 999,999
- ◯ 1,000,000 – 2,000,000
- ◯ Over 2,000,000

● Established city before 1880
• Newly emerging city, 1880–1900
— Urban-industrial core

1880 population
1900 population

0   100   200   300 Miles
0 100 200 300 Kilometers

ATLANTIC OCEAN

GULF OF MEXICO

MAP 18–2   The Growth of American Cities, 1880–1900
Several significant trends stand out on this map. First is the development of an urban-industrial core, stretching from New England to the Midwest, where the largest cities were located. And second is the emergence of relatively new cities in the South and West, reflecting the national dimensions of innovations in industry and transportation.

riphery or in other towns and cities. Banks and insurance companies clustered in such financial centers as Atlanta's Five Points district to service the corporations. Department stores and shops clustered in retail districts in strategic locations along electric trolley lines. It was to these areas that urban residents usually referred when they talked about going "downtown." In the entertainment district, electric lights lit up theaters, dance halls, and restaurants into the night.

As retail and office uses crowded out dwellings from the city center, a new phenomenon emerged: the residential neighborhood. Advances in transportation technology, first the horsedrawn street railway and, by the 1890s, the electric trolley, eased commuting for office workers. Some in the growing and increasingly affluent middle class left the crowded, polluted city altogether to live in new residential suburbs. These people did not abandon the city; they still looked to it for its jobs, schools, libraries, and entertainment,

but they rejected it as a place to live, leaving it to the growing ranks of working-class immigrants and African Americans. This pattern contrasted with that of Europe, where the middle class remained in the city.

The suburb emerged as the preferred place of residence for the urban middle class after 1870. As early as 1873, Chicago boasted nearly 100 suburbs with a combined population of more than 50,000. Smaller cities like Cleveland, Richmond, Memphis, Omaha, and San Francisco also sprouted large suburban communities. The ideals that had promoted modest suburban growth earlier in the nineteenth century—privacy, aesthetics, and home ownership—became increasingly important to the growing numbers of middle-class families after 1880. Consider the Russells of Short Hills, New Jersey. Short Hills lay 18 miles by railroad from New York City. William Russell; his wife, Ella Gibson Russell; and their six children moved there from Brooklyn in the late 1880s, seeking a "pleasant, cultured people whose society we could enjoy" and a cure for Russell's rheumatism. Russell owned and managed a small metal brokerage in New York and enjoyed gardening, reading, and socializing with his new neighbors. Ella Russell cared for their six children with the help of a servant and also found time for several clubs and charities.

The design of the Russell home reflected the principles Catharine Beecher and Harriet Beecher Stowe outlined in their suburban home bible, *American Woman's Home* (1869). The kitchen, according to Beecher and Stowe, should be organized for expedience and hygiene. The home's utilities should be confined to a central core, freeing wall areas for other functions. The new technology of central heating made it unnecessary to divide a house into many small rooms, each with its own fireplace or stove. Taking advantage of this change, Beecher and Stowe recommended that a home's ground floor have fewer but larger rooms, to encourage the family to pursue their individual activities in a common space. Parlors and reception rooms disappeared, along with such former standards as the children's wing, the male "smoking room," and the female parlor.

The once-prevailing view that women were too frail for vigorous exercise was changing. Thus, the entire Russell family was to be found enjoying the tennis, swimming, and skating facilities at the Short Hills Athletic Club. Because the community bordered on undeveloped woodland traversed by trails, "wheel clubs" appeared in the 1880s to organize families for bicycle outings. The emphasis on family togetherness also reflected the changing role of men in late-nineteenth-century society. Women's roles also broadened, as Ella Russell's club work attested.

Suburbs differed, not only from the city, but also from one another. With the growth after 1890 of the electric trolley, elevated rail lines, and other relatively inexpensive forms of commuter travel, suburbs became accessible to a broader spectrum of the middle class. The social structure, architecture, and amenities of suburbs varied, depending on the rail service and distance from the city. The commuter railroad remained popular among people like the Russells who could afford the time and expense of commuting to and from the city center.

The suburb underscored the growing fragmentation of life in and around American cities in the late nineteenth century. Residence, consumer habits, and leisure activities reflected growing social and class divisions. Yet, at the same time, the growing materialism of American society promised a common ground for its disparate ethnic, racial, and social groups.

The New Middle Class

From the colonial era, America's urban middle class had included professionals, physicians, lawyers, ministers, educators, editors, as well as merchants, shopkeepers, and skilled artisans (until they dropped from the middle class in the late nineteenth century). In the late nineteenth century, industrial technology and urban growth expanded the urban middle class to include salespeople, factory supervisors, managers, civil servants, technicians, and a broad range of "white-collar" office workers, such as insurance agents, bank tellers, and legal assistants. This newer middle class set national trends in residential patterns, consumption, and leisure.

The more affluent members of the new middle class, like the Russells, repaired to new subdivisions within and outside the city limits. Simple row houses sheltered the growing numbers of clerks and civil servants who remained in the city. These dwellings contrasted sharply with the crowded one- or two-room apartments that confined the working class. Rents for these apartments ran as much as $3 a week, at a time when few workers made more than $9 or $10.

A Consumer Society

The new middle class transformed America into a consumer society. In earlier times, land had been a symbol of prestige. Now it was consumer goods. And the new industries obliged with a dazzling array of merchandise and technologies. By 1910, the new middle class lived in all-electric homes with indoor plumbing. A typical kitchen might include an electric coffeepot, a hot plate, a chafing dish, and a toaster. The modern city dweller worked by the clock, not by the sun. Eating patterns changed: Cold packaged cereals replaced hot meats at breakfast; fast lunches of Campbell's soup, "a meal in itself," or canned stews weaned Americans from the heavy lunch. Jell-O appeared in the 1890s, touted as America's "most quick and easy" dessert. In Nashville at the same time, Joel Cheek ground and blended coffee beans in his store for customers' convenience. He convinced the city's Maxwell House Hotel to serve his new concoction, and in 1907, when President Theodore Roosevelt visited the hotel and drained his cup, he turned to Cheek and declared that the coffee was "good to the very last drop." A slogan and Maxwell House coffee were born.

Advertising played an important role in the consumer society. Advertisers created demand and developed loyalty for brand-name products. In early-twentieth-century New York, a six-story-high Heinz electric sign was a sensation, especially the 40-foot-long pickle at its top.

The middle class liked anything that saved time: trolleys, trains, electric razors, vacuum cleaners. The telephone replaced the letter for everyday communication; it was quicker and less formal. By 1900, some 1.4 million phones were in service, and many middle-class homes had one.

The middle class liked its news in an easy-to-read form. Urban tabloids multiplied after 1880, led by Joseph Pulitzer's *New York World* and William Randolph Hearst's *New York Journal*. The newspapers organized the news into topical sections, used bold headlines and graphics to catch the eye, ran human interest stories to capture the imagination, inaugurated sports pages to attract male readers, and offered advice columns for women. And they opened their pages to a wide range of attractive advertising, much of it directed to women, who did about 90 percent of the shopping in American cities by 1900.

As the visual crowded out the printed in advertising, newspapers, and magazines, these materials became accessible to a wider urban audience. Although mainly middle class in orientation, the tabloid press drew urban society together with new features such as the comic strip, which first appeared in the 1890s, and heart-rending personal sagas drawn from real life. Immigrants, who might have had difficulty reading small-type newspapers, received their initiation into the mainstream of American society through the tabloids.

In a similar manner, the department store, essentially a middle-class retail establishment, became one of the city's most democratic forums and the focus of the urban downtown after 1890. Originating in the 1850s and 1860s with the construction of retail palaces such as Boston's Jordan Marsh, Philadelphia's Wanamaker & Brown, New York's Lord & Taylor, and Chicago's Marshall Field, the department store came to epitomize the bounty of the new industrial capitalism. At the time of the Philadelphia Exposition in 1876, only 30 or so department stores existed; by 1920, there were thousands. They exuded limitless abundance with their extensive inventories, items for every budget, sumptuous surroundings, and efficient, trained personnel.

At first, most department-store customers were middle-class married women. Not expected to work and with disposable income and flexible schedules, these women had the means and time to wander department store aisles. The stores catered to their tastes, and the current emphasis on home and domesticity, with such items as prefabricated household furnishings, ready-made clothing, toys, and stationery. Industry churned out uniform, high-quality products in abundance, and middle-class salaries absorbed them. Department stores maintained consumers' interest with advertising campaigns arranged around holidays like Easter and Christmas, the seasons, and the school calendar. Each event required new clothing and accessories, and the ready-made clothing industry changed fashions accordingly.

Soon the spectacle and merchandise of the department store attracted shoppers from all social strata, not just the middle class. "The principal cause of the stores' success," one shopper explained in 1892, "is the fact that their founders have understood the necessity of offering a new democracy whose needs and habits" are satisfied "in the cheapest possible way," providing "a taste for elegance and comfort unknown to previous generations." Although many less affluent women came merely to "window-shop" (a new expression inspired by the large plate-glass display windows retailers installed in their stores to attract customers), some came to buy. After 1890, department stores increasingly hired young immigrant women to cater to their growing foreign-born clientele.

The department store, the turn-of-the-century shopping mall, provided inexpensive amusement for young working-class people, especially immigrants. Mary Antin recalled how she and her teenage friends and sister would spend their Saturday nights patrolling "a dazzlingly beautiful palace called a 'department store.'" It was there that Mary and her sister "exchanged our hateful homemade European costumes...for real American machine-made garments, and issued forth glorified in each other's eyes."

By 1900, department stores had added sporting goods and hardware sections and were attracting customers from a wide social spectrum. When Wanamaker's introduced a "bargain room" in 1888, other retail stores, including Filene's famous "Automatic Bargain Basement" in Boston, followed suit.

The Growth of Leisure Activities

The expanding floor space devoted to sporting goods reflected the growth of leisure in urban society. And like other aspects of that society, leisure and recreation both separated and cut across social classes. The leisure activities of the wealthy increasingly removed them from the rest of urban society. For them, the good life required such prerequisites as a mansion on Fifth Avenue, carriages and horses for transportation, a pony for the younger children, a saddle horse for the older ones, and a yacht. As such sports as football became important extracurricular activities at Harvard, Yale, and other elite universities, intercollegiate games became popular occasions for the upper class to congregate and, not incidentally, to discuss business. The elite also gathered at the athletic clubs and country clubs that emerged as open spaces disappeared in the city. High fees and strict membership criteria kept these clubs exclusive. The first country club in the United States was founded in Brookline, Massachusetts, a Boston suburb, in 1882. Country clubs built golf courses for men and tennis courts primarily for women. The clubs offered a suburban retreat, away from the diverse middle- and working-class populations, where the elite could play in privacy.

Middle-class urban residents could not afford country clubs, but they rode electric trolleys to the end of the line to enjoy suburban parks and bicycle and skating clubs. Reflecting the emphasis on family togetherness in late-nineteenth-century America, both men and women participated in these sports. Bicycling in particular became immensely popular. New bikes cost at least $50, putting them beyond the reach of the working class.

If college football was the rage among the elite, baseball was the leading middle-class spectator sport. Organized baseball originated among the urban elite before the Civil War. The middle class took over the sport after the war. Baseball epitomized the nation's transition from a rural to an urban industrial society. Reflecting rural tradition, it was played on an expanse of green, usually on the outskirts of the city. It was leisurely; unlike other games, it had no time limit. Reflecting industrial society, however, it had clearly defined rules and was organized into leagues. Professional leagues were profit-making enterprises, and, like other enterprises, they frequently merged. Initially, most professional baseball games were played on weekday afternoons, making it hard for

Amusement for the masses. Better transportation, more leisure time, and disposable income fueled escapes such as Luna Park in Coney Island, Brooklyn, a place where people could come together and have fun in a relatively controlled environment.

working-class spectators to attend. After merging with the American Association in 1883, the National League adopted some of its innovations to attract more fans, including beer sales, cheap admission, and, despite the objections of Protestant churches, Sunday games.

The tavern, or saloon, was the workingman's club. Typically an all-male preserve, the saloon provided drink, cheap food, and a place to read a newspaper, socialize, and learn about job opportunities. Advances in refrigeration in the 1870s allowed large breweries such as Anheuser-Busch and Pabst to distribute their product nationwide. Alcoholism was a severe problem in cities, especially, though not exclusively, among working-class men, fueling the prohibition movement of the late nineteenth century.

Amusement parks, with their mechanical wonders, were another hallmark of the industrial city. Declining trolley fares made these parks accessible to the working class around 1900. Unlike taverns, they provided a place for working-class men and women to meet and date.

The most renowned of these parks was Brooklyn's Coney Island. In 1897, George C. Tilyou opened Steeplechase Park

on Coney Island. He brought an invention by George Washington Ferris, a giant rotating vertical wheel, equipped with swinging carriages, to the park from Chicago, and the Ferris Wheel quickly became a Coney Island signature. Together with such attractions as mechanical horses and 250,000 of Thomas Edison's light bulbs, Steeplechase dazzled patrons with its technological wonders. It was quickly followed by Luna Park and Dreamland, and the Coney Island attractions became collectively known as "the poor man's paradise." Immigrant entrepreneurs, seeing a good thing, flocked to Coney Island to set up sideshows, pool halls, taverns, and restaurants. One German immigrant opened a small café serving sausages that he named "frankfurters" after his native Frankfurt. Locals called them "Coney Island hots" or "hot dogs" because they resembled the dachshund, a German-bred dog.

After 1900, the wonders of Coney Island began to lure people from all segments of an increasingly diverse city. Sightseers came from around the world. Notables such as Herman Melville, Mark Twain, and even Sigmund Freud (what did he think of Dreamland?) rubbed shoulders with factory workers, domestics, and department store clerks. In much the same manner, baseball was becoming a national pastime as games attracted a disparate crowd of people with little in common but their devotion to the home team.

Increasing materialism had revealed great fissures in American urban society by 1900. Yet places like department stores, baseball parks, and amusement parks provided democratic spaces for some interaction. Newspapers and schools also offered diverse groups the vicarious opportunity to share similar experiences.

The Ideal City

For all its problems, the American city was undeniably the locus of the nation's energy; in some ways, with the passing of the frontier, it had replaced the West in the national imagination as the environment where possibility was boundless. This sense of limitless energy and innovation appeared most notably in urban skylines where skyscrapers reached heavenward as graceful cathedrals of commerce. The tall buildings bespoke a confidence that declared even the sky was not the limit. The profile of the city center reflected what contemporary architect Louis Sullivan asserted: "what the people are within, the buildings express without; and inversely what the buildings are objectively is a sure index of what the people are subjectively."

Few landscapes expressed this ideal better than the 1893 World's Columbian Exposition in Chicago, a World's Fair to celebrate the 400th anniversary of the European discovery of America (though delays caused the Fair to open one year later). But timing was the only aspect of the Fair that was not a smashing success. The Fair demonstrated how with foresight, planning, and copious funds, it was possible to create a safe and esthetic urban environment, quite different from the gritty industrial city just beyond its borders. Dubbed the White City, the exposition epitomized cleanliness, grandeur, beauty, and order in its architecture. A writer for *Harper's* could barely contain himself: "The fair! The fair! Never had the name such significance before. Fairest of all the World's present sights it is. A city of palaces set in spaces of emerald, reflected in shining lengths of water which stretch in undulating lines under flat arches of marble bridges and along banks planted with consummate skill." That it was sheer fantasy, a temporary respite from the reality beyond the gates, did not faze the millions who attended. The White City represented the possibility, and in America, anything was possible.

Conclusion

The new industrial order, the changing nature of work, the massive migrations of populations from the countryside and abroad, and the rise of great cities changed the American landscape in the late nineteenth century. By 1900, the factory worker and the department store clerk were more representative of the new America than the farmer and small shopkeeper. Industry and technology had created thousands of new jobs, but they also eliminated the autonomy many workers had enjoyed and limited their opportunities to advance.

Immigrants thronged to the United States to realize their dreams of economic and religious freedom. They found both to varying degrees but also discovered a darker side to the promise of American life. The great cities thrilled newcomers with their possibilities and their abundance of goods and activities. But the cities also bore witness to the growing divisions in American society. As the new century dawned, the prospects for urban industrial America seemed limitless, yet the stark contrasts that had appeared so vividly inside and outside the Centennial Exposition persisted and deepened.

Still, it would be wrong to depict the nation in 1900 as merely a larger and more divided version of what it had been in 1876. Although sharp ethnic, racial, and class differences persisted, the nation seemed better poised to address them in 1900 than it had a quarter-century earlier. Labor unions, ethnic organizations, government legislation, and new urban institutions promised ways to remedy the worst abuses of the new urban, industrial economy.

Review Questions

1. Were there ways to achieve the benefits of industrialization without its social costs, or did the nation's political and economic systems make that impossible?

2. How did working-class women respond to the new economy? How did their participation and responses differ from that of working-class men?

3. What factors accounted for immigration becoming a global phenomenon during the late nineteenth century?

4. The growing fragmentation of urban life reflected deep divisions in modern urban industrial society. At the same time, there were forces that tended to overcome these divisions. What were these forces, and were they sufficient to bridge the divisions?

5. How did Old World conditions influence Mary Antin's adjustment to American life? Would individuals from other immigrant groups have expressed similar sentiments, or was Mary's reaction specific to her Jewish background?

Key Terms

American Federation of Labor (p. 505)

Chain migration (p. 509)

Collective bargaining (p. 505)

Gilded Age (p. 496)

Gospel of Wealth (p. 503)

Great Migration (p. 515)

Great Uprising (p. 505)

Horatio Alger Stories (p. 504)

Horizontal integration (p. 499)

Hull House (p. 503)

Knights of Labor (p. 505)

Molly Maguires (p. 504)

Nativism (p. 511)

Pogroms (p. 506)

Social Darwinism (p. 504)

Sweatshops (p. 501)

Tenements (p. 503)

Trusts (p. 499)

Vertical integration (p. 499)

Recommended Reading

Blumin, Stuart M. *The Emergence of the Middle Class: Social Experience in the American City, 1760–1900* (1989). Analyzes the key factors in the emergence of the urban middle class, especially in the late nineteenth century, and its impact on urban society and culture.

Bodnar, John. *The Transplanted: A History of Immigrants in Urban America* (1985). An excellent starting point for learning about the diverse immigrant experience in the United States that is also sensitive to conditions in the countries of origin.

Daniels, Roger. *Coming to America: A History of Immigration and Ethnicity in American Life* (1990). Preferred by some to Bodnar's survey. Has the great virtue of covering all im-

migrant groups; the discussion of Asian immigrants is especially good.

Dreiser, Theodore. *Sister Carrie* (1900). One of the best novels to capture life in late-nineteenth-century Chicago and New York. Few detail so clearly the moral and economic dilemmas newcomers faced in the fast-evolving American urban environment.

Higham, John. *Strangers in the Land: Patterns of American Nativism, 1860–1925* (1965). Despite its age, an excellent overview of and introduction to the subject of nativism; especially good in setting the context of nativism in American society and politics.

Where to Learn More

■ **Edison National Historic Site, West Orange, New Jersey.** The site contains the Edison archives, including photographs, sound recordings, and industrial and scientific machinery. Its 20 historic structures dating from the 1880–1887 period include Edison's home and laboratory. www.nps.gov/edis

■ **Pasa al Norte.** This museum, located in El Paso, Texas, serves as the Mexico–United States International Immigration History Center. Its exhibits focus on the importance of El Paso ("the Southwest Ellis Island") as a port-of-entry between the United States and Mexico from the late sixteenth century to the present. Utminers.utep .edu/panihm/default.htm

■ **Missouri Historical Society, St. Louis, Missouri.** The Society displays a long-term exhibition accompanied by public programs called "St. Louis in the Gilded Age,"

which focuses on the changes generated by industrialization and urban development in St. Louis from 1865 to 1900. www.mohistory.org

■ **Angel Island State Park, San Francisco Bay.** Angel Island served as a detention center from 1910 to 1940 for Asian immigrants who were kept there for days, months, and, in some cases, years while immigration officials attempted to ferret out illegal entries. Exhibits depict the era through pictures and artifacts. www.Angelisland.org

■ **Statue of Liberty National Monument and Ellis Island, New York, New York.** More than 12 million immigrants were processed at Ellis Island between 1892 and 1954. The exhibits provide a fine overview of American immigration history during this period. There is an ongoing oral history program as well. www.nps.gov/stli

Study Resources

For study resources for this chapter, go to www.myhistorylab.com and choose *The American Journey*. You will find a wealth of study and review material for this chapter, including pre- and posttests, customized study plan, key term review flash cards, interactive map and document activities, and documents for analysis.

This idealized 1875 engraving presents a harmonious image of western expansion and railroad construction that belies a more complex and disruptive reality, particularly for Native Americans.

Railroad building on the Great Plains, colored engraving, 1875 (Granger Collection 4E239.36).

Transforming the West 19
1865–1890

After a pleasant ride of about six miles we attained a very high elevation, and, passing through a gorge of the mountains, we entered a level, circular valley, about three miles in diameter, surrounded on every side by mountains. The track is on the eastern side of the plain, and at the point of junction extends in nearly a southwest and northeast direction. Two lengths of rails are left for today's work....At a quarter to nine A.M. the whistle of the C.P. [Central Pacific Railroad] is heard, and soon arrives, bringing a number of passengers....Two additional trains arrive from the East. At a quarter to eleven the Chinese workmen commenced leveling the bed of the road with picks and shovels, preparatory to placing the ties....At a quarter past eleven the Governor's train arrived. The engine was gayly decorated with little flags and ribbons, the red, white, and blue. At 12 M. the rails were laid, and the iron spikes driven. The last tie that was laid is 8 feet long, 8 inches wide, and 6 inches thick. It is of California laurel, finely polished, and is ornamented with a silver escutcheon bearing the following inscription: "The last tie laid on the Pacific Railroad, May 10th, 1869."...

The point of contact is 1,085 4/5 miles from Omaha, leaving 690 miles for the C.P. portion of the work. The engine Jupiter, of the C.P., and engine 119, of the U.P.R.R. [Union Pacific Railroad] moved up within thirty feet of each other....Three cheers were given for the Government of the United States, for the railroad, for the President, for the Star Spangled Banner, for the laborers, and for those who furnished the means respectively. The four spikes, two gold and two silver, were furnished by Montana, Idaho, California, and Nevada. They were about seven inches long, and a little larger than the iron spike. Dr. Harkness, of Sacramento, on presenting to Governor Stanford a spike of pure gold, delivered a short and appropriate speech. The Hon. F.A. Tuttle, of Nevada, presented Dr. Durant with a spike of silver, saying: 'To the iron of the East, and the gold of the West, Nevada adds her link of silver to span the continent and wed the oceans.'…The two locomotives then moved up until they touched each other, . . . and at one P.M., under an almost cloudless sky, and in the presence of about one thousand one hundred people, the completion of the greatest railroad on earth was announced.

Andrew J. Russell, "The Completion of the Pacific Railroad," *Frank Leslie's Illustrated Newspaper,* June 5, 1869.

myhistorylab

Personal Journeys Online

- ■ Eugene Chihuahua, *Leaving the West,* 1885. An Apache's account of being forced from his home into imprisonment.

- ■ Emma Hill, *Settling in Kansas,* 1873. A woman's account of pioneer hardships.

- ■ Carl and Fredrik Bergman, *Times Look Quite Promising,*1884-1893. Swedish immigrants describe their experiences in Texas.

Andrew J. Russell's short journey on the morning of May 10, 1869, from Ogden to Promontory Summit, Utah, enabled him to document what he called "the completion of the greatest work of the age, by which this vast continent is spanned, from ocean to ocean, by the iron path of travel and commerce." Russell had already been on the road two years, working as the official Union Pacific photographer. The transcontinental railroad itself was still longer in the making, having been authorized in 1862, but it symbolized the classic American journey, a people and a nation moving westward.

The construction of the transcontinental railroad set a precedent for western development. The two railroads that met in a desolate sagebrush basin were huge corporate enterprises, not individual efforts, and corporations would dominate western growth as much as they did eastern industrialization. The crowd of onlookers had good reason to give three cheers for the federal government, for it played a crucial role in railroad construction, as in virtually all aspects of western development. Congress had authorized the Union Pacific and Central Pacific to build the railroad link, given them the right-of-way for their tracks, and provided huge land grants and financial subsidies.

The railroads' dependence on capital investment, engineering knowledge, technological innovations, and labor skills also typified western development. Their labor forces both reflected and reinforced the region's racial and ethnic diversity. European immigrants, Mexicans, Paiute Indians, both male and female, and especially Chinese, recruited in California and Asia, chiseled the tunnels through the mountains, built the bridges over the gulches, and laid the ties and rails across the plains. But Russell had the Chinese workers step back so as not to appear in the famous photographs he took at Promontory, an indication of the racism that marred so many western achievements.

Laying track as quickly as possible to collect the subsidies awarded by the mile, the railroad corporations adopted callous and reckless construction tactics, resulting in waste, deaths (perhaps as many as a thousand Chinese), and environmental destruction, all consequences that would similarly characterize other forms of economic development in the West. And as with most American undertakings in the West, the construction provoked conflict with the Cheyenne, Sioux, and other tribes. As one railroad official declared, "we've got to clean the damn Indians out or give up building the Union Pacific Railroad."

The most important feature of the railroad, however, was that traffic moved in both directions. The transcontinental and subsequent railroads helped move soldiers, miners, cattle raisers, farmers, merchants, and other settlers into the West, but they also enabled the West to send precious metals, livestock, lumber, and wheat to the growing markets in the East. Thus the railroad both integrated the West into the rest of the nation and made it a crucial part of the larger economic revolution that transformed America after the Civil War.

CHRONOLOGY

1858	Gold is discovered in Colorado, Nevada, and British Columbia.
1860	Gold is discovered in Idaho.
1862	Homestead Act is passed.
	Gold is discovered in Montana.
1864	Militia slaughters Cheyennes at Sand Creek, Colorado.
1867	Cattle drives make Abilene the first cow town.
1868	Fort Laramie Treaty is signed.
1869	First transcontinental railroad is completed.
1872	Canada enacts homestead law.
1874	Gold is discovered in the Black Hills.
	Turkey Red wheat is introduced in Kansas.
	Barbed wire is patented.
1876	Indians devastate U.S. troops in the Battle of Little Bighorn.
1879	Defeat of Araucanian Indians opens the pampas to settlement in Argentina "Exodusters" migrate to Kansas.
1885	Chinese massacred at Rock Springs, Wyoming.
1887	Dawes Act is passed.
1890	Government troops kill 200 Sioux at Wounded Knee, South Dakota.
1892	Mining violence breaks out at Coeur d'Alene, Idaho.
1893	Western Federation of Miners is organized.

Subjugating Native Americans

The initial obstacle to exploiting the West was the people already living there, who used its resources in their own way and held different concepts of progress and civilization. For despite easterners' image of the West as an unsettled wilderness, Native Americans had long inhabited it and had developed a variety of economies and cultures. As whites pressed westward, they attempted to subjugate the Indians, displace them from their lands, and strip them of their culture. Conquest gradually forced Indians onto desolate reservations, but efforts to destroy their beliefs and transform their way of life were less successful.

Tribes and Cultures

Throughout the West, Indians had adapted to their environment, developing subsistence economies ranging from simple gathering to complex systems of irrigated agriculture. Each activity encouraged their sensitivity to the natural world, and each had social and political implications.

This photograph, taken by A. J. Russell, records the celebration at the joining of the Central Pacific and Union Pacific railroads on May 10, 1869, at Promontory Summit, Utah. Railroads transformed the American West, linking the region to outside markets, spurring rapid settlement, and threatening Indian survival.

In the Northwest, abundant food from rich waters and dense forests gave rise to complex and stable Indian societies. During summer fishing runs, the Tillamooks, Chinooks, and other tribes caught salmon that, after being dried in smokehouses, sustained them throughout the year. During the mild winters, they developed artistic handicrafts, elaborate social institutions, and a satisfying religious life.

At the opposite environmental extreme, in the dry and barren Great Basin of Utah and Nevada, Shoshones and Paiutes ate grasshoppers and other insects to supplement their diet of rabbits, mice, and other small animals. Such harsh environments restricted the size, strength, and organizational complexity of societies. Needing to spend most of their time searching for food, these Indians lived in small family groups in flimsy huts rather than established villages. In the Southwest, the Pueblos dwelled in permanent towns of adobe buildings and practiced intensive agriculture. Because tribal welfare depended on maintaining complex irrigation systems, the Zunis, Hopis, and other Pueblos emphasized community solidarity rather than individual ambition. Town living encouraged social stability and the development of effective governments, elaborate religious ceremonies, and creative arts. Navajos, Apaches, and other nomadic tribes in the region relied on sheepherding and hunting.

The most numerous Indian groups lived on the Great Plains. The largest of these tribes were the Lakotas, or Sioux, who ranged from western Minnesota through the Dakotas; the Cheyennes and Arapahos, who controlled much of the central plains between the Platte and Arkansas rivers; and the Comanches, preeminent on the southern plains. Two an-

imals dominated the lives of these peoples: the horse, which enabled them to move freely over the plains and to use the energy stored in the valuable grasses, and the buffalo, which provided meat, hides, bones and horns for tools, and a focus for spiritual life.

The importance of the horse, which had gradually spread northward after its introduction by the Spanish in the sixteenth century, indicates that Indian lives constantly adapted to changing conditions, including the appearance of Europeans and then Americans. Trade with whites, often mediated by other tribes, brought Indians new tools, weapons, and other useful products as well as new opportunities and challenges, but their societies were resilient, thanks especially to procedures, rituals, and beliefs devised over generations to ensure tribal identity and stability.

Clashing values.   Despite their diversity, all tribes emphasized community welfare over individual interest. They based their economies on subsistence rather than profit. They tried to live in harmony with nature to ward off sickness, injury, death, or misfortune. And they were intensely religious, absorbed with the need to establish proper relations with supernatural forces that linked human beings with all other living things. By thus living in what the Navajos called "the blessing way," Indians achieved both physical and spiritual contentment. The connections among these basic values appeared in the frequent religious rituals regulating hunting. The Sioux, for example, performed ceremonies in which they accorded respect to the buffalo's soul, sought its forgiveness for having to kill it, and promised not to be wasteful, so that the animals would not depart and bring starvation on the tribe. These connections also shaped Indians' attitude toward land, which they regarded, like air and water, as part of nature to be held and used communally, not as an individual's personal property from which others could be excluded.

White and Indian cultural values were incompatible. Disdaining Native Americans and their religion, white people condemned them as "savages" to be converted or exterminated. Rejecting the concept of communal property, most settlers demanded land for the exclusive use of ambitious individuals. Ignoring the need for natural harmony, they followed their own culture's goal of extracting wealth from the land for a market economy.

No one expressed these cultural differences better than the great Sioux leader Sitting Bull. Referring to the forces of the spirit world, he declared: "It is through this mysterious power that we too have our being and we therefore yield to our neighbors, even our animal neighbors, the same right as ourselves, to inhabit this land. Yet…[w]e have now to deal with another race.…Possession is a disease with them. These people have made many rules that the rich may break but the poor may not.…They claim this mother of ours, the earth, for their own and fence their neighbors away; they deface her with their buildings.…That nation is like a spring freshet that overruns its banks and destroys all who are in its path. We cannot dwell side by side."

Federal Indian Policy

The government had in the 1830s adopted the policy of separating whites and Indians (see Chapter 10). Eastern tribes were moved west of Missouri and resettled on land then scorned as "the Great American Desert," unsuitable for white habitation and development. This division presumed a permanent frontier with perpetual Indian ownership of western America. It collapsed in the 1840s, when the United States acquired Texas, California, and Oregon, and migrants crossed Indian lands to reach the West Coast. Mormons developed a trail through Indian country in 1847 and settled on Indian lands; gold and silver discoveries beginning in 1848 prompted miners to invade Indian lands. Rather than curbing white entry into Indian country, the government built forts along the overland trails and ordered the army to punish Indians who threatened travelers.

White migration devastated the Indians, already competing among themselves for the limited resources of the Plains. Migrants' livestock destroyed crucial timber and pastures along streams in the semiarid region; trails disrupted buffalo grazing patterns and eliminated buffalo from tribal hunting ranges. The Pawnees in particular suffered from the violation of their hunting grounds. One observer reported that "their trail could be followed by the dead bodies of those who starved to death." The Plains Indians also suffered from diseases the white migrants introduced. Smallpox, cholera, measles, whooping cough, and scarlet fever, for which Indians had no natural immunity, swept through the tribes, killing up to 40 percent of their population. Emigrants along the Platte River routes came across "villages of the dead."

By the early 1850s, white settlers sought to occupy Indian territory. Recognizing that the Great American Desert could support agriculture, they pressed on the eastern edge of the plains and demanded the removal of the Indians. Simultaneously, railroad companies developed plans to lay tracks across the plains. To promote white settlement, the federal government decided to relocate the tribes to separate and specific reserves. In exchange for accepting such restrictions, the tribes were promised annual payments of livestock, clothing, and other materials. To implement this policy, the government negotiated treaties extinguishing Indian rights to millions of acres (see Map 19–1) and ordered the army to keep Indians on their assigned reservations.

These actions alarmed Native Americans. One Cherokee complained of a government official "with a pocket full of money and his mouth full of lies. Some chiefs he will bribe, some he will flatter and some he will make drunk; and the result…will be called a treaty." And the treaties the army enforced were not always what the Indians, however reluctantly, had accepted. White negotiators sometimes omitted from the formal documents provisions that Indians had insisted upon, and at times Congress sharply reduced the annual payments or the size of the reservations promised in the treaties. The commissioner of Indian affairs aptly described the Indians' lot: "By alternate persuasion and force these tribes have been removed, step by step, from mountain to valley, and from river to plain, until they have been pushed halfway across the continent. They can go no further; on the ground they now occupy the crisis must be met, and their future determined."

Warfare and Dispossession

Most smaller tribes accepted the government's conditions, but larger tribes resisted. From the 1850s to the 1880s, warfare engulfed the advancing frontier. Indians sometimes initiated conflict, especially in the form of small raids, but invading Americans bore ultimate responsibility for these wars. As General Philip Sheridan declared of the Indians: "We took away their country and their means of support, broke up their mode of living, their habits of life, introduced disease and decay among them, and it was for this and against this that they made war. Could anyone expect less?"

One notorious example of white aggression occurred in 1864, at Sand Creek, Colorado. Gold discoveries had attracted a flood of white miners and settlers onto land only recently guaranteed to the Cheyennes and Arapahos. Rather than enforcing the Indians' treaty rights, however, the government compelled the tribes to relinquish their lands, except for a small tract designated as the Sand Creek reservation. But white settlers wanted to eliminate the Indian presence altogether. John Chivington, a Methodist minister who had organized Denver's first Sunday school, led a militia force to the Sand Creek camp of a band of Cheyennes under Black Kettle, an advocate of peace and accommodation. An American flag flew over the camp. Under Chivington's orders to "kill and scalp all, big and little," the militia attacked Black Kettle's sleeping camp without warning. With howitzers and rifles, the soldiers fired into the camp and then assaulted any survivors with swords and knives. One white trader later described the helpless Indians: "They were scalped, their brains knocked out; the [white] men used their knives, ripped open women, clubbed little children, knocked them in the head with their guns, beat their brains out, mutilated their bodies in every sense of the word."

The **Sand Creek Massacre** appalled many easterners. The Cheyennes, protested the commissioner of Indian affairs, were "butchered in cold blood by troops in the service of the United States." A congressional investigating committee denounced Chivington for "a foul and dastardly massacre which would have disgraced the veriest savage among those who were the victims of his cruelty." Westerners, however, justified the brutality as a means to

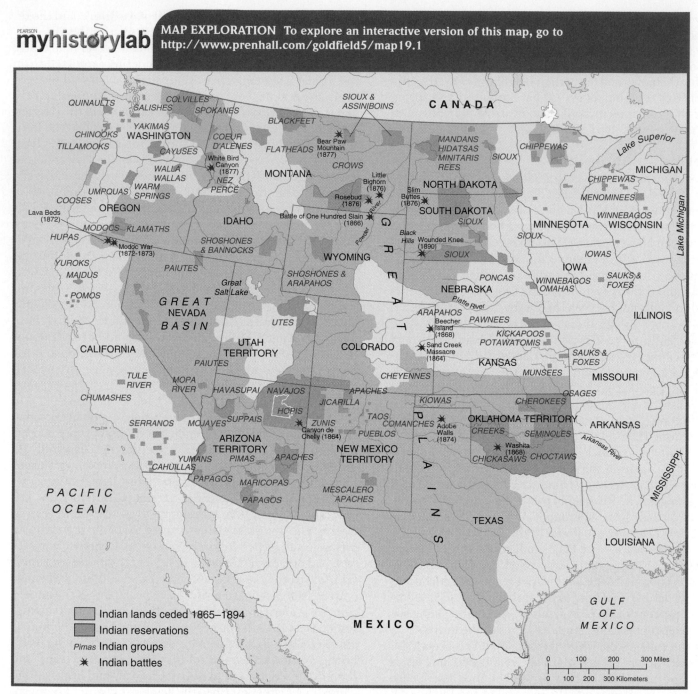

MAP 19–1   Indian Land Cessions, 1860–1894
As white people pushed into the West to exploit its resources, Indians were steadily forced to cede their lands. By 1900 they held only scattered parcels, often in areas considered worthless by white people. Restricted to these reservations, tribes endured official efforts to suppress Indian customs and values.

secure their own opportunities. One western newspaper demanded, "Kill all the Indians that can be killed. Complete extermination is our motto."

Other tribes were more formidable. None was more powerful than the Sioux, whose military skills had been honed in conflicts with other tribes. An army offensive against the Sioux in 1866 failed completely. Entire units de-

serted in fear and frustration; others were crushed by the Sioux. On the Bozeman Trail, in what the Lakotas called the Battle of One Hundred Slain, the Sioux wiped out an army detachment led by a captain who had boasted that he would destroy the Sioux nation. General William T. Sherman, who had marched through Georgia against Confederates, knew that the odds were different in the West. Fifty Plains Indians, he declared, could "checkmate" 3,000 soldiers. General Philip Sheridan calculated that the army suffered proportionately greater losses fighting Indians than either the Union or the Confederacy had suffered in the Civil War.

With the army unable to defeat the Sioux and their allies, and with many easterners shocked by both the military's indiscriminate aggression and the expense of the fighting, the government sued for peace. Describing white actions as "uniformly unjust," a federal peace commission in 1868 negotiated the **second Treaty of Fort Laramie,** in which the United States abandoned the Bozeman Trail and other routes and military posts on Sioux territory, one of the few times Indians forced whites to retreat. The United States also guaranteed the Sioux permanent ownership of the western half of South Dakota and the right to inhabit and hunt in the Powder River country in Wyoming and Montana, an area to be henceforth closed to all white people.

For several years, peace prevailed on the northern plains, but in 1872, the Northern Pacific Railroad began to build westward on a route that would violate Sioux territory. Rather than stopping the railroad, the government sent an army to protect the surveyors. Sherman drew up plans for the war that he expected the construction to provoke. He regarded railroad expansion as the most important factor in defeating the Indians, for it would allow troops to travel as far in a day as they could march in weeks. Other technological developments, from the telegraph to rapid-fire weapons, also undercut the skills of the Indian warrior.

The destruction of the buffalo also threatened Native Americans. From 1872 to 1874, white hunters killed 4 million buffalo. Railroad survey and construction parties disrupted grazing areas, and hunters working for the railroads killed hordes of buffalo, both to feed construction crews and to prevent the animals from obstructing rail traffic. Hide hunters slaughtered even more of the beasts for their skins, leaving the bodies to rot. Reporters found vast areas covered with "decaying, putrid, stinking remains." Federal officials encouraged the buffalo's extermination because it would destroy the Indians' basis for survival.

The climactic provocation of the Sioux began in 1874, when Colonel George A. Custer led an invasion to survey the Black Hills for a military post and to confirm the presence of gold. Thousands of white miners then illegally poured onto Sioux land. Ignoring Sioux demands that the government enforce the Fort Laramie treaty, the army insisted that the Indians leave their Powder River hunting grounds. When the Sioux refused, the army attacked. The Oglala Sioux, under Crazy Horse, repulsed one prong of this offensive at the Battle of the Rosebud in June 1876 and then joined a larger body of Sioux under Sitting Bull and their Cheyenne and Arapaho allies to overwhelm a second American column, under Custer, at the **Battle of the Little Bighorn.**

But the Indians could not follow up their dramatic victory. They had to divide their forces to find fresh grass for their horses and to hunt for food. Not similarly handicapped but supplied and equipped by an industrializing nation, the U.S. Army relentlessly pursued the separate bands to exhaustion. "We have been running up and down in this country, but they follow us from one place to another," lamented Sitting Bull. He led his followers to Canada, but the other bands capitulated in the winter of 1876–1877. In the end, the conquest of the northern plains came, not through any decisive victory, but through attrition and the inability of the traditional Indian economy to support resistance to the technologically and numerically superior white forces.

The defeat of the Sioux nearly completed the Indian Wars. Smaller tribes, among them the Kiowas, Modocs, and Utes, had been overrun earlier. In the Northwest, the Nez Percé resisted in 1877 when the government reneged on its agreement to protect their land. Outwitting and outfighting the larger forces of the U.S. Army over a 1,500-mile retreat toward Canada, the exhausted Nez Percé surrendered after being promised a return to their own land. But the government refused to honor that pledge, too, and imprisoned the tribe in Oklahoma, where more than a third perished within a few years.

In the Southwest, the Navajos and the Comanches were subdued, as the Sioux had been, by persistent pursuit that prevented them from obtaining food. The last to submit

Red Cloud, Oglala Lakota chief in the 1880s. In the 1860s, he led the Sioux to military victory over the United States, forcing the government, in the Treaty of Fort Laramie, to abandon army posts and withdraw from Sioux territory.

were the Apaches, under Geronimo. In 1886, he and 36 followers, facing 5,000 U.S. troops, finally surrendered. Geronimo and other Apaches were sent to a military prison in Florida; the tribes were herded onto barren reservations. The Oglala chief Red Cloud concluded of the white invasion: "They made us many promises, more than I can remember, but they never kept but one. They promised to take our land, and they took it."

Life on the Reservation: Americanization

Conquering the tribes and seizing their land were only the initial objectives of government policy. The next goal was to require Indians to adopt white ways, instilled by education and religion and enforced when necessary by the military. This goal did not involve assimilation but merely "Americanization," an expression of cultural conquest.

The government received aid from many Christian denominations, which had long proposed nonviolent methods of controlling Indians. They helped staff reservations as agents, missionaries, or civilian employees. Protestant philanthropists controlled several private organizations that worked to shape Indian policy, including the Indian Rights Association and the Women's National Indian Association. Reformers wanted to change Indian religious and family life, train Indian children in Protestant beliefs, and force Indians to accept private ownership and market capitalism.

Confined to reservations, Indians were a captive audience for white reformers. Furthermore, with their very survival dependent on government rations and annual payments stipulated by treaties, Indians were "compelled by sheer necessity," as one federal official said, to accept government orders "or starve." One Paiute woman wailed, "Our poor children are crying to us for food, and we are powerless to help the little ones." Government agents of the Bureau of Indian Affairs used their power to undermine tribal authority and destroy traditional Indian government, prohibiting tribal councils from meeting and imprisoning tribal leaders.

White activists sought to destroy Indian religion because it was "pagan" and because it helped Indians resist assimilation. Protestant religious groups persuaded the Bureau of Indian Affairs to frame a criminal code prohibiting tribal religious practices. Established in 1884, the code remained in effect until 1933. It was first invoked to ban the Sun Dance, the chief expression of Plains Indian religion. To enforce the ban, the government withheld rations and disrupted the religious ceremonies that transmitted traditional values.

In 1890, to suppress the Ghost Dance religion, the army even used artillery and killed at least 200 Sioux men, women, and children at Wounded Knee, South Dakota, in what became known as the **Wounded Knee Massacre.**

Missionaries attempted to convert Indians to Christianity but often found them reluctant to accept the creed of their conquerors. As one Crow Indian explained, "We found there were too many kinds of religion among white men for us to understand, and that scarcely any two white men agreed which was the right one to learn. This bothered us a good deal until we saw that the white man did not take his religion any more seriously than he did his laws, and that he kept both of them just … to use when they might do him good in his dealings with strangers. These were not our ways. We kept the laws we made and lived our religion."

The government and religious groups also used education to eliminate Indian values and traditions. They isolated Indian children from tribal influences at off-reservation boarding schools. Troops often seized Indian children for these schools, where they were confined until after adolescence. The schoolchildren were forced to speak English, attend Christian services, and profess white American values (see American Views: Zitkala-Sa's View of Americanization).

Finally, the government and the religious reformers imposed the economic practices and values of white society on Indians. Government agents taught Indian men how to farm and distributed agricultural implements; Indian women were

Dressed in their school uniforms, Indian children sit under the U.S. flag. Government and missionary schools sought to promote "Americanization" and suppress native cultures. Such education, said one member of Congress, "is the solution of the vexed Indian problem."

Western History Collections, University of Oklahoma Library, "Phillips #436."

American Views

Zitkala-Sa's View of Americanization

Zitkala-Sa, or Red Bird, was an 8-year-old Sioux girl when she was taken from her South Dakota reservation in 1884 and placed in a midwestern missionary school, where she encountered what she called the "iron routine" of the "civilizing machine." Here she recalls her first day at the school.

■ What lessons were the missionaries trying to teach Zitkala-Sa by their actions?

■ What lessons did Zitkala-Sa learn?

Soon we were being drawn rapidly away by the white man's horses. When I saw the lonely figure of my mother vanish in the distance, a sense of regret settled heavily upon me....I no longer felt free to be myself, or to voice my own feelings. The tears trickled down my cheeks, and I buried my face in the folds of my blanket. Now the first step, parting me from my mother, was taken, and all my belated tears availed nothing....Trembling with fear and distrust of the palefaces...I was as frightened and bewildered as the captured young of a wild creature....

[At the missionary school,] the constant clash of harsh noises, with an undercurrent of many voices murmuring an unknown tongue, made a bedlam within which I was securely tied. And though my spirit tore itself in struggling for its lost freedom, all was useless....

We were placed in a line of girls who were marching into the dining room....A small bell was tapped, and each of the pupils drew a chair from under the table. Supposing this act meant they were to be seated, I pulled out mine and at once slipped into it from one side. But when I turned my head, I saw that I was the only one seated, and all the rest at our table remained standing. Just as I began to rise, looking shyly around to see how chairs were to be used, a second bell was sounded. All were seated at last, and I had to crawl back into my chair again. I heard a man's voice at one end of the hall, and I looked around to see him. But all others hung their heads over their plates. As I glanced at the long chain of tables, I caught the eyes of a paleface woman upon me. Immediately I dropped my eyes, wondering why I was so keenly watched by the strange woman. The man ceased his mutterings, and then a third bell was tapped. Every one picked up his knife and fork and began eating. I began crying instead, for by this time I was afraid to venture anything more.

But this eating by formula was not the hardest trial in that first day. Late in the morning, my friend Judewin gave me a terrible warning. Judewin knew a few words of English; and she had overheard the paleface woman talk about cutting our long, heavy hair. Our mothers had taught us that only unskilled warriors who were captured had their hair shingled by the enemy. Among our people, short hair was worn by mourners, and shingled hair by cowards!

... I remember being dragged out, though I resisted by kicking and scratching wildly. In spite of myself, I was carried downstairs and tied fast in a chair. I cried aloud, shaking my head all the while until I felt the cold blades of the scissors against my neck, and heard them gnaw off one of my thick braids. Then I lost my spirit....My long hair was shingled like a coward's. In my anguish I moaned for my mother, but no one came to comfort me. Not a soul reasoned quietly with me, as my own mother used to do; for now I was only one of many little animals driven by a herder....

I blamed the hard-working, well-meaning, ignorant [missionary] woman who was inculcating in our hearts her superstitious ideas. Though I was sullen in all my little troubles, as soon as I felt better I was ... again actively testing the chains which tightly bound my individuality like a mummy for burial....

Many specimens of civilized peoples visited the Indian school. The city folks with canes and eyeglasses, the countrymen with sunburnt cheeks and clumsy feet, forgot their relative social ranks in an ignorant curiosity. Both sorts of these Christian palefaces were alike astounded at seeing the children of savage warriors so docile and industrious....

In this fashion many [whites] have passed idly through the Indian schools during the last decade, afterward to boast of their charity to the North American Indian. But few there are who have paused to question whether real life or long-lasting death lies beneath this semblance of civilization.

Source: Zitkala-Sa, "The School Days of an Indian Girl" (1900). Reprinted in *American Indian Stories* (Glorieta, NM.: Rio Grande Press, 1976).

taught household tasks. These tactics reduced the status of Indian women, whose traditional responsibility for agriculture had guaranteed them respect and authority. Nor could men farm successfully on reservation lands that whites had already rejected as unproductive. Whites, however, believed that the real obstacle to economic prosperity for the Indians was their rejection of private property. The Indians' communal values, the reformers argued, inhibited the pursuit of personal success that lay at the heart of capitalism. As one Bureau of Indian Affairs official declared, Indians must be taught to be more "mercenary and ambitious to obtain riches."

To force such values on Indians, Congress in 1887 passed the **Dawes Act,** which divided tribal lands among individual Indians. Complained one Caddo chief to U.S. officials: "You are attempting to change our customs and entail ruin on my people." Western settlers who had no interest in the Indians supported the law because it provided that reservation lands not allocated to individual Indians would be opened to white settlers. Under this "reform," the amount of land held by Indians declined by more than half by 1900.

White acquisition and exploitation of Indian land seemed to be the only constant in the nation's treatment of Native Americans. Assimilation failed, because most Indians clung to their own values and rejected as selfish, dishonorable, and obsessively materialistic those favored by whites. As Big Bear, a chief of the Otoe-Missouria, defiantly declared, "You cannot make white men of us. That is one thing you can't do." But if it was not yet clear what place Native Americans would have in America, it was at least clear by 1900 that they would no longer stand in the way of western development.

Exploiting the Mountains: The Mining Bonanza

Migrants to the West exploited the region's natural resources in pursuit of wealth and success. Some were rewarded; others met tragedy and failure. In either case, the challenges they confronted and the ventures they initiated gave rise to romantic images: the West as a land of adventure, opportunity, and freedom; pioneers as self-reliant individuals. Promoters, artists, and novelists developed these images into a heroic legend that movies, television, and politicians perpet-

uated. All too often, however, reality differed from legend. Opportunities were frequently short-lived and rarely available to all; individualism often gave way to group, corporate, or government action; nature and technology mocked self-reliance. The appeal of the cherished images made the reality harder to bear.

In the later nineteenth century, the West experienced several stages of economic development that transformed the environment, produced economic and social conflict, and integrated the region into the modern national economy. The first stage of development centered on mining, which attracted eager prospectors into the mountains and deserts in search of gold and silver. They founded communities, stimulated the railroad construction that brought further development, and contributed to the disorderly heritage of the frontier (see Map 19–2). But few gained the wealth they expected.

Rushes and Mining Camps

The first important gold rush in the Rocky Mountains came in Colorado in 1859. More than 100,000 prospectors crowded into Denver and nearby mining camps. Simultaneously, the discovery of the famous Comstock Lode in Nevada produced an eastward rush of miners from California and booming mining camps like Virginia City. Strikes in the northern Rockies followed in the 1860s. Boise and Lewiston in Idaho and Helena in Montana became major mining centers, and other camps prospered briefly before fading into ghost towns. The last of the frontier gold rushes came in 1874 on the Sioux reservation in the Black Hills of South Dakota, where the roaring mining camp of Deadwood flourished. Later, other minerals shaped frontier development: silver in Nevada, silver and lead in Colorado and Idaho, silver and copper in Arizona and Montana.

Mining camps were often isolated by both distance and terrain. They frequently consisted only of flimsy shanties, saloons, crude stores, dance halls, and brothels, all hastily built by entrepreneurs. Such towns reflected the speculative, exploitive, and transitory character of mining. And yet they did contribute to permanent settlement by encouraging agriculture, industry, and transportation in the surrounding areas.

The camps had an unusual social and economic structure. Their population was overwhelmingly male. In 1860,

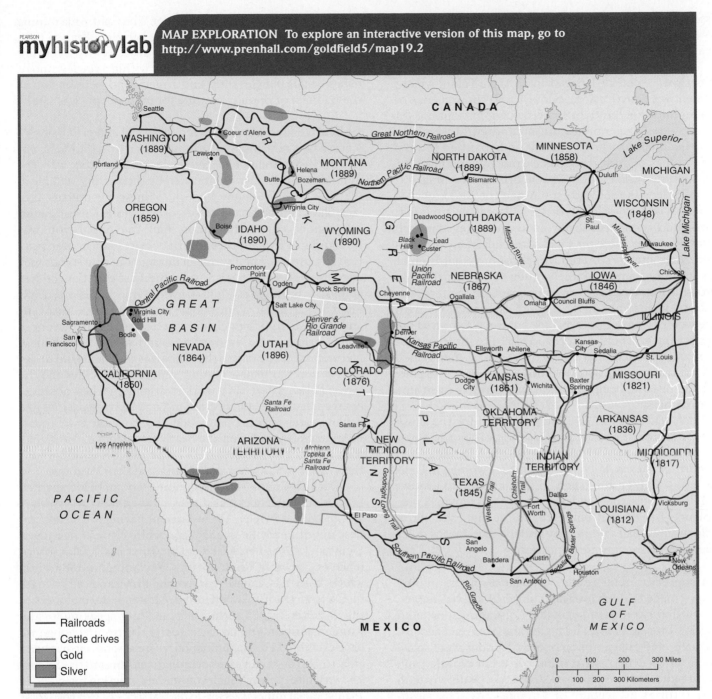

MAP 19–2   **Economic Development of the West: Railroads, Mining, and Cattle, 1860–1900**
The spread of the railroad network across the West promoted economic development by providing access to outside markets
for its resources. The discovery of precious metals often attracted the railroads, but stockraisers had to open cattle trails to
reach the railheads.

for example, about 2,300 men and only 30 women lived in
the Nevada camps of Virginia City and Gold Hill. Women
found far fewer economic opportunities than men did on
the mining frontier. Some became prospectors themselves;
in Montana, women, "skirts hiked up," were reported working claims. But most stayed within conventional domestic

spaces. Several opened lodging houses or hotels. Those with
less capital worked as seamstresses and cooks and took in
washing. The few married women often earned more than
their husbands by boarding other miners willing to pay for
the trappings of family life. When one found that miners
would pay ten dollars for a biscuit made by a woman, she

confessed: "In my dreams that night I saw crowds of bearded miners striking gold from the earth with every blow of the pick, each one seeming to leave a share for me."

Prostitution.   But the largest source of paid employment for women was prostitution, a flourishing consequence of the gender imbalance and the limited economic options for women. As one Denver prostitute later noted, "I went into the sporting life for business reasons and no other. It was a way for a woman in those days to make money and I made it." Mary Josephine Welch, an entrepreneurial Irish immigrant, settled in Helena in 1867 and established the Red Light Saloon, the first of many saloons, dance halls, and brothels that she owned and operated. Most women who engaged in such activities, however, were far less successful. Many who entered brothels already suffered from economic hardship or a broken family. Some Chinese women were virtually sold into prostitution. One California newspaper in the 1870s described a scene resembling antebellum slave auctions, with Chinese women "stripped and paraded onto a platform where prospective buyers could inspect and bid." Prostitution then usually worsened their distress. By the 1890s, as men gained control of the vice trade from the madams, violence, suicide, alcoholism, disease, drug addiction, and poverty overcame most prostitutes.

Public authorities showed little concern for the abuse and even murder of prostitutes, although they fined and taxed "sporting women" to raise revenue. Condemning such moral indifference, middle-class Protestant women in Denver and other cities established "rescue homes" to protect or rehabilitate prostitutes and dance-hall girls from male vice and violence. But their attempts to impose piety and purity had little success; male community leaders valued social order less than they did economic opportunity.

Saloon society.   The gender imbalance in the mining camps also made saloons prevalent among local businesses. An 1879 business census of Leadville, Colorado, reported 10 dry-goods stores, 4 banks, and 4 churches, but 120 saloons, 19 beer halls, and 118 gambling houses. Saloons were social centers in towns where most miners lived in crowded and dirty tents and rooming houses. As Mark Twain wrote in *Roughing It* (1872), his account of Virginia City, "The cheapest and easiest way to become an influential man and be looked up to by the community at large, was to stand behind a bar, wear a cluster-diamond pin, and sell whiskey."

The male-dominated saloon society of the mining camps generated social conflict. One observer of the Montana camps reported that men, "unburdened by families, drink whenever they feel like it, whenever they have money to pay for it, and whenever there is nothing else to do.... Bad manners follow, profanity becomes a matter of course.... Excitability and nervousness brought on by rum help these tendencies along, and then to correct this state of things the pistol comes into play." Disputes over mining claims could be-

come violent, adding to the disorder. The California mining town of Bodie experienced 29 killings between 1877 and 1883, a homicide rate higher than that of any U.S. city a century later. But such killings occurred only within a small group of males, young, single, surly, and armed, who were known as the Badmen of Bodie. Daily life for most people was safe.

Collective violence.   Indeed, personal and criminal violence, which remains popularly associated with the West, was less pervasive than collective violence. This, too, affected mining camps and was aggravated by their ethnic and racial diversity. Irish, Germans, English, Chinese, Australians, Italians, Slavs, and Mexicans, among others, rushed into the mining regions. In many camps, half the population was foreign-born and another fourth consisted of first-generation Americans. The European immigrants who sometimes encountered nativist hostility in the East experienced less animosity in the West, but nonwhite minorities often suffered. In particular, white people frequently drove Mexicans and Chinese from their claims or refused to let them work in higher-paid occupations in the mining camps. The Chinese had originally migrated to the California gold fields and thereafter spread to the new mining areas of the Rockies and the Great Basin, where they worked in mining when possible, operated laundries and restaurants, and held menial jobs like hauling water and chopping wood. In 1870, more than a quarter of Idaho's population and nearly 10 percent of Montana's was Chinese. Where they were numerous, the Chinese built their own communities and maintained their customs.

But racism and fear of economic competition sparked hostility and violence against the Chinese almost everywhere. In Colorado, town leaders boasted of having driven all Chinese out of Leadville by 1879, and white citizens destroyed Denver's Chinatown in 1880. The worst anti-Chinese violence occurred in Rock Springs, Wyoming, in 1885 when whites killed 28 Chinese workers and drove away all 700 residents from the local Chinatown. Although the members of the mob were well known, the grand jury, speaking for the white majority, found no cause for legal action: "Though we have examined a large number of witnesses, no one has been able to testify to a single criminal act committed by any known white person." Such community sanction for violence against racial minorities made mob attacks one of the worst features of the mining camps.

Labor and Capital

New technology had dramatic consequences for both miners and the mining industry. Initially, mining was an individual enterprise in which miners used simple tools, such as picks, shovels, and wash pans, to work shallow surface deposits known as placers. Placer mining attracted prospectors with relatively little capital or expertise, but surface deposits were quickly exhausted. More complex and expensive operations were needed to reach the precious metal buried in the earth.

Opening restaurants and boarding houses, some women earned money from their domestic skills in mining camps.

Hydraulic mining, for example, required massive capital investment to build reservoirs, ditches, and troughs to power high-pressure water cannons that would pulverize hillsides and uncover the mineral deposits. California's North Bloomfield Gravel Mining Company owned hundreds of miles of ditches and used more than a million gallons of water a day to feed its huge water nozzles. Quartz, or lode, mining, sometimes called hard-rock mining, required still more money, technology, and time to sink a shaft into the earth, timber underground chambers and tunnels, install pumps to remove underground water and hoists to lower men and lift out rock, and build stamp mills and smelters to treat the ore.

Such complex, expensive, and permanent operations necessarily came under corporate control. Often financed with eastern or British capital, the new corporations integrated the mining industry into the larger economy. Hard-rock mining produced more complex ores than could be treated in remote mining towns. With the new railroad network, they were shipped to smelting plants as far away as Kansas City and St. Louis and then to refineries in eastern cities. Western ores thus became part of national and international business. The mining industry's increasing development of lower-grade deposits led to greater capital investment and larger operations that employed more workers and machinery.

Effects of corporate mining. Quartz mining thus helped usher the mining frontier into a more stable period. But the new corporate mining had disturbing effects. Its impact on the environment was horrendous. Hydraulic mining washed away hillsides, depositing debris in canyons and valleys to a depth of 100 feet or more, clogging rivers and causing floods, and burying thousands of acres of farmland. Such damage provoked an outcry and eventually led to government regu-

lation. Fewer westerners worried about sterile slag heaps or the toxic fumes that belched from smelters and killed vegetation. They were the signs of progress. "The thicker the fumes," declared one proud Butte newspaper, "the greater our financial vitality."

Corporate mining also hurt miners, transforming them into wage workers with restricted opportunities. "It is useless to say that here all have an equal chance," conceded a Colorado newspaper in 1891. Miners' status declined as new machinery, such as power drills, reduced the need for skilled laborers and enabled employers to hire cheaper workers from eastern and southern Europe. Mining corporations, moreover, did little to protect miners' health or safety. Miners died in cave-ins, explosions, and fires or from the great heat and poisonous gases in underground mines. Others contracted silicosis, lead poisoning, or other diseases or were crippled or killed by machines. Miners called power hoists "man killers" because they frequently crushed and dismembered workers. Investigating the new machinery in 1889, the Montana inspector of mines concluded that "death lurks even in the things which are designed as benefits."

Unions and union busting. To protect themselves, miners organized unions. These functioned as benevolent societies, aiding injured miners or their survivors, establishing hospitals and libraries, and providing an alternative to the saloons with union halls serving as social and educational centers. Unions also promoted miners' interests by striking against wage cuts and campaigning for mine safety. They convinced states to pass mine safety laws and, beginning in the 1880s, to appoint mine inspectors. The chief role of these state officials was, in the words of a Colorado inspector, to decide "How far should an industry be permitted to advance its material welfare at the expense of human life?"

The industry itself, however, often provided the answer to this question, for mining companies frequently controlled state power and used it to crush unions. Thus, in 1892, in the Coeur d'Alene district of Idaho, mining companies locked out strikers and imported a private army, which battled miners in a bloody gunfight. Management next persuaded the governor and the president to send in the state militia and the U.S. Army. State officials then suppressed the strike and the union by confining all union members and their sympathizers in stockades.

Strikes, union busting, and violence continued for years. When mining companies in Utah, Colorado, and Montana pursued the same aggressive tactics of lockouts and wage cuts, the local miners' unions in the West united for strength and

Chinese miners in Idaho operate the destructive water cannons used in hydraulic mining. Technological changes made most miners wage workers for companies

Idaho State Historical Society

self-protection. In 1893, they formed one of the nation's largest and most militant unions, the Western Federation of Miners.

Violence and conflict were attributable not to frontier lawlessness but to the industrialization of the mines. Both management's tactics—blacklisting union members, locking out strikers, obtaining court injunctions against unions, and using soldiers against workers—and labor's response mirrored conditions in the industrial East. In sum, western mining, reflecting the industrialization of the national economy, had been transformed from a small-scale prospecting enterprise characterized by individual initiative and simple tools into a large-scale corporate business characterized by impersonal management, outside capital, advanced technology, and wage labor.

Using the Grass: The Cattle Kingdom

The development of the range-cattle industry opened a second stage of exploitation of the late-nineteenth-century West. It reflected the needs of an emerging eastern urban society, the economic possibilities of the grasslands of the Great Plains, the technology of the expanding railroad network, and the requirements of corporations and capital. It also brought "cow towns" and urban development to the West. The fabled cowboy, though essential to the story, was only a bit player.

Cattle Drives and Cow Towns

The cattle industry originated in southern Texas, where the Spanish had introduced cattle in the eighteenth century. Developed by Mexican ranchers, "Texas longhorns" proved well adapted to the plains grasslands. By the 1860s, they numbered about 5 million head. As industrial expansion in the East and Midwest enlarged the urban market for food, the potential value of Texas steers increased. And the extension of the railroad network into the West opened the possibility of tapping that market. The key was to establish a shipping point on the railroads west of the settled farming regions, a step first taken in 1867 by Joseph McCoy, an Illinois cattle shipper. McCoy selected Abilene, Kansas, in his words "a very small, dead place, consisting of about one dozen log huts." But Abilene was also the western railhead of the Kansas Pacific Railroad and was ringed by lush grasslands for cattle. McCoy bought 250 acres for a stockyard and built stock pens, stables, and a hotel for cowhands. Texans opened the **Chisholm Trail** through Indian Territory to drive their cattle northward to Abilene (see Map 19–2). Within three years, a million and a half cattle reached Abilene, divided into herds of several thousand, each directed by a dozen cowhands on a "long drive" taking two to three months.

Cow town life.   The cattle trade attracted other entrepreneurs who created a bustling town. Bankers prospered enough to convince one reporter in 1873 that "banks are as fat a thing as gold mines." Grocers, tailors, bootmakers, laundresses, barbers, druggists, blacksmiths, lawyers, and hotelkeepers provided consumer goods and services. Entertainments mushroomed: saloons, gambling rooms, dance halls, billiard parlors, and brothels. As both railroads and settlement advanced westward, a series of other cow towns—Ellsworth, Wichita, Dodge City, Cheyenne—attracted the long drives, cattle herds, and urban development.

As with the mining camps, the cow towns' reputation for violence was exaggerated. They adopted gun-control laws, prohibiting the carrying of handguns within city limits, and established police forces to maintain order. The primary duties of law officers were arresting drunks, fixing sidewalks, and collecting fines. The cow towns regulated, rather than prohibited, prostitution and gambling, for merchants viewed these vices as necessary to attract the cattle trade. Thus, the towns taxed prostitutes and gamblers and charged high fees for liquor licenses. By collecting such "sin taxes," Wichita was able to forgo general business taxes, thereby increasing its appeal to prospective settlers.

Not all cow towns became cities like Wichita, which by 1888 boasted of "Fine Educational Institutions, Magnificent Business Blocks, Elegant Residences, and Extensive Manufacturers"; most, like Abilene, dwindled into small towns serving farm populations. But cow towns, again like mining camps, contributed to the growth of an urban frontier. Railroads often determined the location and growth of western cities, providing access to markets for local products, transporting supplies and machinery for residents, and attracting capital for commercial and industrial development. When railroads reached El Paso, Texas, for example, it became a shipping point for cattle but then built its own packinghouses and opened smelters to process Arizona ores. Its Mexican workers clustered in barrios and developed their own religious and social organizations, just as San Francisco's Chinese did in Chinatown or European immigrants did in eastern cities. This urbanization demonstrated how western developments paralleled those in older regions. The West, in fact, had become the most urban region in the nation by 1890, with two-thirds of its population living in communities of at least 2,500 people.

Rise and Fall of Open-Range Ranching

The significance of the long drive to the cow towns faded as cattle raising expanded beyond Texas. Indian removal and extension of the railroads opened land for ranching in Kansas, Nebraska, Wyoming, Colorado, Montana, and the Dakotas. Cattle reaching Kansas were increasingly sold to stock these northern ranges rather than for shipment to the packinghouses. Ranches soon spread across the Great Plains and into the Great Basin, the Southwest, and even eastern Oregon and Washington. This expansion was helped by the initially low investment that ranching required. Calves were cheap, and grass was mostly free. Ranchers did not buy, but merely used, the grazing lands of the open range, which was public land. It sufficed to acquire title to the site for a ranch house and a water source, because controlling access to water in semiarid lands gave effective control of the surrounding public domain. Ranchers thus needed to invest only in horses, primitive corrals, and bunkhouses. Their labor costs were minimal: They hired cowboys in the spring to round up new calves for branding and in the fall to herd steers to market.

By the early 1880s, the high profits from this enterprise and an expanding market for beef attracted speculative capital and reshaped the industry. Eastern and European capital flooded the West, with British investors particularly prominent. Some investors went into partnership with existing ranchers, providing capital in exchange for expertise and management. Wisconsin investors formed the Three Rivers Land and Cattle Company of New Mexico, for example, by buying into a ranch owned by Susan Barber, whom they then employed as general manager. Barber was unusual in the male-dominated industry, but the managerial skills she demonstrated were necessary for success. On a larger scale, British and American corporations acquired, expanded, and managed huge ranches. In 1883, the Swan Land and Cattle Company controlled a tract in Wyoming 130 miles long and 40 to 100 miles wide, with more than 100,000 head of cattle.

Effects of corporate control.   Large companies soon dominated the industry, just as they had gained control of mining. In California, Miller & Lux integrated its extensive cattle raising with meatpacking to emerge as the only agricultural corporation among the nation's 200 largest firms. On the plains, cattle companies often worked together to enhance their power, especially by restricting access to the range and by intimidating small competitors. Some large companies illegally enclosed the open range, building fences to exclude newcomers and minimize labor costs by reducing the number of cowboys needed to control the cattle. One Wyoming newspaper complained: "Some morning we will wake up to find that a corporation has run a wire fence about the boundary lines of Wyoming, and all within the same have been notified to move."

Such tensions sometimes exploded in instances of social violence as serious as those that disrupted the mining

Cowboys gather around the chuck wagon at the XIT Ranch in Texas. Poor pay and arduous work defined the lives of most cowboys.

Global Perspectives

The West Abroad

Americans have always liked to think of the American West as a distinctive region whose prospectors, cowboys, and homesteaders helped shape an exceptional national experience. In fact, however, other countries also experienced comparable developments in the late nineteenth century. While the United States and other countries romanticized their frontier experiences, common environmental, economic, and social forces diminished their distinctiveness.

An obvious demonstration that the frontier was not uniquely American was the interlocking western development in the United States and Canada. The mining frontier crossed the border and included gold rushes in British Columbia from 1858 to 1867 and the Yukon in the 1890s. Canadian goldfields imported California's mining regulations and also followed the pattern of corporate supplanting placer mining. As for cattle raising, one Alberta rancher said in 1884: "We adopted pretty much the same system as was carried on across the border." Ranchers used Canada's public domain for pasture, while cowboys had familiar clothing, work, and wages. Stock associations developed to safeguard ranchers' interests, and gradually big eastern Canadian and British firms dominated the industry.

Like its American counterpart, the Canadian government promoted the construction of a transcontinental railroad, the Canadian Pacific, with land grants and subsidies. It enacted a homestead law providing free land in 1872. It encouraged European immigrants to settle and then witnessed land booms, commercial wheat production, and falling crop prices.

Canada experienced less violence and disorder than the United States, largely because of its Indian policy. Although it too established reservations, Canada treated Indians with respect, created a system of incorruptible agents, and used the North West Mounted Police to prevent the exploitation of Indians by settlers. The Mounted Police also maintained law and order on the mining and ranching frontiers.

While Canada most closely paralleled the American experience, Australia, too, had similarities. Its gold rush began in 1851, attracted miners, technology, and capital from California, and saw violence against Chinese. As in North America, corporate mining soon replaced the original "diggers." In 1861 Australia enacted homestead-type laws to assist small farmers who eventually developed into major wheat producers. And in the 1870s a large-scale pastoral economy, though based on sheep, not cattle, emerged in its vast arid region.

Argentina had no mining frontier, but after suppressing the Araucanian Indians in 1879 to open the pampas to settlement, it developed first a cattle ranching and then an agricultural frontier. Argentine gauchos, like American cowboys, came to symbolize the national character, though they too soon became ranch hands dependent on wages. The government promoted railroad construction in the 1880s, and European immigration helped people the prairies, spurring wheat production and the adoption of the new farming technologies.

■ How might transnational factors such as economic, technological, and demographic changes contribute to understanding the development of the American West in the late nineteenth century?

---

frontier. Attempts by large ranchers to fence off public lands in Texas provoked the Fence-Cutters War of 1883–84. Montana's largest cattlemen organized an armed force known as "Stuart's Stranglers" and, in America's worst vigilante violence, killed over a hundred people they viewed as challenging their power. Less deadly but more famous was the Johnson County War in Wyoming, when large ranchers, their foremen, and hired Texas gunmen set out with a death list of 70 people to eliminate. They murdered three people but met such popular resistance that the U.S. Army had to be called in to save them.

The corporate cattle boom overstocked the range and threatened the industry itself. Overgrazing replaced nutritious grasses with sagebrush, Russian thistle, and other plants that livestock found unpalatable. Droughts in the mid-1880s further withered vegetation and enfeebled the animals. Millions of cattle starved or froze to death in terrible blizzards in 1886 and 1887. These ecological and financial disasters destroyed the open-range cattle industry. The surviving ranchers reduced their operations, restricted the size of their herds, and tried to ensure adequate winter feed by growing hay. To further reduce their dependence on natural vegetation, they introduced drought-resistant sorghum and new grasses; to reduce their dependence on rainfall, they drilled wells and installed windmills to pump water.

Cowhands and Capitalists

One constant in the cattle industry was the cowboy, but his working conditions and opportunities changed sharply over time and corresponded little to the romantic image of a dashing individual free of social constraints. Cowboys' work was hard, dirty, seasonal, tedious, sometimes dangerous, and poorly paid. Many early cowboys were white southerners unwilling or unable to return home after the Civil War. Black cowhands made up perhaps 25 percent of the trail-herd outfits. Many others, especially in Texas and the Southwest, were Mexicans. Indeed, Mexicans developed most of the tools, techniques, and trappings that characterized the cattle industry: from boots, chaps, and the "western" saddle to roundups and roping. Black and Mexican cowboys were often relegated to the more lowly jobs, such as wrangler, a "dust-eater" who herded horses for others to use, but most served as ordinary hands on ranch or trail. As the industry expanded northward, more cowboys came from rural Kansas, Nebraska, and neighboring states.

Initially, in the frontier-ranching phase dominated by the long drive, cowboys were seasonal employees who worked closely with owners. Often the sons or neighbors of ranchers, they frequently expected to become independent stock raisers themselves. They typically enjoyed the rights to "maverick" cattle, or put their own brand on unmarked animals they encountered, and to "run a brand," or to own their own cattle while working for a ranch. These informal rights provided opportunities to acquire property and move up the social ladder.

As ranching changed with the appearance of large corporate enterprises, so did the work and work relationships of cowhands. The power and status of employer and employees diverged, and the cowboys' traditional rights disappeared. Employers redefined mavericking as rustling and prohibited cowhands from running a brand of their own. One cowboy complained that these restrictions deprived a cowhand of his one way "to get on in the world." But that was the purpose: Cowboys were to be workers, not potential ranchers and competitors. To increase labor efficiency, some companies prohibited their cowboys from drinking, gambling, and carrying guns.

Unions and strikes.   Cowboys sometimes responded to these structural transformations the same way skilled workers in the industrial East did, by forming unions and striking.

The first strike occurred in Texas in 1883, when the Panhandle Stock Association, representing large operators, prohibited ranch hands from owning their own cattle and imposed a standard wage. More than 300 cowboys struck seven large ranches for higher wages — $50 rather than $30 per month — and the right to brand mavericks for themselves and to run small herds on the public domain. Ranchers evicted the cowboys, hired scabs, and used the Texas Rangers to drive the strikers from the region.

Other strikes also failed because corporate ranches and their stock associations had great influence and cowhands faced long odds in their efforts to organize. They were isolated across vast spaces and had little leverage in the industry. Members of the Northern New Mexico Cowboys Union, formed in 1886, recognized their weakness. After asking employers for "what we are worth after many years' experience," they conceded, "We are dependent on you."

The transformation of the western cattle industry and its integration into a national economy dominated by corporations thus made the cherished image of cowboy independence and rugged individualism more myth than reality. One visitor to America in the late 1880s commented: "Out in the fabled West, the life of the 'free' cowboy is as much that of a slave as is the life of his Eastern brother, the Massachusetts mill-hand. And the slave-owner is in both cases the same, the capitalist."

Working the Earth: Homesteaders and Agricultural Expansion

Even more than ranching and mining, agricultural growth boosted the western economy and bound it tightly to national and world markets. In this process, the government played a significant role, as did the railroads, science and technology, eastern and foreign capital, and the dreams and hard work of millions of rural settlers. The development of farming produced remarkable economic growth, but it left the dreams of many unfulfilled.

Settling the Land

To stimulate agricultural settlement, Congress passed the most famous land law, the **Homestead Act** of 1862 (see the Overview table, Government Land Policy). The measure offered 160 acres of land free to anyone who would live on the plot and farm it for five years. The act promised opportunity and independence to ambitious farmers. The governor of Nebraska exclaimed, "What a blessing this wise and humane legislation will bring to many a poor but honest and industrious family."

Limits of the Homestead Act.   Despite the apparently liberal land policy, however, prospective settlers found less land open to public entry than they expected. Federal land

Mexican-American ranch family, Mora Valley, New Mexico Territory, 1895. Anglo-dominated development often displaced such families from their traditional lands and turned them into wage-laborers.

Source: Photographic Archives, Palace of the Governors, Museum of New Mexico, Santa Fe, New Mexico.

laws did not apply in much of California and the Southwest, where Spain and Mexico had previously transferred land to private owners. Elsewhere, the government had given away millions of acres to railroads or authorized selling millions more for educational and other purposes. Moreover, other laws provided for easy transfer of public lands to cattle companies, to other corporations exploiting natural resources, and to land speculators.

Thus, settlers in Kansas, Nebraska, Minnesota, and the Dakotas in the late 1860s and early 1870s often found most of the best land unavailable for homesteading and much of the rest remote from transportation facilities and markets. As much as 40 percent of the land in Kansas, for example, was closed to homesteading, which prompted the editor of the *Kansas Farmer* to complain that "the settlement of the state is retarded by land monopolists, corporate and individual." Although 375,000 farms were claimed by 1890 through the Homestead Act, a success by any measure, most settlers had to purchase their land.

The Homestead Act also reflected traditional eastern conceptions of the family farm, which were inappropriate in the West. A farm of 160 acres would have suited conditions in eastern Kansas or Nebraska, but farther west, larger-scale farming was necessary. And the law ignored the need for capital—for machinery, buildings, livestock, and fencing—that was required for successful farming. In 1887 Oregon officials estimated that families needed $800 for such expenses, a significant sum, and California's governor concluded in 1881 that without such capital farming "would bring defeat to the man of humble means."

Promoting settlement. Nevertheless, many interests promoted settlement. Newspaper editors trumpeted the prospects of their region. Land companies, eager to sell their speculative holdings, sent agents through the Midwest and Europe to encourage migration. Steamship companies, hoping to sell transatlantic tickets, advertised the opportunities in the American West across Europe. Religious and ethnic groups encouraged immigration. The Scandinavian Immigration Society generated both publicity and settlers for Minnesota; the Hebrew Emigrant Aid Society established Jewish agricultural colonies in Kansas and North Dakota. On a larger scale, the Mormons organized the Perpetual Emigrating Fund Company, which helped more than 100,000 European immigrants settle in Utah and Idaho. Their agricultural communities, relying on communal cooperation under church supervision, succeeded where individual efforts often failed in developing this region.

Most important, railroad advertising and promotional campaigns attracted people to the West. In 1882 alone, the Northern Pacific distributed more than 630,000 pieces of promotional literature in English, Swedish, Dutch, Danish, and Norwegian. "The glowing accounts of the golden west sent out by the R.R. companies," one pioneer later recalled, had convinced her that "they were doing a noble work to let poor people know there was such a grand haven they could reach." Only later did she realize the railroads' selfish motive. Not only would they profit from selling their huge land reserves to settlers, but a successful agricultural economy would produce crops to be shipped east and a demand for manufactured goods to be shipped west on their lines. The railroads therefore advanced credit to prospective farmers, provided transportation assistance, and extended technical and agricultural advice.

Thus encouraged, migrants poured into the West, occupying and farming more acres between 1870 and 1900 than Americans had in the previous 250 years (see Figure 19–1). Farmers settled in every region (see Map 19–3). Many went to California, Oregon, and Washington, where American development had begun much earlier. Some journeyed into the arid Great Basin and Rocky Mountains or the Southwest, where they often acquired land at the expense of the long-established Mexican population. Most, however, streamed into the Great Plains states, from the Dakotas to Texas.

White migrants predominated in the mass migration, but African Americans initiated one of its most dramatic

OVERVIEW

Government Land Policy

Legislation	Result
Railroad land grants (1850–1871)	Granted 181 million acres to railroads to encourage construction and development
Homestead Act (1862)	Gave 80 million acres to settlers to encourage settlement
Morrill Act (1862)	Granted 11 million acres to states to sell to fund public agricultural colleges
Other grants	Granted 129 million acres to states to sell for other educational and related purposes
Dawes Act (1887)	Allotted some reservation lands to individual Indians to promote private property and weaken tribal values among Indians and offered remaining reservation lands for sale to whites (by 1906, some 75 million acres had been acquired by whites)
Various laws	Permitted direct sales of 100 million acres by the Land Office

episodes, a millenarian folk movement they called the Exodus. Seeking to escape the misery and repression of the post-Reconstruction South, these poor "Exodusters" established several dozen black communities in 1879 in Kansas and Nebraska on the agricultural frontier. The Exodusters, said one observer, "regarded Kansas as a modern Canaan."

Many of the new settlers came from Europe, bringing with them not only their own attitudes toward the land but also special crops, skills, settlement patterns, and agricultural practices. Peasants from Norway, Sweden, and Denmark flocked to Minnesota. Germans, Russians, and Irish put down roots across Texas, Kansas, Nebraska, and the Dakotas. French, Germans, and Italians developed vineyards, orchards, and nurseries in California, where laborers from Japan and Mexico arrived to work in fields and canneries. By 1890, the foreign-born population of North Dakota exceeded 40 percent, and nonnatives made up much of the population in California and other western states. Immigrants often settled together in separate ethnic communities, held together by their church, and attempted to preserve their language and customs rather than be assimilated.

Hispanic losses.   Migrants moved into the West in search of opportunity, which they sometimes seized at the expense of others already there. In the Southwest, Hispanics had long lived in village communities largely outside a commercial economy, farming small tracts of irrigated land and herding sheep on communal pastures. As Anglos, or white Americans, arrived, their political and economic influence undermined traditional Hispanic society. Congress restricted the original Hispanic land grants to only the villagers' home lots and irrigated fields, throwing open most of their common lands to newcomers. Hispanic title was confirmed to only 2 million of the 37.5 million acres at stake. Anglo ranchers and settlers manipulated the federal land system to control these lands. The notorious Santa Fe Ring, a group of lawyers and land speculators, seized millions of acres through fraud and legal chicanery.

Spanish Americans resisted these losses in court or through violence. One militant group, organized as *Las Gorras Blancas* ("the White Caps"), staged night raids to cut fences erected by Anglo ranchers and farmers and to attack the property of railroads, the symbol of the encroaching new order. "Our purpose," they announced, "is to protect the rights of the people in general and especially those of the helpless classes." Anglos condemned these actions, but one federal judge described them as merely "the protests of a

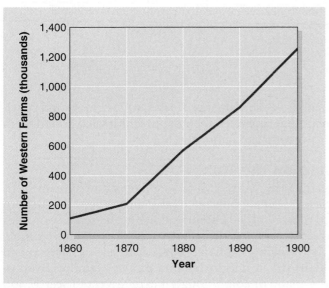

FIGURE 19–1   The Growth of Western Farming, 1860–1900

Indian removal, railroad expansion, and liberal land policies drew farm families into the West from much of Europe as well as the East. Technological innovations like barbed wire and farm machinery soon enabled them to build farms, but economic, social, and environmental challenges remained.

Data Source: Historical Statistics of the United States (1975).

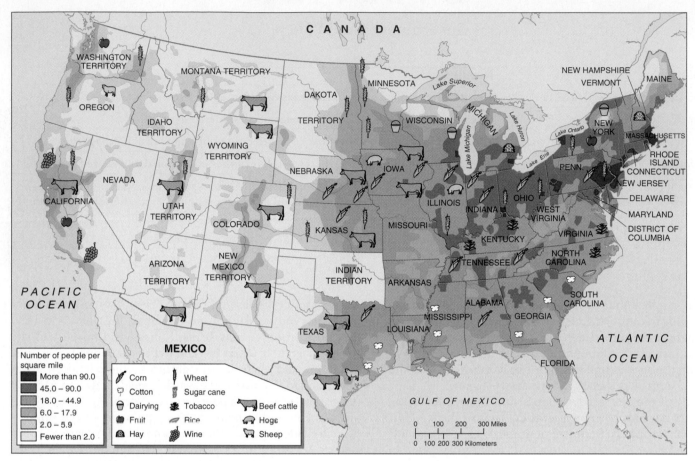

MAP 19–3   **Population Density and Agricultural Land Use in the Late Nineteenth Century**
Economic integration of the West promoted regional agricultural specialization. Stockraising and grain production dominated the more sparsely settled West, while the South grew the labor-intensive crops of cotton, tobacco, and sugar cane, and other areas concentrated on dairy products, fruit, and other crops for nearby urban markets.

simple, pastoral people against the establishment of large landed estates, or baronial feudalism, in their native country." Such resistance, however, had little success.

As their landholdings shrank, Hispanic villagers could not maintain their pastoral economy. Few turned to homesteading, for that would have required dispersed settlement and abandoning the village and its church, school, and other cultural institutions. Thus many Hispanics became seasonal wage laborers in the Anglo-dominated economy, sometimes working as stoop labor in the commercial sugar-beet fields that emerged in the 1890s, sometimes working on the railroads or in the mines. Women also participated in the new labor market. Previously crucial to the subsistence village economy, they now sought wage labor as cooks and domestic servants in railroad towns and mining camps. Such seasonal labor enabled Hispanics to maintain their villages and provided sufficient income to adopt some Anglo technology, such as cook stoves and sewing machines. But if Hispanics retained some cultural autonomy, they had little

influence over the larger processes of settlement and development that restricted their opportunities and bound them to the western and national economy.

Home on the Range

In settling the West, farm families encountered many difficulties, especially on the Great Plains, where they had to adapt to a radically new environment. The scarcity of trees on the plains meant that there was little wood for housing, fuel, and fencing. Until they had reaped several harvests and could afford to import lumber, pioneer families lived in houses made of sod. Though inexpensive and sturdy, sod houses were also dark and dirty. Snakes, mice, and insects often crawled out of the walls and roofs. Describing how a snake would "fall down on the bed," one child noted, "Mother would grab the hoe and there was something doing and after the fight was over Mr. Bull Snake was dragged outside." Small wonder that one Nebraska homesteader recalled that her first sight of a sod house "sickened me."

Women's work.   Within these rough houses, women worked to provide food, clothing, and medicine to ensure the family's survival. Their efforts were greatly constrained by the harsh environment. For fuel, families often had to rely on buffalo or cattle "chips," dried dung, which repelled some newcomers. One farmer reported in 1879 that "it was comical to see how gingerly our wives handled these chips at first. They commenced by picking them up between two sticks, or with a poker. Soon they used a rag, and then a corner of their apron. Finally, growing hardened, a wash after handling them was sufficient. And now? Now it is out of the bread, into the chips and back again—and not even a dust of the hands!" The scarcity of water also complicated women's domestic labor. They often had to transport water over long distances, pulling barrels on "water sleds" or carrying pails on neck yokes. They melted snow for wash water and used the same water over again for different chores. Where possible, they also helped to dig wells by hand.

Some women farmed the land themselves. Single women could claim land under the Homestead Act, and in some areas, women claimants made up 18 percent of the total and succeeded more frequently than men in gaining final title. At times, married women operated the family farm by themselves while their husbands worked elsewhere to earn the money needed for seeds, equipment, and building supplies. In the 1870s, one Dakota woman recounted the demands women faced: "I had lived on a homestead long enough to learn some fundamental things: that while a woman had more independence here than in any other part of the world, she was expected to contribute as much as a man, not in the same way, it is true, but to the same degree; that people who fought the frontier had to be prepared to meet any emergency; that the person who wasn't willing to try anything once wasn't equipped to be a settler."

Isolation and community.   Isolation and loneliness troubled many early settlers on the plains. Women especially suffered because they frequently had less contact with other people than farm men, who conducted their families' business in town and participated in such public activities as political meetings. One farm woman complained that "being cut off from everybody is almost too much for me." Luna Kellie recalled that from her Nebraska farm "there were no houses in sight and it seemed like the end of the world."

Over time, conditions improved. "It does beet all how fast this country is getting up," wrote one South Dakota woman in 1886. "I'm looking round and see two new houses been put up since yesterday." As population increased, women in particular worked to bind isolated households into communities by organizing social activities and institutions. They held fairs, dances, and picnics and established churches, schools, and libraries, thereby gaining both companionship and a sense of purpose.

Sunday school meeting in Custer County, Nebraska, in 1888. Sunday schools were important social as well as religious institutions on the Great Plains, where, as one newspaper reported, rural families often felt like "strangers in a strange land."

Churches, in turn, also promoted community. Indeed, many were "union" churches, open to people of all denominations. In addition to holding religious services, revivals, and camp meetings, churches were often the center of social life, especially by sponsoring sociables and children's organizations. "However great may have been the need for salvation," one plains woman recalled, "the need for recreation was given preference." Nondenominational Sunday schools helped bind together differing nationalities and church preferences, and because they did not require the services of an ordained minister they often enabled women to initiate and lead community activities. Although western ministers often received little social deference—they were called "devil skinners," "Gospel sharks," and "salvation peddlers"—they earned praise for directing eastern relief assistance to destitute settlers in times of drought and for linking them to sympathetic home missionary societies.

Other institutions also encouraged community action. Rural families created their own agricultural cooperatives and other economic and social organizations, like local Grange lodges. External developments also served the rural population. Rural Free Delivery, for example, eventually brought letters, newspapers, magazines, and advertisements to farm families' doorsteps; mail-order companies made available to farm people such helpful goods as stoves, sewing machines, and shoes. After acquiring her first Montgomery Ward catalog in 1885, one Wyoming woman declared it "impossible to exaggerate the importance of . . . this book of wonder." Such changes helped incorporate westerners into the larger society.

FROM THEN TO NOW

The Legacy of Indian Americanization

The assumptions, objectives, and failures of the Americanization policies of the nineteenth century continue to affect American Indians more than a century later. Although periodically modified (see Chapter 25), these policies long persisted, as did their consequences. In the 1970s official investigations reported that the continuing attempts of the Bureau of Indian Affairs to use education to force Indians into an Anglo-American mold "have been marked by near total failure, haunted by prejudice and ignorance." Similarly, the conditions on reservations in the nineteenth century foreshadowed those a century later. Today, Indians rank at the bottom on almost all measures of economic well-being and suffer the highest rates of infant mortality, pneumonia, and suicide. The U.S. Commission on Civil Rights reported in 2003 that Indians endured a "quiet crisis" of poverty, discrimination, and unmet promises.

Indian culture, however, did not succumb to either the pressure to Americanize or these miserable conditions. In the words of a Shoshone writer, "Indian history didn't end in the 1800s. Indian cultures . . . evolve, grow, and continually try to renew themselves." In recent decades, Indian peoples have begun to reclaim their past and assert control over their future. Dramatic protests called attention to serious grievances while Indians also moved to regain control of the institutions that define their cultural identity. They have established community schools and colleges that preserve traditions while opening new opportunities; they have built tribal museums and visitor centers in order to shape the presentation of their histories and cultures. New laws and court decisions have assured Indian religious freedom, land ownership, and water rights. Dramatically symbolizing Indians' success in preserving their cultural heritage and keeping it vibrant for future generations was the 2004 opening of the National Museum of the American Indian in the Mall in Washington, DC. "What we really want visitors to understand," said its director, a Cheyenne, "is that we survived" both conquest and Americanization. "We are still here, making vital contributions."

Indian protesters temporarily seized control of the Bureau of Indian Affairs building in Washington D.C., in 1972.

■ In what ways does the historical experience of Native Americans differ from that of other minority groups in the United States?

A government boarding school, designed to isolate Indian youth from their culture, looms over the old tribal lodgings on the Pine Ridge Reservation in 1891.

PEARSON
myhistorylab

From Then to Now Online

19-1 A government attempt to use schools to control and indoctrinate Indian children.

19-2 A Sioux woman recounts the dramatic impact of the American Indian Movement in the 1970s.

19-3 The director of the Bureau of Indian Affairs apologizes for its callous treatment of Indians in the past.

Farming the Land

Pioneer settlers had to make daunting adjustments to develop the agricultural potential of their new land. Advances in science, technology, and industry made such adjustments possible. The changes not only reshaped the agricultural economy but also challenged traditional rural values and expectations.

Growing crops.   Fencing was an immediate problem, for crops needed protection from livestock. But without timber, farmers could not build wooden fences. Barbed wire, developed in the mid-1870s, solved the problem. By 1900, farmers were importing nearly 300 million pounds of barbed wire each year from eastern and midwestern factories.

The aridity of most of the West also posed difficulties. In California, Colorado, and a few other areas, settlers used streams fed by mountain snow packs to irrigate land. Elsewhere, enterprising farmers developed variants of the "dry farming" practices that the Mormons had introduced in Utah to maximize the limited rainfall. Some farmers erected windmills to pump underground water. The scarce rainfall also discouraged the cultivation of many of the crops that supported traditional general agriculture and encouraged farmers to specialize in a single cash crop for market. Gradually, many plains farmers turned from corn to wheat, especially the drought-resistant Turkey Red variety of hard winter wheat that German Mennonites had introduced into Kansas from Russia. Government agencies and agricultural colleges contributed to the success of such adaptations, and private engineers and inventors also fostered agricultural development. Related technological advancements included grain elevators that would store grain for shipment and load it into rail cars mechanically and mills that used corrugated, chilled-iron rollers rather than millstones to process the new varieties of wheat.

Mechanization and technological innovations made possible the large-scale farming practiced in semiarid regions. Farmers required special plows to break the tough sod, new harrows to prepare the soil for cultivation, grain drills to plant the crop, and harvesting and threshing machines to bring it in. Thanks to more and better machines, agricultural efficiency and productivity shot up. By the 1890s, machinery permitted the farmer to produce 18 times more wheat than hand methods had. Nearly 1,000 corporations were manufacturing agricultural machinery to meet the demands of farmers, who purchased implements in steadily mounting quantities.

Growing tensions.   These developments reflected both the expansion of agriculture and its increasing dependence on the larger society. Western commercial farmers needed the high demand of eastern and midwestern cities and the expanding world market. The rail network provided essential transportation for their crops; the nation's industrial sector produced necessary agricultural machinery. Banks and loan companies extended the credit and capital that allowed farmers to take advantage of mechanization and other new advances; and many other businesses graded, stored, processed, and sold their crops. In short, because of its market orientation, mechanization, and specialization, western agriculture relied on other people or impersonal forces as it was incorporated into the national and international economy.

When conditions were favorable—good weather, good crops, and good prices—western farmers prospered. Too often, however, they faced adversity. The early years of settlement were unusually wet, but even then periodic droughts brought crop failures. Other natural hazards also disrupted production. Especially alarming were plagues of grasshoppers, forming what one woman described as a "cloud so dense that the sun was obscured and the earth was in darkness." Grasshoppers ate crops, clothing, and bedding; they attacked sod houses and chewed woodwork and furniture. Private relief organizations distributed food, clothing, and seed to farm families suffering from droughts and grasshoppers in the 1870s, and state governments and Congress appropriated public funds to combat destitution on the agricultural frontier.

In the late 1880s, drought coincided with a slump in crop prices. The large European market that had encouraged agricultural expansion in the 1870s and early 1880s contracted after 1885, when several nations erected trade barriers to U.S. commodities. More important, America's production competed with that from Argentina, Canada, Australia, and Russia, and a world surplus of grain drove prices steadily downward. The average price of wheat dropped from $1.19 a bushel in 1881 to only $0.49 in 1894; prices for other farm commodities also declined.

Squeezed between high costs for credit, transportation, and manufactured goods and falling agricultural prices, western farmers faced disaster. They responded by lashing back at their points of contact with the new system. They especially condemned the railroads, believing that the companies charged excessive and discriminatory freight rates. Luna Kellie complained of the railroads, "The minute you crossed the Missouri River your fate both soul and body was in their hands. What you should eat and drink, what you should wear, everything was in their hands and they robbed us of all we produced except enough to keep body and soul together and many many times not that."

Farmers censured the grain elevators in the local buying centers. Often owned by eastern corporations, including the railroads, elevators allegedly exploited their local monopoly to cheat farmers by fixing low prices or misrepresenting the quality of wheat. A Minnesota state investigation found that systematic fraud by elevators cost farmers collectively a massive sum. Farmers also denounced the bankers and mortgage lenders who had provided the credit for them to acquire land, equipment, and machinery. Much of the money had come from eastern investors seeking the higher interest rates in the West. With failing crops and falling prices, however, the debt burden proved calamitous for many farmers. Beginning in 1889, many western farms were foreclosed.

Stunned and bitter, western farmers concluded that their problems arose because they had been incorporated into the new system, an integrated economy directed by forces beyond their control. And it was a system that did not work well. "There is," one of them charged, "something radically wrong in our industrial system. There is a screw loose."

Conclusion

In a few decades, millions of people had migrated westward in search of new opportunities. With determination, ingenuity, and hard work they had settled vast areas, made farms and ranches, built villages and cities, brought forth mineral wealth, and imposed their values on the land. These were remarkable achievements, though tempered by the shameful treatment of Indians and the often destructive exploitation of natural resources. But if most westerners took pride in their accomplishments, and a few enjoyed wealth and power, many also grew discontented with the new conditions they encountered as the "Wild" West receded.

The farmers' complaints indicted the major processes by which the West was developed and exploited in the late nineteenth century. Railroad expansion, population movements, eastern investment, corporate control, technological innovations, and government policies had incorporated the region fully into the larger society. Indians experienced this incorporation most thoroughly and most tragically, losing their lands, their traditions, and often their lives; the survivors were dependent on the decisions and actions of interlopers determined to impose "Americanization," the name itself implying the adoption of national patterns.

Cowboys and miners also learned that the frontier merely marked the cutting edge of eastern industrial society. Both groups were wageworkers, often for corporations controlled by eastern capital, and if industrial technology directly affected miners more than cowhands, neither could escape integration into the national economy by managerial decisions, transportation links, and market forces. Most settlers in the West were farmers, but they too learned that their distinctive environment did not insulate them from assimilation into larger productive, financial, and marketing structures.

Western developments, in short, reflected and interacted with those of eastern industrial society. The processes of incorporation drained away westerners' hopes along with their products, and many of the discontented would demand a serious reorganization of relationships and power. Led by angry farmers, they turned their attention to politics and government, where they encountered new obstacles and opportunities.

Review Questions

1. Why was the completion of the first transcontinental railroad, described by Andrew J. Russell, celebrated from Boston to San Francisco? How did western railroads shape the settlement and development of the West and affect the East as well?

2. What factors were most influential in the subjugation of American Indians?

3. What were the major goals of federal Indian policy, and how did they change?

4. How did technological developments affect Indians, miners, and farmers in the West?

5. How did the federal government help transform the West?

6. In what ways did European investors, markets, and migrants influence the development of the American West?

Key Terms

Chisholm Trail (p. 538)

Dawes Act (p. 534)

Homestead Act (p. 541)

Little Bighorn, Battle of the (p. 531)

Sand Creek Massacre (p. 529)

Second Treaty of Fort Laramie (p. 531)

Wounded Knee Massacre (p. 532)

Recommended Reading

Ball, Eve. *Indeh: An Apache Odyssey* (1980). An absorbing collection of the Apaches' own memories of the "Indian wars."

Paul, Rodman W. *The Far West and the Great Plains in Transition* (1988). A valuable survey of regional development that devotes particular attention to mining.

Riley, Glenda. *The Female Frontier: A Comparative View of Women on the Prairie and the Plains* (1988). A useful guide to women's experiences in the West.

Weeks, Philip. *Farewell, My Nation: The American Indian and the United States, 1820–1890*, 2nd ed. (2001). Modern discussion of Indian policy that provides insights into the perspectives of the Indians.

White, Richard. *"It's Your Misfortune and None of My Own": A New History of the American West* (1991). An important and original analysis of the development of the West that highlights environmental, ethnic, labor, and social history.

Wyman, Mark. *Hard Rock Epic: Western Miners and the Industrial Revolution, 1860–1910* (1979). Miners experiencing the dual frontiers of the West and the industrial revolution.

Where to Learn More

■ **Little Bighorn Battlefield National Monument, Crow Agency, Montana.**   The site of Custer's crushing defeat includes a monument to the Seventh Cavalry atop Last Stand Hill. A newly authorized Indian Memorial will include sacred texts, artifacts, and pictographs of the Plains Indians. www.nps.gov/libi/home.htm

■ **National Museum of the American Indian, Smithsonian Institution, Washington DC.**   This spectacular museum opened in 2004 and reflects the world view of Native Americans, with exhibits on spirituality and identity, performances of traditional dances, and important lecture series. www.nmai.si.edu

■ **National Cowboy Hall of Fame, Oklahoma City, Oklahoma.**   This large institution contains an outstanding collection of western art, displays of cowboy and Indian artifacts, and both kitschy exhibitions of the mythic Hollywood West and serious galleries depicting the often hard realities of the cattle industry. Its many public programs also successfully combine fun with learning. www.cowboyhalloffame.org/index2.html

■ **Golden Spike National Historic Site, near Promontory, Utah.**   The completion of the transcontinental railroad here in 1869 is reenacted from May to October, using reproductions of the original locomotives. Visitors can drive the route of the railroad, now a National Backway Byway through abandoned mining and railroad towns, from Promontory to Nevada. Virtual tour, history, and tourist links. www.nps./gov/gosp

Study Resources

For study resources for this chapter, go to www.myhistorylab.com and choose *The American Journey*. You will find a wealth of study and review material for this chapter, including pre- and post-tests, customized study plan, key term review flash cards, interactive map and document activities, and documents for analysis.

In the late nineteenth century, parades like this Republican one in Canton, Ohio, in 1896 were popular features of a participatory political culture dominated by political parties and intense partisanship.

Politics and Government
1877–1900
20

The largest political procession of the season in Fort Wayne, so far, was that of the Republicans Saturday night. They turned out in very large numbers and paraded on the principal streets preparatory to the speaking which came later at the Rifles' armory. The following were in line:

First Regiment Band
Railroad Men's Club
Soldiers' and Sons' Union Club
Tippecanoe Club
Chase Club
Lincoln Club
McKinley Club
Colored Drum Corps
Colored Republicans' Club
Republican Voters

The McKinley Club wore tin hats and the Tippecanoe club carried torches that spouted fire at intervals. One of the prettiest illuminations was the railroad lantern light of the Railroad Men's Republican club. The numerous lights of the colors used in the railway service make as pretty a sight as can be seen anywhere.

Most of the clubs were in fine uniforms and made a grand appearance. Numerous banners and transparencies announcing mottoes of the campaign were carried. One banner bore the words, "Cleveland's record—Glad Lincoln was shot—Pronounced the war a failure."

The great parade was viewed by thousands of people who thronged the streets all along the line of march.

The hall was crowded and the meeting was most enthusiastic. Music was furnished by the band and Emerson quartette of Huntington.... The quartette just took the cake. Anything more enjoyable and mirth-provoking than their glees rendered as they render them would be hard to find. After music by the quartette, which was enthusiastically encored, Dr. Stemen, the presiding officer, introduced the speaker of the evening, Hon. L.R. Stookey, of Warsaw, Ind. Mr. Stookey is a ready and rapid speaker. He paid a glowing tribute to the soldiers, and referred in scathing terms to Grover Cleveland's treatment of them and his insulting vetoes of pension bills. He spoke…[of a law providing for election supervisors at the polls] and what we ask is that it shall apply without limitation north and south whenever there is an attempt or danger of attempt, to deny equal rights of all to cast their free ballot and have it counted as cast.

When he concluded the Emerson quartette gave another selection and responded to an encore. The audience then began to call loudly for "You," "You." Mr. A.J. You, our candidate for congress, was then introduced and made a stirring address. Mr. You has been speaking nearly every day and evening and is holding out first rate and proving himself one of the most popular candidates in the field.

He was repeatedly and enthusiastically cheered during his speech. Another selection by the quartette, and the house resounded with calls for "Brown," "Brown." Rev. W.H. Brown, for years the pastor of the A.M.E. church, of this city, took the platform and, though he protested that the hour was too late to permit another speech, made it clearly evident in the course of a twenty minute speech that the colored people of the country understand the situation and intend to stand by the party that broke the chains and gave freedom to the slave. The meeting then adjourned to music by the Glee club.

Source: *Fort Wayne* (Ind.) *Weekly Gazette*, October 20, 1892.

myhistorylab

Personal Journeys Online

- Susan B. Anthony, *Speech to the National American Woman Suffrage Association*, 1894. Asking Congress for political justice.

- Henry Vincent, *Marching through Iowa*, 1894. The journey of Kelly's "industrial army."

- William Jennings Bryan, 1896. Campaigning across America.

The Fort Wayne Gazette, a fiercely Republican newspaper, proudly reported on the activities of the local Republicans in Indiana during the political campaign in 1892. Their grand torchlight parade through the streets of Fort Wayne, the thronging and enthusiastic crowds, the lengthy and bombastic speeches all illustrate much about U.S. politics in the late nineteenth century. Parties mobilized ardently partisan voters into a politics of participation, which included political clubs, campaign festivities, and record-high turnouts on election day. The pageantry and hoopla made politics a major source of popular entertainment for Republicans and Democrats alike. But the extreme campaign rhetoric and outright misrepresentation of opponents—the Republican insistence that the Democratic presidential candidate, Grover Cleveland, had been pleased by the assassination of Abraham Lincoln matched a Democratic assertion that the "vile, wicked, evil, and odious" Republican candidate was "a bully toward the feeble and a truckler to the powerful"—indicated the intensity of partisan emotions. So did the military-style campaign, with uniformed marchers organized into companies, brigades, and divisions; with signs, slogans, and speeches referring to soldiers and the Civil War; with rallies held in armories. These campaign features also pointed to the enduring importance of the Civil War as a basis for partisan divisions and loyalties and marked electoral politics as a rough-and-tumble masculine business.

At the same time, contemporary issues did matter. The marchers' tin hats were an unmistakable and favorable reference to a controversial Republican tariff law that had so prohibitively taxed foreign tin plate that an American tin-plate-manufacturing industry emerged. Stookey's stump appeal for election supervisors to protect voters' rights at the polls similarly pointed to an important policy issue while hinting at the sometimes violent nature of elections, including the suppression of voters. It also emphasized that suffrage was often a contested issue.

The prominent role of Rev. Brown, the content of his speech, and the participation of the Colored Drum Corps and the Colored Republicans' Club in the parade show

CHRONOLOGY

1867	Patrons of Husbandry (the Grange) is founded.
1869	Massachusetts establishes the first state regulatory commission.
1873	Silver is demonetized in the "Crime of '73."
1874	Woman's Christian Temperance Union is organized.
1875	U.S. Supreme Court, in *Minor v. Happersett,* upholds denial of suffrage to women.
1876	Greenback Party runs presidential candidate.
1877	Rutherford B. Hayes becomes president after disputed election.
	Farmers' Alliance is founded.
	Supreme Court, in *Munn v. Illinois,* upholds state regulatory authority over private property.
1878	Bland-Allison Act requires the government to buy silver.
1880	James A. Garfield is elected president.
1881	Garfield is assassinated; Chester A. Arthur becomes president.
1883	Pendleton Civil Service Act is passed.
1884	Grover Cleveland is elected president.
1886	Supreme Court, in *Wabash v. Illinois,* rules that only the federal government, not the states, can regulate interstate commerce.
1887	Interstate Commerce Act is passed.
1888	Benjamin Harrison is elected president.
1890	Sherman Antitrust Act is passed.
	McKinley Tariff Act is passed.
	Sherman Silver Purchase Act is passed.
	National American Woman Suffrage Association is organized.
	Wyoming enters the Union as the first state with woman suffrage.
1892	People's Party is organized.
	Cleveland is elected to his second term as president.
1893	Depression begins.
	Sherman Silver Purchase Act is repealed.
1894	Coxey's Army marches to Washington.
	Pullman strike ends in violence.
1895	Supreme Court, in *Pollock v. Farmers' Loan and Trust Company,* invalidates the federal income tax.
	Supreme Court, in *United States v. E. C. Knight Company,* limits the Sherman Antitrust Law to commerce, excluding industrial monopolies.
1896	William Jennings Bryan is nominated for president by Democrats and Populists.
	William McKinley is elected president.
1900	Currency Act puts U.S. currency on the gold standard.

that partisan divisions in the United States overlapped with racial, religious, and other social divisions. Black voters, for instance, would "stand by the party that broke the chains and gave freedom to the slave." The journey to the polls, symbolized by the parade through Fort Wayne, invoked the most basic beliefs and values of Americans.

While the *Gazette* lavished praise on the Republican campaign and "our candidate" and ridiculed the opposition, its Democratic counterpart, the *Fort Wayne Sentinel*, extolled the success of the Democratic campaign, the enthusiasm of Democratic crowds, the integrity of Democratic candidates, and the despicable nature of the Republican Party. Such partisanship permeated journalism as well as nearly all aspects of public life, including government agencies, even those sworn to uphold the Constitution, such as Indiana's judiciary. As a crucial swing state, Indiana particularly experienced the influence of political organization and partisanship, but their presence and effects were felt throughout the United States.

These features of late-nineteenth-century politics would eventually be transformed in significant ways. But while they endured, they shaped not only campaigns and elections but also the form and role of government. Only a national crisis in the 1890s would finally cause some Americans to demand more of their political leaders and institutions.

The Structure and Style of Politics

Politics in the late nineteenth century was an absorbing activity. Campaigns and elections expressed social values as they determined who held the reins of government. Political parties dominated political life. They organized campaigns, controlled balloting, and held the unswerving loyalty of most of the electorate. While the major parties worked to maintain a sense of unity and tradition among their followers, third parties sought to activate those the major parties left unserved. Other Americans looked outside the electoral arena to achieve their political goals.

Campaigns and Elections

Political campaigns and elections generated remarkable public participation and enthusiasm. They constituted a major form of entertainment at a time when recreational opportunities were limited. Campaign pageantry absorbed communities large and small. In cities and towns across the nation, as in Fort Wayne, thousands of men in elaborate uniforms marched in massive torchlight parades to demonstrate partisan enthusiasm. Political picnics and camp meetings

served a comparable function in rural areas. Attending party meetings and conventions, listening to lengthy speeches appealing to group loyalties and local pride, gathering at the polls to watch the voting and the counting, celebrating victory and drowning the disappointment of defeat—all these provided social enjoyment and defined popular politics.

The excitement of political contests prompted the wife of Chief Justice Morrison Waite to write longingly on election day, 1876, "I should want to vote all day." But women, though they often identified with a political party, could not vote at all in national elections. Justice Waite himself had just a year earlier written the unanimous opinion of the Supreme Court (in *Minor v. Happersett*) that the Constitution did not confer suffrage on women. Men generally believed that weakness and sentimentality disqualified women from the fierce conflicts of the public realm.

Virtually all men participated in politics. In many states, even immigrants not yet citizens were eligible to vote and flocked to the polls. African Americans voted regularly in the North and irregularly in the South before being disfranchised at the end of the century. Overall, turnout was remarkably high, averaging nearly 80 percent of eligible voters in presidential elections between 1876 and 1900, a figure far greater than ever achieved thereafter (see Figure 20–1).

Political parties mobilized this huge electorate. They kept detailed records of voters, transported them to the polls, saw that they were registered where necessary, and sometimes even paid their poll taxes or naturalization fees to make them eligible. With legal regulations and public machinery for elections negligible, parties dominated the campaigns and elections. Until the 1890s, most states had no laws to ensure secrecy in voting, and balloting often took place in open rooms or on sidewalks. Election clerks and judges were not public officials but partisans chosen by the political parties.

Nor did public authorities issue official ballots. Instead voters used party tickets—strips of paper printed by the parties—listing only the names of the candidates of the party issuing them and varying in size and color. Casting a ballot thus revealed the voter's party allegiance. Tickets were distributed by paid party workers known as peddlers or hawkers, who stationed themselves near the polls, each trying to force his ticket on prospective voters. Contending hawkers contributed greatly to the election day chaos. Fighting and intimidation were so commonplace at the polls that one state supreme court ruled in 1887 that they were "acceptable" features of elections.

As the court recognized, the open and partisan aspects of the electoral process did not necessarily lead to election fraud, however much they shaped the nature of political participation. In these circumstances, campaigns and elections provided opportunities for men to demonstrate publicly their commitment to their party and its values, thereby reinforcing their partisan loyalties.

Nonvoting women, too, often exhibited their partisanship in this exciting political environment. Women wrote

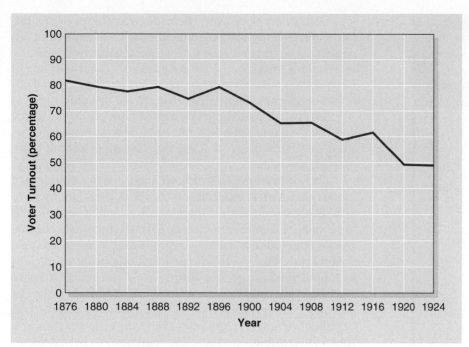

FIGURE 20–1   Voter Turnout in Presidential Elections, 1876–1924
The exciting partisan politics of the late nineteenth century produced very high voter turnouts, but as party competition declined and states enacted more restrictive voter regulations, popular participation in elections fell in the twentieth century.

partisan literature and gave campaign speeches; Anna Dickinson, one of the period's most popular orators, was hired by the Republican National Committee to campaign in the East and Midwest. Sometimes partisan women acted together with men; other times they worked through separate women's organizations. J. Ellen Foster established the Woman's National Republican Association in 1888 and built it into an organizing machine for the Republican Party with numerous state and local clubs. In these partisan groups women discussed and circulated party literature and devised plans to influence elections. Their partisanship was so deeply embedded that they remained loyal Republicans even when the party repudiated woman suffrage. "What discourages me about women," noted suffragist Susan B. Anthony, was that they care more for "[their] political party... than for [their] own political rights."

Partisan Politics

A remarkably close balance prevailed between the two major parties in the elections of this era. Democrats and Republicans had virtually the same level of electoral support, one reason they worked so hard to get out the vote (see Map 20–1). Control of the presidency and Congress shifted back and forth. Rarely did either party control both branches of government at once.

The party balance gave great influence to New York, New Jersey, Ohio, and Indiana, whose evenly divided voters controlled electoral votes that could swing an election either way. Both parties tended to nominate presidential and vice presidential candidates from those states to woo their voters. The parties also concentrated campaign funds and strategy on the swing states. Thus the Republican presidential candidate James Garfield of Ohio commented in 1880: "Nothing is wanting except an immediate and liberal supply of money for campaign expenses to make Indiana certain. With a victory there, the rest is easy." Garfield narrowly carried Indiana by 6,000 votes, and the nation by 9,000 out of 9.2 million cast. His victory was not the outcome of a contest over great issues but of carefully organized, tightly balanced parties mobilizing their supporters.

Party loyalty.   Interrelated regional, ethnic, religious, and local factors determined the party affiliations of most Americans. Economic issues, although important to the politics of the era, generally did not decide party ties. Farmers, for example, despite their many shared economic concerns, affiliated with both major parties. Like religious belief and ethnic identity, partisan loyalty was largely a cultural trait passed from parents to children, a situation that helps to explain the electoral stability of most communities.

Republicans were strongest in the North and Midwest, where they benefited from their party's role as the defender of the Union in the Civil War. "Republicanism in [Iowa] is not a logical conviction," reported one journalist in 1884; "it is a baleful fanaticism.... The war is still in progress in this region.... The women are worse than the men; they are intolerant, ferocious, implacable." But not all northerners voted for the Grand Old Party, or GOP. The Republican Party appealed primarily to old-stock Americans and other Protestants, including those of German and Scandinavian descent. African Americans, loyal to the party that had emancipated and enfranchised the slaves of the South, also supported the GOP where they could vote. Democrats were strongest in the South, where they stood as the defenders of the traditions of the region's white population. But Democrats also drew support in the urban Northeast, especially from Catholics and recent immigrants.

Party identities.   Each major party consisted of a complex coalition of groups with differing traditions and interests. One observer of the Democratic Party in California described it as "a sort of Democratic happy family, like we see in the prairie-dog villages, where owls, rattlesnakes, prairie dogs, and lizards all live in the same hole." This internal diversity often provoked conflict and threatened party stability. To hold its coalition together, each party identified itself

MAP EXPLORATION To explore an interactive version of this map, go to http://www.prenhall.com/goldfield5/map20.1

Elections of 1876–1892

Voted Republican 4–5 times

Voted Democratic 4–5 times

Voted more irregularly

MAP 20–1   The Two-Party Stalemate of the Late Nineteenth Century
Strong parties, staunch loyalties, and an evenly divided electorate made for exciting politics but often stalemated government in the late nineteenth century. Most states voted consistently for one of the major parties, leaving the few swing states like New York and Indiana the scenes of fierce partisan battles.

with a theme that appealed broadly to all its constituents, while suggesting that it was menaced by the members and objectives of the opposing party.

Republicans identified their party with nationalism and national unity and attacked the Democrats as an "alliance between the embittered South and the slums of the Northern cities." They combined a "bloody shirt" appeal to the memories of the Civil War with campaigns for immigration restriction and cultural uniformity. Seeing a threat to American society in efforts by Catholic immigrants to preserve their ethnic and cultural traditions, for example, Republican legislatures in several states in the 1880s and 1890s enacted laws regulating parochial schools, the use of foreign languages, and alcohol consumption. Similarly regarding Mormons as "subversive and treasonous" and engaged in "crime under the guise of religion," Republicans in both Congress and state legislatures enacted measures disfranchising them and otherwise restricting their civil rights.

Democrats portrayed themselves as the party of limited government and "personal liberties," a theme that appealed to both the racism of white southerners and the resentment immigrants felt about the nativist meddling of Republicans. The Democrats' commitment to personal liberties had limits. They supported the disfranchisement of African Americans, the exclusion of Chinese immigrants, and the dispossession of American Indians. Nevertheless, their emphasis on traditional individualism and localism proved popular.

The partisan politics of both major parties culminated in party machines, especially at the local level. Led by powerful bosses, such as the Democrat Richard Croker of New York and the Republican George Cox of Cincinnati, the machines controlled not only city politics but also municipal government. Party activists used well-organized ward clubs to mobilize working-class voters, who were rewarded with municipal jobs and baskets of food or coal doled out by the machine. Such assistance was often necessary, given the lack of public welfare systems, but to buy votes the machine also sold favors. Public contracts and franchises were peddled to businesses whose high bids covered kickbacks to the machine.

Third parties.   The partisan politics of the era left room for several third parties, organized around specific issues or groups. The **Prohibition Party** persistently championed the abolition of alcohol but also supported electoral reforms such as woman suffrage, economic reforms such as railroad regulation and income taxes, and social reforms including improved race relations. Some farmers and workers formed larger but shorter-lived third parties, charging that Republicans and Democrats had failed to respond to economic problems caused by industrialization or, worse still, had deliberately promoted powerful business interests at the expense of ordinary Americans. The **Greenback Party** of the 1870s denounced "the infamous financial legislation which takes all from the many to enrich the few." Its policies of labor reform and currency inflation (to stimulate and democratize the economy) attracted supporters from Maine to Texas. Other significant third parties included the Anti-Monopoly Party, the Union Labor Party, and, most important, the People's or **Populist Party** of the 1890s. Although third parties often won temporary success at the local or regional level, they never permanently displaced the major parties or undermined traditional voter allegiances.

Associational Politics
Much political activity was neither partisan nor electoral. Associations of like-minded citizens, operating as pressure groups, played an increasingly important role in late-nineteenth-century politics. These organizations worked to achieve public policies beneficial to their members. Farmers organized many such groups, most notably the Patrons of Husbandry, known familiarly as the Grange (see Chapter 17).

The Grange rejected partisanship but not politics. This sympathetic cartoon shows a Granger trying to warn Americans blindly absorbed in partisan politics of the dangers of onrushing industrialization.

Established in 1867, with both women and men eligible for membership, the Grange had 22,000 local lodges and nearly a million members by 1875. Its campaign for public regulation of the rates charged by railroads and grain elevators helped convince midwestern states to pass the so-called **Granger laws.** Labor organizations often pursued ambitious political agendas as well. Adopting nonpartisan tactics, the New Jersey Federation of Trades and Labor Unions drafted bills to require improved working conditions, testified before legislative committees, and marshaled delegations of workers to lobby for the measures.

Industrialists also formed pressure groups. Organizations such as the American Iron and Steel Association and the American Protective Tariff League lobbied Congress for high tariff laws and made campaign contributions to friendly politicians of both parties. At the state level business groups used their political clout to block the reform efforts of farmers and workers, sometimes in the legislatures but otherwise in the courts. Declaring that "lawmakers are too frequently influenced by public clamor and agitation for the cure of so-called social wrongs," the Illinois Manufacturers' Association in 1895 persuaded the Illinois Supreme Court to overturn a law establishing the eight-hour day for working women and girls.

A small group of conservative reformers known derisively as **Mugwumps** (the term derives from the Algonquian word for "chief") devoted most of their effort to campaigning for honest and efficient government through civil serv-

ice reform. They organized the National Civil Service Reform League to publicize their plans, lobby Congress and state legislatures, and endorse sympathetic candidates. Other pressure groups focused on cultural politics. The rabidly anti-Catholic American Protective Association, for example, agitated for laws restricting immigration, taxing church property, and inspecting Catholic religious institutions.

Christian lobbyists committed their political energies to demanding laws imposing their view of personal moral behavior. The National Bureau of Reforms described itself as "the channel by which the swift protests, petitions, and letters of the people can be brought to bear in the interest of righteousness upon the lawmakers, both of the nation and the states." It campaigned for laws requiring Sabbath observance (no entertainment, work, or travel on Sundays) and Bible reading in schools, restricting divorce on scriptural grounds, and prohibiting gambling and other "sinful" activities. The greatest success for such Christian lobbyists was the Comstock Law, passed by Congress in 1873, which outlawed the possession or sale of "obscene" materials, including any contraceptive information or devices. Directly affecting the lives of many Americans, the Comstock Law clearly revealed the importance of this type of political activism.

Women as activists.   Women also sought power and influence through associational politics. Susan B. Anthony and others formed groups to lobby Congress and state legislatures for constitutional amendments extending the right to vote to women. The leading organizations merged in 1890 as the **National American Woman Suffrage Association.** Despite the opposition of male politicians of both major parties, suffragists had succeeded by the mid-1890s in gaining full woman suffrage in four western states, Wyoming, Colorado, Idaho, and Utah, and partial suffrage (the right to vote in school elections) in several other states, east and west.

Other women shaped public issues through social service organizations. Although the belief that women belonged in the domestic sphere limited their involvement in electoral politics, it furnished a basis for political action focused on welfare and moral reform. With petition campaigns, demonstrations, and lobbying, women's social service organizations sought to remedy poverty and disease, improve education and recreation, and provide day nurseries for the children of workingwomen. The Illinois Woman's Alliance—organized in 1888 by suffragists, women assemblies of the Knights of Labor, and middle-class women's clubs—investigated the conditions of women and children in workshops and factories and campaigned successfully for protective labor legislation and compulsory school-attendance laws. The Woman's Municipal League, organized in New York City in 1894, described itself as a "political club" concerned with "education, sanitation, public health, and police and fire protection."

Women also combined domesticity and politics in the temperance movement. Alcoholism, widespread in U.S. society, was regarded as a major cause of crime, wife abuse, and

Women lobbying a Congressional committee to support woman suffrage. Susan B. Anthony noted with regret that "to all men women suffrage is only a side issue."

by present standards. The receding governmental activism of the Civil War and Reconstruction years coincided with a resurgent belief in localism and **laissez-faire** policies. In addition, a Congress and presidency divided between the two major parties, a small and inefficient bureaucracy, and judicial restraints joined powerful private interests to limit the size and objectives of the federal government.

The Weak Presidency

The presidency was a weak and restricted institution. The impeachment of President Johnson at the outset of Reconstruction had undermined the office. President Grant clearly subordinated it to the legislative branch by deferring to Congress on appointments and legislation. Other factors contributed as well. The men who filled the office between 1877 and 1897 — Republicans Rutherford B. Hayes (1877–1881), James A. Garfield (1881), and Chester A. Arthur (1881–1885); Democrat Grover Cleveland (1885–1889 and 1893–1897); and Republican Benjamin Harrison (1889–1893) — were all honest and generally capable. Each had built a solid political record at the state or federal level. But they were all conservatives, with a narrow view of the presidency, and proposed few initiatives. The most aggressive of them, Cleveland, used his energy in a singularly negative fashion, vetoing two-thirds of all the bills Congress passed, more than all his predecessors combined. Cleveland once vetoed a relief measure for drought-stricken Texas farmers with the statement that "though the people support the Government, the Government should not support the people." This attitude limited government action.

The presidents of this era viewed their duties as chiefly administrative. They made little effort to reach out to the public or to exert legislative leadership. (See Global Perspectives, Why Great Men Are Not Chosen Presidents.) In 1885, Woodrow Wilson, at the time a professor of history and government, described "the business of the president" as "not much above routine" and concluded that the office might "not inconveniently" be made purely administrative, its occupant a sort of tenured civil servant. (Wilson took a very different view when he became president himself in 1913, helping transform the presidency into a powerful office.)

The presidency was also hampered by its limited control over bureaus and departments, which responded more directly to Congress, and by its small staff, consisting of no more than a half-dozen secretaries, clerks, and telegraphers. As Cleveland complained, "If the President has any great policy in mind or on hand he has no one to help him work it out."

broken homes. The temperance movement thus invoked women's presumed moral superiority to address a real problem that fell within their accepted sphere. The Woman's Christian Temperance Union (WCTU) gained a massive membership by campaigning for restrictive liquor laws. It helped secure prohibition or local-option laws in a dozen states and was particularly successful in persuading legislatures to require temperance education in the public schools.

Under the leadership of Frances Willard, the WCTU built on traditional women's concerns to develop an important critique of American society. Reversing the conventional view, Willard argued that alcohol abuse was a result, not a cause, of poverty and social disorder. Under the slogan of "Home Protection," the WCTU inserted domestic issues into the political sphere with a campaign for social and economic reforms far beyond temperance. It pushed for improved health conditions, reached out to the Knights of Labor to support workplace reforms, and lobbied for federal aid to education, particularly as a means to provide schooling for black children in the South. It eventually supported woman suffrage as well, on the grounds that women needed the vote to fulfill their duty to protect home, family, and morality. The organization further expanded its political activities by establishing an office in Washington, which drafted model legislation, and developing effective lobbying techniques that other special-interest groups have subsequently followed.

The Limits of Government

Despite the popular enthusiasm for partisan politics and the persistent pressure of associational politics, government in the late nineteenth century was neither active nor productive

The Inefficient Congress

Congress was the foremost branch of the national government. It exercised authority over the federal budget, oversaw the cabinet, debated public issues, and controlled legislation. Its members were often state and national party leaders, who were strong-willed and, as one senator conceded, "tolerated no intrusion from the President or from anybody else."

But Congress was scarcely efficient. Its chambers were noisy and chaotic, and members rarely devoted their attention to the business at hand. The repeated shifts in party control impeded effective action. So, too, did the loss of experienced legislators to rapid turnover. In some Congresses, a majority of members were first-termers. Procedural rules, based on precedents from a simpler time and manipulated by determined partisans, hindered congressional action. Some rules restricted the introduction of legislation; others prevented its passage. The most notorious rule required that a quorum be not only present but voting. When the House was narrowly divided along party lines, the minority could block all business simply by refusing to answer when the roll was called.

But as a nationalizing economy required more national legislation, the amount of business before Congress grew relentlessly (see Figure 20–2). The expanding scale of congressional work prompted a gradual reform of procedures and the centralization of power in the Speaker of the House and the leading committees. These changes did not, however, create a coherent program for government action.

The Federal Bureaucracy and the Spoils System

Reflecting presidential weakness and congressional inefficiency, the federal bureaucracy remained small and limited in the late nineteenth century. There were little more than 50,000 government employees in 1871, and three-fourths of them were local postmasters scattered across the nation. Only 6,000, from President Grant to janitors, worked in Washington. The number of federal employees grew to 157,000 by 1891, but it was still the postal service that absorbed most of this increase.

The system for selecting and supervising federal officials had developed gradually in the first half of the century. Known as the spoils system, its basic principle was that victorious politicians awarded government jobs to party workers, often with little regard for qualifications, and ousted the previous employees. Appointees then typically promised part of their salary and time to the political interests of their patron or party. The spoils system played a crucial role in all aspects of politics. It enabled party leaders to strengthen their organizations, reward loyal party service, and attract the political workers needed to mobilize the electorate. Supporters described it as a democratic system that offered opportunities to many citizens and prevented the emergence of an entrenched bureaucracy.

Critics, however, charged that the system was riddled with corruption, abuse, and inefficiency. Rapid turnover bred instability; political favoritism bred incompetence. One secretary of the navy, appointed at the behest of Indiana's Republican machine, was said to have exclaimed during his first official inspection of a ship: "Why, the thing's hollow!" Certainly, the spoils system was ineffective for filling positions that required special clerical skills, such as typing, or scientific expertise like that required by the Weather Bureau (established in 1870) or the U.S. Geological Survey (established in 1879). Even worse, the spoils system absorbed the president and Congress in unproductive conflicts over patronage.

Inconsistent State Government

State governments were more active than the federal government. Considered closer and more responsible to the people, they had long exercised police power and regulatory authority. They collected taxes for education and public works, and they promoted private enterprise and public health. Still, they did little by today's standards. Few people thought it appropriate for government at any level to offer direct help to particular social groups. Some state governments contracted in the 1870s and 1880s, following the wartime activism of the 1860s, and new state constitutions restricted the scope of public authority.

Nonetheless, state governments gradually expanded their role in response to the stresses produced by industrial-

GRAPHIC EXPLORATION To explore an interactive version of this graph, go to http://www.prenhall.com/goldfield5/fig20.2

PEARSON
myhistorylab

FIGURE 20–2 Increase in Congressional Business, 1871–1901

Industrialization, urbanization, and western expansion brought increased demands for government action, but the party stalemate, laissez-faire attitudes, and inefficient public institutions often blocked effective responses.

ization. Following the lead of Massachusetts in 1869, most states had by the turn of the century created commissions to investigate and regulate industry. Public intervention in other areas of the economy soon followed. One observer noted in 1887 that state governments enacted many laws and established numerous state agencies in "utter disregard of the laissez-faire principle." In Minnesota, for example, the state helped farmers by establishing a dairy commission, prohibiting the manufacture or sale of margarine, creating a bureau of animal industry, and employing state veterinarians. In the lumber industry, state officials oversaw every log "from the woods to the saw-mill." State inspectors examined Minnesota's steam boilers, oil production, and sanitary conditions. Other laws regulated railroads, telegraphs, and dangerous occupations, prohibited racial discrimination in inns, and otherwise protected the public welfare.

Not all such agencies and laws were effective, nor were all state governments as diligent as Minnesota's. Southern states, especially, lagged, and one midwesterner complained that his legislature "meets in ignorance, sits in corruption, and dissolves in disgrace every two years." Still, the widening scope of state action represented a growing acceptance of public responsibility for social welfare and economic life and laid the foundation for more effective steps in the early twentieth century.

Public Policies and National Elections

Several great issues dominated the national political arena in the late nineteenth century, including civil service reform, tariffs, and business and financial regulation. Civil service reform attracted relatively little popular interest, but Americans argued passionately about even the smallest details of tariff, regulatory, and financial legislation. Rarely, however, did these issues clearly and consistently separate the major political parties. Instead, they divided each party into factions along regional, interest, and economic lines. As a consequence, these leading issues often played only a small role in determining elections and were seldom resolved by government action.

Civil Service Reform

Reform of the spoils system emerged as a prominent issue during the Hayes administration. The Mugwumps and other reformers wanted a professional civil service, based on merit and divorced from politics. They wanted officeholders to be selected on the basis of competitive written examinations and protected from removal on political grounds. They expected such a system to promote efficiency, economy, and honesty in government. But they also expected it to increase their own influence and minimize that of "mere politicians." As one Baltimore Mugwump said, civil service reform would replace ignorant and corrupt officeholders with "gentlemen . . . who need nothing and want nothing from government except the satisfaction of using their talents," or at least with "sober, industrious . . . middle-class persons who have taken over . . . the proper standards of conduct."

Not all Americans agreed with such haughty views. The *New York Sun* denounced "the proposition that men shall be appointed to office as the result of examinations in book learning and that they shall remain in office during life. . . . We don't want an aristocracy of office-holders in this country." And a midwestern newspaper declared, "A free land develops free men. They will accept no dictation from men who claim superior virtue or superior wisdom."

President Hayes favored civil service reform but did not fully renounce the spoils system. He rewarded those who had helped to elect him, permitted party leaders to name or veto candidates for the cabinet, and insisted that his own appointees contribute funds to Republican election campaigns. But he rejected the claims of some machine leaders and office seekers and struck a blow for change when he fired Chester A. Arthur from his post as New York customs-house collector after an investigation pronounced Arthur's patronage system "unsound in principle, dangerous in practice," and characterized by "ignorance, inefficiency, and corruption."

The weakness of the civil service reformers was dramatically underscored in 1880 when the Republicans, to improve their chances of carrying the crucial state of New York, nominated Arthur for vice president on a ticket headed by James Garfield of Ohio. They won, and Garfield immediately found himself enmeshed in the demands of the unreformed spoils system. He once complained to his wife, "I had hardly arrived before the door-bell began to ring and the old stream of office-seekers began to pour in. . . . All day long it has been a steeple chase, I fleeing and they pursuing." Within a few months of his inauguration in 1881, Garfield was assassinated by a disappointed and crazed office seeker, and Arthur became president.

Public dismay over this tragedy finally spurred changes in the spoils system. In 1883 Congress passed the **Pendleton Civil Service Act,** prohibiting federal employees from soliciting or receiving political contributions from government workers and creating the Civil Service Commission to administer competitive examinations to applicants for government jobs. The act gave the commission jurisdiction over only about 10 percent of federal positions but provided that presidents could extend its authority. And subsequent presidents did so, if sometimes only to prevent their own appointees from being turned out by a succeeding administration. A professional civil service free from partisan politics gradually emerged, strengthening the executive branch's ability to handle its increasing administrative responsibilities.

The new emphasis on merit and skill rather than party ties opened new opportunities to women. Federal clerks were

Why Great Men Are Not Chosen Presidents

U.S. politics and government were subjects of great interest to Europeans. Accustomed to monarchs, prime ministers, parliaments, and efficient civil service bureaucracies, they found perplexing the decentralized U.S. system of federalism, the emphasis on localism and laissez-faire, and the popular frenzy and organizational thrust of partisan politics. Nothing was more fascinating than the character of U.S. political leaders, who seemed to Europeans to be consistently unimaginative and dull. As one noted, "The only thing remarkable about them is that being so commonplace they should have climbed so high."

Lord James Bryce of Great Britain provided the classic European perspective on the U.S. presidency in 1888. "Europeans often ask," Bryce observed, "how it happens that this great office…is not more frequently filled by great and striking men?" This seemed particularly puzzling given that the United States boasted of an open society that rewarded ability, not one bound by the hereditary distinctions of aristocracy.

Most important in explaining the absence of "brilliancy" among U.S. presidents, Bryce ventured, was the political system of the United States, with its party-dominated politics and its limited government.

In America party loyalty and party organization have been hitherto so perfect that any one put forward by the party will get the full party vote if his character is good and his "record," as they call it, unstained.…Even those who admit his mediocrity will vote straight when the moment for voting comes. Besides, the ordinary American voter does not object to mediocrity. He has a lower conception of the qualities requisite to make a statesman than those who direct public opinion in Europe have. He likes his candidates to be sensible, vigorous, and, above all, what he calls "magnetic," and does not value, because he sees no need for, originality or profundity, a fine culture or a wide knowledge.…

After all,…a President need not be a man of brilliant intellectual gifts. Englishmen, imagining him as something like their prime minister, assume that he ought to be a dazzling orator, able to sway legislatures or multitudes, possessed also of the constructive powers that can devise a great policy or frame a comprehensive piece of legislation. They forget that the President does not sit in Congress,…submit bills nor otherwise influence the action of the legislature. His main duties are to be prompt and firm in securing the due execution of the laws and maintaining the public peace.… Eloquence, … imagination, profundity of thought or extent of knowledge…are not necessary.

■ How might the "ordinary American voter" in the late nineteenth century have defended the U.S. political system from Bryce's indictment?

nearly exclusively male as late as 1862, but by the early 1890s, women held a third of the clerical positions in the executive departments in Washington. These workers constituted the nation's first substantial female clerical labor force. Their work in public life challenged the conventional belief that a woman's ability and personality limited her to the domestic sphere. To succeed, clerks had to be assertive and competent, acquire managerial skills, and think of their careers as permanent, not temporary. One woman described her "brain work" as an examiner of accounts in the Interior Department in 1893 as "demanding the closest and most critical attention, together with a great deal of legal and business knowledge."

The Political Life of the Tariff
Americans debated heatedly over tariff legislation throughout the late nineteenth century. This complex issue linked basic economic questions to partisan, ideological, and regional concerns. Tariffs on imported goods provided revenue for the federal government and protected American industry from European competition. They promoted industrial growth but often allowed favored industries to garner high profits. By the 1880s, tariffs covered 4,000 items and generated more revenue than the government needed to carry on its limited operations.

Reflecting its commitment to industry, the Republican Party vigorously championed protective tariffs. Party lead-

561

HER PLATFORM GOING TO PIECES.

"BETWEEN THE TWO I SHALL HAVE A HEAVY FALL."

Political divisions over public policies often occurred within rather than between the major parties. Here the platform of the Democratic party ("Democracy") is splintering because of conflicting interests.

ers also claimed that American labor benefited from tariff protection. "Reduce the tariff, and labor is the first to suffer," declared William McKinley of Ohio. Most Democrats, by contrast, favored tariff reduction, a position that reflected their party's relatively laissez-faire outlook. They argued that lower tariffs would encourage foreign trade and, by reducing the treasury surplus, minimize the temptation for the government to pursue activist policies. They pointed out the discriminatory effects of high tariffs, which benefited some interests, such as certain manufacturers, but hurt others, such as some farmers, while raising the cost of living for all (see the Overview, Arguments in the Tariff Debates).

The differences between the parties, however, were often more rhetorical than substantial. They disagreed only about how high tariffs should be and what interests they should protect. Congressmen of both parties voted for tariffs that would benefit their districts. California Democrats called for protective duties on wool and raisins, products produced in California; Massachusetts Republicans, to aid their state's shoe manufacturers, supported tariffs on shoes but opposed tariffs on leather. A Democratic senator from Indiana, elected on a campaign pledge to reduce tariffs, summed up the prevailing rule succinctly: "I am a protectionist for every interest which I am sent here by my constituents to protect."

In the 1884 campaign, the Republican presidential candidate, James G. Blaine, maintained that prosperity and high employment depended on high tariffs. The Democrats' platform endorsed a lowered tariff, but their candidate, New York governor Grover Cleveland, generally ignored the issue. Unable to address this and other important issues, both parties resorted to scandal mongering. The Democrats exploited Blaine's image as a beneficiary of the spoils system, which convinced the Mugwumps to bolt to Cleveland. Blaine's nomination, resolved the Massachusetts Mugwumps, was "an insult to the conscience of the country." Republicans responded by exposing Cleveland as the father of an illegitimate child. One observer called the election "a more bitter, personal, and disgusting campaign than we have ever seen."

Cleveland continued to avoid the tariff issue for three years after his election, until the growing treasury surplus and rising popular pressure for tariff reduction prompted him to act. He devoted his entire 1887 annual message to attacking the "vicious, inequitable, and illogical" tariff, apparently making it the dominant issue of his 1888 reelection campaign. Once again, however, the distinctive political attribute of the period—intense and organized campaigning between closely balanced parties—forced both Democrats and Republicans to blur their positions. Cleveland proposed a Democratic platform that ignored his recent message and did not even use the word *tariff*. When the party convention adopted a tariff-reduction plank, Cleveland complained bitterly and named high-tariff advocates to manage his campaign. "What a predicament the party is placed in," lamented one Texas Democrat, with tariff reform "for its battle cry and with a known protectionist...as our chairman." Cleveland won slightly more popular votes than his Republican opponent, Benjamin Harrison of Indiana, but Harrison carried the electoral college, indicating the decisive importance of strategic campaigning, local issues, and large campaign funds rather than great national issues.

The triumphant Republicans raised tariffs to prohibitive levels with the McKinley Tariff Act of 1890. McKinley praised the law as "protective in every paragraph and American on every page," but it provoked a popular backlash that helped return the Democrats to power. Still, the Democrats made little effort to push tariff reform. The *Atlanta Constitution* mused about such tariff politics in a bit of doggerel:

It's funny 'bout this tariff, how they've lost it or forgot;
They were rushing it to Congress once; their collars were so hot
They could hardly wait to fix it 'till we harvested a crop;
Was it such a burnin' question that they had to let it drop?

The Beginnings of Federal Regulation

While business leaders pressed for protective tariffs and other public policies that promoted their interests, they otherwise used their great political influence to ensure governmental laissez-faire. Popular pressure nonetheless compelled

OVERVIEW

Arguments in the Tariff Debates

Area Affected	High-Tariff Advocates	Low-Tariff Advocates
Industry	Tariffs promote industrial growth.	Tariffs inflate corporate profits.
Employment	Tariffs stimulate job growth.	Tariffs restrict competition.
Wages and prices	Tariffs permit higher wages.	Tariffs increase consumer prices.
Government	Tariffs provide government revenue.	Tariffs violate the principle of laissez-faire and produce revenues that tempt the government to activism.
Trade	Tariffs protect the domestic market.	Tariffs restrict foreign trade.

Congress to take the first steps toward the regulation of business with the passage of the Interstate Commerce Act in 1887 and the Sherman Antitrust Act in 1890.

The rapid growth of great industrial corporations and their disruptive effects on traditional practices and values profoundly alarmed the public (see Chapter 18). Farmers condemned the power of corporations over transportation facilities and their monopolization of industries affecting agriculture, from those that manufactured farm machinery to those that ran flour mills. Small-business owners suffered from the destructive competition of corporations, workers were exploited by their control of the labor market, and consumers felt victimized by high prices. The result was a growing demand to rein in the corporations.

Popular concern focused first on the railroads, the preeminent symbol of big business. Both farm groups and business shippers complained of discriminatory rates levied by railroads. Consumers condemned the railroads' use of pooling arrangements to suppress competition and raise rates. The resulting pressure was responsible for the Granger laws enacted in several midwestern states in the 1870s to regulate railroad freight and storage rates. At first, the Supreme Court upheld this legislation, ruling in *Munn v. Illinois* (1877) that state governments had the right to regulate private property when it was "devoted to a public use." But in 1886, the Court ruled in *Wabash, St. Louis, and Pacific Railway Company v. Illinois* that only the federal government could regulate interstate commerce. This decision effectively ended state regulation of railroads but simultaneously increased pressure for congressional action. "Upon no public question are the people so nearly unanimous as upon the proposition that Congress should undertake in some way the regulation of interstate business," concluded a Senate committee. With the support of both major parties, Congress in 1887 passed the **Interstate Commerce Act.**

The act prohibited rebates, discriminatory rates, and pooling and established the **Interstate Commerce Commission (ICC)** to investigate and prosecute violations. The ICC was the first federal regulatory agency. But its powers were too limited to be effective. Senator Nelson Aldrich of Rhode Island, a leading spokesman for business interests, described the law as an "empty menace to great interests, made to answer the clamor of the ignorant." Railroads continued their objectionable practices and frustrated the commission by refusing to provide required information and endlessly appealing its orders to a conservative judiciary. In its first 15 years, only one court case was decided in favor of the ICC. Not surprisingly, then, popular dissatisfaction with the railroads continued into the twentieth century. Californian Frank Norris, in his novel *The Octopus* (1901), likened them to "a gigantic parasite fattening upon the lifeblood of an entire commonwealth."

Many people saw railroad abuses as indicative of the dangers of corporate power in general and demanded a broader federal response. As with railroad regulation, the first antitrust laws—laws intended to break up or regulate corporate monopolies—were passed by states. Exposés of the monopolistic practices of such corporations as Standard Oil forced both major parties to endorse national antitrust legislation during the campaign of 1888. In 1890, Congress enacted the **Sherman Antitrust Act** with only a single vote in opposition. But this near unanimity concealed real differences over the desirability and purpose of the law. Although it emphatically prohibited any combination in restraint of trade (any attempt to restrict competition), the law was vaguely written and too weak to prevent abuses. The courts further weakened the act, and presidents of both parties made little effort to enforce it. Essentially still unfettered, large corporations remained a threat in the eyes of many Americans.

The Money Question

Persistent wrangling over questions of currency and coinage made monetary policy the most divisive political issue. President Garfield suggested the complexities of this subject when he wryly declared that a member of Congress had been committed to an asylum after "he devoted himself almost exclusively to the study of the currency, became fully entangled with the theories of the subject, and became insane."

In the 1880s many Americans feared that corporate power had too much influence in government and was endangering popular liberty. The question, as posed by this cartoon, was "What are you going to do about it?"

In 1875, sound money advocates in Congress enacted a deflationary law that withdrew some greenbacks from circulation and required that the remainder be convertible into gold after 1878. This action forced the money issue into electoral politics. Outraged inflationists organized the Greenback Party. They charged that the major parties had "failed to take the side of the people" and instead supported the "great moneyed institutions." The Greenbackers polled more than a million votes in 1878 and elected 14 members of Congress, nearly gaining the balance of power in the House. As the depression faded, however, so did interest in the greenback issue, and the party soon withered.

Despite the sometimes arcane and difficult nature of the money question, millions of Americans adopted positions on it and defended them with religious ferocity.

Creditors, especially bankers, as well as conservative economists and many business leaders favored limiting the money supply. They called this a **sound money** policy and insisted that it would ensure economic stability, maintain property values, and retain investor confidence. Farmers and other debtors complained that this deflationary monetary policy would depress already low crop prices, drive debtors further into debt, and restrict economic opportunities. They favored expanding the money supply to match the country's growing population and economy. They expected this inflationary policy to raise prices, stimulate the economy, reduce debt burdens, and increase opportunities.

The conservative leadership of both major parties supported the sound money policy, but their rank-and-file membership, especially in the West and the South, included many inflationists. As a result, the parties avoided confronting each other on the money issue.

The conflict between advocates of sound money and inflation centered on the use of paper money, or "greenbacks," and silver coinage. The greenback controversy had its roots in the Civil War. To meet its expenses during the war, the federal government issued $450 million in greenbacks, paper money backed only by the credit of the United States, not by gold or silver, the traditional basis of currency. After the war, creditors demanded that the greenbacks be withdrawn from circulation. Debtors and other Americans caught up in the postwar depression favored retaining the greenbacks and even expanding their use.

The silver issue.   Inflationists then turned to the silver issue, which would prove more enduring and disruptive. Historically, the United States had been on a bimetallic standard, using both gold and silver as the basis of its currency. But after the 1840s, the market price of silver rose above the currency value assigned to it by the government. Silver miners and owners began to sell the metal for commercial use rather than to the government for coinage, and little silver money circulated. In 1873, Congress passed a law "demonetizing" silver, thereby making gold the only standard for U.S. currency. Gold-standard supporters hoped that the law would promote international trade by aligning U.S. financial policy with that of Great Britain, which insisted on gold-based currency. But they also wanted to prevent new silver discoveries in the American West from expanding the money supply.

Indeed, silver production soon boomed, flooding the commercial market and dropping the value of the metal. Dismayed miners wanted the Treasury Department to purchase their surplus silver on the old terms and demanded a return to the bimetallic system. More important, the rural debtor groups seeking currency inflation joined in this demand, seeing renewed silver coinage as a means to reverse the long deflationary trend in the economy. Many passionately denounced the "Crime of '73" as a conspiracy of eastern bankers and foreign interests to control the money system to the detriment of ordinary Americans.

Again, both major parties equivocated. Eastern conservatives of both parties denounced silver; southerners and westerners demanded **free silver,** meaning unlimited silver coinage. One New York Democrat complained that western and southern members of his party were "mad as wild Texas steers on this silver dollar business. As we pass each other in the streets they seem to sneer, and hiss through their teeth the words 'gold bug,' and look as if they would like to spit upon [us]." By 1878, a bipartisan coalition succeeded in passing the Bland-Allison Act. This compromise measure required the government to buy and coin at least $2 million of silver a month. However, the government never exceeded the minimum, and the law had little inflationary effect. Republican President Arthur and Democratic President Cleveland recommended repealing the Bland-Allison Act, but the parties avoided the silver issue in their national platforms, fearing its divisive effect.

After hard times hit rural regions in the late 1880s, inflationists secured passage of the Sherman Silver Purchase Act of 1890. The Treasury now had to buy a larger volume of silver and pay for it with treasury notes redeemable in either gold or silver. But this, too, produced little inflation, because the government did not coin the silver it purchased, redeemed the notes only with gold, and, as western silver production increased further, had to spend less and less to buy the stipulated amount of silver. Debtors of both parties remained convinced that the government favored the "classes rather than the masses." Gold-standard advocates (again, of both parties) were even less happy with the law and planned to repeal it at their first opportunity. The division between the two groups was deep and bitter.

The Crisis of the 1890s

In the 1890s, social, economic, and political pressures created a crisis for both the political system and the government. A third-party political challenge generated by agricultural discontent disrupted traditional party politics. A devastating depression spawned social misery and labor violence. Changing public attitudes led to new demands on the government and a realignment of parties and voters. These developments, in turn, set the stage for important political, economic, and social changes in the new century.

Farmers Protest Inequities

The agricultural depression that engulfed the Great Plains and the South in the late 1880s brought misery and despair to millions of rural Americans. Falling crop prices and rising debt overwhelmed many people already exhausted from overwork and alarmed by the new corporate order. "At the age of 52 years, after a long life of toil, economy, and self-denial, I find myself and family virtual paupers," lamented one Kansan. His family's farm, rather than being "a house of refuge for our declining years, by a few turns of the monopolistic crank has been rendered valueless." To a large extent, the farmers' plight stemmed from bad weather and international over-production of farm products. Seeking relief, however, the farmers naturally focused on the inequities of railroad discrimination, tariff favoritism, a restrictive financial system, and apparently indifferent political parties.

Credit inequities.   Angry farmers particularly singled out the systems of money and credit that worked so completely against agricultural interests. Government rules for national banks directed credit into the urbanized North and East at the expense of the rural South and West and prohibited loans on farm property and real estate. As a result, farmers had to turn to other sources of credit and pay higher interest rates. In the West, farmers borrowed from mortgage companies to buy land and machinery, but declining crop prices made it difficult for them to pay their debts, and mortgage foreclosures then crushed the hopes of many. In the South, the credit shortage interacted with the practices of cotton marketing and retail trade to create the sharecropping system, which trapped more and more farmers, black and white, in a vicious pattern of exploitation. Moreover, the government's policies of monetary deflation worsened the debt burden for all farmers.

Freight rates and tariffs.   Farmers protested other features of the nation's economic system as well. Railroad freight rates were two or three times higher in the West and South than in the North and East. The near-monopolistic control of grain elevators and cotton brokerages in rural areas left farmers feeling exploited. Protective tariffs on agricultural machinery and other manufactured goods further raised their costs. The failure of political parties and the government to devise effective regulatory and antitrust measures or to correct the inequities in the currency, credit, and tariff laws capped the farmers' anger. By the 1890s, many were convinced that the nation's economic and political institutions were aligned against them.

Farmers organize.   In response, farmers turned to the **Farmers' Alliance,** the era's greatest popular movement of protest and reform. Originating in Texas, the Southern Farmers' Alliance spread throughout the South and across the Great Plains to the Pacific coast. African American farmers organized the Colored Farmers' Alliance. The Northwestern Farmers' Alliance reached westward and northward from Illinois to Nebraska and Minnesota. In combination, these groups constituted a massive grassroots movement committed to economic and political reform.

The Farmers' Alliance restricted membership to men and women of the "producing class" and urged them to stand "against the encroachments of monopolies and in opposition to the growing corruption of wealth and power." At first, the Alliance organized farmers' cooperatives to market crops and purchase supplies. Although some co-ops worked well, most soon failed because of the opposition of established business interests. Railroads suppressed Alliance grain elevators by refusing to handle their wheat. In Leflore County, Mississippi, when members of the Colored Farmers' Alliance shifted their trade to an Alliance store, local merchants provoked a conflict in which state troops killed 25 black farmers, including the local leaders of the Colored Alliance.

The Alliance also developed ingenious proposals to remedy rural credit and currency problems. In the South, the Alliance pushed the subtreasury system, which called on the government to warehouse farmers' cotton and advance them credit based on its value (see Chapter 17). In the West, the Alliance proposed a system of federal loans to farmers, using land as security. This land-loan scheme, like the subtreasury system, was a political expression of greenbackism; it would have expanded the money supply while providing immediate relief to distressed farmers. These proposals were immensely popular among farmers, but the major parties and Congress rejected them. The Alliance also took up earlier calls for free silver, government control of railroads, and banking reform, again to no avail. Denouncing the indifference of the major parties and the institutions of government, William A. Peffer, the influential editor of the Alliance newspaper the *Kansas Farmer,* declared that the "time has come for action. The people will not consent to wait longer.... The future is full of retribution for delinquents."

The People's Party

In the West, discontented agrarians organized independent third parties to achieve reforms the major parties had ignored. State-level third parties appeared in the elections of 1890 under many names. All eventually adopted the labels "People's" or "Populist," which were first used by a Kansas party formed by members of the Farmers' Alliance, the Knights of Labor, the Grange, and the old Greenback Party. The new party's campaign, marked by grim determination and fierce rhetoric, set the model for Populist politics and introduced many of the movement's leaders. These people, women as well as men, were earnest organizers and powerful orators. One was *Kansas Farmer* editor Peffer. Others included "Sockless Jerry" Simpson, Annie Diggs, and Mary E. Lease.

When hostile business and political leaders attacked the Populist program as socialistic, Lease retorted, "You may call me an anarchist, a socialist, or a communist. I care not, but I hold to the theory that if one man has not enough to eat three times a day and another has $25,000,000, that last man has something that belongs to the first." Lease spoke as clearly against the colonial status experienced by the South and West: "The great common people of this country are slaves, and monopoly is the master. The West and South are bound and prostrate before the manufacturing East."

The Populist parties proved remarkably successful. They gained control of the legislatures of Kansas and Nebraska and won congressional elections in Kansas, Nebraska, and Minnesota. Their victories came at the expense of the Republicans, who had traditionally controlled politics in these states, and contributed to a massive defeat of the GOP in the 1890 midterm elections. Thereafter, Populists won further victories throughout the West. In the mountain states,

A PARTY OF PATCHES.
Grand Balloon Ascension—Cincinnati, May 20th, 1891.

Established interests ridiculed the Populists unmercifully. This hostile cartoon depicts the People's Party as an odd assortment of radical dissidents committed to a "Platform of Lunacy."

where their support came more from miners than from farmers, they won governorships in Colorado and Montana. On the Pacific coast, angry farmers found allies among urban workers in Seattle, Tacoma, Portland, and San Francisco, where organized labor had campaigned for reform since the 1880s. The Populists elected a governor in Washington, congressmen in California, and legislators in all three states. Even in the Southwest, where territorial status limited political activity, Populist parties emerged. In Oklahoma, the party drew support from homesteaders and tenant farmers; in Arizona, from miners and railroad workers; in New Mexico, from small stockraisers and poor Hispanics.

With their new political power, farmers enacted reform legislation in many western states. New laws regulated banks and railroads and protected debtors by capping interest rates and restricting mortgage foreclosures. Others protected unions and mandated improved workplace conditions. Still others made the political system more democratic. Populists were instrumental, for example, in winning woman suffrage in Colorado and Idaho, although the united opposition of Democrats and Republicans blocked their efforts to win it in other states.

In the South, the angry farmers did not initially form third parties but instead attempted to seize control of the dominant Democratic Party by forcing its candidates to pledge support to the Alliance platform. The rural southern electorate then swept these "Alliance Democrats" into office. But most of these Democrats then repudiated their Alliance pledges and remained loyal to their party and its traditional opposition to governmental activism. Betrayed again by the political system, disgruntled Alliance members began organizing their own Populist parties, but they faced obstacles that western farmers did not. A successful challenge to the entrenched Democrats would require the political cooperation of both white and black farmers, but that would expose Populists to demagogic attacks from Democrats for undermining white supremacy, frightening away potential white supporters. The *Baton Rouge Advocate,* for example, warned its readers that the Populists were "the most dangerous and insidious foe of white supremacy."

Some Southern Populists, black and white, did appeal for racial cooperation in political if not social action. In Texas, John B. Rayner, the "silver tongued orator of the colored race," spoke to racially mixed audiences across the state and helped shape the Texas Populist platform calling for "equal justice and protection under the law to all citizens without reference to race, color, or nationality." In Georgia, the Populist leader Tom Watson supported a biracial party organization and counseled white people to accept black people as partners in their common crusade. "You are kept apart," Watson told black and white southerners, "that you may be separately fleeced of your earnings. You are made to hate each other because upon that hatred is rested the keystone of the arch of financial despotism which enslaves you both."

But steeped in racism, most white southerners recoiled from the prospect of interracial unity. And for their part, most black people remained loyal to the Republican Party for its role in abolishing slavery and for the few patronage crumbs the party still threw their way. Moreover, primarily tenants and farm laborers, their interests were not identical to those of white landowning farmers who formed the core of the Populist Party. Unwilling or unable to mobilize black voters and largely unsuccessful in dislodging white voters from the Democratic Party, Populists in the South achieved but limited political success, making significant inroads only in the legislatures of Texas, Alabama, and Georgia, and sending Tom Watson to Congress.

National action.   Populists soon realized that successful reform would require national action. They met in Omaha, Nebraska, on July 4, 1892, to organize a national party and nominated former Greenbacker James B. Weaver for president. The party platform, known as the **Omaha Platform,** rejected the laissez-faire policies of the old parties: "We believe that the powers of government, in other words, of the people, should be expanded...to the end that oppression, injustice, and poverty shall eventually cease in the land." It demanded government ownership of the railroads and the telegraph and telephone systems, a national currency issued by the government rather than by private banks, the subtreasury system, free silver, a graduated income tax, and the redistribution to settlers of land held by railroads and spec-

ulative corporations. Accompanying resolutions endorsed the popular election of senators, the secret ballot, and other electoral reforms to make government more democratic and responsive to popular wishes. When the platform was adopted, "cheers and yells," one reporter wrote, "rose like a tornado from four thousand throats and raged without cessation for 34 minutes, during which women shrieked and wept, men embraced and kissed their neighbors...in the ecstasy of their delirium."

The Populists left Omaha to begin an energetic campaign. Weaver toured the western states and with Mary Lease invaded the Democratic stronghold of the South where some Populists tried to mobilize black voters. Southern Democrats, however, used violence and fraud to intimidate Populist voters and cheat Populist candidates out of office. Some local Populist leaders were murdered, and Weaver was driven from the South. One Democrat confessed that Alabama's Populist gubernatorial candidate "carried the state, but was swindled out of his victory... with unblushing trickery and corruption." Southern Democrats also appealed effectively to white supremacy, undermining the Populist effort to build a biracial reform coalition.

Elsewhere, too, Populists met disappointment. Midwestern farmers unfamiliar with Alliance ideas and organization ignored Populist appeals and stood by their traditional political allegiances. So did most eastern working-class voters, who learned little of the Populist program beyond its demand for inflation, which they feared would worsen their own conditions.

The Populists lost the election but showed impressive support. They garnered more than a million votes, carried several western states, and won hundreds of state offices throughout the West and in pockets of the South. Populist leaders immediately began working to expand their support, to the alarm of both southern Democrats and northern Republicans.

The Challenge of the Depression

The emergence of a significant third-party movement was but one of many developments that combined by the mid-1890s to produce a national political crisis. A harsh and lengthy depression began in 1893, cruelly worsening conditions not only for farmers but for most other Americans. Labor unrest and violence engulfed the nation, reflecting workers' distress but frightening more comfortable Americans. The persistent failure of the major parties to respond to serious problems contributed mightily to the growing popular discontent. Together these developments constituted an important challenge to America's new industrial society and government.

Although the Populists lost in 1892, the election nonetheless reflected the nation's spreading dissatisfaction. Voters decisively rejected President Harrison and the incumbent Republicans in Congress, putting the Democrats in

FROM THEN TO NOW

Political Parties

Few things in contemporary American politics present a sharper contrast to the nineteenth century than the role of political parties. In the late nineteenth century, parties dominated both politics and government, commanding the allegiance of Americans, controlling the selection of candidates, mobilizing voters, providing ballots, running elections, staffing government positions. Today, parties do practically none of these things.

This transformation began at the end of the nineteenth century. Extreme partisanship alienated increasing numbers of voters and prompted states to assert control over elections and parties. Civil service reform steadily reduced party influence in government. So did the evolution of special-interest lobbying groups and the growing reliance in the twentieth century on independent regulatory commissions, rather than partisan legislative committees, to make and implement policies. The introduction and spread of primary elections stripped parties of their control over nominations. Individual candidates now rely more on personal organizations than the party apparatus to manage campaigns and communicate directly to voters through the mass media rather than through party workers. Campaign finance reform laws and the rise of political action committees (PACs) have reduced party control over the funding and direction of campaigns. Finally, declining numbers of Americans identify with a particular party, with nearly half the electorate in favor of making all elections nonpartisan or even of abolishing parties. Fewer and fewer Americans bother to vote, and those who do are much more likely than before to split their ticket, voting for candidates of different parties for different offices. This often results in divided government—with the Congress controlled by one party and the presidency by the other, producing a stalemate that increases public cynicism about parties.

Of course, parties endure and retain some importance. Election laws favor the two established parties, public funds subsidize party activities, Congress and state legislatures continue to rely on party divisions to organize their leadership and committee structures, and party discipline still influences the way legislators vote. But while such institutional factors guarantee the continuation of the two-party system, the parties themselves no longer enjoy the influence they had in the nineteenth century.

■ What are the advantages and the drawbacks of the historical decline of party influence in American political life?

Partisanship asserts its influence in government offices in this 1881 cartoon for civil service reform.

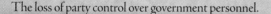
The loss of party control over government personnel.

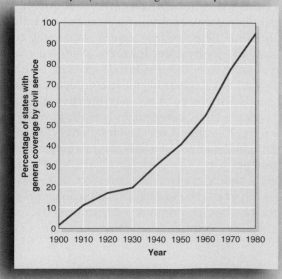

PEARSON
myhistorylab
From Then to Now Online

20-1 *Leaving the Party*. American labor song.

20-2 J. S. Clarkson, *In Defense of Politicians and Parties*, 1891. A leading Republican defends partisan politics and the spoils system.

control of Congress and Grover Cleveland back in the White House. But the conservative Cleveland was almost oblivious to the mounting demand for reform. He delivered an inaugural address championing laissez-faire and rejecting government action to solve social or economic problems.

Cleveland's resolve was immediately tested when the economy collapsed in the spring of 1893. Railroad overexpansion, a weak banking system, tight credit, and plunging agricultural prices all contributed to the disaster. So too did a depression in Europe, which reduced American export markets and prompted British investors to sell their American investments for gold. Hundreds of banks closed, and thousands of businesses, including the nation's major railroads, went bankrupt. By winter, 20 percent of the labor force was unemployed, and the jobless scavenged for food in a country that had no public unemployment or welfare programs. "Never within memory," said one New York minister, "have so many people literally starved to death as in the past few months."

Churches, local charity societies, and labor unions tried to provide relief but were overwhelmed. Most state governments offered little relief beyond encouraging private charity to the homeless. In Kansas, however, the Populist governor insisted that traditional laissez-faire policies were inadequate: "It is the duty of government to protect the weak, because the strong are able to protect themselves." (See American Views, A Populist Views American Government.) Cleveland disagreed and showed little sympathy for the struggling. The functions of the government, he said, "do not include the support of the people."

Appeals for federal action.   If Cleveland and Congress had no idea how the federal government might respond to the depression, other Americans did. Jacob Coxey, a Populist businessman from Ohio, proposed a government public-works program for the unemployed to be financed with paper money. This plan would improve the nation's infrastructure, create jobs for the unemployed, and provide an inflationary stimulus to counteract the depression's deflationary effects. In short, Coxey advocated positive government action to combat the depression. Elements of his plan would be adopted for mitigating economic downturns in the twentieth century; in 1894, it was too untraditional for Congress to consider.

Coxey organized a march of the unemployed to Washington as "a petition with boots on" to support his ideas. **Coxey's Army** of the unemployed, as the excited press dubbed it, marched through the industrial towns of Ohio and Pennsylvania and into Maryland, attracting attention and support. Other armies formed in eastern cities from Boston to Baltimore and set out for the capital. Some of the largest armies organized in the western cities of Denver, San Francisco, and Seattle. Three hundred men in an army from Oakland elected as their commander Anna Smith, who promised to "land my men on the steps of the Capitol at Washington." "I'm not afraid of anything," Smith explained. "I have a woman's heart and a woman's sympathy, and these lead me to do what I have done for these men, even though it may not be just what a woman is expected to do."

Lewis Fry, the organizer of the Los Angeles army, declared: "If the government has a right to make us die in time of war, we have the right to demand of her the right to live in time of peace." Fry's 500 marchers captured a train to cross the Southwest and were feted and fed by townspeople from Tucson to El Paso. When the Southern Pacific uncoupled the train's locomotive and left the marchers stranded without food or water in West Texas, the governor of Texas threatened to hold the railroad responsible for murder "by torture and starvation." Texas citizens quickly raised funds to speed the army on to St. Louis. From there it marched to Washington on foot.

The sympathy and assistance with which Americans greeted these industrial armies reflected more than anxiety over the depression and unemployment. As one economist noted, what distinguished the Populists and Coxeyites from earlier reformers was their appeal for federal action. Their substantial public support suggested a deep dissatisfaction with the failure of the government to respond to social and economic needs.

Nonetheless, the government acted to suppress Coxey. When he reached Washington with 600 marchers, police and soldiers arrested him and his aides, beat sympathetic bystanders in a crowd of 20,000, and herded the marchers into detention camps. Unlike the lobbyists for business and finance, Coxey was not permitted to reach Congress to deliver his statement urging the government to assist "the poor and oppressed."

Protecting big business.   The depression also provoked labor turmoil. In 1894, there were some 1,400 industrial strikes, involving nearly 700,000 workers, the largest number of strikers in any year in the nineteenth century. Cleveland had no response except to call for law and order. One result was the government's violent suppression of the Pullman strike (see Chapter 18).

In a series of decisions in 1895, the Supreme Court strengthened the bonds between business and government. First, it upheld the use of a court-ordered injunction to break the Pullman strike. As a result, injunctions became a major weapon for courts and corporations against labor unions, until Congress finally limited their use in 1932. Next, in *United States v. E. C. Knight Company,* the Court gutted the Sherman Antitrust Act by ruling that manufacturing, as opposed to commerce, was beyond the reach of federal regulation. Finally, the Court invalidated an income tax that agrarian Democrats and Populists had maneuvered through Congress. The conservative Court rejected the reform as an "assault upon capital." A dissenting justice noted that the decision gave vested interests "a power and influence" dangerous to

Jacob Coxey's "Army" of the unemployed marches to Washington, D.C., in 1894. Many such "industrial armies" were organized during the depressed 1890s, revealing dissatisfaction with traditional politics and limited government.

the majority of Americans. Not until 1913, and then only with an amendment to the Constitution, would it be possible to adopt an equitable system of taxation.

Surveying these developments, farmers and workers increasingly concluded that the government protected powerful interests while ignoring the plight of ordinary Americans. Certainly the callous treatment shown workers contrasted sharply with Cleveland's concern for bankers as he managed the government's monetary policy in the depression. Cleveland blamed the economic collapse on the Sherman Silver Purchase Act, which he regarded as detrimental to business confidence and a threat to the nation's gold reserve. He persuaded Congress in 1893 to repeal the law, enraging southern and western members of his own party. These Silver Democrats condemned Cleveland for betraying the public good to "the corporate interests."

Cleveland's policy failed to end the depression. By 1894, the Treasury began borrowing money from Wall Street to bolster the gold reserve. These transactions benefited a syndicate of bankers headed by J. P. Morgan. It seemed to critics that an indifferent Cleveland was helping rich bankers profit from the nation's economic agony. "A set of vampires headed by a financial trust has control of our destiny," cried one rural newspaper.

The Battle of the Standards and the Election of 1896

The government's unpopular actions, coupled with the unrelenting depression, alienated workers and farmers from the Cleveland administration and the Democratic Party. In the off-year elections of 1894, the Democrats suffered the greatest loss of congressional seats in American history. Populists increased their vote by 42 percent, making especially significant gains in the South. In North Carolina, for example, they gained control of the legislature and promptly enacted important electoral, economic, and educational reforms long blocked by the Democrats. But the real beneficiaries of the popular hatred of Cleveland and his policies were the Republicans. Denouncing Cleveland's "utter imbecility," they gained solid control of Congress as well as state governments across the North and West. All three parties began to plan for the presidential election of 1896.

As hard times persisted, the silver issue came to overshadow all others. Some Populist leaders, hoping to broaden the party's appeal, began to emphasize silver rather than the more radical but divisive planks of the Omaha Platform. Many southern and western Democrats, who had traditionally favored silver inflation, also decided to stress the issue, both to undercut the Populists and to distance themselves and their party from the despised Cleveland. They held rallies and conventions across the South and West, distributed silver literature, and argued that free silver would finally end the depression.

McKinley and the Republicans.   William McKinley, governor of Ohio and author of the McKinley Tariff Act of 1890, emerged as the front-runner of a crowd of hopeful Republican presidential candidates. His candidacy benefited particularly from the financial backing and political management of Mark Hanna, a wealthy Ohio industrialist. Hanna thought that McKinley's passion for high tariffs as the key to revived prosperity would appeal to workers as well as to industry and business. As governor, McKinley had reached out to workers by supporting pro-labor legislation and by avoiding the anti-Catholic positions that alienated immigrants from the Republican Party. Nonetheless, he shared Hanna's conviction that government should actively promote business in-

William Jennings Bryan in 1896. A powerful orator of great human sympathies, Bryan was adored by his followers as "the majestic man who was hurling defiance in the teeth of the money power." Nominated three times for the presidency by the Democrats, he was never elected.

terests; he was not Hanna's puppet, as opponents sometimes claimed.

The Republicans nominated McKinley on the first ballot at their 1896 convention. Their platform called for high tariffs but also endorsed the gold standard, placating eastern delegates but prompting several western Silver Republicans to withdraw from the party.

Bryan and the Silverites.   When the Democratic convention met, embattled supporters of the gold standard soon learned that the silver crusade had made them a minority in the party. With a fervor that conservatives likened to "scenes of the French Revolution," the Silver Democrats revolutionized their party. They adopted a platform repudiating Cleveland and his policies and endorsing free silver, the income tax, and tighter regulation of trusts and railroads. A magnificent speech supporting this platform by William Jennings Bryan helped convince the delegates to nominate him for president. Bryan was only 36 years old, but he had already served in Congress, edited an important newspaper, and gained renown for his oratorical skills and popular sympathies.

Holding their convention last, the Populists faced a terrible dilemma. The Democratic nomination of Bryan on a silver platform undercut their hopes of attracting disappointed reformers from the major parties. Bryan, moreover, had already worked closely with Nebraska Populists, who now urged the party to endorse him rather than split the silver vote and ensure the victory of McKinley and the gold standard. Other Populists argued that fusing—joining with the Democrats—would cost the Populists their separate identity and subordinate their larger political principles to the issue of free silver. After anguished discussion, the Populists nominated Bryan for president but named a separate vice presidential candidate, Tom Watson of Georgia, in an effort to maintain their identity. They hoped the Democrats would reciprocate by replacing their nominee with Watson, but the Democrats ignored the overture. The Populists' strength was in the South and West, regions that Bryan would control anyway. They could offer him little help in the battle for the Midwest and East, what Bryan called "the enemy's country."

Money and oratory.   The campaign was intense and dramatic, with each side demonizing the other. Eastern financial and business interests contributed millions of dollars to Hanna's campaign for McKinley. Standard Oil alone provided $250,000, about the same amount as the Democrats' total national expenses. Hanna used these funds to organize an unprecedented campaign. Shifting the emphasis from parades to information, Republicans issued 250 million campaign documents in a dozen languages, warning of economic disaster should Bryan be elected and the bimetallic standard be restored, but promising that McKinley's election would finally end the depression. Republicans were aided by a na-

American Views

A Populist Views American Government

An educator, merchant, and former editor, Lorenzo D. Lewelling became one of the most articulate champions of the Populist Party and its principles. Elected governor of Kansas in 1892, he headed what was heralded as "The First People's Party Government on Earth." On January 9, 1893, Lewelling delivered his inaugural address, in which he declared, "I appeal to the people of this great commonwealth to array themselves on the side of humanity and justice." The following passages from the speech sketch out Lewelling's views of the 1890s and his "dream of the future."

- How does Lewelling's rhetoric reflect the deep divisions of the 1890s?
- What is Lewelling's view of the proper role of government?
- For what does Lewelling criticize the government of the 1890s?
- What does Lewelling mean by his statement that "the rich have no right to the property of the poor"?

The survival of the fittest is the government of brutes and reptiles, and such philosophy must give place to a government which recognizes human brotherhood. It is the province of government to protect the weak, but the government today is resolved into a struggle of the masses with the classes for supremacy and bread, until business, home, and personal integity are trembling in the face of possible want in the family. Feed a tiger regularly and you tame and make him harmless, but hunger makes tigers of men. If it be true that the poor have no right to the property of the rich let it also be declared that the rich have no right to the property of the poor.

It is the mission of Kansas to protect and advance the moral and material interests of all its citizens. It is its especial duty at the present time to protect the producer from the ravages of combined wealth. National legislation has for twenty years fostered and protected the interests of the few, while it has left the South and West to supply the products with which to feed and clothe the world, and thus to become the servants of wealth.

The demand for free coinage has been refused. The national banks have been permitted to withdraw their circulation, and thus the interests of the East and West have been diverged until the passage of the McKinley bill culminated in their diversement. The purchasing power of the dollar has become so great [that] corn, wheat, beef, pork, and cotton have scarcely commanded a price equal to the cost of production.

The instincts of patriotism have naturally rebelled against these unwarranted encroachments of the power of money. Sectional hatred has also been kept alive by the old powers, the better to enable them to control the products and make the producer contribute to the millionaire; and thus, while the producer labors in the field, the shop, and the factory, the millionaire usurps his earnings and rides in gilded carriages with liveried servants....

The problem of today is how to make the State subservient to the individual, rather than to become his master. Government is a voluntary union for the common good. It guarantees to the individual life, liberty, and the pursuit of happiness. The government then must make it possible for the citizen to enjoy liberty and pursue happiness. If the government fails of these things, it fails in its mission....If old men go to the poor-house and young men go to prison, something is wrong with the economic system of the government.

What is the State to him who toils, if labor is denied him and his children cry for bread? What is the State to the farmer who wearily drags himself from dawn till dark to meet the stern necessities of the mortgage on the farm? What is the State to him if it sanctions usury and other legal forms by which his home is destroyed and his innocent ones become a prey to the fiends who lurk in the shadow of civilization? What is the State to the business man, early grown gray, broken in health and spirit by successive failures; anxiety like a boding owl his constant companion by day and the disturber of his dreams by night? How is life to be sustained, how is liberty to be enjoyed, how is happiness to be pursued under such adverse conditions as the State permits if it does not sanction? Is the State powerless against these conditions?

This is the generation which has come to the rescue. Those in distress who cry out from the darkness shall not be heard in vain. Conscience is in the saddle. We have leaped the bloody chasm and entered a contest for the protection of home, humanity, and the dignity of labor.

The grandeur of civilization shall be emphasized by the dawn of a new era in which the people shall reign, and if found necessary they will "expand the powers of government to solve the enigmas of the times." The peo-ple are greater than the law or the statutes, and when a nation sets its heart on doing a great and good thing it can find a legal way to do it.

I have a dream of the future. I have the evolution of an abiding faith in human government, and in the beau-tiful vision of a coming time I behold the abolition of poverty. A time is foreshadowed when the withered hand of want shall not be outstretched for charity; when lib-erty, equality, and justice shall have permanent abiding places in the republic.

Source: *People's Party Paper* (Atlanta), January 20, 1893.

tional press so completely sympathetic that many newspapers not only shaped their editorials but distorted their news sto-ries to Bryan's disadvantage.

Lacking the Republicans' superior resources, the Demo-crats relied on Bryan's superb speaking ability and youthful energy. Bryan was the first presidential candidate to cam-paign systematically, speaking hundreds of times to millions of voters. By contrast, McKinley stayed home in Canton, Ohio, where he conducted a "front porch" campaign. Ex-plaining his refusal to campaign outside Canton, McKinley said, "I might just as well put up a trapeze...and compete with some professional athlete as go out speaking against Bryan." But Hanna brought groups of Republicans from all over the country to visit McKinley every day, and McKinley reiterated his simple promise of prosperity.

In the depression, that appeal proved enough. As the Democratic candidate, Bryan was, ironically, burdened with the legacy of the hated Cleveland administration. The in-tense campaign brought a record voter turnout. McKinley won decisively by capturing the East and Midwest as well as Oregon and California (see Map 20–2). Bryan carried the tra-ditionally Democratic South and the mountain and plains states, where Populists and silverites dominated. He failed to gain support in either the Midwest or the cities of the East. His silver campaign had little appeal to industrial workers. Hanna realized that Bryan was making a mistake in subordi-nating other popular grievances to silver: "He's talking sil-ver all the time, and that's where we've got him."

Bryan immediately wrote a personal account of the cam-paign, which he optimistically titled *The First Battle*. But Bryan and the Democrats would not win subsequent bat-tles, at least not on the issues of the 1890s. The elections of 1894 and 1896 ended the close balance between the major parties. Cleveland's failures, coupled with an economic re-covery in the wake of the election of 1896, gained the Re-

This Republican campaign poster of 1896 depicts William McKin-ley standing on sound money and promising a revival of prosperity. The depression of the 1890s shifted the electorate into the Republi-can column.

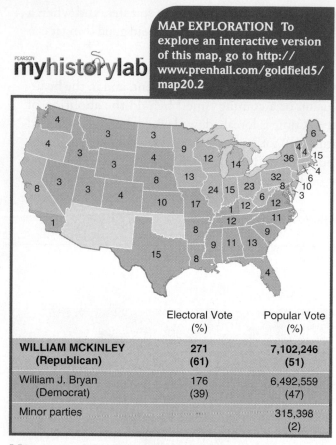

MAP EXPLORATION To explore an interactive version of this map, go to http://www.prenhall.com/goldfield5/map20.2

PEARSON
myhistorylab

	Electoral Vote (%)	Popular Vote (%)
WILLIAM MCKINLEY (Republican)	**271 (61)**	**7,102,246 (51)**
William J. Bryan (Democrat)	176 (39)	6,492,559 (47)
Minor parties		315,398 (2)

MAP 20–2   The Election of 1896
William Jennings Bryan carried most of the rural South and West, but his free silver campaign had little appeal to more urban and industrial regions, which swung strongly to Republican candidate William McKinley.

publicans a reputation as the party of prosperity and industrial progress, firmly establishing them in power for years to come. By contrast, the Democratic Party receded into an ineffectual sectional minority dominated by southern conservatives, despite Bryan's liberal views.

The People's Party simply dissolved. Demoralized by fusion with the Democrats, who had earlier violently repressed them, many southern Populists dropped out of politics. The Democrats' disfranchisement laws, directed at discontented poor white southerners as well as poor black southerners, further undermined the Populists in the South. In the West, the silver tide of 1896 carried many Populists into office, but with their party collapsing, they had no hope of reelection. By 1898, the Populist Party had virtually disappeared. Its reform legacy, however, proved more enduring. The issues it raised would continue to shape state and national politics.

McKinley plunged into his presidency. Unlike his predecessors, he had a definite, if limited, program, consisting of tariff protection, sound money, and overseas expansion. He worked actively to see it through Congress and to shape public opinion, thereby helping establish the model of the mod-

ern presidency. He had promised prosperity, and it returned, although not because of the record high tariff his party enacted in 1897 or the Currency Act of 1900, which firmly established the gold standard. Prosperity returned, instead, because of reviving markets and a monetary inflation that resulted from the discovery of vast new deposits of gold in Alaska, Australia, and South Africa. The silverites had recognized that an expanding industrial economy required an expanding money supply. Ironically, the new inflation was greater than the inflation that would have resulted from free silver. With the return of prosperity and the decline of social tensions, McKinley easily won reelection in 1900, defeating Bryan a second time.

Conclusion

In late-nineteenth-century America, politics and government often seemed at cross-purposes. Political contests were exciting events, absorbing public attention, attracting high voter turnout, and often raising issues of symbolic or substantive importance. Closely balanced political parties commanded the zealous support of their constituents and wielded power and influence. The institutions of government, by contrast, were limited in size, scope, and responsibility. A weakened presidency and an inefficient Congress, hampered by a restrictive judiciary, were often unable to resolve the very issues that were so dramatically raised in the political arena. The persistent disputes over tariff and monetary policy illustrate this impasse. But the issue that most reflected it was civil service reform. The patronage system provided the lifeblood of politics but also disrupted government business.

Localism, laissez-faire, and other traditional principles that shaped both politics and government were becoming increasingly inappropriate for America's industrializing society. New challenges were emerging that state and local governments could not effectively solve on their own. The national nature of the railroad network, for example, finally brought the federal government into the regulatory arena, however imperfectly, with the Interstate Commerce Act of 1887. Both the depression of the 1890s and the popular discontent articulated most clearly by the Populist rejection of laissez-faire underscored the need for change and discredited the limited government of the Cleveland administration.

By the end of the decade, the political system had changed. The Republicans had emerged as the dominant party, ending the two-party stalemate of previous decades. Campaign hoopla in local communities had given way to information-based campaigns directed by and through national organizations. A new, activist presidency was emerging. And the disruptive currency issue faded with the hard times that had brought it forth. Still greater changes were on the horizon. The depression and its terrible social and economic consequences undermined traditional ideas about the responsibilities of government and increased public support for activist policies. The stage was set for the Progressive Era.

Review Questions

1. What social and institutional factors shaped the disorderly nature of elections in the late nineteenth century? How did they operate in U.S. politics?

2. What social and institutional factors determined the role of government? How and why did the role of government change during this period?

3. What factors determined the party affiliation of American voters? Why did so many third parties develop during this era?

4. How might the planks of the Omaha Platform have helped solve farmers' troubles?

5. What factors shaped the conduct and outcome of the election of 1896? How did that contest differ from earlier elections?

Key Terms

Coxey's Army (p. 569)

Farmers' Alliance (p. 565)

Free silver (p. 564)

Granger laws (p. 557)

Greenback Party (p. 556)

Interstate Commerce Act (p. 563)

Interstate Commerce Commission (ICC) (p. 563)

Laissez-faire (p. 558)

Mugwumps (p. 557)

National American Woman Suffrage Association (p. 557)

Omaha Platform (p. 567)

Pendleton Civil Service Act (p. 560)

Populist Party (p. 556)

Prohibition Party (p. 556)

Sherman Antitrust Act (p. 563)

Sound money (p. 564)

Recommended Reading

Cherny, Robert W. *American Politics in the Gilded Age* (1997). An excellent brief analysis, emphasizing the importance of parties in both elections and public policy.

Foster, Gaines M. *Moral Reconstruction: Christian Lobbyists and the Federal Legislation of Morality, 1865-1920* (2002). A suggestive study of the efforts of Christian lobbyists to expand government authority over personal behavior.

Keller, Morton. *Affairs of State: Public Life in Late Nineteenth Century America* (1977). A detailed and fascinating ac-

count of the changing dimensions of government and politics.

McMath, Robert C., Jr. *American Populism: A Social History, 1877–1898* (1993). The best modern history of Populism; balanced and readable.

Summers, Mark. *Party Games: Getting, Keeping, and Using Power in Gilded Age Politics* (2004). A provocative account of the way partisan politicians (mis)shaped politics and public policy.

Where to Learn More

■ **Rest Cottage, Evanston, Illinois.**   Frances Willard's home, from which she directed the Woman's Christian Temperance Union, is carefully preserved as a museum. The Willard Memorial Library contains more memorabilia and papers of Willard and the WCTU. www.wctu.org/house.html

■ **President Benjamin Harrison's Home, Indianapolis, Indiana.**   President Harrison's brick Italianate mansion, completed in 1875, has been completely restored with the family's furniture and keepsakes. The former third-floor ballroom serves as a museum with exhibits of many artifacts of the Harrisons' public and private lives. www.presidentbenjaminharrison.org

■ **Susan B. Anthony House National Historic Landmark, Rochester, New York.**   This modest house was the home of the prominent suffragist and contains Anthony's original furnishings and personal photographs. www.susanbanthonyhouse.org/main.html

■ **Rutherford B. Hayes Presidential Center, Fremont, Ohio.**   This complex contains President Hayes's home, office, and extensive grounds together with an excellent library and museum holding valuable collections of manuscripts, artifacts, and photographs illustrating his personal interests and political career. www.rbhayes.org

Study Resources

PEARSON myhistorylab

For study resources for this chapter, go to www.myhistorylab.com and choose *The American Journey*. You will find a wealth of study and review material for this chapter, including pre- and post-tests, customized study plan, key term review flash cards, interactive map and document activities, and documents for analysis.

The great woman suffrage parade leaves Capitol Hill and heads for the White House, March 3, 1913. Dramatic tactics and careful organizing like those that marked this parade helped secure reform in the Progressive Era.

The Progressive Era
1900–1917
21

Five thousand women, marching in the woman suffrage pageant yesterday, practically fought their way foot by foot up Pennsylvania avenue, through a surging mass of humanity that completely defied the Washington police, swamped the marchers, and broke their procession into little companies. The women, trudging stoutly along under great difficulties, were able to complete their march only when troops of cavalry from Fort Myer were rushed into Washington to take charge of Pennsylvania avenue. No inauguration has ever produced such scenes, which in many instances amounted to little less than riots....

The parade in itself, in spite of the delays, was a great success....As a spectacle the pageant was entrancing. Beautiful women, posing in classic robes, passed in a bewildering array, presenting an irresistible appeal to the artistic, and completely captivating the hundred thousand spectators....

Miss Margaret Foley, bearing aloft a large "Votes for Women" flag, and Mrs. G. Farquhar, carrying an American flag, led the procession....After the float reading, "We Demand an Amendment to the United States Constitution Enfranchising the Women of This Country," came a body of ushers clad in light blue capes....Two large floats...represented the countries in which women are working for equal rights, followed by a large body of women on foot dressed in street clothes, who bore the banners and pennants of scores of suffrage associations throughout the world....The Homemakers...were dressed in long purple robes over their street clothes. Following them came a float, "In Patriotic Service,"...and

Miss Lillian Wald, the walking leader of a large body of women who followed the float, dressed as trained nurses, with gray caps and coats.

Miss Margaret Gage and Maurice Cohen, wearing college gowns with mortar boards, represented "Education," which was followed by nearly 1,000 women of the college section.... A group of young girls in blue capes represented the wage-earners, followed by "A Labor Story," which depicted the crowded condition of tenements, with women and children bending over sewing machines, dirty and disheveled, in squalid quarters.... [Then followed] the women in the government section, all wearing light blue capes,...the business women, dressed in similar manner,...the teachers,...the social workers,...the white and pink costumed delegation of "writers,"...club women and women clergy.

The greatest ovation was given to "General" Rosalie Jones, who led her little band of hikers from New York over rough roads and through snow and rain to march for the "cause."...

But there were hostile elements in the crowd through which the women marched....Passing through two walls of antagonistic humanity, the marchers for the most part kept their temper. They suffered insult and closed their ears to jibes and jeers....

The pageant moved up Pennsylvania avenue with great difficulty and surrounded with some danger. Crowds surged into the streets, completely over-whelming the police and stopping the pageant's progress. Mounted police charged into the crowds, but failed at times to drive them back, even with the free use of clubs. In more than an hour the pageant had moved only ten blocks....

When the surging multitude was driven back in one place it flowed back into the street at another. The pageant slowly moved along, sometimes not more than a dozen feet at a time....

As a result of the unruly spirit of the biggest crowd that ever witnessed a parade on Pennsylvania Avenue, or of the inactivity of the police, who seemed powerless to protect the marching suffragists, the Emergency Hospital last night was filled to overflowing....

Washington Post, March 4, 1913.

myhistorylab

Personal Journeys Online

- Mother Jones, *Marching Against Child Labor,* 1903. Account of Mother Jones leading a group of children to see President Roosevelt.

- Alice Hamilton, *Investigating Industrial Health,* 1943. Hamilton's recollection of her pioneering efforts in Chicago to investigate and improve industrial health conditions.

- Al Smith, *Enacting Reform Legislation,* 1929. Smith's account of overcoming opposition to reform laws in the wake of the Triangle Fire in 1911.

"General" Rosalie Jones's march and the jumbled news accounts from the *Washington Post* reporters convey the intensity of the dramatic woman suffrage parade on March 3, 1913. But the women's difficult journey down Pennsylvania Avenue that day, suggestive of the much longer journey to achieve woman suffrage, illustrated critical features of life in the **Progressive Era.**

Important movements challenged traditional relationships and attitudes—here involving women's role in American life—and often met strong resistance. "Progressives" seeking reforms organized their supporters across lines of class, education, occupation, geography, gender, and, at times, race and ethnicity—as the variety of groups in the suffrage parade demonstrates. Rather than rely on

CHRONOLOGY

1893–1898	Depression grips the nation.
1893	New Zealand establishes woman suffrage.
1894	New Zealand establishes maximum hours and compulsory arbitration.
1898	South Dakota adopts initiative and referendum.
	New Zealand initiates old age pensions.
	National Consumers' League is organized.
1899	Anti-Cigarette League of America is established.
1900	Robert La Follette is elected governor of Wisconsin.
1901	United States Steel Corporation is formed.
	President William McKinley is assassinated; Theodore Roosevelt becomes president.
	Socialist Party of America is organized.
	New York Tenement House Law is enacted.
	Galveston, Texas, initiates the city commission plan.
1902	Antitrust suit is filed against Northern Securities Company.
	McClure's initiates muckraking journalism.
	Mississippi enacts the first direct-primary law.
	National Reclamation Act is passed.
	Roosevelt intervenes in coal strike.
1903	Women's Trade Union League is organized.
1904	National Child Labor Committee is formed.
	Roosevelt is elected president.
1905	Industrial Workers of the World is organized.
1906	Hepburn Act strengthens the Interstate Commerce Commission.
	Meat Inspection Act extends government regulation.
	Pure Food and Drug Act is passed.
1908	*Muller v. Oregon* upholds maximum workday for women.
	William Howard Taft is elected president.
1910	National Association for the Advancement of Colored People is organized.
	Ballinger-Pinchot controversy erupts.
1912	Children's Bureau is established.
	Progressive Party organizes and nominates Roosevelt.
	Woodrow Wilson is elected president.
1913	Sixteenth and Seventeenth Amendments are ratified.
	Underwood-Simmons Tariff Act establishes an income tax.
	Federal Reserve Act creates the Federal Reserve System.
1914	Federal Trade Commission is established.
	Harrison Act criminalizes narcotics.
1915	National Birth Control League is formed.
1916	Keating-Owen Act prohibits child labor.
1917	Congress enacts literacy test for immigrants.
1918	Woman Suffrage is adopted in England.
1919	Eighteenth Amendment is ratified.
1920	Nineteenth Amendment is ratified.

traditional partisan politics, reformers adopted new political techniques, including lobbying and demonstrating, as nonpartisan pressure groups. Reform work begun at the local and state levels—where the suffrage movement had already met some success—inexorably moved to the national level as the federal government expanded its authority and became the focus of political interest. Finally, this suffrage demonstration reveals the exceptional diversity of the progressive movement, for the women were marching, in part, against Woodrow Wilson, who had campaigned for the presidency as a progressive.

However, woman suffrage did not define progressivism. Indeed, in a sense, there was no "progressive movement," for progressivism had no unifying organization, central leadership, or consensus on objectives. Instead, it represented the coalescing of different and sometimes even contradictory movements that sought changes in the nation's social, economic, and political life. But reformers did share certain convictions. They believed that industrialization and urbanization had produced serious social disorders, from city slums to corporate abuses. They believed that new ideas and methods were required to correct these problems. In particular, they rejected the ideology of individualism in favor of broader concepts of social responsibility, and they sought to achieve social order through organization and efficiency. Finally, most progressives believed that government itself, as the organized agent of public responsibility, should address social and economic problems.

Other Americans resisted the progressives' plans. The interaction among the reformers and the conflict with their opponents made the two decades before World War I a period of remarkable ferment and excitement. The progressives' achievements, and their failures, profoundly shaped America.

The Ferment of Reform

The diversity of progressivism reflected the diverse impulses of reform. Reformers responded to the tensions of industrialization and urbanization by formulating programs according to their own interests and priorities. Clergy and professors provided new ideas to guide remedial action. Journalists exposed corporate excesses and government corruption and stirred public demand for reform. Business leaders sought to curtail disorder through efficiency and regulation, while industrial workers struggled to improve the horrible conditions in which they worked and lived. Women organized to protect their families and homes from new threats and even to push beyond domestic issues. Nearly every movement for change encountered fierce opposition. But in raising new issues and proposing new ideas, progressives helped America grapple with the problems of industrial society. (See Overview, Major Progressive Organizations and Groups.)

The Context of Reform: Industrial and Urban Tensions

The origins of progressivism lay in the crises of the new urban-industrial order that emerged in the late nineteenth century. The severe depression and mass suffering of the 1890s, the labor violence and industrial armies, the political challenges of Populism and an obviously ineffective government shattered the complacency many middle-class Americans had felt about their nation and made them aware of social and economic inequities that rural and working-class families had long recognized. Many Americans began to question the validity of social Darwinism and the laissez-faire policies that had justified unregulated industrial growth. They began to reconsider the responsibilities of government and, indeed, of themselves for social order and betterment.

By 1900, returning prosperity had eased the threat of major social violence, but the underlying problems intensified. Big business, which had disrupted traditional economic relationships in the late nineteenth century, suddenly became bigger in a series of mergers between 1897 and 1903, resulting in huge new business combinations. The formation in 1901 of the United States Steel Corporation, the world's largest firm, symbolized this development. Such gigantic corporations threatened to squeeze opportunities for small firms and workers, dominate markets, and raise social tensions. They also inspired calls for public control.

Industrial growth affected factory workers most directly. Working conditions were difficult and often dangerous. Most workers still toiled nine to ten hours a day; steelworkers and textile employees worked 12-hour shifts. Wages were minimal; an economist in 1905 calculated that 60 percent of all adult male breadwinners made less than a living wage. Family survival, then, often required women and children to work, often in the lowest paid, most exploited positions. Southern cotton mills employed children as young as 7; coal mines paid 12-year-old slate pickers 39 cents for a ten-hour day. Poor ventilation, dangerous fumes, open machinery, and the absence of safety programs threatened not only workers' health but their lives as well. Such conditions were gruesomely illustrated in 1911, when a fire killed 146 workers, most of them young women, trapped inside the factory of the Triangle Shirtwaist Company in New York because management had locked the exits. The fire chief found "skeletons bending over sewing machines." The United States had the highest rate of industrial accidents in the world. Half a million workers were injured and 30,000 killed at work each year. These terrible conditions cried out for reform.

OVERVIEW

Major Progressive Organizations and Groups

Group	Activity
Social Gospel movement	Urged churches and individuals to apply Christian ethics to social and economic problems
Muckrakers	Exposed business abuses, public corruption, and social evils through investigative journalism
Settlement House movement	Attempted through social work and public advocacy to improve living and working conditions in urban immigrant communities
National Consumers' League (1898)	Monitored businesses to ensure decent working conditions and safe consumer products
Women's Trade Union League (1903)	United workingwomen and their middle-class allies to promote unionization and social reform
National Child Labor Committee (1904)	Campaigned against child labor
Country Life movement	Attempted to modernize rural social and economic conditions according to urban-industrial standards
National American Woman Suffrage Association	Led the movement to give women the right to vote
Municipal reformers	Sought to change the activities and structure of urban government to promote efficiency and control
Conservationists	Favored efficient management and regulation of natural resources rather than uncontrolled development or preservation

Other Americans saw additional social problems in the continuing flood of immigrants who were transforming America's cities. From 1900 to 1917, more than 14 million immigrants entered the United States. Most of the arrivals were so-called new immigrants from southern and eastern Europe, rather than the British, Irish, Germans, and Scandinavians who had arrived earlier. Several hundred thousand Japanese also arrived, primarily in California, as did increasing numbers of Mexicans. Crowding into urban slums, immigrants overwhelmed municipal sanitation, education, and fire protection services. One Russian described his new life as "all filth and sadness."

Many native-born Americans associated the immigrants with rampant urban crime and disease and with city bosses and government corruption. Ethnic prejudices abounded. In 1902 Woodrow Wilson, then president of Princeton University, declared that Italian and Polish immigrants had "neither skill nor energy, nor any initiative or quick intelligence." Americans of the "Old Stock" often considered the predominantly Catholic and Jewish newcomers a threat to social stability and cultural identity and so demanded programs to reform either the urban environment or the immigrants themselves.

Church and Campus

Many groups, drawing from different traditions and inspirations, responded to these economic and social issues. Reform-minded Protestant ministers were especially influential, creating the **Social Gospel movement,** which sought to introduce religious ethics into industrial relations and appealed to churches to meet their social responsibilities. Washington Gladden, a Congregational minister in Columbus, Ohio, was one of the earliest Social Gospelers. Shocked in 1884 by a bloody strike crushed by wealthy members of his own congregation, Gladden began a ministry to working-class neighborhoods that most churches ignored. He endorsed unions and workers' rights and proposed replacing a cruelly competitive wage system with profit sharing.

A more profound exponent of the Social Gospel was Walter Rauschenbusch, a Baptist minister who had served impoverished immigrants in New York's slums. In his book *Christianity and the Social Crisis* (1907), he argued that Christians should support social reform to alleviate poverty, slums, and labor exploitation. He attacked low wages for transforming workers "into lean, sallow, hopeless, stupid, and vicious young people, simply to enable some group of

Overcome with grief, families of the victims of the Triangle Shirtwaist fire later received from the factory owners $75 for each life lost. Still mourning, family members asked, "Justice, what justice?"

stockholders to earn 10 percent." Such ideas were popularized by Charles Sheldon, a Kansas minister, whose book *In His Steps* sold 23 million copies and called on Americans to act in their daily lives as they believed Jesus Christ would in the same circumstances.

The Social Gospel was part of an emerging liberal movement in American religion. Scholars associated with this movement discredited the literal accuracy of the Bible and emphasized instead its general moral and ethical lessons. As modernists, they abandoned theological dogmatism for a greater tolerance of other faiths and became more interested in social problems. Liberal Protestantism had its Jewish and Catholic counterparts in Reform Judaism and liberal Catholicism, but the Social Gospel movement flowered mainly among Episcopalians, Congregationalists, and Methodists. It climaxed in 1908 in the formation of the Federal Council of Churches of Christ in America. The council, representing 33 religious groups, adopted a program that endorsed welfare and regulatory legislation to achieve social justice. By linking reform with religion (as "applied Christianity," in the words of Washington Gladden), the Social Gospel movement gave progressivism a powerful moral drive that affected much of American life.

The Social Gospel movement provided an ethical justification for government intervention to improve the social order. Scholars in the social sciences also gradually helped turn public attitudes in favor of reform by challenging the laissez-faire views of the social Darwinists and traditional academics. In *Applied Sociology* (1906), Lester Ward called for social progress through rational planning and government intervention rather than through unrestrained and unpredictable competition. Economists rejected laissez-faire principles in favor of state action to accomplish social evolution. Industrialization, declared economist Richard T. Ely, "has brought to the front a vast number of social problems whose

solution is impossible without the united efforts of church, state, and science."

Muckrakers

Journalists also spread reform ideas by developing a new form of investigative reporting known as **muckraking**. Technological innovations had recently made possible the mass circulation of magazines, and editors competed to attract an expanding urban readership. Samuel S. McClure sent his reporters to uncover political and corporate corruption for *McClure's Magazine*. Sensational exposés sold magazines, and soon *Cosmopolitan, Everybody's,* and other journals began publishing investigations of business abuses, dangerous working conditions, and the miseries of slum life.

Muckraking articles aroused indignant public demands for reform. Lincoln Steffens detailed the corrupt links between "respectable" businessmen and crooked urban politicians in a series of articles called "The Shame of the Cities." Ida Tarbell revealed John D. Rockefeller's sordid construction of Standard Oil. Muckraking novels also appeared. *The Octopus* (1901), by Frank Norris, dramatized the Southern Pacific Railroad's stranglehold on California's farmers, and *The Jungle* (1906), by Upton Sinclair, exposed the nauseating conditions in Chicago's meatpacking industry. Surveying the work of such muckrakers in 1906, one newspaper declared, "The public conscience has been awakened and wrong-doers have been stricken with fear. But henceforth the work of exposing evil must be transformed into a steady-going, constructive effort to prevent it."

The Gospel of Efficiency

Many progressive leaders believed that efficiency and expertise could control or resolve the disorder of industrial society. President Theodore Roosevelt praised the "gospel of efficiency." Like many other progressives, he admired the success of corporations in applying management techniques to guide economic growth. Drawing from science and technology as well as from the model of the corporation, many progressives attempted to manage or direct change efficiently. They used scientific methods to collect extensive data and relied on experts for analysis and recommendations. "Scientific management," a concept often used interchangeably with "sound business management," seemed the key to eliminating waste and inefficiency in government, society, and industry. Rural reformers thought that "scientific agriculture" could bring prosperity to the impoverished southern countryside; urban reformers believed that improvements in medical science and the professionalization of physicians through uniform state-licensing standards could eradicate the cities' wretched health problems.

Business leaders especially advocated efficiency, order, and organization. Industrialists were drawn to the ideas of Frederick Taylor, a proponent of scientific management, for cutting factory labor costs. Taylor proposed to increase worker efficiency through imposed work routines, speedups, and mechanization. Workers, Taylor insisted, should "do what they are told promptly and without asking questions.... It is absolutely necessary for every man in our organization to become one of a train of gear wheels." By assigning workers simple and repetitive tasks on machines, Taylorization made their skills expendable and enabled managers to control the production, pace of work, and hiring and firing of personnel. Stripped of their influence and poorly paid, factory workers shared little of the wealth generated by industrial expansion and scientific management. When labor complained, one business leader declared that unions failed "to appreciate the progressivism of the age."

Sophisticated managers of big business saw some forms of government intervention as another way to promote order and efficiency. In particular, they favored regulations that could bring about safer and more stable conditions in society and the economy. Government regulations, they reasoned, could reassure potential consumers, open markets, mandate working conditions that smaller competitors could not provide, or impose systematic procedures that competitive pressures would otherwise undercut.

Labor Demands Its Rights

Industrial workers with different objectives also hastened the ferment of reform. Workers resisted the new rules of efficiency experts and called for improved wages and working conditions and reduced work hours. They and their middle-class sympathizers sought to achieve some of these goals through state intervention, demanding laws to compensate workers injured on the job, curb child labor, and regulate the employment of women. Sometimes they succeeded. After the Triangle Shirtwaist fire, for example, urban politicians with working-class constituencies created the New York State Factory Commission and enacted dozens of laws dealing with fire hazards, machine safety, and wages and hours for women.

Workers also organized unions to improve their lot. The American Federation of Labor (AFL) claimed 4 million members by 1920, recruiting mainly skilled workers, particularly native-born white males. New unions organized the factories and sweatshops where most immigrants and women worked. Despite strong employer resistance, the International Ladies Garment Workers Union (1900) and the Amalgamated Clothing Workers (1914) or-

ganized the garment trades, developed programs for social and economic reforms, and led their members—mostly young Jewish and Italian women—in spectacular strikes. The "Uprising of the 20,000," a 1909 strike in New York City, included months of massive rallies, determined picketing, and police repression. One observer marveled at the women strikers' "emotional endurance, fearlessness, and entire willingness to face danger and suffering."

A still more radical union tried to organize miners, lumberjacks, and Mexican and Japanese farm workers in the West, black dockworkers in the South, and immigrant factory hands in New England. Founded in 1905, the Industrial Workers of the World (IWW), whose members were known as **"Wobblies,"** used sit-down strikes, sit-ins, and mass rallies, tactics adopted by other industrial unions in the 1930s and the civil rights movement in the 1960s. "Respectable people" considered the Wobblies violent revolutionaries, but most of the violence was committed against IWW members. Private employers and public officials used every method, legal and illegal, to destroy the Wobblies, but broader labor unrest nonetheless stimulated the reform impulse.

Extending the Woman's Sphere

Women reformers and their organizations played a key role in progressivism. Women responded not merely to the human suffering caused by industrialization and urbanization but also to related changes in their own status and role. By the early twentieth century, more women than before were working outside the home—in the factories, mills, and sweatshops of the industrial economy and as clerks in stores and offices. In 1910, more than one-fourth of all workers

The campaign against child labor attracted passionate support from many Americans. Here two girls, wearing "Abolish Child Slavery" banners in Yiddish and English, participate in a labor parade in New York City on May 1, 1909.

were women, increasing numbers of them married. Their importance in the workforce and participation in unions and strikes challenged assumptions that woman's "natural" role was to be a submissive housewife. Shrinking family size, labor-saving household equipment, and changing social expectations enabled middle-class women to find more time and opportunities to pursue activities outside the home. Better educated than previous generations, they also acquired interests, information, skills, and confidence relevant to a larger public setting.

The women's clubs that had begun multiplying in the late nineteenth century became seed-beds of progressive ideas in the early twentieth century. Often founded for cultural purposes, women's clubs soon adopted programs for social reform and gave their members a route to public influence. In 1914, an officer of the General Federation of Women's Clubs proudly declared that every cause for social reform had "received a helpful hand from the clubwomen."

Women also joined or created other organizations that pushed beyond the limits of traditional domesticity. "Woman's place is in the home," observed one progressive, but "no longer is the home encompassed by four walls." By threatening healthy and happy homes, urban problems required that women become "social housekeepers" in the community. The National Congress of Mothers, organized in 1897, worried about crime and disease and championed kindergartens, foster-home programs, juvenile courts, and compulsory school attendance.

Led by the crusading Florence Kelley, the National Consumers' League, founded in 1898, tried to protect both women wage earners and middle-class housewives by monitoring stores and factories to ensure decent working conditions and safe products. The Women's Trade Union League (WTUL, founded in 1903) united working women and their self-styled middle-class "allies" to unionize women workers and eliminate sweatshop conditions. Its greatest success came in the 1909 garment workers' strike, when the allies assisted strikers with relief funds, bail money, food supplies, and a public-relations campaign. This cooperation, declared one WTUL official, demonstrated the "sisterhood of women."

Although most progressive women stressed women's special duties and responsibilities as social housekeepers, others began to demand women's equal rights. In 1914, for example, critics of New York's policy of dismissing women teachers who married formed a group called the Feminist Alliance and demanded "the removal of all social, political, economic and other discriminations which are based upon sex, and the award of all rights and duties in all fields on the basis of individual capacity alone." With these new organizations and ideas, women gave important impetus and direction to the reform sentiments of the early twentieth century.

Transatlantic Influences

A major source of America's progressive impulse lay outside its borders. European nations were already grappling with many of the problems that stemmed from industrialization and urbanization, and they provided guidance, examples, and possible solutions. Progressive reformers soon learned that America's political, economic, and social structures made it necessary to modify, adapt, or even abandon these imported ideas, but their influence was obvious.

University study in Europe taught Americans the limits of their traditional laissez-faire attitudes and the possibilities of state action. Trained in Germany, the economist Richard T. Ely returned to academic posts in America to teach that government "is the agency through which we must work." International influences were especially strong in the Social Gospel movement, symbolized by William T. Stead, a British social evangelist, whose idea of a "Civic Church" (a partnership of churches and reformers) captured great attention in the United States. Stead himself went to Chicago to promote "a broad and clear social programme," and his book *If Christ Came to Chicago* helped inspire Sheldon's *In His Steps*. Muckrakers not only exposed American problems but looked for foreign solutions. *McClure's* sent Ray Stannard Baker to Europe in 1900 "to see why Germany is making such progress"; *Everybody's* sent Charles E. Russell around the world in 1905 to describe the social advances in Europe and New Zealand. (See Global Perspectives, The New Zealand Way.)

Institutional connections also linked progressives with European reformers. The American Association for Labor Legislation, for example, was formed in 1905 as an offshoot of the International Association for Labor Legislation, founded in 1900 by French, Belgian, and German social economists. By 1912, American consumer activists, trade unionists, factory inspectors, and feminists regularly participated in international conferences on labor legislation, child welfare, social insurance, and housing reform and returned home with new ideas and strategies. State governments organized commissions to analyze European policies and agencies for lessons that might be applicable in the United States.

Socialism

The growing influence of socialist ideas also promoted the spirit of progressivism. Socialism never attracted a large following in the United States, but its criticism of the industrial economy gained increasing attention in the early twentieth century. American socialists condemned social and economic inequities, criticized limited government, and demanded public ownership of railroads, utilities, and communications. They also campaigned for tax reforms, better housing, factory inspections, and recreational facilities for all.

Muckrakers like Lincoln Steffens and Upton Sinclair were committed socialists, as were some Social Gospel ministers and labor leaders, but the most prominent socialist was the dynamic and engaging Eugene V. Debs. An Indiana labor leader who had converted to socialism while imprisoned for his role in the 1894 Pullman strike, Debs had evangelical energy and a generous spirit. He decried what he saw

Global Perspectives

The New Zealand Way

In its very name, the Progressive Era seems characteristically American, but its major developments were actually part of a worldwide phenomenon in which the peoples of many different nations promoted significant reforms, especially through the expansion of government responsibility and power. While Europeans provided an important range of reform ideas and models for Americans, it was often New Zealand, described by one muckraker as the "practical utopia of the South Seas," that "blazed the world's way" in social and economic reforms.

Small, rural, sparsely populated, only slightly industrialized, and still a colony of Great Britain, New Zealand might seem an unlikely candidate to lead progressive reform, but one American minister predicted in 1900 that "we fool Americans will go on for fifty or seventy-five years before we…undertake what they have already achieved in New Zealand." New Zealanders were less driven by a desire to correct the evils of industrialization and urbanization—poverty, sweatshops, slums, labor exploitation, social conflict—than by a determination to prevent their emergence in the first place. As the charismatic Liberal leader Richard Seddon declared, "If we deal with [these problems] now, the curse of the older countries will never come to New Zealand."

With the election of a Liberal government in 1891, New Zealand launched two decades of reform. It began the serious regulation of working conditions in 1891. In 1894 the General Assembly mandated regular factory inspections and established maximum hours, first for women and then for men, and prohibited child labor in factories. Other laws in the 1890s established minimum wages for women. The Industrial Conciliation and Arbitration Act of 1894 both encouraged unionization and required compulsory arbitration to deal with industrial disputes and assure social peace and progress. A model system of workers' compensation was established in 1901.

New Zealand also pioneered in political and social reform. In 1893 it became the first country to establish woman suffrage in national elections. With one member of the parliament reasoning that "it is the duty of the State to make proper provision for the aged," New Zealand initiated old age pensions in 1898. Early in the twentieth century it expanded state-funded, rather than contributory, pensions to cover widows with children, injured miners, and other groups. Beginning in 1905, it developed public housing programs, providing first rental housing for low-income families and then government loans for the purchase of homes. The Public Health Act of 1900 initiated a series of laws expanding government responsibility for proper sanitation, safe water, vaccinations, and the regulation of food and drugs.

New Zealand reformers urged the United States to follow the "New Zealand Way" and adopt these and other reforms, and many American progressives did look to that small country for guidance. "If a British colony dares to lead," noted one progressive journalist, "surely it is not visionary to expect our Republic to fall in line."

■ What economic, social, and political factors might explain why progressive reform emerged more slowly and less completely in the United States than in New Zealand?

---

as the dehumanization produced by industrial capitalism and hoped for an egalitarian society where everyone would have the opportunity "to develop the best there is in him for his own good as well as the good of society." Even a critical journalist concluded: "There was more of goodness in him than bubbled up in any other American."

In 1901, Debs helped organize the Socialist Party of America; thereafter, he worked tirelessly to attract followers to a vision of socialism deeply rooted in American political and religious traditions. In the next decade, the party won many local elections, especially in Wisconsin and New York, where it drew support from German and Russian immigrants, and in Oklahoma, where it attracted poor tenant farmers.

Most progressives considered socialist ideas too drastic. Nevertheless, socialists contributed importantly to the reform ferment, not only by providing support for reform initiatives but often also by prompting progressives to push for changes to undercut increasingly attractive radical alternatives.

Opponents of Reform

Not all Americans supported progressive reforms, and many people regarded as progressives on some issues opposed change in other areas. Social Gospeler Rauschenbusch, for instance, opposed expanding women's rights. More typically, opponents of reform held consistently traditional attitudes, like the conservatives who saw in feminism the orthodox bogies of "non-motherhood, free love, easy divorce, economic independence for all women, and other demoralizing and destructive theories."

Social Gospelers themselves faced opposition from Protestant traditionalists emphasizing what they termed fundamental beliefs. Particularly strong among evangelical denominations with rural roots, these **fundamentalists** stressed personal salvation rather than social reform. "To attempt reform in the black depths of the great city," said one, "would be as useless as trying to purify the ocean by pouring into it a few gallons of spring water." Indeed, the urban and industrial crises that inspired Social Gospelers to preach reform drove many evangelical leaders to endorse social and political conservatism. The most famous evangelist, the crude but spellbinding Billy Sunday, scorned all reforms but prohibition and denounced labor unions, women's rights, and business regulation as violating traditional values. Declaring that the Christian mission was only to save individual souls, he condemned the Social Gospel as "godless social service nonsense" and attacked its advocates as "infidels and atheists."

Business interests, angered by exposés of corporate abuse and corruption, attacked the muckrakers. Business groups such as the American Bankers' Association accused muckrakers of promoting socialism. Major corporations like Standard Oil created public relations bureaus to improve their image and identify business, not its critics, with the public interest. "The voice of the public," one press agent proclaimed, was "spoken through the Chamber of Commerce." Advertising boycotts discouraged magazines from running critical stories, and credit restrictions forced some muckraking journals to suspend publication. By 1910, the heyday of muckraking was over.

Labor unions likewise encountered resistance. Led by the National Association of Manufacturers, business groups denounced unions as corrupt and radical, hired thugs to disrupt them, organized strikebreaking agencies, and used blacklists to eliminate union activists. The antiunion campaign peaked in Ludlow, Colorado, in 1914, when John D. Rockefeller's Colorado Fuel and Iron Company used armed guards and the state militia to shoot and burn striking workers and their families. The courts aided employers by issuing injunctions against strikes and prohibiting unions from using boycotts, one of their most effective weapons.

Progressives campaigning for government intervention and regulation also met stiff resistance. Many Americans objected to what they considered unwarranted interference in private economic matters. Again, the courts often supported these attitudes. In *Lochner v. New York* (1905), the Supreme Court even overturned a maximum-hours law on the grounds that it deprived employers and employees of their "freedom of contract." Progressives continually struggled against such opponents, and progressive achievements were limited by the persistence and influence of their adversaries.

Reforming Society

With their varied motives and objectives, progressives worked to transform society by improving living conditions, educational opportunities, family life, and social and industrial relations. (See Overview, Major Laws and Constitutional Amendments of the Progressive Era.) They sought what they called social justice, but their plans for social reform sometimes also smacked of social control. Organized women dominated the movement to reform society, but they were supported, depending on the goal, by Social Gospel ministers, social scientists, urban immigrants, labor unions, and even some conservatives eager to regulate personal behavior.

Greene, in New York (N. Y.) Telegram

A WOMAN'S WORK IS NEVER DONE

Women's activism was critically important in reconstructing American life during the Progressive Era. Busily engaged in social housekeeping, Mother America uses corrective legislation to clean the dirty laundry of industrialization and injustice.

OVERVIEW

Major Laws and Constitutional Amendments of the Progressive Era

Legislation	Effect
New York Tenement House Law (1901)	Established a model housing code for safety and sanitation
Newlands Act (1902)	Provided for federal irrigation projects
Hepburn Act (1906)	Strengthened the Interstate Commerce Commission
Pure Food and Drug Act (1906)	Regulated the production and sale of food and drug products
Meat Inspection Act (1906)	Authorized federal inspection of meat products
Sixteenth Amendment (1913)	Authorized a federal income tax
Seventeenth Amendment (1913)	Mandated the direct popular election of senators
Underwood-Simmons Tariff Act (1913)	Lowered tariff rates and levied the first regular federal income tax
Federal Reserve Act (1913)	Established the Federal Reserve System to supervise banking and provide a national currency
Federal Trade Commission Act (1914)	Established the FTC to oversee business activities
Harrison Act (1914)	Regulated the distribution and use of narcotics
Smith-Lever Act (1914)	Institutionalized the county agent system
Keating-Owen Act (1916)	Indirectly prohibited child labor
Eighteenth Amendment (1919)	Instituted prohibition
Nineteenth Amendment (1920)	Established woman suffrage

Settlement Houses and Urban Reform

The spearheads for social reform were settlement houses—community centers in urban immigrant neighborhoods. Reformers created 400 settlement houses, largely modeled after Hull House in Chicago, founded in 1889 by Jane Addams. Settlement houses often reflected the ideals of the Social Gospel. "A simple acceptance of Christ's message and methods," wrote Addams, "is what a settlement should stand for." Yet most were secular institutions, avoiding religion to gain the trust of Catholic and Jewish immigrants.

Most settlements were led and staffed primarily by middle-class young women, seeking to alleviate poverty and do useful professional work when most careers were closed to them. Settlement work did not immediately violate prescribed gender roles because it initially focused on the "woman's sphere"—family, education, domestic skills, and cultural "uplift." Thus settlement workers organized kindergartens and nurseries; taught classes in English, cooking, and personal hygiene; and held musical performances and poetry readings.

However, settlement workers soon saw that the root problem for immigrants was widespread poverty that required more than changes in individual behavior. Unlike earlier reformers, they regarded many of the evils of poverty as products of the social environment rather than of moral weakness. Slum dwellers, Addams sadly noted, suffered from "poisonous sewage, contaminated water, infant mortality, adulterated food, smoke-laden air, juvenile crime, and unwholesome crowding." Thus, settlement workers campaigned for stricter building codes to improve slums, better urban sanitation systems to enhance public health, public parks to revive the urban environment, and laws to protect women and children.

Their crusades for sanitation and housing reform demonstrated the impact that social reformers often had on urban life. Settlement worker Mary McDowell launched a campaign against the open garbage dumps and polluted sewers in Chicago. Drawing upon European innovations in waste disposal, organizing women's groups to hold cleanup campaigns, and using public pressure, McDowell became known as the "Garbage Lady" for her success in improving Chicago's massive environmental problems. Similarly, Lawrence Veiller was convinced by his work at the University Settlement in New York City that "the improvement of the homes of the people was the starting point for everything." Organizing pressure groups to promote tenement house reform, Veiller relied on settlement workers to investigate housing conditions, prepare public exhibits depicting rampant disease in congested slums, and agitate for improvements. Based on their findings, Veiller drafted a new housing code limiting the size of tenements and requiring toilet facilities, ventilation, and fire protection. In 1901, the New York Tenement House Law became a model for other cities. To promote uniform building codes throughout the nation, the tireless Veiller founded the National Housing Association in 1910.

Protective Legislation for Women and Children

While settlement workers initially undertook private efforts to improve society, many reformers eventually concluded that only government intervention could achieve social justice. As Veiller insisted, it was "unquestionably the duty of the state" to enforce justice in the face of "greed on the part of those who desire to secure for themselves an undue profit."

The maiming and killing of children in industrial accidents made it "inevitable," Addams said, "that efforts to secure a child labor law should be our first venture into the field of state legislation." The National Child Labor Committee, organized in 1904, led the campaign to curtail child labor (see Figure 21–1). Reformers documented the problem with extensive investigations and also benefited from the public outrage stirred by socialist John Spargo's muckraking book *The Bitter Cry of the Children* (1906). In 1900, most states had no minimum working age; by 1914, every state but one had such a law. Effective regulation, however, required national action, for many state laws were weak or poorly enforced.

Stiff resistance came from manufacturers who used child labor, conservatives who opposed government action as an intrusion into family life, and some poor parents who needed their children's income. But finally, Congress in 1912 estab-

lished the Children's Bureau to investigate the welfare of children. Julia Lathrop, from Hull House, directed the bureau, the first government agency headed and staffed almost entirely by women. Lathrop and the bureau lobbied Congress and in 1916 saw the passage of the Keating-Owen Act, prohibiting the interstate shipment of goods manufactured by children. The law was weaker than the ones in many states and did not cover most child workers. Even so, the Supreme Court declared the measure unconstitutional.

Social reformers also lobbied for laws regulating the wages, hours, and working conditions of women and succeeded in having states from New York to Oregon pass maximum-hours legislation. After the Supreme Court upheld such laws in *Muller v. Oregon* (1908), 39 states enacted new or stronger laws on women's maximum hours between 1909 and 1917. Fewer states established minimum wages for women. In 1912, Massachusetts created a commission to recommend such wages, and within a year, eight midwestern and western states authorized wage commissions to set binding rates. But few other states followed these examples.

Protective legislation for women posed a troubling issue for reformers. In California, for example, middle-class clubwomen favored protective legislation on the grounds of women's presumed weakness. They wanted to preserve "California's potential motherhood." More radical progressives, as in the socialist-led Women's Trade Union League of Los Angeles, supported such legislation to help secure economic independence and equality in the labor market for women, increase the economic strength of the working class, and serve as a precedent for laws improving conditions for all workers.

Progressive Era lawmakers adopted the first viewpoint. They limited protective legislation to measures reflecting the belief that women needed paternalist protection, even by excluding them from certain occupations. Laws establishing a minimum wage for women, moreover, usually set a wage level below subsistence rates. Rather than assuring women's economic independence, then, protective legislation in practice reinforced women's subordinate place in the labor force.

Protective legislation for male workers scarcely existed. Both lawmakers and judges rebuffed demands for the protection of all workers while approving reforms that endorsed inequality. Only in very dangerous industries did male workers gain much protection, due primarily to the relentless efforts of labor unions. The Western Federation of Miners persuaded several states that the extraordinary occupational hazards of mining—cave-ins, explosions, poisonous gasses, silicosis and other diseases—required laws regulating hours and conditions of work.

Social justice reformers forged the beginnings of the welfare state in further legislation. Prompted by both humanitarian and paternalistic urgings, many states began in 1910 to provide "mothers' pensions" to indigent widows with dependent children. Twenty-one states, led by Wisconsin in 1911, enacted workers' compensation programs, ending the custom of holding workers themselves liable for injuries on the job.

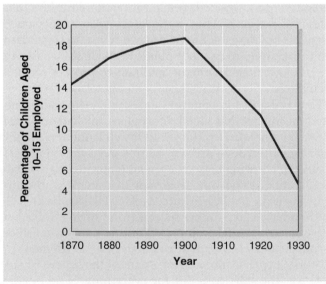

FIGURE 21–1   Child Labor, 1870–1930

Nearly 2 million children worked in factories and fields in 1900, twice as many as in 1870. Progressives' efforts to curtail child labor through laws for compulsory education and a minimum working age encountered resistance, and change came slowly.

Data source: U.S. Bureau of the Census.

Compared to the social insurance programs in western Europe, however, these were feeble responses to the social consequences of industrialization. Proposals for health insurance, unemployment insurance, and old-age pension programs went nowhere. Business groups and other conservative interests curbed the movement toward state responsibility for social welfare.

Reshaping Public Education

Concerns about child labor overlapped with increasing attention to the public schools. The rapid influx of immigrants, as well as the demands of the new corporate workplace, generated interest in education not only as a means of advancement but also as a tool for assimilation and the training of future workers. Middle-class women supported public school reforms. In 1900, for example, women's clubs in North Carolina launched a program to improve school buildings, increase teachers' salaries, and broaden the curriculum. School administrators also pushed for changes, both to upgrade their own profession and to expand their public influence. And some intellectuals predicted that schools themselves could promote social progress and reform. The philosopher John Dewey sketched his plans for progressive education in *The School and Society* (1899).

Between 1880 and 1920, compulsory school attendance laws, kindergartens, age-graded elementary schools, professional training for teachers, vocational education, parent-teacher associations, and school nurses became standard elements in American education. School reformers believed these measures to be both educationally sound and important for countering slum environments. As Jacob Riis contended, the kindergartner would "rediscover... the natural feelings that the tenement had smothered." Others supported the kindergarten as "the earliest opportunity to catch the little Russian, the little Italian, the little German, Pole, Syrian, and the rest and begin to make good American citizens of them." Further socialization came through vocational courses intended to instill discipline in poor students and prepare them to become productive adults.

Public education in the South lagged behind the North. Northern philanthropy and southern reformers brought some improvements after 1900, as per capita expenditures for education doubled, school terms were extended, and high schools spread across the region. But the South frittered away its limited resources on a segregated educational system that shortchanged both races. Black southerners particularly suffered, for the new programs increased the disparity in funding for white and black schools. South Carolina spent 12 times as much per white pupil as per black pupil. Booker T. Washington complained in 1906 that the educational reforms meant "almost nothing so far as the Negro schools are

The famous photographer Lewis Hine used his camera to document child labor. The eleven-year-old boys at this North Carolina textile mill in 1908 earned sixty cents a day.

concerned." As a northern critic observed, "To devise a school system which shall save the whites and not the blacks is a task of such delicacy that a few surviving reactionaries are willing to let both perish together."

Racism also underlay important changes in the schooling of Native Americans. The earlier belief that education would promote equality and facilitate assimilation gave way to a conviction that Indians were inferior and fit merely for manual labor. Educators now rejected the notion of a common school education for Indian children in favor of manual training that would enable Indians to fill menial jobs and whites to "turn their attention to more intellectual employments." Educators also renounced the practice of integrating Indian children into previously all-white classrooms, a policy begun in 1891. The superintendent of the Chilocco, Oklahoma, school believed that the new commitment to practical vocational education "solved the Indian problem," but critics noted that limiting Indian children to a rudimentary and segregated education merely doomed them to the margins of American society.

Challenging Gender Restrictions

Most progressives held fairly conservative, moralistic views about sexuality and gender roles. Margaret Sanger, however, radically challenged conventional ideas about the social role of women. Despite great opposition, she initiated the modern birth control movement. A public-health nurse and an IWW organizer, she soon made the struggle for reproductive rights her personal crusade. Sanger saw in New York's immigrant neighborhoods the plight of poor women worn out from repeated pregnancies or injured or dead from self-induced knitting-needle abortions. Despite federal and state laws against contraceptives, Sanger began promoting birth control as a way to avert such tragedies. In 1914, Sanger published a magazine, *Woman Rebel,* in which she argued that "a woman's body belongs to herself alone. It does not belong to the United States of America or any other government on the face of the earth." Prohibiting contraceptives meant "enforced motherhood," Sanger declared. "Women cannot be on an equal footing with men until they have full and complete control over their reproductive function."

Sanger's crusade attracted support from many women's and labor groups, but it also infuriated those who regarded birth control as a threat to the family and morality. Indicted for distributing information about contraception, Sanger fled to Europe. Other women took up the cause, forming the National Birth Control League in 1915 to campaign for the repeal of laws restricting access to contraceptive information and devices. They had little immediate success, but their cause would triumph in later generations.

Reforming Country Life

Although most progressives focused on the city, others sought to reform rural life, both to modernize its social and economic conditions and to integrate it more fully into the larger society. They worked to improve rural health and sanitation, to replace inefficient one-room schools with modern consolidated ones under professional control, and to extend new roads and communication services into the countryside. To further these goals, President Theodore Roosevelt created the Country Life Commission in 1908. The country lifers had a broad program for social and economic change, involving expanded government functions, activist government agencies staffed by experts, and the professionalization of rural social services.

Agricultural scientists, government officials, and many business interests also sought to promote efficient, scientific, and commercial agriculture. A key innovation was the county-agent system: The U.S. Department of Agriculture and business groups placed an agent in each county to teach farmers new techniques and to encourage changes in the rural social values that had previously spawned the Populist radicalism that most progressives decried. Farmers, it was hoped, would acquire materialistic values and learn "economy, order, . . . patriotism, and a score of other wholesome lessons," as one progressive put it in 1910. The Smith-Lever Act (1914) provided federal subsidies for county agents throughout the country.

Few farmers, however, welcomed these efforts. As one Illinois county agent said in 1915, "Farmers, as a whole, resent exceedingly those forces which are at work with missionary intent trying to uplift them." School consolidation meant the loss of community control of education; good roads would raise taxes and chiefly benefit urban business interests. Besides, most farmers believed that their problems stemmed, not from rural life, but from industrial society and its nefarious trusts, banks, and middlemen. Rural Americans did not want their lives revolutionized.

Even so, rural people were drawn into the larger urban-industrial society during the Progressive Era. Government agencies, agricultural colleges, and railroads and banks steadily tied farmers to urban markets. Telephones and rural free delivery of mail lessened countryside isolation but quickened the spread of city values. Improved roads and the coming of the automobile eliminated many rural villages and linked farm families directly with towns and cities. Consolidated schools wiped out the social center of rural neighborhoods and carried children out of their communities, eventually encouraging an ever-growing migration to the city.

Moral Crusades and Social Control

Moral reform movements, although often appearing misguided or unduly coercive today, generally reflected the progressive hope to protect people in a debilitating environment. In practice, however, these efforts to shape society tended toward social control. Morerover, these efforts often meshed with the restrictive attitudes that conservative Americans held about race, religion, immigration, and morality. The result was widespread attempts to restrict certain groups and control behavior.

Controlling immigrants.   Many Americans wanted to limit immigration for racist reasons. Nativist agitation in California prompted the federal government to secure restrictions on Japanese immigration in 1907. Californians, including local progressives, also hoped to curtail the migration of Mexicans. A Stanford University researcher condemned Mexicans as an "undesirable class," and in 1916 the Los Angeles County supervisors urged the federal government to deport Mexican immigrants.

Nationally, public debate focused on restricting the flow of new immigrants from southern and eastern Europe. Some labor leaders believed that immigration held down wages and impeded unionization; many sociologists thought it created serious social problems; other Americans disliked the newcomers on religious, cultural, or ethnic grounds. Many backed their prejudice with a distorted interpretation of Darwinism, labeling the Slavic and Mediterranean peoples "inferior races." As early as 1894, nativists had organized the Immigration Restriction League, which lobbied for a literacy test for admission, sure that it would "bear most heavily upon the Italians, Russians, Poles, Hungarians, Greeks, and Asiatics, and very lightly or not at all upon English-speaking immigrants or Germans, Scandinavians, and French." Congress enacted a literacy law in 1917.

Other nativists demanded the "Americanization" of immigrants already in the country. The Daughters of the American Revolution sought to inculcate loyalty, patriotism, and conservative values. Settlement workers and Social Gospelers promoted a gentler kind of Americanization through English classes and home mission campaigns, but they too attempted to transfer their own values to the newcomers. The most prominent advocate of Americanization was a stereotypical progressive, Frances Kellor. She studied social work at the University of Chicago, worked in New York settlement houses, wrote a muckraking exposé of employment agencies that exploited women, and became director of the New York Bureau of Immigration. In 1915, she helped organize the National Americanization Committee and increasingly emphasized destroying immigrants' old-country ties and imposing an American culture.

Prohibition.   Closely linked to progressives' worries about immigrants was their campaign for **prohibition.** This movement engaged many of the progressives' basic impulses. Social workers saw liquor as a cause of crime, poverty, and family violence; employers blamed it for causing industrial accidents and inefficiency; Social Gospel ministers condemned the "spirit born of hell" because it impaired moral judgment and behavior. But also important was native-born Americans' fear of new immigrants—"the dangerous classes, who are readily dominated by the saloon." Many immigrants, in fact, viewed liquor and the neighborhood saloon as vital parts of daily life, and so prohibition became a focus of nativist hostility, cultural conflict, and Americanization pressures. In the South, racism also figured prominently. Alexander McKelway, the southern secretary for the National Child Labor Committee, endorsed prohibition as a way to maintain social order and white supremacy. McKelway himself drank, but he helped organize the North Carolina Anti-Saloon League to deny alcohol to African Americans, whom he considered naturally "criminal and degenerate."

Protestant fundamentalists also stoutly supported prohibition, working through the Anti-Saloon League, founded in 1893. Their nativism and antiurban bias surfaced in demands for prohibition to prevent the nation's cities from lapsing into "raging mania, disorder, and anarchy." With most urban Catholics and Jews opposing prohibition—the Central Conference of American Rabbis denounced it as "born of fanaticism"—the Anti-Saloon League justified imposing its reform on city populations against their will: "Our nation can only be saved by turning the pure stream of country sentiment...to flush out the cesspools of cities and so save civilization from pollution."

With these varied motivations, prohibitionists campaigned for local and state laws against the manufacture and sale of alcohol. Beginning in 1907, they proved increasingly successful, especially in the South, Midwest, and Far West. By 1917, 26 states had prohibition laws. Congress then approved the **Eighteenth Amendment,** which made prohibition the law of the land by 1920.

Less controversial were drives to control or prohibit narcotics and cigarettes. Patent (over-the-counter) medicines commonly contained opium, heroin, and cocaine (popularly used for hay fever), and physicians known as "dope doctors" openly dispensed drugs to paying customers. Fears that addiction was spreading in "the fallen and lower classes"—and particularly among black people and immigrants—prompted Congress in 1914 to pass the Harrison Act, prohibiting the distribution and use of narcotics for other than medicinal purposes. The Anti-Cigarette League of America, organized in 1899 and having 300,000 members by 1901, led the charge against cigarettes. Aided by educators and physicians worried about the effect of cigarette smoking on mental and physical health and by business leaders concerned with industrial productivity and efficiency, these activists were encouraged when national organizations of Baptists, Methodists, and Presbyterians all condemned smoking in 1909. They persuaded many states to prohibit the manufacture, sale, or use of cigarettes, but such restrictive laws were rarely enforced and often repealed within a few years.

Suppressing prostitution.   Reformers also sought to suppress the "social evil" of prostitution. Like crowded slums, sweatshops, and child labor, the "vice districts" where prostitution flourished were seen as part of the exploitation and disorder in the industrial cities. Women's low wages as factory workers and domestic servants explained some of the problem, as a muckraking article entitled "The Daughters of the Poor" pointed out. But nativism spurred public concern, as when New York officials insisted that most prostitutes and brothel owners, some of whom "have been

The Flanner House, a black settlement house in Indianapolis, provided the black community with many essential services, including health care. In addition to this baby clinic, pictured in 1918, it established a tuberculosis clinic at a time when the city's public hospitals refused to treat black citizens afflicted with the disease.

seducers of defenseless women all their lives," were foreign-born.

The response to prostitution was typical of progressivism: investigation and exposure, a reliance upon experts—boards of health, medical groups, clergy—for recommendations, and enactment of new laws. The New York City Committee of Fifteen, organized in 1900, investigated prostitution in response to complaints of clergymen and concerns about links among vice districts, urban political machines, and corrupt business interests. Its report dismissed as ineffective the European attempts to regulate prostitution. The progressive solution emerged in state and municipal action abolishing the "red light" districts previously tolerated and in a federal law, the Mann Act of 1910, prohibiting the interstate transport of women "for immoral purposes."

California provided other examples of progressives' interest in social control and moral reform. The state assembly, described by the *San Francisco Chronicle* as "a legislature of progressive cranks," prohibited gambling, cardplaying, and prizefighting. Los Angeles—influenced by the aptly named Morals Efficiency League—banned premarital sex and introduced censorship of art. One critic in 1913 complained that the reformers' "frenzy of virtue" made "Puritanism…the inflexible doctrine of Los Angeles."

For Whites Only?

Racism permeated the Progressive Era. In the South, progressivism was built on black disfranchisement and segregation. Like most white southerners, progressives believed that racial control was necessary for social order and that it enabled reformers to address other social problems. Such reformers also invoked racism to gain popular support for their objectives. In Georgia, for instance, child labor reformers warned that while white children worked in the Piedmont textile mills, black children were going to school: Child labor laws and compulsory school attendance laws were necessary to maintain white supremacy.

Governors Hoke Smith of Georgia and James Vardaman, "the White Chief," of Mississippi typified the link between racism and reform in the South. These men supported progressive reforms but also viciously attacked black rights. Their racist demagogy incited antiblack violence throughout the South. Antiblack race riots, like the one stirred up in Atlanta by Smith's election in 1906, and lynching—defended on the floor of the U.S. Senate by a southern progressive—were part of the system of racial control that made the era a terrible time for African Americans.

Even in the North, race relations deteriorated. Civil rights laws went unenforced, restaurants and hotels excluded black customers, and schools were segregated. A reporter in Pennsylvania found that "this disposition to discriminate against Negroes has greatly increased within the past decade." Antiblack race riots exploded in New York in 1900 and in Springfield, Illinois—Abraham Lincoln's hometown—in 1908.

Black activism.   Although most white progressives promoted or accepted racial discrimination, and most black southerners had to adapt to it, black progressive activism was growing. Even in the South, some African Americans struggled to improve conditions. In Atlanta, for example, black women created progressive organizations and established settlement houses, kindergartens, and daycare centers. With public parks reserved for white people, the Gate City Day Nursery Association built and supervised a playground on the campus of Atlanta Baptist College. The women of the Neighborhood Union, organized in 1908, even challenged the discriminatory policies of Atlanta's board of education, demanding equal facilities and appropriations for the city's black schools. They had only limited success, but their efforts demonstrated a persisting commitment to reform society.

In the North, African Americans more openly criticized discrimination and rejected Booker T. Washington's philosophy of accommodation. Ida Wells-Barnett, the crusading journalist who had fled the South for Chicago (see Chapter 17), became nationally prominent for her militant protests. She fought fiercely against racial injustices, especially school segregation, agitated for woman suffrage, and organized kindergartens and settlement houses for Chicago's black migrants.

Still more important was W. E. B. Du Bois, who campaigned tirelessly against all forms of racial discrimination. In 1905, Du Bois and other black activists met in Niagara Falls, Canada, to make plans to promote political and economic equality. In 1910, this **Niagara Movement** joined with a small group of white reformers, including Jane Addams, to organize the National Association for the Advancement of Colored People. The NAACP sought to overthrow segregation and establish equal justice and educational opportunities. As its director of publicity and research, Du Bois launched an influential magazine, *The Crisis,* to shape public opinion. "Agitate," he counseled, "protest, reveal the truth, and refuse to be silenced." By 1918, the NAACP had 44,000 members in 165 branches. Two generations later, it would successfully challenge the racial discrimination that most early-twentieth-century white progressives either supported or tolerated.

Reforming Politics and Government

Progressives of all kinds worked to reform politics and government. But their political activism was motivated by different concerns, and they sometimes pursued competing objectives. Many wanted to change procedures and institutions to promote greater democracy and responsibility. Others hoped to improve the efficiency of government, eliminate corruption, or increase their own influence. All justified their objectives as necessary to adapt the political system to the nation's new needs.

Carrying ballot boxes on a stretcher to ridicule American pretensions to a healthy democracy without woman suffrage, these activists marched in a dramatic parade in New York City in 1915. Combining such tactics with traditional appeals to patriotism and women's moral purity, woman suffragists eventually achieved the greatest democratic reform of the Progressive Era.

Woman Suffrage

One of the most important achievements of the era was woman suffrage. The movement had begun in the mid-nineteenth century, but suffragists had been frustrated by the prevailing belief that women's proper sphere was the home and the family. Males dominated the public sphere, including voting. Woman suffrage, especially when championed as a step toward women's equality, seemed to challenge the natural order of society, and it generated much opposition, not only among men but among traditionalist-minded women as well.

Most women progressives viewed suffrage as the key issue of the period. Already taking active leadership in broad areas of public affairs—especially by confronting and publicizing social problems and then lobbying legislators and other officials to adopt their proposed solutions—they thought it ridiculous to be barred from the ballot box. But most of all, the vote meant power, both to convince politicians to take seriously their demands for social reforms and to participate fully in electoral as in other forms of politics, thereby advancing the status of women.

In the early twentieth century, suffragists began to outflank their traditional opposition. Under a new generation of leaders, such as Carrie Chapman Catt and Harriot Stanton Blatch, they adopted activist tactics, including parades, mass meetings, and "suffrage tours" by automobile. They also organized by political districts and attracted workingwomen and labor unions. By 1917, the National American Woman Suffrage Association had over 2 million members.

Some suffrage leaders adopted new arguments to gain more support. Rather than insisting on the justice of woman suffrage or emphasizing equal rights, they spoke of the special moral and maternal instincts women could bring to politics if allowed to vote. The suffrage movement now appeared less a radical, disruptive force than a vehicle for extending traditional female benevolence and service to society. Many suffragists, particularly among working-class groups, remained committed to the larger possibilities they saw in suffrage, but the new image of the movement increased public support by appealing to conventional views of women. Noted one Nebraska undergraduate, women students no longer feared "antagonizing the men or losing invitations to parties by being suffragists."

Gradually, the suffrage movement began to prevail (see Map 21–1). In 1910, Washington became the first state since the mid-1890s to approve woman suffrage, followed by California in 1911 and Arizona, Kansas, and Oregon in 1912. Suffragists also mounted national actions, such as the dramatic inaugural parade in March 1913 described at the beginning of this chapter. The violence surrounding that event outraged public opinion, revived interest in a federal constitutional amendment to grant women the vote, and prompted women to send petitions and organize pilgrimages to Washington from across the country. By 1919, thirty-nine states had established full or partial woman suffrage, and Congress finally approved an amendment. Ratified by the states in 1920, the **Nineteenth Amendment** marked a critical advance in political democracy.

Electoral Reform

Other electoral reforms changed the election process and the meaning of political participation. The so-called **Australian ballot** adopted by most states during the 1890s provided for secret voting, freeing voters from intimidation and discouraging vote buying and other corruption. It also replaced the individual party tickets with an official ballot listing all candidates and distributed by public officials. The Australian ballot led to quiet, orderly elections. One Cincinnati editor, recalling the "howling mobs" and chaos at the polls in previous elections, declared, "The political bummer and thug has been relegated to the background…while good citizenship…has come to the front."

Government responsibility for the ballot soon led to public regulation of other parts of the electoral process previously controlled by parties. Beginning with Mississippi in 1902, nearly every state provided for direct primaries to remove nominations from the boss-ridden caucus and convention system. Many states also reformed campaign practices.

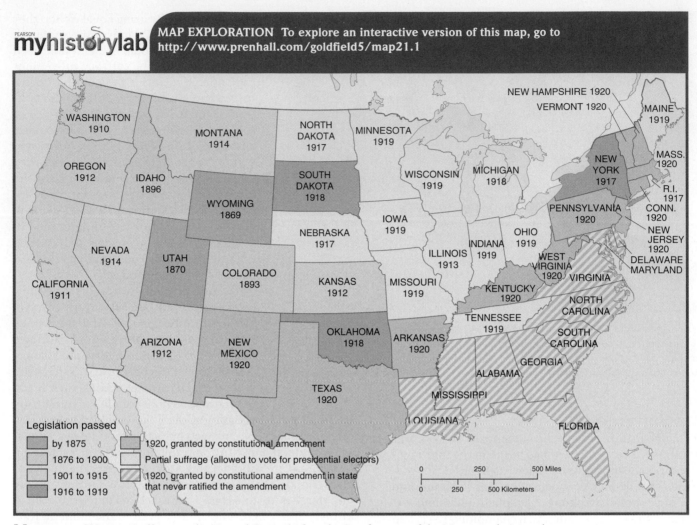

Legislation passed

- by 1875
- 1876 to 1900
- 1901 to 1915
- 1916 to 1919
- 1920, granted by constitutional amendment
- Partial suffrage (allowed to vote for presidential electors)
- 1920, granted by constitutional amendment in state that never ratified the amendment

MAP 21–1   Woman Suffrage in the United States before the Ratification of the Nineteenth Amendment
Beginning with Wyoming in 1869, woman suffrage slowly gained acceptance in the West, but women in the South and much of the East got the ballot only when the Nineteenth Amendment was ratified in 1920.

These reforms weakened the influence of political parties. Their decreasing ability to mobilize voters was reflected in a steady decline in voter participation, from 79 percent in 1896 to 49 percent in 1920 (see Figure 20–1). These developments had ominous implications, for parties and voting had traditionally linked ordinary Americans to their government. As parties slowly contracted, nonpartisan organizations and pressure groups, promoting narrower objectives, gained influence. Thus the National Association of Manufacturers (1895) and the United States Chamber of Commerce (1912) lobbied for business interests; the National Farmers Union (1902), for commercial agriculture; the American Federation of Teachers (1916), for professional educators. Many of these special-interest groups represented the same middle- or upper-class interests that had led the attack on parties. Their organized lobbying would steadily give them greater influence over government and contribute to the declining popular belief in the value of voting or participation in politics.

Disfranchisement more obviously undermined American democracy. In the South, Democrats—progressive and conservative alike—eliminated not only black voters but also many poor white voters from the electorate through poll taxes, literacy tests, and other restrictions. Republicans in the North adopted educational or literacy tests in ten states, enacted strict registration laws, and gradually abolished the right of aliens to vote. These restrictions reflected both the progressives' anti-immigrant prejudices and their obsessions with social control and with purifying politics and "improving" the electorate. Such electoral reforms reduced the political power of ethnic and working-class Americans, often stripping them of their political rights and means of influence.

Municipal Reform

Antiparty attitudes also affected progressives' efforts to reform municipal government, which they regarded as inefficient and corrupt, at least partly because of the power of urban political machines. Muckrakers had exposed crooked alliances between city bosses and business leaders that resulted in wasteful or inadequate municipal services. In some cities, urban reformers attempted to break these alliances and improve conditions for those suffering most from municipal misrule. For example, in Toledo, Ohio, Samuel "Golden Rule" Jones won enough working-class votes to be elected mayor four times despite the hostility of both major parties. Serving from 1897 to 1904, Jones opened public playgrounds and kindergartens, established the eight-hour day for city workers, and improved public services. Influenced by the Social Gospel, he also provided free lodging for the homeless and gave his own salary to the poor. Other reforming mayors fought municipal corruption, limited the political influence of corporations, and championed public ownership of utilities.

More elitist progressives attempted to change the structure of urban government by replacing ward elections, which could be controlled by the neighborhood-based city machine, with at-large elections. To win citywide elections required greater resources and therefore helped swell middle-class influence at the expense of the working class. So did nonpartisan elections, which reformers introduced to weaken party loyalties.

Urban reformers developed two other structural innovations: the city commission and the city manager. Both attempted to institutionalize efficient, businesslike government staffed by professional administrators. By 1920, hundreds of cities had adopted one of the new plans, which business groups often promoted. In Des Moines, for example, the president of the Commercial Club declared that "the professional politician must be ousted and in his place capable businessmen chosen to conduct the affairs of the city." Again, then, reform often shifted political power from ethnic and working-class voters, represented however imperfectly by partisan elections, to smaller groups with greater resources.

Progressive State Government

Progressives also reshaped state government. Some tried to democratize the legislative process, regarding the legislature—the most important branch of state government in the nineteenth century—as ineffective and even corrupt, dominated by party bosses and corporate influences. The Missouri legislature reportedly "enacted such laws as the corporations paid for, and such others as were necessary to fool the people." Populists had first raised such charges in the 1890s and proposed two novel solutions. The **initiative** enabled reformers to propose legislation directly to the electorate, bypassing an unresponsive legislature; the **referendum** permitted voters to approve or reject legislative measures. South Dakota Populists established the first system of "direct legislation" in 1898, and progressives adopted these innovations in 20 other states between 1902 and 1915.

Conservative opponents and procedural difficulties, however, often blocked these reforms or turned them against progressives. In the state of Washington in 1914, an initiative to establish an eight-hour workday was defeated by an electorate alarmed by conservative propaganda, and organized labor had to fight seven referendum measures, such as an antipicketing law, that business interests had promoted.

Other innovations also expanded the popular role in state government. The **Seventeenth Amendment,** ratified in 1913, provided for the election of U.S. senators directly by popular vote instead of by state legislatures. Beginning with Oregon in 1908, ten states adopted the **recall,** enabling voters to remove unsatisfactory public officials from office.

As state legislatures and party machines were curbed, dynamic governors such as Robert La Follette in Wisconsin, Charles Evans Hughes in New York, and Hiram Johnson in California pushed progressive programs into law. Elected governor in 1900, "Fighting Bob" La Follette turned Wisconsin into "the laboratory of democracy." Overcoming fierce opposition from "stalwart" Republicans, La Follette established direct primaries, railroad regulation, the first state income tax, workers' compensation, and other important measures before being elected to the U.S. Senate in 1906. La Follette also stressed efficiency and expertise. The Legislative Reference Bureau that he created to advise on public policy was staffed by university professors. He used regulatory commissions to oversee railroads, banks, and other interests. Most states followed suit, and expert commissions became an important feature of state government, gradually gaining authority at the expense of elected local officials.

"Experts" were presumed to be disinterested and therefore committed to the general welfare. In practice, however, regulators were subject to pressures from competing interest groups, and some commissions became captives of the very industries they were supposed to control. This irony was matched by the contradiction between the expansion of democracy through the initiative and referendum and the increasing reliance on nonelected professional experts to set and implement public policy. Such inconsistencies emphasize the complex mixture of ideas, objectives, and groups that were reshaping politics and government.

Theodore Roosevelt and the Progressive Presidency

When an anarchist assassinated William McKinley in 1901, Theodore Roosevelt entered the White House, and the progressive movement gained its most prominent leader. The son of a wealthy New York family, Roosevelt had pursued a career in Republican politics, serving as a New York legislator, U.S. civil service commissioner, and assistant secretary of the navy. After his exploits in the Spanish-American War (see chapter 22), he was elected governor of New York in 1898 and vice president in 1900. His public life was matched by an active private life, in which he both wrote works of history and obsessively pursued what he called the "strenuous life":

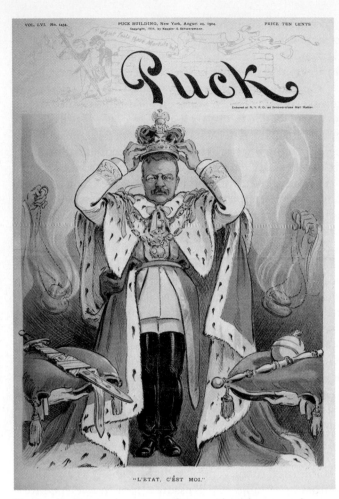

VOL. LVI. No. 1434.   PUCK BUILDING, New York, August 21, 1904.   PRICE TEN CENTS
Copyright, 1904, by Keppler & Schwarzmann.

Entered at N. Y. P. O. as Second-class Mail Matter.

Puck

"L'ETAT, C'EST MOI."

Fearing that Roosevelt was expanding presidential power and usuring Congressional authority, critics depicted him as assuming a monarchical role.

boxing, wrestling, hunting, rowing, even ranching and chasing rustlers in Dakota Territory.

Roosevelt's frenetic activity, aggressive personality, and penchant for self-promotion worried some Americans. Mark Twain fretted that "Mr. Roosevelt is the Tom Sawyer of the political world of the twentieth century; always showing off; always hunting for a chance to show off; in his frenzied imagination the Great Republic is a vast Barnum circus with him for a clown and the whole world for audience." But Roosevelt's flamboyance and ambitions made him the most popular politician of the time and enabled him to dramatize the issues of progressivism and to become the first modern president.

TR and the Modern Presidency

Roosevelt rejected the limited role of Gilded Age presidents. He believed that the president could do anything to meet national needs that the Constitution did not specifically prohibit. "Under this interpretation of executive power," he later recalled, "I did and caused to be done many things not pre-

viously done.... I did not usurp power, but I did greatly broaden the use of executive power." Indeed, the expansion of government power and its consolidation in the executive branch were among his most significant accomplishments.

Rather than defer to Congress, Roosevelt exerted legislative leadership. He spelled out his policy goals in more than 400 messages to Congress, sent drafts of bills to Capitol Hill, and intervened to win passage of "his" measures. Some members of Congress resented his "executive arrogance" and "dictatorship." Roosevelt generally avoided direct challenges to the conservative Old Guard Republicans who controlled Congress, but his activities helped shift the balance of power within the national government.

Roosevelt also reorganized the executive branch. He believed in efficiency and expertise, which he attempted to institutionalize in special commissions and administrative procedures. To promote rational policymaking and public management, he staffed the expanding federal bureaucracy with able professionals. Here, too, he provoked opposition. The president, complained one Republican, was "trying to concentrate all power in Washington... and to govern the people by commissions and bureaus."

Finally, Roosevelt encouraged the development of a personal presidency by exploiting the public's interest in their exuberant young president. He established the first White House press room and skillfully handled the mass media. His endless and well-reported activities, from playing with his children in the White House to wrestling, hiking, and horseback-riding with various notables, made him a celebrity, known as TR or Teddy. The publicity not only kept TR in the spotlight but also enabled him to mold public opinion.

Roosevelt and Labor

One sign of TR's vigorous new approach to the presidency was his handling of a coal strike in 1902. Members of the United Mine Workers Union walked off their jobs, demanding higher wages, an eight-hour day, and recognition of their union. The mine owners closed the mines and waited for the union to collapse. But led by John Mitchell, the strikers held their ranks. The prospect of a freezing winter frightened consumers. Management's stubborn arrogance contrasted with the workers' orderly conduct and willingness to negotiate and hardened public opinion against the owners.

Although his legal advisers told him that the government had no authority to intervene, Roosevelt invited both the owners and the union leaders to the White House and declared that the national interest made government action necessary. Mitchell agreed to negotiate with the owners or to accept an arbitration commission appointed by the president. The owners, however, refused even to speak to the miners and demanded that Roosevelt use the army to break the union, as Cleveland had done in the Pullman strike in 1894.

Roosevelt was not a champion of labor, and he had favored shooting the Pullman strikers. But as president, he believed his role was to mediate social conflict for the public good. Furious with the owners' "arrogant stupidity" and "insulting" attitude toward the presidency, Roosevelt announced that he would use the army to seize and operate the mines, not to crush the union. Questioned about the constitutionality of such an action, Roosevelt bellowed, "To hell with the Constitution when the people want coal." Reluctantly, the owners accepted the arbitration commission they had previously rejected. The commission gave the miners a 10 percent wage increase and a nine-hour day, but not union recognition, and permitted the owners to raise coal prices by 10 percent. Roosevelt described his intervention as simply giving both labor and management a "square deal." It also set important precedents for an active government role in labor disputes and a strong president acting as a steward of the public.

Managing Natural Resources

Federal land policy had helped create farms and develop transportation, but it had also ceded to speculators and business interests much of the nation's forests, mineral deposits, waterpower sites, and grazing lands. Reckless exploitation of these resources alarmed a new generation that believed the public welfare required the **conservation** of natural resources through efficient and scientific management. Conservationists achieved early victories in the Forest Reserve Act (1891) and the Forest Management Act (1897), which authorized the federal government to withdraw timberlands from development and to regulate grazing, lumbering, and hydroelectric sites in the forests (see Map 21–2).

Roosevelt built on these beginnings and on his friendship with Gifford Pinchot to make conservation a major focus of his presidency. Pinchot had been trained in French and German scientific forestry practices. Appointed in 1898 to head the new Division of Forestry (renamed the Forest Service in 1905), he brought rational management and regulation to resource development. With his advice, TR used presidential authority to triple the size of the forest reserves to 150 million acres, set aside another 80 million acres valuable for minerals and petroleum, and establish dozens of wildlife refuges. In 1908, Roosevelt held a White House conference of state and federal officials that led to the creation of the National Conservation Commission, 41 state conservation commissions, and widespread public support for the conservation movement.

Not everyone, of course, agreed with TR's conservationist policies. Some favored **preservation,** hoping to set aside land as permanent wilderness, whereas Roosevelt favored a scientific and efficient rather than uncontrolled use of resources. Pinchot declared, "Wilderness is waste." Preservationists won some victories, saving a stand of California's giant redwoods and helping create the National Park Service in 1916, but more Americans favored the utilitarian emphasis of the early conservationists.

Other interests opposed conservation completely. While some of the larger timber and mineral companies supported conservation as a way to guarantee long-run profits, smaller western entrepreneurs often cared only about quick returns. Many westerners, moreover, resented having easterners make key decisions about western growth and saw conservation as a perpetuation of this colonial subservience. Many ranchers refused to pay federal grazing fees. Colorado arsonists set forest fires to protest the creation of forest reserves.

But westerners were happy to take federal money for expensive irrigation projects that private capital would not underwrite. They favored the 1902 National Reclamation Act, which established what became the **Bureau of Reclamation.** Its engineers were to construct dams, reservoirs, and irrigation canals, and the government was to sell the irrigated lands in tracts no larger than 160 acres. With massive dams and networks of irrigation canals, it reclaimed fertile valleys from the desert, but by not enforcing the 160-acre limitation it helped create powerful corporate farms in the West.

Westerners also welcomed Roosevelt's policies of conservation and rational development when they restricted Indian control of land and resources. Based on racist assumptions that Indians wasted natural resources, these policies sought to break up many reservations to open the land to whites for "efficient" development. Roosevelt also supported irrigation projects on Indian land that diverted Indian rivers to make water available to whites, not only in agriculture but in growing cities like Phoenix. Tribal protests were ignored.

Corporate Regulation

Nothing symbolized Roosevelt's active presidency better than his popular reputation as a "trust buster." TR regarded the formation of large business combinations favorably, but he realized he could not ignore the public anxiety about corporate power. Business leaders and Old Guard conservatives opposed any government intervention in the large trusts, but Roosevelt knew better. "You have no conception of the revolt that would be caused if I did nothing," he said privately. To satisfy popular clamor, ensure social stability, and still retain the economic advantages of big modern corporations, TR proposed to "develop an orderly system, and such a system can only come through the gradually exercised right of efficient government control." Rather than invoking "the foolish antitrust law," he favored government regulation to prevent corporate abuses and defend the public interest. "Misconduct," not size, was the issue. Roosevelt preferred to use government agencies to work with corporations to avoid lawsuits. But he did sue some "bad trusts."

In 1902, the Roosevelt administration filed its most famous antitrust suit, against the Northern Securities Company, a holding company organized by J. P. Morgan to control the railroad network of the Northwest. For TR, this suit was an assertion of government power that reassured a worried public and encouraged corporate responsibility. In 1904, the

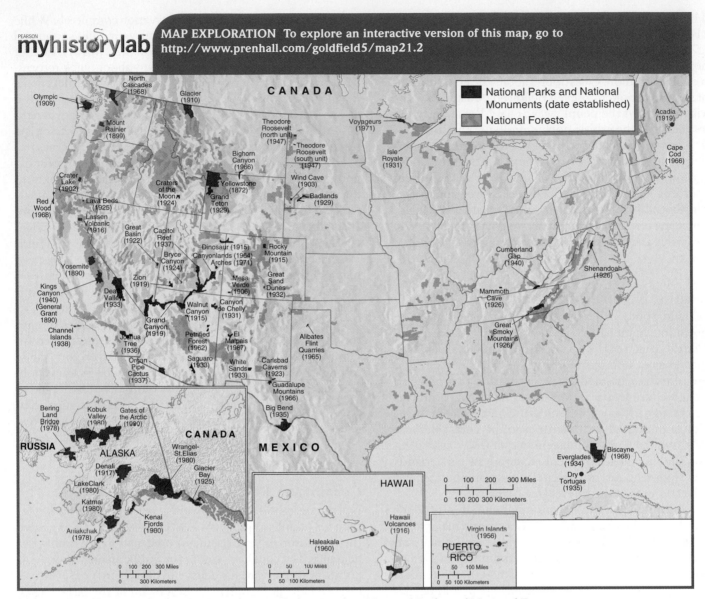

MAP 21–2   The Growth of Federal Reserves, Including Leading National Parks and National Forests
Rapid exploitation of the West prompted demands to preserve its spectacular scenery and protect its remaining forests. In 1872 Yellowstone became the first National Park, and the National Forest system began in the 1890s. Conservation became increasingly important during the Progressive Era but often provoked Western hostility.

Supreme Court ordered the dissolution of the Northern Securities Company. Ultimately, Roosevelt brought 44 antitrust suits against business combinations, but except for a few like Standard Oil, he avoided the giant firms. Many of the cases had inconclusive outcomes, but Roosevelt was more interested in establishing a regulatory role for government than in breaking up big businesses.

Elected president in his own right in 1904 over the colorless and conservative Democratic candidate, Judge Alton B. Parker, Roosevelt responded to the growing popular demand for reform by pushing further toward a regulatory government. He proposed legislation "to work out methods of controlling the big corporations without paralyzing the energies of the business community." In 1906, Congress passed the Hepburn Act, the Pure Food and Drug Act, and the Meat Inspection Act. All three were compromises between reformers seeking serious government control of the industries involved and political defenders and lobbyists of the industries themselves.

The Hepburn Act authorized the Interstate Commerce Commission to set maximum railroad rates. Although a weaker law than many progressives had wanted, it marked the first time the federal government gained the power to set rules for a private enterprise. The two other laws aimed at consumer protection in food and drugs. In part, this legislation reflected public demand, but many business leaders also supported government regulation, convinced that it would expand their markets by certifying the quality of their products and drive their smaller competitors out of business. Thus the laws extended government supervision and regulation over business to protect the public health and safety, but they also served some corporate purposes.

Despite the compromises and weaknesses in the three laws, TR contended that they marked "a noteworthy advance in the policy of securing federal supervision and control over corporations." In 1907 and 1908, he pushed for an eight-hour workday, stock market regulation, and inheritance and income taxes. Republican conservatives in Congress blocked such reforms, and tensions increased between the progressive and conservative wings of the party. Old Guard Republicans thought Roosevelt had extended government powers dangerously, but in fact his accomplishments had been relatively modest because of his need to compromise in Congress. As La Follette noted, Roosevelt's "cannonading filled the air with noise and smoke, which confused and obscured the line of action, but, when the battle cloud drifted by and the quiet was restored, it was always a matter of surprise that so little had really been accomplished."

Taft and the Insurgents

TR handpicked his successor as president: a loyal lieutenant, William Howard Taft. Taft had been a federal judge, governor-general of the Philippines, and secretary of war. Later he would serve as chief justice of the United States. But if Roosevelt thought that Taft would be a successful president, continuing his policies and holding the Republican Party together, he was wrong. Taft's election in 1908, over Democrat William Jennings Bryan in his third presidential campaign, led to a Republican political disaster.

Taft did preside over important progressive achievements. His administration pursued a more active and successful antitrust program than Roosevelt's. He supported the Mann-Elkins Act (1910), which extended the ICC's jurisdiction to telephone and telegraph companies. Taft set aside more public forest lands and oil reserves than Roosevelt had. He also supported a constitutional amendment authorizing an income tax, which went into effect in 1913 under the **Sixteenth Amendment.** One of the most important accomplishments of the Progressive Era, the income tax would provide the means for the government to expand its activities and responsibilities.

Nevertheless, Taft soon alienated progressives and floundered into a political morass. His problems were twofold. First, the Republicans were divided. Midwestern reform Republicans, led by La Follette, clashed with conservative Republicans, led by Senator Nelson Aldrich of Rhode Island. Second, Taft was politically inept. Even his wife complained of his "unfortunate shortcoming of not knowing much and of caring less about the way the game of politics is played." He was unable to mediate between the two Republican factions, and the party split apart.

Reformers wanted to restrict the power of the speaker of the House, "Uncle Joe" Cannon, a reactionary who systematically blocked progressive measures and loudly declared, "I am goddamned tired of listening to all this babble of reform." After seeming to promise support, Taft backed down when conservatives threatened to defeat important legislation. The insurgents in Congress eventually restricted the speaker's powers, but they never forgave what they saw as Taft's betrayal. The tariff also alienated progressives from Taft. He had campaigned in 1908 for a lower tariff to curb inflation—and to the approval of midwestern Republicans. But when they introduced tariff reform legislation, the president failed to support them, and Aldrich's Senate committee added 847 amendments, many of which raised tariff rates. Taft justified his inaction as avoiding presidential interference with congressional business, but this position clashed with TR's example and the reformers' expectations. Progressives concluded that Taft had sided with the Old Guard against real change.

This perception solidified when Taft stumbled into a controversy over conservation. Gifford Pinchot had become embroiled in a complex struggle with Richard Ballinger, Taft's secretary of the interior. Ballinger, who was closely tied to western mining and lumbering interests, favored private development of public lands. When Pinchot challenged Ballinger's role in a questionable sale of public coal lands in Alaska to a J. P. Morgan syndicate, Taft upheld Ballinger and fired Pinchot. Progressives concluded that Taft had repudiated Roosevelt's conservation policies.

The Progressives determined to replace Taft, whom they now saw as an obstacle to reform. In 1911, the National Progressive League organized to champion La Follette for the Republican nomination in 1912. Roosevelt rejected an appeal for support, convinced that a challenge to the incumbent president was both doomed and divisive. Besides, his own position was closer to Taft's than to what he called "the La Follette type of fool radicalism." But Taft's political blunders increasingly angered Roosevelt. Condemning Taft as "disloyal to our past friendship," TR began to campaign for the Republican nomination himself. In 13 state primaries, he won 278 delegates, to only 46 for Taft. But most states did not then have primaries; as a result, Taft was able to dominate the Republican convention and win renomination. Roosevelt's forces formed a third party—the Progressive Party—and nominated the former president. The Republican split almost guaranteed victory for the Democratic nominee, Woodrow Wilson.

Woodrow Wilson and Progressive Reform

The pressures for reform called forth many new leaders. The one who would preside over progressivism's culmination, and ultimately its collapse, was Woodrow Wilson. Elected president in 1912 and 1916, he mediated among differing progres-

A portrait of Woodrow Wilson by Edward Charles Tarbell. A strong president, Wilson led Congress to enact sweeping and significant legislation.

quarreled during Taft's administration, Democrats pushed progressive remedies and achieved major victories in the state and congressional elections of 1910. To improve the party's chances in 1912, Bryan announced that he would step aside. The Democratic spotlight shifted to the governor of New Jersey, Woodrow Wilson.

Wilson combined public eloquence with a cold personality; he balanced a self-righteousness that led to stubborn inflexibility with an intense ambition that permitted the most expedient compromises. Wilson first entered public life as a conservative, steeped in the limited-government traditions of his native South. As president of Princeton University, beginning in 1902, he became a prominent representative of middle-class respectability and conservative causes. In 1910, New Jersey's Democratic bosses selected him for governor to head off the progressives, but once in office, Wilson championed popular reforms and immediately began to campaign as a progressive for the party's 1912 presidential nomination.

Wilson's progressivism differed from that of Roosevelt in 1912. TR emphasized a strong government to promote economic and social order. He defended big business as inevitable and healthy provided that government control ensured that it would benefit the entire nation. Roosevelt called this program the **New Nationalism,** reflecting his belief in a powerful state and a national interest. He also supported demands for social welfare, including workers' compensation and the abolition of child labor.

Wilson was horrified by Roosevelt's vision. His **New Freedom** program rejected what he called TR's "regulated monopoly." Wilson wanted "regulated competition," with the goverment's role limited to breaking up monopolies through antitrust action and preventing artificial barriers like tariffs from blocking free enterprise. Wilson opposed social welfare legislation as paternalistic, reaching beyond the proper scope of the federal government, which he hoped to minimize. (This position, shot back the alarmed Roosevelt, meant the repeal of "every law for the promotion of social and industrial justice.")

Roosevelt's endorsement of social legislation attracted many women into political action. As Jane Addams observed, "their long concern for the human wreckage of industry has come to be considered politics." (See American Views, Jane

sive views to achieve a strong reform program, enlarge the power of the executive branch, and make the White House the center of national politics.

The Election of 1912

Despite the prominence of Roosevelt and La Follette, progressivism was not simply a Republican phenomenon. In Congress, southern Democrats more consistently supported reform measures than Republicans did, and the Democratic leader William Jennings Bryan surpassed Roosevelt as a persistent advocate of significant reform. As the Republicans

American Views

Jane Addams and the Progressive Party

Jane Addams, the founder of Hull House in Chicago, was active not merely in a range of social reform movements but also in nearly every facet of progressive politics. An ardent suffragist, Addams seconded the presidential nomination of Theodore Roosevelt at the founding convention of the Progressive Party in 1912, while a "Jane Addams Chorus" sang "Onward, Christian Soldiers" and "The Battle Hymn of the Republic." In this reminiscence from her second autobiography, Addams describes the convention and her part in the party's campaign that year.

■ Why did settlement workers like Addams see the Progressive Party as the climax to their struggle for social justice?

■ How did Addams's political interests fit into Roosevelt's program of the New Nationalism?

■ How does Addams's rhetoric reflect the moral impulses underlying much of progressive reform?

■ Why does Addams believe that women were attracted to the Progressive Party?

It was in August, 1912, that the Progressive Party was organized.

Suddenly, as if by magic, the city of Chicago became filled with men and women from every state in the Union who were evidently haunted by the same social compunctions and animated by like hopes; they revealed to each other mutual sympathies and memories. They urged methods which had already been tried in other countries, for righting old wrongs and for establishing standards in industry. For three days together they defined their purposes and harmonized their wills into gigantic cooperation....

They believed that the program of social legislation placed before the country by the Progressive Party was of great significance to the average voter quite irrespective of the party which might finally claim his allegiance.

The platform, in the hope that the political organization of the nation might never again get so far away from the life of the people, advocated equal suffrage, direct primaries, the initiative and referendum.... In spite of our belief in our leader [Theodore Roosevelt], I was there, and I think the same was true of many others, because the platform expressed the social hopes so long ignored by the politicians; although we appreciated to the full our good fortune in securing on their behalf the magnetic personality of the distinguished candidate. Perhaps we felt so keenly the uplifting sense of comradeship with old friends and coworkers not only because we had all realized how inadequate we were in small groups but because the very sentiments of compassion and desire for social justice were futile unless they could at last find ex-

pression as an integral part of...government. At any rate, it was evident that measures of industrial amelioration and demands for social justice, so long discussed by small groups, were at last thrust into the stern arena of political action....

The Progressive Convention has been described many times, and perhaps never quite adequately. It was a curious moment of release from inhibitions, and it did not seem in the least strange that reticent men and women should speak aloud of their religious and social beliefs, confident that they would be understood.

The women who identified themselves with the Progressive Convention inevitably experienced moments of heart searching and compunction. It is hard to understand it now, after we have possessed the ballot for a decade and have come to deem it a virtue "to enter politics," but at the moment we felt it necessary to give to the public our reasons for thus identifying ourselves with a political party. We said that when a great party pledges itself to the protection of children, to the care of the aged, to the relief of overworked girls, to the safeguarding of burdened men, it is inevitable that it should appeal to women and should seek to draw upon the great reservoir of their moral energy so long undesired and unutilized in practical politics; that one is the corollary of the other; a program of human welfare, the necessity for women's participation.

The real interest in the measures advocated in the party platform came however during the campaign itself when it was possible to place them before many groups throughout the country. Sometimes the planks in our platform were sharply challenged, but more often regarded with approval and occasionally with enthusiasm. I recall a meeting in Leadville, Colorado, made up altogether of miners who were much surprised to find that politics had anything to do with such affairs. They had always supposed that hours of labor were matters to be fought for and not voted upon. It was very exhilarating to talk to them, and it seemed to me that I had never before realized how slow we had been to place the definite interests of the workingmen in such shape that they could be voted upon. As a campaign speaker I was sent from town to town in both Dakotas, in Iowa, Nebraska, Oklahoma, Colorado, Kansas, and Missouri. The comrade-

ship which a like-minded group always affords, combined with the heartiness of western good will, kept my spirits at high tide in spite of the fatigue of incessant speaking....

The campaign renewed one's convictions that if the community as a whole were better informed as to the ethical implications of industrial wrongs whole areas of life could be saved from becoming brutalized or from sinking into hard indifference....At moments we believed that we were witnessing a new pioneering of the human spirit, that we were in all humility inaugurating an exploration into the moral resources of our fellow citizens.

Source: Jane Addams, *The Second Twenty Years at Hull-House* (New York: Macmillan, 1930).

Addams and the Progressive Party.) The Progressive Party also endorsed woman suffrage, accepted women as convention delegates, and pledged to give women equal representation on party committees. The *New York Times* exaggerated in claiming that the 1912 campaign had become "feminized," but certainly women activists welcomed the opportunity of participating "in party affairs before the vote is won" and thereby "answering forcibly many of the objections to the vote" for women.

Despite his personal popularity, however, TR was unable to add progressive Democrats to the Republicans who followed him into the Progressive Party, and thus was doomed to defeat. Other reform voters embraced the Socialist candidate, Eugene V. Debs, who captured 900,000 votes—6 percent of the total. Taft played little role in the campaign. "I might as well give up as far as being a candidate," he lamented. "There are so many people in the country who don't like me."

Wilson won an easy electoral college victory, though he received only 42 percent of the popular vote and fewer popular votes than Bryan had won in any of his three campaigns (see Map 21–3). Roosevelt came in second, Taft third. The Democrats also gained control of Congress, giving Wilson the opportunity to enact his New Freedom program.

Implementing the New Freedom

As president, Wilson built on Roosevelt's precedent to strengthen executive authority. He proposed a full legislative program and worked forcefully to secure its approval. He held regular conferences with Democratic leaders and had a private telephone line installed between the Capitol and the White House to keep tabs on congressional actions. When necessary, he appealed to the public for support, ruth-

lessly used patronage, or compromised with conservatives. With such methods and a solid Democratic majority, Wilson gained approval of important laws.

Wilson turned first to the traditional Democratic goal of reducing the high protective tariff, the symbol of special privileges for industry. He forced through the **Underwood-Simmons Tariff Act** of 1913, the first substantial reduction in duties since before the Civil War. The act also levied the first income tax under the recently ratified Sixteenth Amendment. Conservatives condemned the "revolutionary" tax, but it was designed simply to compensate for lower tariff rates. The top tax rate paid by the wealthiest was a mere 7 percent.

Wilson next reformed the nation's banking and currency system, which was inadequate for a modernizing economy. A panic in 1907 and a subsequent congressional investigation had dramatized the need for a more flexible and decentralized financial system. Wilson skillfully maneuvered a compromise measure through Congress, balancing the demands of agrarian progressives for government control with the bankers' desires for private control. The **Federal Reserve Act** of 1913 created 12 regional Federal Reserve banks that, although privately controlled, were to be supervised by the Federal Reserve Board, appointed by the president. The law also provided for a flexible national currency and improved access to credit. Serious problems remained, but the new system promoted the progressive goals of order and efficiency and fulfilled Wilson's New Freedom principle of introducing limited government regulation while preserving private business control.

Wilson's third objective was new legislation to break up monopolies. Initially, he supported the Clayton antitrust bill, which prohibited unfair trade practices and sharply restricted holding companies. But when business leaders and other progressives strenuously objected, Wilson reversed himself.

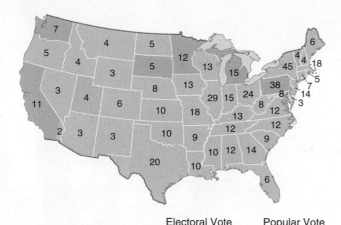

	Electoral Vote (%)	Popular Vote (%)
WOODROW WILSON **(Democrat)**	**435** **(82)**	**6,296,547** **(42)**
Theodore Roosevelt (Progressive)	88 (17)	4,118,571 (27)
William Taft (Republican)	8 (1)	3,486,720 (23)
Eugene Debs (Socialist)	–	900,672 (6)

MAP 21–3   The Election of 1912
The split within the Republican Party enabled Woodrow Wilson to carry most states and become president even though he won only a minority of the popular vote.

Opting for continuous federal regulation rather than for the dissolution of trusts, Wilson endorsed the creation of the **Federal Trade Commission (FTC)** to oversee business activity and prevent illegal restrictions on competition.

The Federal Trade Commission Act of 1914 dismayed many of Wilson's early supporters because it embraced the New Nationalism's emphasis on positive regulation. Roosevelt's 1912 platform had proposed a federal trade commission; Wilson now accepted what he had earlier denounced as a partnership between trusts and the government that the trusts would dominate. Indeed, Wilson's conservative appointments to the FTC ensured that the agency would not seriously interfere with business, and by the 1920s, the FTC had become virtually a junior partner of the business community.

The fate of the Clayton antitrust bill after Wilson withdrew his support reflected his new attitude toward big business. Congressional conservatives gutted the bill with crippling amendments before permitting it to become law in 1914. As one senator complained, "When the Clayton bill was first written, it was a raging lion with a mouth full of teeth. It has degenerated to a tabby cat with soft gums, a plaintive mew, and an anemic appearance. It is a sort of legislative apology to the trusts, delivered hat in hand, and accompanied by assurances that no discourtesy is intended."

These measures indicate the limited nature of Wilson's vision of reform. In fact, he now announced that no further reforms were necessary—astonishing many progressives whose objectives had been completely ignored. Wilson refused to support woman suffrage and helped kill legislation abolishing child labor and expanding credits to farmers. Race relations provided a flagrant instance of Wilson's indifference to issues of social justice. Raised in the South, he believed in segregation and backed the southern Democrats in his cabinet when they introduced formal segregation within the government itself. Government offices, shops, restrooms, and restaurants were all segregated; employees who complained were fired. Federal officials in the South discharged black employees. One Georgia official promised that there would be no more government jobs for African Americans: "A Negro's place is in the cornfield."

The Expansion of Reform

Wilson had won in 1912 only because the Republicans had split. By 1916, Roosevelt had returned to the GOP, and Wilson realized that he had to attract some of TR's former followers. Wilson therefore abandoned his opposition to social and economic reforms and promoted measures he had previously condemned. But he had also grown in the White House and now recognized that some problems could be resolved only by positive federal action.

To assist farmers, Wilson in 1916 convinced Congress to pass the Federal Farm Loan Act. This law, which Wilson himself had earlier rejected twice, provided farmers with federally financed long-term agricultural credits. The Warehouse Act of 1916 improved short-term agricultural credit. The Highway Act of 1916 provided funds to construct and improve rural roads through the adoption of the dollar-matching principle by which the federal government would expand its power over state activities in the twentieth century.

Wilson and the Democratic Congress also reached out to labor. Wilson signed the Keating-Owen Act prohibiting the interstate shipment of products made by child labor. In 1902, Wilson had denounced Roosevelt's intervention in the coal strike, but in 1916 he broke a labor-management impasse and averted a railroad strike by helping pass the Adamson Act establishing an eight-hour day for railroad workers. Wilson also pushed the Kern-McGillicuddy Act, which achieved the progressive goal of a workers' compensation system for federal employees. Together, these laws marked an important advance toward government regulation of the labor market.

Wilson also promoted activist government when he nominated Louis Brandeis to the Supreme Court. Known as "the people's lawyer," Brandeis had successfully defended protective labor legislation before the conservative judiciary. The nomination outraged conservatives, including William Howard Taft and the American Bar Association. Brandeis was the first Jew nominated to the court, and anti-Semitism motivated some of his opponents. Wilson overcame a vicious campaign against Brandeis and secured his confirmation.

FROM THEN TO NOW

The Environmental Movement

Many of the issues that concern environmentalists today were first raised by the conservationists and preservationists of the Progressive Era. Led by Theodore Roosevelt, conservationists favored the planned and regulated management of America's natural resources for the public benefit. In contrast, preservationists—like John Muir, who founded the Sierra Club in 1892—sought to protect wilderness from any development whatsoever. Opposing both were those who championed the uncontrolled development of public lands.

Decades later, public concern over polluted rivers, oil spills, and urban smog gave birth to the environmental movement, which drew on the legacy of both the conservation and preservation movements but had wider interests and broader support than either. Beginning in the 1970s, Congress passed laws to protect endangered species, reduce pollution, limit the use of pesticides, and control hazardous waste. The Environmental Protection Agency became the largest federal regulatory agency.

Again, however, as during the Progressive Era, efforts to protect the environment encountered opposition from proponents of unrestricted development, especially in the West. In the Sagebrush Rebellion in the 1980s, some Westerners condemned "outside" federal regulation and tried to seize control of public lands for private exploitation. One oil company dismissed catastrophic oil spills as merely "Mother Earth letting some oil come out." And four Republican presidents from the West—Californians Richard Nixon and Ronald Reagan and Texans George Bush and George W. Bush, all closely tied to oil and real estate interests—sought in varying degrees to curtail environmental policies, agencies, and budgets, even to deny the existence of global warming, and to oppose environmental protection as inconsistent with economic growth. This repudiation of Theodore Roosevelt's conservationism reflected the shift of the party's base to the sunbelt. As one presidential adviser said, "Conservation is not in the Republican ethic."

Congress, the courts, and the public, however, generally resisted efforts to weaken environmental policy. Debate is sure to continue over the cost and effectiveness of specific policies, but Americans are increasingly inclined to stand with Theodore Roosevelt and John Muir in looking to the federal government for effective action to resolve environmental problems.

■ How do differing economic and political attitudes underlie the conflicting stances of Americans toward environmental issues?

**United Nations
Climate Change Conference**

Former Vice President Al Gore won the Nobel Peace Prize for helping direct attention to the dangers of global warming.

Theodore Roosevelt and John Muir, here on a 1903 camping trip in Yosemite, championed public responsibility for the nation's scenic and other natural resources.

PEARSON
myhistorylab
From Then to Now Online

21-1 Gifford Pinchot, *The Fight for Conservation*, 1910. The man who coined the tern "conservation" defends the movement it describes.

21-2 George L. Knapp, *The Other Side of Conservation*, 1910. A publicist for the opponents of conservation attacks the movement.

By these actions, Wilson brought progressivism to a culmination of sorts and consolidated reformers behind him for a second term. Less than a decade earlier, Wilson the private citizen had assailed government regulation and social legislation; by 1916, he had guided an unprecedented expansion of federal power. His own transformation symbolized the development of progressivism.

Conclusion

In the early twentieth century, progressive reformers responded to the tensions of industrial and urban development by moving to change society and government. Rejecting the earlier emphasis on individualism and laissez-faire, they organized to promote social change and an interventionist state. Programs and laws to protect women, children, and injured workers testified to their compassion; the creation of new agencies and political techniques indicated their interest in order and efficiency; campaigns to end corruption, whether perceived in urban political machines, corporate influence, drunkeness, or "inferior" immigrants, illustrated their self-assured vision of the public good.

Progressivism had its ironies and paradoxes. It called for democratic reforms—and did achieve woman suffrage, direct legislation, and popular election of senators—but helped disfranchise black southerners and northern immigrants. It advocated social justice but often enforced social control. It demanded responsive government but helped create bureaucracies largely removed from popular control. It endorsed the regulation of business in the public interest but forged regulatory laws and commissions that tended to aid business. Some of these seeming contradictions reflected the persistence of traditional attitudes and the need to accommodate conservative opponents; others revealed the progressives' own limitations in vision, concern, or nerve.

Nonetheless, both the successes and the failures of progressivism revealed that the nature of politics and government had changed significantly. Americans had come to accept that government action could resolve social and economic problems, and the role and power of government expanded accordingly. The emergence of an activist presidency, capable of developing programs, mobilizing public opinion, directing Congress, and taking forceful action, epitomized this key development.

These important features would be crucial when the nation fought World War I, which brought new challenges and dangers to the United States. The Great War would expose many of the limitations of progressivism and the naiveté of the progressives' optimism.

Review Questions

1. How and why did the presidency change during the Progressive Era?

2. How did the progressive concern for efficiency affect social reform efforts, public education, government administration, and rural life?

3. How and why did the relationship between business and government change during this time?

4. Why did social reform and social control often intermingle in the Progressive Era? Can such objectives be separate?

5. What factors, old and new, stimulated the reform movements of progressivism?

6. How did the role of women change during the Progressive Era? How did the changes affect progressivism?

7. Why did the demand for woman suffrage provoke such determined support and such bitter opposition, as illustrated by the 1913 parade and riot in Washington, DC?

Key Terms

Australian ballot (p. 595)

Bureau of Reclamation (p. 599)

Conservation (p. 599)

Eighteenth Amendment (p. 593)

Federal Reserve Act (p. 604)

Federal Trade Commission (p. 605)

Fundamentalists (p. 588)

Initiative (p. 597)

Muckraking (p. 584)

New Freedom (p. 602)

New Nationalism (p. 602)

Niagara Movement (p. 594)

Nineteenth Amendment (p. 595)

Preservation (p. 599)

Progressive Era (p. 581)

Prohibition (p. 593)

Recall (p. 597)

Referendum (p. 597)

Seventeenth Amendment (p. 597)

Sixteenth Amendment (p. 601)

Social Gospel Movement (p. 583)

Underwood-Simmons Tariff Act (p. 604)

Wobblies (p. 585)

Recommended Reading

Addams, Jane. *Twenty Years at Hull House* (1910). Jane Addams's own classic story of settlement work.

Baker, Jean H. *Votes for Women* (2002). A valuable collection of essays illuminating themes, activities, and leaders of the woman suffrage movement.

Diner, Steven J. *A Very Different Age: Americans of the Progressive Era* (1998). An engaging survey of the era, stressing social history.

Flanagan, Maureen. *America Reformed: Progressives and Progressivisms* (2007). A valuable new study examining key progressive ideas and how they were implemented in public policy.

Gould, Lewis L. *The Presidency of Theodore Roosevelt* (1991). A balanced and comprehensive account of TR's presidency.

Wiebe, Robert. *The Search for Order, 1877–1920* (1967). A masterful essay that emphasizes the organizational thrust of middle-class progressives.

Where to Learn More

■ **John Muir National Historic Site, Martinez, California.**   The architecture and furnishings of this 17-room house reflect the interests of John Muir, the writer and naturalist who founded the Sierra Club and led the preservationists in the Progressive Era. www.nps.gov/jomu

■ **Sewall-Belmont House National Historic Site, Washington, DC.**   Headquarters of the National Woman's Party, this 200-year-old house on Capitol Hill has memorabilia of the woman suffrage movement, including posters, flags, and photographs of the early marches, and an extensive feminist library focused on the struggle for equal suffrage. Beginning in 1923 Alice Paul campaigned from this building for the Equal Rights Amendment. http://www.sewallbelmont.org

■ **Hull House, Chicago, Illinois.**   This pioneering settlement house is now a museum on the campus of the University of Illinois, Chicago. www.uic.edu/jaddams/hull/hull_house.html

■ **Lower East Side Tenement Museum, New York City, New York.**   A six-story tenement building containing 22 apartments, this museum vividly illustrates the congested and unhealthy living conditions of urban immigrants from the 1870s to the early twentieth century. See www.tenement.org for a virtual tour.

Study Resources

For study resources for this chapter, go to www.myhistorylab.com and choose *The American Journey*. You will find a wealth of study and review material for this chapter, including pre- and post-tests, customized study plan, key term review flash cards, interactive map and document activities, and documents for analysis.

A jubilant Uncle Sam celebrates victory in the Spanish-American War and anticipates the building of an American empire.

Creating an Empire 22
1865–1917

Havana, Cuba October 1901

When the Spanish-American war was declared the United States . . . assumed a position as protector of the interests of Cuba. It became responsible for the welfare of the people, politically, mentally, and morally. The mere fact of freeing the island from Spanish rule has not ended the care which this country should give. . . . The effect will be to uplift the people, gaining their permanent friendship and support and greatly increasing our own commerce. At present there are two million people requiring clothing and food, for but a small proportion of the necessaries of life are raised on the island. It is folly to grow food crops when sugar and tobacco produce such rich revenues in comparison. The United States should supply the Cubans with their breadstuffs, even wine,

fruit, and vegetables, and should clothe the people. . . . The money received for their crops will be turned over in a great measure in buying supplies from the United States. . . .

Naturally the manufacturers of the United States should have precedence in furnishing machinery, locomotives, cars, and rails, materials for buildings and bridges, and the wide diversity of other supplies required, as well as fuel for their furnaces. With the present financial and commercial uncertainty at an end the people of the island will . . . come into the American market as customers for products of many kinds.

The meeting of the Constitutional Convention on November 5th will be an event in Cuban history of the greatest importance, and much will depend upon the action and outcome of this convention as to our future control of the island. . . . I considered it unwise to interfere, and I have made it a settled policy to permit the Cubans to manage every part of their constitution-making. This has been due to my desire to prevent any possible charge of crimination being brought against the United States in the direction of their constitutional affairs. . . .

There is no distrust of the United States on the part of the Cubans, and I know of no widespread antipathy to this country, its people, or its institutions. There are, of course, a handful of malcontents, as there must be in every country. . . .

I could not well conceive how the Cubans could be otherwise than grateful to the United States for its efforts in their behalf. . . . In the brief time since the occupation of the island by American troops the island has been completely rehabilitated—agriculturally, commercially, financially, educationally, and governmentally. This improvement has been so rapid and so apparent that no Cuban could mistake it. To doubt in the face of these facts that their liberators were not still their faithful friends would be impossible.

Major-General Leonard Wood, "The Future of Cuba," *The Independent* 54 (January 23, 1902): 193–194; idem, "The Cuban Convention," *The Independent* 52 (November 1, 1900): 265–266.

myhistorylab

Personal Journeys Online

- Josiah Strong, *Our Country*, 1885. An appeal for Anglo-Saxon imperialism by an American minister.
- Charles Denby, *Shall We Keep the Philippines?*, 1898. An argument for an economic empire by an American diplomat.
- Vincent F. Howard, *Imperialism*, 1900. A poem denouncing the imperialist journey.

General Leonard Wood's reports on Cuba,

then under his control as military governor, captured the complex mixture of attitudes and motives that underlay the journey of the United States from a developing nation to a world power. Plans for economic expansion, a belief in national mission, a sense of responsibility to help others, scarcely hidden religious impulses and racist convictions—all combined in an uneasy mixture of self-interest and idealism.

Wood himself had taken a symbolic journey in American expansionism. His earlier career had been on the American southwestern frontier with the troops chasing the Apache under Geronimo, but in 1898 he and Theodore Roosevelt organized the Rough Riders cavalry to participate in the Spanish-American War in Cuba. As Wood wrote on a transport ship headed for that Spanish colony: "[T]his is the first great expedition our country has sent overseas and marks the commencement of a new era in our relations with the world." Upon Spain's surrender, Cuba came under United States military occupation, and Wood was appointed military governor of the island.

Wood's support for the war was reflected in his activities as a colonial administrator. Convinced of the superiority of American institutions, he favored their expansion.

KEY TOPICS

◆ Why the United States became an imperial power in the 1890s

◆ The Spanish-American War and the colonial empire the United States gained as a result

◆ U.S. involvement in Asia, and the tensions with Japan that resulted

◆ U.S. predominance in the Caribbean and Latin America

The United States had a responsibility, he believed, to uplift those less able. But expansion would promote American interests as well. Thus, Wood brought improved sanitation, schools, and transportation to Cuba, but he instituted these reforms through an authoritarian government and regarded Cubans as backward and incapable of self-government. And at the same time, he expected that American business interests would "naturally" be the beneficiaries of his reorganization of Cuban life. Thus, Wood combined changes that satisfied paternalistic or humanitarian instincts with attempts to incorporate Cuba into America's new commercial empire, fulfilling the traditional colonial role of providing raw materials and serving as a market for American products and capital.

The tension between what a friend of his called the "righteous" and the "selfish" aspects of expanding American influence lay beneath the surface in Wood's reports. His claim that he was not interfering with Cuba's constitutional convention was disingenuous, for he had already undertaken to limit those who could participate as voters or delegates and was even then devising means to restrict the convention's autonomy. And in his repeated insistence that the Cubans were grateful for the intervention of "their faithful friends," the Americans, Wood obviously protested too much: Cubans, as well as Filipinos, Puerto Ricans, and others, rarely perceived American motives or American actions as positively as did Wood and other proponents of American expansion. Victory in the Spanish-American War had provided the United States with an extensive empire, status as a world power, and opportunities and problems that would long shape U.S. foreign policy.

CHRONOLOGY

1861–1869	Seward serves as secretary of state.
1867	United States purchases Alaska from Russia.
1870	Annexation of the Dominican Republic is rejected.
1879	France conquers Algeria.
1881	Naval Advisory Board is created.
1882	Great Britain occupies Egypt.
1887	United States gains naval rights to Pearl Harbor.
1890	Alfred Thayer Mahan publishes *The Influence of Sea Power upon History*.
1893	Harrison signs but Cleveland rejects a treaty for the annexation of Hawaii.
1893–1897	Depression increases interest in economic expansion abroad.
1894–1895	Sino-Japanese War is fought.
1895	United States intervenes in Great Britain–Venezuelan boundary dispute.
	Cuban insurrection against Spain begins.
1896	William McKinley is elected president on an imperialist platform.
1898	Spanish-American War is fought.
	Hawaii is annexed.
	Anti-Imperialist League is organized.
	Treaty of Paris is signed.
1899–1902	Filipino-American War is fought.
1899	Open Door note is issued.
1900	Boxer Rebellion against foreign influence breaks out in China.
1901	Theodore Roosevelt becomes president.
1903	Platt Amendment restricts Cuban autonomy.
	Panama "revolution" is abetted by the United States.
1904	United States acquires the Panama Canal Zone.
	Roosevelt Corollary is announced.
1904–1905	Russo-Japanese War is fought.
1905	Treaty of Portsmouth ends the Russo-Japanese War through U.S. mediation.
1906–1909	United States occupies Cuba.
1907–1908	Gentlemen's Agreement restricts Japanese immigration.
1909	United States intervenes in Nicaragua.
1912–1933	United States occupies Nicaragua.
1914	Panama Canal opens.
1914–1917	United States intervenes in Mexico.
1915–1934	United States occupies Haiti.
1916–1924	United States occupies the Dominican Republic.
1917	Puerto Ricans are granted U.S. citizenship.
1917–1922	United States occupies Cuba.

The Roots of Imperialism

The United States had a long-established tradition of expansion across the continent. Through purchase, negotiation, or conquest, the vast Louisiana Territory, Florida, Texas, New Mexico, California, and Oregon had become U.S. territory. Indeed, by the 1890s, Republican Senator Henry Cabot Lodge of Massachusetts boasted that Americans had "a record of conquest, colonization, and territorial expansion unequalled by any people in the nineteenth century." Lodge now urged the country to build an overseas empire, emulating the European model of **imperialism** based on the acquisition and exploitation of colonial possessions. Other Americans favored a less formal empire, in which United States interests and influence would be ensured through extensive trade and investments rather than through military occupation. Still others advocated a cultural expansionism in which the nation exported its ideals and institutions. All such expansionists could draw from many sources to support their plans. Some cited political, religious, and racial ideas; some were concerned about national security and power; others pointed to economic trends at home and abroad (see Overview, Rationales for Imperialism).

Ideological and Religious Arguments

Scholars, authors, politicians, and religious leaders provided interlocking ideological arguments for the new imperialism. Some intellectuals, for example, invoked social Darwinism, maintaining that the United States should engage in a competitive struggle for wealth and power with other nations. "The survival of the fittest," declared one writer, was "the law of nations as well as a law of nature." As European nations expanded into Asia and Africa in the 1880s and 1890s, seeking colonies, markets, and raw materials, these advocates argued, the United States had to adopt similar policies to ensure national success.

Related to social Darwinism was a pervasive belief in racial inequality and in the superiority of people of English, or Anglo-Saxon, descent. To many Americans, the industrial progress, military strength, and political development of England and the United States were proof of an Anglo-Saxon superiority that carried with it a responsibility to extend the blessings of their rule to less able people. John Fiske, a philosopher and historian, popularized these ideas in his oft-repeated lecture "Manifest Destiny." "The work which the English race began when it colonized North America," Fiske declaimed, "is destined to go on until every land on the earth's surface that is not already the seat of an old civilization shall become English in its language, in its religion, in its political habits and traditions, and to a predominant extent in the blood of its people." As a popular expression put it, colonialism was the "white man's burden," carrying with it a duty to aid and uplift other peoples. Such attitudes led some expansionists to favor imposing American ideas and practices on other cultures regardless of their own values and customs.

The political scientist John W. Burgess, for example, concluded that Anglo-Saxons "must have a colonial policy" and "righteously assume sovereignty" over "incompetent" or "barbaric races" in other lands.

Reflecting this aggressiveness, as well as Darwinian anxieties, some Americans endorsed expansion as consistent with their ideals of masculinity. Forceful expansion would be a manly course, relying upon and building strength and honor among American males. Men who confronted the challenges of empire would thereby improve their ability to compete in the international arena. "Pride of race, courage, manliness," predicted one enthusiast, would be both the causes and the consequences of an assertive foreign policy.

American missionaries also promoted expansionist sentiment. Hoping to evangelize the world, American religious groups increased the number of Protestant foreign missions sixfold from 1870 to 1900. Women in particular organized foreign missionary societies and served in the missions. Missionaries publicized their activities throughout the United States, generating interest in foreign developments and support for what one writer called the "imperialism of righteousness." Abroad they pursued a religious transformation that often resembled a cultural conversion, for they promoted trade, developed business interests, and encouraged westernization through technology and education as well as religion. Sometimes, as in the Hawaiian Islands, American missionaries even promoted annexation by the United States.

Indeed, the American religious press endlessly repeated the themes of national destiny, racial superiority, and religious zeal. The Reverend J. H. Barrows in early 1898 lectured on the "Christian conquest of Asia," suggesting that American Christianity and commerce would cross the Pacific to fulfill "the manifest destiny of the Christian Republic." Missionaries contributed to the imperial impulse by describing their work, as Barrows did, in terms of the conquest of enemy territory. Thus, while missionaries were motivated by what they considered to be idealism and often brought real benefits to other lands, especially in education and health, religious sentiments reinforced the ideology of American expansion.

Strategic Concerns

Other expansionists were motivated by strategic concerns, shaped by what they saw as the forces of history and geography. America's location in the Western Hemisphere, its coastlines on two oceans, and the ambitions and activities of other nations, particularly Germany and Britain, convinced some Americans that the United States had to develop new policies to protect and promote its national security and interests. Alfred Thayer Mahan, a naval officer and president of the Naval War College, emphasized the importance of a strong navy for national greatness in his book *The Influence of Sea Power upon History*. To complement the navy, Mahan proposed that the United States build a canal across the isthmus of Panama to link its coasts, acquire naval bases in the

OVERVIEW

Rationales for Imperialism

Category	Beliefs
Racism and Social Darwinism	The conviction that Anglo-Saxons were racially superior and should dominate other peoples, either to ensure national success, establish international stability, or benefit the "inferior" races by imposing American ideas and institutions on them
Righteousness	The conviction that Christianity, and a supporting American culture, should be aggressively spread among the benighted peoples of other lands
Mahanism	The conviction, following the ideas advanced by Alfred Thayer Mahan, that U.S. security required a strong navy and economic and territorial expansion
Economics	A variety of arguments holding that American prosperity depended on acquiring access to foreign markets, raw materials, and investment opportunities

Caribbean and the Pacific to protect the canal, and annex Hawaii and other Pacific islands to promote trade and service the fleet. The United States must "cast aside the policy of isolation which befitted her infancy," Mahan declared, and "begin to look outward."

Mahanism found a receptive audience. President Benjamin Harrison declared in 1891 that "as to naval stations and points of influence, we must look forward to a departure from the too conservative opinions which have been held heretofore." Still more vocal advocates of Mahan's program were a group of nationalistic Republicans, predominantly from the Northeast. They included politicians like Henry Cabot Lodge and Theodore Roosevelt, journalists like Whitelaw Reid and Albert Shaw, and diplomats and lawyers like John Hay and Elihu Root.

Conscious of European colonialism, these men favored imperial expansion, as Shaw wrote, "for the sake of our destiny, our dignity, our influence, and our usefulness." Roosevelt promoted Mahan's ideas when he became assistant secretary of the navy in 1897, but he was even more militaristic. Praising "the most valuable of all qualities, the soldierly virtues," Roosevelt declared in 1897: "No triumph of peace is quite so great as the supreme triumphs of war." One British observer concluded on the eve of the Spanish-American War that Mahan's influence had served "as oil to the flame of 'colonial expansion' everywhere leaping into life" (see American Views, An Imperialist Views the World).

Even so, Mahan was not solely responsible for the large-navy policy popular among imperialists. Its origins went back to 1881, when Congress established the Naval Advisory Board, which successfully lobbied for larger naval appropriations. An extensive program to replace the navy's obsolete wooden ships with modern cruisers and battleships was well under way by 1890, when Mahan's book appeared. The United States soon possessed the formidable navy the expansionists wanted. This larger navy, in turn, demanded strategic bases and coaling stations. One writer indicated the circular nature of this development by noting in 1893 that Manifest Destiny now meant "the acquisition of such territory, far and near," as would secure "to our navy facilities desirable for the operations of a great naval power."

Economic Designs

One reason for the widespread support for a larger navy was its use to expand and protect America's international trade. Nearly all Americans favored economic expansion through foreign trade. Such a policy promised national prosperity: more markets for manufacturers and farmers, greater profits for merchants and bankers, more jobs for workers. Far fewer favored the acquisition of colonies that was characteristic of European imperialism. (See Global Perspectives, European Colonial Imperialism.) Commercial as opposed to colonial goals were the primary objective. As one diplomat declared in 1890, the nation was more interested in the "annexation of trade" than in the annexation of territory.

The United States had long aggressively fostered American trade, especially in Latin America and East Asia. As early as 1844, the United States had negotiated a trade treaty with China, and ten years later a squadron under Commodore Matthew Perry had forced the Japanese to open their ports to American products. In the late nineteenth century, the dramatic expansion of the economy caused many Americans to favor more government action to open foreign markets to American exports. Alabama Senator John Morgan had the cotton and textiles produced in the New South in mind when he warned in 1882: "Our home market is not equal to the demands of our producing and manufacturing classes and to the capital which is seeking employment.... We must either enlarge the field of our traffic, or stop the business of manufacturing just where it is." More ominous, a naval officer trying to open Korea to U.S. products declared in 1878, "At least one-third of our mechanical and agricultural products are now in excess of our wants, and we must *export* these products or *deport* the people who are creating them."

Emily Hartwell, an American missionary, and her Chinese converts ("Bible Women") in the Foochow Mission in 1902. American missionaries wanted to spread the Gospel abroad but inevitably spread American influence as well. Hartwell used the ethnocentric and militant rhetoric of the imperialism of righteousness in appealing to Americans for money and prayers for her "picket duty on the very outskirts of the army of the Lord."

Exports, especially of manufactured goods, which grew ninefold between 1865 and 1900, did increase greatly in the late nineteenth century. Still, periodic depressions fed the fears of overproduction. The massive unemployment and social unrest that accompanied these economic crises also provided social and political arguments for economic relief through foreign trade.

In the depression of the 1890s, with the secretary of state seeing "symptoms of revolution" in the Pullman strike and Coxey's Army of unemployed workers (see Chapter 20), the interest in foreign trade became obsessive. More systematic government efforts to promote trade seemed necessary, a conclusion strengthened by new threats to existing American markets. In that tumultuous decade, European nations raised tariff barriers against American products, and Japan and the European imperial powers began to restrict commercial opportunities in the areas of China that they controlled. Many American leaders decided that the United States had to adopt decisive new policies or face economic catastrophe.

First Steps

Despite the growing ideological, strategic, and economic arguments for imperialism, the government only fitfully interested itself in foreign affairs before the mid-1890s. It did not pursue a policy of isolationism from international affairs, for the nation maintained normal diplomatic and trade ties and at times vigorously intervened in Latin America and East Asia. But in general the government deferred to the initiative of private interests, reacted haphazardly to outside events,

and did little to create a professional foreign service. In a few bold if inconsistent steps, however, the United States moved to expand its influence.

Seward and Blaine

Two secretaries of state, William H. Seward, secretary under Presidents Abraham Lincoln and Andrew Johnson (1861–1869), and James G. Blaine, secretary under Presidents James Garfield and Benjamin Harrison (1881, 1889–1892), laid the foundation for a larger and more aggressive U.S. role in world affairs. Seward possessed an elaborate imperial vision, based on his understanding of commercial opportunities, strategic necessities, and national destiny. His interest in opening East Asia to American commerce and establishing American hegemony over the Caribbean anticipated the subsequent course of American expansion. Seward purchased Alaska from Russia in 1867, approved the navy's occupation of the Midway Islands in the Pacific, pushed American trade on a reluctant Japan, and repeatedly tried to acquire Caribbean naval bases (see Map 22–1). His policy of expansion, however, as one observer noted, "went somewhat too far and too fast for the public," and many of his plans fizzled. Congressional opposition frustrated his efforts to obtain Haiti and the Dominican Republic and to purchase the Danish West Indies; Colombia blocked his attempt to gain construction rights for a canal across the isthmus of Panama.

Blaine was an equally vigorous, if inconsistent, advocate of expansion. He worked to extend what he called America's "commercial empire" in the Pacific. And he sought to ensure U.S. sovereignty over any canal in Panama, insisting that it be "a purely American waterway to be treated as part of our own coastline." In an effort to induce Latin American nations to import manufactured products from the United States rather than Europe, Blaine proposed a customs union to reduce trade barriers, expecting it to strengthen U.S. control of hemispheric markets. Wary of economic subordination to the colossus of the north, however, the Latin American nations rejected Blaine's plan but did agree to establish what eventually came to be known as the **Pan American Union.** Based in Washington, it helped to promote hemispheric understanding and cooperation.

If U.S. officials were increasingly assertive toward Latin America and Asia, however, they remained little involved in Europe (one secretary of state declared in 1885 that he had no interest in European affairs, which he regarded "with impatience and contempt"). They were wholly indifferent to Africa, which the European powers were then carving up into colonies. In short, despite some important precedents

American Views

An Imperialist Views the World

Theodore Roosevelt, Henry Cabot Lodge, Alfred Thayer Mahan, and other influential imperialists frequently corresponded with one another, expressing their views forcefully if not always in depth. The following excerpts are from Roosevelt's private letters to Lodge and Mahan in 1897, while he was assistant secretary of the navy and before the Spanish-American War.

- In what ways does Roosevelt reflect the influence of Mahan?
- What is Roosevelt's view of war?
- How does Roosevelt view European nations?
- How does he view the independence of other nations in the Western Hemisphere?

I suppose that I need not tell you that as regards Hawaii I take your views absolutely, as indeed I do on foreign policy generally. If I had my way we would annex those islands tomorrow. If that is impossible I would establish a protectorate over them. I believe we should build the Nicaraguan canal at once, and in the meantime that we should build a dozen new battleships, half of them on the Pacific Coast; and these battleships should have a large coal capacity and a consequent increased radius of action....I think President Cleveland's action [in rejecting the annexation of Hawaii] was a colossal crime, and we should be guilty of aiding him after the fact if we do not reverse what he did. I earnestly hope we can make the President [McKinley] look at things our way. Last Saturday night Lodge pressed his views upon him with all his strength.

I agree with all you say as to what will be the result if we fail to take Hawaii. It will show that we either have lost, or else wholly lack, the masterful instinct which alone can make a race great. I feel so deeply about it I hardly dare express myself in full. The terrible part is to see that it is the men of education who take the lead in trying to make us prove traitors to our race.

I fully realize the importance of the Pacific coast....But there are big problems in the West Indies also. Until we definitely turn Spain out of those islands (and if I had my way that would be done tomorrow), we will always be menaced by trouble there. We should acquire the Danish Islands [in the West Indies], and by turning Spain out should serve notice that no strong European power, and especially not Germany, should be allowed to gain a foothold by supplanting some weak European power. I do not fear England; Canada is a hostage for her good behavior.

I wish we had a perfectly consistent foreign policy, and that this policy was that every European power should be driven out of America, and every foot of American soil, including the nearest islands in both the Pacific and the Atlantic, should be in the hands of independent American states, and so far as possible in the possession of the United States or under its protection.

To speak with a frankness which our timid friends would call brutal, I would regard a war with Spain from two standpoints: first, the advisability on the grounds both of humanity and self-interest of interfering on behalf of the Cubans, and of taking one more step toward the complete freeing of America from European dominion; second, the benefit done our people by giving them something to think of which isn't material gain, and especially the benefit done our military forces by trying both the Navy and the Army in actual practice. I should be very sorry not to see us make the experiment of trying to land, and therefore feed and clothe, an expeditionary force [on Cuba], if only for the sake of learning from our own blunders. I should hope that the force would have some fighting to do. It would be a great lesson, and we would profit much by it.

I wish there was a chance that the [U.S. battleship] Maine was going to be used against some foreign power; by preference Germany—but I am not particular, and I'd take even Spain if nothing better offered.

Source: Reprinted by permission of the publisher from *The Letters of Theodore Roosevelt*, Vol. I 1868–1898, selected and edited by Elting E. Morison (Cambridge, MA: Harvard University Press, 1951)

Global Perspectives

European Colonial Imperialism

The United States was not alone in expanding its role in the world. Beginning in the 1870s, leading European nations engaged in a competitive struggle to partition much of Africa and Asia in pursuit of their imperial ambitions. Like Americans, Europeans advanced many justifications for imperialism. Many favored colonies to acquire markets, resources, and investment opportunities; others saw in colonies strategic advantages or international prestige. Some interwove racist and religious attitudes to justify European empire building as "an instrument for the good of humanity."

But advanced industrialization, more than the questionable blessings of religion and race, accounted for European success. Railroads, steamships, and ocean cables facilitated transportation and communication, and modern weaponry easily overcame native resistance. In the Battle of Omdurman in 1898, a British expedition armed with machine guns massacred 11,000 Sudanese tribesmen trying to defend their independence while itself suffering only 28 casualties. Said one observer: "It was not a battle but an execution."

Before the 1870s Africa had largely escaped European colonialism, but within 30 years European powers had divided much of the continent. France gained most of northwestern Africa, conquering Algeria in 1879, occupying Tunisia in 1881, and dividing Morocco with Spain. Britain acquired territory from the Mediterranean Sea to the Cape. To control the area around the Suez Canal, viewed as the empire's lifeline to India, the British occupied Egypt in 1882 and then seized the Sudan. With unimaginable brutality, Belgium's King Leopold colonized the Congo in central Africa. Germany established colonies in southwestern Africa and, like Italy, in East Africa.

European powers also advanced on Asia. To its earlier control of India, Great Britain added Burma and Malaya. France extended its authority over Indochina in the 1880s and 1890s by gaining control of Vietnam and Laos. Russia expanded its empire into contiguous territories, securing Turkestan in Central Asia and then reaching toward East Asia, particularly the Manchurian region of China. Other nations also sought spheres of influence in China, acquiring ports, naval stations, and railroad and mining concessions.

Competitive imperialism risked conflict, between expansive nations as well as with colonized peoples, but such risks did not deter aspiring imperialists. In 1887 the Japanese foreign minister insisted: "We have to establish a new, European-style empire on the edge of Asia." And in 1895 an American leader declared of European imperialism: "The United States must not fall out of the line of march."

■ While many Americans distinguished their foreign policy goals from European imperialism, how might the nation's expansion into the American West and its treatment of Native Americans correspond to such colonialism?

for the future, much of American foreign policy remained undeveloped, sporadic, and impulsive.

Hawaii

Blaine regarded Hawaii as "indispensably" part of "the American system." As early as 1842, the United States had announced its opposition to European control of Hawaii, a key waystation in the China trade and where New England missionaries and whalers were already active. Although Hawaii continued to be ruled by native monarchs, American influence grew, particularly as other Americans arrived to establish sugar plantations and eventually dominate the economy. Treaties in 1875 and 1887 integrated the islands into the American economy and gave the United States control over Pearl Harbor on the island of Oahu. In 1887, the United States rejected a proposal from Britain and France for a joint guarantee of Hawaii's independence and endorsed a new Hawaiian constitution that gave political power to wealthy white residents. The obvious next step was U.S. annexation, which Blaine endorsed in 1891.

A combination of factors soon impelled American planters to bid for annexation. The McKinley Tariff Act of 1890 effectively closed the U.S. market to Hawaiian sugar producers, threatening their economic ruin. At the same

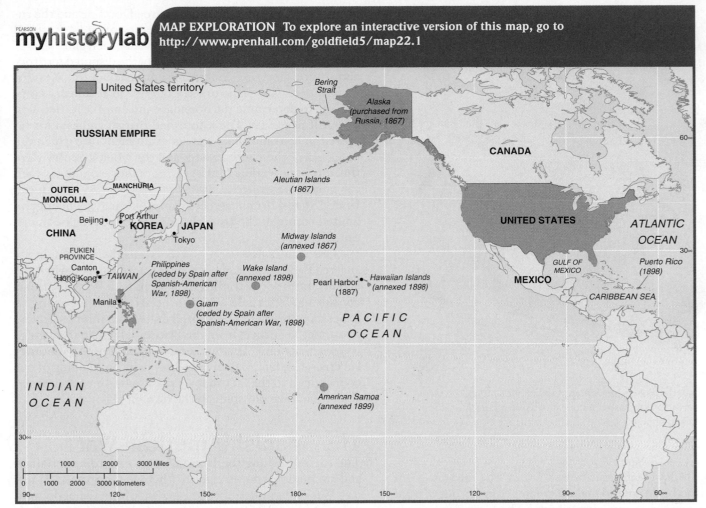

MAP EXPLORATION To explore an interactive version of this map, go to http://www.prenhall.com/goldfield5/map22.1

MAP 22–1   **United States Expansion in the Pacific, 1867–1899**
Pursuing visions of a commercial empire in the Pacific, the United States steadily expanded its territorial possessions as well as its influence there in the late nineteenth century.

time, Queen Liliuokalani moved to restore native control of Hawaiian affairs. To ensure market access and protect their political authority, the American planters decided to seek annexation to the United States. In 1893, they overthrew the queen. John Stevens, the American diplomatic representative, ordered U.S. marines to help the rebels, then declared an American protectorate over the new Hawaiian government, and wired Washington: "The Hawaiian pear is now fully ripe, and this is the golden hour for the United States to pluck it." A delegation from the new provisional government, which did not include any native Hawaiians, went to Washington to draft a treaty for annexation. President Harrison signed the pact but could not get Senate approval before the new Cleveland administration took office.

Grover Cleveland immediately called for an investigation of the whole affair. Soon convinced that "the undoubted sentiment of the people is for the Queen, against the provisional Government, and against annexation," Cleveland apologized to the queen for the "flagrant wrong" done her by the "reprehensible conduct" of U.S. diplomats and troops. But the American-dominated provisional government refused to step down, and Cleveland's rejection of annexation set off a noisy debate in the United States.

Many Republicans strongly supported annexation, which they regarded as merely part of a larger plan of expansion. One eastern Republican manufacturer called for the annexation of Hawaii as the first step toward making the Pacific "an American ocean, dominated by American commercial enterprise for all time." On the West Coast, where California business interests had close ties with the islands, the commercial and strategic value of Hawaii seemed obvious. Reflecting racial imperialism, others argued that annexation would both fittingly reward the enterprising white residents of Hawaii and provide an opportunity to civilize native Hawaiians.

Democrats generally opposed annexation. They doubted, as Missouri Senator George Vest declared, whether the United States should desert its traditional principles and "venture upon the great colonial system of the European

COASTING.
The old horse was too slow for Uncle Sam.

As other imperial powers look on, the United States abandons its traditional principles to rush headlong into world affairs. Uncle Sam would not always find it a smooth ride.

powers." Most Democrats believed that "the mission of our nation is to build up and make a greater country out of what we have, instead of annexing islands." The Hawaiian episode of 1893 thus foreshadowed the arguments over imperialism at the end of the century and emphasized the policy differences between Democrats and the increasingly expansionist Republicans.

Chile and Venezuela

American reactions to developments in other countries in the 1890s also reflected an increasingly assertive national policy and excitable public opinion. In 1891, American sailors on shore leave in Chile became involved in a drunken brawl that left two of them dead, 17 injured, and dozens in jail. Encouraged by a combative navy, President Harrison threatened military retaliation against Chile, provoking an outburst of bellicose nationalism in the United States. Harrison relented only when Chile apologized and paid an indemnity.

A few years later, the United States again threatened war over a minor issue but against a more formidable opponent. Although opposed to annexing Hawaii, President Cleveland adopted an increasingly aggressive policy in Latin America. In 1895, he intervened in a boundary dispute between Great Britain and Venezuela over British Guiana. Cleveland was motivated not only by the long-standing U.S. goal of challenging Britain for Latin American markets but also by ever

more expansive notions of the Monroe Doctrine and the authority of the United States. Secretary of State Richard Olney sent Britain a blunt note (a "twenty-inch gun," Cleveland called it) demanding arbitration of the disputed territory and stoutly asserting American supremacy in the Western Hemisphere. Cleveland urged Congress to establish a commission to determine the boundary and enforce its decision by war if necessary. The astonished British ambassador reported an "extraordinary state of excitement into which the Congress of the United States and the whole country were thrown by the warlike Message…a condition of mind which can only be described as hysterical." As war fever swept the United States, Britain agreed to arbitration, recognizing the limited nature of the issue that so convulsed Anglo-American relations.

Cleveland's assertion of U.S. hemispheric dominance angered Latin Americans, and their fears deepened when the United States decided arbitration terms with Britain without consulting Venezuela, which protested before bowing to American pressure. The United States had intervened less to protect Venezuela from the British bully than to advance its own hegemony. The further significance of the Venezuelan crisis, Captain Mahan noted, lay in its "awakening of our countrymen to the fact that we must come out of our isolation…and take our share in the turmoil of the world."

The Spanish-American War

The forces pushing the United States toward imperialism and international power came to a head in the Spanish-American War. Cuba's quest for independence from the oppressive colonial control of Spain activated Americans' long-standing interest in the island. Many sympathized with the Cuban rebels' yearning for freedom, others worried that disorder in Cuba threatened their own economic and political interests, and some thought that intervention would increase the influence of the United States in the Caribbean and along key Pacific routes to Asian markets. But few foresaw that the war that finally erupted in 1898 would dramatically change U.S. relationships with the rest of the world and give the United States a colonial empire.

The Cuban Revolution

The last major European colony in Latin America, Cuba held an economic potential that attracted American business interests and a strategic significance for any Central American canal. In the late nineteenth century, American investors expanded their economic influence in Cuba, while Cubans themselves rebelled repeatedly but unsuccessfully against increasingly harsh Spanish rule. Cuban discontent erupted again in 1895, when the Cuban patriot José Martí launched another revolt.

The rebellion was a classic guerrilla war, with the rebels controlling the countryside and the Spanish army the towns and cities. American economic interests were seriously affected, for both Cubans and Spaniards destroyed American property and disrupted American trade. The Cleveland administration, motivated as much by a desire to protect American property and establish a safe environment for further investments as by a concern for Cuban rights, urged Spain to adopt reforms. But the brutality with which Spain attempted to suppress the revolt promoted American sympathy for the Cuban insurgents. Determined to cut the rebels off from their peasant supporters, the Spanish herded most civilians into "reconcentration camps," where tens of thousands died of starvation and disease.

American sympathy was further aroused by the sensationalist **yellow press.** To attract readers and boost advertising revenues, the popular press of the day adopted bold headlines, fevered editorials, and real or exaggerated stories of violence, sex, and corruption. A circulation war between William Randolph Hearst's *New York Journal* and Joseph Pulitzer's *New York World* helped stimulate interest in Cuban war. "Blood on the roadsides, blood on the fields, blood on the doorsteps, blood, blood, blood! The old, the young, the weak, the crippled—all are butchered without mercy," the *World* feverishly reported of Cuba. "Is there no nation wise enough, brave enough to aid this blood-smitten land?" Failure to intervene to protect the innocent from Spanish lust and cruelty, insisted the yellow journalists, would be dishonorable and cowardly.

The nation's religious press, partly because it reflected the prejudice of many Protestants against Catholic Spain, also advocated American intervention. One religious newspaper endorsed an American war against Spain as God's instrument for attacking "that system of iniquity, the papacy." Another promised that if war came, "every Methodist preacher will be a recruiting officer" for the military. The *Catholic Herald* of New York sarcastically referred to the "bloodthirsty preachers" of the Protestant churches, but such preachers undeniably influenced American opinion against Spain.

As the Cuban rebellion dragged on, more and more Americans advocated intervention to stop the carnage, protect U.S. investments, or uphold various principles. Expansionists like Roosevelt and Lodge clamored for intervention, but so did their opponents. Populists, for example, sympathized with a people seeking independence from colonial rule and petitioned Congress to support the crusade for Cuban freedom; conservative Democrats hoped that the excitement of intervention and war "might do much towards directing the minds of the people from imaginary ills, the relief of which is erroneously supposed to be reached by 'Free Silver.'" In the election of 1896, both major parties endorsed Cuban independence.

Growing Tensions

In his 1897 inaugural address, President William McKinley outlined an expansionist program ranging from further enlargement of the navy to the annexation of Hawaii and the construction of a Central American canal in Nicaragua, but his administration soon focused on Cuba. McKinley's principal complaint was that chronic disorder in Cuba disrupted American investments and agitated public opinion. Personally opposed to military intervention, McKinley first used diplomacy to press Spain to adopt reforms that would settle the rebellion. Following his instructions, the U.S. minister to Spain warned the Spanish government that if it did not quickly establish peace, the United States would take whatever steps it "should deem necessary to procure this result." In late 1897, Spain modified its brutal military tactics and offered limited autonomy to Cuba. But Cubans insisted on complete independence, a demand that Spain refused to grant.

Relations between the United States and Spain deteriorated. In early 1898, the *New York Journal* published a private letter from a Spanish diplomat that mocked McKinley as "weak and a bidder for the admiration of the crowd." (The *Journal* called the letter "the worst insult to the United States in its history.") McKinley found more troubling the letter's intimation that Spain was not negotiating in good faith. Only days later, on February 15, 1898, the U.S. battleship *Maine* blew up in Havana harbor, killing 260 men. The Spanish were not responsible for the tragedy, which a modern naval inquiry has attributed to an internal accident. But many Americans agreed with Theodore Roosevelt, the assistant secretary of the navy, who called it "an act of dirty treachery on the part of the Spaniards" and told McKinley that only war was "compatible with our national honor." Others demanded war, in the words of an Illinois politician, "if we would uphold our manhood." Thus understandings of appropriate male conduct also influenced decisions as to how the nation should act.

Popular anger was inflamed, but the sinking of the *Maine* by itself did not bring war, though it did restrict McKinley's options and pressure him to be more assertive toward Spain. One newspaper expressed its hope to see "any signs, however faint, of manhood in the White House." Other pressures soon began to build on the president. Increasingly, business interests favored war as less disruptive than a volatile peace that threatened their investments. Senator Lodge reported a consensus "that this situation must end. We cannot go on indefinitely with this strain, this suspense, and this uncertainty, this tottering upon the verge of war. It is killing to business." Further, McKinley feared that a moderate policy would endanger Republican congressional candidates. Again Senator Lodge, although hesitant to suggest "war for political reasons," nevertheless advised McKinley, "If the war in Cuba drags on through the summer with nothing done, we shall go down in the greatest [election] defeat ever known."

At the end of March 1898 (when the French ambassador in Washington reported that "a sort of bellicose fury has seized the American nation"), McKinley sent Spain an ultimatum. He demanded an armistice in Cuba, an end to the reconcentration policy, and the acceptance of American arbitration, which implied Cuban independence. Desperately,

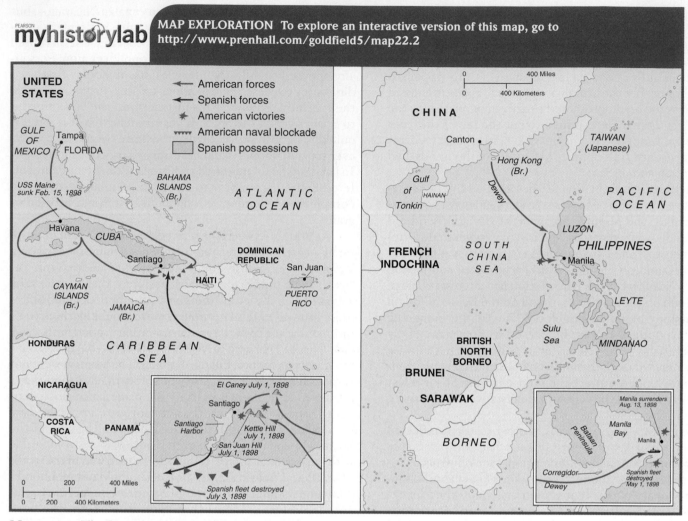

MAP EXPLORATION To explore an interactive version of this map, go to
http://www.prenhall.com/goldfield5/map22.2

MAP 22–2   The Spanish–American War
The United States gained quick victories in both theaters of the Spanish–American War. Its naval power proved decisive, with Commodore Dewey destroying one enemy fleet in the Philippines, and a second U.S. naval force cutting off the Spanish in Cuba.

Spain made concessions, abolishing reconcentration and declaring a unilateral armistice. But McKinley had already begun war preparations, withdrawing American diplomats from Cuba and Spain, ordering the navy to prepare for war, and drafting a war message for Congress. He submitted the message on April 11, asking for authority to use force against Spain "in the name of humanity, in the name of civilization, in behalf of endangered American interests." Congress declared war on Spain on April 25, 1898.

A few national leaders welcomed the war as a step toward imperialism, but there was little popular support for an imperialist foreign policy. Most interventionists were not imperialists, and Congress added the **Teller Amendment** to the war resolution, disclaiming any intention of annexing Cuba and promising that Cubans would govern themselves. Congress also refused to approve either a canal bill or the annexation of Hawaii. Nevertheless, the Spanish-American War did turn the nation toward imperialism.

War and Empire

The decisive engagement of the war took place not in Cuba but in another Spanish colony, the Philippines, and it involved the favored tool of the expansionists, the new navy (see Map 22–2). In 1897, McKinley had approved plans for an attack on the Philippines in the event of war with Spain. Once war was declared, Commodore George Dewey led the U.S. Asiatic squadron into Manila Bay and destroyed the much weaker Spanish fleet on May 1, 1898. This dramatic victory galvanized expansionist sentiment in the United States. The navy had long coveted Manila Bay as a strategic harbor, but other Americans, casting an eye on commercial opportunities in China, saw a greater significance in the victory. With Dewey's triumph, exulted one expansionist, "We are taking our proper rank among the nations of the world. We are after markets, the greatest markets now existing in the world." To expand this foothold in Asia, McKinley ordered troops to the Philippines, postponing the military expedition to Cuba itself.

Theodore Roosevelt and the Rough Riders. Ironically, their horses were left behind in Florida and TR complained of the Army's "Confusion and lack of system and general mismanagement."

popularly associated with the Rough Riders. One war correspondent wrote of the black soldiers' charge: "They followed their leaders up the terrible hill from whose crest the desperate Spaniards poured down a deadly fire of shell and musketry. They never faltered.... Their aim was splendid, their coolness was superb.... The war had not shown greater heroism." Nevertheless, the Rough Riders gained the credit, thanks in part to Roosevelt's self-serving and well-promoted account of the conflict, which one humorist proposed retitling *Alone in Cuba*.

U.S. naval power again proved decisive. In a lopsided battle on July 3, the Spanish squadron in Cuba was destroyed, isolating the Spanish army and guaranteeing its defeat. U.S. forces then seized the nearby Spanish colony of Puerto Rico without serious opposition. Humbled, Spain signed an armistice ending the war on August 12.

Americans were delighted with their military achievements, but the *Philadelphia Inquirer* cautioned, "With peace will come new responsibilities, which must be met. We have colonies to look after and develop."

Dewey's victory also precipitated the annexation of Hawaii, which had seemed unlikely only weeks before. Annexationists now pointed to the islands' strategic importance as stepping stones to Manila. "To maintain our flag in the Philippines, we must raise our flag in Hawaii," the *New York Sun* contended. McKinley himself privately declared, "We need Hawaii just as much and a good deal more than we did California. It is Manifest Destiny." In July, Congress approved annexation, a decision welcomed by Hawaii's white minority. Native Hawaiians solemnly protested this step taken "without reference to the consent of the people of the Hawaiian Islands." Filipinos would soon face the same American imperial impulse.

Military victory also came swiftly in Cuba, once the U.S. Army finally landed in late June. Victory came despite bureaucratic bungling in the War Department, which left the American army poorly led, trained, and supplied. Troops had to fight with antiquated weapons, wear wool uniforms in the sweltering tropics, and subsist on rations they condemned as "embalmed beef." More than 5,000 Americans died of diseases and accidents brought on by such mismanagement; only 379 were killed in battle. State militias supplemented the small regular army, as did volunteer units, such as the famous Rough Riders, a cavalry regiment of cowboys and eastern dandies organized by Leonard Wood and Theodore Roosevelt.

While the Rough Riders captured public attention, other units were more effective. The 10th Negro Cavalry, for example, played the crucial role in capturing San Juan Hill, a battle

The Treaty of Paris

The armistice required Spain to accept Cuban independence, cede Puerto Rico and Guam (a Pacific island between Hawaii and the Philippines) to the United States, and allow the Americans to occupy Manila, pending the final disposition of the Philippines at a formal peace conference. The acquisition of Puerto Rico and Guam indicated the expansionist nature the conflict had assumed for the United States. So did the postponement of the Philippine issue. McKinley knew that delay would permit the advocates of expansion to build public support for annexation. Because the U.S. Army did not capture Manila until after the armistice had been signed, he could not claim the islands by conquest, as Spain pointed out.

McKinley defended his decision to acquire the Philippines with self-righteous imperialist rhetoric, promising to extend Christian influence and American values. But he was motivated primarily by a determination to use the islands to strengthen America's political and commercial position in East Asia. Moreover, he believed the Filipinos poorly suited to self-rule, and he feared that Germany or Japan might seize the Philippines if the United States did not. Meeting in Paris in December, American and Spanish negotiators settled the final terms for peace. Spain agreed—despite Filipino demands for independence—to cede the Philippines to the United States.

The decision to acquire the Philippines sparked a dramatic debate over the ratification of the Treaty of Paris.

Most Americans enthusiastically greeted the declaration of war against Spain. Rallies and parades, such as this "Off to War Parade" in Denver, encouraged the war spirit.

Imperialists invoked the familiar arguments of economic expansion, national destiny, and strategic necessity, while asserting that Americans had religious and racial responsibilities to advance civilization by uplifting backward peoples. The *United States Investor* spoke for business leaders in demanding the Philippines as "a base of operations in the East" to protect American interests in China; other economic expansionists argued that the Philippines themselves had valuable resources and were a market for American goods or warned that "our commercial rivals in the Orient" would grab the islands if the United States did not. The *Presbyterian Banner* spoke for what it termed a nearly unanimous religious press in affirming "the desirability of America's retaining the Philippines as a duty in the interest of human freedom and Christian progress." Conveniently ignoring that most Filipinos were Catholic, the *Baptist Union* insisted, "The conquest by force of arms must be followed up by conquest for Christ." And some imperialists argued that conquering and holding the Philippines as a colony would create among Americans the "physical manhood" and "character of force" presumably necessary in the international Darwinian struggle.

Opponents of the treaty raised profound questions about national goals and ideals. They included such prominent figures as the civil-service reformer Carl Schurz, the steel baron Andrew Carnegie, the social reformer Jane Addams, the labor leader Samuel Gompers, and the author Mark Twain. Their organizational base was the Anti-Imperialist League, which campaigned against the treaty, distributing pamphlets, petitioning Congress, and holding rallies. The League's criticisms reflected a conviction that imperialism was a repu-

diation of the moral and political traditions embodied in the Declaration of Independence. The acquisition of overseas colonies, they argued, conflicted with the nation's commitment to liberty and its claim to moral superiority.

William Jennings Bryan ridiculed the imperialists' arguments of national destiny: "When the desire to steal becomes uncontrollable in an individual he is declared to be a kleptomaniac and is sent to an asylum; when the desire to grab land becomes uncontrollable in a nation we are told that the 'currents of destiny are flowing through the hearts of men.'" Some African Americans derided the rhetoric of Anglo-Saxon superiority that underlay imperialism, and even organized the Black Man's Burden Association to promote Philippine independence.

But other arguments were less high-minded. Many anti-imperialists objected to expansion on the racist grounds that Filipinos were inferior and unassimilable. Gompers feared that cheap Asian labor would undercut the wages and living standards of American workers. The *San Francisco Call,* representing California-Hawaiian sugar interests, wanted no competition from the Philippines.

The debate over the treaty became bitter. Furious at the opponents of empire, Roosevelt called them "little better than traitors." Carl Schurz responded that McKinley himself had earlier termed territorial annexation through conquest "a criminal act of aggression"; the president's seizure of the Philippines, Puerto Rico, and Hawaii, said Schurz, had perverted a legitimate concern for Cuba into "a war of selfish ambition and conquest."

Finally, on February 6, 1899, the Senate narrowly ratified the treaty. All but two Republicans supported the pact; most Democrats opposed it, although several voted in favor after Bryan suggested that approval was necessary to end the war and detach the Philippines from Spain. Thereafter, he hoped, a congressional resolution would give the Filipinos their independence. But by a single vote, the Republicans defeated a Democratic proposal for Philippine independence once a stable government had been established; the United States would keep the islands.

Bryan attempted to make the election of 1900 a referendum on "the paramount issue" of imperialism, promising to free the Philippines if the Democrats won. But other issues determined the outcome. Some of the most ardent anti-imperialists were conservatives who remained loyal to McKinley because they could not tolerate Bryan's economic policies. Republicans also benefited from the prosperity the country experienced under McKinley after the hard 1890s, and they played on the nationalist emotions evoked by the war, especially by nominating the "hero of San Juan Hill," Theodore Roosevelt, for vice president. "If you choose to vote for America, if you choose to vote for the flag for which we fought," Roosevelt said, "then you will vote to sustain the administration of President McKinley." Bryan lost again, as in 1896, and under Republican leadership, the United States became an imperial nation.

Republicans countered William Jennings Bryan's attempt to make imperialism an issue in 1900 by wrapping themselves in patriotism and the American flag. "Take Your Choice," a cartoon from *Judge*, posed President McKinley raising Old Glory over the Philippines with a disheveled and frantic Bryan chopping down the symbol of American pride and power.

Imperial Ambitions: The United States and East Asia, 1899–1917

In 1899, as the United States occupied its new empire, Assistant Secretary of State John Bassett Moore observed that the nation had become "a world power.... Where formerly we had only commercial interests, we now have territorial and political interests as well." American policies to promote these expanded interests focused first on East Asia and Latin America, where the Spanish-American War had provided the United States with both opportunities and challenges. In Asia, the first issue concerned the fate of the Philippines, but looming beyond it were American ambitions in China, where other imperial nations had their own goals.

The Filipino-American War

Filipino nationalists, like the Cuban insurgents, were already fighting Spain for their independence before the sudden American intervention. The Filipino leader, Emilio Aguinaldo, welcomed Dewey's naval victory as the sign of a *de facto* alliance with the United States; he then issued a declaration of independence and proclaimed the Philippine Republic. His own troops captured most of Luzon, the Philippines' major island, before the U.S. Army arrived. But the Filipinos' optimism declined as American officials acted in an increasingly imperious manner toward them, first refusing to meet with the "savages," then insisting that Filipino forces withdraw from Manila or face "forcible action," and finally dismissing the claims of Aguinaldo and "his so-called government." When the Treaty of Paris provided for U.S. ownership rather than independence, Filipinos felt betrayed. Mounting tensions erupted in a battle between American and Filipino troops outside Manila on February 4, 1899, sparking a long and brutal war.

Ultimately, the United States used nearly four times as many soldiers to suppress the Filipinos as it had to defeat Spain in Cuba and, in a tragic irony, employed many of the same brutal methods for which it had condemned Spain. Recognizing that "the Filipino masses are loyal to Aguinaldo and the government which he heads," U.S. military commanders adopted ever harsher measures, often directed at civilians, who were crowded into concentration camps in which perhaps 200,000 died. American troops often made little effort to distinguish between soldiers and noncombatants, viewing all Filipinos with racial antagonism. After reporting one massacre of a thousand men, women, and children, an American soldier declared, "I am in my glory when I can sight my gun on some dark skin and pull the trigger."

Before the military imposed censorship on war news, reporters confirmed U.S. atrocities; one wrote that "American troops have been relentless, have killed to exterminate men, women, and children, prisoners and captives, active insurgents and suspected people, from lads of 10 and up." A California newspaper defended such actions with remarkable candor: "There has been too much hypocrisy about this Philippine business.... Let us all be frank. WE DO NOT WANT THE FILIPINOS. WE DO WANT THE PHILIPPINES. All of our troubles in this annexation matter have been caused by the presence in the Philippine Islands of the Filipinos.... The more of them killed the better. It seems harsh. But they must yield before the superior race."

The overt racism of the war repelled African Americans. John Mitchell, a Virginia editor, condemned all the talk of "white man's burden" as deceptive rhetoric for brutal acts that could not be "defended either in moral or international law." Mitchell argued that white southerners needed missionary work more than freedom-loving Filipinos. "With the government acquiescing in the oppression and butchery of a dark race in this country and the enslaving and slaughtering of a dark race in the Philippines," he concluded, "we think it time to call all missionaries home and have them work on our own people."

Other Americans also denounced the war. The Anti-Imperialist League revived, citing the war as proof of the corrosive influence of imperialism on the nation's morals and principles. Women figured prominently in mass meetings and lobbying efforts to have the troops returned, their moral stature further undercutting the rationale for colonial wars. By 1902, the realities of imperial policy—including American casualties far exceeding those of the Spanish-American War—disillusioned most of those who had clamored to save Cuba.

By that time, however, the American military had largely suppressed the rebellion, and the United States had established a colonial government headed by an American governor general appointed by the president. Filipino involvement in the government was limited on educational and religious grounds. Compared to the brutal war policies, U.S. colonial rule was relatively benign, though paternalistic. William Howard Taft, the first governor general, launched a program that brought the islands new schools and roads, a public health system, and an economy tied closely to both the United States and a small Filipino elite. Independence would take nearly half a century.

China and the Open Door

America's determined involvement in the Philippines reflected its preoccupation with China. By the mid-1890s, other powers threatened prospects for American commercial expansion in China. Japan, after defeating China in 1895, annexed Formosa (Taiwan) and secured economic privileges in the mainland province of Fukien (Fujian); the major European powers then competed aggressively to claim other areas of China as their own **spheres of influence.** In Manchuria, Russia won control of Port Arthur (Lüshun) and the right to construct a railway. Germany obtained a 99-year lease on another Chinese port and mining and railroad privileges on the Shantung (Shandong) Peninsula. The British wrung special concessions in Kowloon, opposite Hong Kong, and in other Chinese provinces, as well as a port facing the Russians in Manchuria. France gained a lease on ports and exclusive commercial privileges in southern China.

These developments alarmed the American business community. It was confident that, given an equal opportunity, the United States would prevail in international trade because of its efficient production and marketing systems. But the creation of exclusive spheres of influence limited the opportunity to compete. In early 1898, business leaders organized the Committee on American Interests in China to lobby Washington to promote American trade in the shrinking Chinese market. The committee persuaded the nation's chambers of commerce to petition the McKinley administration to act. This campaign influenced McKinley's interest in acquiring the Philippines, but the Philippines, in the words of Mark Hanna, were only a "foothold";

China was the real target. The State Department soon reported that, given overproduction for the home market, "the United States has important interests at stake in the partition of commercial facilities in regions which are likely to offer developing markets for its goods. Nowhere is this consideration of more interest than in its relation to the Chinese Empire."

In 1899, the government moved to advance those interests. Without consulting the Chinese, Secretary of State John Hay asked the imperial powers to maintain an **Open Door** for the commercial and financial activities of all nations within their Chinese spheres of influence. Privately, Hay had already approved a plan to seize a Chinese port for the United States, if necessary to join in the partition of China, but equal opportunity for trade and investment would serve American interests far better. It would avoid the expense of military occupation, avert further domestic criticism of U.S. imperialism, and guarantee a wider sphere for American business.

The other nations replied evasively, except for Russia, which rejected the Open Door concept. In 1900, an antiforeign Chinese nationalist movement known as the Boxers laid siege to the diplomatic quarter in Beijing. The defeat of the Boxer Rebellion by a multinational military force, to which the United States contributed troops, again raised the

A FAIR FIELD AND NO FAVOR.
UNCLE SAM: "I'm out for commerce, not conquest."

The United States usually preferred the "annexation of trade" to the annexation of territory. The Open Door policy promised to advance American commercial expansion, but Uncle Sam had to restrain other imperialists with colonial objectives.

prospect of a division of China among the colonial powers. Hay sent a second Open Door note, reaffirming "the principle of equal and impartial trade" and respect for China's territorial integrity.

Despite Hay's notes, China remained a tempting arena for imperial schemes. But the Open Door became a cardinal doctrine of American foreign policy in the twentieth century, a means by which the United States sought to dominate foreign markets. The United States promoted an informal or economic empire, as opposed to the traditional territorial colonial empire identified with European powers. Henceforth, American economic interests expected the U.S. government to oppose any developments that threatened to close other nations' economies to American penetration and to advance "private enterprise" abroad.

Rivalry with Japan and Russia

At the turn of the twentieth century, both the Japanese and the Russians were more deeply involved in East Asia than was the United States. Japan and Russia expressed little support for the Open Door, which they correctly saw as favoring American interests over their own. But in pursuing their ambitions in China, the two countries came into conflict with each other. Alarmed at the threat of Russian expansion in Manchuria and Korea, Japan in 1904 attacked the Russian fleet at Port Arthur and defeated the Russian army in Manchuria.

American sympathies in the Russo-Japanese War lay with Japan, for the Russians were attempting to close Manchuria to foreign trade. President Theodore Roosevelt privately complained that a reluctant American public opinion meant that "we cannot fight to keep Manchuria open." He welcomed the Japanese attack in the belief that "Japan is playing our game." But he soon began to fear that an overwhelming Japanese victory would threaten American interests as much as Russian expansionism did, so he skillfully mediated an end to the war. In the Treaty of Portsmouth in 1905, Japan won control of Russia's sphere of influence in Manchuria, half the Russian island of Sakhalin, and recognition of its domination of Korea.

The treaty marked Japan's emergence as a great power, but, ironically, it worsened relations with the United States. Anti-American riots broke out in Tokyo. The Japanese people blamed Roosevelt for obstructing further Japanese gains and blocking a Russian indemnity that would have helped Japan pay for the war. Tensions were further aggravated by San Francisco's decision in 1906 to segregate Asian and white schoolchildren. Japan regarded this as a racist insult, and Roosevelt worried that "the infernal fools in California" would provoke war. Finally, he persuaded the city to rescind the school order in exchange for his limiting Japanese immigration, which lay at the heart of California's hostility. Under the **Gentlemen's Agreement,** worked out through a series of diplomatic notes in 1907 and 1908, Japan agreed to deny passports to workers trying to come to the United States, and the United States promised not to prohibit Japanese immigration overtly or completely.

The United States and Japan entered into other agreements aimed at calming their mutual suspicions in East Asia but failed to mend the deteriorating relationship. The Taft-Katsura Agreement (1905), the Root-Takahira Agreement (1908), and the Lansing-Ishii Agreement (1917) seemed to trade grudging American acceptance of Japan's special interests in Manchuria and control of Korea for Japanese promises to respect American rule in the Philippines and maintain the Open Door in China. But these agreements were vague, if not contradictory, and produced discord rather than harmony between the two countries.

Increasingly, Japan began to exclude American trade from its territories in East Asia and to press for further control over China. Elihu Root, Roosevelt's secretary of state, insisted that the Open Door and American access had to be maintained but asserted also that the United States did not want to be "a protagonist in a controversy in China with Russia and Japan or with either of them." The problem was that the United States could not sustain the Open Door without becoming a protagonist in China. This paradox, and the unwillingness to commit military force, would plague American foreign policy in Asia for decades.

Imperial Power: The United States and Latin America, 1899–1917

In Latin America, where no major powers directly challenged American objectives as Japan and Russia did in Asia, the United States was more successful in exercising imperial power (see Map 22–3). In the two decades after the Spanish-American War, the United States intervened militarily in Latin America no fewer than 20 times to promote its own strategic and economic interests (see Overview, U.S. Interventions in Latin America, 1891–1933). Policymakers believed that these goals required restricting the influence of European nations in the region, building an isthmian canal under U.S. control, and establishing the order thought necessary for American trade and investments to expand. Intervention at times achieved these goals, but it often ignored the wishes and interests of Latin Americans, provoked resistance and disorder, and aroused lasting ill will.

U.S. Rule in Puerto Rico

Well before 1898, expansionists like James G. Blaine had advocated acquiring Puerto Rico because of its strategic location in the Caribbean. During the Spanish-American War, Roosevelt urged Washington, "Do not make peace until we get" Puerto Rico. Military invasion and the Treaty of Paris brought the island under American control, with mixed consequences. A military government improved transportation and sanitation and developed public health and education.

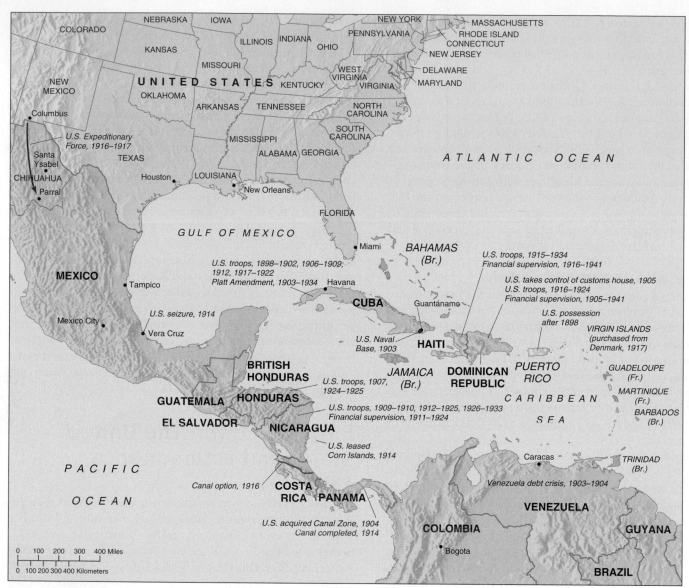

MAP 22-3   The United States in the Caribbean
For strategic and economic reasons, the United States repeatedly intervened in the Caribbean in the first three decades of the twentieth century. Such interventions protected the U.S. claim to dominance but often provoked great hostility among Latin Americans.

But to the dismay of Puerto Ricans, who had been promised that American rule would bestow "the advantages and blessings of enlightened civilization," their political freedoms were curtailed. "We have suffered everything. No liberty, no rights," said José Henna, who had led the resistance to Spanish colonialism. "We are Mr. Nobody from Nowhere."

In 1900, the United States established a civil government, but it was under U.S. control, with popular participation even less than under Spain. In the so-called Insular Cases (1901), the Supreme Court upheld the authority of Congress to establish an inferior status for Puerto Rico as an "unincorporated territory" without promise of statehood. Disappointed Puerto Ricans pressed to end this colonial status, some advocating independence, others statehood or merely

greater autonomy. This division would continue for decades to come. In 1917, the United States granted citizenship and greater political rights to Puerto Ricans, but their island remained an unincorporated territory under an American governor appointed by the president.

Economic development also disappointed most islanders, for American investors quickly gained control of the best land and pursued large-scale sugar production for the U.S. market. The landless peasants struggled to survive as workers on large plantations. By 1929, the new governor—ironically, Theodore Roosevelt, Jr.—found that under the domination of American capital, "poverty was widespread and hunger, almost to the verge of starvation, common." A subsequent investigation concluded that while "the influx

OVERVIEW

U.S. Interventions in Latin America, 1891–1933

Country	Type of Intervention	Year
Chile	Ultimatum	1891–1892
Colombia	Military intervention	1903
Cuba	Occupation	1898–1902, 1906–1909, 1912, 1917–1922
Dominican Republic	Military and administrative intervention	1905–1907
	Occupation	1916–1924
Haiti	Occupation	1915–1934
Mexico	Military intervention	1914, 1916–1917
Nicaragua	Occupation	1912–1925, 1927–1933
Panama	Acquisition of Canal Zone	1904
Puerto Rico	Military invasion and territorial acquisition	1898

of capital has increased the efficiency of production and promoted general economic development," the benefits had gone largely to Americans, not to ordinary Puerto Ricans, whose conditions were "deplorable." Increasingly, they left their homes to seek work in the United States.

Cuba as a U.S. Protectorate

Despite the Teller Amendment, the Spanish-American War did not leave Cuba independent. McKinley opposed independence and distrusted the Cuban rebels. Many Americans considered the Cubans racial inferiors, and one U.S. general in Cuba snorted, "Why those people are no more fit for self-government than gun-powder is for hell." Accordingly, a U.S. military government was established in the island. Only in 1900, when the Democrats made an issue of imperialism, did the McKinley administration move toward permitting a Cuban government and withdrawing American troops. McKinley summoned a Cuban convention to draft a constitution under the direction of the American military governor, General Leonard Wood. Reflecting the continuing U.S. fear of Cuban autonomy, the constitution restricted suffrage on the basis of property and education, leaving few Cubans with the right to vote.

Even so, before removing its troops, the United States wanted to ensure its control over Cuba. It therefore made U.S. withdrawal contingent on Cuba's adding to its constitution the provisions of the **Platt Amendment,** drawn up in 1901 by the U.S. secretary of war. The Platt Amendment restricted Cuba's autonomy in diplomatic relations with other countries and in internal financial policies, required Cuba to lease naval bases to the United States, and most important, authorized U.S. intervention to maintain order and preserve Cuban independence. Cubans resented this restriction on their sovereignty. As General Wood correctly observed,

"There is, of course, little or no independence left Cuba under the Platt Amendment."

Cubans quickly learned that reality when the United States prevented Cuba from extending to the British the same trade privileges that U.S. merchants enjoyed. The Open Door would not apply in the Caribbean, which was to be an American sphere of influence. To preserve that influence, the United States sent troops into Cuba three times between 1906 and 1917 (Roosevelt admitted his recurrent itch to "wipe its people off the face of the earth"). Meanwhile, American property interests in Cuba increased more than fourfold, and American exports to the island increased eightfold from 1898 to 1917.

During their occupations of Cuba, the Americans modernized its financial system, built roads and public schools, and developed a public-health and sanitation program that eradicated the deadly disease of yellow fever. But most Cubans thought that these material benefits did not compensate for their loss of political and economic independence. The Platt Amendment remained the basis of U.S. policy toward Cuba until 1934.

The Panama Canal

The Spanish-American War intensified the long American interest in a canal through Central America to eliminate the lengthy and dangerous ocean route around South America. Its commercial value seemed obvious, but the war emphasized its strategic importance. McKinley declared that a canal was now "demanded by the annexation of the Hawaiian Islands and the prospective expansion of our influence and commerce in the Pacific."

Theodore Roosevelt moved quickly to implement McKinley's commitment to a canal after becoming president in 1901. He was convinced that a strong presidential role was at least as important in foreign affairs as in domestic politics. Neither Congress nor "the average American," he believed, took "the trouble to think carefully or deeply" about international affairs. Roosevelt's canal diplomacy helped establish the assertive presidency that has largely characterized U.S. foreign policy ever since.

First, Roosevelt persuaded Britain to renounce its treaty right to a joint role with the United States in any canal venture. Britain's willingness reflected a growing friendship between the two nations, both wary of Germany's increasing aggressiveness. Where to build the canal was a problem. One possibility was Nicaragua, where a sea-level canal could be built. Another was Panama, then part of Colombia. A canal through Panama would require an elaborate system of locks. But the French-owned Panama Canal Company had been unsuccessfully trying to build a canal in Panama and was now eager to sell its rights to the project before they expired in 1904.

In 1902, Congress directed Roosevelt to purchase the French company's claims for $40 million and build the canal in Panama if Colombia ceded a strip of land across the isthmus on reasonable terms. Otherwise, Roosevelt was to negotiate with Nicaragua for the alternative route. In 1903, Roosevelt pressed Colombia to sell a canal zone to the United States for $10 million and an annual payment of $250,000. Colombia, however, rejected the proposal, fearing the loss of its sovereignty in Panama and hoping for more money. After all, when the Panama Canal Company's rights expired, Colombia could then legitimately collect the $40 million so generously offered the company.

Roosevelt was furious. After threatening "those contemptible little creatures" in Colombia, he began writing a message to Congress proposing military action to seize the isthmus of Panama. Instead of using direct force, however, Roosevelt worked with Philippe Bunau-Varilla, a French official of the Panama Canal Company, to exploit long-smoldering Panamanian discontent with Colombia. Roosevelt's purpose was to get the canal zone, Bunau-Varilla's to get the American money. Roosevelt ordered U.S. naval forces to Panama; from New York, Bunau-Varilla coordinated a revolt against Colombian authority directed by officials of the Panama Railroad, owned by Bunau-Varilla's canal company. The bloodless "revolution" succeeded when U.S. forces prevented Colombian troops from landing in Panama, although the United States was bound by treaty to maintain Colombian sovereignty in the region. Bunau-Varilla promptly signed a treaty accepting Roosevelt's original terms for a canal zone and making Panama a U.S. protectorate, which it remained until 1939. Panamanians themselves denounced the treaty for surrendering sovereignty in the zone to the United States, but the United States took formal control of the canal zone in 1904 and completed construction of the Panama Canal in 1914.

Many Americans were appalled by what the *Chicago American* called Roosevelt's "rough-riding assault upon another republic over the shattered wreckage of international

The *Puck* cartoonist criticizes Theodore Roosevelt's aggressive foreign policy by depicting him in his Rough-Rider uniform and indicating his preference for the crown of European imperialism over the simple American hats of previous presidents.

law and diplomatic usage." But others, as *Public Opinion* reported, wanted a "canal above all things" and were willing to overlook moral questions and approve the acquisition of the canal zone as simply "a business question." Roosevelt himself boasted, "I took the Canal Zone and let Congress debate," but his actions generated resentment among Latin Americans that rankled for decades.

The Roosevelt Corollary

To protect the security of the canal, the United States increased its authority in the Caribbean. The objective was to establish conditions there that would both eliminate any pretext for European intervention and promote American control over trade and investment. The inability of Latin American nations to pay their debts to foreign lenders raised the possibility of European intervention, as evidenced by a German and British blockade of Venezuela in 1903 to secure repayment of debts to European bankers. "If we intend to say hands off to the powers of Europe," Roosevelt concluded, "then sooner or later we must keep order ourselves."

The Panama Canal

On December 31, 1999, almost a century after the United States took control of the Panama Canal Zone, Panama reclaimed it. "The canal is ours," proclaimed Panamanian president Mireya Moscoso, as her country's flag was raised over the canal area, resolving a contentious and complex issue.

From the beginning, Panamanians denounced the 1903 treaty—"the treaty that no Panamanians signed"—that had given the United States a perpetual lease and American sovereignty over a strip of land that divided their country in two. For many decades, the United States rejected the repeated Panamanian demands for an end to this "Yankee colonialism" over the Canal Zone, with one U.S. senator explaining, "We stole it fair and square." But in the 1960s and 1970s, the United States began negotiating the return of the Canal Zone to Panama, motivated less by concerns about Panamanian discontent than by conclusions that the canal was no longer of such strategic significance that the U.S. needed to maintain perpetual control and exclusive jurisdiction over it. Besides, the canal was gradually becoming obsolete, too small to accommodate ever-larger ships.

A treaty in 1978 returned jurisdiction over the Canal Zone to Panama but left the United States responsible for operating and defending the canal until December 31, 1999. During the 1990s, Panama gradually assumed territorial and legal jurisdiction over the canal, with Panamanian administrators and workers assuming responsibilities previously held by Americans. Shortly after celebrating the final transfer of authority, Panamanian officials began planning to modernize the canal, and in 2007 Panama started a massive construction project to double the canal's capacity and thereby facilitate international trade and provide much needed revenue for the country. The new sets of locks are expected to be completed by 2014, one hundred years after the canal first opened.

President Mireya Moscoso celebrated Panama's regaining control of the Canal Zone in 1999.

■ Why did Americans and Panamanians hold such contrasting views of the Canal Zone and its importance?

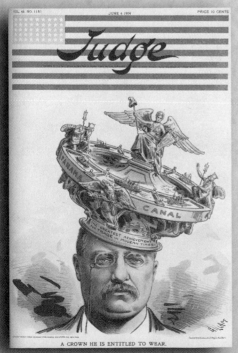

A CROWN HE IS ENTITLED TO WEAR.

Both critics and admirers saw the Panama Canal as topping Roosevelt's imperial crown.

PEARSON
myhistorylab

From Then to Now Online

22-1 Roosevelt Defends His Acquisition of the Panama Canal Zone. 1913. The former president praises his own actions.

22-2 Panama Recovers the Canal Zone 2000. A reporter describes Panama's celebrations over gaining control of the Canal Zone.

Toward that end, in 1904, Roosevelt announced a new policy, the so-called **Roosevelt Corollary** to the Monroe Doctrine. "Chronic wrongdoing," he declared, would cause the United States to exercise "an international police power" in Latin America. The Monroe Doctrine had expressed American hostility to European intervention in Latin America; the Roosevelt Corollary attempted to justify U.S. intervention and authority in the region. Roosevelt invoked his corollary immediately, imposing American management of the debts and customs duties of the Dominican Republic in 1905. Commercial rivalries and political intrigue in that poor nation had created disorder, which Roosevelt suppressed for both economic and strategic reasons. Financial insolvency was averted, popular revolution prevented, and possible European intervention forestalled.

Latin Americans vigorously resented the United States' unilateral claim to authority. By 1907, the so-called Drago Doctrine (named after Argentina's foreign minister) was incorporated into international law, prohibiting armed intervention to collect debts. Still, the United States would continue to invoke the Roosevelt Corollary to advance its interests in the hemisphere. As Secretary of State Elihu Root asserted, "The inevitable effect of our building the Canal must be to require us to police the surrounding premises." He then added, "In the nature of things, trade and control, and the obligation to keep order which go with them, must come our way."

houses. Under the new government, American bankers then gained control of Nicaragua's national bank, railroad, and customs service. To protect these arrangements, U.S. troops were again dispatched in 1912. To control popular opposition to the American client government, the marines remained in Nicaragua for two decades. Military power, not the social and economic improvement promised by dollar diplomacy, kept Nicaragua's minority government stable and subordinate to the United States.

Dollar diplomacy increased American power and influence in the Caribbean and tied underdeveloped countries to the United States economically and strategically. By 1913, American investments in the region reached $1.5 billion, and Americans had captured more than 50 percent of the foreign trade of Costa Rica, Cuba, the Dominican Republic, Guatemala, Haiti, Honduras, Nicaragua, and Panama. But this policy failed to improve conditions for most Latin Americans. U.S. officials remained primarily concerned with promoting American control and extracting American profits from the region. One American diplomat, for instance, casually described a Guatemalan president in whose government San Francisco bankers had invested heavily as a cruel despot who had "the good sense to be civil to our country and its citizens and to keep his cruelties . . . for home consumption." Not surprisingly, dollar diplomacy proved unpopular in Latin America.

Dollar Diplomacy

Roosevelt's successor as president, William Howard Taft, hoped to promote U.S. interests without such combative rhetoric and naked force. He proposed "substituting dollars for bullets"—using government action to encourage private American investments in Latin America to supplant European interests, promote development and stability, and earn profits for American bankers. Under this **dollar diplomacy,** American investments in the Caribbean increased dramatically during Taft's presidency from 1909 to 1913, and the State Department helped arrange for American bankers to establish financial control over Haiti and Honduras.

But Taft did not shrink from employing military force to protect American property or to establish the conditions he thought necessary for American investments. In fact, Taft intervened more frequently than Roosevelt had, with Nicaragua a major target. In 1909, Taft sent U.S. troops there to aid a revolution fomented by an American mining corporation and to seize the Nicaraguan customs

THE BIG STICK IN THE CARIBBEAN SEA

The Roosevelt Corollary proclaimed the intention of the United States to police Latin America. Enforcement came, as this cartoon shows, with Roosevelt and subsequent presidents sending the U.S. Navy to one Caribbean nation after another.

Wilsonian Interventions

Taking office in 1913, the Democrat Woodrow Wilson repudiated the interventionist policies of his Republican predecessors. He promised that the United States would "never again seek one additional foot of territory by conquest" but would instead work to promote "human rights, national integrity, and opportunity" in Latin America. Wilson also named as his secretary of state the Democratic symbol of anti-imperialism, William Jennings Bryan. Their generous intentions were apparent when Bryan signed a treaty with Colombia apologizing for Roosevelt's seizure of the Panama Canal Zone.

Nonetheless, Wilson soon became the most interventionist president in American history. Convinced that the United States had to expand its exports and investments abroad and that U.S. dominance of the Caribbean was strategically necessary, he also held the racist belief that Latin Americans were inferior and needed paternalistic guidance from the United States. In providing that guidance, through military force if necessary, Wilson came close to assuming that American principles and objectives were absolutes, and that different cultural traditions and national aspirations were simply wrong. His self-righteousness and determination to transform the behavior of other peoples led his policies to be dubbed "missionary diplomacy," but they also contained elements of Roosevelt's commitment to military force and Taft's reliance on economic power.

Caribbean interventions. In 1915, Wilson ordered U.S. marines to Haiti. They went, explained Bryan, to restore order and preserve "gravely menaced" American interests. The United States saved and even enhanced those interests by establishing a protectorate over Haiti and drawing up a constitution that increased U.S. property rights and commercial privileges. The U.S. Navy selected a new Haitian president, granting him nominal authority over a client government. Real authority, however, rested with the American military, which controlled Haiti until 1934, protecting the small elite who cooperated with American interests and exploited their own people. As usual, American military rule improved the country's transportation, sanitation, and educational systems, but the forced-labor program that the United States adopted to build such public works provoked widespread resentment. In 1919, marines suppressed a revolt against American domination, killing more than 3,000 Haitians.

Wilson also intervened elsewhere in the Caribbean. In 1916, when the Dominican Republic refused to cede control of its finances to U.S. bankers, Wilson ordered the marines to occupy the country. The marines ousted Dominican officials, installed a military government to rule "on behalf of the Dominican government," and ran the nation until 1924. In 1917, the United States intervened in Cuba, which remained under American control until 1922.

Interfering with Mexico. Wilson also involved himself in the internal affairs of Mexico. The lengthy dictatorship of Porfirio Díaz had collapsed in 1911 in revolutionary disorder. The popular leader Francisco Madero took power and promised democratic and economic reforms that alarmed both wealthy Mexicans and foreign investors, particularly Americans. In 1913, General Victoriano Huerta seized control in a brutal counterrevolution backed by the landed aristocracy and foreign interests. Appalled by the violence of Huerta's power grab and aware that opponents had organized to reestablish constitutional government, Wilson refused to recognize the Huerta government.

Wilson hoped to bring the Constitutionalists to power and "to secure Mexico a better government under which all contracts and business and concessions will be safer than they have been." He authorized arms sales to the forces led by Venustiano Carranza, pressured Britain and other nations to deprive Huerta of foreign support, and blockaded the Mexican port of Vera Cruz. In 1914 Wilson exploited a minor incident to have the marines attack and occupy Vera Cruz. This assault damaged his image as a promoter of peace and justice, and even Carranza and the Constitutionalists denounced the American occupation as unwarranted aggression. After, Carranza toppled Huerta, Wilson shifted his support to Francisco ("Pancho") Villa, who seemed more susceptible to American guidance. But Carranza's growing popular support in Mexico and Wilson's preoccupation with World War I in Europe finally led the United States to grant de facto recognition to the Carranza government in October 1915.

Villa then began terrorizing New Mexico and Texas, hoping to provoke an American intervention that would undermine Carranza. In 1916, Wilson ordered troops under General John J. Pershing to pursue Villa into Mexico, leading Carranza to fear a permanent U.S. occupation of northern Mexico. Soon the American soldiers were fighting the Mexican army rather than Villa's bandits. On the brink of full-fledged war, Wilson finally ordered U.S. troops to withdraw in January 1917 and extended full recognition to the Carranza government. Wilson lamely defended these steps as showing that the United States had no intention of imposing on Mexico "an order and government of our own choosing." That had been Wilson's original objective, however. His aggressive tactics had not merely failed but also embittered relations with Mexico.

Conclusion

By the time of Woodrow Wilson's presidency, the United States had been expanding its involvement in world affairs for half a century. Several themes had emerged from this activity: increasing American domination of the Caribbean, continuing interest in East Asia, the creation of an overseas empire, and the evolution of the United States into a major world power. Underlying these developments were an uneasy mixture of ideas and objectives. The American involvement in the world reflected a traditional, if often misguided, sense of national rectitude and mission. Generous humanitarian impulses vied with ugly racist prejudices as Americans sought both to help other peoples and to direct them toward U.S. concepts of religion, sanitation, capitalist development, and public institutions. American motives ranged from ensuring national security and competing with European colonial powers to the conviction that the United States had to expand its economic interests abroad. But if imperialism, both informal and at times colonial, brought Americans greater wealth and power, it also increased tensions in Asia and contributed to anti-American hostility and revolutionary ferment in Latin America. It also entangled the United States in the Great Power rivalries that would ultimately result in two world wars.

Review Questions

1. After the Spanish-American War, General Leonard Wood asserted that Cubans believed that their American "liberators" were "still their faithful friends." Why might Cubans not have agreed with Wood?

2. What factors, old and new, shaped American foreign policy in the late nineteenth century? How were they interrelated?

3. How were individual politicians and diplomats able to affect America's foreign policy? How were they constrained by governmental institutions, private groups, and public opinion?

4. To what extent was the United States' emergence as an imperial power a break from, as opposed to a culmination of, its earlier policies and national development?

5. How effective were U.S. interventions in Latin America? What were the objectives and consequences?

6. In what ways did the policies of other nations shape the development of American foreign policy?

Key Terms

Dollar diplomacy (p. 632)

Gentlemen's Agreement (p. 627)

Imperialism (p. 614)

Mahanism (p. 615)

Open Door (p. 626)

Pan American Union (p. 616)

Platt Amendment (p. 629)

Roosevelt Corollary (p. 632)

Spheres of Influence (p. 626)

Teller Amendment (p. 622)

Yellow press (p. 621)

Recommended Reading

Beisner, Robert L. *From the Old Diplomacy to the New, 1865–1900*, 2d ed. (1986). An excellent analysis of historiographical issues.

Hoganson, Kristin L. *Fighting for American Manhood: How Gender Politics Provoked the Spanish-American and Philippine-American Wars* (1998). An innovative and provocative book showing how gender concerns influenced U.S. foreign policy.

LaFeber, Walter. *The American Search for Opportunity, 1865–1913* (1993). A fascinating study documenting the disruptive international consequences of America's rise to world power.

LaFeber, Walter. *The New Empire: An Interpretation of American Expansion, 1860–1898* (1963). An influential study that emphasizes economic factors in American foreign policy.

Perez, Louis A., Jr. *The War of 1898: The United States and Cuba in History and Historiography* (1998). A brief book that emphasizes how relations between Cuba and the United States shaped the war and its meaning.

Pletcher, David. *The Diplomacy of Trade and Investment: American Economic Expansion in the Hemisphere, 1865–1900* (1998). Stresses the complex but inconsistent and unsystematic nature of American economic expansion.

Where to Learn More

■ **Mission Houses, Honolulu, Hawaii.**   Built between 1821 and 1841, these buildings were homes and shops of missionaries sent to Hawaii by the American Board of Commissioners for Foreign Missions. Their exhibits include furnishings and memorabilia of a group important in developing American ties with Hawaii. www.missionhouses.org

■ **Funston Memorial Home, Iola, Kansas.**   Operated as a museum by the Kansas State Historical Society, this is the boyhood home of General Frederick Funston, prominent in the Spanish-American War and the Filipino-American War. For a virtual tour, together with military information, political cartoons, Roosevelt correspondence, and Funston links, see http://skyways.lib.ks.us/museums/funston

■ **James G. Blaine House, Augusta, Maine.**   The Executive Mansion of Maine's governor since 1919, this house was formerly Blaine's home and still contains his study and furnishings from the time he served as secretary of state and U.S. senator. http://www.blainehouse.org

Study Resources

For study resources for this chapter, go to www.myhistorylab.com and choose *The American Journey*. You will find a wealth of study and review material for this chapter, including pre- and post-tests, customized study plan, key term review flash cards, interactive map and document activities, and documents for analysis.

SEND THE EAGLE'S ANSWER
MORE SHIPS

UNITED STATES SHIPPING BOARD   EMERGENCY FLEET CORPORATION

In World War I, mobilization of the home front was basic to military success. Government posters exhorted Americans to increase industrial and agricultural production, buy war bonds, and suppress dissent.

America and the Great War 23
1914–1920

The present German submarine warfare against commerce is a warfare against mankind. . . . It is a war against all nations. . . . Each nation must decide for itself how it will meet it. . . . There is one choice we cannot make, we are incapable of making: we will not choose the path of submission and suffer the most sacred rights of our nation and our people to be ignored or violated. . . . The world must be made safe for democracy. Its peace must be planted upon the tested foundations of political liberty.

Excerpted from President Woodrow Wilson's Request for Declaration of War, April 2, 1917.

Woodrow Wilson Presidential Library

If it is important for us to speak and vote our convictions in matters of internal policy, though we may unfortunately be in disagreement with the President, it is infinitely more important for us to speak and vote our convictions when the question is one of peace or war, certain to involve the lives and fortunes of many of our people and, it may be, the destiny of all of them and of the civilized world as well.

Mr. President, many of my colleagues on both sides of this floor have from day to day offered for publication in the *Record* messages and letters received from their constituents. I have received some 15,000 letters and telegrams [and] 9 out of 10 are an unqualified endorsement of my course in opposing war with Germany. . . .

The poor, sir, who are the ones called upon to rot in the trenches, have no organized power, have no press to voice their will upon the questions of peace or war; but, oh, Mr. President, at some time they will be heard.

637

The failure to treat the belligerent nations of Europe alike ... is wholly accountable for our present dilemma. We should not seek to hide our blunder behind the smoke of battle to inflame the mind of our people by half truths into a frenzy of war in order that they may never appreciate the real cause of it until it is too late. I do not believe that our national honor is served by such a course.

Excerpts from Wisconsin Senator Robert M. La Follette's three-hour speech opposing the war, April 4, 1917—Congressional Record—Senate, April 4, 1917, 224–225.

myhistorylab

Personal Journeys Online

- Jane Addams, *Peace and Bread in Time of War*, 1922. Describing the transition of President Wilson from an advocate of peace to one of war.

- Letter from former president Theodore Roosevelt to Sir Edward Grey, 1915. Promoting American preparedness and support of the Allies.

Escorted by the U.S. cavalry on the evening

of April 2, 1917, Woodrow Wilson drove through a misty rain eerily illuminated by searchlights down Pennsylvania Avenue to Capitol Hill to deliver his war address. Throughout the day the Emergency Peace Federation had frantically lobbied Congress, but sentiment in both houses was growing for war. Tension inside and outside the Capitol was palpable. Pro-war Senator Henry Cabot Lodge even punched a protesting pacifist, and mounted police with drawn sabers held back silent crowds as Wilson asked Congress to declare war on Germany, a war, Senator La Follette insisted, that had "no popular support." Even Wilson conceded that the war he requested would sow death, misery, and reaction throughout the nation but also threatened "the firm hand of repression" against disloyalty—anticipating battles at home as well as abroad. When Wilson promised to make the world "safe for democracy," many members of Congress, waving small American flags, broke into cheers, and Senator Lodge personally congratulated Wilson.

Although widely recognized for his oratorical talents, Senator La Follette proved unable to sway the forces for war in Congress. Indeed, his speech aroused such anger in the Senate chamber that he was handed a noose as he exited the room. Both the Senate and the House unanimously supported Wilson's request and the United States entered the war on April 6. Denounced in the press, Senator La Follette and his family were ostracized for his anti-war views, providing a sobering indication of the treatment Americans would face who dared to oppose the war against Germany.

Two years later on July 10, 1919, Wilson made the same journey down Pennsylvania Avenue to Capitol Hill. This time he rode in brilliant sunshine through cheering crowds and flag-decorated streets. He asked the Senate to ratify a peace treaty that most Americans favored and that he promised would prevent future wars. But Wilson's reception in the Senate was chilly; some even refused to stand when he entered the room and many others received the address in silence. Senator Lodge scarcely concealed his hatred of the president or his opposition to the treaty. The hostility in the room apparently affected the president who spoke without his usual eloquence. During the fierce

CHRONOLOGY

1914	World War I begins in Europe.
	President Woodrow Wilson declares U.S. neutrality.
1915	Germany begins submarine warfare.
	Lusitania is sunk.
	Woman's Peace Party is organized.
1916	Sussex Pledge is issued.
	Preparedness legislation is enacted.
	Woodrow Wilson is reelected president.
1917	The February Revolution ends tsarist regime in Russia.
	Germany resumes unrestricted submarine warfare.
	The United States declares war on Germany.
	Selective Service Act establishes the military draft.
	Espionage Act is passed.
	Committee on Public Information, War Industries Board, Food Administration, and other mobilization agencies are established.
	American Expeditionary Force arrives in France.
	East St. Louis race riot erupts.
	Bolshevik Revolution occurs in Russia.
1918	Wilson announces his Fourteen Points.
	Sedition Act is passed.
	Eugene Debs is imprisoned.
	The United States intervenes militarily in Russia.
	Armistice ends World War I.
1919	Paris Peace Conference is held.
	Steel, coal, and other strikes occur.
	Red Scare breaks out.
	Prohibition amendment is adopted.
	Wilson suffers a massive stroke.
1920	Palmer Raids round up radicals.
	League of Nations is defeated in the U.S. Senate.
	Woman suffrage amendment is ratified.
	U.S. troops are withdrawn from Russia.
	Warren Harding is elected president.
1921	United States signs a separate peace treaty with Germany.

political struggle over the treaty that followed, Wilson suffered an incapacitating stroke. The Senate ultimately rejected the treaty and Wilson's peace.

Between these two presidential appearances, Americans experienced the horrors of the Great War, confronting and overcoming challenges but also sacrificing some of their national ideals and aspirations. The war declaration came after a long period in which Americans tried to balance their desires for neutrality and peace with their ambitions for wealth, their sympathies for other countries, and their perceptions of America's security and world role. Not only was the war the United States' first major military conflict on foreign soil, but it also changed American life.

Many of the changes, from increased efficiency to Americanization, reflected prewar progressivism, and the war years did promote some reforms. But the war also diverted reform energies into new channels, subordinated generous impulses to attitudes that were more coercive and strengthened the conservative opposition to reform. The results were often reactionary and contributed to a postwar mood that not only curtailed further reform but also helped defeat the peace treaty upon which so much had been gambled.

Waging Neutrality

Few Americans were prepared for the Great War that erupted in Europe in August 1914, but fewer still foresaw that their own nation might become involved in it. With near unanimity, they supported neutrality. But American attitudes, decisions, and actions, both public and private, undercut neutrality, and the policies of governments in Berlin, London, and Washington drew the United States into the war.

The Origins of Conflict

There had been plenty of warning. Since the 1870s, the competing imperial ambitions of the European powers had led to economic rivalries, military expansion, diplomatic maneuvering, and international tensions. A complex system of alliances divided the continent into two opposing blocs. In central Europe, the expansionist Germany of Kaiser Wilhelm II allied itself with the multinational Austro-Hungarian Empire. Confronting them, Great Britain and France entered into alliances with tsarist Russia. A succession of crises threatened this precarious balance of power, and in May 1914, an American diplomat reported anxiously, "There is too much hatred, too many jealousies." He predicted "an awful cataclysm."

The cataclysm began a month later. On June 28, a Serbian terrorist assassinated Archduke Franz Ferdinand, the heir to the Austro-Hungarian throne, in Sarajevo. With Germany's support, Austria declared war on Serbia on July 28. Russia then mobilized its army against Austria to aid Serbia, its Slavic client state. To assist Austria, Germany declared war on Russia and then on Russia's ally, France. Hoping for a quick victory, Germany struck at France through neutral Belgium; in response, Britain declared war on Germany on August 4. Soon Turkey and Bulgaria joined Germany and Austria to form the **Central Powers**. The **Allies**—Britain, France, and Russia—were joined by Italy and Japan. Britain drew on its empire for resources, using troops from India, Canada, Australia, New Zealand, and South Africa. The war had become a global conflict, waged not only in Europe but also in Africa, the Middle East, and East Asia.

Mass slaughter enveloped Europe as huge armies battled to a stalemate. The British and French faced the Germans along a line of trenches stretching across France and Belgium from the English Channel to Switzerland. Little movement occurred despite great efforts and terrible casualties from artillery, machine guns, and poison gas. The British once suffered 300,000 casualties in an offensive that gained only a few square miles before being pushed back. Machine gunners went into shock at the carnage they inflicted. In the trenches, soldiers suffered in the cold and mud, surrounded by decaying bodies and human waste, enduring lice, rats, and nightmares, and dying from disease and exhaustion. The belligerents subordinated their economies, politics, and cultures to military demands. The Great War, said one German soldier, had become "the grave of nations."

American Attitudes

Although the United States had also competed for markets, colonies, and influence, few Americans had expected this calamity. Most believed that the United States had no vital interest in the war and would not become involved. "Our isolated position and freedom from entangling alliances," noted the *Literary Digest,* "inspire our press with the cheering assurance that we are in no peril of being drawn into the European quarrel." President Wilson issued a proclamation of neutrality and urged Americans to be "neutral in fact as well as in name . . . impartial in thought as well as in action."

However, neither the American people nor their president stayed strictly neutral. German Americans often sympathized with Germany, and many Irish Americans hoped for a British defeat that would free Ireland from British rule. But most Americans sympathized with the Allies. Ethnic, cultural, and economic ties bound most Americans to the British and French. Politically, too, most Americans felt a greater affinity for the democratic Western Allies—tsarist Russia repelled them—than for Germany's more authoritarian government and society. And whereas Britain and the United States had enjoyed a rapprochement since 1895, Germany had repeatedly appeared as a potential rival. Many Americans considered it a militaristic nation, particularly after it violated Belgium's neutrality.

Wilson himself admired Britain's culture and government and distrusted Germany's imperial ambitions. Like other influential Americans, Wilson believed that a German victory would threaten America's economic, political, and perhaps even strategic interests. "England is fighting our fight," he said privately. Secretary of State William Jennings Bryan was genuinely neutral, but most officials favored the Allies. Robert Lansing, counselor of the State Department; Walter Hines Page, the ambassador to England; and Colonel Edward House, Wilson's closest adviser on foreign affairs—all assisted British diplomats, undercut official U.S. protests against British violations of American neutrality, and encouraged Wilson's suspicions of Germany. Early in the war, House wrote to Page, "I cannot see how there can be any serious trouble between England and America, with all of us feeling as we do." House and Lansing assured the Allies privately that "we considered their cause our cause."

British propaganda bolstered American sympathies. British writers, artists, and lecturers depicted the Allies as fighting for civilization against a brutal Germany that mutilated nuns and babies. Although German troops, like most other soldiers, did commit outrages, they were not guilty of the systematic barbarity claimed by Allied propagandists. Britain, however, shaped America's view of the conflict. It cut the only German cable to the United States and censored war news to suit itself. German propaganda directed at American opinion proved so ineffectual that the German ambassador concluded it might as well be abandoned.

Sympathy for the Allies, however, did not mean that Americans favored intervention. The British ambassador complained that it was "useless" to expect any "practical" advantage from the Americans' sympathy, for they had no intention of joining the conflict. Indeed, few Americans doubted that neutrality was the appropriate course and peace the proper goal. The carnage in France solidified their convictions. Wilson was determined to pursue peace as long as his view of national interests allowed.

The Economy of War

Economic issues soon threatened American neutrality. International law permitted neutral nations to sell or ship war matériel to belligerents, and with the economy mired in a recession when the war began, many Americans looked to war orders to spur economic recovery. But the British navy prevented trade with the Central Powers. Only the Allies could buy American goods. Their orders for steel, explosives, uniforms, wheat, and other products, however, pulled the country out of the recession. One journalist rejoiced that "war, for Europe, is meaning devastation and death; for America a bumper crop of new millionaires and a hectic hastening of prosperity revival."

Other Americans worried that this one-sided war trade undermined genuine neutrality. Congress even considered an embargo on munitions. But few Americans supported the idea. One financial journal declared of the Allied war trade: "We need it for the profits which it yields." Whatever its justification, however, the war trade strengthened U.S. ties with the Allies and embittered Germany. As the German ambassador noted, American industry was "actually delivering goods only to the enemies of Germany."

A second economic issue complicated matters. To finance their war purchases, the Allies borrowed from American bankers. Initially, Secretary of State Bryan persuaded Wilson to prohibit loans to the belligerents as "inconsistent with the true spirit of neutrality." But as the importance of the war orders to both the Allies and the American economy became clear, Wilson ended the ban. Secretary of the Treasury William McAdoo argued that it would be "disastrous" not to finance the Allies' purchases, on which "our prosperity is dependent." By April 1917, American loans to the Allies exceeded $2 billion, nearly a hundred times the amount lent to Germany. These financial ties, like the war trade they underwrote, linked the United States to the Allies and convinced Germany that American neutrality was only a formality.

The Diplomacy of Neutrality

The same imbalance characterized American diplomacy. Wilson insisted on American neutral rights but acquiesced in British violations of those rights, while sternly refusing to yield on German actions. Wilson argued that while British violations of international law cost Americans property, markets, and time, German violations cost lives. As the *Boston Globe* noted, the British were "a gang of thieves" and the Germans "a gang of murderers. On the whole, we prefer the thieves, but only as the lesser of two evils."

When the war began, the United States asked belligerents to respect the 1909 **Declaration of London** on neutral rights. Germany agreed to do so; the British refused. Instead, skirting or violating established procedures, Britain blockaded Germany, mined the North Sea, and forced neutral ships into British ports to search their cargoes and confiscate material deemed useful to the German war effort. These British actions infringed U.S. trading rights. Wilson branded Britain's blockade illegal and unwarranted, but by October he had conceded many of America's neutral rights in order to avoid conflict with Britain. This concession reflected both Wilson's English sympathies and the profitable war trade with the Allies. He was also convinced that the Allied cause was vital to America's interests.

The British then prohibited food and other products that Germany had imported during peacetime, thereby interfering further with neutral shipping. Even the British admitted that these steps had no legal justification, and one American official complained privately, "England is playing a . . . high game, violating international law every day." But when the Wilson administration finally protested, it undermined its own position by noting that "imperative necessity" might justify a violation of international law. This statement virtually authorized the British to violate American rights. In January 1915, Wilson yielded further by observing that "no very important questions of principle" were involved in the Anglo-American quarrels over ship seizures and that they could be resolved after the war.

Submarine warfare.   This policy tied the United States to the British war effort and provoked a German response. With its army stalemated on land and its navy no match for Britain's, Germany decided in February 1915 to use its submarines against Allied shipping in a war zone around the British Isles. Neutral ships risked being sunk by mistake, partly because British ships illegally flew neutral flags. Germany maintained that the blockade and the acquiescence of neutral countries in British violations of international law made submarine warfare necessary.

Submarines could not readily follow traditional rules of naval warfare. These rules had been drawn up for surface ships and required them to identify enemy merchant ships and ensure the safety of passengers before attacking. But small and fragile submarines depended on surprise attacks. They could not surface without risking attack, and they were too small to rescue victims of their sinkings. Yet Wilson refused to see the same "imperative necessity" in German tactics that he found in British tactics, and he warned that he would hold Germany responsible for any loss of U.S. lives or property.

In May 1915, a German submarine sank a British passenger liner, the *Lusitania*. It had been carrying arms, and the German embassy had warned Americans against traveling on the ship, but the loss of life—1,198 people, including 128

Americans—caused Americans to condemn Germany. "To speak of technicalities and the rules of war, in the face of such wholesale murder on the high seas, is a waste of time," trumpeted one magazine. Yet only six of a thousand editors surveyed called for war, and even the combative Theodore Roosevelt estimated that 98 percent of Americans still opposed war. Wilson saw that he had to "carry out the double wish of our people, to maintain a firm front in respect of what we demand of Germany and yet do nothing that might by any possibility involve us in the war."

This was a difficult stance. Wilson demanded that Germany abandon its submarine campaign. His language was so harsh that Bryan resigned, warning that by requiring more of Germany than of Britain, the president violated neutrality and threatened to draw the nation into war. Bryan protested Britain's use of American passengers as shields to protect contraband cargo. "This country cannot be neutral and unneutral at the same time," he declared and proposed prohibiting Americans from traveling on belligerent ships. His proposal gained support in the South and West and was introduced as a resolution in both the Senate and the House in February 1916.

Wilson moved to defeat the resolutions, insisting that they impinged on presidential control of foreign policy and on America's neutral rights. In truth, the resolutions abandoned no vital national interest and offered to prevent another provocative incident. Moreover, neither law nor tradition gave Americans the right to travel safely on belligerent ships. Wilson's assertion of such a right committed him to a policy that could only lead to conflict. Of the nation's "double wish," then, Wilson placed more priority on confronting what he saw as a German threat than on meeting the popular desire for peace.

Arguments over submarine warfare climaxed in April 1916. A German submarine torpedoed the French ship *Sussex,* injuring four Americans. Wilson threatened to break diplomatic relations if Germany did not abandon unrestricted submarine warfare against all merchant vessels, enemy as well as neutral. This threat implied war. Germany promised not to sink merchant ships without warning but made its **Sussex Pledge** contingent on the United States' requiring Britain also to adhere to "the rules of international law universally recognized before the war." Wilson's diplomatic victory, then, was hollow. Peace for America would depend on the British adopting a course they had already rejected. As Wilson saw it, however, "any little German lieutenant can put us into the war at any time by some calculated outrage." Wilson's diplomacy had left the nation's future at the mercy of others.

The Battle over Preparedness

The threat of war sparked a debate over military policy. Theodore Roosevelt and a handful of other politicians, mostly northeastern Republicans convinced that Allied victory was in the national interest, advocated what they called **preparedness,** a program to expand the armed forces and establish universal military training. Conservative business groups also joined the agitation. The National Security League, consisting of eastern bankers and industrialists, combined demands for preparedness with attacks on progressive reforms.

But most Americans, certain that their nation would not join the bloody madness, opposed expensive military preparations. Many supported the peace movement. Leading feminists, such as Jane Addams, Charlotte Perkins Gilman, and Carrie Chapman Catt, formed the Woman's Peace Party in 1915, and other organizations, such as the American League to Limit Armaments, also campaigned against preparedness. William Jennings Bryan condemned preparedness as a program for turning the nation into "a vast armory with skull and crossbones above the door." Most opponents agreed that military spending would undermine domestic reform and raise taxes while enriching arms merchants and financiers.

Wilson also opposed preparedness initially, but he reversed his position when the submarine crisis with Germany intensified. He also began to champion military expansion lest Republicans accuse him in the 1916 election of neglecting national defense. In early 1916, he made a speaking tour to generate public support for enlarging the armed forces. Continuing opposition to preparedness, especially in the South and West, forced Wilson to drop his proposal for a national reserve force. Nevertheless, the National Defense Act and the Naval Construction Act increased the strength of the army and authorized a naval construction program. Draped in the flag, Wilson marched at the head of a huge preparedness parade in Washington to celebrate the military program.

The Election of 1916

Wilson's preparedness plans stripped the Republicans of one issue in 1916, and his renewed support of progressive reforms (see Chapter 21) helped to hold Bryan Democrats in line. Wilson continued his balancing act in the campaign itself, at first stressing Americanism and preparedness but then emphasizing peace. The slogan "He Kept Us Out of War" appealed to the popular desire for peace, and the Democratic campaign became one long peace rally. Wilson disliked the peace emphasis but exploited its political appeal. He warned, "The certain prospect of the success of the Republican party is that we shall be drawn, in one form or another, into the embroilments of the European war."

The Republicans were divided. They had hoped to regain their progressive members after Roosevelt urged the Progressive Party to follow him back into the GOP. But many joined the Democratic camp instead, including several Progressive Party leaders, who endorsed Wilson for having enacted the party's demands of 1912. Roosevelt's frenzied interventionism had alienated many midwestern Republicans opposed to preparedness and cost him any chance of gaining the nomination for himself. Instead, the GOP nominated Charles Evans Hughes, a Supreme Court justice and

A preparedness parade winds its way through Mobile, Alabama, on July 4, 1916. By 1916, President Wilson, invoking the spirit of patriotism, had given his support to the preparedness program of military expansion.

University of South Alabama Achives.

former New York governor. The platform denounced Wilson's "shifty expedients" in foreign policy and promised "strict and honest neutrality." Unfortunately for Hughes, Roosevelt's attacks on Wilson for not pursuing a war policy persuaded many voters that the GOP was a war party. The link with Roosevelt kept Hughes from exploiting qualms about Wilson's own lack of neutrality. "If Hughes is defeated," wrote one observer, "he has Roosevelt to thank for it."

The election was the closest in decades (see Map 23–1). When California narrowly went for Wilson, it decided the contest. The results reflected sectional differences, with the South and West voting for Wilson and most of the Northeast and Midwest for Hughes. The desire for peace, all observers concluded, had determined the election.

Descent into War

Still, Wilson knew that war loomed, and he made a last effort to avert it. In 1915 and 1916, he had tried to mediate the European conflict, using Colonel House as a secret intermediary. Now he again appealed for an end to hostilities. In January 1917, he sketched out the terms of what he called a "peace without victory." Anything else, he warned, would only lead to another war. The new world order should be based on national equality and **self-determination,** arms reductions, freedom of the seas, and an international organ-

ization to ensure peace. It was a distinctly American vision.

Neither the Allies nor the Central Powers were interested. Each side had sacrificed too much to settle for anything short of outright victory. Germany wanted to annex territory in eastern Europe, Belgium, and France and to take over Belgian and French colonies in Africa; Austria sought Balkan territory. The Allies wanted to destroy German military and commercial power, weaken the Austro-Hungarian Empire, take Germany's colonies in Africa, and supplant Turkish influence in the Middle East. One British leader denounced Wilson as "the quintessence of a prig" for suggesting that after three years of "this terrible effort," the two sides should accept American principles rather than their own national objectives. Wilson's initiative failed.

To break the deadlock, Germany resumed unrestricted submarine warfare. This decision seemed necessary to the Germans: By 1917, nearly 700 German civilians were dying each day because of the British blockade, far more than the daily toll of British soldiers in the trenches. German generals believed that even if the United States declared war, it could do little more in the short run to injure Germany than it was already doing. German submarines, they hoped, would end the war by cutting the Allies off from U.S. supplies before the United States could send an army to Europe. On January 31, Germany announced its decision to unleash its submarines in a broad war zone.

Wilson commits to war.   Wilson was now virtually committed to a war many Americans opposed. He broke diplomatic relations with Germany and asked Congress to arm American merchant vessels. When the Senate refused, Wilson invoked an antipiracy law of 1819 and armed the ships anyway. Although no American ships had yet been sunk, he also ordered the naval gun crews to fire at submarines on sight. The secretary of the navy warned Wilson that these actions violated international law and were a step toward war; Wilson called his policy "armed neutrality." Huge rallies across America demanded peace.

Several developments soon shifted public opinion. On March 1, Wilson released an intercepted message from the German foreign minister, Arthur Zimmermann, to the German minister in Mexico. It proposed that in the event of war between the United States and Germany, Mexico should ally itself with Germany; in exchange, Mexico would recover its "lost territory in Texas, New Mexico, and Arizona." The Zimmermann note produced a wave of hostility toward Germany

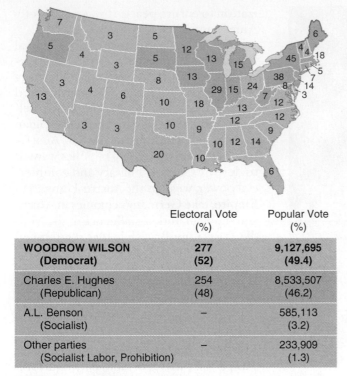

	Electoral Vote (%)	Popular Vote (%)
WOODROW WILSON (Democrat)	**277** **(52)**	**9,127,695** **(49.4)**
Charles E. Hughes (Republican)	254 (48)	8,533,507 (46.2)
A.L. Benson (Socialist)	–	585,113 (3.2)
Other parties (Socialist Labor, Prohibition)	–	233,909 (1.3)

MAP 23–1   The Election of 1916
Woodrow Wilson won reelection in 1916, despite a reunified Republican Party, by sweeping the South and West on campaign appeals to peace and progressive reform.

and increased support for intervention in the war, especially in the Southwest, which had opposed involvement. In addition, the Russian revolution overthrowing the tsarist regime now made Russia "a fit partner" for the United States, according to Wilson. When submarines sank four American freighters in mid-March, anti-German feeling broadened.

On April 2, 1917, Wilson delivered his war message, declaring that neutrality was no longer possible, given Germany's submarine "warfare against mankind." To build support for joining a war that most people had long regarded with revulsion and as alien to American interests, Wilson set forth the nation's war goals as simple and noble. The United States would not fight for conquest or domination but for "the ultimate peace of the world and for the liberation of its peoples." Interventionists were delighted with the decision for war but often distanced themselves from any goal other than promoting national interests. Some progressives who had opposed involvement were won over by Wilson's appeal to idealism.

But others in Congress opposed any involvement in the war. In addition to Senator Robert La Follette's opposition, Senator George Norris of Nebraska condemned the economic motives for American belligerency, crying out, "We are going to war upon the command of gold." Ridiculing Wilson's advocacy of war as a means to promote democracy, House Democratic leader Claude Kitchin of North Carolina

insisted that the American people opposed war and unsuccessfully urged holding a popular referendum on the question.

After vigorous debate, the Senate passed the war resolution 82 to 6 and the House 373 to 50. On April 6, 1917, the United States officially entered the Great War—what Kitchin predicted would be "one vast drama of horrors and blood, one boundless stage upon which will play all the evil spirits of earth and hell."

Waging War in America

Mobilizing for military intervention was a massive undertaking. "It is not an army that we must shape and train for war," announced President Wilson; "it is a Nation." The government reorganized the economy to emphasize centralized management, developed policies to control public opinion and suppress dissent, and transformed the role of government itself. Mobilization often built on the progressives' moralism and sense of mission and their efforts to resolve social and economic problems by government intervention. In other respects, however, the war experience undercut progressive achievements and withered the spirits of reformers. People on the home front, like the soldiers in Europe, would participate in the Great War in many different ways; all would find their lives changed.

Managing the War Economy

Surveying the nation's economy in May 1917, Secretary of War Newton Baker echoed Wilson. War no longer involved merely soldiers and weapons, he said. "It is the conflict of smokestacks now, the combat of the driving wheel and the engine." To harness those factories and machines for the war, federal and state governments developed a complex structure of agencies and controls for every sector of the economy, from industry and agriculture to transportation and labor (see Overview, Major Government Wartime Agencies). Supervised by the Council of National Defense, these agencies shifted resources to war-related enterprises, increased production of goods and services, and improved transportation and distribution.

Organizing industry.   The most important agency was the **War Industries Board (WIB),** established in July 1917 to set industrial priorities, coordinate military purchasing, and supervise business. Led by financier Bernard Baruch, the WIB exercised unprecedented power over industry by setting prices, allocating scarce materials, and standardizing products and procedures to boost efficiency. The number of sizes and styles of plows was reduced by 80 percent; the number of colors of typewriter ribbon dropped from 150 to 5. The WIB even specified how many trunks traveling salesmen could carry and how many stops elevators could make. Yet Baruch was not an industrial dictator; he aimed at business-government integration. The WIB promoted major business interests, helped suspend antitrust laws, and guar-

OVERVIEW

Major Government Wartime Agencies

Agency	Purpose
War Industries Board	Reorganized industry to maximize wartime production
Railroad Administration	Modernized and operated the nation's railroads
Food Administration	Increased agricultural production, supervised food distribution and farm labor
National War Labor Board	Resolved labor-management disputes, improved labor conditions, and recognized union rights as means to promote production and efficiency
Committee on Public Information	Managed propaganda to build public support for the war effort

anteed huge corporate profits. So many business leaders became involved in the WIB that there was a popular outcry against business infiltration of the government, and one corporate executive admitted, "We are all making more money out of this war than the average human being ought to." Some progressives began to see the dangers, and business leaders the advantages, of government economic intervention.

The Railroad Administration also linked business ambitions to the war economy. Under William McAdoo, it operated the nation's railroads as a unified system to move supplies and troops efficiently. Centralized management eliminated competition, permitted improvements in equipment, and brought great profits to the owners but higher prices to the general public. The progressive Republican Senator Hiram Johnson of California protested that the Railroad Administration was "outrageously generous to the railroads and shamefully unjust to the people."

Ensuring food supplies. Equally effective and far more popular was the Food Administration, headed by Herbert Hoover. Hoover had organized relief supplies for war-torn Belgium and now controlled the production and distribution of food for the United States and its allies. He persuaded millions of Americans to accept meatless and wheatless days, so that the Food Administration could feed military and foreign consumers. Half a million women went door to door to secure food-conservation pledges from housewives. City residents planted victory gardens in parks and vacant lots, and President Wilson even pastured sheep on the White House lawn.

Hoover also worked closely with agricultural processors and distributors, ensuring profits in exchange for cooperation. Farmers profited from the war, too. To encourage production, Hoover established high prices for commodities, and agricultural income rose by 30 percent. State and federal governments provided commercial farmers with sufficient farm labor despite the military draft and competition from high-wage war industries. The Food Administration organized the Woman's Land Army to work in the fields.

Most states formed units of the Boys' Working Reserve for agricultural labor. Many southern and western states required "loafers" and "slackers" to work in agriculture. Agribusinesses in the Southwest persuaded the federal government to permit them to import Mexicans to work under government supervision and be housed in special camps.

Overseeing labor relations. The National War Labor Board supervised labor relations. In exchange for labor's cooperation, this agency guaranteed the rights of unions to organize and bargain collectively. With such support, unions sharply increased their membership. The labor board also encouraged improved working conditions, higher wages, and shorter hours. War contracts stipulated an eight-hour day, and by the end of the war, nearly half the nation's workers had achieved the 48-hour week. Wages rose, too, but often only as fast as inflation. These improvements limited labor disputes during the war, and Secretary of War Baker praised labor as "more willing to keep in step than capital." But when such unions as the Industrial Workers of the World did not keep in step, the government suppressed them.

Although these and other government regulatory agencies were dismantled when the war ended, their activities reinforced many long-standing trends in the American economy, from the consolidation of business to the commercialization of agriculture and the organization of labor. They also set a precedent for governmental activism that would prove valuable during the crises of the 1930s and 1940s.

Women and Minorities: New Opportunities, Old Inequities

Women and war work. The reorganization of the economy also had significant social consequences, especially for women and African Americans. In response to labor shortages, public officials and private employers exhorted women to join the work force—"For Every Fighter a Woman Worker"—urged one poster. Women now took jobs previously closed to them. Besides farm work, they built airplanes, produced guns and ammunition, and manufactured tents and cartridge belts. More than 100,000 women worked in munitions plants and 40,000 in the steel industry. Women constituted 20 percent or more of all workers making electrical machinery, leather and rubber goods, and food. They operated drills and lathes, controlled cranes in steel mills, and repaired equipment in machine shops. "One of the lessons from the war," said one manufacturer, "has been to show that women can do exacting work." Harriot Stanton Blatch, a suffragist active in the Food Administration, estimated that a million women had replaced men in industry, where "their drudgery is for the first time paid for."

Many working women simply shifted to other jobs, where their existing skills earned better wages and benefits. The reshuffling of jobs among white women opened new vacancies for black women in domestic, clerical, and industrial employment. As black women replaced white women in the garment and textile industries, social reformers spoke of "a new day for the colored woman worker." But their optimism

With women's labor crucial for the war effort, both government agencies and private industry recruited women for factory work. Here, four women, wearing "womanall" worksuits, pause at their jobs at the Westinghouse Electric Company in 1918.

Hagley Museum and Library, Wilmington Delaware.

was unwarranted. Racial as well as gender segregation continued to mark employment, and wartime improvements were temporary. Federal efforts to prevent pay inequities and sexual harassment in the workplace were halfhearted and subordinated to the goals of efficiency and productivity. And, as one woman said of employers, "As usual, they did not want women to interfere in any way."

Woman suffrage and prohibition. The war did help middle-class women reformers achieve two long-sought objectives: woman suffrage and prohibition. Women's support for the war effort prompted more Americans to support woman suffrage. Emphasizing the national cooperation needed to wage the war, one magazine noted that "arbitrarily to draw the line at voting, at a time when every man and woman must share in this effort, becomes an absurd anomaly." Even Woodrow Wilson finally endorsed the reform, terming it "vital to the winning of the war." Congress approved the suffrage amendment, which was ratified in 1920. Convinced that abstaining from alcohol would save grain and make workers and soldiers more efficient, Congress also passed the Prohibition amendment, which was ratified in 1919.

African Americans and war work. The war also changed the lives of African Americans. The demand for industrial labor caused a huge migration of black people from the rural South, where they had little opportunity, few rights, and no hope. In northern cities, they worked in shipyards, steel mills, and packing houses. Half a million African Americans moved north during the war, doubling and tripling the black populations of Chicago, Detroit, and other industrial cities.

Unfortunately, black people often encountered the kind of racial discrimination and violence in the North that they had hoped to leave behind in the South. Fearful and resentful white people started race riots in northern cities. In East St. Louis, Illinois, where thousands of black southerners sought defense work, a white mob, in July 1917, murdered at least 39 black people, sparing, as an investigating committee reported, "neither age nor sex in their blind lust for blood." Others placed the tragedy in a larger context. The *Literary Digest* noted, "Race-riots in East St. Louis afford a lurid background to our efforts to carry justice and idealism to Europe." And Wilson was told privately that the riot was "worse than anything the Germans did in Belgium."

Financing the War

To finance the war, the government borrowed money and raised taxes. Business interests favored the first course, but southern and western progressives argued that taxation was more efficient and equitable and would minimize war profiteering. Despite conservative and business opposition to progressive taxation, the tax laws of 1917 and 1918 established a graduated tax structure with higher taxes on large incomes,

Black women work in a brickyard for wartime construction. Mobilization opened new jobs for women, but racial subordination and segregation persisted. Black women often performed the hardest and least desirable work.

corporate profits, and wealthy estates. Conservative opposition, however, would frustrate progressives' hopes for permanent tax reforms.

The government raised two-thirds of the war costs by borrowing. Most of the loans came from banks and wealthy investors, but the government also campaigned to sell **Liberty Bonds** to the general public. Celebrities went to schools, churches, and rallies to persuade Americans to buy bonds as their patriotic duty. "Every person who refuses to subscribe," Secretary of the Treasury McAdoo told a California audience, "is a friend of Germany." Using techniques of persuasion and control from advertising and mass entertainment, the Wilson administration thus enlisted the emotions of loyalty, fear, patriotism, and obedience for the war effort.

Conquering Minds

The government also tried to promote a war spirit among the American people by establishing propaganda agencies and enacting legislation to control social attitudes and behavior. This program drew from the restrictive side of progressivism: its impulses toward social control, behavior regulation, and nativism. It also reflected the interests of more conservative forces. The Wilson administration adopted this program of social mobilization because many Americans opposed the war: German Americans with ethnic ties to the Central Powers, Irish Catholics and Russian Jews who condemned the Allies for persecution and repression, Scandinavian immigrants averse to military service, pacifists who recoiled from what Wilson himself called "the most terrible and disastrous of all wars," radicals who denounced the war as capitalist and imperialist, and many others, especially among the rural classes of the South and Midwest, who saw no reason to participate in the distant war.

Government propaganda. To rally Americans behind the war effort, Wilson established the **Committee on Public Information (CPI)** under journalist George Creel. Despite its title, the CPI sought to manipulate, not inform, public opinion. Creel described his goal as winning "the fight for the minds of men, for the 'conquest of their convictions.'" The CPI flooded the country with press releases, advertisements, cartoons, and canned editorials. An average of six pounds of government publicity went each day to every newspaper in California, for example. The CPI made newsreels and war movies to capture public attention. It scheduled 75,000 speakers, who delivered a million speeches to 400 million listeners. Its women's division targeted American women in stereotyped emotional terms. It hired artists to design posters, professors to write pamphlets in 23 languages, and poets to compose war poems for children.

Other government agencies launched similar campaigns. The Woman's Committee of the Council of National Defense established the Department of Educational Propaganda and Patriotic Education. Carrie Chapman Catt dropped her peace activism to head this bureau, in the hope that the war effort would increase support for woman suffrage. The agency worked to win over women who opposed the war, particularly in the rural Midwest, West, and South. It formed women's speakers bureaus, developed programs for community meetings at country schools, and distributed millions of pamphlets.

Government propaganda had three themes: national unity, the loathsome character of the enemy, and the war as a grand crusade for liberty and democracy. Obsessed with national unity and conformity, Creel promoted fear, hatred, and prejudice in the name of a triumphant Americanism. Germans were depicted as brutal, even subhuman, rapists and murderers. The campaign suggested that any dissent was unpatriotic, if not treasonous, and dangerous to national survival. This emphasis on unreasoning conformity helped prompt hysterical attacks on German Americans, radicals, and pacifists.

Suppressing Dissent

The Wilson administration also suppressed dissent, now officially branded disloyalty. For reasons of their own, private interests helped shape a reactionary repression that tarnished the nation's professed idealistic war goals. The campaign also established unfortunate precedents for the future.

Congress rushed to stifle antiwar sentiment. The **Espionage Act** provided heavy fines and up to 20 years in prison for obstructing the war effort, a vague phrase but "omnipotently comprehensive," warned an Idaho senator who opposed the law. In fact, the Espionage Act became a weapon to crush dissent and criticism. Eventually, Congress passed the still more sweeping **Sedition Act of 1918,** which provided severe penalties for speaking or writing against the draft, bond sales, and war production and for criticizing government personnel or policies. Congress emphasized the law's inclusive nature by rejecting a proposed amendment stipulating that "nothing in this act shall be construed as limiting the liberty or impairing the right of any individual to publish or speak what is true, with good motives, and for justifiable ends." Senator Hiram Johnson lamented, "It is war. But, good God, . . . when did it become war upon the American people?"

Postmaster General Albert Burleson banned antiwar or radical newspapers and magazines from the mail, suppressing literature so indiscriminately that one observer said he "didn't know socialism from rheumatism." Even more zealous in attacking radicals and presumed subversives was the reactionary attorney general, Thomas Gregory, who made little distinction between traitors and pacifists, war critics, and radicals. Eugene Debs was sentenced to ten years in prison for a "treasonous" speech in which he declared it "extremely dangerous to exercise the right of free speech in a country fighting to make democracy safe in the world." By war's end, a third of the Socialist Party's national leadership was in prison, leaving the party in a shambles. Other notable radicals imprisoned included Ricardo Flores Magon, a Mexican American labor organizer who was sentenced to 20 years for publishing antiwar material in his Los Angeles Spanish-language newspaper, *Regeneración.*

Gregory also enlisted the help of private vigilantes, including the several hundred thousand members of the reactionary American Protective League, which sought to purge radicals and reformers from the nation's economic and political life. They wiretapped telephones, intercepted private mail, burglarized union offices, broke up German-language newspapers, harassed immigrants, and staged mass raids, seizing thousands of people who they claimed were not doing enough for the war effort.

State and local authorities also suppressed what they saw as antiwar, radical, or pro-German activities. They established 184,000 investigative and enforcement agencies, known as councils of defense or public-safety committees. They encouraged Americans to spy on one another, required people to buy Liberty Bonds, and prohibited teaching German in schools or using the language in religious services and telephone conversations. Indeed, suppression of all things German reached extremes. Germanic names of towns, streets, and people were changed; sauerkraut became liberty

"Beat Back the Hun," a poster to induce Americans to buy Liberty Bonds, demonizes the enemy in a raw, emotional appeal. Liberty bond drives raised the immense sum of $23 billion.

cabbage, and the hamburger the liberty sandwich. In Tulsa, a member of the council of defense killed someone for making allegedly pro-German remarks. The council declared its approval, and community leaders applauded the killer's patriotism. A midwestern official of the Council of National Defense noted, "All over this part of the country men are being tarred and feathered and some are being lynched. . . . These cases do not get into the newspapers nor is an effort ever made to punish the individuals concerned."

Members of the business community exploited the hysteria to promote their own interests at the expense of farmers, workers, and reformers. As one Wisconsin farmer complained, businessmen "now under the guise of patriotism are trying to ram down the farmers' throats things they hardly dared before." On the Great Plains from Texas to North Dakota, the business target was the Nonpartisan League, a radical farm group demanding state control or ownership of banks, grain elevators, and flour mills. Although the League supported the war, oversubscribed bond drives, and had George Creel affirm its loyalty, conservatives depicted it as seditious to block its advocacy of political and economic reforms, including the confiscation of large fortunes to pay for the war. Minnesota's public-safety commission condemned members of the Nonpartisan League as traitors and proposed a "firing squad working overtime" to deal with them. Nebraska's council of defense barred League meetings. Public officials and self-styled patriots broke up the League's meetings and whipped and jailed its leaders.

In the West, business interests targeted labor organizations, especially the Industrial Workers of the World. In Arizona, for example, the Phelps-Dodge Company broke a mine strike in 1917 by depicting the Wobblie miners as bent on war-related sabotage. A vigilante mob, armed and paid by the mining company, seized 1,200 strikers, many of them Wobblies and one-third of them Mexican Americans, and herded them into the desert without food or water. Federal investigators found no evidence of sedition among the miners and reported that the company and its thugs had been inspired, not by "patriotism," but by "ordinary strike-breaking motives." Corporate management was merely "raising the false cry of 'disloyalty'" to suppress workers' complaints.

Nonetheless, the government itself assisted the business campaign. It used the army to break loggers' support for the IWW in the Pacific Northwest, and it raided IWW halls across the country in September 1917. The conviction of nearly 200 Wobblies on charges of sedition in three mass trials in Illinois, California, and Kansas crippled the nation's largest industrial union.

In the end, the government was primarily responsible for the war hysteria. It encouraged suspicion and conflict through inflammatory propaganda, repressive laws, and violation of basic civil rights, by supporting extremists who used the war for their own purposes, and by tolerating mob violence against German Americans. This ugly mood would infect the postwar world.

Waging War and Peace Abroad

While mobilizing the home front, the Wilson administration undertook an impressive military effort to help the Allies defeat the Central Powers. Wilson also struggled to secure international acceptance for his plans for a just and permanent peace.

The War to End All Wars

When the United States entered the war, the Allied position was dire. The losses from three years of trench warfare had sapped military strength and civilian morale. French soldiers mutinied and refused to continue an assault that had cost 120,000 casualties in five days; the German submarine campaign was devastating the British. On the eastern front, the Russian army had collapsed, and the Russian government had gradually disintegrated after the overthrow of the tsarist regime.

What the Allies needed, said French Marshal Joseph Joffre in April 1917, was simple: "We want men, men, men." In May, Congress passed the **Selective Service Act of 1917,** establishing conscription. More than 24 million men eventually registered for the draft, and nearly 3 million entered the army when their numbers were drawn in a national lottery. Almost 2 million more men volunteered, as did more than 13,000 women, who served in the navy and marines. Nearly one-fifth of America's soldiers were foreign-born (Europeans spoke of the "American Foreign Legion"); 367,000 were black. Many Native Americans served with distinction as well; in recognition, Indian veterans were made citizens in 1919, a status extended to all Indians five years later.

Civilians were transformed into soldiers in hastily organized training camps, operated according to progressive principles. Prohibition prevailed in the camps; the poorly educated and largely working-class recruits were taught personal hygiene; worries about sin and inefficiency produced massive campaigns against venereal disease; and immigrants were taught English and American history. Some units were ethnically segregated: At Camp Gordon, Georgia, Italians and Slavs had separate units, with their own officers.

Racial segregation was more rigid, not only in training camps and military units but in assignments as well. The navy assigned black sailors to menial positions, and the army similarly used black soldiers primarily as gravediggers and laborers. But one black combat division was created, and four black regiments fought under French command. France decorated three of these units with its highest citations for valor. White American officers urged the French not to praise black troops, treat black officers as equals, or permit fraternization. But white racism could not diminish the extraordinary record of one of the most famous of the black units in France—the 369th Infantry Regiment, also known as the "Harlem Hellfighters." The 369th spent 191 days in combat and was the first Allied unit to reach the Rhine.

Women were recruited as noncombatant personnel, such as clerks, translators, and switchboard operators, thereby enabling more men to be assigned to combat duty. The navy awarded them equal rank with males performing the same tasks, and they were eligible after the war for veterans benefits. The army was a different story. Although they served in uniform and under military discipline, women had no formal military status, were ineligible for benefits, and often had their skills and contributions devalued. On the eve of a major battle in France, Merle Egan in the U.S. Army Signal Corps, feverishly training soldiers to operate switchboards to help coordinate the massive military buildup, found that some of the men resented taking instructions from a woman. But "when I reminded them that any soldier could carry a gun but the safety of a whole division might depend on the switchboard one of them was operating, I had no more trouble."

Women and War

Assessing the problem of preparedness for the war, U.S. Secretary of the Navy Josephus Daniels asked his counsel "Is there any regulation which specifies that a Navy yeoman be a man?" When the response was no, Daniels directed his subordinates to "enroll women in the naval service as yeomen," adding that "we will have the best clerical assistance the country can provide" and free up men to fight.

Although unable to vote, women clamored for a more active role in the war, and ultimately over 30,000 women joined the military. The Army, however, never formally approved the enlistment of women, and the several hundred women it sent to France as telephone operators were not recognized as veterans until 1978 when they received honorable discharges.

Most women who served in the Great War were nurses; they held no rank and received no benefits but were acknowledged as veterans at war's end. But the Army and Navy Nurse Corps were closed to African American women, who joined the Red Cross in hopes of gaining entry into the military.

The role of women in wartime stirred debate then and now. It was not until the 1990s that women's opportunities in the military changed significantly. By 1994 the military opened up 260,000 new positions for women. Although still prohibited from serving in the infantry or from driving tanks, women took on new responsibilities that increased their risks on the battlefield. But women encountered resistance to their new roles both inside the military and in society as a whole.

The current war in Iraq has rekindled the debate about women in combat. One in every seven troops in Iraq is a woman and more than 70 have been killed, with another 400 wounded. The public debate continues, but this time with a growing awareness that in the Iraqi war, where troops are in short supply and where the frontlines are everywhere, women are indeed "in combat."

HOORAY FOR THE GIRLS

WITH A CAST DRAWN FROM THE JUNIOR RANKS OF NEW YORK SOCIETY. For the benefit of THE AMERICAN COMMITTEE FOR DEVASTATED FRANCE

"I want to be a soldier" was the theme of this popular song describing women's war-time roles.

■ Why has women's role in the military generated so much controversy?

myhistorylab

From Then to Now Online

Woman soldier on patrol in Iraq.

Into action in France.   The first American troops landed in France in June 1917. The American Expeditionary Force (AEF) was commanded by General John J. Pershing, a career officer who had chased Pancho Villa across northern Mexico (see Chapter 22). A gruff stickler for discipline, Pershing wanted to train his soldiers for a full two years before committing them to battle in 1919. But the AEF was rushed across the Atlantic to revive the collapsing morale among the French. Private Leo Bailey recalled that few men in his company had ever discharged a firearm of any kind. "To have sent us to the front at that time would have been murder," he said. "We were woefully ignorant of the basic principles of the soldier." Months of training, under French direction, then followed as the Americans learned about trench warfare: using bayonets, grenades, and machine guns and surviving poison-gas attacks. Finally in October, the 1st Division, the Big Red One, moved into the trenches.

Full-scale American intervention began in the late spring of 1918 (see Map 23–2). General Tasker Bliss asked the French chief of staff, "Well, we have come over here to get killed. Where do you want to use us?" In June, the fresh American troops helped the French repulse a German thrust toward Paris at Château-Thierry. One soldier later recalled: "We saw the long lines of Marines leap from somewhere and start across the wheatfields. . . . As the first wave disappeared over the crest we heard the opening clatter of dozens of machine guns that sprayed our advancing lines. Then we heard some shrieks that made our blood run cold. High above the roar of the artillery and the clatter of machine guns we heard the war cries of the Marines. . . . It seemed less than half an hour before all the machine guns had stopped firing."

Further savage fighting at Belleau Wood blocked the Germans again, prompting a French officer to declare, "You Americans are our hope, our strength, our life." In July, the

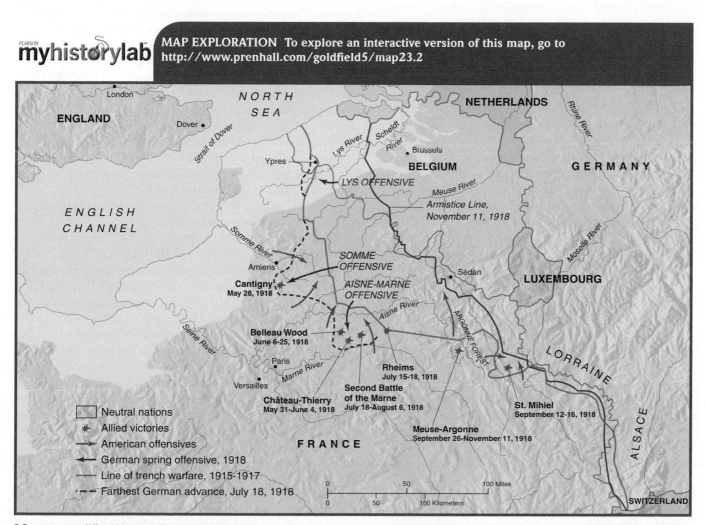

MAP EXPLORATION To explore an interactive version of this map, go to
http://www.prenhall.com/goldfield5/map23.2

MAP 23–2   The Western Front, 1918
After three years of trench warfare, the arrival of large numbers of American troops in 1918 enabled the Allies to launch an offensive that drove back the Germans and forced an armistice.

AEF helped defeat another German advance, at Rheims. The influx of American troops had tipped the balance toward Allied victory. By July 18, the German chancellor later acknowledged, "even the most optimistic among us knew that all was lost. The history of the world was played out in three days."

The Russian front.   In July, Wilson also agreed to commit 15,000 American troops to intervene in Russia. Russia's provisional government had collapsed when the radical **Bolshevik** faction of the communist movement had seized power in November 1917. Under V. I. Lenin, the Bolsheviks signed an armistice with Germany in early 1918, which freed German troops for the summer offensive in France. The Allied interventions were initially designed to reopen the eastern front and later to help overthrow the Bolshevik government.

Lenin's call for the destruction of capitalism and imperialism alarmed the Allied leaders. One Wilson adviser urged the "eradication" of the Russian government. Soon, American and British troops were fighting Russians in an effort to influence Russia's internal affairs. U.S. forces remained in Russia even after Germany surrendered in 1918. They did not leave until 1920. These military interventions failed, but they contributed to Russian distrust of the West.

The Western front.   The Allies were more successful on the western front. Having stopped the German offensive in July, they launched their own advance. The decisive battle began in late September when an American army over 1 million strong attacked German trenches in the Argonne Forest. Many Americans were still inexperienced; some had been drafted only in July and had spent more time traveling than training. Nevertheless, they advanced steadily, despite attacks with poison gas and heavy artillery. Lieutenant Maury Maverick (later a Texas congressman) described the shelling: "We were simply in a big black spot with streaks of screaming red and yellow, with roaring giants in the sky tearing and whirling and roaring." An exploding shell terrified him: "There is a great swishing scream, a smash-bang, and it seems to tear everything loose from you. The intensity of it simply enters your heart and brain, and tears every nerve to pieces."

The battle for the Argonne raged for weeks. A German general reported that his exhausted soldiers faced Americans who "were fresh, eager for fighting, and brave." But he found their sheer numbers most impressive. Eventually, this massive assault overwhelmed the Germans. Despite severe casualties, the AEF had helped the British and French to defeat the enemy. (See American Views, Letter from Albert Smith, October 15, 1918.) With its allies surrendering, its own army in retreat, and revolution breaking out among the war-weary residents of its major cities, Germany asked for peace. On November 11, 1918, an armistice ended the Great War. More than 115,000 Americans were among the 8 million soldiers and 7 million civilians dead.

The Fourteen Points

The armistice was only a step toward final peace. President Wilson had already enunciated America's war objectives on January 8, 1918, in a speech outlining what became known as the Fourteen Points. In his 1917 war message, Wilson had advocated a more democratic world system, and this new speech spelled out how to achieve it. But Wilson also had a political purpose. The Bolsheviks had published the Allies' secret treaties dividing up the expected economic and territorial spoils of the war. Lenin had called for an immediate peace based on the liberation of all colonies, self-determination for all peoples, and the rejection of annexations and punitive indemnities. Wilson's Fourteen Points reassured the American and Allied peoples that they were fighting for more than imperialist gains and offered an alternative to what he called Lenin's "crude formula" for peace.

Eight of Wilson's points proposed creating new nations, shifting old borders, or ensuring self-determination for peoples previously subject to the Austrian, German, or Russian empire. The point about Russia would haunt Wilson after the Allied interventions there began, for it called on all nations to evacuate Russian territory and permit Russia "an unhampered and unembarrassed opportunity for the independent determination of her own political development" under "institutions of her own choosing." Another five points invoked principles to guide international relations: freedom of the seas, open diplomacy instead of secret treaties, reduction of armaments, free trade, and the fair settlement of colonial claims. Wilson's fourteenth and most important point proposed a league of nations to carry out these ideals and ensure international stability.

Wilson and the German government had these principles in mind when negotiating the armistice. The Allies, however, had never explicitly accepted the Fourteen Points, and framing a final peace treaty would be difficult. While Wilson favored a settlement that would promote international stability and economic expansion, he recognized that the Allies sought "to get everything out of Germany that they can." Indeed, after their human and economic sacrifices, Britain and France wanted tangible compensation, not pious principles.

Convinced of the righteousness of his cause, Wilson decided to attend the peace conference in Paris, although no president had ever gone to Europe while in office. But Wilson weakened his position before he even set sail. First, he urged voters to support Democratic candidates in the November 1918 elections to indicate approval of his peace plan. But the electorate, responding primarily to domestic problems like inflation, gave the Republicans control of both houses of Congress. This meant that any treaty would have to be approved by Senate Republicans angry that Wilson had tried to use war and peace for partisan purposes. Second, Wilson refused to consult with Senate Republicans on plans for the peace conference and failed to name important Republicans to the Paris delegation. It was going to be Wilson's treaty, and Republicans would feel no responsibility to approve it.

American soldiers advancing through smoke and shattered trees of the Argonne Forest in October 1918. The Great War was a conflict of relentless attrition, marked by the horrors of poison gas, artillery bombardment, pandemic disease, and what one American called the "unburied dead."

U.S. Army Signal Corps. National Archives III-SC 94980.

The Paris Peace Conference

The peace conference opened on January 18, 1919. Meeting at the Palace of Versailles, the delegations were dominated by the principal Allied leaders: Wilson of the United States, David Lloyd George of Britain, Georges Clemenceau of France, and Vittorio Orlando of Italy. The Central Powers and Bolshevik Russia were excluded. The treaty would be one-sided except to the extent that Wilson could insist on the liberal terms of the Fourteen Points against French and British intransigence. As Clemenceau remarked, "God gave us the Ten Commandments and we broke them. Mr. Wilson has given us the Fourteen Points. We shall see." Wilson himself had broken two of the Fourteen Points before the conference began. He had acquiesced in Britain's rejection of freedom of the seas. And he had sent U.S. troops to intervene in Russia in violation of its right to self-determination.

For months, the conference debated Wilson's other goals and the Allies' demands for compensation and security. Lloyd George later commented, with reference to the self-righteous Wilson and the assertive Clemenceau, "I think I did as well as might be expected, seated as I was between Jesus Christ and Napoleon Bonaparte." Under protest, Germany signed the **Treaty of Versailles** on June 28, 1919. Its terms were far more severe than Wilson had proposed or Germany had anticipated. Germany had to accept sole responsibility for starting the war, a stipulation that all Germans bitterly resented. It was required to pay huge reparations to the Allies,

give up land to France, Poland, Belgium, and Denmark, cede its colonies, limit its army and navy to small self-defense forces, destroy military bases, and promise not to manufacture or purchase armaments.

Wilson gained some acceptance of self-determination. As the German, Austro-Hungarian, Turkish, and Russian empires had collapsed at the end of the war, nationalist groups had proclaimed their independence. On one hand, the peace settlement formally recognized these new nation-states: Poland, Finland, Estonia, Latvia, and Lithuania in eastern Europe and Austria, Hungary, Czechoslovakia, and Yugoslavia in central Europe (see Map 23–3). On the other hand, France, Italy, Romania, and Japan all annexed territory regardless of the wishes of the inhabitants. Germans were placed under Polish control in Silesia and Czech control in Bohemia. Austria was not allowed to merge with Germany. And the conference sanctioned colonialism by establishing a trusteeship system that enabled France, Britain, and Japan to take over German colonies and Turkish territory.

The Allied leaders endorsed the changes in eastern Europe in part because the new states there were anticommunist and would constitute a barrier against Bolshevism. Indeed, the Allies at Versailles were preoccupied with Bolshevik Russia, which one of Wilson's aides called the "black cloud of the east, threatening to overwhelm and swallow up the world." Communist movements in early 1919 in Germany, Austria, and Hungary caused the Allies to fear that "the Russian idea was still rising in power," and they hoped to isolate and weaken Bolshevik Russia. Allied armies were in Russia during the peace conference, and Wilson and the other leaders agreed to provide further aid to fight the Bolsheviks. This hostility to Russia, like the punitive terms for Germany and the concessions to imperial interests, boded ill for a stable and just postwar order. (see Global Perspectives, War and Revolution: The Bolsheviks and the International Community.)

But Wilson hoped that the final section of the Versailles treaty would resolve the flaws of the agreement by establishing his great international organization to preserve peace: the **League of Nations.** The Covenant, or constitution, of the League was built into the treaty. Its crucial feature, Article Ten, bound the member nations to guarantee each other's independence—a provision that was Wilson's concept of collective security. "At least," he told an aide, "we are saving the Covenant, and that instrument will work wonders, bring the blessing of peace, and then when the war psychosis has abated, it will not be difficult to settle all disputes

American Views

Letter from Albert Smith, October 15, 1918

Ultimately numbering over 2 million men, the American troops sent to Europe were organized as the American Expeditionary Forces (AEF) under the command of General Pershing. By August 1918, Pershing had enough troops to form the American First Army, which fought on its own front. In this letter to his brother, Albert Smith describes the largest campaign of the American forces—the Meuse-Argonnne campaign—which proved both decisive and costly for the Allies.

In the struggle, the AEF cooperated with an African American unit under French command, and the campaign produced one of the greatest heroes of World War I: Private Alvin York of Pall Mall, Tennessee, who would receive the Medal of Honor and promotion to sergeant for personally killing 20 Germans and destroying 35 German machine guns.

Smith's letter glowingly refers to the heroic actions of American doughboys—both white and black. Moreover, even as he discourages his own brother from joining the war, he also takes great pride in his own role on the front lines.

- What does Smith's letter illustrate about the impact of total war on soldiers and civilians?
- How does Smith suggest both his confidence about defeating the Germans and his war weariness?
- How did Smith adapt to the new tools of war, especially the use of gas and machine guns?

France
Oct, 15, 1918
Mr. Mcgregor Smith
Cookeville, Tenn.

Dear "Greg";

I received a letter from you a few weeks ago but have not had time to answer for we have been exceedingly busy. We are speedy clearing France of the Huns and making Europe safe for you Kids to come over next spring. This will be the most peaceable country in the world in about sixty days. You just think that you want to come over here we wont need you. I wanted to come over pretty badly and was happy as a lark the day we left New York but that will be nothing to the state of my feeling when I start back to the states. If the Statue of liberty ever sees me again it will have to about face and come down south to find me after she sees me pass going into the harbor at New York on my way home. This is the wettest muddiest country I ever saw, it has been raining steadily for seven weeks. I stepped in a mud hole the other night and went up to my waist in mud and didnt get to change clothes and in fact I haven't changed yet. I haven't changed for over two month and haven't even had my clothes off for that length of time. I have not had a bath for six weeks and none in sight for I haven't the slightest idea of using what little drinking water I get in my canteen for batheing purposes. I shave as often as possible for the beard on my face keeps my Gas mask from being effective and the germans use quite a bit of gas. Gas and machine gun is their only effective weapons. I have been on every front in France. You cant imagine how torn up this country really is. Every where there are wire entanglements and trenches and dug outs. Even out of the war zone there are entanglements and dugouts to protect the civilians from air raids. . . . The hardest fight we were in was in the Argenne [Argonne] Forest. Our batteries were the one that destroyed the machine gun nest at Montfaucon. I was at the Forward observation post the night the barrage was laid during the big drive of the last few weeks. The barrage that night was the heaviest one ever laid in France. I saw every bit of it and saw the infantry go over the top. That certainly was a night that I will always remember. Our doughboy are the greatest men in the world, they certainly have "Fritz" bluffed. During Aug. When we were in a drive against mount Sac [Montsec] the strongest fortified hill in France we supported a regiment of Negro infantry and when they went over the top and up the hill they were saying to them germans "take yo hats off white folks no Kazerade to late now." They sure did slaughter the Huns. The southern boys are certainly hard fighters. The third Tenn. Infantry is the hardest fighting regiment over here. I understand that they have been cited by the British for bravery. At Cambrai they were the Americans that advanced thru the heart of the city and cleared the place of machine guns.

Don't worry about coming over here stay in school that is your service to your country. I am in good health and ready to come home after the war but not before, I will do my bit here. I was appointed for the officers, training camp this month for the third time but refused it, I will go later on in the year I want to stay on the front as long as the war lasts. Be good and study HARD have a good time and write often,

Love to all,

Albert

Corp. Albert P. Smith

Hq. Co. 115 F.A. American Expdt. France

Source: www.historychannel.com/letters/albert_smith.html

that baffle us now." Sailing home, he mused, "Well, it is finished, and, as no one is satisfied, it makes me hope we have made a just peace; but it is all on the lap of the gods."

Waging Peace at Home

Wilson was determined to defeat the opposition to the peace treaty. But many Americans were engaged in their own struggles with the new conditions of a nation suddenly at peace but riven by economic, social, and political conflict. Wilson's battle for the League of Nations would fail tragically. The other conflicts would rage until the election of 1920 restored a normalcy of sorts.

Battle over the League

Most Americans favored the Versailles treaty. A survey of 1,400 newspapers found fewer than 200 opposed. Thirty-three governors and 32 state legislatures endorsed the League of Nations. But when Wilson called for the Senate to accept "the moral leadership . . . and confidence of the world" by ratifying the treaty, he met resistance. Some Republicans wanted to prevent the Democrats from campaigning in 1920 as the party responsible for a victorious war and a glorious peace. But most Republican opponents of the treaty raised serious questions, often reflecting national traditions in foreign relations. Nearly all Democrats favored the treaty, but they were a minority; some Republicans would have to be converted for the treaty to be approved.

Progressive Republican senators, such as Robert La Follette and Hiram Johnson, led one group of opponents. Called the **Irreconcilables,** they opposed participation in the League of Nations, which they saw as designed to perpetuate the power of imperialist countries. Article Ten, they feared, would require the United States to help suppress rebellions in Ireland against British rule or to enforce disputed European borders. Johnson declared, "I am opposed to American boys policing Europe and quelling riots in every new nation's backyard." Most of the Irreconcilables gave priority to restoring civil liberties and progressive reform at home.

A larger group of opponents had reservations about the treaty's provisions. These **Reservationists** were led by Henry Cabot Lodge, the chair of the Senate Foreign Relations Committee. They regarded Article Ten as eroding congressional authority to declare war. They also fretted that the League might interfere with domestic questions, such as immigration laws. Lodge held public hearings on the treaty to rouse and focus opposition. German Americans resented the war-guilt clause; Italian and Polish Americans complained that the

With the defeat of Germany, Americans wanted their soldiers home. And although many returning African-American soldiers were denied celebratory homecomings and would face discrimination and hostility, their role in World War I brought fresh confidence and respect to the African-American community. Few units stirred the patriotism and pride as did the valiant 369th Infantry Regiment, decorated by the French government for heroism and "gallantry under fire." Here African-American friends and families turn out to welcome home the "Men of Bronze," as they were also called.

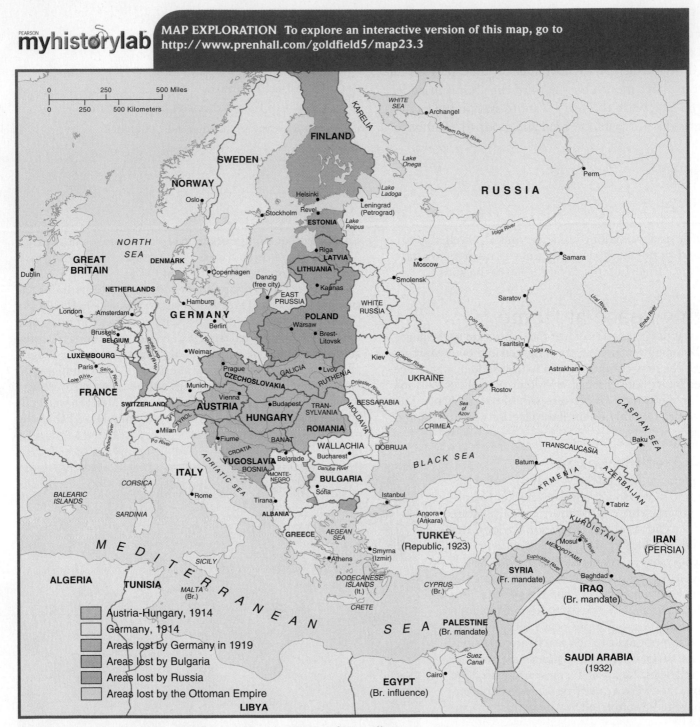

PEARSON
myhistorylab   **MAP EXPLORATION** To explore an interactive version of this map, go to
http://www.prenhall.com/goldfield5/map23.3

MAP 23–3   Europe and the Middle East after the Treaty of Versailles
World War I and the Treaty of Versailles rearranged the borders of Europe and the Middle East. Germany, Russia, and the Austrian and Turkish empires all lost land, and new nations were recognized, but the principle of self-determination was only imperfectly observed.

Global Perspectives

War and Revolution: The Bolsheviks and the International Community

An uneasy amalgam of distinctive nationalities, the Russian Empire at the start of World War I covered vast territories and included 178 million people. A poor, agrarian country, Russia suffered from autocratic tsarist rule. Long-standing economic problems and political aspirations, especially among land-starved peasants, combined to make Russia a cauldron of tensions inflamed by its involvement in the Great War. The Russian army reflected the discontent that plagued the empire; 400,000 soldiers were killed during the first six months of war, and thereafter desertion became a significant problem.

Food shortages provoked protests among peasants and workers—all challenging tsarist rule. Uprisings in February 1917 immobilized Petrograd, the capital, and persuaded the military to mutiny. The February Revolution ended the Romanov dynasty and brought to power a Provisional Government dominated by liberal reformers. Despite recognition and financial aid from its Allies—the United States, France, and Britain—the new government was politically vulnerable and unable to solve the country's pressing problems.

As frustrations mounted, support for the Bolshevik faction of the Communist Party grew. The Bolsheviks envisioned a world without classes or war—a vision that appealed to a war-weary society with a disintegrating economy. In October 1917, the Provisional Government collapsed and the Bolsheviks came to power.

Promising peace, land, and workers' control, the Bolsheviks were led by V. I. Lenin, a lawyer who had worked for a socialist revolution in Russia since the turn of the century. On March 3, 1918, Russia and Germany signed the Treaty of Brest-Litovsk, an armistice that cost Russia significant territory. But Lenin defended the treaty because Germany still occupied large parts of Russia and the counterrevolutionary, or "White," forces were gathering momentum.

The Allies decried both the Bolshevik revolution and the separate peace with Germany, which enabled Germany to strengthen its forces on the western front. Russia's withdrawal from the war emboldened the "Whites," the opponents of the Bolshevik "Reds," and encouraged the Allies to assist them with financial support and troops. But the Allied invasions of Russia were failures, serving only to convince Lenin that the Allies were imperialists bent on overthrowing the world's only socialist state. In the tumultuous postwar period, Lenin's call for workers to overthrow their governments, European and American leaders believed, fed the postwar labor unrest that wracked industrialized nations. Woodrow Wilson fumed that the "poison" of Bolshevism was "running through the veins of the world." Wilson feared that returning African American troops would serve as the "greatest medium in conveying bolshevism to America," but other policymakers targeted aliens, immigrants, and labor activists, culminating in the "Red Scare."

The fears stirred by the Bolshevik Revolution, however, did not provoke similar governmental extremism in either Great Britain or France, both of which would recognize the Soviet Union by 1924. But America, as the British ambassador noted, was singularly "frightened" of the revolution, and the United States would withhold recognition until 1933.

■ What was the impact of the Bolshevik revolution on the war and peace? How did the Allies respond to the Bolsheviks who came to power in Russia in 1917?

treaty did not satisfy the territorial ambitions of Italy and Poland; Irish Americans condemned the treaty's failure to give self-determination to Ireland. Many progressives criticized the treaty's compromises on self-determination, reparations, and colonies. Linking these failures with Wilson's domestic policies, one former supporter concluded; "The administration has become reactionary, and deserves no support from any of us."

Lodge's opposition was shaped by both partisanship and deep personal hostility. "I never expected to hate anyone in politics with the hatred I feel toward Wilson," Lodge confessed. Wilson reciprocated, and when Lodge proposed reservations or amendments to the treaty, Wilson refused to compromise. He proposed "a direct frontal attack" on his opponents. If they wanted war, he said, he would "give them a belly full." In early September 1919, Wilson set out across the country to win popular support for the League. In three weeks, he traveled 8,000 miles and delivered 37 speeches.

In poor health following a bout with influenza, Wilson collapsed in Pueblo, Colorado. Confused and in tears, he mumbled to his secretary, "I seem to have gone to pieces." Taken back to Washington, Wilson on October 2 suffered a massive stroke that paralyzed his left side and left him psychologically unstable and temporarily blind. Wilson's physician and his wife, Edith Galt Wilson, kept the nature of his illness secret from the public, Congress, and even the vice president and cabinet. Rumors circulated that Edith Wilson was running the administration, but she was not. Instead, it was immobilized.

By February 1920, Wilson had partially recovered, but he remained suspicious and quarrelsome. Bryan and other Democratic leaders urged him to accept Lodge's reservations to gain ratification of the treaty. Wilson refused. Isolated and inflexible, he ordered Democratic senators to vote with the Irreconcilables against the treaty as amended by Lodge. On March 19, 1920, the Senate killed the treaty.

Economic Readjustment and Social Conflict

The League was not the only casualty of the struggle to conclude the war. Grave problems shook the United States in 1919 and early 1920. An influenza epidemic had erupted in Europe in 1918 among the massed armies. It now hit the United States, killing perhaps 700,000 Americans, far more than had died in combat. Frightened officials closed public facilities and banned public meetings in futile attempts to stop the contagion.

Meanwhile, the Wilson administration had no plans for an orderly reconversion of the wartime economy, and chaos ensued. The government canceled war contracts and dissolved the regulatory agencies. Noting that "the war spirit of cooperation and sacrifice" had disappeared with the Armistice, Bernard Baruch decided to "turn industry absolutely free" and abolished the War Industries Board as of January 1, 1919. Other agencies followed in such haste that turmoil engulfed the economy.

The government also demobilized the armed forces. The army discharged 600,000 soldiers still in training camps; the navy brought AEF soldiers home from France so fast that it had to expand the troopship fleet to four times its peak size during the war. With no planning or assistance, veterans were hustled back into civilian life. There they competed for scarce jobs with workers recently discharged from the war industries.

As unemployment mounted, the removal of wartime price controls brought runaway inflation. The cost of food, clothing, and other necessities more than doubled over prewar rates. The return of the soldiers caused a serious housing shortage, and rents skyrocketed. Democratic leaders urged Wilson to devote less time to the League of Nations and more to the cost of living and the tensions it unleashed. Farmers also suffered from economic readjustments. Net farm income declined by 65 percent between 1919 and 1921. Farmers who had borrowed money for machinery and land to expand production for the war effort were left impoverished and embittered.

Postwar battles: gender and race.   Women also lost their wartime economic advances. Returning soldiers took away their jobs. Male trade unionists insisted that women go back to being housewives. One New York union maintained that "the same patriotism which induced women to enter industry during the war should induce them to vacate their positions after the war." At times, male workers struck to force employers to fire women and barred women from unions in jobs where union membership was required for employment. "During the war they called us heroines," one woman complained, "but they throw us on the scrapheap now." Indeed, state legislatures passed laws prohibiting women from working in many of the occupations they had successfully filled during the war. By 1919, half of the women newly employed in heavy industry during the war were gone; by 1920, women constituted a smaller proportion of the workforce than they had in 1910.

The postwar readjustments also left African Americans disappointed. During the war, they had agreed with W. E. B. Du Bois to "forget our special grievances and close our ranks shoulder to shoulder with our own white fellow citizens." Participation in the war effort, they had hoped, might be rewarded by better treatment thereafter. Now, the meagerness of their reward became clear.

Housing shortages and job competition interacted with racism in 1919 to produce race riots in 26 towns and cities, resulting in at least 120 deaths. In Chicago, 38 people were killed and more than 500 injured in a five-day riot that began when white thugs stoned to death a black youth swimming too near "their" beach. White rioters then fired a machine gun from a truck hurtling through black neighborhoods. But black residents fought back, no longer willing, the *Chicago Defender* reported, "to move along the line of least resistance as did their sires." The new militancy reflected both their experiences in the military and in industry and their exposure to propaganda about freedom and democracy. Racial conflict was part of a postwar battle between Americans hoping to preserve the new social relations fostered by the war effort and those wanting to restore prewar patterns of power and control. In recognition of both the persistence of white racism and the changed attitudes among African Americans, Du Bois revised his prewar stance, affirming, "We return. We return from fighting. We return fighting."

Fighting for industrial democracy.   Even more pervasive discontents roiled as America adjusted to the postwar world. More than 4 million angry workers launched a wave of 3,600 strikes in 1919. They were reacting not only to the soaring cost of living, which undermined the value of their wages, but also to employers' efforts to reassert their authority and destroy the legitimacy labor had won by its participation in the war effort. The abolition of government controls on industry enabled employers not only to raise prices but also to rescind their recognition of unions and reimpose objectionable working conditions. Employers also protected their rising profits by insisting that wages remain fixed. In response, strikers demanded higher wages, better conditions, and recognition of unions and the right of collective bargaining.

The greatest strike involved the American Federation of Labor's attempt to organize steelworkers, who endured dangerous conditions and 12-hour shifts. When the steel companies refused to recognize the union or even discuss issues, 365,000 workers went out on strike in September 1919. Strikers in Pennsylvania pointed out that they had worked "cheerfully, without strikes or trouble of any kind" during the war to "make the world safe for democracy" and that they now sought "industrial democracy." Employers hired thugs to beat the strikers, used strikebreakers to take their jobs, and exploited ethnic and racial divisions. To undercut support for the workers, management portrayed the strikers as disruptive radicals influenced by Bolshevism. After four months, the strike failed.

Employers used the same tactic to defeat striking coal miners, whose wages had fallen behind the cost of living. Refusing to negotiate with the United Mine Workers, coal operators claimed that Russian Bolsheviks had financed the strike to destroy the American economy. Attorney General Mitchell Palmer secured an injunction against the strike under the authority of wartime legislation. Because the government no longer controlled coal prices or enforced protective labor rules, miners complained bitterly that the war had ended for corporations but not for workers.

Two municipal strikes in 1919 also alarmed the public when their opponents depicted them as revolutionary attacks on the social order. In Seattle, the Central Labor Council called a general strike to support 35,000 shipyard workers striking for higher wages and shorter hours. When 60,000 more workers from 110 local unions also walked out, the city ground to a halt. The strikers behaved peacefully and protected public health and safety by operating garbage and fire trucks and providing food, water, and electricity. Nevertheless, Seattle's mayor, business leaders, and newspapers attacked them as Bolsheviks and anarchists. Threatened with military intervention, the labor council called off the strike, but not before it had caused a public backlash against unions across the nation.

Postwar labor unrest met determined suppression. Here, mounted police attack steelworkers in Pittsburgh in 1919. The strikers were seeking union recognition and an end to twelve-hour days.

In Boston, the police commissioner fired police officers for trying to organize a union to improve their inadequate pay. In response, the police went on strike. As in Seattle, Boston newspapers, politicians, and business leaders attributed the strike to Bolshevism, and Wilson denounced the strike as "a crime against civilization." Massachusetts Governor Calvin Coolidge mobilized the National Guard and gained nationwide acclaim when he stated, "There is no right to strike against the public safety by anybody, anywhere, anytime." The entire police force was fired; many of their replacements were war veterans.

The Red Scare

The strikes contributed to an anti-Bolshevik hysteria that swept the country in 1919. The **Red Scare** reflected fears that the Bolshevik revolution in Russia might spread to the United States. Steeped in the antiradical propaganda of the war years, many Americans were appalled by Russian Bolshevism, described by the *Saturday Evening Post* as a "compound of slaughter, confiscation, anarchy, and universal disorder." Their alarm grew in 1919 when Russia established the Third International to foster revolution abroad, and a few American socialists formed the American Communist Party. But the Red Scare also reflected the willingness of antiunion employers, ambitious politicians, sensational journalists, zealous veterans, and racists to exploit the panic to advance their own purposes.

Fed by misleading reports about Russian Bolshevism and its influence in the United States, the Red Scare reached panic levels by mid-1919. Bombs mailed anonymously to several prominent people on May Day seemed proof enough that a Bolshevik conspiracy threatened America. The Justice Department, Congress, and patriotic organizations like

At the peak of the Red Scare, few major newspapers questioned the wholesale assault on civil liberties and instead placed fears of Bolshevism above rights of individuals, especially workers, immigrants, and radicals. In this 1919 cartoon, the *Philadelphia Inquirer,* using the American flag as a protective cover, registers its support for the exile of radical immigrants and ideas.

In November 1919, Palmer and Hoover began raiding groups suspected of subversion. A month later, they deported 249 alien radicals, including the anarchist Emma Goldman, to Russia. Rabid patriots endorsed such actions. One minister favored deporting radicals "in ships of stone with sails of lead, with the wrath of God for a breeze and with hell for their first port." In January 1920, Palmer and Hoover rounded up more than 4,000 suspected radicals in 33 cities. Often without warrants, they broke into union halls, club rooms, and private homes, assaulting and arresting everyone in sight. People were jailed without access to lawyers; some were beaten into signing false confessions. In Lynn, Massachusetts, 39 people meeting to organize a bakery were arrested for holding a revolutionary caucus. The *Washington Post* declared, "There is no time to waste on hairsplitting over infringement of liberty."

Other Americans began to recoil from the excesses and illegal acts. Assistant Secretary of Labor Louis Post stopped further deportations by demonstrating that most of the arrested were "working men of good character, who are not anarchists or revolutionists, nor politically or otherwise dangerous in any sense." They had been arrested, he said, "for nothing more dangerous than affiliating with friends of their own race, country, and language." Support for the Red Scare withered. Palmer's attempt to inflame public emotion backfired. When his predictions of a violent attempt to overthrow the government on May 1, 1920, came to naught, most Americans realized that no menace had ever existed. They agreed with the *Rocky Mountain News:* "We can never get to work if we keep jumping sideways in fear of the bewhiskered Bolshevik." But if the Red Scare faded in mid-1920, the hostility to immigrants, organized labor, and dissent it reflected would endure for a decade.

The Election of 1920

The Democratic coalition that Wilson had cobbled together on the issues of progressivism and peace came apart after the war. Workers resented the administration's hostility to the postwar strikes. Ethnic groups brutalized by the Americanization of the war years blamed Wilson for the war or condemned his peace settlement. Farmers grumbled about wartime price controls and postwar falling prices. Wartime taxes and the social and economic turmoil of 1919–1920 alienated the middle class. Americans were weary of great crusades and social sacrifices; in the words of Kansas journalist William Allen White, they were

the American Legion joined with business groups to suppress radicalism, real and imagined. The government continued to enforce the repressive laws against Wobblies, socialists, and other dissenters; a Minnesota senator warned that the nation was more imperiled than during the war itself. Indeed, Wilson and Attorney General Mitchell Palmer called for more stringent laws and refused to release political prisoners jailed during the war. State governments harassed and arrested hundreds.

Palmer created a new agency, headed by J. Edgar Hoover, to suppress radicals and impose conformity. Its war on radicalism became the chief focus of the Justice Department. As an ambitious and ruthless bureaucrat, Hoover had participated in the government's assault on aliens and radicals during the war. Now he collected files on labor leaders and other "radical agitators" from Senator Robert La Follette to Jane Addams, issued misleading reports on communist influence in labor strikes and race riots, and contacted all major newspapers "to acquaint people like you with the real menace of evil-thinking, which is the foundation of the Red Movement."

"tired of issues, sick at heart of ideals, and weary of being noble." They yearned for what the Republican presidential candidate, Warren Harding of Ohio, called "normalcy."

The Republican ticket in 1920 symbolized the reassurance of simpler times. Harding was a genial politician who devoted more time to golf and poker than to public policy. An Old Guard conservative, he had stayed with the GOP when Theodore Roosevelt led the progressives out in 1912. His running mate, Calvin Coolidge, governor of Massachusetts, owed his nomination to his handling of the Boston police strike.

Wilson called the election of 1920 "a great and solemn referendum" on the League of Nations, but such lofty appeals fell flat. Harding was ambiguous about the League, and the Democratic national platform endorsed it but expressed a willingness to accept amendments or reservations. The Democratic nominees, James Cox, former governor of Ohio, and the young Franklin D. Roosevelt, Wilson's assistant secretary of the navy, favored the League, but it was not a decisive issue in the campaign.

Harding won in a landslide reflecting the nation's dissatisfaction with Wilson and the Democratic Party. "The Democrats are inconceivably unpopular," wrote Walter Lippmann, a prominent journalist. Harding received 16 million popular votes to Cox's 9 million. Running for president from his prison cell, Socialist Eugene Debs polled nearly a million votes. Not even his closest backers considered Harding qualified for the White House, but, as Lippmann said, the nation's "public spirit was exhausted" after the war years. The election of 1920 was "the final twitch" of America's "war mind."

Conclusion

The Great War disrupted the United States and much of the rest of the world. The initial American policy of neutrality yielded to sentimental and substantive links with the Allies and the pressure of German submarine warfare. Despite popular opposition, America joined the conflict when its leaders concluded that national interests demanded it. Using both military and diplomatic power, Woodrow Wilson sought to bring about a more stable and prosperous world order, with an expanded role for the United States. But the Treaty of Versailles only partly fulfilled his hopes, and the Senate refused to ratify the treaty and its League of Nations. The postwar world order would be unstable and dangerous.

Participation in the war, moreover, had changed the U.S. government, economy, and society. Some of these changes, including the centralization of the economy and an expansion of the regulatory role of the federal government, were already under way; some offered opportunities to implement progressive principles or reforms. Woman suffrage and prohibition gained decisive support because of the war spirit. But other consequences of the war betrayed both progressive impulses and the democratic principles the war was allegedly fought to promote. The suppression of civil liberties, manipulation of human emotions, repression of radicals and minorities, and exploitation of national crises by narrow interests helped disillusion the public. The repercussions of the Great War would linger for years, at home and abroad.

Review Questions

1. Why did Senator Robert La Follette oppose the war against Germany? How did many Americans regard the war and possible U.S. intervention?

2. What were the major arguments for and against U.S. entry into the Great War? What position do you find most persuasive? Why?

3. How and why did the United States shape public opinion in World War I? What were the consequences, positive and negative, of the propaganda of the Committee on Public Information, the Food Administration, and other government agencies?

4. How did the war affect women and minorities?

5. Evaluate the role of Woodrow Wilson at the Paris Peace Conference. What obstacles did he face? How successful was he in shaping the settlement?

6. Discuss the arguments for and against American ratification of the Treaty of Versailles.

Key Terms

Allies (p. 640)

Bolshevik (p. 652)

Central Powers (p. 640)

Committee on Public Information (CPI) (p. 647)

Declaration of London (p. 641)

Espionage Act (p. 648)

Irreconcilables (p. 655)

League of Nations (p. 653)

Liberty Bonds (p. 647)

Preparedness (p. 642)

Red Scare (p. 659)

Reservationists (p. 655)

Sedition Act of 1918 (p. 648)

Selective Service Act of 1917 (p. 649)

Self-determination (p. 643)

Sussex Pledge (p. 642)

Treaty of Versailles (p. 653)

War Industries Board (WIB) (p. 644)

Recommended Reading

Clements, Kendrick A. *The Presidency of Woodrow Wilson* (1992). The best single volume on the Wilson presidency.

Ferrell, Robert H. *Woodrow Wilson and World War I, 1917–1921* (1985). A useful synthesis that emphasizes diplomatic issues.

Kennedy, David M. *Over Here: The First World War and American Society* (1980). Thorough and illuminating discussion of the impact of World War I on American society.

Murray, Robert K. *The Red Scare: A Study in National Hysteria, 1919–1920* (1955). An important early study that retains much value.

Schaffer, Ronald. *America in the Great War: The Rise of the War Welfare State* (1991). An effective and provocative summary that illuminates the expanding role of government.

Zieger, Robert H. *America's Great War: World War I and the American Experience* (2000). A masterful account of the diplomatic, military, and domestic aspects of the war.

Where to Learn More

- **National Infantry Museum, Fort Benning, Georgia.** This sprawling collection of weapons, uniforms, and equipment includes exhibits on World War I. www.benningmwr.com/index.cfm

- **General John J. Pershing Boyhood Home, Laclede, Missouri.** Maintained by the Missouri State Park Board, Pershing's restored nineteenth-century home exhibits some of his personal belongings and papers. www.mostateparks.com/pershingsite.htm

- **Sgt. Alvin C. York Homeplace and State Historic Site, Pall Mall, Tennessee.** The home of America's greatest military hero of World War I contains fascinating artifacts, including York's letters written in the trenches. www.alvincyork.org

- **Wisconsin Veterans Museum, Madison, Wisconsin.** The most stunning museum of its size in the United States, this large building combines impressive collections of artifacts ranging from uniforms to tanks, with substantive exhibits and video programs based on remarkable historical research. It both documents and explains the participation of Wisconsin soldiers in the nation's wars, including the Spanish-American War and World War I. http://museum.dva.state.wi.us

Study Resources

For study resources for this chapter, go to www.myhistorylab.com and choose *The American Journey*. You will find a wealth of study and review material for this chapter, including pre- and post-tests, customized study plan, key term review flash cards, interactive map and document activities, and documents for analysis.

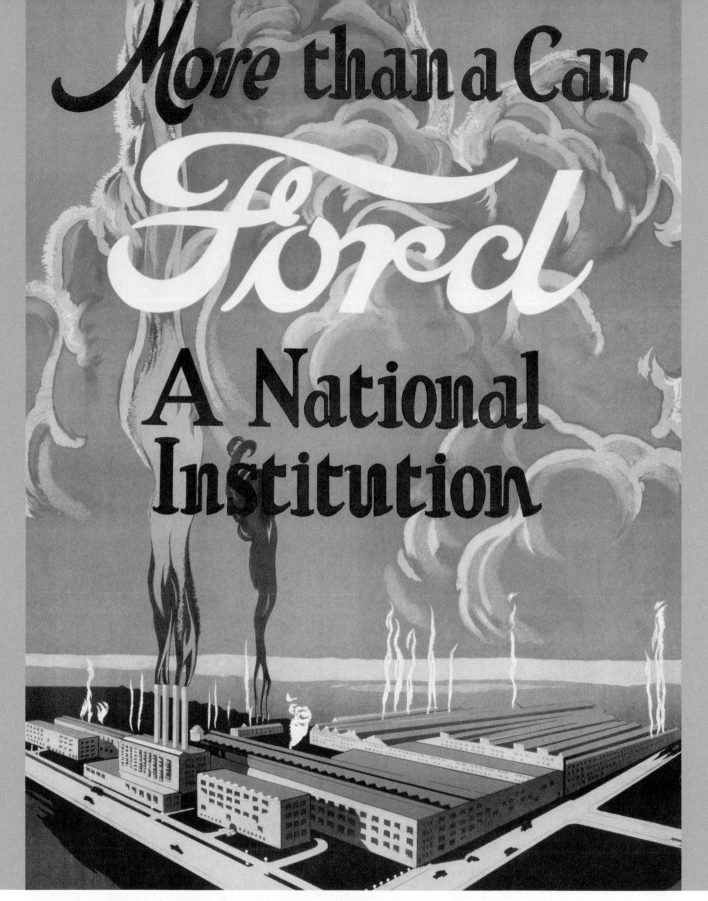

This image celebrates not only the centrality of the automobile but the mammoth size of the Ford enterprise and Henry Ford's vision of mass production in modern American society.

Toward a Modern America
The 1920s 24

Happy times were here again. American industry, adopting Henry Ford's policy of mass production and low prices, was making it possible for everybody to have his share of everything. The newspapers, the statesmen, the economists, all agreed that American ingenuity had solved the age-old problem of poverty. There could never be another depression....

The war had done something to Henry, it had taught him a new way to deal with his fellow men....He became more abrupt in his manner, more harsh in his speech. "Gratitude?" he would say. "There's no gratitude in business. Men work for money."...From now on he was a business man, and held a tight rein on everything. This industry was his, he had made it himself, and what he wanted of the men he hired was that they should do exactly as he told them....

Every worker had to be strained to the uttermost limit, every one had to be giving the last ounce of energy he had in his carcass....They were tired when they started in the morning, and when they quit they were grey and staggering with fatigue, they were empty shells out of which the last drop of juice had been squeezed....

Henry Ford was now getting close to his two million cars a year goal....From the moment the ore was taken out of the ship at the River Rouge plant [in Detroit], through all the processes turning it into steel and shaping it into automobile parts with a hundred-ton press, and putting five thousand parts together into a car which rolled off the assembly line under its own power— all those processes were completed in less than a day and a half!

Some forty-five thousand different machines were now used in the making of Ford cars, in sixty establishments scattered over the United States.…Henry Ford was remaking the roads of America, and in the end he would remake the roads of the world—and line them all with filling stations and hot-dog stands of the American pattern.

Upton Sinclair, *The Flivver King: A Story of Ford-America* (Chicago: Charles H. Kerr, 1999).

myhistorylab

Personal Journeys Online

■ Chicago Daily Tribune, "Capt. Charles Lindbergh, Lone U.S. Flyer, Wings Way from New York to Paris in 33 Hours 29 Minutes," 1927. Photographic essay of Lindbergh's accomplishment.

■ Elsie Johnson McDougald, "The Double Task: The Struggle of Negro Women for Sex and Race Emancipation," 1925. Article attacks racial stereotypes and discusses the diversity among African American women in New York City.

Upton Sinclair, one of America's most famous muckraking journalists, won his greatest recognition with the 1906 publication of his novel *The Jungle*, which graphically depicted the wretched conditions endured by Chicago's immigrant meatpacking workers. In *The Flivver King*, Sinclair again demonstrates his extraordinary ability to weave together a dramatic and historical account of industrial America, as embodied in the rise of the automobile industry and the revolutionizing vision of Henry Ford, the entrepreneur who captured the American mind and symbolized modern America to the world.

"Machinery," proclaimed Henry Ford, "is the new Messiah." Others in the 1920s thought that Ford, too, deserved homage. "Just as in Rome one goes to the Vatican and endeavours to get audience of the Pope," noted a British observer, "so in Detroit one goes to the Ford Works and endeavours to see Henry Ford." Ford had in-

troduced the assembly line at his automobile factory on the eve of World War I, and by 1925 it was turning out a Model T car every ten seconds. The term "mass production" originated in Henry Ford's 1926 description of the system of flow-production techniques popularly called "Fordism." The system symbolized the nation's booming economy: in the 1920s, Europeans used the word *Fordize* as a synonym for *Americanize*. Ford coupled machines and technology with managerial innovations. He established the five-dollar day, twice the prevailing wage in Detroit's auto industry, and slashed the workweek from 48 to 40 hours. These changes, Ford argued, would reduce the costs of labor turnover and boost consumer purchasing power, leading to further profits from mass production.

The assembly line, however, alienated workers, and even Ford himself conceded that the repetitive operations on the line were "so monotonous that it scarcely seems

CHRONOLOGY

1915	Ku Klux Klan is founded anew.
1919	Volstead Act is passed.
1920	Urban population exceeds rural population for the first time.
	Warren Harding is elected president.
	Prohibition takes effect.
	First commercial radio show is broadcast.
	Sinclair Lewis publishes *Main Street*.
1921	Sheppard-Towner Maternity and Infancy Act is passed.
	Washington Naval Conference limits naval armaments.
1922	Fordney-McCumber Act raises tariff rates.
	Sinclair Lewis publishes *Babbitt*.
	Country Club Plaza in Kansas City opens.
1923	Harding dies; Calvin Coolidge becomes president.
1924	National Origins Act sharply curtails immigration.
	Coolidge is elected president.
1925	Scopes trial is held in Dayton, Tennessee.
	F. Scott Fitzgerald publishes *The Great Gatsby*.
1927	Charles A. Lindbergh flies solo across the Atlantic.
1928	Kellogg-Briand Pact is signed.
	Herbert Hoover is elected president.
1929	Ernest Hemingway publishes *A Farewell to Arms*.

possible that any man would care to continue long at the same job." Ford first tried to adapt his mostly immigrant workers to these conditions through an Americanization program. His Education Department taught classes in English, sobriety, obedience, and industrial efficiency to the unskilled laborers entering the factory. After the course, they participated in a symbolic pageant: They climbed into a huge "melting pot," 15 feet across and 7 feet deep. After Ford managers stirred the pot with ten-foot ladles, the workers emerged wearing new clothes and waving American flags—new Americans made for the factory. When the labor market became more favorable to management in the early 1920s, Ford abolished the Education Department and relied on discipline to control workers, determined, as Sinclair observed, to keep "a tight rein on everything." To maximize profits and increase efficiency, Ford even prohibited talking, whistling, sitting, or smoking on the job. Wearing fixed expressions—"Fordization of the face"—workers could communicate only without moving their lips in the "Ford whisper." In keeping with the actions of other employers, Ford also joined the assault on labor organization, banning unions altogether and enlisting the aid of spies and informants to guard against their formation.

But even greater control and higher profits did not satisfy Henry Ford, for, like the 1920s itself, he remained conflicted about the progress he championed—the changes he saw and had helped facilitate. The automobile not only represented the new consumer culture, but it also forever transformed America and Americans—highways, filling stations, and hamburger stands sprang up across the nation, and the car even altered the dating practices of young Americans, alarming some parents and community leaders about what they feared as "bedrooms on wheels." Cars and cigarettes were among the most intensively advertised goods in the 1920s, and for some they

signaled rebellion and freedom. Women in short skirts and the rise of the Jazz Age all contributed to what Ford saw as the evils of the new America. Launching a crusade against the new direction America was headed, Ford decided, according to Sinclair, that "what America needed was to be led back to its past." Embracing nativism and Protestantism, Ford, an ardent anti-Semite, targeted Jewish Americans in his diatribes, blaming them for radicalism and labor organization, and he singled out the "International Jew" for allegedly controlling the international financial community.

Henry Ford and Fordism reflected the complexity of the 1920s. Economic growth and technological innovation were paired with social conflict as traditions were destroyed, values were displaced, and new people were incorporated into a society increasingly industrialized, urbanized, and dominated by big business. Industrial production and national wealth soared, buoyed by new techniques and markets for consumer goods. Business values pervaded society, and government promoted business interests.

But not all Americans prospered. Many workers were unemployed, and the wages of still more were stagnant or falling. Farmers endured grim conditions and worse prospects. Social change brought pleasure to some and deep concern to others. City factories like the Ford Works attracted workers from the countryside, increasing urbanization; rapid suburbanization opened other horizons. Leisure activities flourished, and new mass media promoted modern ideas and stylish products. Workers would have to achieve personal satisfaction through consumption and not production. But such experiences often proved unsettling, and some Americans sought reassurance by imposing their cultural or religious values on everyone around them. The tumultuous decade thus had many unresolved issues, much like the complex personality of Henry Ford himself. And Ford so dominated the age that when college students were asked to rank the greatest people of all time, Ford came in third, behind Christ and Napoleon.

The Economy That Roared

Following a severe postwar depression in 1920 and 1921, the American economy boomed through the remainder of the decade. Gross domestic product soared nearly 40 percent; output per worker-hour, or productivity, rose 72 percent in manufacturing; average per capita income increased by a third. Although the prosperity was not evenly distributed and some sectors of the economy were deeply troubled, most Americans welcomed the industrial expansion and business principles of the New Era.

Boom Industries

Many factors spurred the economic expansion of the 1920s. The huge wartime and postwar profits provided investment capital that enabled business to mechanize. Mass production spread quickly in American industry; machine-made standardized parts and the assembly line increased efficiency and production. Businesses steadily adopted the scientific management principles of Frederick W. Taylor (see Chapter 21). These highly touted systems, though often involving little more than an assembly-line speed-up, also boosted effi-

ciency. The nation more than doubled its capacity to generate electricity during the decade, further bolstering the economy. In factories, electric motors cut costs and improved manufacturing; in homes, electricity spurred demand for new products. Henry Ford was right: Mass production and consumption went hand in hand. Although not one in ten farm families had access to electric power, most other families did by 1929, and many bought electric sewing machines, vacuum cleaners, washing machines, and other labor-saving appliances.

The automobile industry drove the economy. Its productivity increased constantly, and sales rose from about 1.9 million vehicles in 1920 to nearly 5 million by 1929, when 26 million vehicles were on the road (see Figure 24–1). The automobile industry also employed one of every 14 manufacturing workers and stimulated other industries, from steel to rubber and glass. It created a huge new market for the petroleum industry and fostered oil drilling in Oklahoma, Texas, and Louisiana. It launched new businesses, from service stations (over 120,000 by 1929) to garages. It also encouraged the construction industry, a mainstay of the 1920s economy. Large increases in road building and residential housing, prompted by growing automobile ownership and migration to cities and suburbs, provided construction jobs, markets for lumber and other building materials, and profits.

New industries also sprang up. The aviation industry grew rapidly during the 1920s, with government support. The U.S. Post Office subsidized commercial air service by providing air mail contracts to private carriers. Congress then

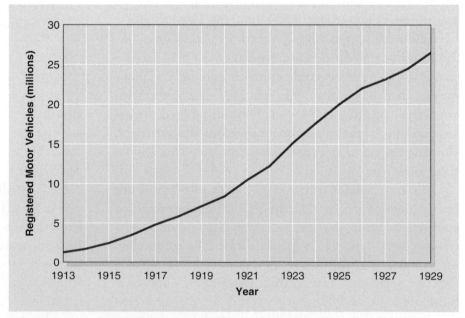

FIGURE 24–1   Registered Motor Vehicles, 1913–1929
The rapid adoption of automobiles shaped the 1920s, stimulating demand for steel and gasoline, encouraging the use of credit, facilitating urbanization, promoting tourism, and suggesting new cultural horizons.

Data Source: U.S. Bureau of Public Roads

authorized commercial passenger service over the mail routes, with regular traffic opening in 1927 between Boston and New York. By 1930, more than 100 airlines crisscrossed America.

The Great War also stimulated the chemical industry. The government confiscated chemical patents from German firms that had dominated the field and transferred them to U.S. companies like DuPont. With this advantage, DuPont in the 1920s became one of the nation's largest industrial firms, a chemical empire producing plastics, finishes, dyes, and organic chemicals. It developed products for the commercial market: enamel for household appliances and automobile finishes, gasoline additives to eliminate engine knocks (many workers died from producing what the *New York World* called "loony gas"), rayon for women's clothing, cellophane to package consumer goods. Led by such successes, the chemical industry became a $4 billion giant employing 300,000 workers by 1929.

The new radio and motion picture industries also flourished. Commercial broadcasting began with a single station in 1920. By 1927, there were 732 stations, and Congress created the Federal Radio Commission to prevent wave-band interference. The rationale for this agency, which was reorganized as the Federal Communications Commission (FCC) in 1934, was that the airwaves belong to the American people and not to private interests. Nevertheless, corporations quickly dominated the new industry. Westinghouse, RCA, and General Electric began opening strings of stations in the early 1920s. Large corporations also ultimately controlled radio manufacturing. Factory-made crystal radio sets became available in 1920, and some 5 million sets were sold by mid-decade. But corporate pressure and patent control eliminated more than 90 percent of the 750 manufacturers by 1927.

The motion-picture industry became one of the nation's five largest businesses, with 20,000 movie theaters selling 100 million tickets a week. Hollywood studios were huge factories, hiring directors, writers, camera crews, and actors to produce films on an assembly-line basis. While Americans watched Charlie Chaplin showcase his comedic genius in such films as *The Gold Rush* (1925), corporations like Paramount were integrating production with distribution and exhibition to maximize control and profit and eliminate independent producers and theaters. The advent of talking movies later in the decade brought still greater profits and power to the major studios, which alone could afford the increased engineering and production costs.

Corporate Consolidation

A wave of corporate mergers, rivaling the one at the turn of the century, swept over the 1920s economy. Great corporations swallowed up thousands of small firms. Particularly significant was the spread of **oligopoly**—the control of an entire industry by a few giant firms. The number of automobile manufacturers dropped from 108 to 44, while only three companies—Ford, General Motors, and Chrysler—produced 83 percent of the nation's cars. Their large-scale, integrated operations eliminated competition from small firms. In the electric light and power industry, nearly 4,000 local utility companies were merged into a dozen holding companies. Mergers also expanded oligopolistic control over other industries. By 1929, the nation's 200 largest corporations controlled nearly half of all nonbanking corporate wealth.

Oligopolies also dominated finance and marketing. Big banks extended their control through mergers and by opening branches. By 1929, a mere 1 percent of the nation's banks controlled half its banking resources. In marketing, national chain stores, such as A&P and Woolworth's, displaced local retailers. With 15,000 grocery stores and an elaborate distribution system, A&P could buy and sell goods for less than the corner grocer.

The corporate consolidation of the 1920s provoked little public fear or opposition. Independent retailers campaigned for local zoning regulations and laws to restrict chain stores, but for the most part, Americans accepted the idea that size brought efficiency and productivity.

Open Shops and Welfare Capitalism

Business also launched a vigorous assault on labor. In 1921, the National Association of Manufacturers organized an **open-shop** campaign to break union-shop contracts, which required all employees to be union members. Denouncing collective bargaining as un-American, businesses described the open shop, in which union membership was not required and usually prohibited, as the "American plan." They forced workers to sign so-called **yellow-dog contracts** that bound them to reject unions to keep their jobs. Business also used boycotts to force employers into a uniform antiunion front. Bethlehem Steel, for example, refused to sell steel to companies employing union labor. Where unions existed, corporations tried to crush them, using spies or hiring strikebreakers.

Some companies advocated a paternalistic system called **welfare capitalism** as an alternative to unions. Eastman Kodak, General Motors, U.S. Steel, and other firms provided medical services, insurance programs, pension plans, and vacations for their workers and established employee social clubs and sports teams. These policies were designed to undercut labor unions and persuade workers to rely on the corporation. Home-financing plans, for instance, increased workers' dependence on the company, and stock ownership plans inculcated business values among employees. Welfare capitalism, however, covered scarcely 5 percent of the workforce and often benefited only skilled workers already tied to the company through seniority. Moreover, it was directed primarily at men. General Electric, for example, dismissed women workers when they married. Women rarely built up enough seniority to obtain vacations and pensions.

Corporations in the 1920s also promoted company unions, management-sponsored substitutes for labor unions. But company unions were usually forbidden to handle wage and hour issues. Their function was to implement company policies and undermine real unionism. General Electric's

An Assembly Line of the Ford Motor Company

Ford Motor Company's assembly line at the River Rouge plant in Detroit. The increasing mechanization of work, linked to managerial and marketing innovations, boosted productivity in the 1920s and brought consumer goods within the reach of far more Americans than before.

State Historical Society of Wisconsin.

management reported that through the company union, "we have been able to educate and secure sympathy and support from a large body of employees who, under the old arrangement of bargaining with [AFL] craft unions, could not have been reached."

Partly because of these pressures, membership in labor unions fell from 5.1 million in 1920 to 3.6 million in 1929. But unions also contributed to their own decline. Conservative union leaders neglected ethnic and black workers in mass-production industries. Nor did they try to organize women, by 1930 nearly one-fourth of all workers. And they failed to respond effectively to other changes in the labor market. The growing numbers of white-collar workers regarded themselves as middle class and beyond the scope of union action.

With increasing mechanization and weak labor unions, workers suffered from job insecurity and stagnant wages. Mechanization, *Fortune* concluded, meant that "from the purely productive point of view, a part of the human race is already obsolete." Unemployment reached 12 percent in 1921 and remained a persistent concern of many working-class Americans during the decade. And despite claims to the contrary, hours were long: The average workweek in manufacturing remained more than 50 hours.

The promise of business to pay high wages proved hollow. Real wages (purchasing power) did improve, but most of the improvement came before 1923 and reflected falling prices more than rising wages. After 1923, American wages stabilized. Henry Ford made no general wage hike after 1919, although his workers would have needed an increase of 65 percent to recover the buying power they had enjoyed in 1914. Indeed, in 1928, Ford lowered wage rates. U.S. Steel also

reduced weekly wages, even while its profits almost doubled between 1923 and 1929. The failure to raise wages when productivity was increasing threatened the nation's long-term prosperity. In short, rising national income largely reflected salaries and dividends, not wages.

Some workers fared worse than others. Unskilled workers, especially southern and eastern Europeans, black migrants from the rural South, and Mexican immigrants, saw their already low wages decline relative to those of skilled workers. Southern workers earned much less than northerners, even in the same industry, and women were paid much less than men even for the same jobs. Male furniture assemblers, for example, earned 56 cents an hour; females only 32 cents. Overall, the gap between rich and poor widened during the decade (see Figure 24–2). By 1929, fully 71 percent of American families earned less than what the U.S. Bureau of Labor Statistics regarded as necessary for a decent living standard. The maldistribution of income meant that eventually Americans would be unable to purchase the products they made.

Consumer credit, rare before the 1920s, expanded during the decade. Credit offered temporary relief by permitting consumers to buy goods on time. General Motors introduced consumer credit on a national basis to create a mass market for expensive automobiles. By 1927, two-thirds of automobiles were purchased on the installment plan. By 1929, providing consumer credit had become the nation's tenth-largest business. Nevertheless, installment loans did not in the long run raise the purchasing power of an income; they simply added interest charges to the price of products.

Sick Industries

Despite the general appearance of prosperity, several "sick" industries dragged on the economy. Coal mining, textile and garment manufacturing, and railroads suffered from excess capacity (too many mines and factories), shrinking demand, low returns, and management-labor conflicts. For example, U.S. coal mines had a capacity of a billion tons, but scarcely half of that amount was needed because of increasing use of oil, natural gas, and hydroelectricity. Using company police, strikebreakers, and injunctions, mine operators broke the United Mine Workers and slashed wages by up to one-third. Unemployment in the industry approached 30 percent; by 1928, a reporter found "thousands of women and children literally starving to death" in Appalachia and the remaining miners held in "industrial slavery."

Similarly, the textile industry coped with overcapacity and declining demand by shifting operations from New En-

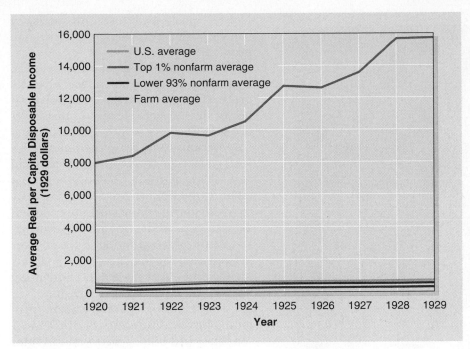

FIGURE 24–2   Growing Income Inequality in the 1920s
Despite the aura of prosperity in the 1920s, the vast majority of Americans received little or no increase in their real income. Farm families dragged the average down further, while the wealthiest Americans doubled their own incomes.

Data Source: Charles Holt, "Who Benefited from the Prosperity of the Twenties?" *Explorations in Economic History,* 14 (1977).

gland to the cheap-labor South, employing girls and young women for 56-hour weeks at 18 cents an hour. Textile companies, aided by local authorities, suppressed strikes in Tennessee and North Carolina. Ella May Wiggins sang of the worries in the mills:

How it grieves the heart of a mother,
You every one must know.
For we can't buy for our children,
Our wages are too low.

Wiggins was murdered by company thugs, leaving behind five small children. The textile industry, despite substandard wages and repressive policies, remained barely profitable.

American agriculture never recovered from the 1921 depression. In 1919, gross farm income amounted to 16 percent of the national income; by 1929, it had dropped to half that. Agricultural problems did not derive from inefficiency or low productivity. Mechanization (especially more tractors) and improved fertilizers and pesticides helped to produce crop surpluses. But surpluses and shrinking demand forced down prices. After the war, foreign markets dried up, and domestic demand for cotton slackened. Moreover, farmers' wartime expansion left them heavily mortgaged in the 1920s. Small farmers, unable to compete with larger, better-capitalized farmers, suffered most. Many lost their land and became tenants or farm hands. By 1930, only 57 percent of

American farmers owned the land they worked, the lowest percentage ever.

Racial discrimination worsened conditions for black and Hispanic tenants, sharecroppers, and farm workers. In the South, African American sharecroppers trapped in grinding poverty endured segregation, disfranchisement, and violence. Mexican immigrants and Hispanic Americans labored as migrant farm workers in the Southwest and California. Exploited by the contract-labor system pervasive in large-scale agriculture, they suffered from poor wages, miserable living conditions, and racism that created, in the words of one investigation, "a vicious circle" from which "few can escape through their own efforts."

By the end of the 1920s, the average per capita income for people on the nation's farms was only one-fourth that of Americans off the farm. "Widespread agricultural disaster," warned one Iowa newspaper, was producing "a highly dangerous situation." Like textile workers in New England and the Piedmont and coal miners in Appalachia, rural Americans suffered in the 1920s.

The Business of Government

The Republican surge in national politics also shaped the economy. In the 1920 election, the Republican slogan was "Less government in business, more business in government." By 1924, Calvin Coolidge, the decade's second Republican president, proclaimed, "This is a business country...and it wants a business government." Under such direction, the federal government advanced business interests at the expense of other objectives.

Republican Ascendancy

Republicans in 1920 had retained control of Congress and put Warren Harding in the White House. Harding was neither capable nor bright. One critic described a Harding speech as "an army of pompous phrases moving over the landscape in search of an idea." But he had a genial touch that contrasted favorably with Wilson. He pardoned Eugene Debs, whom Wilson had refused to release from prison, and he spoke out against racial violence. He also helped shape the modern presidency by supporting the Budget and Accounting Act of 1921, which gave the president authority over the budget and created the Budget Bureau and the General Accounting Office. Moreover, Harding recognized his own limitations and promised to appoint "the best minds" to his cabinet. Some of his appointees were highly accomplished,

Over 6,000,000 motor cars enjoy the enduring beauty...the protection of *DUCO*

But that isn't all! The benefits of *DUCO* are brought to you on any number of things that come into your home!

DuPont became one of the nation's largest industrial corporations in the 1920s by developing new consumer products and marketing them aggressively. This advertisement for Duco automobile finishes blends images of a cathedral and an auto showroom, placing consumerism in a favorable light.

Hoover's goal was to foster prosperity by making business efficient, responsive, and profitable.

Andrew Mellon had a narrower goal. A wealthy banker and industrialist, he pressed Congress to reduce taxes on businesses and the rich. He argued that lower taxes would enable wealthy individuals and corporations to increase their capital investments, thereby creating new jobs and general prosperity. But Mellon's hope that favoring the rich would cause prosperity to trickle down to the working and middle classes proved ill-founded. Nevertheless, despite the opposition of progressives in Congress, Mellon succeeded in lowering maximum tax rates and eliminating wartime excess-profits taxes in 1921.

The Harding administration promoted business interests in other ways, too. The tariff of 1922 raised import rates to protect industry from foreign competition. High new duties on foreign aluminum, for instance, permitted manufacturers—including Mellon's own Alcoa Aluminum—to raise prices by 40 percent. But high tariffs made it difficult for European nations to earn the dollars to repay their war debts to the United States. High rates also impeded American farm exports and raised consumer prices.

The Harding administration aided the business campaign against unions. Attorney General Harry Daugherty secured an injunction against a railroad strike in 1922 and promised to "use the power of the government to prevent the labor unions of the country from destroying the open shop."

The Republicans also curtailed government regulation. By appointing advocates of big business to the Federal Trade Commission and the Federal Reserve Board, among others, Harding made government the collaborator rather than the regulator of business. Progressive Republican Senator George Norris of Nebraska condemned the new appointments, angrily asking, "If trusts, combinations, and big business are to run the government, why not permit them to do it directly rather than through this expensive machinery which was originally honestly established for the protection of the people of the country against monopoly?"

Finally, Harding reshaped the Supreme Court into a still more aggressive champion of business. He named the conservative William Howard Taft as chief justice and matched him with three other justices. All were, as one of them pro-

and two of them, Secretary of Commerce Herbert Hoover and Secretary of the Treasury Andrew Mellon, shaped economic policy throughout the 1920s.

A self-described progressive dedicated to efficiency, Hoover made the Commerce Department the government's most dynamic office. He cemented its ties with the leading sectors of the economy, expanded its collection and distribution of industrial information, pushed to exploit foreign resources and markets, and encouraged innovation. Thanks to his spreading influence, he was often called the secretary of commerce and "assistant secretary of everything else."

claimed, sympathetic to business leaders "beset and bedeviled with vexatious statutes, prying commissions, and government intermeddling of all sorts." The Court struck down much of the government economic regulation adopted during the Progressive Era, invalidated restraints on child labor and a minimum wage law for women, and approved restrictions on labor unions.

Government Corruption

The green light that Harding Republicans extended to private interests led to corruption and scandals. Harding appointed many friends and cronies who saw public service as an opportunity for graft. Attorney General Daugherty's associates in the Justice Department took bribes in exchange for pardons and government jobs. The head of the Veterans Bureau went to prison for cheating disabled veterans of $200 million. Albert Fall, the secretary of the interior, leased petroleum reserves set aside by progressive conservationists to oil companies in exchange for cash, bonds, and cattle for his New Mexico ranch. Exposed for his role in the Teapot Dome scandal, named after a Wyoming oil reserve, Fall became the first cabinet officer in history to go to jail. Daugherty escaped a similar fate by destroying records and invoking the Fifth Amendment.

Harding was appalled by the scandals. "My God, this is a hell of a job!" he told William Allen White. "I have no trouble with my enemies. . . . But my damned friends, . . . they're the ones that keep me walking the floor nights!" Harding died shortly thereafter, probably of a heart attack.

Coolidge Prosperity

On August 3, 1923, Vice President Calvin Coolidge was sworn in as president by his father while visiting his birthplace in rural Vermont, thereby reaffirming his association with traditional values. This image reassured Americans troubled by the Harding scandals. Coolidge's calm appearance hid a furious temper and a mean spirit. Coolidge supported business with ideological conviction. He opposed the activist presidency of the Progressive Era, cultivating instead a deliberate inactivity calculated to lower expectations of government. He endorsed Secretary of the Treasury Mellon's ongoing efforts to reverse the progressive tax policies of the Wilson years and backed Secretary of Commerce Hoover's persistent efforts on behalf of the business community (although he privately sneered at Hoover as the "Wonder Boy").

Like Harding, Coolidge installed business supporters in the regulatory agencies. To chair the Federal Trade Commission he appointed an attorney who had condemned the agency as "an instrument of oppression and disturbance and injury instead of help to business." Under this leadership, the FTC described its new goal as "helping business to help itself," which meant approving trade associations and agreements to suppress competition. This attitude, endorsed by the Supreme Court, aided the mergers that occurred after 1925. The *Wall Street Journal* crowed, "Never before, here or anywhere else, has a government been so completely fused with business."

And Coolidge confined the government's role to helping business. When Congress tried to raise farm prices, Coolidge vetoed the measure as "preposterous" special-interest legislation. One economist said that Coolidge's vetoes revealed "a stubborn determination to do nothing," but they revealed more. For on the same day that Coolidge vetoed assistance to farmers, he raised by 50 percent the tariff on pig iron, thereby increasing manufacturers' profits and farmers' costs for tools. Government action was acceptable for business but not for nonbusiness interests.

"Coolidge prosperity" determined the 1924 election. The Democrats, hopelessly divided, took 103 ballots to nominate the colorless, conservative Wall Street lawyer John W. Davis. A more interesting opponent for Coolidge was Robert La Follette, nominated by discontented farm and labor organizations that formed a new Progressive Party. La Follette campaigned against "the power of private monopoly over the political and economic life of the American people." The Progressive platform demanded government ownership of railroads and utilities, farm assistance, and collective bargaining. The Republicans, backed by immense contributions from business, denounced La Follette as an agent of Bolshevism. The choice, Republicans insisted, was "Coolidge or Chaos." Thus instructed, Americans chose Coolidge, though barely half the electorate bothered to vote.

The Fate of Reform

But progressive reform was not completely dead. Even Harding proposed social welfare measures, and, during the 1921 depression, he convened a conference on unemployment and helped spark voluntary relief. A small group in Congress, led by La Follette and George Norris, attacked Mellon's regressive tax policies and supported measures regulating agricultural processors, protecting workers' rights, and maintaining public ownership of a hydroelectric dam at Muscle Shoals, Alabama, that conservative Republicans wanted to privatize. Yet the reformers' successes were few and often temporary.

The fate of women's groups illustrates the difficulties reformers faced in the 1920s. At first, the adoption of woman suffrage prompted politicians to champion women's reform issues. In 1920, both major parties endorsed many of the goals of the new **League of Women Voters.** Within a year, many states had granted women the right to serve on juries, several enacted equal-pay laws, and Wisconsin adopted an equal-rights law. Congress passed the **Sheppard-Towner Maternity and Infancy Act,** the first federal social-welfare law, in 1921. It provided federal funds for infant and maternity care, precisely the type of protective legislation that the suffragists had described as women's special interest. Women also ran for political office and by 1922 there were fifteen women mayors of small towns throughout the nation.

But thereafter women reformers gained little. As it became clear that women did not vote as a bloc but according to their varying social and economic backgrounds, Congress lost interest in women's issues. In 1929, Congress killed the Sheppard-Towner Act. Nor could reformers gain ratification of a child-labor amendment after the Supreme Court invalidated laws regulating child labor. Conservatives attacked women reformers as "Bolsheviks."

Disagreements and shifting interests also limited the success of women reformers. Led by the National Woman's Party, some feminists campaigned for an Equal Rights Amendment, whereas other reformers feared that it would nullify the progressive laws that protected working women. Such reform organizations as the Consumers' League lost their energy and focus. The General Federation of Women's Clubs, always relatively conservative, promoted home economics and the use of electrical appliances. Indeed, many younger women rejected the public reform focus of progressive feminists. The *Magazine of Business* even maintained that women valued the vacuum cleaner more than the vote. By

1927, the president of the Women's Trade Union League called the decade "hideous in the public life of our people and in the noisy flaunting of cheap hopes and cheaper materialism."

Cities and Suburbs

The 1920 census was the first to report that more Americans lived in urban than in rural areas. The trend toward urbanization accelerated in the 1920s as millions of Americans fled the depressed countryside for the booming cities. This massive population movement interacted with technological innovations to reshape cities, build suburbs, and transform urban life (see Map 24–1).

Expanding Cities

Urbanization affected every region of the country. In absolute terms, the older industrial cities of the Northeast and upper Midwest grew the most, attracting migrants from the

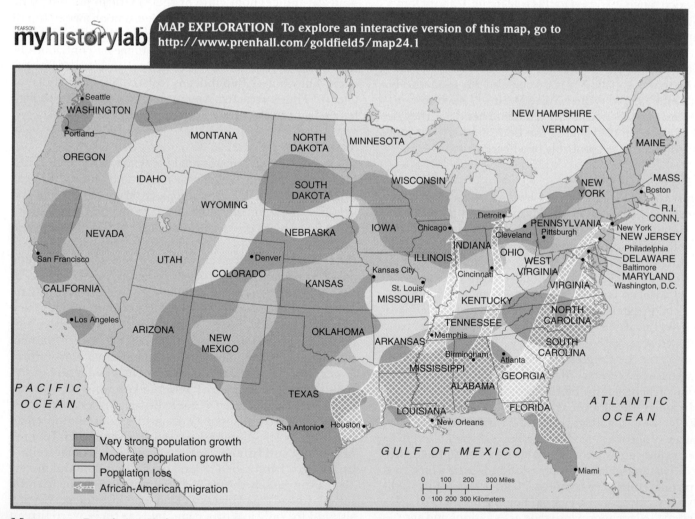

MAP EXPLORATION To explore an interactive version of this map, go to http://www.prenhall.com/goldfield5/map24.1

MAP 24–1   Population Shifts, 1920–1930
Rural Americans fled to the cities during the 1920s, escaping a declining agricultural economy to search for new opportunities. African Americans in particular left the rural South for eastern and midwestern cities, but the urban population also jumped in the West and in the South itself.

rural South and distressed Appalachia. New York remained the nation's foremost metropolis. All the other major cities also grew—none more spectacularly than Detroit, which now had 1.6 million people. The "Motor City" thrived on the booming automobile industry and related industries like glass manufacturing. Old trees and wide lawns gave way to multi-lane highways as apartment houses and parking lots obliterated old Detroit.

Rural southerners also headed for southern cities. In fact, the South was the nation's most rapidly urbanizing region. Migrants from the countryside poured into Atlanta, Birmingham, Memphis, and Houston. Little more than jungle before 1914, Miami became the fastest growing city in the United States during the 1920s—"the Magic City." Not all southerners welcomed urban growth and the values it represented. The novelist Thomas Wolfe cautioned against boosters in Asheville, North Carolina, "who shout 'Progress Progress Progress'—when what they mean is more Ford automobiles, more Rotary Clubs, more Baptist Ladies Social unions.... We are not necessarily four times as civilized as our grandfathers because we go four times as fast in automobiles, because our buildings are four times as tall."

In the West, Denver, Portland, and Seattle (each a regional economic hub) and several California cities grew rapidly. Los Angeles grew by 115 percent and by 1930 was the nation's fifth-largest city, with over 1.2 million people. Although it was the center of California's agricultural wealth and the motion picture industry and one of the world's busiest ports, Los Angeles was also linked to the automobile industry. The southern California oil fields and the demand for gasoline made it the nation's leading refining center.

The population surge transformed the urban landscape. As land values soared, developers built skyscrapers, giving Cleveland, Kansas City, San Francisco, and many other cities modern skylines. By the end of the decade, American cities had nearly 400 skyscrapers taller than 20 stories.

The Great Black Migration

A significant feature of the rural-to-urban movement was the **Great Migration** of African Americans from the South. Like other migrants, they were responding chiefly to economic factors. Southern segregation and violence made migration attractive, but job opportunities made it possible. Prosperity created jobs, and with the decline in European immigration, black workers filled the positions previously given to new immigrants. Though generally the lowest paid and least secure jobs, they were better than sharecropping in the rural South. Black men worked as unskilled or semiskilled laborers; black women became domestics in white homes. The migrants often found adjustment to their new environment difficult. Southern rural black culture clashed with industrial work rhythms and discipline and with urban living. Still, more than 1.5 million African Americans moved to northern cities in the 1920s.

There black ghettos usually developed, more because of prejudice than the wishes of the migrants. Although African Americans, like European immigrants, often wanted to live together to sustain their culture, racist restrictions meant that segregation, not congregation, most shaped their urban community. With thousands of newcomers limited to certain neighborhoods, housing shortages developed. Rapacious landlords charged ever-increasing rents for ever-declining housing. Rents doubled in New York's Harlem during the decade. Racism exacerbated urban poverty; black workers earned less than working-class white workers but had to spend 50 percent more for housing. High rents and low wages forced black families to share inferior and unsanitary housing that threatened their health and safety. In Pittsburgh, only 20 percent of black houses had bathtubs, and only 50 percent had indoor toilets; in another city, an observer wrote that "the State would not allow cows to live in some of these apartments used by colored people."

However, the Great Migration also increased African Americans' racial consciousness, autonomy, and power. In 1928, for instance, black Chicagoans, using the ballot denied to African Americans in the South, elected the first black man to Congress since the turn of the century. Mutual-aid societies and fraternal orders proliferated. Churches were particularly influential. A reporter in 1926 counted 140 black churches in a 150-block area of Harlem. Most of these were "storefront churches" where "cotton-field preachers" provided an emotional and fundamentalist religion familiar to migrants from the rural South.

Another organization also appealed to poor black ghetto dwellers. The Universal Negro Improvement Association (UNIA), organized by Marcus Garvey, a Jamaican immigrant to New York, rejected the NAACP's goal of integration. A black nationalist espousing racial pride, Garvey exhorted black people to migrate to Africa to build a "free, redeemed, and mighty nation." In the meantime, he urged them to support black businesses. UNIA organized many enterprises, including groceries, restaurants, laundries, a printing plant, and the Black Star Steamship Line, intended as a commercial link between the United States, the West Indies, and Africa. UNIA attracted half a million members, the first black mass movement in American history. When Garvey was convicted of mail fraud and deported, however, the movement collapsed.

Racial pride also found expression in the **Harlem Renaissance,** an outpouring of literature, painting, sculpture, and music. Inspired by African American culture and black urban life, writers and artists created works of power and poignancy. The poetry of Langston Hughes reflected the rhythm and mood of jazz and the blues. When a white patron complained that his writing was not "primitive" enough, Hughes responded, "I did not feel the rhythms of the primitive surging through me, and so I could not live and write as though I did. I was Chicago and Kansas City and Broadway and Harlem. And I was not what she wanted me to be." Other

Zora Neale Hurston, folklorist, anthropologist, and novelist, wrote with wit and verve about the African-American South she so closely studied. Part of the dynamic community known as the Harlem Renaissance, Hurston won recognition in 1925 for her short story "Spunk." Her collective work, especially her later novel, *Their Eyes Were Watching God,* both reflected and advanced the creative pulse of what one black intellectual regarded as the first opportunity for African Americans to realize "group expression and self-determination."

leading authors of the Harlem Renaissance who asserted their independence included Claude McKay, who wrote of the black working class in *Home to Harlem* (1928), Zora Neale Hurston, James Weldon Johnson, and Dorothy West.

Barrios

Hispanic migrants also entered the nation's cities in the 1920s, creating their own communities, or barrios. Fifty thousand Puerto Ricans settled in New York, mostly in East ("Spanish") Harlem, where they found low-paying jobs. Far more migrants arrived from Mexico. Although many worked as migrant farm laborers, they often lived in cities in the off-season. Others permanently joined the expanding urban economy in industrial and construction jobs. The barrios, with their own businesses, churches, and cultural organizations, created a sense of permanency.

These communities enabled the newcomers to preserve their cultural values and build social institutions, such as *mutualistas* (mutual aid societies), that helped them obtain credit, housing, and healthcare. But the barrios also reflected the hostility that Hispanics encountered in American cities.

The number of Mexicans in Los Angeles tripled during the 1920s to nearly 100,000, but segregation confined them to East Los Angeles. Other areas of the city, such as El Segundo and Lynwood, boasted of being "restricted to the white race" and having "no Negroes or Mexicans." Los Angeles maintained separate schools for Mexicans, and a social worker reported that "America has repulsed the Mexican immigrant in every step he has taken" toward integration. As new migrants streamed in, conditions in the barrios deteriorated, for few cities provided adequate public services for them. Denver's barrio was described in 1924 as an area "both God and Denver had forgotten," with "no paving, no sidewalks, no sewers."

Some Hispanics fought discrimination. La Orden de Hijos de America ("The Order of the Sons of America"), organized in San Antonio in 1921, campaigned against inequities in schools and the jury system. In 1929, it helped launch the larger League of United Latin American Citizens (LULAC), which would help advance civil rights for all Americans.

The Road to Suburbia

As fast as the cities mushroomed in the 1920s, the suburbs grew twice as fast. Park Ridge outside Chicago, Inglewood outside Los Angeles, Shaker Heights outside Cleveland, and many others expanded by 400 percent. New suburbs arose across the country. Fourteen hundred new subdivisions appeared in Los Angeles County during the 1920s; two-thirds of the new municipal incorporations in Illinois and Michigan were suburbs of Chicago, St. Louis, or Detroit. Some suburbs, such as Highland Park, where Henry Ford built his factory near Detroit, and Fairfield, Alabama, were industrial, but most were havens for the middle and upper classes.

Automobiles created the modern suburb. Nineteenth-century suburbs were small and linear, stretching along the street railway system. The new developments were sprawling and dispersed, for the automobile enabled people to live in formerly remote areas. A single-family house surrounded by a lawn became the social ideal, a pastoral escape from the overcrowded and dangerous city. Many suburbs excluded African Americans, Hispanics, Jews, and working-class people. Shaker Heights, for instance, limited land sales to white buyers and required expensive building materials and professional architects. Suburbanites of more modest means found homes in such places as Westwood, outside Chicago, the "World's Largest Bungalow Development."

Suburbanization and the automobile brought other changes. The government provided federal money to states to build highways, and by the end of the decade, road construction was the largest single item in the national budget. Autos and suburbs also stimulated the growth of new industries. In 1922, J. C. Nichols opened the Country Club Plaza, the first suburban shopping center, in Kansas City; it provided free off-street parking. Department stores and other large retailers began leaving the urban cores for the suburbs, where both parking and more affluent customers were waiting. Drive-in restaurants began with Royce Hailey's Pig Stand in Dallas in 1921. That same year, the first fast-food franchise

Making tortillas—the staple of the Mexican diet—these Mexican American women used stone mortars in the 1920s to grind the corn by hand at the El Sol del Mayo tortilla plant in East Los Angeles. Spurned by Anglo society, Mexican Americans found support, jobs, and community in the barrios where they lived and worked. The barrios also enabled some Mexican Americans, like plant owner Maria Zuevedo, to become small business owners. They provided products and services that satisfied the traditional cultural values of the Mexican community.

chain, White Castle, appeared, with its standardized menu and building, serving hamburgers "by the sack" to Americans in record numbers. Enjoying remarkable success, owners Walt Anderson and Billy Ingram described their volume of sales in one year: "Picture a line of buns, laid side by side, one hundred and sixty-three miles long, forty-one truckloads of hamburger, weighing two tons each, two carloads of onions, three carloads of pickles, ninety-six-hundred five gallon urns of coffee and you have an idea of the output of the White Castle System for the year 1925."

Mass Culture in the Jazz Age

The White Castle chain symbolized a new society and culture. Urbanization and the automobile joined with new systems of distributing, marketing, and communications to mold a mass culture of standardized experiences and interests. Not all Americans participated equally in the new culture, however, and some attacked it.

Advertising the Consumer Society

Advertising and its focus on increasing consumption shaped the new society. President Coolidge considered advertising "the most potent influence in adopting and changing the habits and modes of life, affecting what we eat, what we wear,

and the work and play of the whole nation." A less complacent observer calculated that in 1925, nearly 50 percent more was spent "to educate consumers in what they may or may not want to buy" than on education from grade school through university.

Advertisers exhorted consumers via newspapers, billboards, streetcar signs, junk mail, radio, movies, and even skywriting. They sought to create a single market where everyone, regardless of region and ethnicity, consumed brand-name products. Advertisers attempted to stimulate new wants by ridiculing previous models or tastes as obsolete, acclaiming the convenience of a new brand, or linking the latest fashion with status or sex appeal. "If I wear a certain brand of underwear," observed one critic, "I have the satisfaction of knowing that my fellow-men not so fortunately clad are undoubtedly fouled swine."

The home became a focus of consumerism. Middle- and upper-class women purchased mass-produced household appliances, such as electric irons, toasters, vacuum cleaners, washing machines, and refrigerators. Working-class women bought packaged food, ready-made clothing, and other consumer goods to lighten their workload. Advertisers attempted to redefine the housewife's role as primarily that of a consumer, purchasing goods for her family. To promote sales of clothing and cosmetics, advertising depicted women as concerned with fashion, beauty, and sex appeal. It thus contributed to the declining interest in the larger social issues that the earlier women's movement had raised.

A shifting labor market also promoted mass consumption. The increasing number of white-collar workers had more time and money for leisure and consumption. Factory workers, whose jobs often provided little challenge, less satisfaction, and no prospect for advancement, found in consumption not only material rewards but, thanks to advertisers' claims, some self-respect and fulfillment as stylish and attractive people worthy of attention. Women clerical workers, the fastest growing occupational group, found in the purchase of clothes and cosmetics a sign of social status and an antidote to workplace monotony.

Under the stimulus of advertising, consumption increasingly displaced the traditional virtues of thrift, prudence, and avoidance of debt. Installment buying became common. By 1928, fully 85 percent of furniture, 80 percent of radios, and 75 percent of washing machines were bought on credit. But with personal debt rising more than twice as fast as incomes, even aggressive advertising and the extension of credit could not indefinitely prolong the illusion of a healthy economy.

Leisure and Entertainment

During the 1920s, Americans also spent more on recreation and leisure, important features of the new mass society. Millions of people packed into movie theaters whose ornate style symbolized their social importance. In Chicago, the Uptown boasted a 4,000-seat theater, an infirmary, a nursery, and a restaurant; its turreted façade soared eight stories. Inside was a four-story lobby with twin marble staircases,

The soup for men who eat to win!

MEN with the success-habit eat wisely and well, both. They enjoy Campbell's Tomato Soup regularly and they get from it a sparkle and zest, which tell in the day's work. All of the rich, tonic goodness. All of the famous tomato healthfulness. 12 cents a can.

Advertisements for brand-name products, like this 1929 ad for Campbell's tomato soup, often tried to link simple consumption with larger issues of personal success and achievement.

crystal chandeliers, and an orchestra to entertain people waiting to enter. "It is beyond human dreams of loveliness," exclaimed one ad, "achieving that overpowering sense of tremendous size and exquisite beauty."

Movies helped to spread common values and to set national trends in dress, language, and behavior. Studios made films to attract the largest audiences and fit prevailing stereotypes. Cecil B. De Mille titillated audiences while reinforcing conventional standards with religious epics like *The Ten Commandments* (1923) and *The King of Kings* (1927). Set in ancient times, such movies depicted both sinful pleasures and the eventual triumph of moral order. One Hollywood executive called for "passionate but pure" films that would give "the public all the sex it wants with compensating values for all those church and women groups."

Radio also helped to mold popular culture. The first radio network, the National Broadcasting Company (NBC), was formed in 1926. Soon it was charging $10,000 to broadcast a commercial to a national market. Networks provided standardized entertainment, personalities, and news to Americans across the nation. Radio incorporated listeners

into a national society. Rural residents, in particular, welcomed the "talking furniture" for giving them access to the speeches, sermons, and business information available to city dwellers.

The phonograph, another popular source of entertainment, allowed families to listen to music of their choice in their own homes. The phonograph business boomed. Manufacturers turned out more than 2 million phonographs and 100 million records annually. Record companies promoted dance crazes, such as the Charleston, and developed regional markets for country, or "hillbilly," music in the South and West, as well as a "race market" for blues and jazz among the growing urban population, black and white. The popularity of the trumpet player Louis Armstrong and other jazz greats gave the decade its nickname, the **Jazz Age.**

Jazz derived from African American musical traditions. The Great Migration spread it from New Orleans and Kansas City to cities throughout the nation. Its improvisational and rhythmic characteristics differed sharply from older and more formal music and were often condemned by people who feared that jazz would undermine conventional restraints on behavior. A group in Cincinnati, arguing that the music would implant "jazz emotions" in babies, won an injunction against its performance near hospitals. Middle-class black Chicagoans frowned on jazz and favored "the better class of music." But the symphony conductor Leopold Stokowski defended jazz as the music of modern America: "Jazz has come to stay because it is an expression of the times, of the breathless, energetic, superactive times in which we are living; it is useless to fight against it." (See Global Perspectives, The International Journey of Jazz.)

Professional sports also became more commercialized. Millions of Americans, attracted by the popularity of such celebrities as Babe Ruth of the New York Yankees, crowded into baseball parks to follow major league teams. Ruth treated himself as a commercial commodity, hiring an agent, endorsing Cadillacs and alligator shoes, and defending a salary in 1932 that dwarfed that of President Hoover by declaring, "I had a better year than he did."

Large crowds turned out to watch boxers Jack Dempsey and Gene Tunney pummel each other; those who could not get tickets listened to radio announcers describe each blow. College football attracted frenzied followers among people with no interest in higher education. Universities built huge stadiums—Ohio State's had 64,000 seats. By 1929, the Carnegie Commission noted that the commercialization of college sports had "overshadowed the intellectual life for which the university is assumed to exist."

Other crazes, from flagpole sitting to miniature golf, also highlighted the spread of popular culture and its emphasis on leisure. Another celebrity who captured popular fascination was the aviator Charles Lindbergh, who flew alone across the Atlantic in 1927. In the *Spirit of St. Louis,* a tiny airplane built on a shoestring budget and nearly outweighed by the

Violinist Carroll Dickerson, at the Sunset Café in 1922, led one of the jazz bands that flourished in Chicago's many clubs, pointing up the central role of African Americans in the Jazz Age. *Variety* magazine dubbed Chicago the "hottest café town" in the United States, but the Illinois Vigilance Association despaired that "in Chicago alone" it had "traced the fall of 1,000 girls to jazz music" in just two years.

massive amount of fuel it had to carry, Lindbergh fought bad weather and fatigue for 34 hours before landing to a hero's welcome in Paris. Named its first "Man of the Year" by *Time,* one of the new mass-circulation magazines, Lindbergh won adulation and awards from Americans who still valued the image of individualism.

The New Morality

The promotion of consumption and immediate gratification weakened traditional self-restraint and fed a desire for personal fulfillment. The failure of wartime sacrifices to achieve promised glories deepened Americans' growing disenchantment with traditional values. The social dislocations of the war years and growing urbanization accelerated moral and social change. Sexual pleasure became an increasingly open objective. Popularization of Sigmund Freud's ideas weakened prescriptions for sexual restraint; the growing availability of birth-control information enabled women to enjoy sex with less fear of pregnancy; and movie stars like Clara Bow, known as "the It Girl," and Rudolph Valentino, flaunted sexuality to mass audiences. Traditionalists worried as divorce rates, cigarette consumption, and hemlines went up while respect for parents, elders, and clergy went down. A sociological study of Muncie, Indiana—the nation's "Middletown"—found that "religious life as represented by the churches is less pervasive than a generation ago."

Young people seemed to embody the new morality. Rejecting conventional standards, they embraced the era's frenzied dances, bootleg liquor, smoking, more revealing clothing, and sexual experimentation. They welcomed the freedom

from parental control that the automobile afforded. The "flapper"—a frivolous young woman with short hair and a skimpy skirt who danced, smoked, and drank in oblivious self-absorption—was a major obsession in countless articles bearing such titles as "These Wild Young People" and "The Uprising of the Young." Few people were more alarmed than the president of the University of Florida. "The low-cut gowns, the rolled hose and short skirts are born of the Devil," he cried, "and are carrying the present and future generations to chaos and destruction." But feminists also condemned this symbol of changing standards. "It is sickening," Charlotte Perkins Gilman wrote in 1923, "to see so many of the newly freed abusing that freedom in mere imitation of masculine vice and weakness."

But the new morality was neither as new nor as widespread as its advocates and critics believed. Signs of change had appeared before the Great War in the popularity of new clothing fashions, social values, and public amusements among working-class and ethnic groups. And if it now became fashionable for the middle class to adopt such attitudes and practices, most Americans still adhered to traditional beliefs and values. Legislators in Utah and Virginia, for example, proposed laws requiring hemlines within 3 inches of the ankle and necklines within 3 inches of the throat. The city council in Oshkosh, Wisconsin, passed a law prohibiting partners from "looking into each other's eyes while dancing." Moreover, as Gilman's comment suggests, the new morality offered only a limited freedom. It certainly did not promote social equality for women, who remained subject to traditional double standards, with marriage and divorce laws, property rights, and employment opportunities biased against them.

The Searching Twenties

Many writers rejected what they considered the materialism, conformity, and provincialism of mass culture. Their criticism made the postwar decade one of the most creative periods in American literature. The brutality and hypocrisy of the war stimulated the critics' disillusionment and alienation. What Gertrude Stein called the Lost Generation considered, in the words of F. Scott Fitzgerald, "all Gods dead, all wars fought, all faiths in man shaken." Ernest Hemingway, wounded as a Red Cross volunteer during the war, rejected idealism in his novel *A Farewell to Arms* (1929), declaring that he no longer saw any meaning in "the words sacred, glorious, and sacrifice."

Novelists also turned their attention to American society. In *The Great Gatsby* (1925), Fitzgerald traced the self-deceptions

The International Journey of Jazz

A central part of American culture in the 1920s, jazz expanded its global reach in the decade known for mass production and mass consumerism. Just as Henry Ford sold his Model T cars abroad, jazz musicians took their distinctively American form of music south to Latin America and east to England, France, the Soviet Union, and China.

Jazz caught the imagination of the world. For many at home and abroad, the jarring spontaneity of jazz signaled a new age. It was, according to George Gershwin, the result of "energy stored up in America." For the composer John Alden Carpenter, it represented "the first art innovation originating in America to be accepted seriously in Europe." A German critic could not have agreed more, exclaiming, "Jazz is the expression of a Kultur epoch….Jazz is a musical revelation, a religion, a philosophy of the world, just like Expressionism and Impressionism."

Jazz also had its detractors—both in the United States and abroad. At home, one of the principal architects of mass production, Henry Ford, labeled jazz "musical slush" that encouraged the youth to imitate the "drivel of morons." A noted French poet called jazz "a triumph of barbaric folly," and an English observer worried that jazz—the "aboriginal music of the Negro"—might threaten American music.

Still, the enthusiasm for jazz was so strong that white jazz musicians claimed credit for its origins—at least until the 1930s, when the historical role of African Americans in creating jazz was more fully acknowledged in the United States and Europe. Black musicians had given Europe its first taste of jazz during World War I with James Reese Europe's 369th Division Band. Throughout the 1920s, other African American bands and performers traveled abroad, spreading the international message of jazz while escaping the racism of their home country. Sam Wooding's orchestra toured Europe and the Soviet Union; Herb Flemming's band, the Red Devils, and Benny Peyton's band along with remarkable performers like Josephine Baker dazzled audiences with dance and music in Buenos Aires, Paris, and London.

Jazz underscored to America and the world that an important part of the American heritage derived from an African—not European—heritage. But as the popularity of jazz grew internationally, the music no longer belonged exclusively to Americans, or even African Americans. Other countries appropriated the music and shaped it on their own terms. Still, the origins of jazz—this movement that captured the world's attention—belonged to black musicians who regarded jazz as a special expression of the African American community.

■ How did the influence of jazz affect America domestically and internationally?

---

of the wealthy. Sinclair Lewis ridiculed middle-class society and its narrow business culture in *Babbitt* (1922), whose title character provided a new word applied to the smug and shallow. In 1930, Lewis became the first American to win the Nobel Prize in literature.

Other writers condemned the mediocrity and intolerance of mass society. The critic Harold Stearns edited *Civilization in the United States* (1922), a book of essays. Its depiction of a repressive society sunk in hypocrisy, conformity, and materialism prompted his departure for Paris, where he lived, like Hemingway and Fitzgerald, as an expatriate, alienated from America. H. L. Mencken made his *American Mercury* the leading magazine of cultural dissenters. Conventional and conservative himself, Mencken heaped vitriol on the "puritans," "peasants," and "prehensile morons" he saw everywhere in American life.

When President Coolidge declined an invitation to exhibit American paintings in Paris by declaring that there were none, he seemed to confirm for the critics the boorishness of American society. But many of the critics were as self-absorbed as their targets. When the old progressive muckraker Upton Sinclair complained that he found nothing "constructive" in Mencken's voluminous writings, Mencken was delighted. "Uplift," he retorted, "has damn nigh ruined the country." Fitzgerald claimed to have "no interest in politics at all." Such attitudes dovetailed with the society they condemned.

Culture Wars

Despite the blossoming of mass culture and society in the 1920s, conflicts divided social groups. Some of these struggles involved reactions against the new currents in American life, including technological and scientific innovations, urban growth, and materialism. But movements to restrict immigration, enforce prohibition, prohibit the teaching of evolution, and even sustain the Ku Klux Klan did not have simple origins, motives, or consequences. The forces underlying the culture wars of the 1920s would surface repeatedly in the future (see Overview, Issues in the Culture Wars of the 1920s).

Nativism and Immigration Restriction

For years, many Americans, from racists to reformers, had campaigned to restrict immigration. In 1917, Congress required immigrants to pass a literacy test. But renewed immigration after the war revived the anti-immigration movement, and the propaganda of the war and the Red Scare years generated public support for more restriction. Depicting immigrants as radicals, racial inferiors, religious subversives, or criminals, nativists clamored for congressional action. The Emergency Quota Act of 1921 reduced immigration by about two-thirds and established quotas for nationalities on the basis of their numbers in the United States in 1910. Restrictionists, however, demanded more stringent action, especially against the largely Catholic and Jewish immigrants from southern and eastern Europe. Coolidge himself urged that America "be kept American," by which he meant white, Anglo-Saxon, and Protestant.

Congress adopted this racist rationale in the **National Origins Act of 1924,** which proclaimed its objective to be the maintenance of the "racial preponderance" of "the basic strain of our population." This law restricted immigration quotas to 2 percent of the foreign-born population of each nationality as recorded in the 1890 census, which was taken before the mass immigration from southern and eastern Europe. Another provision, effective in 1929, restricted total annual immigration to 150,000, with quotas that nearly eliminated southern and eastern Europeans. The law also completely excluded Japanese immigrants.

Other actions targeted Japanese residents in America. California, Oregon, Washington, Arizona, and other western states prohibited them from owning or leasing land, and in 1922, the Supreme Court ruled that, as nonwhites, they could never become naturalized citizens. A Japanese newspaper in Los Angeles criticized such actions as be-

To entertain families and friends, the KKK held "Klan Day at the Races," pictured here at Denver's Overland Park Race Track.

traying America's own ideals. Dispirited by the prejudice of the decade, Japanese residents hoped for fulfillment through their children, the **Nisei,** who were American citizens by birth.

Ironically, the Philippines, as a U.S. territory, was not subject to the National Origins Act, and Filipino immigration increased ninefold during the 1920s. Most Filipino newcomers became farm laborers, especially in California, or worked in Alaskan fisheries. Similarly, because the law did not apply to immigrants from the Western Hemisphere, Mexican immigration also grew. Nativists lobbied to exclude Mexicans, but agribusiness interests in the Southwest blocked any restrictions on low-cost migrant labor.

The Ku Klux Klan

Nativism was also reflected in the popularity of the revived Ku Klux Klan, the goal of which, according to its leader, was to protect "the interest of those whose forefathers established the nation." Founded in Georgia in 1915 and modeled on its Reconstruction predecessor, the new Klan was a national, not only a southern, movement and claimed several million members by the mid-1920s. Admitting only native-born white Protestants, the Klan embodied the fears of a traditional culture threatened by social change. Ironically, its rapid spread owed much to modern business and promotional techniques as hundreds of professional recruiters raked in hefty commissions selling Klan memberships to those hoping to defend their way of life.

OVERVIEW

Issues in the Culture Wars of the 1920s

Issue	Proponent view	Opponent view
The new morality	Promotes greater personal freedom and opportunities for fulfillment	Promotes moral collapse
Evolutionism	A scientific advance linked to notions of progress	A threat to religious belief
Jazz	Modern and vital	Unsettling, irregular, vulgar, and primitive
Immigration	A source of national strength from ethnic and racial diversity	A threat to the status and authority of old-stock white Protestants
Great Migration	A chance for African Americans to find new economic opportunities and gain autonomy and pride	A threat to traditional white privilege, control, and status
Prohibition	Promotes social and family stability and reduces crime	Restricts personal liberty and increases crime
Fundamentalism	An admirable adherence to traditional religious faith and biblical injunctions	A superstitious creed given to intolerant interference in social and political affairs
Ku Klux Klan	An organization promoting community responsibility, patriotism, and traditional social, moral, and religious values	A group of religious and racial bigots given to violent vigilantism and fostering moral and public corruption
Mass culture	Increases popular participation in national culture; provides entertainment	Promotes conformity, materialism, mediocrity, spectacle, and relaxation
Consumerism	Promotes material progress and higher living standards	Promotes waste, sterility, and self-indulgence

In part, the Klan was a fraternal order, providing entertainment, assistance, and community for its members. Its picnics, parades, charity drives, and other social and family-oriented activities—perhaps a half-million women joined the Women of the Ku Klux Klan—sharply distinguished the organization from both the small, secretive Klan of the nineteenth century and the still smaller, extremist Klan of the later twentieth century. Regarding themselves as reformers, Klan members supported immigration restriction and Prohibition.

But the Klan also exploited racial, ethnic, and religious prejudices and campaigned against many social groups and what it called "alien creeds." It attacked African Americans in the South, Mexicans in Texas, Japanese in California, and Catholics and Jews everywhere. A twisted religious impulse ran through much of the Klan's organization and activities. It hired itinerant Protestant ministers to spread its message, erected altars and flaming crosses at its meetings, and sang Klan lyrics to the tunes of well-known hymns. One Klan leader maintained that "the Klan stood for the same things as the Church, but we did the things the Church wouldn't do." This included publishing anti-Catholic newspapers, boycotting Catholic and Jewish businesses, and lobbying for laws against parochial schools and for compulsory Bible reading in the public schools. The Klan also resorted to violence. In

1921, for example, a Methodist minister who belonged to the Klan murdered a Catholic priest on his own doorstep, and other Klansmen burned down Catholic churches. The leader of the Oregon Klan insisted that "the only way to cure a Catholic is to kill him."

To the Klan, Catholics and Jews symbolized not merely subversive religions but also the ethnic diversity and swelling urban population that challenged traditional Protestant culture. To protect that culture, the Klan attempted to censor or disrupt "indecent" entertainment, assaulted those it accused of adultery, and terrorized doctors who performed abortions.

While the Klan's appeal seemed rooted in the declining countryside, it also attracted urban residents. Chicago had the largest Klan organization in the nation, with 50,000 members, and Houston, Dallas, Portland, Indianapolis, Denver, and the satellite communities ringing Los Angeles were also Klan strongholds. Urban Klansmen were largely lower or lower middle class, many recently arrived from the country and retaining its attitudes; others were long-term urban residents who feared being marginalized by social changes, especially by competition from immigrants and new ideas.

The Klan also ventured into politics, with some success. But eventually it encountered resistance. In the North, Catholic workers disrupted Klan parades. In the South, too, Klan excesses provoked a backlash. After the Klan in Dallas

Evangelist Aimee Semple McPherson delivering her "Foursquare Gospel" that offered all sinners salvation.

flogged 68 people in a "whipping meadow" along the Trinity River in 1922, respect turned to outrage. Newspapers demanded that the Klan disband, district attorneys began to prosecute Klan thugs, and in 1924 Klan candidates were defeated by a ticket headed by Miriam "Ma" Ferguson, whose gubernatorial campaign called for anti-Klan laws and for the loss of tax exemptions for churches used for Klan meetings. Elsewhere the Klan was stung by revelations of criminal behavior and corruption by Klan leaders, who had been making fortunes pocketing membership fees and selling regalia to followers. The Klan crusade to purify society had bred corruption and conflict everywhere. By 1930, the Klan had nearly collapsed.

Prohibition and Crime

Like the Klan, Prohibition both reflected and provoked social tensions in the 1920s. Reformers had long believed that prohibiting the sale of alcohol would improve social conditions, reduce crime and family instability, increase economic efficiency, and purify politics. They rejoiced in 1920 when the Eighteenth Amendment, prohibiting the manufacture, sale, or transportation of alcoholic beverages, took effect. Congress then passed the **Volstead Act,** which defined the forbidden liquors and established the Prohibition Bureau to enforce the law. But many social groups, especially in urban ethnic communities, opposed Prohibition, and the govern-

ment could not enforce the law where public opinion did not endorse it.

Evasion was easy. By permitting alcohol for medicinal, sacramental, and industrial purposes, the Volstead Act gave doctors, priests, and druggists a huge loophole through which to satisfy their friends' needs. Hearing that the use of sacramental wines had increased by 800,000 gallons under Prohibition, one Protestant leader complained that "not more than one-quarter of this is sacramental—the rest is sacrilegious." City-dwellers made "bathtub gin," and rural people distilled "moonshine." Scofflaws frequented the speakeasies that replaced saloons or bought liquor from bootleggers and rumrunners, who imported it from Canada, Cuba, or Mexico. The limited resources of the Prohibition Bureau often allowed bootleggers to operate openly. Dozens met publicly in a Seattle hotel in 1922 and adopted "fair prices" for liquor and a code of ethics "to keep liquor runners within the limits of approved business methods."

The ethics and business methods of bootleggers soon shocked Americans, however. The huge profits encouraged organized crime, which had previously concentrated on gambling and prostitution, to develop elaborate liquor-distribution networks. Operating outside the law, crime "families" used violence to enforce contracts, suppress competition, and attack rivals. In Chicago, Al Capone's army of nearly a thousand gangsters killed hundreds. Using the profits from bootlegging and new tools like the automobile and the submachine gun, organized crime corrupted city governments and police forces.

Gradually, even many "drys"—people who had initially favored Prohibition—dropped their support, horrified by the boost the amendment gave organized crime and worried about the general disrespect for law that it promoted. A 1926 poll found that four-fifths of Americans wanted to repeal or modify Prohibition. Yet it remained in force because it was entangled in party politics and social conflict. Many rural Protestant Americans saw Prohibition as a symbolic cultural issue. As the comedian Will Rogers said, "Mississippi will vote dry and drink wet as long as it can stagger to the polls." Prohibition represented the ability of rural Protestants to control the newcomers in the expanding cities. Democrats called for repeal in their 1928 and 1932 platforms, and in 1933, 36 states ratified an amendment repealing what Herbert Hoover had called a "noble experiment."

Old-Time Religion and the Scopes Trial

Religion provided another fulcrum for traditionalists attempting to stem cultural change. Protestant fundamentalism, which emphasized the infallibility of the Bible, including the creation story, emerged at the turn of the century as a conservative reaction to religious modernism and the social changes brought by the mass immigration of Catholics and Jews, the growing influence of science and technology, and the secularization of public education. But the fundamentalist crusade to reshape America became formidable only

American Views

Evangelism and the Search for Salvation

Aimee Semple McPherson defied traditional roles for women in becoming one of the most famous evangelical leaders in the United States. Traveling in her "Gospel Car," she crisscrossed the nation reminding her followers that "Jesus Is Coming Soon" and advising them to "Get Ready." In 1923, she opened the Angelus Temple in Los Angeles—a white-domed building large enough for 5,000 followers of what McPherson called the "Foursquare Gospel." A lighted rotating cross on top of the dome could be seen from fifty miles away—a beacon for those who journeyed to her center of "spiritual energy." A charismatic orator, McPherson embraced the theatrics of Hollywood to stir her crowds and raised vast sums of money, or "love gifts," to finance the Temple and its activities. Playing upon the phrase shareholder, McPherson sold doll-house chairs for $25 each, enabling purchasers to be "chair-holders" in the Temple. Though tainted by a mysterious disappearance in 1926, she remained extraordinarily popular, attracting crowds of thousands who sought salvation during times of change and uncertainty. McPherson died in 1944 from an accidental overdose of sleeping pills.

In this excerpt from one of her autobiographies, McPherson describes the growth of the Angelus Temple and her pioneering use of radio to advance her "success in soul winning."

- Why was Aimee Semple McPherson so popular in the 1920s?
- What does her success suggest about the role of religion in American life?
- How do you think evangelicals like McPherson might have viewed the cult of business that also characterized the decade?

From the days the doors opened on January 1, 1923, a mighty spiritual revival surged into Angelus Temple with ever-increasing power and fervor. Eight thousand converts knelt at the altars in the first six months and fifteen hundred believers were immersed in the baptistry. Hundreds were healed and baptized with the Holy Spirit. One thousand young people convenanted together to serve as the Angelus Temple Foursquare Crusaders. And as the weeks and months passed, new outreaches commenced.

In February, the Prayer Tower opened, where prayer has not ceased as men gather in two-hour shifts during the night and women pray during the day, bringing God thousands of requests which come by mail, telephone, and telegraph from all over the world.

Then came the challenge of the radio!…My soul was thrilled with the possibilities this media offered for the spread of gospel. We secured time on a radio station and began broadcasting a few services. But the thought persisted that if Angelus Temple had her own radio station we could broadcast almost all of the meetings!

And God provided through the love gifts of his people for the radio station. In February 1924, KFSG—Kall Four Square Gospel—went on the air, broadcasting the glorious song, "Give the winds a mighty voice, Jesus saves!"…Time and time again converted gamblers, dope addicts, bootleggers, and white-slavery victims rose from knees to send thrilling testimonies out over radio station KFSG as well as to the Temple audience.…For three years I stayed close by Angelus Temple, preaching and teaching many times a week, conducting a daily "Sunshine Hour" broadcast, writing, editing, publishing, and praying for the sick.…The revival swept on and out. Branch churches sprang up in cities and towns. [And the Foursquare gospel] message has become well known around the world.

Source: *Aimee Semple McPherson: The Story of My Life* (Waco, TX: Word Books, 1973).

in the 1920s. Evangelists like Billy Sunday and Aimee Semple McPherson attracted thousands to their revivals across America. Striking and dramatic, McPherson conducted massive faith-healing ceremonies as she promoted her "Foursquare Gospel." (See American Views, Evangelism and the Search for Salvation.)

Fundamentalist groups, colleges, and publications sprang up throughout the nation, especially in the South. The anti-Catholic sentiment exploited by the Klan was but one consequence of fundamentalism's insistence on strict biblical Christianity. A second was the assault on Darwin's theory of evolution, which contradicted literal interpretations of biblical Creation. The Southern Baptist Convention condemned "every theory, evolutionary or other, which teaches that man originated or came by way of lower animal ancestry." Fundamentalist legislators tried to prevent the teaching of evolution in public schools in at least 20 states. In 1923, Oklahoma banned textbooks based on Darwinian theory, and Florida's legislature denounced teaching evolution as "subversive." In 1925, Tennessee forbade teaching any idea contrary to the biblical account of human origins.

Social or political conservatism, however, was not an inherent part of old-time religion. The most prominent antievolution politician, William Jennings Bryan, continued to campaign for political, social, and economic reforms. Never endorsing the Klan, he served on the American Committee on the Rights of Religious Minorities and condemned anti-Semitism and anti-Catholicism. Bryan feared that Darwinism promoted political and economic conservatism. The survival of the fittest, he complained, elevated force and brutality, ignored spiritual values and democracy, and discouraged altruism and reform. How could a person fight for social justice "unless he believes in the triumph of right?"

The controversy over evolution came to a head when the American Civil Liberties Union (ACLU) responded to Tennessee's violation of the constitutional separation of church and state by offering to defend any teacher who tested the antievolution law. John Scopes, a high school biology teacher in Dayton, Tennessee, did so and was arrested. The Scopes trial attracted national attention after Bryan agreed to assist the prosecution and Clarence Darrow, a famous Chicago lawyer and prominent atheist, volunteered to defend Scopes.

Millions of Americans tuned their radios to hear the first trial ever broadcast. The judge, a fundamentalist, sat under a sign urging people to "Read Your Bible Daily." He ruled that scientists could not testify in support of evolution: Because they were not present at the Creation, their testimony would be "hearsay." But he did allow Darrow to put Bryan on the stand as an expert on the Bible. Bryan insisted on the literal truth of every story in the Bible, allowing Darrow to ridicule his ideas and force him to concede that some biblical passages had to be construed symbolically. Though the local jury took only eight minutes to convict Scopes, fundamentalists suffered public ridicule from reporters, including H. L. Mencken, who sneered at the "hillbillies" and "yokels" of Dayton.

But fundamentalism was hardly destroyed, and antievolutionists continued their campaign. New organizations, such as the Bryan Bible League, lobbied for state laws and an antievolution amendment to the Constitution. Three more states forbade teaching evolution, but by 1929 the movement had faltered. Even so, fundamentalism retained religious influence and would again challenge science and modernism in American life (see From Then to Now, The Culture Wars).

Through the historical figures of William Jennings Bryan and Clarence Darrow, the Scopes Trial symbolized the cultural battles of the twenties. And when Darrow (standing) interrogated Bryan on the accuracy of the Bible, the *New York Times* called the exchange the "most amazing courtroom scene in Anglo-American history."

A New Era in the World?

Abroad and at home, Americans in the 1920s sought peace and economic order. Rejection of the Treaty of Versailles and the League of Nations did not foreshadow isolationism. Indeed, in the 1920s, the United States became more deeply involved in international matters than ever before in peacetime. This involvement both produced important successes and sowed the seeds for serious future problems.

War Debts and Economic Expansion

The United States was the world's dominant economic power in the 1920s, changed by the Great War from a debtor to a creditor nation. The loans the United States had made to its allies during the war troubled the nation's relations with Europe throughout the decade. American insistence on repayment angered Europeans, who saw the money as a U.S. contribution to the joint war effort against Germany. Moreover, high American tariffs blocked Europeans from exporting goods to the United States and earning dollars to repay their debts. Eventually, the United States readjusted the terms for repayment, and American bankers extended large loans to Germany, which used the money to pay reparations to Britain and France, whose governments then used the same money to repay the United States. This unstable system depended on a continuous flow of money from the United States.

America's global economic role expanded in other ways as well. Exports, especially of manufactured goods, soared; by 1929, the United States was the world's largest exporter, responsible for one-sixth of all exports. American investment abroad more than doubled between 1919 and 1930. To expand their markets and avoid foreign tariffs, many U.S. companies became **multinational corporations,** establishing branches or subsidiaries abroad. Ford built assembly plants in England, Japan, Turkey, and Canada. International Telephone and Telegraph owned two dozen factories in Europe and employed more overseas workers than any other U.S. corporation.

Other companies gained control of foreign supply sources. American oil companies invested in foreign oil fields, especially in Latin America, where they controlled more than half of Venezuelan production. The United Fruit Company developed such huge operations in Central America that it often dominated national economies. In Costa Rica, the company had a larger budget than the national government.

Europeans and Latin Americans alike worried about this economic invasion; even Secretary of Commerce Herbert Hoover expressed concerns. Multinationals, he warned, might eventually take markets from American manufacturers and jobs from American workers. Business leaders, however, dismissed such reservations.

Hoover's concerns, moreover, did not prevent him from promoting economic expansion abroad. The government worked to open doors for American businesses in foreign countries, helping them to secure access to trade, investment opportunities, and raw materials. Hoover's Bureau of Foreign Commerce opened 50 offices around the world to boost American business. Hoover also pressed the British to give U.S. corporations access to rubber production in the British colony of Malaya. Secretary of State Charles Evans Hughes negotiated access to Iraqi oil fields for U.S. oil companies. The government also authorized bankers and manufacturers to form combinations, exempt from antitrust laws, to exploit foreign markets.

Rejecting War

Although government officials cooperated with business leaders to promote American strategic and economic interests, they had little desire to use force abroad. Popular reaction against the Great War, strengthened by a strong peace movement, constrained policymakers. Having repudiated collective security as embodied in the League of Nations, the United States nonetheless sought to minimize international conflict and promote its national security. In particular, the State Department sought to restrict the buildup of armaments among nations.

At the invitation of President Harding, delegations from nine nations met in Washington at the Washington Naval Conference in 1921 to discuss disarmament. The conference drafted a treaty to reduce battleship tonnage and suspend the building of new ships for a decade. The terms virtually froze the existing balance of naval power, with the first rank assigned to Britain and the United States, followed by Japan and then France and Italy. Japan and the United States also agreed not to fortify their possessions in the Pacific any further and to respect the Open Door in East Asia. Public opinion welcomed the treaty; the U.S. Senate ratified it with only one dissenting vote, and the 1924 Republican platform hailed it as "the greatest peace document ever drawn."

The United States made a more dramatic gesture in 1928, when it helped draft the **Kellogg-Briand Pact.** Signed by 64 nations, the treaty renounced aggression and outlawed war. Without provisions for enforcement, however, it was little more than symbolic. The Senate reserved the right of self-defense, repudiated any responsibility for enforcing the treaty, and maintained U.S. claims under the Monroe Doctrine. These limitations on the treaty, Senator Hiram Johnson noted, "have made its nothingness complete."

Managing the Hemisphere

Senate insistence on the authority of the Monroe Doctrine reflected the U.S. claim to a predominant role in Latin America. The United States continued to dominate the hemisphere to promote its own interests. It exerted its influence through investments, control of the Panama Canal, invocation of the Monroe Doctrine, and, when necessary, military intervention.

In response to American public opinion, the peace movement, and Latin American nationalism, the United States retreated from the extreme gunboat diplomacy of the Progressive Era, withdrawing troops from the Dominican Republic and Nicaragua. Secretary of State Hughes assured Latin Americans that "we covet no territory; we seek no conquest; the liberty we cherish for ourselves we desire for others; and we accept no rights for ourselves that we do not accord to others." But Haiti remained under U.S. occupation throughout the decade, American troops stayed in Cuba and Panama, and the United States directed the financial policies of other Latin American countries. Moreover, it sent the marines into Honduras in 1924 and back to Nicaragua in 1926. Such interventions could establish only temporary stability while provoking further Latin American hostility. "We are hated and despised," said one American businessman in Nicaragua. "This feeling has been created by employing American marines to hunt down and kill Nicaraguans in their own country."

Latin American resentment led to a resolution at the 1928 Inter-America Conference denying the right of any nation "to intervene in the internal affairs of another." The U.S. delegation rejected the measure, but the anger of Latin Americans prompted the Hoover administration to rescind support for the Roosevelt Corollary (see chapter 22), and J. Reuben Clark, chief legal officer of the State Department, drafted the Clark Memorandum. Not published until 1930, this document stated that the Roosevelt Corollary was not a legitimate extension of the Monroe Doctrine and thereby helped prepare the way for the so-called Good Neighbor Policy toward Latin America. Still, the United States did not pledge nonintervention and retained the means, both military and economic, to dominate the hemisphere.

Herbert Hoover and the Final Triumph of the New Era

As the national economy steamed ahead in 1928, the Republicans chose as their presidential candidate Herbert Hoover, a man who symbolized the policies of prosperity and the New Era. Hoover was not a politician—he had never been elected to office—but a successful administrator who championed rational and efficient economic development. A cooperative government, he believed, should promote business interests and encourage corporations to form trade associations to ensure stability and profitability. It should not regulate economic activities. Hoover's stiff managerial image was softened by his humanitarian record and his roots in rural Iowa.

The Democrats, by contrast, chose a candidate who evoked the cultural conflicts of the 1920s. Alfred E. Smith, a four-term governor of New York, was a Catholic, an opponent of Prohibition, and a Tammany politician tied to the immigrant constituency of New York City. He had failed to gain the presidential nomination in 1924, when the party split over prohibition and the Klan, but in 1928 he won the dubious honor of running against Hoover. His nomination plunged the nation into the cultural strife that had divided the Democrats in 1924. Rural fundamentalism, anti-Catholicism, Prohibition, and nativism were crucial factors in the campaign. The fundamentalist assault was unrelenting. Billy

Sunday attacked Smith and the Democrats as "the forces of hell," and a Baptist minister in Oklahoma City warned his congregation, "If you vote for Al Smith, you're voting against Christ and you'll all be damned."

But Hoover was, in certain ways, the more progressive candidate. Sympathetic to labor, sensitive to women's issues, hostile to racial segregation, and favorable to the League of Nations, Hoover had always distanced himself from what he called "the reactionary group in the Republican party." By contrast, despite supporting factory reform and state welfare legislation to benefit his urban working-class constituents, Smith was essentially conservative and as parochial as his most rural adversaries. He responded to a question about the needs of the states west of the Mississippi by asking, "What states *are* west of the Mississippi?"

Although many Americans voted against Smith because of his social background, the same characteristics attracted others. Millions of urban and ethnic voters, previously Republican or politically uninvolved, voted for Smith and laid the basis for the new Democratic coalition that would emerge in the 1930s. In 1928, however, with the nation still enjoying the economic prosperity so closely associated with Hoover and the Republicans, the Democrats were routed (see Map 24–2).

	Electoral Vote (%)	Popular Vote (%)
HERBERT HOOVER (Republican)	**444** **(82)**	**21,391,993** **(58)**
Alfred E. Smith (Democrat)	87 (17)	15,016,169 (41)
Norman Thomas (Socialist)	–	267,835 (1)
Other parties (Socialist Labor, Prohibition)	–	62,890 (–)

MAP 24–2 **The Election of 1928**
The cultural conflicts of the 1920s shaped the 1928 election. Al Smith carried the largest cities, but Herbert Hoover swept most of the rest of the nation, even attracting much of the usually Democratic South.

The Culture Wars

Cultural conflict raged through American society in the 1920s. Nativists demanded immigration restrictions; the Ku Klux Klan played on fears of racial, ethnic, and religious minorities; prohibitionists grappled with the minions of Demon Rum; and Protestant fundamentalists campaigned to prohibit the teaching of evolution in public schools.

Beginning in the 1960s, fueled as before by challenges to traditional values and beliefs—African American demands for civil rights, opposition to the Vietnam War, the women's rights movement and women's growing presence in the workplace, a new wave of immigration (dominated this time by Asians and Latin Americans), the gay rights movement—cultural conflict flared again and continues to burn.

Pro-choice and anti-abortion protesters square off at the pro choice "March for Women's Lives" in the Washington, D.C. Mall in April 2004.

The central battleground of today's culture wars, however, is women's rights, and especially abortion rights. Ever since the Supreme Court ruled in *Roe v. Wade* in 1973 that women had a right to an abortion, opponents have sought to curtail or abolish that right in the name of family values. Antiabortion protests became increasingly violent in the 1980s and 1990s. Although the Supreme Court has upheld *Roe v. Wade* and laws restraining demonstrations at abortion clinics, it has also upheld state laws imposing limits on abortion rights. In 2007, moreover, the Supreme Court reversed its earlier ruling by banning late-term abortions and specifically excluding a woman's health as a factor for consideration.

Gay rights is another battleground in the culture wars. Religious conservatives, again in the name of family values, have sought to counter efforts to extend civil rights protections to gays and lesbians. Same-sex marriage has produced a volatile struggle, igniting public debate and provoking protest and legal challenges.

According to one popular analysis, the antagonists in today's culture wars are, on one side, those who find authority in religious traditions, and, on the other, those who find authority in society and human reason. The war is not over and cultural conflict, motivated by deeply rooted convictions, is likely to remain a persistent undercurrent in American life.

■ What do these cultural conflicts reveal about American society?

PEARSON
myhistorylab

From Then to Now Online

Denouncing the Massachusetts ruling legalizing same-sex marriage, chanting protesters in California invoke "family values" to reaffirm their belief in heterosexual-only unions.

24-1 "White Sheets in Washington, D.C.," 1925. Photograph of 40,000 Ku Klux Klan members marching down Pennsylvania Avenue.

24-2 New York Times, "Great Crowd Hears Aimee McPherson," 1926. Mass congregation of 7,500 followers turn out to hear McPherson's "Four Square Gospel."

24-3 Los Angeles Times, "California Supreme Court Overturns Gay Marriage Ban," 2008. Article discussing the state court decision upholding the legality of same-sex marriage.

In his campaign, Hoover boasted that Republican policies could bring America to "the final triumph over poverty." But 1928 would be the Republicans' final triumph for a long time. The vaunted prosperity of the 1920s was ending, and the country faced a future dark with poverty.

Conclusion

The New Era of the 1920s changed America. Technological and managerial innovations produced giant leaps in productivity, new patterns of labor, a growing concentration of corporate power, and high corporate profits. Government policies, from protective tariffs and regressive taxation to the relaxation of regulatory laws, reflected and reinforced the triumphs of the business elite over traditional cautions and concerns.

The decade's economic developments, in turn, stimulated social change, drawing millions of Americans from the countryside to the cities, creating an urban nation, and fostering a new ethic of materialism, consumerism, and leisure and a new mass culture based on the automobile, radio, the movies, and advertising. This social transformation swept up many Americans but left others unsettled by the erosion of traditional practices and values. The concerns of traditionalists found expression in campaigns for prohibition and against immigration, the revival of the Ku Klux Klan, and the rise of religious fundamentalism. Intellectuals denounced the materialism and conformity they saw in the new social order and fashioned new artistic and literary trends.

But the impact of the decade's trends was uneven. Mechanization increased the productivity of some workers but cost others their jobs; people poured into the cities while others left for the suburbs; Prohibition, intended to stabilize society, instead produced conflict, crime, and corruption; government policies advanced some economic interests but injured others. Even the notion of a "mass" culture obscured the degree to which millions of Americans were left out of the New Era. With no disposable income and little access to electricity, rural Americans scarcely participated in the joys of consumerism; racial and ethnic minorities were often isolated in ghettos and barrios; and many workers faced declining opportunities. Most ominous was the uneven prosperity undergirding the New Era. Although living standards rose for many Americans and the rich expanded their share of the national wealth, more than 40 percent of the population earned less than $1,500 a year and fell below the established poverty level. The unequal distribution of wealth and income made the economy unstable and vulnerable to a disastrous collapse.

Review Questions

1. How did the automobile industry affect the nation's economy and society in the 1920s? In the excerpt from *The Flivver King,* how does Upton Sinclair illustrate the tension between workers and technology even as they both served Henry Ford's vision of mass production and mass consumerism?

2. What factors characterized the boom industries of the 1920s? The sick industries? How accurate is it to label the 1920s the decade of prosperity?

3. What were the underlying issues in the election of 1924? Of 1928? What role did politics play in the public life of the 1920s?

4. What were the chief points of conflict in the culture wars of the 1920s? What were the underlying issues in these clashes? Why were they so hard to compromise?

5. In what ways did the World War experience shape developments in the 1920s?

6. What were the chief features of American involvement in world affairs in the 1920s? To what extent did that involvement constitute a new role for the United States?

Key Terms

Great Migration (p. 675)

Harlem Renaissance (p. 675)

Jazz Age (p. 678)

Kellogg-Briand Pact (p. 686)

League of Women Voters (p. 673)

Multinational corporations (p. 686)

National Origins Act of 1924 (p. 681)

Nisei (p. 681)

Oligopoly (p. 669)

Open shop (p. 669)

Sheppard-Towner Maternity and Infancy Act (p. 673)

Volstead Act (p. 683)

Welfare capitalism (p. 669)

Yellow-dog contracts (p. 669)

Recommended Reading

Braeman, John, Robert Bremner, and David Brody, eds. *Change and Continuity in Twentieth Century America: The 1920s* (1968). Stimulating essays that cover important features of economic, social, and political history.

Dumenil, Lynn. *The Modern Temper: American Culture and Society in the 1920s* (1995). A complex account of cultural clashes and tensions during the 1920s.

Flink, James J. *The Car Culture* (1975). The fascinating history of the automobile and its social impact.

Hawley, Ellis W. *The Great War and the Search for a Modern Order* (1979). A valuable survey emphasizing economic and organizational changes.

Where to Learn More

- **F. Scott and Zelda Fitzgerald Museum, Montgomery, Alabama.** The novelist and his wife lived a short while in this house in her hometown. www.alabamatravel.org/central/szfm.html

- **Herbert Hoover National Historic Site, West Branch, Iowa.** Visitors may tour Hoover's birthplace cottage, presidential library, and museum. www.hoover.archives.gov

- **Henry Ford Museum and Greenfield Village, Dearborn, Michigan.** Among many fascinating exhibits, "The Automobile in American Life" superbly demonstrates the importance of the automobile in American social history. www.hfmgv.org

- **Warren G. Harding House, Marion, Ohio.** Harding's home from 1891 to 1921 is now a museum with period furnishings. www.ohiohistory.org/places/harding

- **Calvin Coolidge Homestead, Plymouth, Vermont.** Operated by the Vermont Division of Historic Sites, the homestead preserves the exact interiors and furnishings from when Coolidge took the presidential oath of office there in 1923. www.calvin-coolidge.org/pages/homestead and www.dhca.state.vt.us./HistoricSites/sites.htm

Study Resources

For study resources for this chapter, go to www.myhistorylab.com and choose *The American Journey*. You will find a wealth of study and review material for this chapter, including pre- and post-tests, customized study plan, key term review flash cards, interactive map and document activities, and documents for analysis.

Anguished faces tell a story of hard work and hard times. Farm families like the Barnetts of Woodward, Oklahoma, struggled throughout the Great Depression to survive on the land.

The Great Depression and the New Deal 1929–1939

25

My mother had two small babies on her hands. When I became sickly, Grandmother Josefa took me home with her, and I never returned to my parents....My grandmother's house was located on the "American" side of town, but there was nothing they could do about it because she was there before anybody else. My grandmother worked very hard; I grew up in the Depression.

When it was time for me to go to school I was assigned to [the] Mexican side of town. We were segregated; [the] Anglo children were sent to Roosevelt and the Mexican children who lived closer to Roosevelt [still] had to go down to Harding. I'll admit, there was a lot of discrimination in those years.

During the Depression my grandmother sewed piecework for the WPA. My dad helped out when he could [and] Uncle Ernesto also worked. He used to dig graves.

The Depression years were very, very hard. I remember seeing the people passing on their way to California.... It hurt me to see the people in their rickety old cars, their clothes in tatters, escaping from the drought and the dust bowls.

Oral Testimony,
Carlotta Silvas Martin

On April 27 [1933], according to the *New York Times*, Paul Schneider, aged forty-four, a sick and crippled Chicago school teacher, shot himself to death. His widow, left with three children, stated that he had not been paid for eight months.... Less than a month after Paul Schneider's discouragement drove him to suicide, the militant action of Chicago teachers—patient no more . . . resulted in the payment of $12,000,000 due them for the last months of 1932. Their pay for the five months of 1933 is still owed them. Five hundred of them are reported to be in asylums and sanitariums as a result of the strain. . . .

These are the conditions facing teachers fortunate enough to be employed. What of the unemployed? . . . "We are always hungry," wrote [one unemployed teacher]. "We owe six months' rent. . . . We live every hour in fear of eviction. . . . My sister, a typist, and I . . . have been out of work for two years. . . . We feel discouraged . . . and embittered. We are drifting, with no help from anyone."

Eunice Langdon,

The Nation, August 16, 1933

I am sitting in the city free employment bureau. It's the women's section. We have been sitting here now for hours. We sit here every day, waiting for a job. There are no jobs. . . .

. . . [W]e don't talk much. . . . There is a kind of humiliation. . . . We look away from each other. We look at the floor.

Meridel LeSueur, "Women

on the Breadlines," 1932

Dear Mrs. Roosevelt,

I am now 15 years old and in the 10th grade. I have always been smart but I never had a chance as all of us is so poor. I hope to complete my education, but I will have to quit school I guess if there is

no clothes can be bought. (Don't think that we are on the relief.) Mother has been a faithful servant for us to keep us together. I don't see how she has made it.

Mrs. Roosevelt, don't think I am just begging, but that is all you can call it I guess. . . . Do you have any old clothes you have throwed back. You don't realize how honored I would feel to be wearing your clothes.

Your friend,

M.I.

Star Route One

Albertville, Ala.

January 1, 1936

"Carlotta Silvas Martin: A Mexican American Childhood during the Depression" and "Meridel LeSueur: The Despair of Unemployed Women," both from Susan Ware, *Modern American Women: A Documentary History* (New York: McGraw-Hill Higher Education, 2002), pp. 162–165, 145–146; Eunice Langdon, "The Teacher Faces the Depression," *Nation* 137 (August 16, 1933): 182–187; Letter to Eleanor Roosevelt, January 1, 1936, www.newdeal.feri.org/eleanor/mi0136.htm

myhistorylab

Personal Journeys Online

- **Letter from Eleanor Roosevelt to Walter White, 1936.** Roosevelt writes against lynching.

- **Paul Taylor, "Again the Covered Wagon,"** *Survey Graphic,* **July 1935.** Article on the migration of "Okies" to California during the Dust Bowl

Carlotta Silvas Martin, Eunice Langdon, and Meridel LeSueur convey some of the trauma of the Great Depression, but no one voice can capture its devastating effect on Americans. The U.S. economy utterly collapsed, leaving millions of people jobless, homeless, or in continual fear of foreclosure, eviction, even starvation. The decade of hard times constituted a journey into desperation and despair. Men, women, children everywhere saw their families and dreams shattered and felt the sting of humiliation as they stood in bread lines or begged for clothes or food scraps. The winter of 1932–1933 was particularly cruel: Unemployment soared and stories of malnutrition and outright starvation made headlines in newspapers throughout the nation. Hunger was so widespread in Kentucky and West Virginia that one relief committee limited its handouts to those who were at least 10 percent below the normal weight for their height. The school teacher who committed suicide lived in the city of Chicago, where, that winter, half the people were without jobs, one-half of the city's property tax bills were left unpaid, and, most striking, one newspaper declared "Starvation Hits 14,000."

Natural disaster accompanied economic crisis in the drought-stricken states of the Great Plains, forcing families to leave their farms. They packed up their meager belongings and took to the road to escape the darkened skies of the "Dust Bowl" in search of anything better. John Steinbeck's novel *The Grapes of Wrath* powerfully portrayed the westward movement of these homeless migrants. The poignant image of "the path of people in flight," as Steinbeck himself called it, also stayed with Carlotta Silvas, who as a young girl saw hungry and half-clothed families pass through her hometown of Superior, Arizona.

The election of Franklin D. Roosevelt, however, lifted spirits and hopes of jobless Americans throughout the nation. They enthusiastically responded to his **New Deal,** taking jobs, as did Carlotta's grandmother, with such programs as the Works Progress Administration (WPA). In unprecedented numbers, they also wrote to both FDR and Eleanor Roosevelt, asking for advice and for assistance for everything from a month's rent money to tide them over to old clothes to wear to school, as did the 15-year-old girl from Alabama. And they also wrote to thank the president and first lady for their compassionate support and leadership. Throughout all such letters ran a common theme: the belief among poor and unemployed Americans that for the first time there were people in the White House who were interested in their welfare, who wanted to eliminate their hardships, and who would listen to their ideas.

The decade of hard times affected people differently. The collapse hit hardest those industries dominated by male workers, leaving mothers and wives with new roles as the family breadwinners, sometimes straining family relationships and men's sense of purpose and respect. Some families drifted apart, while others coped simply by making do. As Carlotta Silvas noted, her "dad helped out when he could." But the pressure for women to take on new economic responsibilities—especially married women—did not escape the wrath of the public. They were roundly condemned as "thieving parasites" and placed in the impossible position of both being forced to work and told they should not hold jobs.

Race and ethnicity further complicated the problems of joblessness and relief. Southern states routinely denied African Americans relief assistance, as did southwestern states for Hispanic Americans. The New Deal failed to overcome most of the traditional attitudes and practices that targeted women and minorities and reinforced local prejudice and segregation. For Carlotta Silvas, that meant walking farther to school—a daily journey that she remembered throughout her life.

Hard times, then, both united and divided the American people. Franklin and Eleanor Roosevelt and the programs of the New Deal brought fresh hope and connected

CHRONOLOGY

1929	Stock market crashes.
1931	Japan invades Manchuria.
1932	Farmers' Holiday Association organizes rural protests in the Midwest.
	Reconstruction Finance Corporation is created to assist financial institutions.
	Bonus Army is routed in Washington, DC.
	Franklin D. Roosevelt is elected president.
1933	Adolf Hitler comes to power in Germany.
	Emergency Banking Act is passed.
	The United States recognizes the Soviet Union.
	Agricultural Adjustment Administration (AAA) is created to regulate farm production.
	National Recovery Administration (NRA) is created to promote industrial cooperation and recovery.
	Federal Emergency Relief Act provides federal assistance to the unemployed.
	Civilian Conservation Corps (CCC) is established to provide work relief in conservation projects.
	Public Works Administration (PWA) is created to provide work relief on large public construction projects.
	Civil Works Administration (CWA) provides emergency winter relief jobs.
	Tennessee Valley Authority (TVA) is created to coordinate regional development.
1934	Securities and Exchange Commission (SEC) is established.
	Indian Reorganization Act reforms Indian policy.
	Huey Long organizes the Share-Our-Wealth Society.
	Democrats win midterm elections.
1935	Supreme Court declares NRA unconstitutional.
	Italy attacks Ethiopia.
	National Labor Relations Act (Wagner Act) guarantees workers' rights to organize and bargain collectively.
	Social Security Act establishes a federal social insurance system.

	Banking Act strengthens the Federal Reserve.
	Revenue Act establishes a more progressive tax system.
	Resettlement Administration is created to aid dispossessed farmers.
	Rural Electrification Administration (REA) is created to help provide electric power to rural areas.
	Soil Conservation Service is established.
	Emergency Relief Appropriation Act authorizes public relief projects for the unemployed.
	Works Progress Administration (WPA) is created.
	Huey Long is assassinated.
1936	Supreme Court declares AAA unconstitutional.
	Roosevelt is reelected president.
	Hitler remilitarizes the Rhineland.
	Roosevelt sails to South America as part of Good Neighbor Policy.
	Sit-down strikes begin.
1937	Chicago police kill workers in Memorial Day Massacre.
	FDR tries but fails to expand the Supreme Court.
	Farm Security Administration (FSA) is created to lend money to small farmers to buy and rehabilitate farms.
	National Housing Act is passed to promote public housing projects.
	"Roosevelt Recession" begins.
1938	Congress of Industrial Organizations (CIO) is founded.
	Germany annexes Austria.
	Fair Labor Standards Act establishes minimum wage and maximum hours rules for labor.
	Roosevelt fails to "purge" the Democratic Party.
	Republicans make gains in midterm elections.
	Munich agreement reached, appeasing Hitler's demand for Sudetenland.
	Kristallnacht, violent pogrom against Jews, occurs in Germany.

Americans to the White House as never before. And although the federal activism of the 1930s achieved neither full recovery nor systematic reform, it restored confidence to many Americans and permanently transformed the nation's responsibility for the welfare of its citizens. By the end of the decade, President Roosevelt was proud of these changes and also frustrated by the persistence of hard times. But he was no longer worried that the economy—indeed the whole of society—teetered on the edge of catastrophe; his gaze now fixed abroad, where even more ominous developments, he believed, threatened the nation's future and security.

Hard Times in Hooverville

The prosperity of the 1920s ended in a stock-market crash that revealed the flaws honeycombing the economy. As the nation slid into a catastrophic depression, factories closed, employment and incomes tumbled, and millions lost their homes, hopes, and dignity. Some protested and took direct action; others looked to the government for relief.

Crash!

The buoyant prosperity of the New Era, more apparent than real by the summer of 1929, collapsed in October, when the stock market crashed. During the preceding two years, the market had hit record highs, stimulated by optimism, easy credit, and speculators' manipulations. Its extraordinary growth captured international attention: the *London Daily Mail* reported that "Wall Street has become another world power, with more authority than the League of Nations." But after peaking in September, it suffered several sharp checks, and on October 29, "Black Tuesday," panicked investors dumped their stocks, wiping out the previous year's gains in one day. Confidence in the economy disappeared, and the slide continued for months, and then years. The market hit bottom in July 1932. By then, the stock of U.S. Steel had plunged from $262 to $22, Montgomery Ward from $138 to $4. Much of the paper wealth of America had evaporated, and the nation sank into the **Great Depression**.

The Wall Street crash marked the beginning of the depression, but it did not cause it. The depression stemmed from weaknesses in the New Era economy. Most damaging was the unequal distribution of wealth and income. Workers' wages and farmers' incomes had fallen far behind industrial productivity and corporate profits; by 1929, the richest 0.1 percent of American families had as much total income as the bottom 42 percent (see Figure 25–1). With more than half the nation's people living at or below the subsistence level, there was not enough purchasing power to maintain the economy.

A second factor was that oligopolies dominated American industries. By 1929, the 200 largest corporations (out of 400,000) controlled half the corporate wealth. Their power led to "administered prices," prices kept artificially high and rigid rather than determined by supply and demand. Because it did not respond to purchasing power, this system not only helped bring on economic collapse but also dimmed prospects for recovery.

Weaknesses in specific industries had further unbalanced the economy. Agriculture suffered from overproduction, declining prices, and heavy debt; so did the coal and textile industries. Increased mechanization in key industries had resulted in significant unemployment even during the 1920s; a 1932 report authorized by President Hoover found that jobless rates had exceeded 10 percent in mass production industries for the period 1923–1928. These difficulties left the economy dependent on a few industries for expansion and

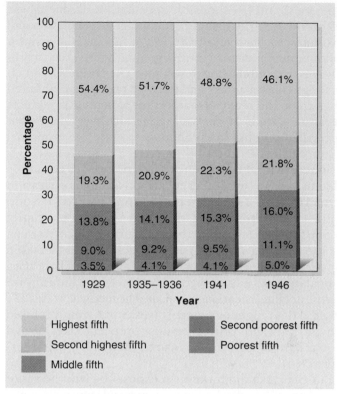

FIGURE 25–1   Distribution of Income in the United States, 1929–1946

An unequal distribution of income contributed to the Great Depression by limiting purchasing power. Only slight changes occurred until after World War II, but other factors gradually stabilized the national economy.

Data Source: U.S. Bureau of the Census.

employment, and these industries could not carry the burden. Banking presented other problems. Poorly managed and regulated, banks had contributed to the instability of prosperity; they now threatened to spread the panic and depression.

International economic difficulties spurred the depression as well. Shut out from U.S. markets by high tariffs, Europeans had depended on American investments to manage their debts and reparation payments from the Great War. The stock market crash dried up the flow of American dollars to Europe, causing financial panics and industrial collapse and making the Great Depression global. In turn, European nations curtailed their imports of American goods and defaulted on their debts, further debilitating the U.S. economy. American exports fell by 70 percent from 1929 to 1932. As foreign markets shrank, so did hopes for economic recovery. (See Global Perspectives, The Worldwide Collapse.)

Government policies also bore some responsibility for the crash and depression. Failure to enforce antitrust laws had encouraged oligopolies and high prices; failure to regulate banking and the stock market had permitted financial recklessness and irresponsible speculation. Reducing tax rates on the wealthy had also encouraged speculation and contributed to the maldistribution of income. Opposition to labor unions and collective bargaining helped keep workers' wages and purchasing power low. The absence of an effective agricultural policy and the high tariffs that inhibited foreign trade and reduced markets for agricultural products hurt farmers. In short, the same governmental policies that shaped the booming 1920s economy also led to economic disaster.

State and local fiscal policies also pointed to economic problems for the 1930s. The expansion of public education and road construction led to higher property taxes in communities throughout the nation, and although per capita tax collection at the federal level actually declined between 1920 and 1929, the tax burden in states and cities increased dramatically. Indeed, state and local taxes rose faster than personal incomes in the 1920s. The real estate industry reported a decline as early as 1926, and homeowners steadily protested their higher property taxes. Some simply refused to pay; in Chicago, protest against property taxes turned into a strike that lasted from 1930 to 1933, nearly bankrupting the city.

But the crash did more than expose the weaknesses of the economy. Business lost confidence and refused to make investments that might have brought recovery. Instead, banks called in loans and restricted credit, and depositors tried to withdraw their savings, which were uninsured. The demand for cash caused banks to fail, dragging the economy down further. And the Federal Reserve Board prolonged the depression by restricting the money supply.

The depression particularly battered farmers. Commodity prices fell by 55 percent between 1929 and 1932, stifling farm income. Cotton farmers earned only 31 percent of the pittance they had received in 1929. Unable to pay their mortgages, many farm families lost their homes and fields. "We have no security left," cried one South Dakota farm woman. "Foreclosures and evictions at the point of sheriff's guns are increasing daily." The dispossessed roamed the byways, highways, and railways of a troubled country.

Urban families were also evicted when they could not pay their rent. Some moved in with relatives; others lived in **Hoovervilles**—the name reflects the bitterness directed at the President—shacks where people shivered, suffered, and starved. Oklahoma City's vast Hooverville covered 100 square miles; one witness described its hapless residents as squatting in "old, rusted-out car bodies," orange crates, and holes in the ground.

Soup kitchens became standard features of the urban landscape, with lines of the hungry stretching for blocks. But charities and local communities could not meet the massive needs, and neither the states nor the federal government had welfare or unemployment compensation programs. To survive, people planted gardens in vacant lots and back alleys and tore apart empty houses or tapped gas lines for fuel. In immigrant neighborhoods, social workers found a "primitive communism" in which people shared food, clothing, and fuel in the belief that "what goes around comes around." Few Americans escaped hard times, but their experiences varied with their circumstances and expectations.

The Depression Spreads

By early 1930, the effects of financial contraction were painfully evident. Factories shut down or cut back, and industrial production plummeted; by 1932, it was scarcely 50 percent of its 1929 level. Steel mills operated at 12 percent of capacity, auto factories at 20 percent. Unemployment skyrocketed, as an average of 100,000 workers a week were fired in the first three years after the crash. By 1932, one-fourth of the labor force was out of work (see Figure 25–2), and the wages of those Americans lucky enough to work fell sharply. Personal income dropped by more than half between 1929 and 1932. Moreover, the depression began to feed on itself in a vicious circle: Shrinking wages and employment cut into purchasing power, causing business to slash production again and lay off workers, thereby further reducing purchasing power.

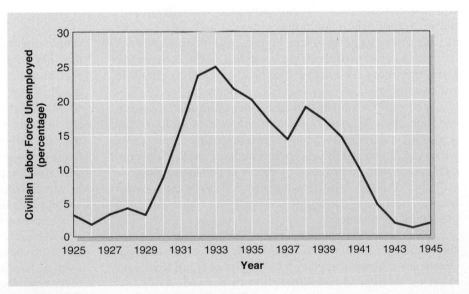

FIGURE 25–2   Unemployment, 1925–1945

Unemployment soared in the early 1930s, spreading distress and overwhelming charities and local relief agencies. Federal programs improved conditions, but only America's entry into World War II really ended the problem.

Data Source: U.S. Bureau of the Census

Homeless Americans gathered in squalid Hoovervilles like this one in Seattle and struggled to survive.

"Women's Jobs" and "Men's Jobs"

The depression affected wage-earning women in complex ways. Although they suffered 20 percent unemployment by 1932, women were less likely than men to be fired. Gender segregation had concentrated women in low-paid service, sales, and clerical jobs that were less vulnerable than the heavy industries where men predominated. But while traditional attitudes somewhat insulated working women, they also reinforced opposition to female employment, especially that of married women. As one Chicago civic organization complained, "They are holding jobs that rightfully belong to the God-intended providers of the household." Nearly every state considered restricting the employment of married women, and the city council of Akron, Ohio, resolved that public agencies and private employers should stop employing wives. Three-fourths of the nation's school systems refused to hire married women as teachers, and two-thirds dismissed female teachers who married. Many private employers, especially banks and insurance companies, also fired married women.

Firing women, however, rarely produced jobs for men, because few men sought positions in fields dominated by women. Men did displace women as teachers, social workers, and librarians, but firing women simply aggravated the suffering of families. Disapproval of female employment implied that women did not deserve equal opportunities and probably stiffened the opposition to opening "men's jobs" to women when women were desperate for work. Despite such hostility, the proportion of married women in the workforce increased in the 1930s as women took jobs to help their families survive, and about one-third of working married women provided the sole support for their families.

Families in the Depression

"I have watched fear grip the people in our neighborhood around Hull House," wrote Jane Addams as the depression deepened in 1931 and family survival itself seemed threatened. Divorce declined because it was expensive, but desertion increased, and people postponed marriage. Birthrates fell. Husbands and fathers, the traditional breadwinners, were often humiliated and despondent when laid off from work. A social worker observed in 1931, "Like searing irons, the degradation, the sheer terror and panic which loss of job brings, the deprivation and the bitterness have eaten into men's souls." A college professor wrote of the suicide of his brother who had been "utterly disheartened by his prolonged search for employment [and] went into a shabby hotel [where he] blew his brains out." He then added, "After nearly thirty years of toil as a college professor, I myself had great difficulty in raising the money to pay for the modest kind of burial befitting the gentleman my brother was. I could not go to his funeral; I could not pay for both the burial expenses and the railway fare." Unemployed men, sociologists reported, "lost much of their sense of time and dawdled helplessly and dully about the streets," dreading to return home. An unemployed Philadelphia man, according to his wife, was "always walking or looking [for work]. The places are so far apart that his feet get sore.... We had to put cotton in the heels of his shoes. Sometimes he don't know where he's walking."

Women's responsibilities, by contrast, often grew. The number of female-headed households increased sharply. Not only did some women become wage earners, but their traditional role as homemakers also gained new significance. To make ends meet, many women sewed their own clothing and raised and canned vegetables, reversing the trend toward consumerism. Some also took on extra work at home. In San Antonio, one in every ten families had boarders, and in Alabama, housewives took in laundry at 10 cents for a week's washload.

The depression also affected children. Some parents sacrificed their own well-being to protect their children. One witness described "the uncontrolled trembling of parents who have starved themselves for weeks so that their children might not go hungry." But children felt the tension and fear, and many went without food. In New York City, 139

The Worldwide Collapse

The Wall Street crash did not immediately provoke widespread alarm at home or abroad. One French observer commented that an "abscess" had been "lanced." British commentators dismissed it as an isolated event and predicted continuing prosperity. President Hoover remained confident well into 1930, even telling a group of religious leaders requesting relief for the unemployed, "You have come sixty days too late. The depression is over."

Still, the stock market collapse did have consequences: It made European borrowing more difficult, especially hurting Germany's failing economy. Without loans from the United States, Germany defaulted on its war debts and faced near bankruptcy. Moreover, the United States accounted for 40 percent of the world's manufactured goods—twice the figure for Germany and England combined in 1929. When the United States slid into depression, the global repercussions were staggering.

The international crisis required global cooperation, but the world's nations responded with various forms of economic nationalism. The United States rejected its role as the lender of the last resort for destitute countries and constructed trade barriers by passing the Smoot-Hawley tariff in 1930. Within months Canada, Mexico, France, Spain, and New Zealand raised their tariffs against American goods. World trade came to a standstill; its volume plummeted by two-thirds between 1929 and 1933.

As the depression deepened, world leaders pointed to external causes and turned to conventional solutions. In the United States, Herbert Hoover claimed that "the hurricane that swept our shores was of European origin" and affirmed the need to balance the budget in hard times. French leaders blamed British monetary policies and blasted the United States for "exporting unemployment" through "mechanization" that replaced workers with machines. The French also regarded a balanced budget as inviolable. In Britain, however, the socialist prime minister, Ramsay MacDonald, faulted capitalism for the collapse, adding "we are not on trial, it is the system under which we live." Britain provided unemployment insurance and public relief. But even MacDonald refused to unbalance the budget to meet the needs of all the jobless. The Japanese finance minister also objected to increased spending for the unemployed.

By 1932, the international crisis had worsened, and the United States and Germany had unemployment rates of 25 and 40 percent, respectively. The German banking system had collapsed in 1931, and the depression helped facilitate the political success of the Nazi Party in 1932. Jobless Germans looted stores and coal yards for food and fuel. As in the United States, working women were targeted as a cause of the depression. One German newspaper declared that "Germany will perish if the women are working and the men are unemployed."

The shockingly high rates of unemployment throughout the world created unprecedented conditions of poverty and despair. And although Americans did not leap from windows during the collapse of the stock market, suicide rates went up in both Germany and the United States during the 1930s. Cases of malnutrition were found in New York, Budapest, and Vienna, among other cities, and relief agencies everywhere were overwhelmed by the needs of the jobless. People lost jobs and homes, creating Hoovervilles in the United States, *bidonvilles* ("tin cities") in France, and the Hungry Mile in Australia. The Great Depression had indeed become global, and, without international cooperation, the unemployed looked to their governments for solutions and support.

■ Why did the U.S. depression become a global crisis and how did world leaders respond?

people, most of them children, died of starvation and malnutrition in 1933. Boys and girls stayed home from school and church because they lacked shoes or clothing; others gave up their plans for college. As hope faded, family conflicts increased. Some parents nagged their children, even considering them burdens. Many teenagers left home, either to escape parental authority or so that younger children would have more to eat. These "juvenile transients" suffered from starvation, exposure, illness, and accidents. The California Unemployment Commission concluded that the depression had left the American family "morally shattered. There is no security, no foothold, no future."

"Last Hired, First Fired"

The depression particularly harmed racial minorities. With fewer resources and opportunities, they were less able than other groups to absorb the economic pain. African Americans were caught in a double bind, reported a sociologist at Howard University in 1932: They were "the last to be hired and the first to be fired." Black unemployment rates were more than twice the white rate, reflecting increased job competition and persistent racism. Jobless white workers now sought the menial jobs traditionally reserved for black workers, such as street cleaning and domestic service. In Atlanta, white citizens paraded with banners denouncing the hiring of black workers "Until Every White Man Has a Job."

Racism also limited the assistance African Americans received. Religious and charitable organizations often refused to care for black people. Local and state governments set higher relief eligibility requirements for blacks than for whites and provided them with less aid. One Memphis resident saw the result of such policies: "Colored men and women with rakes, hoes, and other digging tools, with buckets and baskets, digging around in the garbage and refuse for food." In 1931, African American women in Harlem joined together as the Harlem Housewives League to challenge New York City's race-based unequal distribution of relief. Out of work for longer periods of time and without even modest relief assistance, African Americans were forced to crowd together in already cramped apartments, while still paying exorbitant rents to white landlords. An African American social worker described the despair and poverty of Harlem's residents: "Packed in damp, rat-ridden dungeons, they existed in squalor not too different from that of Arkansas sharecroppers." By 1932, most African Americans were suffering acute privation. "At no time in the history of the Negro since slavery," reported the Urban League, "has his economic and social outlook seemed so discouraging."

Hispanic Americans also suffered. As mostly unskilled workers, they faced increasing competition for decreasing jobs paying declining wages. They were displaced even in the California agricultural labor force, which they had dominated. By the mid-1930s, they made up only a tenth of the state's migratory labor force, which increasingly consisted of white people who had fled the South and the Great Plains. Other jobs were lost when Arizona, California, and Texas barred Mexicans from public works and highway construction jobs. Vigilantes threatened employers who hired Mexicans rather than white Americans.

Economic woes and racism drove nearly half a million Mexican immigrants and their American-born children from the United States. Local authorities in the Southwest, with the blessing of the Department of Labor, urged all Mexicans, regardless of their citizenship status, to return to Mexico and free up jobs and relief assistance for white Americans. To intimidate Mexican residents, the U.S. Immigration Service

The Great Depression made more desperate the plight of Mexican Americans; they faced discrimination and feared deportation. As migrant laborers, they also struggled with the forces of nature as they traveled from field to field in search of work. This Mexican migrant worker holds his new baby with his wife standing at the door's edge. They live in this shack on the edge of a frozen pea field in California.

conducted several raids, rounding up people and demanding immediate proof of citizenship. In 1931, a Los Angeles official announced that tens of thousands of Mexicans "have been literally scared out of southern California." By 1933, Los Angeles County had sent 15 trains filled with 12,000 Mexicans who had been receiving relief back to Mexico. Fear of deportation kept many Mexican American families from seeking relief or even healthcare in Texas.

Protest

Bewildered and discouraged, most Americans reacted to the crisis without protest. Influenced by traditional individualism, many blamed themselves for their plight. But others did act, especially to protect their families. Protests ranged from small desperate gestures like stealing food and coal to more dramatic deeds. In Louisiana, women seized a train to call attention to the needs of their families; in New Jersey, in the "bloodless battle of Pleasantville," 100 women held the city council hostage to demand assistance.

Communists, socialists, and other radicals organized more formal protests. Communists led the jobless into "unemployment councils" that staged hunger marches, demonstrated for relief, and blocked evictions. Mothers facing eviction in Chicago told their children: "Run quick and find the Reds." Socialists built similar organizations, including the People's Unemployment League in Baltimore, which had 12,000 members. Groups of this kind provided protection and assistance. However, local officials often suppressed their protests. In 1932, police fired on the Detroit Unemployment Council as it marched to demand food and jobs, killing four marchers and wounding many more.

Rural protests also broke out. Again, communists organized some of them, as in Alabama, where the Croppers' and Farm Workers' Union mobilized black agricultural laborers in 1931 to demand better treatment. In the Midwest, the Farmers' Holiday Association, organized among family farmers in 1932, stopped the shipment of produce to urban markets, hoping to drive up prices. A guerrilla war broke out as farmers blocked roads and halted freight trains, dumped milk in ditches, and fought bloody battles with deputy sheriffs. Midwestern farmers also tried to prevent foreclosure of their farms. In Iowa, farmers beat sheriffs and mortgage agents and nearly lynched a judge conducting foreclosure proceedings; in Nebraska, a Farmers' Holiday leader warned that if the state did not halt foreclosures, "200,000 of us are coming to Lincoln and we'll tear that new State Capitol Building to pieces."

Herbert Hoover and the Depression

The Great Depression challenged the optimism, policies, and philosophy that Herbert Hoover had carried into the White House in 1929. The president took unprecedented steps to resolve the crisis but shrank back from the interventionist policies activists urged. His failures, personal as well as political and economic, led to his repudiation and to a major shift in government policies.

The Failure of Voluntarism

Hoover fought economic depression more vigorously than any previous president, but he believed that voluntary private relief was preferable to federal intervention. The role of the national government, he thought, was to advise and encourage the voluntary efforts of private organizations, individual industries, or local communities. As secretary of commerce, Hoover had championed trade associations as organizations to achieve economic order and social progress.

Hands in their pockets, hungry men stand numbly in one of New York City's 82 breadlines. Said one observer: "The wretched men, many without overcoats or decent shoes, usually began to line up soon after six o'clock, in good weather or bad, rain or snow."

As president, he persuaded Congress in 1929 to create the Federal Farm Board to promote voluntary agricultural co-operatives to raise farm income without government regulations. After the crash, he tried to apply this voluntarism to the depression.

Hoover obtained pledges from business leaders to maintain employment and wage levels. But most corporations soon repudiated these pledges, slashed wages, and laid off workers. An official of the Bureau of Labor Statistics complained that business leaders "are hell-bent to get wages back to the 1913 level." Hoover himself said, "You know, the only trouble with capitalism is capitalists; they're too damn greedy." Still, he rejected government action.

Hoover also depended on voluntary efforts to relieve the misery caused by massive unemployment. He created the President's Organization for Unemployment Relief to help raise private funds for voluntary relief agencies. Charities and local authorities, he believed, should help the unemployed; direct federal relief would expand government power and undermine the recipients' character. He vetoed congressional attempts to aid the unemployed.

The depression rendered Hoover's beliefs meaningless. Private programs to aid the unemployed scarcely existed. Only a few unions, such as the Amalgamated Clothing Workers, had unemployment funds, and these were soon spent. Company plans for unemployment compensation covered less than 1 percent of workers, revealing the charade of the welfare capitalism of the 1920s. Some business leaders rejected any responsibility. "Even God Almighty never promised anybody that he should not suffer from hunger," snorted the president of the Southern States Industrial Council. Private charitable groups like the Salvation Army, church associations, and ethnic societies quickly exhausted their resources. By 1931, the director of Philadelphia's Federation of Jewish Charities conceded, "Private philanthropy is no longer capable of coping with the situation." Tens of thousands of Philadelphians, he noted, had been reduced to "the status of a stray cat prowling for food.... What this does to the innate dignity of the human soul is not hard to guess."

Nor could local governments cope, and their efforts declined as the depression deepened. New York City provided relief payments of $2.39 a week for an entire family, and other cities much less. By 1932, more than 100 cities made no relief appropriations at all, and the commissioner of charity in Salt Lake City reported that people were sliding toward starvation. Only eight state governments provided even token assistance. Constitutional restrictions on taxes and indebtedness stopped some from responding to the relief crisis. Others lacked the will. Texas refused to issue bonds to fund relief.

Hoover blundered not in first relying on charities and local governments for relief but in refusing to admit that they were inadequate. Even his advisers warned that voluntarism and individual initiative had become obsolete. Both his vision and his efforts fell short.

As the depression worsened, Hoover adopted more activist policies. He persuaded Congress to cut taxes to boost consumers' buying power, and he increased the public works budget. The Federal Farm Board lent money to cooperatives and spent millions trying to stabilize crop prices. Unable to control production, however, the board conceded failure by late 1931. More successful was the Reconstruction Finance Corporation (RFC). Established in January 1932, the RFC lent federal funds to banks, insurance companies, and railroads so that their recovery could "trickle down" to ordinary Americans. Hoover still opposed direct aid to the general public, although he finally allowed the RFC to lend small amounts to state and local governments for unemployment relief.

But these programs satisfied few Americans. "While children starve," cried Pennsylvania's governor, Hoover "intends to let us have just as little relief as possible after the longest delay possible." Far more action was necessary, but Hoover remained committed to voluntarism and a balanced budget. The *New Republic* remarked in wonder: "Strangely enough, though he praises our government as representative and democratic, Mr. Hoover seems to regard most of the positive activities it might undertake as the intrusion of an alien sovereignty rather than the cooperative action of a people." Hoover's ideological limitations infuriated Americans who saw him as indifferent to their suffering and a reactionary

Nearly 20,000 veterans of World War I set out for Washington, D.C., in 1932 to claim a special bonus payment. Setting up camps along the way, they recieved food and sympathy from local supporters.

protector of privileged business interests—an image his political opponents encouraged.

Repudiating Hoover: The 1932 Election

Hoover's treatment of the **Bonus Army** symbolized his unpopularity and set the stage for the 1932 election. In 1932, unemployed veterans of World War I gathered in Washington, demanding payment of service bonuses not due until 1945. Hoover refused to meet with them, and Congress rejected their plan. But 10,000 veterans erected a shantytown at the edge of Washington and camped in vacant public buildings. Hoover decided to evict the veterans, but General Douglas MacArthur exceeded his cautious orders and on July 28 led cavalry, infantry, and tanks against the ragged Bonus Marchers. The troops cleared the buildings and assaulted the shantytown, dispersing the veterans and their families and setting their camp on fire.

This assault provoked widespread outrage. "What a pitiful spectacle is that of the great American Government, mightiest in the world, chasing unarmed men, women, and children with army tanks," commented the *Washington News*. The administration tried to brand the Bonus Marchers as communists and criminals, but subsequent investigations refuted such claims. The incident confirmed Hoover's public image as harsh and insensitive.

In the summer of 1932, with no prospects for victory, Republicans renominated Hoover. Confident Democrats selected Governor Franklin D. Roosevelt of New York, who promised "a new deal for the American people." A distant cousin of Theodore Roosevelt, FDR had prepared for the presidency. Born into a wealthy family in 1882, he had been educated at Harvard, trained in the law, and schooled in politics as a state legislator, assistant secretary of the navy under Wilson, and the Democratic vice presidential nominee in 1920. In 1921, Roosevelt contracted polio, which paralyzed him from the waist down, leaving him dependent on braces or crutches. His struggle with this ordeal gave him greater maturity, compassion, and determination. His continued involvement in politics, meanwhile, owed much to his wife, Eleanor. A social reformer, she became a Democratic activist, organizing women's groups and campaigning across New York. In a remarkable political comeback, FDR was elected governor in 1928 and reelected in 1930.

The 1932 campaign gave scant indication of what Roosevelt's New Deal might involve. The Democratic platform differed little from that of the Republicans, and Roosevelt spoke in vague or general terms. He knew that the election would be a repudiation of Hoover more than an endorsement of himself. Still, observers found clues in Roosevelt's record in New York, where he had created the first state system of unemployment relief and supported social welfare and conservation. More important was his outgoing personality, which radiated warmth and hope in contrast to Hoover's gloom. "If you put a rose in Hoover's hand," said one observer, "it would wilt."

FDR carried every state south and west of Pennsylvania (see Map 25–1). It was the worst rout of a Republican candidate ever (except in 1912, when the party had split). Yet Hoover would remain president for four more months, as the Constitution then required. And in those four months, the depression worsened, spreading misery throughout America. When teachers in Chicago, unpaid for months, fainted in their classrooms from hunger, it symbolized the imminent collapse of the nation. The final blow came in February 1933, when panic struck the banking system. Nearly 6,000 banks had already failed, robbing 9 million depositors of their savings. Desperate Americans rushed to withdraw their funds from the remaining banks, pushing them to the brink. With the federal government under Hoover immobilized, state governments shut the banks to prevent their failure. By March, an eerie silence had descended on the nation. Hoover concluded, "We are at the end of our string."

Launching the New Deal

In the midst of this national anxiety, Franklin D. Roosevelt pushed forward an unprecedented program to resolve the crises of a collapsing financial system, crippling unemployment, and agricultural and industrial breakdown and to promote reform. The early New Deal achieved successes and

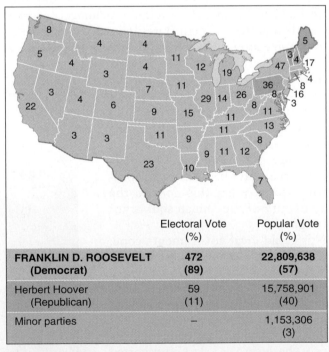

	Electoral Vote (%)	Popular Vote (%)
FRANKLIN D. ROOSEVELT (Democrat)	**472** **(89)**	**22,809,638** **(57)**
Herbert Hoover (Republican)	59 (11)	15,758,901 (40)
Minor parties	—	1,153,306 (3)

MAP 25–1   The Election of 1932
In the midst of the Great Depression, only the most rock-ribbed Republican states failed to turn to Franklin D. Roosevelt and the Democrats for relief. The election of 1932 was a landslide.

OVERVIEW

Major Laws of the Hundred Days

Law	Objective
Emergency Banking Act	Stabilized the private banking system
Agricultural Adjustment Act	Established a farm recovery program based on production controls and price supports
Emergency Farm Mortgage Act	Provided for the refinancing of farm mortgages
National Industrial Recovery Act	Established a national recovery program and authorized a public works program
Federal Emergency Relief Act	Established a national system of relief
Home Owners Loan Act	Protected homeowners from mortgage foreclosure by refinancing home loans
Glass-Steagall Act	Separated commercial and investment banking and guaranteed bank deposits
Tennessee Valley Authority Act	Established the TVA and provided for the planned development of the Tennessee River Valley
Civilian Conservation Corps Act	Established the CCC to provide work relief on reforestation and conservation projects
Farm Credit Act	Expanded agricultural credits and established the Farm Credit Administration
Securities Act	Required full disclosure from stock exchanges
Wagner-Peyser Act	Created a U.S. Employment Service and encouraged states to create local public employment offices

attracted support, but it also had limitations and generated criticism that suggested the need for still greater innovations.

Action Now!

On March 4, 1933, Franklin Delano Roosevelt became president and immediately reassured the American people. He insisted that "the only thing we have to fear is fear itself" and he promised "action, and action now!" Summoning Congress, Roosevelt pressed forward on a broad front. In the first three months of his administration, the famous Hundred Days of the New Deal, the Democratic Congress passed many important laws (see Overview, Major Laws of the Hundred Days).

Roosevelt's program reflected a mix of ideas, some from FDR himself, some from a diverse group of advisers, including academic experts dubbed the "brain trust," politicians, and social workers. It also incorporated principles from the progressive movement, precedents from the Great War mobilization, and even plans from the Hoover administration. Above all, the New Deal was a practical response to the depression. FDR had set its tone in his campaign when he declared, "The country needs, and, unless I mistake its temper, the country demands bold, persistent experimentation.... Above all, try something."

FDR first addressed the banking crisis. On March 5, he proclaimed a national bank holiday, closing all remaining banks. Congress then passed his Emergency Banking Act, a conservative measure that extended government assistance to sound banks and reorganized weak ones. Prompt govern-

ment action, coupled with a reassuring **fireside chat** over the radio by the president, restored popular confidence in the banks. When they reopened on March 13, deposits exceeded withdrawals. "Capitalism," said Raymond Moley of the brain trust, "was saved in eight days." In June, Congress created the **Federal Deposit Insurance Corporation (FDIC)** to guarantee bank deposits up to $2,500.

The financial industry was also reformed. The Glass-Steagall Act separated investment and commercial banking to curtail risky speculation. The Securities Act reformed the sale of stocks to prevent the insider abuses that had characterized Wall Street, and in 1934 the **Securities and Exchange Commission (SEC)** was created to regulate the stock market. Two other financial measures in 1933 created the Home Owners Loan Corporation and the Farm Credit Administration, which enabled millions to refinance their mortgages.

Creating Jobs

Roosevelt also provided relief for the unemployed. The Federal Emergency Relief Administration (FERA) furnished funds to state and local agencies. Harry Hopkins, who had headed Roosevelt's relief program in New York, became its director and one of the New Deal's most important members. FERA spent over $3 billion before it ended in 1935, and by then Hopkins and FDR had developed new programs that provided work rather than just cash. Work relief, they believed, preserved both the skills and the morale of recipients. In the winter of 1933–1934, Hopkins spent nearly

$1 billion to create jobs for 4 million men and women through the Civil Works Administration (CWA). The CWA hired laborers to build roads and airports, teachers to staff rural schools, and singers and artists to give public performances. The Public Works Administration (PWA) provided work relief on useful projects to stimulate the economy through public expenditures. Directed by Harold Ickes, the PWA spent billions from 1933 to 1939 to build schools, hospitals, courthouses, dams, and bridges.

One of FDR's personal ideas, the Civilian Conservation Corps (CCC), combined work relief with conservation. Launched in 1933, the CCC employed 2.5 million young men to work on reforestation and flood-control projects, build roads and bridges in national forests and parks, restore Civil War battlefields, and fight forest fires. The men lived in isolated camps and earned $30 a month, $25 of which had to be sent home. "I'd go anywhere," said one Baltimore applicant. "I'd go to hell if I could get work there." One of the most popular New Deal agencies, the CCC lasted until 1942.

Helping Some Farmers

Besides providing relief, the New Deal promoted economic recovery. In May 1933, Congress established the Agricultural Adjustment Administration (AAA) to combat the depression in agriculture caused by crop surpluses and low prices. The AAA subsidized farmers who agreed to restrict production. The objective was to boost farm prices to parity, a level that would restore farmers' purchasing power to what it had been in 1914. In the summer of 1933, the AAA paid southern farmers to plow up 10 million acres of cotton and midwestern farmers to bury 9 million pounds of pork. Restricting production in hard times caused public outrage. "Farmers are not producing too much," said one critic. "What we have overproduction of is empty stomachs and bare backs." Secretary of Agriculture Henry Wallace defended production controls as analogous to corporations maximizing profits: "Agriculture cannot survive in a capitalistic society as a philanthropic enterprise."

Agricultural conditions improved. Farm prices rose from 52 percent of parity in 1932 to 88 percent in 1935, and gross farm income rose by 50 percent. Not until 1941, however, would income exceed the level of 1929, a poor year for farmers. Moreover, some of the decreased production and increased prices stemmed from devastating droughts and dust storms on the Great Plains. The AAA itself harmed poor farmers while aiding larger commercial growers. As southern planters restricted their acreage, they dismissed tenants and share-croppers, and with AAA payments, they bought new farm machinery, reducing their need for farm labor. A reporter in 1935 found thousands of sharecroppers "along the highways and byways of Dixie,...lonely figures without money, without homes, and without hope."

The Supreme Court declared the AAA unconstitutional in 1936, but new laws established the farm subsidy program for decades to come. Increasing mechanization and scientific agriculture kept production high and farmers dependent on government intervention.

The Flight of the Blue Eagle

The New Deal attempted to revive U.S. industry with the National Industrial Recovery Act (NIRA), which created the National Recovery Administration (NRA). The NRA sought to halt the slide in prices, wages, and employment by suspending antitrust laws and authorizing industrial and trade associations to draft codes setting production quotas, price policies, wages and working conditions, and other business practices. The codes promoted the interests of business generally and big business in particular, but Section 7a of the NIRA guaranteed workers the rights to organize unions and bargain collectively—a provision that John L. Lewis of the United Mine Workers called an Emancipation Proclamation for labor.

Hugh Johnson became director of the NRA. He persuaded business leaders to cooperate in drafting codes and the public to patronize participating companies. The NRA Blue Eagle insignia and its slogan "We Do Our Part" covered

A coal miner greeting Franklin D. Roosevelt in West Virginia in 1932. Roosevelt's promise of a New Deal revived hope among millions of Americans trapped in hard times.

American Views

The Commissioner of the Bureau of Indian Affairs on the New Deal for Native Americans

John Collier, reformer and social worker, served as commissioner of the Bureau of Indian Affairs (BIA) from 1933 until 1945. During his tenure, he radically transformed the agency—long known to be corrupt and hostile to Native Americans—into an organization committed to the preservation of tribal cultures and the restoration of Indian lands. Like other New Dealers, Collier attempted to use the power of the federal government to protect those with limited political power and economic influence—in this case Native Americans.

Collier was extraordinarily successful in promoting the restoration of tribal rights and autonomy and helped ensure that future generations of Indians could reclaim their lands. Yet he was frustrated by Congress's unwillingness to fund the programs he believed necessary for a genuine New Deal for Native Americans. In his 1938 annual report, he calls for greater economic support, arguing that it would be a good investment for the nation. Most important, even as he acknowledges that real changes have occurred since 1933, he points out that there is still much to be done to achieve political autonomy and economic self-sufficiency for American Indians.

- How did Collier describe the treatment of Native Americans, and why did white Americans regard Indians as a "problem" to be eliminated?

- What were the new goals of the Bureau of Indian Affairs?

- How did Collier regard the role of land in Native American society? Why?

- What was the greatest challenge Collier saw for Native Americans in 1938?

For nearly 300 years white Americans, in our zeal to carve out a nation made to order, have dealt with the Indians on the erroneous, yet tragic, assumption that the Indians were a dying race—to be liquidated. We took away their best lands; broke treaties, promises; tossed them the most nearly worthless scraps of a continent that had once been wholly theirs. But we did not liquidate their spirit. The vital spark which kept them alive was hardy. So hardy, indeed, that we now face an astounding and heartening fact.

Actually, the Indians, on the evidence of federal census rolls of the past eight years, are increasing almost twice the rate of the population as a whole.

With this fact before us, our whole attitude toward the Indians has necessarily undergone a profound change. Dead is the centuries-old notion that the sooner we eliminate this doomed race, preferably humanely, the better.... No longer can we naively talk of or think of the "Indian problem."

We, therefore, define our Indian policy somewhat as follows: So productively to use the moneys appropriated by the Congress for Indians as to enable them, on good, adequate land of their own, to earn decent livelihoods and lead self-respecting, organized lives in harmony with their own aims and ideals, as an integral part of American life. This will not happen tomorrow; perhaps not in our lifetime; but with the revitalization of Indian hope due to the actions and attitudes of this government during the last few years, that aim is a probability, and a real one.... So intimately is all of Indian life tied up with the land and its utilization that to think of Indians is to think of land. The two are inseparable. Upon the land and its intelligent use depends the main future of the American Indian.

The Indian feels toward his land, not a mere ownership but a devotion and veneration befitting that what is not only a home but a refuge.... Not only does the Indian's major source of livelihood derive from the land but his social and political organizations are rooted in soil.

Since 1933, the Indian Service has made a concerted effort—an effort which is as yet but a mere beginning—to help the Indian to build back his landholdings to a point where they will provide an adequate basis for a self-sustaining economy, a self-satisfying social organization.

Source: John Collier. Annual Report of the Secretary of the Interior for the Fiscal Year Ended June 30, 1938. From www.historymatters.gmu.edu

workplaces, storefronts, and billboards. Blue Eagle parades marched down the nation's main streets and climaxed in a massive demonstration in New York City.

Support for the NRA waned, however. Corporate leaders used it to advance their own goals and to discriminate against small producers, consumers, and labor. Minnesota's governor, Floyd Olson, condemned the dominance within the NRA of the same selfish business interests he saw as responsible for the depression: "I am not satisfied with hanging a laurel wreath on burglars, thieves, and pirates and calling them code authorities."

Businesses also violated the labor rights specified in Section 7a. Defiant employers viewed collective bargaining as infringing their authority. Employers even used violence to smother unions. The NRA did little to enforce Section 7a, and Johnson, strongly probusiness, denounced all strikes. Workers felt betrayed. Roosevelt tried to reorganize the NRA, but the act remained controversial until the Supreme Court declared it unconstitutional in 1935.

Critics Right and Left

The early New Deal did not end the depression. Recovery was fitful and uneven; millions of Americans remained unemployed. Nevertheless, the New Deal's efforts to grapple with problems, its successes in reducing suffering and fear, and Roosevelt's own skills carried the Democratic Party to victory in the 1934 elections. But New Deal policies also provoked criticism, from both those convinced that too little had been achieved and those alarmed that too much had been attempted.

Despite the early New Deal's probusiness character, conservatives complained that the expansion of government activity and its regulatory role weakened the autonomy of American business. They also condemned the efforts to aid nonbusiness groups as socialistic, particularly the "excessive" spending on unemployment relief and the "instigation" of labor organizing. By 1934, as *Time* magazine reported, "Private fulminations and public carpings against the New Deal have become almost a routine of the business day." Industrialists and bankers organized the American Liberty League to direct attacks on the New Deal. The league distributed over 5 million pamphlets; it also furnished editorials and news stories to newspapers. These critics attracted little popular support, however, and their selfishness antagonized Roosevelt.

More realistic criticism came from the left. In 1932, FDR had campaigned for "the forgotten man at the bottom of the economic pyramid," and some radicals argued that the early New Deal had forgotten the forgotten man. Communists and socialists focused public attention on the poor, especially in the countryside. In California, communists organized Mexican, Filipino, and Japanese farm workers into the Cannery and Agricultural Workers Union; in Arkansas and Tennessee, socialists in 1934 helped organize sharecroppers into the Southern Tenant Farmers Union, protesting the "Raw Deal" they had received from the AAA. Both unions encountered violent reprisals. Growers killed three picketers in California's San Joaquin Valley; in Arkansas, landlords shot union organizers and led vigilante raids on sharecroppers' shacks. This terrorism, however, created sympathy for farmworkers.

Even without the involvement of socialists or communists, labor militancy in 1934 pressed Roosevelt. The number of workers participating in strikes leaped from 325,000 in 1932 (about the annual average since 1925) to 1.5 million in 1934. From dockworkers in Seattle and copper miners in Butte to streetcar drivers in Milwaukee and shoemakers in Boston, workers demanded their rights. Textile workers launched the largest single strike in the nation's history, shutting down the industry in 20 states.

Rebuffing FDR's pleas for fair treatment, employers moved to crush the strikes, often using complaisant police and private strikebreakers. In Minneapolis, police shot 67 teamsters, almost all in the back, as they fled an ambush arranged by employers; in Toledo, company police and National Guardsmen attacked autoworkers with tear gas, bayonets, and rifle fire; in the textile strike, police killed six

New Deal agricultural programs stabilized the farm economy, but not all farmers benefited. Landowners who received AAA payments evicted these black sharecroppers huddled in a makeshift roadside camp in Missouri in 1935.

picketers in South Carolina, and soldiers wounded another 50 in Rhode Island. At times, the workers held their ground, and they often attracted popular support, even in general strikes that paralyzed major cities like San Francisco. But against such powerful opponents, workers needed help to achieve their rights. Harry Hopkins and other New Dealers realized that labor's demands could not be ignored.

Four prominent individuals mobilized popular discontent to demand government action to assist groups neglected by the New Deal. Representative William Lemke of North Dakota, an agrarian radical leader of the Nonpartisan League, called attention to rural distress. Lemke objected to the New Deal's limited response to farmers crushed by the depression. In his own state, nearly two-thirds of the farmers had lost their land through foreclosures. The AAA's strategy of simply restricting production, he thundered, was an "insane policy in the midst of hunger, misery, want, and rags."

Francis Townsend, a California physician, proposed to aid the nation's elderly, many of whom were destitute. The Townsend Plan called for a government pension to every American over the age of 60, provided that the recipient retired from work and spent the entire pension. This scheme promised to extend relief to the elderly, open jobs for the unemployed, and stimulate economic recovery. Townsend attracted people who, in his words, "believe in the Bible, believe in God, cheer when the flag passes by, the Bible Belt solid Americans." Over 5,000 Townsend Clubs lobbied for government action to help the elderly poor.

Father Charles Coughlin, a Catholic priest in the Detroit suburb of Royal Oak, threatened to mobilize another large constituency against the limitations of the early New Deal. Thirty million Americans listened eagerly to his weekly radio broadcasts, which mixed religion with anti-Semitism and demands for social justice and financial reform. Coughlin had condemned Hoover for assisting banks but ignoring the unemployed, and initially he welcomed the New Deal as "Christ's Deal." But after concluding that FDR's policies favored "the virile viciousness of business and finance," Coughlin organized the National Union for Social Justice to lobby for his goals. With support among lower-middle-class, heavily Catholic, urban ethnic groups, Coughlin posed a real challenge to Roosevelt's Democratic Party.

Roosevelt found Senator Huey P. Long of Louisiana still more worrisome. Alternately charming and autocratic, Long had modernized his state with taxation and educational reforms and an extensive public-works program after his election as governor in 1928. Moving to the Senate and eyeing the White House, Long proposed more comprehensive social-welfare policies than the New Deal had envisaged. In 1934, he organized the Share-Our-Wealth Society. His plan to end poverty and unemployment called for confiscatory taxes on the rich to provide every family with a decent income, health coverage, education, and old-age pensions. Long's appeal was enormous. Within months, his organization claimed more than 27,000 clubs and 7 million members.

These dissident movements raised complex issues and simple fears. They built on concerns about the New Deal, both demanding government assistance and fretting about government intrusion. Their programs were often ill-defined or impractical—Townsend's plan would cost more than half the national income; and some of the leaders, like Coughlin and Long, approached demagoguery. Nevertheless, their popularity warned Roosevelt that government action was needed to satisfy reform demands and ensure his reelection in 1936.

Consolidating the New Deal

Responding to the persistence of the depression and political pressures, Roosevelt in 1935 undertook economic and social reforms that some observers have called the Second New Deal. The new measures shifted government action more toward reform even as they still addressed relief and recovery. Nor did FDR's interest in reform simply reflect cynical politics. He had frequently championed progressive measures in the past, and many of his advisers had deep roots in reform movements. After the 1934 elections gave the president an

The New Deal enabled photographers and artists to take to the road to capture images of the nation's dispossessed. This photograph by Dorothea Lange of an 18-year old mother and her child in a migrant labor camp in 1937 illustrates both despair and detachment and conveys the hardship of homelessness and deprivation in the Great Depression.

even more Democratic Congress, Harry Hopkins exulted: "Boys—this is our hour. We've got to get everything we want—a works program, social security, wages and hours, everything—now or never."

Weeding Out and Lifting Up

"In spite of our efforts and in spite of our talk," Roosevelt told the new Congress in 1935, "we have not weeded out the overprivileged and we have not effectively lifted up the underprivileged." To do so, he developed "must" legislation. One of the new laws protected labor's rights to organize and bargain collectively. Drafted by Senator Robert Wagner of New York to replace Section 7a, it received Roosevelt's endorsement only after it was clear that both Congress and the public favored it. The Wagner National Labor Relations Act, dubbed "Labor's Magna Carta," guaranteed workers the right to organize unions and prohibited employers from adopting unfair labor practices, such as firing union activists and forming company unions. The law also set up the National Labor Relations Board (NLRB) to enforce these provisions, protect workers from coercion, and supervise union elections.

Social security.   Of greater long-range importance was the Social Security Act. Other industrial nations had established national social-insurance systems much earlier, but only the Great Depression moved the United States to accept the idea that the federal government should protect the poor and unemployed. Even so, the law was a compromise, framed by a nonpartisan committee of business, labor, and public representatives and then weakened by congressional conservatives. It provided unemployment compensation, old-age pensions, and aid for dependent mothers and children and the blind.

The conservative nature of the law appeared in its stingy benefit payments, its lack of health insurance, and its exclusion of more than one-fourth of all workers, including many in desperate need of protection, such as farm laborers and domestic servants. Moreover, unlike in other nations, the old-age pensions were financed through a regressive payroll tax on both employees and employers rather than through general tax revenues. Thus the new system was more like a compulsory insurance program. Roosevelt conceded as much but defended the taxes on workers as a tactic to protect the reform.

Despite its weaknesses, the Social Security Act was one of the most important laws in American history and Roosevelt was justifiably proud. It provided, he pointed out, "at least some measure of protection to the average citizen and to his family against the loss of a job and against poverty-ridden old age." Moreover, by establishing federal responsibility for social welfare, it inaugurated a welfare system that subsequent generations would expand.

Money, tax, and land reform.   Another reform measure, the Banking Act of 1935, increased the authority of the Federal Reserve Board over the nation's currency and credit system and decreased the power of the private bankers whose irresponsible behavior had contributed to the depression and the appeal of Father Coughlin. The Revenue Act of 1935, passed after Roosevelt assailed the "unjust concentration of wealth and economic power," provided for graduated income taxes and increased estate and corporate taxes. Opponents called it the Soak the Rich Tax, but with its many loopholes, it was scarcely that and was certainly not a redistributive measure such as Huey Long had proposed. Nevertheless, it set a precedent for progressive taxation and attracted popular support.

The Second New Deal also responded belatedly to the environmental catastrophe that had turned much of the Great Plains from Texas to the Dakotas into a Dust Bowl (see Map 25–2). Since World War I, farmers had stripped marginal land of its native grasses to plant wheat. When drought

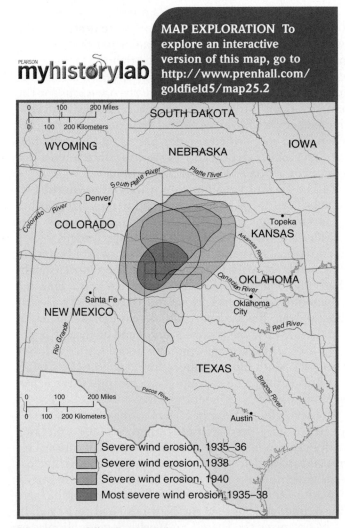

MAP 25–2   The Dust Bowl
Years of overcultivation, drought, and high winds created the Dust Bowl, which most severely affected the southern Great Plains. Federal relief and conservation programs provided assistance, but many residents fled the area, often migrating to California.

FROM THEN TO NOW

Social Security

No politician will "ever scrap my social security program." So predicted FDR when he signed the Social Security Act in 1935. He based his confidence on the provisions in the act that linked benefits to payroll deductions. Because workers contributed to the program, they would feel a "right to collect their pensions and unemployment benefits." But Roosevelt could not have imagined just how successful the Social Security program would become since the 1930s. It now assists 47 million Americans, and, over the next two decades, nearly 80 million Americans will be eligible for benefits. The nation's first "baby boomer," Kathleen Casey-Kirschling, who was born one second after midnight on January 1, 1946, filed to receive Social Security payments beginning January 2008. And there are many baby boomers to follow.

Americans eagerly embraced the Social Security program in the 1930s proudly displaying their Social Security cards and even having their numbers tattooed on their bodies.

But the successful expansion of the program has also called its future into question. Critics of the program may not propose "scrapping" Social Security, but they do advocate a major overhaul. In part, their opposition stems from a backlash against "big government" that emerged in the 1960s and ultimately found its champion in Republican President Ronald Reagan, who declared, "Government is not the solution to our problems; government is the problem." Citing long-term concerns about the program's solvency, these critics call for privatizing the system, enabling contributors to invest their Social Security accounts in the stock market, for example.

President George W. Bush made revamping Social Security the centerpiece of his 2005 State of the Union Address and launched a 60-day nationwide tour to drum up support for Social Security reform. But the American public overwhelmingly rejected his plans for privatization; by June 2005 nearly 65 percent of the American public disapproved of Bush's recommendations for changes in Social Security. Pledging to "fight to keep the security in Social Security," Democrats and even key Republicans challenged the president's "attack" on what many Americans regard as the "most successful program in our country's history."

■ Why does the vast majority of Americans continue to support social security despite the critics of "big government?"

PEARSON myhistorylab
From Then to Now Online

President George W. Bush's campaign to reform Social Security stirred angry protest throughout America.

25-1 "More Security for the American Family," 1936. Government poster advertising the social security program.

25-2 Abraham Epstein, "'Social Security' Under the New Deal," 1935. Critique of the Social Security legislation passed in August 1935.

25-3 *Washington Post*, "Birth of a Salesman: Pitching Social Security," 2005. Article describing President George W. Bush's efforts to revamp the social security program.

and high winds hit the plains in 1932, crops failed, and nothing was left to hold the soil. Dust storms blew away millions of tons of topsoil, despoiling the land and darkening the sky a thousand miles away. Families abandoned their farms in droves. Many of these poor "Okies" headed for California, their plight captured in John Steinbeck's novel, *The Grapes of Wrath* (1939).

In 1935, Roosevelt established the Resettlement Administration to focus on land reform and help poor farmers. Under Rexford Tugwell, this agency initiated soil erosion projects and attempted to resettle impoverished farmers on better land, but the problem exceeded its resources. Congress moved to save the land, if not its people, by creating the Soil Conservation Service in 1935.

Expanding Relief

If reform gained priority in the Second New Deal, relief remained critical. With millions still unemployed, Roosevelt pushed through Congress in 1935 the Emergency Relief Appropriation Act, authorizing $5 billion—at the time the largest single appropriation in American history—for emergency public employment. Roosevelt created the Works Progress Administration (WPA) under Hopkins, who set up work relief programs to assist the unemployed and boost the economy. Before its end in 1943, the WPA gave jobs to 9 million people (more than a fifth of the labor force) and spent nearly $12 billion. Three-fourths of its expenditures went on construction projects that could employ manual labor: The WPA built 125,000 schools, post offices, and hospitals; 8,000 parks; nearly 100,000 bridges; and enough roads and sewer systems to circle the earth 30 times. The WPA laid much of the basic infrastructure on which the nation still relies.

The WPA also developed work projects for unemployed writers, artists, musicians, and actors. "Why not?" said FDR. "They are human beings. They have to live." The Federal Writers' Project put authors to work preparing state guidebooks, writing historical pamphlets, and recording the memories of ex-slaves. The Federal Art Project hired artists to teach art in night schools, prepare exhibits at museums, and paint murals on post office walls. The Federal Theatre Project organized theatrical productions and drama companies that in four years played to 30 million Americans. The Federal Music Project hired musicians to collect and perform folk songs. These WPA programs allowed people to use their talents while surviving the depression, increased popular access to cultural performances, and established a precedent for federal support of the arts. "What has happened and in such a short time is almost incredible," said one reviewer. "From a government completely apathetic to art, we suddenly have a government very art conscious."

The National Youth Administration (NYA), another WPA agency, gave part-time jobs to students, enabling 2 million high school and college students to stay in school, learn skills, and do productive work. At the University of Nebraska, NYA students built an observatory; at Duke University, law student Richard M. Nixon earned 35 cents an hour doing research in the library. Lyndon Johnson, a Texas NYA official, believed that "if the Roosevelt administration had never done another thing, it would have been justified by the work of this great institution for salvaging youth."

The Roosevelt Coalition and the Election of 1936

The 1936 election gave Americans an opportunity to judge FDR and the New Deal. Conservatives alarmed at the expansion of government, business people angered by regulation and labor legislation, and wealthy Americans furious with tax reform decried the New Deal. But they were a minority. Even the presidential candidate they supported, Republican Governor Alf Landon of Kansas, endorsed much of the New Deal, criticizing merely the inefficiency and cost of some of its programs. The New Deal's earlier critics on the left had also lost most of their following. The reforms of 1935 had undercut their arguments, and the assassination of Huey Long in the same year had removed their ablest politician. They formed the Union Party and nominated William Lemke for the presidency, but they were no longer a threat.

The programs and politicians of the New Deal had created an invincible coalition behind Roosevelt. Despite ambivalence about large-scale government intervention, the New Deal's agricultural programs reinforced the traditional Democratic allegiance of white southerners while attracting many western farmers. Labor legislation clinched the active support of the nation's workers; Sidney Hillman of the Amalgamated Clothing Workers promised that his union would campaign for FDR "to see to it that we hold onto the gains labor has won." Middle-class voters, whose homes had been saved and whose hopes had been raised, also joined the Roosevelt coalition.

So did urban ethnic groups, who had benefited from welfare programs and appreciated the unprecedented recognition Roosevelt's administration gave them. FDR named the first Italian American to the federal judiciary, for example, and appointed five times as many Catholics and Jews to government positions as the three Republican presidents had during the 1920s. African Americans voted overwhelmingly Democratic for the first time. Women, too, were an important part of the Roosevelt coalition, and Eleanor often attracted their support as much as Franklin did. As one campaigner said to a roaring crowd in 1936, "Many women in this country when they vote for Franklin D. Roosevelt will also be thinking with a choke in the throat of Eleanor Roosevelt!"

This political realignment produced a landslide. Roosevelt polled 61 percent of the popular vote and the largest electoral vote margin ever recorded, 523 to 8. Landon even lost Kansas, his own state, and Lemke received fewer than 900,000 votes. Democrats also won huge majorities in Congress. Roosevelt's political coalition reflected a mandate for

Eleanor Roosevelt campaigns with FDR in Fremont, Nebraska, in 1935. A visible activist for social and economic reform, she was also politically important in building the powerful Roosevelt coalition. "Previously," said the journalist Ruby Black, "a President's wife acted as if she didn't know that a political party existed."

himself and the New Deal; it would enable the Democrats to dominate national elections for three decades.

The New Deal and American Life

The landslide of 1936 revealed the impact of the New Deal on Americans. Industrial workers mobilized to secure their rights, women and minorities gained increased, if still limited, opportunities to participate in American society, and southerners and westerners benefited from government programs they turned to their own advantage. Government programs changed daily life, and ordinary people often helped shape the new policies.

Labor on the March

The labor revival in the 1930s reflected both workers' determination and government support. Workers wanted to improve their wages and benefits as well as to gain union recognition and union contracts that would allow them to limit arbitrary managerial authority and achieve some control over the workplace. This larger goal provoked opposition

from employers and their allies and required workers to organize, strike, and become politically active. Their achievement was remarkable.

The Second New Deal helped. By guaranteeing labor's rights to organize and bargain collectively, the Wagner Act sparked a wave of labor activism. But if the government ultimately protected union rights, the unions themselves had to form locals, recruit members, and demonstrate influence in the workplace.

At first, those tasks overwhelmed the American Federation of Labor (AFL). Its reliance on craft-based unions and reluctance to organize immigrant, black, and women workers left it unprepared for the rush of industrial workers seeking unionization. More progressive labor leaders saw that industry-wide unions were more appropriate for unskilled workers in mass-production industries. Forming the Committee for Industrial Organization (CIO) within the AFL, they campaigned to unionize workers in the steel, auto, and rubber industries, all notoriously hostile to unions. AFL leaders insisted that the CIO disband and then in 1937 expelled its unions. The militants reorganized as the separate **Congress of Industrial Organizations.** (In 1955, the two groups merged as the AFL-CIO.)

The split roused the AFL to increase its own organizing activities, but it was primarily the new CIO that put labor on the march. It inspired workers previously neglected by organized labor. The CIO's interracial union campaign in the Birmingham steel mills, said one organizer, was "like a second coming of Christ" for black workers, who welcomed the union as a chance for social recognition as well as economic opportunity. The CIO also employed new and aggressive tactics, particularly the sit-down strike, in which workers, rather than picketing outside the factory, simply sat inside the plant, thereby blocking both production and the use of strikebreakers. Conservatives were outraged, but Upton Sinclair said, "For seventy-five years big business has been sitting down on the American people, and now I am delighted to see the process reversed."

The CIO won major victories despite bitter opposition from industry and its allies. The issue was not wages but labor's right to organize and bargain with management. Sit-down strikes paralyzed General Motors in 1937 after it refused to recognize the United Auto Workers. GM tried to force the strikers out of its Flint, Michigan, plants by turning off the heat, using police and tear gas, threatening strikers' families, and obtaining court orders to clear the plant by military force. But the governor refused to order National Guardsmen to attack, and the strikers held out, aided by the Women's Emergency Brigade, working-class women who picketed the building, heckled the police, and smuggled food to the strikers. After six weeks, GM signed a contract with the UAW. Chrysler soon followed suit. Ford refused to recognize the union until 1941, often violently disrupting organizing efforts.

Steel companies also used violence against unionization. In the Memorial Day Massacre in Chicago in 1937, police guarding a plant of the Republic Steel Company fired on strikers and their families, killing ten people as they tried to flee. Scores more were wounded and beaten in a police frenzy so violent that theaters refused to show a newsreel of the event. A Senate investigation found that Republic and other companies had hired private police to attack workers seeking to unionize, stockpiled weapons and tear gas, and corrupted officials. The investigators concluded that "private corporations dominate their employees, deny them their constitutional rights, promote disorder and disharmony, and even set at naught the powers of the government itself." Federal court orders finally forced the companies to bargain collectively.

New Deal labor legislation, government investigations and court orders, and the federal refusal to use force against strikes helped the labor movement secure basic rights for American workers. Union membership leaped from under 3 million in 1932 to 9 million by 1939, and workers won higher wages, better working conditions, and more economic democracy.

Women and the New Deal

As federal programs proliferated in 1933, a Baltimore women's group urged the administration to "come out for a square and new deal for women." Although women did gain increased attention and influence, government and society remained largely bound by traditional values.

New Deal relief programs had a mixed impact on working women. Formal government policy required equal consideration for women and men, but local officials so flouted this requirement that Eleanor Roosevelt urged Harry Hopkins to "impress on state administrators that the women's programs are as important as the men's. They are so apt to forget us!" Women on relief were restricted to women's work—more than half worked on sewing projects, regardless of their skills—and were paid scarcely half what men received. WPA training programs also reinforced traditional ideas about women's work; black women, for example, were trained to be maids, dishwashers, and cooks. Although women constituted nearly one-fourth of the labor force, they obtained only 19 percent of the jobs created by the WPA, 12 percent of those created by the FERA, and 7 percent of those created by the CWA. The CCC excluded women altogether. Still, relief agencies provided crucial assistance to women during the depression.

Other New Deal programs also had mixed benefits for women. Despite demands by the League of Women Voters and the Women's Trade Union League for "equal pay for equal work and equal opportunity for equal ability regardless of sex," many NRA codes mandated lower wage scales for women than for men, which officials justified as reflecting long-established customs. But by raising minimum wages, the NRA brought relatively greater improvement to women, who were concentrated in the lowest paid occupations, than to male workers. The Social Security Act did not cover domestic servants, waitresses, or women who worked in the home, but it did help mothers with dependent children.

Still more significant, the Social Security Act reflected and reinforced prevailing notions about proper roles for men and women. The system was based on the idea that men should be wage earners and women should stay at home as wives and mothers. Accordingly, if a woman worked outside the home and her husband was eligible for benefits, she would not receive her own retirement pension. And if a woman had no husband but had children, welfare authorities would remove her from work-relief jobs regardless of whether she wanted to continue to work, and would give her assistance from the Aid to Dependent Children (ADC) program, which was also created under the Social Security Act. These new programs, then, while providing much-needed assistance, also institutionalized a modern welfare system that segregated men and women in separate spheres and reaffirmed the then popular belief that the success of the family depended on that separation.

Women also gained political influence under the New Deal, although Molly Dewson, the director of the Women's Division of the Democratic Party, exaggerated when she exclaimed, "The change from women's status in government before Roosevelt is unbelievable." Dewson herself exercised considerable political power and helped to shape the party's campaigns. Around Dewson revolved a network of women, linked by friendships and experiences in the National Consumers' League, Women's Trade Union League, and other progressive reform organizations. Appointed to many positions in the Roosevelt administration, they helped develop and implement New Deal social legislation. Secretary of Labor Frances Perkins was the first woman cabinet member and a key member of the network; other women were in the Treasury Department, the Children's Bureau, and relief and cultural programs.

Eleanor Roosevelt was their leader. Described by a Washington reporter as "a cabinet member without portfolio," she roared across the social and political landscape of the 1930s, pushing for women's rights, demanding reforms, traveling across the country, writing newspaper columns and speaking on the radio, developing plans to help unemployed miners in West Virginia and abolish slums in Washington, and lobbying both Congress and her husband. FDR used her as his eyes and ears and sometimes his conscience. He rebuffed her critics with a jaunty, "Well, that is my wife; I can't do anything about her." Indeed, Eleanor Roosevelt had become not merely the most prominent first lady in history

With an appointment in the National Youth Administration, the educator Mary McLeod Bethune was the highest-ranking African-American woman in the Roosevelt administration. She advised FDR on all racial matters and envisioned "dozens of Negro women coming after me, filling positions of trust and strategic importance."

but a force in her own right and a symbol of the growing importance of women in public life.

Minorities and the New Deal

Despite the move of African Americans into the Democratic Party, the New Deal's record on racial issues was limited. Although Roosevelt deplored racial abuses, he never pushed for civil rights legislation, fearing to antagonize southern congressional Democrats whose support he needed. For similar reasons, many New Deal programs discriminated against African Americans. The CCC segregated black workers; NRA codes so often specified lower wages and benefits for black workers relative to white workers or even excluded black workers from jobs that the black press claimed NRA stood for "Negro Run Around" or "Negroes Ruined Again." And racist officials discriminated in allocating federal relief. Atlanta, for instance, provided average monthly relief checks of $32.66 to white people but only $19.29 to black people.

Nonetheless, disproportionately poor and unemployed African Americans did benefit from the New Deal's welfare and economic programs. W. E. B. Du Bois asserted that "large numbers of colored people in the United States would have starved to death if it had not been for the Roosevelt poli-

cies," adding that the New Deal served to sharpen their sense of the value of citizenship by making clear the "direct connection between politics and industry, between government and work, [and] between voting and wages." And key New Dealers campaigned against racial discrimination. Eleanor Roosevelt prodded FDR to appoint black officials, wrote articles supporting racial equality, and flouted segregationist laws. Attacked by white racists, she was popular in the black community. Harry Hopkins and Harold Ickes also promoted equal rights. Ickes, a former president of Chicago's NAACP chapter, insisted that African Americans receive PWA relief jobs in proportion to their share of the population and ended segregation in the Department of the Interior, prompting other cabinet secretaries to follow suit. As black votes in northern cities became important, pragmatic New Dealers also began to pay attention to black needs.

African Americans themselves pressed for reforms. Civil rights groups protested discriminatory policies, including the unequal wage scales in the NRA codes and the CCC's limited enrollment of black youth. African Americans demonstrated against racial discrimination in hiring and their exclusion from federally financed construction projects.

In response, FDR took more interest in black economic and social problems. He prohibited discrimination in the WPA in 1935, and the NYA adopted enlightened racial policies. Roosevelt also appointed black people to important positions, including the first black federal judge. Many of these officials began meeting regularly at the home of Mary McLeod Bethune of the National Council of Negro Women. Dubbed the Black Cabinet, they worked with civil rights organizations, fought discrimination in government, influenced patronage, and stimulated black interest in politics.

The New Deal improved economic and social conditions for many African Americans. Black illiteracy dropped because of federal education projects, and the number of black college students and graduates more than doubled, in part because the NYA provided student aid to black colleges. New Deal relief and public health programs reduced black infant mortality rates and raised life expectancy rates. Conditions for black people continued to lag behind those for white people, and discrimination persisted, but the black switch to the Roosevelt coalition reflected the New Deal's benefits.

Native Americans also benefited from the New Deal. The depression had imposed further misery on a group already suffering from poverty, wretched health conditions, and the nation's lowest educational level. Many New Deal programs had limited applicability to Indians, but the CCC appealed to their interests and skills. More than 80,000 Native Americans received training in agriculture, forestry, and animal husbandry, along with basic academic subjects. CCC projects, together with those undertaken by the PWA and the WPA, built schools, hospitals, roads, and irrigation systems on reservations.

New Deal officials also refocused government Indian policy, which had undermined tribal authority and promoted assimilation by reducing Indian landholding and attacking Indian culture. Appointed commissioner of Indian affairs in 1933, John Collier prohibited interference with Native American religious or cultural life, directed the Bureau of Indian Affairs to employ more Native Americans, and prevented Indian schools from suppressing native languages and traditions.

Collier also persuaded Congress to pass the Indian Reorganization Act of 1934, often called the Indians' New Deal. The act guaranteed religious freedom, reestablished tribal self-government, and halted the sale of tribal lands. It also provided funds to expand Indian landholdings, support Indian students, and establish tribal businesses. But social and economic problems persisted on the isolated reservations, and white missionaries and business interests attacked Collier's reforms as atheistic and communistic. And not all Native Americans supported Collier's reforms, asserting that he, too, stereotyped Indians and their culture, and labeling his efforts as "back-to-the-blanket" policies designed to make Native American cultures historical commodities. Collier himself was disappointed by Congress's refusal to fund his more radical economic programs, acknowledging by the end of the decade that much more needed to be done for Native Americans. (See American Views, The Commissioner of the Bureau of Indian Affairs on the New Deal for Native Americans.)

Hispanic Americans received less assistance from the New Deal. Relief programs aided many Hispanics in California and the Southwest but ignored those who were not citizens. Moreover, local administrators often discriminated against Hispanics, especially by providing higher relief payments to Anglos. Finally, by excluding agricultural workers, neither the Social Security Act nor the Wagner Act gave Mexican Americans much protection or hope. Farm workers remained largely unorganized, exploited, and at the mercy of agribusinesses.

The New Deal: North, South, East, and West

"We are going to make a country," President Roosevelt declared, "in which no one is left out." And with that statement, along with his belief that the federal government must take the lead in building a new "economic constitutional order," FDR ensured that his New Deal programs and policies fanned out throughout the nation, bolstering the stock market and banking in New York, constructing public housing for poor white and African American families in most major cities, and building schools, roads, and bridges in every region of the United States. Ironically, the New Deal also offered special benefits to the South, which was traditionally averse to government activism, and to the West, which considered itself the land of rugged individualism.

The New Deal in the South. The New Deal's agricultural program boosted farm prices and income more in the South than any other region. By controlling cotton production, it also promoted diversification; its subsidies financed mechanization. The resulting modernization helped replace an archaic sharecropping system with an emergent agribusiness. The rural poor were displaced, but the South's agricultural economy advanced.

The New Deal also improved southern cities. FERA and WPA built urban sewer systems, airports, bridges, roads, and harbor facilities. Whereas northern cities had already constructed such facilities themselves—and were still paying off the debts these had incurred—the federal government largely paid for such modernization in the South, giving its cities an economic advantage.

Federal grants were supposed to be awarded to states in proportion to their own expenditures, but while southern politicians welcomed New Deal funds—"I'm gonna grab all I can for the state of Texas," said Governor Lee O'Daniel—they refused to contribute their share of the costs. Nationally, the federal proportion of FERA expenditures was 62 percent; in the South, it was usually 90 percent and never lower than 73 percent. Virginia officials refused to provide even 10 percent, declaring, "It takes people a long time to starve." Some southern cities and counties refused to contribute anything to relief, and Memphis spent less on relief—only 0.1 percent of its budget—than on maintaining public golf courses.

Federal money enabled southern communities to balance their budgets, preach fiscal orthodoxy, and maintain traditional claims of limited government. Federal officials complained about the South's "parasitic" behavior in accepting aid but not responsibility, and even southerners acknowledged the hypocrisy of the region's invocation of state's rights. "We recognize state boundaries when called on to give," noted the *Houston Press,* "but forget them when Uncle Sam is doing the giving."

The federal government had a particularly powerful impact on the South with the **Tennessee Valley Authority (TVA),** launched in 1933 (see Map 25–3). Coordinating activities across seven states, the TVA built dams to control floods and generate hydroelectric power, produced fertilizer, fostered agricultural and forestry development, encouraged conservation, improved navigation, and modernized school and health systems. Private utility companies denounced the TVA as socialistic, but most southerners supported it. Its major drawback was environmental damage that only became apparent later. Over a vast area of the South, it provided electricity for the first time.

The New Deal further expanded access to electricity by establishing the Rural Electrification Administration (REA) in 1935. Private companies had refused to extend power lines into the countryside because it was not profitable, consigning 90 percent of the nation's farms to drudgery and darkness. The REA revolutionized farm life by sponsoring rural nonprofit electric cooperatives. By 1941, 35 percent of American farms had electricity; by 1950, 78 percent. By providing electric power to light and heat homes and barns, pump

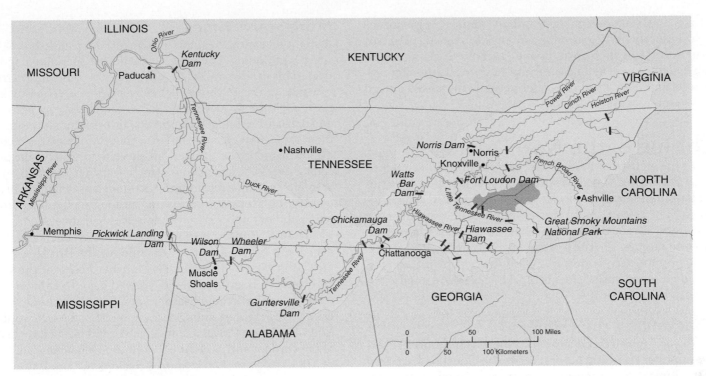

MAP 25-3   The Tennessee Valley Authority
By building dams and hydroelectric power plants, the TVA controlled flooding and soil erosion and generated electricity that did much to modernize a large region of the Upper South.

water, and run refrigerators, washing machines, and radios, one Arkansas newspaper concluded, the REA had made "a reality" of what had been only a "utopian dream."

The New Deal in the West. The New Deal also changed the West. Westerners received the most federal money per capita in welfare, relief projects, and loans. Like southerners, they accepted federal aid and clamored for more. Utah, which received the most federal relief funds per capita, was the nation's "prize 'gimme state,'" said one FERA official. Western farmers and cattle raisers were saved by federal payments, and even refugees from the Dust Bowl depended on relief assistance and medical care in federal camps.

The Bureau of Reclamation, established in 1902, emerged as one of the most important government agencies in the West. It built huge dams to control the western river systems and promote large-scale development. The Hoover Dam on the Colorado River between Nevada and Arizona, completed in 1935; the Grand Coulee Dam on the Columbia River in Washington, finished in 1941; and other giant projects prevented flooding, produced cheap hydroelectric power, and created reservoirs and canal systems to bring water to farms and cities. By furnishing capital and expertise, the government subsidized and stimulated western economic development, particularly the growth of agribusiness.

Westerners welcomed such assistance but rarely shared the federal goals of rational resource management. Instead, they often wanted to continue to exploit the land and re-

sented federal supervision as colonial control. In practice, however, the government worked in partnership with the West's agribusinesses and timber and petroleum industries.

The New Deal and Public Activism

Despite Hoover's fear that government responsibility would discourage local initiative, the 1930s witnessed an upsurge in activism. New Deal programs, in fact, often encouraged or empowered groups to shape public policy. Moreover, because the administration worried about centralization, some federal agencies fostered what New Dealers called "grassroots democracy." The AAA set up committees that ultimately included more than 100,000 people to implement agricultural policy and held referendums on crop controls; local advisory committees guided the various federal arts projects; federal management of the West's public grasslands mandated cooperation with associations of livestock raisers.

At times, local administration of national programs enabled groups to exploit federal policy for their own advantage. Wealthy planters shaped AAA practices at the expense of poor tenant farmers; local control of TVA projects excluded black people. But federal programs often allowed previously unrepresented groups to contest traditionally dominant interests. By requiring that public housing projects be initiated locally, for example, New Deal programs prompted labor unions, religious and civic groups, neighborhood associations, and civil rights groups to form associations to overcome the hostility of realtors and bankers to public housing. Often seeing greater opportunities for participation and influence in federal programs than in city and state governments, community groups campaigned to expand federal authority. In short, depression conditions and New Deal programs actually increased citizen involvement in public affairs.

Ebbing of the New Deal

After his victory in 1936, Roosevelt committed himself to further reforms. "I see one-third of a nation ill-housed, ill-clad, ill-nourished," he declared in his second inaugural address. "The test of our progress is not whether we add more to the abundance of those who have much; it is whether we provide enough for those who have too little." But determined opponents, continuing economic problems, and the president's own misjudgments blocked his reforms and deadlocked the New Deal.

Challenging the Court

Roosevelt regarded the Supreme Court as his most dangerous opponent. During his first term, the Court had declared several important measures unconstitutional. FDR complained that the justices held "horse-and-buggy" ideas about government that prevented the president and Congress from responding to changes. Indeed, most of the justices were elderly conservatives, appointed by Republicans and unsympathetic to an activist federal government. It seemed that the Court would also strike down the Second New Deal.

Emboldened by the 1936 landslide, Roosevelt decided to restructure the federal judiciary. In early 1937, he proposed legislation authorizing the president to name a new justice for each one serving past the age of 70. Additional justices, he said, would increase judicial efficiency. But his real goal was to appoint new justices more sympathetic to the New Deal.

His Court plan led to a divisive struggle. The proposal was perfectly legal: Congress had the authority, which it had used repeatedly, to change the number of justices on the Court. But Republicans and conservative Democrats attacked the plan as a scheme to "pack" the Court and subvert the separation of powers among the three branches of government. Some conservatives called the president a dictator, but even many liberals expressed reservations about the plan or FDR's lack of candor in proposing it.

The Court itself undercut support for FDR's proposal by upholding the Social Security and Wagner acts and minimum-wage legislation. Moreover, the retirement of a conservative justice allowed Roosevelt to name a sympathetic successor. Congress rejected Roosevelt's plan.

Roosevelt's challenge to the Court hurt the New Deal. It worried the public, split the Democratic Party, and revived conservatives. Opponents promptly attacked other New Deal policies, from support for unions to progressive taxation. Henceforth, a conservative coalition of Republicans and southern Democrats in Congress blocked FDR's reforms.

More Hard Times

A sharp recession, beginning in August 1937, added to Roosevelt's problems. The New Deal's deficit spending had reflected his desire to alleviate suffering, not a conviction that it would stimulate economic recovery. As the economy improved in 1936, Roosevelt decided to cut federal expenditures and balance the budget. But private investment and employment remained stagnant, and the economy plunged. A record decline in industrial production canceled the gains of the preceding two years, and unemployment leaped from 7 million to 11 million within a few months. Republicans delighted in attacking the "Roosevelt recession," although it stemmed from retrenchment policies they themselves had advocated.

In 1938, Roosevelt reluctantly increased spending. His decision was based on the principles of the British economist John Maynard Keynes. As Marriner Eccles of the Federal Reserve Board explained, the federal government had to serve as the "compensatory agent" in the economy—it would use deficit spending to increase demand and production when private investment declined, and would raise taxes to pay its debt and cool the economy when business activity became excessive. New appropriations for the PWA and other government programs revived the faltering economy, but neither FDR nor Congress would spend what was necessary to end the depression. Only the vast expenditures for World War II would bring full recovery.

Political Stalemate

The recession interrupted the momentum of the New Deal and strengthened its opponents. In late 1937, their leaders in Congress issued a "conservative manifesto" decrying New Deal fiscal, labor, and regulatory policies. Holding seniority in a Congress malapportioned in their favor, they blocked most of Roosevelt's reforms. None of his must legislation passed a special session of Congress in December. In 1938, Congress rejected tax reforms and reduced corporate taxes.

The few measures that passed were heavily amended. The Fair Labor Standards Act established maximum hours and minimum wages for workers but authorized so many exemptions that one New Dealer asked "whether anyone is subject to this bill." The Farm Tenancy Act established the Farm Security Administration to lend tenant farmers and agricultural laborers money with which to acquire their own land, but appropriations were severely limited. The National Housing Act created the United States Housing Authority to finance slum clearance and public housing projects, but its total funds were less than the amount needed to demolish tenements in New York City alone.

To protect the New Deal, Roosevelt turned again to the public, with whom he remained immensely popular. In the 1938 Democratic primaries, he campaigned against the New Deal's conservative opponents. But FDR could not transfer his personal popularity to the political newcomers he supported. What his foes attacked as a purge failed. Roosevelt lost further political leverage when the Republicans gained 75 seats in the House and seven in the Senate and 13 governorships.

The 1938 elections did not repudiate the New Deal, for the Democrats retained majorities in both houses of Congress. But the Republican revival and the survival of the conservative southern Democrats guaranteed that the New Deal had gone as far as it ever would. With Roosevelt in the White House and his opponents controlling Congress, the New Deal ended in political stalemate.

Good Neighbors and Hostile Forces

Even before FDR's conservative opponents derailed the New Deal, the president felt their impact in the area of foreign policy. Isolationists in Congress counseled against any U.S. involvement in world affairs and appealed to the growing national disillusionment with America's participation in the Great War to support their position.

Responding to the spreading popular belief that World War I had been fought to protect the fortunes of financiers and munitions makers, Republican Senator Gerald Nye established a committee in 1934 to investigate the origins of U.S. involvement in what many Americans now termed the European War. For two years, the Nye Committee sensationally exposed the greed of big business and intimated that President Woodrow Wilson had gone to war to save profits for capitalists—and not democracy for the world. Jobless and homeless Americans reacted angrily to the committee's findings, and public sentiment against fighting another foreign war hardened. Moreover, Roosevelt himself, although not an isolationist, believed that the gravity of the nation's economic depression warranted a primary focus on domestic recovery, and in the early years of his presidency, took few international initiatives.

The actions he did take related directly to salvaging America's desperate economy. As the depression worsened in 1933, American businesses searched for new markets throughout the world, and key business leaders informed FDR that they would welcome the opportunity to expand trade to the Soviet Union. Moscow was also eager to renew ties to the United States, and President Roosevelt extended formal recognition of the Soviet Union in November 1933. His decision was not without controversy; even his own mother denounced him for it. Still worse, the anticipated trade did not occur, although FDR believed that establishing diplomatic ties with the Soviets also served as a warning to Japan and its expansionist appetite.

Enhancing trade opportunities and rescuing the economy from the damage wrought by high tariffs figured prominently in Roosevelt's policies in the Western Hemisphere. In large measure, Roosevelt merely extended the Good Neighbor policy begun by his predecessor. Hoover had abandoned the U.S. policy of interventionism, and by the time he left office in March 1933, all U.S. troops had been removed from Latin America. Still, the Great Depression strained U.S.-Latin American relations, sending economic shock waves throughout Central and South America and, in several instances, helping propel to power ruthless dictators who ruled with iron fists and U.S. support. Moreover, although FDR continued the policy of military nonintervention, his displeasure with the 1933 election of a radical as president of Cuba led him to support a coup there that resulted in the coming to power of the infamous dictator Fulgencio Batista. The Batista era lasted until he was overthrown by Fidel Castro in 1959.

To symbolize that the United States was a "good neighbor," FDR visited the Caribbean in 1934, receiving an enthusiastic reception, and in 1936, he broke new ground by becoming the first U.S. president to sail to South America. He also worked to encourage trade by reducing tariffs. Between 1929 and 1933, the volume of trade worldwide had collapsed by 40 percent and American exports had plummeted by 60 percent. Eager to increase American exports, FDR's secretary of state, Cordell Hull, who, like Roosevelt, believed in the need for lower tariffs, finalized trade agreements with numerous Latin American nations that allowed "most favored nation" status and resulted in sharply increasing U.S. exports to its southern neighbors. Good neighbors were also good trading partners.

Neutrality and Fascism

Outside the hemisphere, during his first term as president, Roosevelt generally followed the policy of avoiding involvement in Europe's political, economic, and social problems. But the aggressive actions of Adolf Hitler in Germany ultimately led Roosevelt to a different position, and in the latter part of the decade, he faced the task of educating the American public, still resentful of U.S. participation in World War I, about the fascist danger that was spreading in Europe.

Hitler came to power in 1933, shortly before FDR entered the White House, and he pledged to restore German pride and nationalism in the aftermath of the Versailles Treaty. As the leader of the National Socialist Workers Party, or Nazis, Hitler established a **fascist government**—a one-party dictatorship closely aligned with corporate interests, committed to a "biological world evolution," and determined to establish a new empire, the Third Reich. He vowed to eliminate Bolshevik radicalism and purify the German "race" through the elimination of those he deemed undesirable, especially targeting Jews, the group Hitler blamed for most, if not all, Germany's ills.

Others aided the spread of fascism. Italian leader Benito Mussolini, who had assumed power in 1922 and envisaged emulating the power and prestige of the Roman Empire, brutally attacked Ethiopia in 1935. The following year, a young fascist military officer, Francisco Franco, led an uprising in Spain, and with the assistance of Italy and Germany, successfully ousted the Spanish Republic and its loyalist supporters

On November 9, 1938, Nazi Germany launched an attack on Jews, destroying their businesses and burning their synagogues. This street scene in Berlin shows the shattered windows of Jewish businesses. Nazi leader Joseph Goebbels recorded the event, known as Kristallnacht, in his diary: "Yesterday: Berlin. There, all proceeded fantastically. One fire after another. It is good that way.... 100 dead. But no German property damaged."

by 1939 to create an authoritarian government. Meanwhile, Hitler implemented his plan of conquest: He remilitarized the Rhineland in 1936, and in 1938 he annexed Austria.

The aggressive actions of Germany and Italy failed to eclipse U.S. fears of becoming involved in another European war. Congress passed Neutrality Acts designed to continue America's trade with its world partners but prohibit the president from taking sides in the mounting European crisis. The first act, passed in 1935, prohibited Americans from traveling to a war zone, banned loans to belligerent nations, and instituted an embargo on armaments to belligerents. In 1936 Congress extended the legislation for another year and then in 1937 made the neutrality prohibitions permanent, with the addition of a "cash-and-carry" provision that required belligerent nations to pay for American goods in advance of shipment. President Roosevelt reluctantly signed the bill into law, but continued to work to heighten public awareness of the dangers of Nazism.

Appeasement and more neutrality.   After annexing Austria, Hitler pushed again in 1938 when he demanded the Sudetenland from Czechoslovakia. The French and the British refused to stand up to Hitler, following instead a policy of appeasement. Meeting in Munich in September 1938, the leaders of England and France abandoned their security obligations to the Czechs, yielding the Sudetenland to Hitler in exchange for a weak promise of no more annexations.

In America, too, the sentiment was for peace at all costs, and isolationism permeated the halls of Congress. Indeed, Hitler himself did not regard the United States as a threat to his expansionist plans: "America," he said in 1939, "is not dangerous to us." Hitler held FDR in low esteem and denounced America as a racially mixed nation of intellectual inferiors. "Transport a German to Kiev," Hitler declared, "and he remains a perfect German. But transplant him to Miami, and you make a degenerate out of him—in other words, an American."

Isolationism compounded by anti-Semitism and by the divisions between the leaders of the American Jewish community combined to ensure that the United States would not become a haven for Jews suffering under Nazi brutality. News of Nazi atrocities against Austrian Jews in 1938 shocked the American press, and Hitler's violent pogrom, known as *Kristallnacht* ("Night of the Broken Glass"), conducted against Jews throughout Germany in November 1938, added fresh proof of Nazi cruelty. Although the United States recalled its ambassador from Berlin to protest the pogrom (in response, Germany recalled its ambassador from Washington), it did not alter its restrictive immigration-quota system, the 1924 National Origins Act, to provide refuge for German Jews. Unchallenged, Hitler pressed on with his campaign of persecution and terror against those he termed "inferior races" and "anti-socials," herding Jews, Slavs, homosexuals, and the handicapped into concentration camps. As early as 1933, Hitler established the first concentration camp at Dachau, and by 1939, camps in Germany held over 25,000 people.

As Europe edged closer to war, the relationship between the United States and Japan, periodically tense in the twentieth century, became more strained. Japan resented U.S. economic interests in East Asia and was offended by the policy of excluding Japanese immigrants. The United States regarded Japan's desires for empire as threatening but also needed Japan as a trading partner, especially in the economically depressed 1930s. Consequently, in September 1931, when Japan seized Manchuria, the United States did little more than denounce the action. Again in 1937, after Japanese troops attacked Chinese forces north of Beijing and outright war began between Japan and China, the United States merely condemned the action. That same year, President Roosevelt denounced "the epidemic of world lawlessness," indicting the aggressiveness of Italy, Germany, and Japan and calling for a "quarantine" of aggressors, but he continued his policy of refusing to risk war with Japan.

Edging Toward Involvement

After the Munich agreement, President Roosevelt moved away from domestic reform toward preparedness for war, fearful that conflict in Europe was unavoidable and determined to revise the neutrality laws. In his State of the Union address in January 1939, FDR explained that America's neutrality laws might "actually give aid to an aggressor and deny it to the victim." By the fall of that year, he had won support for eliminating the prohibition on arms sales and adding armaments to the list of cash-and-carry items—a revision that would enable the United States to provide important assistance to Britain and France in the winter of 1939–1940. Hitler's defiance of the Munich agreement in Czechoslovakia, overrunning Prague by March 1939, merely anticipated his next move toward Poland and also convinced the British and the French that war was imminent.

Conclusion

The Great Depression and the New Deal mark a major divide in American history. The depression cast doubt on the traditional practices, policies, and attitudes that underlay not only the nation's economy but also its social and political institutions and relationships. The New Deal brought only partial economic recovery. However, its economic policies, from banking and securities regulation to unemployment compensation, farm price supports, and minimum wages, created barriers against another depression. The gradual adoption of compensatory spending policies expanded the government's role in the economy. Responding to the failures of private organizations and state and local governments, the federal government assumed the obligation to provide social welfare. The New Deal established pensions for the elderly, aid for dependent mothers and children and the blind, public housing for the poor, and public health services. Although these programs were limited in scope and access, they helped establish a responsible government. "Better the occasional faults of a Government that lives in a spirit of charity," Roosevelt warned, "than the constant omission of a Government frozen in the ice of its own indifference."

Roosevelt also expanded the role of the presidency. As his White House took the initiative for defining public policy, drafting legislation, lobbying Congress, and communicating with the nation, it became the model for all subsequent presidents. Not only was the president's power increased, but Roosevelt made the federal government, rather than state or local governments, the focus of public interest and expectations. Under Hoover, one secretary had handled all the White House mail; under FDR, a staff of 50 was overwhelmed.

Roosevelt and the New Deal also revitalized the Democratic Party, drawing minorities, industrial workers, and previously uninvolved citizens into a coalition with white southerners. The tensions in so broad-based a coalition sometimes prevented effective public policies, but the coalition made the Democrats the dominant national party.

Political constraints explain some of the New Deal's failures. Conservative southern Democrats and northern Republicans limited its efforts to curtail racial discrimination or protect the rural and urban poor. But Roosevelt and other New Dealers were often constrained by their own vision, refusing to consider the massive deficit spending necessary to end the depression or not recognizing the need to end gender discrimination. But if the New Deal did not bring the revolution its conservative critics claimed—it did not redistribute wealth or income—it did change American life.

By the end of the 1930s, as international relations deteriorated, FDR was already considering a shift, as he later said, from Dr. New Deal to Dr. Win-the-War. Reluctant to move beyond public opinion that did not want war and limited by neutrality legislation, FDR cautiously led the nation toward war—this time against an enemy far more threatening than the Great Depression. Ironically, only then would President Roosevelt end the depression that had ravaged the nation for nearly a decade.

Review Questions

1. Why did President Hoover's emphasis on voluntarism fail to resolve the problems of the Great Depression in the United States?

2. Describe the relief programs of the New Deal. What were they designed to accomplish? What were their achievements and their limitations?

3. What were the major criticisms of the early New Deal? How accurate were those charges?

4. How did the policies of the New Deal shape the constituency and the prospects of the Democratic Party in the 1930s?

5. Describe the conflict between management and labor in the 1930s. What were the major issues and motivations? How did the two sides differ in resources and tactics, and how and why did these factors change over time?

6. How did the role of the federal government change in the 1930s? What factors were responsible for the changes?

Key Terms

Bonus Army (p. 704)

Congress of Industrial Organizations (CIO) (p. 713)

Fascist government (p. 719)

Federal Deposit Insurance Corporation (FDIC) (p. 705)

Fireside chat (p. 705)

Great Depression (p. 697)

Hoovervilles (p. 698)

New Deal (p. 695)

Securities and Exchange Commission (SEC) (p. 705)

Tennessee Valley Authority (TVA) (p. 716)

Recommended Reading

Conkin, Paul. *The New Deal,* 3rd ed. (1992). A brief and insightful critique of FDR's programs.

Fraser, Steve, and Gary Gerstle, eds. *The Rise and Fall of the New Deal Order, 1930–1980* (1989). A valuable collection of essays that surveys the New Deal and explores its legacy.

Kennedy, David. *Freedom from Fear: The American People in Depression and War* (1999). The most recent and comprehensive survey of the period.

Leuchtenburg, William. *Franklin D. Roosevelt and the New Deal, 1932–1940* (1963). The best single-volume study of FDR's policies during his first two terms as president.

Where to Learn More

- **Center for New Deal Studies, Roosevelt University, Chicago, Illinois.** The center contains political memorabilia, photographs, papers, and taped interviews dealing with Franklin D. Roosevelt and the New Deal; it also sponsors an annual lecture series about the Roosevelt legacy. www.roosevelt.edu/newdeal/

- **Franklin D. Roosevelt Home and Presidential Library, Hyde Park, New York.** The Roosevelt home, furnished with family heirlooms, and the spacious grounds, where FDR is buried, personalize the president and provide insights into his career. The nearby library has displays and exhibitions about Roosevelt's presidency, and the Eleanor Roosevelt Wing is dedicated to her career. www.fdrlibrary.marist.edu

- **Eleanor Roosevelt National Historic Site, Hyde Park, New York.** These two cottages, where Eleanor Roosevelt worked and, after 1945, lived, contain her furniture and memorabilia. Visitors can also watch a film biography of ER and tour the grounds of this retreat where she entertained personal friends and world leaders. www.nps.gov/elro.

- **New Deal Network.** A valuable guide to the study of the Great Depression and the New Deal with a rich collection of photographs and documents. www.newdeal.feri.org

Study Resources

For study resources for this chapter, go to www.myhistorylab.com and choose *The American Journey*. You will find a wealth of study and review material for this chapter, including pre- and post-tests, customized study plan, key term review flash cards, interactive map and document activities, and documents for analysis.

The United States fought Germany and Japan as part of an alliance known as the United Nations. This government poster shows the flags of the many nations advancing together, the Stars and Stripes, the Union Jack of Great Britain, and the hammer and sickle of the Soviet Union in the most prominent positions.

World War II 1939–1945

26

December, 1942

The scene [under the stadium] at The University of Chicago would have been confusing to an outsider, if he could have eluded the security guards and gained admittance. He would have seen only what appeared to be a crude pile of black bricks and wooden timbers....

Finally, the day came when we were ready to run the experiment. We gathered on a balcony about 10 feet above the floor of the large room in which the structure had been erected. Beneath us was a young scientist, George Weil, whose duty it was to handle the last control rod that was holding the reaction in check....

Finally, it was time to remove the control rods. Slowly, Weil started to withdraw the main control rod. On the balcony, we watched the indicators which measured the neutron count and told us how rapidly the disintegration of the uranium atoms under their neutron bombardment was proceeding.

At 11:35 A.M., the counters were clicking rapidly. Then, with a loud clap, the automatic control rods slammed home. The safety point had been set too low.

It seemed a good time to eat lunch. During lunch everyone was thinking about the experiment but nobody talked much about it.

At 2:30, Weil pulled out the control rod in a series of measured adjustments. Shortly after, the intensity shown by the indicators began to rise at a slow but ever-increasing rate. At this moment we knew that the self-sustaining [nuclear] reaction was under way.

The event was not spectacular, no fuses burned, no lights flashed. But to us it meant that release of atomic energy on a large scale would be only a matter of time.

Enrico Fermi, in *The First Reactor* (Washington, DC: U.S. Department of Energy, 1982).

PEARSON
myhistorylab

Personal Journeys Online

- Patricia Cain Koehler, *Oregon Historical Quarterly* (Fall 1990). Helping to build aircraft carriers during World War II.

- Leon Overstreet in S. L. Sanger, *Working on the Bomb: An Oral History of World War II Hanford* (1995). A construction worker remembers the Manhattan Project.

- Bill Mauldin, in Studs Terkel, *The Good War* (1985). The famous cartoonist explains the origins of his characters Willie and Joe, the typical WWII G.I.s.

Enrico Fermi was describing the first controlled nuclear chain reaction—the critical experiment from which atomic weapons and atomic power would soon develop. Fermi had emigrated to escape the growing political repression of Fascist Italy. In 1938, he had received the Nobel Prize in physics. While in Stockholm, Sweden, to accept the prize, he and his family put secret plans into action and went to the United States rather than return to Italy. In 1942, after the United States joined the ongoing global conflict of World War II, Fermi was put in charge of nuclear fission research at the University of Chicago and played a leading role in efforts to develop an atomic bomb. The following year found Fermi, other atomic scientists, and their families at Los Alamos, a science city that the government built hurriedly on a high plateau in northern New Mexico, where isolation was supposed to ensure secrecy and help the United States win the race with Nazi Germany to develop atomic weapons.

The instant city was a cross between a cheap subdivision and an army camp for deeply engaged but eccentric scientists. "I always pitied our Army doctors for their thankless job," Enrico's wife, Laura Fermi, later wrote: "They had prepared for the emergencies of the battlefields, and they were faced instead with a high-strung bunch of men, women, and children…high-strung because we were too many of a kind, too close to one another, and we were all crackpots." Scientists spent their days designing a bomb that would change world politics and returned to dinners cooked on wood-burning stoves.

The Fermis were not the only family to give Los Alamos a multinational flavor. Laura remembered that it was "all one big family and all one big accent.…Everybody in science was there, both from the United States and from almost all European countries." British and Canadians worked alongside U.S. scientists. So did refugees from Europe, their presence making Los Alamos the most distinguished assemblage of physicists in the world (Laura Fermi later wrote about them in the book *Illustrious Immigrants*). Niels Bohr had fled Denmark to escape the Nazis. Edward Teller was a Hungarian who had studied in Germany. Hans Bethe had left Germany, and Stanislaus Ulam was the only member of his family to survive the Nazi conquest of Poland. Absent were scientists from the Soviet Union, which was bearing the worst of the fighting against Germany but was carefully excluded from the secret of the atomic bomb.

The internationalism of Los Alamos mirrored the larger war effort. Japan's attack on Pearl Harbor in December 1941 thrust the United States into a war that spanned the globe. America's allies against Japan in the Pacific and East Asia included Great Britain, Australia, and China. In Europe, its allies against Nazi Germany and Fascist Italy included Great Britain, the Soviet Union, and

more than 20 other nations. The scientists racing to perfect the atomic bomb knew that victory was far from certain. Germany and Japan had piled one conquest on another since the late 1930s, and they continued to seize new territories in 1942. Allied defeat in a few key battles could have resulted in a standoff or an Axis victory. A new weapon might end the war more quickly or make the difference between victory and defeat.

The war's domestic impacts were as profound as its international consequences. The race to build an atomic bomb was only one part of a vast effort to harness the resources of the United States to the war effort. The war highlighted racial inequalities, gave women new opportunities, and fostered growth in the South and West. By devastating the nation's commercial rivals, compelling workers to retrain and factories to modernize, World War II left the United States dominant in the world economy. It also increased the size and scope of the federal government and built an alliance among the armed forces, big business, and science that helped shape postwar America.

The Dilemmas of Neutrality

Americans in the 1930s wanted no part of another overseas war. According to a 1937 Gallup Poll, 70 percent thought that it had been a mistake for the United States to fight in 1917. Despite two years of German victories and a decade of Japanese aggression against China, opinion polls in the fall of 1941 showed that a majority of voters still hoped to avoid war. President Roosevelt's challenge was to lead the United States toward rearmament and support for Great Britain and China without alarming a reluctant public.

The Roots of War

The roots of World War II can be found in the aftereffects of World War I. The peace settlement created a set of small new nations in eastern Europe that were vulnerable to aggression by their much larger neighbors, Germany and the Soviet Union (more formally, the Union of Soviet Socialist Republics, or USSR). Italy and Japan thought that the Treaty of Versailles had not recognized their stature as world powers. Many Germans were convinced that Germany had been betrayed rather than defeated in 1918. In the 1930s, economic crisis undermined an already shaky political order. Unemployment rose in every country, and the level of international trade dropped by two-thirds. Economic hardship and political instability fueled the rise of right-wing dictatorships that offered territorial expansion by military conquest as the way redress old rivalries, dominate trade, and gain access to raw materials.

CHRONOLOGY

1931	Japan invades Manchuria.
1933	Hitler takes power in Germany.
1935	Congress passes first of three neutrality acts. Italy invades Ethiopia.
1936	Germany and Italy form the Rome-Berlin Axis. Civil war erupts in Spain.
1937	Japan invades China.
1938	Germany absorbs Austria. Munich agreement between Germany, Britain, and France.
1939	Germany and the Soviet Union sign a non-agression pact. Germany absorbs Czechoslovakia. Germany invades Poland; Great Britain and France declare war on Germany.
1940	Germany conquers Denmark, Norway, Belgium, the Netherlands, and France. Japan, Germany, and Italy sign the Tripartite Pact. Germany bombs England in the Battle of Britain. The United States begins to draft men into the armed forces. Franklin Roosevelt wins an unprecedented third term.
1941	The United States begins a lend-lease program to make military equipment available to Great Britain and later the Soviet Union. The Fair Employment Practices Committee is established. Germany invades the Soviet Union. Roosevelt and Churchill issue the Atlantic Charter. Japan attacks U.S. military bases in Hawaii.
1942	American forces in the Philippines surrender to Japan.

	President Roosevelt authorizes the removal and internment of Japanese Americans living in four western states. Naval battles in the Coral Sea and off the island of Midway blunt Japanese expansion. U.S. forces land in North Africa. Soviet forces encircle a German army at Stalingrad. The first sustained and controlled nuclear chain reaction takes place at the University of Chicago.
1943	U.S. and British forces invade Italy, which makes terms with the Allies. Race conflict erupts in riots in Detroit, New York, and Los Angeles. The landing of Marines on Tarawa initiates the island-hopping strategy. U.S. war production peaks. Roosevelt, Churchill, and Stalin confer at Tehran.
1944	Allied forces land in Normandy. The U.S. Navy destroys Japanese sea power in the battles of the Philippine Sea and Leyte Gulf. The Battle of the Bulge is the last tactical setback for the Allies.
1945	Roosevelt, Stalin, and Churchill meet at Yalta to plan the postwar world. The United States takes the Pacific islands of Iwo Jima and Okinawa. Franklin Roosevelt dies; Harry S. Truman becomes president. Germany surrenders to the United States, Great Britain, and the Soviet Union. The United Nations is organized at an international meeting in San Francisco. Potsdam Conference. Japan surrenders after the detonation of atomic bombs over Hiroshima and Nagasaki.

Japanese internal propaganda in the 1930s stressed the need to rebuild Japan's greatness. Japanese nationalists believed that the United States, Britain, and France had treated Japan unfairly after World War I, despite its participation against Germany. They believed that Japan should expel the French, British, Dutch, and Americans from Asia and create a **Greater East Asia Co-Prosperity Sphere,** in which Japan gave the orders and other Asian peoples complied. Seizing the Chinese province of Manchuria to expand an East Asian empire that already included Korea and Taiwan emboldened Japan's military in 1931. A full-scale invasion of China followed in 1937. Japan took many of the key cities and killed tens of thousands of civilians in the "rape of Nanking,"

but failed to dislodge the government of Jiang Jieshi (Chiang Kai-shek) and settled into a war of attrition.

Italian aggression embroiled Africa and the Mediterranean. The Fascist dictator Benito Mussolini had sent arms and troops to aid General Francisco Franco's right-wing rebels in Spain. The three-year civil war, which ended with Franco's victory in 1939, became a bloody testing ground for new German military tactics and German and Italian ambitions against democratic Europe.

In Germany, Adolf Hitler mixed the desire to reassert national pride and power after the defeat of World War I with an ideology of racial hatred. Coming to power by constitutional means in 1933, Hitler quickly consolidated his grip by destroying opposition parties and made himself the German Führer, or absolute leader. Proclaiming the start of a thousand-year Reich ("empire"), he combined the historic German interest in eastward expansion with a long tradition of racialist thought about German superiority. In the Nazi scheme, Germany and other northern European nations ranked above the Slavs of eastern Europe, who were to be pushed aside to provide more territory for a growing German population.

Special targets of Nazi hatred were the Jews, who were prominent in German business and professional life but soon faced persecution aimed at driving them from the country. In 1935, the Nuremberg Laws denied civil rights to Jews and the campaign against them intensified. On November 9, 1938, in vicious attacks across Germany that became known as *Kristallnacht* ("Night of the Broken Glass"), Nazi thugs rounded up, beat, and murdered Jews, smashed property, and burned synagogues. The Nazi government began expropriating Jewish property and excluded Jews from most employment.

Germany and Italy formed the Rome-Berlin Axis in October 1936 and the Tripartite Pact with Japan in 1940, leading to the term **Axis Powers** to describe the aggressor nations. Political dissidents in all three nations had already been suppressed. Mussolini boasted of burying the "putrid corpse of liberty." Politicians in Japan feared assassination if they spoke against the army, and the Thought Police intimidated the public. Hitler's Germany, however, was the most repressive. The Nazi concentration camp began as a device for political terrorism, where socialists and other dissidents and "antisocials"—homosexuals and beggars—could be separated from "pure" Germans. In the camps, the inmates were overworked and abused. Hitler decreed that opponents should disappear into "night and fog." Soon the systematic discrimination and concentration camps would evolve into massive forced-labor camps and then into hellish extermination camps.

Hitler's War in Europe

After annexing Austria through a coup and seizing and slicing up Czechoslovakia, Germany demonstrated the worthlessness of the Munich agreement by invading Poland on September 1, 1939. Britain and France, Poland's allies, declared war on Germany but could not stop the German war machine. Western journalists covering the three-week conquest of Poland coined the term ***Blitzkrieg,*** or "lightning war," to describe the German tactics. Armored divisions with tanks and motorized infantry punched holes in defensive positions and raced forward 30 or 40 miles per day. Dive

bombers blasted defenses. Portable radios coordinated the tanks, trucks, and motorcycles. Ground forces with horse-drawn artillery and supply wagons encircled the stunned defenders.

Hitler's greatest advantage was the ability to attack when and where he chose. From September 1939 to October 1941, Germany marched from victory to victory (see Map 26–1). Striking from a central position against scattered enemies, Hitler chose the targets and timing of each new front: eastward to smash Poland in September 1939; northward to conquer Denmark and Norway in April and May 1940; westward to defeat the Netherlands, Belgium, and France in May and June 1940, an attack that Italy also joined; southward into the Balkans, enlisting Hungary, Romania, and Bulgaria as allies and conquering Yugoslavia and Greece in April and May 1941. Hitler also launched the Battle of Britain in the second half of 1940. German planes bombarded Britain mercilessly, in an unsuccessful effort to pound the British into submission.

Hitler gambled once too often in June 1941. Having failed to knock Britain out of the war, he invaded the Soviet Union. The attack caught the Red Army off guard. Germany and the USSR had signed a nonagression pact in 1939, and the Soviets had helped to dismember Poland. The Soviet dictator Joseph Stalin had disregarded warnings of a German buildup as a British attempt to goad him into war with Germany. Hitler hoped that smashing the USSR and seizing its vast resources would make Germany invincible. From June until December 1941, more than 4 million Germans, Italians, Hungarians, and Romanians pushed through Belarus, Ukraine, and western Russia. They encircled and captured entire Soviet armies. Before desperate Soviet counterattacks

The raspy-voiced Adolf Hitler had a remarkable ability to stir the German people. He and his inner circle made skillful use of propaganda, exploiting German resentment over the country's defeat in World War I and, with carefully staged mass rallies, such as this event in 1938, inspiring an emotional conviction of national greatness.

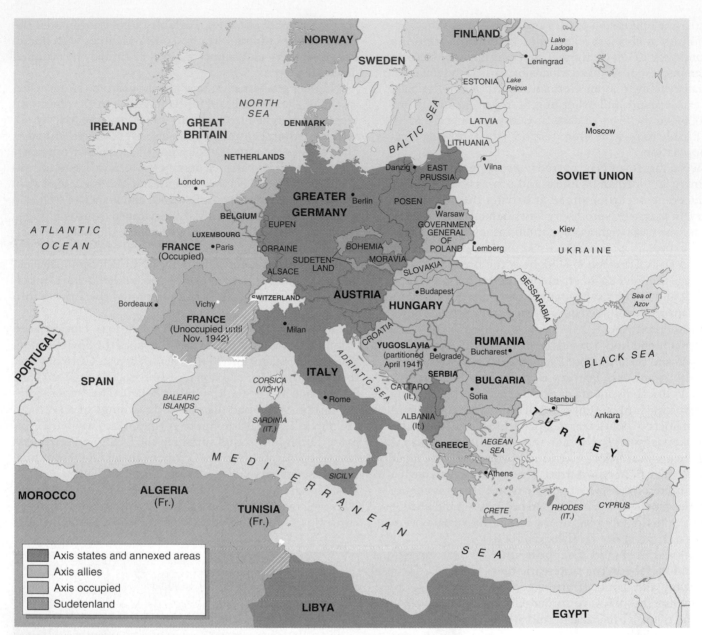

MAP 26–1   Axis Europe, 1941, on the Eve of Hitler's Invasion of the Soviet Union
After almost two years of war, the Axis powers controlled most of Europe, from the Atlantic Ocean to the Soviet border through annexation, military conquest, and alliances. Failure to force Britain to make peace caused Hitler to look eastward in 1941 to attempt the conquest of the Soviet Union.

and a bitter winter stopped the German columns, they had reached the outskirts of Moscow and expected to finish the job in the spring.

Trying to Keep Out

"We Must Keep Out!" shouted the September 7, 1939, *Chicago Daily News*. As war erupted in Europe, most Americans wanted to avoid foreign quarrels. People who opposed intervention in the European conflict were sometimes called isolationists, but they considered themselves realists who remembered the lessons of World War I. For more than two

years after the invasion of Poland, strong sentiment against intervention shaped public debate and limited President Roosevelt's ability to help Britain and its allies.

Much of the emotional appeal of neutrality came from disillusionment with the American crusade in World War I, which had failed to make the world safe for democracy. Many opponents of intervention wanted the United States to protect its traditional spheres of interest in Latin America and the Pacific. The aviator Charles A. Lindbergh spoke for many when he argued that the best way to ensure the safety of the United States was to conserve resources to defend the

Western Hemisphere. Like George Washington, whose Farewell Address they quoted, they wanted to avoid becoming entangled in the perpetual quarrels of the European nations.

Congressional hearings by the Nye committee on munitions manufacturers and financiers had strengthened antiwar leanings. Between 1935 and 1937, Congress had passed five neutrality acts, which forbade arms sales and limited economic relations with nations at war. Other legislation prohibited loans to nations that had not paid their World War I debts (including France and Great Britain). Noninterventionists spanned the political spectrum from left-leaning labor unions to conservative business tycoons like Henry Ford. The country's ethnic variety also complicated U.S. responses. Nazi aggression ravaged the homelands of Americans of Polish, Czech, Greek, and Norwegian ancestry. In contrast, 2.7 million Irish Americans, resentful of centuries of English rule over Ireland, had mixed feelings. More than 5 million German Americans remembered the anti-German sentiment of World War I, while many of the 4.6 million Italian Americans admired Mussolini. Any move to intervene in Europe had to take these different views into account, meaning that Roosevelt had to move slowly and carefully in his effort to align the United States on the side of Britain.

Edging Toward Intervention

Despite the Nazi triumphs, nonintervention had direct emotional appeal. The case for supporting beleaguered Britain and China, by contrast, rested on abstract values like the worth of free societies and free markets. Still, Roosevelt's appeals to democratic values gained support in 1939 and 1940. Radio broadcasts from England describing London under German bombing heightened the sense of imperiled freedom. The importance of open markets also bolstered interventionism. As Roosevelt pointed out, "Freedom to trade is essential to our economic life. We do not eat all the food we produce; we do not burn all the oil we can pump; we do not use all the goods we can manufacture." U.S. business leaders had little doubt that Axis victories would bring economic instability and require crushing defense budgets to protect Fortress America.

Because 85 percent of the American people agreed that the nation should fight only if it was directly attacked, Roosevelt had to chip away at neutrality, educating, arguing, and taking one step at a time. The first step came in October 1939. A month-long congressional debate inspired millions of letters and telegrams in favor of keeping the arms embargo against warring nations. Nevertheless, the lawmakers reluctantly allowed arms sales to belligerent nations on a "cash-and-carry" basis, to avoid expanding European debts. In control of the Atlantic, France and Britain were the only expected customers.

Isolationism and anti-Semitism help to explain why the United States accepted only a few thousand Jewish refugees. American law strictly limited the numbers of Europeans who could enter the United States, and Congress in 1939 declined to authorize the entry outside the quotas of 20,000 Jewish children. Bureaucrats at the State Department blocked entry to "undesirables," such as left-wing opponents of Hitler, and were unsympathetic to Jewish refugees. In 1939, officials turned the passenger ship *St. Louis* away from Miami and forced its 950 German Jewish refugees back to Europe. FDR made small gestures, such as allowing 15,000 German and Austrian refugees, including many scientists and artists, to remain in the United States on visitor permits, but the public supported restrictions on immigration. The consequences of these restrictions would prove tragic later in the war, as the Nazis began systematic genocide of European Jews.

The collapse of France and U.S. rearmament.   Despite the efforts of noninterventionists, in 1940 the United States edged closed to involvement in the war. In May, the Roosevelt administration established the National Defense Advisory Commission and the Council of National Defense to deal with strategic planning for war. The sudden defeat of France, which had survived four years of German attacks in World War I, made the new war seem far more serious. In the summer of 1940, Congress voted to expand the army to 2 million men, build 19,000 new warplanes, and add 150 ships to the navy. Lawmakers approved the nation's first peacetime draft in September, requiring 16.5 million men between the ages of 21 and 35 to register for military service on October 16.

In the same month, the United States concluded a destroyer deal with Britain. The British were desperate for small, maneuverable warships to guard imports of food and war materials against German submarines. The Americans had long wanted additional air and naval bases to guard the approaches to North America. Roosevelt met both needs by trading 50 old destroyers for the use of bases on British territories in the Caribbean, Bermuda, and Newfoundland.

The Election of 1940.   In the presidential election of 1940, foreign policy was secondary. Wendell Willkie, the Republican nominee, unlike many in his party, shared Roosevelt's belief in the importance of aid to Britain. The big campaign issue was therefore whether FDR's unprecedented try for a third term represented arrogance or a legitimate concern for continuity in a time of peril. The election was tighter than in 1932 or 1936, but Roosevelt received 55 percent of the vote. The president pledged that no Americans would fight in a foreign war. But if the United States were attacked, he said privately, the war would no longer be "foreign."

The Brink of War

After the election, FDR and his advisers edged the United States toward stronger support of Britain and put pressure on Japan. In January 1941, Roosevelt proposed the lend-lease program, which allowed Britain to "borrow" military equipment for the duration of the war. Roosevelt compared the program to lending a garden hose to a neighbor whose house had caught fire. Senator Robert Taft of Ohio countered that it was more like lending chewing gum, since you wouldn't want it back after it was used. Behind the scheme was Britain's inability to pay for American goods. "Well, boys," their ambassador explained to a group of reporters, "Britain's broke."

The **Lend-Lease Act** triggered intense political debate. The Committee to Defend America by Aiding the Allies argued the administration's position. In opposition, the strongly isolationist America First Committee claimed that lend-lease would allow the president to declare anything a "defense article." Their spokesperson, Charles Lindbergh, protested that the United States should not surrender weapons that it might need to defend itself. Congress finally passed the measure in March 1941, authorizing the president to lease, lend, or otherwise dispose of arms and other equipment to any country whose defense was considered vital to the security of the United States. The program proved invaluable in aiding Great Britain, to which the United States extended unlimited credit, and later in assisting the Soviet Union.

FDR soon began an undeclared war in the North Atlantic, instructing the navy to report sightings of German submarines to the British. In September, the U.S. destroyer *Greer* clashed with a German submarine. Portraying the incident as German aggression, Roosevelt proclaimed a "shoot on sight" policy for German subs and ordered American ships to escort British convoys to within 400 miles of Britain. In reply, German submarines torpedoed the destroyer *Kearny* on October 17 and sank the destroyer *Reuben James,* with the loss of more than 100 lives, on October 30. After the attack on the *Reuben James,* Congress repealed parts of the Neutrality Act of 1939 to allow U.S. merchant ships to be armed and to carry munitions to Great Britain. The United States was now approaching outright naval war with Germany.

The Atlantic Charter.   With U.S. ships on a war footing in the North Atlantic, Roosevelt and the British prime minister, Winston Churchill, met secretly off Newfoundland in August 1941 to map out military strategy and postwar goals. They agreed that the defeat of Germany was their first priority, and Japan was secondary. Their joint proclamation, known as the **Atlantic Charter,** provided a political umbrella for American involvement in the war. Echoing Woodrow Wilson, Roosevelt insisted on a commitment to oppose territorial conquest, support self-government, promote freedom of the seas, and create a system of economic collaboration. Churchill signed to keep Roosevelt happy, but the document papered over sharp differences between U.S. and British expectations about the future of world trade and European colonial possessions.

Roosevelt's intent in the North Atlantic remains uncertain. Some historians think that he hoped the United States could support Britain short of war. Others believe that he accepted the inevitability of war but hesitated to outpace public opinion (the House of Representatives renewed the military draft in August 1941 by just one vote). In this second interpretation, FDR wanted to eliminate Hitler without going to war if possible, with war if necessary. "I am waiting to be pushed into the situation," he told his secretary of the treasury.

Events in the Pacific.   The final shove came in the Pacific rather than the Atlantic. In 1940, as part of its rearmament program, the United States decided to build a "two-ocean navy." This decision antagonized Japan, prodding it toward a war that most U.S. leaders hoped to postpone or avoid. Through massive investment and national sacrifice, Japan had achieved roughly 70 percent of U.S. naval strength by late 1941. However, America's buildup promised to reduce the ratio to only 30 percent by 1944. Furthermore, the United States was restricting Japan's vital imports of steel, iron ore, and aluminum in an effort to curb its military aggression. In July 1941, after Japan occupied French Indochina, Roosevelt froze Japanese assets in the United States, blocked shipments of petroleum products, and began to build up U.S. forces in the Philippines. These actions caused Japan's rulers to consider war against the United States while Japan still had a petroleum reserve. Both militarily and economically, it looked in Tokyo as if 1942 was Japan's last chance for victory.

The Japanese military made its choice in September. Unless the United States and Britain ended aid to China and acquiesced in Japanese dominance of Southeast Asia—impossible conditions—war preparations would be complete in October. The Japanese General Staff defined its aims as "expelling American, Dutch, and British influences from East Asia, consolidating Japan's sphere of autonomy and security, and constructing a new order in greater East Asia." Japanese war planners never seriously considered an invasion of the United States or expected a decisive victory. They hoped that attacks on American Pacific bases would shock the United States into letting Japan have its way in Asia or at least win time to create impenetrable defenses in the central Pacific.

December 7, 1941

Since 1941, Americans have questioned Roosevelt's foreign policy. If he wanted an excuse for war, was the torpedoing of the *Reuben James* not enough? If he wanted to preserve armed neutrality, why threaten Japan by moving the Pacific fleet from California to Hawaii in 1940 and sending B-17 bombers to the Philippines in 1941? It now seems that Roosevelt wanted to restrain the Japanese with bluff and intimidation, so that the United States could focus on defeating Germany. American moves were intended to be aggressive but measured in the Atlantic, firm but defensive in the Pacific. After July, however, Washington expected a confrontation with Japan over the oil fields and rubber plantations of Southeast Asia. Because the United States had cracked the Japanese codes, it knew by November that Japanese military action was imminent but expected the blow to come in Southeast Asia.

Instead, the Japanese navy launched a surprise attack on American bases in Hawaii. The Japanese fleet sailed a 4,000-mile loop through the empty North Pacific, avoiding

Rationing in Britain

When World War II broke out, Britain depended on imports for the basic necessities of life—two-thirds of its food, all of its petroleum, all of its rubber, all of its tea.

The British government began to ration gasoline in September 1939 and added butter, sugar, meat, and paper to the list of rationed products early in 1940. By the end of the war, half of all foodstuffs were on strict rationing. The Ministry of Food encouraged Britons to make do with foods that could be grown at home, such as potatoes and carrots, "bright treasure dug from the good British earth." One Ministry of Food advertisement tried to put a good light on shortages:

The fishermen are saving lives
By sweeping seas for mines,

So you'll not grumble, 'What no fish?'
When you have read these lines.

Clothing was also controlled because cotton was an import and wool was needed for military uniforms. Styles became simpler by government decree. To save cloth, there would be no wide lapels or turned-up cuffs. Skirts became narrower and shorter.

Shortages continued even after the Allies won the Battle of the Atlantic in 1943 and pushed German submarines away from the vital convoy routes. Until the last year of the war, the average German had a better standard of living than the average Briton. At the same time, many members of the British working class welcomed rationing because it equalized consumption among rich and poor and ensured that the wealthy would not monopolize resources.

Because World War II exhausted the British economy, rationing remained in force long after victory. Clothing came off the list in 1949, but meat only in 1954—a year after the coronation of Queen Elizabeth II ushered in a new era in British history and long after the American economy was launched into a postwar boom.

■ Rationing in the United States was a way to fine-tune the war economy and engage everyday Americans in the war effort, but in Britain it was a necessity for survival. How might this difference have affected the ways in which the two nations approached the postwar world?

merchant shipping and American patrols. Before dawn on December 7, 1941, six Japanese aircraft carriers launched 351 planes in two bombing strikes against Pearl Harbor. When the smoke cleared, Americans counted their losses: eight battleships, eleven other warships, and nearly all military aircraft damaged or destroyed, and 2,403 people killed. They could also count their good fortune. Dockyards, drydocks, and oil storage tanks remained intact because the Japanese admiral had refused to order a third attack. And the American aircraft carriers, at sea on patrol, were unharmed. They proved far more important than battleships as the war developed. Within hours, the Japanese attacked U.S. bases at Guam, Wake Island, and in the Philippines.

Speaking to Congress the following day, Roosevelt proclaimed December 7, 1941, "a date which will live in infamy." He asked for and got a declaration of war against Japan. Hitler and Mussolini declared war on the United States on December 11, following their obligation under the Tripartite Pact. On January 1, 1942, the United States, Britain, the Soviet Union, and 23 other nations subscribed to the principles of the Atlantic Charter and pledged not to negotiate a separate peace.

Holding the Line

When Japan was considering war with the United States and Great Britain in 1940, Admiral Isoroku Yamamoto, the commander of Japan's Combined Fleet, weighed the chances of victory: "If I am told to fight regardless of the consequences, I shall run wild for the first six months or a year, but I have utterly no confidence for the second or third year." The admiral was right. Japan's armies quickly conquered most of Southeast Asia; its navy forced the United States onto the defensive in the central Pacific. As it turned out, Japan's conquests reached their limit after six months, but in early 1942, this was far from clear. At the same time, in Europe, Allied fortunes went from bad to worse. Again, no one knew that German and Italian gains would peak at midyear. Decisive turning points did not come until November 1942, a year after the United States entered the war, and not until the middle of

The Japanese attack on Pearl Harbor shocked the American people. Images of burning battleships confirmed the popular image of Japan as sneaky and treacherous and stirred a desire for revenge. The attack rendered the United States incapable of resisting Japanese aggression in Southeast Asia in early 1942, but it failed to achieve its goal of destroying U.S. naval power in the Pacific.

1943 could the **Allies**—the United States, Britain, the Soviet Union, China, and other nations at war with Germany, Japan, and Italy—begin with confidence to plan for victory.

Stopping Germany

In December 1941, the United States plunged into a truly global war that was being fought on six distinct fronts (see Map 26–2). In North Africa, the British were battling Italian and German armies that were trying to seize the Suez Canal, a critical transportation link to Asia. Along the 1,000-mile **Eastern Front,** Soviet armies held defensive positions as German forces, pushing deeply into Soviet ter-

ritory, reached the outskirts of Moscow and Leningrad (now St. Petersburg). In the North Atlantic, German submarines stalked merchant ships carrying supplies to Britain. In China, Japan controlled the most productive provinces but could not crush Chinese resistance. In Southeast Asia, Japanese troops attacked the Philippines, the Dutch East Indies (now Indonesia), New Guinea, Malaya, and Burma. In the central Pacific, the Japanese fleet confronted the U.S. Navy. With the nation facing danger across both the Atlantic and Pacific oceans, Roosevelt helped Americans understand the global nature of the conflict by calling it the "second world war."

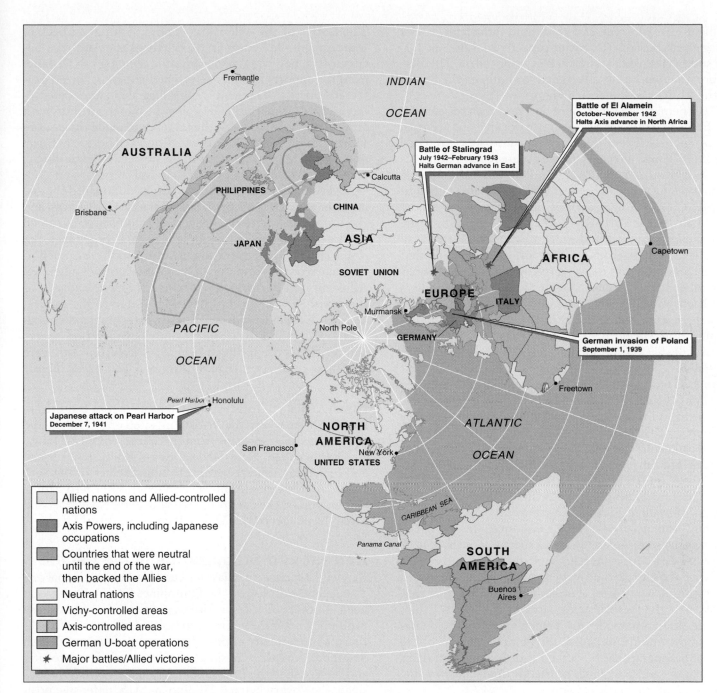

MAP 26–2 A Global War
World War II was truly a global war. As this map indicates, fighting engulfed both sides of the Eurasian continent and spread into the Atlantic, Pacific, and Indian oceans. The United States was the only major belligerent nation that was insulated from the battle fronts by two oceans.

Despite the popular desire for revenge against Japan, the Allies had already decided to defeat Germany first. The reasoning was simple: Germany, with its huge armies, massive industrial capacity, and technological expertise, was far stronger than Japan. Defeat of Japan would not ensure the defeat of Germany, especially if it crushed the Soviet Union or starved Britain into submission. By contrast, a strategy that helped the Soviets and British survive and then destroyed German military power would doom Japan.

The Eastern Front and the Battle of Stalingrad.   The Eastern Front held the key to Allied hopes. In 1941, Germany had seized control of 45 percent of the Soviet population, 47 percent of its grain production, and more than 60 percent of its coal, steel, and aluminum industries. Hitler next sought to destroy the Soviet capacity to wage war, targeting southern Russia, an area rich in grain and oil. The German thrust in 1942 was also designed to eliminate the British from the Middle East.

The scheme was easier to plot on a map than to carry out in the fields of Russia. The German offensive opened with stunning success. Every day's advance, however, stretched supply lines. Tanks ran out of fuel and spare parts. The horses that pulled German supply wagons died for lack of food.

The turning point of the war in Europe came at Stalingrad (present-day Volgograd), an industrial center on the western bank of the Volga River. After initially aiming at the city, German armies turned south toward the Russian oil fields, leaving a dangerous strongpoint on their flank that the German command decided to capture. In September and October 1942, German, Italian, and Romanian soldiers fought their way house by house into the city. At night, the Soviets ferried their wounded across the Volga and brought in ammunition. For both Hitler and Stalin, the city became a test of will that outweighed even its substantial military importance.

The Red Army delivered a counterstroke on November 18 that cut off 290,000 Axis soldiers. Airlifts kept the Germans fighting for more than two additional months, but they surrendered in February 1943. This was the first German mass capitulation, and it came at immense human cost to both sides. The Soviet army suffered more deaths in this battle than the United States did in the entire war. Russians call the hills around Stalingrad "white fields" because human bones still turn up after the spring thaw.

Behind the victory was an extraordinary revival of the Soviet capacity to make war. In the desperate months of 1941, the Soviets dismantled nearly 3,000 factories and rebuilt them far to the east of the German advance in the midst of Siberian winter. As many as 25 million workers and their families followed the factories eastward. As the military took most able-bodied men, Soviet women tilled the fields and worked in the munitions plants. By the time the two armies clashed at Stalingrad, the Soviets were producing four times as many tanks and warplanes as the Germans, portending the outcome of the battles to come.

The Survival of Britain

After the failure of German air attacks in 1940, the British struggled to save their empire and supply themselves with food and raw materials. In World War I, German submarines (known as U-boats, from *Unterseeboot*) had nearly isolated Great Britain. In 1940 and 1941, they tried again. From bases in France, greatly improved U-boats intercepted shipments of oil from Nigeria, beef from Argentina, minerals from Brazil, and weapons from the United States. Through the end of 1941, German "tonnage warfare" sank British, Allied, and neutral merchant vessels faster than they could be replaced.

The Battle of the Atlantic.   The British fought back in what came to be known as the **Battle of the Atlantic.** Between 1939 and 1944, planning and rationing cut Britain's need for imports in half. At sea, the British organized protected convoys. Merchant ships sailing alone were defenseless against submarines. Grouping the merchant ships with armed escorts "hardened" the targets and made them more difficult to find in the wide ocean. Roosevelt's destroyer deal of 1940 and U.S. naval escorts in the western Atlantic in 1941 contributed directly to Britain's survival.

Nevertheless, German submarines dominated the Atlantic in 1942. U-boats operated as far as the Caribbean and the Carolinas, where the dangers of Cape Hatteras forced coastal shipping out to sea. In June 1942, U-boats sank 144 ships, and U-boats operating in "wolfpacks" continued to decimate convoys into 1943. The balance shifted only when Allied aircraft began to track submarines with radar, spot them with searchlights as they maneuvered to the surface, and attack them with depth charges. New sonar systems allowed escort ships to measure submarines' direction, speed, and depth. By the spring of 1943, American shipyards were launching ships faster than the Germans could sink them.

North Africa.   British ground fighting in 1942 centered in North Africa, where the British operated out of Egypt and the Italians and Germans from the Italian colony of Libya. By October 1942, Field Marshal Erwin Rommel's German and Italian forces were within striking distance of the Suez Canal. At El Alamein, however, General Bernard Montgomery forced the enemy to retreat in early November and lifted the danger to the Middle East.

Retreat and Stabilization in the Pacific

Reports from eastern Asia after Pearl Harbor were appalling. The Japanese attack on the Philippines (see Map 26-3) had been another tactical surprise that destroyed most American air power on the ground and isolated U.S. forces. In February, a numerically inferior Japanese force seized British Singapore, until then considered an anchor of Allied strength, and then pushed the British out of Burma. In a three-month siege, they overwhelmed Filipino and U.S. defensive positions on the Bataan peninsula outside Manila; thousands of their captives died of maltreatment on their way to prisoner-of-war camps in what is remembered as the Bataan Death March. On May 6, the last American bastion, the island fortress of Corregidor in Manila Bay, surrendered. The Japanese fleet was virtually undamaged at the end of April, and the Japanese army was triumphant in conquest of European and American territories in Southeast Asia.

The Battles of the Coral Sea and Midway.   The first check to Japanese expansion came on May 7–8, 1942, in the Battle of the Coral Sea, where U.S. aircraft carriers halted a

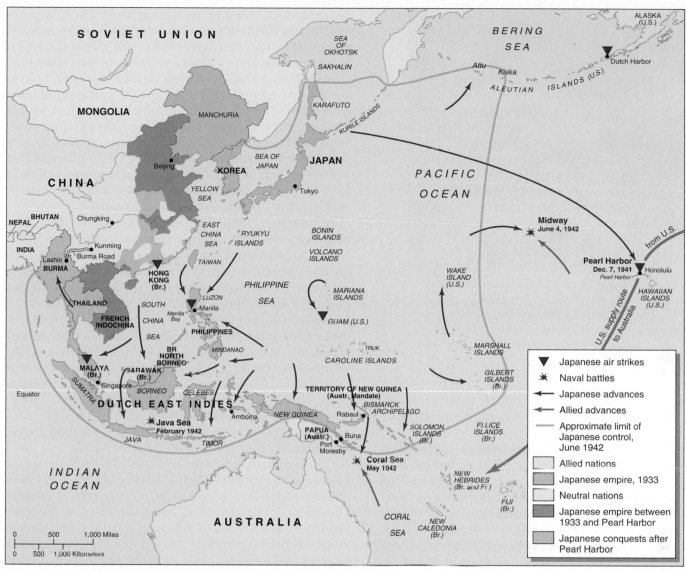

MAP 26–3   World War II in the Pacific, from Pearl Harbor to Midway
The first six months after the Japanese attack on Pearl Harbor brought a string of Japanese victories and conquests in the Pacific, the islands southeast of Asia, and the British colonies of Malaya and Burma. Japan's advance was halted by a standoff battle in the Coral Sea, a decisive U.S. naval victory at Midway, and the length and vulnerability of Japanese supply lines to the most distant conquests.

Japanese thrust toward Australia and confirmed that the U.S. Navy could fight effectively. In June, the Japanese struck at the island of Midway, 1,500 miles northwest of Honolulu. Their goal was to destroy American carrier forces. The plan included a diversionary invasion of the Aleutian Islands (the westernmost parts of Alaska) and a main assault on Midway, to draw the Americans into battle on Japanese terms. Having cracked Japanese radio codes, U.S. forces were aware of the plan and refused the bait. On the morning of June 4, the Japanese and American carrier fleets faced off across 175 miles of ocean, each sending planes to search out the other. U.S. Navy dive bombers found the Japanese fleet and sank or crippled three aircraft carriers in five minutes; another damaged

Japanese carrier sank later in the day. The Battle of Midway ended Japanese efforts to expand in the Pacific.

Mobilizing for Victory

News of the Japanese attack on Pearl Harbor shattered a bright Sunday afternoon. Twelve-year-old Jean Bartlett's family was headed to the movies when news of the attack came over the car radio. Elliott Johnson was eating in a Chinese restaurant in Portland, Oregon, when the proprietor burst from the kitchen with a portable radio; the line was two blocks long by the time he got to the marine recruiting office. In Cincinnati, the enormously popular Andrews Sisters

During the course of World War II, the government limited the consumption of a number of products to reserve supplies of products for the war effort and to prevent demand from pushing up the prices of scarce consumer goods. Shoppers like this woman at a grocery store counter used ration stamps to obtain their share of controlled products.

found that no one had shown up for their Sunday matinee concert. "Where is Pearl Harbor?" Maxine Andrews asked the theater's doorman.

War changed the lives of most Americans. Millions of men and women served in the armed forces, and millions more worked in defense factories. In order to keep track of this staggering level of activity, the number of civilian employees of the federal government quadrupled to 3.8 million, a much greater increase than during the New Deal. Meanwhile, youngsters saved tin foil, collected scrap metal, and followed the freedom-fighting stories of Wonder Woman in the comics. College science students might be recruited to work at scientific espionage against the Nazis. The breadth of involvement in the war effort gave Americans a common purpose that softened the divisions of region, class, and national origin while calling attention to continuing inequalities of race.

Organizing the Economy

The need to fight a global war brought a huge expansion of the federal government. Congress authorized the president to reorganize existing government departments and create new agencies. The War Manpower Commission allocated workers among vital industries and the military. The War Production Board invested $17 billion for new factories and managed $181 billion in war-supply contracts, favoring existing corporations because they had experience in large-scale production.

The Office of Price Administration (OPA) fought inflation with price controls and rationing that began with tires, sugar, and coffee and eventually included meat, butter, gaso-

line, and shoes. "Use it up, wear it out, make it do or do without" was the OPA's slogan. Consumers used ration cards and ration stamps to obtain scarce products. With gasoline scarce, horse-drawn delivery wagons made a comeback, while dads sometimes took over junior's bicycle for commuting to work.

By slowing price increases, the OPA helped convince Americans to buy the war bonds that financed half the war spending. Americans also felt the bite of the first payroll deductions for income taxes as the government secured a steady flow of revenues and soaked up some of the high wages that would have pushed inflation. In total, the federal budget in 1945 was $98 billion, eleven times as large as in 1939, and the national debt had increased more than sixfold.

Industry had reluctantly begun to convert from consumer goods to defense production in 1940 and 1941. By the time of the attack on Pearl Harbor, 25 percent of the national economy was devoted to military needs. Although corporations hated to give up the market for consumer goods, the last passenger car for the duration of the war rolled off the assembly line in February 1942. Existing factories retooled to make war equipment, and huge new facilities turned out thousands of planes and ships. Baltimore, Atlanta, Fort Worth, Los Angeles, and Seattle became centers for aircraft production. New Orleans, Portland, Oregon, and the San Francisco Bay area were shipbuilding centers.

The United States applied mass-production technology to aircraft production at a time when Japan was building warplanes one at a time and Germany in small batches. The most spectacular example was the new Ford plant at Willow Run, Michigan, designed to adapt assembly-line approaches to manufacturing B-24 bombers. Where the typical automobile had 15,000 parts, a B-24 had 1,550,000. The assembly line itself was more than a mile long, starting with four separate tracks that gradually merged into one. By 1943, the plant was delivering ten planes a day. American aircraft workers were twice as productive as their German counterparts and four times more productive than Japanese.

Most defense contracts went to such established industrial states as Michigan, New York, and Ohio, but the relative impact was greatest in the South and West, where the war marked the takeoff of what Americans would later call the Sunbelt (see Map 26–4). Washington, DC, teemed with staff officers, stenographers, and other office workers who helped to coordinate the war effort. Local leaders in cities from Charlotte to Fort Worth to Phoenix saw the war as an economic opportunity and campaigned for defense factories and military bases. Albuquerque, New Mexico, more than doubled in population during the 1940s. War-boom cities, such as San Diego (up 92 percent in population in the 1940s) and Mobile (up 68 percent), bustled with activity and hummed with tension. Factories operated three shifts, movies ran around the clock, and workers filled the streets after midnight.

The hordes of war workers found housing scarce. Workers in Seattle's shipyards and Boeing plants scrounged for

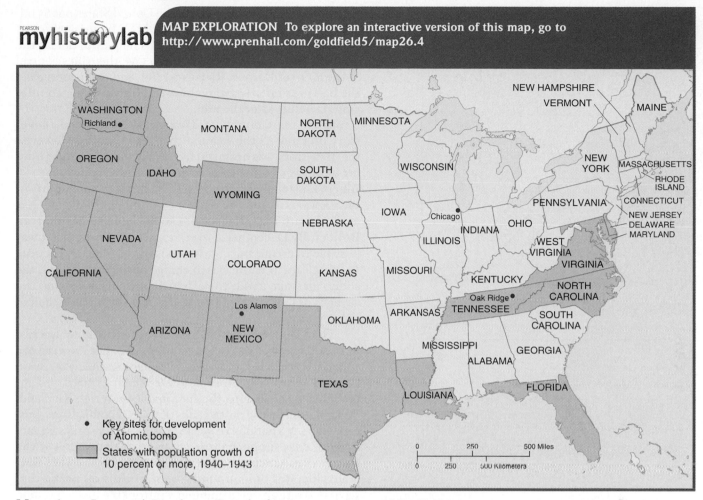

MAP EXPLORATION To explore an interactive version of this map, go to
http://www.prenhall.com/goldfield5/map26.4

MAP 26–4   **States with Population Growth of 10 Percent or More, 1940–1943**
The conversion of U.S. industry to defense production and the headlong expansion of the armed forces pulled Americans to coastal states and cities and to the South, where the mild climate allowed year-round military training.

living space in offices, tents, chicken coops, and rooming houses where "hot beds" rented in shifts. The situation was similar in small towns like Seneca, Illinois, home to a company that normally made river barges. Between June 1942 and June 1945, it built 157 specialized ships to land tanks in amphibious assaults. Thousands of new workers flocked to Seneca. They lined up three deep at the bars with their Friday paychecks. Residents would sometimes find a stranger rolled up in a blanket on their front porch.

The output of America's war industries was staggering (see Figure 26–1). One historian estimates that 40 percent of the world's military production was coming from the United States by 1944. Equally impressive is the 30 percent increase in the productivity of U.S. workers between 1939 and 1945. Surging farm income pulled agriculture out of its long slump. Organized labor offered a no-strike pledge for the duration, assuring that no one could accuse unions of undermining the war effort but limiting the economic gains of some workers and damping the militancy of the CIO. Nev-

ertheless, overall per capita income doubled, and the poorest quarter of Americans made up some of the ground lost during the Great Depression.

The Enlistment of Science

The war reached into scientific laboratories as well as shops and factories. "There wasn't a physicist able to breathe who wasn't doing war work," remembered Professor Philip Morrison. At the center of the scientific enterprise was Vannevar Bush, former dean at the Massachusetts Institute of Technology. As head of the newly established Office of Scientific Research and Development, Bush guided spending to develop new drugs such as antibiotics, blood-transfusion procedures, weapons systems, radar, sonar, and dozens of other military technologies. The scale of research and development dwarfed previous scientific work and set the pattern of massive postwar federal support for science.

The most costly scientific effort was the development of radar, or radio detection and ranging devices. Building on

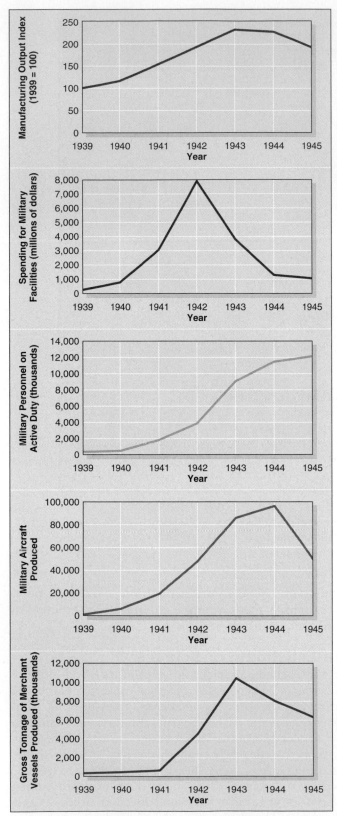

FIGURE 26–1   Making War: The United States Mobilizes, 1939–1945

The U.S. economic mobilization for World War II reached its peak in 1943, the year in which the Allies prepared for the offensives against Germany and Japan that they hoped would end the war. The number of men and women in uniform continued to grow until 1945.

British research on microwaves, the United States put $3 billion into the Radiation Laboratory at MIT. Increasingly compact and sophisticated radar systems helped to defeat the German and Japanese navies and to give the Allies control of the air over Europe. Radar research and engineering laid the basis for microwave technology, transistors, and integrated circuits after the war.

In the summer of 1945, *Time* magazine planned a cover story on radar as the weapon that won the war. However, the *Time* story was upstaged by the atomic bomb, the product of the war's other great scientific effort. As early as 1939, Albert Einstein had written to FDR about the possibility of such a weapon and the danger of falling behind the Germans. In late 1941, Roosevelt established the **Manhattan Project.** By December 2, 1942, scientists proved that it was possible to create and control a sustained nuclear reaction. Because Enrico Fermi was in charge of the experiment, the coded message about the scientific discovery evoked the voyages of Columbus: "The Italian navigator has landed in the new world."

The Manhattan Project moved from theory to practice in 1943. The physicist J. Robert Oppenheimer directed the young scientists at Los Alamos in designing a nuclear-fission bomb. Engineers in other new science cities tried two approaches to producing the fissionable material. Richland, Washington, on the dusty banks of the Columbia River, burgeoned from a handful of peach farmers into a sprawling metropolis that supported the creation of plutonium at the Hanford Engineer Works. Oak Ridge, Tennessee, near Knoxville, was built around gaseous-diffusion plants that separated rare and vital uranium-235 from the more common uranium-238. The two sites were chosen because of the proximity to hydroelectric power from new federal dams on the Columbia and Tennessee rivers, showing continuity from the New Deal to the war effort.

The Manhattan Project ushered in the age of atomic energy. Plutonium from Hanford fueled the first bomb tested at the Trinity site in New Mexico on July 16, 1945. The explosion astonished even the physicists; Oppenheimer quoted from Hindu scriptures in trying to comprehend the results: "Now I am become Death, destroyer of worlds."

Men and Women in the Military

World War II required a more than thirtyfold expansion of the U.S. armed forces from their 1939 level of 334,000 soldiers, sailors, and Marines. By 1945, 8.3 million men and women were on active duty in the army and army air forces and 3.4 million in the navy and Marine Corps, totals exceeded only by the Soviet Union. The military establishment was four times larger than in World War I. Once in the military, sailors and GIs served an average of 33 months. In total, some 350,000 women and more than 16 million men served in the armed forces; 292,000 died in battle, 100,000 survived prisoner-of-war camps, and 671,000 returned wounded.

Most of the Americans in uniform served in support jobs that kept the war machine going. They repaired airplanes and built runways, tracked supplies, and counted coffins. The poet John Ciardi wrote out commendations for valor. Bill Mauldin drew cartoons for the Army newspaper *Stars and Stripes*. As was true in wars throughout history, it was loyalty to the men in their own unit that kept fighting men steady. "The only thing that kept you going was your faith in your buddies," recalled a Marine from the Pacific theater. "You couldn't let 'em down. It was stronger than flag and country."

Native Americans in the military.   Twenty-five thousand American Indians served in the armed forces. Most were in racially integrated units, and Harvey Natcheez, of the Ute tribe, was the first American to reach the center of conquered Berlin. Because the Navajo were one of the few tribes that had not been studied by German anthropologists, the Army Signal Corps decided that their language would be unknown to the Axis armies. Roughly 400 members of the tribe were "code-talkers" who served in Marine radio combat-communication teams in the Pacific theater, transmitting vital information in Navajo.

African Americans in the military.   Approximately 1 million African Americans served in the armed forces during World War II. African American leaders had pressed for a provision in the Selective Service Act to bar discrimination "against any person on account of race or color." But as it had since the Civil War, the army organized black soldiers in segregated units and often assigned them to the menial jobs, such as construction work, and excluded them from combat until manpower shortages forced changes in policy.

The average black soldier encountered discrimination on and off the base. Towns adjacent to army posts were sometimes open to white soldiers but off-limits to blacks. At some southern bases, German prisoners of war watched movies from the first rows along with white GIs while African American soldiers watched from the back. Private Charles Wilson wrote President Roosevelt that Davis-Monthan Army Air Force Base in Tucson was color-coded: Barracks for African Americans were coated with black tar paper, and those for white soldiers sported white paint. Military courts were quick to judge and harshly punish black GIs. It took racially based riots at army bases in North Carolina and Georgia to open up equal (although segregated) access to base recreation facilities.

Despite the obstacles, all-black units, such as the 761st Tank Battalion and the 99th Pursuit Squadron, earned distinguished records. More broadly, the war experience helped to invigorate postwar efforts to achieve equal rights, as had also been true after World War I.

Women in the military.   The nation had a different—but also mixed—reaction to the women who joined the armed forces as army and navy nurses and as members of the WACS (Women's Army Corps), WAVES (Navy), SPARS (Coast Guard), and Marine Corps Women's Reserve. The armed services tried not to change established gender roles. Military officials told Congress that women in uniform could free men for combat. Many of the women hammered at typewriters, worked switchboards, inventoried supplies. Others, however, worked close to combat zones as photographers, code analysts, weather forecasters, radio operators, and nurses. WAC officers battled the tendency of the popular press to call females in the service "girls" rather than "women" or "soldiers" yet emphasized that military service promoted "poise and charm."

The greatest departure from expected roles was the work of the 1,074 members of the Women's Airforce Service Pilots (WASPS), a civilian auxiliary of the Army Air Forces. Many of the WASPS had learned to fly as civilians. From 1942 to 1944, they ferried military aircraft across the country, towed targets for antiaircraft practice, and tested new planes. Caro Bayley, from Springfield, Ohio, lied about her height so that she could pilot B-25s and later flew hazardous runs to test new radar systems. Nevertheless, WASPS were not allowed to carry male passengers, and the group was dissolved when the supply of male pilots caught up with demand.

African Americans served in the military large numbers during World War II. Here a signals company has set up operations in the ruins of an ancient temple in southern Italy.

The Home Front

The war inexorably penetrated everyday life. Residents in war-production cities had to cope with throngs of new workers. Especially in 1941 and 1942, many were unattached males—young men waiting for their draft call and older men without their families. They elbowed long-term residents in stores, snatched seats on the streetcars, and filled restaurants and theaters. Military and defense officials worried about sexually transmitted diseases and pressured cities to shut down their vice districts. At the same time, college officials scrambled to fill their classrooms, especially after the draft age dropped to 18 in 1942. Many colleges and universities responded to federal requests with special training programs for future officers and engineering and technical training for military personnel.

Families in Wartime

Many Americans put their lives on fast forward. Men and women often decided to beat the clock with instant matrimony. Couples who had postponed marriage because of the depression could afford to marry as the economy picked up. War intensified casual romances and heightened the appeal of marriage as an anchor in troubled times. Jewelers worried about running out of wedding rings. Altogether, the war years brought 1.2 million "extra" marriages, compared to the rate for the period 1920–1939.

The war's impact on families was gradual. The draft started with single men, then called up married men without children, and finally tapped fathers in 1943. Left at home were millions of "service wives," whose compensation from the government was $50 per month. Women who followed their husbands to stateside military posts and war factories often met cold welcomes from local residents. Harriet Arnow crafted a sensitive exploration of isolation from friends and family in her novel *The Dollmaker,* about a Kentucky farm woman who accompanied her husband to a Detroit war plant.

The war had mixed effects on children. "Latchkey children" of working mothers often had to fend for themselves, but middle-class kids whose mothers stayed home could treat the war as an interminable scout project, with salvage drives and campaigns to sell war bonds. In the rural Midwest children picked milkweed pods to stuff life jackets; in coastal communities, they participated in blackout drills. Seattle high schools set aside one class period a day for the High School Victory Corps, training boys as messengers for air-raid wardens, while girls knitted sweaters and learned first aid. Between the end of the school day and suppertime, children listened as Captain Midnight, Jack Armstrong, and Hop Harrigan ("America's ace of the airways") fought the Nazis and Japanese on the radio.

Learning About the War

The federal government tried to keep civilians of all ages committed to the war. It encouraged scrap drives and backyard victory gardens and created colorful posters to warn against espionage, inspire women to join the effort, and promote rationing and car-pooling. The government also managed news about the fighting. Censors screened soldiers' letters. Early in the war, they blocked publication of most photographs of war casualties, although magazines such as *Life* were full of strong and haunting images. Worried about flagging commitment, censors later authorized photographs of enemy atrocities to motivate the public.

Government officials had a harder time controlling Hollywood. The Office of War Information wanted propaganda in feature films, but not so heavy-handed that it drove viewers from theaters. Officials told movie directors to tone down car chases because screeching tires implied wasted rubber. War films revealed the nation's racial attitudes, often drawing distinctions between "good" and "bad" Germans but uniformly portraying Japanese as subhuman and repulsive. The most successful films dramatized the courage of the Allies. *Mrs. Miniver* (1942) showed the British transcending class differences in their battle with the Nazis. *So Proudly We Hail* (1943) celebrated the heroism of military nurses in the Philippines.

Women in the Workforce

As draft calls took men off the assembly line, women changed the composition of the industrial workforce. The war gave them new job opportunities that were embodied in the image of Rosie the Riveter. Women made up one-quarter of West

As millions of men entered the armed forces, millions of women went to work. By 1943, federal agencies were actively recruiting women workers. Those who took production-line jobs in shipyards and aircraft factories, such as the woman shown here, received the greatest attention.

WOW

WAAC

WAVE

ARMY NURSE

NAVY NURSE

RED CROSS

She's a WOW
WOMAN ORDNANCE WORKER

The U.S. government developed the image of Rosie the Riveter to encourage women to take war production jobs. This 1942 poster shows a woman worker with the polka-dot bandanna associated with Rosie, and it equates the bandanna with the hats worn by WACS, WAVEs, and other women in the armed services.

Coast shipyard workers and nearly half of Dallas and Seattle aircraft workers. Most women in the shipyards were clerks and general helpers. The acute shortage of welders and other skilled workers, however, opened thousands of lucrative journeyman positions to them. Aircraft companies, which compounded the labor shortage by stubborn "whites only" hiring, developed new power tools and production techniques to accommodate the smaller average size of women workers, increasing efficiency for everyone on the production line.

By July 1944, 19 million women held paid jobs, up 6 million in four years. Women's share of government jobs increased from 19 to 38 percent; they typed and filed in offices, but they also wrote propaganda for the Office of War Information and analyzed intelligence data for the office of Strategic Service. Women's share of manufacturing jobs rose from 22 to 33 percent, many of them as W.O.W.s or Woman Ordnance Workers. Mirroring the sequence in which the military draft took men, employers recruited single women before turning to married women in 1943 and 1944. The federal government assisted female entry into the labor force by funding daycare programs

that served 600,000 children. Some women worked out of patriotism. Many others, however, needed to support their families and already had years of experience in the workforce. As one of the workers recalled of herself and a friend, "We both had to work, we both had children, so we became welders, and if I might say so, damn good ones."

Americans did not know how to respond to the growing numbers of working women. The country needed their labor, but many worried that their employment would undermine families. Employment recruitment posters showed strong, handsome women with rolled-up sleeves and wrenches in hand, but *Life* magazine reassured readers that women in factories could retain their sex appeal. Men and women commonly assumed that women would want to return to the home after victory.

Ethnic Minorities in the War Effort

Mexican American workers made special contributions to the war effort. As defense factories and the military absorbed workers, western farms and railroads faced an acute shortage of workers. In the 1930s, western states had tried to deport Mexican nationals who were competing for scarce jobs. In 1942, however, the United States and Mexico negotiated the *bracero* program, under which the Mexican government recruited workers to come to the United States on six-to-twelve month contracts. More than 200,000 Mexicans worked on U.S. farms under the program, and more than 100,000 worked for western railroads. Although *bracero* workers still faced discrimination, the U.S. government tried to improve working conditions because it wanted to keep public opinion in Latin America favorable to the Allied cause.

The war was a powerful force for the assimilation of Native Americans. Forty thousand moved to off-reservation jobs; they were a key labor force for military supply depots throughout the West. The average cash income of Indian households tripled during the war. Many stayed in cities at its end. The experience of the war accelerated the fight for full civil rights. Congress had made Indians citizens in 1924, in part to recognize their contributions in World War I, but several states continued to deny them the vote. Activists organized the National Congress of American Indians in 1944 and began the efforts that led the U.S. Supreme Court in 1948 to require states to grant voting rights.

African Americans, too, found economic advancement through war jobs. Early in the mobilization, labor leader A. Philip Randolph of the Brotherhood of Sleeping Car Porters worked with Walter White of the NAACP to plan a "Negro March on Washington" to protest racial discrimination by the federal government. To head off a major embarrassment, Roosevelt issued Executive Order 8802 in June 1941, barring racial discrimination in defense contracts and creating the **Fair Employment Practices Committee** (FEPC); the order coined a phrase that reverberated powerfully through the coming decades: "No discrimination on grounds of race, color, creed, or national origin."

AMERICANOS TODOS
★
LUCHAMOS POR LA
VICTORIA

★ AMERICANS ALL ★
LET'S FIGHT FOR VICTORY

The government worked hard to encourage Hispanics to support the war effort, both for their direct contributions and to maintain good relations with Mexico and other Latin America nations.

The FEPC's small staff resolved fewer than half of the employment-discrimination complaints, and white resistance to black coworkers remained strong. In Mobile, New Orleans, and Jacksonville, agreements between shipyards and segregated unions blocked skilled black workers from high-wage jobs. Attempts to overturn discrimination could lead to violence. When the Alabama Dry Dock Company integrated its workforce in May 1943, white workers rioted. Transportation workers in Philadelphia struck the following year to protest upgrading of jobs held by black workers. Nevertheless, African American membership in labor unions doubled, and wartime prosperity raised the average black income from 41 percent of the white average in 1939 to 61 percent by 1950, particularly because labor shortages raised farm wages.

Outside the workplace, African American women found that many voluntary service groups were racially segregated. In response, they formed the Women's Army for National Defense. They did their part by selling war bonds, helping with civil defense, and organizing USO clubs for black soldiers.

Many African Americans saw themselves as engaged in a "Double V" effort for victory against tyranny abroad and victory over racism at home. Economic gains helped. So did the fact that many were able to vote for the first time, either because they had moved to northern states where voting was not racially limited or because they were servicemen serving overseas. The economic and political changes helped to build a base for the civil rights movement that gained momentum in the postwar decades.

Clashing Cultures

As men and women migrated in search of work, they also crossed or collided with traditional boundaries of religion, region, and race. In Charlotte, where military personnel demanded access to recreation on weekends, Southern Baptists had to agree to loosen Sunday closing laws. Farm boys mixed with city slickers, northerners with southerners. "When I woke up the first morning on the troop train in Fulton, Kentucky," recalled one midwesterner, "I thought I was in Timbuktu."

Some of the most troublesome conflicts arose from African American migration out of the South accelerated in the early 1940s. Many of the migrants headed for well-established black neighborhoods in northern cities. Others created new African American neighborhoods in western cities. White southerners and black northerners with different ideas of racial etiquette found themselves side by side in West Coast shipyards. In the Midwest, black migrants from the South and white migrants from Appalachia crowded into cities such as Cincinnati and Chicago, competing for the same high-wage jobs and scarce apartments.

Tensions between black and white residents exploded in at least 50 cities in 1943 alone. New York's Harlem neighborhood erupted in a riot after rumors of attacks on black servicemen. In Detroit, the issue was the boundary between white and black territory. In June 1943, an argument over the use of Detroit's Belle Isle Park set off three days of violence: Twenty-five black people and nine white people died in the most serious racial riot of the war.

Tensions were simultaneously rising between Mexican Americans and Anglos. As the Mexican community in Los Angeles swelled to an estimated 400,000, newspapers published anti-Mexican articles. On June 6, 1943, off-duty sailors and soldiers attacked Latinos on downtown streets and invaded Mexican American neighborhoods. The main targets were so-called *pachucos*—young Chicanos who wore flamboyant "zoot suits" with long, wide-shouldered jackets and pleated, narrow-cuffed trousers, whom the rioters considered delinquents or draft dodgers. The attacks dragged on for a week of sporadic violence against black people and Filipinos as well as Latinos. The assaults were poignantly ironic because 750,000 Mexican Americans served in the armed forces and were the most decorated group relative to their numbers.

Internment of Japanese Americans

On February 19, 1942, President Roosevelt authorized the secretary of war to define restricted areas and remove civilian residents who were threats to national security. The primary targets were 112,000 Japanese Americans in California and parts of Washington, Oregon, and Arizona. Japanese immigrants and their children in the western states had experienced 40 years of hostility because of racial prejudice, fear of the growing power of Japan, and jealousy of their business success. The outbreak of war triggered anti-Japanese hysteria and gave officials an excuse to take action against enemy aliens (immigrants who retained Japanese citizenship) and their American-born children. As the general commanding on the West Coast put it, "A Jap is a Jap. It makes no difference whether he is an American citizen or not."

Most West Coast Japanese were unable to leave because of ties to families and businesses. At the end of April 1942, Japanese in the coastal states were given a week to organize their affairs and report to assembly centers at fairgrounds and armories, where they were housed for several weeks before being moved again to ten internment camps in isolated locations in the western interior (see American Views, Internment of Japanese Americans: Life in Camp Harmony). Here, they were housed in tarpaper barracks, hemmed in by barbed-wire fences, and guarded by military police. The victims reacted to the hardship and stress in different ways. Several thousand second-generation Japanese Americans renounced their citizenship in disgust. But many others demonstrated their loyalty by cooperating with the authorities, finding sponsors who would help them move to other parts of the country, or joining the 442nd Regimental Combat Team, the most decorated American unit in the European war.

Although the U.S. Supreme Court sanctioned the removals in *Korematsu v. United States* (1944), the nation officially recognized its liability for lost property with the Japanese Claims Act of 1948. The nation acknowledged its broader moral responsibility in 1988, when Congress approved redress payments to each of the 60,000 surviving evacuees.

The internment of West Coast Japanese contrasted with the treatment of Japanese Americans by the military government of Hawaii. Despite the greater threat that Japan posed to Hawaii than to California, local residents and officials avoided panic. Hawaii's long history as a multiethnic society made residents disinclined to look for a racial scapegoat. Fewer than 1 percent of Hawaii's Japanese American population of 160,000 were interned. The treatment of

In 1942, the federal government removed Japanese Americans from parts of four western states and interned them in isolated camps scattered through the West.

mainland Japanese Americans also contrasted with the situation of German Americans and Italian Americans. The government interned approximately 11,000 German nationals and German Americans who were explicitly seen as individual threats. Until November 1942, it imposed curfews and travel restrictions on Italians and Italian Americans on the West Coast, but it interned fewer than 2,000. Both numbers were tiny fractions of the total populations.

The End of the New Deal

Roosevelt's New Deal ran out of steam in 1938. The war had reinvigorated his political fortunes by focusing national energies on foreign policy, over which presidents have the greatest power. After the 1942 election left Congress in the hands of Republicans and conservative southern Democrats, lawmakers ignored proposals that war emergency housing be used to improve the nation's permanent housing stock, abolished the National Resources Planning Board, curtailed rural electrification, and crippled the Farm Security Administration. Roosevelt himself declared, at a 1943 press conference, that "Dr. Win-the-War" had replaced "Dr. New Deal."

The presidential election of 1944 raised few new issues of substance. The Republicans nominated Governor Thomas Dewey of New York, who had made his reputation as a crime-fighting district attorney. The Democrats renominated Roosevelt for a fourth term. Missouri Senator Harry S Truman, a tough investigator of American military preparedness, replaced liberal New Dealer Henry Wallace as Roosevelt's running mate. The move appeased southern Democrats and moved the ticket toward the political center.

The most important issue was a fourth term for Roosevelt. Supporters argued that the nation could not afford to change leaders in the middle of a war, but Dewey's vigor and relative youth (he was 20 years younger than FDR) pointed up the president's failing health and energy. Voters gave Roosevelt 432 electoral votes to 99, but the narrowing gap in the popular vote—54 percent for Roosevelt and 46 percent for Dewey—made the Republicans eager for 1948.

War and Peace

In January 1943, the U.S. War Department completed the world's largest office building, the Pentagon. The building housed 23,000 workers along 17.5 miles of corridors. The building provided the space in which military planners could coordinate the tasks of raising and equipping the armed forces that would strike directly at Germany and Japan. Indeed, while Congress was chipping away at federal programs, the war effort was massively expanding the government presence in American life. The gray walls of the Pentagon symbolized a U.S. government that was outgrowing its prewar roots.

Turning the Tide in Europe

The unanswered military question of 1942 and 1943 was when the United States and Britain would open a second front against Germany by attacking across the English Channel. U.S. leaders wanted to justify massive mobilization with a war-winning campaign and to strike across Europe to occupy the heart of Germany. Stalin needed a full-scale invasion of western Europe to divert German forces from the Eastern Front, where Soviet troops were inflicting 90 percent of German battle casualties.

The Allies spent 1943 hammering out war aims and strategies. Meeting in Casablanca in January 1943, Roosevelt and Churchill demanded the unconditional surrender of Italy, Germany, and Japan. The phrase meant that there would be no deals that kept the enemy governments or leaders in power and was an effort to avoid the mistake of ending World War I with Germany intact. Ten months later, the Allied leaders huddled again. Roosevelt and Churchill met with China's Jiang in Cairo and then flew on to meet Stalin in Tehran. Jiang and Stalin could not meet directly because the Soviet Union was neutral in the East Asian war. At Tehran, the United States and Britain promised to invade France within six months. "We leave here," said the three leaders, "friends in fact, in spirit, in purpose."

The superficial harmony barely survived the end of the war. The Soviets had shouldered the brunt of the war for nearly two and a half years, suffering millions of casualties and seeing their nation devastated. Stalin and his generals scoffed at the small scale of early U.S. efforts. Roosevelt's ideal of self-determination for all peoples, embodied in the Atlantic Charter, seemed naive to Churchill, who wanted the major powers to carve out realistic spheres of influence in Europe. Stalin wanted control of eastern Europe to protect the Soviet Union against future invasions and assumed that realistic statesmen would understand.

The Campaign in North Africa.   The United States entered the ground war in Europe with Operation TORCH. Soon after the British victory at El Alamein, British and American troops under General Dwight Eisenhower landed in French Morocco and Algeria on November 8, 1942, against little opposition. (see Map 26–5). These were territories that the Germans had left under a puppet French government after the French military collapse in 1940. German troops that remained in North Africa taught U.S. forces hard lessons in tactics and leadership, but their stubborn resistance ended in May 1943, leaving all of Africa in Allied hands.

Eisenhower had already demonstrated his ability to handle the politics of military leadership, skills he perfected commanding a multinational army for the next two and one-half years. He also chose the right subordinates, giving operational command to Generals Omar Bradley and George Patton. Bradley was low-keyed and rock solid; to relax he worked algebra and calculus problems. Patton was a much flashier figure (he wore a pearl-handled revolver), with a mighty ego and a fierce commitment to victory.

The Invasion of Italy.   The central Mediterranean remained the focus of U.S. and British action for the next year, despite the fact that the hard-pressed Soviets were desperate for their allies to attack the heart of German power in northern Europe. However, the British feared military disaster from a premature landing in across the English Channel and proposed strikes in southern Europe, which Churchill inaccurately called the "soft underbelly" of Hitler's empire. U.S. Army Chief of Staff George Marshall and President Roosevelt agreed to invade Italy in 1943, in part so that U.S. troops could participate in the ground fighting in Europe. Allied forces overran Sicily in July and August, but the Italian mainland proved more difficult. When Sicily fell, the Italian king and army forced Mussolini from power and began to negotiate peace with Britain and America (but not the Soviet Union). In September, the Allies announced an armistice with Italy, and Eisenhower's troops landed south of Naples on September 9. Germany responded by occupying the rest of Italy.

Just as American military planners had feared, the Italian campaign soaked up Allied resources. The mountainous Italian peninsula was one long series of defensive positions, and the Allies repeatedly bogged down. Week after week, the experience of GIs on the line was the same: "You wake up in the mud and your cigarettes are all wet and you have an ache in your joints and a rattle in your chest." The Allies only managed to gain control of two-thirds of Italy before German resistance crumbled in the final weeks of the war.

Soviet Advances and the Battle of Kursk.   Meanwhile, the Soviets recruited, rearmed, and upgraded new armies,

MAP EXPLORATION To explore an interactive version of this map, go to
http://www.prenhall.com/goldfield5/map26.5

MAP 26–5 World War II in Europe, 1942–1945
Nazi Germany had to defend its conquests on three fronts. Around the Mediterranean, American and British forces pushed the
Germans out of Africa and southern Italy, while guerrillas in Yugoslavia pinned down many German troops. On the Eastern Front,
Soviet armies advanced hundreds of miles to drive the German Army out of the Soviet Union and eastern Europe. In June 1944,
U.S. and British landings opened the Western Front in northern France for a decisive strike at the heart of Germany.

American Views

The Internment of Japanese Americans in 1942

In the spring of 1942, the U.S. army ordered Japanese Americans in four western states relocated to internment camps distant from the Pacific Coast. Monica Itoe Sone describes the experience of her Seattle family as they were transferred to temporary quarters—at the state fairgrounds, renamed "Camp Harmony" by the military—before they were moved again to Idaho.

- How do the expectations of *issei* (immigrants who had been born in Japan) differ from those of *nisei* (their American-born children, including the author of this memoir)?
- Why did the U.S. army wait five months after Pearl Harbor before beginning the internment?
- Does the management of the assembly and internment suggest anything about stereotypes of Japanese Americans?

General DeWitt kept reminding us that E day, evacuation day, was drawing near. "E day will be announced in the very near future. If you have not wound up your affairs by now, it will soon be too late."

…On the twenty-first of April, a Tuesday, the general gave us the shattering news. "All the Seattle Japanese will be moved to Puyallup by May 1. Everyone must be registered Saturday and Sunday between 8 A.M. and 5 P.M."

Up to that moment, we had hoped against hope that something or someone would intervene for us. Now there was no time for moaning. A thousand and one details must be attended to in this one week of grace. Those seven days sputtered out like matches struck in the wind, as we rushed wildly about. Mother distributed sheets, pillowcases and blankets, which we stuffed into seabags. Into the two suitcases, we packed heavy winter overcoats, plenty of sweaters, woolen slacks and skirts, flannel pajamas and scarves. Personal toilet articles, one tin plate, tin cup and silverware completed our luggage. The one seabag and two suitcases apiece were going to be the backbone of our future home, and we planned it carefully.

Henry went to the Control Station to register the family. He came home with twenty tags, all numbered "10710," tags to be attached to each piece of baggage, and one to hang from our coat lapels. From then on, we were known as Family #10710. [On the day set for relocation] we climbed into the truck.…As we coasted down Beacon Hill bridge for the last time, we fell silent, and stared out at the delicately flushed, morning sky of Puget Sound.

We drove through bustling Chinatown, and in a few minutes arrived on the corner of Eighth and Lane. This area was ordinarily lonely and deserted but now it was gradually filling up with silent, labeled Japanese.…

Finally at ten o'clock, a vanguard of Greyhound busses purred in and parked themselves neatly along the curb. The crowd stirred and murmured. The bus doors opened and from each, a soldier with rifle in hand stepped out and stood stiffly at attention by the door.…

Newspaper photographers with flash-bulb cameras pushed busily through the crowd. One of them rushed up to our bus, and asked a young couple and their little boy to step out and stand by the door for a shot. They were reluctant, but the photographers were persistent and at length they got out of the bus and posed, grinning widely to cover their embarrassment. We saw the picture in the newspaper shortly after and the caption underneath it read, "japs good-natured about evacuation." Our bus quickly filled to capacity.… The door closed with a low hiss. We were now the Wartime Civil Control Administration's babies.

About noon we crept into a small town…and we noticed at the left of us an entire block filled with neat rows of low shacks, resembling chicken houses. Someone commented on it with awe, "Just look at those chicken houses. They sure go in for poultry in a big way here." Slowly the bus made a left turn, drove through a wire-fenced gate, and to our dismay, we were inside the oversized chicken farm.…

The apartments resembled elongated, low stables about two blocks long. Our home was one room, about 18 by 20 feet, the size of a living room. There was one small window in the wall opposite the one door. It was bare except for a small, tinny wood-burning stove crouching in the center....

I stared at our little window, unable to sleep. I was glad Mother had put up a makeshift curtain on the window for I noticed a powerful beam of light sweeping across it every few seconds. The lights came from high towers placed around the camp where guards with Tommy guns kept a twenty-four hour vigil. I remembered the wire fence encircling us, and a knot of anger tightened in my breast. What was I doing behind a fence like a criminal? If there were accusations to be made, why hadn't I been given a fair trial? Maybe I wasn't considered an American anymore. My citizenship wasn't real, after all. Then what was I? I was certainly not a citizen of Japan as my parents were. On second thought, even Father and Mother...had little tie with their mother country. In their twenty-five years in America, they had worked and paid their taxes to their adopted government as any other citizen.

Of one thing I was sure. The wire fence was real. I no longer had the right to walk out of it. It was because I had Japanese ancestors. It was also because some people had little faith in the ideas and ideals of democracy.

Source: Monica Itoi Sone, *Nisei Daughter* (Seattle: University of Washington Press, 1979).

---

despite enormous losses. They learned to outfight the Germans in tank warfare and rebuilt munitions factories beyond German reach. They also made good use of 17.5 million tons of U.S. lend-lease assistance. As Soviet soldiers recaptured western Russia and Ukraine, they marched in 13 million pairs of American-made boots and ate U.S. rations. They traveled in 78,000 jeeps and 350,000 Studebaker, Ford, and Dodge trucks. "Just imagine how we could have advanced from Stalingrad to Berlin without [lend-lease vehicles]," future Soviet premier Nikita Khrushchev later commented.

The climactic battle of the German-Soviet war erupted on July 5, 1943. The Germans sent 3,000 tanks against the Kursk salient, a huge wedge that the Red Army had pushed into their lines. In 1941 and 1942, such a massive attack would have forced the Soviets to retreat, but now Soviet generals had prepared a defense with 3,000 tanks of their own. With 1 million men actively engaged on each side for more than two weeks, Kursk was the largest pitched battle of the war. It marked the end of the last great German offensive, leaving Germany capable of a fighting retreat but too weak to have any hope of winning the war and expecting an American and British attack across the English Channel.

Operation OVERLORD

On **D-Day**—June 6, 1944—the western Allies landed on the coast of Normandy in northwestern France. Six divisions went ashore from hundreds of attack transports carrying 4,000 landing craft, as vividly dramatized in the film *Saving Private Ryan.* Dozens of warships and 12,000 aircraft provided support. One British and two American airborne divisions dropped behind German positions. When the sun set on the "longest day," the Allies had a tenuous toehold in France. Americans had been waiting for the news. In Montgomery, Alabama, flags appeared along the streets and traffic halted at 5:00 P.M. for buglers from nearby bases and the high school to sound the "call to the colors." At 6:00 P.M. all movie projectors were stopped to allow time for prayer.

The landing finally satisfied Soviet demands for a more balanced war effort, but the next few weeks brought limited success. The Allies secured their beachheads and poured more than a million men and hundreds of thousands of vehicles ashore in the first six weeks. However, the German defenders kept them pinned along a narrow coastal strip. **Operation OVERLORD,** the code name for the entire campaign across northern France, met renewed success in late July and August. U.S. troops improved their fighting skills through "experience, sheer bloody experience." They finally broke through the German lines around the town of St.-Lô and then drew a ring around the Germans that slowly closed on the town of Falaise. The Germans lost a quarter of a million troops.

The German command chose to regroup closer to Germany rather than fight in France. The Allies liberated Paris on August 25; Free French forces (units that had never surrendered to the Nazis) led the entry. The drive toward Germany was the largest U.S. operation of the war. The only impediments appeared to be winter weather and pushing forward enough supplies for the rapidly advancing armies.

The story was similar on the Eastern Front, where the Soviets relentlessly battered one section of the German lines after another. By the end of 1944, the Red Army had entered the Balkans and reached central Poland. The Soviets had suffered as many as 27 million military and civilian deaths and sustained by far the heaviest burden in turning back Nazi tyranny (see Table 26–1).

American, British, and Canadian forces opened the long-awaited second front against Germany on June 6, 1944–D-Day—when tens of thousands of troops landed on the coast of Normandy in France. The landings were the largest amphibious operation ever staged. Although the Germans had expected the landings farther north, their defenses pinned the Allies to a narrow beachhead for several weeks.

Victory and Tragedy in Europe

In the last months of 1944, massive air strikes finally began to reduce German war production, which had actually increased during 1943 and much of 1944. The Americans flew

Table 26–1
Military and Civilian Deaths in World War II

Nation	Victims (millions)
USSR	27
China	10–20
Germany and Austria	6
Poland	6
Japan	2.7
Yugoslavia	1.7
Romania	0.7
France	0.6
Great Britain	0.5
Hungary	0.5
Italy	0.4
Czechoslovakia	0.4
United States	0.3

daylight raids from air bases in Britain with heavily armed B-17s ("Flying Fortresses") and B-24s, ("Liberators") to destroy factories with precision bombing. On August 17, 1943, however, Germans shot down or damaged 19 percent of the bombers that attacked the aircraft factories of Regensburg and the ball-bearing factories of Schweinfurt. The Americans had to seek easier targets.

Gradually, however, the balance shifted. P-51 escort fighter helped B-17s overfly Germany in relative safety after mid-1944. Thousand-bomber raids on railroads and oil facilities began to cripple the German economy. The raids forced Germany to devote 2.5 million workers to air defense and damage repair and to divert fighter planes from the front lines. The air raids cut German military production by one-third through 1944 and destroyed the transportation system. Politics, rather than military need, governed the final great action of the European air war. British and U.S. bombers in February 1945 staged a terror raid on the nonindustrial city of Dresden, packed with refugees, filled with great art, and undefended by the Germans; a firestorm fueled by incendiary bombs and rubble from blasted buildings killed tens of thousands of civilians.

The Battle of the Bulge and the collapse of Germany. Even as the air bombardment intensified, Hitler struck a last blow. Stripping the Eastern Front of armored units, he launched 25 divisions against thinly held U.S. positions in the Ardennes Forest of Belgium on December 16, 1944. He hoped to split U.S. and British forces by capturing the Belgian port of Antwerp. The attack surprised the Americans, and taking advantage of snow and fog that grounded Allied aircraft, the Germans drove a 50-mile bulge into U.S. lines. Although the Americans took substantial casualties, the German thrust literally ran out of gas beyond the town of Bastogne. The Battle of the Bulge never seriously threatened the outcome of the war, but pushing the Germans back through the snow-filled forest gave GIs a taste of the conditions that marked the war in the Soviet Union.

The Nazi empire collapsed in the spring of 1945. American and British divisions crossed the Rhine in March and enveloped Germany's industrial core. The Soviets drove through eastern Germany toward Berlin. On April 25, American and Soviet troops met on the Elbe River. Hitler committed suicide on April 30 in his concrete bunker deep under devastated Berlin, which surrendered to the Soviets on May 2. The Nazi state formally capitulated on May 8.

The Holocaust.

The defeat of Germany revealed appalling evidence of the evil at the heart of the Nazi ideology of racial superiority. After occupying Poland in 1939, the Nazis had transformed concentration camps into forced-labor camps, where overwork, starvation, and disease killed hundreds of thousands of Jews, Gypsies, Poles, Russians, and others the Nazis classed as subhuman. As many as 7 million labor conscripts from eastern and western Europe provided forced labor in fields, factories, mines, and repair crews, often dying on the job from overwork and starvation.

The "final solution" to what Hitler thought of as the "Jewish problem" went far beyond slave labor. The German army in 1941 had gained practice with death by slaughtering hundreds of thousands of Jews and other civilians as it swept across Russia. In the fall of that year, Hitler decided on the total elimination of Europe's Jews. The elite SS, Hitler's personal army within the Nazi Party, in 1942 set out to do his bidding. At Auschwitz, Treblinka, and several other death camps, the SS organized the efficient extermination of up to 6 million Jews and 1 million Poles, Gypsies, and others who failed to fit the Nazi vision of the German master race. Prisoners arrived by forced marches and cattle trains. Those who were not worked or starved to death were herded into gas chambers and then incinerated in huge crematoriums.

The Nazi regime sent slave laborers too weak to continue working on its V-2 rocket project to the Nordhausen concentration camp to die of starvation. When U.S. troops liberated the camp in April 1945, they found more than 3,000 corpses.

The evidence of genocide—systematic racial murder—is irrefutable. Allied officials had begun to hear reports of mass murder midway through the war, but memories of the inaccurate propaganda about German atrocities in World War I made many skeptical. Moreover, the camps were located in the heart of German-controlled territory, areas that Allied armies did not reach until 1945. At Dachau in southwestern Germany, American forces found 10,000 bodies and 32,000 prisoners near death through starvation. Soviet troops who overran the camps in Poland found even more appalling sights—gas chambers as big as barns, huge ovens, the dead stacked like firewood. For more than half a century, the genocide that we now call the **Holocaust** has given the world its most vivid images of inhumanity.

The Pacific War

In the Pacific, as in Europe, the United States used 1943 to probe enemy conquests and to build better submarines, bigger aircraft carriers, and superior planes. Washington divided responsibilities in the Pacific theater. General Douglas MacArthur operated in the islands that stretched between Australia and the Philippines. Admiral Chester Nimitz commanded in the central Pacific. The Allies planned to isolate Japan from its southern conquests. The British moved from India to retake Burma. The Americans advanced along the islands of the southern Pacific to retake the Philippines. With Japan's army still tied down in China, the Americans then planned to bomb Japan into submission.

Racial hatred animated both sides in the Pacific war and fueled a "war without mercy." Americans often characterized Japanese soldiers as vermin. Political cartoons showed Japanese as monkeys or rats, and some Marines had "Rodent Exterminator" stenciled on their helmets. In turn, the Japanese depicted themselves as the "leading race" with the duty to rule the rest of Asia. Japan treated Chinese, Filipinos, and other conquered peoples with contempt and brutality, and the record of Japanese atrocities is substantial. Japanese viewed Americans as racial mongrels and called them demons. Each side expected the worst of the other and frequently lived up to expectations.

The Pacific campaigns of 1944 are often called **island hopping.** Planes from American carriers controlled the air, allowing the navy and land forces to isolate and capture the most strategically located Japanese-held islands while bypassing the rest. The process started in November 1943, when Marines took Tarawa (see Map 26–6). It worked to perfection with the assault on Saipan in June 1944, where U.S. Navy flyers destroyed three Japanese aircraft carriers and hundreds of planes.

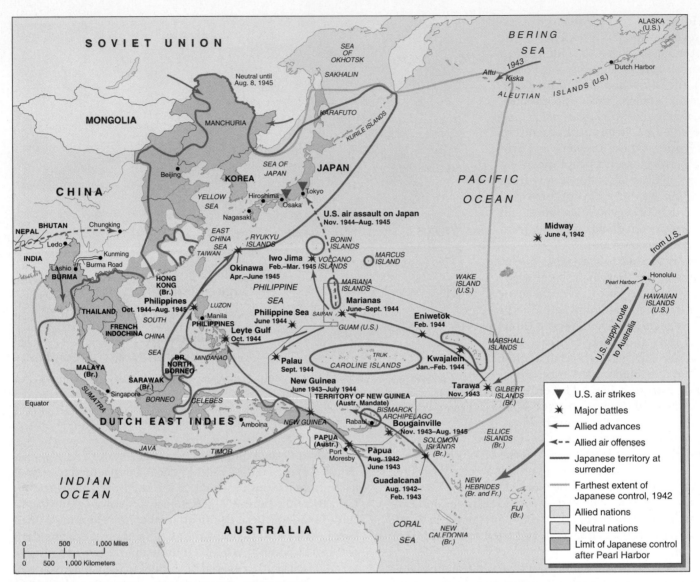

MAP 26–6   World War II in the Pacific, 1942–1945
The Allied strategy against Japan was to cut off Japan's southern conquests by retaking the central Pacific islands, the Philippines, and Burma and then to strike at the Japanese home islands. Submarine warfare and massive air attacks from November 1944 to August 1945 crippled Japan's capacity to wage war. The detonation of atomic bombs over Hiroshima and Nagasaki then forced surrender on August 15, 1945.

MacArthur used a version of the bypass strategy in the Solomon Islands and New Guinea, leapfrogging past Japanese strong points. The invasion of the Philippines repeated the approach by landing on Leyte, in the middle of the island chain. The Philippine campaign also destroyed the last offensive capacity of the Japanese fleet. In the Battle of Leyte Gulf, the U.S. Navy sank four Japanese battleships, four carriers, and ten cruisers. The Japanese home islands were left with no defensive screen against an expected invasion.

During 1943 and 1944, the United States also savaged the Japanese economy. Submarines choked off food, oil, and raw materials bound for Japan and island bases. By 1945, im-

ports to Japan were one-eighth of the 1940 level. Heavy bombing of Japan began in early 1944, using the new long-range B-29. Japan's dense wooden cities were more vulnerable than their German counterparts, and Japanese air defenses were much weaker. A fire-bomb raid on Tokyo on the night of March 9, 1945, killed 124,000 people and left 1 million homeless; it was perhaps the single biggest mass killing of all time. Overall, conventional bombing destroyed 42 percent of Japan's industrial capacity. By the time the United States captured the islands of Iwo Jima and Okinawa in fierce fighting (April–June 1945) and neared the Japanese home islands, Japan's position was hopeless.

Searching for Peace

At the beginning of 1945, the Allies sensed victory. Conferring from February 4 to 11 in the Ukrainian town of Yalta, Roosevelt, Stalin, and Churchill planned for the postwar world. The most important American goal was to enlist the Soviet Union in finishing off the Pacific war. Americans hoped that a Soviet attack on Manchuria would tie down enough Japanese troops to reduce U.S. casualties in invading Japan. Stalin repeated his intent to declare war on Japan within three months of victory in Europe, in return for a free hand in Manchuria.

In Europe, the Allies had decided in 1944 to divide Germany and Austria into French, British, American, and Soviet occupation zones and to share control of Berlin. The Red Army already controlled Bulgaria, Romania, and Hungary, countries that had helped the Germans; Soviet officials were installing sympathetic regimes there. Soviet armies also controlled Poland. The most that Roosevelt could coax from Stalin was a vague pledge to allow participation of non-communists in coalition governments in eastern Europe. Stalin also agreed to join a new international organization, the United Nations (UN), whose foundations were laid at a conference in San Francisco in the spring of 1945. The new organization was intended to correct the mistakes of World War I, when the United States had stayed aloof from the League of Nations and had relied on international treaties without mechanisms of enforcement. American leaders wanted the UN to provide a framework through which the United States could coordinate collective security against potential aggressors while retaining its own military strength as the primary means to preserve the peace.

Conservative critics later charged that the western powers "gave away" eastern Europe at the **Yalta Conference**. In fact, the Soviet Union gained little that it did not already control. In East Asia as well, the Soviets could seize the territories the agreement granted them. Roosevelt may have overestimated his ability to charm Stalin, but the Yalta talks could not undo the results of four years of fighting by the Soviet Army.

Truman and Potsdam.   On April 12, two months after Yalta, Roosevelt died of a cerebral hemorrhage. Harry Truman, the new president, was a shrewd politician, but his experience was limited; Roosevelt had not even told him about the Manhattan Project. Deeply distrustful of the Soviets, Truman first ventured into personal international diplomacy in July 1945 at a British-Soviet-American conference at Potsdam, near Berlin. Most of the sessions debated the future of Germany. The leaders endorsed the expulsion of ethnic Germans from eastern Europe and moved the borders of Poland 100 miles west into historically German territory. Truman also made it clear that the United States expected to dominate the occupation of Japan. Its goal was to democratize the Japanese political system and reintroduce Japan into the international community, a policy that succeeded. The **Potsdam Declaration** on July 26 summarized U.S. policy and gave Japan an opening for surrender. However, the declaration failed to guarantee that Emperor Hirohito would not be tried as a war criminal. The Japanese response was so cautious that Americans read it as rejection.

The atomic bomb.   Secretary of State James Byrnes now urged Truman to use the new atomic bomb, tested just weeks earlier. Japan's ferocious defense of Okinawa had confirmed American fears that the Japanese would fight to the death. Thousands of suicide missions by kamikaze pilots who tried to crash their planes into U.S. warships seemed additional proof of Japanese fanaticism. Prominent Americans were wondering if unconditional surrender was worth another six or nine months of bitter fighting. In contrast, using the bomb to end the conflict quickly would ensure that the United States could occupy Japan without Soviet participation, and the bomb might intimidate Stalin (see Overview, The Decision to Use the Atomic Bomb). In short, a decision not to use atomic weapons was never a serious alternative in the summer of 1945.

The ruins of Hiroshima in the aftermath of the atomic bomb. Atomic bombs, dropped first on Hiroshima and then on Nagasaki in August 1945, instantly destroyed most of each city. Now one airplane could wreak the kind of devastation that massive fire-bombing raids had inflicted on cities such as Hamburg and Tokyo, adding new terror to the idea of total war.

FROM THEN TO NOW

Nuclear Weapons

In 2007, the United States pressed the Communist regime in North Korea to abandon its small but viable nuclear weapons program, worried about Iran's possible plans to develop such weapons, and found itself mired in a war in Iraq whose official reason had been to block Iraqi development or use of nuclear explosives and other weapons of mass destruction.

Those efforts continued more than half a century of work to contain the spread of atomic weapons. Such weapons have not been used in warfare since the two bombs that the United States dropped on Japan, but the fear of nuclear war and efforts to limit the number of nuclear-capable nations has been a constant in American policy and diplomacy. A key step was the Nuclear Non-Proliferation Treaty, signed in 1968 and extended indefinitely in 1995. One hundred eighty nations have agreed not to acquire nuclear weapons, but the power of international opinion was not enough to stop India and Pakistan, bitter rivals in south Asia, from testing their own a-bombs in 1998.

More positively, both the United States and Russia have agreed to limit to total size of their nuclear stockpiles. The United States has helped to pay for dismantling of Russian warheads and their removal from Ukraine and Kazakhstan, both formerly parts of the Soviet Union, although worries about diversion of warheads into the hands of terrorists have provided the plot for adventure novels and movies such as *The Peacemaker* (1998).

G.I.s in November 1951 watch a nuclear test from only six miles away at the Nevada Proving Ground near Las Vegas.

■ In the next chapters, look for points at which the fear of nuclear weapons has influenced U.S. policy toward other nations. What factors have prompted choices of military versus diplomatic responses?

myhistorylab

From Then to Now Online

26-1 Lewis Strauss, and Edward Teller, Deciding on a Nuclear Arms Race, 1949 and 1950. Member of Atomic Energy Commission and leading nuclear scientist urge development of hydrogen bomb.

26-2 Dwight D. Eisenhower, Atoms for Peace, Dec. 8, 1953. Speech to United Nations.

26-3 Federation of American Scientists, 1993. South Africa's decision to give up nuclear weapons.

An inspector from the International Atomic Energy Administration searching for evidence of nuclear weapons production in Iraq, in front of a picture of Iraqi dictator Saddam Hussein.

OVERVIEW

The Decision to Use the Atomic Bomb

Americans have long argued about whether the use of atomic bombs on the Japanese cities of Hiroshima and Nagasaki was necessary to end the war. Several factors probably influenced President Truman's decision to use the new weapon.

Military necessity	After the war, Truman argued that the use of atomic bombs was necessary to avoid an invasion of Japan that would have cost hundreds of thousand of lives. Military planners expected Japanese soldiers to put up the same kind of suicidal resistance in defense of the home islands as they had to American landings in the Philippines, Iwo Jima, and Okinawa. More recently, historians have argued that the Japanese military was near collapse and an invasion would have met far less resistance than feared.
Atomic diplomacy	Some historians believe that Truman used atomic weapons to overawe the Soviet Union and induce it to move cautiously in expanding its influence in Europe and East Asia. Truman and his advisers were certainly aware of how the bomb might influence the Soviet leadership.
Domestic politics	President Roosevelt and his chief military advisers had spent billions on the secret atomic bomb project without the full knowledge of Congress or the American public. The managers of the Manhattan Project may have believed that only proof of its military value would quiet critics and justify the huge cost.
Momentum of war	The United States and Britain had already adopted wholesale destruction of German and Japanese cities as a military tactic. Use of the atomic bomb looked like a variation on fire bombing, not the start of a new era of potential mass destruction. In this context, some historians argue, President Truman's choice was natural and expected.

In early August, the United States dropped two of the three available nuclear bombs on Japan. On August 6, at Hiroshima, the first bomb killed at least 80,000 people and poisoned thousands more with radiation. A second bomb, three days later at Nagasaki, took another 40,000 lives. Japan ceased hostilities on August 14 and surrendered formally on September 2. The world has wondered ever since whether the United States might have defeated Japan without resorting to atomic bombs, but recent research shows that the bombs were the shock that allowed the emperor and peace advocates to overcome military leaders who wanted to fight to the death.

How the Allies Won

The Allies won with economic capacity, technology, and military skill. The ability to outproduce the enemy made victory certain in 1944 and 1945, but it was the ability to outthink and outmaneuver the Axis powers that staved off defeat in 1942 and 1943.

In the spring of 1942, an unbroken series of conquests had given the Axis powers control of roughly one-third of the world's production of industrial raw materials, up from only 5 percent in 1939. But while Germany and Japan struggled to turn these resources into military strength, the Soviet Union accomplished wonders in relocating and rebuilding its manufacturing capacity after the disasters of 1941. The United States, meanwhile, rearmed with astonishing swiftness, accomplishing in one year what Germany had thought would take three. By 1944, the United States was outproducing all of its enemies combined; over the course of the war, it manufactured two-thirds of all the war materials used by the Allies.

The United States and the Soviet Union not only built more planes and tanks than the Axis nations, but they also built better ones. The Soviets developed and mass-produced the T-34, the world's most effective tank. American aircraft designers soon jumped ahead of the Germans. The United States and Britain gained the lead in communication systems, radar, code-breaking capability, and, of course, atomic weapons. Even behind the lines the Allies had the technical advantage. The U.S. and British forces that invaded France were fully motorized, and Soviet forces increasingly so, while the German army still depended on horses to draw supply wagons and artillery.

The Allies learned hard lessons from defeat and figured out how to outfight the Axis. Hitler's generals outsmarted the Soviet military in 1941, Japan outmaneuvered the British and Americans in the first months of the Pacific war, and the German navy came close to squeezing the life from Great Britain in 1942. In 1943 and 1944, the tables were turned. The Russians reexamined every detail of their military procedures and devised new tactics that kept the vast German armies off guard and on the defensive. New ways to fight U-boats in the Atlantic devastated the German submarine service and staved off defeat. Americans in the Pacific utilized the full capacity of aircraft carriers, while Japanese admirals still dreamed of confrontations between lines of battleships.

Finally, the Allies had the appeal of democracy and freedom. The Axis nations were clearly the aggressors. Germany and Japan made bitter enemies by exploiting and abusing the people of the countries they conquered, from Yugoslavia and France to Malaya and the Philippines, and incited local resistance movements. The Allies were certainly not perfect, but they fought for the ideals of political independence and were welcomed as liberators as they pushed back the Axis armies.

Conclusion

World War II changed the lives of tens of millions of Americans. It made and unmade families. It gave millions of women new responsibilities and then sent them back to the kitchen. It put money in pockets that had been emptied by the Great Depression and turned struggling business owners into tycoons. In war zones and behind the lines, it introduced millions of men and women in the armed forces to people and places outside the United States.

Whether on the home front or the fighting front, Americans knew that victory was uncertain, the hard-fought result of public leadership and military effort. Under other leadership, the United States might have stood aside until it was too late to reverse the Axis conquest of Europe and East Asia. The collapse of the Soviet Union or the failure of the North Atlantic convoy system might have made Germany unbeatable. In 1941 and 1942 in particular, Americans faced each day with fear and uncertainty.

The war unified the nation in new ways, while confirming old divisions. People of all backgrounds shared a common cause The war narrowed the distance between native-born, small-town Americans and recent European immigrants from the big cities. The chasms between Protestant, Catholic, and Jewish Americans were far narrower in 1945 than they had been in 1940.

But nothing broke the barriers that separated white and black Americans. Unequal treatment in a war for democracy outraged black soldiers, who returned to fight for civil rights. The uprooting of Japanese Americans was another reminder of racial prejudice. After the war, however, memories of the contrast between the nation's fight against Axis tyranny and the unequal treatment of American citizens fueled a gradual shift of public attitudes that climaxed in the civil rights movements of the 1950s and 1960s.

The United States ended the war as the world's overwhelming economic power. It had put only 12 percent of its population in uniform, less than any other major combatant. For every American who died, 20 Germans and dozens of Soviets perished. Having suffered almost no direct destruction, the United States was able to dictate a postwar economic trading system that favored its interests.

Nevertheless, the insecurities of the war years influenced the United States for decades. A nation's current leaders are often shaped by its last war. Churchill had directed strategy, and Hitler, Mussolini, and Truman had all fought in World War I and carried its memories into World War II. The lessons of World War II would similarly influence the thinking of presidents from Dwight Eisenhower in the 1950s to George H. W. Bush in the 1990s. Even though the United States ended 1945 with the world's mightiest navy, biggest air force, and only atomic bomb, memories of the instability that had followed World War I made its leaders nervous about the shape of world politics.

One result in the postwar era was conflict between the United States and the Soviet Union, whose only common ground had been a shared enemy. After Germany's defeat, their wartime alliance gave way to hostility and confrontation in the Cold War. At home, international tensions fed the pressure for social and political conformity. The desire to enjoy the fruits of victory after 15 years of economic depression and sacrifice made the postwar generation sensitive to perceived threats to steady jobs and stable families. For the next generation, the unresolved business of World War II would haunt American life.

Review Questions

1. What motivated German, Italian, and Japanese aggression in the 1930s? How did Great Britain, the USSR, and other nations respond to the growing conflict?

2. What arguments did Americans make against involvement in the war in Europe, and how deep was anti-intervention sentiment? Why did President Roosevelt and many others believe it necessary to block German and Japanese expansion? What steps did Roosevelt take to increase U.S. involvement short of war?

3. What was the military balance in early 1942? What were the chief threats to the United States and its allies? Why did the fortunes of war turn in late 1942?

4. Assess how mobilization for World War II altered life in the United States. How did the war affect families? How did it shift the regional balance of the economy? What opportunities did it open for women?

5. Did World War II help or hinder progress toward racial equality in the United States? How did the experiences of Japanese Americans, African Americans, and Mexican Americans challenge American ideals?

6. What factors were decisive in the defeat of Germany? How important were Soviet efforts on the Eastern Front, the bomber war, and the British-American landings in France?

7. What was the U.S. strategy against Japan, and how well did it work? What lay behind President Truman's decision to use atomic bombs against Japanese cities?

8. What role did advanced science and technology play in World War II? How did the scientific lead of the United States affect the war's outcome?

Key Terms

Allies (p. 734)

Atlantic Charter (p. 732)

Axis Powers (p. 723)

Battle of the Atlantic (p. 736)

Blitzkrieg (p. 729)

D-Day (p. 749)

Eastern Front (p. 734)

Fair Employment Practices Committee (p. 743)

Greater East Asia Co-Prosperity Sphere (p. 728)

Holocaust (p. 751)

Island hopping (p. 751)

Lend-Lease Act (p. 732)

Manhattan Project (p. 740)

Operation OVERLORD (p. 749)

Potsdam Declaration (p. 753)

Yalta Conference (p. 753)

Recommended Reading

Bailey, Beth, and David Farber. *The First Strange Place: The Alchemy of Race and Sex in World War II Hawaii* (1992). Explores the effects of the war on American ideas about the proper roles of men and women, black people, white people, and Asian Americans.

Hersey, John. *Hiroshima* (1946; rev. edition 1985). Recounts the atomic bombing through the eyes of victims and survivors.

Keegan, John. *The Second World War* (1990). A comprehensive and readable account giving a strong sense of the relative importance of the various fronts.

Sherwin, Martin J. *A World Destroyed: The Atomic Bomb and the Grand Alliance* (1975). Explains why American lead-

ers never seriously considered alternatives to the atomic bomb.

Terkel, Studs. *The Good War: An Oral History of World War II* (1984). Eloquent testimony about the effects of the war on both ordinary and extraordinary Americans.

Tuttle, William. *Daddy's Gone to War: The Second World War in the Lives of America's Children* (1993). Explores the homefront experience through the memories of wartime children.

Yellin, Emily. *Our Mothers' War: American Women and the Home Front during World War II* (2004). Offers fascinating detail on all aspects of women's lives during the war.

Where to Learn More

■ **National Museum of the U.S. Air Force, Dayton, Ohio.** Visitors can walk among World War II fighter planes and bombers, including the B-29 that dropped the atomic bomb on Nagasaki, and learn about the role of aviation in the war. www.wpafb.af.mil/museum

■ **National Museum of the Pacific War, Fredericksburg, Texas.** In the birthplace of Admiral Chester Nimitz, this new museum is an excellent introduction to the war with Japan. www.nimitz-museum.org

■ **Los Alamos County Historical Museum and Bradbury Science Museum, Los Alamos, New Mexico.** The

museum traces the origins of atomic energy for military and civilian uses. Nearby is the Los Alamos County Historical Museum, which gives the feel of everyday life in the atomic town. www.lanl.gov/museum

■ **United States Holocaust Memorial Museum, Washington, DC.** The Holocaust Museum gives visitors a deeply moving depiction of the deadly impact of Nazi ideas in the 1930s and 1940s. The museum's website at www.ushmm.urlorg also explores virtually every facet of the Holocaust experience for Jews during World War II.

Study Resources

For study resources for this chapter, go to www.myhistorylab.com and choose *The American Journey*. You will find a wealth of study and review material for this chapter, including pre- and posttests, customized study plan, key term review flash cards, interactive map and document activities, and documents for analysis.

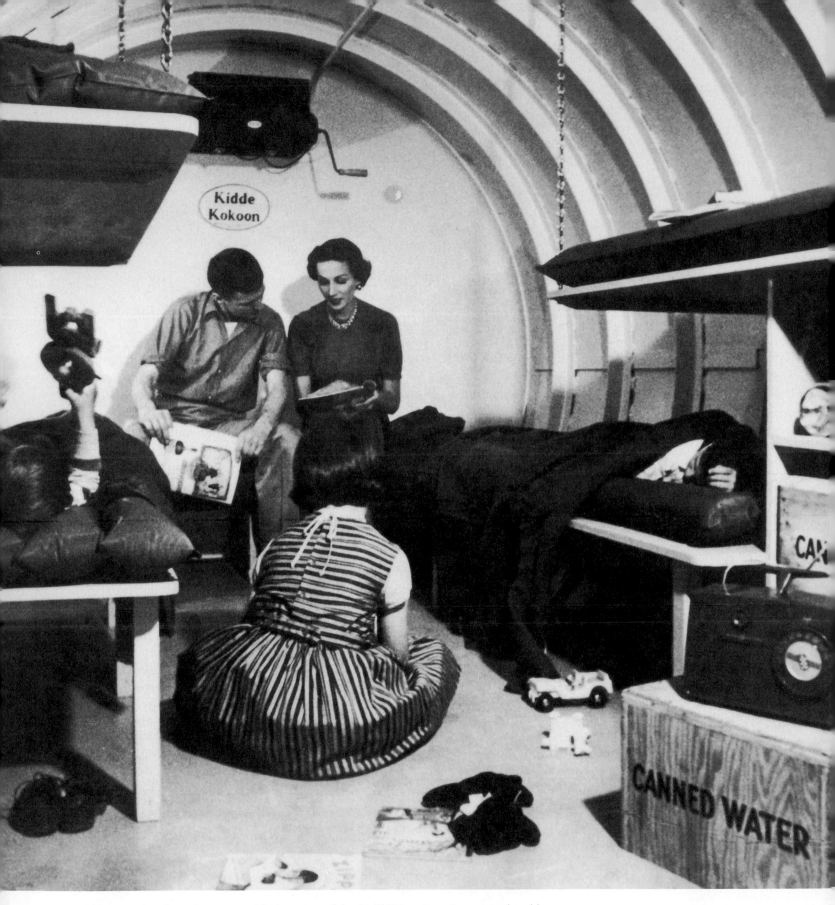

As international tensions rose with the onset of the Cold War, Americans wondered how to prepare for a possible nuclear war. Many families stocked extra food and water and bought a battery-powered radio, but few actually installed backyard bomb shelters like the one being tested by this family in a Long Island suburb not far from Levittown.

The Cold War at Home and Abroad 1946–1952 27

My eyes popped when I got to town hall because the lobby and the stairs leading up to the hearing room were loaded with people. The upstairs hallway was jammed and the room was packed. People were standing along the walls. I remember there were a lot of children, toddlers—some in strollers—and many babies held by men and women. We expected there would be quite a turnout. But the extent of the crowd was a big surprise to me.... The meeting itself was rather brief. There were some speeches. No screaming and yelling the way people do at town meetings today. Everyone was quiet, anxious. I remember one guy in uniform, holding a baby, made a strong statement. These people were desperate. It was very moving. When the decision was announced, the crowd broke into applause.

Levittown was the last place on the planet I thought I would be living. But, as it turned out, we moved there because the house was such a good buy.... We loved living there. I came into work and told [*Newsday* managing editor Alan] Hathway that I would be eating crow for the rest of my days.

Bernadette Rischer Wheeler, in "Levittown at Fifty: Long Island Voices," at www.lihistory.com/specsec/hsvoices.htm; originally published in *Newsday*.

myhistorylab

Personal Journeys Online

- ◼ "This Is How I Keep House," McCalls, April 1949. The routine of a typical Levittown housewife.

- ◼ Eric Hodgins, *Mr. Blandings Builds His Dream House* (1946). A fictional New York advertising agent buys a house in the far edge of suburbia.

- ◼ Atlanta Housing Council, "Proposed Areas for Expansions of Negro Housing in Atlanta, Georgia," Papers of the Atlanta Urban League, Atlanta University Center, Atlanta, Georgia. Reprinted in Andrew Wiese and Becky Nicolaides, *The Suburb Reader* (2006). Atlanta Housing Council suggests ways to continue residential segregation in a growing city.

Bernadette Wheeler was a reporter for *Newsday*, the daily newspaper for the Long Island suburbs of New York, who covered the birth of the new community of Levittown. She remembers the meeting on May 21, 1947, when the local governing board approved construction of the new subdivision. The size of the crowd indicated the severity of the housing shortage after World War II and the intense desire of Americans to return to normal life. After years of hardship, they defined American ideals in terms of economic opportunity and the chance to enjoy national prosperity. Even President Truman replaced the model gun on his White House desk with a model plow. Over the next decade, the residents who moved to Levittown and thousands of other new subdivisions would start the baby boom and rekindle the economy with their purchases of automobiles, appliances, and televisions.

This compelling desire to enjoy the promise of American life after years of sacrifice helps explain why Americans reacted so fiercely to new challenges and threats. They watched as congressional conservatives and President Truman fought over the fate of New Deal programs. More worrisome was the confrontation with the Soviet Union that was soon being called the **Cold War.** Triggered by the Soviet Union's imposition of communist regimes throughout eastern Europe, the Cold War grew into a global contest in which the United States tried to counter Soviet influence around the world. By the time real war broke out in Korea in 1950, many Americans were venting their frustration by blaming international setbacks on internal subversion and trying to root out suspected "reds."

The Cold War began in the late 1940s, but it would shape the United States and the world for another generation. Massive rearmament allowed U.S. presidents to act as international policemen in the name of democratic values—a vast change from the earlier American goal of remaining disengaged from the problems of other nations. Defense spending also reshaped American industry and helped stimulate 25 years of economic growth. The Cold War narrowed the range of political discussion, making many of the left-wing ideas of the 1930s taboo by the 1950s. It also made racial segregation and limits on immigration into international embarrassments and thus nudged the nation to live up to its ideals.

Launching the Great Boom

In 1947, *The Best Years of Our Lives* swept seven Oscars at the Academy Awards. The immensely popular movie dealt squarely with the problems of returning veterans, following three veterans as they tried to readjust to civilian life. The

KEY TOPICS

◆ Post-war shortages and the massive exit of women from the workforce

◆ The beginning of a 25-year economic boom

◆ The beginning of the postwar civil rights movement

◆ The origins of the Cold War

◆ The reelection of Harry Truman

◆ The Korean War and the nuclear arms race

◆ McCarthy and the Second Red Scare

CHRONOLOGY

1944	Servicemen's Readjustment Act (GI Bill) is passed.
1945	United Nations is established.
1946	Employment Act creates Council of Economic Advisers.
	George Kennan sends his "long telegram."
	Winston Churchill delivers his "iron curtain" speech.
1947	Truman Doctrine is announced.
	Truman establishes a federal employee loyalty program.
	Kennan explains containment policy in an anonymous article in *Foreign Affairs*.
	Marshall Plan begins providing economic aid to Europe.
	HUAC holds hearings on Hollywood.
	Taft-Hartley Act rolls back gains of organized labor.
	National Security Act creates National Security Council and Central Intelligence Agency.
1948	Communists stage coup in Czechoslovakia.
	Berlin airlift overcomes Soviet blockade.
	Truman orders desegregation of the armed forces.
	Selective Service is reestablished.
	Truman wins reelection.
1949	North Atlantic Treaty Organization is formed.
	Communist Chinese defeat Nationalists.
	Soviet Union tests an atomic bomb.
	Department of Defense is established.
1950	Senator McCarthy begins his Red hunt.
	Alger Hiss is convicted of perjury.
	Internal Security Act (McCarran Act)
	NSC-68 is drafted and accepted as U.S. policy.
	Korean War begins.
1951	Senate Internal Security Subcommittee begins hearings.
	Truman relieves MacArthur of his command.
	Julius and Ethel Rosenberg are convicted of conspiring to commit espionage.
	Truce talks begin in Korea.
1952	United States tests the hydrogen bomb.
	Eisenhower is elected president.

plot cut between the personal problems of reconnecting with wives and sweethearts and the social challenge of finding meaningful work.

Behind the story line was nagging concern about the future. "Hard times are coming," one character predicts. When World War II ended, Americans feared that demobilization would bring a rerun of the inflation and unemployment that had followed World War I. Indeed, in the first 18 months of peace, rising prices, strife between labor and management, and shortages of everything from meat to automobiles confirmed their anxiety. But in fact, 1947 and 1948 ushered in an economic expansion that lasted for a quarter-century. The resulting prosperity would finance a military buildup and an activist foreign policy. It also supported continuity in domestic politics from the late 1940s to the mid-1960s.

Reconversion Chaos

Japan's sudden surrender took the United States by surprise. Plans called for a two-year phase-out of military spending and a gradual reintroduction of veterans to the domestic economy. Now these plans were obsolete. The Pentagon, already scaling back defense spending, canceled $15 billion in war contracts in the first two days after the Japanese surrender. Public pressure demanded that the military release the nation's 12 million service personnel as rapidly as possible. GIs in Europe and the South Pacific waited impatiently for their turn on slow, crowded troop ships. Even at the rate of 25,000 discharges a day, it took a year to get all of them back to civilian life.

Veterans came home to shortages of food and consumer goods. High demand and short supply meant inflationary pressure, checked temporarily by continuing the Office of Price Administration until October 1946. Meanwhile, producers, consumers, and retailers scrambled to evade price restrictions and scarcities. Farmers sold meat on the black market, bypassing the big packing companies. Automobiles

The Best Years of Our Lives dealt realistically with the problems facing veterans trying to readjust to civilian life. Director William Wyler strove for a feeling of accuracy, shooting on location in Cincinnati and costuming the actors in clothing bought in local stores.

were extremely scarce; the number of vehicles registered in the United States had declined by 4 million during the war. For the privilege of spending a few hundred dollars on a junker, consumers sometimes had to pay used-car dealers for so-called accessories like $150 batteries and $100 lap robes.

A wave of strikes made it hard to retool factories for civilian products. Inflation squeezed factory workers, who had accepted wage controls during the war effort. Since 1941, prices had risen twice as fast as base wages. In the fall of 1945, more and more workers went on strike to redress the balance; the strikes interrupted the output of products from canned soup to copper wire. By January 1946, some 1.3 million auto, steel, electrical, and packinghouse workers were off the job. Strikes in these basic industries shut other factories down for lack of supplies. Presidential committees crafted settlements that allowed steel and auto workers to make up ground lost during the war, but they also allowed corporations to pass on higher costs to consumers. One Republican senator complained of "unionists who fatten themselves at the expense of the rest of us." Bill Nation, who inspected window moldings at a GM plant in Detroit, wondered who the senator was talking about. The strike gave him an hourly raise of 18 cents, pushing his weekly income to $59. After paying for food, housing, and utilities, Bill was left with $13.44 for himself, his wife, and five children to spend on clothes, comic books, and doctor bills.

Economic Policy

The economic turmoil of 1946 set the stage for two major and contradictory efforts to deal more systematically with peacetime economic readjustment. The Employment Act of 1946 and the Taft-Hartley Act of 1947 represented liberal and conservative approaches to the peacetime economy.

The Employment Act was an effort by congressional liberals to ward off economic crisis by fine-tuning government taxation and spending. It started as a proposal for a full-employment bill that would ensure everyone's "right to a useful and remunerative job." Watered down in the face of business opposition, it still defined economic growth and high employment as national goals. It also established the **Council of Economic Advisers** to assist the president. Even this weak legislation, putting the federal government at the center of economic planning, would have been unthinkable a generation earlier.

In the short term, the Employment Act aimed at a problem that did not materialize. Economists had predicted that the combination of returning veterans and workers idled by canceled defense work would bring depression-level unemployment of 8 to 10 million. In fact, more than 2 million women provided some slack by leaving the labor force outright. Federal agencies hastened their departure by publishing pamphlets asking men the pointed question, "Do you want your wife to work after the war?" In addition, a savings pool of $140 billion in bank accounts and war bonds created a huge demand for consumer goods and workers to produce them. Total employment rose rather than fell with the end of the war, and unemployment in 1946–1948 stayed below 4 percent.

From the other end of the political spectrum, the **Taft-Hartley Act** climaxed a ten-year effort by conservatives to reverse the gains made by organized labor in the 1930s. The act passed in 1947 because of anger about continuing strikes. For many Americans, the chief culprit was John L. Lewis, head of the United Mine Workers, who had won good wages for coal miners with a militant policy that included wartime walkouts. In a country that still burned coal for most of its energy, the burly, bushy-browed, and combative Lewis was instantly recognizable, loved by his workers and hated by nearly everyone else. In April 1946, a 40-day coal strike hampered industrial production. The coal settlement was only days old when the nation faced an even more crippling walkout by railroad workers. Truman asked for the unprecedented power to draft strikers into the army; the threat undercut the union and led to a quick and dramatic settlement. Many middle-class Americans were convinced that organized labor needed to be curbed.

In November 1946, Republicans capitalized on the problems of reconversion chaos, labor unrest, and dissatisfaction with Truman. Their election slogan was simple: "Had enough?" The GOP won control of Congress for the first time since the election of 1928, continuing the political trend toward the right that had been apparent since 1938.

Adopted by the now firmly conservative Congress, the Taft-Hartley Act was a serious counterattack by big business against large unions. It outlawed several union tools as "unfair labor practices." It barred the closed shop (the requirement that all workers hired in a given company or plant be union members) and blocked secondary boycotts (strikes against suppliers or customers of a targeted business). The federal government could postpone a strike by imposing a cooling-off period, which gave companies time to stockpile their products. Officers of national unions had to swear that they were not Communists or Communist sympathizers, even though corporate executives had no similar obligation. The bill passed over Truman's veto.

The GI Bill

Another landmark law for the postwar era passed Congress without controversy. The Servicemen's Readjustment Act of 1944 was designed to ease veterans back into the civilian mainstream. Popularly known as the **GI Bill of Rights**, it was one of the federal government's most successful public assistance programs. Rather than pay cash bonuses to veterans, as after previous wars, Congress tied benefits to specific public goals. The GI Bill guaranteed loans of up to $2,000 for buying a house or farm or starting a business, a substantial sum at a time when a new house cost $6,000. The program encouraged veterans to attend college with money for tuition and books plus monthly stipends.

The GI Bill democratized American higher education by making college degrees accessible to men with working-class backgrounds. It brought far more students into higher education than could otherwise have enrolled. In the peak year of 1947, veterans made up half of all college students. "We're all trying to get where we would have been if there hadn't been a war," one veteran attending Indiana University told *Time* magazine. Veterans helped convert the college degree, once available primarily to the socially privileged, into a basic business and professional credential. However, the GI tide unfortunately crowded women out of classrooms, although 60,000 servicewomen did take advantage of educational benefits. Cornell University made room for veterans by limiting women to 20 percent of its entering class; the University of Wisconsin closed its doors to women from out of state. Women's share of bachelor's degrees dropped from 40 percent in 1940 to 25 percent in 1950.

College life in 1946 and 1947 meant close quarters. Universities were unequipped to deal with older or married students. Prefabricated apartments from the wartime atomic-energy project at Richland, Washington, were trucked to college campuses around the West to house newly enrolled veterans. Recycled Quonset huts became as much a part of campus architecture as gothic towers and ivy-covered halls. States rented surplus defense facilities for big-city extension campuses. Many of these campuses evolved into major public universities, such as the University of Illinois at Chicago and Portland State University in Oregon.

Assembly-Line Neighborhoods

Americans faced a housing shortage after the war. In 1947, fully 3 million married couples were unable to set up their own households. Most doubled up with relatives while they waited for the construction industry to respond. Hunger for housing was fierce. Eager buyers lined up for hours and paid admission fees to tour model homes or to put their names in drawings for the opportunity to buy.

The solution started with the federal government and its Veterans Administration (VA) mortgage program. By guaranteeing repayment, the VA allowed veterans to get home-purchase loans from private lenders without a downpayment. Neither the VA program nor the New Deal–era Federal Housing Administration (FHA) mortgage insurance program, however, could do any good unless there were houses to buy. Eyeing the mass market created by the federal programs, innovative private builders devised their own solution. In 1947, William Levitt, a New York builder who had developed defense housing projects, built 2,000 houses for veterans on suburban Long Island. His basic house had 800 square feet of living space in two bedrooms, living room, kitchen, and bath, a 60-by-100-foot lot, and an unfinished attic waiting for the weekend handyman. It was only one-third the size of the typical new house 50 years later, but it gave new families a place to start. There were 6,000 **Levittown** houses by the end of 1948 and more than 17,000 by 1951.

Other successful builders worked on the same scale. They bought hundreds of acres of land, put in utilities for the entire tract, purchased materials by the carload, and kept specialized workers busy on scores of identical houses. Floor plans were square, simple, and easy for semiskilled workers to construct. For the first time, kitchens across America were designed for preassembled cabinets and appliances in standard sizes. "On-site fabrication" was mass production without an assembly line. Work crews in the Los Angeles suburb of Lakewood started a hundred houses a day as they moved down one side of the street and back up the other, digging

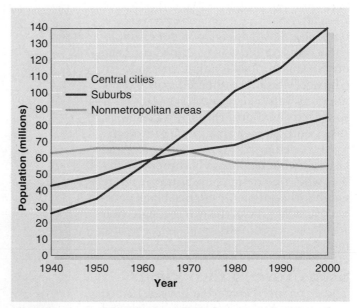

FIGURE 27–1 The Suburbanizing Nation
In the decades after World War II, Americans moved in unprecedented numbers to new communities surrounding established cities in the early 1960s, the combined population of suburban areas passed the populations of large central cities and of smaller towns and rural areas.

foundation trenches, pouring concrete, and working through the dozens of other stages of home building.

From 1946 through 1950, the federal government backed $20 billion in VA and FHA loans, approximately 40 percent of all home-mortgage debt. Housing starts neared 2 million in the peak year of 1950. By the end of the 1940s, 55 percent of American households owned their homes. The figure continued to climb until the 1980s, broadening access to the dream of financial security for many families. All during this time, the suburban population grew much faster than the population of central cities, and the population outside of metropolitan areas actually declined. (see Figure 27–1).

Isolation and discrimination.   Unfortunately, the suburban solution to the housing shortage came with costs. The vast new housing tracts tended to isolate women and children from traditional community life. Moreover, they were of little benefit to African Americans. As the migration of black workers and their families to northern and western cities continued after the war, discrimination excluded them from new housing. As late as 1960, the 82,000 residents of Levittown had no African American neighbors; not until 1957 did a black family move into a second Levittown near Philadelphia. Federal housing agencies and private industry worsened the problem by **redlining** older neighborhoods, which involved withholding home-purchase loans and insurance coverage from inner-city areas that were deemed too risky as investments.

Public and private actions kept African Americans in deteriorating inner-city ghettos. When severe flooding in 1948 drove thousands of African Americans from leftover wartime housing in Portland, Oregon, for example, their only choice was to crowd into the city's small black neighborhood. In Chicago, where an estimated 27,000 black migrants were arriving each year, landlords squeezed them into run-down buildings, subdividing larger apartments into one-room "kitchenette" units, with sinks and hot plates but no private bathrooms. Families who tried to find new homes in white neighborhoods on the edge of black ghettos often met rocks thrown through their windows, firebombs, and angry white mobs.

Steps Toward Civil Rights

The urgent need for decent housing helped to motivate African Americans to demand full rights as citizens. The wartime experience of fighting for freedom abroad while suffering discrimination at home steeled a new generation of black leaders to close the gap between America's ideal of equal-

ity and its performance. As had also been true after World War I, some white Americans held the opposite view, hoping to reaffirm racial segregation. A wave of racist violence surged across the South after the war; special targets were black veterans who tried to register to vote. However, many white Americans felt uneasy about the contradiction between a crusade for freedom abroad and racial discrimination at home.

In this era of rapid change and racial tension, the Truman administration recognized the importance of upholding civil rights for all Americans. Caught between pressure from black leaders and the fear of alienating southern Democrats, the president in 1946 appointed the Committee on Civil Rights, whose report developed an agenda for racial justice that would take two decades to put into effect. The NAACP had already begun a campaign of antisegregation lawsuits, which the Justice Department now began to support. The administration ordered federal housing agencies to modify their racially restrictive policies and prohibited racial discrimination in federal employment. Federal committees began to push for desegregation of private facilities in the symbolically important city of Washington, DC. In an important decision in the case of *Shelley v. Kraemer* (1948), the Supreme Court held that clauses in real estate deeds that forbid selling or renting to minorities could not be enforced in the courts.

The president also ordered "equality of treatment and opportunity" in the armed services in July 1948. The army in particular dragged its feet, hoping to limit black enlistees to

Jackie Robinson, the first black player in modern major league baseball, joined the Brooklyn Dodgers in 1947. He was both personally courageous and an outstanding player. Here he steals home against the Chicago Cubs in 1952.

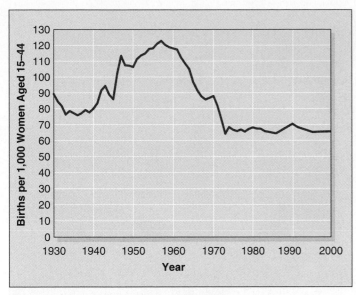

FIGURE 27–2 The Postwar Baby Boom: The U.S. Birthrate. 1930–2000

The baby boom after World War II was the product of high marriage rates and closely spaced children. The generation of Americans born between 1945 and 1960 has strongly affected American society and politics as its members went to school and college, entered the workforce, started their own families, and now have begun to plan for retirement in the twenty-first century.

10 percent of the total. Manpower needs and the record of integrated units in the war in Korea from 1950 to 1953 persuaded the reluctant generals. Over the next generation, African Americans would find the military an important avenue for career opportunities.

Changes in national policy were important for ending racial discrimination, but far more Americans were interested in lowering racial barriers in professional team sports. Americans had applauded individual black champions, such as boxer Joe Louis and sprinter Jesse Owens, but team sports required their members to travel, practice, and play together. The center of attention was Jack Roosevelt ("Jackie") Robinson, a gifted African American athlete, who opened the 1947 baseball season as a member of the Brooklyn Dodgers. Robinson broke the color line that had reserved the modern major leagues for white players. His ability to endure taunting and hostility and still excel on the ballfield opened the door for other African Americans and Latinos. In the segregated society of the 1940s, Robinson found himself a powerful symbol of racial change.

Consumer Boom and Baby Boom

The housing boom was a product of both pent-up demand and a postwar "family boom." Americans celebrated the end of the war with weddings; the marriage rate in 1946 surpassed even its wartime high. Many women who left the labor force opted for marriage, and at increasingly younger ages. By 1950, the median age at which women married would be just over

20 years—lower than at any previous time in the twentieth century. Movies in the 1930s had abounded with independent career women. By the late 1940s, Hollywood reflected new attitudes and social patterns by portraying women as helpless victims or supportive wives and publicizing hard-edged stars, such as Joan Crawford, as homebodies at heart. The United States ended the 1940s with 7 million more married couples than at the decade's start.

New marriages jumpstarted the "baby boom," as did already married couples who decided to catch up after postponing childbearing during the war. In the early 1940s, an average of 2.9 million children per year were born in the United States; in 1946–1950, the average was 3.6 million. Those 3.5 million "extra" babies needed diapers, swing sets, lunch boxes, bicycles, and schoolrooms (see Figure 27–2).

Fast-growing families also needed to stock up on household goods, including revolutionary products like Tide, the first synthetic laundry detergent that appeared on the shelves in 1946. Out of an average household income of roughly $4,000 in 1946 and 1947, a family of four had $300 to $400 a year for furnishings and appliances. A couple who studied *Consumer Reports* might equip its new Levittown kitchen with a Dripolator coffee maker for $2.45 and a

Americans were eager to enjoy the most modern appliances and houses. Manufacturers promoted streamlined kitchens to make life easier for housewives and their families.

Mirro-Matic pressure cooker for $12.95. The thrifty family could get along with a Motorola table radio in brown plastic for under $30; for $100, it could have a massive radio-phonograph combination in a 4-foot console as the centerpiece of a well-equipped living room.

Truman, Republicans, and the Fair Deal

From new radios to new homes to new jobs, the economic gains of the postwar years propelled Americans toward the political center. After 15 years of economic crisis and world war, they wanted to enjoy prosperity. William Levitt tried to humorously capture the American satisfaction with the fruits of free enterprise when he said in 1948 that "no man who owns his house and lot can be a Communist; he has too much to do."

Recognizing this attitude, Harry Truman and his political advisers tried to define policies acceptable to moderate Republicans as well as to Democrats. This meant creating a bipartisan coalition to block Soviet influence in western Europe and defending the core of the New Deal's social and economic agenda at home.

This political package is known as the strategy of the "vital center," after the title of a 1949 book by Arthur Schlesinger, Jr. The book linked anti-communism in foreign policy with efforts to enact inclusive social and economic policies to extend freedom abroad and at home. The vital center reflected the political reality of the Cold War years, when Democrats had to prove that they were tough on communism before they could enact domestic reforms. The approach defined the heart of the Democratic Party for 20 years and found full expression in the administrations of John Kennedy (1961–1963) and Lyndon Johnson (1963–1969).

Truman's Opposition

Truman had unexpected luck in his campaign for a full term as president in 1948. Besides the Republicans, he faced new fringe parties on the far right and far left that allowed him to position himself in the moderate center. The blunt, no-nonsense Missourian entered the campaign an underdog, but he soon looked like the country's best option for steering a steady course.

Harry Truman greets supporters and railroad workers in Pittsburgh at the start of an 18-state campaign tour in June 1948. Truman's grassroots campaign and down-home style helped him pull out an unexpected victory in November 1948.

Truman's opponents represented the left-leaning American Progressive Party, the **Dixiecrats** (officially the States' Rights Democrats), and the Republicans. The Progressive candidate was Henry Wallace, who had been FDR's vice president from 1941 to 1945, before being dumped in favor of Truman; more recently, he had been Truman's secretary of commerce. The Dixiecrat, Governor Strom Thurmond of South Carolina, had bolted the Democratic Party over civil rights. The most serious challenger was the Republican, Thomas Dewey, who had run against Roosevelt in 1944.

Wallace cast himself as the prophet for "the century of the common man." His background as a farm journalist

Gunnar Myrdal, Race Relations, and Cold War Leadership

In 1938, the Swedish social scientist Gunnar Myrdal came to the United States at the invitation of the Carnegie Foundation to study relations between white and black Americans—what people at the time called the "Negro problem." Six years later, he published *An American Dilemma*, a 1,000-page volume with hundreds of additional pages of supporting data. Studying the problems of race relations as a stranger, Myrdal was struck by the basic national values derived from English law and Christian belief, values and opportunities that he termed the "American Creed."

Not since Reconstruction has there been more reason to anticipate fundamental changes in American race relations, changes which will involve a development toward the American ideals....America, relative to all the other branches of Western civilization, is moralistic and "moral-conscious." ...

America feels itself to be humanity in miniature. When in this crucial time the international leadership passes to America, the great reason for hope is that this country has a national experience of united racial and cultural diversity and a national theory, if not a consistent practice, of freedom and equality for all. What America is constantly reaching for is democracy at home and abroad. The main trend in its history is the gradual realization of the American Creed.

In this sense the Negro problem is not only America's greatest failure but also America's incomparably great opportunity for the future. If America should follow its own deepest convictions, its well-being at home would be increased directly. At the same time, America's prestige and power would be increased directly....America can demonstrate that justice, equality and cooperation are possible between white and colored people.

Myrdal's challenge became an important consideration during the Cold War. Washington policymakers realized that the peoples of Africa, Asia, and Latin America were paying close attention to how the nation's white majority treated its black and Hispanic citizens. This concern for America's global reputation helped make otherwise reluctant leaders into supporters of the black civil rights movement and fair treatment of Mexican migrant workers. The admission of multiracial Hawaii as the fiftieth state in 1959 was a challenge to segregationists and was seen as a "bridge to Asia" that carried the message that the United States was welcoming to all peoples.

Gunnar Myrdal, *An American Dilemma* (New York: McGraw-Hill, 1964), pp. lxi, lxx, 1021. (Originally published in 1944)

■ Does the idea of an American Creed help us to understand the international roles of the United States in the twenty-first century?

---

prepared him to deal with domestic policy but not with world affairs. After Truman fired him from the cabinet in 1946 for advocating a conciliatory stance toward the Soviet Union, Wallace continued to denounce U.S. foreign policy. Enthusiastic college crowds raised his sights from "scaring the Democratic Party leftward" to running for president. Most liberal Democrats avoided the Progressive Party; the Communist Party supplied many of Wallace's campaign workers.

Wallace argued that the United States was forcing the Cold War on the Soviet Union and undermining American ideals by diverting attention from poverty and racism at home. He wanted to repeal the draft and destroy atomic weapons. His arguments had merit, for the United States was becoming a militarized society, but Wallace struck most voters as a kook rather than a statesman, and he made skepticism about the Cold War increasingly vulnerable to right-wing attack.

At the other political extreme were the southerners who walked out when the 1948 Democratic National Convention called for full civil rights for African Americans. Mayor Hubert Humphrey of Minneapolis challenged the Democratic

Party "to get out of the shadow of states' rights and walk forthrightly into the bright sunshine of human rights." His speech foreshadowed Humphrey's 20 years of liberal influence in the Democratic Party, culminating in his presidential nomination in 1968.

When the angry southerners met to nominate their own candidate, however, the South's important politicians stayed away. They had worked too long to throw away seniority and influence in Congress and the Democratic Party. Major southern newspapers called the revolt futile and narrowminded. Strom Thurmond claimed that the Dixiecrats were really trying to defend Americans against government bureaucracy, not fighting to preserve racial segregation, but few listened outside the deep South.

Tom Dewey, Truman's real opponent, had a high opinion of himself. He had been an effective governor of New York and represented the moderate eastern establishment within the Republican Party. Fortunately for Truman, Dewey lacked the common touch. Smooth on the outside, he alienated people who should have been his closest supporters. He was a bit of a snob and was an arrogant campaigner, refusing to interrupt his morning schedule to talk to voters.

Dewey was also saddled with the results of the Republican-controlled "do-nothing" 80th Congress (1947–1948). Truman used confrontation with Congress to rally voters who had supported the New Deal. He introduced legislation that he knew would be ignored, and he used his veto even when he knew Congress would override it. All the while he was building a list of campaign issues by demonstrating that the Republicans were obstructionists. Vote for me, Truman argued, to protect the New Deal, or vote Republican to bring back the days of Herbert Hoover.

Whistle-Stopping Across America

The 1948 presidential campaign mixed old and new. For the last time, a major candidate crisscrossed the nation by rail and made hundreds of speeches from the rear platforms of trains. For the first time, national television broadcast the two party conventions, although the primitive cameras showed the handful of viewers little more than talking heads. The Republican campaign issued a printed T-shirt that read "Dew-It With Dewey," the earliest advertising T-shirt in the collections of the Smithsonian Institution.

Truman ran on both character and issues. He was a widely read and intelligent man who cultivated the image of a backslapper. "I'll mow 'em down...and I'll give 'em hell," he told his vice presidential running mate. Crowds across the country greeted him with "Give 'em hell, Harry!" He covered 31,700 miles in his campaign train and gave ten speeches a day. Republicans belittled the small towns and cities he visited, calling them "whistle stops." Democrats made the term a badge of pride for places like Laramie, Wyoming, and Pocatello, Idaho.

Truman brought the campaign home to average Americans. He tied Dewey to inflation, housing shortages, and

fears about the future of Social Security (an issue that Democrats would continue to use into the next century). In industrial cities, he hammered at the Taft-Hartley Act. In the West, he pointed out that Democratic administrations had built dams and helped to turn natural resources into jobs. He called the Republicans the party of privilege and arrogance. The Democrats, he said, offered opportunity for farmers, factory workers, and small business owners.

Truman got a huge boost from Dewey's unwillingness to fight. Going into the fall with a huge lead in the public opinion polls, Dewey sought to avoid mistakes. He packed his speeches with platitudes: "Our streams abound with fish." "You know that your future is still ahead of you." The results astounded the poll takers, who had stopped sampling opinion in mid-October just as a swing to Truman gathered strength. Wallace and Thurmond each took just under 1.2 million votes. Dewey received nearly 22 million popular votes and 189 electoral votes, but Truman won more than 24 million popular votes and 303 electoral votes (see Map 27–1).

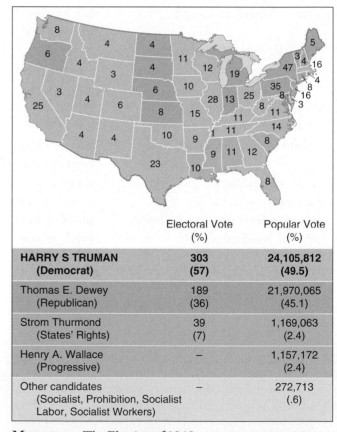

	Electoral Vote (%)	Popular Vote (%)
HARRY S TRUMAN (Democrat)	**303 (57)**	**24,105,812 (49.5)**
Thomas E. Dewey (Republican)	189 (36)	21,970,065 (45.1)
Strom Thurmond (States' Rights)	39 (7)	1,169,063 (2.4)
Henry A. Wallace (Progressive)	–	1,157,172 (2.4)
Other candidates (Socialist, Prohibition, Socialist Labor, Socialist Workers)	–	272,713 (.6)

MAP 27–1   The Election of 1948
Harry Truman won a narrow victory in the presidential election of 1948 by holding many of the traditionally Democratic states of the South and West and winning key industrial states in the Middle West. His success depended on the coalition of rural and urban interests that Franklin Roosevelt had pulled together in the 1930s.

Truman's Fair Deal

Truman hoped to build on the gains of the New Deal. In his State of the Union address in January 1949, he called for a Fair Deal for all Americans. He promised to extend the New Deal and ensure "greater economic opportunity for the mass of the people." Over the next four years, however, conservative Republicans and southern Democrats forced Congress to choose carefully among Truman's proposals, accepting those that expanded existing programs but rejecting new departures. The result was a set of disconnected measures rather than the consistent program that Truman had advocated.

With the Housing Act of 1949, the federal government reaffirmed its concern about families who had been priced out of the private market. Passed with the backing of conservative Senator Robert Taft, "Mr. Republican" to his admirers, the act provided money for local housing agencies to buy, clear, and re-sell land for housing. The intent was to clear "substandard and blighted areas" and replace them with affordable modern apartments. The program never worked as intended because of scanty appropriations, poor design of the replacement housing, and local decisions that concentrated public housing in segregated minority neighborhoods, but it established the goal of decent housing for all Americans.

In 1950, Congress revitalized the weak Social Security program. Benefits went up by an average of 80 percent, and 10.5 million additional people received old-age and survivors' insurance. Most of the new coverage went to rural and small-town people, thus consolidating the broad support that has made it politically difficult to change Social Security ever since, even in the face of projected shortages in the twenty-first century.

Congress rejected other Fair Deal proposals that would remain on the national agenda for decades. A Senate fili-buster killed a permanent Fair Employment Practices Commission to fight racial discrimination in hiring, halting progress toward civil rights. The medical establishment blocked a proposal for national health insurance as "social-istic," leaving the issue to be revisited in the 1960s (with the passage of Medicare and Medicaid) and 1990s (with Bill Clinton's proposals for healthcare reform). The overall message from Truman's second term was clear: Americans liked what the New Deal had given them but were hesitant about new initiatives.

Confronting the Soviet Union

In 1945, the United States and the Soviet Union were allies, victorious against Germany and planning the defeat of Japan. By 1947, they were engaged in a diplomatic and economic confrontation and soon came close to war over the city of Berlin. The business tycoon and presidential adviser Bernard Baruch characterized the conflict in April 1947 as a "cold war," and newspaper columnist Walter Lippmann quickly popularized the term.

Over the next 40 years, the United States and the Soviet Union contested for economic, political, and military influence around the globe. The heart of Soviet policy was to control eastern Europe as a buffer zone against Germany. The centerpiece of American policy was to link the United States, western Europe, and Japan into an alliance of over-whelming economic power. Both sides spent vast sums on conventional military forces and atomic weapons that held the world in a "balance of terror." They also competed for political advantage in Asia and Africa as newly independent nations replaced European colonial empires. For the United States, the Cold War was simultaneously an effort to promote democracy in Europe, maintain a favorable military position in relation to the Soviet Union, and preserve its leadership of the world economy.

Each side in the Cold War thought the worst of the other. Behind the conflicts were Soviet insecurity about an aggressive West and American fear of Communist expansionism. Americans and Soviets frequently interpreted each other's actions in the most threatening terms, turning miscalculations and misunderstandings into crises. A U.S. public that had suffered through nearly two decades of economic depression and war reacted to international problems with frustration and anger. The emotional burdens of the Cold War warped and narrowed a generation of American political life around the requirements of anticommunism.

The End of the Grand Alliance

The Yalta Conference of February 1945 had recognized military realities by marking out rough spheres of influence. The Soviet defeat of Germany on the Eastern Front had made the Soviet Union the only military power in eastern Europe. The American and British attacks through Italy and France had made the Western allies dominant in western Europe and the Mediterranean. The Soviets, Americans, British, and French shared control of defeated Germany, each with its own occupation zone and its own sector of Berlin, the former German capital located inside the Soviet zone. The Western allies had the better of the bargain. Defeated Italy and Japan, whose reconstruction was firmly in Western hands, had far greater economic potential than Soviet-controlled Bulgaria, Romania, or Hungary. In addition, the British, French, and American occupation zones in western Germany held more people and industrial potential than the Russian zone in eastern Germany.

As the victorious powers tried to put their broad agreements into operation, they argued bitterly about Germany and eastern Europe. Was the Soviet Union to dominate eastern Europe as its protective buffer, or was the region to be open to Western economic and political influence? For Poland, Truman and his advisers claimed that Yalta had assumed open elections on the American model. The Soviet Union claimed that Yalta had ensured that any Polish government would be friendly to Soviet interests and acted to guarantee that this would be so.

Facing Soviet intransigence over eastern Europe, Truman decided that the United States should "take the lead in running the world in the way the world ought to be run." One technique was economic pressure. The State Department "mislaid" a Soviet request for redevelopment loans. The United States and Britain objected to Soviet plans to take industrial equipment and raw materials from the western occupation zones in Germany, compensation that the Soviets thought they had been promised.

The United States also tried to involve the Soviet Union and eastern Europe in new international organizations. The Senate approved American membership in the newly organized United Nations (UN) with only two opposing votes, a sharp contrast to its rejection of the League of Nations in 1920. The Washington-based **International Monetary Fund (IMF)** and the **World Bank** were designed to revive international trade. The IMF stabilized national currencies against the short-term pressures of international trade. The World Bank drew on the resources of member nations to make economic development loans to governments for such projects as new dams or agricultural modernization. These organizations ensured that the reviving world economy would revolve around the industrial and technological power of the United States, and they continue to dictate the economic policy of many developing nations into the twenty-first century.

In 1946, the United States presented a plan in the United Nations to control atomic energy. Bernard Baruch suggested that an international agency should oversee all uranium production and research on atomic explosives. The Baruch plan emphasized enforcement and inspections that would have opened the Soviet nuclear effort to American interference, an unacceptable prospect for a nation trying to catch up with the United States by building its own atomic bombs. On-site inspection would remain a problem in arms-control negotiations for the next half-century.

While UN delegates debated the future of atomic energy, American leaders were becoming convinced of Soviet aggressiveness. In February 1946, George Kennan, a senior American diplomat in Moscow, sent a "long telegram" to the State Department. He depicted a Soviet Union driven by expansionist Communist ideology. The Soviets, he argued, would constantly probe for weaknesses in the capitalist world. The best response was firm resistance to protect the Western heartlands.

The British encouraged the same tough stand. Lacking the strength to shape Europe on its own, Great Britain repeatedly nudged the United States to block Soviet influence. Speaking at Westminster College in Missouri in March 1946, Winston Churchill warned that the Soviet Union had dropped an "iron curtain" across the middle of Europe and urged a firm Western response.

Churchill's speech matched the mood in official Washington. Truman's foreign-policy advisers shared the belief in an aggressive Soviet Union, and the president himself saw the world as a series of either-or choices. Administration leaders did not fear an immediate Soviet military threat to the United States, for they knew that World War II had exhausted the Soviet Union. But they knew that the Soviets were strong enough to brush aside the U.S. occupation forces in Germany. Added to military apprehension were worries about political and economic competition. Communist parties in war-ravaged Europe and Japan were exploiting discontent. In Asia and Africa, the allegiance of nationalists who were fighting for independence from European powers remained in doubt. America's leaders worried that much of the Eastern Hemisphere might fall under Soviet control.

Were Truman and his advisers right about Soviet intentions? The evidence is mixed. In their determination to avoid another Munich, Truman and his foreign-policy circle ignored examples of Soviet caution and conciliation. The Soviets withdrew troops from Manchuria in northern China and acquiesced in America's control of defeated Japan. They allowed a neutral but democratic government in Finland and technically free elections in Hungary and Czechoslovakia (although it was clear that Communists would do well there). They demobilized much of their huge army and reduced their forces in eastern Europe.

However, the Soviet regime also acted to justify American fears. The Soviet Union could not resist exerting influence in the Middle East. It pressured Turkey to give it partial control of the exit from the Black Sea. It retained troops in northern Iran until warned out by the United States. The Soviets were ruthless in support of Communist control in Eastern Europe in 1946 and 1947; they aided a Communist takeover in Bulgaria, backed a coup in Romania, and undermined the last non-Communist political opposition in Poland. U.S. policymakers read these Soviet actions as a rerun of Nazi aggression and determined not to let a new totalitarian threat undermine Western power.

The Truman Doctrine and the Marshall Plan

Whatever restraint the Soviet Union showed was too late or too little. Early in 1947, Truman and his advisers acted decisively. The British could no longer afford to back the Greek government that was fighting a civil war against Communists, and U.S. officials feared that a Communist takeover in Greece would threaten the stability of Italy, France, and the Middle East. Truman coupled his case for intervention in Greece with an appeal for aid to neighboring Turkey, which lived under the shadow of the Soviet Union. On March 12, he told Congress that the United States faced a "fateful hour" and requested $400 million to fight Communism in Greece and Turkey and secure the free world. Congress agreed, and the United States became the dominant power in the eastern Mediterranean.

Framing the specific request was a sweeping declaration that became known as the **Truman Doctrine**. The president pledged to use U.S. economic power to help free nations everywhere resist internal subversion or aggression. "It must be the policy of the United States," he said, "to support free peoples who are resisting attempted subjugation by armed minorities or by outside pressures.... I believe that our help should be primarily through economic and financial aid, which is essential to economic stability and orderly political processes."

Meanwhile, Europe was sliding toward chaos. Germany was close to famine after the bitter winter of 1946–1947. Western European nations were bankrupt and unable to import raw materials for their factories. Overstressed medical systems could no longer control tuberculosis and other diseases. Communist parties had gained in Italy, France, and Germany. Winston Churchill, again sounding the alarm, described Europe as "a rubble-heap, a charnel house, a breeding ground of pestilence and hate."

The U.S. government responded with unprecedented economic aid. Secretary of State George C. Marshall announced the European Recovery Plan on June 5, 1947. What the press quickly dubbed the **Marshall Plan** committed the United States to help rebuild Europe. The United States invited Soviet and eastern European participation, but under terms that would have reduced Moscow's control over its satellite economies. The Soviets refused, fearing that the United States wanted to undermine its influence, and instead organized their eastern European satellites in their own association for Mutual Economic Assistance, or Comecon, in 1949. In western Europe, the Marshall Plan was a success. Aid totaled $13.5 billion over four years. It met many of Europe's economic needs and quieted class conflict. The Marshall Plan expanded American influence through cooperative efforts. Because Europeans spent much of the aid on U.S. goods and machinery, and because economic recovery promised markets for U.S. products, business and labor both supported it. In effect, the Marshall Plan created an "empire by invitation," in which Americans and Europeans jointly planned Europe's recovery.

The Americans also micromanaged European politics. In Italy, for example, the U.S. forced the middle-of-the-road Christian Democrats to kick the Italian Communist party out of its governing coalition in return for economic aid. In 1948, Marshall warned the Italians that aid would vanish if they voted Communists into power. The State Department recruited Italian American organizations to pressure relatives in Italy and was relieved when the Christians Democrats won.

U.S. policy in Japan followed the pattern set in Europe. As supreme commander of the Allied Powers, General Douglas MacArthur acted as Japan's postwar dictator. He tried to change the values of the old war-prone Japan through social reform, democratization, and demilitarization. At the end of 1947, however, the United States decided that democracy and pacifism could go too far. Policymakers were fearful of economic collapse and political chaos, just as in Europe. The "reverse course" in occupation policy aimed to make Japan an economic magnet for other nations in East Asia, pulling them toward the American orbit and away from the Soviet Union. MacArthur reluctantly accepted the new policy of "economic crank-up" by preserving Japan's corporate giants and encouraging American investment. At American insistence, the new Japan accepted American bases and created its own "self-defense force" (with no capacity for overseas aggression).

George Kennan summed up the new American policies in the magazine *Foreign Affairs* in July 1947. Writing anonymously as "X," Kennan argued that the Soviet leaders were committed to a long-term strategy of expanding Communism. The proper posture of the United States, he said, should be an equally patient commitment to "firm and vigilant **containment** of Russian expansive tendencies." Kennan warned that the emerging Cold War would be a long conflict, with no quick fixes.

Soviet Reactions

The bold American moves in the first half of 1947 put the Soviet Union on the defensive. In response, Soviet leaders orchestrated strenuous opposition to the Marshall Plan by French and Italian Communists. East of the Iron Curtain, Hungarian Communists expelled other political parties from a coalition government. Bulgarian Communists shot opposition leaders. Romania, Bulgaria, and Hungary signed defense pacts with the Soviet Union.

In early 1948, the Soviets targeted Czechoslovakia. For three years, a neutral coalition government there on the model of Finland had balanced trade with the West with a foreign policy friendly to the Soviet Union. In February 1948, while Russian forces assembled on the Czech border, local Communists took advantage of political bumbling by other members of the governing coalition. Taking control through a technically legal process, they pushed aside Czechoslovakia's democratic leadership and turned the nation into a dictatorship and Soviet satellite within a week.

The climax of the Soviet reaction came in divided Berlin, located 110 miles inside the Soviet Union's East German occupation zone. The city was divided into four sectors: one controlled by the Soviets and three by the United States, Britain, and France. On June 4, 1948, Soviet troops blockaded surface traffic into Berlin, cutting off the U.S., British, and French sectors. The immediate Soviet aim was to block Western plans to merge their three German occupation zones into an independent federal republic (West Germany). Rather than abandon 2.5 million Berliners or shoot their way through, the Western nations responded to the **Berlin blockade** by airlifting supplies to the city. Stalin decided not to intercept the flights. After 11 months, the Soviets abandoned the blockade, making the Berlin airlift a triumph of American resolve.

American Rearmament

The coup in Czechoslovakia and the Berlin blockade shocked American leaders and backfired on the Soviets. The economic assistance strategy of 1947 now looked inadequate. Congress responded in 1948 by reinstating the military draft and increasing defense spending. Much of the money bought new warplanes, as thrifty congressmen decided that air power was the easiest way for the United States to project its military power abroad.

The United States had already begun to modernize and centralize its national security apparatus, creating the institutions that would run foreign policy in the second half of the century. The National Security Act of July 1947 created the **Central Intelligence Agency** (CIA) and the **National Security Council** (NSC). The CIA handled intelligence gathering and covert operations. The NSC assembled top diplomatic and military advisers in one committee. In 1949, legislation also created the Department of Defense to oversee the army, navy, and air force (independent from the army since 1947). The civilian secretary of defense soon began to exercise influence on foreign policy equal to that of the secretary of state. The new post of chairman of the joint chiefs of staff was supposed to coordinate the rival branches of the military.

In April 1949, ten European nations, the United States, and Canada signed the North Atlantic Treaty as a mutual defense pact. American commitments to the **North Atlantic Treaty Organization (NATO)** included military aid and the deployment of U.S. troops in western Europe. As Republican Senator Robert Taft warned in the ratification debate, NATO was the sort of "entangling alliance" that the United States had avoided for 160 years. It was also the insurance policy that western Europeans required if they were to accept the dangers as well as the benefits of a revived West Germany, which was economically and militarily necessary for a strong Europe. In short, NATO was a sort of marriage contract between Europe and the previously standoffish United States. After 1955, its counterpart would be the **Warsaw Pact** for mutual defense among the Soviet Union and its European satellites (see Map 27–2).

Two years later, the United States signed similar but less comprehensive agreements in the western Pacific: the ANZUS Pact with Australia and New Zealand and a new treaty with the Philippines. The alliances reassured Pacific allies that were nervously watching the United States negotiate a unilateral peace treaty with Japan (ignoring the Soviet Union). The United States overcame opposition from nations Japan had attacked in World War II by promising to assist their defense and maintaining military bases in Japan. Taken together, peacetime rearmament and mutual defense pacts amounted to a revolution in American foreign policy.

Cold War and Hot War

The first phase of the Cold War reached a crisis in the autumn of 1949. The two previous years had seen an uneasy equilibrium in which American success in southern and western Europe and the standoff over Berlin (the blockade ended in May 1949) balanced the consolidation of Soviet power in eastern Europe. Now, suddenly, two key events seemed to tilt the world balance against the United States and its allies. In September, Truman announced that the Soviet Union had tested its own atomic bomb. A month later, the Communists under Mao Zedong (Mao Tse-tung) took power in China. The following summer, civil war in Korea sucked the United States into a fierce war with Communist North Korea and China. While Americans studied maps that showed communism spreading across Europe and Asia, their government accelerated a 40-year arms race with the Soviet Union.

Berlin was still a devastated city in 1948. When the Soviet Union closed off ground access to the British, French, and American occupation zones, the city became a symbol of the West's Cold War resolve. Allied aircraft lifted in food, fuel, and other essentials for West Berliners for nearly a year until the Soviets ended the blockade.

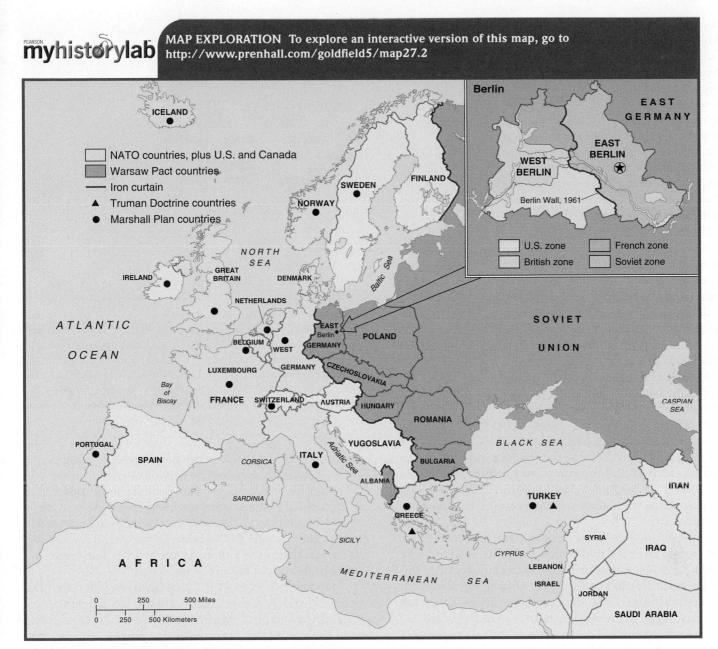

MAP EXPLORATION To explore an interactive version of this map, go to http://www.prenhall.com/goldfield5/map27.2

MAP 27–2   Cold War in Europe
In the late 1940s and 1950s, the Cold War split Europe into rigidly divided western and eastern blocs. Members of NATO allied with the United States to oppose Soviet expansion. The Soviet Union directed the military and foreign policies of members of the Warsaw Pact.

The Nuclear Shadow

Experts in Washington had known that the Soviets were working on an A-bomb, but the news dismayed the average citizen. As newspapers and magazines scared their readers with artists' renditions of the effects of an atomic bomb on New York or Chicago, the shock tilted U.S. nuclear policy toward military uses. In 1946, advocates of civilian control had won a small victory when Congress established the Atomic Energy Commission (AEC). The AEC tried to balance research on atomic power with continued testing of

new weapons. Now Truman told the AEC to double the output of fissionable uranium and plutonium for "conventional" nuclear weapons.

A more momentous decision soon followed. Truman decided in January 1950 to authorize work on the "super" bomb—the thermonuclear fusion weapon that would become the hydrogen bomb (H-bomb). The debate over the "super" pitted a cautious scientific advisory committee and J. Robert Oppenheimer against powerful political figures and a handful of scientists who believed, correctly, that the

Soviets were already at work on a similar weapon. As would be true in future nuclear-defense debates, the underlying question was how much capacity for nuclear destruction was enough.

Nuclear weapons proliferated in the early 1950s. The United States repeatedly tested nuclear fission weapons in Nevada and exploded the first hydrogen bomb in the South Pacific in November 1952. Releasing 100 times the energy of the Hiroshima bomb, the detonation tore a mile-long chasm in the ocean floor. Great Britain became the third nuclear power in the same year. The Soviet Union tested its own hydrogen bomb only nine months after the United States. Americans who remembered the attack on Pearl Harbor now worried that the Soviets might send fleets of bombers over the Arctic to surprise U.S. military forces and smash its cities into radioactive powder.

The nuclear arms race and the gnawing fear of nuclear war multiplied the apprehensions of the Cold War. Under the guidance of the Federal Civil Defense Administration, Americans learned that they should always keep a battery-powered radio and tune to 640 or 1240 on the AM dial for emergency information when they heard air raid sirens. Schoolchildren learned to hide under their desks when they saw the blinding flash of a nuclear detonation.

More insidiously, nuclear weapons development generated new environmental and health problems. Soldiers were exposed to posttest radiation with minimal protection. Nuclear tests in the South Pacific dusted fishing boats with radioactivity and forced islanders to abandon contaminated homes. Las Vegas promoted tests in southern Nevada as tourist attractions, but radioactive fallout contaminated large sections of the West and increased cancer rates among "downwinders" in Utah. Weapons production and atomic experiments contaminated vast tracts in Nevada, Washington, and Colorado and left huge environmental costs for later generations (see Map 27-3).

The Cold War in Asia

Communist victory in China's civil war was as predictable as the Soviet nuclear bomb but no less controversial. The collapse of Jiang Jieshi's Nationalist regime was nearly inevitable, given its corruption and narrow support. Nevertheless, Americans looked for a scapegoat when Jiang's anti-Communist government and remnants of the Nationalist army fled to the island of Taiwan off China's southern coast.

Advocates for Jiang, mostly conservative Republicans from the Midwest and West, were certain that Truman's administration had done too little. "China asked for a sword,"

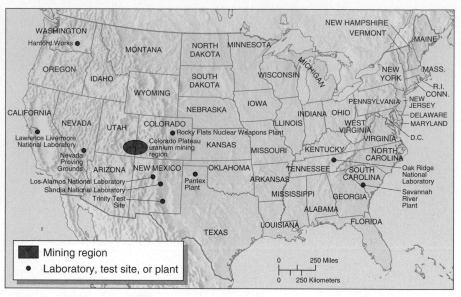

MAP 27-3 **The Landscape of Nuclear Weapons**
The development and production of nuclear weapons was concentrated in the West and South. The World War II sites of Hanford, Los Alamos, and Oak Ridge remained active after the war. Workers at Savannah River, Rocky Flats, and Pantex produced nuclear materials. Scientists and engineers at Lawrence-Livermore and Sandia laboratories designed and assembled weapons that were tested at the Nevada Proving Grounds. Prospectors with Geiger counters swarmed over the canyons of southwestern Colorado and southeastern Utah in a uranium-mining rush in the early 1950s.

complained one senator, "and we gave her a dull paring knife." Critics looked for scapegoats. Foreign Service officers who had honestly analyzed the weakness of the Nationalists were accused of Communist sympathies and hounded from their jobs. The results were tragedy for those unfairly branded as traitors and damage to the State Department, a weakness that would haunt the United States as it became entangled in southeast Asia in the 1950s and 1960s.

Mao's victory expanded a deep fissure between the "Europe first" and "Asia first" approaches to U.S. foreign policy. Both during and after World War II, the United States had made Europe its first priority. Strong voices, however, had persistently argued that America's future lay with China, Japan, and the Pacific nations. Influential senators claimed that the "loss of China" was the disastrous result of putting the needs of England and France above the long-term interests of the United States.

NSC-68 and Aggressive Containment

The turmoil of 1949 led to a comprehensive statement of American strategic goals. In April 1950, the State Department prepared a sweeping report known as **National Security Council Paper 68 (NSC-68).** The document described a world divided between the forces of "slavery" and "freedom" and assumed that the Soviet Union was actively aggressive, motivated by greed for territory and a "fanatic faith" in Communism. To defend civilization itself, said the experts, the United States should use as much force as needed to resist Communist expansion anywhere and everywhere.

FROM THEN TO NOW

NATO

In 2003, the North Atlantic Treaty Organization (NATO) assumed command of the International Security Assistance Force in Afghanistan. The action came two years after the United States responded to the September 11 attacks by attacking that country's Al Qaeda's bases and Taliban regime, and it was one more step in the transformation of NATO after the end of the Cold War.

NATO airstrike against Serb forces in Kosovo in 1999.

When created in 1949, NATO had three purposes. The first was to unite non-communist nations of western Europe in an alliance against the Soviet Union. The second was to formally commit the United States and Canada to the defense of western Europe. The third was to establish a framework that would make the rearmament of West Germany acceptable to other European nations. For the next forty years—until the collapse of eastern European Communism—NATO coordinated western European defense planning and remained a foundation stone of United States foreign policy.

Since the early 1990s, however, a new Europe has meant a new NATO, which has expanded into the former Soviet sphere in eastern Europe over Russian objections. At its fiftieth anniversary summit in 1999, NATO admitted Poland, Hungary, and the Czech Republic, and has since added seven other eastern European nations.

The other change was a redefinition of NATO's mission. In the mid-1990s in southeastern Europe, NATO stepped in belatedly to halt a bitter civil war in Bosnia where Christian Serbs engaged in massacres and deportations of Muslin Bosnians with the goal of creating "ethnically clean" Serbian districts. NATO intervened more quickly in Kosovo in 1999 to stop Serb reprisals against ethnic Albanians in another civil war. With these actions, and with its role in Afghanistan, NATO changed from a purely defensive military alliance to Europe's own police force.

■ What factors might explain why NATO has been the longest lasting of the Cold War military alliances?

PEARSON
myhistorylab

From Then to Now Online

27-1 Clark Clifford, *Memorandum*, March 1948. Recommending formation of a defense alliance that would take form as NATO.

27-2 *Map of NATO*. Expansion from 1949 through 2004.

27-3 *NATO* defines the terrorist actions of September 11 2001 as an attack on all NATO nations.

U.S. tank at Checkpoint Charlie, looking from the American sector of West Berlin toward Communist controlled East Berlin. The sign announces the border in the languages of the four nations that divided control of Germany and Berlin after World War II.

The authors of NSC-68 intended to extend the Truman Doctrine and convince Americans of the threat of the Cold War. They also thought in terms of military solutions. In the original containment policy, Truman and his advisers had hoped to contain the Soviets by diplomacy and by integrating the economies of Europe and Japan with that of the United States. Now that the Soviets had the atomic bomb, however, the American atomic shield might be neutralized. Instead, NSC-68 argued that the United States needed to press friendly nations to rearm and make its former enemies into military allies. It also argued that the nation needed expensive conventional forces to defend Europe on the ground and to react to crises as a "world policeman." NSC-68 thus advocated nearly open-ended increases in the defense budget (which, in fact, tripled between 1950 and 1954).

NSC-68 summed up what many people already believed. Although it was not a public document, its portrait of implacable Communist expansion would have made sense to most Americans; it certainly did to Harry Truman. The outbreak of war in Korea at the end of June 1950 seemed to confirm that Communism was a military threat. The thinking behind the report led the United States to approach the Cold War as a military competition and to view political changes in Africa and Asia as parts of a Soviet plan. The need for a flexible military response became the centerpiece of a U.S. policy of active intervention that led eventually to the jungles of Vietnam in the 1960s. And the report's implied strategy of bankrupting the Communists through competitive defense spending helped destroy the Soviet Union at the end of the 1980s.

War in Korea, 1950–1953

The success of Mao and the Chinese Communists forced the Truman administration to define national interests in eastern Asia and the western Pacific. Most important was Japan, still an industrial power despite its devastating defeat. The United States had denied the Soviet Union any part in the occupation of Japan in 1945 and had shaped a more democratic nation that would be a strong and friendly trading partner. Protected by American armed forces, Japan would be part of a crescent of off-shore strong points that included Alaska, Okinawa, the Philippines, Australia, and New Zealand.

Two questions remained at the start of 1950 (and were still troublesome at the end of the century). One was the future of Taiwan and the remnants of Jiang's regime. Some American policymakers wanted to defend Jiang against the Communists. Others assumed that his tattered forces would collapse and allow Mao to complete the Communist takeover of Chinese territory. The other question was Korea, whose own civil war would soon bring the world to the brink of World War III.

The Korean peninsula is the closest point on the Asian mainland to Japan. With three powerful neighbors—China, Russia, and Japan—Korea had always had to fight for its independence. From 1910 to 1945, it was an oppressed colony of the Japanese Empire. As World War II ended, Soviet troops moved down the peninsula from the north and American forces landed in the south, creating a situation similar to that in Germany. The 38th parallel, which Russians and Americans set as the dividing line between their zones of occupation, became a *de facto* border. The United States in 1948 recognized an independent South Korea, with its capital at Seoul, under a conservative government led by Syngman Rhee. Rhee's support came from large landowners and from a police force trained by the Japanese before 1945. The Soviets recognized a separate North Korea, whose Communist leader, Kim Il Sung, advocated radical social and political

United Nation forces in Korea fought the weather as well as Communist North Koreans and Chinese. Baking summer heat alternated with fierce winters. Snow and cold were a major help to the Chinese when they surprised United States forces in November 1950 and drove American troops such as these southward.

change. Both leaders saw the 38th parallel as a temporary barrier and hoped to unify all Koreans under their own rule. Each crushed political dissent and tried to undermine the other with economic pressure and commando raids.

As early as 1947, the United States had decided that Korea was not essential to American military strategy. Planners assumed that U.S. air power in Japan could neutralize unfriendly forces on the Korean peninsula. In January 1950, Secretary of State Dean Acheson carefully excluded Korea from the primary "defensive perimeter" of the United States but kept open the possibility of international guarantees for Korean security.

On June 25, 1950, North Korea, helped by Soviet equipment and Chinese training, attacked South Korea. The invasion began the **Korean War,** which lasted until 1953 (see Map 27–4). Truman and Acheson believed that Moscow lay behind the invasion. They worried that the attack was a ploy to suck America's limited military resources into Asia before a bigger war came in Europe or the Middle East. Republicans blamed Acheson's speech for inviting an invasion, but the war was really an intensification of an ongoing civil war that Stalin was willing to exploit. In fact, Kim originated the invasion plan because he seemed to be losing the civil war in the south, and he spent a year persuading Stalin to agree to it. Stalin hoped that the conquest of South Korea would force Japan to sign a favorable treaty with the USSR.

American leaders thought that the explosion of a hot war after five years of world tension demanded a military response. As the South Korean army collapsed, Truman committed American ground troops from Japan on June 30. The United States also had the good fortune of securing an endorsement from the United Nations. Because the Soviet Union was boycotting the UN (hoping to force the seating of Mao's People's Republic of China in place of Jiang's government), it could not use its veto when the Security Council asked UN members to help South Korea. The Korean conflict remained officially a United Nations action. Although U.S. Generals Douglas MacArthur, Matthew Ridgway, and Mark Clark ran the show as the successive heads of the UN command, 21 other nations committed military resources in a true multinational coalition.

The Politics of War

Fortunes in the first year of the Korean conflict seesawed three times. The first U.S. combat troops were outnumbered, outgunned, and poorly trained. They could not stop the North Koreans. By early August, the Americans clung to a narrow toehold around the port of Pusan on the tip of the Korean peninsula. As reinforcements arrived, however, MacArthur transformed the war with a daring amphibious counterattack at Inchon, 150 miles behind North Korean lines. The North Korean army was already overextended and exhausted. It collapsed and fled north.

The temptation to push across the 38th parallel and unify the peninsula under Syngman Rhee was irresistible. MacArthur and Washington officials disregarded warnings by China that it would enter the war if the United States tried to reunite Korea by force. U.S. and South Korean troops

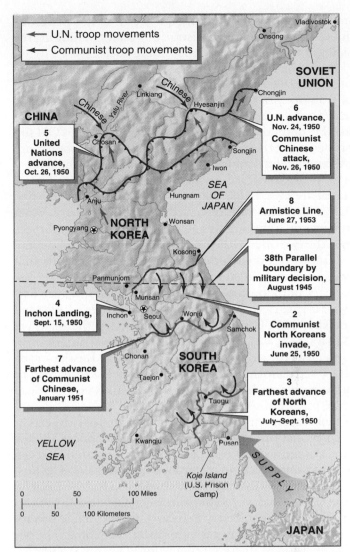

Map 27–4   The Korean War
After rapid reversals of fortune in 1950 and early 1951, the war in Korea settled into stalemate. Most Americans agreed with the need to contain Communist expansion but found it deeply frustrating to fight for limited objectives rather than total victory.

rolled north, drawing closer and closer to the boundary between North Korea and China.

Chinese forces attacked MacArthur's command in late October but then disappeared. MacArthur dismissed the attacks as a token gesture. In fact, they were a final warning. On November 26, the Chinese struck the overextended American columns. They had massed 300,000 troops without detection by American aviation. Their assault drove the UN forces into a two-month retreat that again abandoned Seoul.

Despite his glaring mistake, MacArthur remained in command until he publicly contradicted national policy. In March 1951, with the UN forces again pushing north, Truman prepared to offer a ceasefire that would have preserved the separate nations of South and North Korea. MacArthur tried to preempt the president by demanding that China admit defeat or suffer the consequences. He then published a direct attack on the administration's policy of limiting the Asian war to ensure the security of Europe.

President Truman had no choice. To protect civilian control of the armed forces, he relieved MacArthur of his command on April 11, 1951. The general returned to parades and a hero's welcome when he addressed a joint session of Congress. He quoted a line from an old barracks song: "Old soldiers never die; they just fade away." The song was soon heard on the radio, but Truman remained in charge of the war.

In Korea itself, U.S. and South Korean forces stabilized a strong defensive line that cut diagonally across the 38th parallel. Here the conflict settled into trench warfare. What had started as a civil war was now an international conflict between the two sides in the larger Cold War. UN and Communist armies faced each other across steep bare hills that choked in clouds of summer dust and froze in winter. For two years, boredom alternated with fierce inch-by-inch battles for territory with such names as Heartbreak Ridge and Pork Chop Hill. The war's only glamour was in the air, where the arrival of new F-86 Saberjets in 1952 allowed American pilots to clear the skies of Chinese aviators in Russian-made MIG 15s. Meanwhile, white and black soldiers learned to work together under the pressure of combat (See American Views, Integrating the Army in Korea).

Stabilization of the Korean front ushered in two years of truce negotiations beginning in July 1951, for none of the key actors wanted a wider war. The Chinese were careful to keep their warplanes north of the ground combat zone. The Russians stayed out of the war. The United States learned a painful lesson in 1950 and was willing to accept a divided Korea.

Negotiations stalled over thousands of Chinese prisoners of war who might not want to return to China. The political decision to turn free choice for POWs into a symbol of resistance to Communism left Truman's administration bogged down in a grinding war. Nearly half of the 140,000 U.S. casualties came after the truce talks started. The war was a decisive factor behind the Republican victory in the November 1952 elections and dragged on until June 1953, when an armistice returned the peninsula roughly to its prewar political division, a situation that endured into the twenty-first century.

The blindly ambitious attack into North Korea was one of the great failures of intelligence and strategic leadership in U.S. military history. Nearly everyone in Washington shared the blame. Civilian leaders could not resist the desire to roll back Communism. Truman hoped for a striking victory before the 1950 congressional elections. The Joint Chiefs of Staff failed to effectively challenge a general with MacArthur's heroic reputation. MacArthur himself allowed ambition and wishful thinking to jeopardize his army.

Consequences of the Korean War.   The war in Korea was a preview of Vietnam 15 years later. American leaders propped up an undemocratic regime to defend democracy. Both North Koreans and South Koreans engaged in savage political reprisals as the battlefront shifted back and forth. American soldiers found it hard to distinguish between allied and enemy Koreans. American emphasis on massive firepower led U.S. forces to demolish entire villages to kill single snipers. The air force tried to break North Korean resistance by pouring bombs on cities, power stations, factories, and dams; General Curtis Le May estimated that the bombings killed a million Koreans.

The Korean War had global consequences. It helped to legitimize the United Nations and set a precedent for its peace-keeping role in places like the Middle East. In Washington, it confirmed the ideas underlying NSC-68, with its call for the United States to expand its military and to lead an anti-Communist alliance. Two days after the North Korean invasion, President Truman ordered the Seventh Fleet to interpose between mainland China and the Nationalist Chinese on Taiwan, a decision that guaranteed 20 years of hostility between the United States and China. In the same month, the United States began to aid France's struggle to retain control over its Southeast Asian colony of Indochina, which included Laos, Cambodia, and Vietnam.

In Europe, the United States now pushed to rearm West Germany as part of a militarized NATO and sent troops to Europe as a permanent defense force. It increased military aid to European governments and secured a unified command for the national forces allocated to NATO, a step that made West German rearmament acceptable to other nations of western Europe that remembered 1940. Rearmament also stimulated German economic recovery and bound West Germany to the political and economic institutions of the North Atlantic nations. In 1952, the European Coal and Steel Community marked an important step toward economic cooperation that would evolve into the European Union by the end of the century. Dwight Eisenhower, who had led the Western allies in the invasion of France and Germany, became the new NATO commander in April 1951; his appointment symbolized the American commitment to western Europe.

As the United States expanded its system of military bases in Europe and Asia over the next decade, millions of American service personnel and their families were introduced to other parts of the world by deployments overseas. Until transoceanic jet travel became widely available in the 1960s, America's global defense commitments and alliances were the most important way that Americans learned firsthand about the world.

The Second Red Scare

The Korean War reinforced the second Red Scare, an assault on civil liberties that stretched from the mid-1940s to the mid-1950s and dwarfed the Red Scare of 1919–1920. The Cold War fanned fears of Communist subversion on American soil. Legitimate concerns about espionage mixed with suspicions that Communist sympathizers in high places were helping Stalin and Mao. The scare was also a weapon that the conservative wing of the Republican Party used against the men and women who had built Roosevelt's New Deal (see Overview, The Second Red Scare).

Efforts to root out suspected subversives operated on three tracks. National and state governments established loyalty programs to identify and fire suspect employees. The courts punished members of suspect organizations. Congressional and state legislative investigations followed the whims of committee chairs. Anti-Communist crusaders often relied on dubious evidence and eagerly believed the worst. They also threatened basic civil liberties.

The Communist Party and the Loyalty Program

The Communist Party in the United States was in rapid decline as a political factor after World War II. Many intellectuals had left the party over the Nazi-Soviet Pact in 1939. The wartime glow of military alliance with the Soviet Union helped the party recover to perhaps 80,000 members—still fewer than one in every 1,500 Americans—but the postwar years brought a series of failures. In 1946, Walter Reuther defeated a Communist for the presidency of the huge United Auto Workers union, and other CIO unions froze Communists out of leadership positions, bringing industrial unions into the American mainstream. Communist support for Henry Wallace reduced the party's influence and isolated it from the overwhelming majority of voters.

Nevertheless, Republicans used Red-baiting as a campaign. In 1944 they tried to frighten voters about "commy-democrats" by linking FDR, CIO labor unions, and Communism. Democrats slung their own mud by trying to convince voters that Hitler preferred the Republicans. Two years later, Republican campaigners told the public that the basic choice was "between Communism and Republicanism." Starting a 30-year political career, a young navy veteran named Richard Nixon won a southern California congressional seat by hammering on his opponent's connections to supposedly Communist-dominated organizations.

President Truman responded to the Republican landslide with Executive Order 9835 in March 1947, initiating a loyalty program for federal employees. Truman may have been trying to head off more drastic action by Congress. Nevertheless, Order 9835 was a blunt instrument. It authorized the attorney general to prepare a list of "totalitarian, Fascist, Communist, or subversive" organizations and made membership or even "sympathetic association" with such groups grounds for dismissal. The loyalty program applied to approximately 8 million Americans working for the federal government or defense contractors; similar state laws affected another 5 million.

Loyalty was a moving target. The attorney general's list grew by fits and starts, with often arbitrary additions. Many accusations were just malicious gossip, but allegations stayed in a worker's file even if refuted. Appointment to a new federal job triggered a new investigation, in which officials might pore over the same old material. Many New Dealers and people associated with presumably liberal East Coast institutions were targets. An Interior Department official boasted that he had been especially effective in squeezing out graduates of Harvard and Columbia.

Federal employees worked under a cloud of fear. Would the cooperative store they had once patronized or the protest group they had joined in college suddenly appear on the attorney general's list? Would someone complain that they had disloyal books on their shelves? Loyalty boards asked about religion, racial equality, and a taste for foreign films. They also tried to identify homosexuals, who were thought to be targets for blackmail by foreign agents. The loyalty program resulted in 1,210 firings and 6,000 resignations under Truman and comparable numbers during Dwight Eisenhower's first term from 1953 to 1956.

Naming Names to Congress

Congress was even busier than the executive branch. The congressional hunt for subversives had its roots in 1938, when Congressman Martin Dies, a Texas Democrat, created the Special Committee on Un-American Activities. Originally intended to ferret out pro-Fascists, the Dies Committee evolved into the permanent **House Committee on Un-American Activities (HUAC)** in 1945. It investigated "un-American propaganda" that attacked constitutional government.

One of HUAC's juiciest targets was Hollywood. In the last years before television, the movie industry stood at the height of its capacity to influence public opinion. In 1946, Americans bought an average of 90 million tickets every week. But Hollywood's reputation for loose morals, foreign-born directors, Jewish producers, and left-leaning writers aroused the suspicions of many congressmen. HUAC sought to make sure that no un-American messages were being peddled through America's most popular entertainment.

When the hearings opened in October 1947, studio executives Jack Warner of Warner Brothers and Louis B. Mayer of MGM assured HUAC of their anti-Communism. So did the popular actors Gary Cooper and Ronald Reagan. By contrast, eight screenwriters and two directors—the so-called Hollywood Ten—refused to discuss their past political associations, citing the free-speech protections of the First Amendment to the Constitution. HUAC countered with citations for contempt of Congress. The First Amendment defense failed when it reached the Supreme Court, and the Ten went to jail in 1950.

HUAC changed the politics of Hollywood. Before 1947, it had been fashionable to lean toward the left; even *The Best Years of Our Lives* contained criticism of American society. After the hearings, it was imperative to tilt the other way. Humphrey Bogart apologized for being a "dope" about politics. The government refused to let British-born Charlie Chaplin reenter the United States in 1952 because of his left-wing views. Other actors, writers, and directors found themselves on the Hollywood blacklist, banned from jobs where they might insert Communist propaganda into American movies.

At the start of 1951, the new Senate Internal Security Subcommittee went into action. The McCarran Committee,

OVERVIEW

The Second Red Scare

Type of Anti-Communist Effort	Key Tools	Results
Employee loyalty programs	U.S. attorney general's list of subversive organizations	Thousands of federal and state workers fired, careers damaged
Congressional investigations	HUAC	Employee blacklists, investigation of writers and intellectuals, Hollywood Ten
	McCarran Committee	
	Army-McCarthy hearings	
Criminal prosecutions	Trials for espionage and conspiracy to advocate violent overthrow of the U.S. government	Convictions of Communist Party leaders (1949), Alger Hiss (1950), and Rosenbergs (1951)

named for the Nevada senator who chaired it, targeted diplomats, labor union leaders, professors, and schoolteachers. Both committees turned their investigations into rituals. The real point was not to force personal confessions from witnesses but to badger them into identifying friends and associates who might have been involved in suspect activities.

The only sure way to avoid "naming names" was to respond to every question by citing the Fifth Amendment to the Constitution, which protects Americans from testifying against themselves. When the states adopted the Fifth Amendment in 1791, they wanted to protect citizens against false confessions coerced by intimidation and torture. The ordeal triggered by a congressional subpoena was certainly intimidating. Many Americans assumed that citing the amendment was a sure sign of guilt, not a matter of principle, and talked about Fifth Amendment Communists. "Taking the Fifth" could not protect jobs and reputations.

State legislatures imitated Congress by searching for "Reducators" among college faculty in such states as Oklahoma, Washington, and California. College presidents frequently fired faculty who took the Fifth Amendment. Harvard apparently used its influence to stay out of the newspapers, cutting a deal in which the FBI fed it information about suspect faculty, whom the university quietly fired. More common was the experience of the economics professor fired from the University of Kansas City after testifying before the McCarran Committee. He found it hard to keep any job once his name had been in the papers. A local dairy fired him because it thought its customers might be uneasy having a radical handle their milk bottles.

Subversion Trials

In 1948, the Justice Department indicted the leaders of the American Communist Party under the Alien Registration Act of 1940. Eleven men and women were convicted in 1949 of conspiring to advocate the violent overthrow of the United States government through their speech and publications. Some of

the testimony came from Herbert Philbrick, an advertising manager and FBI informer who had posed as a party member. Philbrick parlayed his appearance into a bestseller titled *I Led Three Lives* and then into a popular television series in which the FBI foiled Communist spies every Friday night.

The case of Alger Hiss soon followed. In 1948, a former Communist, Whittaker Chambers, named Hiss as a Communist with whom he had associated in the 1930s. Hiss, who had held important posts in the State Department, first denied knowing Chambers but then admitted to having known him under another name. He continued to deny any involvement with Communists and sued Chambers for slander. As proof, Chambers revealed microfilms that he had hidden inside a pumpkin on his Maryland farm, and Congressman Richard Nixon quickly announced the discovery. Tests seemed to show that the "pumpkin papers" were State Department documents that had been copied on a typewriter Hiss had once owned. With the new evidence, the Justice Department indicted Hiss for perjury—lying under oath. A first perjury trial ended in deadlock, but a second jury convicted Hiss in January 1950.

Hiss was more important as a symbol than as a possible spy. For more than 40 years, the essence of his case was a matter of faith, not facts. Even his enemies agreed that any documents he might have stolen were of limited importance. What was important, they said, was the sort of disloyalty and "weak thinking" that Hiss represented. Moreover, his smugness as a member of the East Coast establishment enraged them. To his opponents, Hiss stood for every wrong turn the nation had taken since 1932. In contrast, his supporters found a virtue in every trait his enemies hated, from his refined taste to his education at Johns Hopkins University and Harvard Law School. Many supporters believed that he had been framed. Evidence from Soviet records and American intelligence intercepts that became public in the 1990s confirms that he did pass information to the Soviets from the mid-1930s through 1945.

American Views

Integrating the Army in Korea

Racial integration of the armed forces became official policy in 1948, but President Truman's directive was not fully implemented until after the war in Korea. Two veterans of that war—white G.I. Harry Summers and black officer Beverly Scott—recall some of the steps toward integration.

- What do these recollections say about the pervasiveness of racism in mid-century American life?
- How has the experience of minority soldiers changed from the 1950s to the 1990s?

Harry Summers: When they first started talking about integration, white soldiers were aghast. They would say, How can you integrate the army? How do you know when you go to the mess hall that you won't get a plate or a knife or a spoon that was used by a Negro? Or when you go to the supply room and draw sheets, you might get a sheet that a Negro had slept on?...

I remember a night when my rifle company was scheduled to get some replacements. I was in a three-man foxhole with one other guy, and they dropped this new replacement off at our foxhole. The other guy I was in the foxhole with was under a poncho, making coffee. It was bitterly cold. And pitch dark. He got the coffee made, and he gave me a drink, and he took a drink, and then he offered some to this new replacement, who we literally couldn't see, it was that dark.

And the guy said, "No, I don't want any."

"What the hell are you talking about, you don't want any? You got to be freezing to death. Here, take a drink of coffee."

"Well," he said, "you can't tell it now, but I'm black. And tomorrow morning when you find out I was drinking out of the same cup you were using, you ain't gonna be too happy."

Me and this other guy kind of looked at each other.

"You silly son of a bitch," we told him, "here, take the goddam coffee."

Beverly Scott: The 24th Regiment was the only all-black regiment in the division, and as a black officer in an all-black regiment commanded by whites I was always super sensitive about standing my ground. Being a man. Being honest with my soldiers....

Most of the white officers were good. Taken in the context of the times, they were probably better than the average white guy in civilian life. But there was still that patronizing expectation of failure. White officers came to the 24th Regiment knowing or suspecting or having been told that this was an inferior regiment.

[In September 1951, members of the regiment were integrated into other units.]

I was transferred to the 14th [Regiment] and right away I experienced some problems. People in the 14th didn't want anybody from the 24th. I was a technically qualified communications officer, which the 14th said they needed very badly, but when I got there, suddenly they didn't need any commo officers.

Then their executive officer said, "We got a rifle platoon for you. Think you can handle a rifle platoon?"

What the hell do you mean, can I handle a rifle platoon? I was also trained as an infantry officer. He know that. I was a first lieutenant, been in the army six years.... If I had been coming in as a white first lieutenant the question never would have been asked.

Source: Rudy Tomedi, *No Bugles, No Drums: An Oral History of the Korean War* (New York: John Wiley, 1993).

Richard Nixon (right) and the chief investigator for the House Committee on Un-American Activities inspect microfilm of the "pumpkin papers." Hidden inside a pumpkin on the Maryland farm of committee informant Whittaker Chambers, the papers helped convict Alger Hiss of perjury. Nixon's role in pursuing Hiss launched a political career that took him to the White House.

1950. In a rambling speech in Wheeling, West Virginia, he latched on to the issue of Communist subversion. Although no transcript of the speech survives, he supposedly stated, "I have here in my hand a list of 205 that were known to the Secretary of State as being members of the Communist Party and who, nevertheless, are still working and shaping the policy of the State Department." In the following days, the 205 Communists changed quickly to 57, to 81, to 10, to 116. McCarthy's rise to fame climaxed with an incoherent six-hour speech to the Senate. He tried to document the charges by mixing previously exposed spies with people who no longer worked for the government or who had never worked for it. Over the next several years, his speeches were aimed at moving targets, full of multiple untruths. He threw out so many accusations, true or false, that the facts could never catch up.

The Senate disregarded McCarthy, but the public heard only the accusations, not the lack of evidence. Senators treated McCarthy as a crude outsider in their exclusive club, but voters in 1950 turned against his most prominent opponents. Liberal politicians ran for cover; conservatives were happy for McCarthy to attract media attention away from HUAC and the McCarran Committee. In 1951, McCarthy even called George Marshall, then serving as secretary of defense, an agent of Communism. The idea was ludicrous. Marshall was one of the most upright Americans of his generation, the architect of victory in World War II, and a key contributor to the stabilization of Europe. Nevertheless, McCarthy was so popular that the Republicans featured him at their 1952 convention and their presidential candidate, Dwight Eisenhower, conspicuously failed to defend Marshall, who had been chiefly responsible for Eisenhower's fast-track career.

The case of Julius and Ethel Rosenberg represented a similar test of belief. In 1950, the British arrested nuclear physicist Klaus Fuchs, who confessed to passing atomic secrets to the Soviets when he worked at Los Alamos in 1944 and 1945. The "Fuchs spy ring" soon implicated the Rosenbergs, New York radicals of strong beliefs but limited sophistication. Convicted in 1951 on the vague charge of conspiring to commit espionage, they were sent to the electric chair in 1953 after refusing to buy a reprieve by naming other spies.

As with Alger Hiss, the government had a plausible but not airtight case. After their trial, the Rosenbergs became a cause for international protest. Their small children became pawns and trophies in political demonstrations, an experience recaptured in E. L. Doctorow's novel *The Book of Daniel* (1971). There is no doubt that Julius Rosenberg was a convinced Communist. It is likely that he was part of the Soviet spy ring, but he probably did not pass atomic secrets. Ethel Rosenberg was charged, in the words of FBI director J. Edgar Hoover, "as a lever" to pressure her husband into naming his confederates.

McCarthy's personal crudeness made him a media star but eventually undermined him. Given control of the Senate Committee on Government Operations in 1953, he investigated dozens of agencies from the Government Printing Office to the Army Signal Corps. Early in 1954, he investigated an army dentist with a supposedly subversive background. The back-and-forth confrontation led to two months of televised hearings. The cameras brought political debates into living rooms and put McCarthy's bullying style on trial. "Have you no decency?" asked the army's lawyer, Joseph Welch, at one point.

The end came quickly. McCarthy's "favorable" rating in the polls plummeted. The comic strip *Pogo* began to feature a foolishly menacing figure with McCarthy's face named Simple J. Malarkey. The U.S. Senate finally voted 67 to 22 in December 1954 to condemn McCarthy for conduct "unbecoming a Member of the Senate." When he died in 1957, he

Senator McCarthy on Stage

The best-remembered participant in the second Red Scare was Senator Joseph McCarthy of Wisconsin. Crude, sly, and ambitious, McCarthy had ridden to victory in the Republican landslide of 1946. His campaign slogan, "Congress needs a tail gunner," claimed a far braver war record than he had earned. He burst into national prominence on February 9,

Senator Joe McCarthy used press releases and carefully managed congressional committee hearings to attack suspected Communists, although he had almost no hard information. At the Army-McCarthy hearings in June 1954, he clashed with attorney Joseph Welch. Here Welch listens as McCarthy points to Oregon on a map that supposedly showed Communist Party organization in the United States.

had been repudiated by the Senate and ignored by the media that had built him up.

Understanding McCarthyism

The antisubversive campaign that everyone now calls **McCarthyism,** however, died a slower death. Legislation, such as the Internal Security Act (1950) and the Immigration and Nationality Act (1952), remained as tools of political repression. HUAC continued to mount investigations as late as the 1960s.

Fear of Communist subversion reached deep into American society. In the early 1950s, Cincinnati's National League baseball team was trying out a new name; harking back to its origins as the Red Stockings, the team now became the "Redlegs," not the "Reds." The brief revision of baseball history was one example of how the fear of Communists spread from Washington through the grassroots. Cities and states required loyalty oaths from their employees; Ohio even required oaths from recipients of unemployment compensation.

In retrospect, at least four factors made Americans afraid of Communist subversion. One was the legitimate concern about atomic spies. The Soviet Union had developed an extensive espionage network in the early 1940s. More than a few U.S.

officials passed on secret information, although there was not the vast interlocking conspiracy that some critics feared. A second was an undercurrent of anti-Semitism and nativism, for many labor organizers and Communist Party members (like the Rosenbergs) had Jewish and eastern European backgrounds. Third was southern and western resentment of the nation's Ivy League elite. Most general, finally, was a widespread fear that the world was spinning out of control. Many people sought easy explanations for global tensions. It was basically reassuring if Soviet and Chinese Communist successes were the result of American traitors rather than of Communist strengths.

Partisan politics mobilized the fears and resentments into a political force. From 1946 through 1952, the conservative wing of the Republican Party used the Red Scare to attack New Dealers and liberal Democrats. HUAC, the McCarran Committee, and McCarthy were all tools for bringing down the men and women who had been moving the United States toward a more active government at home and abroad. The Republican elite used McCarthy until they won control of the presidency and Congress in 1952, and then abandoned him.

The broader goal of the second Red Scare was conformity of thought. Many of the professors and bureaucrats targeted for investigation had indeed been Communists or interested in Communism, usually in the 1930s and early 1940s. Most saw it as a way to increase social justice, and they sometimes excused the failures of Communism in the Soviet Union. Unlike the handful of real spies, however, they were targeted not for actions but for ideas. The investigations and loyalty programs were efforts to ensure that Americans kept any left-wing ideas to themselves.

Conclusion

In the face of confrontation over Berlin, fighting in Korea, and growing numbers of nuclear weapons, the Cold War stayed cool because each side achieved its essential goals. The Soviet Union controlled eastern Europe, while the United States built increasingly strong ties with the NATO nations and Japan. Although the result was a stalemate, it nevertheless absorbed huge shares of Soviet and American resources and conditioned the thinking of an entire generation.

The shift from prewar isolationism to postwar internationalism was one of the most important changes in the nation's history. To many of its advocates, internationalism represented a commitment to spread political democracy to other nations. As the 1950s and 1960s would show, the results often contradicted the ideal when the United States forcibly imposed its will on other peoples. Even as the results overseas fell short of the ideal, however, the new internationalism highlighted and helped change domestic racial attitudes.

The Truman years saw the implementation of a national security policy that dominated the next half-century. The armed forces were strong but subordinate to the civilian administration through the National Security Council and Department of Defense. The expansion of the close alliance between scientific research and defense needs that had begun with World War II augmented the national defense capacity. The United States led an international system of collective security based on mutual defense treaties, contributing financial assistance and sophisticated weapons while its allies helped to provide the military manpower.

These same years also brought increasing stability within the nation. The economic chaos of 1946 faded quickly. By identifying liberalism at home with anti-Communism abroad, Truman's efforts to define a vital center helped protect the New Deal. Americans in the early 1950s could be confident that New Deal and Fair Deal programs to expand economic opportunity and increase economic security were permanent, if incomplete, setting the stage for new social activism in the 1960s. If the Republicans had won in 1948, they might have dismantled the New Deal. By 1952, both presidential candidates affirmed the consensus that placed economic opportunity at the center of the national agenda. The suburban housing boom seemed to turn the dream of prosperity into reality for millions of families.

Despite the turmoil and injustice of the second Red Scare and deep worries about nuclear war, the United States emerged from the Truman years remarkably prosperous. It was also more secure from international threats than many nervous Americans appreciated. The years from 1946 to 1952 set the themes for a generation that believed that the United States could do whatever it set its mind to: end poverty, land an astronaut on the moon, thwart Communist revolutions in other countries. There was a direct line from Harry Truman's 1947 declaration that the United States would defend freedom around the world to John Kennedy's 1961 promise that the nation would bear any burden necessary to protect free nations from Communism. As the world moved slowly toward greater stability in the 1950s, Americans were ready for a decade of confidence.

Review Questions

1. As described in the opening of the chapter, what housing choices were available after World War II? How did these choices reshape American cities? How did the postwar readjustment create a suburban society?

2. What were the key differences between Harry Truman and congressional Republicans about the legacy of the New Deal? Why did regulating labor unions become a central domestic issue in the late 1940s? Why did Truman manage to win the presidential election of 1948 despite starting as an underdog?

3. How did the postwar years expand opportunity for veterans and members of the working class? How did they limit opportunities for women? How did they begin to challenge racial inequities in American society?

4. What foreign policy priorities did United States set after 1945? To what extent did the United States achieve its most basic objectives? How did mutual mistrust fuel and deepen the Cold War?

5. How did the Cold War change character in 1949 and 1950? What were key actions by the Soviet Union and China, and how did the United States respond? What was the effect of the chaotic fighting in Korea on U.S. domestic politics and diplomacy?

6. What factors motivated an increasingly frantic fear of domestic subversion in the late 1940s and early 1950s? Who were the key actors in the second Red Scare? What was its long-term impact on American society?

7. How did the continuation and expansion of the nation's global commitments after 1945 affect life in the United States?

Key Terms

Berlin blockade (p. 771)

Central Intelligence Agency (p. 771)

Cold War (p. 760)

Containment (p. 771)

Council of Economic Advisers (p. 762)

Dixiecrats (p. 766)

GI Bill of Rights (p. 763)

House Committee on Un-American Activities (HUAC) (p. 779)

International Monetary Fund (IMF) (p. 770)

Korean War (p. 777)

Levittown (p. 763)

Marshall Plan (p. 771)

McCarthyism (p. 791)

National Security Council (p. 772)

National Security Council Paper 68 (NSC-68) (p. 774)

North Atlantic Treaty Organization (NATO) (p. 772)

Redlining (p. 764)

Taft-Hartley Act (p. 762)

Truman Doctrine (p. 770)

Warsaw Pact (p. 772)

World Bank (p. 770)

Recommended Reading

Boyer, Paul. *By the Bomb's Early Light: American Thought and Culture at the Dawn of the Atomic Age* (1985). Examines the mixture of hopes and fears with which Americans greeted the arrival of the atomic age, giving detailed attention to popular culture as well as national policy.

Fried, Richard. *The Russians Are Coming! The Russians Are Coming! Propaganda and Patriotism in Cold War America* (1998). Explores how the Cold War shaped everyday life.

Goulden, Joseph C. *The Best Years, 1945–1950* (1976). A very readable portrayal of the ways in which Americans adjusted to the postwar years, drawing heavily on contemporary magazine accounts.

Leffler, Melvyn. *A Preponderance of Power: National Security, the Truman Administration, and the Cold War* (1992). Pro-

vides a balanced interpretation of responsibility for the Cold War in a detailed but readable account of American policy.

McCullough, David. *Truman* (1992). A readable and sympathetic biography of the thirty-third president.

Navasky, Victor. *Naming Names* (1980). The impact of HUAC on Hollywood and the entertainment industry, told by a strong opponent of the committee.

Rampersad, Arnold. *Jackie Robinson* (1997). Presents Jackie Robinson as a pioneer of racial integration on and off the ballfield.

Stueck, William. *Rethinking the Korean War: A New Diplomatic and Strategic History* (2002). An up-to-date analysis of the global impact of the war in Korea.

Where to Learn More

■ **Harry S Truman National Historical Site, Library, and Museum, Independence, Missouri.**   The museum has exhibits on Truman's political career and U.S. history during his administration. Also in Independence is the Harry S Truman Courtroom and Office, with exhibits on his early career. www.nps.gov/hstr

■ **General Douglas MacArthur Memorial, Norfolk, Virginia.**   The MacArthur Memorial in downtown Nor-

folk commemorates the career of a key figure in shaping the postwar world. www.macarthurmemorial.org

■ **United Nations Headquarters, New York, New York.** A tour of the United Nations complex in New York is a reminder of the new organizations for international cooperation that emerged from World War II. www.un.org

Study Resources

For study resources for this chapter, go to www.myhistorylab.com and choose *The American Journey.* You will find a wealth of study and review material for this chapter, including pre- and post-tests, customized study plan, key term review flash cards, interactive map and document activities, and documents for analysis.

On August 28, 1963, Rev. Martin Luther King, Jr. delivered his famous "I have a dream" speech to the March on Washington for Jobs and Freedom. The address was a climactic moment in the civil rights movement, encapsulating the optimism of decades of struggle, but the March on Washington also papered over emerging divisions that would become apparent later in the 1960s.

The Confident Years 1953–1964

28

The first day I was able to enter Central High School [in Little Rock, Arkansas, September 23, 1957], what I felt inside was terrible, wrenching, awful fear. On the car radio I could hear that there was a mob. I knew what a mob meant and I knew that the sounds that came from the crowd were very angry. So we entered the side of the building, very, very fast. Even as we entered there were people running after us, people tripping other people. There has never been in my life any stark terror or any fear akin to that. I'd only been in the school a couple of hours and by that time it was apparent that the mob was just overrunning the school. Policemen were throwing down their badges and the mob was getting past the wooden sawhorses because the police would no longer fight their own in order to protect us. So we were all called into the principal's office, and there was great fear that we would not get out of this building. We were trapped. And I thought, Okay, so I'm going to die here, in school.... Even the adults, the school officials, were panicked, feeling like there was no protection.... [A] gentleman, who I believed to be the police chief, said ... "I'll get them out." And we were taken to the basement of this place. And we were put into two cars, grayish blue Fords. And the man instructed the drivers, he said, "Once you start driving, do not stop." And he told us to put our heads down. This guy revved up his engine and he came up out of the bowels of this building, and as he came up, I could just see hands reaching across this car, I could hear the yelling, I could see guns, and he was told not to stop. "If you hit somebody, you keep rolling, 'cause the kids are

dead." And he did just that, and he didn't hit anybody, but he certainly was forceful and aggressive in
the way he exited this driveway, because people tried
to stop him and he didn't stop. He dropped me off at
home. And I remember saying, "Thank you for the
ride," and I should've said, "Thank you for my life."

Melba Patillo Beals, in Henry Hampton and Steve Frayer, eds.,
*Voices of Freedom: An Oral History of the Civil Rights Movement
from the 1950s through the 1980s* (New York: Bantam, 1990).

myhistorylab

Personal Journeys Online

- Diane Nash, Interview in Mathew Allman, *The New Negro*, 1961. The civil rights sit-in movement in Nashville in 1960.

- Suzette Miller, in Staughton Lynd, *Nonviolence in America*, 1966. Grass roots civil rights efforts in Mississippi in 1961.

Melba Pattillo was one of the nine African American students who entered previously all-white Central High in the fall of 1957. Her enrollment in the high school, where she managed to last through a year of harassment and hostility, was a symbolic step in the journey toward greater racial equality in U.S. society. School integration in Little Rock implemented the U.S. Supreme Court decision in the case of *Brown v. Board of Education* in 1954, which declared that racially segregated schools violated the mandate that all citizens receive equal protection of the law. The violence with which some white residents of Little Rock responded, and the courage of the students, marked one of the key episodes in the civil rights revolution that spanned roughly a decade from the *Brown* decision to the Voting Rights Act of 1965.

The struggle for full civil rights for all Americans was rooted in national ideals, but it was also shaped by the continuing tensions of the Cold War. President Dwight Eisenhower acted against his own inclinations and sent federal troops to keep the peace in Little Rock in part because he worried about public opinion in other nations. As the United States and the Soviet Union maneuvered for influence in Africa and Asia, domestic events sometimes loomed large in foreign relations. Few Americans questioned the rightness or necessity of contesting the

Cold War—or of America's ultimate triumph. This consensus gave U.S. policy an overarching goal of containment but also narrowed American options by casting issues at home and abroad in terms of the U.S.-Soviet rivalry.

Melba Pattillo's life after Little Rock also reveals something about the increasing economic opportunities available to most Americans. She graduated from San Francisco State University, earned a master's degree from Columbia University, and worked as a television reporter and writer. San Francisco State was part of the great expansion of higher education that helped millions of Americans move into middle-class jobs and neighborhoods. The prosperous years from 1953 to 1964 spread the economic promise of the 1940s across American society. Young couples could afford large families and new houses. Labor unions grew conservative because cooperation with big business offered immediate gains for their members.

Despite challenges at home and abroad, Americans were fundamentally confident during the decade after the Korean War. They expected corporations to use scientific research to craft new products for eager customers and medical researchers to conquer diseases. When the USSR challenged U.S. preeminence and launched the first artificial space satellite in 1957, Americans responded with shock followed by redoubled efforts to regain what they considered their rightful world leadership in science and technology.

A Decade of Affluence

Americans in the 1950s believed in the basic strength of the United States. Television's *General Electric Theater* was third in the ratings in 1956–1957. Every week, its host, Ronald Reagan, a popular Hollywood lead from the late 1930s, stated, "At General Electric, progress is our most important product." It made sense to his viewers. Large, technologically sophisticated corporations were introducing new marvels: Orlon sweaters and Saran Wrap, long-playing records, and Polaroid cameras. As long as the United States defended free enterprise, Reagan told audiences on national speaking tours, the sky was the limit.

CHRONOLOGY

1953	CIA-backed coup returns Shah Reza Pahlevi to power in Iran.
	Soviet Union detonates hydrogen bomb.
1954	Vietnamese defeat the French; Geneva conference divides Vietnam.
	United States and allies form SEATO.
	Supreme Court decides *Brown v. Board of Education of Topeka*.
	CIA overthrows the government of Guatemala.
	China provokes a crisis over Quemoy and Matsu.
1955	Salk polio vaccine is announced.
	Black citizens boycott Montgomery, Alabama, bus system.
	Soviet Union forms the Warsaw Pact.
	AFL and CIO merge.
1956	Interstate Highway Act is passed.
	Soviets repress Hungarian revolt.
	Israel, France, and Britain invade Egypt.
1957	U.S. Army maintains law and order in Little Rock after violent resistence to integration of Central High School.
	Soviet Union launches *Sputnik,* world's first artificial satellite.
1958	United States and Soviet Union voluntarily suspend nuclear tests.
1959	Fidel Castro takes power in Cuba.
	Nikita Khrushchev visits the United States.
1960	U-2 spy plane shot down over Russia.
	Sit-in movement begins in Greensboro, North Carolina.

1961	Bay of Pigs invasion fails.
	Kennedy establishes the Peace Corps.
	Vienna summit fails.
	Freedom rides are held in the Deep South.
	Berlin crisis leads to construction of the Berlin Wall.
1962	John Glenn orbits the earth.
	Cuban missile crisis brings the world to the brink of nuclear war.
	Michael Harrington publishes *The Other America*.
1963	Civil rights demonstrations rend Birmingham.
	Civil rights activists march in Washington.
	Betty Friedan publishes *The Feminine Mystique*.
	Limited Test Ban Treaty is signed.
	Ngo Dinh Diem is assassinated in South Vietnam.
	President Kennedy is assassinated.
1964	Civil Rights Act is passed.
	Freedom Summer is organized in Mississippi.
	Office of Economic Opportunity is created.
	Gulf of Tonkin Resolution is passed.
	Wilderness Act marks new direction in environmental policy.
1965	Medical Care Act establishes Medicare and Medicaid.
	Elementary and Secondary Education Act extends direct federal aid to local schools.
	Selma-Montgomery march climaxes era of nonviolent civil rights demonstrations.
	Voting Rights Act suspends literacy tests for voting.

Many Americans valued free enterprise and family life as part of the anti-Communist crusade. Social and intellectual conformity ensured a united front. Congress established Loyalty Day in 1955. National leaders argued that strong families were bulwarks against Communism and that churchgoing inoculated people against subversive ideas. Under the lingering cloud of McCarthyism, the range of political ideas that influenced government policy was narrower than in the 1930s and 1940s. Nevertheless, critics began to voice the discontents that exploded in the 1960s and 1970s.

What's Good for General Motors

Dwight Eisenhower presided over the prosperity of the 1950s. Both Democrats and Republicans had courted him as a presidential candidate in 1948. Four years later, he picked the Republicans because he wanted to make sure that the party remained committed to NATO and collective security in Europe rather than retreat into isolationism. He easily defeated the Democratic candidate, Adlai Stevenson, the moderately liberal governor of Illinois. Stevenson was a thoughtful politician, a witty campaigner, and a favorite in academic circles. He also carried Truman's negative legacy of domestic policy confrontation, the hated war in Korea, and the "loss" of China, and he had no chance of winning.

Eisenhower and the politics of the middle.   Over the next eight years, Eisenhower claimed the political middle for Republicans. Publicists tried a variety of labels for his domestic views: "progressive moderation," "New Republicanism," "dynamic conservatism." Satisfied with postwar America, Eisenhower accepted much of the New Deal but saw little need for further reform. In a 1959 poll, liberals considered him a fellow liberal and conservatives thought him a conservative. Eisenhower's first secretary of defense, "Engine Charlie" Wilson, had headed General Motors. At his Senate confirmation hearing, he proclaimed, "For years, I thought what was good for the country was good for General Motors and vice versa." Wilson's statement captured a central theme of the 1950s. Not since the 1920s had Americans been so excited about the benefits of big business. When *Fortune* magazine began in 1957 to publish an annual list of the 500 largest U.S. corporations, it tapped a national fascination with America's productive capacity.

The new prosperity.   The economy in the 1950s gave Americans much to like. Between 1950 and 1964, output grew by a solid 3.2 percent per year. Automobile production, on which dozens of other industries depended, neared 8 million vehicles per year in the mid-1950s. Less than 1 percent of new car sales were imports, and people avidly awaited each year's new models from Detroit, pondering their preferences for a gull-winged Chevrolets or a fantastically finned DeSoto.

American workers in the 1950s had more disposable income than ever before. Their productivity, or output per worker, increased steadily. Average compensation per hour of work rose faster than consumer prices in nine of eleven years

from 1953 to 1964. Rising productivity made it easy for corporations to share gains with large labor unions. The steel and auto industries set the pace with contracts that gave their workers a middle-class way of life. In turn, labor leaders lost interest in making radical changes in American society. In 1955, the older and politically more conservative American Federation of Labor absorbed the younger Congress of Industrial Organizations. The new AFL-CIO positioned itself as a partner in prosperity and foe of Communism at home and abroad.

For members of minority groups with regular industrial and government jobs, the 1950s were also economically rewarding. Detroit, Dayton, Oakland, and other industrial cities offered them factory jobs at wages that could support a family. Black people worked through the Urban League, the National Association of Colored Women, and other race-oriented groups to secure fair-employment laws and jobs with large corporations. Many Puerto Rican migrants to New York found steady work in the Brooklyn Navy Yard. Mexican American families in San Antonio benefited from maintenance jobs at the city's military bases. Steady employment allowed black people and Latinos to build strong community institutions and vibrant neighborhood business districts.

However, there were never enough family-wage jobs for all of the African American and Latino workers who continued to move to northern and western cities. Many Mexican Americans were still migrant farm laborers and workers in nonunionized sweatshops. Minority workers were usually the first to suffer from the erosion of some industrial jobs and the shift of other jobs to new suburban factories that were isolated from minority neighborhoods. Black unemployment crept upward to twice the white rate, laying the seeds of frustration that would burst forth in the 1960s.

Native Americans faced equally daunting prospects. To cut costs and accelerate assimilation, Congress pushed the policy of termination between 1954 and 1962. The government sold tribal land and assets, distributed the proceeds among tribal members, and terminated its treaty relationship with the tribe. Applied to such tribes as the Klamaths in Oregon and the Menominees in Wisconsin, termination gave thousands of Indians one-time cash payments but cut them adrift from the security of tribal organizations. The Bureau of Indian Affairs encouraged Indians to move to large cities, but jobs were often unavailable. The new urban populations would nourish growing militancy among Native Americans in the 1960s and 1970s.

Reshaping Urban America

If Eisenhower's administration opted for the status quo on many issues, it nevertheless reshaped U.S. cities around an agenda of economic development. In 1954, Congress transformed the public housing program into urban renewal. Cities used federal funds to replace low-rent businesses and run-down housing on the fringes of their downtowns with new hospitals, civic centers, sports arenas, office towers,

Daly City, south of San Francisco, typified the mass-produced suburbs that housed the growing postwar middle class. It was the inspiration for the satirical song, "Little Boxes."

Cold War. The roads would be wide and strong enough for trucks hauling military hardware; they were also supposed to make it easy to evacuate cities in case of a Soviet attack.

Although the first interstate opened in Kansas in 1956, most of the mileage came into use in the 1960s and 1970s. Interstates halved the time of city-to-city travel. They were good for General Motors, the steel industry, and the concrete industry, requiring the construction equivalent of 60 Panama Canals. The highways promoted long-distance trucking at the expense of railroads. They also wiped out hundreds of homes per mile when they plunged through large cities. As with urban renewal, the bulldozers most often plowed through African American or Latino neighborhoods, where land was cheap and white politicians could ignore protests. Some cities, such as Miami, used the highways as barriers between white and black neighborhoods.

Interstates accelerated suburbanization. The beltways or perimeter highways that began to ring most large cities made it easier and more profitable to develop new subdivisions and factory sites than to reinvest in city centers. Federal grants for sewers and other basic facilities further cut suburban costs. Continuing the pattern of the late 1940s, suburban growth added a million new single-family houses per year.

and luxury apartments. Urban renewal temporarily revitalized older cities in the Northeast and Midwest that were already feeling the competition of the fast-growing South and West. *Fortune* in 1956 concluded that some of the largest cities were the best run—Cincinnati, New York, Philadelphia, Detroit, Milwaukee.

Only a decade later, the same cities would top the list of urban crisis spots, in part because of accumulating social costs from urban renewal. The bulldozers often leveled minority neighborhoods in the name of downtown expansion. Urban renewal displaced Puerto Ricans in New York, African Americans in Atlanta and Norfolk, Mexican Americans in Denver. Los Angeles demolished the seedy Victorian mansions of Bunker Hill, just northwest of downtown, for a music center and bank towers. A mile to the north was Chavez Ravine, whose Mexican American population lived in substandard housing but maintained a lively community. When conservative opposition blocked plans for public housing, the residents were evicted, and Dodger Stadium was built. Here as elsewhere, urban showplaces rose at the expense of minority groups.

The Eisenhower administration also revolutionized American transportation. Americans had long dreamed of something better than two-lane highways that routed motorists through the stop-and-go traffic of cities and trapped them behind creeping trucks. By the early 1950s, they were fed up with roads designed for Model A Fords: They wanted to enjoy their new V-8 engines and the 50 million new cars sold between 1946 and 1955. The solution was the **Federal Highway Act of 1956,** creating a national system of interstate and defense highways. The legislation wrapped a program to build 41,000 miles of freeways in the language of the

Comfort on Credit

Prosperity transformed spending habits. The 1930s had taught Americans to avoid debt. The 1950s taught them to buy on credit. Families financed their new houses with 90 percent Federal Housing Administration (FHA) mortgages and 100 percent Veterans Administration (VA) mortgages. They filled the rooms by signing installment contracts at furniture and appliance stores and charging the drapes and carpeting on department-store credit cards. The value of consumer debt, excluding home mortgages, tripled from 1952 to 1964.

New forms of marketing facilitated credit-based consumerism. The first large-scale suburban shopping center was Northgate in Seattle, which assembled all the elements of the full-grown mall—small stores facing an interior corridor between anchor department stores and surrounded by parking. By the end of the decade, developers were building malls with 1 million square feet of shopping floor. At the start of the 1970s, the universal credit card (Visa, MasterCard) made shopping even easier.

Surrounding the new malls were the servants and symbols of America's car culture. Where cities of the early twentieth century had been built around public transportation—streetcars and subways—those of the 1950s depended on pri-

Global Perspectives

Consumer Society in Europe

In 1958, the French comedian Jacques Tati made the film *Mon Oncle* ("My Uncle"), depicting the plight of a befuddled middle-aged Frenchman trying to cope with the high-tech lifestyle of his sister and her businessman husband. Their house is angular and modern, unlike his rickety walk-up apartment. Their chairs are modern, low-slung, and uncomfortable. Their kitchen is full of sleek and mysterious appliances. Their money comes from a plastics factory whose production line also baffles the hapless hero.

The film was an early reaction to the headlong development of consumer society in western Europe. In the late 1940s, Europe was still a miserable place, with war damage to be repaired and shortages of basic goods. Fifteen years later, it was a showplace of prosperity and modern design. Both Italians and Germans talked about their "economic miracle." German industrial production rose by 250 percent in the 1950s, and the rest of western Europe was not far behind. Just as in the United States, a booming domestic economy raised wages and consumption.

Americans experienced the European boom through a wave of new, stylishly designed products that began to appear in upscale stores—household appliances from Germany, typewriters from Italy and Switzerland, textiles from Finland, elegant furniture from Denmark, sports cars from Germany, England, and Italy. The millionth Volkswagen Beetle rolled off the assembly line in 1955; the total number of Beetles eventually topped that of the Model T Ford. For average Europeans, the boom meant a new apartment or duplex in a suburban "new town," money to buy an automobile, and enough left over for a vacation. Meanwhile, new glass-sheathed office buildings shoved their way into old city centers.

By the early 1960s, European filmmakers could depict a continent that was no longer lagging behind the United States. One of the points of Ian Fleming's James Bond novels and films, such as *Goldfinger* (1964), was brand-name snobbery. *Red Desert* (1964) dramatized its story of personal alienation against a backdrop of Italian industry depicted in the stark primary colors of modern design. *Blow-Up* (1966) gave Americans a window into fashionable swinging England.

According to historian Lizabeth Cohen, the United States after World War II became a "consumer's republic" that defined mass consumption as the solution to social and economic problems. During America's confident years, western Europe was not far behind.

- How did European prosperity fit into the aims of U.S. foreign policy after World War II?

---

vate automobiles. Interstate highways sucked retail business from small-town main streets to interchanges on the edge of town. Nationally franchised motels and fast-food restaurants sprang up along suburban shopping strips, pioneered by Holiday Inn (1952) and McDonald's (nationally franchised in 1955). By shopping along highways rather than downtown, suburban whites also opted to minimize contact with people of other races.

More extreme than the mall were entirely new environments for high-intensity consumption and entertainment that appeared in the Southwest. Mobster Bugsy Siegel transformed Las Vegas with the Flamingo Hotel in 1947. Other hotel-casinos soon turned Vegas into a middle-class adult fantasy land. Disneyland was Las Vegas for the whole family, a walk-through fantasy designed to outperform wide-screen movies as a "real" experience. Opening in Orange County, California, in 1955, Disneyland offered a carefully tended environment that was as safe as a shopping mall and as artificial as Las Vegas—a never-ending state fair without the smells and dust.

The spread of automobiles took Americans to more places than Disneyland. The tacit pact between large corporations and labor unions meant that more workers had two-week vacations and time to take to their families on the road. Between 1954 and 1963, the number of visits to National Parks doubled to more than 100 million and visits to National Forests nearly tripled. Route 66 from Chicago to Los Angeles was celebrated in song. On television from 1956 to 1963, variety show hostess Dinah Shore tied the nation's best-selling car to the appeal of vacationing as she belted out the jingle "Drive your Chevrolet through the USA, America's the greatest land of all."

The New Fifties Family

Family life in the Eisenhower years departed from historic patterns. Prosperity allowed children to finish school and young adults to marry right after high school. Young women faced strong social pressure to pursue husbands rather than careers; women went to college, people said, to get the "Mrs." degree rather than the B.A. In a decade when the popular press worried about "latent homosexuality," single men were suspect. The proportion of single adults reached its twentieth-century low in 1960. At all social levels, young people married quickly and had an average of three children spaced closely together, adding to the number of baby boomers whose needs would influence American society into the twenty-first century. Family activities replaced the street corner for kids and the neighborhood tavern for men. Strong families, said experts, defended against Communism by teaching American values.

The impact of television.   Television was made to order for the family-centered fifties. By 1960, fully 87 percent of households had sets (see Figure 28–1). Popular entertainment earlier had been a communal activity; people saw movies as part of a group, cheered baseball teams as part of a crowd. TV was watched in the privacy of the home.

Television programming was up for grabs. Experts hoped that 90-minute dramas would elevate popular taste, but

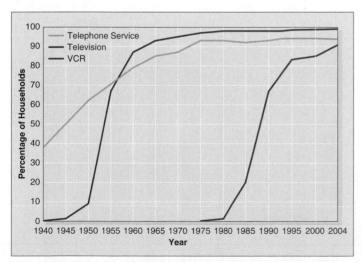

FIGURE 28–1   Households with Telephones, Televisions, and VCRs

American life in the twentieth century was transformed by a sequence of electronic consumer goods, from telephones to laptop computers. Entertainment items (televisions and videocassette recorders) spread even more rapidly among consumers than did the home telephone.

Data Source: *Statistical Abstract of the United States.*

Middle class women in the 1950s faced conflicting pressures and messages. The popular media idealized the woman whose life revolved around her house and family. As this magazine cover suggests, however, that image was as much a myth as a reality. Despite real limitations on available careers, increasing numbers of women entered the labor force and made necessary contributions to their families' incomes—while daydreaming about getting help with never-ending household tasks.

Day Dreaming by Constantin Alajalov. © 1959 SEPS; Licensed by Curtis Publishing Co., Indianapolis, Ind. All rights reserved. www.curtispublishing.com

morning talk shows, quiz shows, and puppet shows like *Howdy Doody* were common in the early days because they were cheap to produce. Variety hours recycled old vaudeville formats. Soap operas, 15-minute newscasts, and Saturday morning adventure shows were adapted straight from radio.

Situation comedies were the most successful programs. Viewers liked continuing characters who resolved everyday problems in half an hour. A few shows dealt with characters outside the middle-class mainstream, such as the bus driver and sewer worker played by Jackie Gleason and Art Carney on *The Jackie Gleason Show* and *The Honeymooners* (1952–1957). Most successful shows depicted the ideal of family togetherness. Lucille Ball and Desi Arnaz in *I Love Lucy* (1951–1955) started a family and left New York for suburbia. The families on *The Adventures of Ozzie and Harriet* (1952–1966), *Father Knows Best* (1954–1962), and *Leave It to Beaver* (1957–1962) were white, polite, and happy. The Nelsons, Andersons, and Cleavers bore northern European names and lived in single-family houses with friendly neighbors. Thousands of school-aged baby boomers wondered why their families didn't have good times like the families on the picture tube.

Stay-at-home moms and working women.   The 1950s extended the stay-at-home trend of the postwar years. Women gave up some of their earlier educational gains. Their share of new college degrees and professional jobs fell. Despite millions of new electrical appliances, the time spent on housework increased. Magazines proclaimed that proper families maintained distinct roles for dad and mom, and mom was urged to find fulfillment in a well-scrubbed house and children. While television programming helped limit women's roles by power of example, TV actresses assured readers that they were housewives first and career women second.

In fact, far from allowing women to stay home as housewives, family prosperity in the 1950s often depended on their earnings. The number of employed women reached new highs. By 1960, nearly 35 percent of all women held jobs, including 7.5 million mothers with children under 17 (see Figure 28–2). The pressures of young marriages, large families, and economic needs interacted to erode some of the assumptions behind the idealized family and laid the groundwork for dramatic social changes in the 1960s and 1970s.

Inventing Teenagers

Teenagers in the 1950s joined adults as consumers of movies, clothes, and automobiles. Advertisers tapped and expanded the growing youth market by promoting a distinct "youth culture," an idea that became omnipresent in the 1960s and 1970s. While psychologists pontificated on the special problems of adolescence, many cities matched their high schools to the social status of their students: college-prep curricula for middle-class neighborhoods, vocational and technical schools for future factory workers, and separate schools or tracks for African Americans and Latinos. "Maturity" in middle-class high schools meant self-confidence and leadership; at vocational schools, it meant neatness and respect for authority. In effect, the schools trained some children to be doctors and officers and others to be mechanics and enlisted men.

All teenagers shared rock-and-roll, a new music of the mid-1950s that adapted black urban rhythm-and-blues for a white mass market. Rhythm-and-blues was the hard-edged and electrified offspring of tra-

ditional blues and gospel music. In turn, rock music augmented its black roots by drawing vitality from poor white southerners familiar with country and western music (Buddy Holly, Elvis Presley), Hispanics (Richie Valens), and, in the 1960s, the British working class (the Beatles). Record producers played up the association between rock music and youthful rebellion. The 1955 movie *Blackboard Jungle* depicted juvenile delinquency to the music of Bill Haley's "Rock Around the Clock." Elvis Presley's meteoric career, launched in 1956 with "Heartbreak Hotel," depended both on his skill at blending country music with rhythm-and-blues and the sexual suggestiveness of his stage act. The music allowed black performers like Chuck Berry and Ray Charles to "cross over" to mainstream pop music.

Technological changes helped rock split off from adult pop music. Portable phonographs and 45-rpm records let kids listen to rock-and-roll in their own rooms. Car radios and transistor radios (first marketed around 1956) let disc jockeys reach teenagers outside the home. The result was separate music for young listeners and separate advertising for teenage consumers, the roots of the teenage mall culture of the next generation.

The raucous sounds and rebellious lyrics of early rock and roll gave adult authorities even more reason to emphasize social conformity. Schools, churches, and elected officials responded with dress codes, campaigns against sinful comic books, and worry about juvenile delinquency. Young people responded by crowding movie theaters for *Rebel Without a Cause*

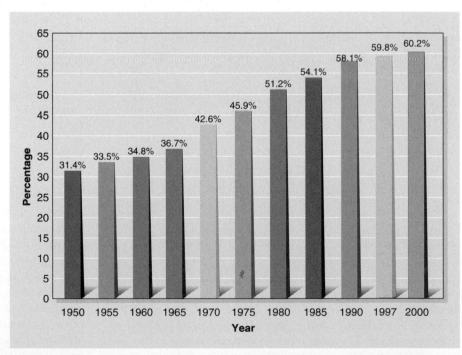

FIGURE 28–2   Working Women as a Percentage of All Women, 1950–2000
The proportion of American women who are part of the labor force (working or looking for work) has increased steadily since 1950, with the fastest increase between 1965 and 1985.

(1955), in which James Dean played an anguished teenager in stifling suburbia. Outside the realm of mass entertainment, the Beats were coming together in San Francisco, where novelists like Jack Kerouac, poets like Gary Snyder, artists, and musicians drifted in and out of the City Lights bookstore. They attracted national attention in 1955 when Allen Ginsberg first chanted his poem "Howl," with its blistering attack on stifling materialism.

Turning to Religion

Leaders from Dwight Eisenhower to FBI Director J. Edgar Hoover advocated churchgoing as an antidote for Communism. Regular church attendance grew from 48 percent of the population in 1940 to 63 percent in 1960. Moviegoers flocked to biblical epics: *The Robe* (1953), *The Ten Commandments* (1956), and *Ben-Hur* (1959). *Newsweek* talked about the "vast resurgence of Protestantism," and *Time* claimed that "everybody knows that church life is booming in the U.S."

In his first years as a star, Elvis Presley brought new energy to the world of popular music.
Frank Driggs/Archive Photos

The situation was more complex. Growing church membership looked impressive at first, but the total barely kept pace with population growth. In some ways, the so-called return to religion was new. Congress created new connections between religion and government when it added "under God" to the Pledge of Allegiance in 1954 and required currency to bear the phrase "In God We Trust" in 1955.

Radio and television preachers added a new dimension to religious life. Bishop Fulton J. Sheen brought vigorous anti-Communism and Catholic doctrine to millions of TV viewers who would never have entered a Catholic church. Norman Vincent Peale blended popular psychology with Protestantism, presenting Jesus Christ as "the greatest expert on human nature who ever lived." His book *The Power of Positive Thinking* (1952) sold millions of copies.

Another strand in the religious revival was found in the revitalized evangelical and fundamentalist churches. During the 1950s, the theologically and socially conservative Southern Baptists passed the Methodists as the largest Protestant denomination. The evangelist Billy Graham continued the grand American tradition of the mass revival meeting. In auditoriums and stadiums, he preached personal salvation in words that everyone could understand. Graham was a pioneer in the resurgence of evangelical Christianity that gradually shifted the tone of American religious life by stressing an individual approach to belief and social issues. "Before we can solve the economic, philosophical, and political problems in the world," he said, "pride, greed, lust, and sin are going to have to be erased."

African American churches were community institutions as well as religious organizations. With limited options for enjoying their success, the black middle class joined prestigious churches. Black congregations in northern cities swelled in the postwar years. Prestigious black churches thrived and often supported extensive social service programs. In southern cities, churches were centers for community pride and training grounds for the emerging civil rights movement.

Other important changes to come in American religion had their roots in the 1950s and early 1960s. Boundaries between many Protestant denominations blurred as church leaders emphasized national unity, paving the way for the ecumenical movement and denominational mergers. Supreme Court decisions sowed the seeds for later political activism among evangelical Christians. In *Engel v. Vitale* (1962), the Court ruled that public schools could not require children to start the school day with group prayer. *Abington Township v. Schempp* (1963) prohibited devotional Bible reading in the schools. Such decisions alarmed many evangelicals; within two decades, school prayer would be a central issue in national politics.

The Gospel of Prosperity

Writers and intellectuals often marveled at the prosperity of Eisenhower's America. For scholars and journalists who had grown up during the Great Depression, the lack of economic hardship was the big story. William H. Whyte, Jr., searched American corporations for the changing character of the United States in *The Organization Man* (1956). The historian David Potter brilliantly analyzed Americans in *People of Plenty* (1954), contending that their national character had been shaped by the abundance of natural resources. In *The Affluent Society* (1958), economist John Kenneth Galbraith predicted that the challenge of the future would be to ensure the fair distribution of national wealth.

At times in these years, production and consumption outweighed democracy in the American message to the world. Officially, Americans argued that abundance was a natural by-product of a free society. In fact, it was easy to present prosperity as a goal in itself, as Vice President Richard Nixon did when he represented the United States at a technology exposition in Moscow in 1959. The U.S. exhibit included 21 models of automobiles and a complete six-room ranch house. In its "miracle kitchen," Nixon engaged Soviet Communist Party chairman Nikita Khrushchev in a carefully planned "kitchen debate." The vice president claimed that the "most important thing" for Americans was "the right to choose": "We have so many different manufacturers and many different kinds of washing machines so that the housewives have a choice."

Khrushchev heard a similar message when he visited the United States in September 1959. His itinerary started with a helicopter ride over rush-hour Washington to show the ubiquity of individually owned automobiles. He went to a farm in Coon Rapids, Iowa, a machine shop in Pittsburgh, and Hollywood movie studios. Although Khrushchev never believed that ordinary workers had miracle kitchens, he returned to Moscow knowing that America meant "business."

The Underside of Affluence

The most basic criticism of the ideology of prosperity was the simplest—that affluence concealed vast inequalities. Michael Harrington had worked among the poor before writing *The Other America* (1962). He reminded Americans about the "underdeveloped nation" of 40 to 50 million poor people who had missed the last two decades of prosperity. The poor were walled off in urban and rural backwaters. They were old people living on stale bread in bug-infested hotels. They were white families in the valleys of Appalachia, African Americans in city ghettos who could not find decent jobs, and Hispanic migrant workers whose children went for months without a glass of milk.

If Harrington found problems at the bottom of U.S. society, C. Wright Mills found dangers in the way that the Cold War distorted American society at the top. *The Power Elite* (1956) described an interlocking alliance of big government, big business, and the military. The losers in a permanent war economy, said Mills, were economic and political democracy. His ideas would reverberate in the 1960s during the Vietnam War.

Other critics targeted the alienating effects of consumerism and the conformity of homogeneous suburbs. Journalists indicted suburban society with coined terms like

Movie actor James Dean died in an automobile accident shortly after completing *Rebel Without a Cause*. His tragic death and his depiction of alienated youth made him a symbol of dissatisfaction with the middle-class 1950s.

"slurb" and books like *The Crack in the Picture Window* (1957) and *The Split Level Trap* (1961). Sociologist David Riesman saw suburbia as the home of "other-directed" individuals who lacked inner convictions. Although much of the antisuburban rhetoric was based on intellectual snobbery rather than research, it represented significant dissent from the praise of affluence.

There was far greater substance to the increasing dissatisfaction among women, who faced conflicting images of the perfect woman in the media. On one side was the comforting icon of Betty Crocker, the fictional spokeswoman for General Mills who made housework and cooking look easy. On the other side were sultry sexpots like Marilyn Monroe and the centerfold women of *Playboy* magazine, which first appeared in 1953. Women wondered how to be both Betty and Marilyn. In 1963, Betty Friedan's book *The Feminine Mystique* recognized that thousands of middle-class housewives were seething behind their picture windows. It followed numerous articles in *McCall's, Redbook,* and the *Ladies' Home Journal* about the unhappiness of college-educated women who were expected to find total satisfaction in kids and cooking. Friedan repackaged the message of the women's magazines along with the results of a survey of her Smith College classmates, who were then entering their forties. What Friedan called "the problem that has no name" was a sense of personal emptiness. "I got up one morning," remembered Geraldine Bean, "and I got my kids off to school. I went in to comb my hair and wash my face, and I stood in front of the bathroom mirror crying…because at eight-thirty in the morning I had my children off to school. I had my housework done. There was absolutely nothing for me to do the rest of the day." She went on to earn a Ph.D. and win election to the board of regents of the University of Colorado.

The United States exhibit at a technology exposition in Moscow in 1959 displayed a wide range of American consumer goods, from soft-drink dispensers to sewing machines. It included a complete six-room ranch house with an up-to-date kitchen where, in a famous encounter dubbed the "kitchen debate," Vice President Richard Nixon and Soviet Communist Party chairman Nikita Khrushchev disputed the merits of capitalism and Communism.

Facing off with the Soviet Union

Americans got a reassuring new face in the White House in 1953, but not new policies toward the world. As had been true since 1946, the nation's leaders weighed every foreign policy decision for its effect on the Cold War. The United States pushed ahead in an arms race with the Soviet Union, stood guard on the borders of China and the Soviet empire, and judged political changes in Latin America, Africa, and Asia for their effect on the global balance of power.

U.S. and Soviet actions created a bipolar world that mimicked the effects of a magnet on a scattering of iron filings. The two poles of a magnet draw some filings into tightly packed clusters, pull others into looser alignments pointing toward one pole or the other, and leave a few in the middle unaffected. In the later 1950s and early 1960s, the United States and the USSR were the magnetic poles. Members of NATO, the Warsaw Pact, and other formal alliances made up the tight clusters. The third world of officially uncommitted nations felt the influence of both blocs, sometimes aligning with one or the other and sometimes struggling to remain neutral.

Why We Liked Ike

In the late twentieth century, few leaders were able to master both domestic policy and foreign affairs. Some presidents, such as Lyndon Johnson, were more adept at social problems than diplomacy. By contrast, Richard Nixon and George H. W. Bush were more interested in the world outside the United States.

Dwight Eisenhower was also a "foreign-policy president." As a general, he had understood that military power should serve political ends. He had helped to hold together the alliance that defeated Nazi Germany and built NATO into an effective force in 1951–1952. He then sought the Republican nomination, he said, to ensure that the United States would keep its international commitments. He sealed his victory in 1952 by emphasizing his foreign-policy expertise, telling a campaign audience that "to bring the Korean war to an early and honorable end…requires a personal trip to Korea. I shall make that trip…I shall go to Korea."

What makes Eisenhower's administration hard to appreciate is that many of its accomplishments were things that did not happen. Eisenhower refused to dismantle the social programs of the New Deal. He exerted American political and military power around the globe but avoided war. Preferring to work behind the scenes, he knew how to delegate authority and keep disagreements private.

In his "hidden-hand" presidency, Eisenhower sometimes masked his intelligence. It helped his political agenda if Americans thought of him as a smiling grandfather. He was the first president to have televised news conferences and knew how to manipulate them. The "Ike" whose face smiled from "I Like Ike" campaign buttons and who gave rambling, incoherent answers at White House press conferences knew exactly what he was doing—controlling information and keeping the opposition guessing. When his press secretary advised him to duck questions at one press conference, Ike replied, "Don't worry, I'll just confuse them." He was easily reelected in 1956, when Americans saw no reason to abandon competent leadership.

A Balance of Terror

The backdrop for U.S. foreign policy was the growing capacity for mutual nuclear annihilation. The rivalry between the United States and the USSR was played out within a framework of deterrence, the knowledge that each side could launch a devastating nuclear attack. The old balance of power had become a balance of terror.

The Eisenhower administration's doctrine of **massive retaliation** took advantage of America's superior technology while economizing on military spending. Eisenhower and his advisers worried that matching the land armies of China and the Soviet Union would inflate the role of the federal government in American society (see Figure 28–3). Eisenhower compared uncontrolled military spending to crucifying humankind on a "cross of iron." "Every gun that is fired," he warned, "every warship launched, every rocket fired signifies…a theft from those who hunger and are not fed, those who are cold and not clothed." The administration concentrated military spending where the nation already had the greatest advantage—on atomic weapons. In response to any serious attack, the United States would direct maximum force against the homeland of the aggressor. Secretary of State Dulles called for "a maximum deterrent at a bearable cost." Reporters translated the policy as "more bang for the buck."

The massive-retaliation doctrine treated nuclear weapons as ordinary or even respectable. It put European and American cities on the frontline in the defense of Germany, for it meant that the United States would react to a Soviet conventional attack on NATO by dropping nuclear bombs on the Soviet Union, which would presumably retaliate in kind. The National Security Council in 1953 made reliance on "massive retaliatory damage" by nuclear weapons official policy.

The doctrine grew even more fearful as the Soviet Union developed its own hydrogen bombs. The chairman of the Atomic Energy Commission terrified the American people by mentioning casually that the Soviets could now obliterate New York City. Dozens of nuclear weapons tests in the late 1950s made the atomic threat immediate. So did signs for air-raid shelters posted on downtown buildings and city-wide air-raid drills. Radioactivity carried by fallout from the tests appeared in milk supplies in the form of the isotope strontium 90. Stories about

handfuls of survivors groping through the ruins of atomic war filled popular literature.

The Soviet Union added to the worries about atomic war by launching the world's first artificial satellite. On the first Sunday of October 1957, Americans discovered that *Sputnik*—Russian for "satellite"—was orbiting the earth. The Soviets soon lifted a dog into orbit while U.S. rockets fizzled on the pad. Soviet propagandists claimed that their technological "first" showed the superiority of Communism, and Americans wondered if the United States had lost its edge. Schools beefed up science courses and began to introduce the "new math," Congress passed the National Defense Education Act to expand college and postgraduate education, and the new **National Aeronautics and Space Administration (NASA)** took over the satellite program in 1958.

The crisis was more apparent than real. Eisenhower had rejected the use of available military rockets for the U.S. space program in favor of developing new launch vehicles, and he overlooked the symbolic impact of *Sputnik*. He thus built himself into a political box, for the combination of Soviet rocketry and nuclear capacity created alarm about a missile gap. The Soviet Union was said to be building hundreds of intercontinental ballistic missiles (ICBMs) to overwhelm American air defenses designed to intercept piloted bombers. By the early 1960s, critics charged, a do-nothing administration would have put the United States in peril. Although there was no such gap, Eisenhower was unwilling to reveal secret information that might have allayed public anxiety.

Containment in Action

Someone who heard only the campaign speeches in 1952 might have expected sharp foreign-policy changes under Eisenhower, but there was more continuity than change.

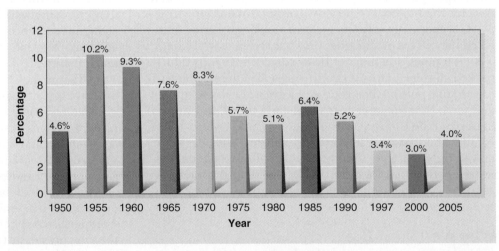

FIGURE 28–3   Defense Spending as a Percentage of Gross Domestic Product, 1950–2005. Defense spending has been an important force for economic development and innovation. The impact of the defense budget on the domestic economy was greatest in the mid-1950s, at the height of the Cold War. Lesser peaks came during the Vietnam War in the late 1960s and the Reagan administration defense buildup in the early 1980s.

Data Source: *Statistical Abstract of the United States.*

Schoolchildren in the 1950s regularly practiced taking cover in case of atomic attack. If there was warning, they were to file into interior hallways, crouch against the walls, and cover their heads with their jackets as protection against flying glass. If they saw the blinding flash of an atomic explosion without warning, they were to "duck and cover" under their school desks.

John Foster Dulles, Eisenhower's secretary of state, had attacked the Democrats as defeatists and appeasers. He demanded that the United States liberate eastern Europe from Soviet control and encourage Jiang Jieshi to attack Communist China. Warlike language continued after the election. In 1956, Dulles proudly claimed that tough-minded diplomacy had repeatedly brought the United States to the verge of war: "We walked to the brink and looked it in the face. We took strong action." Critics protested that "brinkmanship" endangered the entire world.

In fact, Eisenhower viewed the Cold War in the same terms as Truman. He worried about the "sullen weight of Russia" pushing against smaller nations and saw a world caught between the incompatible values of freedom and communism, but caution replaced campaign rhetoric about "rolling back" Communism. Around the periphery of the Communist nations, from eastern Asia to the Middle East to Europe, the United States accepted the existing sphere of Communist influence but attempted to block its growth, a policy most Americans accepted.

The U.S. worldview assumed both the right and the need to intervene in the affairs of other nations, especially countries in Latin America, Asia, and Africa. Policymakers saw these nations as markets for U.S. products and sources of vital raw materials. When political disturbances arose in these states, the United States blamed Soviet meddling to justify U.S. intervention. If Communism could not be rolled back in eastern Europe, the CIA could still undermine anti-American governments in the third world. The Soviets themselves took advantage of local revolutions even when they did not instigate them; in doing so they confirmed Washington's belief that the developing world was a game board on which the superpowers carried on their rivalry by proxy.

Twice during Eisenhower's first term, the CIA subverted democratically elected governments that seemed to threaten U.S. interests. In Iran, which had nationalized British and U.S. oil companies in an effort to break the hold of Western corporations, the CIA in 1953 backed a coup that toppled the government and helped the young shah, as the reigning monarch was called, to gain control. The shah then cooperated with the United States, but his increasingly repressive regime would lead to his overthrow in 1979 and deep Iranian resentment of the United States. In Guatemala, the leftist government was threatening the United Fruit Company. When the Guatemalans accepted weapons from the Communist bloc in 1954, the CIA imposed a regime friendly to U.S. business (see Map 28–1).

For most Americans in 1953, democracy in Iran was far less important than ending the war in Korea and stabilizing relations with China. Eisenhower declined to escalate the Korean War by blockading China and sending more U.S. ground forces. Instead, he positioned atomic bombs on Okinawa, only 400 miles from China. The nuclear threat, along with the continued cost of the war on both sides, brought the Chinese to a truce that left Korea divided into two nations.

The following year, China began to shell the small islands of Quemoy and Matsu, from which the Nationalist Chinese on Taiwan were launching commando raids on the mainland. Again, Secretary Dulles rattled the atomic saber, and China stopped the attacks. Evidence now suggests that Washington misread the situation. Mao's "theatrical" shelling was a political statement, not a prelude to military assault. Stepping to the "brink of war" did not deter Chinese aggression, because China never planned to attack.

Halfway around the world, there was a new crisis when three U.S. friends—France, Britain, and Israel—ganged up on Egypt. France was angry at Egyptian support for revolutionaries in French Algeria. Britain was even angrier at Egypt's nationalization of the British-dominated Suez Canal. And Israel wanted to weaken its most powerful Arab enemy. On October 29, 1956, Israel attacked Egypt. A week later, British and French forces attempted to seize the canal.

Although the United States had been the first nation to recognize Israel in 1948, the relationship was much less close

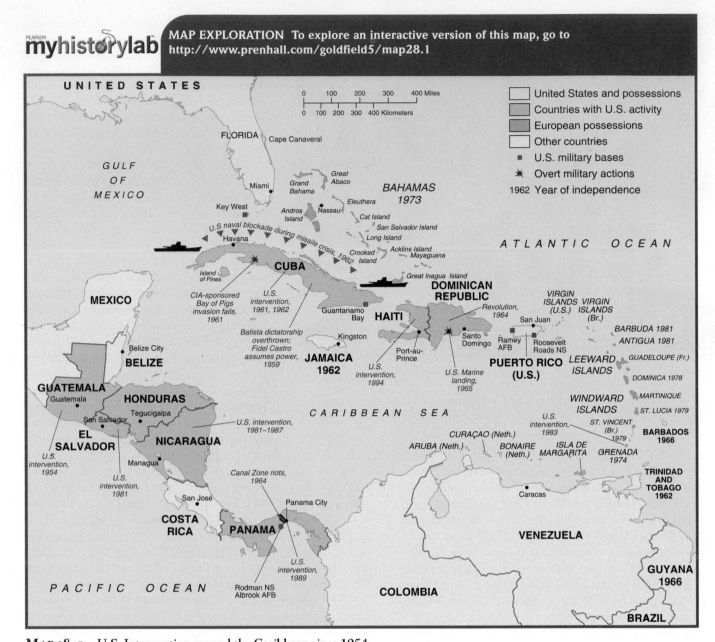

MAP EXPLORATION To explore an interactive version of this map, go to
http://www.prenhall.com/goldfield5/map28.1

MAP 28–1   U.S. Intervention around the Caribbean since 1954
The United States has long kept a careful eye on the politics of neighboring nations to the south. In the second half of the twentieth century, the United States frequently used military assistance or force to influence or intervene in Caribbean and Central American nations. The purpose has usually been to counter or undermine left-leaning governments; some interventions, as in Haiti, have been intended to stabilize democratic regimes.

than it would become. The U.S. forced a quick cease-fire, partly to maintain its standing with oil-producing Arab nations. Because Egypt blocked the canal with sunken ships, the war left Britain and France dependent on American oil that Eisenhower would not provide until they left Egypt. Resolution of the crisis involved one of the first uses of peacekeeping troops under the United Nations flag.

In Europe, Eisenhower accepted the status quo because conflicts there could result in nuclear war. In 1956, challenges to Communist rule arose in East Germany, Poland, and Hungary and threatened to break up the Soviet empire. The Soviets replaced liberal Communists in East Germany while accepting a more liberal leader in Poland. In Hungary, however, reformers took the fatal step of proposing to quit the Warsaw Pact. Open warfare broke out when the Soviet army rolled across the border to preserve the Soviet empire. Hungarian freedom fighters in Budapest used rocks and firebombs against Soviet tanks for several days, while pleading in vain for Western aid. NATO would not risk war with the USSR. Tens of thousands of Hungarians died, and 200,000 fled when the Soviets crushed the resistance.

Global Standoff

The Soviet Union, China, and the United States and its allies were all groping in the dark as they maneuvered for influence in the 1950s and 1960s. In one international crisis after another, each player misinterpreted the other's motivations and diplomatic signals. Now that documents from both sides of the Cold War are becoming available, historians have realized what dangerously different meanings the two sides gave to their confrontations between 1953 and 1964.

A good example is the U-2 spy plane affair of 1960, which derailed progress toward nuclear disarmament. The Kremlin was deeply worried that West Germany and China might acquire nuclear bombs. Washington wanted to reduce military budgets and nuclear fallout. Both countries voluntarily suspended nuclear tests in 1958 and prepared for a June 1960 summit meeting in Paris, where Eisenhower intended to negotiate a test ban treaty. But on May 1, 1960, Soviet air defenses shot down an American U-2 aircraft over the heart of Russia and captured the pilot, Francis Gary Powers. The cover story for the U-2 was weather research, but the frail-looking black plane was a CIA operation. Designed to soar above the range of Soviet antiaircraft missiles, information obtained by U-2s had assured American officials that there was no missile gap.

When Moscow trumpeted the news of the plane's downing, Eisenhower took personal responsibility in hopes that Khrushchev would accept the U-2 as an unpleasant reality of international espionage. Unfortunately, the planes meant something very different to the Soviets, touching their festering sense of inferiority. They had stopped protesting the flights in 1957, because they saw complaints as demeaning. The Americans thought their silence signaled acceptance. Khrushchev had staked his future on good relations with the United States; when Eisenhower refused to apologize in Paris, Khrushchev stalked out. Disarmament was set back for years because the two sides had such different understandings of the same events.

The most important aspect of Eisenhower's foreign policy was continuity. Despite militant rhetoric, the administration pursued containment as defined under Truman. The Cold War consensus, however, prevented the United States from seeing the nations of the developing world on their own terms. By viewing every independence movement and social revolution as part of the competition with Communism, U.S. leaders created unnecessary problems. In the end, Eisenhower left troublesome and unresolved issues—upheaval in Latin America, civil war in Vietnam, tension in Germany, the nuclear arms race—for his successor, John Kennedy, who wanted to confront international Communism even more vigorously. (see American Views, Two Presidents Assess the Implications of the Cold War).

John F. Kennedy and the Cold War

John Kennedy was a man of contradictions. Many Americans recall his presidency (1961–1963) as a golden age, but they are more taken by his memory than they were by Kennedy himself. A Democrat who promised to get the country moving again, he presided over policies whose direction was set under Eisenhower. Despite stirring rhetoric about leading the nation toward a **New Frontier** of scientific and social progress, he recorded his greatest failures and successes in the continuing Cold War.

The Kennedy Mystique

Kennedy won the presidency over Richard Nixon in a cliff-hanging election that was more about personality and style than about substance (see Map 28–2). Both candidates were determined not to yield another inch to Communism. The charming and eloquent Kennedy narrowly skirted scandal for a sexually promiscuous personal life. Well publicized as

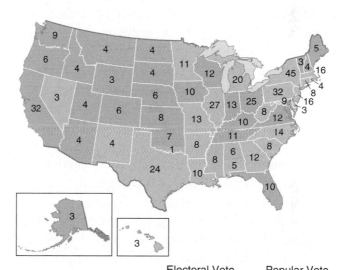

	Electoral Vote (%)	Popular Vote (%)
JOHN F. KENNEDY (Democrat)	**303** **(56)**	**34,226,731** **(49.9)**
Richard M. Nixon (Republican)	219 (41)	34,108,157 (49.7)
Other	15 (3)	197,029 (.4)

Note: Fifteen electors voted for Harry Byrd, although he had not been an active candidate. Minor party candidates took a tiny percentage of the popular vote.

MAP 28–2 The Election of 1960
The presidential election of 1960 was one of the closest in American history. John Kennedy's victory depended on his appeal in northern industrial states with large Roman Catholic populations and his ability to hold much of the traditionally Democratic South. Texas, the home state of his vice-presidential running mate, Lyndon Johnson, was vital to the success of the ticket.

American Views

Two Presidents Assess the Implications of the Cold War

In speeches two days apart in January 1961, outgoing President Dwight Eisenhower and incoming President John Kennedy offered contrasting interpretations of America's Cold War crusade. Eisenhower spoke with concern about the effects of defense spending on American society. Kennedy promised an unlimited commitment of resources to achieve national goals.

- Why did Kennedy define the American mission to the world so broadly?
- What changes in the 1950s led Eisenhower to warn about the dangers of pursuing that mission?
- Do the selections show basic agreement or disagreement about the goals of national policy?

Dwight D. Eisenhower
Farewell Address, January 18, 1961

Our military organization today bears little relation to that known by any of my predecessors in peacetime.... This conjunction of an immense military establishment and a large arms industry is new in the American experience. The total influence—economic, political, even spiritual—is felt in every city, every State house, every office of the federal government. We recognize the imperative need for this development. Yet we must not fail to comprehend its grave implications....

In the councils of government, we must guard against the acquisition of unwarranted influence, whether sought or unsought, by the military-industrial complex. The potential for the disastrous rise of misplaced power exists and will persist. We must never let the weight of this combination endanger our liberties or democratic processes. We should take nothing for granted. Only an alert and knowledgeable citizenry can compel the proper meshing of the huge industrial and military machinery of defense with our peaceful methods and goals.

John F. Kennedy
Inaugural Address, January 20, 1961

Let the word go forth from this time and place, to friend and foe alike, that the torch has been passed to a new generation of Americans—born in this century, tempered by war, disciplined by a hard and bitter peace, proud of our ancient heritage—and unwilling to witness or permit the slow undoing of those human rights to which this nation has always been committed, and to which we are committed today at home and around the world.

Let every nation know, whether it wishes us well or ill, that we shall pay any price, bear any burden, meet any hardship, support any friends, oppose any foe to assure the survival and the success of liberty.

---

a hero from World War II, he tempered ruthless ambition with respect for public service. His forthright campaigning allayed voter concern about his Roman Catholicism. Nixon had wider experience and was a shrewd tactician, but he was also self-righteous and awkward. Eisenhower had wanted to drop Nixon as vice president in 1956 and gave him only lukewarm support in 1960—when a reporter asked Eisenhower to cite important decisions to which Nixon had contributed, Ike replied, "Give me a week and I might think of one."

Television was crucial to the outcome. The campaign featured the first televised presidential debates. In the first session, Nixon actually gave better replies, but his nervousness and a bad makeup job turned off millions of viewers, who admired Kennedy's energy. Nixon never overcame the setback, but the race was tight, with tiny margins in crucial states giving Kennedy the victory. His televised inauguration was the perfect setting for an impassioned plea for national unity: "My fellow Americans," he challenged, "ask not what your country can do for you—ask what you can do for your country."

Kennedy brought dash to the White House. His beautiful and refined wife, Jackie, made sure to seat artists and writers next to diplomats and businessmen at White House dinners. Kennedy's staff and large family played touch football, not golf. No president had shown such verve since Teddy Roosevelt. People began to talk about Kennedy's "charisma," his ability to lead by sheer force of personality. In fact, the image of a fit, vigorous man concealed the reality that he was

For many Americans in the early 1960s, John and Jacqueline Kennedy and their two children represented the ideal family, although the carefully posed pictures with happy smiles concealed the president's severe health problems and deep rifts in the marriage.

ized American investments, and thousands of Cubans fled to the United States.

When 1,400 anti-Castro Cubans landed at Cuba's **Bay of Pigs** on April 17, 1961, they were following a plan prepared by the Eisenhower administration. The CIA had trained and armed the invaders and convinced Kennedy that the landing would trigger spontaneous uprisings. But when Kennedy refused to commit U.S. armed forces to support them, Cuban forces captured the attackers.

Kennedy followed the Bay of Pigs debacle with a hasty and ill-thought-out summit meeting with Khrushchev in Vienna in June. Poorly prepared and nearly incapacitated by agonizing back pain, Kennedy made little headway. Khrushchev saw no need to bargain and subjected him to intimidating tirades. "He just beat the hell out of me," Kennedy told a reporter. Coming after Kennedy's refusal to salvage the Bay of Pigs by military intervention, the meeting left the Soviets with the impression that the president was weak and dangerously erratic.

To exploit Kennedy's perceived vulnerability, the Soviet Union renewed tension over Berlin, deep within East Germany. The divided city served as an escape route from Communism for hundreds of thousands of East Germans. Khrushchev now threatened to transfer the Soviet sector in Berlin to East Germany, which had no treaty obligations to France, Britain, or the United States. If the West had to deal directly with East Germany for access to Berlin, it would have to recognize a permanently divided Germany. Kennedy sounded the alarm: He doubled draft calls, called up reservists, and warned families to build fallout shelters. Boise, Idaho, families paid $100 for a share in a community shelter with its own power plant and hospital. Outside New York, Art Carlson and his son Claude put up a prefabricated steel shelter in four hours; Sears planned to sell the same model for $700.

Rather than confront the United States directly, however, the Soviets and East Germans on August 13, 1961, built a wall around the western sectors of Berlin while leaving the access route to West Germany open. The **Berlin Wall** thus isolated East Germany without challenging the Western allies in West Berlin itself. In private, Kennedy accepted the wall as a clever way to stabilize a dangerous situation: "A wall," he said, "is a hell of a lot better than a war." Tensions remained high for months as the two sides tested each other's resolve. Berlin remained a point of East-West tension until East German Communism collapsed in 1989 and Berliners tore down the hated wall.

battling severe physical ailments that demanded constant medical attention and often left him with debilitating pain.

Behind the glamorous façade, Kennedy remained a puzzle. One day, Kennedy could propose the Peace Corps, which gave thousands of idealistic young Americans a chance to help developing nations; another day, he could approve plots to assassinate Fidel Castro. Visitors who expected a shallow glad-hander were astonished to meet a sharp, hard-working man who was eager to learn about the world. One savvy diplomat commented, "I have never heard of a president who wanted to know so much."

Kennedy's Mistakes

Kennedy and Khrushchev perpetuated similar problems. Talking tough to satisfy their more militant countrymen, they repeatedly pushed each other into a corner, continuing the problems of mutual misunderstanding that had marked the 1950s. When Khrushchev promised, in January 1961, to support "wars of national liberation," he was really fending off Chinese criticism. But Kennedy overreacted in his first State of the Union address by asking for more military spending.

Three months later, Kennedy fed Soviet fears of American aggressiveness by sponsoring an invasion of Cuba. At the start of 1959, Fidel Castro had toppled the corrupt dictator Fulgencio Batista, who had made Havana infamous for Mafia-run gambling and prostitution. Castro then national-

Getting into Vietnam

U.S. involvement in Vietnam, located in Southeast Asia on the southern border of China, dated to 1949–1950. After World War II ended, France had fought to maintain its colonial rule there against rebels who combined Communist ideology with fervor for national independence under the leadership of Ho Chi Minh. Although the United States supported independence of most other European colonies, the triumph of Mao Zedong in China and the Korean War caused policymakers to see Vietnam as another Cold War conflict. The United States picked up three-quarters of the costs. Nevertheless, the French military position collapsed in 1954 after Vietnamese forces overran the French stronghold at Dien Bien Phu. The French had enough, and President Eisenhower was unwilling to join another Asian war. A Geneva peace conference "temporarily" divided Vietnam into a Communist north and a non-Communist south and scheduled elections for a single Vietnamese government.

The United States then replaced France as the supporter of the pro-Western Vietnamese in the south. Washington's client was Ngo Dinh Diem, an anti-Communist from South Vietnam's Roman Catholic elite. U.S. officials encouraged Diem to put off the elections and backed his efforts to construct an independent South Vietnam. Ho meanwhile consolidated the northern half as a communist state that claimed to be the legitimate government for all Vietnam. The United States further reinforced containment in Asia by bringing Thailand, the Philippines, Pakistan, Australia, New Zealand, Britain, and France together in the **Southeast Asia Treaty Organization (SEATO)** in 1954 (see Map 28–3).

Another indirect consequence of the Vienna summit was the growing U.S. entanglement in South Vietnam, where Kennedy saw a chance to take a firm stand and reassert America's commitment to containment. In the countryside, Communist insurgents known as the **Viet Cong** were gaining strength. The anti-Communist leader, Diem, controlled the cities with the help of a large army and a Vietnamese elite that had worked with the French. The United States stepped up its supply of weapons and sent advisers, including members of one of Kennedy's military innovations, the Army Special Forces Group (Green Berets).

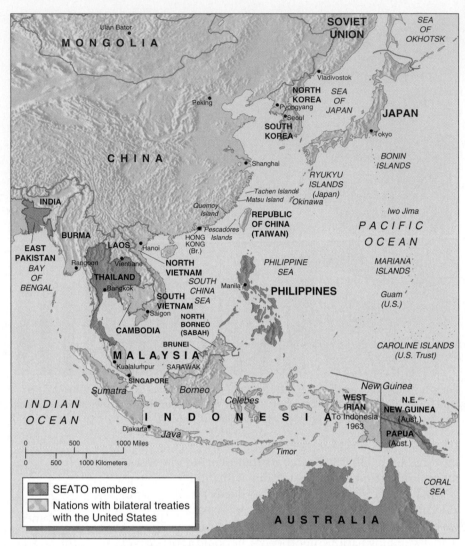

MAP 28–3   SEATO and Other East Asian Countries with Ties to the United States

In East Asia and the western Pacific, the United States in the 1950s constructed a series of alliances to resist Soviet and Chinese Communist influence.

U.S. aid did not work. Despite overoptimistic reports and the help of 16,000 U.S. troops, Diem's government by 1963 was losing the loyalty—the "hearts and minds"—of many South Vietnamese. North Vietnamese support for the Viet Cong canceled the effect of U.S. assistance. Diem courted a second civil war by violently crushing opposition from Vietnamese Buddhists. Kennedy's administration tacitly approved a coup on November 1 that killed Diem and his brother and installed an ineffective military junta.

Missile Crisis: A Line Drawn in the Waves

The escalating tensions of 1961 in Southeast Asia, the Caribbean, and Germany were a prelude to the crisis that came closest to triggering a nuclear war. In the summer of 1962, congressional Republicans had hounded Kennedy about the Soviet military presence in Cuba. On October 15, reconnaissance photos revealed Soviets at work on launching sites from which nuclear missiles could hit the United States. Top officials spent five exhausting and increasingly desperate days sorting through the options. Doing nothing was never considered: The missiles would be a political disaster and a threat to national security. A full-scale invasion of Cuba was not feasible on short notice, and "surgical" air strikes were technically impossible. Either sort of military operation would kill hundreds of Soviet personnel and force Moscow to react. Secretary of Defense Robert McNamara suggested demanding removal of the missiles and declaring a naval "quarantine" against the arrival of further offensive weapons. A blockade would buy time for diplomacy.

Kennedy imposed the blockade in a terrifying speech on Monday, October 22. He emphasized the "deceptive" deployment of the Russian missiles and raised the specter of nuclear war. Americans would have been even more afraid had they known that some of the missiles were operational and that Soviets in Cuba were authorized to use them in self-defense. While Khrushchev hesitated, Soviet ships circled outside the quarantine line. On Friday, Khrushchev offered to withdraw the missiles in return for a U.S. pledge not to invade Cuba. On Saturday, a second communication nearly dashed this hopeful opening by raising a new complaint about U.S. missiles on the territory of NATO allies. The letter was the result of pressure by Kremlin hard-liners and Khrushchev's own wavering. Kennedy decided to accept the first letter and ignore the second. The United States pledged not to invade Cuba and secretly promised to remove obsolete Jupiter missiles from Turkey. Khrushchev accepted these terms on Sunday, October 28.

Why did Khrushchev risk the Cuban gamble? One reason was to protect Castro as a symbol of Soviet commitment to anti-Western regimes in the developing world. Americans hated the Castro government out of proportion to its geopolitical importance, but they rightly feared that Cuba would try to export revolution throughout Latin America. Kennedy had tried to preempt Castroism in 1961 by launching the **Alliance for Progress,** an economic-development program for Latin America that tied aid to social reform. However, the United States had also orchestrated the Bay of Pigs invasion and funded a CIA campaign to sabotage Cuba. High U.S. officials were not contemplating a full-scale invasion, but Castro and Khrushchev had reason to fear the worst.

Khrushchev also hoped to redress the strategic balance. As Kennedy discovered on taking office, the United States actually led the world in the deployment of strategic missiles. Intermediate-range rockets gave the USSR a nuclear club over western Europe, but in October 1962, the Soviet Union had fewer than 50 ICBMs to aim at the United States and China. The United States was creating a defensive triad of 1,000 land-based Minuteman missiles, 500 long-range bombers, and 600 Polaris missiles on nuclear submarines targeted on the USSR. The strategic imbalance had sustained NATO during the Berlin confrontation, but 40 launchers in Cuba with two warheads each would have doubled the Soviet capacity to strike at the United States.

Soviet missiles in Cuba thus flouted the Monroe Doctrine and posed a real military threat. Kennedy and Khrushchev had also backed each other into untenable positions. In September, Kennedy had warned that the United States could not tolerate Soviet offensive weapons in Cuba, never dreaming that they were already there. Had Khrushchev acted openly (as the United States had done when it placed missiles in Turkey), the United States would have been hard pressed to object under international law. By acting in secret and breaking previous promises, the Soviets outsmarted themselves. When the missiles were discovered, Kennedy had to act.

In the end, both sides were cautious. Khrushchev backed down rather than fight. Kennedy fended off hawkish advisers who wanted to destroy Castro. The world had trembled, but neither nation wanted war over "the missiles of October."

Science and Foreign Affairs

The two superpowers competed through science as well as diplomacy. When Kennedy took office, the United States was still playing catch-up in space technology. A Russian, Yuri Gagarin, was the first human to orbit the earth, on April 12, 1961. American John Glenn did not match Gagarin's feat until February 1962. Kennedy committed the United States to placing a U.S. astronaut on the moon by 1970. The decision narrowed a multifaceted scientific and military program to a massive engineering project that favored the economic capacity of the United States.

The Soviet Union and the United States were also fencing about nuclear weapons testing. After the three-year moratorium, both resumed tests in 1961–1962. The United States started with underground tests to minimize fallout, but then followed with atmospheric detonations. Renewed testing let the Russians show off huge hydrogen bombs with yields of 20 and 30 megatons—roughly 1,000 times the power of the bombs dropped on Japan. Both nations worked on multiple-targetable warheads, antiballistic missiles, and other innovations that might destabilize the balance of terror.

After the missile crisis showed his toughness, however, Kennedy had enough political maneuvering room to respond to pressure from liberal Democrats and groups like Women Strike for Peace and the Committee for a Sane Nuclear Policy by giving priority to disarmament. In July 1963, the United States, Britain, and the USSR signed the **Limited Test Ban Treaty,** which outlawed nuclear testing in the atmosphere, in outer space, and under water, and invited other nations to join in. A more comprehensive treaty was impossible because the Soviet Union refused the on-site inspections the United States deemed necessary to distinguish underground tests from earthquakes. France and China, the other nuclear powers, refused to sign, and the treaty did not halt weapons development, but it was the most positive achievement of Kennedy's foreign policy and a step toward later disarmament treaties.

Righteousness like a Mighty Stream: The Struggle for Civil Rights

Supreme Court decisions are based on abstract principles, but they involve real people. One was Linda Brown of Topeka, Kansas, a third-grader whose parents were fed up with sending her past an all-white public school to attend an all-black school a mile away. The Browns volunteered to help the NAACP challenge Topeka's school segregation by trying to enroll Linda in their neighborhood school, beginning a legal case that reached the Supreme Court. On May 17, 1954, the Court decided ***Brown v. Board of Education of Topeka,*** opening a new civil rights era. Led by the persuasive power of the new chief justice, Earl Warren, the Court unanimously reversed the 1896 case of *Plessy v. Ferguson* by ruling that sending black children to "separate but equal" schools denied them equal treatment under the Constitution. When Linda Brown's father heard the news, his eyes filled with tears, and he said, "Thanks be to God."

The *Brown* decision made the growing effort to secure equal legal treatment for African Americans an inescapable challenge to American society. The first phase of the civil rights struggle built from the Supreme Court's decision in 1954 to a vast gathering at the Lincoln Memorial in 1963. In between, African Americans chipped away at the racial seg-regation of schools, universities, and public facilities with marches, boycotts, sit-ins, and lawsuits, forcing segregated communities to choose between integration and violent defiance. In the two years following the 1963 March on Washington, the federal government passed landmark legislation.

Getting to the Supreme Court

The *Brown* decision climaxed a 25-year campaign to reenlist the federal courts on the side of equal rights (see Overview, Civil Rights: The Struggle for Racial Equality). The work began in the 1930s when Charles Hamilton Houston, dean of Howard University's law school, trained a corps of civil rights lawyers. Working on behalf of the NAACP, he hoped to erode *Plessy* by suits focused on interstate travel and professional graduate schools (the least defensible segregated institutions, because states seldom provided alternatives). In 1938, Houston's student Thurgood Marshall, a future Supreme Court justice, took over the NAACP job. He and other NAACP lawyers such as Constance Baker Motley risked personal danger crisscrossing the South to file civil rights lawsuits wherever a local case emerged. In 1949, Motley was the first black lawyer to argue a case in a Mississippi courtroom since Reconstruction.

Efforts in the 1940s and early 1950s, often fueled by the experience of World War II soldiers, had important successes. In *Smith v. Allwright* (1944), the Supreme Court invalidated the all-white primary, a decision that led to increased black voter registration in many southern communities. With new political power, and often with the cooperation of relatively progressive white leaders, blacks fought for specific improvements, such as equal pay for teachers or the hiring of black police officers.

The *Brown* case combined lawsuits from Delaware, Virginia, South Carolina, the District of Columbia, and Kansas. In each instance, students and families braved community pressure to demand equal access to a basic public service. Chief Justice Earl Warren brought a divided Court to unanimous agreement. Viewing public education as central for the equal opportunity that lay at the heart of American values, the Court weighed the consequences of segregated school systems and concluded that separate meant unequal. The reasoning fit the temper of a nation that was proud of making prosperity accessible to all.

Brown also built on efforts by Mexican Americans in the Southwest to assert their rights of citizenship. After World War II, Latino organizations such as the League of United Latin American Citizens battled

Elizabeth Eckford, one of the first black students to attend Central High in Little Rock, Arkansas, in 1957, enters the school amid taunts from white students and bystanders.

Civil Rights: The Struggle for Racial Equality

Area of Concern	Key Actions	Results
Public school integration	Federal court cases	*Brown v. Board of Education of Topeka* (1954) Enforcement by presidential action, Little Rock (1957)
		Follow-up court decisions, including mandatory busing programs
Equal access to public facilities	Montgomery bus boycott (1955)	Civil Rights Act of 1964
	Lunch counter sit-ins (1960)	
	Freedom rides (1961)	
	Birmingham demonstrations (1963)	
	March on Washington (1963)	
Equitable voter registration	Voter registration drives, including Mississippi Summer Project (1964) Demonstrations and marches, including Selma to Montgomery march (1965)	Voting Rights Act of 1965

job discrimination and ethnic segregation. In 1946, Mexican American parents sued five Orange County, California school districts that systematically placed their children in separate schools. In the resulting case of *Mendez v. Westminster*, federal courts prohibited segregation of Mexican American children in California schools as a violation of the equal protection clause of the Fourteenth Amendment. Eight years later, the Supreme Court forbade Texas from excluding Mexican Americans from juries. These cases provided precedents for the Court's decision in *Brown* and subsequent civil rights cases.

Deliberate Speed

Racial segregation by law was largely a southern problem, the legacy of Jim Crow laws (see Chapter 17). The civil rights movement therefore focused first on the South, allowing Americans elsewhere to think of racial injustice as a regional issue.

Southern responses to *Brown* revealed regional differences. Few southern communities desegregated schools voluntarily, for to do so undermined the entrenched principle of a dual society. Their reluctance was bolstered in 1955 when the Supreme Court allowed segregated states to carry out the 1954 decision "with all deliberate speed" rather than immediately. The phrase recognized that the courts had limited powers to enforce broad decisions and allowed communities to find reasons for delay; Thurgood Marshall later commented, "I've finally figured out what 'all deliberate speed' means. It means slow."

The following year, 101 southern congressmen and senators issued the **Southern Manifesto,** which asserted that the Court decision was unconstitutional. President Eisenhower privately deplored the desegregation decision, which

violated his sense of states' rights and upset Republican attempts to gain southern votes; he called both those who resisted the decision and those who wanted to enforce it "extremists." At the same time, many in Washington knew that racial discrimination offered, in the worlds of Dean Acheson, "the most effective kind of ammunition" for Soviet propaganda.

Eisenhower's distaste for racial integration left the Justice Department on the sidelines. Courageous parents and students had to knock on schoolhouse doors, often carrying court orders. Responses varied: school districts in border states, such as Maryland, Kentucky, and Oklahoma, desegregated relatively peacefully; farther south, African American children often met taunts and violence.

The first crisis came in Little Rock, Arkansas, in September 1957. The city school board admitted nine African Americans, including Melba Pattillo, to Central High, while segregationist groups, such as the White Citizens Council, stirred up white fears. Claiming he feared violence, Governor Orval Faubus surrounded Central High with the National Guard and turned the new students away. Under intense national pressure, Faubus withdrew the Guard. The black students entered the school, but a howling mob forced the police to sneak them out after two hours. Fuming at the governor's defiance of federal authority, Eisenhower reluctantly nationalized the National Guard and sent in the 101st Airborne Division to keep order. Eight of the students endured a year of harassment in the hallways of Central.

Virginians in 1958–1959 tried avoidance rather than confrontation. Massive resistance was a state policy that required local school districts to close rather than accept black

Students from North Carolina A&T, an all-black college, began the lunch-counter sit-in movement in February 1960. Here four students sit patiently in the Greensboro Woolworth's without being served. Participants wore their best clothes and suffered politely through days of verbal and sometimes physical abuse.

students. When court orders to admit 19 black students triggered the shutdown of four high schools and three junior highs in Norfolk, white parents tried to compensate with private academies and tutoring, but it was soon apparent that a modern community could not dismantle public education. Norfolk's leaders realized that no large business was going to locate in a city whose claim to fame was the "lost class of '59," and Virginia's elite privately welcomed federal court decisions that got them off the hook by striking down their own law.

Change came slowly to state universities. Border states desegregated colleges and professional schools with few incidents. Again, the story was different in the lower South. In 1956, the University of Alabama admitted Autherine Lucy under court order but then expelled her before she could attend classes. In September 1962, James Meredith tried to enter the University of Mississippi, igniting a riot that the state refused to control. Because the governor directly defied the federal courts and broke promises to the administration, President Kennedy sent in the army. A year later, Governor George Wallace of Alabama grabbed headlines by "standing in the schoolhouse door" to prevent integration of the University of Alabama, gaining a national

prominence that culminated in a third-party candidacy for president in 1968.

The breakthrough in school integration did not come until the end of the 1960s, when the courts rejected further delays, and federal authorities threatened to cut off education funds. As late as 1968, only 6 percent of African American children in the South attended integrated schools. By 1973, the figure was 90 percent. Attention thereafter shifted to northern communities, whose schools were segregated, not by law, but by the divisions between white and black neighborhoods and between white suburbs and multiracial central cities, a situation known as *de facto* segregation.

Public Accommodations

The civil rights movement also sought to integrate public accommodations. Most southern states separated the races in bus terminals and movie theaters. They required black riders to take rear seats on buses. They labeled separate restrooms and drinking fountains for "colored" users. Hotels denied rooms to black people, and restaurants refused them service.

The struggle to end segregated facilities started in Montgomery, Alabama. On December 1, 1955, Rosa Parks, a seamstress who worked at a downtown department store, refused to give up her bus seat to a white passenger and was arrested. Parks acted spontaneously, but she was part of a network of civil rights activists who wanted to challenge segregated buses and was the secretary of the Montgomery NAACP. As news of her action spread, the community institutions that enriched southern black life went into action. The Women's Political Council, a group of college-trained black women, initiated a mass boycott of the privately owned bus company. Alabama State College professor Jo Ann Robinson worked through the night to mimeograph 52,500 flyers and enlisted students to spread them through the city. Martin Luther King, Jr., a 26-year-old pastor, led the boycott. He galvanized a mass meeting with a speech that quoted the biblical prophet Amos: "We are determined here in Montgomery to work and fight until justice runs down like water, and righteousness like a mighty stream."

Montgomery's African Americans organized their boycott in the face of white outrage. A car pool substituted for the buses despite police harassment. As the boycott survived months of pressure, the national media began to pay attention. After nearly a year, the Supreme Court agreed that the bus segregation law was unconstitutional.

Victory in Montgomery depended on steadfast African American involvement. Leaders included Ralph Abernathy, other black preachers, and faculty members from Alabama State College. Participants cut across the class lines that had divided black southerners. Success also revealed the discrepancy between white attitudes in the Deep South and national opinion. For white southerners, segregation was a local concern best defined as a legal or constitutional matter. For other Americans, it was increasingly an issue of the South's deviation from national moral norms.

The Montgomery boycott won a local victory and made King famous, but it did not propel immediate change. King formed the **Southern Christian Leadership Conference (SCLC)** and sparred with the NAACP about community-based versus court-based civil rights tactics, but four African American college students in Greensboro, North Carolina, started the next phase of the struggle. On February 1, 1960, they put on jackets and ties and sat down at the segregated lunch counter in Woolworth's, waiting through the day without being served. Their patient courage brought more demonstrators; within two days, 85 students packed the store. Nonviolent sit-ins spread throughout the South.

The sit-ins had both immediate and long-range effects. In such comparatively sophisticated border cities as Nashville, Tennessee, sit-ins integrated lunch counters. Elsewhere, they precipitated white violence and mass arrests. Like soldiers on a battlefield, nervous participants in sit-ins and demonstrations drew strength from one another. "If you don't have courage," said one young woman in Albany, Georgia, "you can borrow it." King welcomed nonviolent confrontation. SCLC leader Ella Baker, one of the movement's most important figures, helped the students form a new organization, the **Student Nonviolent Coordinating Committee (SNCC).**

The year 1961 brought "freedom rides" to test the segregation of interstate bus terminals. The idea came from James Farmer of the **Congress of Racial Equality (CORE),** who copied a little-remembered 1947 Journey of Reconciliation that had tested the integration of interstate trains. Two buses carrying black and white passengers met only minor problems in Virginia, the Carolinas, and Georgia, but Alabamians burned one of the buses and attacked the riders in Birmingham, where they beat demonstrators senseless and clubbed a Justice Department observer. The governor and police refused to protect the freedom riders. The riders traveled into Mississippi under National Guard protection but were arrested at the Jackson bus terminal. Despite Attorney General Robert Kennedy's call for a cooling-off period, freedom rides continued through the summer. The rides proved that African Americans were in charge of their own civil rights revolution.

The March on Washington, 1963

John Kennedy was a tepid supporter of the civil rights movement and entered office with no civil rights agenda. Since entering politics in Massachusetts, he had been strong on rhetoric and symbolic gestures but weak on follow through. He appointed segregationist judges to mollify southern congressmen and would have preferred that African Americans stop disturbing the fragile Democratic Party coalition. As Eisenhower did at Little Rock, Kennedy intervened at the University of Mississippi in 1962 because of a state challenge to federal authority, not to further racial justice.

In the face of the slow federal response, the SCLC concentrated for 1963 on rigidly segregated Birmingham. April began with sit-ins and marches that aimed to integrate lunch counters, restrooms, and stores and secure open hiring for some clerical jobs. Birmingham's commissioner of public safety, Bull Connor, used fire hoses to blast demonstrators against buildings and roll children down the streets. When demonstrators fought back, his men chased them with dogs. Continued marches brought the arrest of hundreds of children. King's "Letter from Birmingham City Jail" stated the case for protest: "We have not made a single gain in civil rights without determined legal and nonviolent pressure.... Freedom is never voluntarily given by the oppressor; it must be demanded by the oppressed."

The Birmingham demonstrations were inconclusive. White leaders accepted minimal demands on May 10 but delayed enforcing them. Antiblack violence continued, including a bomb that killed four children in a Birmingham church. Meanwhile, the events in Alabama had forced President Kennedy to board the freedom train with an eloquent June 11 speech and to send a civil rights bill to Congress. "Are we to say... that this is the land of the free, except for Negroes, that we have no second-class citizens, except Negroes...? Now the time has come for the nation to fulfill its promise."

On August 28, 1963, a rally in Washington transformed African American civil rights into a national cause. A quarter of a million people, black and white, marched to the Lincoln Memorial. The day gave Martin Luther King, Jr., a national pulpit. His call for progress toward Christian and American goals had immense appeal. Television cut away from afternoon programs for his "I Have a Dream" speech.

The March on Washington demonstrated the mass appeal of civil rights and its identification with national values. It also papered over growing tensions within the civil rights movement. In the mid-1960s a growing militancy split the civil rights effort and moved younger African Americans, as well as Latinos and Native Americans, to emphasize their own distinct identities within American society.

Religious Belief and Civil Rights

Although *Brown* and other civil rights court decisions drew on the secular Constitution, much of the success of the southern civil rights movement came from grassroots Christianity. A century earlier, the abolitionist crusade had drawn much of its power from evangelistic revival movements. Now in the 1950s and 1960s, black southerners drew on prophetic Christianity to forge and act on a vision of a just society. Religious conviction and solidarity provide courage in the face of opposition.

At the same time, most white Christians understood that segregation contradicted the message of the Bible. The two largest religious groups in the South, the Presbyterian Church of the United States and the Southern Baptist Convention, took public stands in favor of desegregation in the mid-1950s. Revival leader Billy Graham shared a pulpit with Martin Luther King, Jr., in 1957 and insisted against local laws that his revival services be integrated. The opponents of civil rights thus lacked the moral support of the South's most fundamental cultural institutions.

In this context, it was no accident that black churches were organizing centers for civil rights work. King named his organization the Southern Christian Leadership Conference with clear intent and purpose. His famous speech in Washington drew on religious imagery and ended: "Free at last! Free at last! Thank God almighty, we are free at last!"

"Let Us Continue"

The two years that followed King's speech mingled despair and accomplishment. The optimism of the March on Washington shattered with the assassination of John Kennedy in November 1963. In 1964 and 1965, however, President Lyndon Johnson pushed through Kennedy's legislative agenda and much more in a burst of government activism unmatched since the 1930s. Federal legislation brought victory to the first phase of the civil rights revolution, launched the **War on Poverty,** expanded health insurance and aid to education, and opened an era of environmental protection.

After being attacked and dispersed by Alabama state police as they attempted a fifty-three mile march from Selma to Montgomery, Alabama, civil rights demonstrators regrouped. Under the glare of national press coverage, Alabama authorities let the march proceed. Here the leaders—including Martin Luther King, Jr., Coretta Scott King, Hosea Williams, Bayard Rustin, and Ralph Bunche—enter Montgomery.

Dallas, 1963

In November 1963, President Kennedy visited Texas to raise money and patch up feuds among Texas Democrats. On November 22, the president's motorcade took him near the Texas School Book Depository building in Dallas, where Lee Harvey Oswald had stationed himself at a window on the sixth floor. When Kennedy's open car swung into the sights of his rifle, Oswald fired three shots that wounded Texas Governor John Connally and killed the president. As doctors vainly treated the president in a hospital emergency room, Dallas police arrested Oswald. Vice President Lyndon Johnson took the oath of office as president on Air Force One while the blood-spattered Jacqueline Kennedy looked on. Two days later, as Oswald was being led from one jail cell to another, Jack Ruby, a Texas nightclub owner, killed him with a handgun in full view of TV cameras.

Lee Oswald was a 24-year-old misfit. He had served in the Marines and worked maintaining U-2 spy planes before defecting to the Soviet Union, which he found to be less than a workers' paradise. He returned to the United States after three years with a Russian wife and a fervent commitment to Fidel Castro's Cuban revolution. It was later learned that he had tried to shoot a right-wing general in 1963. He visited the Soviet and Cuban embassies in Mexico City in September trying to drum up a job, but neither country thought him worth hiring.

Some Americans believe there is more to the story. Why? One possibility is the expectation that important events should have great causes. Oswald seems too insignificant to be responsible on his own for the murder of a charismatic president. The sketchy job done by the Warren Commission, appointed to investigate the assassination, also bred doubts. The commission hurried to complete its work before the 1964 election. It also sought to assure Americans that Kennedy had not been killed as part of a Communist plot. The Warren Commission calmed fears in the short run but left loose ends that have fueled conspiracy theories.

All of the theories remain unproved. Until they are, logic holds that the simplest explanation is usually the best. Oswald was a social misfit with a grievance against U.S. society. Ruby was an impulsive man who told his brother on his deathbed that he thought he had done the country a favor. Like Presidents Garfield and McKinley before him, Kennedy died at the hands of one unbalanced man acting alone.

War on Poverty

Five days after the assassination, Lyndon Johnson claimed Kennedy's progressive aura for his new administration. "Let us continue," he told the nation, promising to implement Kennedy's policies. In fact, Johnson was vastly different from Kennedy. He was a professional politician who had reached the top through Texas politics and congressional infighting. As Senate majority leader during the 1950s, he had built a web of political obligations and friendships. Johnson's presence on the ticket in 1960 had helped to elect Kennedy by attracting southern voters, but the Kennedy entourage loathed him. He lacked Kennedy's polish and easy relations with the eastern elite. He knew little about foreign affairs but was a master of domestic politics. Johnson's upbringing in rural Texas shaped a man who was endlessly ambitious, ruthless, and often personally crude, but also deeply committed to social equity. He had entered public life with the New Deal in the 1930s and believed in its principles. Johnson, not Kennedy, was the true heir of Franklin Roosevelt. African American writer Ralph Ellison called him "the greatest American president for the poor and for the Negroes."

Johnson inherited a domestic agenda that the Kennedy administration had defined but not enacted. Kennedy's New Frontier had met the same fate as Truman's Fair Deal. Initiatives in education, medical insurance, tax reform, and urban affairs had stalled or been gutted by conservatives in Congress.

Kennedy's farthest-reaching initiative was rooted in the acknowledgment that poverty was a persistent U.S. problem. Michael Harrington's study *The Other America* became an unexpected bestseller. As poverty captured public attention, Kennedy's economic advisers devised a community action program that emphasized education and job training, a national service corps, and a youth conservation corps. They prepared a package of proposals to submit to Congress in 1964 that focused on social programs intended to alter behaviors that were thought to be passed from generation to generation, thus following the American tendency to attribute poverty to the personal failings of the poor.

Johnson made Kennedy's antipoverty package his own. Adopting Cold War rhetoric, he declared "unconditional war on poverty." The core of Johnson's program was the **Office of Economic Opportunity (OEO)**. Established under the direction of Kennedy's brother-in-law R. Sargent Shriver in 1964, the OEO operated the Job Corps for school dropouts, the Neighborhood Youth Corps for unemployed teenagers, the Head Start program to prepare poor children for school, and VISTA (Volunteers in Service to America), a domestic Peace Corps. OEO's biggest effort went to Community Action Agencies. By 1968, more than 500 such agencies provided health and educational services. Despite flaws, the War on Poverty improved life for millions of Americans.

Civil Rights, 1964–1965

Johnson's passionate commitment to economic betterment accompanied a commitment to civil rights. In Johnson's view,

"President Lyndon Johnson was a crafty and sometimes ruthless politician, but he also had a deep personal commitment to solving problems of poverty and inequality in American society."

segregation not only deprived African Americans of access to opportunity but also distracted white southerners from their own poverty and underdevelopment. As he complained in a speech in New Orleans, southern leaders ignored the region's economic needs in favor of racial rabble-rousing.

One solution was the **Civil Rights Act of 1964,** which Kennedy had introduced but which Johnson got enacted. The law prohibited segregation in public accommodations, such as hotels, restaurants, gas stations, theaters, and parks, and outlawed employment discrimination on federally assisted projects. It also created the Equal Employment Opportunity Commission (EEOC) and included gender in the list of categories protected against discrimination, a provision whose consequences were scarcely suspected in 1964.

Even as Congress was debating the 1964 law, **Freedom Summer** moved political power to the top of the civil rights agenda. Organized by SNCC, the Mississippi Summer Freedom Project was a voter-registration drive that sent white and black volunteers to the small towns and back roads of Mississippi. The target was a political system that used rigged literacy tests and intimidation to keep black southerners from voting. In Mississippi in 1964, only 7 percent of eligible black citizens were registered voters. Local black activists had laid the groundwork for a registration effort with years of courageous effort through the NAACP and voter leagues. Now an increasingly militant SNCC took the lead. The explicit goal was to increase the number of African American voters. The tacit intention was to attract national attention by putting middle-class white college students in the line of fire. Freedom Summer gained 1,600 new voters and taught 2,000 children in SNCC-run Freedom Schools at the cost of beatings, bombings, church arson, and the murder of three project workers.

Another outgrowth of the SNCC effort was the Mississippi Freedom Democratic Party (MFDP), a biracial coalition that bypassed Mississippi's all-white Democratic Party, followed state party rules, and sent its own delegates to the 1964 Democratic convention. To preserve party harmony, President Johnson refused to expel the "regular" Mississippi Democrats and offered instead to seat two MFDP delegates and enforce party rules for 1968. The MFDP walked out, seething with anger. Fannie Lou Hamer, a MFDP delegate who had already suffered in the struggle for voting rights, remembered, "We learned the hard way that even though we had all the law and all the righteousness on our side—that white man is not going to give up his power to us. We have to build our own power."

Freedom Summer and political realities both focused national attention on voter registration. Lyndon Johnson and Martin Luther King, Jr., agreed on the need for federal voting legislation when King visited the president in December 1964 after winning the Nobel Peace Prize. For King, power at the ballot box would help black southerners to take control of their own communities. For Johnson, voting reform would fulfill the promise of American democracy. It would also benefit the Democratic Party by replacing with black voters the white southerners who were drifting toward the anti-integration Republicans.

The target for King and the SCLC was Dallas County, Alabama, where only 2 percent of eligible black residents were registered, compared with 70 percent of white residents. Peaceful demonstrations started in January 1965. By early February, jails in the county seat of Selma held 2,600 black people whose offense was marching to the courthouse to demand the vote. The campaign climaxed with a march from Selma to the state capital of Montgomery. SNCC leader John Lewis remembered, "I don't know what we expected. I think maybe we thought we'd be arrested and jailed, or maybe they wouldn't do anything to us. I had a little knapsack on my shoulder with an apple, a toothbrush, toothpaste, and two books in it: a history of America and a book by [Christian theologian] Thomas Merton."

On Sunday, March 7,500 marchers crossed the bridge over the Alabama River, to meet a sea of state troopers. The troopers gave them two minutes to disperse and then attacked on foot and horseback "as if they were mowing a big field." The attack drove the demonstrators back in bloody confusion while television cameras rolled.

As violence continued, Johnson addressed a joint session of Congress to demand a voting-rights law: "Our mission is at once the oldest and the most basic of this country: to right wrong, to do justice, to serve man." He ended with the refrain of the civil rights movement: "We shall overcome." By opening the political process to previously excluded citizens, the Voting Rights Act was as revolutionary and far-reaching as the Nineteenth Amendment, which guaranteed women the right to vote, and the Labor Relations Act of 1935, which recognized labor unions as the equals of corporations.

Johnson signed the **Voting Rights Act** on August 6, 1965. The law outlawed literacy tests and provided for federal voting registrars in states where registration or turnout in 1964 was less than 50 percent of the eligible population. It applied initially in seven southern states. Black registration in these states jumped from 27 percent to 55 percent within the first year. In 1975, Congress extended coverage to Hispanic voters in the Southwest. The Act required new moderation from white leaders, who had to satisfy black voters, and it opened the way for black and Latino candidates to win positions at every level of state and local government. In the long run, the Voting Rights Act climaxed the battle for civil rights and shifted attention to the continuing problems of economic opportunity and inequality.

War, Peace, and the Landslide of 1964

Lyndon Johnson was the peace candidate in 1964. Johnson had maintained Kennedy's commitment to South Vietnam. On the advice of such Kennedy holdovers as Defense Secretary Robert McNamara, he stepped up commando raids and naval shelling of North Vietnam, on the assumption that North Vietnam controlled the Viet Cong. On August 2, North Vietnamese torpedo boats attacked the U.S. destroyer *Maddox* in the Gulf of Tonkin while it was eavesdropping on North Vietnamese military signals. Two days later, the *Maddox* and the *C. Turner Joy* reported another torpedo at-

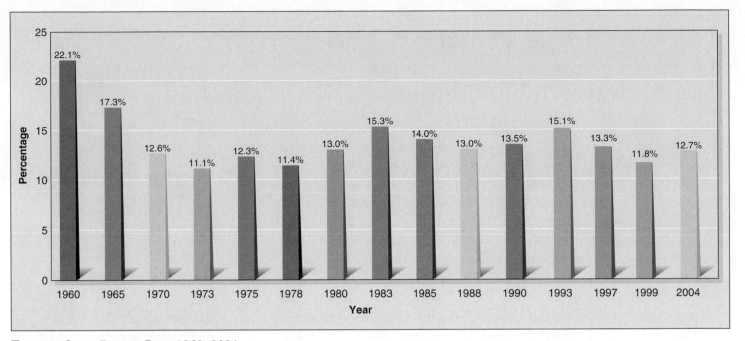

FIGURE 28–4   Poverty Rate, 1960–2004
With the improvement of federal health insurance, assistance for the elderly, and antipoverty programs, the proportion of Americans living in poverty dropped dramatically in the later 1960s. It began to inch upward again in the 1980s, when the priorities of the federal government shifted.

Data Source: *Statistical Abstract of the United States.*

tack (probably false sonar readings). Johnson ordered a bombing raid in reprisal and asked Congress to authorize "all necessary measures" to protect U.S. forces and stop further aggression. Congress passed the **Gulf of Tonkin Resolution** with only two nay votes, effectively authorizing the president to wage undeclared war.

Johnson's militancy paled beside that of his Republican opponent. Senator Barry Goldwater of Arizona represented the new right wing of the Republican Party, which was drawing strength from the South and West. Goldwater wanted minimal government interference in free enterprise and aggressive confrontation with Communism. Campaign literature accurately described him as "a choice, not an echo." He declared that "extremism in the defense of liberty is no vice," raising visions of vigilantes and mobs. Goldwater's campaign made Johnson look moderate. Johnson pledged not "to send American boys nine or ten thousand miles from home to do what Asian boys ought to be doing for themselves" while Goldwater proposed an all-out war.

The election was a landslide. Johnson's 61 percent of the popular vote was the greatest margin ever recorded in a presidential election. Democrats racked up two-to-one majorities in Congress. For the first time in decades, liberal Democrats could enact their domestic program without begging votes from conservative southerners or Republicans, and Johnson could achieve his goal of a **Great Society** based on freedom and opportunity for all.

The result was a series of measures that Johnson pushed through Congress before the Vietnam War eroded his polit-

ical standing and distracted national attention. The National Endowment for the Arts and the National Endowment for the Humanities seemed uncontroversial at the time but would later become the focus of liberal and conservative struggles over the character of American life. The Wilderness Act (1964), which preserved 9.1 million acres from development, would prove another political battlefield in the face of economic pressures in the next century.

The goal of increasing opportunity for all Americans stirred the president most deeply. As he told a July 1965 news conference, "When I was young, poverty was so common that we didn't know it had a name. An education was something that you had to fight for.... It is now my opportunity to help every child get an education, to help every Negro and every American citizen have an equal opportunity, to have every family get a decent home, and to help bring healing to the sick and dignity to the old." The Elementary and Secondary Education Act was the first general federal aid program for public schools, allocating $1.3 billion for textbooks and special education. The Higher Education Act funded low-interest student loans and university research facilities. The Medical Care Act created **Medicare,** federally funded health insurance for the elderly, and **Medicaid,** which helped states offer medical care to the poor. The Appalachian Regional Development Act funded economic development in the depressed mountain counties of 12 states from Georgia to New York and proved a long-run success.

It is sometimes said that the United States declared war on poverty and lost. In fact, the nation came closer to winning

FROM THEN TO NOW

Medical Research on Polio and AIDS

When Dr. Jonas Salk announced an effective vaccine for polio on April 12, 1955, the United States gained a new hero. In the confident mid-1950s, the polio vaccine seemed another proof of America's ability to improve the world.

Fear of polio haunted American families after World War II. Most Americans knew at least one child who hobbled through life on crutches and metal leg braces. Hospitals filled with new cases every summer—58,000 in 1952 alone. Many children clung to life inside iron lungs, metal cylinders that pumped air in and out of a hole in the throat.

Salk's announcement was welcome news. A generation later, President Ronald Reagan would list the polio vaccine with the steam engine and the silicon chip as one of the great modern discoveries.

Scientists first identified a new disease pattern, acquired immune deficiency syndrome (AIDS), in 1981. The name described the symptoms resulting from the human immunodeficiency virus (HIV), which destroys the body's ability to resist disease. Worldwide the HIV death toll was 2.9 million by 2006 and nearly 40 million people were living with HIV.

Polio has been eradicated in Europe and the Americas, but it continued to ravage Africa into the twenty-first century.

HIV/AIDS triggers many of the same intense emotions as polio. It strikes people in their prime and gradually wastes their strength. At the same time, HIV/AIDS remains as daunting scientifically as it has been politically volatile. In 2002, the federal budget allocated $2.8 billion for HIV/AIDS research and another $10 billion for prevention and treatment programs in the United States and other nations, amounts vastly greater than the funds spent fighting polio. If Salk's success confirmed American confidence in the 1950s, the global struggle against HIV and AIDS mirrors the complexity of the twenty-first century.

■ How has the scale and funding for medical and scientific research changed since the 1950s?

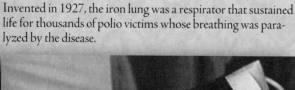

Invented in 1927, the iron lung was a respirator that sustained life for thousands of polio victims whose breathing was paralyzed by the disease.

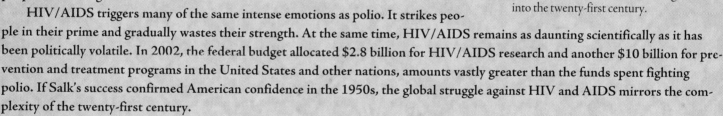
myhistorylab

From Then to Now Online

28-1 Marilynne Rogers, *Coping with Polio* (1996). The author describes her experiencing battling polio in 1949, when she was nine years old.

28-2 Centers for Disease Control and Prevention, *Current Trends Update on Acquired Immune Deficiency Syndrome (AIDS)—United States* (1982). The federal report that first used the term AIDS.

28-3 New York Chapter of ACT UP, excerpts from New Members Packet. The AIDS Coalition to Unleash Power (ACT-UP) used radical activist tactics to push for greater efforts at AIDS research and treatment.

28-4 World Health Organization, *AIDS Epidemic Update* (2006). Data on the spread of AIDS in different parts of the world.

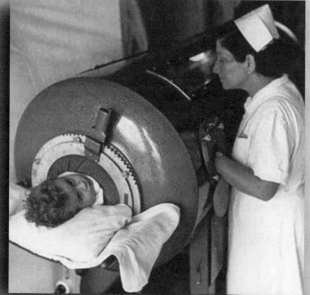

the war on poverty than it did the war in Vietnam. New or expanded social insurance and income-support programs, such as Medicare, Medicaid, Social Security, and food stamps, cut the proportion of poor people from 22 percent of the American population in 1960 to 13 percent in 1970 (see Figure 28.4). Infant mortality dropped by a third because of improved nutrition and better access to healthcare for mothers and children. Taken together, the political results of the 1964 landslide moved the United States much closer to the vision of an end to poverty and racial injustice.

Conclusion

The era commonly remembered as the 1950s stretched from 1953 to 1964. Consistent goals guided U.S. foreign policy through the entire period, including vigilant anti-Communism and the confidence to intervene in trouble spots around the globe. At home, the Supreme Court's *Brown* decision introduced a decade-long civil rights revolution that reached its emotional peak with the March on Washington and its political climax with the Civil Rights Act (1964) and Voting Rights Act (1965). However, many patterns of personal behavior and social relations remained unchanged. Women faced similar expectations from the early fifties to the early sixties. Churches showed more continuity than change.

In retrospect, it is remarkable how widely and deeply the Cold War shaped U.S. society. Fundamental social institutions, such as marriage and religion, got extra credit for their contributions to anti-Communism. The nation's long tradition of home-grown radicalism was virtually silent in the face of the Cold War consensus. Even economically meritorious programs like more money for science and better roads went down more easily if linked to national defense.

But the consistency and stability of the 1950s were fragile. The larger world was too complex to fit forever within the narrow framework of bipolar conflict. American society was too disparate and dynamic for Cold War conformity. In the later 1960s and the 1970s, contradictions burst through the surface of the American consensus. Foreign competitors, resource scarcities, and environmental damage diminished economic abundance and sapped national confidence. Nations from Vietnam to Iran refused to cooperate with U.S. plans for the world. Corrupt politicians threatened the constitutional order.

Under these pressures, the national consensus splintered after 1964. Some members of minority groups turned their backs on integration. Some younger Americans dropped out of mainstream society to join the aptly named counterculture. Others sought the security of religious commitment and community. Perhaps most divisively, "hawks" battled "doves" over Vietnam. If civil rights and Cold War had been the defining issues for the fifties, Vietnam would define the sixties, which stretched from 1965 to 1974.

Review Questions

1. What were the sources of prosperity in the 1950s and 1960s? How did prosperity shape cities, family life, and religion? What opportunities did it create for women and for young people? How did it affect the American role in the world? Why did an affluent nation still need a war on poverty in the 1960s?

2. What assumptions about the Soviet Union shaped U.S. foreign policy? What assumptions about the United States shaped Soviet policy? What did American leaders think was at stake in Vietnam, Berlin, and Cuba?

3. Who initiated and led the African American struggle for civil rights? What role did the federal government play? What were the goals of the civil rights movement? Where did it succeed, and in what ways did it fall short?

4. How did the growth of nuclear arsenals affect international relations? How did the nuclear shadow affect U.S. politics and society?

5. In what new directions did Lyndon Johnson take the United States? Were there differences between the goals of the New Frontier and the Great Society?

6. Why was school integration the focus of such strong conflict? How did the work of Mexican Americans and African Americans support the same goal of equal access to education?

7. How did religious belief shape American society in the Eisenhower and Kennedy years?

Key Terms

Alliance for Progress (p. 805)

Bay of Pigs (p. 803)

Berlin Wall (p. 803)

Brown v. Board of Education of Topeka (p. 806)

Civil Rights Act of 1964 (p. 812)

Congress of Racial Equality (CORE) (p. 809)

Federal Highway Act of 1956 (p. 791)

Freedom Summer (p. 812)

Great Society (p. 813)

Gulf of Tonkin Resolution (p. 813)

Limited Test Ban Treaty (p. 805)

Massive retaliation (p. 798)

Recommended Reading

Beschloss, Michael. *May-Day: Eisenhower, Khrushchev, and the U-2 Affair* (1986). The drama and confusion of the U-2 affair are used to interpret the meaning of the Cold War for the United States and the Soviet Union.

Bugliosi, Vincent. *Reclaiming History: The Assassination of President John F. Kennedy* (2007). An exhaustive refutation of conspiracy theories.

Chappell, David L. *A Stone of Hope: Black Prophetic Religion and the Death of Jim Crow* (2004). Examines the way that religion shaped the actions of white and black southerners.

Graebner, William. *Coming of Age in Buffalo* (1990). In words and pictures, places the complexity of teenage life in the 1950s within the American patterns of class and race.

Halberstam, David. *The Fifties* (1993). Provides a readable and detailed account of political and social change.

Harrington, Michael. *The Other America* (1962). Published early in the Kennedy years, an impassioned study that reminded Americans of continuing economic inequality and helped launch the War on Poverty.

Posner, Gerald. *Case Closed* (1993). A detailed analysis of John Kennedy's death that refutes the most popular conspiracy theories.

Rorabaugh, William J. *Kennedy and the Promise of the Sixties* (2002). A sympathetic account of Kennedy and changes in American society.

White, Theodore. *The Making of the President, 1960* (1961). A vivid account of the issues and personalities of the 1960 campaign.

Williams, Juan. *Eyes on the Prize: America's Civil Rights Years, 1954–1965* (1988). A graphic and fast-moving account of the civil rights movement, written in conjunction with a PBS television series.

Wolfe, Tom. *The Right Stuff* (1979). An irreverent account of the early years of the U.S. space program that captures the atmosphere of the 1950s and early 1960s.

Where to Learn More

- **National Air and Space Museum, Washington, DC.** Part of the Smithsonian Institution's complex of museums in Washington, the Air and Space Museum is the richest source for artifacts and discussion of the American space program. www.nasm.edu.

- **Kansas Cosmosphere, Hutchinson, Kansas.** A rich collection of artifacts and equipment from the U.S. space program. www.cosmo.org.

- **Sixth Floor Museum, Dallas, Texas.** Occupying the sixth floor of the former Texas School Book Depository building, exhibits examine the life, death, and legacy of John F. Kennedy. www.jfk.org.

- **Birmingham Civil Rights Institute Museum, Birmingham, Alabama.** This museum and archive deal with the background of southern racial segregation, civil rights activism, and the 1963 demonstrations in Birmingham. www.bcri.bham.al.us

- **Martin Luther King, Jr., National Historical Site, Atlanta, Georgia.** The birthplace and grave of Reverend King are the nucleus of a park set in the historic black neighborhood of Auburn. www.nps.gov/malu

- **National Civil Rights Museum, Memphis, Tennessee.** Located in the Lorraine Motel, where Martin Luther King, Jr., was killed, the museum traces the participants, background, and effects of key events in the civil rights movement. www.civilrightsmuseum.org

- **National Afro-American Museum and Cultural Center, Wilberforce, Ohio.** The exhibit "From Victory to Freedom: Afro-American Life in the Fifties" looks at home, family, music, and religion. www.ohiohistory.org/places/afroam

- **John F. Kennedy Library and Museum, Boston, Massachusetts.** Exhibits offer a sympathetic view of Kennedy's life and achievements. www.cs.umb.edu/jfklibrary

Study Resources

For study resources for this chapter, go to www.myhistorylab.com and choose *The American Journey*. You will find a wealth of study and review material for this chapter, including pre- and posttests, customized study plan, key term review flash cards, interactive map and document activities, and documents for analysis.

1968 was a year of escalating violence and disorder, from the Tet. Offensive in Vietnam to political assassinations and riots in American cities. Many of the tensions converged and exploded
in August during the Democratic Party convention in Chicago, where 20,000 law enforcement
officials and National Guard were mobilized to face thousands of antiwar demonstrators. Public order collapsed on the night of August 28, when police attacked demonstrators trying to
march to the convention center.

Shaken to the Roots 29
1965–1980

Contact light! O.K., engine stop....Houston, Tranquility Base here. The Eagle has landed!...We opened the hatch and Neil, with me as navigator, began backing out of the tiny opening [in the Lunar Module *Eagle*]. It seemed like a small eternity before I heard Neil say, "That's one small step for man...one giant leap for mankind." In less than fifteen minutes I was backing awkwardly out of the hatch onto the surface to join Neil, who, in the tradition of all tourists, had his camera ready to photograph my arrival.

I took off jogging to test my maneuverability. The exercise gave me an odd sensation and looked even more odd when I later saw the films of it. With bulky suits on, we seemed to be moving in slow motion....At one point, I remarked that the surface was "Beautiful, beautiful. Magnificent desolation." I was struck by the contrast between the starkness of the shadows and the desert-like barrenness of the rest of the surface. It ranged from dusty gray to light tan and was unchanging except for one startling sight: our LM sitting there with its black, silver and bright yellow-orange thermal coating shining brightly in the otherwise colorless landscape.

During a pause in experiments, Neil suggested we proceed with the flag....To our dismay the staff of the pole wouldn't go far enough into the lunar surface....I dreaded the possibility of the American flag collapsing into the lunar dust in front of the television camera.

Edgar Cortright, ed., *Apollo Expeditions to the Moon* (Washington: NASA SP 350, 1975).

myhistorylab

Personal Journeys Online

- *Easy Rider*, 1969. Fantasies of escape from 1960s America in a popular movie.

- Craig McNamara, interview in Joan Morrison and Robert K. Morrison, *From Camelot to Kent State: The Sixties Experience in the Words of Those Who Lived It*, 1987. Antiwar protest and the generation gap in 1968.

- Reies Lopez Tijerina, "Letter from the Santa Fe Jail," reprinted in *A Documentary History of the Mexican Americans*, ed. by Wayne Moquin, 1971. A Hispanic civil rights manifesto from 1969.

- "Bill Gates and Paul Allen Talk," *Fortune*, 132, October 2, 1995, pp 69–72. Copyright(c) 1995 *Fortune*. Microsoft founders recall the early ways.

Buzz Aldrin and Neil Armstrong, on July 20, 1969, completed the longest journey that anyone had yet taken. Landing the *Apollo 11* lunar module on the surface of the moon climaxed a five-day trip across the quarter-million miles separating the earth from the moon. Six and a half hours after the landing, Armstrong and Aldrin were the first humans to walk on the moon's surface.

The *Apollo 11* expedition combined science and Cold War politics. The American flag waving on the lunar surface was a symbol of victory in one phase of the space race between the United States and the Soviet Union. NASA had been working since 1961 to meet John F. Kennedy's goal of a manned trip to the moon before the end of the decade. After the *Apollo 11* expedition, U.S. astronauts made five more trips to the moon between 1969 and 1972, which helped to restore the nation's standing as the world's scientific and technological leader.

Even with the excitement of *Apollo*'s success, however, the United States was increasingly shaken and divided in the later 1960s and 1970s. The failure to win an easy victory in Vietnam eroded the nation's confidence and fueled bitter divisions about the nation's goals. Most Americans had agreed about the goals of the Cold War, the benefits of economic growth, and the value of equal opportunity. Stalemate in Southeast Asia, political changes in third-world countries, and an oil supply crisis in the 1970s challenged U.S. influence in the world. Frustrated by the slow progress toward racial equality, many minority Americans advocated separation rather than integration, helping to plunge the nation's cities into crisis, while other Americans began to draw back from some of the objectives of racial integration.

Political scandals, summarized in three syllables, "Watergate," undercut faith in government. Fifteen years of turmoil forced a grudging recognition of the limits to American military power, economic capacity, governmental prerogatives, and even the ideal of a single American dream.

The End of Consensus

Pleiku is a town in Vietnam 240 miles north of Saigon (now Ho Chi Minh City). In 1965, Pleiku was the site of a South Vietnamese army headquarters and U.S. military base. At 2:00 A.M. on February 7, Viet Cong attacked the U.S. base, killing eight Americans and wounding a hundred. The national security adviser, McGeorge Bundy (in Saigon on a fact-finding visit), Ambassador Maxwell Taylor, and General William Westmoreland, the commander of U.S. forces South Vietnam, all recommended a retaliatory air strike against North Vietnam. President Johnson concurred, and navy bombers roared off aircraft carriers in Operation FLAMING DART. A month later, Johnson ordered a full-scale air offensive codenamed ROLLING THUNDER.

The attack at Pleiku triggered plans that were waiting to be put into effect since the Gulf of Tonkin resolution the previous summer. The official reason for the bombing was to pressure North Vietnam to negotiate an end to the war. As the South Vietnamese government lost control of the countryside, air strikes on North Vietnam looked like an easy way to redress the balance. In the back of President Johnson's mind were the need to prove his toughness and the mistaken assumption that China was aggressively backing North Vietnam.

The air strikes pushed the United States over the line from propping up the South Vietnamese government to leading the war effort. A president who desperately wanted a way out of Southeast Asia kept adding U.S. forces. Eventually, the war in Vietnam would distract the United States from the goals of the Great Society and drive Johnson from office. It hovered like a shadow

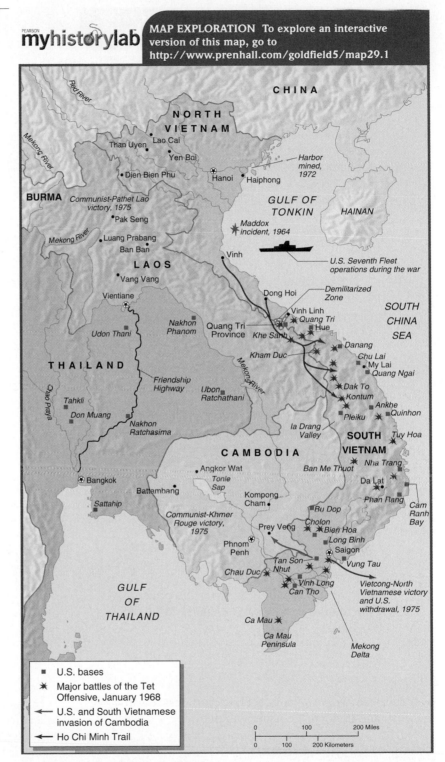

MAP EXPLORATION To explore an interactive version of this map, go to http://www.prenhall.com/goldfield5/map29.1

MAP 29–1   The War in Vietnam
The United States attacked North Vietnam with air strikes but confined large-scale ground operations to South Vietnam and Cambodia. In South Vietnam, U.S. forces faced both North Vietnamese army units and Viet Cong rebels, all of whom received supplies by way of the so-called Ho Chi Minh Trail, named for the leader of North Vietnam. The coordinated attacks on cities and towns throughout South Vietnam during the Tet Offensive in 1968 surprised the United States.

CHRONOLOGY

1962	Rachel Carson publishes *Silent Spring*.
	Port Huron Statement launches Students for a Democratic Society.
	Supreme Court limits vocal prayer in schools in *Engel* v. *Vitale*
1965	Congress approves Wilderness Act.
	Malcolm X is assassinated.
	Residents of Watts neighborhood in Los Angeles riot.
	Immigration Reform Act allows increased immigration from outside Europe
1967	African Americans riot in Detroit and Newark.
1968	Viet Cong launches Tet Offensive.
	James Earl Ray kills Martin Luther King, Jr.
	Lyndon Johnson declines to run for reelection.
	SDS disrupts Columbia University.
	Sirhan Sirhan kills Robert Kennedy.
	Peace talks start between the United States and North Vietnam.
	Police riot against antiwar protesters during the Democratic National Convention in Chicago.
	Richard Nixon is elected president.
1969	Neil Armstrong and Buzz Aldrin walk on the moon.
1970	United States invades Cambodia.
	National Guard units kill students at Kent State and Jackson State universities.
	Earth Day is celebrated.
	Environmental Protection Agency is created.
1971	*New York Times* publishes the secret Pentagon Papers.
	President Nixon freezes wages and prices.
	Plumbers unit is established in the White House.
1972	Nixon visits China.

	United States and Soviet Union adopt SALT I.
	Operatives for Nixon's reelection campaign break into Democratic headquarters in the Watergate complex in Washington, DC.
1973	Paris accords end direct U.S. involvement in South Vietnamese war.
	United States moves to all-volunteer armed forces.
	Watergate burglars are convicted.
	Senate Watergate hearings reveal the existence of taped White House conversations.
	Spiro Agnew resigns as vice president, is replaced by Gerald Ford.
	Arab states impose an oil embargo after the third Arab-Israeli War.
1974	Nixon resigns as president, is succeeded by Gerald Ford.
1975	Communists triumph in South Vietnam.
	United States, USSR, and European nations sign the Helsinki Accords.
1976	Jimmy Carter defeats Gerald Ford for the presidency.
1978	Carter brings the leaders of Egypt and Israel to Camp David for peace talks.
	U.S. agrees to transfer control of the Panama Canal to Panama.
1979	SALT II agreement is signed but not ratified.
	OPEC raises oil prices.
	Three Mile Island nuclear plant comes close to disaster.
	Iranian militants take U.S. embassy hostages.
1980	Iranian hostage rescue fails.
	Soviet troops enter Afghanistan.
	Ronald Reagan defeats Jimmy Carter for the presidency.

over the next two presidents, set back progress toward global stability, and divided the American people.

Deeper into Vietnam

Lyndon Johnson faced limited options in Vietnam (see Map 29–1). The pervasive American determination to contain Communism and Kennedy's previous commitments there hemmed Johnson in. Advisers persuaded him that controlled military escalation—a middle course between withdrawal and all-out war—could secure Vietnam. They failed to understand the extent of popular opposition to the official gov-

ernment in Saigon and the willingness of North Vietnam to sacrifice to achieve national unity.

ROLLING THUNDER put the United States on the up escalator to war. Because an air campaign required ground troops to protect bases in South Vietnam, U.S. Marines landed on March 8. Over the next four months, General Westmoreland wore away Johnson's desire to contain U.S. involvement. More bombs, a pause, an offer of massive U.S. aid—nothing brought North Vietnam to the negotiating table. Meanwhile, defeat loomed. Johnson dribbled in new forces and expanded their mission from base security to com-

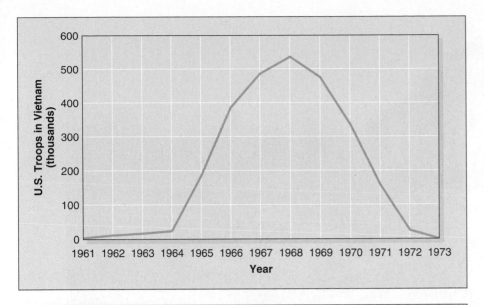

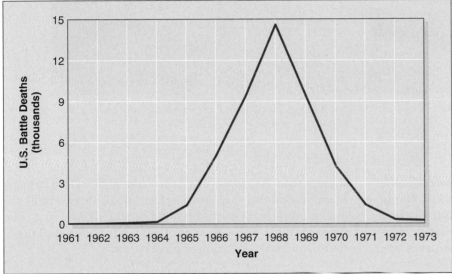

FIGURE 29–1   The United States in Vietnam
American involvement in Vietnam grew slowly during the Kennedy administration from 1961 to 1963, expanded rapidly under Lyndon Johnson from 1964 to 1968, and fell just as rapidly under Richard Nixon from 1969 to 1973. The Nixon Doctrine tried to substitute American weapons and equipment for American military personnel but failed to prevent a North Vietnamese victory in 1975 after United States withdrawal.

Statistical Abstract of the United States

The U.S. strategy on the ground was **search and destroy.** As conceived by Westmoreland, sophisticated surveillance and heavily armed patrols were used to locate enemy detachments, which could then be destroyed by air strikes, artillery, and reinforcements carried in by helicopter. The approach made sense when the opposition consisted of North Vietnamese troops and large Viet Cong units. It worked well in the sparsely populated Ia Drang Valley, where the First Air Cavalry chewed up North Vietnamese regulars in November 1965.

However, most opponents were not North Vietnamese divisions but South Vietnamese guerrillas. The Viet Cong avoided set-piece battles. Instead, they forced the United States to make repeated sweeps through farms and villages. The enemy was difficult for Americans to recognize among farmers and workers, making South Vietnamese society itself the target. The U.S. penchant for massive firepower killed thousands of Vietnamese and made millions refugees. Because the South Vietnamese government was unable to secure areas after American sweeps, the Viet Cong often reappeared after the Americans had crashed through a district.

The U.S. air war also had limited results. Pilots dropped a vast tonnage of bombs on the Ho Chi Minh Trail, a network of supply routes from North Vietnam to South Vietnam through the mountains of neighboring Laos. Despite the bombing, thousands of workers converted rough paths into roads that were repaired as soon as they were damaged. The air assault on North Vietnam itself remained "diplomatic," intended to force North Vietnam to stop intervening in the South Vietnamese civil war. Since North Vietnam's leadership considered North and South to be one country, the American goal was unacceptable. Attacking North Vietnam's poorly developed economy, the United States soon ran out of targets. The CIA estimated that it cost nearly $10 to inflict every $1 of damage.

Voices of Dissent

At home, protest against the war quickly followed the commitment of U.S. combat forces. In the 1950s, dissenters on the left had been too intimidated by McCarthyism to protest overcommitment to the Cold War. Now a coalition of experienced

bat. On July 28, he finally gave Westmoreland doubled draft calls and an increase in U.S. combat troops from 75,000 to 275,000 by 1966 (see Figure 29–1).

Johnson's decision turned a South Vietnamese war into a U.S. war. Secretary of Defense McNamara was clear about the change: "We have relied on South Vietnam to carry the brunt. Now we would be responsible for a satisfactory military outcome." At the end of 1967, U.S. forces in South Vietnam totaled 485,000; they reached their maximum of 543,000 in August 1969.

The city of Hue suffered severe damage in the Tet Offensive and its aftermath. Here refugees return to the rubble of bombed-out houses.

Getty Images Inc.—Hulton Archive Photos

antiwar workers and new college activists openly challenged the Cold Warriors. The first national antiwar march took place in Washington on April 17, 1965. Twenty-five thousand people picketed the White House, assembled at the Washington Monument for speeches by Senator Ernest Gruening of Alaska (one of the two dissenting votes on the Gulf of Tonkin Resolution) and African American leaders, and walked up the Mall to the Capitol.

One group of opponents consisted of "realists" who argued that the war was a mistake. Foreign policy expert Hans Morgenthau, for example, fully supported anti-Soviet containment in Europe but maintained that the United States had no vital interests in South Vietnam. Policymakers in Washington, he said, were misreading the situation, wasting U.S. lives and resources, and weakening the American presence in regions such as Europe that were truly important to national security. Respected figures like the Cold War strategist George Kennan joined in the dissent. Senator J. William Fulbright held well-publicized hearings in 1966 and 1967, at which respectable critics of the war could state their case to a national audience, and published *The Arrogance of Power* (1967), a book arguing that even the United States needed to recognize limits on its vast political and military power.

Martin Luther King, Jr. offered one of the strongest condemnations of the war in a speech at New York's Riverside Church on April 4, 1967. He decried the diversion of re-

sources from domestic programs to the military, the impacts of the war on the people of Vietnam, and what he saw as the poisonous effects of warfare on the soul of America. The speech was a deeply Christian argument for policies of negotiation and reconciliation in place of war.

From protest to confrontation.   In 1966 and 1967, antiwar activity changed from respectful protest to direct confrontations with what protesters called the war machine. Protesters lay down in front of trains carrying munitions. Representatives of Women Strike for Peace journeyed to North Vietnam to explore possible solutions. Religious groups such as the American Friends Service Committee tried to dispense medical and humanitarian aid even-handedly in both North Vietnam and South Vietnam.

The tone of the debate became nastier. Johnson and his associates ridiculed the dissenters (for example, Fulbright became "Halfbright" among the administration's inner circle). Protesters chanted "Hey, hey, LBJ! How many kids did you kill today?" Much of the anger was directed at the military draft administered by the **Selective Service System.** In theory, the Selective Service picked the young men who could best serve the nation as soldiers and deferred induction of those with vital skills. As the war expanded, the administration tried to hold the allegiance of the middle class by finding ways to exempt their sons from service in Vietnam.

In October 1967, 100,000 people marched on the Pentagon to protest the war in Vietnam.

rupted its operations by invading draft-board offices and trying to burn files or douse them with animal blood. Resistance mounted throughout the decade. By the end of 1969, over half the men drafted in California were refusing to show up, and prosecutions for draft evasion would peak in 1972 at nearly 5,000.

The popular media portrayed the conflicting visions of the Vietnam War. Barry McGuire's "Eve of Destruction" climbed the charts. Folksinger Phil Ochs sang "I Ain't Marching Anymore." "And it's one, two, three, what are we fighting for?" sang Country Joe and the Fish. Supporters countered with an aging John Wayne in the movie *The Green Berets*. Country singer Merle Haggard spoke for many small-town Americans who supported the war in "Okie from Muskogee" (where they didn't burn draft cards).

Full-time college enrollment was good for a deferment; so was the right medical diagnosis from the right doctor. As a result, draftees and enlistees tended to be small-town and working-class youth. They were also young. The average GI in World War II had been in his mid-twenties; the typical soldier in Vietnam was 19 or 20. Women who served as military nurses tended to come from the same small-town and working-class backgrounds where patriotism was unquestioned. The resentment created by the draft was an important wedge that began to erode the long-standing alliance between working-class Americans and the Democratic Party.

Military service also deepened the gap between blacks and whites. The black community supplied more than its share of combat soldiers. In 1965, when African Americans made up 11 percent of the nation's population, 24 percent of the soldiers who died in Vietnam were black. This disparity forced the Defense Department to revise its combat assignments so that the racial impact was more equal in later years. Martin Luther King, Jr., joined the protest in 1967. King called the war a moral disaster whose costs weighed most heavily on the poor and a new form of colonialism that was destroying Vietnamese society.

Draft resistance provided a direct avenue for protest against the war. Some young men burned the small paper cards that indicated their selective service classification, causing Congress to enact steep penalties for the act. Several thousand moved to Canada, to spend a decade or more in exile. Thousands of others described their religious and ethical opposition to war in applications for conscientious-objector classification. Much smaller numbers went to jail for refusing to cooperate in any way with the Selective Service System. And a handful of activists, including the Catholic priests Daniel Berrigan and Philip Berrigan, directly dis-

New Left and Community Activism

The antiwar movement was part of a growing grassroots activism that took much of its tone from the university-based **Students for a Democratic Society (SDS).** The group was important for its ideas, not its size. Its Port Huron Statement, adopted in 1962, called for grassroots action and participatory democracy. Building on the ideas of such 1950s dissenters as C. Wright Mills, SDS tried to harness youthful disillusionment about consumerism, racism, and imperialism. It wanted to counter the trends that seemed to be turning Americans into tiny cogs in the machinery of big government, corporations, and universities. SDS thought of itself as a "New Left" that was free from the doctrinal squabbles that hampered the old left of the 1930s and 1940s.

Many of the original SDS leaders were also participants in the civil rights movement. The same was true of Mario Savio, founder of the **Free Speech Movement (FSM)** at the University of California at Berkeley in 1964. Savio hoped to build a multi-issue "community of protest" around the idea of "a free university in a free society." FSM protests climaxed with a December sit-in that led to 773 arrests and stirred protest on other campuses.

What SDS wanted to do with its grassroots organizing resembled the federal community-action programs associated with the war on poverty. The **Model Cities Program** (1966) invited residents of poor neighborhoods to write their own plans for using federal funds to improve local housing, education, health services, and job opportunities. Model Cities assemblies challenged the racial bias in programs like urban renewal and helped train community leaders.

In the 1970s and 1980s, when SDS was long gone and the Model Cities Program was fading, the lessons of grassroots reform would still be visible in alternative organizations and

Writer Ken Kesey and the self-defined Merry Pranksters toured the country in a brightly painted bus, parked here in San Francisco's Golden Gate Park. They sometimes threw open parties where they served punch laced with psychedelic drugs in the hope of inciting radical social change.

but not living like social reformers or revolutionaries. The musical *Hair* (1968) and the film *Easy Rider* (1969) harnessed their social ferment to the box office as mass culture absorbed the youth culture.

Within the youth culture was a smaller and more intense counterculture that added Eastern religion, social radicalism, and evangelistic belief in the drug LSD. The Harvard professor Timothy Leary and the writer Aldous Huxley claimed that hallucinogenic or psychedelic drugs, such as mescaline and LSD, would swing open the "doors of perception." Rock lyrics began to reflect the drug culture in 1966 and 1967, and young people talked about Leary's advice to "tune in, turn on, and drop out." San Francisco's Haight-Ashbury district became a national mecca for hippies in 1967's "Summer of Love," and hippie districts sprang up around university campuses across the country.

The cultural rebels of the late 1950s and early 1960s had been trying to combine personal freedom with new social arrangements. Many hippies were more interested in altering their minds with drugs than with politics or poetry. Serious exploration of societal alternatives was left for the minority who devoted themselves to the political work of the New Left, communal living, women's liberation, and other movements.

political movements that strengthened democracy from the bottom up. Activists staffed food cooperatives, free clinics, women's health groups, and drug-counseling centers across the country. Community-based organization was a key element in self-help efforts by African Americans, Asian Americans, and Latinos. Neighborhood associations and community-development corporations that provided affordable housing and jobs extended the "backyard revolution" into the 1980s and beyond. Social conservatives, such as anti-abortionists, used the same techniques on behalf of their own agendas.

Youth Culture and Counterculture

The popular context for the serious work of the New Left was the growing youth culture and **counterculture.** Millions of young people in the second half of the 1960s expressed their alienation from American society by sampling drugs or chasing the rainbow of a youth culture. Some just smoked marijuana, grew long hair, and listened to psychedelic rock. Others plunged into ways of life that scorned their middle-class backgrounds. The middle-aged and middle-class ignored the differences and dubbed the rebellious young "hippies."

The youth culture took advantage of the nation's prosperity. It was consumerism in a tie-dyed T-shirt. A high point was the 1969 Woodstock rock festival in New York State, a weekend of "sex, drugs, and rock-and-roll" for 400,000 young people. But Woodstock was an excursion, not a life-altering commitment. Members of the Woodstock Generation were consumers in a distinct market niche, dressing

Sounds of Change

The youth culture was shaped by films and philosophers, by pot and poets, but above all by music. Many changes in American society are mirrored in the abrupt shift from the increasingly complacent rock-and-roll of the early 1960s to the more provocative albums of mid-decade: Bob Dylan's *Highway 61 Revisited* (1965), the Beatles *Rubber Soul* (1965) and *Sergeant Pepper's Lonely Hearts Club Band* (1967), the Jefferson Airplane's *Surrealistic Pillow* (1967). The songs were still aimed at popular success, but the musicians were increasingly self-conscious of themselves as artists and social critics.

At the start of the decade, the African American roots of rock-and-roll were unmistakable, but there was no social agenda. Elvis Presley and the Everly Brothers kept the messages personal, and there was no reason to anticipate any departure from popular music's normal concerns about love and loss. Music that criticized American society initially found a much smaller audience through the folk-music revival in a few big cities and university campuses. Folksingers like the long-established Pete Seeger and the younger Joan Baez drew on black music, white country music, and old labor-organizing songs to keep alive dissenting voices.

OVERVIEW

Why Were We in South Vietnam?

U.S. leaders offered a number of justifications for U.S. military involvement in Vietnam. Here are some of the key arguments, with points that supported or questioned the explanation.

To Prop Up a Domino:		Communist success in South Vietnam would undermine pro-American regimes in adjacent nations, which would topple like a row of dominoes,
	Pro	The firm U.S. stand contributed to an anti-Communist coup in Indonesia in 1965 and encouraged pro-American interests in Thailand and the Philippines.
	Con	Detailed knowledge of each nation in Southeast Asia shows that their own histories and internal issues were far more important in determining their futures than was U.S. action in Vietnam.
To Contain China:		China's Communist regime wanted to expand its control throughout Asia.
	Pro	The People's Republic of China was hostile to the United States, as shown in the Korean War, and had a long history of trying to control Vietnam.
	Con	North Vietnam had closer ties to the Soviet Union than to China and played the two Communist nations against each other to preserve its independence from China.
To Defeat Aggression:		South Vietnam was an independent nation threatened by invasion.
	Pro	The major military threat to South Vietnam after 1965 came from the growing presence of the North Vietnamese army, and U.S. military intervention was necessary to counter that invasion.
	Con	The conflict in South Vietnam originated as a civil war within South Vietnam. Moreover, South and North Vietnam were a single nation, artificially divided in 1954, so that North Vietnam was trying to reunify rather than invade South Vietnam.
To Protect Democracy:		South Vietnam was a democratic nation that deserved U.S. support.
	Pro	South Vietnam had an emerging middle class and an opportunity to develop democratic institutions.
	Con	South Vietnam was never a true democracy, ruled first by civilian dictator Ngo Dinh Diem and then a series of military strongmen.

Then, in an artistic revolution, the doors opened to a new kind of rock music. The Beatles capitalized on their immense popularity to begin a career of artistic experimentation. They also opened the way for such hard-edged British bands as the Rolling Stones and The Who to introduce social criticism and class consciousness into rock lyrics. San Francisco's new psychedelic-rock scene took its name from drugs, such as LSD, and centered on shows at the Fillmore Auditorium, where performers in 1966 included the Jefferson Airplane, the Grateful Dead, and Buffalo Springfield. The Texan Janis Joplin came to San Francisco to draw on black musical styles after reading the Beat writers who had celebrated the city's jazz and racial openness.

Bob Dylan, a folksinger with an acoustic guitar, "went electric" at the Newport, Rhode Island, folk festival in 1965 and further transformed the music scene. Songs like "Blowin' in the Wind" and "Like a Rolling Stone" were personal and political at the same time; Dylan's music was musically exciting and socially critical in a way that expressed much of the discontent of American young people. Dylan paved the way for later singers like Bruce Springsteen and Kurt Cobain.

The transformation of rock in the mid-1960s invited far more explicit treatment of sex and illegal drugs than was pre-viously accepted in pop music. Jim Morrison and The Doors, Lou Reed and the Velvet Underground, and Jimi Hendrix exploded onto the scene in 1967. Their driving rhythms and sexually aggressive stage personalities blended the tensions of big cities with influences from white rock and roll and black rhythm and blues. Hendrix spanned the greatest distance from ghetto blues clubs of the 1950s to the mass market of the late 1960s, with albums such as *Are You Experienced* (1967). By 1972, both Morrison and Hendrix were dead of hard living and drug abuse. Meanwhile, *Rolling Stone* magazine had published its first issue in November 1967, giving the new sounds a forum for serious analysis.

Communes and Cults

Out of the half-secular, half-spiritual vision of the counterculture came people who not only dropped out of mainstream institutions but also tried to drop into miniature societies built on new principles. Thousands of Americans in the late 1960s and 1970s formed "intentional communities" or "communes." Their members usually tried to combine individual freedom and spontaneity with cooperative living. Upper New England, the Southwest, and the northern Pacific coast were commune country. Rural communes usually located on marginal land too poor to support commercial farming;

At the Newport (Rhode Island) Jazz Festival in 1963, Joan Baez and Bob Dylan performed as folksingers who worked in the tradition of protest songs. Two years later in Newport, Dylan shocked the popular music world by replacing his acoustic instrument with an amplified guitar and backup and jump-starting a fruitful blending of folk, country, and rock music into radical new sounds.

members pored over *The Whole Earth Catalog* (1968) to figure out how to live on the land.

Communes were artificial families, financed by inheritances, food stamps, and handicraft sales. Many suffered from the same inequality between men and women that was fueling the feminist revolt. Like natural families, they were emotional hothouses that often most collapsed because their members had incompatible goals.

However, a number of communes were serious endeavors. Some tried to follow spiritual leadings from Christianity or Buddhism. Thousands of smaller and less conspicuous urban communes whose members occupied large old houses pursued experiments in socialism, environmentalism, or feminism. Such efforts helped to spread the ideas of organic farming, cooperative land ownership, and low-consumption environmentalism that would move into the mainstream.

The Feminist Critique

The growing dissatisfaction of many women with their domestic roles helped set the stage for a revived feminism that was another result of the ferment of the 1960s. Important steps in this revival included the Presidential Commission on the Status of Women in 1961; the addition of gender as one of the categories protected by the Civil Rights Act of 1964 (see Chapter 28), and creation of the National Organization for Women (NOW) in 1966.

Mainstream feminism targeted unequal opportunity in the job market. Newspapers in the early 1960s segregated help-wanted ads by sex, listing "Girl Friday" jobs in one column and professional work in another. College-educated baby boomers encountered "glass ceilings" and job discrimination. Throughout the mid-1960s and 1970s, activists battled to open job categories to women, who battled for equal pay for everyone with equal qualifications and responsibilities.

Changes in sexual behavior paralleled efforts to equalize treatment in the workplace. More reliable methods of contraception, especially birth-control pills introduced in the early 1960s, gave women greater control over childbearing. In some ways a replay of ideas from the 1920s, a new sexual revolution eroded the double standard that expected chastity of women but tolerated promiscuity among men. One consequence was a singles culture that accepted sexual activity between unmarried men and women.

More radical versions of the feminist message came from women who had joined the civil rights and antiwar movements only to find themselves working the copy machine and the coffeemaker while men plotted strategy. Radicals caught the attention of the national media with a demonstration against the 1968 Miss America pageant. Protesters crowned a sheep as Miss America and encouraged women to make a statement by tossing their bras and makeup in the trash.

Women's liberation took off as a social and political movement in 1970 and 1971 as influential books probed the roots of the inequality between men's and women's opportunities. Women shared their stories and ideas in small "consciousness-raising" sessions. *Ms.* magazine gave the movement a national voice in 1972. Within a few years, millions of women had recognized events and patterns in their lives as discrimination based on gender. The feminist movement, and specific policy measures related to it, put equal rights and the fight against sexism (a word no one knew before 1965) on the national agenda and gradually changed how Americans thought about the relationships between men and women. Feminists focused attention on rape as a crime of violence and called attention to the burdens the legal system placed on rape victims. In the 1980s and 1990s, they also challenged sexual harassment in the workplace, gradually refining the boundaries between acceptable and unacceptable behavior.

Coming Out

The new militancy among gay men and lesbians drew on several of the social changes of the late 1960s and 1970s. Willingness to acknowledge and talk about nonstandard sexual behavior was part of a change in public values. Tactics of political pressure came from the antiwar and civil rights movements. The timing, with a series of key events from 1969 to 1974, coincided with that of women's liberation.

Gay activism spread from big cities to small communities, from the coasts to Middle America. New York police had long harassed gay bars and their customers. When police raided Manhattan's Stonewall Inn in June 1969, however, patrons fought back in a weekend of disorder. The **Stonewall Rebellion** was a catalyst for homosexuals to assert themselves as a political force. San Francisco also became a center of gay life. Openly gay poets and artists were prominent in the city's avant-garde circles. By the late 1970s, the city had more than 300 business and social-gathering places identified as gay and lesbian.

With New Yorkers and San Franciscans as examples, more and more gay men and lesbians "came out," or went public about their sexual orientation. They published newspapers, organized churches, and lobbied politicians for protection of basic civil rights such as equal access to employment, housing, and public accommodations. They staged "gay pride" days and marches. In 1974, the American Psychiatric Association eliminated homosexuality from its official list of mental disorders.

Cities Under Stress

In the confident years after World War II, big cities had an upbeat image. The typical movie with a New York setting opened with a shot of the towering Manhattan skyline and plunged into the bustling business or theater district. By the 1970s, however, slums and squalid back streets dominated popular imagery. *The French Connection* (1971) followed a drug dealer from Fifth Avenue to empty and menacing warehouses. *Klute* (1971) and *Taxi Driver* (1976) took moviegoers through the twilight world of prostitution. Television cop shows repeated the message that cities had become places of random and frequent violence.

Diagnosing an Urban Crisis

Popular entertainment reflected Americans' growing discomfort with their cities. The nation entered the 1960s with the assumption that urban problems were growing pains. Exploding metropolitan areas needed money for streets, schools, and sewers. Politicians viewed the difficulties of central cities as by-products of exuberant suburban growth, which left outmoded downtowns in need of physical redevelopment. In mid-decade, however, TV networks and news magazines began to run stories about "Battlefield, USA" and "Crisis in the Cities" that described cities as sinking under racial violence, crime, and unemployment.

Central cities had a special burden in caring for the domestic poor. Baltimore, for example, had 27 percent of the Maryland population in 1970 but 66 percent of the state's welfare recipients. Impoverished and often fragmented families needed schools to serve as social-work agencies as well as educational institutions. Poor people with no other access to healthcare treated city hospital emergency rooms as the family doctor.

Many urban problems were associated with the "second ghettos" created by the migration of 2.5 million African Americans from southern farms to northern and western cities in the 1950s and 1960s. By 1970, one-third of all African Americans lived in the 12 largest cities, crowding into ghetto neighborhoods dating from World War II.

Postwar black migrants found systems of race relations that limited their access to decent housing, the best schools, and many unionized jobs. Many families arrived just in time to face the consequences of industrial layoffs and plant closures in the 1970s and 1980s. Already unneeded in the South because of the mechanization of agriculture, the migrants found themselves equally unwanted in the industrial North, caught in decaying neighborhoods and victimized by crime.

The residential ghetto trapped African American families that tried to follow the expectations of mainstream society. Because ghettos grew block by block, middle-class black families had to pioneer as intruders into white neighborhoods and then see ghetto problems crowd in behind them. Their children faced the seductions of the street, which became increasingly violent with the spread of handguns and trade in illegal drugs.

Central cities faced additional financial problems unrelated to poverty and race. Many of their roads, bridges, fire stations, and water mains were 50 to 100 years old by the 1960s and 1970s, and they were wearing out. Closure of the elevated West Side Highway along the Hudson River in Manhattan after huge chunks fell out of the roadway symbolized a spreading urban problem. Decay of urban utility and transportation systems was a by-product of market forces and public policy. Private developers often borrowed money saved through northeastern bank accounts, insurance policies, and pension funds to finance new construction in sunbelt suburbs. The defense budget pumped tax dollars from the old industrial cities into the South and West.

High local taxes in older cities were one result, for the American system of local government demands that cities and the poor help themselves. By the early 1970s, the average resident of a central city paid roughly twice the state and local taxes per $1,000 of income as the average suburbanite. As Mayor Moon Landrieu of New Orleans commented, "We've taxed everything that moves and everything that stands still; and if anything moves again, we tax that, too."

Conflict in the Streets

African Americans and Hispanics who rioted in city streets in the mid-1960s were fed up with the lack of job opportunities, with substandard housing, and with crime. Prominent black writers, such as James Baldwin in *The Fire Next Time* (1963), had warned of the mounting anger. Suddenly the fires were real. Riots in Rochester, Harlem, and Brooklyn in July 1964 opened four years of racial violence. Before they subsided, the riots had scarred most big cities and killed 200 people, most of them African Americans.

The explosion of the Watts neighborhood in Los Angeles fixed the danger of racial unrest in the public mind. Trouble started on August 11, 1965, when a white highway-patrol officer arrested a young African American for drunken driving. Loud complaints drew a crowd, and the arrival of Los Angeles police turned the bystanders into an angry mob that attacked passing cars. Rioting, looting, and arson spread through Watts for two days until the National Guard cordoned off the trouble spots and occupied the neighborhood on August 14 and 15.

The outburst frightened white Americans. In most previous race riots, whites had used violence to keep blacks "in their place." In Watts, blacks were the instigators. The primary targets were the police and ghetto businesses that had reputations for exploiting their customers. The National Advisory Commission on Civil Disorders concluded in 1968 that most property damage was the "result of deliberate attacks on white-owned businesses characterized in the Negro community as unfair or disrespectful." In short, the riots were protests about the problems of ghetto life.

After Watts, Americans expected "long hot summers" and got them. Scores of cities suffered riots in 1966, including a riot by Puerto Ricans in Chicago that protested the same problems blacks faced. The following year, the worst violence was in Newark, New Jersey, and in Detroit, where 43 deaths and blocks of blazing buildings stunned television viewers.

Few politicians wanted to admit that African Americans and Hispanics had serious grievances. Their impulse was to blame riffraff and outside agitators—"lawbreakers and mad dogs," to quote future California governor Ronald Reagan. This theory was wrong. Almost all participants were neighborhood residents. Except that they were younger, they were representative of the African American population, and their violence came from the frustration of rising expectations. Despite the political gains of the civil rights movement, unemployment remained high, and the police still treated all blacks as potential criminals. The urban riots were political actions to force the problems of African Americans onto the national agenda.

Minority Self-Determination

Minority separatism and demands for self-determination tapped the same anger that fueled the urban riots. Drawing on a long heritage of militancy (such as armed resistance during racial riots), activists challenged the central goal of the civil rights movement, which sought full integration and participation in American life. The phrase **Black Power** summed up the new alternative. The term came from frustrated SNCC leader Stokely Carmichael in 1966: "We've been saying freedom for six years— and we ain't got nothing. What we're going to start saying now is 'Black Power'!"

The slogans of Black Power, Brown Power, and Red Power spanned goals that ran from civil rights to cultural pride to revolutionary separatism. They were all efforts by minorities to define themselves through their own heritage and backgrounds, not simply by looking in the mirror of white society. Thus they questioned the American assumption that everyone wanted to be part of the same homogeneous society.

Expressions of Black Power. Black Power translated many ways—control of one's own community through the voting machine, celebration of the African American heritage, creation of a parallel society that shunned white institutions. Its intellectual roots reached back to Marcus Garvey and included admiration for anti-colonial nationalism in Africa and Asia. At the personal level, it was a synonym for black pride. In the political realm it pointed toward the successful campaigns of Richard Hatcher in Gary, Indiana, and Carl Stokes in Cleveland, the first African Americans elected mayors of large northern cities.

Black Power also meant increased interest in the **Nation of Islam,** or Black Muslims, who combined a version of Islam with radical separatism. They called for self-discipline, support of black institutions and businesses, and total rejection of whites. The Nation of Islam appealed to blacks who saw no future in integration. It was strongest in northern cities, such as Chicago, where it offered an alternative to the life of the ghetto streets.

In the early 1960s, Malcolm X emerged as a leading Black Muslim. Growing up as Malcolm Little, he was a street-wise

Malcolm X arrives home in New York after his house was bombed on February 14, 1965. He would be assassinated a week later.

Members of the Black Panthers assemble outside the Alameda County Courthouse in Oakland, California on July, 15, 1968, when Panther leader Huey Newton goes on trial for killing a police officer.

criminal until he converted to the Nation of Islam in prison. After his release, Malcolm preached that blacks should stop letting whites set the terms by which they judged their appearance, communities, and accomplishments. He emphasized the African cultural heritage and economic self-help and proclaimed himself an extremist for black rights. In the last year of his life, however, he returned from a pilgrimage to Mecca willing to consider limited acceptance of whites. Rivals within the movement assassinated him in February 1965, but his ideas lived on in *The Autobiography of Malcolm X*.

The **Black Panthers** pursued similar goals. Bobby Seale and Huey Newton grew up in the Oakland, California, area and met as college students. They saw African American ghettos as internal colonies in need of self-determination. They created the Panthers in 1966, began to carry firearms, and recruited Eldridge Cleaver as the group's chief publicist.

The Panthers asserted their equality. They shadowed police patrols to prevent mistreatment of African Americans and carried weapons into the California State Legislature in May 1967 to protest gun control. As Seale recalled, the goal was "to read a message to the world" and use the press to "blast it across the country." The Panthers also promoted community-based self-help efforts, such as a free-breakfast program for school children and medical clinics, and ran political candidates.

In contrast to the rioters in Watts, the Panthers had a political program, if not the ability to carry it through. The movement was shaken when Newton was convicted of manslaughter for killing a police officer and Cleaver fled to Algeria. Panther chapters imploded when they attracted thugs and shakedown artists as well as visionaries. Nevertheless, the Panthers survived as a political party into the 1970s. Former Panther Bobby Rush entered Congress in 1992.

Hispanic activism in the Southwest. Latinos in the Southwest developed their own Brown Power movement in the late 1960s. Led by Reies López Tijerina, Hispanics in rural New Mexico demanded the return of lands that had been lost to Anglo Americans despite the guarantees of the Treaty of Guadalupe Hidalgo in 1848. Tijerina's "Letter from the Santa Fe Jail" denounced the "rich people from outside the state with their summer homes and ranches" and "all those who have robbed the people of their land and culture for 120 years." Mexican Americans in the 1970s organized for political power in southern Texas communities where they were a majority. In Denver, Rodolfo Gonzales established the Crusade for Justice. His "Plan for the Barrio" emphasized Hispanic cultural traditions, community control of schools, and economic development.

The best-known Hispanic activism combined social protest with the crusading spirit of earlier labor union organizing campaigns. Cesar Chavez organized the multiracial United Farm Workers (UFW) among Mexican American agricultural workers in California in 1965. Chavez was committed both to nonviolent action for social justice and to the labor movement. UFW demands included better wages and safer working conditions, such as less exposure to pesticides. UFW vice president Dolores Huerta spoke for the special needs of women who labored in the fields. Because farm workers were not covered by the National Labor Relations Act of 1935, the issue was whether farm owners would recognize the union as a bargaining agent and sign a contract. Chavez supplemented work stoppages with national boycotts against table grapes, lettuce, and certain brands of wine, making *la huelga* ("the strike") into *la causa* for urban liberals. Rival organizing by the Teamsters Union and the short attention span of the national public gradually undermined the UFW's initial success. Nevertheless, Chavez's dogged toughness and self-sacrifice gave both Chicanos and the country a new hero.

Latino political activism had strong appeal for young people. Ten thousand young Chicanos stormed out of Los Angeles high schools in March 1968 to protest poor education and racist teachers. Some students organized as Brown Berets to demand more relevant education and fairer police treatment. Many rejected assimilation in favor of community self-determination and began to talk about *la raza* ("the people"), whose language and heritage descended from centuries of Mexican history. "Chicano" itself was a slang term with insulting overtones that was now adopted as a badge of pride and cultural identity.

Native Americans assert their identity. Native Americans also fought both for equal access to American society

Dolores Huerta and Cesar Chavez confer at the 1973 convention of the United Farm Workers. Chavez and Huerta tried to build a union that welcomed workers of all ethnic backgrounds, but the UFW leaders were largely Hispanic, and the union took much of its symbolism from the Mexican heritage shared by most of its members.

and to preserve cultural traditions through tribal institutions. Congress in 1968 restored the authority of tribal law on reservations. Three years later the Alaska Native Claims Settlement Act granted native Alaskans 44 million acres and $963 million to settle claims for their ancestral lands. Legally sophisticated tribes sued for compensation and enforcement of treaty provisions, such as fishing rights in the Pacific Northwest. Larger tribes established their own colleges, such as Navajo Community College (1969) and Oglala Lakota College (1971). Navajo Community College, said its catalog, "exists to fulfill many needs of the Navajo people.... It provides a place where Navajo history and culture can be studied and learned; it provides training in the skills necessary for many jobs on the reservation which today are held by non-Navajos."

A second development was media-oriented protests that asserted Red Power. One of the earliest was a series of "fish-ins" in which Indians from Washington state, helped by the multi-tribal National Indian Youth Council, exercised treaty-based fishing rights in defiance of state regulations. Native American students gained national attention by seizing the abandoned Alcatraz Island for a cultural and educational center (1969–1971). Indians in Minneapolis created the **American Indian Movement (AIM)** in 1968 to increase economic opportunity and stop police mistreatment. AIM participated in the cross-country Broken Treaties Caravan, which climaxed by occupying the Bureau of Indian Affairs in Washington in 1972. AIM also allied with Sioux traditionalists on the Pine Ridge Reservation in South Dakota against the tribe's elected government. In 1973, they took over the village of Wounded Knee, where the U.S. Army in 1890 had massacred 300 Indians. They held out for 70 days before leaving peacefully. Since these events of the early 1970s, Indians have continued to assert their distinctiveness within American society.

Suburban Independence: The Outer City

In the mid-1960s, the United States became a suburban nation. The 1970 census found more people living in the suburban counties of metropolitan areas (37 percent) than in central cities (31 percent) or in small towns and rural areas (31 percent). Just after World War II, most new suburbs had been bedroom communities that depended on the jobs, services, and shopping of central cities. By the late 1960s, suburbs were evolving into "outer cities," whose inhabitants had little need for the old central city. The *New York Times* in 1978 found that 40 percent of the residents of New York's Long Island and New Jersey suburbs visited the city fewer than three times a year, and most denied that they were part of the New York area. For them, suburban malls and shopping strips were the new American Main Street and suburban communities the new Middle America.

Suburban economic growth and political influence. Suburbs captured most new jobs, leaving the urban poor with few opportunities for employment. In the 15 largest metropolitan areas, the number of central city jobs fell by 800,000 in the 1960s, while the number of suburban jobs rose by 3.2 million. The shift from rail to air for business travel accentuated suburban job growth. Sales representatives and executives could arrive at airports on the edge of town rather than at railroad stations at the center and transact business without ever going downtown. By the 1970s, every major airport had a fringe of hotels, office parks, and corporate offices. Around many cities, suburban retailing, employment, and services fused into so-called edge cities, such as the Galleria Post Oak district in Houston and the Tysons Corner area in northern Virginia. Suburban rings gained a growing share of public facilities intended to serve the entire metropolitan area. As pioneered in California, community colleges served the suburban children of the baby boom. Many of the new four-year schools that state university systems added in the 1960s and early 1970s were also built for suburbanites, from George Mason University and the University of

Armed confrontation between militant Indians and state and federal law enforcement at Wounded Knee, S.D. in 1973 recalled the decades of warfare between plains tribes and the U.S. army in the previous century.

though integration through busing occurred peacefully in dozens of cities, many white people resented the practice. Working-class students who depended on public schools found themselves on the front lines of integration, while many middle-class families switched to private education. For many Americans, the image of busing for racial integration was fixed in 1975, when white citizens in Boston reacted with violence against black students who were bused to largely white high schools in the South Boston and Charlestown neighborhoods. The goal of equal opportunity clashed with equally strong values of neighborhood, community, and ethnic solidarity.

Because the Supreme Court also ruled that busing programs normally stopped at school-district boundaries, suburbs with independent districts escaped school integration. One result was to make busing self-defeating, for it led white families to move out of the integrating school district. Others placed their children in private academies, as happened frequently in the South. Busing also caused suburbanites to defend their political independence fiercely. In Denver, for example, a bitter debate lasted from 1969 until court-ordered busing in 1974. By-products included incorporation or expansion of several large suburbs and a state constitutional amendment that blocked further expansion of the city boundaries (and thus of the Denver school district).

Maryland—Baltimore County in the Washington-Baltimore area to California State University campuses at Northridge and Fullerton. The California Angels in baseball and New York Islanders in hockey gave suburban regions exclusive claims to their own major league sports franchises.

Suburban political power grew along with economic clout. In 1962, the Supreme Court handed down a landmark decision in the case of ***Baker v. Carr***. Overturning laws that treated counties or other political subdivisions as the units to be represented in state legislatures, *Baker* required that legislative seats be apportioned on the basis of population. The principle of "one person, one vote" broke the stranglehold of rural counties on state governments, but the big beneficiaries were not older cities, but fast-growing suburbs. By 1975, suburbanites held the largest block of seats in the House of Representatives—131 suburban districts, 130 rural, 102 central city, and 72 mixed. Reapportionment in 1982, based on the 1980 census, produced a House that was even more heavily suburban.

School busing controversies.   School integration controversies in the 1970s reinforced a tendency for suburbanites to separate themselves from city problems. In ***Swann v. Charlotte-Mecklenburg Board of Education*** (1971), the U.S. Supreme Court held that crosstown busing was an acceptable solution to the *de facto* segregation that resulted from residential patterns within a single school district. When school officials around the country failed to achieve racial balance, federal judges ordered their own busing plans. Al-

The Year of the Gun, 1968

Some years are turning points that force society to reconsider its basic assumptions. In 1914, the violence of World War I undermined Europe's belief in progress. In 1933, Americans had to rethink the role of government. In 1968, mainstream Americans increasingly turned against the war in Vietnam, student protest and youth counterculture turned ugly, and political consensus shattered.

The Tet Offensive

The longer the Vietnam War continued and the less interest that China or the Soviet Union showed in it, the less valid the conflict seemed to the American people. It looked more and more like a war for pride, not national security.

The Viet Cong's Tet Offensive on January 30, 1968, undermined that pride. At the end of 1967, U.S. officials were overconfidently predicting victory. They also fell for a North Vietnamese feint by committing U.S. forces to the defense of Khe Sanh, a strongpoint near the North-South border. The defense was a tactical success for the United States but thinned its forces elsewhere in South Vietnam. Then, at the beginning of Tet, the Vietnamese New Year, the Viet Cong attacked 36 of 44 provincial capitals and the national capital, Saigon. They hit the U.S. embassy and reached the runways of Tan Son Nhut air base. If the United States was winning, the Tet offensive should not have been possible.

As a military effort, the attacks failed. U.S. and South Vietnamese troops repulsed the attacks and cleared the cities. But the offensive was a psychological blow that convinced the American public that the war was quicksand. Television coverage of the Tet battles made the bad publicity worse. During World War II, officials had censored pictures from the front. Images from Vietnam went directly to the evening news; it was a "living room war" that gave immediacy to abstract arguments over policy and strategy. At least until Tet, the commentary from network news anchors had supported the U.S. effort, but the pictures undermined civilian morale. Viewers could hear cigarette lighters clicking open to set villages in flames. A handful of images stayed in people's memories—a Buddhist monk burning himself to death in protest; a child with flesh peeled off by napalm; a South Vietnamese official executing a captive on the streets of Saigon.

In the wake of the Tet crisis, General Westmoreland's request for 200,000 more troops forced a political and military reevaluation. Clark Clifford, a dedicated Cold Warrior, was the new secretary of defense. Now he had second thoughts. Twenty "wise men"—the big names of the Cold War—told the president that the war was unwinnable on terms acceptable to America's allies and to many Americans. By devouring resources and souring relations with other nations, it endangered rather than enhanced American security. Most scholars have agreed with this assessment. Tet and its aftermath had shown U.S. military superiority but highlighted the nation's inability to translate tactical advantage into political success in South Vietnam or the United States. The best option, the wise men told LBJ, was disengagement. "He could hardly believe his ears," Clifford remembered.

LBJ's Exit

The president was already in political trouble. After other prominent Democrats held back, Minnesota's liberal Senator Eugene McCarthy had decided to challenge Johnson in the presidential primaries. Because he controlled the party organizations in two-thirds of the states, Johnson did not need the primary states for renomination and ignored the first primary in New Hampshire. With enthusiastic college students staffing his campaign, McCarthy won a startling 42 percent of the popular vote and 20 of 24 delegates in the New Hampshire primary. The vote was a protest against Johnson's Vietnam policy rather than a clear mandate for peace. Nevertheless, the vote proved that the political middle would no longer hold.

By showing Johnson's vulnerability, New Hampshire also drew Robert Kennedy into the race. The younger brother of the former president, Kennedy inspired both fervent loyalty and strong distaste. In the 1950s, he had worked for Senator Joe McCarthy and had initially been a reluctant supporter of civil rights during his brother's administration. He was arrogant and abrasive, but also bright and flexible. More than other mainstream politicians of the 1960s, he touched the hearts of Hispanic and African American voters as well as the white working class. He had left his position as attorney general to win election to the Senate from New York in 1964. Now he put the Kennedy mystique on the line against a man he despised.

Facing political challenges and an unraveling war, on March 31, 1968, Johnson announced a halt to most bombing of North Vietnam, opening the door for peace negotiations that formally began in May 1969. He then astounded the country by withdrawing from the presidential race. It was a statesmanlike act by a man who had been consumed by a war he did not want, had never understood, and could not end. As he told an aide, the war made him feel like a hitchhiker in a hailstorm: "I can't run, I can't hide, and I can't make it stop." Hoping to save his domestic program, he served out his term with few friends and little credit for his accomplishments.

Violence and Politics: King, Kennedy, and Chicago

Johnson's dramatic withdrawal was followed by the violent disruption of U.S. politics through assassination and riot. On

GIs evacuate a wounded comrade from fighting near the border between Vietnam and Cambodia.

Red Spring, 1968

Columbia University in New York City was in turmoil in the spring of 1968. Its African American students and its SDS chapter had several grievances. One was the university's cooperation with the Pentagon-funded Institute for Defense Analysis. Another was its plan to build a gymnasium on park land that might better serve the residents of Harlem. Some students wanted changes in university policy, others a confrontation that would recruit new radicals. They occupied five university buildings, including the library and the president's office, for a week in April until police evicted them. A student strike and additional clashes with the authorities lasted until June.

The "battle of Morningside Heights" (the location of Columbia) generated banner headlines in the United States, but it was tame when compared to events in Europe. During the same "red spring," demonstrations and revolts by angry university students and workers created upheaval on both sides of the Iron Curtain.

In the months that followed the Tet crisis, much of the industrial world was in ferment. Students rioted in Italy and Berlin over rigid university systems, the Vietnam War, and the power of multinational corporations. Workers and students protested against the Franco regime in Spain. In Paris, student demonstrations against the Vietnam War turned into attacks on the university system and the French government. Students fought police in the Paris streets in the first days of May with the approval of a majority of Parisians. Radical industrial workers called a general strike. The government nearly toppled before the disturbance subsided.

Grassroots rebellion also shook the Soviet grip on eastern Europe. University students in Poland protested the stifling of political discussion. Alexander Dubcek, the new leader of the Czech Communist Party, brought together students and the middle class around reforms that caused people to talk about the "Prague Spring"—a blossoming of democracy inside the Soviet bloc. Here the changes went too far. As Czechs pressed for more and more political freedom, the Soviet Union feared losing control of one of its satellites. On August 21, 500,000 troops from the USSR and other Warsaw Pact nations rolled across the border and forced Czechoslovakia back into line.

■ **What common factors might help explain student unrest on both sides of the Iron Curtain?**

April 4, 1968, an ex-convict, James Earl Ray, shot and killed Martin Luther King, Jr., as he stood on the balcony of a Memphis motel. King's death was the product of pure racial hatred, and it triggered a climactic round of violence in black ghettos. Fires devastated the West Side of Chicago and downtown Washington, DC. The army guarded the steps of the Capitol, ready to protect Congress from its fellow citizens.

The shock of King's death was still fresh when another political assassination stunned the nation. On June 5, Robert Kennedy won California's primary election. He was still behind Vice President Hubert Humphrey in the delegate count but coming on strong. As Kennedy walked out of the ballroom at his headquarters in the Ambassador Hotel in Los Angeles, a Jordanian immigrant named Sirhan Sirhan put a bullet in his brain. Sirhan may have wanted revenge for America's tilt toward Israel in that country's victorious Six-Day War with Egypt and Jordan in 1967.

Kennedy's death ensured the Democratic nomination for Humphrey, a liberal who had loyally supported Johnson's war policy. After his nomination, Humphrey faced the Republican Richard Nixon and the Independent George Wallace. Nixon positioned himself as the candidate of the political middle. Wallace appealed to southern whites and working-class northerners who feared black militancy and hated "the ivory-tower folks with pointy heads."

Both got great help from the Democratic Convention, held in Chicago on August 26–29. While Democrats feuded among themselves, Chicago Mayor Richard Daley and his police department monitored antiwar protesters. The National Mobilization Committee to End the War in Vietnam drew from the New Left and from older peace activists—sober and committed people who had fought against nuclear weapons in the 1950s and the Vietnam War throughout the 1960s. They wanted to embarrass the Johnson-Humphrey administration by marching to the convention hall on nomination night. Mixed in were the Yippies (the term supposedly stood for Youth International Party, but the idea of hippies making yippie! came first and the word later). The Yippies planned to attract young people to Chicago with the promise of street theater, media events, and confrontation that would puncture the pretensions of the power structure. To the extent they had a program, it was to use the youth culture to attract converts to radical politics.

The volatile mix was ready for a spark. On August 28, the same night that Democratic delegates were nominating Humphrey, tensions exploded in a police riot. Protesters and Yippies had congregated in Grant Park, across Michigan Avenue from downtown hotels. Undisciplined police waded into the crowds with clubs and tear gas. Young people fought back with rocks and bottles. Television caught the hours of violence that ended when the National Guard separated police from demonstrators. On the convention floor, Senator Abraham Ribicoff of Connecticut decried "Gestapo tactics" on the streets of Chicago. Mayor Daley shouted back obscenities. For Humphrey, the convention was a catastrophe, alienating liberal Democrats and associating Democrats with disorder in the public mind.

The election was closer than Humphrey had any right to hope (see Map 29–2). Many Americans who liked Wallace's message were unwilling to vote for a radical third party. Nixon appealed to the white middle class and claimed that he had a secret plan to end the war. He also used increasing fears about crime and street violence as a "wedge issue" to split worried white voters from the Democrats. Humphrey picked up strength in October after he separated himself from Johnson's war policy. Election day gave Wallace 13.5 percent of the popular vote, Humphrey 42.7 percent of the popular vote and 191 electoral votes, and Nixon 43.4 percent of the popular vote and 301 electoral votes.

The Wallace candidacy was a glimpse of the future. The national media saw Wallace in terms of bigotry and a backlash against civil rights, getting only part of the story. Many of Wallace's northern backers were unhappy with both parties. Liberal on economic issues but conservative on family and social issues, many of these working-class voters evolved into "Reagan Democrats" by the 1980s. In the South, Wallace was a transitional choice for conservative voters who would eventually transfer their allegiance from the Democratic to the Republican Party.

Nixon, Watergate, and the Crisis of the Early 1970s

The new president was an unlikely politician, ill at ease in public and consumed by a sense of inferiority. A product of small-town California, he felt rejected by the eastern elite. After losing a 1962 race for governor of California, he announced that he was quitting politics and that the press would no longer have Dick Nixon "to kick around." In 1968, he skill-

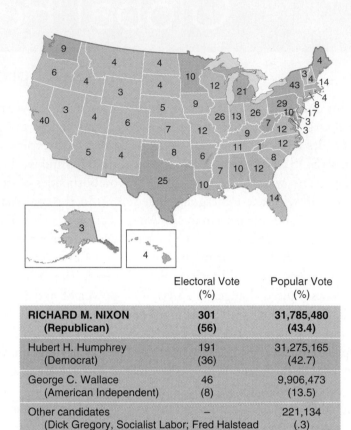

	Electoral Vote (%)	Popular Vote (%)
RICHARD M. NIXON (Republican)	**301** **(56)**	**31,785,480** **(43.4)**
Hubert H. Humphrey (Democrat)	191 (36)	31,275,165 (42.7)
George C. Wallace (American Independent)	46 (8)	9,906,473 (13.5)
Other candidates (Dick Gregory, Socialist Labor; Fred Halstead and Paul Boutelle, Socialist Workers; Eugene McCarthy, Peace and Freedom; E. Harold Munn and Rolland E. Fisher, Prohibition)	–	221,134 (.3)

MAP 29–2   The Election of 1968
Richard Nixon won the presidency with the help of George Wallace, the American Independent Party candidate. Wallace won several southern states, offering an alternative to white southerners unhappy with the Democratic Party but not yet prepared to vote Republican. He also drew northern working-class votes away from Hubert Humphrey and thus helped Nixon to take several midwestern states.

fully sold a "new Nixon" to the media. Seven years later, the press was his undoing as it uncovered the Watergate scandal.

Nixon's painful public presence and dishonesty have tended to obscure his administration's accomplishments. He reduced tensions in the Cold War. He reluctantly upgraded civil rights enforcement, set goals for minority hiring by federal contractors, and presided over impressive environmental legislation.

Getting Out of Vietnam, 1969–1975

After 1968, things got worse in Southeast Asia before they got better. Nixon had no secret plan to end the war. Opposition intensified with the revelation that U.S. soldiers in March 1968 had slaughtered hundreds of men, women, and children in the South Vietnamese village of My Lai after failing to find any Viet Cong. This crime accentuated the dehumanizing power of war and showed how far the United States was straying from its ideals. William Calley, who had been in immediate command, eventually served ten years in military prison. Protests at home culminated in 1969 with the Vietnam Moratorium on October 15, when 2 million protesters joined rallies across the country.

Disaffection also mounted in Vietnam. Racial tensions sapped morale on the front lines. Troops lost discipline, took drugs, and hunkered down waiting for their tours of duty to end, and the high command had to adapt its code of justice to keep an army on the job.

Nixon and Vice President Spiro Agnew responded by trying to isolate the antiwar opposition, but Nixon also reduced the role of U.S. ground forces. He claimed that his policies represented "the great silent majority of my fellow Americans." Agnew blamed bad morale on journalists and intellectuals—on "nattering nabobs of negativism" and "an effete corps of impudent snobs." The administration arranged for a "spontaneous" attack by construction workers on antiwar protesters in New York. The hard-hat counterattack was a cynically manipulated symbol, but Nixon and Agnew tapped genuine anger about failure in Asia and rapid change in U.S. society.

The New Left had already split into factions. Many activists continued to focus on peace work, draft resistance, and other efforts to link radical and liberal agendas. About a hundred angry SDS members, however, declared themselves the Weather Underground in 1969, taking their name from a Bob Dylan lyric ("You don't need a weatherman to know which way the wind blows"). They tried to disrupt Chicago and Washington with window-smashing "days of rage." Three Weatherpeople accidentally blew themselves up with a homemade bomb in New York in 1970. Others robbed a Boston bank to get money for the revolution. Still others bombed a University of Wisconsin building and killed a student.

"Vietnamization" and the secret war against Cambodia. Nixon's secretary of defense, Melvin Laird, responded to the antiwar sentiment with "Vietnamization," withdrawing U.S. troops as fast as possible without undermining the South Vietnamese government. In July 1969, the president announced the **Nixon Doctrine.** The United States would help other countries fight their wars with weapons and money but not with soldiers. The policy substituted machines for men. Americans rearmed and enlarged the South Vietnamese army and surreptitiously bombed Communist bases in neutral Cambodia.

The secret war against Cambodia culminated on April 30, 1970, with an invasion. The aim was to smash Viet Cong and North Vietnamese bases to allow time to rebuild the South Vietnamese army. Americans who had hoped that the war was fading away were outraged. Students shut down hundreds of colleges. At Kent State University in Ohio, the National Guard was called in to maintain order. Taunts, tossed bottles, and the recent record of violence put them on edge. On May 4, one unit fired on a group of young people and killed four of them. At Jackson State University in Mississippi, two students were killed when troops fired on their dormitory.

Stalemate and cease-fire.   The Cambodian "incursion" extended the military stalemate in Vietnam to U.S. policy. Beginning in December 1969, a new lottery system for determining the order of draft calls by birthdate let two-thirds of young men know they would not be drafted. In December 1970, Congress repealed the Gulf of Tonkin Resolution and prohibited the use of U.S. ground troops outside South Vietnam. Cambodia, however, was already devastated. The U.S. invasion had destabilized its government and opened the way for the bloodthirsty Khmer Rouge, who killed millions of Cambodians in the name of a working-class revolution. Vietnamization continued; only 90,000 U.S. ground troops were still in Vietnam by early 1972. A final air offensive in December smashed Hanoi into rubble and helped to force four and a half years of peace talks to a conclusion.

The cease-fire began on January 27, 1973. It confirmed U.S. withdrawal from Vietnam. North Vietnamese and Viet Cong forces would remain in control of the territory they occupied in South Vietnam, but they were not to be reinforced or substantially reequipped. The United States promised not to increase its military aid to South Vietnam. There were no solid guarantees for the South Vietnamese government. Immediately after coming to terms with North Vietnam, Nixon suspended the draft in favor of an all-volunteer military.

In 1975, South Vietnam collapsed. Only the U.S. presence had kept its political, ethnic, and religious factions together. For the first two years after the Paris agreement, North Vietnam quietly rebuilt its military capacity. In the spring of 1975, it opened an offensive, and South Vietnamese morale evaporated. Resistance crumbled so rapidly that the United States had to evacuate its embassy in Saigon by helicopter while frantic Vietnamese tried to join the flight.

Nixon and the Wider World

To his credit, Richard Nixon took U.S. foreign policy in new directions even while he was struggling to escape from Vietnam and Cambodia. Like Dwight Eisenhower before him, Nixon's reputation as an anti-Communist allowed him to improve relations with China and the Soviet Union. Indeed, he hoped to distract the American people from frustration in Southeast Asia with accomplishments elsewhere.

Nixon and Henry Kissinger, his national security adviser (and later secretary of state), shared what they considered a realistic view of foreign affairs. For both men, foreign policy was not about crusades or moral stands. It was about the balance of world economic and military power and securing the most advantageous agreements, alliances, and military positions. In particular, they hoped to trade improved relations with China and the Soviet Union for help in settling the Vietnam War.

Since 1950, the United States had acted as if China did not exist, refusing economic relations and insisting that the

Nationalist regime on Taiwan was the legitimate Chinese government. But the People's Republic of China was increasingly isolated within the Communist world. In 1969, it almost went to war with the Soviet Union. Nixon was eager to take advantage of Chinese-Soviet tension. Secret talks led to an easing of the American trade embargo in April 1971 and a tour of China by a U.S. table-tennis team. Kissinger then arranged for Nixon's startling visit to Mao Zedong in Beijing in February 1972.

Playing the "China card" helped to improve relations with the Soviet Union. The Soviets needed increased trade with the United States and a counterweight to China, the United States was looking for help in getting out of Vietnam, and both countries wanted to limit nuclear armaments. In 1969, the Senate came within one vote of stopping the development of defensive antiballistic missiles (ABMs). Opponents feared that strong antimissile defenses would encourage the idea that a nation could launch a first strike and survive the retaliation. Nixon treated the ABM program as a bargaining chip. Protracted negotiations led to the **Strategic Arms Limitation Treaty (SALT)** that Nixon signed in Moscow in May 1972. The agreements blocked the creation of extensive ABM systems but failed to limit bombers, cruise missiles, or multiple independently targeted warheads on single missiles.

Diplomats used the French word ***détente*** to describe the new U.S. relations with China and the Soviet Union. *Détente* means an easing of tensions, not friendship or alliance. It facilitated travel between the United States and China. It allowed U.S. farmers to sell wheat to the Soviets. More broadly, *détente* implied that the United States and China recognized mutual interests in Asia and that the United States acknowledged the Soviet Union as an equal in world affairs. *Détente* made the world safer.

Courting Middle America

Nixon designed domestic policy to help him win reelection. His goal was to solidify his "Middle American" support. The strategy targeted the growing populations of the South and the suburbs, as well as blue-collar voters who were ready to abandon the Democrats for law-and-order Republicans.

The Nixon White House preferred to ignore troubled big cities. Spokesmen announced that the urban crisis was over and dismantled the urban initiatives of Johnson's Great Society, even though such programs as Model Cities had never been given enough money. Instead, Nixon tilted federal assistance to the suburbs. The centerpiece of his **New Federalism** was General Revenue Sharing (1972), which passed federal funds directly to local governments with no limits on use. By 1980, it had transferred more than $18 billion to the states and more than $36 billion to local governments. Revenue sharing was a suburban-aid program. Its no-strings grants supplemented the general funds of every full-service government, whether a city of 2 million or a suburban town of 500.

Nixon pursued the southern strategy through the symbolism of Supreme Court nominations. His first nominees were Clement Haynsworth of Florida and G. Harrold Carswell of Alabama. Although the Senate rejected both as unqualified, the nominations nonetheless gave Nixon a reputation as a champion of the white South. He hoped to move cautiously in enforcing school desegregation, but a task force led by Secretary of Labor George Shultz crafted an approach that allowed substantial desegregation. In this instance, as elsewhere with his domestic policies, Nixon was inflammatory in speeches but moderate in action, increasing the funding of federal civil rights agencies.

Oil, OPEC, and Stagflation

One of the most troublesome domestic issues was inflation. The cost of living began to outpace wages in the late 1960s. Economists saw the situation as a classic example of "demand-pull" inflation, in which too many dollars from government and consumer spending were chasing too few goods and services. One of the causes was LBJ's decision to fight in Vietnam without tax increases until 1968. An income tax cut in 1969, supported by both parties, made the situation worse. Inflation eroded the value of savings and pensions. It also made U.S. goods too expensive for foreign buyers and generated a trade deficit that placed pressures on the international value of the dollar.

In August 1971, Nixon detached the dollar from the gold standard. The Treasury would no longer sell gold at $35 an ounce, a practice that had made the dollar the anchor around which other currencies fluctuated. The dollar could now float in value relative to other currencies, making U.S. exports more competitive but undercutting the nation's ability to lead global economic policy. Nixon took the action without consulting America's allies, even though it triggered drastic readjustments of international markets. It was an example of the political expediency with which he sometimes operated.

The U.S. economy took another hit from inflation in 1973–1974. This time it was "cost-push" inflation, in which a price increase for one key product raises the cost of producing other items. The main cause was the sharp increase in the price of energy, an input to every product and service. Angry at U.S. support for Israel in the Arab-Israeli War of October 1973, Arab nations imposed an embargo on oil exports that lasted from October 1973 to March 1974. The shortages eased when the embargo ended, but the **Organization of Petroleum Exporting Countries (OPEC)** had challenged the ability of the industrial nations to dictate world economic policy.

While Nixon searched for short-term political advantage, underlying problems of the U.S. economy went untreated. After 30 years at the top, the United States could no longer dominate the world economy by itself. The newly found power of OPEC was obvious. Just as important was the surging industrial capacity of Germany and Japan, which now had economies as modern as that of the United States.

FROM THEN TO NOW

Energy Worries

After a generation of postwar prosperity, the United States in the 1970s consumed more energy per person than any other nation. The OPEC oil embargo of 1973–1974 was a wake-up call that hit home in daily life. Gasoline and heating oil became scarce and expensive. Long lines at gas pumps and hurried rationing systems (such as allowing half the nation to fill their gas tanks on odd-numbered days and the other half on even-numbered days) panicked auto-dependent Americans.

Wind power generators near San Diego, among the many wind farms that began to cover windy hillsides across the American West in the new century.

One response was to change personal habits to use less energy. Americans switched off lights, turned down thermostats, and put on sweaters. Consumers compared the efficiency ratings of appliances. Congress required states to enforce a fuel-saving highway speed limit of 55 miles per hour to get federal highway funds and enacted the first fuel economy standards for automobiles. The fuel efficiency of the average new car doubled from 14 miles per gallon in 1973 to 28 miles per gallon by the late 1980s, and more efficient imports captured a third of the U.S. car market by 1980.

A parallel response was to experiment with new energy sources. Oil companies tried to squeeze more petroleum out of abandoned wells and searched for new oil fields in the northern Rockies. Huge strip mining operations tackled coal deposits in isolated areas like Wyoming that had previously been too far from markets. Homeowners put solar panels on their roofs to heat water. The federal government funneled money into energy research as scientists experimented with wind power and solar generation of electricity.

The pressure on oil supplies eased in the 1980s and 1990s. Even as petroleum imports passed domestic production in 1996, many Americans forgot about energy policy until the new century brought new crises—first rolling electrical blackouts in California, then surging gasoline prices from 2006 to the present. The responses would be similar—changes in personal choices like a surge of interest in hybrid automobiles, federal intervention about fuel efficiency, and a boom in alternative energy sources like wind power.

■ What are differences and similarities in the causes of energy price increases between the 1970s and recent years?

PEARSON myhistorylab

From Then to Now Online

Motorists line up for scarce supplies of gasoline in 1979, when political upheaval in Iran created the second energy crisis and gasoline shortage of the 1970s.

29.1 Energy Information Agency, "Petroleum Prices from 1970 to 2006." A compilation of petroleum price movements from the U.S. Department of Energy.

29.2 Jimmy Carter, "The President's Proposed Energy Policy" (April 18, 1977). President Carter used this televised speech to argue for a comprehensive and long-range energy program.

29.3 R. James Woolsey, Amory B. Lovins, and L. Hunter Lovins, "Energy Security It Takes More Than Drilling" (March 29, 2002). Writing in The Christian Science Monitor, energy experts Amory Lovins and Hunter Lovins and former CIA Director James Woolsey argue for combining energy conservation with alternative sources.

Declining rates of saving and investment in industrial capacity seemed to put the United States in danger of following the British road to economic obsolescence and second-level status. Indeed, a new term entered the popular vocabulary in 1971: *Stagflation* was the painful combination of stagnant economic growth, high unemployment, and inflation that matched no one's economic theory but everyone's daily experience.

Americans as Environmentalists

In the turbulent 1970s, Americans found one issue they could agree on. In the 1970s, resource conservation grew into a multifaceted environmental movement. Environmentalism dealt with serious problems. It was broad enough for both scientific experts and activists, for both Republican Richard Nixon and Democrat Jimmy Carter.

After the booming 1950s, Americans had started to pay attention to "pollution," a catchall for the damage that advanced technologies and industrial production did to natural

The first Earth Day in 1970 tapped growing concern about the environment. It helped turn the technical field of pollution control into the broad-based environmental movement.

systems. Rachel Carson's *Silent Spring* in 1962 pushed pollution onto the national agenda. Carson, a well-regarded science writer, described the side effects of DDT and other pesticides on animal life. In her imagined future, spring was silent because all the birds had died of pesticide poisoning. Her book resonated with many suburbanites, who realized that urban sprawl was creating a quiet environmental crisis, providing housing and shopping centers at the cost of bulldozed forests and farms, polluted streams, and smog-choked skies. Other side effects of the industrial economy made banner headlines. An offshore oil well polluted the beaches of Santa Barbara, California, in 1969. Fire danced across the Cuyahoga River in Cleveland when industrial discharges ignited.

Environmentalism gained strength among Americans in 1970. On April 22, 10,000 schools and 20 million other people took part in Earth Day, an occasion first conceived by Wisconsin Senator Gaylord Nelson. Earth Day gained a grassroots following in towns and cities across the country. New York closed Fifth Avenue to automobiles for the day. Companies touted their environmental credentials.

The American establishment had been looking for a safe and respectable crusade to divert the idealism and discontent of the 1960s. Now the mainstream media discovered the ravaged planet. So did a politically savvy president. An expedient proenvironmental stance might attract some of the antiwar constituency. Nixon had already signed the National Environmental Policy Act on January 1, 1970, and later in the year created the **Environmental Protection Agency (EPA)** to enforce environmental laws. The rest of the Nixon administration brought legislation on clean air, clear water, pesticides, hazardous chemicals, and endangered species (see Overview, The Environmental Decades) that made environmental management and protection part of governmental routine. The Carter years brought more attention to environmental cleanup with the Superfund program and the set-aside of huge tracts of land in Alaska for national parks and wildlife refuges.

As Americans became more aware of human-caused environmental hazards, they realized that minority and low-income communities had more than their share of problems. In the Louisiana petrochemical belt along the Mississippi River, African Americans often lived downstream and downwind. Landfills and waste disposal sites were frequently located near minority neighborhoods. In Buffalo, white working-class residents near the Love Canal industrial site discovered in 1978 that an entire neighborhood was built on land contaminated by decades of chemical dumping. Activists sought to understand the health effects and force compensation, paving the way for the Superfund cleanup legislation (see American Views, Grassroots Community Action).

From Dirty Tricks to Watergate

The **Watergate** crisis pivoted on Richard Nixon's character. Despite his solid political standing, Nixon saw enemies everywhere and overestimated their strength. Subordinates learned during his first administration that the president

OVERVIEW

The Environmental Decades

Administration	Focus of Concern	Legislation
Johnson	Wilderness and wildlife	Wilderness Act (1964)
		National Wildlife Refuge System (1966)
		Wild and Scenic Rivers Act (1968)
Nixon	Pollution control and endangered environments	National Environmental Policy Act (1969)
		Environmental Protection Agency (1970)
		Clean Air Act (1970)
		Occupational Safety and Health Act (1970)
		Water Pollution Control Act (1972)
		Pesticide Control Act (1972)
		Coastal Zone Management Act (1972)
		Endangered Species Act (1973)
Ford	Energy and hazardous materials	Toxic Substances Control Act (1976)
		Resource Conservation and Recovery Act (1976)
Carter	Energy and hazardous materials	Energy Policy and Conservation Act (1978)
		Comprehensive Emergency Response, Compensation, and Liability Act (Superfund) (1980)
	Parks and wilderness	Alaska National Interest Lands Conservation Act (1980)

would condone dishonest actions—"dirty tricks"—if they stood to improve his political position. In 1972 and 1973, dirty tricks grew from a scandal into a constitutional crisis when Nixon abused the power of his office to cover up wrongdoing and hinder criminal investigations.

The chain of events that undermined Nixon's presidency started with the **Pentagon Papers.** In his last year as secretary of defense, Robert McNamara had commissioned a report on the U.S. road to Vietnam. The documents showed that the country's leaders had planned to expand the war even while they claimed to be looking for a way out. In June 1971, one of the contributors to the report, Daniel Ellsberg, leaked it to the *New York Times.* Its publication infuriated Nixon.

In response, the White House compiled a list of journalists and politicians who opposed Nixon. As one White House staffer, John Dean, put it, the president's men could then "use the available federal machinery [Internal Revenue Service, FBI] to screw our political enemies." Nixon set up a special investigations unit in the White House. Two former CIA employees, E. Howard Hunt and G. Gordon Liddy, became the chief "plumbers," as the group was known because its job was to prevent leaks of information. The plumbers contributed to an atmosphere of lawlessness in the White House. They

cooked up schemes to embarrass political opponents and ransacked the office of Ellsberg's psychiatrist.

Early in 1972, Hunt went to work for CREEP—the Committee to Re-Elect the President—while Liddy took another position on the presidential staff. CREEP had already raised millions and was hatching plans to undermine Democrats with rumors and pranks. Then, on June 17, 1972, five inept burglars hired with CREEP funds were caught breaking into the Democratic National Committee office in Washington's Watergate apartment building. The people involved knew that an investigation would lead back to the White House. Nixon felt too insecure to ride out what would probably have been a small scandal. Instead, he initiated a coverup. On June 23, he ordered his assistant H. R. Haldeman to warn the FBI off the case with the excuse that national security was involved. Nixon compounded this obstruction of justice by arranging a $400,000 bribe to keep the burglars quiet.

The coverup worked in the short run. As mid-level officials from the Justice Department pursued their investigation, the public lost interest in what looked more like slapstick than a serious crime. Nixon's opponent in the 1972 election was South Dakota Senator George McGovern, an impassioned opponent of the Vietnam War. McGovern was

American Views

Grassroots Community Action

In the 1950s, a major chemical company closed a waste dump in Niagara Falls, New York. The site, known as Love Canal, was soon surrounded by a park, school, and hundreds of modest homes. Residents put up with noxious odors and seepage of chemical wastes until 1978, when they learned that the state health department was concerned about the health effects on small children and pregnant women. Over the next two years, residents battled state and federal bureaucracies and reluctant politicians for accurate information about the risks they faced and then for financial assistance to move from the area (often their homes represented their only savings). In October 1980, President Carter signed a bill to move all of the families permanently from the Love Canal area.

One of the leaders of the grassroots movement was housewife Lois Gibbs. The following excerpts from her story show her increasing sophistication as a community activist, starting by ringing doorbells in 1978 and ending with national television exposure in 1980. Although the Love Canal case itself was unusual, community-based organizations in all parts of the country learned the tactics of effective action in the 1960s and 1970s.

- What public programs in the 1960s and 1970s gave citizens experience in grassroots action?
- How might the Internet change the tactics of community organizing?

Knocking on Doors

I decided to go door-to-door with a petition. It seemed like a good idea to start near the school, to talk to the mothers nearest it. I had already heard that a lot of the residents near the school had been upset about the chemicals for the past couple of years. I thought they might help me. I had never done anything like this....I was afraid a lot of doors would be slammed in my face, that people would think I was some crazy fanatic. But I decided to do it anyway...and knocked on my first door. There was no answer. I just stood there, not knowing what to do. It was an usually warm June day and I was perspiring. I thought: What am I doing here? I must be crazy. People are going to think I am. Go home, you fool! And that's just what I did.

It was one of those times when I had to sit down and face myself. I was afraid of making a fool of myself, I had scared myself, and I had gone home. When I got there, I sat at the kitchen table with my petition in my hand, thinking. Wait. What if people do slam doors in your face? People may think you're crazy. But what's more important—what people think or your child's health? Either you're going to do something or you're going to have to admit you're a coward and not do it....The next day, I went out on my own street to talk to people I knew. It was a little easier to be brave with them. If I could convince people I knew—friends—maybe it would be less difficult to convince others....I went to the back door, as I always did when I visited a neighbor. Each house took about twenty or twenty-five minutes....

Phil Donahue and Political Action

The *Phil Donahue Show* called. They wanted us to appear on their June 18 show. The reaction in the office was different this time, compared to the show in October 1978. In October, everyone was excited. "Phil Donahue—wow!" Now, residents reacted differently. "Donahue. That's great press. Now we'll get the politicians to move!"...Now our people looked at the show as a tool to use in pushing the government to relocate us permanently. By this time we understood how politicians react to public pressure, how to play the political game. We eagerly agreed to go, and found forty other residents to go with us....[After arriving in Chicago] We then planned how we would handle the *Phil Donahue Show*.... We had to get the real issues across. Each resident was assigned an issue. One told of the chromosome tests. Another was to concentrate on her multiple miscarriages.

Another was to ask for telegrams from across the country to the White House in support of permanent relocation. I coached them to get their point in, no matter the question asked. For example, if Donahue asked what you thought of the mayor, and your assignment was to discuss miscarriages, you should answer: "I don't like the mayor because I have had three miscarriages and other health problems, and he won't help us." Or: "My family is sick, and the mayor won't help us. That's why we need people to send telegrams to the White House for permanent relocation."…The residents were great! Each and every one followed through with our plan.

Source: Lois Marie Gibbs, as told to Murray Levine, *Love Canal: My Story* (Albany: State University of New York Press, 1982), pp. 12–13, 161–64.

honest, intelligent, and well to the left of center on such issues as the defense budget and legalization of marijuana. He did not appeal to the white southerners and blue-collar northerners whom Nixon and Agnew were luring from the Democrats. An assassination attempt that took George Wallace out of national politics also helped Nixon win in a landslide.

The coverup began to come apart with the trial of the Watergate burglars in January 1973. Federal Judge John Sirica used the threat of heavy sentences to pressure one burglar into a statement that implied that higher-ups had been involved. Meanwhile, the *Washington Post* was linking Nixon's people to dirty tricks and illegal campaign contributions. The White House scrambled to find a defensible story. White House Counsel John Dean, who coordinated much of the effort, reported to Nixon in March that the scandal and coverup had become a "cancer on the presidency." Nixon was aware of many of the actions that his subordinates had undertaken. He now began to coach people on what they should tell investigators, claimed his staff had lied to him, and tried to set up Dean to take the fall.

In the late spring and early summer, attention shifted to the televised hearings of the Senate's Select Committee on Presidential Campaign Activities. Its chair was Sam Ervin of North Carolina, whose down-home style masked a clever mind. A parade of White House and party officials described their parts in the affair, often accusing each other and revealing the plumbers and the enemies list. The real questions, it became obvious, were what the president knew and when he knew it. It seemed to be John Dean's word against Richard Nixon's.

A bombshell turned the scandal into a constitutional crisis. A mid-level staffer told the committee that Nixon had made tape recordings of his White House conversations. Both the Senate and the Watergate special prosecutor, Archibald Cox, subpoenaed the tapes. Nixon refused to give them up, citing executive privilege and the separation of powers. In late October, after he failed to cut a satisfactory deal, he fired his attorney general and the special prosecutor. This "Saturday-night massacre" caused a storm of protest, and many Americans thought that it proved that Nixon had something to hide. In April 1974, he finally released edited transcripts of the tapes, with foul language deleted and key passages missing; he claimed that his secretary had accidentally erased crucial material. Finally, on July 24, 1974, the U.S.

Supreme Court ruled unanimously that Nixon had to deliver 64 tapes to the new special prosecutor.

Opposition to the president now spanned the political spectrum from Barry Goldwater to liberal Democrats, and Congress began impeachment proceedings. On July 27, the House Judiciary Committee took up the specific charges. Republicans joined Democrats in voting three articles of impeachment: for hindering the criminal investigation of the Watergate break-in, for abusing the power of the presidency by using federal agencies to deprive citizens of their rights, and for ignoring the committee's subpoena for the tapes. Before the full House could vote on the articles of impeachment and send them to the Senate for trial, Nixon delivered the tapes. One of them contained the "smoking gun," direct evidence that Nixon had participated in the coverup on June 23, 1972, and had been lying ever since. On August 8 he announced his resignation, effective the following day.

Watergate was two separate but related stories. On one level, it was about individuals who deceived or manipulated the American people. Nixon and his cronies wanted to win too badly to play by the rules and repeatedly broke the law. Nixon paid for his overreaching ambition with the end of his political career; more than 20 others paid with jail terms. On another level, the crisis was a lesson about the Constitution. The separation of powers allowed Congress and the courts to rein in a president who had spun out of control. The Ervin Committee hearings in 1973 and the House Judiciary Committee proceedings in 1974 were rituals to assure Americans that the system still worked. Nevertheless, the sequence of political events from 1968 to 1974 disillusioned many citizens.

The Ford Footnote

Gerald Ford was the first president who had not been elected as either president or vice president. Ford was Nixon's appointee to replace Spiro Agnew, who had resigned and pleaded no contest to charges of bribery and income tax evasion in 1973 as Watergate was gathering steam. Ford was competent but unimaginative. His first major act was his most controversial—the pardon of Nixon for "any and all crimes" committed while president. Since Nixon had not yet been indicted, the pardon saved him from future prosecution. To many Americans, the act looked like a payoff. Ford insisted that the purpose was to clear the decks so that the nation could think about the future rather than the past. He also offered clemency to thousands of draft resisters.

Ford's administration presided over the collapse of South Vietnam in 1975, but elsewhere in the world, *détente* continued. U.S. diplomats joined the Soviet Union and 30 other European nations in the capital of Finland to sign the **Helsinki Accords.** The agreements called for increased commerce between the Eastern and Western blocs and for human-rights guarantees. They also legitimized the national boundaries that had been set in eastern Europe in 1945.

At home, the federal government did little new during Ford's two and a half years in office. The economy slid into recession, unemployment climbed above 10 percent, inflation diminished the value of savings and wages. Ford beat back Ronald Reagan for the Republican presidential nomination, but he was clearly vulnerable.

His Democratic opponent was a political enigma. James Earl Carter, Jr., had been a navy officer, a farmer, and the governor of Georgia. He was one of several new-style politicians who transformed southern politics in the 1970s. Carter and the others left race-baiting behind to talk like modern New Dealers, emphasizing that whites and blacks both needed better schools and economic growth. He appealed to Democrats as someone who could reassemble LBJ's political coalition and return the South to the Democratic Party. In his successful campaign, Carter presented himself as an alternative to party hacks and Washington insiders (see Map 29–3).

Jimmy Carter: Idealism and Frustration in the White House

Johnson and Nixon had both thought of themselves as outsiders even after nearly 30 years in national politics. Carter was the real thing, a stranger to the national policy establishment that revolves around Washington think tanks and New York law firms. As an outsider, Carter had one great advantage: freedom from the narrow mindset of experts who talk only to each other. However, he lacked both the knowledge of key political players and the experience to resolve legislative gridlock.

The new president's personal background compounded his problems. Intellectuals found this devout Baptist hard to fathom. Labor leaders and political bosses did not know what to make of a farmer from the deep South. The national press was baffled. It was only after his presidency, when Americans took a clear look at Carter's moral character, that they decided they liked what they saw.

Even had he been the most skilled of politicians, however, Carter took office with little room to maneuver. Watergate bequeathed him a powerful and self-satisfied Congress and a combative press. OPEC oil producers, Islamic fundamentalists, and Soviet generals followed their own agendas. The American people themselves were fractionalized and quarrelsome, uneasy with the new advocacy of equality for women, uncertain as a nation whether they

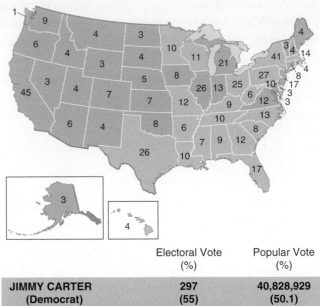

	Electoral Vote (%)	Popular Vote (%)
JIMMY CARTER **(Democrat)**	**297** **(55)**	**40,828,929** **(50.1)**
Gerald R. Ford (Republican)	240 (45)	39,148,940 (47.9)
Ronald Reagan	1	–
Other candidates (McCarthy, Independent; Libertarian)	–	1,575,459 (2.1)

MAP 29–3   The Election of 1976
Georgian Jimmy Carter ran in 1976 as an outsider to Washington politics. He capitalized on a reputation as a progressive governor and on the Watergate scandal, which had damaged the Republican Party.

shared the same values and goals. Carter's attempt to govern like a preacher, with appeals to moral principles, did more to reveal divisions than establish common ground.

Carter, Energy, and the Economy

Carter was refreshingly low-key. After his inauguration, he walked from the Capitol to the White House, as Jefferson had. He preferred sweaters to tuxedos and signed official documents "Jimmy." He tended to tell the public what he thought rather than what pollsters said the people wanted to hear.

Carter's approach to politics reflected his training as an engineer. He was analytical, logical, and given to breaking a problem into its component parts. He was better at working with details than at defining broad goals. He filled his cabinet with experts rather than with political operators. He failed to understand the importance of personalities and was uncomfortable with compromise. He did not seem to understand the basic rules of Washington politics. For example, he and his cabinet officers developed policies and made appointments without consulting key congressional committee chairs.

The biggest domestic problem remained the economy, which slid into another recession in 1978. Another jump in oil prices helped make 1979 and 1980 the worst years for inflation in the postwar era. Interest rates surged past 20 percent as the Federal Reserve tried to reduce inflation by squeezing business and consumer credit. Carter himself was a fiscal conservative whose impulse was to cut federal spending. This course worsened unemployment and alienated liberal Democrats, who wanted to revive the Great Society.

Carter simultaneously proposed a comprehensive energy policy. He asked Americans to make energy conservation the moral equivalent of war—to accept individual sacrifices for the common good. Congress created the Department of Energy but refused to raise taxes on oil and natural gas to reduce consumption. However, the Energy Policy and Conservation Act (1978) did encourage alternative energy sources to replace foreign petroleum. Big oil companies poured billions of dollars into western Colorado to squeeze a petroleum substitute from shale. Solar energy research prospered.

However, antinuclear activism blocked one obvious alternative to fossil fuels. The antinuclear movement had started with concern about the ability of the Atomic Energy Commission to monitor the safety of nuclear-power plants and about the disposal of spent fuel rods. In the late 1970s, activists staged sit-ins at the construction sites of nuclear plants. A near-meltdown at the Three Mile Island nuclear plant in Pennsylvania in March 1979 stalemated efforts to expand nuclear-power capacity. Utilities were soon worrying about the cost of shutting down and dismantling their old nuclear plants rather than trying to build new ones.

When the OPEC price hikes undermined the inflation-fighting effort in the summer of 1979, Carter told the nation that a "moral and spiritual crisis" demanded a rebirth of the American spirit. The public did not know whether he had preached a sermon or given them marching orders. A cabinet reshuffle a few days later was supposed to show that he was firmly in charge. Instead, the media painted the president as inconsistent and incompetent.

Carter's problems were both personal and structural. In effect, opinion leaders had decided by 1979 that he was not capable of leading the nation and then interpreted every action as confirming that belief. There was also the practical problem of trying to hold the loyalty of Democratic liberals while attracting middle-of-the-road voters.

Closed Factories and Failed Farms

Ford and Carter both faced massive problems of economic transition that undercut their efforts to devise effective government programs. Here is how novelist John Updike described the fictional city of Brewer, Pennsylvania, at the start of the 1970s:

> Railroads and coal made Brewer. Everywhere in this city…structures speak of expended energy. Great shapely stacks that have not issued smoke for half a century.… The old textile plants given over to discount clothing outlets teeming with a gimcrack cheer of banners FACTORY FAIR and slogans Where a Dollar Is Still a Dollar.… All

this had been cast up in the last century by what now seem giants, in an explosion of iron and brick still preserved intact in this city where the sole new buildings are funeral parlors and government offices.

Updike's Brewer was like dozens of specialized industrial cities that fell behind a changing economic world in the 1970s and 1980s. Industrial decay stalked such "gritty cities" as Allentown, Pennsylvania; Trenton, New Jersey; and Gary, Indiana. Communities whose workers had made products in high volume for a mass market found that technological revolutions made them obsolete. When radial tires replaced bias-ply tires, Akron rubber workers paid the price. Merchants who replaced mechanical cash registers with electronic models left Dayton with block after block of outmoded factories. Asian steelmakers undercut the aging mills of Pittsburgh and Birmingham. Critics renamed the old manufacturing region of the Northeast and Middle West the Rustbelt in honor of its abandoned factories.

Stories of **deindustrialization** were similar in small cities like Springfield, Ohio, and large cities like Cleveland. Springfield lost 10,000 manufacturing jobs and 4,000 people during the 1970s, suffered unemployment of 17 percent, and needed $30 million in public subsidies to keep its largest factory going in 1982. Cleveland had built a century of prosperity on oil refining, steel, and metalworking; the metropolitan area had grown from 1.3 million in 1940 to 2.1 million in 1970. In the 1970s, however, it lost 165,000 people. As high-paying jobs in unionized industries disappeared, sagging income undermined small businesses and neighborhoods. Falling tax revenue brought the city to the verge of bankruptcy in 1978; bankers forced public service cuts and tax increases, which meant further job losses.

Outmoded facilities and foreign competition undermined the competitiveness of much of the nation's heavy manufacturing in the 1970s and 1980s. Many older factories were closed and abandoned, lending the name Rustbelt to the old industrial heartland.

Plant closures were only one facet of business efforts to increase productivity by substituting machinery for employees. Between 1947 and 1977, American steelmakers doubled output while cutting their workforce from 600,000 to 400,000. High interest rates and a strong dollar made U.S. exports too expensive and foreign imports cheap, forcing American manufacturers to cut costs or perish.

Despite the despairing headlines, some older industries and their workers found new roles in the sink-or-swim environment of technological and international competition. Buffalo, New York, lost much of its steel industry but retained smaller and more flexible factories making diverse products. The auto industry went through a similar cycle of crisis and response. Prosperity in the 1950s had led automobile executives to believe that they knew how to manipulate U.S. consumers. Booming imports of well-made Toyotas and Hondas and customer demand for smaller cars destroyed their complacency in the fuel-short 1970s. In response, Ford, Chrysler, and finally General Motors tried to remake themselves on the Japanese model as lean and flexible manufacturers. They cast off old plants, workers, and executives, started over, often in new locations, and forced Japanese companies to shift production to U.S. localities and workers.

Parallel to the decline of heavy industry was the continuing transformation of American agriculture from small family enterprises to corporate agribusinesses. Agriculture was a national success story in the aggregate, but one accompanied by many human and environmental costs. The early 1970s brought an unexpected boom in farming. Crop failures and food shortages around the world in 1972 and 1973 expanded markets and pushed up prices for U.S. farm products. For a few years, agriculture looked like the best way for the United States to offset the high cost of imported oil. But the boom was over by the 1980s, when global commodity prices slumped. Farmers found themselves with debts they could not cover. Farm bankruptcies in Iowa reached levels unseen since the 1930s, and rock stars staged "Farm Aid" concerts to raise money to fend off foreclosures.

The boom of the 1970s was thus a brief interruption in the long-term transformation of U.S. agriculture. The number of farms slid from 4 million in 1960 to 2.4 million in 1980 and 1.9 million in 2000. Many farmers sold out willingly, glad to escape from drudgery and financial insecurity. Others could not compete in an agricultural system that favored large-scale production by demanding large amounts of capital for equipment and fertilizer. By 2000, fewer than 2 percent of American workers made their living from farming.

Building a Cooperative World

Despite troubles on the home front, Carter's first two years brought foreign-policy successes that reflected a new vision of a multilateral world. As a relative newcomer to international politics, Carter was willing to work with African, Asian, and Latin American nations on a basis of mutual respect. Carter appointed Andrew Young—an African American from Georgia with long experience in the civil rights movement—

Egyptian President Anwar al-Sadat, U.S. President Jimmy Carter, and Israeli Prime Minister Menachem Begin share a symbolic handshake after the signing of a peace treaty between Egypt and Israel on August 26, 1979. The treaty codified the historic agreement that the leaders had hammered out at Camp David, Maryland, in September 1978.

as ambassador to the United Nations, where he worked effectively to build bridges to third-world nations. Carter convinced the Senate in 1978 to approve treaties to transfer control of the Panama Canal to Panama by 2000, removing a sore point in relations with Latin America.

Carter's moral convictions were responsible for a new concern with human rights around the globe. He criticized the Soviet Union for prohibiting free speech and denying its citizens the right to emigrate, angering Soviet leaders, who did not expect the human rights clauses of the Helsinki Accords to be taken seriously. Carter was also willing to criticize some (but not all) American allies. He withheld economic aid from South Africa, Guatemala, Chile, and Nicaragua, which had long records of human rights abuses. In Nicaragua, the change in policy helped left-wing Sandinista rebels topple the Somoza dictatorship.

The triumph of the new foreign policy was the **Camp David Agreement** between Egypt and Israel. Carter risked his reputation and credibility in September 1978 to bring Egyptian President Anwar al-Sadat and Israeli Prime Minister Menachem Begin together at Camp David, the presidential retreat. He refused to admit failure and dissuaded the two leaders from walking out. A formal treaty was signed in Washing-

The Iran hostage crisis reflected intense anti-American feelings in Iran and provoked an equally bitter anti-Iranian reaction in the United States. Fifty-two of the more than 60 U.S. embassy employees first seized were held for 444 days, giving the United States a painful lesson about the limits on its ability to influence events around the world.

ton on March 26, 1979. The pact normalized relations between Israel and its most powerful neighbor and led to Israel's withdrawal from the Sinai Peninsula. It was a vital prelude to further progress toward Arab-Israeli peace in the mid-1990s.

New Crises Abroad

The Cold War was a noxious weed that détente trimmed but did not uproot. In the last two years of Carter's administration, it sprang back to life around the globe and smothered the promise of a new foreign policy. The Soviets ignored the human-rights provisions of the Helsinki Accords. Soviet advisers or Cuban troops intervened in African civil wars. At home, Cold Warriors who had never accepted détente found it easier to attack Carter than Nixon.

The failure of SALT II. Carter inherited negotiations for SALT II—a strategic arms-limitation treaty that would have reduced both the U.S. and Soviet nuclear arsenals— from the Ford administration. SALT II met stiff resistance in the Senate. Opponents claimed it would create a "window of vulnerability" in the 1980s that would invite the Soviets to launch a nuclear first strike. Carter tried to counter criticism by stepping up defense spending, starting a buildup that would accelerate under Ronald Reagan.

Hopes for SALT II vanished on December 24, 1979, when Soviet troops entered Afghanistan, a technically neutral Muslim nation on the southern border of the Soviet Union. A pro-Soviet government had fallen into factional strife, while tribespeople, unhappy with modernization, were mounting increasing resistance. One of the factions invited intervention by the Soviets, who quickly installed a client government. The situation resembled the U.S. involvement in South Vietnam. Similar, too, was the inability of Soviet forces to suppress the Afghan guerrillas, who had American weapons and controlled the mountains. In the end, it took the Soviets a decade to find a way out.

The Iranian Hostage Crisis. The final blow to Carter's foreign policy came in Iran. Since 1953, the United States had strongly backed Iran's monarch, Shah Reza Pahlevi. The shah modernized Iran's economy, but his feared secret police jailed and tortured political opponents. U.S. aid and oil revenues helped him build a large army, but the Iranian middle class despised his authoritarianism, and Muslim fundamentalists opposed the Westernizing influence of modernization. A revolution toppled the shah at the start of 1979.

The upheaval installed a nominally democratic government, but the Ayatollah Ruhollah Khomeini, a Muslim cleric who hated the United States, exercised real power. Throughout 1979, Iran grew increasingly anti-American. After the United States allowed the exiled shah to seek medical treatment in New York, a mob stormed the U.S. embassy in Tehran on November 4, 1979, and took more than 60 Americans hostage. They demanded that Carter surrender the shah. Television brought pictures of blindfolded hostages and anti-American mobs burning effigies of Uncle Sam and wrapping American flags around garbage. The administration tried economic pressure and diplomacy, but Khomeini had no desire for accommodation. When Iran announced in April 1980 that the hostages would remain in the hands of the militants rather than be transferred to the government, Carter ordered an airborne rescue. Even a perfectly managed effort would have been difficult. The hostages were held in the heart of a city of 4 million hostile Iranians, hundreds of miles from the nearest aircraft carrier and thousands of miles from U.S. bases. Hampered by lack of coordination among the military services, the attempt turned into a fiasco that added to the national embarrassment and a feeling of powerlessness. The United States and Iran finally reached agreement on the eve of the 1980 election. The hostages gained their freedom after 444 days, at the moment Ronald Reagan took office as the new president.

The hostage crisis consumed Jimmy Carter the way that Vietnam had consumed Lyndon Johnson. It gripped the public and stalemated other issues. For weeks, Carter limited public appearances to statements in the White House Rose Garden. The public blamed him for problems literally beyond his control, for failing to use military force, and then for using it and failing. Carter's tragedy was that "his" Iranian crisis was the fruit of policies hatched by the Eisenhower administration and pursued by every president since then, all of whom had overlooked the shah's despotic government because of his firm anti-Communism.

After 30 years in which the United States had viewed the entire world as a Cold War battlefield, Carter was willing to accept the developing world on its own terms. His human-rights efforts showed that evangelical religious convictions could be tied to progressive aims. He wanted to avoid supporting oppressive regimes, but the past was too burdensome. Iranian rage at past policies of the sort Carter hoped to change destroyed his ability to direct a new course. After he left office, his continuing work for peace and humanitarian efforts would earn him the Nobel Peace Prize in 2002.

Conclusion

In the mid-1970s, Americans encountered real limits to national capacity. From 1945 to 1973, they had enjoyed remarkable prosperity. That ended in 1974. Long lines at gas stations showed that prosperity was fragile. Cities and regions felt the costs of obsolete industries. Environmental damage caused many Americans to reconsider the goal of economic expansion.

The nation also had to recognize that it could not run the world. American withdrawal from Vietnam in 1973 and the collapse of the South Vietnamese government in 1975 were defeats; the United States ended up with little to show for a long and painful war. SALT I stabilized the arms race, but it also recognized that the Soviet Union was an equal. The American nuclear arsenal might help deter a third world war, but it could not prevent the seizure of hostages in Iran.

These challenges came amid deep economic and social changes in the United States. The ways Americans made their livings and the range of opportunities they faced were in flux. The nation finished the 1970s more egalitarian than it had been in the early 1960s but also more divided. More citizens had the opportunity to advance economically and to seek political power, but there were deepening fissures between social liberals and cultural conservatives, old and new views about roles for women, rich and poor, whites and blacks. In 1961, John Kennedy had called on his fellow citizens to "bear any burden, pay any price" to defend freedom. By 1980, the nation had neither the economic capacity to pay any price nor the unity to agree on what burdens it should bear.

Review Questions

1. Why did the United States fail to achieve its objectives in Vietnam? What factors limited President Johnson's freedom of action there? How did the Tet Offensive affect U.S. policy? How did antiwar protests in the United States influence national policy?

2. How did racial relations change between 1965 and 1970? What were the relationships between the civil rights movement and minority separatism? What were the similarities and differences between African American, Latino, and Native American activism?

3. In what ways was 1968 a pivotal year for U.S. politics and society? How was it influenced by global events?

4. What were the implications of *détente?* Why did the Cold War reappear in the late 1970s? How and why did U.S. influence over the rest of the world change during the 1970s?

5. How did Richard Nixon's political strategy respond to the growth of the South and West? How did it respond to the shift of population from central cities to suburbs?

6. How did the backgrounds of Presidents Johnson, Nixon, and Carter shape their successes and failures as national leaders?

7. What political and constitutional issues were at stake in the Watergate scandal? How did it change American politics?

8. Why was the space race important for the United States? How did it strengthen the alliance between American science, government, and industry?

Key Terms

American Indian Movement (AIM) (p. 832)

Baker v. Carr (p. 833)

Black Panthers (p. 831)

Black Power (p. 830)

Camp David Agreement (p. 846)

Counterculture (p. 825)

Deindustrialization (p. 845)

Détente (p. 838)

Environmental Protection Agency (EPA) (p. 840)

Free Speech Movement (FSM) (p. 825)

Helsinki Accords (p. 844)

Model Cities Program (p. 825)

Nation of Islam (p. 830)

New Federalism (p. 838)

Nixon Doctrine (p. 837)

Organization of Petroleum Exporting Countries (Opec) (p. 838)

Pentagon Papers (p. 841)

Search and destroy (p. 821)

Selective Service System (p. 823)

Stonewall Rebellion (p. 829)

Strategic Arms Limitation Treaty (SALT) (p. 838)

Students for a Democratic Society (SDS) (p. 824)

Swann v. Charlotte-Mecklenburg Board of Education (p. 833)

Watergate (p. 840)

Recommended Reading

Appy, Christian. *Patriots: The Vietnam War Remembered from All Sides* (2003). Summarizes interviews with American and Vietnamese officials and veterans.

Caute, David. *Year of the Barricades* (1988). Tour the events of 1968 on both sides of the Atlantic.

Emerson, Gloria. *Winners and Losers* (1976). The impact of the war in Vietnam on American society is told through the stories of individuals changed by the war.

Farber, David. *Chicago '68* (1988); *Medium Cool* (1969), directed by Haskell Wexler. Farber's book contrasts the perspectives and language of city officials and protesters.

Wexler's film captures the tension of Chicago in the hot summer through the eyes of a reporter.

Halberstam, David. *October 1964* (1994). Halberstam uses the baseball season of 1964 and the World Series between the St. Louis Cardinals and New York Yankees to encapsulate the impact of changing racial relations on American society.

Karnow, Stanley. *Vietnam: A History* (1983). This comprehensive history of American involvement in Vietnam details the collapse of French rule and early U.S. relations with Vietnam.

Where to Learn More

■ **Lyndon B. Johnson National Historical Park, Johnson City, Texas.**   Johnson's ranch, southwest of Austin, gives visitors a feeling for the open landscape in which Johnson spent his early years. www.nps.gov/lypo

■ **Vietnam Veterans Memorial, Washington, DC.**   A simple wall engraved with the names of the nation's Vietnam War dead is testimony to one of the nation's most divisive wars. www.nps.gov/vive

■ **Richard Nixon Library and Birthplace, Yorba Linda, California.**   Exhibits trace Nixon's political career and related world events with a sympathetic interpretation. www.nixonfoundation.org/index.shtml

■ **Titan Missile Museum, Green Valley, Arizona.**   The Green Valley complex near Tucson held 18 Titan missiles. They were deactivated after SALT I, and the complex is now open to visitors. www.pimaair.org/titan_01.htm.

Study Resources

For study resources for this chapter, go to www.myhistorylab.com and choose *The American Journey*. You will find a wealth of study and review material for this chapter, including pre- and post-tests, customized study plan, key term review flash cards, interactive map and document activities, and documents for analysis.

Freeway traffic near San Jose, California reflects the development of the Silicon Valley electronics industry, the ongoing suburban trend, and the continued shift of population and economic activity to the Sunbelt region of the West and South.

The Reagan Revolution and a Changing World

30
1981–1992

The Khmer Rouge marched into the city [Phnom Penh, the capital of Cambodia], dressed in black. Young Khmer Rouge [Marxist revolutionary] soldiers, eight or ten years old, were dragging their rifles, which were taller than them. The whole city, more than two million people was forced out of their homes into the streets. My family walked until we reached Mao Tse-Tung Boulevard, the main boulevard in Phnom Penh. All the population of the city was gathered there. The Khmer Rouge were telling everyone to leave the city.

Although my two middle children were safe in France, my oldest and youngest daughters were close be-side me. Parika was only seven. Mealy, who was nineteen, carried her infant son. I kept my children huddled together. As soon as a parent let go, a child would be lost in the huge crowd. And the Khmer Rouge kept ordering everybody, "You must go forward." They shot their guns in the air. Even during the middle of the night the procession was endless. The Khmer Rouge kept shooting and we kept moving forward.

Recently I saw the movie *Doctor Zhivago*, about the Russian Revolution. If you compare that to what happened in Phnom Penh, the movie is only on a very small scale. Even *Killing Fields* only gives you part of the idea of

851

what happened in Cambodia. The reality was much more incredible.

Each night, when we came back to the village from working in the fields, Mom would say, "Children, let's all go to sleep." She would quietly warn me that the wood had eyes and ears. She'd say, "It's nine o'clock now. Go to sleep. There is nothing else to do but work. All the men are gone in our family." Mom was actually saying for the Khmer Rouge spies to hear, "They are only girls. Don't kill them. We are the only members left of the family." We were lying to them about our identity. It was a horrible game.

If you hid your identity, that meant you wanted your past forgotten. We had changed from people who were intellectual, who used to think independently. You became humiliated, allowed to live only as a slave. We were accepted into the United States thanks to my husband's military service. My daughters and I flew to the United States on July 4, 1979. As we landed, I thought, "This is real freedom."

I've found that America is a country where people have come from all over the world. You do your job, you get paid like anybody else, and you're accepted. But Cambodians I know in France, like my sister, feel differently. People are not accepted if they are not French.

But in America you're part of the melting pot. In 1983, I came to Los Angeles for my daughter Monie's wedding. I decided to stay. Long Beach has the largest concentration of Cambodians in the country. I called the community center in Long Beach. They said they had no job openings. So I decided to get involved in running a store. Donut shops are very American.

All that refugees have is our work, our dreams. Do I still hurt from what happened in the past? When I opened my mouth to tell you my story, I don't know where my tears came from. My daughters don't like to talk about the past in Cambodia. They want to forget and think about their future. They ask me why I would talk about the past with anybody. I said, "The past cannot be erased from my memory."

Celia Noup, in Al Santoli, *New Americans: An Oral History* (New York, 1988).

myhistorylab

Personal Journeys Online

- Jubilee Lau, "Chinese and Proud of It," 1996. From Hong Kong to Idaho in the 1980s.
- Richard Rodriguez, Hunger of Memory, 1982. Learning English in an immigrant household.
- Ana Cabellero, 1980s. Mexican American Generations in El Paso. Interview in Al Santoli, *New Americans*, 1988.

Celia Noup taught school for 20 years in Cambodia, which borders on South Vietnam. In 1975, after a long civil war, the Communist Khmer Rouge insurgents took over Cambodia's capital, Phnom Penh, and forced its inhabitants into the countryside to work in the fields. Four years later, Noup managed to make her way to a refugee camp in neighboring Thailand and then to the United States. Here she joined hundreds of thousands of other refugees who arrived in the later 1970s and 1980s from war-devastated nations such as Cambodia, Vietnam, Laos,

KEY TOPICS

◆ Economic and social change during the Reagan administration

◆ The changing balance of American regions

◆ The rise of conservative thought

◆ The collapse of the Soviet Union and the end of the Cold War

◆ Instability and war in the Middle East

◆ Changes in the legal standing of women

◆ Conflict over family values and religious beliefs

Ethiopia, and Afghanistan. Within a decade, she was working from 5:00 A.M. to 7:00 P.M. in her own donut shop near the Los Angeles airport and worrying about helping her children buy houses.

Celia Noup's life shows some of the ways that new waves of immigration from Asia, Latin America, and Africa have changed the United States over the last generation. Immigrants fueled economic growth in the 1980s and 1990s with their labor and their drive to succeed in business. They revitalized older neighborhoods in cities from coast to coast and changed the ethnic mix of major cities. And they created new racial tensions that found their way into national political debates about immigration and into open conflict in places such as Miami and Los Angeles.

Noup's story is also a reminder of the drawn-out consequences of the U.S. involvement in Vietnam and the long shadow of the Cold War. The Cambodian civil war was fueled by reactions to the Vietnamese war and the U.S. invasion of Cambodia in 1969. American refugee policy was humanitarian but also political, opening the door to people fleeing Communist regimes but holding it shut against refugees from right-wing dictatorships. In Washington, foreign policy decisions in the 1980s started with the desire of a new administration to reaffirm American toughness after failures in Vietnam and ended with the astonishing evaporation of the Cold War.

By the end of Ronald Reagan's presidency (1981–1989), new rules governed domestic affairs as well as international relations. Since World War II, politics had followed a well-thumbed script. Lessons about full employment and social services that were accepted in 1948 still applied in 1968 or 1972. In the 1980s, however, Americans

CHRONOLOGY

1973	*Roe v. Wade:* Supreme Court strikes down state laws banning abortion in the first trimester of pregnancy.
1980	Ronald Reagan is elected president.
1981	Economic Recovery and Tax Act, reducing personal income tax rates, is passed.
	Reagan breaks strike by air traffic controllers.
	AIDS is recognized as a new disease.
1982	Nuclear freeze movement peaks.
	United States begins to finance Contra rebels against the Sandinista government in Nicaragua.
	Equal Rights Amendment fails to achieve ratification.
1983	241 Marines are killed by a terrorist bomb in Beirut, Lebanon.
	Strategic Defense Initiative introduced.
	United States invades Grenada.
1984	Reagan wins reelection.
1985	Mikhail Gorbachev initiates economic and political reforms in the Soviet Union.
1986	Tax Reform Act is adopted.
1987	Congress holds hearings on the Iran-Contra scandal.
	Reagan and Gorbachev sign the Intermediate Nuclear Force treaty.
1988	George H. W. Bush is elected president.
1989	Communist regimes in eastern Europe collapse; Germans tear down Berlin Wall.
	Financial crisis forces federal bailout of many savings and loans.
	United States invades Panama to capture General Manuel Noriega.
1990	Iraq invades Kuwait; and United States sends forces to the Persian Gulf.
	West Germany and East Germany reunite.
	Americans with Disabilities Act is adopted.
1991	Persian Gulf War: Operation Desert Storm drives the Iraqis from Kuwait.
	Soviet Union dissolves into independent nations.
	Strategic Arms Reduction Treaty (START) is signed.
1992	Acquittal of officers accused of beating Rodney King triggers Los Angeles riots.

decided to reverse the growth of federal government responsibilities that had marked both Republican and Democratic administrations since the 1930s. By the 1990s, the center of U.S. politics had shifted substantially to the right, and even a liberal Democrat like Bill Clinton would sound like an Eisenhower Republican.

The backdrop to the political changes were massive readjustments in the American economy that began in the 1970s with the decline of heavy industry and then continued to shift employment from factory jobs to service jobs in the 1980s (Celia Noup's small shop was part of the service economy). The ideology of unregulated markets celebrated economic success and made "yuppies," or young urban professionals, the center of media attention; some of the yuppies probably grabbed a donut on their way to catch a flight from Los Angeles to New York to help close a deal. But behind the lifestyle stories was a troubling reality: a widening gap between the rich and poor. The result by 1992 was a nation that was much more secure in the world than it had been in 1980, but also more divided against itself.

Reagan's Domestic Revolution

Political change began in 1980, when Ronald Reagan and running his mate, George H.W. Bush, rode American discontent to a decisive victory in the presidential election (see Map 30–1). Building on a conservative critique of American policies and developing issues that Jimmy Carter had placed on the national agenda, Reagan presided over revolutionary changes in U.S. government and policies. He was a "Teflon president" who managed to take credit for successes but avoid blame for problems, and he rolled to a landslide reelection in 1984 and set the stage for George Bush's victory in 1988. The consequences of his two terms included an altered role for government, powerful but selective economic growth, and a shift of domestic politics away from bread-and-butter issues toward moral or lifestyle concerns.

An unresolved question is whether Ronald Reagan planned an economic revolution or simply presided over changes initiated by others. Most memoirs by White House insiders suggest the latter; so do journalists who titled books about the Reagan administration *Sleepwalking through History, The Acting President,* and *The Role of a Lifetime.* Even if Reagan was acting out a role scripted by others, however, his policies moved forward, and he was a hit at the polling places. Americans, worried about inflation at home and declining power abroad, elected Reagan by voting *against* Jimmy Carter in 1980, but they enthusiastically voted *for* Reagan in 1984.

Reagan's Majority

Ronald Reagan reinvented himself several times on his unusual journey to the White House. A product of small-town

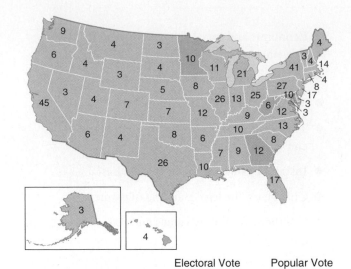

	Electoral Vote (%)	Popular Vote (%)
RONALD REAGAN (Republican)	**489** **(91)**	**43,201,220** **(50.9)**
Jimmy Carter (Democrat)	49 (9)	34,913,332 (41.2)
John B. Anderson (Independent)	–	5,581,379 (6.6)
Other candidates (Libertarian)	–	921,299 (1.1)

MAP 30–1   The Election of 1980
Ronald Reagan won in a landslide in 1980. Independent candidate John Anderson took more votes from Jimmy Carter than from Reagan, but Reagan's personal magnetism was a powerful political force. His victory confirmed the shift of the South to the Republican Party.

Illinois, he succeeded in Hollywood in the late 1930s as a romantic lead actor while adopting the liberal politics common at the time. After World War II, he moved rapidly to the political right as a spokesman for big business. For several years, he traveled the country under the sponsorship of the General Electric Company, giving a standard speech that extolled the virtues of free enterprise. He entered politics with a rousing conservative speech at the 1964 Republican convention and then accepted the invitation of wealthy California Republicans to run for governor in 1966. In two terms in that office, he offered little formal leadership but spoke for a state and then a nation that were drifting toward more conservative values and expectations.

With a common touch that made him a favorite for a sizable segment of the public, Reagan tapped into the nostalgia for a simpler America. Although he was 69 when elected, his status as a movie and television personality made him seem up-to-date. His Hollywood background made it easy for him to use popular films to make his points. He once threatened to veto legislation by challenging Congress with Clint Eastwood's "Make my day." Many blockbuster movies reinforced two of Reagan's messages. One was the importance of direct

Ronald Reagan and his wife, Nancy, celebrate Reagan's inauguration as president.

confrontation with bad guys, ranging from terrorists (*Die Hard*) to drug dealers (*Lethal Weapon*). The second was the incompetence of government bureaucracies, whose elitist mistakes could only be set right by tough individuals like the movie heroes Dirty Harry Callahan and John Rambo.

Some of Reagan's most articulate support came from anti-Communist stalwarts of both parties, who feared that the United States was losing influence in the world. Despite Jimmy Carter's tough actions in 1979 and 1980 and increased defense spending, such conservatives had not trusted him to do enough. The inability to free the hostages in Iran grated. The Panama Canal and SALT II treaties seemed to give away American power. Soviet military buildup, charged the critics, was creating a "window of vulnerability," a dangerous period when the Soviet Union might threaten the United States with a first strike by nuclear weapons.

Other Reagan voters directed their anger at government bureaucracies. Wealthy entrepreneurs from the fast-growing South and West believed that Nixon-era federal offices, such as the Environmental Protection Agency and the Occupational Safety and Health Administration, were choking their businesses in red tape. Many of these critics had amassed new fortunes in oil, real estate, and retailing and hated the taxes that funded social programs.

Christian conservatives worried that social activists were using the federal courts to alter traditional values. Jimmy Carter, a member of the Southern Baptist church, had won a clear majority among white evangelical voters in 1976, but Reagan's contrasting position on school prayer and abortion gave him the edge in 1980 and made him the overwhelming preference of conservative Christian voters in 1984.

In many ways, the two groups were mismatched. Christian moralists had little in common with the high-rolling hedonists and Hollywood tycoons with whom Reagan rubbed shoulders. But they shared a deep distrust of the federal establishment.

Foreign policy activists and opponents of big government would have been unable to elect Reagan without disaffected blue-collar and middle-class voters who deserted the Democrats. Reagan's campaign hammered on the question "Are you better off than you were four years ago?" Democrats faced a special dilemma with the deepening tension between working-class white voters and black voters. They needed both groups to win but found white blue-collar voters deeply alienated by affirmative action and busing for school integration. When pollsters read white Detroiters a statement from Robert Kennedy that called on Americans to recognize special obligations to black citizens who had endured racial discrimination, responses were vehement: "I can't go along with that!" "That's bull!" The same sorts of voters worried about inflation and blamed their difficulties on runaway government spending.

A further Democratic challenge was Ronald Reagan's personal appeal. The new president won over many Americans by surviving a 1981 assassination attempt in fine spirits. Reagan's popularity compounded the Democrats' inability to excite younger voters. The mid-1980s consistently showed that roughly two-thirds of people in their twenties and early thirties were choosing the Republicans as the party of energy and new ideas, leaving the Democrats to the middle-aged and elderly.

In the election of 1984, Democrats sealed their fate by nominating Walter Mondale, who had been vice president under Carter. Mondale was earnest, honest, and dull. Reagan ran on the theme "It's Morning in America," with the message that a new age of pride and prosperity had begun. Mondale assumed that Americans cared enough about the exploding federal deficit that Reagan's defense spending had produced to accept an across-the-board tax increase. With the economy growing and inflation now in check, most voters did not want Mondale to remind them of long-range financial realities, and Reagan won reelection with 98 percent of the electoral votes. His election confirmed that the American public found conservative ideas increasingly attractive.

The New Conservatism

Reagan's approach to public policy drew on conservative intellectuals who offered a coherent critique of the New Deal–New Frontier approach to U.S. government. Some of the leading figures were journalists and academics who had embraced the ideas of the "vital center" a generation earlier (see Chapter 27). Now they feared that the antiwar movement had undermined the anti-Communist stance and that social changes were corrupting mainstream values. *Commentary* magazine became a platform for these combative neoconservative arguments. *The Public Interest* was a new magazine for conservative or skeptical academic writers.

Downsizing the Great Society.   Worries about big government permeated the critique of domestic policy. Edward

As the movie character John Rambo, actor Sylvester Stallone in the early 1980s gave voice to American frustrations with the country's place in the world. The Rambo movies clearly distinguished the good guys from the bad guys and suggested that stronger determination could have brought victory in Vietnam.

Banfield's radical ideas about the failures of the Great Society set the tone of the neoconservative analysis. In *The Unheavenly City* (1968), he questioned the basic idea of public solutions for social problems. He argued that inequality is based on human character and rooted in the basic structure of society; government action can only solve problems that require better engineering, such as pollution control, better highways, or the delivery of explosives to military targets. Government's job, said Banfield, was to preserve public order, not to right wrongs or encourage unrealistic expectations.

Other conservative writers elaborated Banfield's ideas. The most influential was Charles Murray, whose 1984 book, *Losing Ground,* tried to do for neoconservative domestic policy what Michael Harrington's *The Other America* had done for liberal policy. Murray's basic argument was simple: Welfare assistance hurt more than it helped, by encouraging dependency and discouraging individual efforts at self-improvement. Despite massive antipoverty and welfare efforts since 1965, he contended, poverty, minority unemployment, and deviant behavior had increased rather than decreased. The blame, he said, must lie in the welfare programs themselves. Scholars have shown that Murray's book distorts the evidence and makes flawed arguments, but it had a major impact on political debates.

Free market utopians.   Another strand of conservative argument came from free market utopians. After years of stagflation, Americans were eager to hear that unleashing free markets would trigger renewed prosperity. The *Wall Street Journal* evolved from a narrow business newspaper into a national conservative forum by devoting its editorial page to outspoken versions of neoconservatism. Politicians such as Congressman Jack Kemp built support for specific steps to cut economic regulation and encourage business enterprise.

The common themes of the conservative critique were simple: Free markets work better than government programs; government intervention does more harm than good; government assistance saps the initiative of the poor. In 1964, three-quarters of Americans had trusted Washington "to do what is right." By 1980, three-quarters were convinced that the federal government wasted tax money. The neoconservatives offered the details to support Reagan's own summary: "Government is not the solution to our problems; government is the problem." The cumulative effect of the neoconservative arguments was to trash the word "liberal" and convince many Americans that labor unions and minorities were "special interests" but that oil tycoons, defense contractors, and other members of Reagan's coalition were not.

The conservative cause found support in new "think tanks" and political lobbying organizations. Many conservatives were convinced that university faculty members were hopelessly liberal. In response, wealthy businesspeople funded alternative organizations, such as the Manhattan Institute, the Heritage Foundation, and the American Enterprise Institute, where conservative analysts could develop policy proposals and opinion pieces for newspapers. The result was to shift the terms of political discussion substantially in a conservative direction between 1975 and 1990.

Conservative political savvy.   Conservatives promoted their ideology with new political tactics. Targeted mailings raised funds and mobilized voters with emotional appeals while bypassing the mass media, with their supposed preference for mainstream or liberal policies. Conservative organizers also knew how to use radio call-in shows to spread their message. Such appeals contrasted with the Democrats's reliance on more traditional ways to get out the vote through personal contacts and labor unions. Through the 1980s, Democrats repeatedly found themselves blindsided by creative Republican campaign tactics.

Reaganomics: Deficits and Deregulation

The heart of the 1980s revolution was the **Economic Recovery and Tax Act of 1981 (ERTA),** which reduced personal income tax rates by 25 percent over three years. The explicit goal was to stimulate business activity by lowering taxes overall and slashing rates for the rich. Cutting the government's total income by $747 billion over five years, ERTA meant less money for federal programs and more money in the hands of consumers and investors to stimulate economic growth.

Reagan's first budget director, David Stockman, later revealed a second goal. ERTA would lock in deficits by "pulling the revenue plug." Because defense spending and Social Security were untouchable, Congress would find it impossible to create and fund new programs without cutting old ones. Compared with spending patterns in effect in 1980, the Reagan administration also shifted $70 billion per year from domestic to military programs. The first year's tax reductions were accompanied by cuts of $40 billion in federal aid to mass transit, school lunches, and similar programs. If Americans still wanted social programs, they could enact them at the local or state level, but Washington would no longer pay.

The second part of the economic agenda was to free capitalists from government regulations, in the hope of increasing business innovation and efficiency. The **deregulation** revolution built on a head start from the 1970s. A federal antitrust case had split the unified Bell System of AT&T and its subsidiaries into seven regional telephone companies and opened long-distance service to competition. Congress also deregulated air travel in 1978. During the first 40 years of commercial air service, the Federal Aviation Administration had matched airlines and routes (treating air service like a public utility); deregulation now allowed air carriers to start and stop service at will, resulting in cheaper and more frequent air service for major hubs and poorer and more expensive service for small cities. Economists tend to be satisfied that the net gains have outweighed the costs.

Environmental regulation and federal lands. Corporate America used the Reagan administration to attack environmental legislation as "strangulation by regulation." Reagan's new budgets sliced funding for the Environmental Protection Agency. Vice President Bush headed the White House Task Force on Regulatory Relief, which delayed or blocked regulations on hazardous wastes, automobile emissions, and exposure of workers to chemicals on the job.

Most attention, however, went to the controversial appointment of a Colorado lawyer, James Watt, as secretary of the interior. Watt had long worked to open up federal lands in the West to more intensive development. He was sympathetic to a western movement known as the **Sagebrush Rebellion,** which wanted the vast federal land holdings in the West transferred to the states for less environmental protection and more rapid economic use. He once blamed air pollution on natural emissions from trees and compared environmentalists to Nazis and Bolsheviks. Federal resource agencies sold trees to timber companies at a loss to the Treasury, expanded offshore oil drilling, and expedited exploration for minerals.

Deregulation of the banking industry. The early 1980s also transformed American financial markets. Savings and loans had traditionally been conservative financial institutions that funneled individual savings into safe home mortgages. Under new rules, they began to compete for deposits by offering high interest rates and reinvesting the money in much riskier commercial real estate. By 1990, the result was a financial crisis in which bad loans destroyed hundreds of S&Ls, especially in the Southwest. American taxpayers were left to bail out depositors to the tune of hundreds of billions of dollars to prevent a collapse of the nation's financial and credit system.

With the deregulation of financial markets, corporate consolidations and mergers flourished. Corporate raiders raised money with "junk bonds"—high-interest, high-risk securities—and snapped up profitable and cash-rich companies that could be milked of profits and assets. The merger mania channeled capital into paper transactions rather than investments in new equipment and products. Another effect was to damage the economies of small and middle-sized communities by transferring control of local companies to outside managers.

In the short term, the national economy boomed in the mid-1980s. Deregulated credit, tax cuts, and massive deficit spending on defense fueled exuberant growth. The decade as a whole brought nearly 20 million new jobs, especially for professional and managerial workers, office support staff, salespeople, and workers providing personal services. Inflation dipped to 3 percent per year. The stock market mirrored the overall prosperity; the Dow Jones average of blue-chip industrial stock prices more than tripled from August 1982 to August 1987.

Crisis for Organized Labor

The flip side of the economic boom was another round in the Republican offensive against labor unions. Reagan set the tone when he fired more than 11,000 members of the Professional Air Traffic Controllers Organization for violating a no-strike clause in their hiring agreements. He claimed to be enforcing the letter of the law, but the message to organized labor was clear. For many years, corporations had hesitated to hire permanent replacements for striking workers. With Reagan's example, large companies, such as Hormel and Phelps-Dodge, chose that option, undercutting the strike as an effective union strategy. During the Reagan administration, the National Labor Relations Board and other federal agencies also weakened collective bargaining by their interpretation of labor-management regulations.

Decline of union membership and blue-collar jobs. Organized labor counted a million fewer members at the end of Reagan's administration in 1989 than in 1964, even though the number of employed Americans had nearly doubled. Many unions that had been the mainstays of the labor movement in the Roosevelt and Truman years found themselves in trouble, saddled with leaders who were unable to cope with the restructuring of the economy. As union membership declined and unions struggled to cope with the

The working-class family depicted on the television show *Roseanne* offered viewers a glimpse of the problems facing many Americans in an era of economic change marked by deindustrialization and the rise of service jobs.

dustrial satellite of Chicago, Roseanne and Dan Conner struggle to raise a family on the income from a series of jobs as small business owner, assembly-line worker, waitress, skilled laborer. The lifelong unionized factory job is a thing of the past as the shifting economy makes it hard to accumulate savings and stay ahead of the financial crises of normal life, let alone keep kids in college. A telling statistic about the problems of the real equivalents of the Conners was the increase in personal bankruptcy filings from roughly 300,000 per year in the early 1980s to 1,200,000 per year by the later 1990s.

In the 1950s and 1960s, increasing productivity, expanding markets for U.S. goods, and strong labor unions had made it possible for factory workers to enter the middle class. In an era of deindustrialization, however, companies replaced blue-collar workers with machinery or shifted production to nonunion plants. The corporate merger mania of the 1980s added to instability when takeover specialists loaded old companies with new debt, triggering efforts to cut labor costs, sell off plants, or raid pension funds for cash to pay the interest. Manufacturing employment in the 1980s declined by nearly 2 million jobs, with the expansion of high-tech manufacturing concealing much higher losses in traditional industries. In sum, while corporate merger specialists steered their BMWs along the fast lane to success, displaced mill hands drove battered pickups along potholed roads to nowhere.

changing economy, corporations seized the opportunity to demand wage rollbacks and concessions on working conditions as trade-offs for continued employment, squeezing workers in one plant and then using the settlement to pressure another. Workers in the 1970s and 1980s faced the threat that employers might move a factory to a new site elsewhere in the United States or overseas. Or a company might sell out to a new owner, who could close a plant and reopen without a union contract. One 16-year-old described the changes in the grocery chain where her father had worked for 26 years: "They're letting people go with no feelings for how long they've worked there, just lay 'em off. It's sad. He should be getting benefits after all these years and all the sacrifices he's made. Now they're almost ready to lay him off without a word."

Another cause for shrinking union membership was the overall decline of blue-collar jobs, from 36 percent of the American workforce in 1960 to roughly 25 percent at the end of the 1990s. Unionization of white-collar workers made up only part of the loss from manufacturing. Unions were most successful in recruiting government workers, such as police officers, teachers, and bus drivers. By the late 1980s, the American Federation of State, County, and Municipal Employees had twice the membership of the United Steel Workers. In the private sector, however, many white-collar jobs were in small firms that were difficult to organize.

Impact of economic restructuring.   Popular culture's best take on the problems of blue-collar America was the television situation comedy *Roseanne* (1988–1997). Living in an in-

An Acquisitive Society

The new prosperity fueled lavish living by the wealthy and a fascination with the "lifestyles of the rich and famous." The television show of the same name, which premiered in 1984, offered its viewers glimpses of "champagne wishes" and "caviar dreams" as lived by entertainment stars and business tycoons. Prime-time soap operas flourished, bringing to the small screen stories of intrigue among the rich folks of fast-growing Texas in *Dallas* (1978–1991), Colorado in *Dynasty* (1981–1989), and California in *Knots Landing* (1979–1993). With a few exceptions, even the "middle class" in television sitcoms enjoyed lives available only to the top 20 percent of Americans.

The national media in the early 1980s discovered yuppies, or young urban professionals, who were both a marketing category and a symbol of social change. These upwardly mobile professionals supposedly defined themselves by elitist consumerism. Middle-line retailers like Sears had clothed Americans for decades and furnished their homes. With the help of catalog shopping, status-seeking consumers now flocked to such upscale retailers as Neiman-Marcus and Bloomingdale's. Yuppie as a marketing category meanwhile

"They're museum quality!"

This 1993 cartoon contrasting a yuppie couple and a family dressed as hippies makes two points. While highlighting the rapid changes in American styles and tastes from the 1970s to the 1990s, it also satirizes the supposed yuppie tendency to value everything as a commodity or "collectible."

© The New Yorker Collection from CartoonBank.com/CORBIS

New movements in popular music reacted to the acquisitive 1980s. Punk rock pared rock-and-roll to its basics, lashing out at the emptiness of 1970s disco sound. Punk music influenced grunge bands such as Nirvana, which expressed alienation from consumerism. Hip-hop originated among African Americans and Latinos in New York, soon adding the angry and often violent lyrics of rap. Rap during the 1980s was about personal power and sex, but it also dealt with social inequities and deprivation and tapped some of the same anger and frustration that had motivated black power advocates in the 1960s. When it crossed into mainstream entertainment, it retained a hard-edged "attitude" that undercut any sense of complacency about an inclusive American society.

Mass Media and Fragmented Culture

On June 1, 1980, CNN Cable News Network gave television viewers their first chance to watch news coverage 24 hours a day. Newscasters Bernard Shaw and Mary Alice Williams brought instant information to an initial audience of 1.7 million subscribers; a decade later, CNN had hundreds of millions of viewers in more than 75 countries. Business executives in Zurich, college students in Nairobi, and farmers in Omaha all tuned in to the version of world events pulled together in CNN's Atlanta headquarters. CNN made a global reputation with live reporting on the pro-democracy protests of Chinese students in Beijing in 1989. When American bombs began to fall on Baghdad in January 1991, White House officials watched CNN to find out how their war was going.

Fourteen months after CNN went on the air, another new cable channel, MTV: Music Television, started broadcasting. By the time it reached the key New York and Los Angeles markets in January 1983, MTV's round-the-clock programming of music videos had created a new form of popular art and advertising. With its own programming aimed at viewers aged 18 to 34, MTV inspired Nickelodeon for kids and VH-1 for baby boomers.

CNN, MTV, and the rest of cable television reflected both the fragmentation of American society in the 1980s and 1990s and the increasing dependence on instant communication. As late as 1980, ordinary Americans had few choices for learning about their nation and world: virtually identical newscasts on NBC, CBS, and ABC and similar stories in *Time* and *Newsweek* helped to create a common understanding. Fifteen years later, they had learned to surf through dozens of cable channels in search of specialized programs and were

spawned variations, such as "buppie" for black urban professional. It was difficult for most Americans to feel much sympathy for the family in a *New York Times* profile in 1987 who had difficulty making ends meet on $600,000 a year.

Far richer than even such atypical yuppies were wheeler-dealers who made themselves into media stars of finance capitalism. The autobiography of Lee Iacocca, who had helped revive the fortunes of the Chrysler Corporation, was a bestseller in 1984, portraying the corporate executive as hero. *Forbes* magazine began to publish an annual list of the nation's 400 richest people. Long before his television show, real-estate developer Donald Trump made himself a celebrity with a well-publicized personal life and a stream of projects crowned with his name: office tower, hotel, casino. Before he admitted to violating the law against profiting from insider information, the corporate-merger expert Ivan Boesky had told a business-school audience, "Greed is all right. You shouldn't feel guilty," epitomizing an era of big business takeovers driven by paper profits rather than underlying economic fundamentals. In his bestselling novel *The Bonfire of the Vanities* (1987), Tom Wolfe depicted a New York where the art dealers and stockbrokers of glitzy Manhattan meet the poor of the devastated South Bronx only through an automobile accident, to their mutual incomprehension and ruin.

beginning to explore the amazing variety of the World Wide Web (see Chapter 31). Hundreds of magazines for niche markets had replaced the general-circulation periodicals of the postwar generation. Vast quantities of information were more easily available, but much of it was packaged for a subdivided marketplace of specialized consumers.

Poverty amid Prosperity

Federal tax and budget changes had different effects on the rich and poor (see Figure 30–1). Popular attention to the lifestyles of upscale Manhattan and Beverly Hills obscured the economic realities for many Americans. Those in the top fifth increased their share of after-tax income relative to everyone else during the 1980s, and the richest 1 percent saw their share of all privately held wealth grow from 31 percent to 37 percent. The 1981 tax cuts also came with sharp increases in the Social Security tax, which hit lower-income workers the hardest. The tax changes meant that the average annual income of households in the bottom 20 percent *declined* and that many actually paid higher taxes.

The budget changes that fueled conspicuous consumption put pressure on American cities. Cities and their residents absorbed approximately two-thirds of the cuts in the 1981–1982 federal budget. Provisions for accelerated depre-

ciation (tax write-offs) of factories and equipment in the 1981 tax act encouraged the abandonment of center-city factories in favor of new facilities in the suburbs. One result was a growing jobs-housing mismatch. There were often plenty of jobs in the suburbs, but the poorer people who most needed the jobs were marooned in city slums and dependent on public transit that seldom served suburban employers.

Federal tax and spending policies in the 1980s decreased the security of middle-class families. As the economy continued to struggle through deindustrialization, average wage rates fell in the 1980s when measured in real purchasing. The squeeze put pressure on traditional family patterns and pushed into the workforce women who might otherwise have stayed home. Even with two incomes, many families found it hard to buy a house because of skyrocketing prices in urban markets and sky-high interest rates. The national home ownership rate actually fell for the first time in almost 50 years, from 66 to 64 percent of American households. Many Americans no longer expected to surpass their parents' standard of living.

Corporate downsizing and white-collar jobs.   Lower-paying office jobs fell under the same sorts of pressure as factory jobs with the increasing reliance of banks, telephone companies, and credit card companies on automation. Increasing numbers of clerical and office workers in organizations of all sorts, from corporations to universities, were "temps" who shifted from job to job. The shift toward temporary and part-time workers not only kept wages low but also allowed less spending on health insurance and other benefits.

The chill of corporate downsizing hit white-collar families most heavily toward the end of the 1980s. Big business consolidations delivered improved profits by squeezing the ranks of middle managers as well as assembly-line workers. With fewer workers to supervise and with new technologies to collect and distribute information, companies could complete their cost cutting by trimming administrators. Takeovers sometimes meant the elimination of the entire management and support staff of target companies. In the 1950s, a college graduate could sign on with a large corporation like IBM or General Motors, advance through the ranks, and expect to retire from the same company. Now the expectation of a job for life looked dubious; AT&T, for one example, eliminated 76,000 jobs—one-fifth of its total—between 1985 and 1989. Those white-collar workers whose jobs survived clung to them more firmly than ever. The combined result was to clog the ladder of economic opportunity for college graduates, making the cab-driving Ph.D. and the *barrista* with the B.A. popular clichés.

Increase in the poverty rate.   At the lower end of the economic ladder, the proportion of Americans living in poverty increased. After declining steadily from 1960 to a low of 11 percent in 1973, the poverty rate climbed back to the 13 to 15 percent range. Although the economy in the 1980s created lots of new jobs, half of them paid less than poverty-level wages. Conservative critics began to talk about an underclass of Americans permanently outside the mainstream

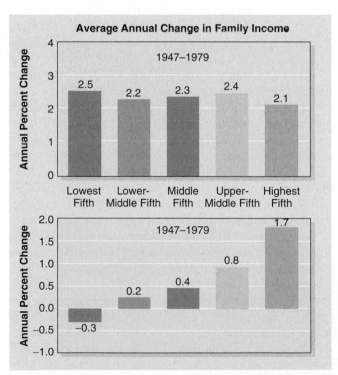

Average Annual Change in Family Income

FIGURE 30–1   Changes in Real Family Income, 1980–1990

In the 1980s, the poor got poorer, the middle class made slight gains, and the most affluent 20 percent of the American people did very well. Tax changes that helped well-off households were one factor. Another factor was the erosion of family-wage jobs in manufacturing.

FROM THEN TO NOW

Women and Office Work

In the twenty-first century, women filled the majority of U.S. office-based jobs. More women than men worked as office managers, receptionists, insurance agents, bookkeepers, and the myriad of other desk-and-computer occupations. This employment pattern that most Americans take for granted is the product of 140 years of gradual change triggered initially by wartime crisis.

Before the Civil War, American women were might be domestic servants, mill operatives, and schoolteachers, but they were not office workers. Clerks were men, sometimes settled into lower-status white-collar careers and sometimes learning a business from the inside before rising into management. They copied letters and documents by hand, traced orders, and kept financial records.

The federal government took the lead in expanding office employment for women during and after the Civil War. These women are working at the Treasury Department.

The Civil War sharply increased the flow of government paperwork while diverting young men into military service. The U.S. Treasury Department in Washington responded in 1862 by hiring women to sort and package federal bonds and currency. Despite concerns about the moral implications of mixing men and women in the same offices, the Treasury found women cheap and reliable workers. By 1870, several hundred women worked in Washington's federal offices.

Women's office jobs expanded with the growth of the national economy and its increasing flows of information. New technologies—telephones, typewriters—meant increasing demand for routine office work. Filling much of the need for desk workers were middle-class women, whose literacy was often guaranteed by the high school diplomas that went disproportionately to women in the later nineteenth century. As women workers filled new downtown skyscrapers, the central districts of large cities lost some of their rough edges and grew more respectable as centers of shopping and entertainment. The division of labor that characterized the first half of the twentieth century was in place. Until recent decades, it was usually men who determined what was to be said, but women who transcribed, transmitted, recorded, and filed their messages.

■ The division between "men's work" and "women's work" changed sharply in the later nineteenth century. What are similarities and differences with the changes in men's and women's work in the later twentieth century?

PEARSON myhistorylab

The Mary Tyler Moore Show, broadcast 1970–1977, was a pioneer in its focus on unmarried career woman "Mary Richards," a television news producer played by Mary Tyler Moore.

From Then to Now Online

30-1 American Historical Association, *Do You Want Your Wife to Work after the War?* (1945). Prepared by the American Historical Association in cooperation with the U.S. Army, this pamphlet responded to the extraordinary increase in working women and to fears of a renewed depression and job scarcity with the war's end.

30-2 Heidi Hartman, Vicky Lovell, and Misha Werschkul, *Women in the Economy* (2004). Researchers at the Institute for Women's Policy Research analyze trends in women's employment and wages.

economy because of poor education, drug abuse, or sheer laziness. In fact, talk of an underclass was a way to avoid confronting the realities of limited economic opportunity. Most of the nation's millions of poor people lived in households with employed adults. In 1992, fully 18 percent of all full-time jobs did not pay enough to lift a family of four out of poverty, a jump of 50 percent over the proportion of underpaid jobs in 1981. One of the biggest barriers to better employment was not a disinterest in work, but rather the isolation of many job seekers in poverty neighborhoods without access to suburban jobs or the informal social networks that are the best way to find good employment.

The wage gap and the feminization of poverty.   Nor could most women, even those working full-time, expect to earn as much as men. In the 1960s and 1970s, the average working woman earned just 60 percent of the earnings of the average man (see Figure 30–2). Only part of the wage gap could be explained by measurable factors, such as education or experience. The gap narrowed in the 1980s and 1990s, with women's earnings rising to 75 percent of men's by 2003. About half of the change was the result of bad news—the decline of earnings among men as high-wage factory jobs dis-

appeared. The other half was the positive result of better-educated younger women finding better jobs. Indeed, women earned 57 percent of the four-year college degrees awarded in 2002 (up from 38 percent in 1960) and 47 percent of first professional degrees (up from 3 percent).

Nevertheless, the low earning capacity of women with limited educations meant that women were far more likely than men to be poor. Women constituted nearly two-thirds of poor adults at the end of the 1980s. Only 6 percent of married-couple households were below poverty level, but 32 percent of households headed by a woman without a husband present were poor. The feminization of poverty and American reliance on private support for child rearing also meant that children had a higher chance of living in poverty than adults and that poor American children were worse off than their peers in other advanced nations.

Homelessness in America.   Falling below even the working poor were growing numbers of homeless Americans. Large cities have always had transient laborers, derelict alcoholics, and voluntarily homeless hobos. In the 1980s, several factors made homelessness more visible and pressing. A new approach to the treatment of the mentally ill reduced

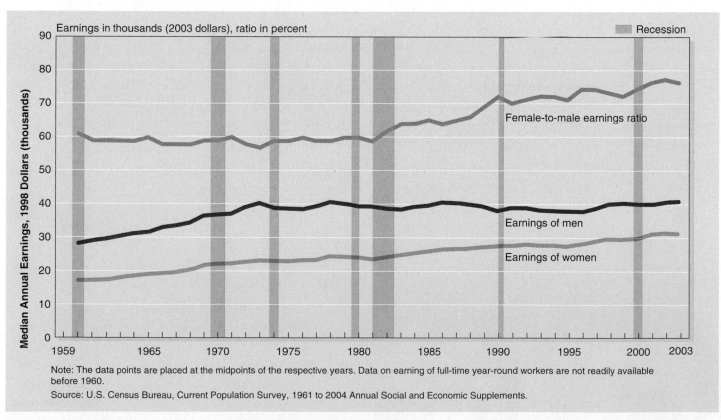

Note: The data points are placed at the midpoints of the respective years. Data on earning of full-time year-round workers are not readily available before 1960.

Source: U.S. Census Bureau, Current Population Survey, 1961 to 2004 Annual Social and Economic Supplements.

FIGURE 30–2   Comparison of Men's and Women's Earnings, 1960–2003
U.S. Census data show that the median earnings of women who worked full time and year round compared to those of men. Since the 1960s, the gap between women and men has narrowed. One reason is better pay for jobs traditionally held by women, but another has been the declining earning power of men without college educations. Nevertheless, the gender gap in earning power remains an important economic issue.

the population of mental hospitals from 540,000 in 1960 to only 140,000 in 1980. Deinstitutionalized patients were supposed to receive community-based treatment, but many ended up on the streets and in overnight shelters. New forms of self-destructive drug abuse, such as crack addiction, joined alcoholism. A boom in downtown real estate destroyed old skid-row districts with their bars, missions, and dollar-a-night hotels.

These factors tripled the number of permanently homeless people during the early and middle 1980s, from 200,000 to somewhere between 500,000 and 700,000. Twice or three times that many may have been homeless for part of a given year. For every person in a shelter on a given night, two people were sleeping on sidewalks, in parks, in cars, and in abandoned buildings. Because homeless people made middle-class Americans uncomfortable, it was reassuring to assume they were outsiders attracted by local conditions, such as tolerant attitudes (as some claimed in Seattle) or mild climate (as some claimed in Phoenix). In fact, few of the down-and-out have the resources to move from town to town. Bag ladies, panhandlers, working people, and yuppies were all parts of the same communities, neighbors in the broadest sense.

Consolidating the Revolution: George Bush

In 1988 George H. W. Bush, Reagan's vice president for eight years, won the presidential election with 56 percent of the popular vote and 40 out of 50 states. Bush's view of national and world politics reflected a background in which personal connections counted. He was raised as part of the New England elite, built an oil business in Texas, and then held a series of high-level federal appointments. As someone who had survived 20 years of bureaucratic infighting, his watchword was prudence. Using a comparison from baseball, Bush described himself as the sort of guy who would play the averages and "bunt 'em over" rather than go for the big inning.

Michael Dukakis, the Democratic nominee in 1988, was a dry-as-dust, by-the-numbers manager who offered the American people "competence." The Bush campaign director, Lee Atwater, looked for hot-button issues that could fit onto a three-by-five card. He found that Dukakis as governor of Massachusetts had delayed cleanup of Boston Harbor, favored gun control, and vetoed a bill requiring schoolchildren to recite the Pledge of Allegiance (arguing

An affluent family pedals past a group of homeless people in Santa Barbara, California. In the 1980s a combination of rising housing prices and the closing of most mental hospitals pushed increasing numbers of Americans onto the streets. Estimates of the number of homeless Americans in the late 1980s ranged from 300,000 to 3 million, depending on the definition of homelessness and the political goals of the estimator.

correctly that it would be overturned in the courts). Even more damaging, Massachusetts officials had allowed a murderer named Willie Horton a weekend furlough from prison, during which he committed a brutal rape. Pro-Bush advertisements tapped into real worries among the voters—fear of crime, racial tension (Horton was black), eroding social values. George Bush, despite his background in prep schools and country clubs, came out looking tough as nails, while the Democrats looked inept.

The ads locked Bush into a rhetorical war on crime and drugs that was his major domestic policy. Americans had good cause to be worried about public safety, but most were generally unaware that the likelihood of becoming the target of a violent crime had leveled off and would continue to fall in the 1990s or that crime was far worse in minority communities than elsewhere, in part due to gang- and drug-related activities.

The Bush administration stepped up the fight against illegal drugs, and the federal drug-control budget tripled. In the early 1980s, a quarter of federal prison inmates were in jail for drug offenses. Longer sentences, mandatory jail time, and tougher parole terms for drug crimes pushed the proportion over 50 percent by 1990. The United States tried to stop the flow of cocaine by blockading its borders with airplanes, sea patrols, and specially trained dogs at airport customs lines. Casual and middle-class use of cocaine and marijuana began to decline in the mid-1980s. Drug use and drug sales were increasingly a problem of poor and minority neighborhoods.

George Bush believed that Americans wanted government to leave them alone. He ignored a flood of new ideas from entrepreneurial conservatives, such as HUD Secretary Jack Kemp. The major legislation from the Bush administration was a transportation bill that shifted federal priorities from highway building toward mass transit and the **Americans with Disabilities Act** (1990) to prevent discrimination against people with physical handicaps. In the areas of crime and healthcare, however, Bush's lack of leadership left continuing problems.

The same attitude produced weak economic policies. The national debt had amounted to 50 percent of personal savings in 1980 but swelled to 125 percent by 1990. The massive budget deficits of the 1980s combined with growing trade deficits to turn the United States from an international creditor to a debtor nation. When Reagan took office, foreigners owed the United States and its citizens the equivalent of $2,500 for every American family. When Bush took office, the United States had used up its foreign assets and become the world's biggest debtor, with liabilities that averaged $7,000 per family. After pledging no new taxes in his campaign, Bush backed into a tax increase in 1990. A strong leader might have justified the taxes to the nation, but voters found it hard to forget the president's waffling and attempts to downplay the importance of his decision.

The most conspicuous domestic event of the Bush administration—the "Rodney King riot" of April 1992 in Los Angeles—was a reminder of the nation's inattention to the problems of race and poverty. Rodney King was a black motorist who had been savagely clubbed and kicked by police officers while being arrested after a car chase on March 3, 1991. A nearby resident captured the beating on videotape from his apartment. Within two days, the tape was playing and replaying on national television. The grainy pictures shocked the nation and confirmed African Americans' worst fears about biased police behavior. Early the next year, the four officers stood trial for unjustified use of force before a suburban jury. The televised trial and the unexpected verdict of not guilty on April 29 stirred deep anger that escalated into four days of rioting.

The disorder revealed multiple tensions among ethnic groups and was far more complex than the Watts outbreak of 1965 (see Chapter 29). African Americans from south-central Los Angeles participated, but so did Central American and Mexican immigrants in adjacent districts, who accounted for about one-third of the 12,000 arrests. The disorder spread south to Long Beach and north to the edge of upscale neighborhoods in Westwood and Beverly Hills. Rioters assaulted the downtown police headquarters, city hall, and the *Los Angeles Times* building. As in 1965, some targets were white passers-by and symbols of white authority. But members of competing minority groups were also victims as angry black people targeted hundreds of Korean-owned and Vietnamese-owned shops as symbols of economic discrimina-

After a jury acquitted the police officers involved in the beating of motorist Rodney King in April 1992, much of Los Angeles erupted in rioting that left much smoldering buildings and revealed deep racial and economic tensions.

tion. Four days of disorder left 58 people dead, mostly African Americans and Latinos.

The Second (Short) Cold War

Ronald Reagan entered office determined to reassert U.S. leadership in world affairs and not to lose the Cold War. He considered the Soviet Union not a coequal nation with legitimate world interests but an "evil empire," like something from the *Star Wars* movies. After the era of détente, global tensions had started to mount in the late 1970s. They were soon higher than they had been since the 1960s. But by the end of Reagan's two terms, unexpected changes were rapidly bringing the Cold War to an end, and George Bush faced a radically new set of foreign policy issues.

Confronting the Soviet Union

Who renewed the Cold War after Nixon's diplomacy of *détente* and Carter's early efforts at negotiation? The Soviets had pursued military expansion in the 1970s, triggering the fear that they might stage a nuclear Pearl Harbor. The Soviet Union in 1980 was supporting Marxist regimes in civil wars in Angola, Ethiopia, Nicaragua, and especially Afghanistan, where its 1980 intervention led to a decade of costly and futile military occupation. Were these actions parts of a careful plan? Or did they result from the Cold War inertia of a rudderless nation that reacted to situations one at a time? Given the aging Soviet leadership and the economic weaknesses revealed in the late 1980s, it makes more sense to see the Soviets as muddling along rather than executing a well-planned global strategy.

On the American side, Reagan's readiness to confront "the focus of evil in the modern world" reflected the views of many conservative supporters that the Soviet Union was a monolithic and ideologically motivated foe bent on world conquest. In hindsight, some Reaganites claim that the administration's foreign policy and massive increases in defense spending were part of a deliberate and coordinated scheme to check a Soviet offensive and bankrupt the Soviet Union by pushing it into a new arms race. It is just as likely, however, that the administration's defense and foreign policy initiatives were a set of discrete but effective decisions.

The Reagan administration reemphasized central Europe as the focus of superpower rivalry, just as it had been in the 1950s and early 1960s. To counter improved Soviet armaments, the United States began to place cruise missiles and mid-range Pershing II missiles in Europe in 1983. NATO governments approved the action, but it frightened millions of their citizens. By the mid-1980s, many Europeans saw the United States as the dangerous and aggressive force in world affairs and the Soviet Union as the voice of moderation—international attitudes that continue to this day.

The controversy over new missiles was part of new thinking about nuclear strategy. Multiple warheads on U.S. missiles already allowed Washington to target 25,000 separate places in the Soviet Union. National Security Directive D-13 (1981) set forth a new doctrine that it might be possible to fight and win a nuclear war despite its enormous costs. A reactivated civil defense program also suggested that the United States was serious about nuclear war. All Americans needed for survival, said one administration official, were "enough shovels" to dig fallout shelters.

Escalation of the nuclear arms race reinvigorated the antiwar and antinuclear movement in the United States as well as Europe. Drawing on the experience of the antiwar movement, the nuclear-freeze campaign caught the imagination of many Americans in 1981 and 1982. It sought to halt the manufacture and deployment of new atomic weapons by the great powers. The movement gained urgency when distinguished scientists argued that the smoke and dust thrown up by an atomic war would devastate the ecology of the entire globe by triggering "nuclear winter." Nearly a million people turned out for a nuclear-freeze rally in New York in 1982. Hundreds of local communities endorsed the freeze or took the symbolic step of declaring themselves nuclear-free zones.

In response, Reagan announced the **Strategic Defense Initiative (SDI),** or Star Wars program, in 1983. SDI was to deploy new defenses that could intercept and destroy ballistic missiles as they rose from the ground and arced through space. Ideas included superlasers, killer satellites, and clouds of projectiles to rip missiles to shreds before they neared their targets. All of the technologies were untested; some existed only in the imagination. Few scientists thought that SDI could work. Many arms control experts thought that defensive systems were dangerous and destabilizing, because strong defenses suggested that a nation might be willing to risk a nuclear exchange. Nevertheless, President Reagan found SDI appealing, for it offered a way around the balance of terror.

Risky Business: Foreign Policy Adventures

The same administration that sometimes seemed reckless in its grand strategy also took risks to assert U.S. influence in global trouble spots to block or roll back Soviet influence. Reagan asserted America's right to intervene anywhere in the world to support local groups fighting against Marxist governments. The assumption underlying this assertion, which later became known as the **Reagan Doctrine,** was that Soviet-influenced governments in Asia, Africa, and Latin America needed to be eliminated if the United States was to win the Cold War.

Nevertheless, Reagan kept the United States out of a major war and backed off in the face of serious trouble. Foreign interventions were designed to achieve symbolic victories rather than change the global balance of power. The exception was the Caribbean and Central America, the "backyard" where the United States had always claimed an overriding interest and where left-wing action infuriated Reagan's conservative supporters.

On October 25, 1983, for example, U.S. troops invaded the small independent Caribbean island of Grenada. A left-leaning government had invited Cuban help in building an airfield, which the United States feared would turn into a Cuban military base. Two thousand American troops overcame Cuban soldiers thinly disguised as construction workers, "rescued" American medical students, and put a more sympathetic and locally popular government in power.

Intervention and covert activities in Central America.

The Reagan administration attributed political turmoil in Central America to Soviet influence and to arms and agitators from Soviet-backed Cuba. Between 1980 and 1983, the United States sent more military aid to conservative governments and groups in Central America than it had during the previous 30 years. Indeed, Central America became the focus of a secret foreign policy operated by the CIA and then by National Security Council (NSC) staff, since a Democratic Congress was not convinced of the danger. The CIA and the NSC engaged not just in espionage but in direct covert operations. The chief target was Nicaragua, the Central American country where leftist Sandinista rebels had overthrown the Somoza dictatorship in 1979. Reagan and his people were determined to prevent Nicaragua from becoming "another Cuba," especially when Sandinistas helped left-wing insurgents in neighboring El Salvador. In the early 1980s, Reagan approved CIA plans to arm and organize approximately 10,500 so-called Contras, from the remnants of Somoza's national guard. From bases in Honduras, the Contras harassed the Sandinistas with sabotage and raids. Reagan called the Contras "freedom fighters," listened to stories of their exploits, and hunched over maps to follow their operations in detail. Meanwhile, Americans with different views aided refugees from the war zones of Central America through the church-based sanctuary movement ("sanctuary" could imply both legal economic assistance and direct defiance of efforts to deport refugees).

The Reagan administration bent the law to support its covert effort to overthrow the Sandinista regime. An unsympathetic Congress blocked U.S. funding for the Contras. In response, CIA director William Casey directed Lieutenant Colonel Oliver North of the National Security Council staff to illegally organize aid from private donors. The arms pipeline operated until a supply plane was shot down in 1986. The Contras failed as a military effort, but the civil war and international pressure persuaded the Sandinistas to allow free elections that led to a democratic, centrist government.

The war against drugs.

The American war against drugs was simultaneously shaping U.S. policy in the Caribbean and straining relations with Latin America. The United States pressured Colombia and Peru to uproot coca plants grown by poor farmers. As president, George Bush parlayed the war on drugs into war on Panama during his first year in office, extending the American tradition of ousting uncooperative governments around the Caribbean. General Manuel Noriega, the Panamanian strongman, had once been on the CIA payroll. He had since turned to international drug sales in defiance of United States antismuggling efforts. On December 20, 1989, American troops invaded Panama, hunted down Noriega, and brought him back to stand trial in the United States on drug-trafficking charges. A handful of Americans and thousands of Panamanians died, many of them civilians caught in the crossfire.

Intervention in the Middle East.

If the results of intervention in Nicaraugua and Panama were mixed, intervention in the Middle East was a failure. In 1982 Israel invaded Lebanon, a small nation to its north, to clear Palestinian guerrillas from its borders and set up a friendly Lebanese government. The Israeli army bogged down in a civil war between Christian Arabs and Muslims. Reagan sent U.S. Marines to preserve the semblance of a Lebanese state and provide a face-saving exit for Israel. Although the Marines arrived in Beirut to interpose themselves between Israeli tanks and the Lebanese, they remained on an ill-defined "presence mission" that angered Arabs and motivated terrorist actions against Israel and the United States by Islamic radicals. In October 1983, a terrorist car bomb killed 241 Marines in their barracks. The remainder were soon gone, confirming the Syrian observation that Americans were "short of breath" when it came to Middle East politics. The debacle in Lebanon undermined U.S.-backed peace initiatives in the Middle East. Continuing terrorist acts such as taking Americans hostage, bombing cruise ships, and sabotaging airliners were aimed at inhibiting U.S. support of Israel.

The Iran-Contra Affair.

Even less effective were the Reagan administration's secret efforts to sell weapons to Iran in return for Iranian help in securing the release of Americans held hostage by pro-Iranian Islamic radicals in Lebanon. The United States in 1985 joined Israel in selling 500 antitank missiles to Iran, then embroiled in a long, bitter war with Iraq. The deal followed stern public pronouncements that the United States would never negotiate with terrorists and considered Iran's religious leaders to be backers of international terrorism. It also violated the official trade embargo against Iran, which had been in place since the U.S. embassy seizure in 1979. In May 1986, National Security adviser Robert McFarlane flew to Iran for more arms-for-hostages talks, carrying a chocolate cake and a Bible autographed by Reagan to present to the Iranian leader Ayatollah Khomeini. The pro-Iranian radicals released several hostages, but others were soon taken. When the deals came to light in 1986 and congressional hearings were held in the summer of 1987, Americans were startled to learn that Colonel North had funneled millions of dollars from the arms sales to the Nicaraguan Contras in a double evasion of the law.

As had been true with Watergate, the Iran-Contra affair was a two-sided scandal. First was the blatant misjudgment of operating a secret, bumbling, and unlawful foreign policy that depended on international arms dealers and ousted Nicaraguan military officers. Second was a concerted effort to cover up the illegal and unconstitutional actions. North shredded relevant documents and lied to Congress. In his final report in 1994, Special Prosecutor Lawrence Walsh found that President Reagan and Vice President Bush were aware of much of what had gone on and had participated in efforts to withhold information and mislead Congress.

U.S. policy in Asia.   American policy in Asia was a refreshing contrast with practices in Central America and the Middle East. In the Philippines, American diplomats helped push corrupt President Ferdinand Marcos out and opened the way for a popular uprising to put Corazon Aquino in office. Secretary of State George Shultz made sure that the United States supported popular democracy while reassuring the Philippine military. In South Korea, the United States similarly helped ease out an unpopular dictator by firmly supporting democratic elections that brought in a more popular but still pro-American government.

Embracing *Perestroika*

Thaw in the Cold War started in Moscow as Soviet leaders sought to salvage a system under severe economic stress. Mikhail Gorbachev became general secretary of the Communist Party in 1985, when the Soviet Union was trapped in the sixth year of its failed attempt to control Afghanistan. Gorbachev was the picture of vigor compared to his three elderly predecessors. A master of public relations who charmed western Europe's leaders and public, he was also a modernizer in a long Russian tradition that stretched back to Tsar Peter the Great in the eighteenth century. Gorbachev startled Soviet citizens by urging *glasnost,* or political openness, with free discussion of issues and relaxation of controls on the press. He followed by setting the goal of *perestroika,* or restructuring of the painfully bureaucratic Soviet economy that was falling behind capitalist nations. His hope was that market-oriented reforms would help the Soviet Union keep up with the United States.

Gorbachev decided that he needed to reduce the crushing burden of Soviet defense spending if the Soviet Union was to have any chance of modernizing. During Reagan's second term, the Soviets offered one concession after another in a drive for arms control. They agreed to cut the number of land-based strategic weapons in half. They gave up their demand for an end to SDI research. In negotiations on conventional forces in Europe, they accepted bigger cuts for the Warsaw Pact nations than for NATO. They even agreed to on-site inspections to control chemical weapons.

Reagan had the vision (or audacity) to embrace the new Soviet position. He cast off decades of belief in the dangers of Soviet Communism and took Gorbachev seriously. One of his reasons for SDI had been his personal belief that the abolition of nuclear weapons was better than fine-tuning the balance of terror. Now he was willing to forget his own rhetoric. He frightened his own staff when he met with Gorbachev in the summer of 1986 and accepted the principle of deep cuts in strategic forces. Reagan explained that when he railed against the evil empire, he had been talking about Brezhnev and the bad old days; Gorbachev and *glasnost* were different.

In the end, Reagan negotiated the **Intermediate Nuclear Force Agreement (INF)** over the strong objections of the CIA and the Defense Department. INF was the first true nuclear-disarmament treaty (see Overview, Controlling Nuclear Weapons: Four Decades of Effort). Previous agreements had only slowed the growth of nuclear weapons; they were "speed limits" for the arms race. The new pact matched Soviet SS-20s with U.S. cruise missiles as an entire class of weapons that would be destroyed, with on-site inspections for verification.

Crisis and Democracy in Eastern Europe

President Bush loved to run the world by Rolodex. When someone's name came up at a formal dinner, he was likely to grab a phone and call the person. When Congress was heading in the wrong direction, he started dialing senators and representatives. When a crisis threatened world peace, he would start chatting with presidents and prime ministers. He viewed diplomacy as a series of conversations and friendships among leaders, not the reconciliation of differing national interests.

Mikhail Gorbachev, holding the child, hosted a summit meeting with President Reagan in Moscow in May 1988. Their smiles ignored the lack of progress toward disarmament beyond the Intermediate Nuclear Force Agreement of the previous year.

OVERVIEW

Controlling Nuclear Weapons: Four Decades of Effort

Limiting the testing of nuclear weapons	Limited Test Ban Treaty (1963)	Banned nuclear testing in the atmosphere, ocean, and outer space.
	Comprehensive Test	Banned all nuclear tests, including underground tests.
	Ban Treaty (1996)	Rejected by U.S. Senate in 1999.
Halting the spread of nuclear weapons	Nuclear Non- Proliferation Treaty (1968)	Pledged five recognized nuclear nations (United States, Soviet Union, Britain, France, China) to pursue disarmament in good faith, and 140 other nations not to acquire nuclear weapons.
	Strategic Arms Limitation Treaty (SALT I, 1972)	Limited the number of nuclear-armed missiles and bombers maintained by the United States and Soviet Union. Closely associated with U.S.-Soviet agreement to limit deployment of antiballistic missile systems to one site each.
	Strategic Arms Limitation Treaty (SALT II, 1979)	Further limited the number of nuclear-armed missiles and bombers. Not ratified but followed by Carter and Reagan administrations.
Reducing the number of nuclear weapons	Intermediate Nuclear Force Agreement (1987)	Required the United States to eliminate 846 nuclear armed cruise missiles, and the Soviet Union to eliminate 1,846 SS-20 missiles.
	Strategic Arms Reduction Treaty (START I, 1991)	By July 1999, led to reductions of approximately 2,750 nuclear warheads by the United States and 3,725 warheads by the nations of the former USSR.
	Strategic Arms Reduction Treaty (START II, 1993)	Set further cuts in nuclear arsenals. Ratified by Russia in April 2000. Russia withdrew in 2002 after the U.S. abandoned the Anti-Ballistic Missile Treaty.
	Strategic Offensive Reductions (2002)	Russia and the United States each agree to deploy no more than 1,700–2,200 strategic nuclear warheads.

Data Source: Arms Control Association.

As a believer in personal diplomacy, George Bush based much of his foreign policy on his changing attitudes toward Mikhail Gorbachev. He started lukewarm, talking tough to please the Republican right wing. Bush feared that Gorbachev, by instituting reforms that challenged the entrenched Communist Party leaders, was being imprudent: one of the worst things he could say about another leader. Before 1989 was over, however, the president had decided that Gorbachev was OK. For the next two years, the United States pushed the prodemocratic transformation of eastern Europe while being careful not to gloat in public or damage Gorbachev's position at home. Bush tried not to push the Soviet Union too hard and infuriate Russian hard-liners. "I don't want to do something that would inadvertently set back the progress," Bush said. Later asked whether the United States had a new foe after the end of the Cold War, Bush answered without hesitation, "The enemy is unpredictability. The enemy is instability."

The end of Communist regimes in Eastern Europe. The people of eastern Europe overcame both U.S. and Soviet caution. Gorbachev had urged his eastern European allies to emulate *perestroika* to free their economies from stifling controls and proclaimed what his Foreign Ministry called the "Sinatra doctrine," alluding to the ballad "My Way" popularized by Frank Sinatra. Each Communist nation could "do it its way" without fearing the Soviet tanks that had crushed change in Hungary in 1956 and Czechoslovakia in 1968. Instead of careful economic liberalization, the Warsaw Pact system collapsed. Poland held free elections in June 1989,

Hungary adopted a democratic constitution in October, and prodemocracy demonstrations then forced out Communist leaders in other eastern European countries. When East Germans began to flee westward through Hungary, the East German regime bowed to mounting pressure and opened the Berlin Wall on November 9. By the end of 1989, there were new democratic or non-Communist governments in Czechoslovakia, Romania, Bulgaria, and East Germany. These largely peaceful revolutions destroyed the military and economic agreements that had harnessed the satellites to the Soviet economy (the Warsaw Pact and Comecon). The Soviet Union swallowed hard, accepted the loss of its satellites, and slowly withdrew its army from eastern Europe.

German reunification and the dissolution of the Soviet Union.   Events in Europe left German reunification as a point of possible conflict. Soviet policy since 1945 had sought to prevent the reemergence of a strong, united Germany that might again threaten its neighbors. West German Chancellor Helmut Kohl removed one obstacle when he reassured Poland and Russia that Germany would seek no changes in the boundaries drawn after World War II. By July 1990, the United States and the Soviet Union had agreed that a reunited Germany would belong to NATO. The decision satisfied France and Britain that a stronger Germany would still be under the influence of the Western allies. In October, the two Germanies completed their political unification, although it would be years before their mismatched economies functioned as one. Reunification was the last step in the diplomatic legacy of World War II.

The final act in the transformation of the Soviet Union began with a failed coup against Mikhail Gorbachev in August 1991. The Soviet Union had held free elections in 1989. Now Gorbachev scheduled a vote on a new constitution that would decrease the power of the central government. Old-line Communist bureaucrats who feared the change arrested Gorbachev in his vacation house and tried to take over the government apparatus in Moscow. They turned out to be bumblers and drunks who had not secured military support and even failed to take over radio and television stations. Boris Yeltsin, president of the Russian Republic, organized the resistance. Muscovites flocked to support Yeltsin and defied tank crews in front of the Russian parliament building. Within three days, the plotters themselves were under arrest.

The coup hastened the fragmentation of the Soviet Union. Before the month was out, the Soviet parliament banned the Communist Party. Gorbachev soon resigned. Previously suppressed nationalist feelings caused all 15 component republics of the Soviet Union to declare their independence. The superpower Union of Soviet Socialist Republics ceased to exist. Russia remained the largest and strongest of the new states, followed by Ukraine and Kazakhstan.

The wall that divided East from West Berlin from 1962 to 1989 was a hated symbol of the Cold War. When the Communist government of East Germany collapsed in November 1989, jubilant Berliners celebrated the opening of the wall and the reuniting of the divided city.

The end of the Cold War leaves the historical assessment of the last half-century of U.S. foreign policy open to debate. Analysts agree that the relentless pressure of American defense spending helped bankrupt and undermine the Soviet Union. It is an open question whether this defense spending also weakened the U.S. economy and America's ability to compete in the world marketplace. Some scholars see the demise of the Soviet empire as ultimate justification for 40 years of Cold War. Dissenters argue the opposite—that the collapse of European Communism shows that American leaders had magnified its threat. Before we can choose among these views, we need to wait for scholars to explore Russian archives and develop a fuller history of Soviet Cold War policy to place alongside our understanding of U.S. policy (see Overview, Why Did the Cold War End?).

The Persian Gulf War

On August 2, 1990, President Saddam Hussein of Iraq seized the small neighboring oil-rich country of Kuwait. The quick conquest gave Iraq control of 20 percent of the world's oil production and reserves. President Bush demanded unconditional withdrawal, enlisted European and Arab allies in an anti-Iraq coalition, and persuaded Saudi Arabia to accept substantial U.S. forces to protect it against Iraqi invasion. Within weeks, the Saudis were host to tens of thousands of U.S. soldiers and hundreds of aircraft.

The background for Iraq's invasion was a simmering dispute over border oil fields and islands in the Persian Gulf. Iraq was a dictatorship that had just emerged from an immensely costly eight-year war with Iran. Saddam Hussein had depended on help from the United States and Arab nations in this war, but Iraq was now economically exhausted. Kuwait was a small, rich nation whose ruling dynasty enjoyed few friends but plenty of oil royalties. The U.S. State Department had signaled earlier in 1990 that it might support some concessions by Kuwait in its dispute with Iraq. Saddam Hussein read the signal as an open invitation to do what he wanted; having been favored in the past by the United States, he probably expected denunciations but no military response.

The Iraqis gave George Bush a golden opportunity to assert America's world influence. The Bush administration was concerned that Iraq might target oil-rich Saudi Arabia. The importance of Middle Eastern oil helped to enlist France and Britain as military allies and to secure billions of dollars from Germany and Japan. Iraq had antagonized nearly all its neighbors. The collapse of Soviet power and Gorbachev's interest in cooperating with the United States meant that the Soviets would not interfere with U.S. plans.

Bush and his advisers offered a series of justifications for U.S. actions. First, and most basic, were the desire to punish armed aggression and the presumed need to protect Iraq's other neighbors. In fact, there was scant evidence of Iraqi preparations against Saudi Arabia. The buildup of U.S. air power plus effective economic sanctions would have accomplished both protection and punishment. Sanctions and diplo-

matic pressure might also have brought withdrawal from most or all of Kuwait. However, additional American objectives—to destroy Iraq's capacity to create nuclear weapons and to topple Saddam's regime—would require direct military action.

The Persian Gulf itself offered an equally golden opportunity to the U.S. and allied armed forces. Here were no tangled jungles, invisible guerrillas, or civilians caught in a civil war. The terrain was open and nearly uninhabited. The enemy had committed regular forces to traditional battle in open land outside Iraq's cities, where the superiority of American equipment and training would be telling. Indeed, the United States could try out the tactics of armored maneuver and close land-air cooperation that the Pentagon had devised to protect Germany against Soviet invasion.

Bush probably decided on war in October, eventually increasing the number of American troops in Saudi Arabia to 580,000. The United States stepped up diplomatic pressure by securing a series of increasingly tough United Nations resolutions that culminated in November 1990 with Security Council Resolution 678, authorizing "all necessary means" to liberate Kuwait. The president convinced Congress to

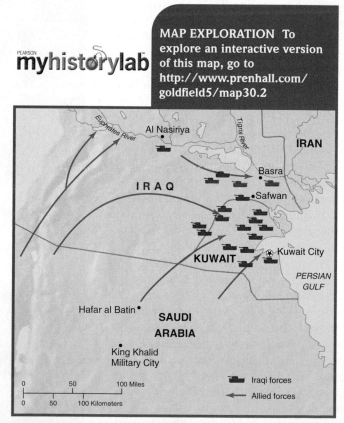

MAP 30–2   The Persian Gulf War

Ground operations against Iraq in the Persian Gulf War followed six weeks of aerial bombardment. The ground attack, which met quick success, was a multinational effort by the United States, Britain, France, Saudi Arabia, and other Arab nations threatened by an aggressive Iraq. The war freed Kuwait from Iraqi occupation but stopped before forcing a change in Iraq's government.

OVERVIEW

Why Did the Cold War End?

Commentators have offered a number of explanations for the rapid failure of the USSR and the collapse of Soviet power at the end of the 1980s. All of these factors made contributions to the complex unraveling of the Cold War.

Economic exhaustion:	The United States in the late 1970s embarked on a great modernization and expansion of its military forces. The USSR exhausted its economy and revealed its technical backwardness by trying to keep pace. Gorbachev's policy of *perestroika* was an attempt to reduce the bureaucratic inertia of the economy.
Failure of leadership:	The Soviet Union in the 1970s and early 1980s was governed by unimaginative bureaucrats. A closed elite that thought only of preserving their privileges and authority could not adapt to a changing world. The policy of *glasnost* was an effort to encourage new ideas.
Intervention in Afghanistan:	The disastrous intervention in Afghanistan revealed the limits of Soviet military power. It alienated the large Muslim population of the USSR and brought disillusionment with the incompetence of Soviet leaders.
Triumph of democratic ideas:	As political discussion became more free, the appeal of democratic ideas took on its own momentum, especially in eastern European satellite nations such as East Germany, Czechoslovakia, and Poland.
Power of nationalism:	The collapse of the Soviet empire was triggered by the resurgence of national sentiments throughout the Soviet empire. National sentiments fueled the breakaway of the eastern European satellite nations such as Hungary, Romania, and Poland. Nationalism also broke up the USSR itself as 14 smaller socialist republics declared independence from the Russian-dominated Union.

agree to military action under the umbrella of the UN. The United States ignored compromise plans floated by France and last-minute concessions from Iraq.

War began one day after the UN's January 15 deadline for Iraqi withdrawal from Kuwait. **Operation Desert Storm** opened with massive air attacks on command centers, transportation facilities, and Iraqi forward positions. The air war destroyed 40 to 50 percent of Iraqi tanks and artillery by late February. The attacks also seriously hurt Iraqi civilians by disrupting utilities and food supplies.

Americans found the **Persian Gulf War** fascinating. They bought millions of Middle East maps to follow the conflict. They watched CNN's live transmission of Baghdad under bombardment. They read about Stealth fighter bombers that were invisible to radar and about precision-guided missiles (although most of the damage came from traditional bombing and low-tech A-10 antitank aircraft).

The 40-day rain of bombs was the prelude to a ground attack (see Map 30–2). Despite Saddam Hussein's threats that the coalition faced the "mother of all battles," the Iraqi military made the land war easy. They concentrated their forces near the Persian Gulf in Kuwait because they expected an amphibious landing near Kuwait City and a direct strike north along the coast. Instead, the allies moved 235,000 U.S., French, and British soldiers far into the interior. On February 24, 1991, these forces swept into Iraq in a great arc. Americans, Saudis, Syrians, and Egyptians advanced directly to liberate Kuwait. A cease-fire came 100 hours after the start of the ground war.

The Iraqis had been driven out of Kuwait, but the relatively slow advance of the left wing failed to prevent many of the Iraqi troops from escaping. Allied forces suffered only 240 deaths in action, compared to perhaps 100,000 for the Iraqis.

Bush directed Desert Storm with the "Vietnam syndrome" in mind, believing that Americans were willing to accept war only if it involved overwhelming U.S. force and ended quickly. The United States hoped to replace Saddam Hussein without disrupting Iraqi society. Instead, the 100-hour war incited armed rebellions against Saddam in southern Iraq by Shiites, a group within the Muslim religion whose adherents comprise a majority in Iraq, and in the north by the ethnically distinct Kurds. Because Bush and his advisers were unwilling to get embroiled in a civil war or commit the United States to occupy all of Iraq, they stood by while Saddam crushed the uprisings. In one sense, the United States won the war but not the peace. Saddam Hussein became a hero to many in the Islamic world simply by remaining in power. In another sense, Bush had accomplished exactly what he wanted: the restoration of the status quo. In 2002, however, President George W. Bush (his son, elected in 2000), made a change in the Iraqi regime a centerpiece of U.S. foreign policy.

Growth in the Sunbelt

The rise in military and defense spending from the late 1970s through the early 1990s and the Persian Gulf War was one of the most powerful sources of growth in the **Sunbelt,** the southern and western regions of the United States. Americans had discovered this "new" region in the 1970s. Kevin Phillips's book *The Emerging Republican Majority* (1969) first popularized the term "Sunbelt." Phillips pointed out that people and economic activity had been flowing southward and westward since World War II, shifting the balance of power away from the Northeast. Sections of the South and West, historically controlled from the northeastern industrial core, have developed as independent centers of economic change.

The Sunbelt was a region of conservative voting habits where Republicans solidified their status as a majority party, a process continuing to the present. In the 1990s, the region's economic power was reflected in a conservative tone in both the Republican and Democratic parties and in the prominence of southern political leaders. Indeed, the career of George Bush, who got his start in New England but gained his greatest success as a new Texan, epitomized the political trend (see Map 30–3).

The rise of the Sunbelt, which is anchored by Florida, Texas, and California, reflected the leading economic trends of the 1970s and 1980s, including military spending, immigration from Asia and Latin America, and recreation and retirement spending. Corporations liked the business climate of the South, which had weak labor laws, low taxes, and generally low costs of living and doing business.

New factories dotted the southern landscape, often in smaller towns rather than cities. General Motors closed factories in Flint, Michigan, but invested in a new Saturn plant in Spring Hill, Tennessee. In contrast to troubled industrial cities in the Northeast and Midwest, cities like Orlando, Charlotte, Atlanta, Dallas, and Phoenix enjoyed headlong prosperity. Houston, with sprawling growth, business spinoffs from NASA, and purring air-conditioners epitomized the booming metropolitan areas of the South and West. It was "the place that scholars flock to for the purpose of seeing what modern civilization has wrought."

The Defense Economy

The Vietnam buildup and reinvestment in the military during the Carter (1977–1981) and Reagan (1981–1989) adminis-

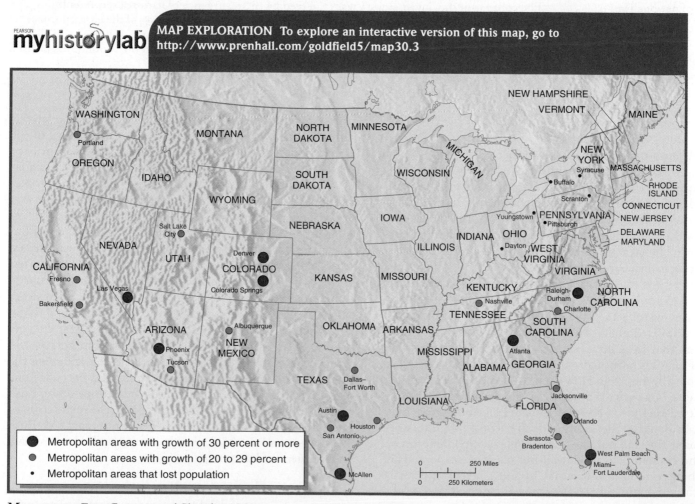

MAP EXPLORATION To explore an interactive version of this map, go to http://www.prenhall.com/goldfield5/map30.3

Legend:
● Metropolitan areas with growth of 30 percent or more
● Metropolitan areas with growth of 20 to 29 percent
• Metropolitan areas that lost population

MAP 30–3   Fast-Growing and Shrinking Metropolitan Areas, 1990–2000
In the 1990s, boom cities were found in the Southeast, the Southwest, and on the West Coast. In contrast, the large metropolitan areas that lost population were all in Ohio, New York, or Pennsylvania, the area hardest hit by the decline of jobs in established manufacturing industries.

Global Perspectives

Disney in Tokyo and Paris

Tokyo Disneyland opened in 1983 as the first Disney theme park outside the United States. Designed by Walt Disney Imagineering, it copied California's original Disneyland and Florida's Walt Disney World. It includes the classic Disneyland features of Adventureland, Westernland, Tomorrowland, and Fantasyland (complete with a Cinderella Castle that looks just like its Florida counterpart).

Tokyo Disney was been enormously successful from the start. It has consistently attracted huge crowds. For many years was the most popular theme park in the world, and developers have added Tokyo DisneySea to keep visitors coming back.

If Japanese immediately took to Tokyo Disneyland, Europeans were much less excited by the Euro Disney Resort that opened east of Paris in 1992. Critics complained about the strict rules for workers. Intellectuals criticized the invasion of American popular culture into the heart of Europe. It took several years, and new attractions like De la Terre à la Lune (Space Mountain), to bring in enough visitors to put the project in the black.

The contrasting experiences demonstrate the close affinities between American and Japanese pop culture. Japanese monster movies of the 1950s, including Godzilla, King of Monsters, and his various opponents, earned money in both Japan and the United States. The huge Japanese animation, or anime, industry that developed after World War II drew on Disney cartoon style. It developed into an economic powerhouse of comic books, TV series, video games, and spinoff toys that made fortunes for Sony, Nintendo, and other companies. Pokemon, which began as a children's game for handheld computers, grew into a marketing phenomenon that made the cover of *Time* magazine.

This exchange of entertainment and consumer products has been part of the increasingly close engagement between the economies of the United States and East Asia. Its roots lie in the democratic revival of Japan after World War II and in the opening of political relations between the United States and the People's Republic of China in the 1970s. It has grown into a huge field of investment and exchange of everything from sneakers to steel, comic book artists to centerfielders.

■ **What are some reasons for the contrasting ways that Japan and France have responded to Disney theme resorts?**

---

trations fueled the growth of the Sunbelt. Over the 40 years from the Korean conflict to the Persian Gulf War, the United States made itself the mightiest military power ever known. Military bases and defense contractors remolded the economic landscape, as mild winters and clear skies for training and operations helped the South and West attract more than 75 percent of military payrolls.

Big cities and small depended on defense spending. Southern California thrived on more than 500,000 jobs in the aircraft industry. Lockheed's huge Burbank plant drew thousands of families to the new suburbs of the San Fernando Valley; McDonnell-Douglas shaped the area around Los Angeles International Airport. Twelve thousand smaller firms and a third of the area's jobs depended on defense spending. A thousand miles away, visitors to Colorado Springs could drive past sprawling Fort Carson and visit the new Air Force Academy, opened in 1958. Sunk deep from view was the North American Air Defense Command headquarters beneath Cheyenne Mountain west of the city.

Defense spending underwrote the expansion of American science and technology. Nearly one-third of all engineers worked on military projects. Large universities, such as MIT, the University of Michigan, the California Institute of Technology, and Stanford, were leading defense contractors. The modern electronics business started in New York, Boston, and the San Francisco Bay area with research and development for military uses, such as guided-missile controls. California's Silicon Valley grew with military sales long before it turned to consumer markets. The space component of the aerospace industry was equally reliant on the defense economy, with NASA spending justified by competition with the Soviet Union. NASA's centers were scattered across the South: launch facilities at the Kennedy Space Center in Cape Canaveral, Florida; research labs at Huntsville, Alabama; and Houston's Manned Spacecraft Center as the control center for space exploration.

Americans from Around the World
Few Americans anticipated the effects of the **Immigration and Nationality Act of 1965,** which transformed the ethnic mix of the United States and helped to stimulate the Sunbelt boom. The new law initiated a change in the composi-

tion of the American people by abolishing the national quota system in effect since 1924. Quotas had favored immigrants from western Europe and limited those from other parts of the world. The old law's racial bias contradicted the self-proclaimed role of the United States as a defender of freedom, and immigration reform was part of the propaganda battle of the Cold War. The new law gave preference to family reunification and welcomed immigrants from all nations equally. The United States also accepted refugees from Communism outside the annual limits.

Immigration reform opened the doors to Mediterranean Europe, Latin America, and Asia. Legal migration to the United States surged from 1.1 million in 1960–1964 to nearly 4 million for 1990–1994. Nonlegal immigrants may have doubled the total number of newcomers in the 1970s and early 1980s. Not since World War I had the United States absorbed so many new residents. By the early 1990s, legal immigration accounted for 37 percent of all U.S. population growth, compared with 10 percent before 1965. Meanwhile, over 2 million nonlegal immigrants had taken advantage of the Immigration Reform and Control Act of 1986 to legalize their presence in the United States.

Immigration changed the nation's ethnic mix. Members of officially defined ethnic and racial minorities accounted for 25 percent of Americans in 1990 and 30 percent in 2000 (see Table 30.1). Roughly 28 million Americans had been born in other countries according to the 2000 census, or 10.4 percent of the population. This was lower than the high of 14.7 percent in 1910 but a great increase from the low of 4.7 percent in 1970. One-third of the foreign born were from Latin America and one-fourth were from Asia.

The largest single group of new Americans came from Mexico. The long border has facilitated easy movement from south to north. Especially in the border states of Texas, New Mexico, Arizona, and California, permanent immigrants have mingled with tourists, family members on visits, temporary workers, and other workers without legal permission to enter the United States. Mexican Americans were the largest minority group in many southwestern and western states in the later twentieth century. They were transforming neighborhoods in Chicago and other midwestern cities and changing everything from politics to the Catholic Church.

The East Coast has especially welcomed migrants from the West Indies and Central America. Many Puerto Ricans, who hold U.S. citizenship, came to Philadelphia and New York in the 1950s and 1960s. The 110th Street subway station in East Harlem marked the center of *El Barrio de Nueva York* for the city's 600,000 Puerto Ricans. Other countries sending large numbers of immigrants include Haiti, the Dominican Republic, Guatemala, Honduras, Nicaragua, El Salvador, and Jamaica. Cuban refugees from Castro's regime concentrated in Miami and in major cities such as Chicago and New York.

Another great immigration has occurred eastward across the Pacific. Chinese, Filipinos, Koreans, Samoans, and other Asians and Pacific Islanders constituted only 6 percent of newcomers to the United States in 1965 but nearly half of all arrivals in 1990. The number of ethnic Chinese in the United States jumped from a quarter of a million in 1965 to 1,645,000 in 1990. Immigrants from Taiwan, Hong Kong, and the People's Republic created new Chinatowns in Houston and San Diego and crowded into the historic Chinatowns of New York and San Francisco.

The most publicized Asian immigrants were refugees from Indochina after the Communist victory in 1975. The first arrivals tended to be highly educated professionals who had worked with the Americans. Another 750,000 Vietnamese, Laotians, and Cambodians arrived after 1976 by way of refugee camps in Thailand, as did Celia Noup. Most settled on the West Coast. The San Francisco Bay area, for example, had more than a dozen Vietnamese-language newspapers, magazines, and cable television programs.

In addition to southeast Asians, political conflicts and upheavals sent other waves of immigrants to the United States. Many Iranians fled the religious regime that took power in their country in the late 1970s, at the same time that Ethiopians were fleeing a nation shattered by drought, civil war, and doctrinaire Marxism. To escape repression in the Soviet Union, Jews and conservative Christians came to the United States in the 1980s, and the collapse of Communism in the Soviet Union opened the door for more Russians, Ukrainians, Romanians, and other eastern Europeans.

Recent immigrants have found both economic possibilities and problems. On the negative side, legal and illegal immigration has added to the number of nonunion workers. By one estimate, two-thirds of the workers in the Los Angeles garment trade were undocumented immigrants. Most worked for small, nonunion firms in basements and storefronts, without health insurance or pensions. But a positive

Table 30–1
Major Racial and Ethnic Minorities in the United States

	1960 Population (in millions)	Percentage of total	2000 Population (in millions)	Percentage of total
American Indians	0.5	0.3	2.5	0.9
Asians and Pacific Islanders	1.1	0.6	10.6	3.7
African Americans	18.9	10.5	34.7	12.3
Hispanics	not available		35.3	12.5

contrast was the abundance of opportunities for talent and ambition in the expanding economy of the mid-1980s and 1990s. The 130,000 Vietnamese immigrants of 1975 now have an average income above the national figure. Asians and Pacific islanders by 2000 constituted 22 percent of the students in California's public universities. Like earlier European immigrants, many newcomers have opened groceries, restaurants, and other businesses that serve their own group before expanding into larger markets. Juan Fernandez found it easier to set up a successful car repair shop in Gary, Indiana, than in Guadalajara, Mexico, because his fellow immigrants preferred a Spanish-speaking mechanic. Asian-born business owners filled retail vacuums in central city neighborhoods abandoned by chain stores. One Korean told a typical story: "A friend of mine came over with his family. He invested a few dollars in a vegetable stand in downtown Manhattan. He and his sons got up early, went to the market early. He took some of his earnings and invested in a candy store. Then he bought two more vegetable and fruit stands. Their kids work hard too and they make a lot of money."

Old Gateways and New

The new immigration from Asia, Latin America, and the Caribbean had its most striking effects in coastal and border cities. New York again became a great mixing bowl of the U.S. population. By 1990, some 28 percent of the population of New York City was foreign-born, compared to 42 percent at the height of European immigration in 1910. ZIP code 11373 in northern Queens was reportedly the most diverse neighborhood in the world.

Just as important was the transformation of southern and western cities into gateways for immigrants from Latin America and Asia. Los Angeles emerged as "the new Ellis Island" that rivaled New York's historic role in receiving immigrants. As *Time* magazine put it in 1983, the arrival of more than 2 million immigrants in greater Los Angeles altered "the collective beat and bop of L.A." In 1960, a mere 1 percent of the Los Angeles County population was Asian and 11 percent was Hispanic. By 2000, the figures for the area's population of 9.5 million were 12 percent Asian and 45 percent Hispanic. The sprawling neighborhoods of East Los Angeles make up the second-largest Mexican city in the world. New ethnic communities appeared in Los Angeles suburbs: Iranians in Beverly Hills, Chinese in Monterey Park, Japanese in Gardena, Thais in Hollywood, Samoans in Carson, Cambodians in Lakewood. One hundred languages are spoken among students entering Los Angeles schools.

New York and Los Angeles are world cities as well as immigrant destinations. Like London and Tokyo, they are capitals of world trade and finance, with international banks and headquarters of multinational corporations. They have the country's greatest concentrations of international lawyers, accounting firms, and business consultants. The deregulation of international finance and the explosive spread of instant electronic communication in the 1980s confirmed their importance as global decision centers (see Table 30–2).

Similar factors have turned Miami into an economic capital of the Caribbean. A quarter-million Cuban businessmen, white-collar workers, and their families moved to the United States between 1959 and 1962 to escape Castro's socialist government. New "freedom flights" carried 150,000 additional Cubans to the United States from 1966 to 1973, and a third round added 125,000 in 1980. Most of the newcomers stayed in South Florida. By the late 1970s Cubans owned about one-

Table 30–2

Global Cities

Ranked by Population in 2005 (population in millions)		Ranked as Economic Decision Centers
Tokyo, Japan	35.2	1. London
Cuidad de Mexico	19.4	2. New York
New York	18.7	3. Hong Kong
Sao Paulo, Brazil	18.3	4. Paris
Mumbai, India	18.2	5. Tokyo
Delhi, India	15.0	6. Singapore
Shanghai, China	14.5	7. Chicago
Kolkata, India	14.3	8. Milan
Jakarta, Indonesia	13.2	9. Los Angeles
Buenos Aires, Argentina	12.6	10. Toronto
Dhaka, Bangladesh	12.4	11. Madrid
Los Angeles	12.3	12. Amsterdam

Sources: UN Department of Economic and Social Affairs/Population Division, *World Urbanization Prospects: The 2005 Revision*; Peter J. Taylor and Robert Lang, "U.S. Cities in the 'World City Network," The Brookings Institution, February 2005.

third of the area's retail stores and many of its other businesses. Their success in business made Miami a major Latino market and helped to attract millions of Latin American tourists and shoppers. Access to the Caribbean and South America also made Miami an international banking and commercial center with hundreds of offices for corporations engaged in U.S.–Latin American trade.

Cross-border communities in the Southwest, such as El Paso, Texas, and Juarez, Mexico, or San Diego, California, and Tijuana, Mexico, are "Siamese twins joined at the cash register." Employees with work permits commute from Mexico to the United States. American popular culture flows southward. Bargain hunters and tourists pass in both directions. A shopping center near San Diego made 60 percent of its sales to Mexicans.

Both nations have promoted the cross-border economy. The Mexican government in the mid-1960s began to encourage a "platform economy" by allowing companies on the Mexican side of the border to import components and inputs duty-free as long as 80 percent of the items were re-exported and 90 percent of the workers were Mexicans. The intent was to encourage U.S. corporations to locate assembly plants south of the border. Such *maquila* industries were able to employ lower-wage workers and avoid strict antipollution laws (leading to serious threats to public health on both sides of the border). From the Gulf of Mexico to the Pacific Ocean, 1,800 *maquiladora* plants employed half a million workers. North of the border, U.S. factories supplied components under laws that meshed with the Mexican regulations.

The Graying of America

Retirees were another factor contributing to the growth of the Sunbelt. Between 1965 and 2000, the number of Americans aged 65 and over jumped from 18.2 million to 35 million, or 12.4 percent of the population. For the first time, most Americans could expect to survive into old age. The "young old" are people in their sixties and seventies who remain sharp, vigorous, and financially secure because of private pensions, Social Security, and Medicare. The "old old" are the 9 million people in their eighties and nineties who often require daily assistance, although data show that improved medical services have made such Americans healthier and more self-sufficient than they were ten or twenty years ago.

Older Americans have become a powerful voice in public affairs. They tend to vote against local taxes but fight efforts to slow the growth of Social Security, even though growing numbers of the elderly are being supported by a relatively smaller proportion of working men and women. By the 1990s, observers noted increasing resentment among younger Americans, who fear that public policy is biased against the needs of those in their productive years. In turn, the elderly fiercely defend the programs of the 1960s and 1970s that have kept many of them from poverty. Protecting Medicare and Social Security was one of the Democrats' best campaign issues in 1996 and 2000, after Republicans suggested cuts in spending growth.

Retired Americans changed the social geography of the United States. Much growth in the South and Southwest has been financed by money earned in the Northeast and Midwest and transferred by retirees. Florida in the 1980s absorbed nearly 1 million new residents aged 60 or older. California, Arizona, Texas, the Carolinas, and the Ozark Mountains of Missouri and Arkansas have all attracted retirees, many of them in age-segregated communities such as Sun City near Phoenix.

Values in Collision

In 1988, two very different religious leaders sought a presidential nomination. Pat Robertson's campaign for the Republican nomination tapped deep discontent with the changes in American society since the 1960s. A television evangelist, Robertson used the mailing list from his *700 Club* program to mobilize conservative Christians and push the Republican Party further to the right on family and social issues. Jesse Jackson, a civil rights leader and minister from Chicago, mounted a grassroots campaign with the opposite goal of moving the Democratic Party to the left on social and economic policy. Drawing on his experience in the black civil rights movement, he assembled a "Rainbow Coalition" that included labor unionists, feminists, and others whom Robertson's followers feared. Both Jackson and Robertson used their powerful personalities and religious convictions to inspire support from local churches and churchgoers.

In diagnosing social ills, Robertson pointed to the problems of individual indulgence, while Jackson pointed to racism and economic inequality. Their sharp divergence expressed differences in basic values that divided Americans in the 1980s and beyond. In substantial measure, the conflicts were rooted in the social and cultural changes of the 1960s and 1970s that had altered traditional institutions, especially the 1950s ideal of a "Ward and June Cleaver" family. Changes in roles and expectations among women and new openness about gay and lesbian sexuality were particularly powerful in dividing U.S. churches and politics.

Women's Rights and Public Policy

The women's liberation movement of the 1960s achieved important gains when Congress wrote many of its goals into law in the early 1970s. Title IX of the Educational Amendments (1972) to the Civil Rights Act prohibited discrimination by sex in any educational program receiving federal aid. The legislation expanded athletic opportunities for women and slowly equalized the balance of women and men in faculty positions. In the same year, Congress sent the Equal Rights Amendment (ERA) to the states for ratification. The amendment read, "Equal rights under the law shall not be denied or abridged by the United States or by any state on account of sex." More than 20 states ratified in the first few months. As conservatives who wanted to preserve traditional family patterns rallied strong opposition, however, the next dozen states ratified only after increasingly tough battles in state legislatures. The ERA then stalled, three states short, until the time limit for ratification expired in 1982.

Abortion rights and the conservative backlash.   In January 1973, the U.S. Supreme Court expanded the debate about women's rights with the case of ***Roe v. Wade***. Voting 7 to 2, the Court struck down state laws forbidding abortion in the first three months of pregnancy and set guidelines for abortion during the remaining months. Drawing on the earlier decision of *Griswold v. Connecticut,* which dealt with birth control, the Court held that the Fourteenth Amendment includes a right to privacy that blocks states from interfering with a woman's right to terminate a pregnancy. The Supreme Court later upheld congressional limitations on the use of federal funds for abortion in *Webster v. Reproductive Health Services* (1989) and allowed some state restrictions in *Planned Parenthood v. Casey* (1992). Nevertheless, the *Roe* decision remained in place.

These changes came in the context of increasingly sharp conflict over the feminist agenda. Both the ERA and *Roe* stirred impassioned support and equally passionate opposition that pushed the two major political parties in opposite directions. Behind the rhetoric were male fears of increased job competition during a time of economic contraction and concern about changing families. Also fueling the debate was a deep split between the mainstream feminist view of women as fully equal individuals and the contrary conservative belief that women had a special role as anchors of families, an updating of the nineteenth-century idea of separate spheres. For conservative politicians, the ERA was a good "wedge issue" that could help split religious conservatives from the Democratic Party. The debate about abortion drew on the same issue of women's relationship to families but added strong religious voices, particularly the formal opposition of the Roman Catholic Church to abortion. The arguments tapped such deep emotion that the two sides could not even agree on a common language, juxtaposing a right to life against rights to privacy and freedom of choice.

Women in the workforce.   The most sweeping change in the lives of American women did not come from federal legislation or court cases, but from the growing likelihood that a woman would work outside the home. In 1960, some 32 percent of married women were in the labor force; 40 years later, 61 percent were working or looking for work (along with 69 percent of single women). Federal and state governments slowly responded to the changing demands of work and family with new policies, such as a federal childcare tax credit.

More women entered the workforce as inflation in the 1970s and declining wages in the 1980s eroded the ability of families to live comfortable lives on one income. Between 1979 and 1986, fully 80 percent of married households saw the husband's income fall in constant dollars. The result, headlined the *Wall Street Journal* in 1994: "More Women Take Low-Wage Jobs Just So Their Families Can Get By."

A second reason for the increase in working women from 29 million in 1970 to 66 million in 2000 was the broad shift from manufacturing to service jobs, reducing demand for factory workers and manual laborers and increasing the need for such "women's jobs" as data-entry clerks, reservation agents, and nurses. Indeed, the U.S. economy still divides job categories by sex. There was some movement toward gender-neutral hiring in the 1970s because of legal changes and the pressures of the women's movement. Women's share of lawyers more than quadrupled, of economists more than tripled, and of police detectives more than doubled. Nevertheless, job types were more segregated by sex than by race in the 1990s.

AIDS and Gay Activism

After the increasing openness about sexual orientation in the 1970s, the character of life in gay communities took an abrupt turn in the 1980s when a new worldwide epidemic emerged. Scientists identified a new disease pattern, **acquired immune deficiency syndrome (AIDS),** in 1981. The name described the symptoms resulting from infection by the human immunodeficiency virus (HIV), which destroys the body's ability to resist disease. HIV is transferred through blood and semen. In the 1980s, the most frequent American victims were gay men and intravenous drug users.

The AIDS Quilt, displayed in Washington in October 1992, combined individual memorials to AIDS victims into a powerful communal statement. The quilt project reminded Americans that AIDS had penetrated every American community.

Many in the gay community believed that the public health response was inadequate because of prejudice against them and used aggressive and sometimes outrageous tactics to pressure the government to increase funding and speed the approval process for new drugs. According to AIDS researcher Anthony Fauci, AIDS activists changed the practice of medicine in the United States for the better by giving patients greater control of their own treatment.

A decade later, it was clear that HIV/AIDS was a national and even global problem. By the end of 2005, AIDS had been responsible for 550,000 deaths in the United States, and transmission to heterosexual women was increasing. The U.S. Centers for Disease Control and Prevention estimated roughly 40,000 new cases of HIV infection per year at the beginning of the twenty-first century, bringing the total of infected Americans to around 1,200,000. Once a problem of big cities, HIV infection had spread to every American community and had helped to change American attitudes about the process of dying through the spread of hospices for the care of the terminally ill. Meanwhile, the toll of AIDS deaths in other parts of the world, particularly eastern Africa, dwarfed that in the United States and made it a world health crisis (see From Then to Now, Chapter 28 page 814).

By the 1990s, Americans were accustomed to open discussion of gay sexuality, if not always accepting of its reality. Television stars and other entertainers could "come out" and retain their popularity. So could politicians in certain districts. Tony Kushner's drama *Angels in America* (1993) won national prizes for its intense exploration of the impact of AIDS on an ordinary American community. On the issue of gays in the military, however, Congress and the Pentagon were more cautious, accepting a policy that made engaging in homosexual acts, though not sexual orientation itself, grounds for discharge.

Churches in Change

Americans picture mining frontiers as rip-roaring places, where a handful of women hold the fort while the men work hard, drink deep, and carry on. Modern Grand Junction, Colorado, however, is far less exciting. Between 1980 and 1984, efforts to develop the oil-shale resources of western Colorado pushed the population of Grand Junction from 60,000 to 80,000. Hopes were high and money was easy, but there was also a boom in religion. Newcomers to Grand Junction, a fast-changing city within a rapidly evolving society, searched for family stability and a sense of community by joining established congregations and organizing new churches. The telephone book in 1985 listed 28 mainline Protestant and Catholic churches, 24 Baptist churches (reflecting the Oklahoma and Texas roots of many oil workers), five more liberal churches (e.g., Unitarian), and more than 50 Pentecostal, Bible, and Evangelical churches. Nearly a dozen Christian schools supplemented the public schools.

Grand Junction's religious bent is typical of the contemporary United States, where religion is prominent in daily lives, institutions, and public policy debates. Americans take their search for spiritual grounding much more seriously than do citizens of other industrial nations. Roughly half of privately organized social activity (such as charity work) is church related. In the mid-1970s, 56 percent of Americans said that religion was "very important" to them, compared to only 27 percent of Europeans. Moreover, religious belief is an important source of political convictions and basis for political action (see American Views, The Religious Imperative in Politics).

As the Grand Junction statistics also suggest, the mainline Protestant denominations that traditionally defined the center of American belief were struggling after 1970. The United Methodist Church, the Presbyterian Church U.S.A., the United Church of Christ, and the Episcopal Church battled internally over the morality of U.S. foreign policy, the role of women in the ministry, and the reception of gay and lesbian members. They were strengthened by an ecumenical impulse that united denominational branches divided by ethnicity or regionalism. However, they gradually lost their position among American churches, perhaps because ecumenism diluted the certainty of their message. Liberal Protestantism has historically been strongest in the slow-growing Northeast and Midwest.

By contrast, evangelical Protestant churches have benefitted from the direct appeal of their message and from strong roots in the booming Sunbelt. Members of evangelical churches (25 percent of white Americans) now outnumber the members of mainline Protestant churches (20 percent). Major evangelical denominations include Baptists, the Church of the Nazarene, and the Assemblies of God. Fundamentalists, defined by a belief in the literal truth of the Bible, are a subset of evangelicals. So are 8 to 10 million Pentecostals and charismatics, who accept "gifts of the spirit," such as healing by faith and speaking in tongues.

Outsiders knew evangelical Christianity through "televangelists." Spending on religious television programming rsoe from $50 million to $600 million by 1980. The "electronic church" built on the radio preaching and professional revivalism of the 1950s. By the 1970s it reached 20 percent of American households. Most Americans recognized the big four. Oral Roberts had a television show and Oral Roberts University in Oklahoma. Pat Robertson had the Christian Broadcasting Network in Virginia. Jerry Falwell claimed leadership of the politically active Moral Majority (see American Views, The Religious Imperative in Politics). Jim and Tammy Faye Bakker had grant plans for real estate developments before their efforts collapsed in fraud.

Evangelical churches emphasized religion as an individual experience focused on personal salvation. Unlike many of the secular and psychological avenues to fulfillment, however, they also offered communities of faith that might stabilize fragmented lives. The conservative nature of their theology and social teaching in a changing society offered certainty that was especially attractive to many younger families.

Another important change in national religious life has been the continuing Americanization of the Roman Catholic Church following the Second Vatican Council in 1965, in which church leaders sought to respond to postwar indus-

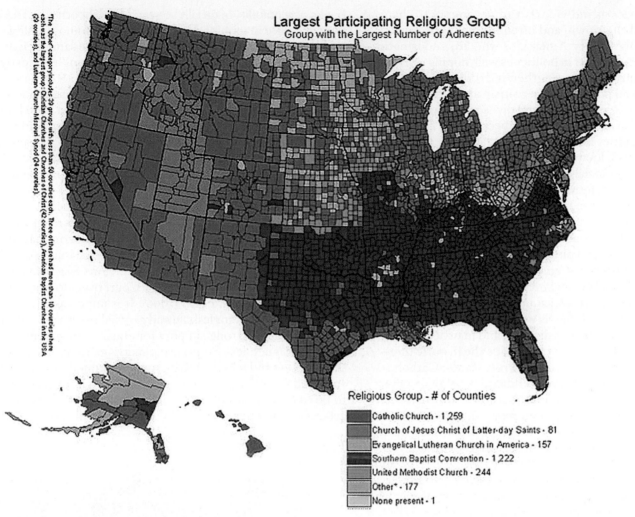

Largest Participating Religious Group
Group with the Largest Number of Adherents

Religious Group - # of Counties

- Catholic Church - 1,259
- Church of Jesus Christ of Latter-day Saints - 81
- Evangelical Lutheran Church in America - 157
- Southern Baptist Convention - 1,222
- United Methodist Church - 244
- Other* - 177
- None present - 1

The "Other" category includes 39 groups with less than 80 counties each. Three of these had more than 10 counties where each was the largest group: Christian Churches and Churches of Christ (42 counties), American Baptist Churches in the USA (29 counties), and Lutheran Church–Missouri Synod (24 counties).

MAP 30–4   Religious Geography of the United States
Differences in dominant religious groups in the United States reflect the history of immigration (Lutherans in the upper Middle West, Roman Catholics in the Northeast and Southwest), internal migration (the concentration of Mormons in and near Utah), and cultural differences between North and South.

Glenmary Research Institute

trial society. In the United States, Roman Catholicism moved toward the center, helped by the popularity of John Kennedy and by worldly success that made Catholics the economic peers of Protestants. Even as the tight connection between Catholicism and membership in European immigrant communities gradually faded, Asian and Latino immigrants brought new vigor to many parishes, and many inner-city churches have been centers for social action. Church practice lost some of its distinctiveness; celebrating Mass in English rather than Latin was an important move toward modernization, but it also sparked a conservative counter-effort to preserve the traditional liturgy. Traditional and nontraditional Catholics also disagree about whether priests should be allowed to marry and other adaptations to American culture.

The new globalization of American society simultaneously increased the nation's religious diversity and confirmed the dominant position of Christianity. Many immigrants from Asia and Africa have come with their native religious beliefs.

There are now hundreds of Hindu temples and thousands of Buddhist centers. More than a million Muslims now worship in mosques that are found in every major city. In total, the proportion of Americans who identify themselves with non-Christian religions grew from 3 percent in 1990 to 4 percent in 2001. Over the same period, however, the proportion identifying with a Christian group or denomination grew from 86 to 87 percent. Indeed, many recent immigrants are Christians: Roman Catholics from Vietnam and the Philippines, Protestants from Korean, evangelicals from the former Soviet Union, Catholics and evangelicals from Latin America.

Culture Wars

In the 1950s and 1960s, Americans argued most often over foreign policy, racial justice, and the economy. Since the 1980s, they have also quarreled over beliefs and values, especially as the patterns of family life have become more varied. In the course of these quarrels, religious belief has heavily influenced politics as individuals and groups try to shape America around their own, and often mutually conflicting, ideas of the godly society. Americans who are undogmatic in religion are often liberal in politics as well, hoping to lessen economic inequities and strengthen individual social freedom. Religious and political conservatism also tend to go together. To some degree, this cultural division runs all the way through American society, dividing liberal North from conservative South, cities from small towns, and college professors from Kiwanis Club members.

The division on social issues is related to theological differences within Protestantism. The "conservative" emphasis on personal salvation and the literal truth of the Bible expresses itself in a desire to restore "traditional" social patterns. Conservatives worry that social disorder occurs when people follow personal impulses and pleasures. In contrast, the "liberal" or "modern" emphasis on the universality of the Christian message restates the Social Gospel with its call to build the Kingdom of God through social justice and may recognize divergent pathways toward truth. Liberals worry that greed in the unregulated marketplace creates disorder and injustice.

The cultural conflict also transcends the historic three-way division of Americans among Protestants, Catholics, and Jews. Instead, the conservative-liberal division now cuts through each group. For example, Catholic reformers, liberal Protestants, and Reform Jews may find agreement on issues of cultural values despite theologies that are worlds apart. The same may be true of conservative Catholics, fundamentalist Protestants, and Orthodox Jews.

Conservatives initiated the culture wars, trying to stabilize what they fear is an American society spinning out of control because of lack of self-discipline and sexual indulgence. In fact, the evidence on the sexual revolution is mixed. Growing numbers of teenagers reported being sexually active in the 1970s, but the rate of increase tapered off in the 1980s. The divorce rate began to drop after 1980. Births to teenagers dropped after 1990, and the number of two-parent families increased. Sexual advice and self-help books proliferated, with such titles as *Open Marriage* (1972) and *The Joy of Sex* (1972), but most adults remained staid and monogamous, according to data from 1994. Perhaps the logical extension of reading about sex in the 1970s was an astonishing eagerness to talk about sex in the 1990s, a decade when soap-opera story lines and talk shows covered everything from family violence to exotic sexual tastes.

The explosion of explicit attention to sexual behavior set the stage for religiously rooted battles over two sets of issues. One cluster revolved around so-called family values, questioning the morality of access to abortion, the acceptability of homosexuality, and the roles and rights of women. A second set of concerns has focused on the supposed role of public schools in undermining morality through sex education, unrestricted reading matter, nonbiblical science, and the absence of prayer. The Supreme Court decisions in 1962 and 1963 that prohibited vocal prayer and devotional Bible reading in public schools were targets for many. Opinion polls show clear differences among religious denominations on such issues as censorship of library

books, acceptability of racially segregated neighborhoods, freedom of choice in terminating pregnancy, and homosexuality.

Not all issues of the culture wars carry the same weight. Censorship of art exhibits and library collections has mostly been an issue for political grandstanding. U.S. senators grabbed headlines in 1989 by attacking the National Endowment for the Arts for funding "obscene" art, but a local jury in Cincinnati later proved tolerant of sexually explicit images in a photographic exhibition. Efforts to restrict legal access to abortion mobilized thousands of right to life advocates in the late 1980s and early 1990s, but illegal acts remained the work of a radical fringe.

A culturally conservative issue with great popular appeal in the early 1990s was an effort to prevent states and localities from protecting homosexuals against discrimination. Under the slogan "No special rights," antigay measures passed in Cincinnati, Colorado, and communities in Oregon in 1993 and 1994, only to have the Supreme Court overturn the Colorado law in *Romer v. Evans* (1996). It is important to note that public support for lesbian and gay civil rights varies with different issues (strong support for equal employment opportunity, much less for granting marriage rights to same-sex couples) and whether the issues are framed in terms of specified rights for gays or in terms of the right of everyone to be free from government interference with personal decisions, such as living arrangements and sexual choices.

In December 1993, the U.S. Supreme Court heard arguments on whether states could require protesters to remain a certain distance from abortion clinics. These antiabortion and proabortion protesters revealed the deep divisions over this and other issues in the culture wars.

American Views

The Religious Imperative in Politics

The strong religious faith of many Americans frequently drives them to different stands on political issues. The first of these two documents, a letter by Jerry Falwell to potential supporters of the Moral Majority, reflects the politically conservative outlook of many evangelical Christians. Falwell is pastor of the Thomas Road Baptist Church in Lynchburg, Virginia. He founded the Moral Majority, a conservative religious lobbying and educational organization, in 1979 and served as its president until 1987, the year he wrote the letter reprinted here. The organization was especially important for voter registration efforts among conservative Christians. The second document, from an open letter issued by the Southside United Presbyterian Church in Tucson in 1982, expresses the conviction of other believers that God may sometimes require civil disobedience to oppose oppressive government actions. The letter explains the church's reasons for violating immigration law to offer sanctuary to refugees from repressive Central American regimes supported by the United States.

- How do Falwell and the Southside Presbyterian Church define the problems that demand a religious response?
- Are there any points of agreement?
- How does each statement balance the claims of God and government?

From the Reverend Jerry Falwell:

I believe that the overwhelming majority of Americans are sick and tired of the way that amoral liberals are trying to corrupt our nation from its commitment to freedom, democracy, traditional morality, and the free enterprise system. And I believe that the majority of Americans agree on the basic moral values which this nation was founded upon over 200 years ago.

Today we face four burning crises as we continue in this Decade of Destiny—the 1980s—loss of our freedom by giving in to the Communists; the destruction of the family unit; the deterioration of the free enterprise system; and the crumbling of basic moral principles which has resulted in the legalizing of abortion, widespread pornography, and a drug problem of epidemic proportions.

That is why I went to Washington, D.C., in June of 1979, and started a new organization, The Moral Majority. Right now you may be wondering: "But I thought Jerry Falwell was the preacher on the Old-Time Gospel Hour television program?"

You are right. For over twenty-four years I have been calling the nation back to God from the pulpit on radio and television. But in recent months I have been led to do more than just preach. I have been compelled to take action.

I have made the commitment to go right into the halls of Congress and fight for laws that will save America.

I will still be preaching every Sunday on the Old-Time Gospel Hour and I still must be a husband and father to my precious family in Lynchburg, Virginia.

But as God gives me the strength, I must do more. I must go into the halls of Congress and fight for laws that will protect the grand old flag for the sake of our children and grandchildren.

From Southside United Presbyterian Church:

We are writing to inform you that Southside Presbyterian Church will publicly violate the Immigration and Nationality Act, Section 274 (A).

We take this action because we believe the current policy and practice of the United States Government with regard to Central American refugees is illegal and immoral. We believe our government is in violation of the 1980 Refugee Act and international law by continuing to arrest, detain, and forcibly return refugees to the terror, persecution, and murder in El Salvador and Guatemala.

We believe that justice and mercy require the people of conscience to actively assert our God-given right to aid anyone fleeing from persecution and murder.

We beg of you, in the name of God, to do justice and love mercy in the administration of your office. We ask that "extended voluntary departure" be granted to refugees from Central America and that current deportation proceedings against these victims be stopped.

Until such time, we will not cease to extend the sanctuary of the church. Obedience to God requires this of us all.

Sources: Gary E. McCuen, ed., *The Religious Right* (Hudson, WI, G. E. McCuen, 1989); Ann Crittenden, *Sanctuary* (New York, Weidenfeld & Nicolson, 1988).

Conclusion

Americans entered the 1980s searching for stability. The 1970s had brought unexpected and uncomfortable change. Soviet actions in Asia and Africa seemed to be destabilizing the world. The memory of defeat in Vietnam left a bitter taste, and hostages in Tehran seemed to signal the end to U.S. global postwar dominance. Energy crises, inflation, and boarded-up factories eroded purchasing power and undermined confidence in the future. Traditional values seemed under siege. Ronald Reagan's presidential campaign played to these insecurities by promising to revitalize the older ways of life and restore the United States to its former influence.

Taken as a whole, the years from 1981 through 1992 brought transformations that redirected the course of American life. Because many changes were associated with national policy choices, it is fair to call this the era of the Reagan revolution. The astonishing collapse of the Soviet Union ended 40 years of Cold War. New political leadership in Washington reversed the 50-year expansion of federal government programs to deal with economic and social inequities. Prosperity alternated with recessions that shifted the balance between regions. The stock market rode a roller coaster, familiar corporate names vanished, and the national media made temporary heroes of business tycoons. Economic inequality increased after narrowing for a generation at the same time that more and more leaders proclaimed that unregulated markets could best meet social needs. Middle-class Latinos and African Americans made substantial gains, while many other minority Americans sank deeper into poverty.

At the same time, it is important to recognize that every revolution has its precursors. Intellectuals have been clarifying the justifications for Reagan administration actions since the 1960s. The Reagan-Bush years extended changes that began in the 1970s, particularly the conservative economic policies and military buildup of the troubled Carter administration. In retrospect, the growing weakness of the USSR should also have been apparent in the same decade, had not the United States been blinded by its fear of Communist power. Intervention in the Persian Gulf amplified U.S. policies that had been in place since the CIA intervened in Iran in 1953. The outbreak of violence in Los Angeles after the Rodney King verdict showed that race relations were as tense as they had been in the 1960s.

In 1992, the United States stood as the undisputed world power. Its economy was poised for a surge of growth at the same time that rivals such as Japan were mired in economic crisis. It was the leader in scientific research and the development of new technologies. Its military capacities far surpassed those of any rival and seemed to offer a free hand in shaping the world—capacities that would be tested and utilized in the new century.

Review Questions

1. Is it accurate to talk about a Reagan Revolution in U.S. politics? Did Reagan's presidency change the economic environment for workers and business corporations? How did economic changes in the 1980s affect the prospects of the richest and poorest Americans?

2. How did American ideas about the proper role of government change during the 1980s? What were the basis of these changes?

3. What caused the breakup of the Soviet Union and the end of the Cold War? Did U.S. foreign policy under Reagan and Bush contribute significantly to the withdrawal of Soviet power from eastern Europe? Did the collapse of the USSR show the strength of the United States and its allies or the weakness of Soviet Communism?

4. How did the United States use military force during the Reagan and Bush administrations? Did military actions achieve the expected goals?

5. What were some of the important economic trends that shifted American growth toward the Sunbelt (South and West)? How has immigration from other nations affected the different American regions?

6. What changes in family roles and sexual behavior became divisive political issues? How have churches responded to cultural changes? What are some of the ways in which churches and religious leaders have tried to influence political decisions?

7. How did U.S. military involvement in southeast Asia in the 1960s continue to affect American society for decades to come?

Key Terms

Acquired immune deficiency syndrome (AIDS) (p. 877)

Americans with Disabilities Act (p. 864)

Deregulation (p. 857)

Economic Recovery and Tax Act of 1981 (ERTA) (p. 856)

Glasnost (p. 887)

Immigration and Nationality Act of 1965 (p. 873)

Intermediate Nuclear Force Agreement (INF) (p. 867)

Operation Desert Storm (p. 871)

Persian Gulf War (p. 871)

Perestroika (p. 867)

Reagan Doctrine (p. 865)

Roe v. Wade (p. 877)

Sagebrush Rebellion (p. 857)

Strategic Defense Initiative (SDI) (p. 865)

Sunbelt (p. 871)

Recommended Reading

Anderson, Elijah. *Streetwise: Race, Class, and Change in an Urban Community* (1990). A deeply troubling portrait of the culture of the streets in the Philadelphia ghetto during the 1980s.

Beschloss, Michael, and Strobe Talbott. *At the Highest Levels* (1993). A dramatic narrative of the last years of the Cold War, based on detailed interviews with American and Soviet participants.

Coutin, Susan Bibler. *The Culture of Protest: Religious Activism and the U.S. Sanctuary Movement* (1993). Examining foreign policy from the grassroots, sympathetically portrays the meanings that participants in the sanctuary movement gave their actions.

Edsall, Thomas Byrne, and Mary D. Edsall. *Chain Reaction: The Impact of Race, Rights, and Taxes on American Politics* (1991). Argues that the Democratic Party has systematically alienated its working-class supporters.

Fitzgerald, Frances. *Way Out There in the Blue: Reagan, Star Wars, and the End of the Cold War* (2000). A detailed analysis of the technical weaknesses and political appeal of strategic missile defense.

Liebow, Elliot. *Tell Them Who I Am: The Lives of Homeless Women* (1993). A sensitive depiction of street people and bag ladies as complex individuals coping with personal problems and economic crisis.

Phillips, Kevin. *Boiling Point: Democrats, Republicans, and the Decline of Middle-Class Prosperity* (1992). Expresses the belief that the economic policies of the Reagan and Bush administrations systematically harmed working- and middle-class families.

Rubin, Lillian. *Families on the Fault Line: America's Working Class Speaks about the Family, the Economy, Race, and Ethnicity* (1994). Interviews with American families about their efforts to cope with economic and social change.

Wills, Garry. *Reagan's America: Innocents at Home* (1987). A biography critical of Reagan's ideas but insightful about his personality.

Where To Learn More

■ **Ronald Reagan Boyhood Home, Dixon, Illinois.** The home where Reagan lived from 1920 to 1923 tells relatively little about Reagan himself but a great deal about the small-town context that shaped his ideas. www.ronaldreaganhome.com

■ **The Intermediate Nuclear Force Agreement (INF).** The full-text document of the INF agreement between the United States and the Soviet Union, the first true nuclear-disarmament treaty. http://www.state.gov/www/global/arms/treaties/inf1.html

■ **The Gulf War.** See video clips from the Canadian Broadcasting Corporation that provide a running narrative of the military crisis and war. http:archives.cbc.ca/war_conflict/1991_gulf_war/.

Study Resources

For study resources for this chapter, go to www.myhistorylab.com and choose *The American Journey*. You will find a wealth of study and review material for this chapter, including pre- and post-tests, customized study plan, key term review flash cards, interactive map and document activities, and documents for analysis.

The terrorist attack on the World Trade Center on September 11, 2001, brought a spontaneous outpouring of efforts to assist the victims. The collapse of the World Trade Center towers killed hundreds of emergency workers. This New York City firefighter looks toward the collapsing buildings where many of his co-workers perished.

Complacency, Crisis, and Global Reengagement

31

1993–2008

I'm a firefighter for the FDNY [Fire Department New York]. I had gotten off the night before....My friend woke me up early that morning to borrow my car to take his sick cat to the vet....I was up so I went to my local bagel store for my coffee and paper...when I heard a lady scream a plane had hit the Trade Center....I thought since it was a beautiful day that perhaps a Cessna with the pilot having a heart attack had accidentally done this....I ran home to put the TV on....as soon as I saw what damage was done I knew this wasn't any Cessna....my god people were jumping...phone rang it was a fellow from my station and he hadn't turned his TV on yet....I screamed to him to turn his #*#* TV on....

When the second plane hit...I said goodbye and told him I was going in....I jumped in my car and was off to the races....the highway was closed...but open for us.

... I had the gas pedal to the floor as I headed toward the city looking out my window I see both towers burning...when I hear a rumble and see the south tower #2 fall....I have to get my gear so I pull off the highway going down the on ramp...arriving at the firehouse everyone's in shock and we know we gotta get there now to help....as we're getting ready to leave the 2nd tower fell....we commandeer a bus and we're off....

We arrived at a staging area and then finally got the ok to go in....who's in charge?...Shoes, papers, and dust are everywhere....we wait til [building] 7 collapses....chief gets us into the site by going thru the financial center and bam there we are....pieces of the outside wall sticking out of the highway....cars on fire...buses gutted....I saw numerous acts of courage that day both civilian and uniformed....the looks on the faces of the people coming out of the city that day will haunt me forever...everyone was the same color....dust white....women

crying....men crying....we...must never forget the men and women that died that day....their sacrifice will live on for generations to come....

John McNamara, Story \#400, The September 11 Digital Archive, 13 April 2002, http://911digitalarchive.org/stories/details/400

myhistorylab

Personal Journeys Online

- Anthony Fernandez III, "Remembering the Oklahoma City Bombing," 2007. A search and rescue worker describes the background of the picture on page 899.

- Dawn Shurmaitis, 2001. Volunteering in the aftermath of the September 11, 2001 attack.

John McNamara was one of the many off-duty New York City firefighters who rushed to the World Trade Center after the terrorist attack on September 11, 2001. Hijacking four commercial jetliners, the terrorists crashed one plane into the Pentagon and one into each of the twin towers of the World Trade Center, 110-story buildings that housed 50,000 workers at the peak of the workday. Like John McNamara, tens of millions of Americans were jolted out of morning routines by riveting television coverage of the burning towers and watched in horror as first one tower and then the other disintegrated into itself. September 11 was an occasion for terror and courage. Passengers on the fourth plane fought the hijackers and made sure that it crashed in the Pennsylvania mountains rather than hit a fourth target. Altogether, 479 police officers, firefighters, and other emergency workers died in the collapse of the towers. Thousands of volun-

teers rushed to assist rescue efforts or contribute to relief efforts. The total confirmed death toll was 2,752 in New York, 184 at the Pentagon, and 40 in Pennsylvania.

The attacks, masterminded by the Al-Qaeda network of Muslim extremists, ended a decade of prosperity at home and complacency about the place of the United States in the world. In their aftermath, as Americans noticed millions of Muslim neighbors and tried to balance civil liberties against national security, they realized how diverse the nation had become. For most of the 1990s, prosperity had allowed politics to focus on social issues, such as healthcare and education, as well as on bitterly partisan but often superficial battles over personalities and presidential behavior. However, the terrorists attacked buildings that were symbols of the nation's economic and military power. The aftermath deepened a business recession that had followed a decade of growth spurred by new technologies. At the same time, the vulnerability of the targets undermined Americans' sense of security and isolation from world problems, underscored the global reach of terrorism, and made understanding its sources more necessary than ever.

Politics of the Center

In Bill Clinton's race for president in 1992, the "war room" was the decision center where Clinton and his staff planned tactics and countered Republican attacks. On the wall was a sign with a simple message: "It's the economy, stupid." The short sentence was a reminder that victory lay in emphasizing everyday problems that George H. W. Bush had neglected. Clinton promised economic leadership and stressed the need for private investment to create jobs. He promised to reduce government bureaucracy and the deficit, touted the value of stable families, and talked about healthcare and welfare reform. His message revealed an insight into the character of the United States in the 1990s. What mattered most were down-to-earth issues, not the distant problems of foreign policy, which seemed to have little urgency after the end of the Cold War. As voters worried about the changing economy and its social consequences, they were eager for leaders who promised practical responses. The mid-1990s brought erratic swings between the two major parties, but the most reliable position was the center.

Bill Clinton's election, first term, and reelection in 1996 showed the attraction of pragmatic policies and the political center in a two-party system. In his first inaugural address in January 1993, Clinton pledged "an end to the era of deadlock and drift and a new season of American renewal." What he found in his first four years in office was an equilibrium that resulted in narrow, bipartisan victories and defeats. In 1996, voters showed that they liked the nation's break from an activist government by keeping the balance of a Democratic White House and Republican Congress, and the presidential election of 2000 proved to be the closest in history.

CHRONOLOGY

1969	First version of Internet (ARPAnet) launched.
1980	CNN begins broadcasting.
1991	World Wide Web launched.
1992	Bill Clinton elected president.
1993	Congress approves the North American Free Trade Agreement (NAFTA).
	Congress adopts Family Leave Act.
1994	Independent Counsel Kenneth Starr begins investigation of Bill and Hillary Clinton. Paula Jones files sexual harassment lawsuit against Bill Clinton.
	Republicans sweep to control of Congress.
	Federal government temporarily shuts down for lack of money.
1995	United States sends peacekeeping troops to Bosnia.
1996	Clinton wins a second term as president.
1998	Paula Jones lawsuit dismissed.
	House of Representatives impeaches Clinton.
1999	Senate acquits Clinton of impeachment charges.
	United States leads NATO intervention in Kosovo.
2000	George W. Bush defeats Al Gore in nation's closest presidential election.
2001	Congress passes massive ten-year tax reduction.
	United States refuses to agree to Kyoto Treaty to limit global warming.
	Terrorists crash airliners into World Trade Center and Pentagon.
	U.S. military operations oust Taliban regime in Afghanistan.
	Congress passes U.S. PATRIOT Act to combat domestic terror.
2002	United States and Russia agree to cut number of deployed nuclear warheads.
	Congress creates Department of Homeland Security.
	United Nations Security Council passes resolution requiring Iraq to allow open inspections of weapons systems.
2003	U.S. and British troops invade Iraq and topple government of Saddam Hussein.
	Supreme Court allows limited forms of affirmative action in university admissions.
2004	George W. Bush reelected as president.
2005	Hurricane Katrina devastates New Orleans
	Iraq adopts new constitution.
2006	Democrats regain narrow edge in Congress.
2008	John McCain and Barack Obama compete for Presidency.

The Election of 1992: A New Generation

Every 15 to 20 years, a new group of voters and leaders comes to power, driven by the desire to fix the mess that the previous generation left behind. The men and women who came of age during World War II learned to accept the need to struggle and the expectation of success. Their attitudes shaped the Cold War, dynamic conservatism, the New Frontier, and foreign policy under Johnson and Nixon. The conservative agenda for Ronald Reagan's and George H. W. Bush's administrations arose from the disillusion and crises of the late 1960s and 1970s, shaping leaders who believed that the answer was to turn the nation's social and economic problems over to the market while asserting America's influence and power around the world.

The mid-1990s brought another generation into the political arena. The members of "Generation X" came of voting age with deep worries about the foreclosing of opportunities. They worried that previous administrations had ignored growing economic divisions and let the competitive position of the United States deteriorate. The range of suggested solutions differed widely—individual moral reform, a stronger labor movement, leaner competition in world markets—but the generational concern was clear.

This generational change made 1992 one of the most volatile national elections in decades. A baby boomer and successful governor of Arkansas who was not widely known nationally, Democrat Bill Clinton decided that George H.W. Bush was vulnerable when more senior Democrats opted to pass on the contest. His campaign for the nomination overcame minimal name recognition, accusations of womanizing, and his use of a student deferment to avoid military service in Vietnam. Clinton made sure that the Democrats fielded a full baby boomer (and southern) ticket by choosing as his running mate the equally youthful Tennessean Albert Gore, Jr., who had served in the Senate for two terms and was widely known for his book on the environment, *Earth in the Balance.*

Bush, the last politician of the World War II generation to gain the White House, won renomination by beating back the archconservative Patrick Buchanan, who claimed that the last 12 years had been a long betrayal of true conservatism. The Republican National Convention in Houston showed how important cultural issues had become to the Republican Party. The party platform conformed to the beliefs of the Christian right. Buchanan delivered a startling speech that called for right-thinking Americans to crusade against unbelievers. Buchanan's divisive comments were a reminder of the multiple ways that religious belief was reshaping U.S. politics.

The wild card was the Texas billionaire Ross Perot, whose independent campaign started with an appearance on a television talk show. Perot loved flip charts, distanced himself from professional politicians, and claimed to talk sense to the American people. He also tried to occupy the political center, appealing to the middle of the middle-class—small business owners, middle managers, and professionals who had approved of Reagan's antigovernment rhetoric but distrusted his corporate cronies. In May, Perot outscored both Bush and Clinton in opinion polls, but his behavior became increasingly erratic. He withdrew from the race and then reentered after floating stories that he was the target of dark conspiracies.

Bush campaigned as a foreign policy expert. He expected voters to reward him for the end of the Cold War, but he ignored anxieties about the nation's direction at home. His popularity had surged immediately after the Persian Gulf War, only to fall rapidly as the country became mired in a recession. In fact, voters in November 1992 ranked the economy first as an issue, the federal budget deficit second, health care third, and foreign policy eighth. Clinton hammered away at economic concerns, appealing to swing voters, such as suburban independents and blue-collar Reagan Democrats. He presented himself as the leader of new, pragmatic, and livelier Democrats. He put on sunglasses and played the saxophone on a late-night talk show. His campaign theme song came from Fleetwood Mac, a favorite rock group of thirty-something Americans: "Don't stop thinking about tomorrow.... Yesterday's gone. Yesterday's gone."

Election day gave the Clinton-Gore ticket 43 percent of the popular vote, Bush 38 percent, and Perot 19 percent. Clinton held the Democratic core of northern and midwestern industrial states and loosened the Republican hold on the South and West (see Map 31–1). Millions who voted for Perot were casting a protest vote for "none of the above" and against "politics as usual" rather than hoping for an actual

Despite personal flaws, Bill Clinton was enormously effective as a political campaigner.

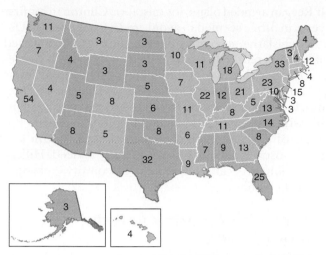

	Electoral Vote (%)	Popular Vote (%)
BILL CLINTON **(Democrat)**	**370** **(69)**	**43,728,275** **(43.2)**
George Bush (Republican)	168 (31)	38,167,416 (37.7)
H. Ross Perot (United We Stand, America)	–	19,237,247 (19.0)

MAP 31–1   The Election of 1992
Bill Clinton defeated George H. W. Bush in 1992 by reviving the Democratic Party in the industrial Northeast and enlisting new Democratic voters in the western states, where he appealed both to Hispanic immigrants and to people associated with fast-growing high-tech industries. He won reelection in 1996 with the same pattern of support. However, the coalition was an unstable combination of "Old Democrats," associated with older industries and labor unions, and "New Democrats," favoring economic change, free trade, and globalization.

Perot victory. Clinton ran best among voters over 65, who remembered FDR and Harry Truman, and voters under 30.

Policing the World

Although Clinton was much more interested in domestic policies, he inherited a confused expectation that the United States could use its military and economic power to keep the world on an even keel and counter ethnic hatred without incurring serious risks to itself. During the administration's first years, U.S. diplomats helped broker an Israel-PLO accord that gave Palestinians self-government in Gaza and the West Bank, only to watch extremists on both sides undermine the accords and plunge Israel into a near–civil war by 2002. The United States in 1994 used diplomatic pressure to persuade North Korea to suspend building nuclear weapons, temporarily calming a potentially explosive trouble spot. The world also benefitted from a gradual reduction of nuclear arsenals and from a 1996 treaty to ban the testing of nuclear weapons.

Elsewhere in the world, Clinton used military power with caution. Given the national distaste for overseas entanglements, he responded far more effectively than critics expected. He inherited a U.S. military presence in Somalia (in northeastern Africa) because of a post-election decision by President Bush; he withdrew U.S. forces when their humanitarian mission of guarding food relief to starving Somalis was overshadowed by the need to take sides in a civil war. Clinton intervened decisively in Haiti to restore an elected president.

Bosnia and Kosovo.   Clinton reluctantly committed the United States to a multinational effort to end the bloody civil war in ethnically and religiously divided Bosnia in 1995. In the early 1990s, the former Communist nation of Yugoslavia, in southeastern Europe, fragmented into five independent nations: Slovenia, Macedonia, Croatia, Bosnia, and Yugoslavia (the name retained by the predominantly Serbian nation with its capital at Belgrade). Bosnia, divided both ethnically and religiously between Christians and Muslims, erupted in bitter civil war. Christian Serbs, supported by Belgrade, engaged in massacres and deportations of Muslim Bosnians with the goal of creating "ethnically clean" Serbian districts. Too late to stop most bloodshed, NATO troops after 1995 enforced a brittle peace accord and a division of territory into Bosnian and Serb sectors under a shaky federated government.

The U.S. military revisited the same part of Europe in 1999, when the United States and Britain led NATO's intervention in Kosovo. The overwhelming majority of people in this Yugoslav province were ethnic Albanians who had chafed under the control of the Serb-controlled Yugoslav government. When a Kosovar independence movement began a rebellion, Yugoslav president Slobodan Milosevic responded with brutal repression that threatened to drive over 1 million ethnic Albanians out of the province. To protect the Kosovars, NATO in March 1999 began a bombing campaign that targeted Yugoslav military bases and forces in Kosovo. In June, Yugoslavia agreed to withdraw its troops and make way for a multinational NATO peacekeeping force with 50,000 troops from Britain, France, Germany, Italy, the Netherlands, and the United States, marking a measured success for U.S. policy.

The reinvention of NATO.   To satisfy Russia, the peacekeeping force that entered Kosovo in June was technically a U.S. operation, but it was a reinvented NATO that negotiated with Yugoslavia. Fifty years earlier, the North Atlantic Treaty Organization had been created for three purposes. The first was to unite non-Communist nations of western Europe in an alliance against the Soviet Union. The second was to formally commit the United States and Canada to the defense of western Europe by placing substantial U.S. military forces in Europe. The third was to establish a framework that would make the rearmament of West Germany acceptable to other European nations. For the next 40 years—until the collapse of eastern European Communism—NATO coordinated western European defense planning and remained a foundation stone of United States foreign policy.

The new NATO is a product of the new Europe of the 1990s. A key step was expansion into the former Soviet sphere in eastern Europe. In 1999, NATO formally admitted Poland, Hungary, and the Czech Republic over the objections of Russia. Three years later, NATO agreed to give Russia a formal role in discussions about a number of its policy decisions, further eroding the barriers of the Cold War, and it added another seven nations of eastern Europe in 2004.

Clinton's Neoliberalism   Domestic policy attracted Clinton's greatest interest, and his first term can be divided into two parts. In 1993–1994, he worked with a slim Democratic majority in Congress to modernize the U.S. economy, taking advantage of an economic upturn that lasted for most of the decade. In 1995 and 1996, however, he faced solid Republican majorities, the result of an unanticipated Republican tide in the November 1994 elections.

The heart of Clinton's agenda was an effort to make the United States economy more equitable domestically and more competitive internationally. These goals marked Clinton as a **neoliberal** who envisioned a partnership between a leaner government and a dynamic private sector. Steps to "reinvent" government cut federal employment below Reagan administration levels. A new tax bill reversed some of the inequities of the 1980s by increasing taxes on the weathiest 1.2 percent of households. An improved college student-aid program spread benefits to more students by allowing direct federal loans. In early 1993, Clinton pushed through the Family and Medical Leave Act, which provided up to 12 weeks of unpaid leave for workers with newborns or family emergencies and had been vetoed twice by George H.W. Bush.

Clinton's biggest setback was the failure of comprehensive healthcare legislation. The goals seemed simple at first: containment of healthcare costs and extension of basic medical insurance from 83 percent of Americans under age 65 to 100 percent. In the abstract, voters agreed that something needed to be done. So did individuals like the 25-year-old photographer's assistant who found herself facing cancer surgery without savings or health insurance: "I work full-time, and because it's a very small business, we don't get any benefits. . . . It just devastated everybody financially. And that shouldn't happen. That's the American dream that's lost."

Clinton appointed his wife, Hillary Rodham Clinton, to head the healthcare task force. Many found this an inappropriate role for a first lady. The plan that emerged from the White House ran to 1,342 pages of complex regulations, with something for everyone to dislike. Senior citizens worried about limits on Medicare spending. Insurance companies did not want more regulations. Businesses did not want the costs of insuring their workers. Taxpayers liked the idea of wider medical insurance coverage but not the idea of paying for it through higher taxes or rationing of medical services. Thus the reform effort went nowhere.

If Reagan avoided blame for mistakes, Clinton in his first two years in office seemed to avoid credit for successes. Despite his legislative accomplishments, the press emphasized his difficulty in reaching decisions. Perhaps because he sometimes started with absolute statements and positions, what might in another leader have looked like a willingness to compromise looked like waffling in Clinton. Both the president and his wife attracted extreme and bitter hatred from the far right, of a sort previously reserved for Franklin and Eleanor Roosevelt and the Kennedy family. Indeed, Hillary Rodham Clinton became a symbol of discomfiting changes in American families.

Contract with America and the Election of 1996

Conservative political ideology and personal animosity against the Clintons were both part of the background for an extraordinary off-year election in 1994, in which voters defeated dozens of incumbents and gave Republicans control of Congress. For most of 1995, the new speaker of the House, Newt Gingrich of Georgia, dominated political headlines as he pushed the **Contract with America,** the official Republican campaign platform for the 1994 elections, which called for a revolutionary reduction in federal responsibilities.

Clinton lay low and let the new Congress attack environmental protections, propose cuts in federal benefits for the elderly, and try to slice the capital-gains tax to help the rich. As Congress and president battled over the budget, congressional Republicans refused to authorize interim spending and forced the federal government to shut down for more than three weeks between November 1995 and January 1996. Gingrich was the clear loser in public opinion, both for the shutdowns and for his ideas. Democrats painted Gingrich and his congressional allies as a radical fringe who wanted to gut Medicare and Medicaid, undermine education, punish legal immigrants, and sell off national parks—core values and programs that most Americans wanted to protect.

After the budget confrontations, 1996 brought a series of measures to reward work—a centrist position acceptable to most Americans. The minimum wage increased. Congress made pension programs easier for employers to create and made health insurance portable when workers changed jobs. After tough negotiations, Clinton signed bipartisan legislation to "end welfare as we know it." **Temporary Assistance to Needy Families (TANF)** replaced Aid to Families with Dependent Children (AFDC). TANF had strict requirements that aid recipients by seeking work or be enrolled in schooling, and it set a time limit on assistance. By 2001, the number of public-assistance recipients had declined 58 percent from its 1994 high, but there are doubts that many of the former recipients have found jobs adequate to support their families.

Clinton's reelection in 1996 was a virtual replay of 1992. His opponent, Robert Dole, represented the World War II generation of politicians. The Republican Party was uncertain whether to stress free markets or morality. The party tried to paper over its uneasy mix of traditional probusiness and socially moderate country-club Republicans, radical proponents of unregulated markets, and religious conservatives increasingly active in politics. Evangelicals dominated many state parties, but they made many traditional party regulars uncomfortable and carried few statewide elections. The Republicans thus displayed many of the internal fractures that characterized U.S. society as a whole.

Because the nation was prosperous and at peace, and because Clinton had claimed the political center and sounded like Dwight Eisenhower, the results were never in doubt. Clinton became the first Democratic president to be elected to a second term since Franklin Roosevelt. The Clinton-Gore ticket took 70 percent of the electoral votes and 49 percent of the popular vote (versus 41 percent for Dole and 9 percent for a recycled Ross Perot). Clinton easily won the Northeast, the industrial Midwest, and the Far West; Hispanic voters alienated by anti-immigrant rhetoric from the Republicans helped Clinton also take the usually Republican states of Florida and Arizona.

The election confirmed that voters liked the pragmatic center. They were cautious about the radical free-market advocates on the extreme right, showing little interest in having Republicans actually put the Contract with America into practice. They were equally unimpressed by liberal advocates of extensive entitlements on the European model. What voters wanted was to continue the reduction of the federal role in domestic affairs that had begun in the 1980s without damaging social insurance programs.

The Dangers of Everyday Life

Part of the background for the sometimes vicious politics of mid-decade was a sense of individual insecurity and fear of violence that coexisted with an economy that was booming in some sectors but still leaving many Americans behind.

Random violence and domestic terrorism.   One after another, headlines and news flashes proclaimed terrifying random acts of violence. The greatest losses of life came in Waco, Texas, and in Oklahoma City. On April 19, 1993, federal agents raided the fortified compound of the Branch Davidian cult outside Waco after a 51-day siege. The raid triggered a fire, probably set from inside, that killed more than 80 people. On the second anniversary of the Waco raid, Timothy McVeigh packed a rented truck with explosive materials and detonated it in front of the federal office building in downtown Oklahoma City, presumably as revenge against what he considered an oppressive government. The blast collapsed the entire front of the nine-story building and killed 169 people.

In April 1999, two high school students in Littleton, Colorado, took rifles and pipe bombs into Columbine High School to kill 12 classmates, a teacher, and themselves; schools in Arkansas and Oregon experienced similar terror from gun-wielding students. A national manhunt in 1997 captured Ted Kaczynski, the so-called Unabomber, who since 1978 had

Search and rescue worker Anthony Fernandez and rescue dog Aspen pause during the search through the ruins of the Oklahoma City federal building after its bombing by domestic terrorists in 1995.

mailed more than a dozen bombs to college professors and airlines as protest against an industrialized economy.

Gun control.   Workplace assassins, schoolroom murders, and domestic terrorism invigorated efforts to monitor access to firearms. The Brady Handgun Violence Prevention Act, passed in 1994, took its name from James Brady, President Reagan's first press secretary, who was seriously injured in the 1981 attempt to kill the president. The act set up a waiting period and background checks for purchases of firearms from retailers, pawnshops, and licensed firearm dealers. Congress also debated detailed restrictions on certain types of weapons, such as assault rifles and particularly lethal types of ammunition. Police forces and urban residents tended to favor such laws, while rural representatives opposed them.

Gun control was political dynamite, for Americans have drastically differing understandings of the Second Amendment, which states: "A well regulated militia, being necessary to the security of a free State, the right of the people to keep and bear arms, shall not be infringed." The powerful National

Rifle Association, the major lobby for gun owners and manufacturers, now argued that the amendment establishes an absolute individual right. Federal courts for many decades interpreted the Second Amendment to apply to the possession of weapons in connection with citizen service in a government-organized militia. In June 2008, however, the Supreme Court in *District of Columbia v. Heller* struck down Washington, D.C.'s absolute ban on the ownership or possession of handguns. The majority in the 5-4 decision argued that the Second Amendment implied an individual right to own firearms. However, it left most state and federal firearms laws intact by allowing restrictions on individual categories of weapons and regulations on acquisition and use that fall short of prohibitions.

Crime and the war on drugs.   Conservatives, including many gun-ownership absolutists, put their faith in strict law enforcement as the best route to public security. The 1990s saw numerous states adopt "three-strike" measures that drastically increased penalties for individuals convicted of a third crime. One result was an explosive growth of the prison industry. Mandatory minimum sentencing caused Louisiana's prison population to grow by 50 percent between 1994 and 2001. Mississippi legislation that severely restricted the possibility of parole caused an even greater jump in the state's prison population from 10,700 in 1994 to 37,700 in 2001. States diverted funds from education and healthcare to build and staff more prisons. The number of people serving sentences of a year or longer in state and federal prisons grew from 316,000 in 1980 to 740,000 in 1990 and 1,422,000 in 2004, with another 714,000 being held for shorter periods in local jails. By 2007, one in every 99.1 adults was behind bars.

The war on drugs, begun in the 1980s, was the biggest contributor to the prison boom. As the drug war dragged on through the 1990s, the federal government poured billions of dollars into efforts to stop illegal drugs from crossing the Mexican border or from landing by boat or airplane. The United States intervened in South American nations that produced cocaine, particularly Peru and Colombia, aiding local military efforts to uproot crops and battle drug lords. Meanwhile, aggressive enforcement of domestic laws against drug possession or sales filled U.S. prison cells. The antidrug campaign fell most heavily on minorities. Connecticut, for example, required mandatory sentences for selling or possessing drugs within two-thirds of a mile of a school, daycare center, or public housing project. Because these criteria encompassed nearly all the neighborhoods in Hartford and New Haven with large minority populations, minority offenders arrested on drug charges were nine times more likely than white offenders to end up in jail.

In fact, crime fell steadily for a decade after reaching a peak in 1991. The rate of violent crime (murder, rape, robbery, aggravated assault) fell by 33 percent from 1991 to 2000, including a 36 percent drop in the number of murders. The rate of major property crimes (burglary, larceny-theft, and motor vehicle theft) fell by 30 percent over the same period. Easing fears combined with escalating costs to cause some states to rethink the reliance on prison terms. California voters adopted a measure that provides for treatment rather than prison for many drug offenders. A handful of states adopted measures legalizing marijuana for medical use. Other states, ranging from Mississippi to Connecticut to North Dakota, softened some of their sentencing laws.

Debating the death penalty.   Governor George Ryan of Illinois was elected in 1998 as a conservative Republican. In January 2003, this small-town businessman emptied death row in the Illinois prison system by commuting the death sentences of 167 convicted murderers to prison terms of life or less. He asserted that his review of individual cases had led him to doubt the justice of the death-penalty system as a whole, which he said is "haunted by the demons of error—error in determining guilt and error in determining who among the guilty deserves to die." Ryan's extraordinary action reflected a wider uncertainty about the fair application of capital punishment that came from cases in which the new technique of DNA testing showed mistaken convictions, revelations about incompetent defense attorneys, and evidence of malfeasance by prosecuting attorneys in withholding evidence that might have exonerated defendants accused of murder.

Specific discussion of flaws in the application of the death penalty reveals basic disagreements about the best approach to public order. Thirty-eight of the 50 states impose the death penalty, although sixteen states have not carried out an execution since 1976. The majority of Americans have accepted capital punishment as a flawed but necessary defense for society. In the presidential campaign of 2000, George W. Bush cited the record number of executions that had taken place in Texas while he was governor as evidence of his toughness against crime. He was confident, he said, that "everybody who has been put to death has been guilty of the crime charged."

In contrast, a passionate minority thinks that capital punishment is a tool so bent and blunted as to be worse than useless. They point out that the deterrent effect of capital punishment is weak at best; murder rates are often higher in death-penalty states than in similar states without the penalty. They note that African Americans and Latinos receive the death penalty far more often than whites charged with the same crimes. The nation's Roman Catholic bishops in 1999 joined with the National Council of Synagogues to condemn the death penalty as contrary to teachings about the sanctity of human life. In *Atkins v. Virginia* (2002), the Supreme Court forbade the execution of mentally retarded persons. In 2005, a divided Court in *Roper v. Simmons* prohibited the execution of anyone who committed the crime for which sentenced while younger than 18. The debate about capital punishment exemplifies the fault lines that divide

Americans as they try to balance the demands of justice and public order.

Morality and Partisanship

If the economy was the fundamental news of the later 1990s, Bill Clinton's personal life was the hot news. In 1998 and 1999, the United States was riveted by revelations about the president's sex life, doubts about his integrity, and debates about his fitness for high office. Years of rumors, innuendos, and lawsuits culminated in 1999 in the nation's second presidential impeachment trial. To his enemies, Clinton's behavior seemed one more example of disregard for law and morality, while his supporters found the entire issue to be nothing but partisan politics.

The president's problems began in 1994 with the appointment of a special prosecutor to investigate possible fraud in the **Whitewater** development, an Arkansas land promotion in which Bill and Hillary Clinton had invested in the 1980s. The probe by Kenneth Starr, the independent counsel, however, expanded into a wide-ranging investigation that encompassed the firing of the White House travel-office staff early in 1993, the suicide of White House aide Vincent Foster, and the sexual behavior of the president. Meanwhile, Paula Jones had brought a lawsuit claiming sexual harassment by then-governor Clinton while she was a state worker in Arkansas. The investigation of Whitewater brought convictions of several friends and former associates of the Clintons, but no evidence pointing decisively at either Bill or Hillary Clinton.

The legal landscape changed in January 1998, with allegations about an affair between the president and Monica Lewinsky, a former White House intern. Lewinsky admitted to the relationship privately and then to Starr's staff after the president had denied it in a sworn deposition for the Paula Jones case. This opened Clinton to charges of perjury and obstruction of justice. Although a federal judge dismissed Jones's suit in April, the continued unfolding of the Lewinsky affair treated the nation to a barrage of personal details about Bill Clinton and to semantic debates over what exactly constituted "having sex." The affair certainly revealed deep flaws in Clinton's character and showed his willingness to shade the truth. Newspaper editorials, radio talk shows, and politicians debated whether such flaws were relevant to his ability to perform his constitutional duties.

In the fall of 1998, the Republican leaders who controlled Congress decided that Clinton's statements and misstatements justified initiating the process of impeachment. In December, the majority on the House Judiciary Committee recommended four articles of impeachment, or specific charges against the president, to the House of Representatives. By a partisan vote, the full House approved two of the charges and forwarded them to the Senate. The formal trial of the charges by the Senate began in January 1999 and ended on February 12. Moderate Republicans joined Democrats, thereby ensuring that the Senate would fall far short of the two-thirds majority required for conviction and removal from office. Article 1, charging that the president had perjured himself, failed by a vote of 45 to 55. Article 2, charging that he had obstructed justice, failed by a vote of 50 to 50.

Why did Congressional Republicans pursue impeachment to the bitter end? It was clear by the end of 1998 that a majority of Americans strongly disapproved of Clinton's conduct but did not think that his personal behavior merited removal from office (see Overview, Presidential Impeachment). The 1998 election, which reduced the Republican majority in the House and resulted in the resignation of Newt Gingrich, confirmed the opinion polls. At the same time, 25 to 30 percent of Americans remained convinced that Clinton was a disgrace whose presence in the White House demeaned the nation. It was not so much that they disliked his policies, which were often quite conservative, but that they felt that his personal flaws and sins made him unfit to lead and represent the nation and deprived him of the moral authority necessary to inspire its people. In other words, although anti-Clinton people were a powerful force within the Republican Party and impeachment was certainly motivated by politics, it was also another battle in America's continuing culture wars.

A New Economy?

Within months of the impeachment trial, Americans had a new worry. In the closing months of 1999, many people stocked up on canned food and kerosene, powdered milk, ammunition, and cash. They were preparing to survive, not foreign invasion or natural disaster, but rather the possible collapse of the global computer network. Europeans called the problem the "millennium bug," Americans the "Y2K" problem (for Year 2000). In the early years of computers, memory space was precious, causing programmers to designate dates with only the last two digits of the year (thus, "82" for 1982). In the mid-1990s, many realized that such programs might treat the year 2000 as 1900, or might choke in electronic confusion, throwing information systems into chaos. While a small army of programmers worked to rewrite and repair the software, the media offered a steady diet of dire stories that urged preparations—just in case.

In fact, almost nothing happened. The software patches worked. Americans on the evening of December 31, 1999, could watch the progression of millennium celebrations and fireworks from Singapore to Rome and then to London as midnight swept westward across the globe. Since civilization did not collapse in Asia and Europe, North Americans could greet midnight with a sigh of relief.

In larger perspective, the Y2K worries illustrate how much the American economy had changed in the preceding decade, and how mysterious the changes seemed. More than ever, it was a global economy. And, unlike any time in the

Presidential Impeachment

Andrew Johnson, 1868	Charges:	Failure to comply with Tenure of Office Act requiring congressional approval to fire cabinet members.
	Political Lineup:	Radical Republicans against Johnson; Democrats and moderate Republicans for him.
	Actions:	Tried and acquitted by Senate.
	Underlying Issues:	Johnson's opposition to Republican plans for reconstruction of southern states after the Civil War.
Richard Nixon, 1974	Charges:	Obstruction of justice in Watergate investigation, abuse of power of federal agencies for political purposes, refusal to recognize congressional subpoena.
	Political Lineup:	Democrats and many Republicans against Nixon.
	Actions:	Charges approved by House committee; Nixon resigned before action by the full House of Representatives.
	Underlying Issues:	Nixon's construction of a secret government and his efforts to undermine integrity of national elections.
Bill Clinton, 1999	Charges:	Perjury and obstruction of justice in the investigation of sexual-misconduct allegations by Paula Jones.
	Political Lineup:	Conservative Republicans against Clinton; Democrats and some moderate Republicans for him.
	Actions:	Tried and acquitted by Senate.
	Underlying Issues:	Republican frustration with Clinton's ability to block their agenda; deep concern about Clinton's character and moral fitness for presidency.

past, it was an economy that depended on electronic computing to manage and transmit vast quantities of data. The impact of the electronic revolution was still being absorbed into the structures and routines of everyday life as Americans put Y2K behind them and looked to a new century.

The Prosperous 1990s

From 1992 through 2000, Americans enjoyed nine years of continuous economic expansion. Unemployment dropped from 7.2 percent in 1992 to 4.0 percent at the start of 2000 as American businesses created more than 12 million new jobs. Key states like California rebounded from economic recession with new growth driven by high-tech industries, entertainment, and foreign trade. The stock market soared during the nineties; rising demand for shares in established blue-chip companies and new **Internet** firms swelled the value of individual portfolios, retirement accounts, and pension funds. The rate of home ownership rose after declining for 15 years. Prosperity also trickled down to Americans at the bottom of the economic ladder. The proportion of Americans in poverty dropped to 12 percent in 1999, and the gap between rich and poor began to narrow (slightly) for the first time in two decades.

The economic boom was great news for the federal budget. Tight spending and rising personal income turned perennial deficits into surpluses for 1998, 1999, and 2000. Reduced borrowing by the U.S. Treasury resulted in low interest rates, which further fueled corporate expansion and consumer spending. Both political parties anticipated a growing surplus for the next decade and debated whether to offer massive tax cuts, buy down the national debt, or shore up Social Security and Medicare. In 1997, Clinton signed a deficit-reduction bill that seemed to promise fiscal stability.

Behind the statistics were substantial gains in the efficiency of the U.S. economy. International rivals, especially Japan, experienced severe economic slumps in the mid-1990s. In the United States, in contrast, by the end of the decade the productivity of manufacturing workers was increasing more than 4 percent per year, the highest rate in a generation. Part of the gain was the payoff from the painful business restructuring and downsizing of the 1970s and 1980s. Another cause was improvements in efficiency from the full incorporation of personal computers and electronic communication into everyday life and business practice.

It remains to be seen whether the growth of the 1990s marked the beginning of a new wave of sustained economic expansion like earlier waves triggered by technological innovation. Until now, such waves have followed 50-year cycles that begin with a 30-year period of rapid expansion followed by two decades of consolidation and slow growth. From 1945 to 1974, for example, the automobile and aerospace industries helped Europe, Japan, and the United States enjoy an era of sustained growth that was followed by two decades of painful economic readjustment and problems. In the later 1990s, fast-growing information-based industries such as electronic communications, software, biotechnology, and medicine may have jump-started another era of prosperity, although many individual technology companies failed in 2001 and 2002; the dotcom bust dragged down the stock market for several years.

The Service Economy

At the beginning of the twenty-first century, the United States was an economy of services. As fewer Americans drove tractors and toiled on assembly lines, more became service workers. The service sector includes everyone not directly involved in producing and processing physical products. Service workers range from lawyers to hair stylists, from police officers who write traffic tickets to theater employees who sell movie tickets. In 1965, services already accounted for more than half of American jobs. By the end of the 1990s, their share rose to more than 75 percent.

Service work varies greatly. At the bottom of the scale are minimum-wage jobs held mostly by women, immigrants, and the young, such as cleaning people, childcare workers, hospital orderlies, and fast-food workers. These positions offer little in terms of advancement, job security, or benefits. In contrast, many of the best new jobs are in information industries. Teaching, research, advertising, mass communications, and professional consulting depend on producing and manipulating information. All of these fields have grown. They add to national wealth by creating and applying new ideas rather than by supplying standardized products and services.

The information economy flourishes in large cities with libraries, universities, research hospitals, advertising agencies, and corporate headquarters. New York's bankers and stockbrokers made Manhattan an island of prosperity in the 1980s. Pittsburgh, with major universities and corporate headquarters, made the transition to the information economy even while its steel industry failed. A good benchmark of a brain-powered economy is whether more than a quarter of the adults (people aged 25 or over) have finished college. The District of Columbia, with its high-priced lawyers and lobbyists, ranked first in 2005, with 47 percent. Next were Connecticut and Massachusetts (37 percent), followed closely by Maryland, New Jersey, and Colorado.

The rise of the service economy had political consequences. Rapid expansion of jobs in state and local government triggered popular revolts against state taxes that started in 1978 with passage of California's Proposition 13, which limited property taxes, and continued into the 1990s. Another growth industry was healthcare. Spending on medical and health services amounted to 15 percent of the gross domestic product in 2000, up from 5 percent in 1960. The need to share this huge expense fairly was the motivation for Medicare and Medicaid in the 1960s and the search for a national health insurance program in the 1990s and beyond.

The High-Tech Sector

The epitome of the "sunrise" economy was electronics, which grew hand-in-glove with the defense budget. The first computers in the 1940s were derived in part from wartime code-breaking efforts. In the 1950s, IBM got half its revenues from air defense computers and guidance systems for B-52 bombers. "It was the Cold War that helped IBM make itself the king of the computer business," commented the company's president, Thomas J. Watson. Employment in computer manufacturing rose in the mid-1960s with the expansion of mainframe computing. Large machines from IBM, Honeywell, NCR, and other established corporations required substantial support facilities and staff and were used largely by universities, government agencies, and corporations. In the 1970s, new companies began to build smaller, specialized machines for such purposes as word processing. One cluster of firms sprang up outside Boston around Route 128, benefitting from proximity to MIT and other Boston-area universities. California's **Silicon Valley,** north of San Jose, took off with corporate spinoffs and civilian applications of military technologies and benefitted from proximity to Stanford University.

Seattle in the 1980s and 1990s prospered from the globalizing economy and the rise of the information industries. Only old-timers noticed the disappearance of fish canneries and lumber mills. Taking their place were Boeing, which fueled an international travel revolution; Microsoft, which made Seattle a high-tech capital; and the many foreign companies that used Seattle's port for access to the U.S. market.

Invention of the microprocessor in 1971 kicked the industry into high gear. The farmlands of Santa Clara County, California, became a "silicon landscape" of neat one-story factories and research campuses. In 1950, the county had 800 factory workers. In 1980, it had 264,000 manufacturing workers and 3,000 electronics firms; 20 years later, San Jose had the highest average annual pay of any metropolitan area. Related hardware and microchip factories spread the industry throughout the West, to such cities as Austin, Dallas, Phoenix, Portland, Boise, and Salt Lake City.

The electronics boom was driven by extraordinary improvements in computing capacity. At the start of the microcomputer era, Intel co-founder Gordon Moore predicted that the number of transistors on a microchip would double every 18 months, with consequent increases in performance and drops in price. "Moore's Law" worked at least through the opening of the new century as producers moved from chips with 5,000 transistors to ones with 50,000,000. The practical result was a vast increase in the capacities and portability of computers. The "portable" Osborne and Apple computers of the early 1980s were suitcase-sized packages with limited hard drives and tiny memories. Twenty years later, when students and business travelers pulled out their laptops at every opportunity, the first generation of personal computers were as outmoded as a Spanish galleon in an age of nuclear submarines.

The computer industry generated an accompanying software industry as a major component of information-technology employment. Every computer needs a complexly coded operating system, word-processing programs, spreadsheet programs, file-reading programs, Internet browsers, and, of course, games. Seattle-based Microsoft parlayed an alliance with IBM into a dominant position that eventually triggered federal antitrust action. Other software firms rose and fell with innovative and then outmoded programs. Software-writing skills also spawned a new world of multimedia entertainment. A sequence of new films, such as *The Matrix* (1999), repeatedly pushed the possibilities of combining computer simulation and live action.

Personal computers and consumer electronics became part of everyday life in the 1990s. Automakers built computers into their cars to diagnose engine problems; high-end models added global positioning systems for drivers too hurried to unfold a map. New buildings came with "smart" climate-control systems. Busy people replaced their appointment books with hand-held personal organizers. In 2005, 80 percent of adults reported that they had Internet access at home or work, up from around 14 percent in 1996, and nearly all of them had used it in the previous month. It took radio 38 years and television 13 years before 50 million Americans tuned in; the Internet reached the same level of use in four years. Children aged 10 to 14 used computers more frequently than any other age group, and nine out of ten could access the Internet at home or at school. The most networked state was Alaska, where computers helped to make up for vast distances and isolating winters.

An Instant Society

The spread of consumer electronics helped to create an "instant society." Americans in the 1990s learned to communicate by e-mail and to look up information on the **World Wide Web.** No longer did messages incur the delays of the postal system or the costs of long-distance telephone calls. Students could avoid inconvenient trips to the library to look up information in books because it was so much quicker to search the Web. (Many of the data for this section on the new economy were compiled in just that way.) The United States was increasingly a society that depended on instant information and expected instant results.

The Internet grew out of concerns about defense and national security. Its prototype was ARPAnet (for Advanced Research Projects Administration of the Defense Department), intended to be a communication system that could survive nuclear attack. As the Internet evolved into a system that connected universities and national weapons laboratories, the Pentagon gave up control in 1984. Through the 1980s, it was used mainly by scientists and academics to share data and communicate by e-mail. The World Wide Web, created in 1991, expanded the Internet's uses by allowing organizations and companies to create websites that placed political and commercial information only a few clicks away from wired consumers. Addresses with the .com suffix soon outnumbered those with .edu, .gov, and .org. The equally rapid expansion of bandwidth allowed web pages filled with pictures and graphics to replace the text-only sites of the 1980s. By the start of the new century, Web surfers could find vast quantities of material, from Paris hotel rates to pornography, from song lyrics to stock prices.

Instant satisfaction was one of the principles behind the boom of dotcom businesses in 1998, 1999, and 2000. Many were services that repackaged information for quick access. Others were essentially on-line versions of mail order catalogs, but capable of listing hundreds of thousands of items. Still others were instant-delivery services designed to save consumers a trip to the video store or minimart. Although many of the dotcom companies crashed in 2001, they can be viewed as extensions of ongoing trends in retailing and services. Americans in 2000 spent 48 cents on meals out for every 52 cents spent on food to eat at home, paying for the convenience of quick meals without preparation and cleanup time. Automatic-teller machines had been a convenience when introduced in the early 1980s, but they were a necessity 20 years later, when Americans expected to be able to pull cash from their bank accounts 168 hours a week rather than find a bank open perhaps 30 hours a week.

Mobile telephones, or cell phones, were part of the same instant society. They exploited underutilized radio bands and communication satellites to allow wireless conversations among cells—geographic areas linked by special microwave broadcasting towers. Technological changes again drove demand. The chunky car phone built into a vehicle gave way to sleek handheld devices the size of *Star Trek* communicators. Wireless phone companies originally sold their phones as emergency backups and business necessities, just as wired telephones had been sold in the first years of the twentieth century. The 5 million cell phone subscribers of 1990 had exploded to 208 million in 2005. The phone had become ubiquitous, beeping in concerts and classrooms, in buses and on street corners. In the disaster of September 11, 2001, portable phones utilizing satellite links offered some final communications from passengers on hijacked airliners.

Meanwhile the twenty-first century Internet had become another inescapable method of communication. Direct travel reservation sites pushed travel agencies out of business. Young people found and kept friends with MySpace and Facebook. Columns of classified ads in newspapers shrank as craigslist expanded. Listings on eBay competed with face-to-face garage sales, and businesses invested in websites rather than Yellow Pages display ads.

In the World Market

Instant access to business and financial information accelerated the globalizing of the American economy. Expanding foreign commerce had become a deliberate goal of national policy with the General Agreement on Tariffs and Trade (GATT) in 1947. GATT regularized international commerce after World War II and helped to secure one of the goals of World War II by ensuring that world markets remained open to American industry. The Trade Expansion Act in 1962 authorized President Kennedy to make reciprocal trade agreements to cut tariffs by up to 50 percent so as to keep American companies competitive in the new European Common Market. Although both measures were aimed at trade with Europe, they also helped to expand American commerce across the Pacific.

With the help of national policy and booming economies overseas, the value of U.S. imports and exports more than doubled, from 7 percent of the gross domestic product in 1965 to 16 percent in 1990—the largest percentage since World War I. Americans in the 1970s began to worry about a "colonial" status, in which the United States exported food, lumber, and minerals and imported automobiles and television sets. By the 1980s, foreign economic competitiveness and trade deficits, especially with Japan, became issues of national concern that continued into the new century, when China and India were emerging as the newest competitors.

The effects of international competition were more complex than "Japan-bashers" acknowledged. Mass-production industries, such as textiles and aluminum, suffered from cheaper and sometimes higher-quality imports, but many specialized industries and services, such as Houston's oil equipment and exploration firms, thrived. Globalization also created new regional winners and losers. In 1982, the United States began to do more business with Pacific nations than with Europe.

The politics of trade.   More recent steps to expand the global reach of the U.S. economy were the **North American Free Trade Agreement (NAFTA)** in 1993 and a new worldwide GATT approved in 1994. Negotiated by Republican George Bush and pushed through Congress in 1993 by Democratic Bill Clinton, NAFTA combined 25 million Canadians, 90 million Mexicans, and 250 million U.S. consumers in a single "common market" similar to that of western Europe. This enlarged free-trade zone was intended to open new markets and position the United States to compete more effectively against the European Community and Japan. The agreement may have been a holdover from the Bush years, but it matched Clinton's ideas about reforming the American economy.

NAFTA was a hard pill for many Democrats, and it revived the old debate between free traders and protectionists. Support was strongest from businesses and industries that sought foreign customers, including agriculture and electronics. Opponents included organized labor, communities already hit by industrial shutdowns, and environmentalists worried about lax controls on industrial pollution in Mexico. In contrast to the nineteenth-century arguments for protecting infant industries, new industries now looked to foreign markets, whereas uncompetitive, older firms hoped for protected domestic markets. The readjustments from NAFTA have produced obvious pain in the form of closed factories or farms made unprofitable by cheaper imports, while its gains are less visible—a new job here, larger sales there.

The **World Trade Organization (WTO),** which replaced GATT in 1996, became the unexpected target of a global protest movement. Seattle officials, committed to promoting Seattle as a world-class city, lobbied hard to get the 1999 WTO meeting. With finance and foreign affairs ministers and heads of government expected to attend, it would give Seattle world attention. Instead, it gave the city a headache. Fifty thousand protesters converged on the meeting, held from November 30 to December 4, 1999. Most demonstrators were peaceful, but several hundred started a rampage through downtown that triggered a massive overreaction by unprepared police.

The battle of Seattle was part of an international movement. Large demonstrations followed against the International Monetary Fund in Washington in 2000 and against a WTO meeting in Genoa, Italy, in 2001. Protesters were convinced that the WTO is a tool of transnational corporations that flout local labor and environmental protections in the name of "free trade" that benefits only the wealthy nations and their businesses. WTO defenders pointed to the long-term effects of open trade in raising net production in the world economy and thereby making more wealth available for developing nations. Opponents asserted, in turn, that such wealth never reaches the workers and farmers in those nations. American opponents demanded that U.S. firms, such as sportswear companies, that make their products overseas make sure that their overseas workers have decent living conditions and wages.

American Views

Relief Work in Africa

In the early twenty-first century, thousands of Americans work in other countries for relief and reconstruction organizations such as the Peace Corps, CARE, and Mercy Corps, and thousands more do similar work under the sponsorship of religious groups. In 2003, Peggy Senger Parsons, an evangelical Quaker minister and trauma counselor from "far off Planet America" spent several months in the small African nation of Burundi, trying to help residents develop strategies for dealing with the impacts of civil war and endemic criminal violence. Here are some excerpts from her blog.

- What does Peggy Parsons's experience suggest about the spread of American culture around the world?

- How does the level of personal safety in a nation such as Burundi compare to that in the United States?

- What questions does Parsons's experience raise about the challenges of building peace and democracy in troubled and divided nations?

- How might religiously based work in other countries differ from efforts sponsored by the U.S. government, such as with the Peace Corps? How might it be the same?

We function in Swahili and French, mine bad and hers good....I have been in the company of four children who have been giving me language and cultural tutorials, which I exchanged for introducing them to the Beatles.

Pavement is a subjective concept in Burundi. Traffic is extremely real. We fly in a zig zag pattern through cars, trucks, bicycles, and lots of little children. If you notice a lack of angels in America, it is because they are all in Burundi keeping the babies from being killed on the road....And in four days I am totally immune to the sight of guys with automatic weapons. My host says that he cannot tell a rebel from a Burundi soldier and sometimes neither can they.

We have a night watchman...we live in a walled compound and he is there to keep us safe. His only weapon is a whistle. The children tell me that if there is trouble he whistles, and all the nearby watchmen whistle and then come running to help. Then I met Gadi the moneychanger. He walks around with rolls of money as big as softballs in every pocket and he does not carry a gun. He has a quiet gentle confidence that reminds me of every wiseguy I ever met in Chicago. I do not know what happens if you jump a moneychanger—but it must be bad enough that nobody tries. Some things are very familiar.

My traumatology students are amazing. They have come from great distances and at great sacrifice to study with me....Many of the terms I need to use have no equivalent. I have learned the face that my translator makes when I give her a hard one. She signals for me to stop, and the students confer and when a consensus is reached about a newly coined phrase someone shouts *Voila!* And we have a new psychological term. My students were interviewed on Burundi National Radio. The reporter came on the second day to do a quick filler piece and stayed all afternoon and then asked to join the class. He carries a huge reel-to-reel recorder. The voices of these students went out to 22 million listeners this morning in Burundi, Congo, Rwanda, and Tanzania. They were fabulous explaining the effects of trauma and how they themselves had been helped in the class. On Friday my class thanked me for telling them the truth and for bringing them the best of myself. They compared me to a Jonah "who did not run away but ran towards her call," can't get better pay than that.

I was not prepared for the fact that my trauma class students would be such recent victims [many bearing fresh wounds from beatings or torture]. Thursday there was a bit of shooting outside of the teaching compound.

I had to be told what it was—a "thump" and then a "tat, tat, tat." But it was quiet after that and we resume. After a long morning of brain physiology and learning about the left brain functions, my translator said, "Peggy have mercy on them—they say they need to sing." And so they did, all Christian music. I taught them "We Shall Overcome" and told them about Dr. King and we marched around the room singing that "I do believe, deep in my heart, that Burundi will have peace one day."

Tourism and travel.   In the 1960s, "jet set" referred to a handful of the idle rich who could treat the world as their playground. Forty years later, nearly everyone was part of the jet set. In 2000, Americans made 27 million visits to other countries in addition to 34 million visits to Canada and Mexico, an 80 percent increase in just the 1990s. At the same time, the United States received 25 million visitors from Canada and Mexico and 26 million from other nations. California, Florida, New York, Hawaii, and Nevada were the top destinations. The number of foreign students studying in the United States passed the half-million mark in 2000. Meanwhile, American college students with the necessary financial resources had come to expect a semester or year abroad as part of their studies.

In addition to temporary visitors, 4 million Americans lived and worked abroad in 2000. Some had retired to Mexico or Spain. Some were military personnel or worked for the State Department. Many more worked for multinational corporations, represented nonprofit organizations, or served as medical and religious missionaries (see American Views, Relief Work in Africa). Americans might supervise the mass production of American brands in Asian factories. They might also work building houses or coordinating relief aid in Afghanistan, counseling victims of genocide in Burundi, or assisting city planners in Tadzhikistan.

Broadening Democracy

Closely related to the changes in the American economy were the changing composition of the American people and the continued emergence of new participants in U.S. government. Bill Clinton's first cabinet, in which three women and four minority men balanced seven white men, recognized the makeup of the American population and marked the maturing of minorities and women as distinct political constituencies. The first cabinet appointed by George W. Bush in 2001 included four minority men and four women, one of whom was Asian American. In both administrations, the new prominence of women and minorities in the national government followed years of growing success in cities and states.

Americans in 2000

The federal census for the year 2000 found 281,400,000 Americans in the 50 states, District of Columbia, and Puerto Rico (and probably 2–3 million more residents were not counted).

The increase from 1990 was 13.2 percent, or 32,700,000. It was the largest ten-year population increase in U.S. history, evidence of the nation's prosperity and its attractiveness for immigrants. More than 12 percent of Americans had been born in other countries, the highest share since 1920 (Table 31–1). One third of all Americans lived in four states: California, Texas, New York, and Florida. These were the key prizes in presidential elections. Their regulations and consumer preferences conditioned national markets for products ranging from automobiles to textbooks.

The West grew the fastest. The super boom states were Nevada (66 percent growth), Arizona (40 percent), Colorado (31 percent), Utah (30 percent), and Idaho (29 percent). Fast growth implies young populations, and the states with the lowest average ages were all western: Utah, Alaska, Idaho, and Texas. The Southwest and South also had the fastest growing metropolitan areas. Las

Protests against the WTO have united environmentalists and labor unions, interests that are often in opposition over domestic issues.

Global Perspectives

Working 24/7 in Bangalore

Bangalore is a beautiful city in the highlands of southern India. Its cool climate attracted retired British officials in the days of the British Empire, leaving a legacy of Victorian parks and wide boulevards. After India achieved independence in 1947, the new government made Bangalore a center for scientific research, leaving a legacy of four universities, dozens of technical schools, and a home-grown high-tech industry. In the 1990s, U.S. electronics companies began to establish branches and subsidiaries to take advantage of the concentration of talent, creating a new suburban landscape of technology parks and gated residential neighborhoods with a strong resemblance to Silicon Valley.

The logical extension came in the twenty-first century. Computers and telephone lines have brought Bangalore, Delhi, and other Indian cities into instant contact with American businesses and consumers. Enough U.S. companies have outsourced their customer-service operations to India to become a comic-strip joke.

The development is a logical extension of the global economy. India represents the world's second-largest concentration of English speakers after the United States. Its high-quality educational system produces a million college graduates a year. Many of them are glad to work for U.S. companies at pay that is cheap by U.S. standards but good by comparison with other opportunities in India.

Any kind of routine customer service can be outsourced—telephone catalog sales, billing and debt collection, credit card marketing, help lines for Internet providers, technical support for computer manufacturers. Tens of thousands of simple income tax returns are now processed in India each year. An American accountant scans in a customer's tax information, an Indian accountant logs on and fills out the return, the American accountant prints it out for signature.

The magic of electronics and the 12-hour time differential allow Indians to do specialized work while Americans sleep. Hospitals can transit MRIs to be read in India and get the results the next morning. Publishers can send files to be formatted and proofread while authors and editors sleep. Software companies can transmit code to be debugged overnight.

There is both a light side and a serious side to this 24/7 economy. It is amusing to learn that Indian workers practice American accents and take "phone names" that sound American; CBS reported that one young woman named Sangita becomes "Julia" because Julia Roberts is her favorite actress. But it is also important to understand that distance scarcely matters when an economy's important products take the form of information, and that information flows back and forth across the oceans linking the United States to the world in ways not seen in earlier centuries.

■ In twenty-first century, is the English language the most important asset of the American economy?

Vegas topped them all with an increase of 83 percent. Among large metro areas with over 500,000 people in 2000, all 20 of the fastest growing of were in the West and Southeast.

In contrast, parts of the American midlands grew slowly. Rural counties continued to empty out in Appalachia and across the Great Plains as fewer and fewer Americans were needed for mining and farming or for the small towns associated with those industries. No state lost population, but North Dakota and West Virginia had ten-year gains of only 1 percent.

Another important trend was increasing ethnic and racial diversity (Table 31–2). Hispanics were the fastest growing group in the U.S. population. Indeed, the number of Hispanics in 2000 (35.2 million) surprised many officials and matched the number of African Americans. Although immigrants concentrated in the coastal and border states, Hispanics and Asian Americans were also spreading into interior states. Asians and Hispanics who had been in the United States for some time showed substantial economic success. Non-Hispanic whites are now a minority in California at 47 percent, in the District of Columbia, in Hawaii, and in New Mexico.

The changing ethnicity of the American people promises to be increasingly apparent in coming decades. Immigrants tend to be young adults who are likely to form families, and birth rates have been high among Hispanics and Asian Amer-

Table 31–1	
Immigrants 1991–2005, by Continent and by Twenty Most Important Countries of Origin	
Total	14,083,000
North America	5,657,000
Mexico	3,127,000
Dominican Republic	469,000
El Salvador	359,000
Cuba	300,000
Haiti	270,000
Jamaica	250,000
Canada	227,000
Guatemala	183,000
Asia	4,557,000
Philippines	773,000
India	729,000
China	708,000
Vietnam	576,000
Korea	267,000
Pakistan	191,000
Iran	167,000
Europe	2,067,000
Poland	234,000
Ukraine	232,000
Russia	218,000
United Kingdom	214,000
South America	912,000
Colombia	225,000
Africa	697,000
Oceania	76,000

Source: *Statistical Abstract of the United States.*

Table 31–2	
States with Highest Proportions of Minority Residents in 2000 (percentage of total population)	
Hispanic	
New Mexico	42%
California	32%
Texas	32%
Arizona	25%
Nevada	20%
Asian and Pacific Islander	
Hawaii	51%
California	11%
Washington	6%
New Jersey	6%
New York	6%
Black	
Mississippi	36%
Louisiana	33%
South Carolina	30%
Georgia	29%
Maryland	28%
American Indian	
Alaska	16%
New Mexico	10%
South Dakota	8%
Oklahoma	8%
Montana	6%

icans. The result is a sort of multiethnic baby boom. In 1972, at the peak of the post–World War II baby boom, 80 percent of elementary and high school students were non-Hispanic whites. By 1999 the figure was 63 percent and falling. Over the coming decades, the effects of ethnic change will be apparent not only in schools but also in the workplace, popular culture, and politics.

Women from the Grassroots to Congress

The increasing prominence of women and family issues in national politics was a steady, quiet revolution that bore fruit in the 1990s, when the number of women in Congress more than doubled. In 1981, President Reagan appointed Arizona judge Sandra Day O'Connor to be the first woman on the United States Supreme Court. In 1984, Walter Mondale chose New York Congresswoman Geraldine Ferraro as his vice presidential candidate. In 1993 Clinton appointed the second woman to the Supreme Court, U.S. Appeals Court judge Ruth Bader Ginsburg. Clinton appointee Janet Reno was the first woman to serve as attorney general, and Madeleine K. Albright the first to serve as secretary of state. George W. Bush continued to break new ground by naming Condoleezza Rice as his national security advisor in 2001 and as secretary of state in 2005.

Political gains for women at the national level reflected their growing importance in grassroots politics. The spreading suburbs of postwar America were "frontiers" that required concerted action to solve immediate needs like adequate schools and decent parks. Because pursuit of such community services was often viewed as "woman's work" (in contrast to the "man's work" of economic development), postwar metropolitan areas offered numerous opportunities for women to engage in volunteer civic work, learn political skills, and run for local office. Moreover, new cities and suburbs had fewer established political institutions, such as political machines and strong parties; their politics were open to energetic women. The entry of more women into politics is a bipartisan affair. Important support and training grounds are the League of Women Voters, which does nonpartisan studies of basic issues, and the National Women's Political Caucus, designed to support women candidates of both parties. Most women in contemporary politics have been more liberal than men—a difference that political scientists attribute to women's interest in the practical problems of schools, neighborhoods, and two-earner families. But women's grassroots mobilization, especially through evangelical churches, has also strengthened groups committed to conservative social values.

Regional differences have affected women's political gains. The West has long been the part of the country most open to women in state and local government and in business. Several western states granted voting rights to women before the adoption of the Nineteenth Amendment. More recently, Westerners have been more willing than voters in the East or South to choose women as mayors of major cities and as members of state legislatures. Many of the skills learned from politics were also useful as women played a growing role in professional and managerial occupations (see Map 31–2).

In 1991, the nomination of Judge Clarence Thomas, an African American, to the U.S. Supreme Court ensured that everyone knew that the terms of U.S. politics were changing. Because of his conservative positions on social and civil rights issues, Thomas was a controversial nominee. Controversy deepened when law professor Anita Hill accused Thomas of harassing her sexually while she served on his staff at the Equal Employment Opportunity Commission. The accusations led to riveting hearings before a U.S. Sen-

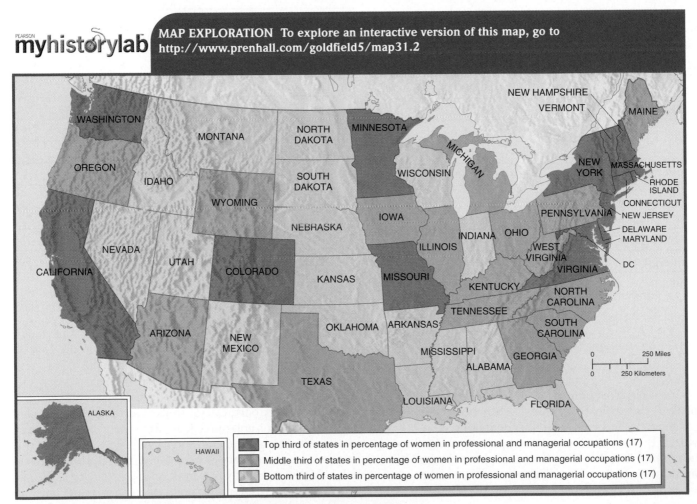

MAP EXPLORATION To explore an interactive version of this map, go to http://www.prenhall.com/goldfield5/map31.2

Top third of states in percentage of women in professional and managerial occupations (17)

Middle third of states in percentage of women in professional and managerial occupations (17)

Bottom third of states in percentage of women in professional and managerial occupations (17)

MAP 31–2 Women in Professional and Managerial Occupations, 2001
Some parts of the nation are more inviting to women-owned businesses than are others. The western and Great Lakes states, with histories of innovative politics, stand out as supportive of business opportunities for women.

Bureau of Labor Statistics, 2003. Compiled by Institute for Women's Policy Research.

ate committee. Critics tried to discredit Hill with vicious attacks on her character, and the committee failed to call witnesses who could have supported her claims. The public was left with Hill's plausible but un-proved allegations and Thomas's equally vigorous but unproved denials. The Sen-ate confirmed Thomas to the Supreme Court. Partisans on each side continued to believe the version that best suited their preconceptions and agendas.

Whatever the merits of her charges, Hill's badgering by skeptical senators an-gered millions of women. In the shadow of the hearings, women made impressive gains in the 1992 election, which pushed women's share of seats in the 50 state legislatures above 20 percent. The number of women in the U.S. Senate jumped from two to seven (and grew further to eleven Democrats and five Republicans in 2007). Bill Clinton ap-pointed women to 37 percent of the 500 or

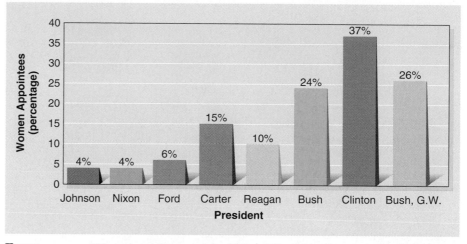

FIGURE 31–1   Women as a Percentage of Initial High-Level Presidential Appoint-ments: Lyndon Johnson to George W. Bush
By the 1990s, Americans were willing to accept women in positions that would have been reserved for men only in earlier decades, such as attorney general, secretary of state, and national security advisor.

so high-level jobs in the White House and federal depart-ments. That is far higher than Jimmy Carter's 15 percent or Lyndon Johnson's 4 percent, and also above George W. Bush's 26 percent of initial appointments (see Figure 31–1). The num-ber of women serving as federal judges grew from 48 in 1981 to more than 200—roughly a quarter of the total.

Women have influenced national politics as voters as well as candidates and cabinet members. Since the 1980s, voting patterns have shown a gender gap. Women in the 1990s identified with the Democratic Party and voted for its candidates at a higher rate than men. The reasons include concerns about the effect of government spending cuts and interest in measures to support families rather than in con-servative rhetoric. This gender gap has helped keep Demo-crats competitive and dampened the nation's conservative swing on social issues.

Minorities at the Ballot Box

The changing makeup of the American populace also helped black and Latino candidates for public office to increased success. After the racial violence of the 1960s, many black people turned to local politics to gain control of their own communities. The first black mayor of a major twentieth-century city was Carl Stokes in Cleveland in 1967. The 1973 election brought victories for Tom Bradley in Los Angeles, Maynard Jackson in Atlanta, and Coleman Young in Detroit. By 1983, three of the nation's four largest cities had black mayors. In 1989, Virginia made Douglas Wilder the first black governor in any state since Reconstruction.

The election of a minority mayor was sometimes more important for its symbolism than for the transfer of real power. Efforts to restructure the basis of city council elec-tions, however, struck directly at the balance of power. Most

mid-sized cities stopped electing city councils by wards or districts during the first half of the twentieth century. Voting at large shifted power away from geographically concentrated ethnic groups. It favored business interests that claimed to speak for the city as a whole but could assign most of the costs of economic growth to older and poorer neighborhoods.

In the 1970s, minority leaders and community activists realized that a return to district voting could convert neigh-borhood segregation from a liability to a political resource. As amended in 1975, the federal Voting Rights Act allowed minorities to use the federal courts to challenge at-large vot-ing systems that diluted the impact of their votes. Blacks and Mexican Americans used the act to reestablish city council districts in the late 1970s and early 1980s in city after city across the South and Southwest.

The political rebalancing meant that local leaders faced strong pressures to ensure equitable distribution of the ben-efits and burdens of growth. Newly empowered minorities began to press for a fair share of an expanding economic pie. In San Antonio and Denver, for example, young Hispanic politicians brought new ideas into city government in the 1980s. Henry Cisneros of San Antonio defeated a represen-tative of the downtown establishment in 1981, and in Den-ver, Federico Peña ousted a 16-year incumbent with the help of an army of volunteers. Both men ran on platforms of planned growth and later served in Clinton's cabinet. Pro-gressive African American mayors in other cities included Dennis Archer in Detroit and Andrew Young in Atlanta, lead-ers who won on positive platforms of growth and equity and who mended fences with business leaders. Meanwhile, Wash-ington state elected a Chinese American as governor, and Hawaii elected Japanese American, native Hawaiian, and Fil-ipino American governors.

As leadership opportunities for African Americans have increased in recent decades, they have gained positions of influence in a growing range of activities. In the field of foreign policy, for example, President George W. Bush choose Colin Powell as secretary of state and Condoleezza Rice as national security advisor. Here Powell (second from left) and Rice (right) observe a White House meeting between Bush and United Nations Secretary General Kofi Annan.

Rights and Opportunities

The increasing presence of Latinos and African Americans in public life highlighted a set of troublesome questions about the proper balance between equal rights and equal opportunities. Was government justified in seeking to equalize outcomes as well as starting points? More broadly, was the United States to be a unitary society in which everyone assimilated to a single culture and adhered to a single set of formal and informal rules, or might it be a plural society in which different groups accepted different goals and behaviors? The debates at the end of the twentieth century replayed many of the questions that European immigration raised at the century's beginning.

Illegal Immigration and Bilingual Education   One issue is the economic impact of illegal immigration. Advocates of tight borders assert that illegal immigrants take jobs away from legal residents and eat up public assistance. Many studies, however, find that illegal immigrants fill jobs that nobody else wants. Over the long run, high employment levels among immigrants mean that their tax contributions through sales taxes and Social Security taxes and payroll deductions more than pay for their use of welfare, food stamps, and unemployment benefits, which illegal immigrants are often afraid to claim for fear of calling attention to themselves. Nevertheless, high immigration can strain local government budgets even if it benefits the nation as a whole. Partly for this reason, 60 percent of California voters approved **Proposition 187** in 1994, cutting off access to state-funded public education and healthcare for illegal immigrants.

A symbolic issue was the degree to which American institutions should accommodate non–English speakers. Referendums in Alaska (1996) and Utah (2000) raised to 26 the number of states that declared English their official language. The measures ranged from general statements to specific prohibitions on printing forms and ballots in multiple languages. California voters in 1998 banned bilingual public education, a system under which children whose first language was Spanish or another "immigrant" tongue were taught for several years in that language before shifting to English-language classrooms. Advocates of bilingual education claimed that it eased the transition into American society, but opponents said that it blocked immigrant children from fully assimilating into American life.

The issue of illegal immigration simmered in the 1990s, but exploded in the new century. As the total of undocumented immigrants reached 11 to 12 million by best estimates, many

At the national level, minorities gradually increased their representation in Congress. Ben Nighthorse Campbell of Colorado, a Cheyenne, brought a Native American voice to the U.S. Senate in 1992. The number of African Americans in the House of Representatives topped 40 after 1992, with the help of districts drawn to concentrate black voters. Even after a series of Supreme Court cases invalidated districts drawn with race as the "predominant factor," however, African Americans held most of their gains, while the number of Latino members of Congress rose to 26 by 2007 (see Figure 31–2).

In struggling for political influence, recent immigrants have added new panethnic identities to their national identities. In the nineteenth century, English-speaking Americans looked at European immigrants from widely separated regions and backgrounds and saw "Italians" or "Jews." In turn, newcomers found economic and political strength by making common cause across their differences, molding identities as ethnic groups within the U.S. context. Newer immigrants have gone through a parallel process. Hispanic activists revived the term "Chicano" to bridge the gap between recent Mexican immigrants and Latinos whose families had settled in the Southwest before the American conquest in 1848. Great gaps of experience and culture separated Chinese, Koreans, Filipinos, and Vietnamese, but they gained political recognition and influence if they dealt with other Americans as "Asians." Native Americans have similarly downplayed tribal differences in efforts to secure better opportunities for Indians as a group.

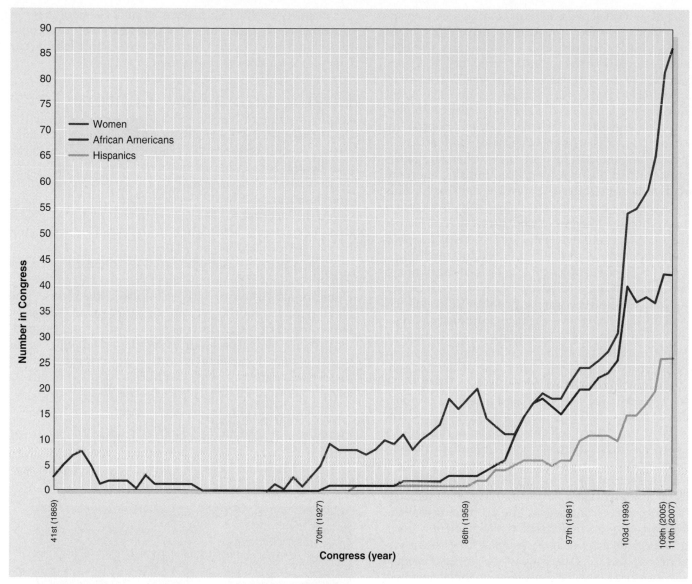

FIGURE 31–2 Minorities and Women in Congress, 1869–2005
The number of African Americans, Hispanics, and women serving in the House of Representatives and Senate increased rapidly in the 1980s and early 1990s and more slowly in the middle 1990s. The increases reflected changing attitudes, the impact of the Voting Rights Act, and decades of political activism at the grassroots.

Americans became increasingly concerned about a porous southern border. Unlike early eras of concern about immigration that had usually coincided with economic downturns, the new immigration worries came in an era of economic prosperity. In 2007, the president and leaders in both political parties were blindsided when a carefully constructed compromise over immigration policy failed because of public outcry over provisions that many voters interpreted as amnesty for rule-breaking.

Affirmative Action   An equally divisive issue was a set of policies that originated in the 1960s as **affirmative action,** a phrase that first appeared in executive orders issued by Presidents Kennedy and Johnson. The initial goal was to re-

quire businesses that received federal contracts to "take affirmative action to ensure that applicants are employed, and that employees are treated during employment without regard for their race, creed, color, or national origin." By the 1970s, many states and cities had adopted similar policies for hiring their own employees and choosing contractors and extended affirmative action to women as well as minorities. Colleges and universities used affirmative-action policies in recruiting faculty and admitting students.

As these efforts spread, the initial goal of nondiscrimination evolved into expectations and requirements for active ("affirmative") efforts to achieve greater diversity among employees, students, or contractors. Government agencies began to set aside a small percentage of contracts for woman-owned or minority-owned firms. Cities actively worked to hire more minority police officers and firefighters. Colleges made special efforts to attract minority students. The landmark court case about affirmative action was **University of California v. Bakke** (1978). Alan Bakke was an unsuccessful applicant to the medical school at the University of California at Davis. He argued that the university had improperly set aside 16 of 100 places in its entering class for minority students, thereby engaging in reverse discrimination against white applicants. In a narrow decision, the U.S. Supreme Court ordered Bakke admitted because the only basis for his rejection had been race. At the same time, the Court stated that race or ethnicity could legally be one of several factors considered in college and university admissions as long as a specific number of places were not reserved for minorities.

In 1996, California voters took grassroots action, approving a ballot measure to eliminate state-sponsored affirmative action. One effect was to prohibit state-funded colleges and universities from using race or ethnicity as a factor in deciding which applicants to admit. In the same year, the Supreme Court let stand a lower-court ruling in *Hopwood v. Texas,* which had forbidden the University of Texas to consider race in admission decisions. The number of black freshmen in the University of Texas dropped by half in 1997 and the number of blacks and Hispanics among first-year law students by two-thirds. The results were similar at the University of California at Berkeley, where the number of blacks among entering law students dropped from twenty to one.

Affirmative action has come under such close scrutiny and attack because it is a lightning rod for disagreements about the character of American society. The problem is that the goal of diversity seems to conflict with the fundamental American value of individual opportunity. In opinion polls, a majority of Americans reject the idea that past injustice and unequal opportunity can justify special consideration for all members of a group. Instead, they believe that individual merit and qualifications should be the sole basis for getting into school or getting a job, and that such factors as SAT scores and civil service exams can measure such qualifications. Others argue that the merit system is severely flawed, that students from poor families lack the advantages at home and at school that give upper-middle-class and wealthy students a head start for success. Affirmative action, they argue, helps to level the field. Nevertheless, many minorities worry that affirmative action undermines their success by suggesting that they received jobs or contracts by racial preference rather than merit.

In 2003, the Supreme Court affirmed the basic principle of affirmative action in two cases involving admission to the University of Michigan. Aided by supporting statements filed by major corporations and by members of the U.S. military, the Court found that promoting ethnic and racial diversity among students constitutes a compelling state interest, and it approved narrowly tailored affirmative-action programs that weigh race and ethnicity along with other admissions criteria on an individual basis. But four years later, a differ-ent majority on the Court rejected public school plans in Seattle and Lexington, Kentucky, that took race into account in deciding how to match students and schools, leaving the larger issue for further court cases.

Edging into a New Century

On the evening of November 7, 2000, CBS-TV made the kind of mistake that journalists dread. Relying on questions put to a sample of voters after they cast their ballots in the presidential contest between Albert Gore, Jr., and George W. Bush, the CBS newsroom first projected that Gore would win Florida and likely the election, then reversed itself and called the election for Bush, only to find that it would be days or even weeks before the votes in several pivotal states, including Florida, could be certified.

The miscue was reminiscent of the premature *Chicago Tribune* headline in November 1948 that proclaimed "Dewey Beats Truman" when the actual results were the reverse. The inability to predict the outcome in 2000 was an indication of the degree to which Americans were split down the middle in their political preferences and their visions for the future. The United States entered the twenty-first century both divided and balanced, with extremes of opinion revolving around a center of basic goals and values.

The 2000 Election

On November 8, 2000, the day after their national election, Americans woke up to the news that neither Republican George W. Bush nor Democrat Albert Gore, Jr., had a major-

In November 2002, Linda Sanchez (left) and Loretta Sanchez celebrate Linda's election to Congress from Los Angeles County. Loretta had won a Congressional seat from Orange County in 1996, and Linda's victory made them the first sisters to serve simultaneously in the House of Representatives.

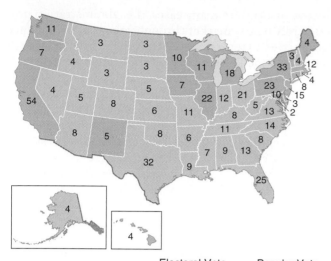

	Electoral Vote (%)	Popular Vote (%)
GEORGE W. BUSH (Republican)	**271** **(50.4)**	**50,459,624** **(47.9)**
Albert Gore (Democrat)	266 (49.4)	51,003,328 (48.4)
Ralph Nader (Green)	–	2,882,985 (2.7)
Other candidates	–	1,066,482 (1.0)

Map 31–3   The Election of 2000
In the nation's closest presidential election, Democrat Al Gore was most successful in the Northeast and Far West, while George W. Bush swept the South and won most of the Great Plains states. Green Party candidate Ralph Nader took most of his votes from Gore, and, in an ironic twist, helped to swing the election to Bush.

ity of votes in the electoral college. For the next five weeks, they woke every day to the same news. Although Gore held a lead in the popular vote (about 340,000 votes out of more than 100 million cast), both candidates needed a majority in Florida to win its electoral votes and the White House. After protracted protests about voting irregularities and malfunctioning voting equipment, politically divided Floridians engaged in an on-again off-again recount in key counties. The U.S. Supreme Court finally preempted the state process and ordered a halt to recounting on December 12 by the politically charged margin of 5 to 4. The result was to make Bush the winner in Florida by a few hundred votes and the winner nationwide by 271 electoral votes to 267 (see Map 31–3).

The heart of the controversy involved how to read Florida's punchcard ballots. Americans learned a new word, *chad,* for the little paper ovals that get punched out. How should election officials count dangling chads that were partially detached? What should they do with ballots where the chad was dimpled but not punched through? Until the Supreme Court put an end to the discussion, teams of officials struggled through recounts. Both parties put their own spin on the process. Republicans framed the issue as "following the

rules," while Democrats framed it as "making every vote count." It is difficult to know who "really" won Florida. There is good evidence that African American voters, who strongly favored Gore, were turned away in disproportionate numbers because of technical challenges to their registration. In one county, a ballot with a particularly poor design probably caused several thousand mistaken votes for a minor candidate rather than Gore. But recounts by teams of newspaper reporters came to different conclusions about who might have won, depending on what criteria were used to accept or reject disputed punchcard ballots. In the aftermath, each side could claim to have won, but the Supreme Court ruling and Bush's inauguration made the point irrelevant.

The outcome of the election showed a nation that was paradoxically divided around a strong center. The votes showed basic differences between the parties. Gore appealed especially to residents of large cities, to women, to African Americans, and to families struggling to make it economically. Bush appealed to people from small towns, to men, and to members of households that had benefitted the most from the prosperity of the Clinton era. These were divisions that had marked the two parties since the 1930s, and their persistence was a reminder of the nation's diversity of opinions and values. The nation also divided regionally, with Gore strong in the Northeast, upper Middle West, and Pacific Coast, Bush in the South, Ohio Valley, Great Plains, and Rocky Mountain states.

At the same time, both Bush, governor of Texas and son of President George H. W. Bush (1989–93), and Gore, vice president for the previous eight years, targeted their campaigns at middle Americans. Each offered to cut taxes, downsize the federal government, and protect Social Security, differing in the details rather than the broad goals. In trying to claim the political middle, they reflected the successful political message of the Clinton administration. Voters also shaved the Republican control of Congress to razor-thin margins, further undermining any chance of radical change in either a conservative or a liberal direction. To those on the political left and right who had hoped for new directions for the nation, it looked like a formula for paralysis; for the majority of Americans, it looked like stability.

Reaganomics Revisited

Despite the message of stability, the Bush administration took the Republican return to executive power as an opportunity to tilt domestic policy abruptly to the right. In effect, the new administration decided it had a mandate for change and acted boldly to implement its goals. Following the example of Ronald Reagan, Bush made massive tax cuts the centerpiece of his first months in office. By starting with proposals for ten-year cuts so large that two generations of federal programs were threatened, Bush and congressional Republicans forced the Democrats to "compromise" on reductions far higher than the economy could probably support. The resulting cuts to income taxes and estate taxes were projected to total $1,350 billion over the decade, with one-third of the benefits going to families earning more than

Despite sophisticated exit polls and computer-based voting models, the 2000 presidential election was too close to call in the hours—and then the weeks—after the voting ended. The Chicago Sun-Times *reflected the suspense and confusion in the news media, trying four different headlines as the lead see-sawed between George W. Bush and Albert Gore, Jr.*

$200,000. The federal budget quickly plunged into the red, undoing the careful political balancing and fiscal discipline of the Clinton administration. Deficits were $375 billion in 2003, $413 billion in 2004, $319 billion in 2005, and $248 billion in 2006, with more of the same forecast for the rest of the decade. Nevertheless, the administration seemed likely to achieve its goal of making the tax cuts permanent after the 2004 elections gave Republicans their biggest margins in Congress since 1929 and Americans became accustomed to the new rules.

The Bush team also moved quickly to deregulate the economy. It opened many of the environmental and business regulations of the last two decades to reconsideration—from arsenic standards in drinking water to protection for wetlands to the pollution controls required

of electric utilities. In many cases, the administration proposed to rely on the market through voluntary compliance and incentives to replace regulations. Vice President Dick Cheney developed a new production-oriented energy policy in consultation with energy companies but not with environmental or consumer groups. The collapse of the energy-trading company Enron in a hailstorm of criticism over deceptive accounting and shady market manipulations to create an energy crisis in California in early 2000 slowed the push to deregulate. In turn, Enron proved to be the first of many companies that had to restate earnings in 2002, depressing the stock market and raising questions about the ethics of big business and business accounting practices. Stock market declines and the evaporation of retirement savings for many workers raised doubts about the solidity of the 1990s boom and helped to hold down economic growth for a third year.

Education policy, a centerpiece of Bush's image as an innovator from his service as governor of Texas, was another legislative front. Tough battles with Congress resulted in compromise legislation, reminiscent of the 1990s, that included national testing standards, as Bush wanted, balanced by more federal funding. More important for both education and religion was the narrow decision by the Supreme Court in *Zelman v. Simmons-Harris* (2002) to uphold the use of taxpayer-funded assistance, or vouchers, to help students attend religious schools. By declaring that both religious and secular institutions can compete for government money as long as it is channeled through individuals who made "true private choices" about how to spend it, the court continued a two-decade trend to narrow the constitutional prohibition on the "establishment of religion."

Downsized Diplomacy

Strong conservatives had long criticized subordinating U.S. authority and freedom of action to international agreements. The new Bush administration heeded this criticism and brought a revolutionary approach to foreign affairs. The administration repeatedly adopted unilateral or bilateral policies in preference to the complexities of negotiations with an entire range of nations.

In his first 18 months, Bush opted out of a series of treaties and negotiations on global issues, sometimes despite years of careful bargaining. In each case he pointed to specific flaws or problems, but the goal was to reduce restrictions on U.S. business and its military. The administration undercut efforts to implement the Convention on Biological Warfare because of possible adverse effects on drug companies. It refused to sign on to efforts to reduce the international trade in arma-

Table 31–3		
Economic Inequality: 2003		
	Percent of Families in Poverty	**Median Household Money Income**
White	10.2	$45,631
Black	24.1	$29,645
Asian	10.1	$55,699
Hispanic origin	21.8	$32,997
Native born	11.5	$44,347
Foreign born	16.6	$37,499

Source: U.S. Census

George W. Bush used his Texas ranch to escape the pressures of Washington and to cultivate his down-to-earth image.

ments, declined to acknowledge a new International Criminal Court that is designed to try war criminals, and ignored an international compact on the rights of women in deference to cultural conservatives. Most prominently, it refused to accept the Kyoto Agreement, aimed at combating the threat of massive environmental change through global warming resulting from the carbon dioxide released by fossil fuels, dismissing a growing scientific consensus on the problem.

In the field of arms control, Bush entered office with the intention of ending the 1972 treaty that had limited the deployment of antimissile defenses by the United States and Russia in order to stabilize the arms race. The treaty had been a cornerstone of national security policy. Despite the objection of Russia, however, he formally withdrew from the treaty in December 2001. In its place he revived Ronald Reagan's idea of a Strategic Defense Initiative with proposals for new but unproven technologies to protect the United States against nuclear attacks by "rogue states." This argument was supported in 2002 by North Korea's revelation that it was pursuing a nuclear weapons program, even though it had agreed not to do so in 1994. Bush also decided not to implement the START II treaty, which had been one of the major accomplishments of his father's term as president. In its place, he worked directly to improve relations with Russia and negotiated a bilateral agreement to reduce substantially the number of nuclear warheads that Russia and the United States actively deploy (while pressing for the development of new tactical nuclear weapons). A new U.S. policy that explicitly claimed the right to act militarily to preempt potential threats confirmed the go-it-alone approach.

Paradoxes of Power

The United States in the twenty-first century faced the paradox of power: the enormous economic, military, and technological capacity that allowed it to impose its will on other nations did not extend to an ability to prevent anti-American actions by deeply enraged individuals.

In the 1990s, the U.S. economy had surged while Japan stagnated, Europe marked time, and Russia verged on economic collapse. The U.S. economy in the early twenty-first century was twice the size of Japan's; California alone had economic capacity equal to France or Britain. America's lead was nurtured by research and development spending equal to that of the next six countries combined. The U.S. military budget exceeded the total military spending of the next dozen nations. The United States had the world's only global navy and a huge edge in military technology.

But the United States remained vulnerable. Huge trade deficits, massive oil imports, and a falling dollar in the early years of the new century underlined its economic vulnerability. Overseas, terrorist attacks by Islamic radicals killed 19 American soldiers at military housing in Saudi Arabia in 1996 and 17 sailors on the destroyer *Cole* while in port in the Arab nation of Yemen in 2000. Bombs at the U.S. embassies in Kenya and Tanzania in 1998 killed more than 200 people. These bombings followed the detonation of explosives in the basement garage of the World Trade Center in New York in February 1993, killing six people. New acts of terror remained a constant threat—realized in an appalling manner on September 11, 2001.

September 11, 2001

The men who hijacked four commercial jetliners on the morning of September 11 were part of the Al-Qaeda network of terrorists coordinated by Osama Bin-Laden. A Saudi Arabian businessman who had turned against the United States because of its role in the Gulf War and its support for Israel, Bin-Laden was probably the brains behind the attacks on the U.S. military and on diplomats overseas and the earlier blast at the World Trade Center. Operating from exile in Afghanistan, he now masterminded the new and spectacular assault. The first hijacked plane hit the North Tower of the World Trade Center at 8:46 A.M. eastern time, and the second plane hit the South Tower at 9:30. As flames billowed upward, the South Tower disintegrated at 10:05 and the North Tower at 10:28. Each building took only ten seconds to fall in on itself, but television replays burned the image into the national memory.

The events of September 11 were an enormous shock to the American people, but worries about escalating terrorism were not new. Security specialists such as Defense Secretary William Cohen had been sounding the alarm through the 1990s. The U.S. Commission on National Security/21st Century, appointed by President Clinton, had included detailed warnings in its February 2001 report, although the new

Firefighters work in the rubble of one of the World Trade Center towers soon after its destruction on September 11, 2001.

administration had ignored its recommendations to reorganize federal homeland security. The problem, however, had been to connect broad concerns to specific threats. After September 11, there were reports of information-gathering failures by the FBI and CIA, to be investigated by a commission appointed by President Bush at the end of 2002. However, it is always enormously difficult to separate and correlate key points in the vast flood of information that flows through law-enforcement and intelligence agencies. Experts call this the problem of discerning real "signals" in the "noise" of information. It is much easier to read the warnings after an event has occurred than to pick out the essential data before the unexpected happens—something as true about the attack on Pearl Harbor, for example, as about the attack of 9–11.

Security and Conflict

On September 12, President George W. Bush called the Pentagon and World Trade Center attacks "acts of war." Three days later, Congress passed a Joint Resolution that gave the president sweeping powers "to use all necessary and appropriate force against those nations, organizations, or persons

he determines planned, authorized, committed, or aided the terrorist attacks that occurred on September 11, 2001." Only one member voted against the resolution—the same level of agreement that the nation showed after December 7, 1941.

The government response in the United States was a hodge-podge of security measures and arrests. Air travelers found endless lines and stringent new screening procedures, watched over by army reservists called to duty by the president. Federal agents detained more than 1,000 terrorist suspects, mostly men from the Middle East, releasing some but holding hundreds without charges, evidence, or legal counsel. President Bush also declared that "enemy combatants" could be tried by special military tribunals, although domestic and international protest caused the administration to agree to more legal safeguards than originally planned. Congress passed the **PATRIOT Act** (Providing Appropriate Tools Required to Intercept and Obstruct Terrorists) in late October, which gave federal authorities substantial new capacity to conduct criminal investigations, in most provisions for the next three to five years. These included the power to request "roving" wiretaps of individuals rather than single telephones, obtain nationwide search warrants, tap information in computerized records, and detain foreigners without filing charges for up to a week. These measures raised a number of concerns about the protection of civil liberties, as noted by the several dozen members of Congress who voted against the act. The law would be renewed in 2006 with a few added provisions to protect basic constitutional and political rights.

In November 2002, Congress approved a massive reorganization of the federal government to improve security at home. The new Department of Homeland Security includes the Immigration and Naturalization Service, Customs Service, Coast Guard, Secret Service, federal airport security workers, bioterrorism experts, and many others. With 170,000 employees, it is the second-largest federal agency, after the Defense Department. In 2004 Congress adopted a package of reforms to improve intelligence gathering and analysis, creating the position of director of national intelligence to oversee the CIA and report directly to the president.

In contrast to the suppression of dissent during World War I or the internment of Japanese Americans during World War II, Americans in 2001 and 2002 were careful on the home front. The leaders and supporters of the War on Terror reacted to dissenting voices, particularly those from a pacifist tradition, with caustic remarks rather than repression. Censorship consisted of careful management of the news and stonewalling of requests under the Freedom of Information Act rather than direct censorship of speech and the press. Violations of civil liberties have affected individuals rather than entire groups. President Bush made an important gesture soon after September 11 by appearing at a mosque and arguing against blanket condemnation of Muslims. Ethnic profiling has resulted in heightened suspicion and surveillance of Muslims, selective enforcement of immigration laws on visitors from 20 Muslim nations, and detention of several hundred U.S. residents of Middle Eastern origin, rather than incarceration of entire ethnic groups.

In the months after 9-11, the military response overseas focused on Afghanistan, where the ruling Taliban regime was harboring Bin-Laden. Afghanistan had been wracked by civil war since the invasion by the Soviet Union in 1979. The Taliban, who came to power after the Soviet withdrawal and civil war, were politically and socially repressive rulers with few international friends. U.S. bombing attacks on Taliban forces began in early October 2001, and internal opposition groups in Afghanistan threw the Taliban out of power by December. Bin-Laden, however, escaped with the aid of mountainous terrain and the confusion of war. The United States and NATO allies were left with an uncertain commitment to rebuild a stable Afghanistan, which remained an active war zone where resurgent Taliban activity in 2007 and 2008 threatened previous gains. The Al-Qaeda network and sympathetic groups remained active around the world with bombings in places as distant as Indonesia and Kenya.

Iraq and Conflicts in the Middle East

Even while the United States was intervening in Afghanistan, the administration was extending its attention to other nations that supported or condoned anti-American terrorists or had the potential to produce chemical, biological, or nuclear weapons of mass destruction. George Bush named North Korea, Iran, and Iraq as an "axis of evil" for these reasons, and then focused on Iraq. After the Gulf War, Iraq had grudgingly accepted a United Nations requirement that it eliminate such weapons, but gradually made UN inspections impossible. This resistance caused Bush to make the overthrow of Iraq's ruthless dictator, Saddam Hussein, the center of foreign policy. In effect, he declared one small, possibly dangerous nation to be the greatest menace the United States faced. In the meantime, North Korea created a further crisis by actively pursuing its atomic weapons program with the threat of additional war. However, it did enter into talks with China, Japan, Russia, South Korea, and the United States and agreed in 2007 to suspend its nuclear weapons program under international supervision and took initial steps toward compliance in 2008 — an example of the potential of persistent and patient diplomacy.

In addition to the direct fallout from the Persian Gulf War, the background to the deep-seated tensions in the Middle East included U.S. support of Israel amidst the deterioration of relations between Israel and the Arab Palestinians in territories occupied by Israel since 1967. The United States has consistently backed Israel since the 1960s. The cornerstones of U.S. policy have been the full endorsement of Israel's right to exist with secure borders and agreement on the right of Palestinians to a national state — in effect, a policy of coexistence. The United States helped to broker an Israel-Egypt peace agreement in 1977 and agreements pointing toward an independent Palestinian state in the 1990s. But hardline Israeli governments have repeatedly taken advantage of U.S. support from the 1980s in Lebanon (see Chapter 30) to the present.

In 2001–2002, the United States watched from the sidelines as the Israeli-Palestinian agreements for transition to a Palestinian state fell apart. Palestinian extremists and suicide bombers and an Israeli government that favored military responses locked each other into a downward spiral that turned into civil war. As a result, many Arabs identify the United States as an enemy of Arab nations and peoples. Israel's decision in 2005 to withdraw from the Gaza Strip and transfer authority there to the Palestinian government was a step toward resolution that unfortunately led to radical takeover there in 2007-08. The deep and long unsolvable Israel-Palestinian conflict helps to explain anti-American terrorism among Arabs, and sometimes other Muslims.

In the spring and summer of 2002, the administration escalated threats of unilateral intervention to change the Iraqi regime and began preparations for a second war in the Persian Gulf region. On October 10, Congress authorized preemptive military action against Iraq. However, international pressure from unenthusiastic allies and from other Arab nations persuaded Bush to put diplomacy ahead of war and devote two months to making his case at the United Nations. On November 8, the UN Security Council unanimously adopted a compromise resolution that gave Iraq three and a half months to allow full and open inspections before military action might be considered. In the following months, UN inspectors searched Iraqi military sites while the United States built up forces in the Middle East in preparation for war. On March 17, 2003, Bush suspended further diplomatic efforts, and on March 19 a full scale U.S.-British invasion of Iraq began (see Map 31–4).

The war to overthrow Saddam Hussein was a success as a large-scale military operation. Heavy bombing disrupted the communications and command systems for Iraq's armed forces, while the technological superiority of the U.S. armed forces overwhelmed them. Coalition forces encountered pockets of resistance from Iraqi army units, but the battles failed to stop the steady push northward from the Persian Gulf. U.S. troops took control of Baghdad without the door-to-door fighting that many had feared. On May 1, 2003, President Bush declared "mission accomplished" — that U.S. and British forces now controlled Iraq and major combat operations in Iraq were over.

Peace proved far more difficult than war. Reconstruction of damaged bridges, roads, water systems, and electrical systems took far longer than expected and many basic services were still fragile or nonexistent four years after the U.S. invasion. Meanwhile, American troops and relief workers were the continuing targets of car bombs, booby-trapped highways, mortar attacks, and similar guerrilla

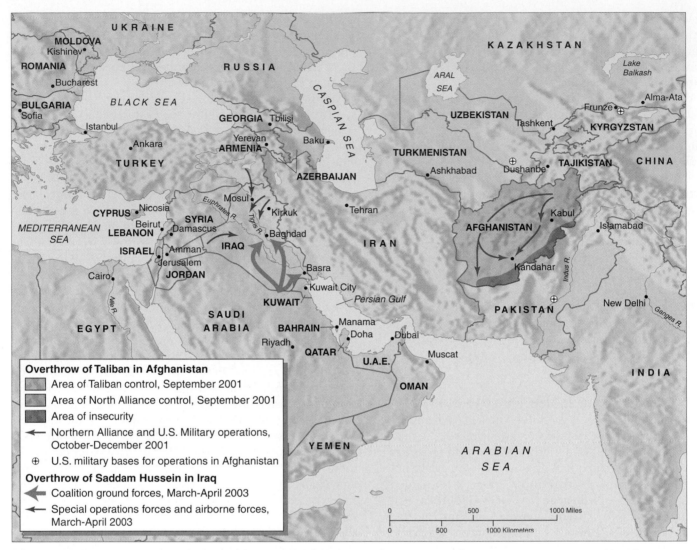

MAP 31–4   Beginning in 2001, the United States engaged in major and continuous military operations in western Asia. Operation Enduring Freedom in late 2001 deposed the Taliban regime in Afghanistan and installed a democratic government in Kabul and vicinity, although the mountainous southeastern border of Afghanistan remained insecure into 2005. The United States, Britain, and other coalition allies invaded Iraq in March, 2003 and defeated the regular Iraqi military in less than a month. However, guerilla insurgency and terrorism continued to challenge the U.S. presence.

resistance. By July 2008, more than 4,100 U.S. soldiers had died in Iraq, over 90 percent of them after the president declared victory.

By 2007, a consensus had emerged among both critics of the war and realistic supporters that the United States had overthrown Saddam without any clear plan for next steps. Because of decisions by Secretary of Defense Donald Rumsfeld, the occupation force was inadequate in size from the start—a deficiency that a "surge" of additional U.S. forces in 2007 could not fully remedy. U.S. officials dismantled the Iraqi army and police, putting 650,000 unemployed but armed men onto the streets. The decision to shut down state industries and purge members of Saddam's political party from low-level government jobs like schoolteachers created massive unemployment. The result was the decimation of

Iraq's middle class, a collapse of living standards, and the creation of roughly two million refugees who fled Iraq's new chaos for neighboring nations.

The aftermath of the war also created political problems for George Bush. A systematic search found no active production facilities or stockpiles for chemical, nuclear, or biological weapons of mass destruction. In October 2004, the final report of the U.S. bomb hunters concluded that Saddam has disbanded his chemical and nuclear weapons efforts after 1991, refuting one of the basic justifications for the war. The continuing necessity to mobilize National Guard and reserve units met heavy criticism. The need to keep an occupying army in Iraq stretched the military close the breaking point at exactly the same time that the Taliban showed renewed strength in Afghanistan.

After the defeat of the Iraqi army in 2003, U.S. forces faced continuing challenges and casualties from a stubborn resistance from anti-American insurgents.

2004 and After

Wars past and present were the pivotal issue in the 2004 election. George W. Bush argued for staying the course with the same administration. Democratic candidate John Kerry had a liberal voting record as a Massachusetts senator and decorations for meritorious service in Vietnam, but central to the Republican campaign were attacks on the veracity of his war record. A wild card was the issue of same-sex marriage. Courts in Massachusetts and politicians in Oregon and San Francisco decided that legal marriage could not be denied to same-sex couples. Their actions mobilized religious and cultural conservatives and led to successful ballot measures banning same-sex marriage in 11 states.

Bush won a solid although not overwhelming victory that helped Republicans extend their lead in Congress. Commentators liked to talk about a nation divided on issues of morality between Democratic "blue states" and Republican "red states" (colors drawn from television maps of election results). In fact, many states remained closely divided and only three shifted from one party to the other (New Hampshire to Kerry, and Iowa and New Mexico to Bush). Pundits also claimed that Bush used the issue of "moral values," including opposition to same-sex marriage, to mobilize voters, but he did not do any better among regular church-goers in 2004 than in 2000.

After the election, Bush reaffirmed his commitment to a U.S. presence in Iraq, where a deeply divided nation held elections for a new government early in 2005. Kurds from northern Iraq and Shiite Muslims from southern Iraq voted in large numbers and formed a coalition govern-ment. Participation was much lower among Sunni Muslims in central Iraq, who had benefitted most from Saddam Hussein's regime and who were the heart of continued guerrilla resistance to the United States occupation forces. The same divisions were evident in October when Iraqis approved a new constitution that met Shiite and Kurdish desires for greater autonomy but left many Sunnis dissatisfied. Those tensions played into the hands of militants who kept the level of violence among Iraqis high. In mid-2007, Congress concluded that the new Iraqi government had failed to meet most of the benchmarks that would have indicated progress toward normalcy in that devastated country, although progress was shown in 2008. Meanwhile, U.S. coalition allies such as Britain were quietly packing and leaving Iraq to its American conquerors.

As the nation worried about the open-ended commitment in Iraq, it received a devastating reminder of vulnerability. At the end of August 2005, hurricane Katrina devastated the Gulf Coast. It first seemed to spare New Orleans, much of which lies below sea level, but its backlash breached levees that protected the city. Much of the city and its surroundings flooded. Tens of thousands of residents who had not evacuated found themselves trapped in homes or huddled in the Superdome. The slowness and inadequacy of the emergency response raised serious doubts about the effectiveness of the Department of Homeland Security and its Federal Emergency Management Agency and revealed the deep fault

The flooding from Hurricane Katrina devastated huge expanses of low income neighborhoods in New Orleans.

Hurricane Katrina had its most devastating impact on the poor neighborhoods of New Orleans, where many residents lacked the ability to evacuate. Instead, thousands of families had to make their way to temporary shelter in the Superdome and other makeshift refuges.

lines that still separate the poor from the larger society—exacerbated in New Orleans by the fact that most of the poor residents were African American. Two years after the disaster, only 60 percent of the city's pre-Katrina residents had stayed or returned, and large sections of the city had seen only sporadic rebuilding. Behind the growing discussion about whether and how to rebuild New Orleans on its vulnerable site was a larger problem of continuing inequality.

Iraq and Katrina combined to deal Republicans a blow in the 2006 Congressional elections, in which Democrats regained effective control of Congress for the first time in 12 years. The results reflected the reality that the red state/blue state division of 2000 and 2004 had been poised on a knife's edge, ready to tilt toward one party or the other. Through 2007, as candidates of both parties jockeyed for presidential nominations, important domestic issues like immigration policy, health insurance, and the future of social security remained unresolved. Federal courts began to cautiously consider the basic issues of civil liberties raised by the PATRIOT Act and, even more, by the unilateral actions of the Bush administration in claiming free rein to deal with persons suspected as terrorists. And there was no clear consensus in Congress or the nation about the best steps in Iraq—whether a quick exit or a long-term U.S. occupation would do more damage to Iraq itself, to the U.S. military, and to U.S. standing in the world.

In September 2008, Americans faced a presidential election campaign with two improbable candidates. The Republicans nominated John McCain, an Arizona senator who had been a prisoner of war during the Vietnam War and who cultivated a reputation as a maverick. Nevertheless, he outlasted more mainstream candidates to win his party's nomination. Democrats had a hard-fought contest between Hillary Rodham Clinton, who hoped to be the first woman nominated for President by a major party, and Barack Obama, an Illinois senator who became the first African American nominee. Whatever the outcome of the election in November, Obama's nomination was a milestone in the long, often painful history of race relations in America.

Conclusion

If there was a dominant theme that ran through the changes and challenges of the 1990s and early 2000s, it was interconnection. The Internet, e-mail, and cell phones brought instant communication. The national economy was more and more deeply engaged with the rest of the world through trade, investment, travel, and immigration. Corporate mismanagement affected far more people than before because of pensions and savings invested in the stock market.

The nation's growing diversity—closely connected to its internationalized economy—was reflected in the political gains of African Americans and Hispanics, as well as women. The same diversity fueled battles over affirmative action and language politics. It underlay the effort to increase security against terrorism without endangering the civil liberties of Muslim Americans.

Despite what some might have wished, Americans also found that they could not always isolate the nation from the problems and conflicts that wracked much of the rest of the world. The Clinton administration joined international peacekeeping efforts in Bosnia and Kosovo. The Bush administration chose to ignore several international agreements, but still sought the cover of United Nations approval for action against Iraq (although it largely disregarded international opinion in its pursuit of the war).

Beyond its growing military commitments, the United States in the first years of the twenty-first century was deeply connected to the world. Travel, work and study abroad—and foreign tourists, workers, and students in the United States—improved American understanding of other nations. But the ease and volume of travel and trade also brought problems and fears. Many Americans had long worried that the United States was being flooded by illegal immigrants, and the revelation that some of the 9-11 terrorists had learned to fly in U.S. training schools compounded fears of a porous border. A ballooning national debt and fast-growing trade deficits reduced the

FROM THEN TO NOW

America's Mission to the World

On April 2, 1917, President Woodrow Wilson addressed Congress and asked for a declaration of war against Germany. Germany's decision to engage in unrestricted submarine warfare had made than nation the enemy of international law and morality

Wilson argued the need for the United States to protect its citizens, but he also proclaimed a crusade to make "the world safe for democracy." Wilson's idealism echoed repeatedly through the twentieth century—in Franklin Roosevelt's proclamation of the Four Freedoms, in John Kennedy's claim that Americans would "bear any burden" in the defense of liberty, in Jimmy Carter's emphasis on advancing human rights in other nations.

But the clearest echo came in January 2005, in the second inaugural address of George W. Bush. Like Wilson, Bush proclaimed that the United States has a mission and destiny to actively and tirelessly extend democracy throughout the world. "It is the policy of the United States to seek and support the growth of democratic movements and institutions in every nation and culture, with the ultimate goal of ending tyranny in our world. America's influence is considerable and we will use it confidently."

U.S. President George W. Bush delivers his inauguration speech January, 2005.

■ In what circumstances might a sense of mission enhance the effectiveness of U.S. foreign policy? When might it create problems?

PEARSON myhistorylab

From Then to Now Online

31-1 Senator Henry Cabot Lodge, *Speech in Washington, D.C.*, 1919. Cabot Lodge sets forth his opposition to U.S. membership in League of Nations.

31-2 John F. Kennedy, *Inaugural Address*, 1961. Kennedy on national mission to the World.

31-3 Jimmy Carter, *Commencement Speech at Notre Dame University*, 1977. Carter talks about human rights and foreign policy.

President Woodrow Wilson called on Congress to formalize a state of war between the revolution that had overthrown the Czar in Russia and also promised "a firm band of stern repression" against any disloyalty at home—a prelude to substantial curtailment of free speech in the United States for the duration of the war.

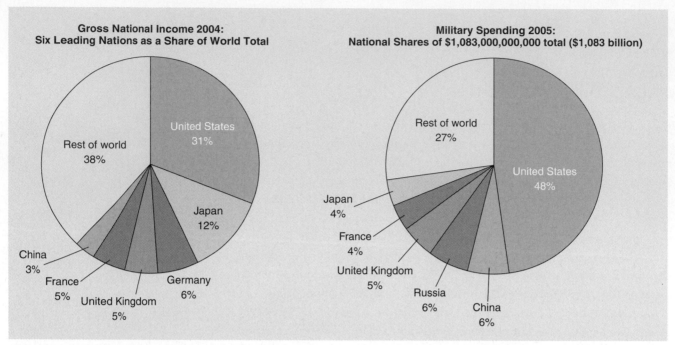

FIGURE 31–3   The United States in the Global Economy

Sources: World Bank, World Economic Development Report 2006; Center for Arms Control and Non-Proliferation (www.armscontrolcenter.org)

purchasing power of the dollar and made the economy dependent on investment from abroad. Hovering in the background was the issue of massive climate change—global warming—that was caused or accelerated by the massive use of fossil fuels whose combustion adds carbon dioxide to the atmosphere. As the Nobel Peace Prize committee recognized in 2007, when it honored the work of an international panel of scientists as well as former vice-president Al Gore efforts to publicize the issue, global warming is a truly international problem that cannot be solved within national boundaries or politics.

The events of September 11 sparked a renewed sense of national unity, at least in the short run. Stories of heroism were inspiring, as was the outpouring of volunteers and contributions for rescue and relief efforts. As the nation slowly settled back into routines, however, the devastation of hurricane Katrina revealed continuing divisions that undercut the full promise of American life. The question that remained was whether Americans could sustain and build an inclusive and unified nation under the pressures of economic uncertainty, threats of terrorism, and war.

Review Questions

1. Was the U.S. political system more polarized and divided in 1992 than in 1980? How did religiously conservative Americans understand issues of foreign relations and economic policy? How did religiously liberal Americans understand the same issues? What was the gender gap in national politics in the 1990s? Why were Republicans unable to appeal to most black and Hispanic voters in 1992?

2. What were Bill Clinton's major policy accomplishments? Do these represent liberal, moderate, or conservative positions?

3. What was the Contract with America? What are other examples of a conservative political trend in the 1990s?

4. What issues were involved in Clinton's impeachment? How does the impeachment compare with the challenges to Presidents Andrew Johnson and Richard Nixon?

5. Did the U.S. economy undergo fundamental changes in the 1990s? What has been the impact of the computer revolution? Of the growing importance of world markets?

6. What new directions did George W. Bush establish for U.S. domestic and foreign policy?

7. How did the terrorist attacks of September 11, 2001, change life in the United States? How did ordinary Americans respond at the time and since the attacks?

8. What or some of the reasons why the experience of the United States in reconstructing Iraq after 2003 has differed from its experience in Japan and Germany after World War II?

Key Terms

Affirmative action (p. 905)

Contract with America (p. 890)

Internet (p. 894)

Neoliberal (p. 890)

North American Free Trade Agreement (NAFTA) (p. 897)

PATRIOT Act (p. 910)

Proposition 187 (p. 904)

Silicon Valley (p. 895)

Temporary Assistance for Needy Families (TANF) (p. 890)

University of California v. Bakke (p. 906)

Whitewater (p. 893)

World Trade Organization (WTO) (p. 897)

World Wide Web (p. 896)

Recommended Reading

Berman, William C. *From the Center to the Edge: A History of the Clinton Presidency* (2001). An assessment of the Clinton administration in historical perspective.

Friedman, Thomas. *The World Is Flat* (2005). A challenging assessment of the increasing integration of the world economy.

Langewiesche, William. *The Atomic Bazaar: The Rise of the Nuclear Poor* (2007). The world context for national concerns about the spread of nuclear weapons.

Mitchell, William. *E-Topia: Urban Life, Jim, But Not As We Know It* (2000). An evaluation of the impact of new electronic communications on the American economy and society.

Packer, George. *The Assassin's Gate: America in Iraq* (2005). A supporter of American intervention in Iraq analyzes missteps before and after the war.

Posner, Richard A. *An Affair of State: The Investigation, Trial and Impeachment of President Clinton* (1999). An even-handed account of the Clinton-Lewinsky scandal that finds few heroes.

Where to Learn More

■ **Oklahoma City National Memorial Center Museum, Oklahoma City, OK.** Exhibits about the federal building bombing and its impact on the community. www.oklahomacitynationalmemorial.org

Study Resources

For study resources for this chapter, go to www.myhistorylab.com and choose *The American Journey*. You will find a wealth of study and review material for this chapter, including pre- and posttests, customized study plan, key term review flash cards, interactive map and document activities, and documents for analysis.

APPENDIX

THE DECLARATION OF INDEPENDENCE

When in the course of human events it becomes necessary for one people to dissolve the political bands which have connected them with another and to assume, among the powers of the earth, the separate and equal station to which the laws of nature and of nature's God entitle them, a decent respect to the opinions of mankind requires that they should declare the causes which impel them to the separation.

We hold these truths to be self-evident, that all men are created equal; that they are endowed by their Creator with certain unalienable rights; that among these are life, liberty, and the pursuit of happiness. That, to secure these rights, governments are instituted among men, deriving their just powers from the consent of the governed; that, whenever any form of government becomes destructive of these ends, it is the right of the people to alter or to abolish it, and to institute a new government, laying its foundation on such principles, and organizing its powers in such form, as to them shall seem most likely to effect their safety and happiness. Prudence, indeed, will dictate that governments long established should not be changed for light and transient causes; and, accordingly, all experience hath shown that mankind are more disposed to suffer, while evils are sufferable, than to right themselves by abolishing the forms to which they are accustomed. But when a long train of abuses and usurpations, pursuing invariably the same object, evinces a design to reduce them under absolute despotism, it is their right, it is their duty, to throw off such government and to provide new guards for their future security. Such has been the patient sufferance of these colonies, and such is now the necessity which constrains them to alter their former systems of government. The history of the present King of Great Britain is a history of repeated injuries and usurpations, all having, in direct object, the establishment of an absolute tyranny over these States. To prove this, let facts be submitted to a candid world:

He has refused his assent to laws the most wholesome and necessary for the public good.

He has forbidden his governors to pass laws of immediate and pressing importance, unless suspended in their operation till his assent should be obtained; and, when so suspended, he has utterly neglected to attend to them.

He has refused to pass other laws for the accommodation of large districts of people, unless those people would relinquish the right of representation in the legislature, a right inestimable to them and formidable to tyrants only.

He has called together legislative bodies at places unusual, uncomfortable, and distant from the depository of their public records, for the sole purpose of fatiguing them into compliance with his measures.

He has dissolved representative houses, repeatedly for opposing, with manly firmness, his invasions on the rights of the people.

He has refused, for a long time after such dissolutions, to cause others to be elected; whereby the legislative powers, incapable of annihilation, have returned to the people at large for their exercise; the state remaining, in the meantime, exposed to all the danger of invasion from without and convulsions within.

He has endeavored to prevent the population of these States; for that purpose, obstructing the laws for naturalization of foreigners, refusing to pass others to encourage their migration hither, and raising the conditions of new appropriations of lands.

He has obstructed the administration of justice by refusing his assent to laws for establishing judiciary powers.

He has made judges dependent on his will alone for the tenure of their offices and the amount and payment of their salaries.

He has erected a multitude of new offices and sent hither swarms of officers to harass our people and eat out their substance.

He has kept among us, in time of peace, standing armies, without the consent of our legislatures.

He has affected to render the military independent of, and superior to, the civil power.

He has combined with others to subject us to a jurisdiction foreign to our Constitution and unacknowledged by our laws, giving his assent to their acts of pretended legislation—

For quartering large bodies of armed troops among us;

For protecting them by mock trial, from punishment for any murders which they should commit on the inhabitants of these States;

For cutting off our trade with all parts of the world;

For imposing taxes on us without our consent;

For depriving us, in many cases, of the benefit of trial by jury;

For transporting us beyond seas to be tried for pretended offences;

For abolishing the free system of English laws in a neighboring province, establishing therein an arbitrary government, and enlarging its boundaries, so as to render it at once an example and fit instrument for introducing the same absolute rule into these colonies;

For taking away our charters, abolishing our most valuable laws, and altering, fundamentally, the powers of our governments.

For suspending our own legislatures and declaring themselves invested with power to legislate for us in all cases whatsoever.

He has abdicated government here by declaring us out of his protection and waging war against us.

He has plundered our seas, ravaged our coasts, burnt our towns, and destroyed the lives of our people.

He is, at this time, transporting large armies of foreign mercenaries to complete the works of death, desolation, and tyranny already begun with circumstances of cruelty and perfidy scarcely paralleled in the most barbarous ages, and totally unworthy the head of a civilized nation.

He has constrained our fellow citizens, taken captive on the high seas, to bear arms against their country, to become the executioners of their friends and brethren, or to fall themselves by their hands.

He has excited domestic insurrections amongst us and has endeavored to bring on the inhabitants of our frontiers, the merciless Indian savages, whose known rule of warfare is an undistinguished destruction of all ages, sexes, and conditions.

In every stage of these oppressions, we have petitioned for redress in the most humble terms; our repeated petitions have been answered only by repeated injury. A prince whose character is thus marked by every act which may define a tyrant is unfit to be the ruler of a free people.

Nor have we been wanting in attention to our British brethren. We have warned them, from time to time, of attempts made by their legislature to extend an unwarrantable jurisdiction over us. We have reminded them of the circumstances of our emigration and settlement here. We have appealed to their native justice and magnanimity, and we have conjured them, by the ties of our common kindred, to disavow these usurpations, which would inevitably interrupt our connections and correspondence. They, too, have been deaf to the voice of justice and consanguinity. We must, therefore, acquiesce in the necessity which denounces our separation, and hold them, as we hold the rest of mankind, enemies in war, in peace, friends.

We, therefore, the representatives of the United States of America, in general Congress assembled, appealing to the Supreme Judge of the world for the rectitude of our intentions, do, in the name and by the authority of the good people of these colonies, solemnly publish and declare, that these united colonies are, and of right ought to be, free and independent states: that they are absolved from all allegiance to the British Crown, and that all political connection between them and the state of Great Britain is, and ought to be, totally dissolved; and that, as free and independent states, they have full power to levy war, conclude peace, contract alliances, establish commerce, and to do all other acts and things which independent states may of right do. And, for the support of this declaration, with a firm reliance on the protection of Divine Providence, we mutually pledge to each other our lives, our fortunes, and our sacred honor.

THE CONSTITUTION OF THE UNITED STATES OF AMERICA

We the people of the United States, in order to form a more perfect union, establish justice, insure domestic tranquillity, provide for the common defense, promote the general welfare, and secure the blessings of liberty to ourselves and our posterity, do ordain and establish this Constitution for the United States of America.

Article I
Section 1. All legislative powers herein granted shall be vested in a Congress of the United States, which shall consist of a Senate and House of Representatives.

Section 2. 1. The House of Representatives shall be composed of members chosen every second year by the people of the several States, and the electors in each State shall have the qualifications requisite for electors of the most numerous branch of the State legislature.

2. No person shall be a representative who shall not have attained to the age of twenty-five years, and been seven years a citizen of the United States, and who shall not, when elected, be an inhabitant of that State in which he shall be chosen.

3. Representatives and direct taxes[1] shall be apportioned among the several States which may be included within this Union, according to their respective numbers, which shall be determined by adding to the whole number of free persons, including those bound to service for a term of years,

---

Note: This version of the Constitution has been edited to conform to present-day punctuation and usage standards. In addition, paragraphs within sections have been numbered for ease of reference.

---

[1]See the Sixteenth Amendment.

and excluding Indians not taxed, three fifths of all other persons.[2] The actual enumeration shall be made within three years after the first meeting of the Congress of the United States, and within every subsequent term of ten years, in such manner as they shall by law direct. The number of representatives shall not exceed one for every thirty thousand, but each State shall have at least one representative; and until such enumeration shall be made, the State of New Hampshire shall be entitled to choose three, Massachusetts eight, Rhode Island and Providence Plantations one, Connecticut five, New York six, New Jersey four, Pennsylvania eight, Delaware one, Maryland six, Virginia ten, North Carolina five, South Carolina five, and Georgia three.

4. When vacancies happen in the representation from any State, the executive authority thereof shall issue writs of election to fill such vacancies.

5. The House of Representatives shall choose their speaker and other officers; and shall have the sole power of impeachment.

Section 3. 1. The Senate of the United States shall be composed of two senators from each State, chosen by the legislature thereof,[3] for six years; and each senator shall have one vote.

2. Immediately after they shall be assembled in consequence of the first election, they shall be divided as equally as may be into three classes. The seats of the senators of the first class shall be vacated at the expiration of the second year, of the second class at the expiration of the fourth year, and of the third class at the expiration of the sixth year, so that one third may be chosen every second year; and if vacancies happen by resignation, or otherwise, during the recess of the legislature of any State, the executive thereof may make temporary appointments until the next meeting of the legislature, which shall then fill such vacancies.[4]

3. No person shall be a senator who shall not have attained to the age of thirty years, and been nine years a citizen of the United States, and who shall not, when elected, be an inhabitant of that State for which he shall be chosen.

4. The Vice President of the United States shall be President of the Senate, but shall have no vote, unless they be equally divided.

5. The Senate shall choose their other officers, and also a president pro tempore, in the absence of the Vice President, or when he shall exercise the office of the President of the United States.

6. The Senate shall have the sole power to try all impeachments. When sitting for that purpose, they shall be on oath or affirmation. When the President of the United States is tried, the chief justice shall preside: and no person shall

be convicted without the concurrence of two thirds of the members present.

7. Judgment in cases of impeachment shall not extend further than to removal from office, and disqualification to hold and enjoy any office of honor, trust or profit under the United States: but the party convicted shall nevertheless be liable and subject to indictment, trial, judgment and punishment, according to law.

Section 4. 1. The times, places, and manner of holding elections for senators and representatives, shall be prescribed in each State by the legislature thereof; but the Congress may at any time by law make or alter such regulations, except as to the places of choosing senators.

2. The Congress shall assemble at least once in every year, and such meeting shall be on the first Monday in December, unless they shall by law appoint a different day.

Section 5. 1. Each House shall be the judge of the elections, returns and qualifications of its own members, and a majority of each shall constitute a quorum to do business; but a smaller number may adjourn from day to day, and may be authorized to compel the attendance of absent members, in such manner, and under such penalties as each House may provide.

2. Each House may determine the rules of its proceedings, punish its members for disorderly behavior, and, with the concurrence of two thirds, expel a member.

3. Each House shall keep a journal of its proceedings, and from time to time publish the same, excepting such parts as may in their judgment require secrecy; and the yeas and nays of the members of either House on any question shall, at the desire of one fifth of those present, be entered on the journal.

4. Neither House, during the session of Congress, shall, without the consent of the other, adjourn for more than three days, nor to any other place than that in which the two Houses shall be sitting.

Section 6. 1. The senators and representatives shall receive a compensation for their services, to be ascertained by law, and paid out of the Treasury of the United States. They shall in all cases, except treason, felony, and breach of the peace, be privileged from arrest during their attendance at the session of their respective Houses, and in going to and returning from the same; and for any speech or debate in either House, they shall not be questioned in any other place.

2. No senator or representative shall, during the time for which he was elected, be appointed to any civil office under the authority of the United States, which shall have been created, or the emoluments whereof shall have been increased, during such time; and no person holding any office under the United States shall be a member of either House during his continuance in office.

---

[2]See the Fourteenth Amendment.
[3]See the Seventeenth Amendment.
[4]See the Seventeenth Amendment.

Section 7. 1. All bills for raising revenue shall originate in the House of Representatives; but the Senate may propose or concur with amendments as on other bills.

2. Every bill which shall have passed the House of Representatives and the Senate, shall, before it become a law, be presented to the President of the United States; If he approves he shall sign it, but if not he shall return it, with his objections, to that House in which it shall have originated, who shall enter the objections at large on their journal, and proceed to reconsider it. If after such reconsideration two thirds of that House shall agree to pass the bill, it shall be sent, together with the objections, to the other House, by which it shall likewise be reconsidered, and if approved by two thirds of that House, it shall become a law. But in all such cases the votes of both Houses shall be determined by yeas and nays, and the names of the persons voting for and against the bill shall be entered on the journal of each House respectively. If any bill shall not be returned by the President within ten days (Sundays excepted) after it shall have been presented to him, the same shall be a law, in like manner as if he had signed it, unless the Congress by their adjournment prevent its return, in which case it shall not be a law.

3. Every order, resolution, or vote to which the concurrence of the Senate and the House of Representatives may be necessary (except on a question of adjournment) shall be presented to the President of the United States; and before the same shall take effect, shall be approved by him, or being disapproved by him, shall be repassed by two thirds of the Senate and House of Representatives, according to the rules and limitations prescribed in the case of a bill.

Section 8. 1. The Congress shall have the power

1. To lay and collect taxes, duties, imposts, and excises, to pay the debts and provide for the common defense and general welfare of the United States; but all duties, imposts, and excises shall be uniform throughout the United States.

2. To borrow money on the credit of the United States;

3. To regulate commerce with foreign nations, and among the several States, and with the Indian tribes;

4. To establish a uniform rule of naturalization, and uniform laws on the subject of bankruptcies throughout the United States;

5. To coin money, regulate the value thereof, and of foreign coin, and fix the standard of weights and measures;

6. To provide for the punishment of counterfeiting the securities and current coin of the United States;

7. To establish post offices and post roads;

8. To promote the progress of science and useful arts, by securing for limited times to authors and inventors the exclusive right to their respective writings and discoveries;

9. To constitute tribunals inferior to the Supreme Court;

10. To define and punish piracies and felonies committed on the high seas, and offenses against the law of nations;

11. To declare war, grant letters of marque and reprisal, and make rules concerning captures on land and water;

12. To raise and support armies, but no appropriation of money to that use shall be for a longer term than two years;

13. To provide and maintain a navy;

14. To make rules for the government and regulation of the land and naval forces;

15. To provide for calling forth the militia to execute the laws of the Union, suppress insurrections and repel invasions;

16. To provide for organizing, arming, and disciplining the militia, and for governing such part of them as may be employed in the service of the United States, reserving to the States respectively, the appointment of the officers, and the authority of training the militia according to the discipline prescribed by Congress;

17. To exercise exclusive legislation in all cases whatsoever, over such district (not exceeding ten miles square) as may, by cession of particular States, and the acceptance of Congress, become the seat of the government of the United States, and to exercise like authority over all places purchased by the consent of the legislature of the State in which the same shall be, for the erection of forts, magazines, arsenals, dockyards, and other needful buildings; and

18. To make all laws which shall be necessary and proper for carrying into execution the foregoing powers, and all other powers vested by this Constitution in the government of the United States, or any department or officer thereof.

Section 9. 1. The migration or importation of such persons as any of the States now existing shall think proper to admit, shall not be prohibited by the Congress prior to the year one thousand eight hundred and eight, but a tax or duty may be imposed on such importation, not exceeding ten dollars for each person.

2. The privilege of the writ of habeas corpus shall not be suspended, unless when in cases of rebellion or invasion the public safety may require it.

3. No bill of attainder or ex post facto law shall be passed.

4. No capitation, or other direct, tax shall be laid, unless in proportion to the census or enumeration herein-before directed to be taken.[5]

5. No tax or duty shall be laid on articles exported from any State.

6. No preference shall be given by any regulation of commerce or revenue to the ports of one State over those of another: nor shall vessels bound to, or from, one State be obliged to enter, clear, or pay duties in another.

7. No money shall be drawn from the treasury, but in consequence of appropriations made by law; and a regular statement and account of the receipts and expenditures of all public money shall be published from time to time.

---

[5]See the Sixteenth Amendment.

8. No title of nobility shall be granted by the United States: and no person holding any office of profit or trust under them, shall, without the consent of the Congress, accept of any present, emolument, office, or title, of any kind whatever, from any king, prince, or foreign State.

Section 10. 1. No State shall enter into any treaty, alliance, or confederation; grant letters of marque and reprisal; coin money; emit bills of credit; make any thing but gold and silver coin a tender in payment of debts; pass any bill of attainder, ex post facto law, or law impairing the obligation of contracts, or grant, any title of nobility.

2. No State shall, without the consent of the Congress, lay any imposts or duties on imports or exports, except what may be absolutely necessary for executing its inspection laws: and the net produce of all duties and imposts laid by any State on imports or exports, shall be for the use of the treasury of the United States; and all such laws shall be subject to the revision and control of the Congress.

3. No State shall, without the consent of the Congress, lay any duty of tonnage, keep troops, or ships of war in time of peace, enter into any agreement or compact with another State, or with a foreign power, or engage in war, unless actually invaded, or in such imminent danger as will not admit of delay.

Article II

Section 1. 1. The executive power shall be vested in a President of the United States of America. He shall hold his office during the term of four years, and, together with the Vice President, chosen for the same term, be elected, as follows:

2. Each State shall appoint, in such manner as the legislature thereof may direct, a number of electors, equal to the whole number of senators and representatives to which the State may be entitled in the Congress: but no senator or representative, or person holding any office of trust or profit under the United States, shall be appointed an elector.

The electors shall meet in their respective States, and vote by ballot for two persons, of whom one at least shall not be an inhabitant of the same State with themselves. And they shall make a list of all the persons voted for, and of the number of votes for each; which list they shall sign and certify, and transmit sealed to the seat of the government of the United States, directed to the president of the Senate. The president of the Senate shall, in the presence of the Senate and House of Representatives, open all the certificates, and the votes shall then be counted. The person having the greatest number of votes shall be the President, if such number be a majority of the whole number of electors appointed; and if there be more than one who have such majority, and have an equal number of votes, then the House of Representatives shall immediately choose by ballot one of them for President; and if no person have a majority, then from the five highest on the list the said House shall in like manner choose

the President. But in choosing the President, the votes shall be taken by States, the representation from each State having one vote; a quorum for this purpose shall consist of a member or members from two thirds of the States, and a majority of all the States shall be necessary to a choice. In every case after the choice of the President, the person having the greatest number of votes of the electors shall be the Vice President. But if there should remain two or more who have equal votes, the Senate shall choose from them by ballot the Vice President.[6]

3. The Congress may determine the time of choosing the electors, and the day on which they shall give their votes; which day shall be the same throughout the United States.

4. No person except a natural born citizen, or a citizen of the United States, at the time of the adoption of this Constitution, shall be eligible to the office of President; neither shall any person be eligible to the office who shall not have attained to the age of thirty-five years, and been fourteen years a resident within the United States.

5. In case of the removal of the President from office, or of his death, resignation, or inability to discharge the powers and duties of the said office, the same shall devolve on the Vice President, and the congress may by law provide for the case of removal, death, resignation or inability, both of the President and Vice President, declaring what officer shall then act as President, and such officer shall act accordingly until the disability be removed, or a President shall be elected.

6. The President shall, at stated times, receive for his services a compensation which shall neither be increased nor diminished during the period for which he shall have been elected, and he shall not receive within that period any other emolument from the United States, or any of them.

7. Before he enter on the execution of his office, he shall take the following oath or affirmation:—"I do solemnly swear (or affirm) that I will faithfully execute the office of President of the United States, and will to the best of my ability, preserve, protect and defend the Constitution of the United States."

Section 2. 1. The President shall be commander in chief of the army and navy of the United States, and of the militia of the several States, when called into the actual service of the United States; he may require the opinion in writing, of the principal officer in each of the executive departments, upon any subject relating to the duties of their respective offices, and he shall have power to grant reprieves and pardons for offenses against the United States, except in cases of impeachment.

2. He shall have power, by and with the advice and consent of the Senate, to make treaties, provided two thirds of the senators present concur; and he shall nominate, and by

---

[6]Superseded by the Twelfth Amendment.

and with the advice and consent of the Senate, shall appoint ambassadors, other public ministers and consuls, judges of the Supreme Court, and all other officers of the United States, whose appointments are not herein otherwise provided for, and which shall be established by law; but the Congress may by law vest the appointment of such inferior officers, as they think proper, in the President alone, in the courts of laws, or in the heads of departments.

3. The President shall have power to fill up all vacancies that may happen during the recess of the Senate, by granting commissions which shall expire at the end of their next session.

Section 3. He shall from time to time give to the Congress information of the state of the Union, and recommend to their consideration such measures as he shall judge necessary and expedient; he may, on extraordinary occasions, convene both Houses, or either of them, and in case of disagreement between them with respect to the time of adjournment, he may adjourn them to such time as he shall think proper; he shall receive ambassadors and other public ministers; he shall take care that the laws be faithfully executed, and shall commission all the officers of the United States.

Section 4. The President, Vice President, and all civil officers of the United States, shall be removed from office on impeachment for, and conviction of, treason, bribery, or other high crimes and misdemeanors.

Article III
Section 1. The judicial power of the United States shall be vested in one Supreme Court, and in such inferior courts as the Congress may from time to time ordain and establish. The judges, both of the Supreme and inferior courts, shall hold their offices during good behavior, and shall, at stated times, receive for their services, a compensation, which shall not be diminished during their continuance in office.

Section 2. 1. The judicial power shall extend to all cases, in law and equity, arising under this Constitution, the laws of the United States, and treaties made, or which shall be made, under their authority;—to all cases of admiralty and maritime jurisdiction;—to controversies to which the United States shall be a party;[7]—to controversies between two or more States;—between a State and citizens of another State;—between citizens of different States;—between citizens of the same State claiming lands under grants of different States, and between a State, or the citizens thereof, and foreign States, citizens or subjects.

2. In all cases affecting ambassadors, other public ministers and consuls, and those in which a State shall be party, the Supreme Court shall have original jurisdiction. In all the other cases before mentioned, the Supreme Court shall have appellate jurisdiction, both as to law and fact, with such exceptions, and under such regulations as the Congress shall make.

3. The trial of all crimes, except in cases of impeachment, shall be by jury; and such trial shall be held in the State where the said crimes shall have been committed; but when not committed within any State, the trial shall be such place or places as the congress may by law have directed.

Section 3. 1. Treason against the United States shall consist only in levying war against them, or in adhering to their enemies, giving them aid and comfort. No person shall be convicted of treason unless on the testimony of two witnesses to the same overt act, or on confession in open court.

2. The Congress shall have power to declare the punishment of treason, but no attainder of treason shall work corruption of blood, or forfeiture except during the life of the person attained.

Article IV
Section 1. Full faith and credit shall be given in each State to the public acts, records, and judicial proceedings of every other State. And the Congress may by general laws prescribe the manner in which such acts, records and proceedings shall be proved, and the effect thereof.

Section 2. 1. The citizens of each State shall be entitled to all privileges and immunities of citizens in the several States.[8]

2. A person charged in any State with treason, felony, or other crime, who shall flee from justice, and be found in another State, shall on demand of the executive authority of the State from which he fled, be delivered up to be removed to the State having jurisdiction of the crime.

3. No person held to service or labor in one State under the laws thereof, escaping into another, shall, in consequence of any law or regulation therein, be discharged from such service or labor, but shall be delivered up on claim of the party to whom such service or labor may be due.[9]

Section 3. 1. New States may be admitted by the Congress into this Union; but no new State shall be formed or erected within the jurisdiction of any other State, nor any State be formed by the junction of two or more States, or parts of States, without the consent of the legislatures of the States concerned as well as of the Congress.

2. The Congress shall have power to dispose of and make all needful rules and regulations respecting the territory or other property belonging to the United States; and nothing in this Constitution shall be so construed as to prejudice any claims of the United States, or of any particular State.

Section 4. The United States shall guarantee to every State in this Union a republican form of government, and shall

---

[7]See the Eleventh Amendment.

[8]See the Fourteenth Amendment, Sec.1.
[9]See the Thirteenth Amendment.

protect each of them against invasion; and on application of the legislature, or of the executive (when the legislature cannot be convened) against domestic violence.

Article V

The Congress, whenever two thirds of both Houses shall deem it necessary, shall propose amendments to this Constitution, or, on the application of the legislatures of two thirds of the several States, shall call a convention for proposing amendments, which in either case shall be valid to all intents and purposes, as part of this Constitution, when ratified by the legislatures of three fourths of the several States, or by conventions in three fourths thereof, as the one or the other mode of ratification may be proposed by the Congress; Provided that no amendment which may be made prior to the year one thousand eight hundred and eight shall in any manner affect the first and fourth clauses in the ninth section of the first article; and that no State, without its consent, shall be deprived of its equal suffrage in the Senate.

Article VI

1. All debts contracted and engagements entered into, before the adoption of this Constitution, shall be as valid against the United States under this Constitution, as under the Confederation.[10]

2. This Constitution, and the laws of the United States which shall be made in pursuance thereof; and all treaties made, or which shall be made, under the authority of the United States, shall be the supreme law of the land; and the judges in every State shall be bound thereby, any thing in the Constitution or laws of any State to the contrary notwithstanding.

3. The senators and representatives before mentioned, and the members of the several State legislatures, and all executive and judicial officers, both of the United States and of the several States, shall be bound by oath or affirmation to support this Constitution; but no religious test shall ever be required as a qualification to any office or public trust under the United States.

Article VII

The ratification of the conventions of nine States shall be sufficient for the establishment of this Constitution between the States so ratifying the same.

Done in Convention by the unanimous consent of the States present the seventeenth day of September in the year of our Lord one thousand seven hundred and eighty-seven, and of the independence of the United States of America the twelfth. In witness whereof we have hereunto subscribed our names.

[Signatories' names omitted]

---

[10]See the Fourteenth Amendment, Sec.4.

Articles in addition to, and amendment of, the Constitution of the United States of America, proposed by Congress, and ratified by the legislatures of the several States, pursuant to the fifth article of the original Constitution.

Amendment I

[First ten amendments ratified December 15, 1791]
Congress shall make no law respecting an establishment of religion, or prohibiting the free exercise thereof; or abridging the freedom of speech, or of the press; or the right of the people peaceably to assemble, and to petition the government for a redress of grievances.

Amendment II

A well regulated militia, being necessary to the security of a free State, the right of the people to keep and bear arms, shall not be infringed.

Amendment III

No soldier shall, in time of peace be quartered in any house, without the consent of the owner, nor in time of war, but in a manner to be prescribed by law.

Amendment IV

The right of the people to be secure in their persons, houses, papers, and effects, against unreasonable searches and seizures, shall not be violated, and no warrants shall issue, but upon probable cause, supported by oath or affirmation, and particularly describing the place to be searched, and the persons or things to be seized.

Amendment V

No person shall be held to answer for a capital or otherwise infamous crime, unless on a presentment or indictment of a grand jury, except in cases arising in the land or naval forces, or in the militia, when in actual service in time of war or public danger; nor shall any person be subject for the same offense to be twice put in jeopardy of life or limb; nor shall be compelled in any criminal case to be a witness against himself, nor be deprived of life, liberty, or property, without due process of law; nor shall private property be taken for public use, without just compensation.

Amendment VI

In all criminal prosecutions, the accused shall enjoy the right to a speedy and public trial, by an impartial jury of the State and district wherein the crime shall have been committed, which district shall have been previously ascertained by law, and to be informed of the nature and cause of the accusation; to be confronted with the witnesses against him; to have compulsory process for obtaining witnesses in his favor, and to have the assistance of counsel for his defense.

Amendment VII

In suits at common law, where the value in controversy shall exceed twenty dollars, the right of trial by jury shall be preserved, and no fact tried by a jury shall be otherwise reexamined in any court of the United States, than according to the rules of the common law.

Amendment VIII

Excessive bail shall not be required, nor excessive fines imposed, nor cruel and unusual punishments inflicted.

Amendment IX

The enumeration in the Constitution of certain rights shall not be construed to deny or disparage others retained by the people.

Amendment X

The powers not delegated to the United States by the Constitution, nor prohibited by it to the States, are reserved to the States respectively, or to the people.

Amendment XI [January 8, 1798]

The judicial power of the United States shall not be construed to extend to any suit in law or equity, commended or prosecuted against one of the United States by citizens of another State, or by citizens or subjects of any foreign State.

Amendment XII [September 25, 1804]

The electors shall meet in their respective States, and vote by ballot for President and Vice President, one of whom, at least, shall not be an inhabitant of the same State with themselves; they shall name in their ballots the person voted for as President, and in distinct ballots, the person voted for as Vice President, and they shall make distinct lists of all persons voted for as President and of all persons voted for as Vice President, and of the number of votes for each, which lists they shall sign and certify, and transmit sealed to the seat of the government of the United States, directed to the President of the Senate;—The President of the Senate shall, in the presence of the Senate and House of Representatives, open all the certificates and the votes shall then be counted;—The person having the greatest number of votes for President, shall be the President, if such number be a majority of the whole number of electors appointed; and if no person have such majority, then from the persons having the highest numbers not exceeding three on the list of those voted for as President, the House of Representatives shall choose immediately, by ballot, the President. But in choosing the President, the votes shall be taken by States, the representation from each State having one vote; a quorum for this purpose shall consist of a member or members from two thirds of the States, and a majority of all the States shall be necessary to a choice. And if the House of Representatives shall not choose a Pres-

ident whenever the right of choice shall devolve upon them, before the fourth day of March next following, then the Vice President shall act as President, as in the case of the death or other constitutional disability of the President. The person having the greatest number of votes as Vice President shall be the Vice President, if such number be a majority of the whole number of electors appointed, and if no person have a majority, then from the two highest numbers on the list, the Senate shall choose the Vice President; a quorum for the purpose shall consist of two thirds of the whole number of Senators, and a majority of the whole number shall be necessary to a choice. But no person constitutionally ineligible to the office of President shall be eligible to that of Vice President of the United States.

Amendment XIII [December 18, 1865]

Section 1. Neither slavery nor involuntary servitude, except as a punishment for crime whereof the party shall have been duly convicted, shall exist within the United States, or any place subject to their jurisdiction.

Section 2. Congress shall have power to enforce this article by appropriate legislation.

Amendment XIV [July 28, 1868]

Section 1. All persons born or naturalized in the United States, and subject to the jurisdiction thereof, are citizens of the United States and of the State wherein they reside. No State shall make or enforce any law which shall abridge the privileges or immunities of citizens of the United States; nor shall any State deprive any person of life, liberty, or property, without due process of law; nor deny to any person within its jurisdiction the equal protection of the laws.

Section 2. Representatives shall be apportioned among the several States according to their respective numbers, counting the whole number of persons in each State, excluding Indians not taxed. But when the right to vote at any election for the choice of electors for President and Vice President of the United States, representatives in Congress, the executive and judicial officers of a State, or the members of the legislature thereof, is denied to any of the male inhabitants of such State, being twenty-one years of age, and citizens of the United States, or in any way abridged, except for participating in rebellion, or other crime, the basis of representation there shall be reduced in the proportion which the number of such male citizens shall bear to the whole number of male citizens twenty-one years of age in such State.

Section 3. No person shall be a senator or representative in Congress, or elector of President and Vice President, or hold any office, civil or military, under the United States, or under any State, who having previously taken an oath, as a member of Congress, or as an officer of the United States, or as a member of any State legislature, or as an executive or judicial officer of any State, to support the Constitution of the United States, shall have engaged in insurrection or rebellion against the same, or given aid or comfort to the enemies thereof. But Congress may by a vote of two thirds of each House, remove such disability.

Section 4. The validity of the public debt of the United States, authorized by law, including debts incurred for payment of pensions and bounties for services in suppressing insurrection or rebellion; shall not be questioned. But neither the United States nor any State shall assume or pay any debt or obligation incurred in aid of insurrection or rebellion against the United States, or any claim for the loss or emancipation of any slave; but all such debts, obligations, and claims shall be held illegal and void.

Section 5. The Congress shall have the power to enforce, by appropriate legislation, the provisions of this article.

Amendment XV [March 30, 1870]
Section 1. The right of citizens of the United States to vote shall not be denied or abridged by the United States or by any State on account of race, color, or previous condition of servitude.

Section 2. The Congress shall have power to enforce this article by appropriate legislation.

Amendment XVI [February 25, 1913]
The Congress shall have power to lay and collect taxes on incomes, from whatever source derived, without apportionment among the several States, and without regard to any census or enumeration.

Amendment XVII [May 31, 1913]
The Senate of the United States shall be composed of two senators from each State, elected by the people thereof, for six years; and each senator shall have one vote. The electors in each State shall have the qualifications requisite for electors of the most numerous branch of the State legislature.

When vacancies happen in the representation of any State in the Senate, the executive authority of such State shall issue writs of election to fill such vacancies: Provided, That the legislature of any State may empower the executive thereof to make temporary appointments until the people fill the vacancies by election as the legislature may direct.

This amendment shall not be so construed as to affect the election or term of any senator chosen before it becomes valid as part of the Constitution.

Amendment XVIII[11] [January 29, 1919]
After one year from the ratification of this article, the manufacture, sale, or transportation of intoxicating liquors within, the importation thereof into, or the exportation thereof from the United States and all territory subject to the jurisdiction thereof for beverage purposes is thereby prohibited.

The Congress and the several States shall have concurrent power to enforce this article by appropriate legislation.

This article shall be inoperative unless it shall have been ratified as an amendment to the Constitution by the legislatures of the several States, as provided in the constitution, within seven years from the date of the submission hereof to the States by Congress.

Amendment XIX [August 26, 1920]
The right of citizens of the United States to vote shall not be denied or abridged by the United States or by any State on account of sex.

Congress shall have the power to enforce this article by appropriate legislation.

Amendment XX [January 23, 1933]
Section 1. The terms of the President and Vice President shall end at noon on the 20th day of January and the terms of Senators and Representatives at noon on the 3d day of January, of the years in which such terms would have ended if this article had not been ratified; and the terms of their successors shall then begin.

Section 2. The Congress shall assemble at least once in every year, and such meeting shall begin at noon on the 3d day of January, unless they shall by law appoint a different day.

Section 3. If, at the time fixed for the beginning of the term of President, the President-elect shall have died, the Vice President-elect shall become President. If a President shall not have been chosen before the time fixed for the beginning of his term, or if the President-elect shall have failed to qualify, then the Vice President-elect shall act as President until a President shall have qualified; and the Congress may by law provide for the case wherein neither a President-elect nor a Vice President-elect shall have qualified, declaring who shall then act as President, or the manner in which one who is to act shall be selected, and such person shall act accordingly until a President or Vice President shall have qualified.

Section 4. The Congress may by law provide for the case of the death of any of the persons from whom, the House of

---

[11]Repealed by the Twenty-first Amendment.

Representatives may choose a President whenever the right of choice shall have devolved upon them, and for the case of the death of any of the persons from whom the Senate may choose a Vice President whenever the right of choice shall have devolved upon them.

Section 5. Sections 1 and 2 shall take effect on the 15th day of October following the ratification of this article.

Section 6. This article shall be inoperative unless it shall have been ratified as an amendment to the Constitution by the legislatures of three-fourths of the several States within seven years from the date of its submission.

Amendment XXI [December 5, 1933]
Section 1. The Eighteenth Article of amendment to the Constitution of the United States is hereby repealed.

Section 2. The transportation or importation into any State, Territory, or possession of the United States for delivery or use therein of intoxicating liquors in violation of the laws thereof, is hereby prohibited.

Section 3. This article shall be inoperative unless it shall have been ratified as an amendment to the Constitution by conventions in the several States, as provided in the Constitution, within seven years from the date of the submission thereof to the States by the Congress.

Amendment XXII [March 1, 1951]
No person shall be elected to the office of the President more than twice, and no person who has held the office of President, or acted as President, for more than two years of a term to which some other person was elected President shall be elected to the office of the President more than once.

But this article shall not apply to any person holding the office of President when this article was proposed by the Congress, and shall not prevent any person who may be holding the office of President, or acting as President, during the term within which this article becomes operative from holding the office of President or acting as President during the remainder of such term.

This article shall be inoperative unless it shall have been ratified as an amendment to the Constitution by the legislatures of three-fourths of the several States within seven years from the date of its submission to the States by the Congress.

Amendment XXIII [March 29, 1961]
Section 1. The District constituting the seat of Government of the United States shall appoint in such manner as the Congress may direct.

A number of electors of President and Vice President equal to the whole number of Senators and Representatives in Congress to which the District would be entitled if it were a State, but in no event more than the least populous State; they shall be in addition to those appointed by the States, but they shall be considered, for the purposes of the election of President and Vice President, to be electors appointed by a State; and they shall meet in the District and perform such duties as provided by the twelfth article of amendment.

Section 2. The Congress shall have power to enforce this article by appropriate legislation.

Amendment XXIV [January 23, 1964]
Section 1. The right of citizens of the United States to vote in any primary or other election for President or Vice President, for electors for President or Vice President, or for Senator or Representative in Congress, shall not be denied or abridged by the United States or any State by reason of failure to pay any poll tax or other tax.

Section 2. The Congress shall have power to enforce this article by appropriate legislation.

Amendment XXV [February 10, 1967]
Section 1. In case of the removal of the President from office or of his death or resignation, the Vice President shall become President.

Section 2. Whenever there is a vacancy in the office of the Vice President, the President shall nominate a Vice President who shall take office upon confirmation by a majority of both Houses of Congress.

Section 3. Whenever the President transmits to the President pro tempore of the Senate and the Speaker of the House of Representatives his written declaration that he is unable to discharge the powers and duties of his office, and until he transmits to them a written declaration to the contrary, such powers and duties shall be discharged by the Vice President as Acting President.

Section 4. Whenever the Vice President and a majority of either the principal officers of the executive departments or of such other body as Congress may by law provide, transmit to the President pro tempore of the Senate and the Speaker of the House of Representatives their written declaration that the President is unable to discharge the powers and duties of his office, the Vice President shall immediately assume the powers and duties of the office as Acting President.

Thereafter, when the President transmits to the President pro tempore of the Senate and the Speaker of the House of Representatives his written declaration that no inability exists, he shall resume the powers and duties of his office unless the Vice President and a majority of either the principal officers of the executive departments or of such other body as Congress may by law provide, transmit within four days to the President pro tempore of the Senate and the Speaker of the House of Representatives their written declaration that the President is unable to discharge the powers and duties of his office. Thereupon Congress shall decide the issue, assembling within forty-eight hours for that purpose if not in session. If the Congress, within twenty-one days after receipt of the latter written declaration, or, if Congress is not in session, within twenty-one days after Congress is required to assemble, determines by two-thirds vote of both Houses that the President is unable to discharge the powers and duties of his office, the Vice President shall continue to discharge the same as Acting President; otherwise, the President shall resume the powers and duties of his office.

Amendment XXVI [June 30, 1971]

Section 1. The right of citizens of the United States who are eighteen years of age or older to vote shall not be denied or abridged by the United States or by any State on account of age.

Section 2. The Congress shall have power to enforce this article by appropriate legislation.

Amendment XXVII[12] [May 7, 1992]

No law, varying the compensation for services of the Senators and Representatives, shall take effect until an election of Representatives shall have intervened.

---

[12]James Madison proposed this amendment in 1789 together with the ten amendments that were adopted as the Bill of Rights, but it failed to win ratification at the time. Congress, however, had set no deadline for its ratification, and over the years—particularly in the 1980s and 1990s—many states voted to add it to the Constitution. With the ratification of Michigan in 1992 it passed the threshold of 3/4ths of the states required for adoption, but because the process took more than 200 years, its validity remains in doubt.

PRESIDENTIAL ELECTIONS

Year	Number of States	Candidates	Party	Popular Vote*	Electoral Vote†	Percentage of Popular Vote
1789	11	GEORGE WASHINGTON	No party designations		69	
		John Adams			34	
		Other Candidates			35	
1792	15	GEORGE WASHINGTON	No party designations		132	
		John Adams			77	
		George Clinton			50	
		Other Candidates			5	
1796	16	JOHN ADAMS	Federalist		71	
		Thomas Jefferson	Democratic-Republican		68	
		Thomas Pinckney	Federalist		59	
		Aaron Burr	Democratic-Republican		30	
		Other Candidates			48	
1800	16	THOMAS JEFFERSON	Democratic-Republican		73	
		Aaron Burr	Democratic-Republican		73	
		John Adams	Federalist		65	
		Charles C. Pinckney	Federalist		64	
		John Jay	Federalist		1	
1804	17	THOMAS JEFFERSON	Democratic-Republican		162	
		Charles C. Pinckney	Federalist		14	
1808	17	JAMES MADISON	Democratic-Republican		122	
		Charles C. Pinckney	Federalist		47	
		George Clinton	Democratic-Republican		6	
1812	18	JAMES MADISON	Democratic-Republican		128	
		DeWitt Clinton	Federalist		89	
1816	19	JAMES MONROE	Democratic-Republican		183	
		Rufus King	Federalist		34	
1820	24	JAMES MONROE	Democratic-Republican		231	
		John Quincy Adams	Independent-Republican		1	
1824	24	JOHN QUINCY ADAMS	Democratic-Republican	108,740	84	30.5
		Andrew Jackson	Democratic-Republican	153,544	99	43.1
		William H. Crawford	Democratic-Republican	46,618	41	13.1
		Henry Clay	Democratic-Republican	47,136	37	13.2
1828	24	ANDREW JACKSON	Democrat	647,286	178	56.0
		John Quincy Adams	National Republican	508,064	83	44.0
1832	24	ANDREW JACKSON	Democrat	687,502	219	55.0
		Henry Clay	National Republican	530,189	49	42.4
		William Wirt	Anti-Masonic	33,108	7	2.6
		John Floyd			11	
1836	26	MARTIN VAN BUREN	Democrat	765,483	170	50.9
		William H. Harrison	Whig		73	
		Hugh L. White	Whig		26	
		Daniel Webster	Whig	739,795	14	49.1
		W. P. Mangum	Whig		11	

* Percentage of popular vote given for any election year may not total 100 percent because candidates receiving less than 1 percent of the popular vote have been omitted.

† Prior to the passage of the Twelfth Amendment in 1904, the electoral college voted for two presidential candidates; the runner-up became Vice-President. Data from Historical Statistics of the United States, Colonial Times to 1957 (1961), pp. 682–683, and The World Almanac.

PRESIDENTIAL ELECTIONS (CONTINUED)

Year	Number of States	Candidates	Party	Popular Vote	Electoral Vote	Percentage of Popular Vote
1840	26	WILLIAM H. HARRISON	Whig	1,274,624	234	53.1
		Martin Van Buren	Democrat	1,127,781	60	46.9
1844	26	JAMES K. POLK	Democrat	1,338,464	170	49.6
		Henry Clay	Whig	1,300,097	105	48.1
		James G. Birney	Liberty	62,300		2.3
1848	30	ZACHARY TAYLOR	Whig	1,360,967	163	47.4
		Lewis Cass	Democrat	1,222,342	127	42.5
		Martin Van Buren	Free Soil	291,263		10.1
1852	31	FRANKLIN PIERCE	Democrat	1,601,117	254	50.9
		Winfield Scott	Whig	1,385,453	42	44.1
		John P. Hale	Free Soil	155,825		5.0
1856	31	JAMES BUCHANAN	Democrat	1,832,955	174	45.3
		John C. Frémont	Republican	1,339,932	114	33.1
		Millard Fillmore	American ("Know Nothing")	871,731	8	21.6
1860	33	ABRAHAM LINCOLN	Republican	1,865,593	180	39.8
		Stephen A. Douglas	Democrat	1,382,713	12	29.5
		John C. Breckinridge	Democrat	848,356	72	18.1
		John Bell	Constitutional Union	592,906	39	12.6
1864	36	ABRAHAM LINCOLN	Republican	2,206,938	212	55.0
		George B. McClellan	Democrat	1,803,787	21	45.0
1868	37	ULYSSES S. GRANT	Republican	3,013,421	214	52.7
		Horatio Seymour	Democrat	2,706,829	80	47.3
1872	37	ULYSSES S. GRANT	Republican	3,596,745	286	55.6
		Horace Greeley	Democrat	2,843,446	*	43.9
1876	38	RUTHERFORD B. HAYES	Republican	4,036,572	185	48.0
		Samuel J. Tilden	Democrat	4,284,020	184	51.0
1880	38	JAMES A. GARFIELD	Republican	4,453,295	214	48.5
		Winfield S. Hancock	Democrat	4,414,082	155	48.1
		James B. Weaver	Greenback-Labor	308,578		3.4
1884	38	GROVER CLEVELAND	Democrat	4,879,507	219	48.5
		James G. Blaine	Republican	4,850,293	182	48.2
		Benjamin F. Butler	Greenback-Labor	175,370		1.8
		John P. St. John	Prohibition	150,369		1.5
1888	38	BENJAMIN HARRISON	Republican	5,447,129	233	47.9
		Grover Cleveland	Democrat	5,537,857	168	48.6
		Clinton B. Fisk	Prohibition	249,506		2.2
		Anson J. Streeter	Union Labor	146,935		1.3
1892	44	GROVER CLEVELAND	Democrat	5,555,426	277	46.1
		Benjamin Harrison	Republican	5,182,690	145	43.0
		James B. Weaver	People's	1,029,846	22	8.5
		John Bidwell	Prohibition	264,133		2.2
1896	45	WILLIAM McKINLEY	Republican	7,102,246	271	51.1
		William J. Bryan	Democrat	6,492,559	176	47.7

*Because of the death of Greeley, Democratic electors scattered their votes.

PRESIDENTIAL ELECTIONS (CONTINUED)

Year	Number of States	Candidates	Party	Popular Vote	Electoral Vote	Percentage of Popular Vote
1900	45	WILLIAM McKINLEY	Republican	7,218,491	292	51.7
		William J. Bryan	Democrat; Populist	6,356,734	155	45.5
		John C. Woolley	Prohibition	208,914		1.5
1904	45	THEODORE ROOSEVELT	Republican	7,628,461	336	57.4
		Alton B. Parker	Democrat	5,084,223	140	37.6
		Eugene V. Debs	Socialist	402,283		3.0
		Silas C. Swallow	Prohibition	258,536		1.9
1908	46	WILLIAM H. TAFT	Republican	7,675,320	321	51.6
		William J. Bryan	Democrat	6,412,294	162	43.1
		Eugene V. Debs	Socialist	420,793		2.8
		Eugene W. Chafin	Prohibition	253,840		1.7
1912	48	WOODROW WILSON	Democrat	6,296,547	435	41.9
		Theodore Roosevelt	Progressive	4,118,571	88	27.4
		William H. Taft	Republican	3,486,720	8	23.2
		Eugene V. Debs	Socialist	900,672		6.0
		Eugene W. Chafin	Prohibition	206,275		1.4
1916	48	WOODROW WILSON	Democrat	9,127,695	277	49.4
		Charles E. Hughes	Republican	8,533,507	254	46.2
		A. L. Benson	Socialist	585,113		3.2
		J. Frank Hanly	Prohibition	220,506		1.2
1920	48	WARREN G. HARDING	Republican	16,143,407	404	60.4
		James M. Cox	Democrat	9,130,328	127	34.2
		Eugene V. Debs	Socialist	919,799		3.4
		P. P. Christensen	Farmer-Labor	265,411		1.0
1924	48	CALVIN COOLIDGE	Republican	15,718,211	382	54.0
		John W. Davis	Democrat	8,385,283	136	28.8
		Robert M. La Follette	Progressive	4,831,289	13	16.6
1928	48	HERBERT C. HOOVER	Republican	21,391,993	444	58.2
		Alfred E. Smith	Democrat	15,016,169	87	40.9
1932	48	FRANKLIN D. ROOSEVELT	Democrat	22,809,638	472	57.4
		Herbert C. Hoover	Republican	15,758,901	59	39.7
		Norman Thomas	Socialist	881,951		2.2
1936	48	FRANKLIN D. ROOSEVELT	Democrat	27,752,869	523	60.8
		Alfred M. Landon	Republican	16,674,665	8	36.5
		William Lemke	Union	882,479		1.9
1940	48	FRANKLIN D. ROOSEVELT	Democrat	27,307,819	449	54.8
		Wendell L. Willkie	Republican	22,321,018	82	44.8
1944	48	FRANKLIN D. ROOSEVELT	Democrat	25,606,585	432	53.5
		Thomas E. Dewey	Republican	22,014,745	99	46.0
1948	48	HARRY S. TRUMAN	Democrat	24,105,812	303	49.5
		Thomas E. Dewey	Republican	21,970,065	189	45.1
		J. Strom Thurmond	States' Rights	1,169,063	39	2.4
		Henry A. Wallace	Progressive	1,157,172		2.4
1952	48	DWIGHT D. EISENHOWER	Republican	33,936,234	442	55.1
		Adlai E. Stevenson	Democrat	27,314,992	89	44.4

PRESIDENTIAL ELECTIONS (CONTINUED)

Year	Number of States	Candidates	Party	Popular Vote	Electoral Vote	Percentage of Popular Vote
1956	48	DWIGHT D. EISENHOWER	Republican	35,590,472	457*	57.6
		Adlai E. Stevenson	Democrat	26,022,752	73	42.1
1960	50	JOHN F. KENNEDY	Democrat	34,227,096	303†	49.9
		Richard M. Nixon	Republican	34,108,546	219	49.6
1964	50	LYNDON B. JOHNSON	Democrat	42,676,220	486	61.3
		Barry M. Goldwater	Republican	26,860,314	52	38.5
1968	50	RICHARD M. NIXON	Republican	31,785,480	301	43.4
		Hubert H. Humphrey	Democrat	31,275,165	191	42.7
		George C. Wallace	American Independent	9,906,473	46	13.5
1972	50	RICHARD M. NIXON‡	Republican	47,165,234	520**	60.6
		George S. McGovern	Democrat	29,168,110	17	37.5
1976	50	JIMMY CARTER	Democrat	40,828,929	297***	50.1
		Gerald R. Ford	Republican	39,148,940	240	47.9
		Eugene McCarthy	Independent	739,256		
1980	50	RONALD REAGAN	Republican	43,201,220	489	50.9
		Jimmy Carter	Democrat	34,913,332	49	41.2
		John B. Anderson	Independent	5,581,379		
1984	50	RONALD REAGAN	Republican	53,428,357	525	59.0
		Walter F. Mondale	Democrat	36,930,923	13	41.0
1988	50	GEORGE H. W. BUSH	Republican	48,901,046	426****	53.4
		Michael Dukakis	Democrat	41,809,030	111	45.6
1992	50	BILL CLINTON	Democrat	43,728,275	370	43.2
		George Bush	Republican	38,167,416	168	37.7
		H. Ross Perot	United We Stand, America	19,237,247		19.0
1996	50	BILL CLINTON	Democrat	45,590,703	379	49.0
		Robert Dole	Republican	37,816,307	159	41.0
		H. Ross Perot	Reform	7,866,284		8.0
2000	50	GEORGE W. BUSH	Republican	50,459,624	271	47.9
		Albert Gore, Jr.	Democrat	51,003,328	266	49.4
		Ralph Nader	Green	2,882,985		2.7

*Walter B. Jones received 1 electoral vote.
† Harry F. Byrd received 15 electoral votes.
‡ Resigned August 9, 1974: Vice President Gerald R. Ford became President.
** John Hospers received 1 electoral vote.
*** Ronald Reagan received 1 electoral vote.
**** Lloyd Bentsen received 1 electoral vote.

DEMOGRAPHICS OF THE UNITED STATES

POPULATION GROWTH

Year	Population	Percent Increase
1630	4,600	
1640	26,600	478.3
1650	50,400	90.8
1660	75,100	49.0
1670	111,900	49.0
1680	151,500	35.4
1690	210,400	38.9
1700	250,900	19.2
1710	331,700	32.2
1720	466,200	40.5
1730	629,400	35.0
1740	905,600	43.9
1750	1,170,800	29.3
1760	1,593,600	36.1
1770	2,148,100	34.8
1780	2,780,400	29.4
1790	3,929,214	41.3
1800	5,308,483	35.1
1810	7,239,881	36.4
1820	9,638,453	33.1
1830	12,866,020	33.5
1840	17,069,453	32.7
1850	23,191,876	35.9
1860	31,443,321	35.6
1870	39,818,449	26.6
1880	50,155,783	26.0
1890	62,947,714	25.5
1900	75,994,575	20.7
1910	91,972,266	21.0
1920	105,710,620	14.9
1930	122,775,046	16.1
1940	131,669,275	7.2
1950	151,325,798	14.5
1960	179,323,175	18.5
1970	203,302,031	13.4
1980	226,542,199	11.4
1990	248,718,301	9.8
2000	281,421,906	13.1

Source: Historical Statistics of the United States (1975); Statistical Abstract by the United States (2001).
Note: Figures for 1630–1780 include British colonies within limits of present United States only; Native American population included only in 1930 and thereafter. Figures before 1790 are estimates.

WORK FORCE

Year	Total Number Workers (1000s)	Farmers as % of Total	Women as % of Total	% Workers in Unions
1810	2,330	84	(NA)	(NA)
1840	5,660	75	(NA)	(NA)
1860	11,110	53	(NA)	(NA)
1870	12,506	53	15	(NA)
1880	17,392	52	15	(NA)
1890	23,318	43	17	(NA)
1900	29,073	40	18	3
1910	38,167	31	21	6
1920	41,614	26	21	12
1930	48,830	22	22	7
1940	53,011	17	24	27
1950	59,643	12	28	25
1960	69,877	8	32	26
1970	82,049	4	37	25
1980	106,940	3	43	23
1990	125,840	3	45	16
2000	140,863	2	47	12

Source: Historical Statistics of the United States (1975); Statistical Abstract of the United States (2001).

VITAL STATISTICS
(IN THOUSANDS)

Year	Births	Deaths	Marriages	Divorces
1800	55	(NA)	(NA)	(NA)
1810	54.3	(NA)	(NA)	(NA)
1820	55.2	(NA)	(NA)	(NA)
1830	51.4	(NA)	(NA)	(NA)
1840	51.8	(NA)	(NA)	(NA)
1850	43.3	(NA)	(NA)	(NA)
1860	44.3	(NA)	(NA)	(NA)
1870	38.3	(NA)	9.6 (1867)	0.3 (1867)
1880	39.8	(NA)	9.1 (1875)	0.3 (1875)
1890	31.5	(NA)	9.0	0.5
1900	32.3	17.2	9.3	0.7
1910	30.1	14.7	10.3	0.9
1920	27.7	13.0	12.0	1.6
1930	21.3	11.3	9.2	1.6
1940	19.4	10.8	12.1	2.0
1950	24.1	9.6	11.1	2.6
1960	23.7	9.5	8.5	2.2
1970	18.4	9.5	10.6	3.5
1980	15.9	8.8	10.6	5.2
1990	16.7	8.6	9.8	4.7
1997	14.6	8.6	8.9	4.3

Source: Historical Statistics of the United States (1975); Statistical Abstract of the United States (1999).

POPULATIONS BY RACIAL GROUPS AND HISPANIC ORIGINS (IN THOUSANDS)

Year	White	Black	Indian	Asian/Pacific Islander	Other Race*	Hispanic Origin**
1790	3,172	757	(NA)	(NA)	(NA)	(NA)
1800	4,306	1,002	(NA)	(NA)	(NA)	(NA)
1820	7,867	1,772	(NA)	(NA)	(NA)	(NA)
1840	14,196	2,874	(NA)	(NA)	(NA)	(NA)
1860	26,923	4,442	(NA)	(NA)	(NA)	(NA)
1880	43,403	6,581	(NA)	(NA)	(NA)	(NA)
1900	66,809	8,834	(NA)	(NA)	(NA)	(NA)
1910	81,732	9,828	(NA)	(NA)	(NA)	(NA)
1920	94,821	10,463	(NA)	(NA)	(NA)	(NA)
1930	110,287	11,891	(NA)	(NA)	(NA)	(NA)
1940	118,215	12,866	(NA)	(NA)	(NA)	(NA)
1950	134,942	15,042	(NA)	(NA)	(NA)	(NA)
1960	158,832	18,872	(NA)	(NA)	(NA)	(NA)
1970	178,098	22,581	(NA)	(NA)	(NA)	(NA)
1980	194,713	26,683	1,420	3,500	6,758	14,609
1990	208,727	30,511	1,959	7,273	9,805	22,354
2000	211,461	34,658	2,476	10,642	22,185	35,603

Source: U.S. Bureau of the Census, U.S. Census of Population: 1940, vol. II, part 1, and vol. IV, part 1; 1950, vol. II, part 1; 1960, vol. I, part 1; 1970, vol. I, part B; and Current Population Reports, P25-1095 and P25-1104; Statistical Abstract of the United States (2001).
* Other or multiple race as self-identified.
** Hispanic population may be of any race.

THE ECONOMY AND FEDERAL SPENDING

Year	Gross National Product (GNP) (in billions)	Foreign Trade (in millions)		Balance of Trade	Federal Budget (in billions)	Federal Surplus/Deficit (in billions)	Federal Debt (in billions)
		Exports	Imports				
1790	(NA)	$ 20	$ 23	$ −3	$ 0.004	$ +0.00015	$ 0.076
1800	(NA)	71	91	−20	0.011	+0.0006	0.083
1810	(NA)	67	85	−18	0.008	+0.0012	0.053
1820	(NA)	70	74	−4	0.018	−0.0004	0.091
1830	(NA)	74	71	+3	0.015	+0.100	0.049
1840	(NA)	132	107	+25	0.024	−0.005	0.004
1850	(NA)	152	178	−26	0.040	+0.004	0.064
1860	(NA)	400	362	−38	0.063	−0.01	0.065
1870	$ 7.4	451	462	−11	0.310	+0.10	2.4
1880	11.2	853	761	+92	0.268	+0.07	2.1
1890	13.1	910	823	+87	0.318	+0.09	1.2
1900	18.7	1,499	930	+569	0.521	+0.05	1.2
1910	35.3	1,919	1,646	+273	0.694	−0.02	1.1
1920	91.5	8,664	5,784	+2,880	6.357	+0.3	24.3
1930	90.7	4,013	3,500	+513	3.320	+0.7	16.3
1940	100.0	4,030	7,433	−3,403	9.6	−2.7	43.0
1950	286.5	10,816	9,125	+1,691	43.1	−2.2	257.4
1960	506.5	19,600	15,046	+4,556	92.2	+0.3	286.3
1970	992.7	42,700	40,189	+2,511	195.6	−2.8	371.0
1980	2,631.7	220,783	244,871	+24,088	590.9	−73.8	907.7
1990	5,524.5	394,030	494,042	−101,012	1,251.8	−220.5	3,233.3
2000	9,958.7	1,068,397	1,438,086	−369,689	1,788.8	+236.4	5,629.0

Source: U.S. Office of Management and Budget, Budget of the United States Government, annual; Statistical Abstract of the United States (2001).

IMMIGRATION TO THE UNITED STATES SINCE 1820 (BY DECADE)

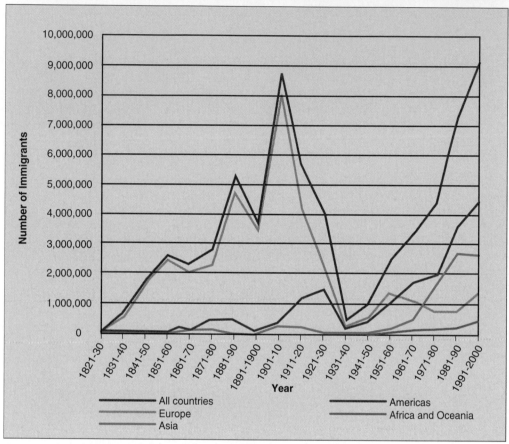

Source: Statistical Yearbook of the Immigration and Naturalization Service, 2001.

GLOSSARY

Affirmative Action A set of policies to open opportunities in business and education for members of minority groups and women by allowing race and sex to be factors included in decisions to hire, award contracts, or admit students to higher education programs.

AIDS (Acquired immune deficiency syndrome) A complex of deadly pathologies resulting from infection with the human immunodeficiency virus (HIV).

Alliance for Progress Program of economic aid to Latin America during the Kennedy administration.

Allies In World War I, Britain, France, Russia, and other belligerent nations fighting against the **Central Powers** but not including the United States, which insisted upon being merely an associated nation. In World War II, the Allies fighting the **Axis Powers** included the United States as well as the Soviet Union, Great Britain, France, China, and other nations.

American Federation of Labor (AFL) Union formed in 1886 that organized skilled workers along craft lines and emphasized a few workplace issues rather than a broad social program.

American Indian Movement (AIM) Group of Native American political activists who used confrontations with the federal government to publicize their case for Indian rights.

Americans with Disabilities Act Legislation in 1992 that banned discrimination against physically handicapped persons in employment, transportation, and public accommodations.

Atlanta Compromise Booker T. Washington's policy accepting segregation and **disfranchisement** for African Americans in exchange for white assistance in education and job training.

Atlantic Charter Statement of common principles and war aims developed by President Franklin Roosevelt and British Prime Minister Winston Churchill at a meeting in August 1941.

Australian ballot Secret voting and the use of official ballots rather than party tickets.

Axis Powers The opponents of the United States and its allies in World War II. The Rome–Berlin Axis was formed between Germany and Italy in 1936 and included Japan after 1940.

Baker v. Carr U.S. Supreme Court decision in 1962 that allowed federal courts to review the apportionment of state legislative districts and established the principle that such districts should have roughly equal populations ("one person, one vote").

Battle of the Atlantic The long struggle between German submarines and the British and U.S. navies in the North Atlantic from 1940 to 1943.

Bay of Pigs Site in Cuba of an unsuccessful landing by fourteen hundred anti-Castro Cuban refugees in April 1961.

Berlin blockade Three-hundred-day Soviet blockade of land access to United States, British, and French occupation zones in Berlin, 1948–1949.

Berlin Wall Wall erected by East Germany in 1961 and torn down in 1989 that isolated West Berlin from the surrounding areas in Communist-controlled East Berlin and East Germany.

Black codes Laws passed by states and municipalities denying many rights of citizenship to free blacks before the Civil War. Also, during the **Reconstruction era,** laws passed by newly elected southern state legislatures to control black labor, mobility, and employment.

Black Panthers Political and social movement among black Americans, founded in Oakland, California, in 1966 and emphasizing black economic and political power.

Black Power Philosophy emerging after 1965 that real economic and political gains for African-Americans could come only through self-help, **self-determination,** and organizing for direct political influence. Latinos and Native Americans developed their own versions as Brown Power and Red Power, respectively.

Blitzkrieg German war tactic in World War II ("lightning war") involving the concentration of air and armored firepower to punch and exploit holes in opposing defensive lines.

Bolshevik Member of the communist movement in Russia that established the Soviet government after the 1917 Russian Revolution; hence, by extension, any radical or disruptive person or movement seeking to transform economic and political relationships.

Bonus Army A group of unemployed veterans who demonstrated in Washington for the payment of service bonuses, only to be dispersed violently by the U.S. Army in 1932.

Brown v. Board of Education of Topeka Supreme Court decision in 1954 that declared that "separate but equal" schools for children of different races violated the **Constitution.**

Bureau of Reclamation Federal agency established in 1902 providing public funds for irrigation projects in arid regions; played a major role in the development of the West by constructing dams, reservoirs, and irrigation systems, especially beginning in the 1930s.

Camp David Agreement Agreement to reduce points of conflict between Israel and Egypt, hammered out in 1977 with the help of U.S. President Jimmy Carter.

carpetbaggers Pejorative term to describe Northern transplants to the South, many of whom were Union soldiers who stayed in the South after the war.

Central Intelligence Agency (CIA) Agency that coordinates the gathering and evaluation of military and economic information on other nations, established in 1947.

Central Powers Germany and its World War I allies Austria, Turkey, and Bulgaria.

Chain migration Process common to many immigrant groups whereby one family member brings over other family members, who in turn bring other relatives and friends and occasionally entire villages.

Chisholm Trail The route followed by Texas cattle raisers driving their herds north to markets at Kansas railheads.

Civil Rights Act of 1964 Federal legislation that outlawed discrimination in public accommodations and employment on the basis of race, skin color, sex, religion, or national origin.

Cold War The political and economic confrontation between the Soviet Union and the United States that dominated world affairs from 1946 to 1989.

Collective bargaining Representatives of a union negotiating with management on behalf of all members.

Colored Farmers' Alliance An organization of southern black farmers formed in Texas in 1886 in response to the **Southern Farmers' Alliance,** which did not accept black people as members.

Committee on Public Information (CPI) Government agency during World War I that sought to shape public opinion in support of the war effort through newspapers, pamphlets, speeches, films, and other media.

Compromise of 1877   The Congressional settling of the 1876 election which installed Republican Rutherford B. Hayes in the White House and gave Democrats control of all state governments in the South.

Congressional Reconstruction   Name given to the period 1867–1870 when the Republican-dominated Congress controlled **Reconstruction Era** policy. It is sometimes known as Radical Reconstruction, after the radical faction in the **Republican party.**

Congress of Industrial Organizations   An alliance of industrial unions that spurred the 1930s organizational drive among the mass-production industries.

Congress of Racial Equality (CORE)   Civil rights group formed in 1942 and committed to nonviolent civil disobedience, such as the 1961 "freedom rides."

Conservation   The efficient management and use of natural resources, such as forests, grasslands, and rivers, as opposed to **preservation** or uncontrolled exploitation.

Containment   The policy of resisting further expansion of the Soviet bloc through diplomacy and, if necessary, military action, developed in 1947–48.

Contract with America   Platform on which many Republican candidates ran for Congress in 1994. Associated with House Speaker Newt Gingrich, it proposed a sweeping reduction in the role and activities of the federal government.

Council of Economic Advisers   Board of three professional economists established in 1946 to advise the president on economic policy.

Counterculture   Various alternatives to mainstream values and behaviors that became popular in the 1960s, including experimentation with psychedelic drugs, communal living, a return to the land, Asian religions, and experimental art.

Coxey's Army   A protest march of unemployed workers, led by Populist businessman Jacob Coxey, demanding inflation and a public works program during the depression of the 1890s.

Dawes Act   An 1887 law terminating tribal ownership of land and allotting some parcels of land to individual Indians with the remainder opened for white settlement.

D-Day   June 6, 1944, the day of the first paratroop drops and amphibious landings on the coast of Normandy, France, in the first stage of **Operation OVERLORD** during World War II.

Declaration of London   Statement drafted by an international conference in 1909 to clarify international law and specify the rights of neutral nations.

Deindustrialization   The process of economic change involving the disappearance of outmoded industries and the transfer of factories to new low-wage locations, with devastating effects in the Northeast and Middle West, especially in the 1970s and 1980s.

Deregulation   Reduction or removal of government regulations and encouragement of direct competition in many important industries and economic sectors.

Disfranchisement   The use of legal means to bar individuals or groups from voting.

Dollar diplomacy   The U.S. policy of using private investment in other nations to promote American diplomatic goals and business interests.

Eastern Front   The area of military operations in World War II located east of Germany in eastern Europe and the Soviet Union.

Economic Recovery and Tax Act of 1981 (ERTA)   A major revision of the federal income tax system.

Eighteenth Amendment   Constitutional revision, ratified in 1919 and repealed in 1933, that prohibited the manufacture or sale of alcohol in the United States.

Environmental Protection Agency (EPA)   Federal agency created in 1970 to oversee environmental monitoring and cleanup programs.

Espionage Act of 1917   Law whose vague prohibition against obstructing the nation's war effort was used to crush dissent and criticism during World War I.

Fair Employment Practice Committee (FEPC)   Federal agency established in 1941 to curb racial discrimination in war production jobs and government employment.

Farmers' Alliance   A broad mass movement in the rural South and West during the late nineteenth century, encompassing several organizations and demanding economic and political reforms; helped create the **Populist party.**

Fascist   Subscribing to a philosophy of governmental dictatorship that merges the interests of the state, armed forces, and big business; associated with the dictatorship of Italian leader Benito Mussolini between 1922 and 1943 and also often applied to Nazi Germany.

Federal Deposit Insurance Corporation (FDIC)   Government agency that guarantees bank deposits, thereby protecting both depositors and banks.

Federal Highway Act of 1956   Measure that provided federal funding to build a nationwide system of interstate and defense highways.

Federalism   The sharing of powers between the national government and the states.

Federal Reserve Act   The 1913 law that revised banking and currency by extending limited government regulation through the creation of the Federal Reserve System.

Federal Trade Commission (FTC)   Government agency established in 1914 to provide regulatory oversight of business activity.

Field Order No. 15   Order by General William T. Sherman in January 1865 to set aside abandoned land along the southern Atlantic coast for forty-acre grants to freedmen; rescinded by President Andrew Johnson later that year.

Fifteenth Amendment   Passed by Congress in 1869, guaranteed the right of American men to vote, regardless of race.

Fireside chats   Speeches broadcast nationally over the radio in which President Franklin Roosevelt explained complex issues and programs in plain language, as though his listeners were gathered around the fireside with him.

Fourteenth Amendment   Constitutional amendment passed by Congress in April 1866 incorporating some of the features of the **Civil Rights Act of 1866.** It prohibited states from violating the civil rights of its citizens and offered states the choice of allowing black people to vote or losing representation in Congress.

Freedmen's Bureau   Agency established by Congress in March 1865 to provide social, educational, and economic services, advice, and protection to former slaves and destitute whites; lasted seven years.

Freedom Summer   Voter registration effort in rural Mississippi organized by black and white civil rights workers in 1964.

Free silver   Philosophy that the government should expand the money supply by purchasing and coining all the silver offered to it.

Free Speech Movement (FSM)   Student movement at the University of California, Berkeley, formed in 1964 to protest limitations on political activities on campus.

Fundamentalists   Religious conservatives who believe in the literal accuracy and divine inspiration of the Bible; the name derives from an influential series of pamphlets, *The Fundamentals* (1909–1914).

Gentlemen's Agreement   A diplomatic agreement in 1907 between Japan and the United States curtailing but not abolishing Japanese immigration.

GI Bill of Rights   Legislation in June 1944 that eased the return of veterans into American society by providing educational and employment benefits.

Gilded Age   Term applied to late-nineteenth-century America that refers to the shallow display and worship of wealth characteristic of the period.

Glasnost   Russian for "openness," applied to Mikhail Gorbachev's encouragement of new ideas and easing of political repression in the Soviet Union.

Gospel of Wealth   Thesis that hard work and perseverance lead to wealth, implying that poverty is a character flaw.

Grandfather clause   Rule that required potential voters to demonstrate that their grandfathers had been eligible to vote; used in some southern states after 1890 to limit the black electorate, as most black men's grandfathers had been slaves.

Grange   The National Grange of the Patrons of Husbandry, a national organization of farm owners formed after the Civil War.

Granger laws   State laws enacted in the Midwest in the 1870s that regulated rates charged by railroads, grain elevator operators, and other middlemen.

Great Depression   The nation's worst economic crisis, extending throughout the 1930s, producing unprecedented bank failures, unemployment, and industrial and agricultural collapse and prompting an expanded role for the federal government.

Great Migration   The mass movement of African Americans from the rural South to the urban North, spurred especially by new job opportunities during World War I and the 1920s.

Great Society   Theme of Lyndon Johnson's administration, focusing on poverty, education, and civil rights.

Great Uprising   Unsuccessful railroad strike of 1877 to protest wage cuts and the use of federal troops against strikers; the first nationwide work stoppage in American history.

Greenback party   A third party of the 1870s and 1880s that garnered temporary support by advocating currency inflation to expand the economy and assist debtors.

Harlem Renaissance   A new African-American cultural awareness that flourished in literature, art, and music in the 1920s.

Helsinki Accords   Agreement in 1975 among NATO and Warsaw Pact members that recognized European national boundaries as set after World War II and included guarantees of human rights.

Holocaust   The systematic murder of millions of European Jews and others deemed undesirable by Nazi Germany.

Homestead Act   Law passed by Congress in May 1862 providing homesteaders (mainly in the West) with 160 acres of free land in exchange for improving the land (as by cultivating it and erecting a house) within five years of the grant.

Hooverville   Shantytown, sarcastically named after President Hoover, in which unemployed and homeless people lived in makeshift shacks, tents, and boxes. Hoovervilles cropped up in many cities in 1930 and 1931.

Horatio Alger Stories   A series of best-selling tales about young rags-to-riches heroes first published in 1867 stressing the importance of neat clothes, cleanliness, thrift, and hard work. The books also highlighted the importance of chance in getting ahead and the responsibility of those better off to serve as positive role models.

horizontal integration   The merger of competitors in the same industry.

Hull House   Chicago **settlement house** that became part of a broader neighborhood revitalization project led by Jane Addams.

Immigration and Nationality Act of 1965   Federal legislation that replaced the national quota system for immigration with overall limits of 170,000 immigrants per year from the Eastern Hemisphere and 120,000 per year from the Western Hemisphere.

Imperialism   The policy and practice of exploiting nations and peoples for the benefit of an imperial power either directly through military occupation and colonial rule or indirectly through economic domination of resources and markets.

Initiative   Procedure by which citizens can introduce a subject for legislation, usually through a petition signed by a specific number of voters.

Intermediate Nuclear Force Agreement (INF)   Disarmament agreement between the United States and the Soviet Union under which an entire class of missiles would be removed and destroyed and on-site inspections would be permitted for verification.

International Monetary Fund (IMF)   International organization established in 1945 to assist nations in maintaining stable currencies.

Internet   The system of interconnected computers and servers that allows the exchange of e-mail, posting of web sites, and other means of instant communication.

Interstate Commerce Act   The 1887 law that expanded federal power over business by prohibiting pooling and discriminatory rates by railroads and establishing the first federal regulatory agency, the **Interstate Commerce Commission.**

Interstate Commerce Commission (ICC)   The first federal regulatory agency, established in 1887 to oversee railroad practices.

Irreconcilables   Group of U.S. senators adamantly opposed to ratification of the **Treaty of Versailles** after World War I.

Jazz Age   The 1920s, so called for the popular music of the day as a symbol of the many changes taking place in the mass culture.

Jim Crow laws   Segregation laws that became widespread in the South during the 1890s, named for a minstrel show character portrayed satirically by white actors in blackface.

Kellogg-Briand Pact   1928 international treaty that denounced aggression and war but lacked provisions for enforcement.

Knights of Labor   Labor union that included skilled and unskilled workers irrespective of race or gender; founded in 1869, peaked in the 1880s, and declined when its advocacy of the eight-hour workday led to violent strikes in 1886.

Ku Klux Klan   Perhaps the most prominent of the vigilante groups that terrorized black people in the South during **Reconstruction Era,** founded by Confederate veterans in 1866.

Laissez-faire   The doctrine that government should not intervene in the economy, especially through regulation.

League of Nations   International organization created by the **Versailles Treaty** after World War I to ensure world stability.

League of Women Voters   Group formed in 1920 from the National American Woman Suffrage Association to encourage informed voting and social reforms.

Lend-Lease   Program begun in 1941 through which the U.S. transferred military equipment to Britain and other World War II allies.

Liberty Bonds   Interest-bearing certificates sold by the U.S. government to finance the American World War I effort.

Little Bighorn, Battle of the   Battle in which Colonel George A. Custer and the Seventh Cavalry were defeated by the Sioux and Cheyennes under Sitting Bull and Crazy Horse in Montana in 1876.

Lost Cause   The phrase many white Southerners applied to their Civil War defeat. They viewed the war as a noble cause but only a temporary setback in the South's ultimate vindication.

Lynching   Execution, usually by a mob, without trial.

Mahanism   The ideas advanced by Alfred Thayer Mahan, stressing U.S. naval, economic, and territorial expansion.

Manhattan Project   The effort, using the code name Manhattan Engineer District, to develop an atomic bomb under the management of the U.S. Army Corps of Engineers during World War II.

Massive retaliation   Popular name for the military doctrine adopted in the 1950s, whereby the U.S. promised to respond to any attack on itself or its allies with massive force, including nuclear weapons.

McCarthyism   Anticommunist attitudes and actions associated with Senator Joe McCarthy in the early 1950s, including smear tactics and innuendo.

Medicaid   Supplementary medical insurance for the poor, financed through the federal government; program created in 1965.

Medicare   Basic medical insurance for the elderly, financed through the federal government; program created in 1965.

Model Cities Program   Effort to target federal funds to upgrade public services and economic opportunity in specifically defined urban neighborhoods between 1966 and 1974.

Molly Maguires   Secret labor organization of mostly Irish miners in the Pennsylvania anthracite coal region in the decade after the Civil War. Named after a woman who led a massive protest against landlords in Ireland in the 1840s, the Maguires carried out selective murders of coal company officials until an infiltrator exposed the group in 1877 and its leaders were arrested, tried, and executed.

Muckraking Journalism exposing economic, social, and political evils, so named by Theodore Roosevelt for its "raking the muck" of American society.

Mugwumps Elitist and conservative reformers who favored **sound money** and limited government and opposed tariffs and the **spoils system.**

Multinational corporation Firm with direct investments, branches, factories, and offices in a number of countries.

National Aeronautics and Space Administration (NASA) Federal agency created in 1958 to manage American space flights and exploration.

National American Woman Suffrage Association The organization, formed in 1890, that coordinated the ultimately successful campaign to achieve women's right to vote.

National Origins Act A 1924 law sharply restricting immigration on the basis of immigrants' national origins and discriminating against southern and eastern Europeans and Asians.

National Security Council (NSC) The formal policymaking body for national defense and foreign relations, created in 1947 and consisting of the president, the secretary of defense, the secretary of state, and others appointed by the president.

National Security Council Paper 68 (NSC-68) Policy statement that committed the United States to a military approach to the **Cold War.**

Nation of Islam Religious movement among black Americans that emphasizes self-sufficiency, self-help, and separation from white society.

Nativist/Nativism Favoring the interests and culture of native-born inhabitants over those of immigrants.

Neoliberal Advocate of or participant in the effort to reshape the **Democratic party** for the 1990s around a policy emphasizing economic growth and competitiveness in the world economy.

New Deal The economic and political policies of the Roosevelt administration in the 1930s.

New Federalism President Richard Nixon's policy to shift responsibilities for government programs from the federal level to the states.

New Freedom Woodrow Wilson's 1912 program for limited government intervention in the economy to restore competition by curtailing the restrictive influences of trusts and protective tariffs, thereby providing opportunities for individual achievement.

New Frontier John F. Kennedy's domestic and foreign policy initiatives, designed to reinvigorate a sense of national purpose and energy.

New Nationalism Theodore Roosevelt's 1912 program calling for a strong national government to foster, regulate, and protect business, industry, workers, and consumers.

Niagara Movement African-American group organized in 1905 to promote racial integration, civil and political rights, and equal access to economic opportunity.

Nineteenth Amendment Constitutional revision that in 1920 established women citizens' right to vote.

Nisei U.S. citizens born of immigrant Japanese parents.

Nixon Doctrine In July, 1969, President Nixon described a new American policy toward Asia, in which the U.S. would honor treaty commitments but would gradually disengage and expect Asian nations to handle military defense on their own.

North American Free Trade Agreement (NAFTA) Agreement reached in 1993 by Canada, Mexico, and the United States to substantially reduce barriers to trade.

Office of Economic Opportunity (OEO) Federal agency that coordinated many programs of the **War on Poverty** between 1964 and 1975.

Oligopoly An industry, such as steel making or automobile manufacturing, that is controlled by a few large companies.

Omaha Platform The 1892 platform of the **Populist party** repudiating laissez-faire and demanding economic and political reforms to aid distressed farmers and workers.

Open Door American policy of seeking equal trade and investment opportunities in foreign nations or regions.

Open shop Factory or business employing workers whether or not they are union members; in practice, such a business usually refuses to hire union members and follows antiunion policies.

Operation Desert Storm Code name for the successful offensive against Iraq by the United States and its allies in the Persian Gulf War (1991).

Operation OVERLORD U.S. and British invasion of France in June 1944 during World War II.

Organization of Petroleum Exporting Countries (OPEC) Cartel of oil-producing nations in Asia, Africa, and Latin America that gained substantial power over the world economy in the mid- to late 1970s by controlling the production and price of oil.

Pan American Union International organization originally established as the Commercial Bureau of American Republics by Secretary of State James Blaine's first Pan-American Conference in 1889 to promote cooperation among nations of the Western Hemisphere through commercial and diplomatic negotiations.

Patriot Act Federal legislation adopted in 2001, in response to the terrorist attacks of September 11, intended to facilitate anti-terror actions by federal law enforcement and intelligence agencies.

Pendleton Civil Service Act A law of 1883 that reformed the **spoils system** by prohibiting government workers from making political contributions and creating the Civil Service Commission to oversee their appointment on the basis of merit rather than politics.

Pentagon Papers Classified Defense Department documents on the history of the United States' involvement in Vietnam, prepared in 1968 and leaked to the press in 1971.

Perestroika Russian for "restructuring," applied to Mikhail Gorbachev's efforts to make the Soviet economic and political systems more modern, flexible, and innovative.

Persian Gulf War War (1991) between Iraq and a U.S. led coalition that followed Iraq's invasion of Kuwait and resulted in the expulsion of Iraqi forces from that country.

Platt Amendment A stipulation the United States had inserted into the Cuban constitution in 1901 restricting Cuban autonomy and authorizing U.S. intervention and naval bases.

Pogroms Government-directed attacks against Jewish citizens, property, and villages in tsarist Russia beginning in the 1880s; a primary reason for Russian Jewish migration to the United States.

Poll tax A tax imposed on voters as a requirement for voting. Most southern states imposed poll taxes after 1900 as a way to disfranchise black people; the measures also restricted the white vote.

Populist Party A major third party of the 1890s, also known as the **People's Party.** Formed on the basis of the **Southern Farmers' Alliance** and other reform organizations, it mounted electoral challenges against the Democrats in the South and the Republicans in the West.

Potsdam Declaration Statement issued by the United States during a meeting of U.S. President Harry Truman, British Prime Minister Winston Churchill, and Soviet Premier Joseph Stalin held at Potsdam, near Berlin, in July 1945 to plan the defeat of Japan and the future of eastern Europe and Germany. In it, the United States declared its intention to democratize the Japanese political system and reintroduce Japan into the international community and gave Japan an opening for surrender.

Preparedness   Military buildup in preparation for possible U.S. participation in World War I.

Preservation   Protecting forests, land, and other features of the natural environment from development or destruction, often for aesthetic appreciation.

Progressive Era   The period of the twentieth century before World War I when many groups sought to reshape the nation's government and society in response to the pressures of industrialization and urbanization.

Prohibition   A ban on the production, sale, and consumption of liquor, achieved temporarily through state laws and the Eighteenth Amendment.

Prohibition Party   A venerable third party still in existence that has persistently campaigned for the abolition of alcohol but has also introduced many important reform ideas into American politics.

Proposition 187   California legislation adopted by popular vote in California in 1994, which cuts off state-funded health and education benefits to undocumented or illegal immigrants.

Reagan Doctrine   The policy assumption that Soviet-influenced governments in Asia, Africa, and Latin America needed to be eliminated if the United States was to win the Cold War.

Recall   The process of removing an official from office by popular vote, usually after using petitions to call for such a vote.

Red Scare   Post–World War I public hysteria over **Bolshevik** influence in the United States directed against labor activism, radical dissenters, and some ethnic groups.

Redeemers   Southern Democrats who wrested control of governments in the former Confederacy, often through electoral fraud and violence, from Republicans beginning in 1870.

Referendum   Submission of a law, proposed or already in effect, to a direct popular vote for approval or rejection.

Reservationists   Group of U.S. senators favoring approval of the **Treaty of Versailles,** the peace agreement after World War I, after amending it to incorporate their reservations.

Roe v. Wade   U.S. Supreme Court decision in 1973 that disallowed state laws prohibiting abortion during the first three months (trimester) of pregnancy and established guidelines for abortion in the second and third trimesters.

Roosevelt Corollary   President Theodore Roosevelt's policy asserting U.S. authority to intervene in the affairs of Latin American nations; an expansion of the **Monroe Doctrine.**

Sagebrush Rebellion   Political movement in the western states in the early 1980s that called for easing of regulations on the economic use of federal lands and the transfer of some or all of those lands to state ownership.

SALT   Strategic Arms Limitation Treaty signed in 1972 by the United States and the Soviet Union to slow the nuclear arms race.

Sand Creek Massacre   The near annihilation in 1864 of Black Kettle's Cheyenne band by Colorado troops under Colonel John Chivington's orders to "kill and scalp all, big and little."

Scalawags   Southern whites, mainly small landowning farmers and well-off merchants and planters, who supported the southern **Republican Party** during **Reconstruction** for diverse reasons; a disparaging term.

Search and destroy   U.S. military tactic in South Vietnam, using small detachments to locate enemy units and then massive air, artillery, and ground forces to destroy them.

Second Treaty of Fort Laramie   The treaty acknowledging U.S. defeat in the Great Sioux War in 1868 and supposedly guaranteeing the Sioux perpetual land and hunting rights in South Dakota, Wyoming, and Montana.

Securities and Exchange Commission (SEC)   Federal agency with authority to regulate trading practices in stocks and bonds.

Sedition Act of 1918   Broad law restricting criticism of America's involvement in World War I or its government, flag, military, taxes, or officials.

Segregation   A system of racial control that separated the races, initially by custom but increasingly by law during and after **Reconstruction.**

Selective Service Act of 1917   The law establishing the military draft for World War I.

Selective Service System   Federal agency that coordinated military conscription before and during the Vietnam War.

Self-determination   The right of a people or nation to decide on its own political allegiance or form of government without external influence.

Settlement house   A multipurpose structure in a poor neighborhood that offered social welfare, educational, and homemaking services to the poor or immigrants; usually under private auspices and directed by middle-class women.

Seventeenth Amendment   Constitutional change that in 1913 established the direct popular election of U.S. senators.

Sharecropping   Labor system that evolved during and after **Reconstruction** whereby landowners furnished laborers with a house, farm animals, and tools and advanced credit in exchange for a share of the laborers' crop.

Sheppard-Towner Maternity and Infancy Act of 1921   The first federal social welfare law; funded infant and maternity health care programs in local hospitals. Social Gospel movement: An effort by leading Protestants to apply religious ethics to industrial conditions and thereby alleviate poverty, slums, and labor exploitation.

Sherman Antitrust Act   The first federal antitrust measure, passed in 1890; sought to promote economic competition by prohibiting business combinations in restraint of trade or commerce.

Silicon Valley   The region of California between San Jose and San Francisco that holds the nation's greatest concentration of electronics firms.

Sixteenth Amendment   Constitutional revision that in 1913 authorized a federal income tax.

Slaughterhouse cases   Group of cases resulting in one sweeping decision by the U.S. Supreme Court in 1873 that contradicted the intent of the **Fourteenth Amendment** by decreeing that most citizenship rights remained under state, not federal, control.

Social Darwinism   The application of Charles Darwin's theory of biological evolution to society, holding that the fittest and the wealthiest survive, the weak and the poor perish, and government action is unable to alter this "natural" and beneficial process.

Solid South   The one-party (Democratic) political system that dominated the South from the 1890s to the 1950s.

Sound money   Misleading slogan that referred to a conservative policy of restricting the money supply and adhering to the gold standard.

Southeast Asia Treaty Organization (SEATO)   Mutual defense alliance signed in 1954 by the United States, Britain, France, Thailand, Pakistan, the Philippines, Australia, and New Zealand.

Southern Christian Leadership Conference (SCLC)   Black civil rights organization founded in 1957 by Martin Luther King, Jr., and other clergy.

Southern Farmers' Alliance   The largest of several organizations that formed in the post-Reconstruction South to advance the interests of beleaguered small farmers.

Southern Homestead Act   Largely unsuccessful law passed in 1866 that gave black people preferential access to public lands in five southern states.

Southern Manifesto   A document signed by 101 members of Congress from southern states in 1956 that argued that the Supreme Court's decision in **Brown v. Board of Education of Topeka** itself contradicted the **Constitution.**

Sphere of influence   A region dominated and controlled by an outside power.

Stonewall Rebellion   On June 27, 1969, patrons fought back when police raided the gay Stonewall Inn in New York; the name refers to that event and to the increase in militancy by gay Americans that it symbolizes.

Strategic Defense Initiative (SDI) President Reagan's program, announced in 1983, to defend the United States against nuclear missile attack with untested weapons systems and sophisticated technologies; also known as "Star Wars."

Student Nonviolent Coordinating Committee (SNCC) Black civil rights organization founded in 1960 and drawing heavily on younger activists and college students.

Students for a Democratic Society (SDS) The leading student organization of the New Left of the early and mid-1960s.

Subtreasury plan A program promoted by the **Southern Farmers' Alliance** in response to low cotton prices and tight credit. Farmers would store their crop in a warehouse (or "subtreasury") until prices rose, in the meantime borrowing up to 80 percent of the value of the stored crops from the government at a low interest rate.

Sunbelt The states of the American South and Southwest.

***Sussex* Pledge** Germany's pledge during World War I not to sink merchant ships without warning, on the condition that Britain also observe recognized rules of international law.

Swann v. Charlotte-Mecklenburg Board of Education U.S. Supreme Court decision in 1971 that upheld cross-city busing to achieve the racial integration of public schools.

Sweatshops Small, poorly ventilated shops or apartments crammed with workers, often family members, who pieced together garments.

Taft-Hartley Act Federal legislation of 1947 that substantially limited the tools available to labor unions in labor–management disputes.

Teller Amendment A congressional resolution adopted in 1898 renouncing any American intention to annex Cuba.

Temporary Assistance for Needy Families (TANF) Federal program created in 1996 to replace earlier welfare programs to aid families and children; it involves explicit work requirements for receiving aid and places a time limit on benefits.

Tenement Four- to six-story residential dwelling, once common in New York and certain other cities, built on a tiny lot without regard to providing ventilation or light.

Tennessee Valley Authority (TVA) Federal regional planning agency established to promote **conservation,** produce electric power, and encourage economic development in seven southern states.

Tenure of Office Act Passed by the Republican controlled Congress in 1867 to limit presidential interference with its policies, the Act prohibited the president from removing certain officeholders without the Senate's consent. President Andrew Johnson, angered at which he believed as an unconstitutional attack on presidential authority, deliberately violated the act by firing Secretary of War Edwin M. Stanton. The House responded by approving articles of impeachment against a president for the first time in American history.

Truman Doctrine President Harry Truman's statement in 1947 that the United States should assist other nations that were facing external pressure or internal revolution; an important step in the escalation of the **Cold War.**

Underwood-Simmons Tariff Act The 1913 reform law that lowered tariff rates and levied the first regular federal income tax.

Union League A **Republican party** organization in northern cities that became an important organizing device among freedmen in southern cities after 1865.

United States v. Cruikshank Supreme Court ruling of 1876 that overturned the convictions of some of those responsible for the Colfax Massacre, ruling that the Enforcement Act applied only to violations of black rights by states, not individuals.

University of California v. Bakke U.S. Supreme Court case in 1978 that allowed race to be used as one of several factors in college and university admission decisions but made rigid quotas unacceptable.

Versailles, Treaty of The treaty ending World War I and creating the **League of Nations.**

Vertical integration The consolidation of numerous production functions, from the extraction of the raw materials to the distribution and marketing of the finished products, under the direction of one firm.

Viet Cong Communist rebels in South Vietnam who fought the pro-American government established in South Vietnam in 1954.

Volstead Act The 1920 law defining the liquor forbidden under the Eighteenth Amendment and giving enforcement responsibilities to the Prohibition Bureau of the Department of the Treasury.

Voting Rights Act Legislation in 1965 that overturned a variety of practices by which states systematically denied voter registration to minorities.

War Industries Board (WIB) The federal agency that reorganized industry for maximum efficiency and productivity during World War I.

War on Poverty Set of programs introduced by Lyndon Johnson between 1963 and 1966 designed to break the cycle of poverty by providing funds for job training, community development, nutrition, and supplementary education.

Watergate A complex scandal involving attempts to cover up illegal actions taken by administration officials and leading to the resignation of President Richard Nixon in 1974.

Welfare capitalism A paternalistic system of labor relations emphasizing management responsibility for employee well-being. While providing some limited benefits, its function was primarily to forestall the formation of unions or public intervention.

Whitewater Arkansas real estate development in which Bill and Hillary Clinton were investors; several fraud convictions resulted from investigations into Whitewater, but evidence was not found that the Clintons were involved in wrong-doing.

Wobblies Popular name for the members of the Industrial Workers of the World (IWW).

Women's Christian Temperance Union (WCTU) National organization formed after the Civil War dedicated to prohibiting the sale and distribution of alcohol.

World Trade Organization International organization that sets standards and practices for global trade, and the focus of international protests over world economic policy in the late 1990s.

World Wide Web Since 1991, the Web has expanded the use of the Internet by allowing organizations and companies to create websites that place political and commercial information only a few clicks away from wired consumers.

Wounded Knee Massacre The U.S. Army's brutal winter massacre in 1890 of at least two hundred Sioux men, women, and children as part of the government's assault on the tribe's Ghost Dance religion.

Yalta Conference Meeting of U.S. President Franklin Roosevelt, British Prime Minister Winston Churchill, and Soviet Premier Joseph Stalin held in February 1945 to plan the final stages of World War II and postwar arrangements.

Yellow-dog contracts Employment agreements binding workers not to join a union.

Yellow press A deliberately sensational journalism of scandal and exposure designed to attract an urban mass audience and increase advertising revenues.

BIBLIOGRAPHY

Chapter 1

Native American Cultures

Bragdon, Kathleen J. *Native People of Southern New England, 1500–1650* (1996).

Clendinnen, Inga. *Aztecs: An Interpretation* (1991).

Fagan, Brian M. *Ancient North America: The Archaeology of a Continent*, 4th ed. (2005).

Milner, George. *The Cahokia Chiefdom: The Archaeology of a Mississippian Society* (1998).

Rouse, Irving. *The Tainos: Rise and Decline of the People Who Greeted Columbus* (1992).

West African Society

Bohannan, Paul, and Philip Curtin. *Africa and Africans*, 3rd ed. (1988).

Iliffe, John. *Africans: The History of a Continent* (1995).

Reader, John. *Africa: A Biography of the Continent* (1998).

Europe in the Age of Discovery

Canny, Nicholas. *Making Ireland British, 1580–1650* (2000).

Cantor, Norman F. *In the Wake of the Plague: The Black Death and the World It Made* (2001).

Cipolla, Carlo M. *Guns, Sails, and Empire: Technological Innovation and the Early Phases of European Expansion, 1400–1700* (1965).

Lewis, Bernard. *Cultures in Conflict: Christians, Muslims, and Jews in the Age of Discovery* (1995).

Marty, Martin. *Martin Luther: A Penguin Life* (2004).

McDermott, James. *Martin Frobisher: Elizabethan Privateer* (2001).

Scammell, G. V. *The First Imperial Age: European Overseas Expansion, c. 1400–1715* (1989).

Conquest and Colonization

Andrews, Kenneth R. *Trade, Plunder, and Settlement: Maritime Enterprise and the Genesis of the British Empire, 1480–1630* (1984).

Crosby, Alfred W., Jr. *Ecological Imperialism: The Biological Expansion of Europe, 900–1900* (1986).

De Las Casas, Bartolomé. *Short Account of the Destruction of the Indies* (several editions).

Eccles, W. J. *France in America*, rev. ed. (1990).

Elliott, J. H. *Empires of the Atlantic World: Britain and Spain in America 1492–1830* (2006).

Hudson, Charles. *Knights of Spain, Warriors of the Sun: Hernando de Soto and the South's Ancient Chiefdoms* (1997).

Kamen, Henry. *Empire: How Spain Became a World Power, 1492–1763* (2003).

Kupperman, Karen Ordahl. *Roanoke: The Abandoned Colony* (1984).

Seed, Patricia. *Ceremonies of Possession in Europe's Conquest of the New World 1492–1640* (1995).

Weber, David J. *Bárbaros: Spaniards and Their Savages in the Age of Enlightenment* (2006).

Chapter 2

New France

Choquette, Leslie. *Frenchmen into Peasants: Modernity and Tradition in the Peopling of French Canada* (1997).

Eccles, W. J. *Essays on New France* (1987).

Moogk, Peter. *La Nouvelle France: The Making of French Canada—A Cultural History* (2000).

New Netherland

Israel, Jonathan. *The Dutch Republic: Its Rise, Greatness, and Fall, 1477–1806* (1995).

Price, J. L. *The Dutch Republic in the Seventeenth Century* (1998).

Shorto, Russell. *The Island at the Center of the World: The Epic Story of Dutch Manhattan, the Forgotten Colony That Shaped America* (2004).

Chesapeake Society

Horn, James. *A Land As God Made It: Jamestown and the Birth of America* (2005).

Krugler, John. *English and Catholic: The Lords Baltimore in the Seventeenth Century* (2004).

Kupperman, Karen Ordahl. *The Jamestown Project* (2007).

Townsend, Camilla. *Pocahontas and the Powhatan Dilemma* (2004).

New England

Bremer, Francis J. *John Winthrop: America's Forgotten Founding Father* (2003).

Cave, Alfred. *The Pequot War* (1996).

Morgan, Edmund S. *Puritan Dilemma: The Story of John Winthrop* (1958).

Philbrick, Nathaniel. *Mayflower: A Story of Courage, Community, and War* (2006).

Ulrich, Laurel Thatcher. *Good Wives: Image and Reality in the Lives of Women in Northern New England, 1650–1750* (1982).

The West Indies

Beckles, Hilary. *White Servitude and Black Slavery in Barbados, 1627–1715* (1989).

Gragg, Larry. *Englishmen Transplanted: The English Colonization of Barbados, 1627–1660* (2003).

Mintz, Sidney. *Sweetness and Power: The Place of Sugar in Modern History* (1985).

The Restoration Colonies

Dunn, Richard S., and Mary Maples Dunn, eds. *The World of William Penn* (1986).

Goodfriend, Joyce D. *Before the Melting Pot: Society and Culture in Colonial New York City, 1664–1730* (1992).

Levy, Barry. *Quakers and the American Family: British Settlement in the Delaware Valley* (1988).

Merwick, Donna. *Death of a Notary: Conquest and Change in Colonial New York* (1999).

Weir, Robert. *Colonial South Carolina: A History* (1983).

Chapter 3
Indians and Europeans

Anderson, Virginia. *Creatures of Empire: How Domestic Animals Transformed Early America* (2004).

Calloway, Colin. *New Worlds for All: Indians, Europeans, and the Remaking of Early America* (1997).

Cronon, William. *Changes in the Land: Indians, Colonists, and the Ecology of New England* (1983).

Drake, James. *King Philip's War: Civil War in New England, 1675–1676* (2000).

Gallay, Alan. *The Indian Slave Trade: The Rise of the English Empire in the American South, 1670–1717* (2003).

Greer, Allan. *Mohawk Saint: Catherine Tekakwitha and the Jesuits* (2004).

Knaut, Andrew L. *The Pueblo Revolt of 1680: Conquest and Resistance in Seventeenth-Century New Mexico* (1995).

Kupperman, Karen. *Indians and English: Facing Off in Early America* (2000).

Merrell, James H. *Into the American Woods: Negotiators on the Pennsylvania Frontier* (1999).

Merwick, Donna. *The Shame and the Sorrow: Dutch-Amerindian Encounters in New Netherland* (2006).

Silverman, David. *Faith and Boundaries: Colonists, Christianity, and Community among the Wampanoag Indians of Martha's Vineyard, 1600–1871* (2005).

Steele, Ian K. *Warpaths: Invasions of North America* (1994).

Washburn, Wilcomb E. *The Governor and the Rebel: A History of Bacon's Rebellion in Virginia* (1957).

White, Richard. *The Middle Ground: Indians, Empires, and Republics in the Great Lakes Region, 1650–1815* (1991).

Africans in America

Breen, T. H., and Stephen Innes. *"Myne Owne Ground": Race and Freedom on Virginia's Eastern Shore, 1640–1676* (1980).

Davis, David Brion. *Inhuman Bondage: The Rise and Fall of Slavery in the New World* (2006).

Jordan, Winthrop. *White over Black: American Attitudes toward the Negro, 1550–1812* (1968).

Lepore, Jill. *New York Burning: Liberty, Slavery, and Conspiracy in Eighteenth-Century Manhattan* (2005).

Littlefield, Daniel. *Rice and Slaves: Ethnicity and the Slave Trade in Colonial South Carolina* (1981).

Morgan, Philip. *Slave Counterpoint: Black Culture in the Eighteenth-Century Chesapeake & Lowcountry* (1998).

Mullin, Michael. *Africa in America: Slave Acculturation and Resistance in the American South and the British Caribbean, 1736–1831* (1994).

Parent, Anthony S. *Foul Means: The Formation of a Slave Society in Virginia, 1660-1740* (2006).

Wood, Betty. *The Origins of American Slavery: Freedom and Bondage in the English Colonies* (1997).

Labor Systems and European Immigration

Bailyn, Bernard. *The Peopling of British North America: An Introduction* (1986).

Bailyn, Bernard. *Voyagers to the West: A Passage in the Peopling of America on the Eve of the Revolution* (1986).

Baseler, Marilyn. *"Asylum for Mankind": America 1607–1800* (1998).

DeWolfe, Barbara, ed. *Discoveries of America: Personal Accounts of British Emigrants to America in the Revolutionary Era* (1997).

Ekirch, A. Roger. *Bound for America: The Transportation of British Convicts to the Colonies, 1718–1775* (1987).

Griffin, Patrick. *The People with No Name: Ireland's Ulster Scots, America's Scots Irish, and the Creation of a British Atlantic World, 1689–1764* (2001).

Innes, Stephen, ed. *Work and Labor in Early America* (1988).

Otterness, Philip. *Becoming German: The 1709 Palatine Migration to New York* (2004).

Roeber, A. G. *Palatines, Liberty, and Property: German Lutherans in Colonial British America* (1993).

Salinger, Sharon V. *"To Serve Well and Faithfully": Labor and Indentured Servants in Pennsylvania, 1682–1800* (1987).

Wokeck, Marianne. *Trade in Strangers: The Beginnings of Mass Migration to North America* (1999).

Chapter 4
Colonial Economic Development

McCusker, John and Kenneth Morgan, eds. *The Early Modern Atlantic Economy* (2001).

Steele, Ian K. *The English Atlantic, 1675–1740: An Exploration of Communication and Community* (1986).

Walton, Gary M., and James F. Shepherd. *The Economic Rise of Early America* (1979).

Waterhouse, Richard. *A New World Gentry: The Making of a Merchant and Planter Class in South Carolina, 1670–1770* (1989).

Religion, Society, and Culture in Early America

Bonomi, Patricia. *Under the Cope of Heaven: Religion, Society, and Politics in Colonial America* (1986).

Boyer, Paul, and Stephen Nissenbaum. *Salem Possessed: The Social Origins of Witchcraft* (1974).

Butler, Jon. *Becoming America: The Revolution before 1776* (2000).

Chaplin, Joyce. *The First Scientific American: Benjamin Franklin and the Pursuit of Genius* (2006).

Dayton, Cornelia Hughes. *Women before the Bar: Gender, Law, & Society in Connecticut, 1639–1789* (1995).

Hall, Gwendolyn Midlo. *Africans in Colonial Louisiana: The Development of Afro-Creole Culture in the Eighteenth Century* (1992).

Herndon, Ruth. *Unwelcome Americans: Living on the Margin in Early New England* (2001).

Isaac, Rhys. *The Transformation of Virginia, 1740–1790* (1982).

May, Henry. *The Enlightenment in America* (1976).

Norton, Mary Beth. *In the Devil's Snare: The Salem Witchcraft Crisis of 1692* (2002).

Colonial and Imperial Politics

Bailyn, Bernard. *The Origins of American Politics* (1968).

Brewer, John. *The Sinews of Power: War, Money, and the English State, 1688–1783* (1989).

Bushman, Richard. *King and People in Provincial Massachusetts* (1985).

Lovejoy, David S. *The Glorious Revolution in America, 1660–1692* (1972).

McConville, Brendan. *The King's Three Faces: The Rise and Fall of Royal America, 1688–1776* (2006).

Morgan, Edmund S. *Inventing the People: The Rise of Popular Sovereignty in England and America* (1988).

Nash, Gary B. *The Urban Crucible: The Northern Seaports and the Origins of the American Revolution*, abr. ed. (1986).

Shannon, Timothy. *Indians and Colonists at the Crossroads of Empire: The Albany Congress of 1754* (1999).

The Expansion of Empires

Barr, Juliana. *Peace Came in the Form of a Woman: Indians and Spaniards in the Texas Borderlands* (2007).

Bond, Bradley, ed. *French Colonial Louisiana and the Atlantic World* (2005).

DuVal, Kathleen. *The Native Ground: Indians and Colonists in the Heart of the Continent* (2006).

Hinderaker, Eric, and Peter Mancall. *At the Edge of Empire: The Backcountry in British North America* (2003).

Hofstra, Warren. *The Planting of New Virginia: Settlement and Landscape in the Shenandoah Valley* (2004).

Richter, Daniel. *Ordeal of the Longhouse: The Peoples of the Iroquois League in the Era of European Colonization* (1992).

Usner, Daniel H., Jr. *Indians, Settlers, and Slaves in a Frontier Exchange Economy: The Lower Mississippi Valley before 1783* (1992).

Weber, David J. *The Spanish Frontier in North America* (1992).

Imperial Warfare

Black, Jeremy. *Britain as a Military Power, 1688–1815* (1999).

Calloway, Colin. *The Scratch of a Pen: 1763 and the Transformation of America* (2006).

Jennings, Francis. *Empire of Fortune: Crowns, Colonies, and Tribes in the Seven Years' War in America* (1988).

Merritt, Jane. *At the Crossroads: Indians and Empires on a Mid-Atlantic Frontier, 1700–1763* (2003).

Steele, Ian K. *Betrayals: Fort William Henry and the "Massacre"* (1990).

Titus, James. *The Old Dominion at War: Society, Politics, and Warfare in Late Colonial Virginia* (1991).

Chapter 5
Imperial Reorganization

Alden, John R. *John Stuart and the Southern Colonial Frontier: A Study of Indian Relations, War, Trade, and Land Problems in the Southern Wilderness, 1754–1775* (1944, 1966).

Alexander, John K. *Samuel Adams: America's Revolutionary Politician* (2002).

Anderson, Fred. *Crucible of War: The Seven Years' War and the Fate of Empire in British North America, 1754–1766* (2000).

Barrow, Thomas C. *Trade and Empire: The British Customs Service in Colonial America, 1660–1775* (1967).

Bonwick, Colin. *The American Revolution* (1991).

Brooke, John. *King George III* (1972).

Cashin, Edward J. *William Bartram and the American Revolution on the Southern Frontier* (2000).

Dowd, Gregory. *War Under Heaven: Pontiac, the Indian Nations, and the British Empire* (2002).

Hatley, Tom. *The Dividing Paths: Cherokees and South Carolinians through the Era of Revolution* (1993).

Langford, Paul. *A Polite and Commercial People: England, 1727–1783* (1989).

Oliphant, John. *Peace and War on the Anglo-Cherokee Frontier, 1756–63* (2001).

Richter, Daniel. *Facing East from Indian Country: A Native History of Early America* (2001).

Shy, John. *Toward Lexington: The Role of the British Army in the Coming of the American Revolution* (1965).

Snapp, J. Russell. *John Stuart and the Struggle for Empire on the Southern Frontier* (1996).

Weber, David J. *The Spanish Frontier in North America* (1992).

White, Richard. *The Middle Ground: Indians, Empires, and Republics in the Great Lakes Region, 1650–1815* (1991).

American Reactions

Breen, Timothy H. *The Marketplace of Revolution: How Consumer Politics Shaped American Independence* (2004).

Brown, Richard D. *Revolutionary Politics in Massachusetts: The Boston Committee of Correspondence and the Towns, 1772–1774* (1970).

Brown, Richard M. *The South Carolina Regulators* (1963).

Calhoon, Robert M. *Dominion and Liberty: Ideology in the Anglo-American World, 1660–1801* (1994).

Countryman, Edward. *A People in Revolution: The American Revolution and Political Society in New York, 1760–1790* (1981).

Egnal, Marc. *A Mighty Empire: The Origins of the American Revolution* (1988).

Ekirch, Robert A. *"Poor Carolina": Politics and Society in Colonial North Carolina, 1729–1776* (1981).

Greene, Jack P. *Negotiated Authorities: Essays in Colonial Political and Constitutional History* (1994).

Greene, Jack P. *Understanding the American Revolution: Issues and Actors* (1995).

Hoerder, Dirk. *Crowd Action in Revolutionary Massachusetts, 1765–1780* (1977).

Jensen, Merrill. *The Founding of a Nation: A History of the American Revolution, 1763–1776* (1968).

Klein, Rachel N. *Unification of a Slave State: The Rise of the Planter Class in the South Carolina Backcountry, 1760–1808* (1990).

Knollenberg, Bernhard. *Origin of the American Revolution, 1759–1766* (1960).

Krawczynski, Keith. *William Henry Drayton: South Carolina Revolutionary Patriot* (2001).

Kurtz, Stephen G., and James H. Hutson, eds. *Essays on the American Revolution* (1973).

Labaree, Benjamin W. *The Boston Tea Party* (1964).

Maier, Pauline. *From Resistance to Revolution: Colonial Radicals and the Development of American Opposition to Britain, 1765–1776* (1972).

Maier, Pauline. *The Old Revolutionaries: Political Lives in the Age of Samuel Adams* (1980).

Morgan, Edmund S. *The Birth of the Republic, 1763–1789*, 3rd ed. (1992).

Morgan, Edmund S., and Helen M. Morgan. *The Stamp Act Crisis: Prologue to Revolution* (1963, 1995).

Nash, Gary B. *The Urban Crucible: The Northern Seaports and the Origins of the American Revolution* (1986).

Pole, J. R., and Jack P. Greene, eds. *A Companion to the American Revolution* (2000, 2003).

Reid, John P. *Constitutional History of the American Revolution: The Power to Tax* (1987).

Ryerson, Richard A. *"The Revolution Is Now Begun": The Radical Committees of Philadelphia, 1765–1776* (1978).

Thomas, Peter D. G. *The Townshend Duties Crisis: The Second Phase of the American Revolution, 1767–1773* (1987).

Ubbelohde, Carl. *The Vice-Admiralty Courts and the American Revolution* (1960).

Whittenburg, James P. "Planters, Merchants, and Lawyers: Social Change and the Origins of the North Carolina Regulation," *William and Mary Quarterly*, 34 (1977), 214–238.

Wood, Gordon S. *The Americanization of Benjamin Franklin* (2004).

Zobel, Hiller B. *The Boston Massacre* (1970).

The Road to Revolution

Ammerman, David. *In the Common Cause: American Response to the Coercive Acts of 1774* (1974).

Brown, Wallace. *The Good Americans: The Loyalists in the American Revolution* (1969).

Calhoon, Robert M. *The Loyalists in Revolutionary America, 1760–1781* (1973).

Clark, J. C. D. *The Language of Liberty, 1660–1832: Political Discourse and Social Dynamics in the Anglo-American World* (1994).

Doll, Peter. *Revolution, Religion, and National Identity: Imperial Nationalism in British North America, 1745–1795* (2000).

Holton, Woody. *Forced Founders: Indians, Debtors, Slaves, and the Making of the American Revolution in Virginia* (1999).

McCullough, David. *John Adams* (2001).

Nelson, William H. *The American Tory* (1961).

Rakove, Jack N. *The Beginnings of National Politics: An Interpretive History of the Continental Congress* (1979).

Young, Alfred F. *The Shoemaker and the Tea Party: Memory and the American Revolution* (1999).

Chapter 6
The Outbreak of War and the Declaration of Independence

Calhoon, Robert M. *The Loyalists in Revolutionary America, 1760–1781* (1973).

Conway, Stephen. *The War of American Independence, 1775–1783* (1995).

Ellis, Joseph. *American Sphinx: The Character of Thomas Jefferson* (1996).

Fischer, David H. *Paul Revere's Ride* (1994).

Foner, Eric. *Tom Paine and Revolutionary America*, 2nd ed. (2004).

Higginbotham, Don. *George Washington: Uniting a Nation* (2002).

Higginbotham, Don. *The War of American Independence: Military Attitudes, Policies, and Practice, 1763–1789* (1971).

Maier, Pauline. *American Scripture: Making the Declaration of Independence* (1997).

Middlekauff, Robert. *The Glorious Cause: The American Revolution, 1763–1789*, 2nd ed. (2005).

The Combatants

Billias, George A., ed. *George Washington's Generals* (1964).

Billias, George A., ed. *George Washington's Opponents: British Generals and Admirals in the American Revolution* (1969).

Frey, Sylvia R. *The British Soldier in America: A Social History of Military Life in the Revolutionary Period* (1981).

Gardiner, Robert. *Navies and the American Revolution, 1775–1783* (1996).

Glatthaar, Joseph T., and James Kirby Martin. *Forgotten Allies: The Oneida Indians and the American Revolution* (2006).

Mayer, Holly A. *Belonging to the Army: Camp Followers and Community during the American Revolution* (1996).

Neimeyer, Charles P. *America Goes to War: A Social History of the Continental Army* (1996).

Royster, Charles. *A Revolutionary People at War: The Continental Army and American Character, 1775–1783* (1979).

Wright, Robert K. *The Continental Army* (1984).

Young, Alfred F. *Masquerade: The Life and Times of Deborah Sampson, Continental Soldier* (2004).

The War in the North

Bodle, Wayne K. *The Valley Forge Winter: Civilians and Soldiers in War* (2002).

Fischer, David H. *Washington's Crossing* (2004).

Gruber, Ira D. *The Howe Brothers and the American Revolution* (1972).

Kwasny, Mark V. *Washington's Partisan War, 1775–1783* (1996).

Martin, James Kirby. *Benedict Arnold, Revolutionary Hero: An American Warrior Reconsidered* (1997).

Rosswurm, Steven. *Arms, Country, and Class: The Philadelphia Militia and "Lower Sort" during the American Revolution, 1775–1783* (1987).

The War Widens

Buchanan, John. *The Road to Guilford Courthouse: The American Revolution in the Carolinas* (1999).

Frey, Sylvia R. *Water from the Rock: Black Resistance in a Revolutionary Age* (1991).

Graymont, Barbara. *The Iroquois in the American Revolution* (1972).

Mintz, Max. *Seeds of Empire: The American Revolutionary Conquest of the Iroquois* (1999).

O'Donnell, James H. *Southern Indians in the American Revolution* (1973).

Wickwire, Franklin, and Mary Wickwire. *Cornwallis: The American Adventure* (1970).

The American Victory

Dull, Jonathan R. *A Diplomatic History of the American Revolution* (1985).

Martin, James K., and Mark E. Lender. *A Respectable Army: The Military Origins of the Republic, 1763–1789* (1982).

Peckham, Howard H. *The Toll of Independence: Engagements and Battle Casualties of the American Revolution* (1974).

The War and Society

Berkin, Carol. *Revolutionary Mothers: Women in the Struggle for America's Independence* (2005).

Buel, Richard, Jr. *Dear Liberty: Connecticut's Mobilization for the Revolutionary War* (1980).

Calloway, Colin G. *The American Revolution in Indian Country: Crisis and Diversity in Native American Communities* (1995).

Hodges, Graham Russell, ed. *The Black Loyalist Directory: African Americans in Exile after the American Revolution* (1996).

Hoffman, Ronald, and Peter J. Albert, eds. *The Transforming Hand of Revolution: Reconsidering the American Revolution as a Social Movement* (1995).

Hoffman, Ronald, and Peter J. Albert. *Women in the Age of the American Revolution* (1989).

Kerber, Linda. *Women of the Republic: Intellect and Ideology in Revolutionary America* (1980).

Massey, Gregory. *John Laurens and the American Revolution* (2000).

Norton, Mary Beth. *Liberty's Daughters: The Revolutionary Experience of American Women, 1750–1800* (1980).

Ward, Harry M. *The War for Independence and the Transformation of American Society* (1999).

Wood, Gordon S. *The Radicalism of the American Revolution* (1999).

Young, Alfred F., ed. *The American Revolution: Explorations in the History of American Radicalism* (1976).

Chapter 7
The New Order of Republicanism

Block, Ruth H. *Visionary Republic: Millennial Themes in American Thought, 1756–1800* (1985).

Carr, Jacqueline Barbara. *After the Siege: A Social History of Boston, 1775–1800* (2005).

Frey, Sylvia R. *Water from the Rock: Black Resistance in a Revolutionary Age* (1991).

Gellman, David N. *Emancipation of New York: The Politics of Slavery and Freedom, 1777–1827* (2006).

Kerber, Linda. *Women of the Republic* (1980).

Kelley, Mary, *Learning to Stand & Speak: Women, Education, and Public Life in America's Republic* (2006).

Miller, Martha R. *The Needle's Eye: Women and Work in the Age of Revolution* (2006).

Purcell, Sarah J. *Sealed With Blood: War, Sacrifice, and Memory in Revolutionary America* (2002).

Wood, Gordon. *The Radicalism of the American Revolution* (1992).

Problems at Home

Davis, Joseph L. *Sectionalism in American Politics, 1774–1787* (1977).

Ferguson, E. James. *The Power of the Purse: A History of American Public Finance, 1776–1790* (1961).

Hoffman, Ronald L., and Peter Albert, eds., *Sovereign States in an Age of Uncertainty* (1981).

Main, Jackson Turner. *Political Parties Before the Constitution* (1973).

Onuf, Peter S. *The Origins of the Federal Republic* (1983).

Richards, Leonard L. *Shays's Rebellion: The American Revolution's Final Battle* (2002).

Diplomatic Weaknesses

Hoxie, Frederick E., Ronald Hoffman, and Peter J. Albert, eds. *Native Americans and the Early Republic* (1999).

Ritcheson, Charles T. *Aftermath of Revolution: British Policy toward the United States, 1783–1795* (1969).

Van Alstyne, Richard W. *The Rising American Empire* (1980).

Toward a New Nation

Beard, Charles. *An Economic Interpretation of the Constitution* (1913).

Brown, Roger H. *Redeeming the Republic: Federalists, Taxation, and the Origins of the Constitution* (1993).

Duncan, Christopher M. *The Anti-Federalists and Early American Political Thought* (1995).

Edling, Max M. *A Revolution in Favor of Government: Origins of the U.S. Constitution and the Making of the American State* (2003).

Gillespie, Michael Allen, and Michael Lienesch, eds. *Ratifying the Constitution* (1989).

McDonald, Forrest. *Novus Ordo Seclorum: The Intellectual Origins of the Constitution* (1985).

McGuire, Robert A. *To Form a More Perfect Union: A New Economic Interpretation of the United States Constitution* (2003).

Chapter 8
Washington's America

Aron, Stephen. *How the West Was Lost: The Transformation of Kentucky from Daniel Boone to Henry Clay* (1996).

Cayton, Andrew R. L. *Frontier Republic: Ideology and Politics in the Ohio Country, 1780–1825 (1989).*

Harvey, Tamara, and Greg O'Brien, eds. *George Washington's South* (2004).

McColley, Robert. *Slavery and Jeffersonian Virginia* (1964).

Nash, Gary B. *Forging Freedom: The Formation of Philadelphia's Black Community, 1720–1840* (1988).

Newman, Simon P. *Parades and the Politics of the American Street* (1997).

Smith, Billy G. The *"Lower Sort": Philadelphia's Laboring People, 1750–1800* (1990).

Ulrich, Laurel Thatcher. *A Midwife's Tale: The Life of Martha Ballard, Based on Her Diary 1785–1812* (1990).

Wallace, Anthony F. C. *The Death and Rebirth of the Seneca* (1970).

White, Richard. *The Middle Ground: Indians, Empires, and Republics in the Great Lakes Region, 1650-1815* (1991).

Wood, Betty. *Women's Work, Men's Work: The Informal Slave Economies of Lowcountry Georgia* (1995).

Forging a New Government

Chernow, Ron. *Alexander Hamilton* (2004).

Cunliffe, Marcus. *George Washington: Man and Monument* (1958).

Ketcham, Ralph. *Presidents above Party: The First American Presidency, 1789–1829* (1984).

Kohn, Richard H. *Eagle and Sword: The Federalists and the Creation of the Military Establishment in America, 1783–1802* (1975).

Phelps, Glenn A. *George Washington and American Constitutionalism* (1993).

Ellis, Joseph J. *Founding Brothers: The Revolutionary Generation* (2000).

The Emergence of Parties

Appleby, Joyce. *Capitalism and a New Social Order: The Republican Vision of the 1790s* (1984).

Buel, Richard Jr., *Securing the Revolution: Ideology in American Politics, 1789–1815* (1972).

Branson, Susan. *Those Fiery Frenchified Dames: Women and Political Culture in Early National Philadelphia* (2001).

Cunningham, Noble E., Jr. *The Jeffersonian Republicans: The Formation of Party Organization, 1789–1801* (1957).

De Conde, Alexander. *Entangling Alliance: Politics and Diplomacy under George Washington* (1958).

Slaughter, Thomas P. *The Whiskey Rebellion: Frontier Epilogue to the American Revolution* (1986).

Young, Alfred F. *The Democratic Republicans of New York: The Origins, 1763–1797* (1967).

The Last Federalist Administration

Dauer, Manning. *The Adams Federalists* (1953).

Ferling, John E. *Adams vs. Jefferson: The Tumultuous Election of 1800 (2004).*

Kurtz, Stephen G. *The Presidency of John Adams: The Collapse of Federalism, 1795–1800* (1957).

Sharp, Roger. *American Politics in the Early Republic: The New Nation in Crisis* (1993).

Smith, James M. *Freedom's Fetters: The Alien and Sedition Laws and American Civil Liberties,* rev. ed. (1966).

Stinchcombe, William. *The XYZ Affair* (1980).

Chapter 9
Jefferson's Presidency

Ackerman, Bruce. *The Failure of the Founding Fathers: Jefferson, Madison, and the Rise of Presidential Democracy* (2005).

Ambrose, Stephen. *Undaunted Courage: Meriwether Lewis, Thomas Jefferson, and the Opening of the American West* (1996).

Banning, Lance. *The Jeffersonian Persuasion: Evolution of a Party Ideology* (1978).

Ben-Atar, Doron S. *The Origins of Jeffersonian Commercial Policy and Diplomacy* (1993).

Dunn, Susan. *Jefferson's Second Revolution: The Election Crisis of 1800 and the Triumph of Republicanism* (2004).

Fischer, David Hackett. *The Revolution of American Conservatism: The Federalist Party in the Era of Jeffersonian Democracy* (1965).

Kennon, Donald R., ed. *A Republic for the Ages: The United States Capitol and the Political Culture of the Early Republic* (1999).

Kukla, Jon. *A Wilderness So Immense: The Louisiana Purchase and the Destiny of America* (2003).

McDonald, Forrest. *The Presidency of Thomas Jefferson* (1976).

Shankman, Andrew. *Crucible of American Democracy: The Struggle to Fuse Egalitarianism and Capitalism in Jeffersonian Pennsylvania* (2004).

Smelser, Marshall. *The Democratic Republic, 1801–1815* (1968)

Young, James Sterling. *The Washington Community, 1800–1828* (1966).

Madison and the Coming of War

Brown, Roger H. *The Republic in Peril* (1964).

Dowd, Gregory Evans. *A Spirited Resistance: The North American Indian Struggle for Unity, 1745–1815* (1992).

Edmunds, R. David. *The Shawnee Prophet* (1983) and *Tecumseh and the Quest for Indian Leadership* (1984).

Owsley, Frank Lawrence, Jr., and Gene H. Smith. *Filibusters and Expansionists: Jeffersonian Manifest Destiny* (1997).

Perkins, Bradford. *Prologue to War: England and the United States, 1805–1812* (1961).

Rutland, Robert A. *Madison's Alternatives: The Jeffersonian Republicans and the Coming of War* (1975).

The War of 1812

Banner, James M. *To the Hartford Convention: The Federalists and the Origins of Party Politics in the Early Republic, 1789–1815* (1967).

Gribbin, William. *The Churches Militant: The War of 1812 and American Religion* (1973).

Horsman, Reginald. *The War of 1812* (1969).

Stagg, J. C. A. *Mr. Madison's War: Politics, Diplomacy, and Warfare in the Early Republic, 1783–1830* (1983).

Watts, Steven. *The Republic Reborn: War and the Making of Liberal America* (1987).

The Era of Good Feelings

Bemis, Samuel Flagg. *John Quincy Adams and the Foundations of American Foreign Policy* (1949).

Cunningham, Noble E., Jr. *The Presidency of James Monroe* (1996).

Livermore, Shaw. *The Twilight of Federalism: The Disintegration of the Federalist Party, 1815–1830* (1962).

May, Ernest R. *The Making of the Monroe Doctrine* (1975).

White, G. Edward. *The Marshall Court and Cultural Change, 1815–1835* (1991).

The Breakdown of Unity

Forbes, Robert Pierce. *The Missouri Compromise and its Aftermath: Slavery and the Meaning of America* (2007).

Rothbard, Murray N. *The Panic of 1819: Reactions and Policies* (1962).

Chapter 10
The Egalitarian Impulse

Butler, Jon. *Awash in a Sea of Faith: Christianizing the American People* (1990).

Hargreaves, Mary W. M. *The Presidency of John Quincy Adams* (1985).

Hatch, Nathan O. *The Democratization of American Christianity* (1989).

Peterson, Merrill D., ed. *Democracy, Liberty, and Property: The State Constitutional Conventions of the 1820s* (1966).

Tocqueville, Alexis de. *Democracy in America,* ed. Phillips Bradley, 2 vols. (1845).

Williamson, Chilton. *American Suffrage from Property to Democracy, 1760–1860* (1960).

Jackson's Presidency

Cole, Donald B. *The Presidency of Andrew Jackson* (1993).

Ellis, Richard E. *The Union at Risk: Jacksonian Democracy, States' Rights, and the Nullification Crisis* (1987).

Freehling, William W. *Prelude to Civil War: The Nullification Controversy in South Carolina, 1816–1836* (1966).

Magliocca, Gerald N. *Andrew Jackson and the Constitution: The Rise and Fall of Generational Regimes* (2007).

Perdue, Theda. *The Cherokee Nation and the Trial of Tears* (2007).

Rogin, Michael Paul. *Fathers and Children: Andrew Jackson and the Subjugation of the American Indian* (1975).

Schlesenger, Arthur, Jr. *The Age of Jackson* (1945).

Wallace, Anthony F. C. *The Long, Bitter Trail: Andrew Jackson and the Indians* (1993).

Ward, John William. *Andrew Jackson: Symbol for an Age* (1955).

Van Buren and Hard Times

McFaul, John M. *The Politics of Jacksonian Finance* (1972).

McGrane, Reginald Charles. *The Panic of 1837* (1924).

Sharp, Roger. *The Jacksonians versus the Banks: Politics in the States after the Panic of 1837* (1970).

Temin, Peter. *The Jacksonian Economy* (1969).

Wilson, Major L. *The Presidency of Martin Van Buren* (1984).

The Rise of the Whig Party

Ashworth, John. *"Agrarians" and "Aristocrats": Party Political Ideology in the United States, 1837–1846* (1983).

Howe, Daniel Walker. *The Political Culture of the American Whigs* (1979).

Kohl, Lawrence Frederick. *The Politics of Individualism: Parties and the American Character in the Jacksonian Era* (1989).

McCormick, Richard P. *The Second American Party System* (1966).

Peterson, Merrill. *The Great Triumvirate: Webster, Clay, and Calhoun* (1987).

The Whigs in Power

Brock, William R. *Parties and Political Conscience* (1979).

Holt, Michael F. *The Rise and Fall of the American Whig Party* (1999).

Merk, Frederick. *Slavery and the Annexation of Texas* (1972).

Peterson, Norma Louis. *The Presidencies of William Henry Harrison and John Tyler* (1990).

Remini, Robert V. *Henry Clay: Statesman for the Union* (1991).

Chapter 11
The Lower South

Bowman, Shearer. *Masters and Lords: Mid-19th Century U.S. Planters and Prussian Junkers* (1993).

Fogel, Robert W., and Stanley Engerman. *Time on the Cross: The Economics of American Negro Slavery* (1974).

Ford, Lacy K., Jr. *Origins of Southern Radicalism: The South Carolina Upcountry, 1800–1860* (1988).

Lockley, Timothy J. *Lines in the Sand: Race and Class in Lowcountry Georgia, 1750–1860* (2001).

McCurry, Stephanie. *Masters of Small Worlds* (1995).

Morris, Christopher. *Becoming Southern: The Evolution of a Way of Life, Warren County and Vicksburg, Mississippi, 1770–1860* (1995).

Rothman, Adam. *Slave Country: American Expansion and the Origins of the Deep South* (2005).

Scarborough, William Kauffman. *Masters of the Big House: Elite Slaveholder's of are Mid-Nineteenth-Century South* (2003).

Thornton, J. Mills, III. *Politics and Power in a Slave Society* (1978).

Vlach, John Michael. *The Planter's Prospect: Privilege and Slaves in Plantation Paintings* (2002).

Wright, Gavin. *The Political Economy of the Cotton South* (1978).

The Upper South

Allmendinger, David F. *Ruffin: Family and Reform in the Old South* (1990).

Bailey, Fred Arthur. *Class and Tennessee's Confederate Generation* (1987).

Crofts, David W. *Old Southampton: Politics and Society in a Virginia County, 1834–1869* (1992)

Dunn, Susan. *Dominion of Memories: Jefferson, Madison, and the Decline of Virginia* (2007).

Fields, Barbara J. *Slavery and Freedom on the Middle Ground: Maryland during the Nineteenth Century* (1985).

McKenzie, Robert Tracey. *One South or Many? Plantation Belt and Upcountry in Civil War Era Tennessee* (1994).

Tadman, Michael. *Speculators and Slaves: Masters, Traders, and Slaves in the Old South* (1989).

Slave Life and Culture

Blassingame, John W. *The Slave Community: Plantation Life in the Antebellum South* (1972).

Camp, Stephanie M. H. *Closer to Freedom: Enslaved Women and Everyday Resistance in the Plantation South* (2004).

Dew, Charles B. *Bond of Iron: Master and Slave at Buffalo Forge* (1994).

Gates, Henry Louis, Jr., ed. *The Bondwoman's Narrative* (2002).

Gutman, Herbert G. *The Black Family in Slavery and Freedom, 1750–1925* (1974).

Kaye, Anthony E. *Joining Places: Slave Neighborhoods in the Old South* (2007).

Kolchin, Peter. *Unfree Labor: American Slavery and Russian Serfdom* (1987).

McLaurin, Melton A. *Celia, a Slave* (1991).

Penningroth, Dylan. *The Claims of Kinfolk: African American Property and Community in the Nineteenth-Century South* (2003).

Starobin, Robert. *Industrial Slavery in the Old South* (1970).

Wade, Richard C. *Slavery in the Cities* (1964).

Free Society

Berlin, Ira. *Slaves without Masters: The Free Negro in the Antebellum South* (1974).

Bolton, Charles C. *Poor Whites of the Antebellum South* (1994).

Bynum, Victoria E. *Unruly Women: The Politics of Social and Sexual Control in the Old South* (1992).

Cecil-Fronsman, Bill. *Common Whites: Class and Culture in Antebellum North Carolina* (1992).

Fox-Genovese, Elizabeth. *Within the Plantation Household: Black and White Women of the Old South* (1988).

Harris, J. William. *Plain Folk and Gentry in a Slave Society* (1985).

Owsley, Frank. *Plain Folk in the South* (1949).

The Proslavery Argument

Bailey, David L. *Shadow on the Church: Southwestern Evangelical Religion and the Issue of Slavery, 1783–1860* (1985).

Fredrickson, George M. *The Black Image in the White Mind* (1971).

Genovese, Eugene D., and Fox-Genovese, Elizabeth. *The Mind of the Master Class: History and Faith in the Southern Slaveholders' Worldview* (2005).

Jenkins, W. S. *Pro-Slavery Thought in the Old South* (1935).

Mathews, Donald G. *Religion in the Old South* (1977).

McKivigan, John R., and Mitchell Snay, eds. *Religion and the Antebellum Debate over Slavery* (1998).

Snay, Mitchell. *Gospel of Disunion: Religion and Separatism in the Antebellum South* (1993).

Chapter 12
Industrial Change and Urbanization

Anbinder, Tyler. *Five Points* (2001).

Bernstein, Peter L. *Wedding of the Waters: The Erie Canal and the Making of a Great Nation* (2005).

Blumin, Stuart M. *The Emergence of the Middle Class: Social Experience in the American City, 1760–1900* (1989).

Bushman, Richard L. *The Refinement of America: Persons, Houses, Cities* (1992).

Cochran, Thomas C. *Frontiers of Change: Early Industrialization in America* (1981).

Dublin, Thomas. *Women at Work: The Transformation of Work and Community in Lowell, Massachusetts, 1826–1860* (1979).

Handlin, Oscar. *Boston's Immigrants: A Study of Acculturation*, rev. ed. (1959).

Horowitz, Morton J. *The Transformation of American Law, 1790–1860* (1977).

Johnson, Paul E. *A Shopkeeper's Millennium: Society and Revivals in Rochester, New York, 1815–1837* (1978).

Laurie, Bruce. *Artisans into Workers: Labor in Nineteenth-Century America* (1989).

Pessen, Edward. *Riches, Class, and Power before the Civil War* (1973).

Roediger, David. *The Wages of Whiteness: Race and the Making of the American Working Class* (1991).

Ryan, Mary. *Cradle of the Middle Class: The Family in Oneida County, New York, 1790–1865* (1981).

Stansel, Christine. *City of Women: Sex and Class in New York, 1789–1860* (1986).

Steinberg, Theodore. *Nature Incorporated: Industrialization and the Waters of New England* (1991).

Wade, Richard C. *The Urban Frontier* (1964).

Wilentz, Sean. *Chants Democratic: New York City and the Rise of the American Working Class, 1790–1865* (1984).

Reform and Moral Order

Burin, Eric. *Slavery and the Peculiar Solution: A History of the American Colonization Society* (2005).

Cott, Nancy F. *The Bonds of Womanhood: "Woman's Sphere" in New England, 1780–1835* (1977).

Cross, Whitney R. *The Burned-Over District: The Social and Intellectual History of Enthusiastic Religion in Western New York, 1800–1850* (1950).

Epstein, Barbara Leslie. *The Politics of Domesticity: Women, Evangelicalism, and Temperance in Nineteenth-Century America* (1981).

Foster, Charles I. *An Errand of Mercy: The Evangelical United Front* (1960).

Ginzberg, Lori D. *Women and the Work of Benevolence: Morality, Politics, and Class in the 19th-Century United States* (1990).

Hanley, Mark Y. *Beyond a Christian Commonwealth: The Protestant Quarrel with the American Republic, 1830–1860* (1994).

Horowitz, Helen L. *Rereading Sex: Battles over Sexual Knowledge and Suppression in Nineteenth-Century America* (2002).

Smith-Rosenberg, Carroll. *Religion and the Rise of the American City* (1971).

Rorabaugh, W. J. *The Alcoholic Republic* (1979).

Walters, Ronald A. *American Reformers, 1815–1860* (1978).

Winn, Kenneth H. *Exiles in a Land of Liberty: Mormons in America, 1830–1846* (1989).

Wosh, Peter J. *Spreading the Word: The Bible Business in Nineteenth-Century America* (1994).

Institutions and Social Improvement

Capper, Charles, and Conrad Edick Wright, eds. *Transient and Permanent: The Transcendentalist Movement and Its Contexts* (1999).

Grob, Gerald N. *Mental Institutions in America: Social Policy to 1875* (1973).

Guarneri, Carl J. *The Utopian Alternative: Fourierism in Nineteenth-Century America* (1991).

Hirsh, Adam Jay. *The Rise of the Penitentiary* (1992).

Kaestle, Carl F. *Pillars of the Republic: Common Schools and American Society, 1780–1860* (1983).

Katz, Michael B. *In the Shadow of the Poorhouse: A Social History of Welfare in America* (1986).

Rothman, David. *The Discovery of the Asylum: Social Order and Disorder in the New Republic* (1971).

Abolitionism and Women's Rights

Basch, Norma. *In the Eyes of the Law: Women, Marriage, and Property in Nineteenth-Century New York* (1982).

Cutter, Barbara. *Domestic Devils, Battlefield Angels: The Radicalism of American Womanhood 1830–1865* (2003).

Hewitt, Nancy A. *Women's Activism and Social Change: Rochester, New York, 1822–1872* (1984).

Isenberg, Nancy. *Sex and Citizenship in Antebellum America* (1998).

Jeffrey, Julie Roy. *The Great Silent Army of Abolitionism: Ordinary Women in the Antislavery Movement* (1998).

Litwack, Leon F. *North of Slavery: The Negro in the Free States, 1790–1860* (1961).

Lumpkin, Katharine Du Pre. *The Emancipation of Angelina Grimké* (1974).

McKivigan, John R. *The War against Proslavery Religion: Abolitionism and the Northern Churches, 1830–1865* (1984).

Newman, Richard S. *The Transformation of American Abolitionism: Fighting Slavery in the Early Republic* (2002).

Rael, Patrick. *Black Identity and Black Protest in the Antebellum North* (2002).

Richards, Leonard L. *The Slave Power: The Free North and Southern Domination, 1780–1860* (2000).

Ripley, C. Peter, Finkenbine, Roy E., Hembree, Michael E., and Yacovone, Donald., eds. *Witness for Freedom: African-American Voices on Race, Slavery, and Emancipation* (1993).

Salerno, Beth A., *Sister Societies: Women's Antislavery Organizations in Antebellum America* (2005).

Chapter 13
The Agricultural Frontier

Cashin, Joan E. *A Family Venture: Men and Women on the Southern Frontier* (1991).

Faragher, John Mack. *Sugar Creek: Life on the Illinois Prairie* (1986).

Hudson, John C. *Making the Corn Belt: A Geographical History of Middle-Western Agriculture* (1994).

Moore, John Hebron. *The Emergence of the Cotton Kingdom in the Old Southwest: Mississippi, 1770–1860* (1987).

Rohrbough, Malcolm J. *The Trans-Appalachian Frontier: People, Societies, and Institutions, 1775–1850* (1978).

Stoll, Steven. *Larding the Lean Earth: Soil and Society in Nineteenth-Century America* (2002).

The Frontier of the Plains Indians

Clark, Malcolm, Jr. *Eden Seekers: The Settlement of Oregon, 1810–1862* (1981).

Goetzmann, William H. *Exploration and Empire: The Explorer and Scientist in the Winning of the American West* (1966).

Jeffrey, Julie R. *Frontier Women: The Trans-Mississippi West, 1840–1880* (1979).

Moore, John H., ed. *The Political Economy of the North American Indians* (1993).

Unruh, John. *The Plains Across: The Overland Emigrations and the Trans-Mississippi West, 1840–1860* (1979).

Utley, Robert M. *A Life Wild and Perilous: Mountain Men and the Paths to the Pacific* (1997).

West, Elliott. *The Way to the West: Essays on the Central Plains* (1995).

White, Richard. *The Roots of Dependency: Subsistence, Environment, and Social Change Among the Choctaws, Pawnees, and Navajos* (1983).

The Mexican Borderlands

Acuña, Rudolfo. *Occupied America: A History of Chicanos* (1988).

Anderson, Gary Clayton. *The Conquest of Texas: Ethnic Cleansing in the Promised Land* (2005).

Arrington, Leonard J. *Great Basin Kingdom: An Economic History of the Latter-Day Saints, 1830–1900*, New ed. (2005).

Gonzales, Manuel G. *Mexicanos: A History of Mexicans in the United States* (1999).

Lack, Paul D. *The Texas Revolutionary Experience: A Political and Social History, 1835–1836* (1992).

Lecompte, Janet. *Pueblo, Hardscabble, Greenhorn: The Upper Arkansas, 1832–1856* (1978).

Phillips, George Harwood. *Indians and Intruders in Central California, 1769–1849* (1993).

Roberts, Randy, and James L. Olsen, *A Line in the Sand: The Alamo in Blood and Memory* (2001).

Tijerina, Andres. *Tejanos and Texas under the Mexican Flag, 1821–1836* (1994).

Topping, Gary, ed. *Utah Historians and the Reconstruction of Western History* (2003).

Weber, David J. *The Mexican Frontier, 1821–1846: The American Southwest under Mexico* (1982).

Politics, Expansion, and War

Griswold del Castillo, Richard. *The Treaty of Guadalupe Hidalgo: A Legacy of Conflict* (1990).

Eisenhower, John S. D. *So Far from God: The U.S. War with Mexico* (1989).

Foos, Paul W. *A Short, Offhand, Killing Affair: Soldiers and Social Conflict during the Mexican-American War* (2002).

Henderson, Timothy J. *A Glorious Defeat: Mexico and its War with the United States* (2007).

Hietala, Thomas R. *Manifest Design: American Aggrandizement in Late Jacksonian America* (1985).

Horsman, Reginald. *Race and Manifest Destiny: The Origins of American Racial Anglo-Saxonism* (1981).

Johannsen, Robert W. *To the Halls of Montezuma: The Mexican War in the American Imagination* (1985).

Merle, Frederic. *Manifest Destiny and Mission in American History* (1963).

Sellers, Charles G. *James K. Polk: Continentalist, 1843–1846* (1966).

Silbey, Joel H. *Storm over Texas: The Annexation Controversy and the Road to Civil War* (2005).

Chapter 14
Slavery in the Territories

Berwanger, Eugene H. *The Frontier against Slavery: Western Anti-Negro Prejudice and the Slavery Extension Controversy* (1967).

Hamilton, Holman. *Prologue to Conflict: The Crisis and Compromise of 1850* (1966).

Hedrick, Joan D. *Harriet Beecher Stowe: A Life* (1993).

Johnson, Susan Lee. *Roaring Camp: The Social World of the California Gold Rush* (2000).

Morrison, Michael E. *Slavery and the American West: The Eclipse of Manifest Destiny and the Coming of the Civil War* (1997).

Peterson, Merrill. *The Great Triumvirate: Webster, Clay, and Calhoun* (1987).

Quarles, Benjamin. *Black Abolitionists* (1969).

Rohrbough, Malcolm J. *Days of Gold: The California Gold Rush and the American Nation* (1997).

Political Realignment

Anbinder, Tyler. *Nativism and Slavery: The Northern Know-Nothings and the Politics of the 1850s* (1992).

Carwardine, Richard J. *Evangelicals and Politics in Antebellum America* (1993).

Cooper, William J., Jr. *The South and the Politics of Slavery, 1828–1856* (1978).

Fehrenbacher, Don E. *Slavery, Law, and Politics: The Dred Scott Case in Historical Perspective* (1981).

Foner, Eric. *Free Soil, Free Labor, Free Men: The Ideology of the Republican Party before the Civil War* (1970).

Gienapp, William E. *The Origins of the Republican Party, 1852–1856* (1987).

Holt, Michael F. *The Fate of their Country: Politicians, Slavery Extension, and the Coming of the Civil War* (2004).

Howe, Daniel Walker. "The Evangelical Movement and Political Culture in the North during the Second Party System," *Journal of American History*, 77 (March 1991): 1216–1239.

Johannsen, Robert W., ed. *The Lincoln-Douglas Debates of 1858* (1965).

Long, Kathryn Teresa. *The Revival of 1857–58: Interpreting an American Religious Awakening* (1998).

Rawley, James A. *Race and Politics: "Bleeding Kansas" and the Coming of the Civil War* (1969).

SenGupta, Ganja. *For God and Mammon: Evangelicals and Entrepreneurs, Masters and Slaves in Territorial Kansas, 1854–1860* (1996).

von Frank, Albert J. *The Trials of Anthony Burns: Freedom and Slavery in Emerson's Boston* (1998).

Wolff, Gerald W. *The Kansas-Nebraska Bill: Party, Section, and the Coming of the Civil War* (1977).

The Road to Disunion

Banks, Russell. *Cloudsplitter* (1997).

Barney, William L. *The Road to Secession: A New Perspective on the Old South* (1972).

Current, Richard N. *Lincoln and the First Shot* (1963).

Dew, Charles B. *Apostles of Disunion: Southern Secession Commissioners and the Causes of the Civil War* (2001).

Helper, Hinton Rowan. *The Impending Crisis of the South: How to Meet It* (1857).

Johnson, Michael P., and James L. Roark, eds. *No Chariot Let Down: Charleston's Free People of Color on the Eve of the Civil War* (1984).

Levine, Bruce. *Half Slave and Half Free: The Roots of Civil War* (2005).

McCardell, John. *The Idea of a Southern Nation: Southern Nationalists and Southern Nationalism, 1830–1860* (1979).

Snay, Michael. *Gospel of Disunion: Religion and Separatism in the Antebellum South* (1993).

Thornton, J. Mills. *Politics and Power in a Slave Society: Alabama, 1800–1860* (1978).

Walther, Eric H. *The Fire-Eaters* (1992).

Chapter 15
Mobilization, North and South

Cooper, William J. *Jefferson Davis: American* (2000).

Davis, William C. *"A Government of Our Own": The Making of the Confederacy* (1994).

Donald, David. *Lincoln* (1995).

Grant, Ulysses S. *Personal Memoirs of U.S. Grant* (1885, 1996).

Royster, Charles. *The Destructive War: William Tecumseh Sherman, Stonewall Jackson, and the Americans* (1991).

Schultz, Jane E. *Women at the Front: Hospital Workers in Civil War America* (2004).

Thomas, Emory M. *Robert E. Lee: A Biography* (1995).

Watkins, Sam R. *"Co. Aytch": A Confederate Memoir of the Civil War* (1882; 2003).

The Early War, 1861–1862

Bierce, Ambrose. *Civil War Stories* (1909; 1994).

Cooling, Benjamin Franklin. *Forts Henry and Donelson: The Key to the Confederate Heartland* (1988).

Daniel, Larry J. *Shiloh: The Battle That Changed the Civil War* (1997).

Fellman, Michael. *Inside War: The Guerrilla Conflict in Missouri during the Civil War* (1989).

Linderman, Gerald F. *Embattled Courage: The Experience of Combat in the American Civil War* (1989).

McPherson, James M. *What They Fought For, 1861–1865* (1994).

Robertson, James I. *Stonewall Jackson: The Man, the Soldier, the Legend* (1997).

Turning Points, 1862–1863

Berlin, Ira, et al., eds. *Freedom: A Documentary History of Emancipation, 1861–1867*, Ser. 1, Vol. 1: *The Destruction of Slavery* (1985).

Josephy, Alvin M., Jr. *The Civil War in the American West* (1993).

McFeely, William S. *Grant: A Biography* (1981).

Quarles, Benjamin. *The Negro in the Civil War* (1953).

Reardon, Carol. *Pickett's Charge in History and Memory* (1997).

Sears, Stephen W. *Landscape Turned Red: The Battle of Antietam* (1983).

Shaara, Michael. *The Killer Angels: A Novel* (1974).

Smith, David Paul. *Frontier Defense in the Civil War: Texas' Rangers and Rebels* (1992).

Striner, Richard, *Father Abraham: Lincoln's Relentless Struggle to End Slavery* (2006).

Wills, Garry. *Lincoln at Gettysburg: The Words That Remade America* (1992).

War Transforms the North

Baker, Kevin. *Paradise Alley: A Novel* (2002)

Mitchell, Reid. *The Vacant Chair: The Northern Soldier Leaves Home* (1993).

Neely, Mark E., Jr. *The Fate of Liberty: Abraham Lincoln and Civil Liberties* (1991).

Pryor, Elizabeth B. *Clara Barton: Professional Angel* (1987).

Richardson, Heather Cox. *The Greatest Nation of the Earth: Republican Economic Policies during the Civil War* (1997).

The Confederacy Disintegrates

Ash, Stephen V. *When the Yankees Came: Conflict and Chaos in the Occupied South, 1861–1865* (1995).

Campbell, Edward D. C., Jr., and Kym S. Rice, eds. *A Woman's War: Southern Women, Civil War, and the Confederate Legacy* (1996).

Clinton, Catherine, and Nina Silber, eds. *Divided Houses: Gender and the Civil War* (1992).

Durden, Robert F. *The Gray and the Black: The Confederate Debate on Emancipation* (1972).

Edwards, Laura. *Scarlett Doesn't Live Here Anymore: Southern Women in the Civil War Era* (2000).

Faust, Drew Gilpin. *Mothers of Invention: Women of the Slaveholding South in the American Civil War* (1996).

Frazier, Charles. *Cold Mountain* (1997).

Grimsley, Mark. *The Hard Hand of War: Union Policy Toward Southern Civilians, 1861–1865* (1995).

Woodward, C. Vann, ed. *Mary Chesnut's Civil War* (1981).

The Union Prevails

Beringer, Richard E., Herman Hattaway, Archer Jones, and William N. Still, Jr. *Why the South Lost the Civil War* (1986).

Glatthaar, Joseph T. *The March to the Sea and Beyond* (1985).

Rubin, Anne Sarah. *A Shattered Nation: The Rise and Fall of the Confederacy, 1861–1868* (2005).

Chapter 16
White Southerners and the Ghosts of the Confederacy

Blight, David W. *Race and Reunion: The Civil War in American Memory* (2001).

Edwards, Laura F. *Gendered Strife and Confusion: The Political Culture of Reconstruction* (1997).

Goldfield, David, *Still Fighting the Civil War: The American South and Southern History* (2002).

More Than Freedom: Black African-American Aspirations in 1865

Berlin, Ira, et al. *Freedom: A Documentary History of Emancipation, 1861–1867. The Wartime Genesis of Free Labor: The Lower South* (1990).

Cimbala, Paul A., and Randall M. Miller, eds. *The Freedmen's Bureau and Reconstruction: A Reconsideration* (1999).

Fitzgerald, Michael W. *The Union League Movement in the Deep South: Politics and Agricultural Change during Reconstruction* (1989).

Gutman, Herbert G. *The Black Family in Slavery and Freedom, 1750–1925* (1976).

Hahn, Steven. *A Nation under Our Feet: Black Political Struggles in the Rural South from Slavery to the Great Migration* (2003).

Jaynes, Gerald. *Branches without Roots: The Genesis of the Black Working Class in the American South, 1862–1882* (1986).

Jones, Jacqueline. *Labor of Love, Labor of Sorrow: Black Women, Work, and the Family from Slavery to the Present* (1985).

Kolchin, Peter. *Unfree Labor: American Slavery and Russian Serfdom* (1990).

Rabinowitz, Howard N. *Race Relations in the Urban South, 1865–1890* (1978).

Rabinowitz, Howard N., ed. *Southern Black Leaders of the Reconstruction Era* (1982).

Stowell, David W. *Rebuilding Zion: The Religious Reconstruction of the South, 1863–1877* (1998).

Thornbrough, Emma Lou., ed. *Black Reconstructionists* (1972).

Williamson, Joel. *After Slavery: The Negro in South Carolina during Reconstruction, 1861–1877* (1965).

Federal Reconstruction, 1865–1870

Benedict, Michael Les. *A Compromise of Principle: Congressional Republicans and Reconstruction, 1863–1869* (1974).

Harris, William C. *With Charity for All: Lincoln and the Restoration of the Union* (1997).

McFeely, William S. *Grant: A Biography* (1981).

Moneyhon, Carl H. *Republicanism in Reconstruction Texas* (1980).

Perman, Michael. *Reunion without Compromise: The South and Reconstruction, 1865–1868* (1973).

Rose, Willie Lee. *Rehearsal for Reconstruction: The Port Royal Experiment* (1964).

Summers, Mark W. *Railroads, Reconstruction, and the Gospel of Prosperity: Aid Under the Radical Republicans, 1865–1877* (1984).

Trefousse, Hans. *The Radical Republicans: Lincoln's Vanguard for Racial Justice* (1969).

Counter-Reconstruction, 1870–1874

Blum, Edward J. *Reforging the White Republic: Race, Religion, and American Nationalism, 1865–1898* (2005).

Current, Richard N. *Those Terrible Carpetbaggers: A Reinterpretation* (1988).

Hogue, James. *Uncivil War: Five New Orleans Street Battles and the Rise and Fall of Radical Reconstruction* (2006).

Perman, Michael. *The Road to Redemption: Southern Politics, 1869–1879* (1984).

Rable, George C. *But There Was No Peace: The Role of Violence in the Politics of Reconstruction* (1984).

Trelease, Allen W. *White Terror: The Ku Klux Klan Conspiracy and Southern Reconstruction* (1971).

Redemption, 1874–1877

Campbell, Randolph B. *Grass-Roots Reconstruction in Texas, 1865–1880* (1997).

Lemann, Nicholas. *Redemption: The Last Battle of the Civil War* (2006).

Richardson, Heather Cox. *The Death of Reconstruction: Race, Labor, and Politics in the Post–Civil War North, 1865–1901* (2001).

Woodward, C. Vann. *Reunion and Reaction: The Compromise of 1877 and the End of Reconstruction* (1951).

The Failed Promise of Reconstruction

Franklin, John Hope. *Reconstruction after the Civil War* (1961).

Ransom, Roger L., and Richard Sutch. *One Kind of Freedom: The Economic Consequences of Emancipation* (1977).

Richardson, Heather Cox. *West from Appomattox: The Reconstruction of America after the Civil War* (2007).

Stampp, Kenneth M. *The Era of Reconstruction, 1865–1877* (1965).

Chapter 17
The Newness of the New South

Billings, Dwight B. Jr. *Planters and the Making of a "New South"* (1979).

Burton, Orville Vernon. *In My Father's House Are Many Mansions: Family and Community in Edgefield County, South Carolina* (1985).

Carlton, David L. *Mill and Town in South Carolina, 1880–1920* (1980).

Clark, Thomas D. *Pills, Petticoats, and Plows: The Southern Country Store* (1944).

Davis, Harold E. *Henry Grady's New South: Atlanta, a Brave and Beautiful City* (1990).

Doyle, Don H. *New Men, New Cities, New South: Atlanta, Nashville, Charleston, Mobile, 1860–1910* (1990).

Durden, Robert F. *The Dukes of Durham, 1865–1929* (1975).

Eller, Ronald D. *Miners, Millhands, and Mountaineers: Industrialization of the Appalachian South, 1880–1920* (1982).

Hall, Jacqueline Dowd, et al. *Like a Family: The Making of a Southern Cotton Mill World* (1987).

Hearden, Patrick J. *Independence and Empire: The New South's Cotton Mill Campaign, 1865–1901* (1982).

Horwitz, Tony, *Confederates in the Attic: Dispatches from the Unfinished Civil War* (1998).

Lewis, W. David, *Sloss Furnaces and the Rise of the Birmingham District: An Industrial Epic* (1994).

Russell, James M. *Atlanta, 1847–1890: City Building in the Old South and the New* (1988).

Tilley, Nannie M. *The R. J. Reynolds Tobacco Company* (1985).

Wright, Gavin, *Old South, New South: Revolutions in the Southern Economy since the Civil War* (1986).

The Southern Agrarian Revolt

Barnes, Donna. *Farmers in Rebellion: The Rise and Fall of the Southern Farmers' Alliance and People's Party in Texas* (1987).

Barr, Alwyn. *Reconstruction to Reform: Texas Politics, 1876–1906* (1971).

Daniel, Pete. *Breaking the Land: The Transformation of Cotton, Tobacco and Rice Cultures since 1880* (1985).

Hahn, Steven. *The Roots of Southern Populism: The Transformation of the Georgia Upcountry, 1850–1890* (1983).

McMath, Robert, Jr. *The Populist Vanguard: A History of the Southern Farmers' Alliance* (1975).

Minnix, Kathleen. *Laughter in the Amen Corner: The Life of Evangelist Sam Jones* (1993).

Newby, I. A. *Plain Folk in the New South: Social Change and Cultural Persistence, 1880–1915* (1989).

Ownby, Ted. *Subduing Satan: Religion, Recreation, and Manhood in the Rural South, 1865–1920* (1990).

Ransom, Roger, and Richard Sutch. *One Kind of Freedom: The Economic Consequences of Emancipation* (1977).

Wallenstein, Peter. *From Slave South to New South: Public Policy in Nineteenth-Century Georgia* (1987).

Webb, Samuel L. *Two-Party Politics in the One-Party South: Alabama's Hill Country, 1874–1920* (1997).

Wiener, Jonathan. *Social Origins of the New South: Alabama, 1860–1885* (1978).

Woodman, Harold D. *King Cotton and His Retainers: Financing and Marketing the Cotton Crop of the South, 1800–1925* (1968).

Woodward, C. Vann. *Tom Watson: Agrarian Rebel* (1938).

Women in the New South

Bernhard, Virginia, et al., eds. *Southern Women: Histories and Identities* (1992).

Enstam, Elizabeth York. *Women and the Creation of Urban Life: Dallas, Texas, 1843–1920* (1998).

Friedman, Jean E. *The Enclosed Garden: Women and Community in the Evangelical South, 1830–1900* (1985).

Gilmore, Glenda Elizabeth. *Gender and Jim Crow: Women and the Politics of White Supremacy in North Carolina, 1896–1920* (1996).

Green, Elna C. *Southern Strategies: Southern Women and the Woman Suffrage Question* (1997).

Higginbotham, Evelyn Brooks. *Righteous Discontent: The Women's Movement in the Black Baptist Church, 1880–1920* (1993).

Hunter, Tera W. *To Joy My Freedom: Southern Black Women's Lives and Labors after the Civil War* (1997).

Lumpkin, Katharine DuPre. *The Making of a Southerner* (1947).

McArthur, Judith N. *Creating the New Woman: The Rise of Southern Women's Progressive Culture in Texas, 1893–1918* (1998).

McDowell, John P. *The Social Gospel in the South: The Woman's Home Mission Movement in the Methodist Episcopal Church, South, 1886–1939* (1982).

Scott, Anne Firor. *The Southern Lady: From Pedestal to Politics, 1830–1930* (1970).

Sims, Anastatia. *The Power of Femininity in the New South: Women's Organizations and Politics in North Carolina, 1880–1930* (1997).

Terrell, Mary Church. *A Colored Woman in a White World* (1980).

Thomas, Mary Martha. *The New Woman in Alabama: Social Reforms and Suffrage, 1890–1920* (1992).

Turner, Elizabeth Hayes. *Women, Culture, and Community: Religion and Reform in Galveston, 1880–1920* (1997).

Wheeler, Marjorie Spruill. *New Women of the New South: The Leaders of the Woman Suffrage Movement in the Southern States* (1993).

Settling the Race Issue

Ayers, Edward L. *Vengeance and Justice: Crime and Punishment in the Nineteenth-Century American South* (1984).

Beatty, Bess. *A Revolution Gone Backwards: The Black Response to National Politics, 1876–1896* (1987).

Blum, Edward J. *Reforging the White Republic: Race, Religion, and American Nationalism, 1865–1898* (2005).

Brundage, W. Fitzhugh. *Lynching in the New South: Georgia and Virginia, 1880–1930* (1993).

Cell, John W. *The Highest Stage of White Supremacy: The Origins of Segregation in South Africa and the American South* (1982).

Clayton, Bruce. *The Savage Ideal: Intolerance and Intellectual Leadership in the South, 1890–1914* (1972).

Dailey, Jane. *Before Jim Crow: The Politics of Race in Postemancipation Virginia* (2000).

Greenwood, Janette Thomas. *Bittersweet Legacy: The Black and White "Better Classes" in Charlotte, 1850–1910* (1994).

Hale, Grace Elizabeth. *Making Whiteness: The Culture of Segregation in the South, 1890–1940* (1998).

Harlan, Louis R. *Booker T. Washington: The Making of a Black Leader, 1856–1901* (1972).

Kantrowitz, Stephen. *Ben Tillman and the Reconstruction of White Supremacy* (2000).

Kenzer, Robert C. *Enterprising Southerners: Black Economic Success in North Carolina, 1865–1915* (1997).

Kousser, J. Morgan, *The Shaping of Southern Politics: Suffrage Restriction and the Establishment of the One-Party South, 1880–1910* (1974).

Letwin, Daniel. *The Challenge of Interracial Unionism: Alabama Coal Miners, 1878–1921* (1998).

Litwack, Leon F. *Trouble in Mind: Black Southerners in the Age of Jim Crow* (1998).

Lofgren, Charles A. *The "Plessy" Case: A Legal-Historical Interpretation* (1987).

Meier, August. *Negro Thought in America, 1880–1915: Racial Ideologies in the Age of Booker T. Washington* (1963).

Prather, H. Leon. *We Have Taken a City: The Wilmington Racial Massacre and Coup of 1898* (1989).

Silber, Nina. *The Romance of Reunion: Northerners and the South* (1993).

Tolnay, Stewart E., and E. M. Beck. *A Festival of Violence: An Analysis of Southern Lynchings, 1882–1930* (1995).

Weare, Walter B. *Black Business in the New South: A Social History of the North Carolina Mutual Life Insurance Company* (1973).

Woodward, C. Vann. *The Strange Career of Jim Crow* (1955).

Chapter 18
New Industry

Bazerman, Charles. *The Languages of Edison's Light* (1999).

Bellamy, Edward. *Looking Backward* (1888).

Benson, Susan Porter. *Counter Cultures: Saleswomen, Managers, and Customers in American Department Stores, 1890–1940* (1986).

Boris, Eileen. *Home to Work: Motherhood and the Politics of Industrial Homework in the United States* (1994).

Buder, Stanley. *Pullman: An Experiment in Industrial Order and Community Planning, 1880–1930* (1967).

Chernow, Ron. *Titan: The Life of John D. Rockefeller, Sr.* (1998).

Davies, Marjorie. *Woman's Place Is at the Typewriter, 1870–1930* (1982).

Dye, Nancy Schrom. *As Equals and as Sisters: Feminism, the Labor Movement, and the Women's Trade Union League of New York* (1981).

Gilfoyle, Timothy J. *City of Eros: New York City, Prostitution, and the Commercialization of Sex, 1790–1920* (1992).

Gutman, Herbert. *Work, Culture, and Society in Industrializing America* (1976).

Katzman, David M. *Seven Days a Week: Women and Domestic Service in Industrializing America* (1978).

Kaufman, Stuart. *Samuel Gompers and the Origins of the American Federation of Labor, 1848–1896* (1973).

Kessler-Harris, Alice. *Out to Work: A History of Wage-Earning Women in the United States* (1982).

Lane, James B. *Jacob A. Riis and the American City* (1974).

Montgomery, David. *The Fall of the House of Labor: The Workplace, the State, and American Labor Activism, 1865–1925* (1987).

Morris, Charles R. *Tycoons: How Andrew Carnegie, John D. Rockefeller, and J.P. Morgan Invented the American Supereconomy* (2005).

Salvatore, Nick. *Eugene V. Debs: Citizen and Socialist* (1982).

Sinclair, Upton. *The Jungle* (1906).

Stromquist, Shelton. *A Generation of Boomers: The Pattern of Railroad Labor Conflict in Nineteenth-Century America* (1987).

Tentler, Leslie Woodcock. *Wage-Earning Women: Industrial Work and Family Life, 1900–1930* (1979).

New Immigrants

Blanck, Dag. *Becoming Swedish-American: The Construction of an Ethnic Identity in the Augustana Synod, 1860–1917* (1997).

Cahan, Abraham. *The Rise of David Levinsky* (1917).

Camarillo, Albert. *Chicanos in a Changing Society: From Mexican Pueblos to American Barrios in Santa Barbara and Southern California, 1848–1930* (1979).

Chen, Yong. *Chinese San Francisco, 1850–1943: A Trans-Pacific Community* (2000).

Clark, Dennis. *The Irish in Philadelphia: Ten Generations of Urban Experience* (1973).

Daniels, Roger. *Not Like Us: Immigrants and Minorities in America, 1890–1924* (1997).

Daniels, Roger. *Guarding the Golden Door: American Immigration Policy and Immigrants since 1882* (2004).

Diner, Hasia. *Erin's Daughters in America* (1983).

Gabaccia, Donna. *From Sicily to Elizabeth Street: Housing and Social Change among Italian Immigrants, 1880–1930* (1984).

Glenn, Evelyn Nakano. *Issei, Nisei, War Bride: Three Generations of Japanese American Women in Domestic Service* (1986).

Howe, Irving. *World of Our Fathers* (1976).

Ignatiev, Noel. *How the Irish Became White* (1995).

Jacobson, Matthew Frye. *Whiteness of a Different Color: European Immigrants and the Alchemy of Race* (1998).

Jacobson, Matthew Frye. *Barbarian Virtues: The United States Encounters Foreign Peoples at Home and Abroad, 1876–1917* (2000).

Kessner, Thomas. *The Golden Door: Italian and Jewish Immigrant Mobility in New York City, 1880–1915* (1977).

Kraut, Alan M. *The Huddled Masses: The Immigrant in American Society, 1880–1921* (1982).

Kusmer, Kenneth. *A Ghetto Takes Shape: Black Cleveland, 1870–1930* (1976).

Lerda, Valeria Gennaro, ed. *From "Melting Pot" to Multiculturalism: The Evolution of Ethnic Relations in the United States and Canada* (1990).

Modell, John. *The Economics and Politics of Racial Accommodation: The Japanese of Los Angeles, 1900–1942* (1977).

Roediger, David R. *The Wages of Whiteness: Race and the Making of the American Working Class* (rev. ed. 1999).

Reimers, David M. *Other Immigrants: The Global Origins of the American People* (2004).

Smith, Betty. *A Tree Grows in Brooklyn* (1943).

Stewart, Kenneth L., and Arnoldo De Leon. *Not Room Enough: Mexicans, Anglos, and Socio-Economic Change in Texas, 1850–1900* (1993).

Wong, K. Scott, and Sucheng Chan, eds. *Claiming America: Constructing Chinese American Identities during the Exclusion Era* (1998).

Yezierska, Anzia. *Bread Givers: A Novel: A Struggle between a Father of the Old World and a Daughter of the New* (1925; new ed. 1975).

New Cities

Barth, Gunther. *Instant Cities: Urbanization and the Rise of San Francisco and Denver* (1975).

Barth, Gunther. *City People: The Rise of Modern City Culture in Nineteenth-Century America* (1982).

Beckert, Sven. *The Monied Metropolis: New York City and the Consolidation of the American Bourgeoisie, 1850–1896* (2001).

Bluestone, Daniel. *Constructing Chicago* (1991).

Bolotin, Norman and Christine Laing. *The World's Columbian Exposition: The Chicago World's Fair of 1893* (1992).

Burrows, Edwin G., and Mike Wallace. *Gotham: A History of New York City to 1898* (1998).

Couvares, Francis G. *The Remaking of Pittsburgh: Class and Culture in an Industrializing City, 1877–1919* (1984).

Deutsch, Sarah. *Women and the City: Gender, Space, and Power in Boston, 1870–1940* (2000).

Fishman, Robert. *Bourgeois Utopias: The Rise and Fall of Suburbia* (1987).

Foy, Jessica, and Thomas J. Schlereth, eds. *American Home Life, 1880–1930: A Social History of Spaces and Services* (1991).

Hayden, Dolores. *Building Suburbia: Green Fields and Urban Growth, 1820–2000* (2004).

Hood, Clifton. *722 Miles: The Building of the Subways and How They Transformed New York* (1993).

Jackson, Kenneth T. *Crabgrass Frontier: The Suburbanization of the United States* (1985).

Kasson, John F. *Amusing the Millions: Coney Island at the Turn of the Century* (1978).

Peiss, Kathy. *Cheap Amusements: Working Women and Leisure in Turn-of-the-Century New York* (1986).

Platt, Harold L. *The Electric City: Energy and the Growth of the Chicago Area, 1880–1930* (1991).

Rosenzweig, Roy. *Eight Hours for What We Will: Workers and Leisure in an Industrial City, 1870–1920* (1983).

Sklar, Kathryn Kish. *Catharine Beecher: A Study of Domesticity* (1973).

Warner, Sam Bass, Jr. *Streetcar Suburbs: The Process of Growth in Boston, 1870–1900* (1962).

Wright, Gwendolyn. *Moralism and the Model Home: Domestic Architecture and Cultural Conflict in Chicago, 1873–1913* (1980).

Chapter 19
General Studies

Armitage, Susan, and Elizabeth Jameson, eds. *The Women's West* (1987).

Butler, Anne M. *Daughters of Joy, Sisters of Misery: Prostitutes in the American West* (1985).

Cronon, William. *Nature's Metropolis: Chicago and the Great West* (1991).

Hine, Robert V. *Community on the American Frontier: Separate But Not Alone* (1980).

Jameson, Elizabeth, and Susan Armitage, eds. *Writing the Range: Race, Class, and Culture in the Women's West* (1997).

Jeffrey, Julie Roy. *Frontier Women* (1998).

Limerick, Patricia Nelson. *The Legacy of Conquest* (1987).

Milner, Clyde A., Carol A. O'Connor, and Martha A. Sandweiss, eds. *The Oxford History of the American West* (1994).

Pascoe, Peggy. *Relations of Rescue: The Search for Female Moral Authority in the American West* (1990).

Riley, Glenda. *A Place to Grow: Women in the American West* (1992).

Robbins, William G. *Colony and Empire: The Capitalist Transformation of the American West* (1994).

West, Elliott. *The Way to the West* (1995).

Worster, Donald. *Rivers of Empire: Water, Aridity, and the Growth of the American West* (1985).

Native Americans

Adams, David W. *Education for Extinction: American Indians and the Boarding School Experience* (1995).

Hoxie, Frederick E. *A Final Promise: The Campaign to Assimilate the Indians, 1880–1920* (2001).

Hutton, Paul. *Phil Sheridan and His Army* (1985).

Iverson, Peter. *Diné: A History of the Navajos* (2002).

Josephy, Alvin M., Jr. *The Nez Percé Indians and the Opening of the Northwest* (1965).

Larson, Robert W. *Red Cloud: Warrior-Statesman of the Lakota Sioux* (1997).

McDonnell, Janet. *The Dispossession of the American Indian* (1991).

Ostler, Jeffrey. *The Plains Sioux and U.S. Colonialism from Lewis and Clark to Wounded Knee* (2004).

Price, Catherine. *The Oglala People, 1841–1879* (1996).

Utley, Robert M. *The Lance and the Shield: The Life and Times of Sitting Bull* (1994).

West, Elliott. *The Contested Plains: Indians, Goldseekers, and the Rush to Colorado* (1998).

Wishart, David. *An Unspeakable Sadness: The Dispossession of the Nebraska Indians* (1994).

Wooster, Robert. *The Military and United States Indian Policy, 1865–1903* (1988).

The Mining Bonanza

Aiken, Katherine G. *Idaho's Bunker Hill: The Rise and Fall of a Great Mining Company* (2005).

Emmons, David. *The Butte Irish: Class and Ethnicity in an American Mining Town* (1989).

James, Ronald, and Elizabeth Raymond, eds. *Comstock Women: The Making of a Mining Community* (1998).

Lingenfelter, Richard. *The Hardrock Miners: A History of the Mining Labor Movement in the American West, 1863–1893* (1974).

Marks, Paula M. *Precious Dust: The American Gold Rush Era* (1994).

Paul, Rodman W. *Mining Frontiers of the Far West, 1848–1880* (1963).

Peterson, Richard H. *The Bonanza Kings: The Social Origins and Business Behavior of Western Mining Entrepreneurs* (1977).

Petrik, Paula. *No Step Backward: Women and Family on the Rocky Mountain Mining Frontier, Helena, Montana* (1987).

Rohrbough, Malcolm. *Aspen: The History of a Silver-Mining Town* (2000).

Smith, Duane A. *Mining America: The Industry and the Environment* (1987).

West, Elliott. *The Saloon on the Rocky Mountain Mining Frontier* (1979).

Zhu, Liping. *A Chinaman's Chance: The Chinese on the Rocky Mountain Mining Frontier* (1997).

The Cattle Kingdom

Atherton, Lewis. *The Cattle Kings* (1961).

Carlson, Paul. *The Cowboy Way* (2000).

Dale, Edward. *The Range Cattle Industry* (1969).

Dary, David. *Cowboy Culture* (1981).

Durham, Philip, and Everett L. Jones. *The Negro Cowboys* (1965).

Dykstra, Robert. *The Cattle Towns* (1968).

Gressley, Gene M. *Bankers and Cattlemen* (1966).

Haywood, C. Robert. *Victorian West: Class and Culture in Kansas Cattle Towns* (1991).

Igler, David. *Industrial Cowboys: Miller & Lux and the Transformation of the Far West* (2001).

Miner, H. Craig. *Wichita: The Early Years, 1865–1880* (1982).

Skaggs, Jimmy M. *The Cattle Trailing Industry* (1973).

Walker, Don D. *Clio's Cowboys* (1981).

The Expansion of Agriculture

Bogue, Allan G. *Money at Interest: The Farm Mortgage on the Middle Border* (1955).

Fite, Gilbert. *The Farmers' Frontier, 1865–1900* (1966).

Garceau, Dee. *The Important Things of Life: Women, Work, and Family in Sweetwater County, Wyoming* (1997).

Handy-Marchello, Barbara. *Women of the Northern Plains: Gender and Settlement on the Homestead Frontier* (2005).

Isern, Thomas. *Bull Threshers and Bindlestiffs: Harvesting and Threshing on the North American Plains* (1990).

Miner, H. Craig. *West of Wichita: Settling the High Plains of Kansas, 1865–1890* (1986).

Nelsen, Jane Taylor, ed. *Prairie Populist: The Memoirs of Luna Kellie* (1992).

Painter, Nell. *Exodusters: Black Migration to Kansas after Reconstruction* (1976).

Pisani, Donald J. *Water, Land, and Law in the West* (1996).

Shannon, Fred A. *The Farmer's Last Frontier: Agriculture, 1860–1897* (1945).

Ethnic and Cultural Frontiers

Camarillo, Albert. *Chicanos in a Changing Society* (1979).

Chan, Sucheng. *This Bittersweet Soil: The Chinese in California Agriculture* (1986).

Deutsch, Sarah. *No Separate Refuge: Culture, Class, and Gender on an Anglo-Hispanic Frontier in the American Southwest* (1987).

Garcia, Mario T. *Desert Immigrants: The Mexicans of El Paso, 1880–1920* (1981).

Gjerde, Jon. *From Peasants to Farmers: The Migration from Balestrand, Norway, to the Upper Midwest* (1985).

McQuillan, D. Aidan. *Prevailing over Time: Ethnic Adjustment on the Kansas Prairies, 1875–1925* (1990).

Takaki, Ronald. *Strangers from a Different Shore: A History of Asian Americans* (1989).

Chapter 20
The Structure and Style of Politics

Argersinger, Peter H. *Structure, Process, and Party* (1992).

Baker, Paula. *The Moral Frameworks of Public Life: Gender, Politics, and the State in Rural New York* (1991).

Bordin, Ruth. *Frances Willard: A Biography* (1986).

Edwards, Rebecca. *Angels in the Machinery: Gender in American Party Politics* (1997).

Gallman, J. Matthew. *America's Joan of Arc: The Life of Anna Elizabeth Dickinson* (2006).

Goldberg, Michael. *An Army of Women: Gender and Politics in Gilded Age Kansas* (1997).

Gustafson, Melanie Susan. *Women and the Republican Party* (2001).

Keyssar, Alexander. *The Right to Vote: The Contested History of Democracy in the United States* (2000).

Kleppner, Paul. *The Third Electoral System, 1853–1892* (1979).

McCormick, Richard L. *The Party Period and Public Policy* (1986).

McGerr, Michael. *The Decline of Popular Politics: The American North, 1865–1928* (1988).

Mead, Rebecca J. *How the Vote Was Won: Woman Suffrage in the Western United States* (2004).

Schneirov, Richard. *Labor and Urban Politics* (1998).

Shafer, Byron, and Anthony Badger. *Contesting Democracy* (2001).

Silbey, Joel. *The American Political Nation, 1838–1893* (1991).

The Limits of Government

Aron, Cindy. *Ladies and Gentlemen of the Civil Service: Middle-Class Workers in Victorian America* (1987).

Brock, William R. *Investigation and Responsibility: Public Responsibility in the United States, 1865–1900* (1984).

Calhoun, Charles W. *The Republican Party and the Southern Question, 1869–1900* (2006).

Campbell, Ballard C. *Representative Democracy: Public Policy and Midwestern Legislatures in the Late Nineteenth Century* (1980).

Hoogenboom, Ari. *Rutherford B. Hayes: Warrior and President* (1996).

Sklar, Kathryn Kish. *Florence Kelley and the Nation's Work: The Rise of Women's Political Culture* (1995).

Skowronek, Stephen. *Building a New American State: The Expansion of National Administrative Capacities* (1982).

Thompson, Margaret S. *The "Spider Web": Congress and Lobbying* (1985).

White, Leonard D. *The Republican Era* (1958).

Public Policies and National Elections

Hoogenboom, Ari. *Outlawing the Spoils: A History of the Civil Service Movement, 1865–1883* (rev. ed., 1982).

Marcus, Robert D. *Grand Old Party: Political Structure in the Gilded Age, 1880–1896* (1971).

Morgan, H. Wayne. *From Hayes to McKinley* (1969).

Reitano, Joanne. *The Tariff Question in the Gilded Age: The Great Debate of 1888* (1995).

Ritter, Gretchen. *Goldbugs and Greenbacks: The Antimonopoly Tradition and the Politics of Finance* (1997).

Socolofsky, Homer E., and Allan B. Spetter. *The Presidency of Benjamin Harrison* (1987).

Sproat, John. *The Best Men: Liberal Reformers in the Gilded Age* (1968).

Summers, Mark. *Rum, Romanism, and Rebellion: The Making of a President, 1884* (2000).

The Crisis of the 1890s

Argersinger, Peter H. *The Limits of Agrarian Radicalism* (1995).

Cantrell, Gregg. *Feeding the Wolf: John B. Rayner and the Politics of Race* (2001).

Glad, Paul. *McKinley, Bryan, and the People* (1964).

Goodwyn, Lawrence. *The Populist Moment* (1978).

Kazin, Michael. *A Godly Hero: The Life of William Jennings Bryan* (2006).

Kousser, J. Morgan. *The Shaping of Southern Politics* (1974).

Larson, Robert W. *Populism in the Mountain West* (1986).

McSeveney, Samuel. *The Politics of Depression* (1972).

Miller, Worth Robert. *Oklahoma Populism* (1987).

Ostler, Jeffrey. *Prairie Populism* (1993).

Postel, Charles. *The Populist Vision* (2007).

Ross, William G. *A Muted Fury: Populists, Progressives, and Labor Unions Confront the Courts* (1994).

Schneirov, Richard, Shelton Stromquist, and Nick Salvatore. *The Pullman Strike and the Crisis of the 1890s* (1999).

Schwantes, Carlos A. *Coxey's Army: An American Odyssey* (1985).

Shaw, Barton. *The Wool-Hat Boys: Georgia's Populist Party* (1984).

Welch, Richard. *The Presidencies of Grover Cleveland* (1988).

Chapter 21
The Ferment of Reform

Blair, Karen. *The Clubwoman as Feminist: True Womanhood Redefined, 1868–1914* (1980).

Brown, Victoria Bissell. *The Education of Jane Addams* (2003).

Chesler, Ellen. *Woman of Valor: The Life of Margaret Sanger* (1992).

Cohen, Nancy. *The Reconstruction of American Liberalism, 1865–1914* (2002).

Coleman, Peter. *Progressivism and the World of Reform* (1987).

Cott, Nancy. *The Grounding of Modern Feminism* (1987).

Curtis, Susan. *A Consuming Faith: The Social Gospel and Modern American Culture* (1991).

Danbom, David B. *"The World of Hope": Progressives and the Struggle for an Ethical Public Life* (1987).

Dubofsky, Melvyn. *We Shall Be All: A History of the Industrial Workers of the World* (1969).

Flanagan, Maureen. *Seeing with Their Hearts: Chicago Women and the Vision of the Good City* (2002).

Marsden, George. *Fundamentalism and American Culture* (1980).

McArthur, Judith N. *Creating the New Woman: The Rise of Southern Women's Progressive Culture in Texas* (1998).

McGerr, Michael. *A Fierce Discontent: The Rise and Fall of the Progressive Movement in America* (2003).

Peiss, Kathy. *Cheap Amusements: Working Women and Leisure in Turn-of-the-Century New York* (1986).

Rodgers, Daniel. *Atlantic Crossings: Social Politics in a Progressive Age* (1998).

Salvatore, Nick. *Eugene V. Debs: Citizen and Socialist* (1982).

Shore, Elliott. *Talkin' Socialism: J. A. Wayland and the Role of the Press in American Radicalism* (1988).

Sklar, Kathryn Kish. *Florence Kelley and the Nation's Work* (1995).

Wheeler, Margaret Spruill. *New Women of the New South* (1993).

Reforming Society

Barron, Hal S. *Mixed Harvest: The Second Great Transformation in the Rural North* (1997).

Boyer, Paul. *Urban Masses and Moral Order in America* (1978).

Carson, Mina. *Settlement Folk: Social Thought and the American Settlement Movement* (1990).

Crocker, Ruth H. *Social Work and Social Order* (1992).

Danbom, David. *The Resisted Revolution: Urban America and the Industrialization of Agriculture* (1979).

Davis, Allen F. *American Heroine: The Life and Legend of Jane Addams* (1973).

Davis, Allen F. *Spearheads of Reform: The Social Settlements and the Progressive Movement* (1968).

Derickson, Alan. *Workers' Health, Workers' Democracy* (1988).

Deverell, William, and Tom Sitton. *California Progressivism Revisited* (1994).

Dorsett, Lyle. *Billy Sunday and the Redemption of Urban America* (1991).

Dye, Nancy S. *As Equals and as Sisters: Feminism, the Labor Movement, and the Women's Trade Union League of New York* (1980).

Frankel, Noralee, and Nancy S. Dye. *Gender, Class, Race, and Reform in the Progressive Era* (1991).

Gorn, Elliott. *Mother Jones: The Most Dangerous Woman in America* (2001).

Hamm, Richard. *Shaping the Eighteenth Amendment* (1995).

Ladd-Taylor, Molly. *Mother-Work: Women, Child Welfare, and the State, 1890–1930* (1994).

Lindenmeyer, Kriste. *A Right to Childhood: The U.S. Children's Bureau and Child Welfare* (1997).

Link, William A. *The Paradox of Southern Progressivism* (1992).

Lubove, Roy. *The Progressives and the Slums* (1962).

Muncy, Robyn. *Creating a Female Dominion in American Reform, 1890–1935* (1991).

Nelson, Daniel. *Frederick W. Taylor and the Rise of Scientific Management* (1980).

Payne, Elizabeth Anne. *Reform, Labor, and Feminism: Margaret Dreier Robins and the Women's Trade Union League* (1988).

Southern, David. *The Progressive Era and Race: Reaction and Reform* (2005).

Tate, Cassandra. *Cigarette Wars: The Triumph of "The Little White Slaver"* (1999).

Timberlake, James. *Prohibition and the Progressive Movement* (1963).

Willrich, Michael. *City of Courts: Socializing Justice in Progressive Era Chicago* (2003).

Reforming Politics and Government

Allswang, John M. *The Initiative and Referendum in California* (2000).

Buenker, John D. *Urban Liberalism and Progressive Reform* (1973).

DuBois, Ellen Carol. *Harriot Stanton Blatch and the Winning of Woman Suffrage* (1997).

Goebel, Thomas. *A Government by the People: Direct Democracy in America* (2002).

Graham, Sara Hunter. *Woman Suffrage and the New Democracy* (1996).

Grantham, Dewey. *Southern Progressivism* (1983).

Gustafson, Melanie S. *Women and the Republican Party* (2001).

Johnston, Robert D. *The Radical Middle Class: Populist Democracy and the Question of Capitalism in Progressive Era Portland, Oregon* (2003).

Kousser, J. Morgan. *The Shaping of Southern Politics* (1974).

McCormick, Richard L. *From Realignment to Reform: Political Change in New York State, 1893–1910* (1983).

McGerr, Michael E. *The Decline of Popular Politics* (1986).

Mead, Rebecca J. *How the Vote Was Won: Woman Suffrage in the Western United States* (2004).

Pegram, Thomas. *Partisans and Progressives* (1992).

Reynolds, John F. *Testing Democracy: Electoral Behavior and Progressive Reform in New Jersey* (1988).

Schiesl, Martin. *The Politics of Efficiency: Municipal Administration and Reform in America* (1977).

Thelen, David P. *The New Citizenship: Origins of Progressivism in Wisconsin* (1972).

Unger, Nancy. *Fighting Bob La Follette: The Righteous Reformer* (2000).

Wright, James E. *The Progressive Yankees: Republican Reformers in New Hampshire* (1987).

Theodore Roosevelt and the Progressive Presidency

Blum, John M. *The Republican Roosevelt* (1954).

Brands, H. W. *T.R.: The Last Romantic* (1997).

Burton, David. *The Learned Presidency: Theodore Roosevelt, William Howard Taft, Woodrow Wilson* (1988).

Dalton, Kathleen. *Theodore Roosevelt: A Strenuous Life* (2002).

Hays, Samuel P. *Conservation and the Gospel of Efficiency: The Progressive Conservation Movement* (1962).

Keller, Morton. *Regulating a New Economy* (1990).

Kolko, Gabriel. *The Triumph of Conservatism* (1963).

Morris, Edmund. *Theodore Rex* (2002).

Rauchway, Eric. *Murdering McKinley: The Making of Theodore Roosevelt's America* (2003).

Righter, Robert. *The Battle over Hetch Hetchy* (2005).

Sanders, Elizabeth. *Roots of Reform: Farmers, Workers, and the American State* (1999).

Sklar, Martin. *The Corporate Reconstruction of American Capitalism* (1988).

Woodrow Wilson and Progressive Reform

Blum, John M. *Woodrow Wilson and the Politics of Morality* (1956).

Clements, Kendrick A. *The Presidency of Woodrow Wilson* (1992).

Cooper, John Milton, Jr. *The Warrior and the Priest: Woodrow Wilson and Theodore Roosevelt* (1983).

Gould, Lewis L. *Reform and Regulation: American Politics from Roosevelt to Wilson* (1996).

Hecksher, August. *Woodrow Wilson* (1991).

Link, Arthur. *Woodrow Wilson and the Progressive Era* (1954).

Livingston, James. *Origins of the Federal Reserve System* (1986).

Sarasohn, David. *The Party of Reform: Democrats in the Progressive Era* (1989).

Thompson, John A. *Woodrow Wilson* (2002).

Urofsky, Melvin. *Louis D. Brandeis and the Progressive Tradition* (1981).

Chapter 22
The Roots of Imperialism

Anderson, David L. *Imperialism and Idealism: American Diplomats in China, 1861–1898* (1985).

Anderson, Stuart. *Race and Rapprochement: Anglo-Saxonism and Anglo-American Relations, 1895–1904* (1981).

Crapol, Edward P. *James G. Blaine: Architect of Empire* (2000).

Hearden, Patrick J. *Independence and Empire: The New South's Cotton Mill Campaign, 1865–1901* (1982).

Hill, Patricia R. *The World Their Household: The American Woman's Foreign Mission Movement and Cultural Transformation, 1870–1920* (1985).

Hunt, Michael H. *Ideology and U.S. Foreign Policy* (1987).

Hunter, Jane. *The Gospel of Gentility: American Women Missionaries in Turn-of-the-Century China* (1984).

Jacobson, Matthew Frye. *Barbarian Virtues: The United States Encounters Foreign Peoples at Home and Abroad* (2000).

Paolino, Ernest. *The Foundations of the American Empire: William Henry Seward and U.S. Foreign Policy* (1973).

Plesur, Milton. *America's Outward Thrust: Approaches to Foreign Affairs, 1865–1890* (1971).

Rosenberg, Emily S. *Spreading the American Dream: American Economic and Cultural Expansion, 1890–1945* (1982).

Shulman, Mark R. *Navalism and the Emergence of American Seapower, 1882–1893* (1995).

Widenor, William. *Henry Cabot Lodge and the Search for an American Foreign Policy* (1980).

Williams, William A. *The Roots of the Modern American Empire* (1969).

The Spanish-American War

Challener, Richard. *Admirals, Generals, and American Foreign Policy, 1889–1914* (1973).

Cosmas, Graham A. *An Army for Empire: The United States Army and the Spanish-American War* (1971).

Dobson, John. *Reticent Expansionism: The Foreign Policy of William McKinley* (1988).

Gatewood, Willard B. Jr. *Black Americans and the White Man's Burden, 1898–1903* (1975).

Gould, Lewis L. *The Spanish-American War and President McKinley* (1982).

Healy, David F. *U.S. Expansionism: The Imperialist Urge in the 1890s* (1970).

Linderman, Gerald. *The Mirror of War: American Society and the Spanish-American War* (1974).

McCartney, Paul T. *Power and Progress: American National Identity, the War of 1898, and the Rise of American Imperialism* (2006).

Milton, Joyce. *The Yellow Journalists* (1989).

Morgan, H. Wayne. *America's Road to Empire: The War with Spain and Overseas Expansion* (1965).

Offner, John. *An Unwanted War: The Diplomacy of the United States and Spain Over Cuba* (1992).

Schoonover, Thomas. *Uncle Sam's War of 1898 and the Origins of Globalization* (2003).

Trask, David R. *The War with Spain in 1898* (1981).

Anti-Imperialism

Beisner, Robert L. *Twelve against Empire: The Anti-Imperialists, 1898–1900* (1968).

Osborne, Thomas J. *"Empire Can Wait": American Opposition to Hawaiian Annexation, 1893–1898* (1981).

Schirmer, Daniel B. *Republic or Empire: American Resistance to the Philippine War* (1972).

Tompkins, E. Berkeley. *Anti-Imperialism in the United States: The Great Debate, 1890–1920* (1970).

Imperial Ambitions: The United States and East Asia, 1899–1917

Cohen, Warren I. *America's Response to China* (1989).

Gates, John M. *Schoolbooks and Krags: The United States Army in the Philippines* (1973).

Hunt, Michael H. *The Making of a Special Relationship: The U.S. and China to 1914* (1983).

Iriye, Akira. *Pacific Estrangement: Japanese and American Expansion, 1897–1911* (1972).

Kramer, Paul A. *The Blood of Government: Race, Empire, the United States, and the Philippines* (2006).

Linn, Brian. *The Philippine War, 1899–1902* (2000).

McCormick, Thomas. *China Market: America's Quest for Informal Empire* (1967).

Miller, Stuart. *"Benevolent Assimilation": The American Conquest of the Philippines, 1899–1903* (1982).

Pletcher, David M. *The Diplomacy of Involvement: American Economic Expansion across the Pacific, 1784–1900* (2001).

Welch, Richard E. *Response to Imperialism: The United States and the Philippine-American War* (1979).

Imperial Power: The United States and Latin America, 1899–1917

Beale, Howard K. *Theodore Roosevelt and the Rise of America to World Power* (1956).

Benjamin, Jules. *Hegemony and Development: The United States and Cuba, 1890–1934* (1977).

Calder, Bruce. *The Impact of Intervention: The Dominican Republic during the U.S. Occupation of 1916 to 1924* (1984).

Carr, Raymond. *Puerto Rico: A Colonial Experiment* (1984).

Carrion, Arturo Morales. *Puerto Rico* (1983).

Cooper, John M., Jr. *The Warrior and the Priest: Woodrow Wilson and Theodore Roosevelt* (1983).

Eisenhower, John. *The United States and the Mexican Revolution, 1913–1917* (1993).

Healy, David F. *Drive to Hegemony: The United States in the Caribbean, 1898–1917* (1988).

Hitchman, James. *Leonard Wood and Cuban Independence, 1898–1902* (1971).

LaFeber, Walter. *Inevitable Revolutions: The United States in Central America* (1993).

LaFeber, Walter. *The Panama Canal* (1990).

Langley, Lester. *The Banana Wars: An Inner History of the American Empire, 1900–1934* (1983).

McCullough, David. *The Path between the Seas: The Creation of the Panama Canal* (1977).

Millett, Allan R. *The Politics of Intervention: The Military Occupation of Cuba, 1906–1909* (1968).

Perez, Louis A., Jr. *Cuba under the Platt Amendment, 1902–1934* (1986).

Chapter 23
General Studies
Chambers, John Whiteclay II. *The Tyranny of Change* (1992).

Clayton, James D., and Anne Sharp Wells. *America and the Great War, 1914–1920* (1998).

Cooper, John M., Jr. *Pivotal Decades: The United States, 1900–1920* (1990).

Gilbert, Martin. *The First World War: A Complete History* (1994).

Hawley, Ellis W. *The Great War and the Search for a Modern Order* (1992).

Lyons, Michael J. *World War I: A Short History* (1994).

Wynn, Neil. *From Progressivism to Prosperity: World War I and American Society* (1986).

Diplomacy of Neutrality, War, and Peace
Ambrosius, Lloyd. *Woodrow Wilson and the American Diplomatic Tradition* (1987).

Bailey, Thomas A., and Paul B. Ryan. *The Lusitania Disaster* (1975).

Burk, Kathleen. *Britain, America, and the Sinews of War* (1985).

Coogan, John. *The End of Neutrality* (1981).

Cooper, John M., Jr. *Breaking the Heart of the World: Woodrow Wilson and the Fight for the League of Nations* (2001).

Foglesong, David S. *America's Secret War against Bolshevism: United States Intervention in the Russian Civil War, 1917–1920* (1995).

Gardner, Lloyd. *Safe for Democracy: The Anglo-American Response to Revolution, 1913–1923* (1984).

Gregory, Ross. *The Origins of American Intervention in the First World War* (1971).

Kaufman, Burton I. *Efficiency and Expansion: Foreign Trade Organization in the Wilson Administration* (1974).

Knock, Thomas J. *To End All Wars: Woodrow Wilson and the Creation of the League of Nations* (1992).

Levin, N. Gordon, Jr. *Woodrow Wilson and World Politics: America's Response to War and Revolution* (1968).

Levine, Lawrence W. *Defender of the Faith: William Jennings Bryan, the Last Decade* (1965).

May, Ernest R. *The World War and American Isolation, 1914–1917* (1966).

McFadden, David W. *Alternative Paths: Soviets and Americans, 1917–1920* (1993).

Stone, Ralph A. *The Irreconcilables* (1970).

Thompson, John A. *Woodrow Wilson* (2002).

Walworth, Arthur. *Wilson and the Peacemakers* (1986).

The Military
Barbeau, A. E., and Florette Henri. *The Unknown Soldiers: Black American Troops in World War I* (1974).

Bristow, Nancy. *Making Men Moral: Social Engineering during the Great War* (1996).

Chambers, John Whiteclay II. *To Raise an Army* (1987).

Coffman, Edward M. *The Hilt of the Sword: The Career of Peyton C. March* (1966).

Mead, Gary. *Doughboys: America and the First World War* (2000).

Patton, Gerald W. *War and Race: The Black Officer in the American Military* (1981).

Stallings, Laurence. *The Doughboys: The Story of the AEF, 1917–1918* (1963).

Trask, David. *The AEF and Coalition Warmaking, 1917–1918* (1993).

Vandiver, Frank E. *Black Jack: The Life and Times of John J. Pershing* (1977).

Zeiger, Susan. *In Uncle Sam's Service: Women Workers with the American Expeditionary Force, 1917–1919* (1999).

Wartime Economy and Society
Breen, William J. *Uncle Sam at Home: Civilian Mobilization, Wartime Federalism, and the Council of National Defense, 1917–1919* (1984).

Britten, Thomas. *American Indians in World War I: At Home and at War* (1997).

Brown, Carrie. *Rosie's Mom: Forgotten Women Workers of the First World War* (2002).

Connor, Valerie. *The National War Labor Board* (1983).

Cuff, Robert D. *The War Industries Board: Business-Government Relations during World War I* (1973).

Danbom, David. *The Resisted Revolution: Urban America and the Industrialization of Agriculture* (1979).

DeBauche, Leslie M. *Reel Patriotism: The Movies and World War I* (1997).

Greenwald, Maurine Weiner. *Women, War, and Work: The Impact of World War I on Women Workers in the United States* (1980).

Haydu, Jeffrey. *Making American Industries Safe for Democracy* (1997).

Henri, Florette. *Black Migration: The Movement North, 1900–1920* (1975).

Koistinen, Paul. *Mobilizing for Modern War: The Political Economy of American Warfare, 1865–1919* (1997).

Luebke, Frederick C. *Bonds of Loyalty: German-Americans and World War I* (1974).

McCartin, Joseph A. *Labor's Great War: The Struggle for Industrial Democracy and the Origins of Modern American Labor Relations, 1912–1921* (1997).

Rudwick, Elliot M. *Race Riot at East St. Louis, July 2, 1917* (1964).

Thompson, John A. *Reformers and War: American Progressive Publicists and the First World War* (1987).

Vaughn, Stephen L. *Holding Fast the Inner Lines: Democracy, Nationalism, and the Committee on Public Information* (1980).

Wartime Dissent and Repression

Early, Frances R. *A World without War: How U.S. Feminists and Pacifists Resisted World War I* (1997).

Gibbs, Christopher. *The Great Silent Majority: Missouri's Resistance to World War I* (1989).

Kennedy, Kathleen. *Disloyal Mothers and Scurrilous Citizens: Women and Subversion during World War I* (1999).

Morlan, Robert. *Political Prairie Fire: The Nonpartisan League, 1915–1922* (1955).

Peterson, H. C., and Gilbert Fite. *Opponents of War, 1917–1918* (1957).

Preston, William, Jr. *Aliens and Dissenters: Federal Suppression of Radicals, 1903–1933* (1963).

Weinstein, James. *The Decline of Socialism in America* (1967).

Postwar Conflict

Brody, David. *Labor in Crisis: The Steel Strike of 1919* (1965).

Coben, Stanley A. *A. Mitchell Palmer, Politician* (1963).

Ellsworth, Scott. *Death in a Promised Land: The Tulsa Race Riot of 1921* (1992).

Frank, Dana. *Purchasing Power: Consumer Organizing, Gender, and the Seattle Labor Movement. 1919–1929* (1994).

Noggle, Burl. *Into the Twenties: The United States from Armistice to Normalcy* (1974).

Theoharis, Athan, and John Stuart Cox. *The Boss: J. Edgar Hoover and the Great American Inquisition* (1988).

Tuttle, William M., Jr. *Race Riot: Chicago in the Red Summer of 1919* (1970).

Chapter 24
General Studies

Hicks, John D. *Republican Ascendancy, 1921–1933* (1960).

Leuchtenberg, William. *The Perils of Prosperity* (1958).

Parrish, Michael E. *Anxious Decades: America in Prosperity and Depression, 1920–1941* (1992).

Perrett, Geoffrey. *America in the Twenties* (1982).

Economic Developments

Argersinger, Jo Ann E. *Making the Amalgamated: Gender, Ethnicity, and Class in the Baltimore Clothing Industry* (1999).

Bernstein, Irving L. *The Lean Years: A History of the American Worker, 1920–1933* (1960).

Flink, James J. *The Automobile Age* (1988).

Kessler-Harris, Alice. *Out to Work: A History of Wage-Earning Women* (1982).

Marchand, Roland. *Creating the Corporate Soul: The Rise of Public Relations and Corporate Imagery in American Big Business* (1998).

Meyer, Stephen III. *The Five Dollar Day: Labor Management and Social Control in the Ford Motor Company* (1981).

Smulyan, Susan. *Selling Radio: The Commercialization of American Broadcasting, 1920–1934* (1994).

Strasser, Susan. *Satisfaction Guaranteed: The Making of the American Mass Market* (1989).

Zahavi, Gerald. *Workers, Managers, and Welfare Capitalism* (1988).

Politics and Government

Burner, David. *Herbert Hoover: A Public Life* (1979).

Clements, Kendrick A. *Hoover, Conservation, and Consumerism: Engineering the Good Life* (2000).

Craig, Douglas B. *After Wilson: The Struggle for the Democratic Party* (1992).

Hawley, Ellis W., ed. *Herbert Hoover as Secretary of Commerce* (1981).

LaFeber, Walter. *Inevitable Revolutions: The United States in Central America* (1984).

Lichtman, Allan J. *Prejudice and the Old Politics: The Presidential Election of 1928* (1979).

Lowitt, Richard. *George W. Norris: The Persistence of a Progressive* (1971).

McCoy, Donald R. *Calvin Coolidge* (1967).

Murray, Robert. *The Politics of Normalcy* (1973).

Perry, Elisabeth Israels. *Belle Moskowitz: Feminine Politics & The Exercise of Power in the Age of Alfred E. Smith* (1987).

Schulzinger, Robert D. *The Making of the Diplomatic Mind* (1975).

Trani, Eugene P., and David L. Wilson. *The Presidency of Warren G. Harding* (1977).

Wilson, Joan Hoff. *American Business and Foreign Policy, 1920–1933* (1968).

Wilson, Joan Hoff. *Herbert Hoover: Forgotten Progressive* (1975).

Cities and Suburbs

Deutsch, Sarah. *No Separate Refuge: Culture, Class, and Gender on an Anglo-Hispanic Frontier in the American Southwest* (1987).

Garcia, Juan. *Mexicans in the Midwest, 1900–1932* (1996).

Goldfield, David. *Cotton Fields and Skyscrapers* (1982).

Gottlieb, Peter. *Making Their Own Way: Southern Blacks' Migration to Pittsburgh, 1916–30* (1987).

Hogan, David Gerard. *Selling 'em by the Sack: White Castle and the Creation of American Food* (1997).

Jackson, Kenneth T. *Crabgrass Frontier: The Suburbanization of the United States* (1985).

Lewis, Earl. *In Their Own Interests: Race, Class, and Power in Twentieth-Century Norfolk, Virginia* (1991).

Osofsky, Gilbert. *Harlem: The Making of a Ghetto* (1968).

Romo, Ricardo. *East Los Angeles: History of a Barrio* (1983).

Teaford, John C. *Cities of the Heartland* (1993).

Worley, William. *J. C. Nichols and the Shaping of Kansas City* (1990).

Society and Culture

Alexander, Charles C. *The Ku Klux Klan in the Southwest* (1965).

Blee, Kathleen M. *Women and the Klan: Racism and Gender in the 1920s* (1991).

Clark, Norman. *Deliver Us from Evil: An Interpretation of American Prohibition* (1976).

Coben, Stanley. *Rebellion against Victorianism* (1991).

Cott, Nancy F. *The Grounding of American Feminism* (1987).

Ewen, Stuart. *Captains of Consciousness: Advertising and the Social Roots of the Consumer Culture* (1976).

Fass, Paula. *The Damned and the Beautiful: American Youth in the 1920s* (1977).

Flanagan, Maureen A. *Seeing With Their Hearts: Chicago Women and the Vision of the Good City, 1871–1933* (2002).

Hobson, Fred. *Mencken: A Life* (1994).

Huggins, Nathan. *Harlem Renaissance* (1971).

Jackson, Kenneth T. *The Ku Klux Klan in the City* (1967).

Jacobson, Matthew Frye. *Whiteness of a Different Color: European Immigrants and the Alchemy of Race* (1998).

Laird, Pamela Walker. *Advertising Progress: American Business and the Rise of Consumer Marketing* (1998).

Latham, Angela J. *Posing a Threat: Flappers, Chorus Girls, and Other Brazen Perfomers of the American 1920s* (2000).

Lawrence, Bruce B. *Defenders of God: The Fundamentalist Revolt against the Modern Age* (1989).

Levine, Lawrence W. *Defender of the Faith: William Jennings Bryan, the Last Decade, 1915–1925* (1965).

Lewis, David L. *When Harlem Was in Vogue* (1981).

Maclean, Nancy. *Behind the Mask of Chivalry: The Making of the Second Ku Klux Klan* (1994).

May, Lary. *Screening Out the Past: The Birth of Mass Culture and the Motion Picture Industry* (1980).

Moore, Leonard. *Citizen Klansmen: The Ku Klux Klan in Indiana* (1991).

Muncy, Robyn. *Creating a Female Dominion in American Reform* (1991).

Ogren, Kathy H. *The Jazz Revolution: Twenties America and the Meaning of Jazz* (1989).

Payne, Elizabeth A. *Reform, Labor, and Feminism: Margaret Dreier Robins and the Women's Trade Union League* (1988).

Pegram, Thomas R. *Battling Demon Rum: The Struggle for a Dry America, 1800–1933* (1998).

Rader, Benjamin G. *American Sports: From the Age of Folk Games to the Age of Spectators* (1983).

Sklar, Robert. *Movie-Made America: A Cultural History of American Movies* (1994).

Stein, Judith. *The World of Marcus Garvey* (1986).

Wiggins, David. *Sport in America* (1995).

Chapter 25
Hard Times in Hooverville

Bernstein, Michael. *The Great Depression* (1987).

Blackwelder, Julia Kirk. *Women of the Depression: Caste and Culture in San Antonio* (1984).

Chafe, William H. *The American Woman, 1920–1970* (1972).

Galbraith, John Kenneth. *The Great Crash: 1929* (1989).

Garraty, John. *The Great Depression* (1986).

Kelley, Robin D. G. *Hammer and Hoe: Alabama Communists during the Great Depression* (1990).

Klein, Maury. *Rainbow's End: The Crash of 1929* (2001).

McElvaine, Robert. *The Great Depression: America, 1929–1941* (1984).

Mullins, William. *The Depression and the Urban West Coast, 1929–1933* (1991).

Reisler, Mark. *By the Sweat of Their Brow: Mexican Immigrant Labor in the United States* (1976).

Scharf, Lois. *To Work and to Wed: Female Employment, Feminism, and the Great Depression* (1980).

Shover, John. *Cornbelt Rebellion: The Farmers' Holiday Association* (1965).

Herbert Hoover and the Depression

Burner, David. *Herbert Hoover: A Public Life* (1979).

Daniels, Roger. *The Bonus March* (1971).

Fausold, Martin L. *The Presidency of Herbert C. Hoover* (1985).

Hamilton, David E. *From New Day to New Deal: American Farm Policy from Hoover to Roosevelt* (1991).

Lisio, Donald. *The President and Protest* (1974).

Romasco, Albert. *The Poverty of Abundance: Hoover, the Nation, the Depression* (1965).

Schwartz, Jordan A. *Interregnum of Despair* (1970).

Watkins, T. H. *The Hungry Years: A Narrative History of the Great Depression in America* (1999).

Wilson, Joan Hoff. *Herbert Hoover: Forgotten Progressive* (1975).

Launching the New Deal

Badger, Anthony J. *The New Deal: The Depression Years, 1933–1940* (1989).

Bernstein, Irving. *Turbulent Years: A History of the American Worker, 1933–1941* (1970).

Blackorby, Edward C. *Prairie Rebel: William Lemke* (1963).

Brinkley, Alan. *Voices of Protest: Huey Long, Father Coughlin, and the Great Depression* (1982).

Conrad, David. *The Forgotten Farmers: The Story of the Sharecroppers in the New Deal* (1965).

Freidel, Frank. *Franklin D. Roosevelt: A Rendezvous with Destiny* (1990).

Grubbs, Donald H. *Cry from the Cotton: The Southern Tenant Farmers Union and the New Deal* (1971).

Hawley, Ellis. *The New Deal and the Problem of Monopoly* (1966).

Leuchtenburg, William. *The FDR Years* (1995).

Ribuffo, Leo P. *The Old Christian Right: The Protestant Far Right from the Great Depression to the Cold War* (1983).

Romasco, Albert. *The Politics of Recovery: Roosevelt's New Deal* (1983).

Saloutos, Theodore. *The American Farmer and the New Deal* (1982).

Williams, T. Harry. *Huey Long* (1969).

Consolidating the New Deal

Allswang, John. *The New Deal and American Politics* (1978).

Andersen, Kristi. *The Creation of a Democratic Majority* (1979).

Berkowitz, Edward D. *America's Welfare State* (1991).

Biles, Roger. *A New Deal for the American People* (1991).

Gamm, Gerald. *The Making of New Deal Democrats* (1989).

Gordon, Colin. *New Deals: Business, Labor, and Politics in America* (1994).

McCoy, Donald R. *Landon of Kansas* (1966).

McJimsey, George. *Harry Hopkins* (1987).

The New Deal and American Life

Argersinger, Jo Ann E. *Toward a New Deal in Baltimore: People and Government in the Great Depression* (1988).

Barnard, John. *Walter Reuther and the Rise of the Auto Workers* (1983).

Biles, Roger. *The South and the New Deal* (1994).

Cohen, Lisabeth. *Making a New Deal: Industrial Workers in Chicago* (1990).

Faue, Elizabeth. *Community of Suffering and Struggle: Women, Men, and the Labor Movement in Minneapolis* (1991).

Fine, Sidney. *Sitdown: The General Motors Strike of 1936–1937* (1969).

Fraser, Steven. *Labor Will Rule: Sidney Hillman and the Rise of American Labor* (1991).

Gregory, James. *American Exodus: The Dust Bowl Migration and Okie Culture in California* (1989).

Gutierrez, David G. *Walls and Mirrors: Mexican Americans, Mexican Immigrants, and the Politics of Ethnicity* (1995).

Kelly, Laurence C. *The Assault on Assimilation: John Collier and the Origins of Indian Policy Reform* (1983).

Lichtenstein, Nelson. *The Most Dangerous Man in Detroit: Walter Reuther and the Fate of American Labor* (1995).

Lowitt, Richard. *The New Deal and the West* (1984).

Mink, Gwendolyn. *The Wages of Motherhood: Inequality in the Welfare State, 1917–1942* (1995).

Sitkoff, Harvard. *A New Deal for Blacks* (1978).

Smith, Douglas L. *The New Deal in the Urban South* (1988).

Stock, Catherine. *Main Street in Crisis: The Great Depression and the Old Middle Class on the Northern Plains* (1992).

Taylor, Graham. *The New Deal and American Indian Tribalism* (1980).

Ware, Susan. *Beyond Suffrage: Women in the New Deal* (1981).

Ware, Susan. *Holding Their Own: American Women in the 1930s* (1982).

Worster, Donald. *Dust Bowl* (1979).

Worster, Donald. *Rivers of Empire* (1985).

Zieger, Robert. *The CIO, 1935–1955* (1995).

Zieger, Robert. *John L. Lewis* (1988).

Ebbing of the New Deal

Brinkley, Alan. *The End of Reform: New Deal Liberalism in Recession and War* (1995).

Cole, Wayne. *Roosevelt and the Isolationists, 1932–1945* (1983).

Dallek, Robert. *Franklin Delano Roosevelt and American Foreign Policy, 1932–1945* (1979).

Davis, Kenneth S. *FDR: Into the Storm, 1937–1940* (1993).

Heinrichs, Waldo. *Threshold of War: Franklin D. Roosevelt and American Entry into World War II* (1988).

Leff, Mark. *The Limits of Symbolic Reform: The New Deal and Taxation* (1984).

Lipstadt, Deborah E. *Beyond Belief: The American Press and the Coming of the Holocaust, 1933–1945* (1986).

Mettler, Suzanne. *Dividing Citizens: Gender and Federalism in New Deal Public Works* (1998).

Patterson, James T. *Congressional Conservatism and the New Deal* (1967).

Patterson, James T. *The New Deal and the States* (1969).

Storrs, Landon R. Y. *Civilizing Capitalism: The National Consumers' League, Women's Activism, and Labor Standards in the New Deal Era* (2000).

Chapter 26
The Politics of War

Dallek, Robert. *Franklin D. Roosevelt and American Foreign Policy, 1932–1945* (1979).

Doenecke, Justus D. *Storm on the Horizon: The Challenge to American Intervention, 1939–1941* (2000).

Iriye, Akira. *Power and Culture: The Japanese-American War, 1941–1945* (1981).

Kimball, Warren. *The Juggler: Franklin Roosevelt as Wartime Statesman* (1991).

Reynolds, David. *From Munich to Pearl Harbor: Roosevelt, America, and the Origins of the Second World War* (2001).

Schneider, James. *Should America Go to War? The Debate over Foreign Policy in Chicago, 1939–1941* (1989).

Military Operations

Beevor, Anthony. *Stalingrad* (1998).

Chappell, John D. *Before the Bomb: How Americans Approached the Pacific War* (1997).

Keegan, John. *Six Armies in Normandy; From D-Day to the Liberation of Paris* (1982).

Morrison, Samuel Eliot. *The Two-Ocean War: A Short History of the United States Navy in the Second World War* (1963).

Prange, Gordon. *At Dawn We Slept: The Untold Story of Pearl Harbor* (1981).

Spector, Ronald H. *Eagle against the Sun: The American War with Japan* (1985).

Syrett, David. *The Defeat of the German U-Boats: The Battle of the Atlantic* (1994).

Tuchman, Barbara W. *Stillwell and the American Experience in China, 1911–1945* (1970).

Weinberg, Gerhard. *A World at Arms: A Global History of World War II* (1994).

The Experience of War

Ambrose, Stephen. *Citizen Soldiers: The U.S. Army from the Normandy Beaches to the Bulge to the Surrender of Germany, June 7, 1944–May 7, 1945* (1997).

Cameron, Craig M. *American Samurai: Myth, Imagination, and the Conduct of Battle in the First Marine Division, 1941–1951* (1994).

Doubler, Michael. *Closing with the Enemy: How GIs Fought the War in Europe, 1944–1945* (1994).

Fussell, Paul. *Wartime: Understanding and Behavior in the Second World War* (1989).

Leinbaugh, Harold P., and John D. Campbell. *The Men of Company K: The Autobiography of a World War II Rifle Company* (1985).

Manchester, William. *Goodbye Darkness: A Memoir of the Pacific War* (1980).

Moore, Christopher Paul. *Fighting for America: Black Soldiers—the Unsung Heroes of World War II* (2005).

Schrijvers, Peter. *The Crash of Ruin: American Combat Soldiers in Europe during World War II* (1996).

Sledge, E. B. *With the Old Breed at Peleliu and Okinawa* (1981).

Mobilizing the Home Front

Blum, John M. *V Was for Victory: Politics and American Culture during World War II* (1976).

Dew, Stephen. *The Queen City at War: Charlotte, North Carolina during World War II* (2001).

Doherty, Thomas. *Projections of War: Hollywood, American Culture, and World War II* (1994).

Goodwin, Doris Kearns. *No Ordinary Time: Franklin and Eleanor Roosevelt, the Home Front in World War II* (1994).

Johnson, Marilynn. *The Second Gold Rush* (1993).

Koppes, Clayton, and Gregory Black. *Hollywood Goes to War* (1987).

Lichtenstein, Nelson. *Labor's War at Home: The CIO in World War II* (1983).

Nash, Gerald. *The American West Transformed: The Impact of the Second World War* (1985).

Newton, Wesley P. *Montgomery in the Good War: Portrait of a Southern City, 1939–1946* (2000).

O'Neill, William L. *A Democracy at War: America's Fight at Home and Abroad in World War II* (1993).

Polenberg, Richard. *War and Society: The United States, 1941–1945* (1972).

Rhodes, Richard. *The Making of the Atomic Bomb* (1986).

Vatter, Harold. *The U.S. Economy in World War II* (1985).

Women and the War Effort

Anderson, Karen. *Wartime Women: Sex Roles, Family Relations, and the Status of Women during World War II* (1981).

Campbell, D'Ann. *Women at War with America: Private Lives in a Patriotic Era* (1984).

Hartmann, Susan. *The Home Front and Beyond: American Women in the 1940s* (1982).

Kesselman, Amy. *Fleeting Opportunities: Women in Portland and Vancouver Shipyards during World War II and Reconversion* (1990).

Litoff, Judy Barrett. *We're in This War Too: World War II Letters of American Women in Uniform* (1994).

Racial Attitudes and U.S. Policy

Daniels, Roger. *Concentration Camps U.S.A.: Japanese Americans and World War II* (1971).

Dower, John. *War without Mercy: Race and Power in the Pacific War* (1986).

Capeci, Dominic J., Jr. *Race Relations in Wartime Detroit: The Sojourner Truth Controversy of 1942* (1984).

Pagán, Jose Obregón. *Murder at Sleepy Lagoon: Zoot Suits, Race and Riot in Wartime Los Alamos* (2004).

Wyman, David S. *The Abandonment of the Jews: America and the Holocaust, 1941–1945* (1984).

Chapter 27
Foreign and Military Policy

Behrman, Greg. *The Most Noble Adventure: The Marshall Plan and the Time When America Helped Save Europe* (2007).

Beisner, Robert. *Dean Acheson: A Life in the Cold War* (2006).

Gaddis, John L. *The United States and the Cold War* (1992).

Herken, Greg *The Winning Weapon: The Atomic Bomb in the Cold War, 1945–1950* (1980).

Hogan, Michael. *Cross of Iron: Harry S Truman and the Origins of the National Security State, 1945–1954* (1998).

Hogan, Michael. *The Marshall Plan* (1987).

Lawrence, Mark. *Assuming the Burden: Europe and the American Commitment to War in Vietnam* (2005).

Le Feber, Walter. *America, Russia, and the Cold War* (1985).

May, Ernest R. ed. *American Cold War Strategy: Interpreting NSC-68* (1993).

Offner, Arnold. *Another Such Victory: President Truman and the Cold War* (2002).

Paterson, Thomas G. *On Every Front: The Making of the Cold War* (1979).

Rhodes, Richard. *Dark Sun: The Making of the Hydrogen Bomb* (1995).

Schaller, Michael. *The American Occupation of Japan* (1985).

York, Herbert F. *The Advisors: Oppenheimer, Teller and the Super* (1976).

Zubok, Vladislav, and Constantine Pleshkanov. *Inside the Kremlin's Cold War: From Stalin to Khrushchev* (1996).

Korean War

Cumings, Bruce. *The Origins of the Korean War* (1981, 1990).

Foot, Rosemary. *The Wrong War: American Policy and the Dimensions of the Korean Conflict, 1950–1953* (1985).

James, D. Clayton. *Refighting the Last War: Command and Crisis in Korea, 1950–1953* (1992).

Kaufman, Burton I. *The Korean War: Challenges in Crisis, Credibility, and Command* (1986).

Stueck, William. *The Korean War: An International History* (1995).

Society and Politics at Home

Gillon, Steven. *Politics and Vision: The ADA and American Liberalism* (1987).

Goldman, Eric F. *The Crucial Decade and After: America, 1945–1960* (1960).

Hamby, Alonzo. *A Man of the People: A Life of Harry Truman* (1995).

Kelly, Barbara M. *Expanding the American Dream: Building and Rebuilding Levittown* (1993).

Lubell, Samuel. *The Future of American Politics* (1952).

McCoy, Donald R., and Richard Ruetten. *Quest and Response: Minority Rights and the Truman Administration* (1973).

Meyerowitz, Joanne, ed. *Not June Cleaver: Women and Gender in Postwar America* (1994).

Patterson, James. *Mr. Republican: A Biography of Robert A. Taft* (1972).

Randall, Gregory. *America's Original G.I. Town: Park Forest, Illinois* (2000).

Rosswurm, Steven. *The CIO's Left-Led Unions* (1992)

White, Graham, and John Maze. *Henry A. Wallace: His Search for a New World Order* (1995).

Wright, Gwendolyn. *Building the Dream: A Social History of Housing in America* (1981).

Red Scare

Caute, David. *The Great Fear* (1978).

Fried, Richard. *Nightmare in Red: The McCarthy Era in Perspective* (1990).

Griffith, Robert. *The Politics of Fear: Joseph R. McCarthy and the Senate* (1970).

Klehr, Harvey, and John Earl Haynes. *Verona: Decoding Soviet Espionage in America* (1999).

Kutler, Stanley. *The American Inquisition* (1982).

Schrecker, Ellen. *Many Are the Crimes: McCarthyism in America* (1998).

Sibley, Katherine. *Red Spies in America: Stolen Secrets and the Dawn of the Cold War* (2004).

Theoharis, Athan, and John Stuart Cox. *The Boss: J. Edgar Hoover and the Great American Inquisition* (1988).

White, G. Edward. *Alger Hiss's Looking-Glass Wars: The Covert Life of a Soviet Spy* (2004).

Whitfield, Stephen. *The Culture of the Cold War* (1996).

Chapter 28
The Eisenhower Presidency

Ambrose, Stephen E. *Ike's Spies: Eisenhower and the Espionage Establishment* (1981).

Bowie, Robert, and Richard Immerman. *Waging Peace: How Eisenhower Shaped an Enduring Cold War Strategy* (1998).

Brands, H. W. *Cold Warriors: Eisenhower's Generation and American Foreign Policy* (1988).

Divine, Robert. *Eisenhower and the Cold War* (1981).

Dudziak, Mary. *Cold War Civil Rights: Race and the Image of American Democracy* (2000).

Greenstein, Fred. *The Hidden-Hand Presidency: Eisenhower as Leader* (1982).

Hixson, Walter. *Parting the Curtain: Propaganda, Culture and the Cold War* (1997).

Pach, Chester. *The Presidency of Dwight David Eisenhower* (1991).

Plummer, Brenda Gayle. *A Rising Wind: Black Americans and U.S. Foreign Affairs, 1935–1960* (1996).

Science, Politics, and Society

Divine, Robert. *The Sputnik Challenge* (1993).

Grossman, Andrew. *Neither Dead nor Red: Civil Defense and American Political Development during the Early Cold War* (2001).

Kleidman, Robert. *Organizing for Peace: Neutrality, the Test Ban, and the Freeze* (1993).

McDougall, Walter. *The Heavens and the Earth: A Political History of the Space Age* (1985).

McEnaney, Laura. *Civil Defense Begins at Home: Militarization Meets Everyday Life in the Fifties* (2000).

Olshansky, David. *Polio: An American Story* (2005).

Rhodes, Richard. *Arsenal of Folly: The Making of the Nuclear Arms Race* (2007).

Smith, Jane. *Patenting the Sun* (1990).

Titus, M. Costandina. *Bombs in the Backyard: Atomic Testing and American Politics* (1986).

Winkler, Allan. *Life under a Cloud: American Anxiety about the Atom* (1993).

The Politics of Growth

Abbott, Carl. *The New Urban America: Growth and Politics in Sunbelt Cities* (1986).

Cohen, Lizabeth. *A Consumers' Republic: The Politics of Mass Consumption in Postwar America* (2003).

Jackson, Kenneth. *The Crabgrass Frontier* (1985).

McQuaid, Kim. *Uneasy Partners: Big Business in American Politics, 1945–1990* (1993).

O'Neill, William L. *American High: The Years of Confidence, 1945–1960* (1986).

Rose, Mark. *Interstate: Express Highway Politics* (1990).

Sugrue, Thomas. *The Origins of the Urban Crisis: Race and Inequality in Postwar Detroit* (1996)

Teaford, Jon. *The Rough Road to Renaissance: Urban Revitalization in America* (1990).

Family Life and Culture

Altshuler, Glenn. *All Shook Up: How Rock 'n' Roll Changed America* (2003).

Altschuler, Glenn, and David Grossvogel. *Changing Channels: America in "TV Guide"* (1992).

Dierenfeld, Bruce. *The Battle over School Prayer: How Engle v. Vitale Changed America* (2007).

Doherty, Thomas. *Cold War, Cool Medium: Television, McCarthyism, and American Culture* (2003)

Horowitz, Daniel. *Vance Packard and American Social Criticism* (1994).

Jamison, Andrew, and Ron Eyerman. *Seeds of the Sixties* (1994).

Kaledin, Eugenia. *Mothers and More: American Women in the 1950s* (1984).

May, Elaine Tyler. *Homeward Bound: American Families in the Cold War Era* (1988).

Rupp, Leila, and Verta Taylor. *Survival in the Doldrums: The American Women's Rights Movement, 1945 to the 1960s* (1987).

Weiss, Jessica. *To Have and To Hold: Marriage, the Baby Boom, and Social Change* (2000).

Whyte, William. *The Organization Man* (1956).

The Early 1960s

Beschloss, Michael. *The Crisis Years: Kennedy and Khrushchev, 1960–1963* (1991).

Dallek, Robert. *An Unfinished Life: John F. Kennedy, 1917–1963* (2003).

Freedman, Lawrence. *Kennedy's Wars: Berlin, Cuba, Laos, and Vietnam* (2001).

Giglio, James. *The Presidency of John F. Kennedy* (1991).

Goldberg, Robert Alan. *Barry Goldwater* (1995).

Hoffman, Elizabeth Cobbs. *All You Need Is Love: The Peace Corps and the Spirit of the 1960s* (1998).

Kearns, Doris. *Lyndon Johnson and the American Dream* (1976).

Logeval, Fredrik. *Choosing War: The Last Chance for Peace and the Escalation of War in Vietnam* (1999).

Moise, Edward. *Tonkin Gulf and the Escalation of the Vietnam War* (1996).

Patterson, James T. *America's Struggle against Poverty, 1900–1985* (1986).

Stern, Mark. *Calculating Visions: Kennedy, Johnson, and Civil Rights* (1992).

Wyden, Peter. *Bay of Pigs: The Untold Story* (1979).

Struggles for Equal Rights

Acuña, Rodolfo. *Occupied America: A History of Chicanos* (1988).

Arsenault, Raymond. *Freedom Riders: 1961 and the Struggle for Racial Justice* (2006).

Branch, Taylor. *Parting the Waters: America in the King Years, 1954–1963* (1988).

Burner, Eric. *And Gently He Shall Lead Them: Robert Parris Moses and Civil Rights in Mississippi* (1994).

Chafe, William. *Civilities and Civil Rights: Greensboro, North Carolina, and the Black Struggle* (1980).

Dittmer, John. *Local People: A History of the Mississippi Movement* (1994).

Egerton, John. *Speak Now against the Day: The Generation before the Civil Rights Movement in the South* (1994).

Garrow, David. *Bearing the Cross: Martin Luther King Jr. and the Southern Christian Leadership Conference* (1986).

Goldman, Roger, and David Gallen. *Thurgood Marshall: Justice for All* (1993).

Halberstam, David. *The Children* (1998).

Hogan, Wesley. *Many Minds, One Heart, SNCC's Dream for a New America* (2007).

Huckaby, Elizabeth. *Crisis at Central High: Little Rock, 1957–1958* (1980).

Kirk, John. *Redefining the Color Line: Black Activism in Little Rock, 1940–1970* (2002).

Klarman, Michael. *From Jim Crow to Civil Rights: The Supreme Court and the Struggle for Racial Equality* (2004).

Kluger, Richard. *Simple Justice: The History of Brown v. Board of Education* (1976).

Marsh, Charles. *God's Long Summer: Stories of Faith and Civil Rights* (1998).

McWhorter, Diane. *Carry Me Home: Birmingham, Alabama: The Climactic Battle of the Civil Rights Revolution* (2000).

Mills, Kay. *This Little Light of Mine: The Life of Fannie Lou Hamer* (1993).

Payne, Charles. *I've Got the Light of Freedom: The Organizing Tradition and the Mississippi Freedom Struggle* (1995).

Ramsky, Barbara. *Ella Baker and the Black Freedom Movement* (2005).

Sitkoff, Harvard. *The Struggle for Black Equality; 1954–1992* (1992).

Thornton, J. Mills III. *Dividing Line: Municipal Politics and the Struggle for Civil Rights in Montgomery, Birmingham and Selma* (2002).

Chapter 29

Overviews

McQuaid, Kim. *The Anxious Years: America in the Vietnam-Watergate Era* (1989).

Blum, John Morton. *Years of Discord: American Politics and Society, 1961–1974* (1991).

Farber, David, *The Age of Great Dreams* (1994).

War in Vietnam

Appy, Christian. *Working-Class War: American Combat Soldiers and Vietnam* (1993).

Auster, Albert, and Leonard Quart. *How the War Was Remembered: Hollywood and Vietnam* (1988).

Buzzanco, Robert. *Masters of War* (1996).

Fitzgerald, Frances. *Fire on the Lake* (1972).

Kimball, Jeffrey. *Nixon's Vietnam War* (1998).

Levy, David W. *The Debate over Vietnam* (1991).

Schulzinger, Robert. *A Time for War: The United States and Vietnam, 1941–1975* (1997).

Shawcross, William. *Sideshow: Kissinger, Nixon, and the Destruction of Cambodia* (1979).

Sheehan, Neil. *A Bright Shining Lie: John Paul Vann and America in Vietnam* (1988).

Van De Mark, Brian. *Into the Quagmire: Johnson and the Escalation of the Vietnam War* (1991).

Van Devanter, Lynda. *Home before Morning* (1984).

Wells, Tom. *The War Within: America's Battle over Vietnam* (1994).

Young, Marilyn. *The Vietnam Wars, 1945–1990* (1991).

The Revolt of the Young

Anderson, Terry. *The Movement and the Sixties* (1995).

Bates, Tom. *Rads: The 1970 Bombing of the Army Math Research Center at the University of Wisconsin and Its Aftermath* (1992).

Breines, Wini. *Community and Organization in the New Left, 1962–1968* (1982).

Evans, Sara. *Personal Politics: The Roots of Women's Liberation in the Civil Rights Movement and the New Left* (1979).

Foley, Michael. *Confronting the War Machine: Draft Resistance during the Vietnam War* (2003).

Gitlin, Todd. *The Sixties: Years of Hope, Days of Rage* (1987).

Lyons, Paul. *The People of This Generation: The Rise and Fall of the New Left in Philadelphia* (2003).

Miller, James. *"Democracy Is in the Streets": From Port Huron to the Siege of Chicago* (1987).

Perry, Charles. *The Haight-Ashbury* (1985).

Rorabaugh, William. *Berkeley at War* (1989).

Sale, Kirkpatrick. *SDS* (1973).

Minority Rights and Minority Separatism

Countryman, Matthew, *Up South: Civil Rights and Black Power in Philadelphia* (2005).

Duberman, Martin, *Stonewall* (1993).

Giddings, Paula, and Cornel West, *Regarding Malcolm X* (1994).

Joseph, Peniel. *Waiting 'Til the Midnight Hour: A Narrative History of Black Power in America* (2006).

Mathiesson, Peter. *In the Spirit of Crazy Horse* (1983).

Padilla, Felix. *Puerto Rican Chicago* (1987).

Smith, Paul Chait, and Robert Allen Warrior. *Like a Hurricane: The Indian Movement from Alcatraz to Wounded Knee* (1996).

Thomas, Piri. *Down These Mean Streets* (1967).

Van Deburg, William L. *New Day in Babylon: The Black Power Movement and American Culture, 1965–1975* (1993).

Foreign Policy in the 1970s

Bill, James A. *The Eagle and the Lion: The Tragedy of American-Iranian Relations* (1988).

Garthoff, Raymond. *Détente and Confrontation* (1985).

Isaacson, Walter. *Kissinger: A Biography* (1992).

Le Feber, Walter. *The Panama Canal: The Crisis in Historical Perspective* (1978).

Nelson, Keith. *The Making of Détente* (1995).

Quando, William B. *Camp David: Peacemaking and Politics* (1986).

Schulzinger, Robert. *Henry Kissinger: Doctor of Diplomacy* (1989).

Smith, Gaddis. *Morality, Reason, and Power* (1986).

Talbot, Strobe. *Endgame: The Inside Story of SALT II* (1979).

Watergate and Politics in the Nixon Years

Carter, Dan T. *The Politics of Rage: George Wallace, the Origins of the New Conservatism, and the Transformation of American Politics* (1996).

Flamm, Michael. *Law and Order: Street Crime, Civil Unrest, and the Crisis of Liberalism in the 1960s* (2005).

Hoff, Joan. *Nixon Reconsidered* (1994).

Kotlowski, Dean. *Nixon's Civil Rights: Politics, Principles, and Policy* (2002).

Kutler, Stanley. *The Wars of Watergate* (1990).

Olson, Keith. *Watergate: The Presidential Scandal That Shook America* (2003).

Schudson, Michael. *Watergate in American Memory: How We Remember, Forget, and Reconstruct the Past* (1992).

Small, Melvin. *The Presidency of Richard Nixon* (1999).

Jimmy Carter and His Presidency

Carter, Jimmy. *Keeping Faith: Memoirs of a President* (1982).

Farber, David. *Taken Hostage: The Iran Crisis and America's First Encounter with Radical Islam* (2004).

Hargrove, Erwin C. *Jimmy Carter as President: Leadership and the Politics of the Public Good* (1988).

Jones, Charles O. *The Trusteeship Presidency: Jimmy Carter and the United States Congress* (1988).

Kaufman, Burton I. *The Presidency of James Earl Carter, Jr.* (1993).

Miller, William Lee. *Yankee from Georgia: The Emergence of Jimmy Carter* (1978).

Environmental Politics

Gottlieb, Robert. *Forcing the Spring: The Transformation of the American Environmental Movement* (1993).

Hays, Samuel. *Beauty, Health, and Permanence: Environmental Politics in the United States, 1955–1985* (1987).

Rome, Adam. *The Bulldozer in the Countryside: Suburban Sprawl and the Rise of American Environmentalism* (2001).

Sale, Kirkpatrick. *The Green Revolution: The American Environmental Movement, 1962–1992* (1993).

Chapter 30
Economic Change: Opportunity and Inequality

Beam, Frank, and Gillian Stevens. *American's Newcomers and the Dynamics of Diversity* (2003).

Duneier, Mitchell. *Slim's Table: Race, Respectability, and Masculinity* (1992).

Ehrenreich, Barbara. *Fear of Falling: The Inner Life of the Middle Class* (1989).

Hacker, Andrew. *Two Nations: Black and White, Separate, Hostile, Unequal* (1992).

Levy, Frank. *The New Dollars and Dreams: American Incomes and Economic Change* (1998).

Markusen, Ann, et al. *The Rise of the Gunbelt: The Military Remapping of Industrial America* (1991).

Spain, Daphne, and Suzanne Bianchi. *Balancing Act: Motherhood, Marriage and Employment among American Women* (1996).

Stewart, James B. *Den of Thieves* (1991).

Wilson, William Julius. *The Truly Disadvantaged* (1967).

Zukin, Sharon. *Loft Living: Culture and Capital in Urban Change* (1982).

The New Conservatism

Bennett, William. *The De-Valuing of America: The Fight for Our Culture and Our Children* (1992).

Critchlow, Donald. *Phyllis Schlafly and Grassroots Conservatism: A Woman's Crusade* (2005).

Edwards, Lee. *The Conservative Revolution: The Movement That Remade America* (1999).

Ehrman, John. *The Rise of Neo-Conservative Intellectuals and Foreign Affairs, 1945–1994* (1995).

Hoeveler, J. David, Jr. *Watch on the Right: Conservative Intellectuals in the Reagan Era* (1991).

Katz, Michael. *The Undeserving Poor: From the War on Poverty to the War on Welfare* (1989).

Kintz, Linda. *Between Jesus and the Market: The Emotions That Matter in Right-Wing America* (1997).

Kristol, Irving. *Neoconservatism: The Autobiography of an Idea* (1995).

Lowi, Theodore J. *The End of the Republican Era* (1995).

Murray, Charles. *Losing Ground: American Social Policy, 1950–1980* (1984).

Politics, Society, and the Mass Media

Denisoff, R. Serge. *Inside MTV* (1988).

Flournoy, Don. *CNN World Report: Ted Turner's International News Coup* (1992).

Gitlin, Todd. *Watching Television* (1987).

Goodwin, Andrew. *Dancing in the Distraction Factory: Music Television and Popular Culture* (1992).

Mills, Nicolaus. *Culture in an Age of Money* (1990).

Military and Foreign Policy

Allin, Dana H. *Cold War Illusions: America, Europe, and Soviet Power, 1969–1989* (1998).

Cortright, David. *Peace Works: The Citizen's Role in Ending the Cold War* (1993).

Draper, Theodore. *A Very Thin Line* (1991).

Freedman, Lawrence, and Efraim Karsh. *The Gulf Conflict, 1990–1991: Diplomacy and the New World Order* (1993).

Friedberg, Aaron L. *In the Shadow of the Garrison State: America's Anti-Statism and the Cold War* (2000).

Gaddis, John L. *Now We Know: Rethinking Cold War History* (1997).

Graubard, Stephen. *Mr. Bush's War* (1992).

Hogan, Michael J., ed. *The End of the Cold War: Its Meaning and Implications* (1992).

Smith, Christian. *Resisting Reagan: The U.S. Central American Peace Movement* (1997).

Tucker, Robert W., and David C. Hendrickson. *The Imperial Temptation: The New World Order and America's Purposes* (1992).

Wirls, Daniel. *Buildup: The Politics of Defense in the Reagan Era* (1992).

Politics and Politicians in the 1980s

Anderson, Martin. *Revolution* (1989).

Berman, William. *America's Right Turn: From Nixon to Bush* (1994).

Clavel, Pierre, and Wim Wiewel, eds., *Harold Washington and the Neighborhoods* (1991).

Diggins, John. *Ronald Reagan: Fate, Freedom, and the Making of History* (2007).

Gallon, Steven M. *The Democrats' Dilemma: Walter F. Mondale and the Liberal Legacy* (1992).

Greene, John Robert. *The Presidency of George Bush* (2000).

Johnson, Haynes. *Sleepwalking through History: America in the Reagan Years* (1991).

Pemberton, William. *Exit with Honor: The Life and Presidency of Ronald Reagan* (1997).

Schaller, Michael. *Reckoning with Reagan: American and Its President in the 1980s* (1992).

Sloan, John W. *The Reagan Effect: Economics and Presidential Leadership* (1999).

Stockman, David. *The Triumph of Politics: How the Reagan Revolution Failed* (1986).

Chapter 31
The New Economy

Castells, Manuel. *The Internet Galaxy: Reflections on the Internet, Business, and Society* (2001).

Gilpin, Robert. *Global Political Economy* (2001).

Kidder, Tracy. *The Soul of a New Machine* (1981).

Micklethwait, John, and Adrian Wooldridge. *A Future Perfect: The Challenge and Hidden Promise of Globalization* (2000).

Markusen, Ann, Peter Hall, and Amy Glasmeier. *High-Tech America: The What, How, Why and When of the Sunrise Industries* (1986).

Moody, Kim. *Workers in a Lean World: Workers in the International Economy* (1997)

Sassen, Saskia. *The Global City* (1991).

Wallace, James, and Jim Erickson. *Hard Drive: Bill Gates and the Making of the Microsoft Empire* (1993).

Wresch, William. *Disconnected: Haves and Have-Nots in the Information Age* (1996).

Politics

Balz, Dan, and Ronald Brownstein. *Storming the Gates: Protest Politics and the Republican Revival* (1996).

Barber, Benjamin. *The Truth of Power: Intellectual Affairs in the Clinton White House* (2001).

Colburn, David, and Jeffrey Adler, eds. *African-American Mayors: Race, Politics and the American City* (2001).

Dionne, E. J., Jr. *Why Americans Hate Politics* (1991).

Gillman, Howard. *The Votes That Counted: How the Courts Decided the 2000 Presidential Election* (2001).

Maraniss, David. *First in His Class: The Biography of Bill Clinton* (1996).

Rae, Nicol, and Colton Campbell. *Impeaching Clinton: Partisan Strife on Capitol Hill* (2003).

Renshon, Stanley. *High Hopes: The Clinton Presidency and the Politics of Ambition* (1998).

Rozell, Mark, and Clyde Wilcox. *Second Coming: The New Christian Right in Virginia Politics* (1996).

Sunstein, Cass, and Richard Epstein. *The Vote: Bush, Gore, and the Supreme Court* (2001).

The Iraq War and Foreign Policy

Baker, James A., III, and Lee Hamilton. *The Iraq Study Group Report* (2006).

Holmes, Stephen. *The Matador's Cape: America's Reckless Response to Terror* (2007).

Keegan, John. *The Iraq War* (2004).

The 9/11 Commission Report: The Final Report of the National Commission on Terrorist Attacks upon the United States (2004).

Ricks, Thomas. *Fiasco: The American Military Adventure in Iraq* (2006).

Social Issues

Anderson, Terry. *The Pursuit of Fairness: A History of Affirmative Action* (2004).

Baldwin, Peter, *Disease and Democracy: The Industrial World Faces AIDS* (2005).

Bowen, William, and Derek Bok. *The Shape of the River: The Long-Term Consequences of Considering Race in College and University Admissions* (1998).

Cohen, Michael Lee. *The Twenty-Something American Dream* (1993).

Cornell, Saul. *A Well Regulated Militia: The Founding Fathers and the Origins of Gun Control in America* (2006).

Linenthal, Edward. *The Unfinished Bombing: Oklahoma City in American Memory* (2001).

Weiss, Michael J. *The Clustered World: How We Live, What We Buy, and What It Means about Who We Are* (2000).

The New American Landscape

Abbott, Carl. *Greater Portland: Urban Life and Landscape in the Pacific Northwest* (2001).

Blackford, Mansel. *Fragile Paradise: The Impact of Tourism on Maui* (2001).

Calthorpe, Peter, and William Fulton. *The Regional City* (2001).

Ford, Larry. *Metropolitan San Diego* (2004).

Riebsame, William, et al. *Atlas of the New West* (1997).

Rothman, Hal. *Neon Metropolis: How Las Vegas Started the Twenty-First Century* (2002).

Warner, Sam Bass, Jr. *Greater Boston: Adapting Regional Traditions to the Present* (2001).

CREDITS

CHAPTER 16 Courtesy of the Library of Congress, 432; The Granger Collection, New York., 437; The Granger Collection, New York., 438; Austin History Center, Austin Public Library / PICA 05496, 440; Courtesy of the Library of Congress, 441; The Granger Collection, New York., 445; Courtesy of the Library of Congress, 448; General Research & Reference Division, Schomberg Center for Research in Black Culture, The New York Public Library. Astor, Lenox and Tilden Foundations, 449; Michael Elazier, Congressional Black Caucus, June 1999, 449; Courtesy of the Library of Congress, 451; Courtesy of the Library of Congress, 453; Courtesy of the Library of Congress, 455; Courtesy of the Library of Congress, 457.

CHAPTER 17 Courtesy of the Library of Congress, 464; T. E. Armitstead Collection, University of South Alabama Archives, 473; Valentine Museum/Richmond History Center, 475; Courtesy of the Library of Congress, 477; Courtesy of the Library of Congress, 480; The Granger Collection, New York, 481; The Ohio Historical Society, 482; North Carolina Mutual Life Insurance Company, 485; West Point Museum Collections, USMA, 486; AP Wide World Photos, 486; Courtesy of the Library of Congress, 488.

CHAPTER 18 Courtesy of the Library of Congress, 492; W. Louis Sonntag, Jr., "The Bowery at Night", watercolor, 1895. Copyright Museum of the City of New York. 32.275.2, 498; Ford Motor Company, 499; Courtesy of the Library of Congress, 501; Getty Images Inc. - Hulton Archive Photos, 503; 22 Baxter Street Court. The Jacob A. Riis Collection, Museum of the City of New York., 503; The Granger Collection, New York, 505; (c) Tetra images/Getty Images, 507; Courtesy of the Nebraska State Historical Society, 510; Courtesy of the Library of Congress, 511; Courtesy of The Bancroft Library. University of California, Berkeley, 513; Brown Brothers, 515; Culver Pictures, Inc., 520.

CHAPTER 19 The Granger Collection, New York, 524; Union Pacific Historical Collection, 528; Denver Public Library, Western History Collection, Call Number : B-115, 531; Western History Collections, University of Oklahoma Libraries. Phillips Collection 357, 532; Western History Collections, University of Oklahoma Libraries, 537; Chinese mining laborers, Idaho, 76-119.2/A, Idaho State Historical Society., 538; Courtesy of the Library of Congress, 539; Courtesy Photographic Archives, Palace of the Governors, Museum of New Mexico, Santa Fe, New Mexico / DCA Negative No.:22468, 542; Courtesy of the Nebraska State Historical Society, 545; (c) Bettmann/CORBIS All Rights Reserved, 546.

CHAPTER 20 Reproduced from the collections of the Ohio Historical Society Archives/Library, 550; The Granger Collection, New York, 557; Courtesy of the Library of Congress, 558; provided courtesy HarpWeek., LLC, 562; Courtesy of the Library of Congress, 564; Kansas State Historical Society, 566; (c) Stock Montage, 2004, 568; Courtesy of the Library of Congress, 570; Culver Pictures, 571; The Granger Collection, New York, 573.

CHAPTER 21 Brown Brothers, 578; Kheel Center, Cornell University, Ithaca, NY 14853-3901, 584; Courtesy of the Library of Congress, 585; Kheel Center, Cornell University, Ithaca, NY 14853-3901, 588; Courtesy of the Library of Congress, 591; Indiana Historical Society, A70, 593; Courtesy of the Library of Congress, 595; provided courtesy HarpWeek., LLC, 598; Courtesy of the Library of Congress, 602; Portrait #65, Courtesy of the Bancroft Library, University of California, Berkeley., 606; (c) JEWEL SAMAD/AFP/Getty Images, 606.

CHAPTER 22 The Granger Collection, New York, 610; Courtesy of the Library of Congress, 616; (c) Bettmann/CORBIS, 620; Courtesy of the Library of Congress, 623; Denver Public Library, Western History Collection, Call Number: RH-234, 624; Courtesy of the Library of Congress, 625; (c) Stock Montage, 2004, 626; provided courtesy HarpWeek., LLC, 630; provided courtesy HarpWeek., LLC, 631; AP Photo/John Moore, 631; The Granger Collection, New York, 632.

CHAPTER 23 Corbis/Bettmann, 636; University of South Alabama Archives, 643; Photograph courtesy of the Hagley Museum and Library, Wilmington, Delaware, 646; National Archives and Records Administration, 647; The Granger Collection, New York, 648; John Hay Library, Brown University, 650; Getty Images Inc. - Hulton Archive Photos, 653; National Archives and Records Administration, 655; The Granger Collection, New York, 660.

CHAPTER 24 (c) Swim Ink/CORBIS, 664; Wisconsin Historical Society/WHi-5020, 670; By Permission of DuPont Automotive, 672; Courtesy of the Library of Congress, 676; Security Pacific Collection / Los Angeles Public Library, 677; By permission of Campbell Soup Company, 678; Frank Driggs Collection, 679; The Denver Public Library, Western History Collection, The Harry M. Rhoads Photograph Collection, Call Number Rh-460, 681; AP Wide World Photos, 683; Getty Images, Inc., 685; (c) Stephen Boitano/Reuters/Corbis, 688; (c) David McNew/Getty Images, Inc., 688.

CHAPTER 25 Getty Images, Inc., 692; University of Washington Libraries, Special Collections, Lee 20102, 699; Courtesy of the Library of Congress, 701; Culver Pictures, Inc. / SuperStock, 702; Courtesy of the Library of Congress, 703; Corbis/Bettmann, 706; Corbis/Bettmann, 708; Courtesy of the Library of Congress, 709; The Denver Public Library, Western History Collection, The Harry M. Rhoads Photograph Collection, Call Number Rh-557, 711; Corbis/Bettmann, 713; Courtesy of the Library of Congress, 715; UPI/CORBIS-BETTMANN, 720.

CHAPTER 26 U.S. Air Force, 724; Bildarchiv PreuBischer Kulturbesitz, Berlin, 729; National Archives and Records Administration, 734; (c) Bettmann/CORBIS, 738; National Archives and Records Administration, 741; Poster Collection / Hoover Institution Archives, 742; Poster Collection / Hoover Institution Archives, 743; Reprinted with Permission of the Dallas Morning News, 744; Courtesy of the Library of Congress, 745; (c) Bettmann/CORBIS, 750; National Archives and Records Administration, 751; Getty Images, Inc – Liaison, 753; Corbis/Bettmann, 754; Peter Arnold, Inc., 754.

CHAPTER 27 Getty Images/Time Life Pictures, 758; RKO Radio Pictures/Hulton Archive, 762; Corbis/Bettmann, 764; The Granger Collection, New York, 765; AP Wide World Photos, 766; Charles Fenno Jacobs/Getty Images, Inc., 772; Getty Images Inc. - Hulton Archive Photos, 775; AP Wide World Photos, 775; National Archives and Records Administration, 776; Corbis/Bettmann, 782; (c) Bettmann/CORBIS, 783.

CHAPTER 28 AP Wide World Photos, 786; Photo Researchers, Inc., 791; "Day dreaming" by Constantin Alajalov. (c) 1959 SEPS: Liscened by Curtis Publishing Co., Indianapolis, IN. All rights reserved. www.curtispublishing.com, 793; Getty Images Inc. - Hulton Archive Photos, 795; Picture Desk, Inc./Kobal Collection, 796; Magnum Photos, Inc., 797; Ruth Sondak, 799; Cecil Stoughton, White House/John Fitzgerald Kennedy Library, Boston, 803; AP Wide World Photos, 806; News & Record Library/ John G. Moebes, 808; (c)1976, Matt Herron/Take Stock-Images of Change, 810; UPI/CORBIS-BETTMANN, 811; Copyright (WHO) World Health Organization, 814; Courtesy of Remote Medicine, 814.

CHAPTER 29 Jeffery Blankfort /Jeroboam, 818; Getty Images Inc. - Hulton Archive Photos, 824; Corbis/Bettmann, 825; Black Star, 826; AP Wide World Photos, 828; Corbis/Bettmann, 830; (c) Bettmann/CORBIS All Rights Reserved, 831; Walter P. Reuther Library, Wayne State University, 832; Agence France Presse/Getty Images, 833; Corbis/Bettmann, 834; Corbis/Bettmann, 839; Getty Images, Inc., 839; Black Star, 840; (c) Vince Streano / CORBIS All Rights Reserved, 845; (c) Wally McNamee/CORBIS, 846; SIPA Press, 847.

CHAPTER 30 Peter Arnold, Inc., 850; Corbis/Bettmann, 855; Photofest, 856; Corbis/Bettmann, 858; (c)The New Yorker Collection 2008 Koren from cartoonbank.com. All Rights Reserved., 859; National Archives and Records Administration, 861; Corbis/Bettmann, 861; P. F. Bentley/PFPIX.COM, 863; PhotoEdit Inc., 864; AP Wide World Photos, 867; Corbis/Sygma, 869; Black Star, 877; AP Wide World Photos, 880.

CHAPTER 31 James Natchway/VII (detail), 884; (c) IRA WYMAN/CORBIS SYGMA, 888; AP Wide World Photos, 891; Corbis Digital Stock, 895; Agence France Presse/Getty Images, 899; Stephen Jaffe Photography, 904; (c) Reuters/CORBIS, 906 AP Wide World Photos, 908; (c) DAEMMRICH BOB/CORBIS SYGMA, 909; AP Wide World Photos, 910; Getty Images, Inc., 913; AP Wide World Photos, 913; (c) Michael Ainsworth / Dallas Morning News / CORBIS All Rights Reserved, 914; Library of Congress, 915 .

INDEX